DATE DUE

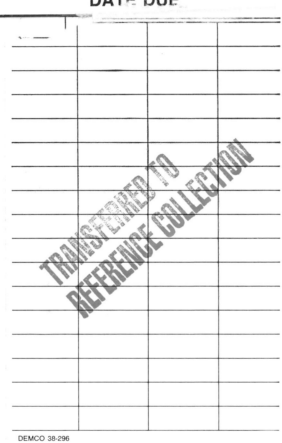

DEMCO 38-296

The United States Army

A Dictionary

*Garland Reference Library
of Social Science*

(Vol. 602)

The Garland Series on U.S.Military Affairs
Bruce W. Watson, Editor-in-Chief

THE GARLAND SERIES ON U.S. MILITARY AFFAIRS presents complete reference coverage of selected military, intelligence, and national security subjects. Beginning with the volume on military intelligence, the multivolume series will discuss these subjects with particular emphasis on contemporary affairs.

_____

Other books in the series:

United States Intelligence:
An Encyclopedia

The United States Air Force:
A Dictionary

The United States Navy:
A Dictionary

Command, Control, and
Communications

_____

UNITED STATES ARMY

A Dictionary

Edited by
Peter Tsouras
Bruce W. Watson
Susan M. Watson

GARLAND PUBLISHING, INC. • NEW YORK & LONDON
1991

The information in this dictionary is based on the research of the authors and does not represent the positions or policies of any agency or department of the U.S. government. The information was derived from unclassified publications and sources and is intended neither to confirm nor to deny, officially or unofficially, the views of the U.S. government.

Library of Congress Cataloging-in-Publication Data

The United States Army : a dictionary / edited by Peter Tsouras, Bruce M. Watson, Susan M. Watson.
   p. cm. — (Garland reference library of the social sciences ; vol. 602)
   Includes bibliographical references.
   ISBN 0-8240-5348-6 (alk. paper)
   1. United States. Army—Encyclopedias. I. Tsouras, Peter. II. Watson, Bruce W.
III. Watson, Susan M., 1943– . IV. Series: Garland reference library of social science ; v. 602.
UA25.U49 1991
355'.00973—dc20   90-41172
                                         CIP

Contents

This dictionary is dedicated with great respect and affection to Brigadier General Richard Eaton, U.S. Army (Retired), whose example of leadership, humanity, and moral courage to the officers and men of the 2nd Brigade, 3rd Infantry Division, was a beacon of hope and inspiration. As the U.S. Army staggered out of the Vietnam era on the point of moral dissolution in the hands of a host of timid careerists, Dick Eaton stood out as a modern knight, *sans peur et sans reproche*. He established a standard of what the Army could be to a generation of bitterly disillusioned junior officers, who in their own ways were to carry some of his fire with them throughout the Army.

Acknowledgments

This dictionary could not have been written without the cheerful forbearance of Patricia Tsouras, who allowed her dining room table to be confiscated as a work table for months on end, and the cheerful professionalism of Major Patricia Tsouras, Chemical Corps, U.S. Army Reserve, who reviewed the entries for nuclear, biological, and chemical (NBC) warfare terminology to insure that the most recent doctrinal changes had been incorporated. We also thank the Army reservists in the Civil Affairs community, Colonel Hlib Hayuk and Major Glen Siegal, for their help in insuring that the book contains the current terminology in the rapidly evolving world of Civil Affairs.

We are also indebted to many for the production of this book. We would like to thank Bruce, Junior and Jennifer Watson for their hours of proofreading and other help. We would like to thank Susan M.O. Watson, who spent days helping us prepare and edit this book. We are most thankful for her kind assistance. Finally, we thank our youngest daughter, Ella, for her patience.

Peter Tsouras
Bruce W. Watson
Susan M. Watson

Introduction

—How to Use This Dictionary

This dictionary is an academic reference for the serious researcher of the U.S. Army. It discusses the major terms and entities currently in use. Its scope is the post-World War II period, with an emphasis on the present.

This book is divided into the following major sections:

—Acronyms.

The U.S. military has a penchant, indeed a mania, for acronyms. The list of acronyms that we have prepared includes all the acronyms used in this work, and stands as an important reference for acronym definitions.

—Entries.

The entries are listed alphabetically, and we have cross-referenced them extensively to further assist in the reader's research.

Acronyms

— A —

A²C²	Army Airspace Command and Control
AA	(1) Antiaircraft
	(2) Attack Assessment
AAA	Antiaircraft Artillery
AAAOB	Antiaircraft Artillery Order of Battle
AAB	Air Assault Brigade
AADC	Area Air Defense Commander
AADS	Army Air Defense Staff
AAF	Army Airfield
AAFES	Army and Air Force Exchange Service
AAG	Army Artillery Group
AAGS	Army Air-Ground System
AAH	Advanced Attack Helicopter
AAI	Authorized Active Inventory
AAICV	Armored Amphibious Infantry Combat Vehicle
AALC	Amphibious Assault Landing Craft
AAM	Air-to-Air Missile
AAMG	Antiair Machine Gun
AAO	Army Acquisition Objective
AAP	Allied Publication (NATO)
AAR	After Action Review
AARS	Advanced Airborne Radar System
AAS	(1) Amphibious Area Study
	(2) Area Analysis Study
AAT	Army Assault Team
AAW	Antiair Warfare
AAWC	Antiair Warfare Coordinator
ABC	(1) Air Battle Captain
	(2) Atomic, Biological, and Chemical
ABM	Antiballistic Missile
ABN	Airborne
ABNCP	Airborne Command Post
AC	Aircraft

ACA	Airspace Coordination Area
ACB	Armored Cavalry Brigade
ACC	(1) Airspace Control Center
	(2) Area Coordination Center
	(3) Army Communications Command
	(4) Army Component Commander
ACCS	Automated Command and Control System
ACE	(1) Allied Command Europe
	(2) Armored Combat Earthmover
ACF	Area Coverage File
ACFT	Aircraft
ACG	Area Coordination Group
ACINT	Acoustical Intelligence
ACL	Allowable Cabin Load
ACOUSTINT	Acoustical Intelligence
ACP	(1) Air Control Point
	(2) Alternate Command Post
ACR	Armored Cavalry Regiment
ACRV	Armored Command Reconnaissance Vehicle
ACS	Armored Cavalry Squadron
ACSB	Amphibious Contingency Support Brief
ACSI	Assistant Chief of Staff, Intelligence (U.S. Army) (Now, Deputy Chief of Staff, Intelligence, U.S. Army)
ACV	Armored Command Vehicle
AD	(1) Active Duty
	(2) Air Defense
	(3) Armored Division
	(4) Artillery Division
ADA	(1) Air Defense Action
	(2) Air Defense Artillery
ADC	(1) Aide de Campe
	(2) Area Damage Control
	(3) Assistant Division Commander
ADCC	Air Defense Control Center
ADE	Assistant Division Officer

ADIZ	Air Defense Identification Zone	**AIRES**	Advanced Imagery Requirements and Exploitation System
ADL	Active Duty List		
ADM	Atomic Demolition Munition	**AIRLO**	Air Liaison Officer
ADMIN	Administration	**AIS**	Army Intelligence Survey
ADOA	Air Defense Operations Area	**AIT**	Advanced Individual Training
ADOR	Active Duty Date of Rank	**AJOPS**	Army Joint Operations Planning System
ADP	Automatic Data Processing		
ADPS	Automated Data Processing System	**AK**	(Soviet "Kalashnikov" Family of Assault Rifles)
ADS	Automated Data System	**AKA**	Also Known As
ADT	Active Duty for Training	**ALCOP**	Alternate Command Post
AE	Assault Echelon	**ALFA**	Advanced Liaison Forward Area
AEB	Aerial Exploitation Battalion	**ALO**	Air Liaison Officer
AEV	Armored Engineer Vehicle	**ALOC(s)**	Air Line(s) of Communications
AEW	(1) Aerial Electronic Warfare	**AM**	Ante Meridian
	(2) Airborne Early Warning	**AMAB**	Air Mobile Assault Brigade
AEW&C	Airborne Early Warning and Control	**AMC**	(1) Air Mission Commander
			(2) Airspace Management Center
AF	Air Force		
AFAP	Artillery Fired Atomic Projectile		(3) Army Materiel Command (Formerly DARCOM)
AFCENT	Allied Forces Central Europe		
AFNORTH	Allied Forces Northern Europe (NATO Command)	**AME**	Airspace Management Element
		AMLS	Airspace Management Liaison Section
AFOE	Assault Follow-on Echelon		
AFSA	Armed Forces Security Agency	**AMMO**	Ammunition
AFSAC	Armed Forces Security Agency Council	**AMOPS**	Army Mobilization and Operations Planning
AFSOUTH	Allied Forces Southern Europe (NATO Command)	**AMSC**	Advanced Military Studies Course
AFV	Armored Fighting Vehicle	**AO**	(1) Action Officer
AG	Adjutant General		(2) Aerial Observer
AGI	Annual General Inspection	**AOI**	Area of Interest
AGM	Air-to-Ground Missile	**AOP**	Area of Probability
AGOS	Air-Ground Operations System	**AOR**	Area of Responsibility
AGR	Active Guard/Reserve	**AP**	Armor Piercing
AGZ	Actual Ground Zero	**APB**	Antipersonnel Bomb
AH	Alternate Headquarters	**APC**	(1) Area of Positive Control
AHLO	Attack Helicopter Liaison Officer		(2) Armored Personnel Carrier
		APCC	Aerial Port Control Center
AI	Air Interdiction	**APDS**	Automated Personnel Data Systems
AIA	Army Intelligence Agency		
AID	Army Information Digest	**APERS**	Antipersonnel
AIFV	Armored Infantry Fighting Vehicle	**APFSDS**	Armor-Piercing, Fin-Stabilized, Discarding Sabot
AIMAA	(U.S. Army) Armor Infantry, Mechanized Air Assault, and Airborne	**AP-I**	Armor-Piercing Incendiary
		APL	Army Promotion List
AIMP	Army Intelligence Management Plan	**APM**	Army Program Memorandum
		APO	(1) Air Post Office
AIPD	Army Institute for Professional Development		(2) Army Post Office
		APPROX	Approximately

AR	(1) Action Required		**AR 7 PSY GP**	Army 7th Psychological Operations Group
	(2) Advanced Readiness			
	(3) Army Regulation		**AR 361 CAB**	Army 361st Civil Affairs Brigade
ARAAV	Armored Reconnaissance Airborne Assault Vehicle		**AR 488 MID**	Army 488th Military Intelligence Detachment
AR ACSI	Army Assistant Chief of Staff for Intelligence		**AR 500 MIG**	Army 500th Military Intelligence Group
AR ARDC	Army Armament Research and Development Command		**AR 501 MIG**	Army 501th Military Intelligence Group
ARC	Armored Reconnaissance Carrier		**ARTEP**	Army Training and Evaluation Program
AREUR	Army Europe		**AS**	(1) Aerial Surveillance
AREUR DCSI	Army Europe Deputy Chief of Staff, Intelligence			(2) Area Security
			ASA	Army Security Agency
ARFCOS	Armed Forces Courier Service		**ASAC**	All-Source Analysis Center
ARLANT	(U.S.) Army Forces, Atlantic Command		**ASAP**	As Soon As Possible
			ASARC	Army Systems Acquisition Review Council
ARLEA	Army Logistics Evaluation Agency		**ASARS**	Advanced Synthetic Aperture Radar System
ARLO	Air Reconnaissance Liaison Officer		**ASAS**	All-Source Analysis System
ARM	Antiradiation Missile		**ASAT**	Antisatellite
ARMA	Army Attache		**ASEP**	Advanced Skills Education Program
ARMD	Armored			
AR MIA	Army Missile Intelligence Agency		**ASGOBS**	Army Standard Ground Order of Battle System
AR MICOM	Army Missile Command		**ASL**	Authorized Stockage List
AR MIIA	Army Medical Intelligence and Information Agency		**ASM**	Air-to-Surface Missile
			ASOC	(1) Air Support Operations Center
ARMLO	Army Liaison Officer			
AR MSIC	Army Missile and Space Intelligence Center			(2) All-Source Analysis Center
			ASP	Ammunition Supply Point
ARNG	Army National Guard		**ASPIC**	Armed Services Personnel Interrogation Center
ARNGUS	(U.S.) Army National Guard			
ARRCOM	Army Armament Readiness Command		**ASPJ**	(U.S.) Airborne Self-Protection Jammer
ARRS	Aerial Reconnaissance Reporting System		**ASSIST**	Army System for Standard Intelligence Support Terminals
ARSA	Annual Reevaluation of Safe Areas		**ASU**	(Soviet Airborne Self-Propelled Antitank Gun)
ARTEP	Army Training and Evaluation Program		**ASubjScd**	Army Subject Schedule
ARTOPO	Army Topographic Command		**ASV**	Armored Support Vehicle
ARTY	Artillery		**AT**	(1) Annual Training
ARV	(1) Armored Reconnaissance Vehicle			(2) Antitank
			ATBM	Antitactical Ballistic Missile
	(2) Army Recovery Vehicle		**ATC**	(Mini-Armored Troop Carrier (Riverine Warfare Craft))
AR 193 INF BR	Army 193 Infantry Brigade			
AR 2 INF DIV	Army 2nd Infantry Division		**ATGM**	Antitank Guided Missile
AR 2 PSY GP	Army 2nd Psychological Operations Group		**ATIPS**	Automated Threat Intelligence Production System (U.S. Army)
AR 4 PSY GP	Army 4th Psychological Operations Group		**ATM**	Antitank Missile

ATP	(1) Allied Tactical Publication (NATO)
	(2) Ammunition Transfer Point
	(3) Army Training Program
	(4) Army Training Publication
ATRS	Advanced Tactical Reconnaissance System
ATS	Army Training System
ATT	Army Training Test
AUTODIN	Automatic Digital Network
AUTOSEVO COM	Automatic Secure Voice Communications
AUTOVON	Automatic Voice Network
AUTUMN FORGE	(NATO Exercise)
AUXCP	Auxiliary Command Post
AV	Armored Vehicle
AVF	All Volunteer Force
AVIM	Aviation Intermediate Maintenance
AVLB	Armored Bridge-Laying Vehicle
AVUM	Aviation Unit Maintenance
AW	Automatic Weapon(s)
AWACS	Airborne Early Warning and Control System
AWADS	Adverse Weather Aerial Delivery System
AWC	(U.S.) Army War College
AWOL	Absent Without Leave
AWOP	(1) Absent Without Pay
	(2) Automated Weaponeering Optimization Program
AWS	Air Weather Service
AWX	All Weather
AZ	Azimuth

— B —

BAG	Battalion Artillery Group
BAI	Battlefield Air Interdiction
BAO	Basic Attack Option
BAQ	Basic Allowance for Quarters
BARP	Brigade Assessment and Recovery Personnel
BAS	Basic Allowance Subsistence
BASS	Battlefield Surveillance System
BCC	Battlefield Circulation Control
BCT	Basic Combat Training
BDA	Battle Damage Assessment

BDE	Brigade
BDP	Base Development Plan
BE	Basic Encyclopedia
BETA	Battlefield Exploitation and Target Acquisition
BFOV	Broad Field of View
BFV	Bradley Fighting Vehicle
BFVS-TOW	Bradley Fighting Vehicle System-Tube-Launched, Optically Tracked, Wire-Guided (Missile) Subsystem
BGPHES	Battle Group Passive Horizon Extension System
BGW	Battlefield Guided Weapon
BI	Background Investigation
BICC	Battlefield Information Coordination Center
BLOS	Base Line of Sight
BLSS	Base Level Self-Sufficiency Spares
BLT	Battalion Landing Team
BM	(Soviet Truck-Mounted Multiple Rocket Launcher)
BMD	(1) Ballistic Missile Defense
	(2) (Soviet Airborne Combat Vehicle)
BMEWS	Ballistic Missile Early Warning System
BMNT	Beginning Morning Nautical Twilight
BMP	(Soviet Armored Infantry Combat Vehicle)
BN	Battalion
BOQ	Bachelor Officers' Quarters
BOT	Burst on Target
BP	Battle Position
BPA	Blanket Purchase Agreement
BPS	Basic Psychological Operations Study
BRAVE SHIELD	(U.S. Air Force and U.S. Army Joint Tactical Exercise)
BRDM	(Soviet Wheeled Amphibious Armored Reconnaissance Vehicle)
BRET	Bistatic Reflected Energy Target
BRIGHT STAR	(U.S. Central Command Exercise)
BRL	Bomb Release Line
BRP	Bomb Release Point
BRU	Bomb Release Unit

BSA	Brigade Support Area
BSD	Battlefield Surveillance Device
BSEP	Basic Skills Education Program
BT	Basic Training
BTF	Battalion Task Force
BTR	(Soviet Armored Personnel Carrier)
BY	Budget Year

— C —

C	Confidential
C³	Command, Control and Communications
C³CM	Command, Control, and Communications Counter-measures
C³I	Command, Control, Communications, and Intelligence
C³NET	Command, Control, and Communications Network
C³S	Command, Control, and Communications Systems
C-C³	Counter Command, Control, and Communications
CA	(1) Civil Affairs
	(2) Covert Action
	(3) Cryptanalysis
CAA	Concepts Analysis Agency (U.S. Army)
CAB	Compartmented Address Book
CAC	(1) Collection Advisory Center
	(2) Combined Arms Center
CACDA	Combined Arms Combat Development Activity
C&C or C²	Command and Control
CARG	Crisis Action Review Group
CAS	(1) Close Air Support
	(2) Crisis Action System
CAS³	Combined Arms and Services Staff School
CAST	Combined Arms and Services Training
CAT	(1) Combined Arms Team
	(2) Crisis Action Team
CATF	Commander, Amphibious Task Force
CATIS	Computer-Aided Tactical Information System
CAV	Cavalry
CBM	Confidence Building Measure(s)

CBR	Chemical, Biological, and Radiological
CBU	Cluster Bomb Unit
CBW	Chemical and Biological Warfare
CCC	Command and Control Center
CCD	(1) Camouflage, Concealment, and Deception
	(2) Charged Coupled Device
CCI	Controlled Communications Security Item
CCM	Counter-Countermeasures
CCP	Communications Checkpoint
CCT	Combat Control Team
CD	(1) Certificate of Destruction
	(2) Committee on Disarmament
	(3) Controlled Dissemination
	(4) Corps of Engineers
CDM	Chemical Downwind Message
CE	(1) Civil Engineer
	(2) Corps of Engineers (U.S. Army)
	(3) Cost Effectiveness
	(4) Counterespionage
	(5) Current Exploitation
C-E	Communications-Electronics
CEB	Clothing Exchange and Bath
CED	(1) Collection, Exploitation, and Dissemination
	(2) Captured Enemy Document
CEN	Center
CENTAG	Central Army Group (NATO)
CENTCOM	(U.S.) Central Command
CENTLANT	Central Sub-Area of Eastern Atlantic Area
C-EO	Communications-Electronics Officer
C-EOI	Communications-Electronics Operation Instructions
CEP	Circular Error Probable
CESS	Contingency Exploitation Support System
CETA	Controlled Environment Tests and Analyses
CEV	Combat Engineering Vehicle
CEWI	Combat Electronic Warfare Intelligence
CFA	(1) Combined Field Army (Korea)
	(2) Covering Force Area
CFC	Combined Field Command (Korea)

CFL	Coordinated Fire Lines
CFV	Cavalry Fighting Vehicle
CFX	Command Field Exercise
CG	(1) Commanding General
	(2) Consolidated Guidance
CGF	Central Group of Forces (Soviet Forces in Czechoslovakia)
CGSOC	Command and General Staff Officer Course
CHAN	Channel
CHECKERED FLAG	(U.S.-Host Nation Exercise)
CHEMWARN	Chemical Strike Warning
C-HUMINT	Counter-Human Intelligence
CI	Counterintelligence
CIC	(1) Combat Information Center
	(2) Combined Interrogation Center
	(3) Counterintelligence Corps
CIFAX	Enciphered Facsimile
CIIC	Current Intelligence and Indications Center
CIK	Crypto-Ignition Key
CILOP	Conversion in Lieu of Procurement
CIMEX	Civil Military Exercise
C-IMINT	Counter-Imagery Intelligence
CINC	Commander-in-Chief
CINCCFC	Commander-in-Chief, Combined Forces Command, Korea
CINCCENT	Commander-in-Chief, Allied Forces Central Europe (NATO)
CINCCHAN	Commander-in-Chief, Channel
CINCEUR	Commander-in-Chief, U.S. Forces Europe
CINCLANT	Commander-in-Chief, Atlantic
CINCNORTH	Commander-in-Chief, Allied Forces Northern Europe (NATO)
CINCPAC	Commander-in-Chief, Pacific
CINCSOUTH	Commander-in-Chief, Southern Command
CINCUNC	Commander-in-Chief, United Nations Command, Korea
CINCUS AREUR	Commander-in-Chief, U.S. Army, Europe
CIP	(1) Consolidated Intelligence Program

	(2) Country Information Package
	(3) Critical Intelligence Parameter
CI Staff	Counterintelligence Staff
CIT	Counterintelligence Team
CITS	(U.S.) Central Command Imagery Transmission System
CJCS	Chairman, Joint Chiefs of Staff
CJTF	Commander, Joint Task Force
CLF	Commander Landing Force
CM	(1) Collection Management
	(2) Countermeasures
	(3) Memorandum by the Chairman, Joint Chiefs of Staff
CMAC	Contingency Maintenance Allocation Chart
CM&D	Collection Management and Dissemination
CMD	Command
CMEC	Captured Material Exploitation Center
CMO	(1) Civil Military Operations
	(2) Collection Management Office
CMT	Crisis Management Team
CO	(1) Commanding Officer
	(2) Company
COCKED PISTOL	(U.S. Exercise Defense Condition)
COCOM	Coordinating Committee
COFAPIII	Commissioned Officer Force Alignment Plan III
COHORT	Cohesion Operational Readiness Training
COIN	Counterinsurgency
COLLATERAL	(All national security information protected under the provisions of an Executive Order and for which special intelligence community compartmentation standards have not been formally established.)
COMINT	Communications Intelligence
COMJAM	Communications Jamming
COMJTF	Commander, Joint Task Force
COMM	Communication
COMMZ	Communications Zone

COMSEC	(1) Communications Security
	(2) Office of Communications Security
COMSSTOCS	Contingency Support Stocks
COMUSFK	Commander, U.S. Forces, Korea
COMUS FORCARIB	Commander, U.S. Forces, Caribbean
COMUSJ	Commander, U.S. Forces, Japan
CONPLAN	Contingency Plan
CONTIC	Continental Army Command Intelligence Center
CONUS	Continental United States
COOP	Contingency of Operations Plan
COP	Command Operation Post
COR	(1) Central Office of Record
	(2) Command Operationally Ready
CoS	Chief of Staff
COSCOM	Corps Support Command
CP	(1) Command Post
	(2) Contingency Planning
CPBS	Capabilities Programming and Budgeting System
CPE	Conventional Planning and Execution
CPX	Command Post Exercise
CR	Crisis Relocation
CRB	Contingency Reference Book
CRC	Control and Reporting Center
CRESTED EAGLE	(U.S. European Command Field Training Exercise)
CRYPTA	Cryptanalysis
CS	(1) Combat Support
	(2) Countersabotage
CSA	(1) Central Supplies Agency (of NATO)
	(2) Chief of Staff, Army
	(3) Cognizant Secure Authority
	(4) Corps Storage Area
CSAM	Chief of Staff, Army Memorandum
CSAR	Combat Search and Rescue
CSCE	Conference on Security and Cooperation in Europe
CSE	(1) Communications Security Establishment
	(2) Cryptologic Support Element
CSG	(1) Chairman's Staff Group
	(2) Combat Support Group
	(3) Cryptologic Support Group
C-SIGINT	Counter-Signals Intelligence
CSM	Command Sergeant Major
CSMO	Cryptologic Support to Military Operations
CSO	Composite Signals Organization
CSP	Crisis Staffing Procedures
CSR	Controlled Supply Rate
CSS	Combat Service Support
CST	Combat Support Training
CT	Counterterrorism
CTA	Central Technical Authority
CTG	Commander, Task Group
CTOC	Corps Tactical Operations Center
CTT	Common Task Test
CUCV	Commercial Utility and Cargo Vehicle
CUSRPG	Canadian-U.S. Regional Planning Group (NATO)
CVRT	Combat Vehicle (Reconnaissance, Tracked)
CW	(1) Carrier Wave
	(2) Chemical Warfare
	(3) Continuous Wave
CWI	Conventional Weapon Index
CY	Calendar Year
CZ	(1) Combat Zone
	(2) Convergent Zone

— D —

DA	Department of the Army
DACG/ AACG	Departure Airfield Control Group/Arrival Airfield Control Group
DAIPR	Department of the Army In-Process Review Programs
DAO	Division Ammunition Officer
DARCOM	Department of the Army Materiel Development and Readiness Command (now Army Materiel Command)
DASC	Direct Air Support Center
DAT	Direct Action Team
DCA	(1) Defense Communications Agency
	(2) Defensive Counter Air

DCPC	Direct Combat Probability Coding
DCPCP	Direct Combat Probability Coding Policy
DCSRDA	Deputy Chief of Staff for Research, Development, and Acquisition, Department of the Army Materiel Development and Readiness Command
DE	Damage Estimation
DECON	Decontamination
DEDAC	Deception and Denial Analysis Committee
DEFCON	(1) Defense Condition
	(2) Defense Readiness Condition
DEFSMAC	Defense Special Missile and Astronautics Center
DEN	Distant Early Warning
DEPEX	Deployment Exercise
DEPSECDEF	Deputy Secretary of Defense
DEROS	Date Eligible to Return from Overseas
DET	Detachment
DEW	Distant Early Warning
DF	Direction Finding
DG	Defense Guidance
DGZ	(1) Designated Ground Zero
	(2) Desired Ground Zero
DIA	Defense Intelligence Agency
DIGOB	Defense Intelligence Ground Order of Battle
DIN	Died in Hospital
DIOBS	Defense Intelligence Order of Battle System
DIRDIA	Director, Defense Intelligence Agency
DIRNSA/ CHCSS	Director, National Security Agency/Chief, Central Security Service
DIS	Defense Investigative Service
DISCOM	Division Support Command
DISPLAY	(NATO Southern Flank Exercise DETERMINATION)
DISUM	Daily Intelligence Summary
DIV	Division
DJS	Director, Joint Staff
DJSM	Director, Joint Staff Memorandum
DLA	Defense Logistics Agency

DLIC	Detachment Left in Contact
DMA	Defense Mapping Agency
DMZ	Demilitarized Zone
DNA	Defense Nuclear Agency
DOA	Date of Arrival
DOB	(1) Date of Birth
	(2) Depth of Burst
DOD	(1) Date of Death
	(2) Date of Departure
	(3) Department of Defense
DODIIS	Department of Defense Intelligence Information System
DOI	(1) Date of Information
	(2) Duration of Illumination
DOR	Date of Rank
DOS	Date of Separation
DOW	Died of Wounds
DPI	Desired Point of Impact
DPOB	Date, Place of Birth
DROS	Date Returned from Overseas
DRU	Direct Reporting Unit
DS	Direct Support
DSA	(1) Defense Supply Agency
	(2) Direct Service Activities (Signals Intelligence)
	(3) Directed Search Area
	(4) Division Support Area
DSARC	Defense Systems Acquisition Review Council
DSE	Direct Support Element
DSG	Designated
DSS	Direct Support System
DSU	Direct Support Unit
DTED	Digital Terrain Elevation Data
DTG	Date-Time Group
DTOC	Division Tactical Operations Center
DZ	Drop Zone
DZ/LZ/RZ	Drop/Landing/Recovery Zone
DZS	Drop Zone Study

— E —

EA	Emergency Action(s)
EAC	Echelon Above Corps
EACIC	Echelon Above Corps Intelligence Center

EAD	Echelon Above Division
E&E	Evasion and Escape
EAP	(1) Emergency Action Plan
	(2) Emergency Action Procedure(s)
EASTLANT	Eastern Atlantic Command
ECCM	Electronic Counter-Countermeasures
ECG	Emergency Coordination Group
ECM	Electronic Countermeasures
E-DAY	(Start Day of an Exercise)
E&E	Escape and Evasion
EECT	End Evening Civil Twilight
EEFI	Essential Elements of Friendly Information
EEI	Essential Elements of Information
EENT	End Evening Nautical Twilight
EES	Emergency Evacuation Study
EFTO	Encrypted for Transmission Only
EI	Effectiveness Index
ELECTRO-OPINT	Electro-Optical Intelligence
ELINT	Electronic Intelligence
ELOS	Extended Line of Sight
ELSEC	Electronic Security
EM	(1) Electromagnetic
	(2) Enlisted Man
EMC	Electromagnetic Capability
EMCON	Emission Control
EMGTN	Equivalent Megatonnage
EMI	Electromagnetic Interference
EML	Environmental and Morale Leave
EMP	Electromagnetic Pulse
EMR	Electromagnetic Reconnaissance
EMSEC	(1) Emanations Security
	(2) Emissions Security
EMT	Equivalent Megatonnage
EMV	Electromagnetic Vulnerability
ENDEX	End Date of Exercise
EO	(1) Electro-optics
	(2) Executive Order
EOB	Electronic Order of Battle
EOD	Explosive Ordinance Disposal
EPM	End Point Marker
EPW	Enemy Prisoner of War
ER	(1) Electronic Reconnaissance
	(2) Enhanced Radiation

ERA	Extended Range Ammunition
ERADCOM	Electronic Research and Development Command
ERD/EDD	Equipment Requirements Data/ Equipment Density Data
ERP	Effective Power (Radiated)
ERPSL	Essential Repair Parts Stockage List
ERW	Enhanced Radiation Weapon
ES	Exposed Site
ESC	Equipment Serviceability Criteria
ESM	Electronic Warfare Support Measures
ETA	(1) Equivalent Target Area
	(2) Estimated Time of Arrival
ETC	Estimated Time of Completion
ETD	Estimated Time of Departure
ETI	Estimated Time of Impact
ETM	Extension Training Materials
ETS	Expiration Term of Service
ETUT	Enhanced Tactical User Terminal
EUCOM	European Command
EUSA	Eighth United States Army, Korea
EVAC	Evacuation
EVS	Electronic Visual Communications
EW	(1) Early Warning
	(2) Electronic Warfare
EWC	Electronic Warfare Center
EW/GCI	Early Warning/Ground Controlled Intercept
EWIR	Electronic Warfare Integrated Reprogramming
EXOPLAN	Exercise Operations Plan
EXPLAN	Exercise Plan
EXSUM	Executive Summary
EZ	Extraction Zone

— F —

FA	Field Artillery
FAAR	Forward Area Alerting Radar
FAASV	Field Artillery Ammunition Support Vehicle
FAC	Forward Air Controller
FADE OUT	(U.S. Exercise Defense Condition)

FAE	Fuel Air Explosive
FAI	Fuel Air Incendiary Concussion Bomb
FAM	Full Army Mobilization War Reserves
FAMP	Foreign Army Materiel Production
FAO	Foreign Area Officer
FARP	Forward Arming and Refueling Point
FARRP	Forward Area Rearming and Refueling Point
FASC	Forward Area Support Center
FAST	Forward Area Support Team
FAST PACE	(U.S. Exercise Defense Condition)
FBS	Forward-Based Systems
FC	Fire Control
FCI	Foreign Counterintelligence
FCL	Final Coordination Line
FCX	Fire Coordination Exercise
FCZ	Forward Combat Zone
FDC	Fire Direction Center
FEBA	Forward Edge of the Battle Area
FEZ	Fighter Engagement Zone
FFA	Free-Fire Area
FFAC	Forward-Forward Air Controller
FI	Foreign Intelligence
FIS	Foreign Instrumentation Signals
FISINT	Foreign Instrumentation Signals Intelligence
FIST	Fire Support Team
FISTV	Fire Support Team Vehicle
FLINTLOCK	(European Special Forces Operations Exercise)
FLIR	Forward-Looking Infrared System
FLO	Fighter Liaison Officer
FLOT	Forward Line of Own Troops
FLR	Forward-Looking Radar
FM	(1) Field Manual
	(2) Foreign Materiel
	(3) Frequency Modulation
FMA	Foreign Materiel Acquisition
FME	Foreign Materiel Acquisition
FNU	First Name Unknown
FO	Forward Observer
FOB	Forward Operational Base
FOBS	Fractional Orbital Bombardment System

FOC	(1) Final Operational Capabilities
	(2) Full Operational Capability
FOD	Foreign Object Damage
FOP	Forward Observation Post
FORGE	Force Generation
FORMAT	Foreign Materiel
FORSCOM	(U.S. Armed) Forces Command
FORSIC	(Army) Forces Command Intelligence Center
FORSIG	(Army) Forces Command Intelligence Group
FORSTAT	Force Status and Identity Report
FOUO	For Official Use Only
FOV	Field of Vision
FP	Fire Position
FPE	Force Planning Estimate
FPF	Final Protective Fire
FPL	Fire Protective Line
FRAGO	Fragmentary Order
FRCOA	Friendly Courses of Action
FRN	Force Requirements Number
FSCC	Fire Support Coordination Center
FSCL	Fire Support Coordination Line
FSCOORD	Fire Support Coordinator
FSD	(1) Field Support Division
	(2) Frequency Spectrum Designation
FSE	Fire Support Element
FSHB	Fallout Safe Height Burst
FSMA	Fire Support Mission Area
FSO	Fire Support Officer
FSOP	Field Standing Operating Procedure
FSTC	Foreign Science and Technology Center (U.S. Army)
FSV	Fire Support Vehicle
FTC	Fast Time Constant (Electronic Counter-Countermeasures)
FTI	Fixed Target Indicator
FTS	Full-time Support
FTX	Field Training Exercise
FUWOB	Forward Unconventional Warfare Operations Base
FV	Fighting Vehicle
FWVP	Fallout Wind Vector Plot
FX	Field Exercise
FY	Fiscal Year
FYDP	Five-Year Defense Program
FYI	For Your Information

— G —

G2	(Army Intelligence)
G3	(Army Operations)
GA	Ground Attack
GAD	Guards Artillery Division
GADT	Ground/Air Defense Threat
GALLANT KNIGHT	(Central Command Exercise)
GAMO	Ground and Amphibious Military Operations
GBL	Ground-Based Laser
GBU	Guided Bomb Unit
GCA	Ground-Controlled Approach
GCE	Ground Combat Element
GCI	Ground Controlled Intercept
GCP	Ground Controlled Processor
GD	Guard
GDS	General Declassification Schedule
GENSER	General Service (Communications)
GEOREF	(A worldwide position reference system that may be applied to any map or chart graduated in latitude and longitude regardless of projection.)
GEP	Ground Entry Point
GIC	Garbarit International de Chargement (International Loading Gauge)
GL	Grenade Launcher
GLCM	Ground-Launched Cruise Missile
GLLD	(U.S.) Ground Laser Locator Designator (For Copperhead)
GLO	Ground Liaison Officer
GM	Guided Missile
GMF	Ground Mobile Forces
GMRD	Guards Motorized Rifle Division (Soviet)
GMT	Greenwich Mean Time
GND	Ground
GOB	Ground Order of Battle
GOR	General Operational Requirement
GP	(1) General Purpose (2) Group
GPF	General Purpose Forces

GPH	Gallons Per Hour
GPS	Global Positioning System
GROFIS	Ground Forces Intelligence Study
GRREG	Graves Registration
GS	(1) General Schedule (2) General Service (3) General Staff (4) General Support (5) Geological Survey
GSE	Ground Support Equipment
GSF	(1) Ground Support Fighter (2) Group of Soviet Forces
GSP	General Strike Plan
GSR	(1) General Support Reinforcing (2) Ground Surveillance Radar
GSRS	(U.S.) General Support Rocket System
GSSB	General Supply Support Base
GVLLD	Ground/Vehicle Laser Locator Designator
GW	Guided Weapon
GWC	Global Weather Control
GWIP	Global Weather Intercept System
GZ	Ground Zero

— H —

HAA	Helicopter Alighting Area
HAB	(1) High Airburst (2) High Altitude Bombing (3) High Altitude Burst
HALO	High Altitude Low Opening
HARV	Harassment Vehicle (Drone)
HE	High Explosive
HEAT	High-Explosive Antitank
HEI	High-Explosive Incendiary
HEL	High-Energy Laser
HELW	High-Energy Laser Weapons
HEP	High-Explosive Plastic
HERT	Headquarters Emergency Relocation Team
HET	Heavy Equipment Transporter
HF	High Frequency
HF/DF	High Frequency/Direction Finding
HH&S	Headquarters and Headquarters Service

HHC	Headquarters and Headquarters Company
HHD	Headquarters and Headquarters Detachment
HHOC	Headquarters, Headquarters and Operations Company
HHT	Headquarters and Headquarters Troop
HHW	Higher High Water
HIDACZ	High Density Airspace Control Zone
HIMAD	High-to-Medium Altitude Air Defense
HJ	HONEST JOHN (U.S. Surface-to-Surface Rocket)
HLA/DZ	Helicopter Landing Area/Drop Zone
HLA/DZS	Helicopter Landing Area/Drop Zone Study
HLW	Higher Low Water
HLZ	Helicopter Landing Zone
HMF	Handbook of Military Forces
HMMWV	High Mobility, Multipurpose, Wheeled Vehicle
HN	Host Nation
HNS	Host Nation Support
HOB	Height of Burst
HOJ	Home on Jam
HOTPHOTO REP	Hot Photographic Interpretation Report
HOTSIT	Hot Situation Message
HP	(1) Headquarters Pamphlet
	(2) Horsepower
HPT	High Payoff Target
HQ	Headquarters
HQDA	Headquarters, Department of the Army
HQJTF	Headquarters, Joint Task Force
HRR	High Resolution Radar
H&S	Headquarters and Service
HTF	How to Fight
HTKP	Hard Target Kill Potential
HTLD	High Technology Light Division
HUMINT	Human Intelligence
HVAP	High Velocity Armor Piercing
HVAPFSDS	High Velocity, Armor-Piercing Fin-Stabilized Discarding Sabot
HVF	Highly Volatile Fuel
HVT	High Value Target
HW	High Water

HWY	Highway
HZ	Hertz

— I —

IA	Imagery Analysis
IAGC	Instantaneous Automatic Gain Control
IAMS	Individual Aerial Mobility System
I & E	Interrogation and Exploitation
I & W	Indications and Warning
IASSA	Intelligence and Security Command Automated Systems Support Activity
IAW	In Accordance With
IBI	Interview-Oriented Background Investigation
IC	Intelligence Collection
ICAF	Industrial College of the Armed Forces
ICBM	Intercontinental Ballistic Missile
ICC	Integrated Communications Center
ICD	Imitative Communications Deception
ICF	Intelligence Collection Flight
ICM	(1) Improved Conventional Munition(s)
	(2) Intelligence Collection Management
ICM/MM	Intelligence Collection Management/ Mission Management
ICOD	Intelligence Cut-Off Date
ICPR	Initial Common Point of Reference
ICR	Intelligence Collection Requirement
ICTF	Interagency Crisis Task Force
ICV	Infantry Combat Vehicle
ID	(1) Identification
	(2) Infantry Division
IDAD	Internal Defense and Development
IDT	Inactive Duty Training
IE	Intelligence Estimate
IED	Imitative Electronic Deception
IET	Initial Entry Training
IEW	Intelligence and Electronic Warfare
IFF	Identification, Friend or Foe

IFFN	Identification, Friend or Foe or Neutral
IFV	Infantry Fighting Vehicle
IG	Inspector General
IHE	Insensitive High Explosive
II	(1) Imagery Interpretation
	(2) Imagery Interpreter
IIC	Imagery Interpretation Center
IICT	Interagency Intelligence Committee on Terrorism
IIG	Imagery Intelligence Group
IIPD/ITAC	Army Imagery Intelligence Production Division
IIR	Intelligence Information Report
IMA	Individual Mobilization Augmentee
IMC	Instrument Meteorological Conditions
IMINT	Imagery Intelligence
INSCOM	Intelligence and Security Command (U.S. Army)
INSIG	Army Intelligence and Security Command Intelligence Group
INST	Instruction
INTEL	Intelligence
INTG	Interrogation
INTREP	Intelligence Report
INTSUM	Intelligence Summary
IO	Intelligence Officer
IOC	Initial Operating Capability
IPB	Intelligence Preparation of the Battlefield
IPIR	Initial Programmed Interpretation Report
IPR	Intelligence Production Requirement
IPS	Intelligence Production Section
IPSP	Intelligence Priorities for Strategic Planning
IPW	Prisoner of War Interrogation
IPWIC	Interagency Prisoner of War Ad Hoc Committee
IR	(1) Induced Radiation
	(2) Information Requirements
	(3) Infrared
	(4) Initial Radiation
	(5) Intelligence Report
	(6) Intelligence Requirement
IRA	Intelligence-Related Activities
IRBM	Intermediate-Range Ballistic Missile
IRCM	Infrared Countermeasures
IRINT	Infrared Intelligence
IROP	Infrared Optical Intelligence
ISD	Information Services Division (Foreign Science and Technology Center, U.S. Army)
ITAC	(1) Intelligence and Threat Analysis Center (U.S. Army)
	(2) International Threat Analysis Center
	(3) Intelligence Tracking Analysis and Correlation
ITACIES	Interim Tactical Imagery Exploitation System (U.S. Army)
ITAD/ITAC	(Army) Intelligence and Threat Analysis Detachment
ITEP	(1) Individual Training Evaluation Program
	(2) Integrated Threat Evaluation Program
	(3) Interim Tactical Electronic Intelligence Processor (U.S. Army)
ITF	Intelligence Task Force
ITIC-PAC	Intelligence and Security Command Theater Intelligence Center—Pacific
ITP	(1) Individual Training Plan
	(2) Intelligence Town Plan
ITPP	Individual Training Plan Proposal
ITT	Interrogator Translator Team
ITV	Improved Tube-Launcehd, Optically Tracked, Wire-Guided (Missile) Vehicle

—J—

JAAT	Joint Air Attack Team
JAG	Judge Advocate General
JAN	Joint Army, Navy
JANAPs	Joint Army-Navy-Air Force Publications
JATF	Joint Amphibious Task Force
JATO	Jet-Assisted Takeoff
JCRC	Joint Casualty Resolution Center
JCS	Joint Chiefs of Staff

JDA	Joint Deployment Agency
JDC	Joint Deployment Community
JDS	Joint Deployment System
JFM	Joint Force Memorandum (Replaced by Joint Program Assesment Memorandum)
JIEP	Joint Intelligence Estimate for Planning
JIF	Joint Interrogation Facilities
JILE	Joint Intelligence Liaison Element
JINTACCS	Joint Interoperability Tactical Command and Control System
JIO	Joint Intelligence Organization
JLRSA	Joint Long-Range Strategic Appraisal
JLRSS	Joint Long-Range Strategic Study
JMA	Joint Mobilization Augmentation
JMEM	Joint Munitions Effectiveness Manual
JMP	Joint Manpower Program
JOA	Joint Operations Area
JOC	Joint Operations Center
JOG	Joint Operations Graphic
JOIA	Joint Operational Intelligence Agency
Joint STARS	Joint Surveillance and Target Attack Radar System
JOPS	Joint Operational Planning System
JPAM	Joint Program Assessment Memorandum
JS	Joint Staff
JSAM	Joint Security Assistance Memorandum
JSCP	Joint Strategic Capabilities Plan
J-SEAD	Joint Suppression of Enemy Air Defenses
JSOP	Joint Strategic Objectives Plan
JSPD	Joint Strategic Planning Document
JSPDSA	Joint Strategic Planning Document Supporting Analysis
JSPS	Joint Strategic Planning System
JSTPS	Joint Strategic Target Planning Staff
JSW	Directorate for Indications and Warning (DIA)
JTA	Joint Table of Allowances

JTD	Joint Table of Distribution (Manning Authorization for a Joint Organization)
JTENS	Joint Service Tactical Exploitation of National Systems
JTF	Joint Task Force
JTFHQ	Joint Task Force Headquarters
JTFP	Joint Tactical Fusion Program
JTIDS	Joint Tactical Information Distribution System
JTL	Joint Target List
JTX	Joint Training Exercise
JUWC	Joint Unconventional Warfare Command
JUWTF	Joint Unconventional Warfare Task Force

— K —

KHZ	Kilohertz
KIA	Killed in Action
KIA-BNR	Killed in Action-Body Not Recovered
KILOD	Killed in the Line of Duty
KIQ	Key Intelligence Questions
KIR	Key Intelligence Requirements
KM	Kilometer
KM/HR	Kilometers Per Hour
KN	Knot
KP	Kitchen Police
KPH	Kilometers Per Hour
KT	(1) Kiloton (2) Knot
KTAS	Knots True Air Speed
KW	Kilowatt
KWH	Kilowatt Hours

— L —

LAA	Limited Access Authorization
LANTCOM	Atlantic Command
LAPES	Low-Altitude Parachute Extraction System
LARS	Light Artillery Rocket System
LASER	Light Amplification by Stimulated Emission of Radiation
LASINT	Laser Intelligence

LASP	Low-Altitude Surveillance Platform	LW	Low Water
LAW	Light Antitank Weapon	LZ	Landing Zone
LC	Line of Contact		
LCC	Land Component Commander		

— **M** —

LD	(1) Line of Departure		
	(2) Linear Disposition	M	(1) Mach
LD/LC	Line of Departure/Line of Contact		(2) Meter
LE	Linear Error	MAAG	Military Assistance Advisory Group
LF	(1) Launch Facility	MAC	Military Airlift Command
	(2) Low Frequency	MACOM	(1) Major Army Command
LFX	Live Fire Exercise		(2) Major Command
LGB	Laser-Guided Bomb	MAD	(1) Magnetic Anomaly Detector
LHW	Lower High Water		(2) Mutual Assured Destruction
LIC	Low-Intensity Conflict	MAF	Marine Amphibious Force
LIMDIS	Limited Distribution	MAG	(1) Marine Airlift Group
LL	(1) Landline		(2) Military Advisory Group
	(2) Latent Lethality		(3) Military Assistance Group
	(3) Light Line	MAGIC	Maritime Air Ground Intelligence Cell
LLLTV	Low Light Level Television	MAGIIC	Mobile Army Ground Imagery Interpretation Center
LLW	Lower Low Water		
LNO	Limited Nuclear Option	MAGIS	Marine Air-Ground Intelligence System
LNU	Last Name Unknown		
LO	(1) Law and Order	MAGTF	Marine Air-Ground Task Force
	(2) Liaison Officer	MAINT	Maintenance
	(3) Low Observables	MAJ	Major
LOB	Line of Bearing	MAJCOM	Major Command
LOC	Line of Communication	M&A	Management and Analysis
LOI	Letter of Instruction	MANPAD	Man Portable Air Defense
LOS	Line of Sight	MANPADS	Man Portable Air Defense System
LOTs	Logistics Over-the-Shore (Operations)		
LOW	(1) Launch on Warning	MAO	Major Attack Option
	(2) Law of War	MAP	(1) Military Assistance Plan
LP	Listening Post		(2) Military Assistance Program
LP/OPs	Listening Posts/Observation Posts	MARDIS	Modernized Army Research and Development Information System
LRR	Long-Range Reconnaissance		
LRRP	Long-Range Reconnaissance Patrol	MARS	Military Affiliate Radio System
		MASH	Mobile Army Surgical Hospital
LRSP	Long-Range Surveillance Plan	MASINT	Measurement and Signature Intelligence
LRTNF	Long-Range Theater Nuclear Force		
		MATSYM	Material Symbol
LSD	(1) Landing Ship Dock	MBA	Main Battle Area
	(2) Least Separation Distance	MBFR	Mutual and Balanced Force Reduction
LTC	Lieutenant Colonel (Army)		
LUA	Launch Under Attack	MBO	Management by Objectives
LVTE-1	Landing Vehicle, Tracked, Engineer, Model 1	MBT	Main Battle Tank

MC	(1) Military Committee
	(2) Military Construction (Appropriation)
	(3) Multichannel
MCC	(1) Mobile Command Center
	(2) Movement Control Center
MCD	Manipulative Communications Deception
MCE	Maximum Credible Event
MCG	Magneto Cumulative Generator
MCHAN	Multichannel
MCN	Mission Control Number
MCP	Mobile Command Post
MCR	Military Command Region
MCRB	Military Costing Review Board
MCSF	Mobile Cryptologic Support Facility
MD	Military District
MDCI	Multidisciplinary Counterintelligence
MDLX	Military Demarcation Line Extended
MDSP	Master Deployment Security Plan
MDW	Military District of Washington
MECH	(1) Mechanical
	(2) Mechanized
MECH MAINT	Mechanical Maintenance
MED	Manipulative Electronic Deception
MEDEVAC	Medical Evacuation
MEDINT	Medical Intelligence
MEECN	Minimum Essential Emergency Communications Network
MEMO	(1) Mission-Essential Maintenance Only
	(2) Mission-Essential Maintenance Operation
MENS	(1) Mission Element Needs Statement
	(2) Mission Essential Needs Statement
MER	Maximum Effective Range
MERADCOM	Mobile Equipment Research and Development Command (U.S. Army)
MERIT	Military Exploitation of Reconnaissance and Intelligence Technology
MERPL	Mission-Essential Repair-Parts List
METL	Mission Essential Task List

METT-T	Mission, Enemy, Terrain, Troops, and Time Available
MEZ	Missile Engagement Zone
MF	Medium Frequency
MFP	Major Force Program
MFL	Master Force List
MFR	(1) Memorandum for the Record
	(2) Mutual Force Reduction
MG	Machine Gun
MGID	Military Geographic Information and Documentation
MGS	Mission Ground Station
MHD	Magnetohydrodynamics
MHE	Mechanized Handling Equipment
MHW(N)(S)	Mean High Water (Nears) (Springs)
MHZ	Megahertz
MI	(1) Mechanized Infantry
	(2) Military Intelligence
MIA	(1) Missile Intelligence Agency
	(2) Missing in Action
MICOM	Missile Command (U.S. Army)
MICV	Mechanized Infantry Combat Vehicle
MID	(1) Military Intelligence Detachment
	(2) Military Intelligence Division
MIG	(1) Military Intelligence Group
	(2) Military Intelligence Guide
MIIA	Medical Intelligence Information Agency (now AFMIC)
MIIDS	Military Intelligence Integrated Data System
MIJI	Meaconing, Intrusion, Jamming, and Interference
MILAN	(International Antitank Guided-Missile System)
MILES	Multiple Integrated Laser Engagement System
MILGP	Military Group
MILPO	Military Personnel Office
MILSAT(COM)	Military Satellite (Communications)
MILSTAR	(U.S. Military Communications Satellite Program)
MILSTRIP	Military Standard Requisitioning and Issue Procedure
MILSTAMP	Military Standard Transportation and Movement Procedures

MIPR	Military Interdepartmental Purchase
MIRV	Multiple Independently Targetable Reentry Vehicle
MIS	(1) Management Information System
	(2) Military Intelligence Service
	(3) Military Intelligence Summary
MISREP	Mission Report
MIT	Mobile Interrogation Team
MITS	Monthly Intelligence Summary (Army Intelligence and Threat Analysis Detachment)
MLR	Main Line of Resistance
MLRS	Multiple Launch Rocket System
MMC	Materiel Management Center
MNU	Middle Name Unknown
MO	Morale Operations
MOA	Memorandum of Agreement
MOBPOI	Mobilization Programs of Instruction
MOBTDA	Mobilization Table of Distribution and Allowances
MOP	Memorandum of Policy
MOPP	Mission-Oriented Protective Posture
MOS	Military Occupational Specialty
MOU	Memorandum of Understanding
MOUT	Military Operations on Urbanized Terrain
MP	Military Police
MPD	Maximum Permissible Dose
MPL	Mandatory Parts List
MPRC	Multipurpose Range Complex
MR	Motorized Rifle
MRB	Motorized Rifle Battalion
MRBM	Medium-Range Ballistic Missile
MRC	(1) Military Region Command
	(2) Motorized Rifle Company
	(3) Movement Report Center
MRD	Motorized Rifle Division
MRDC	Missile Research and Development Command (U.S. Army)
MRE	Meal Ready to Eat
MRF	Minimum Risk Force
MRL	Multiple Rocket Launcher
MRLOGAEUR	Minimum Required Logistics Augmentation Europe
MRLS	Multiple Rocket Launcher System
MRMN	Military Road Maneuver Network
MRN	Military Road Network
MRP	Motorized Rifle Platoon
MRR	(1) Minimum Risk Routes
	(2) Motorized Rifle Regiment
MRR/LLTR	Minimum Risk Routes/Low-Level Transit Routes
MRS	(1) Motorized Rifle Squad
	(2) Movement and Reinforcement Study
MRV	(1) Medium Recovery Vehicle
	(2) Multiple Reentry Vehicle
MSA	Military Strength Assessment
MSC	Military Sealift Command
MSD	Minimum Safe Distance
MSEL	Master Scenario Events List
MSIC	Missile and Space Intelligence Center (Huntsville, Alabama)
MSL	Missile
MSN	Mission
MSN CON	Mission Control
MSR	(1) Main Supply Route
	(2) Missile Site Radar
MST	(1) Maintenance Support Team
	(2) Mutual Security Treaty
MT	(1) Megaton
	(2) Metric Ton
	(3) Motor Transport
MTBF	Mean Time Between Failures
MTF	Medical Treatment Facility
MTI	Moving Target Indicators
MTL	Mean Tide Level
MT-LB	(Soviet Tracked Vehicle)
MTMC	Military Traffic Management Command
MTOE	Modified Table of Organization and Equipment
MTR	Motorized
MTT	(1) Military Training Team
	(2) Mobile Training Team
MTTR	Mean Time to Repair
MTZ	Motorized Infantry
MUTA	Multiple Unit Training Assembly
MW/AA	Missile Warning/Attack Assessment
MWL	Mean Water Level

— N —

N/A	Nonapplicable
NAA	North Atlantic Alliance
NAC	(1) National Agency Check
	(2) No Apparent Change
	(3) North Atlantic Council (NATO)
NADGE	North Atlantic Treaty Organization Air Defense Ground Environment
NAFA	Nonappropriated Fund Activity
NAI	Named Areas of Interest
NATO	North Atlantic Treaty Organization
NBC	Nuclear/Biological/ Chemical
NBCWRS	Nuclear/Biological/Chemical Warning and Reporting System
NC	No Change
NCA	National Command Authority
NCO	Noncommissioned Officer
NCOA	(1) Noncommissioned Officers' Academy
	(2) Noncommissioned Officers' Association
NCOES	Noncommissioned Officer Education System
NCOIC	Noncommissioned Officer in Charge
NCP	Nuclear Contingency Plan
NCS	Net Control Station
NDA	National Defense Area
NDU	National Defense University
NEA	Northeast Asia
NEACP	National Emergency Airborne Command Post
NEMVAC/ NISH	Noncombatant Emergency and Evacuation Intelligence Support Handbook
NEO	Noncombatant Evacuation Operation
NFA	No-Fire Area
NFI	(1) No Further Information
	(2) Not Further Identified
NFIP	National Foreign Intelligence Program
NG	National Guard
NICP	National Inventory Control Point
NLT	Not Later Than
NMCC	National Military Command Center
NMCM	Not Mission Capable Maintenance
NMCS	(1) National Military Command System
	(2) Not Mission Capable Supply
NMI	No Middle Initial
NMIC	National Military Intelligence Center
NMN	No Middle Name
NMP	National Maintenance Point
NMS	New Manning System
NO	Number
NOD	Night Observation Device
NOFORN	Not Releasable to Foreign Nationals
NOIWON	National Operations and Intelligence Watch Officers' Net
NORM	Not Operationally Ready, Maintenance
NORTHAG	Northern Army Group
NPE	Nuclear Planning and Execution
NRT	Near Real Time
NSA	National Security Agency
NSWP	Non-Soviet Warsaw Pact
NTC	National Training Center
NTI	National Tactical Interface
NTM	National Technical Means
NUCINT	Nuclear Intelligence
NUDET	(1) Nuclear Detection
	(2) Nuclear Detonation
NW	Nuclear Warfare
NWC	National War College
NWLE	Nuclear Weapons Logistic Element

— O —

O/A	On or About
OA	(Directorate for Operations and Attaches, Defense Intelligence Agency)
OAG	Operations Advisory Group
O&M	Operation and Maintenance
O and M	Operation and Maintenance (Appropriation)

O and M, A	Operation and Maintenance (Army)
OAS	(1) Offensive Air Support
	(2) Officer Accession System
OB	Order-of-Battle
OBE	Overtaken by Events
OBJ	Objective
OBSN	Observation
OBSUM	Order of Battle Summary
OCONUS	Outside Continental United States
OCR	Optical Character Reader
OCS	Officer Candidate School
ODCSOPS	Deputy Chief of Staff for Operations, Plans, Headquarters, Department of the Army
ODJS	Office of the Director, Joint Staff
OEG	Operational Exposure Guide
OHD	Over-the-Horizon Detection Radar
OHD-B	Over-the-Horizon Radar Backscatter
OIC	Officer in Charge
OIR	(1) Operational Intelligence Requirement
	(2) Other Intelligence Requirements
OJCS	Organization of the Joint Chiefs of Staff
OJT	On-the-Job Training
OLC	Oak Leaf Cluster
OMPF	Official Military Personnel File
OP	(1) Observation Post
	(2) Operations
	(3) Outpost
OPCON	Operational Control
OPFOR	Opposing Forces
OPINTEL	Operational Intelligence
OPLAN	Operations Plan
OP/LP	Observation Post/Listening Post
OPORD or	
OPORDER	Operation(al) Order
OPR	Office of Primary Responsibility
OPS	(1) Operational Project Stocks
	(2) Operations
OPSEC	Operation(al) Security
OPTEVFOR	Operational Test and Evaluation Force
OPTINT	Optical Intelligence
ORE	Operational Readiness Evaluation

ORF	Operational Readiness Float
ORI	Operational Readiness Inspection
ORP	Objective Rally Point
ORT	Operational Readiness Training
ORTT	Operational Readiness Training Test
OSUT	One-station Unit Training
OTEA	Operational Test and Evaluation Agency (U.S. Army)
OTH	Over-the-Horizon
OTH-R	Over-the-Horizon-Radar
OTH-T	Over-the-Horizon-Targeting
OT Line	Observer-Target Line
OUO	Official Use Only
OWRMS	Other War Reserve Materiel Stocks

— P —

PAL	Permissive Action Link
PAMIS	Psychological Operations Automated Management Information System
P&A	Personnel and Administrative
PAO	Public Affairs Officer
PARMIS	Peacetime Airborne Reconnaissance Management Information System
PARPRO	Peacetime Airborne Reconnaissance Program
PB	Particle Beam
PBO	Property Book Officer
PBW	Particle Beam Weapon
PCA	Point of Closest Approach
PCM	Pulse Code Modulation
PCS	Permanent Change of Station
PD	(1) Passive Detection
	(2) Point of Departure
	(3) Priority Designator
	(4) Probability of Damage
	(5) Pulse Duration
PDMS	Point Defense Missile Systems
PEAS	Psychological Operations Effectiveness Analysis Subsystem
PED	Promotion Eligibility Date
PEH	Probable Error in Height
PERINTSUM	Periodic Intelligence Summary

PERS	Personnel
PESM	Passive Electronic Support Measures
PFADS	Psychological Operations Foreign Area Data Sub-system
PFOD	Presumptive Finding of Death
PGM	Precision-Guided Munitions
PHOTINT	Photographic Intelligence
PI	(1) Photographic Interpretation
	(2) Photographic Interpreter
PKO	Peace-Keeping Operation
PL	Phase Line
PLA	Plain-Language Address
PLRS	Position Locating and Reporting System
PLSS	(U.S.) Precision Location Strike System
PLT	Platoon
PM	(1) Post Meridian (After Noon)
	(2) Preventive Maintenance
	(3) Preventive Medicine
	(4) Prime Mover
	(5) Provost Marshal
PMOS	Primary Military Occupational Specialty
PMR	Primary Mission Readiness
PNIO	Priority National Intelligence Objective
PNL	Prescribed Nuclear Load
POB	Place of Birth
POC	(1) Point of contact
	(2) Program of Cooperation
POD	Port of Debarkation
POL	Petroleum, Oils, and Lubricants
POMCUS	Prepositioned Organizational Materiel Configured in Unit Sets
POTUS	President of the United States
POV	Privately Owned Vehicle
POW	Prisoner of War
PP	Proficiency Pay
PPB	Planning, Programming, and Budgeting
PPBS	Planning, Programming, and Budgeting System
PPG	Planning and Programming Guidance (Replaced by the Consolidated Guidance)
PPGM	Planning and Programming Guidance Memorandum
PPI	Pulse Position Indicator

PQT	Professional Qualification Test
PR	Periodic Reinvestigation
PRF	Pulse Repetition Frequency
PRI	Pulse Repetition Interval
PRIMOB	Priority Mobilization War Reserves
PSI	Pounds Per Square Inch
PSP	Pierced Steel Planking
PSS	Personnel Services Support
PSYOP	Psychological Operations
PSYOPGP	Psychological Operations Group
PTL	Primary Target Line
PUP	Pop-up Point (Army Aviation)
PV	Physical Vulnerability
PVDS	Physical Vulnerability Data Sheets
PW	(1) Prisoner(s) of War
	(2) Pulse Width
PW/CI/DET	Prisoners of War/Civilian Internees/Detainees
PWRMS	Prepositioned War Materiel Stocks
PWRS	Prepositioned War Reserve Stock
PX	Post Exchange
PY	Program Year
PZ	Pickup Zone

— Q —

Q&A	Question and Answer
QC	Quality Control
QM	Quartermaster
QPQ	Quid Pro Quo
Q/R	Query/Response
QRC	Quick Reaction Capability
QRG	Quick Response Graphic
QRR	Quick Reaction Requirement
QRT	Quick Reaction Task
QSR	Quick Strike Reconnaissance
QSS	Quick Supply Store
QUICKFIX	(Airborne HF/VHF intercept direction finding and jamming system.)
QUICKLOOK	(Airborne noncommunications emitter location and identification systems.)

— R —

R	(1) Reinforcing
	(2) River
RA	(1) Regular Army
	(2) Restricted Area
RABFAC	Radar Beacon Forward Air Controller
RACO	Rear Area Combat Operations
RAD	Radiation Absorbed Dose
RADAR	Radio Detection and Range
RADAREXREP	Radar Exploitation Report
RADC	Rome Air Development Center
RADCOM	Radio Communications
RADINT	Radar Intelligence
RADREL	Radio Relay
RAG	(1) Regimental Artillery Group
	(2) River Assault Group
RAIDS	Rapid Access Imagery Dissemination System
RAM	(1) Radar Absorbent Materials
	(2) Random Access Memory
	(3) Rolling Airframe Missile
R&C	Review and Comment
R&D	Research and Development
R&R	Rest and Recuperation
RAOC	Rear Area Operations Center
RAP	(1) Rear Area Protection
	(2) Remedial Action Projects
	(3) Rocket-Assisted Projectile
RAPLN	Regular Army Promotion List Number
RAS	Rear Area Security
RATT	Radio Teletypewriter/Teleprinter
RB	Rear Battle
RB/ER	Reduced Blast/Enhanced Radiation
RC	(1) Radio-Controlled
	(2) Required Capability
	(3) Reserve Component
RCA	Riot Control Agent
RCC	Regional Control Center
RCN	Reconnaissance
RCS	Radar Cross Section
RCV	Receive Only Station
RCZ	Rear Combat Zone
RD	(1) Radius of Damage
	(2) Restricted Data
RDA	Research, Development, Acquisition

RDC	Rapid Deployment Capability
RDF	(1) Radio Direction Finder(ing)
	(2) Rapid Deployment Force
RDFDB	Radio Direction Finding Data Base
RDJTF	Rapid Deployment Joint Task Force
RDT&E	Research, Development, Test, and Evaluation
REALTRAIN	Realistic Training
REC	Radioelectronic Combat
RECA(T)	Residual Capability Assessment (Team)
RECCE	Reconnaissance
RECCEXREP	Reconnaissance Exploitation Report
RECI	Radar Emitter Classification Identification (System)
RECON	Reconnaissance
REDCOM	Readiness Command
REDCON	Readiness Condition
REFORGER	(1) (U.S. Deployment and Field Training Exercise)
	(2) (EUCOM Field Training Exercise)
REGT	Regiment
REMAB	Remote Marshalling Base
REMS	Remotely Employed Sensors
REP	(1) Range Error Probable
	(2) Reserve Exploitation Program
REPRO	Reproduction
REPSHIP	Report of Shipment
REW(S)	Radio Electronic Warfare (Service)
REXMIT	Retransmission
RF	Radio Frequency
RFA	Restrictive Fire Area
RFL	Restrictive Fire Line
RFP	Restrictive Fire Plan
RFPW	Radio Frequency Pulse Weapon
RIF	(1) Reconnaissance in Force
	(2) Reduction in Force
RINT	Radar Intelligence
RL	Rocket Launcher
RLT	Regimental Landing Team
RO	Reporting Officer
ROA	Route of Advance
ROB	Radar Order of Battle
ROE	Rules of Engagement
RORO	Roll-on/Roll-off (Ship)
ROTC	Reserve Officer Training Corps

ROU	Radius of Uncertainty
ROUND HOUSE	(U.S. Exercise Defense Condition)
RPM	(1) Revolutions Per Minute
	(2) Rounds Per Minute
RPMA	Real Property Maintenance Activities
RPV	Remotely Piloted Vehicle
RR	Ready Reserve
RRF	Ready Reserve Force
RS	Radiation Status
RSR	Required Supply Rate
RSUTA	Regularly Scheduled Unit Training Assembly
RT	(1) Radio Telephone
	(2) Radius of Target
	(3) Real Time
RTASS	Remote Tactical Airborne Signals Intelligence System
RUM	Resource and Unit Monitoring
RV	Radius of Vulnerability
RW	Radiological Warfare
RWI	Radio Wire Integration
RWO	Reconnaissance Watch Officer
RZ	Recovery Zone

— S —

SA	(1) Signals Analysis
	(2) Situation Analysis
	(3) Surface-to-Air (used to identify Soviet surface-to-air missiles, such as SA-7/ GRAIL.))
SAB	Subject As Above
SAC	Strategic Air Command
SACEUR	Supreme Allied Commander, Europe
SACLANT	Supreme Allied Commander, Atlantic
SAEDA	Subversion and Espionage Against the Army
SAF	Security Assistance Force
SAIB	Safe Area Intelligence Brief
SAM	Surface-to-Air Missile
S&P	Stake and Platform (Semitrailers)
S&T or S&TI	Scientific and Technical Intelligence

SAO	(1) Select Attack option
	(2) Special Access Only
	(3) Special Activities Office(r) (Obsolete term)
SAPAS	Semiautomatic Population Analysis System
SASP	Special Ammunition Supply Point
SBI	Special Background Investigation
SBI-PR	Special Background Investigation-Periodic Reinvestigation
SC	Signal Corps
SCI	(1) Sensitive Compartmented Information
	(2) Special Compartmented Intelligence
SCIF	Sensitive Compartmented Information Facility
SCIMITAR	System for Countering Interdiction Missiles and Target Radars
SCOPES	Squad Combat Operations Exercise Simulated
SCS	Special Contingency Stockpile
SDOB	Scaled Depth of Burst
SEAD	Suppression of Enemy Air Defenses
SEC	Section
SECDEF	Secretary of Defense
SEP	September
SEP BDE	Separate Brigade
SER	Service
SERE	Survival, Evasion, Resistance, and Escape (Training)
SF	(1) Special Forces
	(2) Standard Form
SFG	Special Forces Group
SFOB	Special Forces Operational Base
SFOD-D	First Special Forces Operational Detachment-Delta
SFR	Statement of Functional Requirement
SGT	Sergeant
SHF	Super High Frequency
SHORAD	Short-Range Air Defense
SHORADEZ	Short-Range Air Defense Engagement Zone
SI	Special Intelligence
SICR	Specific Intelligence Collection Requirement

SIGINT	Signals Intelligence
SIGSEC	Signals Security
SIOP	Single Integrated Operational Plan
SI/SAO	Special Intelligence/Special Activities Office
SITMAP	Situation Map
SITREP	Situation Report
SJA	Staff Judge Advocate
SJOT	Supervised On-the-Job Training
SLAR	Side-Looking Airborne Radar
SLF	Super Low Frequency
SLOC	Sea Line of Communication
SLR	Side-Looking Radar
SMEB	Significant Military Exercise Brief
SMO	Support to Military Operations
SMOS	Secondary Military Occupational Specialty
SO	Special Operations
SOD	(1) Special Operations Detachment
	(2) Special Operations Division
SOF	Special Operations Forces
SOFA	Status of Forces Agreement
SOLID SHIELD	(U.S. Joint Exercise)
SOP	(1) Senior Officer Present
	(2) Standard Operating Procedure
	(3) Standing Operating Procedure
SOTA	Signals Intelligence Operational Tasking Authority
SOUTHCOM	Southern Command
SOW	Statement of Work
SP	Start Point
SPA	Special Psychological Operations Analysis
SPECAT	Special Category
SPF	Special Purpose Forces
SPINTCOMM	Special Intelligence Communications
SPIREP	Spot Intelligence Report
SPS	Special Psychological Operations Study
SQD	Squad
SQT	Skill Qualification Test
SRAM	(U.S.) Short-Range Attack Missile
SRBM	Short-Range Ballistic Missile
SRD	(1) Special Research Detachment (U.S. Army)

	(2) System Requirements Document
SRT	Special Reaction Team
SSAN	Social Security Number
SSG	Special Security Group
SSI	Specialty Skill Identifier
SSJ	Self-Screening Jamming
SSM	Surface-to-Surface Missile
SSMO	Signals Intelligence Support to Military Operations
SSO	Special Security Officer
SSSC	Self-Service Supply Center
STANAG	Standardization Agreement
STANO	Surveillance, Target Acquisition, Night Observation
STARTEX	Start Date of an Exercise
STL	Secondary Target Line
STOL	Short Takeoff and Landing
STOVL	Short Takeoff, Vertical Landing
STP	Soldier's Training Publication
SUPIR	Supplemental Programmed Interpretation Report
SURVL	Surveillance
SVC	Service
SW	Short Wave
SWA	(1) Southwest Africa
	(2) Southwest Asia
SWAL	Shallow Water Attack Craft, Light
SWAM	Shallow Water Attack Craft, Medium
SWC	(1) Special Warfare Center (U.S. Army)
	(2) Special Warfare Craft
SWCL	Special Warfare Craft, Light
SWCM	Special Warfare Craft, Medium
SWI	Special Weather Intelligence
SWO	(1) Senior Watch Officer
	(2) Staff Weather Officer
SYS	System

— T —

T	Tank
TA	(1) Tank Army
	(2) Target Analysis
	(3) Terrain Avoidance
	(4) Theater Army
	(5) Traffic Analysis
TAACOM	Theater Army Area Command
TAADS	The Army Authorization Documents System
TAC	(1) Tactical Air Command
	(2) Terrain Analysis Center (U.S. Army)
TACA	Tactical Air Controller, Airborne
TACAIR	Tactical Air
TACAMO	(U.S. Air Relay Communication System)
TACAN	(Ultra High Frequency) Tactical Air Navigation
TACC	Tactical Air Control Center
TACCP	Tactical Command Post
TACCS	Tactical Airborne Command and Control and Surveillance
TACCTA	Tactical Commander's Terrain Analysis
TACE	Tactical Air Coordination Element
TACIES	Tactical Imagery Exploitation System
TACINT or TACINTEL	Tactical Intelligence
TACOPS	Tactical Air Combat Operations Staff
TACP	Tactical Air Control Party
TACREP	Tactical Report
TACS	Tactical Air Control System
TAD	Temporary Additional Duty
TADC	Tactical Air Direction Center
TADIL	Tactical Data Information Link
TADS	(1) Tactical Air Defense System
	(2) Target Acquisition and Designation System
TADS/PNVS	Target Acquisition Designation Sight and Pilot Night Vision Sensor
TAF	Tactical Air Force
TAG	Target Actions Group
TAMCA	Theater Army Movement Control Agency

TAMIS	Training Ammunition Management Information System
TAMMC	Theater Army Materiel Management Center
TAMMS	The Army Maintenance Management System
T&A	Transcription and Analysis
TAOC	Tactical Air Operations Center
TAOR	Tactical Area of Responsibility
TAP	Terrain Analysis Program
TAPM	Total Army Personnel Model
TAPS	Technical Analysis Positions System
TAS	(1) Tactical Airlift Squadron
	(2) Traffic Analysis Survey
TASES	Tactical Airborne Signals Exploitation System
TASM	Tactical Air-to-Surface Missile
TAT	(1) Tactical Analysis Team
	(2) Target Area Tactics
	(3) Terrorist Action Team
TAVR	Territorial and Army Volunteer Reserve
TB	Tank Battalion
TBM	Tactical Ballistic Missile
TC	(1) Tank Company
	(2) Training Circular
	(3) Transportation Corps
TCAC	Technical Control and Analysis Center
TCAE	Technical Control and Analysis Element
TCAS	Technical Control and Analysis Section
TCC	Telecommunications Center
TCF	Tactical Combat Forces
TCF	Traffic Control Point
TCT	Tactical Commander's Terminal
TD	(1) Tank Destroyer
	(2) Tank Division
	(3) Transmitter-Distributor
TDA	Table of Distribution and Allowances
TDDP	Tactical Defense Dissemination Program
TDDS	Tactical Defense Dissemination System
TDF	Tactical Data Facsimile
TDI	Target Data Inventory
TDS	Target Data Sheet
TDY	Temporary Duty

TE	(1) Tactical Exploitation	**TGS**	Transportable Ground System
	(2) Task Element	**TGW**	Terminal Guidance Warhead
T&E	Test and Evaluation	**THREATCON**	Threat Condition
TEA	Tactical Exploitation Assessment	**TI**	(1) Target Indicator
TEAMPACK	(U.S. Ground-Based Signal		(2) Target Intelligence
	Intelligence Sensor)		(3) Technical Intelligence
TEAMS	Trend and Error Analysis	**TIAP**	Theater Intelligence Architec-
	Methodology System		ture Program
TEAM SPIRIT	(U.S. Exercise)	**TIARA**	Tactical Intelligence and
TEB	Tactical Exploitation Battalion		Related Activities
TEC	Training Extension Course	**TICC**	Tactical Information Communi-
TECCE	Tactical Exploitation Collection		cations Center
	and Coordination Element	**TIDL**	Tactical Imagery Data Link
TEDS	Tactical Expendable Drone	**TIES**	Tactical Information Exchange
	System		System
TEL	Transporter-Erector-Launcher	**TIG**	Tactical Intelligence Group
TELECOM	Telecommunications	**TIHB**	Target Intelligence Handbook
TELEFAC	Telecommunications Facility	**TIIF**	Tactical Imagery Interpretation
	Vulnerability Study		Facility
TELINT	Telemetry Intelligence	**TIM**	Target Intelligence Material
TEMPEST	(A term referring to technical	**TIP**	Target Intelligence Package
	investigations for compro-	**TIPE**	Tactical Intelligence Product
	mising emanations from		Enhancement
	electrically operated	**TIPI**	Tactical Information Processing
	information processing		and Interpretation System
	equipment. Such tests are	**TIPP**	Target Intelligence Production
	conducted in support of		Plan
	emanations and emission	**TIRSAG**	Tactical Intelligence, Reconnais-
	security.)		sance,
TENCAP	Tactical Exploitation of National		Surveillance Action Group
	Capabilities	**TIS**	Tactical Intelligence Squadron
TEP	Tactical Electronics Intelligence	**TISS**	Tactical Intelligence Support
	Processor		Staff
TERCOM	Terrain Contour Matching	**TI/TTR**	Target Illumination/Target
TEREC	Tactical Electronic Reconnais-		Tracking Radar
	sance	**TJ**	Terajoules
TERPES	(1) Tactical Electronic Recon-	**TJS**	Tactical Jamming System
	naissance and Exploitation	**TM**	(1) Tactical Missile
	Segment		(2) Team
	(2) Tactical Electronic Recon-		(3) Technical Manual
	naissance Processing and		(4) Threat Manager
	Evaluation System	**TMDE**	Test Measurement and Diagnos-
TEWT	Tactical Exercise Without		tic Equipment
	Troops	**TMF**	Theater Managment Force
TF	Task Force	**TMRD**	Transportation Movement
TFC	Tactical Fusion Center		Requirements Data
TFCC	Tactical Flag Command Center	**TNF**	Theater Nuclear Forces
TFR	Terrain Following Radar	**TO**	Theater of Operations
TG	Task Group	**TOA**	(1) Table of Allowance
TGIF	Transportable Ground Intercept		(2) Time of Arrival
	Facility	**TO&E**	Table of Organization and
TGPF	Transportable Ground		Equipment
	Processing Facility		

TOC	Tactical Operations Center	TSCO	Top Secret Control Officer
TOE	(1) Table of Organization and Equipment	TSCR	Time-Sensitive Collection Requirement
	(2) Time of Entry	TSCW	Top Secret Codeword
TOPCAT	Tactical Operations Planner for Collection, Analysis and Tasking	TSD	Technical Services Division
		TSDS	Tactical Signals Intelligence Data Support
TOT	(1) Time on Target	TSE	Target Support Element
	(2) Time of Transmission	TSEC	Telecommunications Security
TOW	Tube-Launched, Optically Tracked, Wire-Guided (Missile)	TSG	The Surgeon General
		TSM	Technical Surveillance Measures
TP	Target Practice (Rounds)	TSRS	Tactical Support Reconnaissance System
TPFDD	Time-Phased Force and Deployment Data (List)	TSSS or TS³	(1) Tactical Simulator Study Support
TPFDL	Time-Phased Force and Deployment List		(2) Time-Sensitive Support System
TPTRL	Time-Phased Transportation Requirements List	TT	(1) Target Track
TPU	Troop Program Unit		(2) Time on Target
TR	Tank Regiment	TTC	Terminal Throughput Capacity
T-R	Transmit-Receive	TTI	Tactical Target Illustrations
TRADOC	(U.S. Army) Training and Doctrine Command	TTM	Tactical Target Materials
TRAILBLAZER	(U.S. Ground-Based Signal Intelligence Sensor)	TTMC	Tactical Target Materials Catalog
TRAM	Target Recognition and Attack Multisensor	TTMP	Tactical Target Materials Program
TRANS	Transportation	TTY	Teletypewriter
TRANS/ANAL	Transcription and Analysis	TU	Task Unit
TRANSEC	Transmission Security	TUCHA	Type Unit Data (File)
TREDS	Tactical Reconnaissance Exploitation Demonstration System	TUHTKP	Time Urgent Hard Target Kill Potential
		TV	(1) Target Vulnerability
TRIGS	TR-1 Ground Station		(2) Television
TRI-TAC	(U.S. Joint Tactical Communications Program)		(3) Theater of War (Soviet)
		TVD	Theater of Military Operations (Soviet)
TRP	Target Reference Point		
TRS	Tactical Reconnaissance Squadron	TW/AA	Tactical Warning and Attack Assessment
TRV	Tactical Recovery Vehicle		
TRW	Tactical Reconnaissance Wing		
TS	Top Secret		
TSB	Training Support Base		**— U —**
TSC	(1) Tactical Support Center		
	(2) Technical Support Center	U&S	Unified and Specified (Command)
	(3) Top Secret Control		
TSCIXS	Tactical Support Center Information Exchange System	UCMJ	Uniformed Code of Military Justice
		UDIR	U.S. Army, Europe, Daily Intelligence Report
TSCM	Technical Surveillance Countermeasures	UDL	Unit Designation List

UE	Unit Equipment
UFR	Unfunded Requirement
UGS	Unattended Ground Sensors
UHF	Ultra High Frequency
UI	(1) Unidentified
	(2) Unit of Issue
UIC	Unit Identification Code
ULF	Ultra Low Frequency
UMOP	Unintentional Modulation on Pulse
UMS	Unit Manning System
URBBO	Urban Area Boundary File
URBPOP	Urban Population File
US	United States (of America)
USA	(1) United States Army
	(2) United States of America
USACC	U.S. Army Communications Command
USAIA	U.S. Army Intelligence Agency
USAIC	U.S. Army Intelligence Command
USAICE	U.S. Army Intelligence Center, Europe
USAICS	U.S. Army Intelligence Center and School
USAINSCOM	U.S. Army Intelligence and Security Command
USAINTA	U.S. Army Intelligence Agency
USAINTC	U.S. Army Intelligence Command
USAISD	United States Army Intelligence School
USAITAC	U.S. Army Threat Analysis Center
USAR	U.S. Army Reserve
USARC	U.S. Army Reserve Center
USAREUR	U.S. Army, Europe
USARJ	U.S. Army, Japan
USARRED	U.S. Army Forces Readiness Command
USARS	U.S. Army Regimental System
USARSA	U.S. Army School of the Americas
USASA	U.S. Army Security Agency
USATAC	U.S. Army Terrain Analysis Center
USATC	United States Air Target Chart
USCENTCOM	U.S. Central Command
USCINCENT	Commander-in-Chief, U.S. Central Command
USCINCEUR	Commander-in-Chief, U.S.

	European Command
USCINCLANT	Commander-in-Chief, Atlantic Command
USCINCPAC	Commander-in-Chief, Pacific Command
USCINC REDCOM	Commander-in-Chief, U.S. Readiness Command
USCINCSO	Commander-in-Chief, U.S. Southern Command
USCINC SPACE	Commander-in-Chief, U.S. Space Command
USCOM EASTLANT	U.S. Commander, Eastern Atlantic
USEUCOM	U.S. European Command
USFJ	U.S. Forces, Japan
USFK	U.S. Forces, Korea
USG	U.S. Government
USLANTCOM	U.S. Atlantic Command
USMA	U.S. Military Academy
USPACOM	U.S. Pacific Command
USREDCOM	U.S. Readiness Command
USSOCOM	U.S. Special Operations Command
USSOUTH- COM	U.S. Southern Command
USSPACECOM	U.S. Space Command
USTRANSCOM	U.S. Transportation Command
UTA	Unit Training Assembly
UTC	Unit Type Code
UTIC	U.S. Army, Europe, Tactical Intelligence Center
UTM	Universal Transverse Mercator Grid
UTTAS	Utility Tactical Transport Aircraft System
UV	(1) Ultraviolet
	(2) Unique Variable
UW	Unconventional Warfare
UWOA	Unconventional Warfare Operational Area

— V —

VF	Voice Frequency
VHF	Very High Frequency
VIN	Vehicle Identification Number

VIP	(1) Variable Incentive Payment
	(2) Very Important Person
	(3) Visual Input Processor
VISINT	Visual Intelligence
VLF	Very Low Frequency
VN	Vulnerability Number
VOR	Very High Frequency Omnidirectional Range
VORTAC	Collocated Very High Frequency Omnidirectional Range and Ultra High Frequency Tactical Air Navigation
VPK	Vehicles Per Kilometer
VPM	Vehicles Per Mile
VRBM	Variable-Range Ballistic Missile
V/STOL	Vertical/Short Takeoff and Landing
VTOL	Vertical Takeoff and Landing
VTR	Tracked Recovery Vehicle
VULREP	Vulnerability Report

— W —

WAG	World Area Grid
WARM	War Reserve Mode
WARSL	War Reserve Stockage List
WASPMS	Wide-Angle Side Penetrating System
WASSO	Worldwide Military Command and Control System Automated Data Processing Systems Security Officer
WATCHCON	Watch Condition
WATS	Wide Area Telecommunications System
WB	Wide Band
WBGT	Wet-Bulb-Globe-Temperature
WDCS	Weapons Data Correlation System
WE	Weather
WESTCOM	(U.S. Army) Western Command
WESTLANT	Western Atlantic Area
WEZ	Weapon Engagement Zone
WIA	Wounded in Action
WICS	Worldwide Intelligence Communications System
WIN	Worldwide Military Command and Control System Intercomputer Network

WINE	Warning and Indications in Europe
WINK	Warning in Korea
WINTEL	Warning Notice-Intelligence Sources and Methods Involved
WINTEX	Winter Exercise
WMX	Worldwide Military
WO	Work Order
WP	(1) Warsaw Pact
	(2) White Phosphorus (Rounds)
WPC	(1) Warsaw Pact Countries
	(2) Word Processing Center
WPM	Words Per Minute
WRM	War Reserve Material
WRMS	War Reserve Material Stocks
WRS	(1) War Reserve Stocks
	(2) Weapons Recommendation Sheet
WRSA	War Reserve Stocks for Allies
WRSK	War Readiness Spares Kits
WSAP	Weapons System Acquisition Program
WSEP	Weapon System Evaluation Program
WSI/L	War Supporting Industries and Logistics
WSRO	Weapon System Replacement Operations
WWIMS	Worldwide Warning Indicator Monitoring System
WWMCCS	Worldwide Military Command and Control System
WX	Weather

— X —

XMTR	Transmitter
XO	Executive Officer
XPLT	Exploitation

— Z —

Z	Zulu Time
ZI	Zone of Interior

THE
DICTIONARY

—**AH-1S COBRA**, which saw extensive combat in Vietnam, is a single-engine, two-seat, attack helicopter. In its original "G" configuration, it was an excellent weapon against enemy personnel and lightly armored vehicles, but it had no capability against tanks. The tube-launched optically-tracked wire-guided (TOW) missile was mated with the AH-1 to produce the TOW/Cobra, or AH-1S. The AH-1S began service in 1977; the fully modernized version is operational in Europe and Korea. The Cobra, while an effective weapon system, is limited in performance and is largely limited to use in fair weather. In addition, the TOW missile is wire guided, and the launching aircraft must keep the target in its sights until missile impact, tending to expose the aircraft to enemy missile and gunfire. These and other performance, lethality, and survivability considerations led the Army to begin the AH-64 Apache program. The Cobra, however, remained in service in a complementary role after fielding of the Apache. The Cobra's primary mission is to destroy armored vehicles, but it is also equipped with Hydra 70 multipurpose submunition rockets and 20-mm cannons, which are effective against other targets. *See also:* AH-64 Apache, Armed Helicopter.

References

Department of Defense, U.S. Army. *U.S. Army Policy Statement, 1988.* Washington, DC: Headquarters, Department of the Army, 1988.

—**AH-64 APACHE** is a quick-reacting antitank weapon system. Terrain limitations and an unfavorable U.S.-Soviet balance in armor dictate the need for a system that can fly quickly to the heaviest enemy penetration and destroy, disrupt, or delay the attack long enough for friendly armor and ground units to reach the scene. The Apache is designed to fight worldwide. It is armed with laser-designated Hellfire missiles and equipped with a target acquisition designation sight and pilot night vision sensor, which permits its two-man crew to navigate and attack in

darkness and in adverse weather conditions. Although the principal mission of the Apache is to destroy enemy armor, it is also lethal against a variety of other targets because it is quipped with a 30-mm chain gun and Hydra 70 rockets. When it was deployed in 1985, the Apache became the Army's primary attack helicopter, complementing the Cobra, which was already in the field. *See also:* AH-1S Cobra, Armed Helicopter.

References

Department of Defense, U.S. Army. *U.S. Army Policy Statement, 1988.* Washington, DC: Headquarters, Department of the Army, 1988.

—**AT4 LIGHTWEIGHT MULTIPURPOSE WEAPON SYSTEM** is a shoulder-launched disposable antiarmor system issued as a round of ammunition as needed to individual soldiers.

References

Department of Defense, U.S. Army. *U.S. Army Policy Statement, 1988.* Washington, DC: Headquarters, Department of the Army, 1988.

—**ABATIS** is a vehicular obstacle constructed by felling trees one to two meters above the ground on both sides of a road so that they fall, interlocked, toward the expected direction of the enemy's approach. The trees remain attached to the stumps, at 45-degree angles to the road, and the obstacle should be at least 75 meters in depth to be most effective.

References

Department of Defense, U.S. Army. *Operational Terms and Symbols.* Field Manual FM 101-5-1. Washington, DC: Headquarters, Department of the Army, 1985.

—**ABORT.** (1) Abort is a failure to accomplish a mission for any reason other than enemy action. It can occur at any point from the time an operation is initiated until the participants arrive at their destination. (2) Abort is to discontinue an aircraft takeoff run or launch.

References

Department of Defense, Joint Chiefs of Staff. *Department of Defense Dictionary of Military and Related Terms.* Washington, DC: GPO, 1986

—**ABOVE AND BEYOND THE CALL OF DUTY** occurs when a person voluntarily does something that, had he not done it, he would not be justly censured for failure to perform his duty. It usually includes the acceptance of danger or extraordinary responsibilities with praiseworthy fortitude and exemplary courage. In its highest form, it involves the voluntary acceptance of additional danger and risk of life. *See also:* Valor.

References

Department of Defense, U.S. Army. *Military Awards.* Army Regulation AR 672-5-1. Washington, DC: Headquarters, Department of the Army, 1984.

—**ABOVE THE ZONE** is a promotion eligibility category of the officer or warrant officer promotion zone being considered. Those in the above the zone category are officers eligible for promotion and whose dates of rank are senior to other officers in the promotion zone. Officers are normally considered for promotion over a period of years. Most officers are selected while in zone. However, some officers are passed over because of quotas or performance. These officers are reconsidered when they are above zone. A few officers are selected yearly from above zone. *See also:* Active Duty Date of Rank, Below the Zone, Zone of Consideration.

References

Department of Defense, U.S. Army. *Promotion of Officers on Active Duty.* Army Regulation AR 624-100. Washington, DC: Headquarters, Department of the Army, 1984.

—**ABOVEGROUND MAGAZINES** are magazines that are aboveground, except for standard and nonstandard earth-covered magazines. *See also:* Magazine.

References

Department of Defense, U.S. Army. *Ammunition and Explosives Safety Standards.* Army Regulation AR 385-64. Washington, DC: Headquarters, Department of the Army, 1987.

—**ABSENT WITHOUT LEAVE (AWOL)** is absence from one's appointed or other place of duty, or from one's unit, or organization, where one is required to be at the time prescribed.

References

Department of Defense, U.S. Army. *Dictionary of United States Army Terms.* Army Regulation AR 310-25. Washington, DC: Headquarters, Department of the Army, 1986.

—**ABSOLUTE DEVIATION** is the shortest distance between the center of the target and the point where the projectile hits or bursts.

References

Department of Defense, U.S. Army. *Dictionary of United States Army Terms.* Army Regulation AR 310-25. Washington, DC: Headquarters, Department of the Army, 1986.

—**ABSOLUTE DUD** is a nuclear weapon that fails to explode when launched or when it impacts on a target. *See also:* Nuclear Warfare.

References

Department of Defense, Joint Chiefs of Staff. *Department of Defense Dictionary of Military and Related Terms.* Washington, DC: GPO, 1986.

—**ABSOLUTE ERROR.** (1) An absolute error is the shortest distance between the center of impact or the center of burst of a group of shots and the point of impact or burst of a single shot within the group. (2) An absolute error is the error of a sight consisting of its error in relation to a master service sight with which it was tested, including the known error of the master service sight. Relative error, which is part of absolute error, includes only the error of a sight in relation to a master service sight.

References

Department of Defense, U.S. Army. *Dictionary of United States Army Terms.* Army Regulation AR 310-25. Washington, DC: Headquarters, Department of the Army, 1986.

—**ABSORBED DOSE** is the amount of energy imparted by nuclear (or ionizing) radiation to a unit mass of absorbing material. The unit is the centigray, which was formerly called a rad. *See also:* Nuclear Warfare, Whole Body Dose.

References

Department of Defense, U.S. Army. *NBC Operations.* Field Manual FM 3-100. Washington, DC: Headquarters, Department of the Army, 1985.

—**ACCEPTANCE TRIAL** is a test conducted by the nominated representatives of the eventual military users of a weapon to determine if the manufacturer has met the specified performance requirements. *See also:* Adaptability Test.

References

Department of Defense, Joint Chiefs of Staff. *Department of Defense Dictionary of Military and Related Terms.* Washington, DC: GPO, 1986.

—**ACCESS**, as applied to nuclear weapons, means physical access in a manner that allows a nuclear detonation to occur. "Access" in this context relates to the physical ability to perform detailed circuit modification or retrofit on the internal components of nuclear weapons so that official duties in authorized facilities and units can be performed. *See also:* Nuclear Warfare.

References

Department of Defense, U.S. Army. *Dictionary of United States Army Terms.* Army Regulation AR 310-25. Washington, DC: Headquarters, Department of the Army, 1986.

—**ACCESS AUTHORIZATION** is a formal act required to certify that a person, who has been screened and approved for access to classified information, is authorized to have access to such information. This act is normally a security briefing or an indoctrination, at which the person is cautioned concerning the responsibilities of having access to such information, told the meaning of the different classification levels, and provided other security- and counterintelligence-related information. The individual is then asked to sign a nondisclosure statement in which he agrees not to divulge the information to anyone who is not cleared for access or does not need to know the information. *See also:* Access Suspension, Access to Classified Information, Background Investigation.

References

Department of Defense, Joint Chiefs of Staff. *Department of Defense Dictionary of Military and Related Terms.* Washington, DC: GPO, 1986.

—**ACCESS SUSPENSION** is a security term. It is the temporary removal of one's access to classified information because of a circumstance or incident involving the individual and possibly having a bearing on the individual's eligibility for access. *See also:* Access Authorization.

References

Department of Defense, Joint Chiefs of Staff. *Department of Defense Dictionary of Military and Related Terms.* Washington, DC: GPO, 1986.

—**ACCESS TO CLASSIFIED INFORMAITON** is the ability or opportunity to obtain knowledge of classified information. Persons have access to classified information if they are permitted to gain knowledge of the information or if they are in a place where they would be expected to gain such knowledge. Persons do not have access to classified information by being in a place where classified information is kept if security measures prevent them from gaining knowledge of the information. *See also:* Access Authorization.

References

Department of Defense, Joint Chiefs of Staff. *Department of Defense Dictionary of Military and Related Terms.* Washington, DC: GPO, 1986.

—**ACCESS ZONE** is an area from the traveled route to the beginning of the contact zone of a crossing site. *See also*: Contact Zone.

References

Department of Defense, Joint Chiefs of Staff. *Department of Defense Dictionary of Military and Related Terms.* Washington, DC: GPO, 1986.

—**ACCESSORY EQUIPMENT** is nonexpendable equipment that has been fixed in place or attached to a craft, vehicle, or other equipment that may be removed without impairing or affecting the basic function of the object to which it was fastened. *See also:* Nonexpendable Supplies and Material.

References

Department of Defense, U.S. Army. *Dictionary of United States Army Terms.* Army Regulation AR 310-25. Washington, DC: Headquarters, Department of the Army, 1986.

—**ACCIDENTAL ATTACK** is an unintended attack that occurs without deliberate national design. It is a direct result of a random event.

References

Department of Defense, Joint Chiefs of Staff. *Department of Defense Dictionary of Military and Related Terms.* Washington, DC: GPO, 1986.

—**ACCOLADE** is a written, Presidential certificate recognizing service by personnel who died or were wounded in action between 1917 and 1918, or who died in service between 1941 and 1947, or who died of wounds received in Korea between June 27, 1950, and July 27, 1954. Service of civilians who died overseas or as result of injury or disease contracted while serving in a civilian capacity with the U.S. Armed Forces during the dates and/or in areas prescribed is also recognized. *See also:* Valor.

References

Department of Defense, U.S. Army. *Dictionary of United States Army Terms*. Army Regulation AR 310-25. Washington, DC: Headquarters, Department of the Army, 1986.

—**ACCOMPANYING SUPPLIES.** (1) Accompanying supplies are the initial issue of items needed to sustain an operating unit until continuing resupply can begin. Accompanying supplies include the prescribed loads. Normally, a fifteen-day level of supplies is authorized so that the unit can sustain itself during combat or until resupply occurs. (2) Accompanying supplies are all supplies carried by units and individual soldiers during deployment to, and redeployment from, an objective area or a training exercise area.

References

Department of Defense, U.S. Army. *Operational Terms and Symbols*. Field Manual FM 101-5-1. Washington, DC: Headquarters, Department of the Army, Oct. 1985.

————. *Repair Parts Supply for a Theater of Operations*. Field Manual FM 29-19. Washington, DC: Headquarters, Department of the Army, 1985.

—**ACCORDION EFFECT** is used to describe the repeated spreading out and bunching up of vehicles that are in a convoy during road marches. *See also:* Vehicle Distance.

References

Department of Defense, U.S. Army. *Attack Helicopter Operations*. Field Manual FM 17-50. Washington, DC: Headquarters, Department of the Army, 1984.

—**ACCOUNTABILITY.** (1) Accountability is the obligation, imposed by law, lawful order, or regulation, of a person to keep an accurate record of property, documents, or funds. The person having this obligation may or may not have possession of the property, documents, or funds. Accountability is primarily concerned with maintaining records; responsibility is concerned with custody, care, and safekeeping. (2) Accountability is the obligation imposed upon a security control officer to keep an accurate record of the documents and materials that he possesses and the people in his organization who have been cleared for access to classified material or have been indoctrinated into compartmented intelligence programs. *See also:* Accountable Officer.

References

Department of Defense, Joint Chiefs of Staff. *Department of Defense Dictionary of Military and Related Terms*. Washington, DC: GPO, 1986.

Department of Defense, U.S. Army. *Commander's Handbook for Property Accountability at the Unit Level*. Field Manual FM 10-14-1. Washington, DC: Headquarters, Department of the Army, 1984.

—**ACCOUNTABLE OFFICER** is an individual required to maintain accounting, including records of property and funds, whether public or quasi-public. The accountable officer may or may not have physical possession of the property or funds. *See also:* Responsible Officer.

References

Department of Defense, U.S. Army. *Dictionary of United States Army Terms*. Army Regulation AR 310-25. Washington, DC: Headquarters, Department of the Army, 1986.

—**ACCOUNTABLE STRENGTH** applies to all personnel assigned by competent orders to the reporting unit regardless of duty status. It includes personnel present for duty, absent from duty, in transit to duty, and in transit from duty. *See also:* Actions Strength.

References

Department of Defense, U.S. Army. *Dictionary of United States Army Terms*. Army Regulation AR 310-25. Washington, DC: Headquarters, Department of the Army, 1986.

—**ACCOUTERMENT** are items (e.g., medals, ribbons, insignia, badges, emblems, tabs, and tapes) that Army personnel are authorized to wear on their uniforms.

References

Department of Defense, U.S. Army. *Wear and Appearance of Army Uniforms and Insignia*. Army Regulation AR 670-1. Washington, DC: Headquarters, Department of the Army, 1986.

—**ACCUMULATION FACTOR.** Assuming a constant admission rate of one patient per day during a specific estimated period (and none thereafter), accumulation factor is the expected number of patients remaining (occupying beds) at a particular level of hospitalization at the end of each consecutive period. Accumulation factors are available for each patient classification and for different evacuation policies. *See also:* Medical Treatment.

References
Department of Defense, U.S. Army. *Planning for Health Service Support.* Field Manual FM 8-55. Washington, DC: Headquarters, Department of the Army, 1985.

—**ACCURACY LIFE** is the estimated average number of rounds that a particular weapon can fire before its tube becomes so warm that its accuracy tolerance is exceeded.

References
Department of Defense, U.S. Army. *Dictionary of United States Army Terms.* Army Regulation AR 310-25. Washington, DC: Headquarters, Department of the Army, 1986.

—**ACCURACY OF FIRE** is the precision of fire and is measured by the closeness of a grouping of shots at and around the center of the target.

References
Department of Defense, Joint Chiefs of Staff. *Department of Defense Dictionary of Military and Related Terms.* Washington, DC: GPO, 1986.

—**ACKNOWLEDGE** is a directive from the originator of a communication requiring the addressee(s) to advise him that the communication has been received and understood. *See also:* Acknowledgement, Wilco.

References
Department of Defense, U.S. Army. *Operational Terms and Symbols.* Field Manual FM 101-5-1. Washington, DC: Headquarters, Department of the Army, 1985.

—**ACKNOWLEDGEMENT** is a message from the addressee informing the originator that his communication has been received and understood. *See also:* Acknowledge.

References
Department of Defense, U.S. Army. *Operational Terms and Symbols.* FM 101-5-1. Washington, DC: Headquarters, Department of the Army, 1985.

—**ACOUSTICAL INTELLIGENCE (ACOUSTINT or ACINT)** is intelligence information derived from analyzing acoustic waves that are radiated intentionally or unintentionally by the target into the surrounding medium. *See also:* Intelligence.

References
Department of Defense, Joint Chiefs of Staff. *Department of Defense Dictionary of Military and Related Terms.* Washington, DC: GPO, 1986.

Department of Defense, U.S. Army. *Counterintelligence.* Field Manual FM 34-60. Washington, DC: Headquarters, Department of the Army, 1985.

—**ACQUIRE.** (1) When applied to acquisition radars, acquire is the process of detecting the presence and location of a target in sufficient detail to identify it. (2) When applied to tracking radars, acquire is the process of positioning a radar beam so that a target is in that beam, permitting the effective employment of weapons. *See also:* Target.

References
Department of Defense, Joint Chiefs of Staff. *Department of Defense Dictionary of Military and Related Terms.* Washington, DC: GPO, 1986.

—**ACQUISITION** is the purchasing, renting, leasing, or otherwise obtaining of personnel, services, supplies, and equipment from authorized sources as prescribed by the Defense Acquisition Regulation.

References
Department of Defense, U.S. Army. *Ammunition and Explosives Safety Standards.* Army Regulation AR 385-64. Washington, DC: Headquarters, Department of the Army, 1987.

—**ACTION** is a command ordering weapon crews to prepare to fire in any direction designated by the leader. *See also:* Action Station, Actions on Contact.

References
Department of Defense, U.S. Army. *Dictionary of United States Army Terms.* Army Regulation AR 310-25. Washington, DC: Headquarters, Department of the Army, 1986.

—**ACTION STATION** is the assigned position to be taken by an individual in an air attack. *See also:* Action.

References
Department of Defense, U.S. Army. *Dictionary of United States Army Terms.* Army Regulation AR 310-25. Washington, DC: Headquarters, Department of the Army, 1986.

—**ACTIONS ON CONTACT** is used to describe what happens when a moving unit sees the enemy for the first time or receives fire from the enemy. *See also:* Action.

References
Department of Defense, U.S. Army. *The Rifle Squads (Mechanized) and Light Infantry.* Training Circular TC 7-1. Washington, DC: Headquarters, Department of the Army, 1976.

—**ACTIONS STRENGTHS** are the strengths specified by departmental actions (e.g., letters or personnel allotment vouchers) that govern the number of individuals authorized by specific units (table of organization and equipment) and for table of distribution unit authorized strengths for nonpermanent party personnel based upon current Department of the Army policies and trends. These strengths represent the current authorized strengths of organizations and personnel and constitute the basic data for measuring actions to be taken as prescribed by the troop program and troop list. *See also:* Accountable Strength.

References
Department of Defense, U.S. Army. *Dictionary of United States Army Terms.* Army Regulation AR 310-25. Washington, DC: Headquarters, Department of the Army, 1986.

—**ACTIVATE** is to create by official order a unit, post, camp, base, or shore activity that had previously been constituted and designated by a name, number, or both, so that it can be organized to function in its assigned capacity. *See also:* Active Installation.

References
Department of Defense, Joint Chiefs of Staff. *Department of Defense Dictionary of Military and Related Terms.* Washington, DC: GPO, 1986.

—**ACTIVATED MINE** is a mine having a secondary fuze that causes detonation when the mine is moved or otherwise interfered with. *See also:* Mine Warfare.

References
Department of Defense, U.S. Army. *Dictionary of United States Army Terms.* Army Regulation AR 310-25. Washington, DC: Headquarters, Department of the Army, 1986.

—**ACTIVATOR WELL** (secondary fuze well) is a well in a mine that accommodates an activator (secondary fuze) or, specifically, an antihandling device. *See also:* Mine Warfare.

References
Department of Defense, U.S. Army. *Mine/Countermine Operations at the Company Level.* Field Manual FM 20-32. Washington, DC: Headquarters, Department of the Army, 1976.

—**ACTIVE AIR DEFENSE** is a direct defensive action taken to destroy attacking enemy aircraft or missiles or to nullify or reduce the effectiveness of their attack. It includes the use of aircraft, interceptor missiles, air defense artillery, nonair defense weapons in an air defense role, and counter-countermeasures.

References
Department of Defense, U.S. Army. *Air Defense Artillery Deployment: Chaparral/Vulcan/Stinger.* Field Manual FM 44-3. Washington, DC: Headquarters, Department of the Army, 1984.
————. *Operational Terms and Symbols.* Field Manual FM 101-5-1. Washington, DC: Headquarters, Department of the Army, 1985.

—**ACTIVE ARMY.** The U.S. Army consists of: (1) regular Army soldiers on active duty; (2) Army National Guard of the United States and Army Reserve soldiers on active duty (other than for training or in an active Guard/Reserve status); (3) Army National Guard soldiers in the service of the United States pursuant to call; and (4) all persons appointed, enlisted, or inducted into the U.S. Army without component. *See also:* Active Guard/Reserve, Army Composition, Army National Guard, United States Army, United States Army Reserve.

References
Department of Defense, U.S. Army. *Dictionary of United States Army Terms.* Army Regulation AR 310-25. Washington, DC: Headquarters, Department of the Army, 1986.

—**ACTIVE BALLISTIC MISSILE DEFENSE** is direct defensive action taken to intercept and destroy an enemy attack of ballistic missiles. It includes but is not limited to the use of antiballistic missiles and electronic countermeasures. *See also:* Nuclear Warfare.

References
Department of Defense, U.S. Army. *Dictionary of United States Army Terms.* Army Regulation AR 310-25. Washington, DC: Headquarters, Department of the Army, 1986.

—**ACTIVE DEFENSE.** (1) Active defense is the use of limited offensive action and counterattacks to deny access to a contested area or position to the enemy. (2) Active defense, when used by mechanized and armor units, is designed to fight against a highly mobile force. It is intended to wear down the attacker by confronting him continuously and in-depth with combined-arms teams and task forces from mutually supporting battle positions. *See also:* Passive Defense.

References

Department of Defense, Joint Chiefs of Staff. *Department of Defense Dictionary of Military and Related Terms.* Washington, DC: GPO, 1986.

Department of Defense, U.S. Army. *The Infantry Rifle Company (Infantry, Airborne, Air Assault, Ranger).* Field Manual FM 7-10. Washington, DC: Headquarters, Department of the Army, 1982.

—**ACTIVE DUTY** is full-time duty in the active military service of the United States and applies to all active military service regardless of its duration or purpose. *See also:* Above the Zone, Active Duty Credit, Active Duty Date of Rank, Active Duty for Training, Active Duty List, Active Federal Military Service.

References

Department of Defense, U.S. Army. *Enlisted Personnel Management System.* Army Regulation AR 600-200. Washington, DC: Headquarters, Department of the Army, 1984.

———. *Officer Assignment Policies, Details, and Transfers.* Army Regulation AR 614-100. Washington, DC: Headquarters, Department of the Army, 1984.

———. *Promotion of Officers on Active Duty.* Army Regulation AR 624-100.Washington, DC: Department of the Army, 1984.

—**ACTIVE DUTY CREDIT** applies to soldiers who are credited with having completed two, three, or four years of active duty when they serve to within 90 days of the two-, three-, or four-year period. *See also:* Active Duty.

References

Department of Defense, U.S. Army. *Officer Assignment Policies, Details, and Transfers.* Army Regulation AR 614-100. Washington, DC: Headquarters, Department of the Army, 1984.

———. *Promotion of Officers on Active Duty.* Army Regulation AR 624-100. Washington, DC: Headquarters, Department of the Army, 1984.

—**ACTIVE DUTY DATE OF RANK (ADOR)** is the date used to determine the relative seniority of officers of the same grade in which each officer is serving on the active duty list in the U.S. Army. This date is not necessarily the same as the date established for other purposes (e.g., entitlement to pay and allowances). It is the date that shows

active federal service in a grade and establishes an officer's eligibility for promotion. *See also:* Active Duty.

References

Department of Defense, U.S. Army. *Enlisted Personnel Management System.* Army Regulation AR 600-200. Washington, DC: Headquarters, Department of the Army, 1984.

———. *Promotion of Officers on Active Duty.* Army Regulation AR 624-100. Washington, DC: Headquarters, Department of the Army, 1984.

—**ACTIVE DUTY FOR TRAINING (ADT)** is a tour of duty used to train members of the Reserve components in order to provide trained units and qualified persons to fill the needs of the Armed Forces in time of war, national emergency or when the national security requires. It includes annual training, special tours of active duty for training, school tours, and the initial tour performed by nonprior service enlistees. The tour of duty returns to nonactive duty status when the period of active duty for training is completed. *See also:* Active Duty.

References

Department of Defense, Joint Chiefs of Staff. *Department of Defense Dictionary of Military and Related Terms.* Washington, DC: GPO, 1986.

—**ACTIVE DUTY LIST (ADL)** is a list by seniority of all commissioned officers on active duty in the U.S. Army, except for Reserve officers in certain capacities, some of the faculty at the U.S. Military Academy, retired officers on active duty, and students at the Uniformed Services University of Health Services. *See also:* Active Duty.

References

Department of Defense, U.S. Army. *Dictionary of United States Army Terms.* Army Regulation AR 310-25. Washington, DC: Headquarters, Department of the Army, 1986.

———. *Promotion of Officers on Active Duty.* Army Regulation AR 624-100. Washington, DC: Headquarters, Department of the Army, 1984.

—**ACTIVE FEDERAL MILITARY SERVICE** is all periods of active duty and active Guard/Reserve service. *See also:* Active Duty.

References

Department of Defense, U.S. Army. *Dictionary of United States Army Terms.* Army Regulation AR 310-25. Washington, DC: Headquarters, Department of the Army, 1986.

————. *Military Awards*. Army Regulation AR 672-5-1. Washington, DC: Headquarters, Department of the Army, 1984.

—**ACTIVE GUARD/RESERVE (AGR)** refers to paid Guardsmen and Reservists who are on active duty solely to provide full-time support to Reserve components.

References

Department of Defense, U.S. Army. *Dictionary of United States Army Terms*. Army Regulation AR 310-25. Washington, DC: Headquarters, Department of the Army, 1986.

—**ACTIVE INSTALLATION** is an installation in continuous use by Active Army organizations. *See also:* Activate.

References

Department of Defense, U.S. Army. *Dictionary of United States Army Terms*. Army Regulation AR 310-25. Washington, DC: Headquarters, Department of the Army, 1986.

—**ACTIVE MINE** is a mine to be actuated when a signal sent by the mine is reflected by a target. *See also:* Mine Warfare.

References

Department of Defense, Joint Chiefs of Staff. *Department of Defense Dictionary of Military and Related Terms*. Washington, DC: GPO, 1986.

—**ACTIVE NATIONAL GUARD** is composed of the units and members of the Army and Air National Guard of the several states, the Commonwealth of Puerto Rico, and the District of Columbia. It is federally recognized by law and is authorized to have equipment and to engage in regularly scheduled training activities, other than federal service. *See also:* Active Guard/Reserve.

References

Department of Defense, U.S. Army. *Dictionary of United States Army Terms*. Army Regulation AR 310-25. Washington, DC: Headquarters, Department of the Army, 1986.

—**ACTIVE PREVENTATIVE PROGRAM** (against terrorism) consists of the deliberate, low-visibility, clandestine, and/or overt actions that deter or lessen the effectiveness of planned or actual acts of terrorism. This program can include political, social, economic, psychological, military, or a combination of these actions. *See also:* Terrorism Counteraction.

References

Department of Defense, U.S. Army. *Dictionary of United States Army Terms*. Army Regulation AR 310-25. Washington, DC: Headquarters, Department of the Army, 1986.

—**ACTIVE SECURITY MEASURES** include outposts, stand-to, and patrols. The company commander may require that each platoon have a specified number of ouposts. If he does not, the platoon leaders decide each platoon needs. There should be at least one outpost per platoon; in close terrain or during periods of limited visibility, there may be one per squad. *See also:* Stand-To.

References

Department of Defense, U.S. Army. *The Infantry Rifle Company (Infantry, Airborne, Air Assault, Ranger)*. Field Manual FM 7-10. Washington, DC: Headquarters, Department of the Army, 1982.

—**ACTIVE STANO (SURVEILLANCE, TARGET ACQUISITION, NIGHT OBSERVATION) DEVICE** is an instrument that projects energy to detect targets. Because this and other active devices (e.g., radar and active infrared devices) project invisible light, electronic impulses, or other energy, they can be detected by the enemy if it has detection devices. If STANO devices are not properly used, they can reveal friendly positions.

References

Department of Defense, U.S. Army. *The Infantry Rifle Company (Infantry, Airborne, Air Assault, Ranger)*. Field Manual FM 7-10. Washington, DC: Headquarters, Department of the Army, 1982.

—**ACTIVE STATUS** refers to a Reserve component member who is not in the inactive National Guard, on an inactive status list, or in the retired reserve.

References

Department of Defense, U.S. Army. *Dictionary of United States Army Terms*. Army Regulation AR 310-25. Washington, DC: Headquarters, Department of the Army, 1986.

————. *Promotion of Officers on Active Duty*. Army Regulation AR 624-100. Washington, DC: Headquarters, Department of the Army, 1984.

—**ACTIVITY.** (1) An activity is a unit, organization, or installation (e.g., a reception center or redistribution center) that performs a function or mission. (2) An activity is a function or a mission (e.g., recruiting or schooling). *See also:* Establishment.

References
Department of Defense, Joint Chiefs of Staff. *Department of Defense Dictionary of Military and Related Terms.* Washington, DC: GPO, 1986.

—**ACTUAL GROUND ZERO** is the point on the surface of the earth at, or vertically below or above, the center of where a nuclear detonation is actually located. *See also*: Nuclear Warfare.

References
Department of Defense, Joint Chiefs of Staff. *Department of Defense Dictionary of Military and Related Terms.* Washington, DC: GPO, 1986.

—**ACTUATE** is to operate a mine-firing mechanism by influence or by a series of influences so that all the requirements of the mechanism for firing, or for registering a target count, are met. *See also:* Mine Warfare.

References
Department of Defense, Joint Chiefs of Staff. *Department of Defense Dictionary of Military and Related Terms.* Washington, DC: GPO, 1986.

—**ACTUATED MINE** is a mine whose detecting element has been operated and has either electrically signaled a control station or caused the mine to explode. *See also:* Mine Warfare.

References
Department of Defense, U.S. Army. *Dictionary of United States Army Terms.* Army Regulation AR 310-25. Washington, DC: Headquarters, Department of the Army, 1986.

—**ACUTE RADIATION DOSE** is the total ionizing radiation dose received at one time and over a sufficiently short period so that death results. *See also:* Whole Body Dose.

References
Department of Defense, Joint Chiefs of Staff. *Department of Defense Dictionary of Military and Related Terms.* Washington, DC: GPO, 1986.

—**ADAPTABILITY TEST** is a test that ascertains the adaptability of a standardized item of equipment to a particular unit or organization. This test differs from a user test, which is conducted prior to standardization and tests the suitability of the equipment for service. *See also:* Acceptance Trial.

References
Department of Defense, U.S. Army. *Dictionary of United States Army Terms.* Army Regulation AR 310-25. Washington, DC: Headquarters, Department of the Army, 1986.

—**ADD**, in artillery or gunfire support, is a correction used by an observer or spotter to indicate that an increase in range along a spotting line is desired.

References
Department of Defense, U.S. Army. *Operational Terms and Symbols.* Field Manual FM 101-5-1. Washington, DC: Headquarters, Department of the Army, 1985.

—**ADDITIONAL MOS (MILITARY OCCUPATIONAL SPECIALTY)** is a MOS (other than a primary, secondary, or career progression MOS) awarded to a person. *See also:* Additional Skill Identifier.

References
Department of Defense, U.S. Army. *Enlisted Personnel Management System.* Army Regulation AR 600-200. Washington, DC: Headquarters, Department of the Army, 1984.

—**ADDITIONAL SKILL IDENTIFIER** identifies specialized skills that are closely related to and are in addition to those required by an individual's military occupational specialty. *See also:* Additional MOS.

References
Department of Defense, U.S. Army. *Enlisted Personnel Management System.* Army Regulation AR 600-200. Washington, DC: Headquarters, Department of the Army, 1984.

———. *Individual Military Education and Training.* Army Regulation AR 350-1. Washington, DC: Headquarters, Department of the Army, 1987.

—**ADDITIONAL TRAINING ASSEMBLIES** are inactive duty training periods authorized so that personnel can participate in specialized training or in support of training. These are in addition to the training assemblies attended as a part of unit training. *See also*: United States Army Reserve.

References
Department of Defense, Joint Chiefs of Staff. *Department of Defense Dictionary of Military and Related Terms.* Washington, DC: GPO, 1986.

—**ADJUST** is an order to the observer or spotter to initiate an adjustment on a designated target. *See also:* Adjust Fire, Adjustment of Fire.

References

Department of Defense, Joint Chiefs of Staff. *Department of Defense Dictionary of Military and Related Terms.* Washington, DC: GPO, 1986.

—**ADJUST FIRE.** In artillery support, adjust fire is (1) an order or request to initiate an adjustment to fire or (2) a method of control transmitted in the call for fire by the observer or spotter to indicate that he will control the adjustment. *See also:* Adjust, Adjustment of Fire.

References

Department of Defense, Joint Chiefs of Staff. *Department of Defense Dictionary of Military and Related Terms.* Washington, DC: GPO, 1986.

—**ADJUSTED ELEVATION**, based upon firing, is computed to place the center of impact on the target.

References

Department of Defense, U.S. Army. *Dictionary of United States Army Terms.* Army Regulation AR 310-25. Washington, DC: Headquarters, Department of the Army, 1986.

—**ADJUSTED RANGE.** (1) Adjusted range is range corresponding to adjusted elevation. (2) Adjusted range is a range setting, based on firing, computed in order to place the center of impact on the target.

References

Department of Defense, U.S. Army. *Dictionary of United States Army Terms.* Army Regulation AR 310-25. Washington, DC: Headquarters, Department of the Army, 1986.

—**ADJUSTING POINT** is a distinctive terrain feature or some portion of the target, at or near the center of the area, upon which the observer wishes to place fire. *See also:* Observing Point.

References

Department of Defense, U.S. Army. *Dictionary of United States Army Terms.* Army Regulation AR 310-25. Washington, DC: Headquarters, Department of the Army, 1986.

—**ADJUSTMENT.** *See:* Adjustment of Fire.

—**ADJUSTMENT OF FIRE** is a process used in artillery to obtain a correct bearing, range, and height of burst (if time fuzes are used) when engaging a target by observed fire. *See also:* Absolute Deviation, Absolute Error, Accuracy of Fire, Add, Adjust; Adjust Fire; Adjusted Elevation, Adjusted Range, Spot.

References

Department of Defense, Joint Chiefs of Staff. *Department of Defense Dictionary of Military and Related Terms.* Washington, DC: GPO, 1986.

Department of Defense, U.S. Army. *Fire Support in Combined Arms Operations.* Field Manual FM 6-20. Washington, DC: Headquarters, Department of the Army, 1983.

—**ADJUTANT GENERAL (AG)** (Primary staff responsibility, Assistant Chief of Staff, G1) is responsible for operational, technical, and training responsibilities for personnel, administrative, and postal services, and morale support activities. *See also:* G-1, Assistant Chief of Staff, Personnel.

References

Department of Defense, U.S. Army. *Staff Organization and Operations.* Field Manual FM 101-5. Washington, DC: Headquarters, Department of the Army, 1984.

—**ADJUTANT'S CALL** is a bugle call announcing that the adjutant is about to form the guard, battalion, or regiment for a ceremony.

References

Department of Defense, U.S. Army. *Dictionary of United States Army Terms.* Army Regulation AR 310-25. Washington, DC: Headquarters, Department of the Army, 1986.

—**ADMINISTRATION.** (1) Administration is the management and execution of all military matters not included in strategy and tactics. (2) Administration is the internal management of units. *See also:* Administrative Chain of Command.

References

Department of Defense, Joint Chiefs of Staff. *Department of Defense Dictionary of Military and Related Terms.* Washington, DC: GPO, 1986.

—**ADMINISTRATIVE CHAIN OF COMMAND** is the normal chain of command for administration. *See also:* Chain of Command, Operational Chain of Command.

References

Department of Defense, Joint Chiefs of Staff. *Department of Defense Dictionary of Military and Related Terms.* Washington, DC: GPO, 1986.

—**ADMINISTRATIVE CONTROL** is the direction or exercise of authority over subordinate or other organizations in respect to administrative matters (e.g., personnel management, supply, services) and other matters not included in the operational missions of the subordinate or other organizations. *See also:* Control, Operational Command, Operational Control.

References

Department of Defense, Joint Chiefs of Staff. *Department of Defense Dictionary of Military and Related Terms.* Washington, DC: GPO, 1986.

—**ADMINISTRATIVE LOADING** is a loading system that gives primary consideration to achieving maximum use of troop and cargo space without regard to tactical considerations. Equipment and supplies must be unloaded and sorted before they can be used. *See also:* Combat (Tactical) Loading (Cross-Loading), Loading.

References

Department of Defense, Joint Chiefs of Staff. *Department of Defense Dictionary of Military and Related Terms.* Washington, DC: GPO, 1986.

—**ADMINISTRATIVE/LOGISTIC ORDER** is the order that gives the commander's plan for supply, transportation, maintenance, evacuation, hospitalization, personnel, and other administrative and logistic details to include marshaling. *See also:* Administrative/Logistics Plan.

References

Department of Defense, U.S. Army. *USA/USAF Doctrine for Joint Airborne and Tactical Airlift Operations.* Field Manual FM 100-27. Washington, DC: Headquarters, Department of the Army, 1985.

—**ADMINISTRATIVE/LOGISTICS PLAN** applies to combat service support operations. It is based upon the command's operational requirements, as determined by appropriate estimates. When put into effect, it is the administrative/logistics order. *See also:* Administrative/Logistic Order.

References

Department of Defense, U.S. Army. *Staff Organization and Operations.* Field Manual FM 101-5. Washington, DC: Headquarters, Department of the Army, 1984.

—**ADMINISTRATIVE MAP** contains graphically recorded information pertaining to administrative matters (e.g., supply and evacuation installations, personnel installations, medical facilities, collecting points for stragglers and prisoners of war, training bivouacs, service and maintenance areas, main supply roads, traffic circulation, boundaries, and other details necessary to show the administrative situation). *See also:* Map.

References

Department of Defense, Joint Chiefs of Staff. *Department of Defense Dictionary of Military and Related Terms.* Washington, DC: GPO, 1986.

Department of Defense, U.S. Army. *Health Service Support in a Communications Zone (Test).* Field Manual FM 8-21. Washington, DC: Headquarters, Department of the Army, 1981.

—**ADMINISTRATIVE NET** is radio, wire, or a combined radio and wire system of communication by which administrative traffic is sent to various headquarters and units. *See also*: Communications Net.

References

Department of Defense, U.S. Army. *Dictionary of United States Army Terms.* Army Regulation AR 310-25. Washington, DC: Headquarters, Department of the Army, 1986.

—**ADMINISTRATIVE PLAN** is a plan proposed for handling the traffic, supply, evacuation, and other administrative details of operations of a unit. It must be based upon a survey of the situation, (the administrative estimate) and is put into effect by the administrative order. *See also:* Administrative/Logistic Order.

References

Department of Defense, U.S. Army. *Dictionary of United States Army Terms.* Army Regulation AR 310-25. Washington, DC: Headquarters, Department of the Army, 1986.

—**ADMINISTRATIVE RESTRICTION** is a form of command restraint through which a commanding officer may, within his discretion and without imposing arrest, administratively restrict an accused person to specified areas of military command with the further provision that the accused will participate in all military duties and activities of his organization while he is under restraint. Violations of such administrative restrictions are punishable, as are breaches of punitive restriction. *See also:* Restriction.

References

Department of Defense, U.S. Army. *Dictionary of United States Army Terms.* Army Regulation AR 310-25. Washington, DC: Headquarters, Department of the Army, 1986.

—**ADMINISTRATIVE SUPPORT EQUIPMENT** is equipment not essential to the performance of assigned operational missions and tasks. It includes administrative equipment (e.g., office machines, drinking fountains, laundries, and movie projectors). *See also:* Auxiliary Equipment, Primary Weapons and Equipment.

References

Department of Defense, U.S. Army. *Dictionary of United States Army Terms.* Army Regulation AR 310-25. Washington, DC: Headquarters, Department of the Army, 1986.

—**ADVANCE** is a request from a spotter to indicate his desire that the illuminating projectile be burst earlier in relation to the subsequent bursts of high explosive projectiles.

References

Department of Defense, Joint Chiefs of Staff. *Department of Defense Dictionary of Military and Related Terms.* Washington, DC: GPO, 1986.

—**ADVANCE BY BOUNDS** is to move forward in a series of separate advances, usually from cover to cover or from one point of observation to the next. *See also:* Advance by Echelon.

References

Department of Defense, U.S. Army. *Dictionary of United States Army Terms.* Army Regulation AR 310-25. Washington, DC: Headquarters, Department of the Army, 1986.

—**ADVANCE BY ECHELON** is an advance by separate elements of a command moving at different times. *See also:* Advance by Bounds.

References

Department of Defense, U.S. Army. *Dictionary of United States Army Terms.* Army Regulation AR 310-25. Washington, DC: Headquarters, Department of the Army, 1986.

—**ADVANCE DEPOT** is a supply point in the forward part of the communications zone in a theater of operations, ahead of the intermediate and base depots. *See also:* Depot.

References

Department of Defense, U.S. Army. *Dictionary of United States Army Terms.* Army Regulation AR 310-25. Washington, DC: Headquarters, Department of the Army, 1986.

—**ADVANCE DETACHMENT** is the leading element of, and set out from, an advanced guard. *See also:* Advance Party.

References

Department of Defense, U.S. Army. *Dictionary of United States Army Terms.* Army Regulation AR 310-25. Washington, DC: Headquarters, Department of the Army, 1986.

—**ADVANCE GUARD.** (1) An advance guard is a detachment sent ahead of the main force: to insure its uninterrupted advance; to protect the main body against surprise; to facilitate the advance by removing obstacles and repairing roads and bridges; and to cover the deployment of the main body if it is committed to action. (2) An advance guard for a stationary force deploys forward and defends, while an advance guard for a moving force develops the situation along specific routes or axes of advance to prevent the premature deployment of the main body. (3) An advance guard is the security element operating to the front of a moving force. *See also:* Advance Guard Reserve, Advance Guard Support.

References

Department of Defense, U.S. Army. *Cavalry.* Field Manual FM 17-95. Washington, DC: Headquarters, Department of the Army, 1977.

———. *Operational Terms and Symbols.* Field Manual FM 101-5-1. Washington, DC: Headquarters, Department of the Army, 1985.

—**ADVANCE GUARD RESERVE** is the second of the two main parts of an advance guard (the other is the advance guard support). It protects the main force and is itself protected by the advance guard support. Small advance guards do not have reserves. *See also:* Advance Guard, Advance Guard Support.

References

Department of Defense, Joint Chiefs of Staff. *Department of Defense Dictionary of Military and Related Terms.* Washington, DC: GPO, 1986.

—**ADVANCE GUARD SUPPORT** is the first of two main parts of an advance guard (the other is the advance guard reserve). It consists of three smaller elements, in order from front to rear: the advance guard point, the advance party, and the support proper. The advance guard support protects the advance guard reserve. *See also:* Advance Guard, Advance Guard Reserve.

References
Department of Defense, Joint Chiefs of Staff. *Department of Defense Dictionary of Military and Related Terms.* Washington, DC: GPO, 1986.

—**ADVANCE OFFICER** is an officer designated by the commander to precede the column by a distance sufficient to reconnoiter the route of march and to select alternate routes or detours if required; to instruct and place guides and route markers, where appropriate; to notify authorities of the approach of the column; and to receive instructions or changes to instructions at highway regulation points. This officer may also command the advance party. *See also:* Advance Party.

References
Department of Defense, U.S. Army. *Dictionary of United States Army Terms.* Army Regulation AR 310-25. Washington, DC: Headquarters, Department of the Army, 1986.

—**ADVANCE PARTY** is a security element of the advance guard. It is sent out from, and precedes, the advance guard support on the march. It sends forward, and is preceded by, the advance guard point. *See also:* Advance Officer.

References
Department of Defense, U.S. Army. *Dictionary of United States Army Terms.* Army Regulation AR 310-25. Washington, DC: Headquarters, Department of the Army, 1986.

—**ADVANCE TO CONTACT** is an offensive operation designed to gain or reestablish contact with the enemy. *See also:* Approach March, Movement to Contact.

References
Department of Defense, U.S. Army. *Operational Terms and Symbols.* Field Manual FM 101-5-1. Washington, DC: Headquarters, Department of the Army, 1985.

—**ADVANCED BASE** is a base located in or near a theater of operations. Its primary mission is to support military operations.

References
Department of Defense, U.S. Army. *Dictionary of United States Army Terms.* Army Regulation AR 310-25. Washington, DC: Headquarters, Department of the Army, 1986.

Poyer, David. *The Med.* New York: St. Martin's Press, 1988.

—**ADVANCED INDIVIDUAL TRAINING (AIT)** is skill training enlisted personnel receive after they have completed basic training in order to qualify them for a military occupational specialty and to teach them to perform the basics of their jobs before they report to their units. *See also:* Basic Training.

References
Department of Defense, U.S. Army. *Dictionary of United States Army Terms.* Army Regulation AR 310-25. Washington, DC: Headquarters, Department of the Army, 1986.

———. *Individual Military Education and Training.* Army Regulation AR 350-1. Washington, DC: Headquarters, Department of the Army, 1987.

—**ADVANCED LEAVE** is an authorized absence granted to an individual before it is accrued or earned. It is granted with the reasonable expectation that the person will earn and pay back the advance during the remaining period of his active duty enlistment. *See also:* Annual Leave.

References
Department of Defense, U.S. Army. *Leaves and Passes.* Army Regulation AR 630-5. Washington, DC: Headquarters, Department of the Army, 1984.

—**ADVANCED MILITARY STUDIES COURSE (AMSC)** was established at the Command and General Staff College, Fort Leavenworth, Kansas, in 1983. It provides a broad education in the art and science of war at the tactical and operational levels. It goes beyond the Command and General Staff Officer Course in practical application. Annually, 48 officers enroll in this one-year course. Following their academic program, AMSC graduates complete an internship assignment as operational planners at the division or corps staff level. It is the Army's concept that AMSC graduates will seed the force with operational experts of exceptional competence.

References
Department of Defense, U.S. Army. *U.S. Army Policy Statement, 1988.* Washington, DC: Headquarters, Department of the Army, 1988.

—**ADVERSE WEATHER** is weather in which military operations are generally restricted or impeded. *See also:* Marginal Weather.

References
Department of Defense, Joint Chiefs of Staff. *Department of Defense Dictionary of Military and Related Terms.* Washington, DC: GPO, 1986.

—**ADVERSE WEATHER AERIAL DELIVERY SYSTEM (AWADS)** is the precise delivery of personnel, equipment, and supplies during adverse weather, using a self-contained aircraft instrumentation system without artificial ground assistance or use of ground navigation aids. *See also*: Adverse Weather.

References

Department of Defense, U.S. Army. *USA/USAF Doctrine for Joint Airborne and Tactical Airlift Operations*. Field Manual FM 100-27. Washington, DC: Headquarters, Department of the Army, 1985.

—**AERIAL OBSERVER** is an individual whose primary mission is to observe or take photographs from an aircraft in order to adjust indirect fires or to obtain military information. *See also:* Aerial Reconnaissance.

References

Department of Defense, U.S. Army. *Fire Support in Combined Arms Operations*. Field Manual FM 6-20. Washington, DC: Headquarters, Department of the Army, 1984.

—**AERIAL OBSERVER'S ADJUSTMENT** is the correcting of fires by an observer in an airborne vehicle. *See also:* Aerial Reconnaissance.

References

Department of Defense, U.S. Army. *Fire Support in Combined Arms Operations*. Field Manual FM 6-20. Washington, DC: Headquarters, Department of the Army, 1984.

—**AERIAL PHOTOGRAPH, COMPOSITE,** is a photograph taken with one camera having one principal lens and two surrounding and oblique lenses that are symmetrically placed. The photographs from all lenses can be rectified in the printing process so that the photographs can be assembled as verticals with the same scale. Composite photography minimizes the distortion that occurs when a single, vertically positioned camera is used. *See also:* Aerial Photograph, Oblique; Aerial Photograph, Vertical; Aaerial Reconnaissance; Aerial Photographic Mosaic.

References

Reeves, Robert; Anson, Abraham; and Landen, David. *Manual of Remote Sensing*. Falls Church, VA: American Society of Photogrammetry, 1975.

—**AERIAL PHOTOGRPAH, OBLIQUE,** is a photograph taken with the camera axis directed between the horizontal and the vertical. *High oblique* is an oblique photograph in which the apparent horizon is shown; *low oblique* is one in which the apparent horizon is not shown. *See also:* Aerial Photograph, Composite; Aerial Reconnaissance.

References

Reeves, Robert; Anson, Abraham; and Landen, David. *Manual of Remote Sensing*. Falls Church, VA: American Society of Photogrammetry, 1975.

—**AERIAL PHOTOGRAPH, VERTICAL,** is an aerial photograph taken when the optical axis of the camera is approximately perpendicular to the earth's surface and the film is as horizontal as possible. *See also:* Aerial Photograph, Composite; Aerial Reconnaissance.

References

Reeves, Robert; Anson, Abraham; and Landen, David. *Manual of Remote Sensing*. Falls Church, VA: American Society of Photogrammetry, 1975.

—**AERIAL PHOTOGRAPH MOSAIC** is a combination of two or more overlapping prints to form a single picture. Mosaics can be valuable in providing an updated picture of a large area to supplement map data. Usually, vertical photographs, which produce map-like results, are used. However, oblique photographs can be used to produce a panorama. *See also:* Aerial Photograph, Composite; Aerial Reconnaissance.

References

Department of Defense, U.S. Army. *Intelligence Imagery*. Field Manual FM 34-55. Washington, DC: Headquarters, Department of the Army, 1985.

—**AERIAL PORT CONTROL CENTER (APCC)** is the agency responsible for managing and controlling aerial port resources. The APCC is responsible for the receipt and dissemination of all airlift requirements received from the airlift control center as the joint force commander agent.

References

Department of Defense, U.S. Army. *USA/USAF Doctrine for Joint Airborne and Tactical Airlift Operations*. Field Manual FM 100-27. Washington, DC: Headquarters, Department of the Army, 1985.

—**AERIAL RECONNAISSANCE** is a means of obtaining information by aerial photography or by visual observation from the air. *See also:* Aerial

Observer; Aerial Observer's Adjustment; Aerial Photograph, Composite; Aerial Photograph, Oblique; Aerial Photograph, Vertical; Aerial Photographic Mosaic; Aerial Surveillance; Basic Cover (Photogrammetry); Fan Camera Photography; Image; Image Interpreter; Imagery; Imagery Annotation; Imagery Exploitation; Imagery Intelligence; Imagery Interpretation; Imagery Interpreter; Initial Photo Interpretation Report; Initial Programmed Interpretation Report; Oblique Air Photograph; Photogrammetry; Photographic Coverage; Photographic Flight Line; Photographic Intelligence; Photographic Interpretation; Photographic Interpreter; Photographic Reading; Photographic Scale; Photographic Strip; Photography; Photomap; Reconnaissance Photography; Report, Photographic Interpretation; Stereoscopic Cover; Stereoscopic Pair; Stereoscopic Vision; Stereoscopy; Strike Photography; Tri-Camera Photography.

References

Department of Defense, U.S. Army. *Intelligence Imagery*. Field Manual FM 34-55. Washington, DC: Headquarters, Department of the Army, 1985.

Reeves, Robert; Anson, Abraham; and Landen, David. *Manual of Remote Sensing*. Falls Church, VA: American Society of Photogrammetry, 1975.

—**AERIAL SURVEILLANCE** is the systematic observation of air, surface, or subsurface areas by visual, electronic, photographic, or other means for intelligence purposes. Normally, surveillance mission is performed by a large-area coverage sensor (e.g., radar) or by visual observation from higher altitudes so that a large ground area can be covered at all times. *See also:* Aerial Reconnaissance.

References

Department of Defense, U.S. Army. *Intelligence Imagery*. Field Manual FM 34-55. Washington, DC: Headquarters, Department of the Army, 1985.

—**AFFILIATED UNIT** is a reserve component unit sponsored by an Active Army unit to improve readiness to a degree whereby the affiliated unit, after mobilization, may deploy with the sponsoring unit. *See also:* United States Army Reserve.

References

Department of Defense, U.S. Army. *Dictionary of United States Army Terms*. Army Regulation AR 310-25. Washington, DC: Headquarters, Department of the Army, 1986.

—**AFFILIATION** is the close and continuous association or identification of a soldier with a single regiment or institution. *See also:* Regimental Affiliation.

References

Department of Defense, U.S. Army. *Army Forces Training*. Army Regulation AR 350-41. Washington, DC: Headquarters, Department of the Army, 1986.

—**AFFILIATION PROGRAM** is a Department of the Army program that provides for planning, equipping, and training selected Reserve component battalions to achieve a degree of readiness whereby they might deploy as part of an Active Army division. *See also:* Affiliated Unit.

References

Department of Defense, U.S. Army. *Dictionary of United States Army Terms*. Army Regulation AR 310-25. Washington, DC: Headquarters, Department of the Army, 1986.

—**AFTER ACTION REVIEWS (AARs)** should occur at the conclusion of all training events and exercises. In AARs, which provide training as substantive as the activity itself, commanders determine whether the exercise objectives were accomplished based upon appropriate input from staffs, controllers, evaluators, umpires, and opposing forces. *See also:* Exercise.

References

Department of Defense, U.S. Army. *How to Conduct Training Exercises*. Field Manual FM 25-4. Washington, DC: Headquarters, Department of the Army, 1984.

—**AGENCY.** (1) An agency is a separate table of distribution and allowances organization under the direct supervision of Headquarters, Department of the Army. An agency's function can be described as having either a staff support or field operating mission. (2) An agency is a unit or organization that has primary responsibility for performing duties or functions as representative of, and within the assigned authority of, the headquarters to which it is subordinate. *See also:* Staff Support Agency.

References

Department of Defense, U.S. Army. *Dictionary of United States Army Terms*. Army Regulation AR 310-25. Washington, DC: Headquarters, Department of the Army, 1986.

—**AGENCY OF SIGNAL COMMUNICATION** is a facility that has the necessary personnel and equipment to provide signal communication.

References

Department of Defense, U.S. Army. *Dictionary of United States Army Terms*. Army Regulation AR 310-25. Washington, DC: Headquarters, Department of the Army, 1986.

————. *Tactical Single Channel Radio Communications Techniques*. Field Manual FM 24-18. Washington, DC: Headquarters, Department of the Army, 1984.

—**AGILITY** is the ability of friendly forces to act faster than the enemy. It is the first prerequisite for seizing and holding the initiative and such greater quickness permits the rapid concentration of friendly strength against enemy vulnerabilities. This must be done repeatedly so that by the time the enemy reacts to one action, another has taken place, disrupting its plans and leading to late, uncoordinated, and piecemeal responses. It is this process of successive concentration against a locally weaker or unprepared enemy that enables smaller forces to disorient, fragment, and eventually defeat much larger opposing forces.

References

Department of Defense, U.S. Army. *Staff Organization and Operations*. Field Manual FM 101-5. Washington, DC: Headquarters, Department of the Army, 1984.

—**AGREED POINT** is a predetermined point on the ground, identifiable from the air, used when aircraft assist in fire adjustment.

References

Department of Defense, Joint Chiefs of Staff. *Department of Defense Dictionary of Military and Related Terms*. Washington, DC: GPO, 1986.

—**AID MAN** is an enlisted individual of the Army Medical Department, attached to a company, battery, platoon, or troop, who gives emergency medical care and performs other health service functions. *See also:* Medical Treatment.

References

Department of Defense, U.S. Army. *Dictionary of United States Army Terms*. Army Regulation AR 310-25. Washington, DC: Headquarters, Department of the Army, 1986.

—**AID STATION** is a medical treatment facility where medical care, limited health service, and the sorting and disposition of the sick, injured,

and wounded are accomplished under the technical supervision of a medical officer. *See also:* Medical Treatment.

References

Department of Defense, U.S. Army. *Dictionary of United States Army Terms*. Army Regulation AR 310-25. Washington, DC: Headquarters, Department of the Army, 1986.

—**AIDE-DE-CAMP (ADC)** is an individual who performs duties as directed by the general officer. These duties vary according to the directions of each general officer based upon his position, rank, experiences, the size and duties of the military staff, and the number of people who are authorized on his personal staff.

References

Department of Defense, U.S. Army. *Staff Organization and Operations*. Field Manual FM 101-5. Washington, DC: Headquarters Department of the Army, 1983.

—**AIMING CIRCLE** is an instrument for measuring horizontal and vertical angles that is used for survey and for similar work in connection with artillery or machine-gun fire. It is equipped with a magnetic needle so that magnetic azimuths can be set off or read.

References

Department of Defense, U.S. Army. *Dictionary of United States Army Terms*. Army Regulation AR 310-25. Washington, DC: Headquarters, Department of the Army, 1986.

—**AIMING GROUP** is a pattern made on a surface by a series of pencil marks that test the ability of a soldier to sight a gun properly. The soldier directs a small disk target to be moved until it is aligned with the sights of a gun in a fixed position. The position of the disk is marked by a pencil dot made through the hole in the disk. Three such dots make up an aiming group.

References

Department of Defense, U.S. Army. *Dictionary of United States Army Terms*. Army Regulation AR 310-25. Washington, DC: Headquarters, Department of the Army, 1986.

—**AIMING POINT.** (1) An aiming point is an object or point on which the sight of a weapon is laid for direction, or on which an observer orients his observing instrument. (2) An aiming point is the point used by an air bombardier or pilot to determine the point of release of bombs, rockets, mines, or torpedoes.

References
Department of Defense, U.S. Army. *Dictionary of United States Army Terms.* Army Regulation AR 310-25. Washington, DC: Headquarters, Department of the Army, 1986.

—**AIMING POST** is a striped rod used as an aiming point for a gun.

References
Department of Defense, U.S. Army. *Dictionary of United States Army Terms.* Army Regulation AR 310-25. Washington, DC: Headquarters, Department of the Army, 1986.

—**AIR ADJUSTMENT** is the correction of gunfire based upon air observation.

References
Department of Defense, U.S. Army. *Dictionary of United States Army Terms.* Army Regulation AR 310-25. Washington, DC: Headquarters, Department of the Army, 1986.

—**AIR ASSAULT** involves operations in which air assault forces (i.e., combat, combat support, and combat service support), using the firepower, mobility, and total integration of helicopter assets in their ground or air roles, maneuver on the battlefield under the control of the ground or air maneuver commander to engage and destroy enemy forces.

References
Department of Defense, U.S. Army. *Operational Terms and Symbols.* Field Manual FM 101-5-1. Washington, DC: Headquarters, Department of the Army, 1985.

—**AIR AXIS OF ADVANCE,** for aviation elements, is a general air route from an assembly area or forward assembly area to a holding area or battle position. It may lead into the attack route for an attack element. It is broad, and elements using the axis are free to use terrain fighting techniques and specific routes according to the threat and the tactical situation. The air axis of advance can be established in conjunction with air corridors. *See also:* Air Corridor, Attack Route, Flight Route.

References
Department of Defense, U.S. Army. *Attack Helicopter Operations.* Field Manual FM 17-50. Washington, DC: Headquarters, Department of the Army, 1984.

—**AIR BATTLE CAPTAIN (ABC)** is an Army officer designated by the attack helicopter company commander to direct and orchestrate the battle from a scout helicopter. He is the ground commander's subordinate for directing the attack helicopter team supporting fires and for coordinating attack helicopters and close air support aircraft when they are working the same target array. *See also:* Attack Helicopter.

References
Department of Defense, U.S. Army. *Attack Helicopter Operations.* Field Manual FM 17-50. Washington, DC: Headquarters, Department of the Army, 1984.

—**AIR BATTLE MANAGEMENT** is a fundamental task of air defense command and control and airspace management that encompasses the principles for the control and coordination of both tactical air and ground-based air defense resources. Air battle management is exercised through positive and procedural methods.

References
Department of Defense, U.S. Army. *U.S. Army Air Defense Artillery Employment.* Field Manual FM 44-1. Washington, DC: Headquarters, Department of the Army, 1983.

—**AIR CONTROL POINT (ACP)** is an easily identifiable point on the terrain or an electronic navigational aid used to provide the necessary control during air movement. Air control points are generally designated at each point where the flight route makes a definite change in direction and at any other point deemed necessary for timing or control of the operation.

References
Department of Defense, U.S. Army. *Attack Helicopter Operations.* Field Manual FM 17-50. Washington, DC: Headquarters, Department of the Army, 1984.

———. *Dictionary of United States Army Terms.* Army Regulation AR 310-25. Washington, DC: Headquarters, Department of the Army, 1986.

———. *Operational Terms and Symbols.* Field Manual FM 101-5-1. Washington, DC: Headquarters, Department of the Army, 1985.

—**AIR CORRIDOR** is a restricted air route specified for use by friendly aircraft and protects them from being fired on by friendly forces. *See also:* Air Control Point, Communications Checkpoint.

References

Department of Defense, U.S. Army. *Air Defense Artillery Deployment: Chaparral/Vulcan/Stinger.* Field Manual FM 44- 3. Washington, DC: Headquarters, Department of the Army, 1984.

———. *Attack Helicopter Operations.* Field Manual FM 17-50. Washington, DC: Headquarters, Department of the Army, 1984.

———. *Operational Terms and Symbols.* Field Manual FM 101-5-1. Washington, DC: Headquarters, Department of the Army, 1985.

—**AIR DEFENSE ACTION (ADA) AREA** is an area and the airspace above it within which friendly aircraft or air defense action weapons are normally given precedence to operate except under specified conditions. This type of air defense operations area is primarily used to minimize mutual interference between friendly aircraft and ADA weapon systems. ADA areas that have been prioritized for ADA weapons are similar to restricted operations areas for aircraft except that ADA areas are normally in effect longer. *See also:* Air Defense Area.

References

Department of Defense, U.S. Army. *Patriot Battalion Operations.* Field Manual FM 44-15. Washington, DC: Headquarters, Department of the Army, 1984.

—**AIR DEFENSE AREA.** (1) An air defense area is a specifically defined airspace for which air defense must be planned and provided. This type of air defense operations area is primarily used for airspace control, but may also be used to define any area within which air defense action units are operating. (2) Overseas, an air defense area is a specifically defined airspace for which air defense must be planned and provided. (3) In the United States, an air defense area is an airspace of defined dimensions that has been designated by the appropriate agency within which airborne vehicles must be controlled in the interest of national security during an air defense emergency. *See also:* Air Defense Operations Area.

References

Department of Defense, U.S. Army. *Patriot Battalion Operations.* Field Manual FM 44-15. Washington, DC: Headquarters, Department of the Army, 1984.

—**AIR DEFENSE ARTILLERY CONTROLLER** is an air defense artillery officer located at the sector control center who provides information concerning activities at the sector control center to the Army air defense commander. *See also:* Air Defense Artillery Fire Unit.

References

Department of Defense, U.S. Army. *Dictionary of United States Army Terms.* Army Regulation AR 310-25. Washington, DC: Headquarters, Department of the Army, 1986.

—**AIR DEFENSE ARTILLERY DEFENDED AREA** is an air defense restricted area to which friendly aircraft are denied access except under certain specified conditions. *See also:* Air Defense Artillery Prohibited Area, Air Defense Restricted Area.

References

Department of Defense, U.S. Army. *Dictionary of United States Army Terms.* Army Regulation AR 310-25. Washington, DC: Headquarters, Department of the Army, 1986.

—**AIR DEFENSE ARTILLERY FIRE UNIT** is the smallest group of personnel and equipment of a particular air defense weapon system capable of conducting a complete engagement from detection to destruction.

References

Department of Defense, U.S. Army. *Dictionary of United States Army Terms.* Army Regulation AR 310-25. Washington, DC: Headquarters, Department of the Army, 1986.

—**AIR DEFENSE ARTILLERY METHODS OF CONTROL** are procedures by which the fires of air defense weapon systems are supervised in a particular defense. Theater rules or unit standing operating procedures may specify or imply use of either the centralized or decentralized method of control, or circumstances may force autonomous operations. *See also:* Air Defense Controller.

References

Department of Defense, U.S. Army. *Dictionary of United States Army Terms.* Army Regulation AR 310-25. Washington, DC: Headquarters, Department of the Army, 1986.

—**AIR DEFENSE ARTILLERY NEUTRALIZATION** is the destruction or reduction of effectiveness of air defense artillery units by direct measures or through electronic countermeasures.

References

Department of Defense, U.S. Army. *Dictionary of United States Army Terms.* Army Regulation AR 310-25. Washington, DC: Headquarters, Department of the Army, 1986.

—**AIR DEFENSE ARTILLERY OPERATIONS DETACHMENT** is an Army air defense artillery unit organized to operate the Army Air Defense Command Post.

References

Department of Defense, U.S. Army. *Dictionary of United States Army Terms.* Army Regulation AR 310-25. Washington, DC: Headquarters, Department of the Army, 1986.

—**AIR DEFENSE ARTILLERY OPERATIONS OFFICER** is the representative of the commander of all air defense artillery units operating in a defense. He supervises all air defense operations in the Army Air Defense Command Post. *See also:* Air Defense Artillery Operations.

References

Department of Defense, U.S. Army. *Dictionary of United States Army Terms.* Army Regulation AR 310-25. Washington, DC: Headquarters, Department of the Army, 1986.

—**AIR DEFENSE ARTILLERY PROHIBITED AREA** is an airspace to which friendly aircraft are denied access under all conditions. *See also:* Air Defense Artillery Defended Area, Air Defense Restricted Area.

References

Department of Defense, U.S. Army. *Dictionary of United States Army Terms.* Army Regulation AR 310-25. Washington, DC: Headquarters, Department of the Army, 1986.

—**AIR DEFENSE BATTLE ZONE** is a volume of airspace surrounding an air defense fire unit or defended area, extending to a specified altitude and range, in which the fire unit commander engages and destroys targets not identified as friendly under criteria established by higher headquarters. *See also:* Air Defense Action Area.

References

Department of Defense, Joint Chiefs of Staff. *Department of Defense Dictionary of Military and Related Terms.* Washington, DC: GPO, 1986.

—**AIR DEFENSE COMMAND** is the authority and responsibility for the air defense of a designated area. *See also:* Air Defense Commander.

References

Department of Defense, Joint Chiefs of Staff. *Department of Defense Dictionary of Military and Related Terms.* Washington, DC: GPO, 1986.

—**AIR DEFENSE COMMANDER** is a duly appointed commander responsible for the air defense of a designated area. *See also:* Air Defense Command.

References

Department of Defense, Joint Chiefs of Staff. *Department of Defense Dictionary of Military and Related Terms.* Washington, DC: GPO, 1986.

—**AIR DEFENSE CONDITIONS OF READINESS** are the means used by specified authorities to maintain the air defenses at a state of preparedness compatible with the real or apparent imminence of attack. "Defense readiness condition" and "defense readiness posture" are frequently used in relation to conditions of readiness. In response to each condition of readiness, the Army air defense commander prescribes a required state of alert for each air defense artillery unit under his command. *See also:* Air Defense Commander.

References

Department of Defense, U.S. Army. *Dictionary of United States Army Terms.* Army Regulation AR 310-25. Washington, DC: Headquarters, Department of the Army, 1986.

—**AIR DEFENSE CONTROL** is control from the ground or ship of all elements engaging in active air defense. *See also:* Air Defense Artillery Controller.

References

Department of Defense, U.S. Army. *Dictionary of United States Army Terms.* Army Regulation AR 310-25. Washington, DC: Headquarters, Department of the Army, 1986.

—**AIR DEFENSE CONTROL CENTER** is the principal information, communications, and operations center from which all aircraft, antiaircraft operations, air defense artillery, guided missiles, and air warning functions of a specific air defense area are supervised and coordinated. *See also:* Combat Information Center.

References

Department of Defense, Joint Chiefs of Staff. *Department of Defense Dictionary of Military and Related Terms.* Washington, DC: GPO, 1986.

—**AIR DEFENSE CONTROLLER** is a person charged with the specific responsibility of controlling (by radio, radar, or other means) aircraft used in air defense. *See also:* Air Defense Artillery Controller.

References

Department of Defense, U.S. Army. *Dictionary of United States Army Terms.* Army Regulation AR 310-25. Washington, DC: Headquarters, Department of the Army, 1986.

—**AIR DEFENSE DIRECTION CENTER** is an installation capable of performing air surveillance, interception control, and direction of allocated air defense weapons within an assigned sector of responsibility. It may also have an identification capability. *See also:* Air Defense Control Center.

References

Department of Defense, Joint Chiefs of Staff. *Department of Defense Dictionary of Military and Related Terms.* Washington, DC: GPO, 1986.

—**AIR DEFENSE DIVISION** is a geographic subdivision of an air defense region. *See also:* Air Defense Sector.

References

Department of Defense, Joint Chiefs of Staff. *Department of Defense Dictionary of Military and Related Terms.* Washington, DC: GPO, 1986.

—**AIR DEFENSE EMERGENCY** is an emergency condition, declared either by the Commander in Chief, North American Aerospace Defense Command or the Commander in Chief, Aerospace Defense Command, that exists when an attack upon the continental United States, Alaska, Canada, or U.S. installations in Greenland by hostile aircraft or missiles is probable, imminent, or taking place.

References

Department of Defense, Joint Chiefs of Staff. *Department of Defense Dictionary of Military and Related Terms.* Washington, DC: GPO, 1986.

—**AIR DEFENSE GROUND ENVIRONMENT** is the network of ground radar sites and command and control centers within a specific theater of operations that are used to tactically control air defense operations.

References

Department of Defense, Joint Chiefs of Staff. *Department of Defense Dictionary of Military and Related Terms.* Washington, DC: GPO, 1986.

—**AIR DEFENSE IDENTIFICATION ZONE (ADIZ).** (1) An air defense identification zone is a predetermined airspace within which the identification, location, and control of aircraft is required. The most famous ADIZ is off the U.S. East Coast. It has been the scene of numerous unannounced intrusions by Soviet reconnaissance aircraft going to or from Cuba. (2) ADIZ is a type of air defense operations area normally used for airspace control. Areas within an ADIZ are normally characterized by extremely stringent hostile criteria and weapons control statuses. In wartime, the ADIZ is usually bounded by the fire support coordination line and the forward edge of the battle area/forward line of own troops. Friendly aircraft begin minimum risk procedures at the fire support coordination line when returning to friendly airspace. *See also:* Air Defense Operations Area.

References

Department of Defense, U.S. Army. *Patriot Battalion Operations.* Field Manual FM 44-15. Washington, DC: Headquarters, Department of the Army, 1984.

—**AIR DEFENSE MISSION AREA** relates to detecting and engaging the air threat with ground fire systems. Air defense systems must protect all ground fire elements, including troop formations, depots, lines of communication, air bases, key command and control facilities, and other vital assets. *See also:* Air Defense Operations Area.

References

Department of Defense, U.S. Army. *Staff Organization and Operations.* Field Manual FM 101-5. Washington, DC: Headquarters, Department of the Army, 1984.

—**AIR DEFENSE OPERATIONS AREA (ADOA)** is an area and the airspace above it within which procedures are established to minimize mutual interference between air defense and other operations. These designations can include the air defense action area, air defense area, and air defense identification zone. *See also:* Air Defense Action Area, Air Defense Identification Zone.

References

Department of Defense, U.S. Army. *Patriot Battalion Operations.* Field Manual FM 44-15. Washington, DC: Headquarters, Department of the Army, 1984.

—**AIR DEFENSE PRIORITIES** are the commander's list of selected force assets ordered by importance that are to be defended by the supporting air defense action commander. *See also:* Air Defense Commander.

References

Department of Defense, U.S. Army. *Patriot Battalion Operations.* Field Manual FM 44-15. Washington, DC: Headquarters, Department of the Army, 1984.

————. *U.S. Army Air Defense Artillery Employment Hawk.* Field Manual FM 44-90. Washington, DC: Headquarters, Department of the Army, 1983.

—**AIR DEFENSE READINESS** is an operational status requiring air defense forces to maintain a higher than ordinary preparedness for a short time. *See also:* Air Defense Conditions of Readiness.

References

Department of Defense, Joint Chiefs of Staff. *Department of Defense Dictionary of Military and Related Terms.* Washington, DC: GPO, 1986.

—**AIR DEFENSE REGION** is a geographical subdivision of an air defense area. *See also:* Air Defense Area.

References

Department of Defense, Joint Chiefs of Staff. *Department of Defense Dictionary of Military and Related Terms.* Washington, DC: GPO, 1986.

—**AIR DEFENSE RESTRICTED AREA** is an airspace in which special restrictive measures are employed to prevent or minimize interference between friendly forces. *See also:* Air Defense Artillery Defended Area, Air Defense Artillery Prohibited Area.

References

Department of Defense, U.S. Army. *Dictionary of United States Army Terms.* Army Regulation AR 310-25. Washington, DC: Headquarters, Department of the Army, 1986.

—**AIR DEFENSE SECTOR** is a geographical subdivision of an air defense region. *See also:* Air Defense Division.

References

Department of Defense, Joint Chiefs of Staff. *Department of Defense Dictionary of Military and Related Terms.* Washington, DC: GPO, 1986.

—**AIR DEFENSE WARNINGS** reflect the degree of air raid probability according to the following codes:

- **YELLOW**—Air attack probable. Hostile aircraft and/or missiles are en route toward an air defense division/sector, or unknown aircraft and/or missiles suspected to be hostile are en route toward or are within an air defense division/sector.
- **RED**—Air attack imminent or in progress. Hostile aircraft and/or missiles are within an air defense division/sector or are in the immediate vicinity of an air defense division/sector with high probability of entering the division/sector.
- **WHITE**—Air attack not probable. This code may be declared before or after *yellow* or *red*. The initial declaration of an air defense emergency will automatically establish a condition of air defense warning other than white for purposes of security control of air traffic.

See also: Air Defense Conditions of Readiness.

References

Department of Defense, U.S. Army. *Operational Terms and Symbols.* Field Manual FM 101-5-1. Washington, DC: Headquarters, Department of the Army, 1985.

—**AIR DEFENSE WEAPON CONTROL CASE** is a method used to control employment of nuclear warheads in air defense. *See also:* Nuclear Warfare.

References

Department of Defense, U.S. Army. *Dictionary of United States Army Terms.* Army Regulation AR 310-25. Washington, DC: Headquarters, Department of the Army, 1986.

—**AIR DEFENSE WEAPONS CONTROL STATUS** is the degree of fire control imposed on Army units having assigned, attached, or organic air defense weapons. The weapons control status terms normally used are the following:

- **Weapons free.** Weapons may be fired at any aircraft *not positively identified as friendly.* This is the least restrictive of the weapons controls.
- **Weapons tight.** Weapons may be fired ONLY at aircraft *positively identified as hostile* according to the prevailing hostile criteria.
- **Weapons hold.** Weapons are NOT TO BE FIRED except in self-defense.

See also: Air Defense Control.

References
Department of Defense, U.S. Army. *Operational Terms and Symbols.* Field Manual FM 101-5-1. Washington, DC: Headquarters, Department of the Army, 1985.

—**AIR DELIVERY.** *See:* Airdrop.

—**AIR FORCE PERSONNEL WITH THE ARMY** are all military personnel of the Air Force attached by departmental orders for specific tours of duty with organizations of the Department of the Army. They are charged to Air Force command strength.

References
Department of Defense, U.S. Army. *Dictionary of United States Army Terms.* Army Regulation AR 310-25. Washington, DC: Headquarters, Department of the Army, 1986.

—**AIR INSTALLATION** is a command installation providing facilities for housing, training, and related activities necessary for the Air Forces, exclusive of modification centers, aircraft assembly plants, and aircraft parts plants. *See also:* Air-Ground Operations System.

References
Department of Defense, U.S. Army. *Dictionary of United States Army Terms.* Army Regulation AR 310-25. Washington, DC: Headquarters, Department of the Army, 1986.

—**AIR INTERDICTION (AI).** (1) Air interdiction involves air operations that are conducted to destroy, neutralize, or delay the enemy's military potential before it can be used effectively against friendly forces. It is conducted at distances sufficiently removed from friendly forces that detailed integration of each air mission with the fire and movement of friendly forces is not required. (2) AI operations delay, disrupt, divert, or destroy an enemy's military potential before it can be used effectively against friendly forces. These combat operations are performed at distances sufficiently removed from friendly surface forces that detailed integration of specific actions with the fire and movement of friendly forces is normally not required. AI attacks are usually executed against enemy surface forces; movement networks (including lines of communication); command, control, and communications networks; and combat supplies. Interdiction of the enemy can delay the arrival or buildup of forces and supplies, disrupt the enemy's scheme

of operation and control of forces, divert valuable enemy resources to other uses, and destroy forces and supplies. *See also:* Air-Ground Operations System.

References
Department of Defense, U.S. Army. *Attack Helicopter Operations.* Field Manual FM 17-50. Washington, DC: Headquarters, Department of the Army, 1984.

———. *Operational Terms and Symbols.* Field Manual FM 101-5-1. Washington, DC: Headquarters, Department of the Army, 1985.

———. *Operations.* Field Manual FM 100-5. Washington, DC: Headquarters, Department of the Army, 1986.

—**AIR LANDING FACILITY** is the minimum essential facility that can reasonably be constructed in an airhead to permit the continuous air landing of aircraft. The term denotes facilities less elaborate than an airfield. *See also:* Air-Ground Operations System.

References
Department of Defense, U.S. Army. *Dictionary of United States Army Terms.* Army Regulation AR 310-25. Washington, DC: Headquarters, Department of the Army, 1986.

—**AIR LANDING SITE** is a location that could be made into an airstrip or airfield. *See also:* Air-Ground Operations System.

References
Department of Defense, U.S. Army. *Route Reconnaissance and Classification.* Field Manual FM 5-36. Washington, DC: Headquarters, Department of the Army, 1985.

—**AIR LIAISON OFFICER (ALO)** is the senior Air Force officer at each tactical air control party. He advises the Army commander and his staff on the capabilities, limitations, and employment of tactical air operations. He operates the Air Force request net, coordinates close air support missions with the fire support element, and assists in planning the simultaneous employment of air and surface fires. He supervises the forward air controllers and assists the fire support team in directing air strikes in the absence of a forward air controller. *See also:* Tactical Air Control Party.

References
Department of Defense, U.S. Army. *Route Reconnaissance and Classification.* Field Manual FM 5-36. Washington, DC: Headquarters, Department of the Army, 1985.

—AIR LINE OF COMMUNICATION (ALOC) is a system that provides air shipments (regardless of their priority) of selected supplies. *See also:* Sea Line of Communication.

References

Department of Defense, U.S. Army. *Repair Parts Supply for a Theater of Operations.* Field Manual FM 29-19. Washington, DC: Headquarters, Department of the Army, 1985.

—AIR MANEUVER FORCES are combat aviation units that operate in the ground environment. They engage targets by fire from covered and concealed positions. Their operations are similar to ground combat operations in that they tailor their movements to the terrain and use suppressive fires. These units are integrated into the ground force commander's tactical plan. They can control terrain by denying the enemy its use by aerial direct fire for limited periods of time. *See also:* Combat Maneuver Forces.

References

Department of Defense, U.S. Army. *Attack Helicopter Operations.* Field Manual FM 17-50. Washington, DC: Headquarters, Department of the Army, 1984.

———. *Operational Terms and Symbols.* Field Manual FM 101-5-1. Washington, DC: Headquarters, Department of the Army, 1985.

—AIR MISSION COMMANDER (AMC). Operations of aviation elements providing air assault support are controlled by the commander of the largest supporting aviation unit. He is designated the AMC. *See also:* Air Mobile Operations.

References

Department of Defense, U.S. Army. *Operational Terms and Symbols.* Field Manual FM 101-5-1. Washington, D.C.: Headquarters, Department of the Army, 1985.

—AIR MOBILE FORCES are the ground combat, supporting, and air vehicle units required to conduct an air mobile operation. *See also:* Air Mobile Operations.

References

Department of Defense, Joint Chiefs of Staff. *Department of Defense Dictionary of Military and Related Terms.* Washington, DC: GPO, 1986.

—AIR MOBILE OPERATIONS are operations in which combat forces and their equipment move about the battlefield in air vehicles in order to engage in combat. These forces are under the control of the ground force commander. *See also:* Air Mission Commander, Air Mobile Forces, Air Mobile Support Party, Air Mobility, Air Movement Operations, Air Movement Phase.

References

Department of Defense, Joint Chiefs of Staff. *Department of Defense Dictionary of Military and Related Terms.* Washington, DC: GPO, 1986.

—AIR MOBILE SUPPORT PARTY is an Army task organization formed for use in a landing zone to facilitate the assault landing and interim logistical support of elements of the landing zone. *See also:* Air Mobile Operations.

References

Department of Defense, U.S. Army. *Dictionary of United States Army Terms.* Army Regulation AR 310-25. Washington, DC: Headquarters, Department of the Army, 1986.

—AIR MOBILITY is the capability of air mobile forces to move by air vehicles while retaining the ability to engage in ground combat. *See also:* Air Mobile Operations.

References

Department of Defense, Joint Chiefs of Staff. *Department of Defense Dictionary of Military and Related Terms.* Washington, DC: GPO, 1986.

—AIR MOVEMENT OPERATIONS are activities that use airlift assets, primarily helicopters, to move combat, combat support forces, and/or equipment whose primary purpose is *not* to engage and destroy enemy forces. *See also:* Air Mobile Operations.

References

Department of Defense, U.S. Army. *Operational Terms and Symbols.* Field Manual FM 101-5-1. Washington, DC: Headquarters, Department of the Army, 1985.

—AIR MOVEMENT PHASE is the transit phase of an airborne, air assault, or air movement operation that begins with the takeoff of loaded aircraft from departure areas and ends with the delivery of units to their drop zones or landing zones. *See also:* Air Mobile Operations.

References

Department of Defense, U.S. Army. *Operational Terms and Symbols.* Field Manual FM 101-5-1. Washington, DC: Headquarters, Department of the Army, 1985.

—**AIR MOVEMENT PLAN** is a plan prepared jointly by ground and airlift units. It covers the phase of an airborne, air assault, or air movement operation from the time units have loaded aircraft until they arrive at the objective area. The schedule indicates loading times at specific departure airfields or pickup zones, takeoff time, flight routes, order of flight, and arrival time over drop zones or landing zones. Usually, it is published as an annex to the operation plan. *See also*: Ground Tactical Plan, Landing Plan.

References
Department of Defense, U.S. Army. *Dictionary of United States Army Terms.* Army Regulation AR 310-25. Washington, DC: Headquarters, Department of the Army, 1986.

———. *Operational Terms and Symbols.* Field Manual FM 101-5-1. Washington, DC: Headquarters, Department of the Army, 1985.

—**AIR OBSERVER** is an individual whose primary mission is to observe or take photographs from an aircraft in order to adjust indirect fires or to obtain military information. *See also:* Air Observer's Adjustment.

References
Department of Defense, U.S. Army. *Fire Support in Combined Arms Operations.* Field Manual FM 6-20. Washington, DC: Headquarters, Department of the Army, 1983.

—**AIR OBSERVER'S ADJUSTMENT** is the correcting of fires by an air observer who is in an airborne vehicle.

References
Department of Defense, U.S. Army. *Fire Support in Combined Arms Operations.* Field Manual FM 6-20. Washington, DC: Headquarters, Department of the Army, 1983.

—**AIR SECTOR OPERATIONS CENTER.** (1) An air sector operations center is a section, organic to the air defense brigade and an augmentation to the air defense group, that establishes liaison with the Air Force tactical air control center to obtain early warning and identification and to coordinate the commitment of air defense weapons. (2) An air sector operations center is a section, organic to the air defense brigade and an augmentation to the air defense group, that establishes liaison with the Air Force tactical air defense weapons. *See also:* Air-Ground Operations System.

References
Department of Defense, U.S. Army. *Dictionary of United States Army Terms.* Army Regulation AR 310-25. Washington, DC: Headquarters, Department of the Army, 1986.

—**AIR SIGNAL** is a signal from an aircraft used to communicate between air and ground forces when a radio cannot be used. It may be made by dipping the wing, dropping a flame, or firing fireworks that give off an intense colored light. *See also:* Air-Ground Operations System.

References
Department of Defense, U.S. Army. *Dictionary of United States Army Terms.* Army Regulation AR 310-25. Washington, DC: Headquarters, Department of the Army, 1986.

—**AIR STRIKE** is an attack on specific targets by fighter, bomber, or attack aircraft. *See also:* Air-Ground Operations System.

References
Department of Defense, U.S. Army. *Air Defense Artillery Deployment: Chaparral/Vulcan/Stinger.* Field Manual FM 44-3. Washington, DC: Headquarters, Department of the Army, 1984.

———. *Operational Terms and Symbols.* Field Manual FM 101-5-1. Washington, DC: Headquarters, Department of the Army, 1985.

—**AIR SUPERIORITY** is dominance in, or control of, the air to the degree that friendly land, sea, and air forces can operate at specific times and places without prohibitive interference by enemy air forces.

References
Collins, John M. *U.S.-Soviet Military Balance, 1980-1985.* Washington, DC: Congressional Research Service, 1985.

—**AIR SUPPORT** is all forms of support given by air forces to forces on land or at sea. *See also:* Air-Ground Operations System.

References
Department of Defense, U.S. Army. *Operational Terms and Symbols.* Field Manual FM 101-5-1. Washington, DC: Headquarters, Department of the Army, 1985.

—**AIR SUPPORT OPERATIONS CENTER (ASOC)** is the Air Force element that interfaces with the corps tactical operations center. It serves as a focal and contact point for joint air-land operations at the corps level. The ASOC plans, coordinates, and directs the tactical air support of the ground forces. It is subordinate to the tactical air control center and provides fast reaction to immediate requests for close air support. Normally, the ASOC is collocated with a corps tactical operations center, but it can also be deployed with an independent operating division or brigade. An ASOC is primarily concerned with the exchange between air and ground forces of combat data concerning the planning, coordination, and execution of tactical air support ground operations. Provisions are made within the ASOC for G2 and G3 air representation as required for multiservice operations. *See also:* Air-Ground Operations System.

References

Department of Defense, U.S. Army. *Fire Support in Combined Arms Operations.* Field Manual FM 6-20. Washington, DC: Headquarters, Department of the Army, 1983.

———. *Operational Terms and Symbols.* Field Manual FM 101-5-1. Washington, DC: Headquarters, Department of the Army, 1985.

—**AIR TACTICAL OBSERVER** is an officer trained as an air observer whose function is to observe from an aircraft in flight and report on the movement and disposition of friendly and enemy forces. *See also:* Air-Ground Operations System.

References

Department of Defense, U.S. Army. *Dictionary of United States Army Terms.* Army Regulation AR 310-25. Washington, DC: Headquarters, Department of the Army, 1986.

—**AIR TASK FORCE** is a group of air, ground, and service units that carry out air missions as outlined in a plan. *See also:* Air-Ground Operations System.

References

Department of Defense, U.S. Army. *Dictionary of United States Army Terms.* Army Regulation AR 310-25. Washington, DC: Headquarters, Department of the Army, 1986.

—**AIR TRAFFIC CONTROL FACILITY** is a service component airspace control facility involved in air traffic control in the area of operations. *See also:* Airspace Control.

References

Department of Defense, U.S. Army. *Airspace Management and Army Air Traffic in a Combat Zone.* Field Manual FM 1-60. Washington, DC: Headquarters, Department of the Army, 1977.

—**AIR TRAFFIC IDENTIFICATION** involves using electronic devices, operational procedures, visual observation, and/or flight plan correlation to identify and locate aircraft that are flying within the airspace control area. *See also:* Airspace Control.

References

Department of Defense, U.S. Army. *Airspace Management and Army Air Traffic in a Combat Zone.* Field Manual FM 1-60. Washington, DC: Headquarters, Department of the Army, 1977.

—**AIR TRANSPORTABLE UNIT** is a unit, other than an airborne unit, whose equipment has been adapted for air movement. *See also:* Air-Ground Operations System.

References

Department of Defense, U.S. Army. *Operational Terms and Symbols.* Field Manual FM 101-5-1. Washington, DC: Headquarters, Department of the Army, 1985.

—**AIRBORNE.** (1) Airborne is applied to personnel or equipment transported by air (e.g., airborne artillery). (2) Airborne applies to materials that are being, or are designed to be, transported by aircraft (as distinguished from weapons and equipment that are installed in and remain part of the aircraft). (3) Airborne is the state of an aircraft, from the instant it becomes entirely sustained by air until it ceases to be sustained. A lighter-than-air aircraft is not considered airborne when it is attached to the ground, except that moored balloons are airborne whenever they are sent aloft. *See also:* Airborne Assault Weapon, Airborne Beacon, Airborne Command Post, Airborne Force, Airborne Force Commander, Airborne Force Liaison Officer, Airborne Operation, Airborne Units, Airborne Vehicle, Air Transportable Unit.

References

Department of Defense, Joint Chiefs of Staff. *Department of Defense Dictionary of Military and Related Terms.* Washington, DC: GPO, 1986.

Department of Defense, U.S. Army. *Air Cavalry Combat Brigade.* Field Manual FM 17-47. Washington, DC: Headquarters, Department of the Army, 1982.

—**AIRBORNE ASSAULT WEAPON** is an unarmored, mobile, full-tracked gun that provides a mobile antitank capability for airborne troops. Airborne assault weapons can be airdropped. *See also:* Airborne.

References

Department of Defense, Joint Chiefs of Staff. *Department of Defense Dictionary of Military and Related Terms.* Washington, DC: GPO, 1986.

—**AIRBORNE BEACON** is an infrared light transmitter used to assist in the reorganization of forces at night. It is also used to mark drop and landing zones.

References

Department of Defense, U.S. Army. *Dictionary of United States Army Terms.* Army Regulation AR 310-25. Washington, DC: Headquarters, Department of the Army, 1986.

—**AIRBORNE COMMAND POST** is a suitably equipped aircraft used by the commander to control his forces.

References

Department of Defense, U.S. Army. *Operational Terms and Symbols.* Field Manual FM 101-5-1. Washington, DC: Headquarters, Department of the Army, 1985.

—**AIRBORNE FORCE** is a force composed of ground and air units that have been organized, equipped, and trained for primary delivery by airdrop or by airlanded techniques into an area. *See also:* Airborne Force Commander.

References

Department of Defense, U.S. Army. *Operational Terms and Symbols.* Field Manual FM 101-5-1. Washington, DC: Headquarters, Department of the Army, 1985.

—**AIRBORNE FORCE COMMANDER** is the senior commander of all Army airborne units engaged in a specific airborne operation.

References

Department of Defense, U.S. Army. *USA/USAF Doctrine for Joint Airborne and Tactical Airlift Operations.* Field Manual FM 100-27. Washington, DC: Headquarters, Department of the Army, 1985.

—**AIRBORNE FORCE LIAISON OFFICER** is an officer who is the representative of the airborne units and who works with the Air Force on airfields used for airborne operations.

References

Department of Defense, Joint Chiefs of Staff. *Department of Defense Dictionary of Military and Related Terms.* Washington, DC: GPO, 1986.

—**AIRBORNE OPERATION** is an operation involving the air movement of combat forces into an objective area and their logistic support for executing a tactical or a strategic mission. The means used may be any combination of airborne units, air transportable units, and transportable aircraft, depending on the mission and the overall situation.

References

Department of Defense, Joint Chiefs of Staff. *Department of Defense Dictionary of Military and Related Terms.* Washington, DC: GPO, 1986.

Department of Defense, U.S. Army. *Air Cavalry Combat Brigade.* Field Manual FM 17-47. Washington, DC: Headquarters, Department of the Army, 1982.

—**AIRBORNE TROOPS** are ground units that have a primary mission of making assault landings from the air. *See also:* Troops.

References

Department of Defense, Joint Chiefs of Staff. *Department of Defense Dictionary of Military and Related Terms.* Washington, DC: GPO, 1986.

Department of Defense, U.S. Army. *Air Cavalry Combat Brigade.* Field Manual FM 17-47. Washington, DC: Headquarters, Department of the Army, 1982.

—**AIRBORNE UNITS** are Army units that have been organized, equipped, and trained primarily for making assault landings from the air.

References

Department of Defense, U.S. Army. *USA/USAF Doctrine for Joint Airborne and Tactical Airlift Operations.* Field Manual FM 100-27. Washington, DC: Headquarters, Department of the Army, 1985.

—**AIRBORNE VEHICLE** is any air platform that is in flight.

References

Department of Defense, U.S. Army. *Dictionary of United States Army Terms.* Army Regulation AR 310-25. Washington, DC: Headquarters, Department of the Army, 1986.

—**AIRBURST** is an explosion of a bomb or a projectile above the surface (as distinguished from an explosion on contact with the surface or after penetration).

References

Department of Defense, Joint Chiefs of Staff. *Department of Defense Dictionary of Military and Related Terms.* Washington, DC: GPO, 1986.

—**AIRCRAFT CREW** consists of the pilot/gunner and copilot/gunner.

References

Department of Defense, U.S. Army. *Ammunition and Explosives Safety Standards*. Army Regulation AR 385-64. Washington, DC: Headquarters, Department of the Army, 1987.

—**AIRCRAFT PASSENGER TRANSPORT OPERA-TIONS** are operations conducted to apply explosives Q-D tables. They are defined as passenger transport traffic involving military dependents and civilians other than those who are employed by, or are working directly for, Department of Defense components.

References

Department of Defense, U.S. Army. *Ammunition and Explosives Safety Standards*. Army Regulation AR 385-64. Washington, DC: Headquarters, Department of the Army, 1987.

—**AIRCRAFT SERVICING** is the refueling of aircraft with consumables (e.g., fuel, oil, and compressed gases) to predetermined levels, pressures, quantities, or weights.

References

Department of Defense, U.S. Army. *Dictionary of United States Army Terms*. Army Regulation AR 310-25. Washington, DC: Headquarters, Department of the Army, 1986.

—**AIRCRAFT SURVIVABILITY** is the capability of an aircraft to withstand enemy actions, materiel deterioration, or the effects of natural phenomena that singularly or collectively cause it to lose its capability to perform the mission(s) for which it is designed.

References

Department of Defense, U.S. Army. *Dictionary of United States Army Terms*. Army Regulation AR 310-25. Washington, DC: Headquarters, Department of the Army, 1986.

—**AIRCRAFT TURNAROUND** is the replenishing of an aircraft with consumable or expendable stores and equipment to render it fit for immediate operational readiness. *See also:* Aircraft Servicing.

References

Department of Defense, U.S. Army. *Dictionary of United States Army Terms*. Army Regulation AR 310-25. Washington, DC: Headquarters, Department of the Army, 1986.

—**AIRCRAFT VULNERABILITY MEASUREMENT** is the measure of the factors affecting vulnerability to include built-in protective devices, design criteria, stability, reliability, retaliatory weaponry, and air crew proficiency. *See also:* Aircraft Survivability.

References

Department of Defense, U.S. Army. *Dictionary of United States Army Terms*. Army Regulation AR 310-25. Washington, DC: Headquarters, Department of the Army, 1986.

—**AIRDROP.** (1) Airdrop is the unloading of personnel or materiel from an aircraft in flight. (2) Airdrop is a method of delivering supplies and equipment from aircraft to ground elements. As a rule, airdrop is a joint effort between Army and Air Force elements. Air Force airlift aircraft carry the airdrop items to the target area and effect delivery. Both Air Force and Army personnel support the operation on the ground. The airdrop categories are freedrop, low-velocity, high-velocity, and high-altitude low-opening. *See also:* Air Movement Phase.

References

Department of Defense, U.S. Army. *Operational Terms and Symbols*. Field Manual FM 101-5-1. Washington, DC: Headquarters, Department of the Army, 1985.

———. *USA/USAF Doctrine for Joint Airborne and Tactical Airlift Operations*. Field Manual FM 100-27. Washington, DC: Headquarters, Department of the Army, 1985.

—**AIRDROP EQUIPMENT** is special equipment used to airdrop personnel, supplies, and equipment. *See also:* Airdrop.

References

Department of Defense, U.S. Army. *Dictionary of United States Army Terms*. Army Regulation AR 310-25. Washington, DC: Headquarters, Department of the Army, 1986.

—**AIRFIELD** is an area designed for aircraft takeoff and landing. It has the normal air-support facilities (e.g., hangars, fuel storage areas, and outbuildings). *See also:* Air-Ground Operations System.

References

Department of Defense, U.S. Army. *Route Reconnaissance and Classification*. Field Manual FM 5-36. Washington, DC: Headquarters, Department of the Army, 1985.

—**AIRFIELD HELIPORT** is an area designed and prepared to accommodate landing and takeoff of aircraft and helicopters. See also: Air-Ground Operations System.

References

Department of Defense, U.S. Army. *Dictionary of United States Army Terms*. Army Regulation AR 310-25. Washington, DC: Headquarters, Department of the Army, 1986.

—**AIR-GROUND LIAISON CODE** is a set of symbols for a limited number of words, phrases, and sentences used for communications between air and ground forces. These symbols can be given by radio, telephone, blinker, or strips of cloth called air-ground liaison panels. *See also:* Air-Ground Operations System.

References

Department of Defense, U.S. Army. *Dictionary of United States Army Terms*. Army Regulation AR 310-25. Washington, DC: Headquarters, Department of the Army, 1986.

—**AIR-GROUND OPERATIONS SYSTEM (AGOS)** is an Army-Air Force system that provides the ground commander with the means to receive, process, and forward the requests of subordinate ground commanders for air support missions and to rapidly disseminate information and intelligence. It includes the personnel, equipment, procedures, and techniques that make up the Army air-ground system and the U.S. Air Force tactical air control system. *See also:* Army Air-Ground System.

References

Department of Defense, U.S. Army. *Attack Helicopter Operations*. Field Manual FM 17-50. Washington, DC: Headquarters, Department of the Army, 1984.

—**AIRHEAD.** (1) An airhead is a designated area in a hostile or threatened territory that, when secured, permits the delivery (airdropped or airlanded) of forces and supplies and provides maneuver space for operations. Normally, it is the area that is seized in the assault phase of an airborne or air assault operation. (2) An airhead is a designated location in an area of operations used as a base for supply and evacuation by air. *See also*: Beachhead, Bridgehead.

References

Department of Defense, U.S. Army. *Operational Terms and Symbols*. Field Manual FM 101-5-1. Washington, DC: Headquarters, Department of the Army, 1985.

—**AIRHEAD LINE** is a line described or portrayed in an operation order the marks the outside limit of the part of the airhead that is to be denied to the enemy. *See also*: Airhead.

References

Department of Defense, U.S. Army. *Dictionary of United States Army Terms*. Army Regulation AR 310-25. Washington, DC: Headquarters, Department of the Army, 1986.

————. *Operational Terms and Symbols*. Field Manual FM 101-5-1. Washington, DC: Headquarters, Department of the Army, 1985.

—**AIRLAND BATTLE** is the Army's operational concept outlining an approach to military operations that is based upon securing or retaining the initiative and exercising it aggressively to defeat the enemy. Two concepts—extending the battlefield and integrating conventional, nuclear, chemical, and electronic means—Are combined to describe a battlefield where the enemy is attacked to the full depth of its formations. See also: AirLand Battle Doctrine, AirLand Operation, AirLand Supply, AirLand Units.

References

Department of Defense, U.S. Army. *U.S. Army Air Defense Artillery Employment*. Field Manual FM 44-1. Washington, DC: Headquarters, Department of the Army, 1983.

—**AIRLAND BATTLE DOCTRINE.** (1) According to the U.S. Army Posture Statement for Fiscal Year 1988, AirLand Battle doctrine is "the rationale that guides the Army in how it fights. It provides the logic, in conjunction with an analysis of the threat, for the development of forces to meet national security missions. AirLand Battle recognizes the joint nature of modern warfare and has been a catalyst among military professionals, stimulating discussions of the present and future dimensions of military power. One of AirLand Battle's contributions to American military thought has been the reintroduction of the operational art in the conduct of war as the focus of military activity between tactics and strategy."

AirLand Battle seeks to exploit the full potential of U.S. and allied forces by synchronizing all combat means. The doctrine is rooted in time-tested theories and principles, is forward-looking and adaptable to changing technologies, and can accommodate a variety of worldwide situations.

AirLand Battle emphasizes securing the initiative and exploiting it vigorously to defeat the enemy. This is achieved by throwing the enemy off balance with powerful initial blows from unexpected directions and following up rapidly to prevent its recovery.

To ensure unity of effort and success in combat, all three areas of operations (deep, close, and rear) are interrelated parts of one battle. Deep operations are designed to shape conditions in which future close operations will be conducted. Close operations are designed to engage the enemy in close combat to defeat it. Rear operations are designed to assure freedom of maneuver, continuity of operations, and uninterrupted service support. Friendly forces, as a result of synchronized close, rear, and deep operations, can seize the initiative and make the best use of all available combat power.

AirLand Battle emphasizes the use of conventional weapons. It also provides for nuclear and chemical operations, but only after specific authorization by U.S. National Command Authorities.

The Army seldom fights alone. Since 1983, the U.S. Air Force has agreed to use AirLand Battle doctrine in conjunction with its Aerospace Operational doctrine as the basis for joint combat operations. When Army forces are deployed in allied or coalition operations, AirLand Battle doctrine is adaptable to allied political and military guidelines, procedures, and operations plans. AirLand Battle is compatible with and complementary to NATO's strategy and operational concepts to include the Follow-on Forces Attack concept for deep operations.

(2) The Army states:

AirLand Battle doctrine describes the Army's approach to generating and applying combat power at the operational and tactical levels. It is based on securing or retaining the initiative and exercising it aggressively to accomplish the mission. The object of all operations is to impose the Army's will upon the enemy to achieve its purposes. To do this it must throw the enemy off balance with a powerful blow from an unexpected direction, follow up rapidly to prevent his recovery, and continue operations aggressively to achieve the higher commander's goals. The best results are obtained when powerful blows are struck against critical units or areas whose loss will degrade the coherence of enemy operations in depth, and thus most rapidly and economically accomplish the mission. From the enemy's point of view, these operations must be rapid, unpredictable, violent, and disorienting. The pace must be fast enough to prevent him from taking effective counteractions.

The U.S. Army's basic fighting doctrine is called AirLand Battle. It reflects the structure of modern warfare, the dynamics of combat power, and the application of the classical principles of war to contemporary battlefield requirements. It is called AirLand Battle in recognition of the inherently three-dimensional nature of modern warfare. All ground actions above the level of the smallest engagements are strongly affected by the supporting air operations of one or both combatants. *See also*: AirLand Battle.

References

Department of Defense, U.S. Army. *Fire Support in Combined Arms Operations*. Field Manual FM 6-20. Washington, DC: Headquarters, Department of the Army, 1983.

————. *Operations*. Field Manual FM 100-5. Washington, DC: Headquarters, Department of the Army, 1986.

—AIRLAND OPERATION involves an air movement in which personnel and supplies are airlanded at a designated destination for further deployment of units and personnel and further distribution of supplies. *See also:* AirLand Battle.

References

Department of Defense, U.S. Army. *Dictionary of United States Army Terms*. Army Regulation AR 310-25. Washington, DC: Headquarters, Department of the Army, 1986.

————. *USA/USAF Doctrine for Joint Airborne and Tactical Airlift Operations*. Field Manual FM 100-27. Washington, DC: Headquarters, Department of the Army, 1985.

—AIRLAND SUPPLY is the supply or resupply by air to ground units in which aircraft hover or are landed and are unloaded onto the ground. *See also:* AirLand Battle.

References

Department of Defense, U.S. Army. *Dictionary of United States Army Terms*. Army Regulation AR 310-25. Washington, DC: Headquarters, Department of the Army, 1986.

—AIRLAND UNITS are units, other than airborne units, that are transported by aircraft in an airborne operation and that are disembarked from hovering or landed aircraft. *See also:* AirLand Battle.

References

Department of Defense, U.S. Army. *Dictionary of United States Army Terms.* Army Regulation AR 310-25. Washington, DC: Headquarters, Department of the Army, 1986.

—**AIRLANDED** is an operation in which personnel and materiel are moved by air and are disembarked or unloaded after the aircraft has landed or while the helicopter is hovering.

References

Department of Defense, U.S. Army. *Operational Terms and Symbols.* Field Manual FM 101-5-1. Washington, DC: Headquarters, Department of the Army, 1985.

—**AIRLIFT CONTROL CENTER** is a command and control center that is usually in the main operating base where most of the tactical aircraft are based. It plots resource assets and allocations to meet mission requirements. A part of the Airlift Task Force and a subcommand of the major Air Force component, it is established before employment in contingency operations. *See also:* Airlift Missions.

References

Department of Defense, U.S. Army. *Operational Terms and Symbols.* Field Manual FM 101-5-1. Washington, DC: Headquarters, Department of the Army, 1985.

—**AIRLIFT MISSIONS** deploy, employ, and/or support conventional operations and unconventional warfare, and sustain military forces. Airlift is performed in peacetime and in war. In combat, airlift projects power through airdropping, extracting, and airlanding ground forces and supplies. Through mobility operations, the joint or combined force commander can maneuver fighting forces to exploit an enemy's weaknesses. In combat support missions, airlift provides logistics support by transporting personnel and equipment. In peacetime, airlift enhances national objectives by providing military assistance and supporting civilian relief programs.

Airlift may be performed from a strategic or an operational/tactical perspective. Strategic (intertheater) airlift transcends the boundary of any one theater and is executed under the central direction of a higher authority. In contrast, operational/tactical intratheater airlift is performed within a theater of operations and supports theater objectives by rapidly and responsively moving personnel and supplies. *See also:* Airlift Control Center.

References

Department of Defense, U.S. Army. *Operational Terms and Symbols.* Field Manual FM 101-5-1. Washington, DC: Headquarters, Department of the Army, 1985.

—**AIRSPACE CONTROL** is a service provided within the combat zone that contributes to combat effectiveness by promoting safe, efficient, and flexible use of the airspace. It is provided to permit operational flexibility in the controlled airspace, while the authority to approve, disapprove, or deny combat operations is vested only in the joint force commander. *See also:* Airspace control Area, Airspace control Authority, Airspace Control Boundary, Airspace Control Center, Airspace Control Facility, Airspace Control Sector, Airspace Control Sector Authority, Airspace Control System, Airspace Coordination, Airspace Coordination Area, Airspace Management, Airspace Management Center, Airspace Management Element, Airspace Management Liaison Section, Airspace Restricted Area, Airspace Restrictions.

References

Department of Defense, U.S. Army. *Airspace Management and Army Air Traffic in a Combat Zone.* Field Manual FM 1-60. Washington, DC: Headquarters, Department of the Army, 1977.

—**AIRSPACE CONTROL AREA** is airspace laterally defined by the boundaries of a joint force area of operations. The airspace control area can be subdivided into airspace control sectors. *See also:* Airspace Control.

References

Department of Defense, U.S. Army. *Airspace Management and Army Air Traffic in a Combat Zone.* Field Manual FM 1-60. Washington, DC: Headquarters, Department of the Army, 1977.

—**AIRSPACE CONTROL AUTHORITY** is a service component commander who has been designated by the joint force commander to plan and coordinate airspace control matters concerning the operations of the airspace control system in the airspace control area. He is usually the Air Force Component Commander/Commander, U.S. Air Forces. *See also:* Airspace Control.

References

Department of Defense, U.S. Army. *Airspace Management and Army Air Traffic in a Combat Zone.* Field Manual FM 1-60. Washington, DC: Headquarters, Department of the Army, 1977.

—**AIRSPACE CONTROL BOUNDARY** is a lateral limit of an airspace control area, airspace restriction, or high-density airspace control zone.

References

Department of Defense, U.S. Army. *Airspace Management and Army Air Traffic in a Combat Zone*. Field Manual FM 1-60. Washington, DC: Headquarters, Department of the Army, 1977.

—**AIRSPACE CONTROL CENTER (ACC)**, an element within the tactical air control center, includes component service liaison and is responsible for planning and establishing rules and procedures for the coordinated and integrated use of airspace by all component forces.

References

Department of Defense, U.S. Army. *Airspace Management and Army Air Traffic in a Combat Zone*. Field Manual FM 1-60. Washington, DC: Headquarters, Department of the Army, 1977.

—**AIRSPACE CONTROL FACILITY** provides airspace control in the combat zone. These facilities can include the airspace control center, airspace management center, air traffic control facilities, airspace management elements, air defense command posts, and other elements of the tactical air control system. *See also:* Airspace Control.

References

Department of Defense, U.S. Army. *Airspace Management and Army Air Traffic in a Combat Zone*. Field Manual FM 1-60. Washington, DC: Headquarters, Department of the Army, 1977.

—**AIRSPACE CONTROL SECTOR** is a subdivision of the airspace control area. It is designated by the airspace control authority, who has duly considered service component airspace control capabilities and requirements. *See also:* Airspace Control.

References

Department of Defense, U.S. Army. *Airspace Management and Army Air Traffic in a Combat Zone*. Field Manual FM 1-60. Washington, DC: Headquarters, Department of the Army, 1977.

—**AIRSPACE CONTROL SECTOR AUTHORITY** is the individual designated by the airspace control authority as coordinating authority for airspace control within an airspace control sector. *See also:* Airspace Control.

References

Department of Defense, U.S. Army. *Airspace Management and Army Air Traffic in a Combat Zone*. Field Manual FM 1-60. Washington, DC: Headquarters, Department of the Army, 1977.

—**AIRSPACE CONTROL SYSTEM** consists of the organization, personnel, facilities, policies, and procedures required to prevent collisions between aircraft, aircraft and obstructions to flight, and aircraft and surface-launched weapons; and to promote the safe, efficient, and flexible use of airspace. *See also:* Airspace Control.

References

Department of Defense, U.S. Army. *Airspace Management and Army Air Traffic in a Combat Zone*. Field Manual FM 1-60. Washington, DC: Headquarters, Department of the Army, 1977.

—**AIRSPACE COORDINATION** maximizes joint force effectiveness without hindering the combat power of either service. Friendly aircraft must be able to enter, depart, and move within the area of operations free of undue restrictions, while supporting fires and remotely piloted vehicle flights continue uninterrupted. The tempo and complexity of modern combat rule out a system that requires time-consuming coordination. To be simple and flexible, the U.S. airspace coordination system operates under a concept of management by exception. See also: Airspace Control.

References

Department of Defense, U.S. Army. *Staff Organization and Operations*. Field Manual FM 101-5. Washington, DC: Headquarters, Department of the Army, 1984.

—**AIRSPACE COORDINATION AREA (ACA)** is a block of airspace in the target area in which friendly aircraft are reasonably safe from friendly surface fires. Occasionally, it may be a formal measure (a three-dimensional box in the sky). More often, it is informal. The purpose of the ACA is to allow the simultaneous attack of targets near each other by multiple fire support means, one of which normally is air. Formal ACAs are usually established by a separate brigade or higher level command. Informal ACAs may be established as low as the task force level. *See also:* Airspace Control.

References

Department of Defense, U.S. Army. *Attack Helicopter Operations.* Field Manual FM 17-50. Washington, DC: Headquarters, Department of the Army, 1984.

———. *Dictionary of United States Army Terms.* Army Regulation AR 310-25. Washington, DC: Headquarters, Department of the Army, 1986.

———. *Fire Support in Combined Arms Operations.* Field Manual FM 6-20. Washington, DC: Headquarters, Department of the Army, 1983.

———. *Operational Terms and Symbols.* Field Manual FM 101-5-1. Washington, DC: Headquarters, Department of the Army, 1985.

—**AIRSPACE MANAGEMENT** is the coordination, integration, and regulation of the use of an airspace of defined dimensions. *See also:* Airspace Control.

References

Department of Defense, U.S. Army. *Air Defense Artillery Deployment: Chaparral/Vulcan/Stinger.* Field Manual FM 44-3. Washington, DC: Headquarters, U.S. Army, 1984.

———. *Airspace Management and Army Air Traffic in a Combat Zone.* Field Manual FM 1-60. Washington, DC: Headquarters, Department of the Army, 1977.

—**AIRSPACE MANAGEMENT CENTER (AMC)** is an element within a control and reporting center that includes a component service liaison that is responsible for continuously coordinating, regulating, and integrating the component services' air operations in accordance with the rules established by the airspace control center. *See also:* Airspace Control.

References

Department of Defense, U.S. Army. *Airspace Management and Army Air Traffic in a Combat Zone.* Field Manual FM 1-60. Washington, DC: Headquarters, Department of the Army, 1977.

—**AIRSPACE MANAGEMENT ELEMENT (AME)** is a functional component of Army elements within the corps or division tactical operations centers involved with coordinating, integrating, and regulating the actions of Army airspace users with those of non-Army users. It coordinates directly with Air Force elements that are integrated into each tactical operations center. *See also:* Airspace Control.

References

Department of Defense, U.S. Army. *Air Defense Artillery Deployment: Chaparral/Vulcan/Stinger.* Field Manual FM 44-3. Washington, DC: Headquarters, Department of the Army, 1984.

———. *Fire Support in Combined Arms Operations.* Field Manual FM 6-20. Washington, DC: Headquarters, Department of the Army, 1983.

—**AIRSPACE MANAGEMENT LIAISON SECTION (AMLS)** is an agency staffed with representatives from all the service components involved with and responsible to the airspace control authority for planning, coordinating, and integrating the activities related to air control. *See also:* Airspace Control.

References

Department of Defense, U.S. Army. *Airspace Management and Army Air Traffic in a Combat Zone.* Field Manual FM 1-60. Washington, DC: Headquarters, Department of the Army, 1977.

—**AIRSPACE RESTRICTED AREA** is an airspace with specific dimensions designated by the airspace control authority, within which the flight of aircraft is restricted in accordance with certain specified conditions. *See also:* Airspace Control.

References

Department of Defense, U.S. Army. *Airspace Management and Army Air Traffic in a Combat Zone.* Field Manual FM 1-60. Washington, DC: Headquarters, Department of the Army, 1977.

—**AIRSPACE RESTRICTIONS** are special measures applied to segments of an airspace of defined dimensions. *See also:* Airspace Control.

References

Department of Defense, U.S. Army. *Airspace Management and Army Air Traffic in a Combat Zone.* Field Manual FM 1-60. Washington, DC: Headquarters, Department of the Army, 1977.

—**AIRSTRIP** is a runway that does not have the facilities normally expected of an airfield. *See also:* Airfield.

References

Department of Defense, U.S. Army. *Route Reconnaissance and Classification.* Field Manual FM 5-36. Washington, DC: Headquarters, Department of the Army, 1985.

—**ALERT.** (1) Alert is readiness for action, defense, or protection. (2) An alert is a warning signal of a real or threatened danger (e.g., an air attack). (3) An alert is the period of time during which troops stand by in response to an alarm. (4) Alert is to forewarn; to prepare for action. (5) An alert is a warning received by a unit or a headquarters that forewarns of an impending operational mission. *See also:* Air Defense Warnings, Warning Orders.

References
Department of Defense, Joint Chiefs of Staff. *Department of Defense Dictionary of Military and Related Terms.* Washington, DC: GPO, 1986.

—**ALERT FORCE** is a specialized force maintained in a special degree of readiness. *See also:* Alert Order.

References
Department of Defense, Joint Chiefs of Staff. *Department of Defense Dictionary of Military and Related Terms.* Washington, DC: GPO, 1986.

—**ALERT ORDER** is a formal directive issued by the Joint Chiefs of Staff. It reflects a decision by National Command Authorities that U.S. military forces may be required, provides essential guidance for planning in the prevailing situation, and marks the outset of execution planning.

References
Department of Defense, U.S. Army. *Planning Logistics Support for Military Operations.* Field Manual FM 701-58. Washington, DC: Headquarters, Department of the Army, 1987.

—**ALIGNMENT** is the arrangement of several elements on the same line.

References
Department of Defense, U.S. Army. *Drills and Ceremonies.* Field Manual FM 22-5. Washington, DC: Headquarters, Department of the Army, 1986.

—**ALL ARMS AIR DEFENSE WEAPON** is an air defense weapon assigned to, or employed by, two or more of the combat arms.

References
Department of Defense, U.S. Army. *Dictionary of United States Army Terms.* Army Regulation AR 310-25. Washington, DC: Headquarters, Department of the Army, 1986.

—**ALL CLEAR SIGNAL** is a prearranged signal to indicate that danger from the attack of enemy aircraft, mechanized forces, submarines, or other hazard has passed.

References
Department of Defense, U.S. Army. *Dictionary of United States Army Terms.* Army Regulation AR 310-25. Washington, DC: Headquarters, Department of the Army, 1986.

—**ALL SOURCE ANALYSIS CENTER (ASOC)** is a facility containing the people, hardware, software, and communications necessary to perform all source analysis, collection, operations security, and electronic warfare planning and management support. *See also:* Sensitive Compartmented Information Facility.

References
Department of Defense, U.S. Army. *Support Operations: Echelons Above Corps.* Field Manual FM 100-16. Washington, DC: Headquarters, Department of the Army, 1986.

—**ALL-AROUND SECURITY** is the surrounding of a facility or an installation with various security measures.

References
Department of Defense, U.S. Army. *Military Police Team, Squad, Platoon Combat Operations.* Field Manual FM 19-4. Washington, DC: Headquarters, Department of the Army, 1984.

—**ALLOCATED MANPOWER** is the military and civilian manpower spaces authorized by a modification table of organization and equipment/tables of distribution and allowances proponent by manpower decisions. These decisions carry out or amend the manpower program published in the program and budget guidance. The decisions are consolidated in quarterly manpower vouchers. Military manpower is allocated by identity (i.e., officer, warrant officer, enlisted, and Army Nurse Corps and Army Medical Specialist Corps). Civilian manpower is allocated by direct hire, foreign national, and other categories subject to control. These allocations represent employment ceilings for each category of personnel. *See also:* Table of Organization and Equipment.

References
Department of Defense, U.S. Army. *Dictionary of United States Army Terms.* Army Regulation AR 310-25. Washington, DC: Headquarters, Department of the Army, 1986.

—**ALLOCATION.** (1) An allocation is the apportionment of a definite quantity of supplies, space, services, personnel, or productive facility for a specified use. (2) An allocation is an authorization issued by the Comptroller of the Army to specified major headquarters or agencies for purposes of financing operations at subordinate echelons through suballocation or allotment. See *also:* Obligation Authority.

References

Department of Defense, U.S. Army. *Dictionary of United States Army Terms.* Army Regulation AR 310-25. Washington, DC: Headquarters, Department of the Army, 1986.

—**ALLOCATION** (NUCLEAR) is the apportionment of specific numbers and types of nuclear weapons to a commander for a stated period as a planning factor for use in developing war plans. (Additional authority is required for the actual deployment of allocated weapons to locations desired by the commander to support his war plans. Expenditures of these weapons are not authorized until released by proper authority.) *See also*: Nuclear Warfare.

References

Department of Defense, Joint Chiefs of Staff. *Department of Defense Dictionary of Military and Related Terms.* Washington, DC: GPO, 1986.

—**ALLOCATION OF FORCES** is the designation of specific units and other resources to subordinate commands to carry out a given tactical scheme. This designation may include assignment, attachment, operational control, or direct support, direct support reinforcing, and general support. *See also*: Assignment, Attachment, Direct Support, General Support, Operational Control.

References

Department of Defense, U.S. Army. *Operational Terms and Symbols.* Field Manual FM 101-5-1. Washington, DC: Headquarters, Department of the Army, 1985.

—**ALLOCATION** (TACTICAL AIR SUPPORT FORCES) is the translation by the tactical air control center of the apportionment decision into total numbers of sorties by aircraft type that are available for each operation or task. *See also:* Apportionment, Tactical Air Operations.

References

Department of Defense, U.S. Army. *Attack Helicopter Operations.* Field Manual FM. 17-50 Washington, DC: Headquarters, Department of the Army, 1984.

————. *Operational Terms and Symbols.* Field Manual FM 101-5-1. Washington, DC: Headquarters, Department of the Army, 1985.

—**ALLOCATION** (TRANSPORTATION). (1)An allocation is the apportionment by a designated authority of the available transport capability to users. (2) Allocation is an action by a general operating agency making funds allocated or suballocated to it available to another office, generally one subordinate to it, for obligation by the latter. (3) Allocation is a specific authorization of personnel by number to a command, organization, or unit. *See also:* Obligation Authority.

References

Department of Defense, Joint Chiefs of Staff. *Department of Defense Dictionary of Military and Related Terms.* Washington, DC: GPO, 1986.

—**ALL-OTHERS TOUR** is the length of duty authorized at a specific location for soldiers who are not accompanied by command-sponsored dependents. *See also:* Tour of Duty.

References

Department of Defense, U.S. Army. *Dictionary of United States Army Terms.* Army Regulation AR 310-25. Washington, DC: Headquarters, Department of the Army, 1986.

—**ALLOTMENT** is a specified portion of the pay of military personnel voluntarily authorized to be paid to another person or to an institution.

References

Department of Defense, U.S. Army. *Dictionary of United States Army Terms.* Army Regulation AR 310-25. Washington, DC: Headquarters, Department of the Army, 1986.

—**ALLOWABLE CABIN LOAD (ACL)** is the amount of cargo and number of passengers, determined by weight, cubic displacement, and distance, that can be transported in a specific aircraft.

References

Department of Defense, U.S. Army. *USA/USAF Doctrine for Joint Airborne and Tactical Airlift Operations.* Field Manual FM 100-27. Washington, DC: Department of the Army, 1985.

—**ALLOWANCE.** (1) An allowance is money, or its equivalent, furnished in addition to the prescribed rates of pay. An allowance is given to provide for expenses for which a soldier's pay is considered inadequate (e.g., expenses for travel, quarters, clothing, and subsistence). (2) An allowance is a prescribed number of items of supply or equipment provided for an individual or organization.

References

Department of Defense, U.S. Army. *Dictionary of United States Army Terms.* Army Regulation AR 310-25. Washington, DC: Headquarters, Department of the Army, 1986.

—**ALL-PURPOSE HAND-HELD WEAPON** is a lightweight, hand-held, small-arms weapon capable of projecting munitions required to engage area and point-type targets. *See also:* Small Arms.

References

Department of Defense, Joint Chiefs of Staff. *Department of Defense Dictionary of Military and Related Terms.* Washington, DC: GPO, 1986.

—**ALOC (AIR LINE OF COMMUNICATIONS) SUPPLY** is the airlift of nearly all repair parts and selected maintenance items to the theater. *See also*: Air Line of Communication.

References

Department of Defense, U.S. Army. *Repair Parts Supply for a Theater of Operations.* Field Manual FM 29-19. Washington, DC: Headquarters, Department of the Army, 1985.

—**ALTERNATE COMMAND POST (ACP)** may be organized or designated to insure continuity of operations during displacements or in the event of serious damage to the command post facility. The alternate command post may be a subordinate headquarters or it may be partially or fully equipped and manned. *See also*: Command Post.

References

Department of Defense, U.S. Army. *Operational Terms and Symbols.* Field Manual FM 101-5-1. Washington, DC: Headquarters, Department of the Army, 1985.

—**ALTERNATE POSITION.** (1) An alternate position is the space a weapon, unit, or individual occupy when the primary position becomes untenable or unsuitable for carrying out a task.

The alternate position is located so that the individual can continue to fulfill his original task. (2) An alternate position is a space located generally adjacent to the primary position from which a weapon, a unit, or an individual can perform the original task when the primary position becomes untenable or unsuitable. (3) An alternate position is a space or area to the front, flank, or slightly to the rear of the primary position. It must let the platoon cover the same sector of fire as the primary position. It may be forward of the primary position, with less concealment, to be occupied if the platoon is driven out of the primary position by enemy fire or assault. *See also:* Primary Position, Successive Positions, Supplementary Position.

References

Department of Defense, U.S. Army. *Air Defense Artillery Deployment: Chaparral/Vulcan/Stinger.* Field Manual FM 44-3. Department of the Army, 1984.

———. Dictionary *of United States Army Terms.* Army Regulation AR 310-25. Washington, DC: Headquarters, Department of the Army, 1986.

———. *The Infantry Rifle Company (Infantry, Airborne, Air Assault, Ranger).* Field Manual FM 7-10. Washington, DC: Headquarters, Department of the Army, 1982.

—**ALTERNATE SITE** is a prepared, predesignated location to which all or portions of a civilian or military headquarters may be evacuated. It should be capable of rapid activation and expansion. This applies principally to national level organizations. *See also:* Alternate Command Post.

References

Department of Defense, U.S. Army. *Planning Logistics Support for Military Operations.* Field Manual FM 701-58. Washington, DC: Headquarters, Department of the Army, 1987.

—**ALTERNATE SPECIALTY** is a second area of concentration, in addition to the commissioned officer's professional development and utilization, that is assigned by Headquarters, Department of the Army.

References

Department of Defense, U.S. Army. *Dictionary of United States Army Terms.* Army Regulation AR 310-25. Washington, DC: Headquarters, Department of the Army, 1986.

—**ALTERNATE TRAVERSING FIRE** is a method of covering a target that has both width and depth by firing a succession of traversing groups whose normal range dispersion provides in-depth distribution.

References

Department of Defense, U.S. Army. *Dictionary of United States Army Terms.* Army Regulation AR 310-25. Washington, DC: Headquarters, Department of the Army, 1986.

—**ALTITUDE** (ARMY AVIATION) indicates a vertical position in respect to the observer's perceived horizontal reference plane. The following terms indicate altitudes that are relative to the observer:

- **LEVEL**—appears to be at the same altitude as the observer.
- **HIGH**—is above the observer's level reference plane.
- **LOW**—is below the observer's reference plane.

See also: Airbattle Management.

References

Department of Defense, U.S. Army. *Air-to-Air Combat.* Field Manual FM 1-107. Washington, DC: Headquarters, Department of the Army, 1984.

—**AMBULANCE** is a vehicle (e.g., frontline, field, metropolitan, or bus ambulance) specifically designed and equipped to provide transportation and permit en route medical care and treatment to patients. It has appropriate Red Cross markings. It may be utilized for transporting medical supplies and equipment and medical personnel on a medical mission. *See also:* Medical Treatment.

References

Department of Defense, U.S. Army. *Dictionary of United States Army Terms.* Army Regulation AR 310-25. Washington, DC: Headquarters, Department of the Army, 1986.

—**AMBUSH** is a surprise attack by fire from a concealed position or positions on a moving or temporarily halted enemy. *See also:* Area Ambush, Armor Ambush, Point Ambush.

References

Department of Defense, U.S. Army. *Operational Terms and Symbols.* Field Manual FM 101-5-1. Washington, DC: Headquarters, Department of the Army, 1985.

—**AMBUSH FORCE** is the unit that establishes a surprise attack. *See also:* Assault Element, Security Element.

References

Department of Defense, U.S. Army. *The Rifle Squads (Mechanized and Light Infantry).* Training Circular TC 7-1. Washington, DC: Headquarters, Department of the Army, 1976.

—**AMBUSH SITE** is the terrain on which a surprise attack is planned to occur. It is positioned along the target's expected avenue of approach. *See also:* Ambush, Point Ambush

References

Department of Defense, U.S. Army. *The Rifle Squads (Mechanized and Light Infantry).* Training Circular TC 7-1. Washington, DC: Headquarters, Department of the Army, 1976.

—**AMERICAN NATIONAL RED CROSS** is an autonomous quasi-governmental agency, supported by the people, and operating in accordance with the Geneva Convention and a congressional charter. Under federal laws and military regulations, it acts in matters pertaining to the well-being and morale of members of the Armed Forces, wherever they are stationed, and their families. The American Red Cross is further charged to provide national and international relief in disasters and to devise and carry out measures for their prevention. Its activities also include instruction in first aid, water safety, and home nursing; a blood program; a youth program; and the training and assignment of volunteers to work in health and welfare programs. Its emblem is a red cross on a white background. Under the Geneva Convention, the International Committee of the Red Cross, a neutral Swiss body, exerts efforts to assure that the rights of prisoners of war are properly observed and serves as an intermediary between governments and Red Cross societies in time of war or international tension. *See also:* Medical Treatment.

References

Department of Defense, U.S. Army. *Dictionary of United States Army Terms.* Army Regulation AR 310-25. Washington, DC: Headquarters, Department of the Army, 1986.

—**AMMUNITION** is a device charged with explosives; propellants; pyrotechnics; initiating composition; or nuclear, biological, or chemical material (including demolitions) for defensive or offensive actions. *See also:* Other entries under Ammunition.

References

Department of Defense, Joint Chiefs of Staff. *Department of Defense Dictionary of Military and Related Terms.* Washington, DC: GPO, 1986.

Department of Defense, U.S. Army. *Ammunition Handbook.* Field Manual FM 9-13. Washington, DC: Headquarters, Department of the Army, 1981.

—**AMMUNITION AND EXPLOSION AREA** is a designated area set aside from other portions of an installation. It is used to develop, manufacture, maintain, store, or handle ammunition and explosives.

References

Department of Defense, U.S. Army. Ammunition *and Explosives Safety Standards.* Army Regulation AR 385-64. Washington, DC: Headquarters, Department of the Army, 1987.

—**AMMUNITION AND EXPLOSIVES** include (but are not limited to) all items of ammunition; liquid and solid propellants; high and low explosives; guided missiles; warheads; devices; pyrotechnics; chemical agents; and components and substances associated with these items, which present a real or potential hazard to life and property.

References

Department of Defense, U.S. Army. *Ammunition and Explosives Safety Standards.* Army Regulation AR 385-64. Washington, DC: Department of the Army, 1987.

———. *Ammunition Handbook.* Field Manual FM 9-13. Washington, DC: Headquarters, Department of the Army, 1981.

—**AMMUNITION AND EXPLOSIVES AIRCRAFT CARGO AREA** is an area specifically designated for unloading or loading transportation-configured ammunition and explosives from or onto aircraft and for parking aircraft loaded with such ammunition.

References

Department of Defense, U.S. Army. *Ammunition and Explosives Safety Standards.* Army Regulation AR 385-64. Washington, DC: Headquarters, Department of the Army, 1987.

———. *Ammunition Handbook.* Field Manual FM 9-13. Washington, DC: Headquarters, Department of the Army, 1981.

—**AMMUNITION AND TOXIC MATERIAL OPEN SPACE** is an area especially prepared for storing explosive ammunition and toxic material. For reporting purposes, it does not include the surrounding area that is restricted for storage because of safety factors. It includes barricades and improvised coverings.

References

Department of Defense, Joint Chiefs of Staff. *Department of Defense Dictionary of Military and Related Terms.* Washington, DC: GPO, 1986.

—**AMMUNITION BARRICADE** is a structure consisting essentially of concrete, earth, metal, or wood, constructed so as to reduce or confine the blast effect or fragmentation of an explosive.

References

Department of Defense, U.S. Army. *Dictionary of United States Army Terms.* Army Regulation AR 310-25. Washington, DC: Headquarters, Department of the Army, 1986.

—**AMMUNITION BELT.** (1) An ammunition belt is a fabric or metal band with loops for cartridges that are fed from it into a machine gun or other automatic weapon (i.e., a feed belt). (2) An ammunition belt is a belt with loops or pockets for carrying cartridges or clips of cartridges (i.e., a cartridge belt).

References

Department of Defense, U.S. Army. Dictionary of *United States Army Terms.* Army Regulation AR 310-25. Washington, DC: Headquarters, Department of the Army, 1986.

—**AMMUNITION CLIP** is a device that holds rounds of ammunition for loading into certain automatic and semiautomatic weapons.

References

Department of Defense, U.S. Army. *Dictionary of United States Army Terms.* Army Regulation AR 310-25. Washington, DC: Headquarters, Department of the Army, 1986.

—**AMMUNITION CREDIT** is the authority given to an organization to draw a specified quantity of ammunition during a specified period for a particular use. Ammunition credits are not used in the combat zone below the Army level.

References

Department of Defense, U.S. Army. *Dictionary of United States Army Terms.* Army Regulation AR 310-25. Washington, DC: Headquarters, Department of the Army, 1986.

—**AMMUNITION DAY OF SUPPLY** is the estimated quantity of conventional ammunition required per day to sustain operations in an active theater. It is expressed in terms of rounds per weapon per day for ammunition items fired by weapons, and in terms of other units of measure for bulk allotment ammunition items.

References
Department of Defense, U.S. Army. *Dictionary of United States Army Terms*. Army Regulation AR 310-25. Washington, DC: Headquarters, Department of the Army, 1986.

—**AMMUNITION EXPENDITURE** is the consumption of ammunition by an organization. For record purposes, with certain exceptions (e.g., nuclear weapons and designated missile items), ammunition is considered expended when it is issued to the user. Special ammunition is considered expended when both a supporting ordnance special ammunition unit and the fire direction center have been notified of the fact by a delivery unit.

References
Department of Defense, U.S. Army. *Dictionary of United States Army Terms*. Army Regulation AR 310-25. Washington, DC: Headquarters, Department of the Army, 1986.

—**AMMUNITION HANDLER.** (1) An ammunition handler is one whose primary duty is to handle and service ammunition. (2) An ammunition handler is a soldier who prepares ammunition for firing and who, as a member of a weapons crew, assists in the final delivery of ammunition to the loader.

References
Department of Defense, U.S. Army. *Dictionary of United States Army Terms*. Army Regulation AR 310-25. Washington, DC: Headquarters, Department of the Army, 1986.

—**AMMUNITION IDENTIFICATION CODE** superseded the code symbol formerly assigned to each ammunition item to identify it and to facilitate the supply of ammunition to the field. An example is P5HBA. The first two characters refer to the pertinent ordnance catalogue; the remaining three characters refer to the weapon group, type and model, and packaging.

References
Department of Defense, U.S. Army. *Dictionary of United States Army Terms*. Army Regulation AR 310-25. Washington, DC: Headquarters, Department of the Army, 1986.

—**AMMUNITION IN HANDS OF TROOPS** is ammunition included in the prescribed basic load and the authorized excesses to it. This ammunition is under the physical control of the using unit and may be located in unit supply dumps, in unit rolling reserves, and at weapons positions.

References
Department of Defense, U.S. Army. *Dictionary of United States Army Terms*. Army Regulation AR 310-25. Washington, DC: Headquarters, Department of the Army, 1986.

—**AMMUNITION LIFT CAPABILITY** is the ability of an ammunition unit to move ammunition and is expressed in terms of tons of ammunition per day that can be lifted.

References
Department of Defense, U.S. Army. *Dictionary of United States Army Terms*. Army Regulation AR 310-25. Washington, DC: Headquarters, Department of the Army, 1986.

—**AMMUNITION MAINTENANCE** is all actions taken to retain ammunition in or to restore it to a serviceable condition. Such actions include inspecting, testing, servicing, replacing, repairing, and renovating.

References
Department of Defense, U.S. Army. *Dictionary of United States Army Terms*. Army Regulation AR 310-25. Washington, DC: Headquarters, Department of the Army, 1986.

—**AMMUNITION MODIFICATION** is the alteration of ammunition or missile items as a result of engineering changes (e.g., replacing components that do not involve the extensive facilities and equipment required for renovation).

References
Department of Defense, U.S. Army. *Dictionary of United States Army Terms*. Army Regulation AR 310-25. Washington, DC: Headquarters, Department of the Army, 1986.

—**AMMUNITION MODULAR STORAGE SYSTEM** is used to store ammunition on pads within earth-barricaded areas called cells. These cells are joined to form modules, which can be constructed to form module blocks.

References
Department of Defense, U.S. Army. Dictionary of United States Army Terms. Army Regulation AR 310-25. Washington, DC: Headquarters, Department of the Army, 1986.

—**AMMUNITION OFFICER** is the officer designated within a command to assist in providing adequate staff supervision of ammunition activities (e.g., receipt, storage, surveillance, classification, issue, and related endeavors).

References

Department of Defense, U.S. Army. *Dictionary of United States Army Terms.* Army Regulation AR 310-25. Washington, DC: Headquarters, Department of the Army, 1986.

—**AMMUNITION PIT** is a hole or trench in the ground where ammunition is temporarily stored. An ammunition pit is usually near the weapon from which the ammunition will be fired.

References

Department of Defense, U.S. Army. *Dictionary of United States Army Terms.* Army Regulation AR 310-25. Washington, DC: Headquarters, Department of the Army, 1986.

—**AMMUNITION REQUIRED SUPPLY RATE** is the amount of ammunition expressed in terms of rounds per weapons per day for ammunition fired from weapons, and in terms of other units of measure per day for bulk allotment items estimated to be required to sustain operations of designated force without restriction for a specified time. Tactical commanders use this rate to state their requirements for ammunition to support planned tactical operations at specific intervals. It is submitted through command channels and is consolidated at each echelon. It is considered by each commander in determining the controlled supply rate within his command.

References

Department of Defense, U.S. Army. *Dictionary of United States Army Terms.* Army Regulation AR 310-25. Washington, DC: Headquarters, Department of the Army, 1986.

—**AMMUNITION SUPPLY INSTALLATION** is an organized locality that maintains stock records and operates for the reception, classification, storage, and issue of ammunition. The term includes depots, ammunition supply points, railheads, truckheads, dumps, distributing points, and all other installations where ammunition is received, stored, classified, or issued.

References

Department of Defense, U.S. Army. *Dictionary of United States Army Terms.* Army Regulation AR 310-25. Washington, DC: Headquarters, Department of the Army, 1986.

—**AMMUNITION SUPPLY POINT (ASP)** is a forward location where ammunition is distributed to using units on an area basis or distributed by a using unit to individuals or subordinate units.

References

Department of Defense, U.S. Army. *Operational Terms and Symbols.* Field Manual FM 101-5-1. Washington, DC: Headquarters, Department of the Army, 1985.

—**AMMUNITON TRAIN** is an organization of personnel and equipment whose main function is transporting ammunition.

References

Department of Defense, U.S. Army. *Dictionary of United States Army Terms.* Army Regulation AR 310-25. Washington, DC: Headquarters, Department of the Army, 1986.

—**AMMUNITION TRANSFER POINT (ATP)** is a point established in the brigade support area to reduce the travel distances of resupply vehicles. Initial stockage for each brigade ATP is positioned on corps support command stake and platform semitrailers and consists of high volume/high tonnage items as determined by the division ammunition officer and the division commander.

References

Department of Defense, U.S. Army. Operational Terms *and Symbols.* Field Manual FM 101-5-1. Washington, DC: Headquarters, Department of the Army, 1985.

—**AMPHIBIOUS ASSAULT** is the principal type of amphibious operation that involves establishing a force on a hostile shore. *See also:* Amphibious Operation.

References

Department of Defense, Joint Chiefs of Staff. *Department of Defense Dictionary of Military and Related Terms.* Washington, DC: GPO, 1986.

—**AMPHIBIOUS FORCE.** (1) An amphibious force is a naval force and landing force, together with supporting forces that are trained, organized, and equipped for amphibious operations. (2) In naval usage, an amphibious force is the administrative title of the amphibious type command of a fleet. *See also:* Amphibious Operation.

References

Department of Defense, Joint Chiefs of Staff. *Department of Defense Dictionary of Military and Related Terms.* Washington, DC: GPO, 1986.

—**AMPHIBIOUS OPERATION** is an attack launched from the sea by naval and landing forces against a hostile shore. It may be conducted: to conduct further land combat operations; to obtain a site for advanced bases; or to deny the enemy the use of an area or facilities. An amphibious operation is one of the more potent capabilities available to a theater commander, as the invasions of Normandy and Inchon demonstrated. Its usefulness stems from the mobility and flexibility of the amphibious task force and its ability to surprise. The U.S. Army has a collateral responsibility for planning and executing joint amphibious operations. *See also*: Amphibious Assault, Amphibious Force, Amphibious Ships, Amphibious Tank, Amphibious Task Force, Amphibious Task Group, Amphibious Vehicle, Amphibious Withdrawal.

References

Department of Defense, U.S. Army. *Army Forces in Amphibious Operations*. Field Manual FM 31-12. Washington, DC: Headquarters, Department of the Army, 1961.

Department of Defense, U.S. Army. *Staff Organization and Operations*. Field Manual FM 101-5. Washington, DC: Headquarters, Department of the Army, 1984.

—**AMPHIBIOUS SHIPS** are naval ships specifically designed to transport, land, and support forces in amphibious assault operations. They are capable of loading and unloading forces and equipment without external assistance. *See also:* Amphibious Operation.

References

Collins, John M. *U.S.-Soviet Military Balance, 1980-1985*. Washington, DC: Congressional Research Service, 1985.

Department of Defense, U.S. Army. *Army Forces in Amphibious Operations*. Field Manual FM 31-12. Washington, DC: Headquarters, Department of the Army, 1961.

—**AMPHIBIOUS TANK** is a vehicle mounting a howitzer or cannon, capable of delivering direct or indirect fire from the water as well as from ashore and used to provide early supporting fires in amphibious operations.

References

Department of Defense, U.S. Army. *Army Forces in Amphibious Operations*. Field Manual FM 31-12. Washington, DC: Headquarters, Department of the Army, 1961.

—**AMPHIBIOUS TASK FORCE** is a task organization that conducts an amphibious operation. It always includes Navy forces and a landing force, with their organic aviation.

References

Department of Defense, U.S. Army. *Army Forces in Amphibious Operations*. Field Manual FM 31-12. Washington, DC: Headquarters, Department of the Army, 1961.

—**AMPHIBIOUS TASK GROUP** is a subordinate force formed within an amphibious task force. It is composed of a naval attack group and a landing group. *See also:* Amphibious Task Force.

References

Department of Defense, U.S. Army. *Army Forces in Amphibious Operations*. Field Manual FM 31-12. Washington, DC: Headquarters, Department of the Army, 1961.

—**AMPHIBIOUS VEHICLE** is a wheeled or tracked vehicle capable of operating on land and water.

References

Department of Defense, Joint Chiefs of Staff. *Department of Defense Dictionary of Military and Related Terms* Washington, DC: GPO, 1986.

—**AMPHIBIOUS WITHDRAWAL** is an operation involving the removal in naval ships or craft of land forces from a hostile shore.

References

Department of Defense, Joint Chiefs of Staff. *Department of Defense Dictionary of Military and Related Terms*. Washington, DC: GPO, 1986.

—**ANALYSIS OF THE AREA OF OPERATIONS** is a comprehensive study to determine the effects of the area of operations on enemy and friendly operations. It includes an analysis of weather, terrain, and other factors (e.g., economy, sociology, or religion) throughout the commander's area of interest and is a basis for developing specific friendly courses of action and for determining enemy capabilities (courses of action) in commander and staff estimates. The analysis allows the commander and staff to see the battlefield in width, depth, height/airspace, and time dimensions. *See also:* Area of Operations.

References

Department of Defense, U.S. Army. *Staff Organization and Operations*. Field Manual FM 101-5. Washington, DC: Headquarters, Department of the Army, 1984.

—**ANCILLARY FACILITIES** supplement the existing facilities at a particular location by providing specific minimum requirements for supporting reinforcing forces.

References

Department of Defense, Joint Chiefs of Staff. *Department of Defense Dictionary of Military and Related Terms*. Washington, DC: GPO, 1986.

—**ANGELS** (ARMY AVIATION) are the altitude of friendly aircraft in thousands of feet.

References

Department of Defense, U.S. Army. *Air-to-Air Combat*. Field Manual FM 1-107. Washington, DC: Headquarters, Department of the Army, 1984.

—**ANGLE OF ATTACK** is the angle between a longitudinal reference line on the aircraft and the velocity vector relative to the ambient undisturbed air.

References

Department of Defense, U.S. Army. *Dictionary of United States Army Terms*. Army Regulation AR 310-25. Washington, DC: Headquarters, Department of the Army, 1986.

—**ANGLE OF DEPRESSION** is the vertical angle between the horizontal and the axis of the bore of the gun when the gun is aimed below the horizontal.

References

Department of Defense, U.S. Army. *Dictionary of United States Army Terms*. Army Regulation AR 310-25. Washington, DC: Headquarters, Department of the Army, 1986.

—**ANGLE OF TRAVERSE.** (1) An angle of traverse is the horizontal angle through which a gun can be turned on its mount. (2) An angle of traverse is the angle between the lines from a gun to the right and left limits of the front that is covered by its fire (i.e., the angle through which it is traversed).

References

Department of Defense, U.S. Army. *Dictionary of United States Army Terms*. Army Regulation AR 310-25. Washington, DC: Headquarters, Department of the Army, 1986.

—**ANNEX** is a document appended to an operation order or other document to clarify it and to give further details. *See also:* Operation Order.

References

Department of Defense, Joint Chiefs of Staff. *Department of Defense Dictionary of Military and Related Terms*. Washington, DC: GPO, 1986.

—**ANNUAL GENERAL INSPECTIONS (AGIs)** provide commanders with a periodic assessment of the operational and administrative effectiveness of their commands. The heads of Department of the Army agencies and commanders of Army field commands and installations who are authorized an inspector general on their staff are responsible for annually inspecting all elements of their commands, installations, or activities. The overall annual general inspection objectives are to: (1) evaluate management procedures and practices pertaining to personnel, administration, materiel, and fund sources; (2) identify problems, situations, or circumstances that impair mission performance and isolate their causes; and (3) determine the command or activity best suited for corrective actions and evaluate the adequacy of past corrective actions. *See also*: Inspection.

References

Department of Defense, U.S. Army. *Dictionary of United States Army Terms*. Army Regulation AR 310-25. Washington, DC: Headquarters, Department of the Army, 1986.

————. *Organizational Maintenance Operations*. Field Manual FM 29-2. Washington, DC: Headquarters, Department of the Army, 1984.

—**ANNUAL LEAVE** is the 30 days of authorized absence granted to an individual yearly and is charged to his account. It is also called ordinary leave.

References

Department of Defense, U.S. Army. *Leaves and Passes*. Army Regulation AR 630-5. Washington, DC: Headquarters, Department of the Army, 1984.

—**ANNUAL TRAINING (AT)** is the minimal period of annual active duty for training or annual field training a member performs each year to satisfy the annual training requirement that is associated with a Reserve component assignment. It may be performed during one consecutive period or in increments of one or more days, depending on mission requirements. See *also*: Active Duty for Training.

References

Department of Defense, U.S. Army. *Dictionary of United States Army Terms*. Army Regulation AR 310-25. Washington, DC: Headquarters, Department of the Army, 1986.

—**ANTIAIRCRAFT OPERATIONS CENTER** is the tactical headquarters of an antiaircraft commander. It is the agency that collects and evaluates information, disseminates intelligence for aircraft defense, and exercises operational control over subordinate units.

References

Department of Defense, Joint Chiefs of Staff. *Department of Defense Dictionary of Military and Related Terms.* Washington, DC: GPO, 1986.

—**ANTICROP AGENT** is a living organism or chemical used to cause disease or damage to selected food or industrial crops. *See also:* Biological Warfare, Chemical Warfare.

References

Department of Defense, U.S. Army. *NBC Operations.* Field Manual FM 3-100. Washington, DC: Headquarters, Department of the Army, 1985.

—**ANTIHANDLING DEVICE** is found only on antitank mines. It is any device that activates a mine when the mine is lifted, moved, or disturbed. *See also:* Mine Warfare.

References

Department of Defense, U.S. Army. *Mine/Countermine Operations at the Company Level.* Field Manual FM 20-32. Washington, DC: Headquarters, Department of the Army, 1976.

—**ANTIMATERIEL AGENT** is a living organism or chemical used to cause deterioration of, or damage to, selected materiel. *See also:* Biological Warfare, Chemical Warfare.

References

Department of Defense, U.S. Army. *NBC Operations.* Field Manual FM 3-100. Washington, DC: Headquarters, Department of the Army, 1985.

—**ANTIMATERIEL AMMUNITION** are projectiles that have a high explosive filler and are fuzed to explode when they hit the target. The two types of antimateriel munitions are high explosive and high-explosive plastic. The conventional high-explosive antitank round for the 152-mm gun/launcher is considered a multipurpose round and may, therefore, be used as an antimateriel round. *See also:* Antipersonnel Ammunition, High Explosive.

References

Department of Defense, U.S. Army. *Dictionary of United States Army Terms.* Army Regulation AR 310-25. Washington, DC: Headquarters, Department of the Army, 1986.

—**ANTIPERSONNEL AMMUNITION.** Antipersonnel rounds are filled with many subprojectiles that disperse in the target area. They are used primarily against massed troops who are in the open. The two types of antipersonnel projectiles are canister and beehive. *See also:* Antimateriel Ammunition.

References

Department of Defense, U.S. Army. *Dictionary of United States Army Terms.* Army Regulation AR 310-25. Washington, DC: Headquarters, Department of the Army, 1986.

—**ANTIPERSONNEL MINE** is a mine designed to cause casualties to personnel. The two categories of antipersonnel mines are local effect antipersonnel mines and extended effect antipersonnel mines. *See also:* Mine Warfare.

References

Department of Defense, U.S. Army. *Mine/Countermine Operations at the Company Level.* Field Manual FM 20-32. Washington, DC: Headquarters, Department of the Army, 1976.

—**ANTIPLANT AGENT** is a microorganism or chemical that can kill, disease, or damage plants. *See also:* Biological Warfare, Chemical Warfare.

References

Department of Defense, U.S. Army. *NBC Operations.* Field Manual FM 3-100. Washington, DC: Headquarters, Department of the Army, 1985.

—**ANTITANK HELICOPTER** is a helicopter designed for use in an antitank role. *See also:* Attack Helicopter.

References

Department of Defense, Joint Chiefs of Staff. *Department of Defense Dictionary of Military and Related Terms.* Washington, DC: GPO, 1986.

Department of Defense, U.S. Army. *Tactics, Techniques, and Concepts of Antiarmor Warfare.* Field Manual FM 23-3. Washington, DC: Headquarters, Department of the Army, 1972.

—**ANTITANK MINE** is a mine designed to immobilize or destroy a tank. *See also:* Mine.

References

Department of Defense, Joint Chiefs of Staff. *Department of Defense Dictionary of Military and Related Terms.* Washington, DC: GPO, 1986.

Department of Defense, U.S. Army. *Tactics, Techniques, and Concepts of Antiarmor Warfare.* Field Manual FM 23-3. Washington, DC: Headquarters, Department of the Army, 1972.

—**ANTITERRORISM** involves defensive measures used to reduce the vulnerability of personnel, family members, facilities, and equipment to terrorist acts. This includes the collection and analysis of information to accurately assess the magnitude of the threat. *See also:* Terrorism Counteraction.

References

Department of Defense, U.S. Army. *The Army Terrorism Counteraction Program.* Army Regulation AR 525-13. Washington, DC: Headquarters, Department of the Army, 1988.

—**ANTIWITHDRAWAL DEVICE** is a device used in bombs, made integrally with the fuze, that will set off the fuze and subsequently set off the bomb upon attempts to withdraw the fuze. *See also:* Fuze (Specify Type).

References

Department of Defense, U.S. Army. *Dictionary of United States Army Terms.* Army Regulation AR 310-25. Washington, DC: Headquarters, Department of the Army, 1986.

—**APPORTIONMENT** is the determination and the assignment of the total expected effort by percentage and/or by priority that should be devoted to the various air operations and/or geographic areas for a specified period of time. *See also:* Allocation.

References

Department of Defense, U.S. Army. *Attack Helicopter Operations.* Field Manual FM 17-50. Washington, DC: Headquarters, Department of the Army, 1984.

————. *Dictionary of United States Army Terms.* Army Regulation AR 310-25. Washington, DC: Headquarters, Department of the Army, 1986.

————. *Operational Terms and Symbols.* Field Manual FM 101-5-1. Washington, DC: Headquarters, Department of the Army, 1985.

—**APPROACH MARCH** is an advance of a combat unit when direct contact with the enemy is imminent. Troops are fully or partially deployed. The approach march ends when contact with the enemy is made or when the attack position is occupied. *See also:* Advance to Contact.

References

Department of Defense, Joint Chiefs of Staff. *Department of Defense Dictionary of Military and Related Terms.* Washington, DC: GPO, 1986.

—**APPROVED FORCES** are forces specified in the Secretary of Defense Five-Year Plan.

References

Department of Defense, U.S. Army. *Dictionary of United States Army Terms.* Army Regulation AR 310-25. Washington, DC: Headquarters, Department of the Army, 1986.

—**APPURTENANCES** are devices (e.g., stars, letters, numerals, or clasps) worn on the suspension ribbon of a medal or on the ribbon bar. They indicate that the award has been earned more than once, participation in specific events, or other distinguishing characteristics of the award. *See also:* Accouterment.

References

Department of Defense, U.S. Army. *Wear and Appearance of Army Uniforms and Insignia.* Army Regulation AR 670-1. Washington, DC: Headquarters, Department of the Army, 1986.

—**AREA AIR DEFENSE COMMANDER (AADC).** Within an overseas unified command, subordinate unified command, or joint task force, one commander is assigned overall responsibility for air defense. Normally, this commander is the Air Force component commander. Representation from the other service components involved are provided, as appropriate, to the AADC's headquarters. *See also:* Air Defense Area.

References

Department of Defense, Joint Chiefs of Staff. *Department of Defense Dictionary of Military and Related Terms.* Washington, DC: GPO, 1986.

—**AREA AMBUSH** is a surprise attack in which the ambush patrol is deployed at multiple, related point ambushes. *See also:* Ambush, Point Ambush.

References

Department of Defense, U.S. Army. *The Infantry Rifle Company (Infantry, Airborne, Air Assault, Ranger).* Field Manual FM 7-10. Washington, DC: Headquarters, Department of the Army, 1982.

—**AREA COMMAND.** (1) An area command is a command composed of one or more of the armed services, designated to operate in a specific geographical area, which are placed under a single commander (e.g., under the Commander of a Unified Command, Area Commander). (2) An area command, in unconventional warfare, is the organizational structure established within an unconventional warfare operational area to command and control resistance forces. Usually, it integrates the Special Forces operational detachment and the resistance force. *See also:* Command.

References

Department of Defense, Joint Chiefs of Staff. *Department of Defense Dictionary of Military and Related Terms.* Washington, DC: GPO, 1986.

Department of Defense, U.S. Army. *Dictionary of United States Army Terms.* Army Regulation AR 310-25. Washington, DC: Headquarters, Department of the Army, 1986.

—**AREA COORDINATION CENTER (ACC)** is a combined civil-military headquarters that may be formed at subnational, state, and local levels to achieve a coordinated and unified internal defense and development effort at each level within a nation. *See also:* Civil Military Cooperation.

References

Department of Defense, U.S. Army. *Staff Organization and Operations.* Field Manual FM 101-5. Washington, DC: Headquarters, Department of the Army, 1984.

—**AREA COORDINATION GROUP (ACG)** is a composite organization that includes representatives of local military, paramilitary, and other governmental agencies and their U.S. counterparts and is responsible for planning and coordinating internal defense and development operations. *See also:* Area Coordination Center.

References

Department of Defense, Joint Chiefs of Staff. *Department of Defense Dictionary of Military and Related Terms.* Washington, DC: GPO, 1986.

—**AREA COVERAGE** is religious support (including unit and denominational coverage) provided by unit ministry teams to all personnel within a specific geographic area. *See also:* Chaplain.

References

Department of Defense, U.S. Army. *The Chaplain and Chaplain Assistant in Combat Operations.* Field Manual FM 16-5. Washington, DC: Headquarters, Department of the Army, 1984.

—**AREA COVERAGE TEAM** is a unit ministry team that is on call to provide additional religious support to forward units during emergency or high stress situations or to units in rear areas. *See also:* Chaplain.

References

Department of Defense, U.S. Army. *The Chaplain and Chaplain Assistant in Combat Operations.* Field Manual FM 16-5. Washington, DC: Headquarters, Department of the Army, 1984.

—**AREA DAMAGE CONTROL (ADC)** are measures taken before, during, and after hostile actions or natural or man-made disasters to reduce the probability of damage and to minimize its effects. *See also:* Area Damage Control Capabilities Analysis.

References

Department of Defense, U.S. Army. *Civil Affairs Operations.* Field Manual FM 41-10. Washington, DC: Headquarters, Department of the Army, 1985.

—**AREA DAMAGE CONTROL (ADC) CAPABILITIES ANALYSIS** is an analysis conducted to determine the potential of a unit, base, base cluster, command, or specified force, including host nation forces and assets where appropriate, to assist or reinforce during ADC restorative operations.

References

Department of Defense, U.S. Army. *Civil Affairs Operations.* Field Manual FM 41-10. Washington, DC: Headquarters, Department of the Army, 1985.

—**AREA DEFENSE** is usually conducted to deny the enemy access to specific terrain for a specified time. It is a posture designed for defending a broad area. Airborne defense resources have primary responsibility for providing area air defenses. In an area defense, no particular asset receives defense priority. *See also:* Point Defense.

References

Department of Defense, U.S. Army. *U.S. Army Air Defense Artillery Employment Hawk.* Field Manual FM 44-90. Washington, DC: Headquarters, Department of the Army, 1983.

—**AREA FIRE** is fire delivered on a prescribed area. The term generally applies to neutralization fire but is used regardless of the tactical purpose of the fire.

References

Department of Defense, U.S. Army. *Dictionary of United States Army Terms.* Army Regulation AR 310-25. Washington, DC: Headquarters, Department of the Army, 1986.

—**AREA FUZE** is a fuze that will actuate when a target enters the area surveyed by the fuze. *See also:* Fuze (Specify Type).

References

Department of Defense, U.S. Army. Mine/*Countermine Operations at the Company Level*. Field Manual FM 20-32. Washington, DC: Headquarters, Department of the Army, 1976.

—**AREA HEALTH SERVICE SUPPORT** is health service support delineated by a specific geographic area of responsibility. It includes provisions for health services for organizations (and individuals) located within this area that do not have their own organic health service capability or support. *See also:* Medical Treatment.

References

Department of Defense, U.S. Army. *Health Service Support in a Communications Zone (Test)*. Field Manual FM 8-21. Washington, DC: Headquarters, Department of the Army, 1981.

—**AREA OF CONCENTRATION** identifies a requirement or need and an officer who has the requisite area of expertise (subdivision) within a branch or functional area. An officer may possess and serve in more than one area of concentration.

References

Department of Defense, U.S. Army. *Commissioned Officer Professional Development and Utilization*. Department of the Army Pamphlet 600-3. Washington, DC: Headquarters, Department of the Army, 1986.

———. *Dictionary of United States Army Terms*. Army Regulation AR 310-25. Washington, DC: Headquarters, Department of the Army, 1986.

———. *Officer Assignment Policies, Details, and Transfers*. Army Regulation AR 614-100. Washington, DC: Headquarters, Department of the Army, 1984.

—**AREA OF INFLUENCE.** (1) An area of influence, in the Army tactical intelligence sense, is an area where enemy forces that affect current operations are located. (2) An area of influence is a geographical area wherein a commander is directly capable of influencing operations by maneuver or fire support systems that are normally under his command or control. *See also:* Area of Interest.

References

Department of Defense, U.S. Army. *Intelligence Analysis*. Field Manual FM 34-3. Washington, DC: Headquarters, Department of the Army, 1986.

———. *Military Intelligence Battalion (CEWI) (Operations) (Corps)*. Field Manual FM 34-21. Washington, DC: Headquarters, Department of the Army, 1982.

———. *Operational Terms and Symbols*. Field Manual FM 101-5-1. Washington, DC: Headquarters, Department of the Army, 1985.

—**AREA OF INTELLIGENCE RESPONSIBILITY** is an Army tactical intelligence term for a sector assigned to a commander. It is his responsibility to provide intelligence on the sector if he has the means to do so. *See also:* Area of Responsibility.

References

Department of Defense, U.S. Army. *Dictionary of United States Army Terms*. Army Regulation 310-25. Washington, DC: Headquarters, Department of the Army, 1986.

—**AREA OF INTEREST.** (1) An area of interest is where enemy forces that have the potential to affect friendly future operations are located. (2) An area of interest is the area of concern to the commander, including the area of influence, areas adjacent thereto, and areas extending into enemy territory, that affect the objectives of current and planned operations. This area also includes areas occupied by enemy forces that could jeopardize the accomplishment of the mission. *See also:* Area of Influence.

References

Department of Defense, U.S. Army. *Intelligence Analysis*. Field Manual FM 34-3. Washington, DC: Headquarters, Department of the Army, 1986.

———. *Military Intelligence Battalion (CEWI) (Operations) (Corps)*. Field Manual FM 34-21. Washington, DC: Headquarters, Department of the Army, 1982.

———. *Operational Terms and Symbols*. Field Manual FM 101-5-1. Washington, DC: Headquarters, Department of the Army, 1985.

—**AREA OF MILITARILY SIGNIFICANT FALLOUT** is an area in which radioactive fallout affects the ability of military units to carry out their normal mission. *See also:* Nuclear Warfare.

References

Department of Defense, Joint Chiefs of Staff. *Department of Defense Dictionary of Military and Related Terms*. Washington, DC: GPO, 1986.

—**AREA OF NORTHERN OPERATIONS** is a region of variable width in the Northern Hemisphere that lies north of the 50 degrees isotherm—A line along which the average temperature of the warmest four-month period of the year does not exceed 50 degrees Fahrenheit. Mountain regions located outside of this area are included in this category of operations, provided that these same temperature conditions exist.

References

Department of Defense, Joint Chiefs of Staff. *Department of Defense Dictionary of Military and Related Terms.* Washington, DC: GPO, 1986.

—**AREA OF OPERATIONS** is a specific part of a war theater in which offensive or defensive military operations are waged to fulfill an assigned mission. Such areas are assigned to commanders, for which they have responsibility and in which they have authority to conduct military operations. *See also:* Area of Responsibility.

References

Department of Defense, U.S. Army. *Intelligence Analysis.* Field Manual FM 34-3. Washington, DC: Headquarters, Department of the Army, 1986.

———. *Operational Terms and Symbols.* Field Manual FM 101-5-1. Washington, DC: Headquarters, Department of the Army, 1985.

—**AREA OF RESPONSIBILITY (AOR)** is a defined area of land for which the commander of the area responsible for developing and maintaining installations, controlling movement, and conducting tactical operations involving troops under his control; the commander is also given the parallel authority to exercise these functions.

References

Department of Defense, U.S. Army. *Operational Terms and Symbols.* Field Manual FM 101-5-1. Washington, DC: Headquarters, Department of the Army, 1985.

—**AREA OF WAR** is an area of land, sea, and air that is, or may become, directly involved in the operations of war.

References

Department of Defense, Joint Chiefs of Staff. *Department of Defense Dictionary of Military and Related Terms.* Washington, DC: GPO, 1986.

—**AREA ORIENTED** applies to units or personnel whose organizations, mission, training, and equipment are based upon projected operational deployment to a specific geographical area.

References

Department of Defense, U.S. Army. *Dictionary of United States Army Terms.* Army Regulation AR 310-25. Washington, DC: Headquarters, Department of the Army, 1986.

—**AREA RECONNAISSANCE** is a directed effort to obtain detailed information concerning the terrain or enemy activity within a prescribed area (e.g., a town, ridge line, woods, or other feature) that is critical to operations. *See also:* Route Reconnaissance, Zone Reconnaissance.

References

Department of Defense, U.S. Army. *Operational Terms and Symbols.* Field Manual FM 101-5-1. Washington, DC: Headquarters, Department of the Army, 1985.

—**AREA SECURITY (AS)** is a military police mission that includes area reconnaissance, rear battle operations, security of designated personnel, unit convoys, facilities, and main supply route critical points. *See also:* Area Security Force.

References

Department of Defense. U.S. Army. *Operational Terms and Symbols.* Field Manual FM 101-5-1. Washington, DC: Department of the Army, 1985.

—**AREA SECURITY FORCE.** The requirements of an area security force are delineated by the headquarters assigning the mission. Area security operations are normally associated with rear battle operations. Rear battle forces neutralize or destroy enemy forces to defeat enemy attacks in the rear area. *See also:* Rear Battle Response Forces, Security Operations.

References

Department of Defense, U.S. Army. *Operational Terms and Symbols.* Field Manual FM 101-5-1. Washington, DC: Headquarters, Department of the Army, 1985.

—**AREA SUPPLY SUPPORT ACTIVITY** is a supply distribution activity assigned responsibility for storing and distributing supplies for a specific geographical area.

References

Department of Defense, U.S. Army. *Dictionary of United States Army Terms.* Army Regulation AR 310-25. Washington, DC: Headquarters, Department of the Army, 1986.

—**AREA SURVEY,** in unconventional warfare, is conducted on the ground through physical reconnaissance and the exploitation of all sources of information to verify and update the information previously obtained from area studies.

References

Department of Defense, U.S. Army. *Civil Affairs Operations.* Field Manual FM 41-10. Washington, DC: Headquarters, Department of the Army, 1985.

————. *U.S. Army Operational Concept for Special Operations Forces.* TRADOC PAM 525-34. Washington, DC: Headquarters, Department of the Army, 1984.

—**AREA TARGET** is a target that consists of an area rather than a single point.

References

Department of Defense, Joint Chiefs of Staff. *Department of Defense Dictionary of Military and Related Terms.* Washington, DC: GPO, 1986.

—**ARM.** (1) An arm is a weapon used in war. (2) An arm is a supply aircraft, naval ship, tank or armored vehicle, or personnel with prescribed stores of ammunition, bombs, and other armament items that make it ready for combat service. (3) An arm is a branch of the Army primarily concerned with combat and combat support missions. (4) To arm is to make ammunition ready for detonation (e.g., by removing the safety devices or aligning the explosive elements in the explosive train of a fuze).

References

Department of Defense, U.S. Army. *Dictionary of United States Army Terms.* Army Regulation AR 310-25. Washington, DC: Headquarters, Department of the Army, 1986.

—**ARMAMENT ERROR** concerns the dispersion of shots from a gun. It is the deviation of any shot from the center of impact of a series of shots from a gun after all errors of personnel and adjustment have been accounted for.

References

Department of Defense, U.S. Army. *Dictionary of United States Army Terms.* Army Regulation AR 310-25. Washington, DC: Headquarters, Department of the Army, 1986.

—**ARMED AMMUNITION** is an explosive device that is ready to be activated. *See also:* Ammunition.

References

Department of Defense, U.S. Army. *Dictionary of United States Army Terms.* Army Regulation AR 310-25. Washington, DC: Headquarters, Department of the Army, 1986.

—**ARMED FORCES** are the military forces of a nation or a group of nations.

References

Department of Defense, Joint Chiefs of Staff. *Department of Defense Dictionary of Military and Related Terms.* Washington, DC: GPO, 1986.

—**ARMED FORCES CENSORSHIP** is the examination and control of personal communications to or from persons in the Armed Forces of the United States and persons accompanying or serving with the Armed Forces of the United States. *See also:* Military Censorship.

References

Department of Defense, U.S. Army. *Dictionary of United States Army Terms.* Army Regulation AR 310-25. Washington, DC: Headquarters, Department of the Army, 1986.

—**ARMED FORCES COURIER** is an officer or enlisted member of E-7 or above of the U.S. Armed Forces who is assigned to perform Armed Forces Courier Service duties and is identified by possession of an Armed Forces Courier Service Identification Card (ARF-COS Form 9). *See also:* Courier.

References

Department of Defense, Joint Chiefs of Staff. *Department of Defense Dictionary of Military and Related Terms.* Washington, DC: GPO, 1986.

—**ARMED FORCES COURIER SERVICE (ARFCOS)** is a joint service of the Army, Navy, and Air Force with the Chief of Staff of the Army as Executive Agent. The service provides a means of securely and rapidly transmitting classified and other material that requires protection by a military courier. *See also:* Armed Forces Courier.

References

Bamford, James. *The Puzzle Palace: A Report on America's Most Secret Agency.* New York: Penguin Books, 1983.

—**ARMED FORCES COURIER STATION** is an Army, Navy, or Air Force activity that has been approved by the respective military department and officially designated by Headquarters,

Armed Forces Courier Service, for accepting, processing, and dispatching Armed Forces Courier Service material. *See also:* Armed Forces Courier.

References
Department of Defense, Joint Chiefs of Staff. *Department of Defense Dictionary of Military and Related Terms.* Washington, DC: GPO, 1986.

—**ARMED FORCES INTELLIGENCE** is a general intelligence term for information dealing with foreign armed forces, their personnel, training programs, equipment, bases, capabilities, disposition, manpower levels, and all other pertinent aspects of their strengths and liabilities. It is the integrated study of the organized land, sea, and air forces, both actual and potential, of foreign nations. *See also:* Intelligence.

References
Clauser, Jerome K., and Weir, Sandra M. *Intelligence Research Methodology.* State College, PA: HRB-Singer, 1975.

Department of Defense, U.S. Army. *Dictionary of United States Army Terms.* Army Regulation AR 310-25. Washington, DC: Headquarters, Department of the Army, 1986.

—**ARMED FORCES OF THE UNITED STATES** denotes collectively all components of the Army, Navy, Air Force, Marine Corps, and Coast Guard. *See also:* United States Armed Forces.

References
Department of Defense, U.S. Army. *Dictionary of United States Army Terms.* Army Regulation AR 310-25. Washington, DC: Headquarters, Department of the Army, 1986.

—**ARMED HELICOPTER** is a helicopter fitted with weapons or weapons systems.

References
Department of Defense, Joint Chiefs of Staff. *Department of Defense Dictionary of Military and Related Terms.* Washington, DC: GPO, 1986.

—**ARMED RECONNAISSANCE** is an air intelligence term for an air mission that is flown to locate and attack targets of opportunity in assigned areas and along ground communications routes. Armed reconnaissance is unique in that its mission is not to attack specific targets. *See also*: Intelligence.

References
Department of Defense, U.S. Army. *Dictionary of United States Army Terms.* Army Regulation AR 310-25. Washington, DC: Headquarters, Department of the Army, 1986.

—**ARMED SERVICES** are the active and reserve component forces of any country, excluding paramilitary elements (e.g., internal security troops), which are designed, equipped, and trained to deter, deflect, or defeat hostile powers. U.S. Armed Services include the Army, Navy, Air Force, Marine Corps, and Coast Guard.

References
Collins, John M. *U.S.-Soviet Military Balance, 1980-1985.* Washington, DC: Congressional Research Service, 1985.

—**ARMED SERVICES MEDICAL REGULATING OFFICE** is a jointly staffed organization that coordinates all intertheater patient evacuation. It designates the continental U.S. hospital that each patient will be evacuated to. *See also*: Medical Treatment.

References
Department of Defense, U.S. Army. *Support Operations: Echelons Above Corps.* Field Manual FM 100-16. Washington, DC: Headquarters, Department of the Army, 1986.

—**ARMING**, as it applies to explosives, weapons, and ammunition, is the changing from a safe condition to a state of readiness for initiation.

References
Department of Defense, Joint Chiefs of Staff. *Department of Defense Dictionary of Military and Related Terms.* Washington, DC: GPO, 1986.

—**ARMOR.** (1) In mounted warfare, the tank is the primary offensive weapon. Its firepower, protection from enemy fire, and speed create the shock effect necessary to disrupt the enemy's operations and to defeat it. Tanks can destroy enemy armored vehicles, infantry, and antitank guided missile units. They can break through suppressed defenses, exploit the success of an attack by striking deep into the enemy's rear areas, and pursue defeated enemy forces. Armored units can also blunt enemy attacks and launch counterattacks as part of a defense. Armored units have several significant limitations. They are vulnerable in close terrain (e.g., forests and cities) and in limited visibility conditions.

They cannot cross most rivers and swamps without bridging, and they require substantial logistical support. Armor units are also slow to deploy strategically because their weight and the amount of equipment require deployment by sea. (2) Armor is the protective covering, especially metal plates, used on tanks and motor vehicles. (3) Armor is a branch of the Army. *See also*: Armorer, and the entries under Armor and Armored.

References

Department of Defense, U.S. Army. *Dictionary of United States Army Terms*. Army Regulation AR 310-25. Washington, DC: Headquarters, Department of the Army, 1986.

———. *Staff Organization and Operations*. Field Manual FM 101-5. Washington, DC: Headquarters, Department of the Army, 1983.

—**ARMOR AMBUSH.** The purpose of an armor ambush is to destroy one (sometimes two) armored vehicles. The Dragon is normally the major armor-destroying weapon used in a squad-size armor ambush. If the terrain is so thick that fields of fire are very short and armor movement is very restricted, light antitank weapons may be the primary weapon. *See also:* Ambush.

References

Department of Defense, U.S. Army. *The Rifle Squads (Mechanized and Light Infantry)*. Training Circular TC 7-1. Washington, DC: Headquarters, Department of the Army, 1976.

—**ARMOR-DEFEATING AMMUNITION** are projectiles that use either kinetic or chemical energy to destroy armored targets.

References

Department of Defense, U.S. Army. *Dictionary of United States Army Terms*. Army Regulation AR 310-25. Washington, DC: Headquarters, Department of the Army, 1986.

—**ARMOR GROUP** is a field army unit designed to exercise command, control, and supervise one or more separate tanks, armored infantry, and armored cavalry battalions assigned to a corps or field army.

References

Department of Defense, U.S. Army. *Dictionary of United States Army Terms*. Army Regulation AR 310-25. Washington, DC: Headquarters, Department of the Army, 1986.

—**ARMOR PIERCING AND ARMOR PIERCING INCENDIARY** rounds are a category of direct fire projectile. They are designed to penetrate armor plate and other types of homogenous steel. Armor piercing projectiles have a special jacket encasing a hard core of penetrating rod, which is designed when fired with high accuracy to penetrate at an angle very close to the perpendicular to the target. Incendiary projectiles are used principally to penetrate a target and ignite its contents. They are used effectively against fuel supplies and storage areas. *See also:* Armor Piercing Capped.

References

Department of Defense, U.S. Army. *Survivability*. Field Manual FM 5-103. Washington, DC: Headquarters, Department of the Army, 1985.

—**ARMOR PIERCING CAPPED** applies to armor piercing projectiles that have a face hardened steel cap over the head.

References

Department of Defense, U.S. Army. *Dictionary of United States Army Terms*. Army Regulation AR 310-25. Washington, DC: Headquarters, Department of the Army, 1986.

—**ARMOR SWEEP** is a raid or other limited attack without terrain objective by a rapidly moving armor unit through or across enemy-controlled territory. An armor sweep may be conducted for reconnaissance in force, destruction or capture of personnel or materiel, or to harass or disrupt enemy plans and operations.

References

Department of Defense, U.S. Army. *Dictionary of United States Army Terms*. Army Regulation AR 310-25. Washington, DC: Headquarters, Department of the Army, 1986.

—**ARMOR THICKNESS** is expressed in millimeters, followed by the angle of slope from the vertical expressed in degrees.

References

Department of Defense, U.S. Army. *Dictionary of United States Army Terms*. Army Regulation AR 310-25. Washington, DC: Headquarters, Department of the Army, 1986.

—**ARMORED ARTILLERY.** (1) Armored artillery consists of self-propelled artillery weapons that are completely or partially armored. (2) Armored artillery are artillery units equipped with armored artillery weapons and appropriate armored auxiliary vehicles, and are organized primarily to function with armored units.

References

Department of Defense, U.S. Army. *Dictionary of United States Army Terms.* Army Regulation AR 310-25. Washington, DC: Headquarters, Department of the Army, 1986.

—**ARMORED CAVALRY (AC)** consists of combat units that are characterized by a high degree of mobility, fire-power, shock action, and multiple flexible communications. The units are especially designed to execute reconnaissance, security, combat, or economy of force operations using organic surface and air modes of transport.

References

Department of Defense, U.S. Army. *Dictionary of United States Army Terms.* Army Regulation AR 310-25. Washington, DC: Headquarters, Department of the Army, 1986.

—**ARMORED CAVALRY SQUADRON.** Cavalry is a combat maneuver force of combined arms mounted in ground and aerial vehicles that is uniquely organized and equipped for its mission. It is trained to find the enemy in order to prevent the friendly main body from being engaged under adverse circumstances and to provide, within its capability, security for the main body. Cavalry organization and employment exemplify two essential requisites for battle: (1) the need to find the enemy and develop the situation with the least force possible and (2) the need to provide reaction time and maneuver space with a force tailored to leave the bulk of combat power in the main body available for employment at the time and place of decision. The armored cavalry squadron is organized with three ground troops and an air cavalry troop. Cavalry often conducts offensive, defensive, and delay operations. It is particularly suited for economy of force missions.

References

Department of Defense, U.S. Army. *Armored and Mechanized Division Operations.* Field Manual FM 71-100. Washington, DC: Headquarters, Department of the Army, 1978.

—**ARMORED INFANTRY** is a field Army unit designed to close and destroy the enemy by fire and maneuver, to repel hostile assault in close combat, and to provide support for tanks.

References

Department of Defense, U.S. Army. *Dictionary of United States Army Terms.* Army Regulation AR 310-25. Washington, DC: Headquarters, Department of the Army, 1986.

—**ARMORED PERSONNEL CARRIER (APC)** is a lightly armored, highly mobile, full-tracked vehicle, amphibious and air-droppable, used primarily for transporting personnel and their individual equipment during tactical operations. Production modifications or application of special kits permits its use as a mortar carrier, command post, flame thrower, antiaircraft artillery chassis, or limited recovery vehicle.

References

Department of Defense, Joint Chiefs of Staff. *Department of Defense Dictionary of Military and Related Terms.* Washington, DC: GPO, 1986.

—**ARMORED RECONNAISSANCE AIRBORNE ASSAULT VEHICLE (ARAAV)** is a lightly armored, mobile, full-tracked vehicle serving as the main reconnaissance vehicle in infantry and airborne operations and as the principal assault weapon of airborne troops.

References

Department of Defense, Joint Chiefs of Staff. *Department of Defense Dictionary of Military and Related Terms.* Washington, DC: GPO, 1986.

—**ARMORED VEHICLE** is a wheeled or track-laying vehicle, with an armored hull or body. It may have major armament. It is used in combat, for security purposes, and for transporting cargo.

References

Department of Defense, U.S. Army. *Dictionary of United States Army Terms.* Army Regulation AR 310-25. Washington, DC: Headquarters, Department of the Army, 1986.

—**ARMORER** is one who services and makes repairs on small arms and performs duties necessary to keep small arms ready for use.

References

Department of Defense, U.S. Army. *Dictionary of United States Army Terms.* Army Regulation AR 310-25. Washington, DC: Headquarters, Department of the Army, 1986.

—**ARMY.** (1) The U.S. Army consists of the Regular Army, Army of the United States, Army National Guard of the United States, and the United States Army Reserve. (2) Army is an inclusive term for the land military forces of a nation. (3) An army is a large administrative and tactical unit of the forces consisting of two or more Army corps and supporting troops. *See also*: Battalion, Brigades, Company, Corps, Division, Platoon, Regiment, Squad.

References

Department of Defense, U.S. Army. *Dictionary of United States Army Terms*. Army Regulation AR 310-25. Washington, DC: Headquarters, Department of the Army, 1986.

—**ARMY ACQUISITION OBJECTIVE** is the quantity of an item of equipment or ammunition required to equip the U.S. Army-approved force and to sustain that force, together with specified allies, in wartime from D-Day through the period prescribed at the support level directed in the latest Secretary of Defense Consolidated Guidance.

References

Department of Defense, U.S. Army. *Dictionary of United States Army Terms*. Army Regulation AR 310-25. Washington, DC: Headquarters, Department of the Army, 1986.

—**ARMY AIR DEFENSE COMMAND.** (1) An Army Air Defense Command is a command composed of a headquarters battery and two or more brigades of air defense artillery. (2) An Army Air Defense Command is also a command established by the U.S. Army to command all air defense forces allocated to the air defense of the United States. (3) An Army Air Defense Command can be a major subordinate command of the U.S. theater army, collocated with army groups and established by existing operational requirements. *See also:* Army Air Defense Command Post.

References

Department of Defense, U.S. Army. *Dictionary of United States Army Terms*. Army Regulation AR 310-25. Washington, DC: Headquarters, Department of the Army, 1986.

—**ARMY AIR DEFENSE COMMAND POST** is the tactical headquarters of an Army air defense commander.

References

Department of Defense, Joint Chiefs of Staff. *Department of Defense Dictionary of Military and Related Terms*. Washington, DC: GPO, 1986.

—**ARMY AIRCRAFT** is an aircraft under the jurisdiction of the Army. *See also*: Army Aviation.

References

Department of Defense, U.S. Army. *Dictionary of United States Army Terms*. Army Regulation AR 310-25. Washington, DC: Headquarters, Department of the Army, 1986.

—**ARMY AIR-GROUND SYSTEM (AAGS)** is the Army system that provides for interface between Army and the tactical air support agencies of other services in planning, evaluating, processing, and coordinating air support requirements and operations. It is not a separate organization, but is the Army system that is integrated with the Air Force Tactical Air Control System and is superimposed on the Army and Air Force organizations. These systems consist of an aggregate of men, procedures, and equipment found within the existing commands and are organized to perform specific functions of tactical airlift and air support. Their functions are absorbed into the existing staff organizations at each echelon of command.

References

Department of Defense, U.S. Army. *Attack Helicopter Operations*. Field Manual FM 17-50. Washington, DC: Headquarters, Department of the Army, 1984.

———. *USA/USAF Doctrine for Joint Airborne and Tactical Airlift Operations*. Field Manual FM 100-27. Washington, DC: Headquarters, Department of the Army, 1985.

—**ARMY AIRSPACE COMMAND AND CONTROL** (A^2C^2) is the effort necessary to coordinate airspace users for concurrent employment in the accomplishment of assigned missions. *See also:* Army Airspace Command and Control Element.

References

Department of Defense, U.S. Army. *Operational Terms and Symbols*. Field Manual FM 101-5-1. Washington, DC: Headquarters, Department of the Army, 1985.

—**ARMY AIRSPACE COMMAND AND CONTROL** (A^2C^2) **ELEMENT** is an Army element within the corps A^2C^2 element, the division A^2C^2 element, and the separate brigade A^2C^2 element tactical operations centers that is responsible for coordinating, integrating, and regulating airspace within the organization's area of territorial responsibility. It coordinates directly with Air Force elements and functional Army elements (air defense artillery, Army aviation, fire support element) working within each tactical operation center.

References

Department of Defense, U.S. Army. *Operational Terms and Symbols*. Field Manual FM 101-5-1. Washington, DC: Headquarters, Department of the Army, 1985.

—**ARMY AND AIR FORCE EXCHANGE SERVICE (AAFES)** is a service that provides to authorized patrons merchandise and services of necessity and convenience that are not furnished from federal appropriations.

References

Department of Defense, U.S. Army. *Dictionary of United States Army Terms*. Army Regulation AR 310-25. Washington, DC: Headquarters, Department of the Army, 1986.

—**ARMY AND AIR FORCE POSTAL SERVICE** consists of postal services operated and maintained by the Departments of the Army and the Air Force to provide unified postal services (i.e., acceptance, transmission, handling, and delivery of mail; sale of postage stamps and stamped paper; and issuance and payment of money orders) for the two departments in areas where the U.S. civil postal service does not operate and where military situations require.

References

Department of Defense, U.S. Army. *Dictionary of United States Army Terms*. Army Regulation AR 310-25. Washington, DC: Headquarters, Department of the Army, 1986.

—**ARMY AND MARINE CORPS CLASSIFICATION** is a systematic method for classifying Army and Marine Corps land force structure, manpower, and materiel programs. The system is designed for strategic and operational planning at Office, Secretary of Defense, Joint Chiefs of Staff, and Service staff levels. It also is a means of displaying force structure guidance for major Army commands.

References

Department of Defense, U.S. Army. *Dictionary of United States Army Terms*. Army Regulation AR 310-25. Washington, DC: Headquarters, Department of the Army, 1986.

—**ARMY ASSAULT TEAM (AAT)** is a small infantry unit assigned on a mission basis during airborne assault operations to accompany and provide security to an Air Force combat control team as it accomplishes its mission.

References

Department of Defense, U.S. Army. *USA/USAF Doctrine for Joint Airborne and Tactical Airlift Operations*. Field Manual FM 100-27. Washington, DC: Headquarters, Department of the Army, 1985.

—**ARMY ATTACHE** is a member of the Defense Attache Office, which is a part of a U.S. embassy. The Army Attache performs attache duties as they pertain to his service and his military specialty.

References

Department of Defense, U.S. Army. *Dictionary of United States Army Terms*. Army Regulation AR 310-25. Washington, DC: Headquarters, Department of the Army, 1986.

Laubenthal, Sanders A. "Preparing 'the Team': Defense Attache Training." *DIC Newsletter* (Winter 1986): 1-4.

—**(THE) ARMY AUTHORIZATION DOCUMENTS SYSTEM (TAADS)** is an automated system designed to centralize control of personnel and equipment.

References

Department of Defense, U.S. Army. *Organizational Maintenance Operations*. Field Manual FM 29-2. Washington, DC: Headquarters, Department of the Army, 1984.

—**ARMY AVIATION** includes the personnel, aircraft, and allied aircraft equipment organically assigned to Army organizations by the appropriate tables of organization and equipment, tables of distribution, tables of allowances, or other competent authority.

References

Department of Defense, U.S. Army. *Dictionary of United States Army Terms*. Army Regulation AR 310-25. Washington, DC: Headquarters, Department of the Army, 1986.

—**ARMY BASE** is a base or a group of installations for which a local commander is responsible. It consists of the facilities necessary for supporting Army activities, including security, internal lines of communication, utilities, plants and systems, and real property for which the Army has been operating responsibility.

References

Department of Defense, Joint Chiefs of Staff.
*Department of Defense Dictionary of Military and
Related Terms.* Washington, DC: GPO, 1986.

—**ARMY COLLEGE** is an Army school that conducts officer professional development education courses. *See also:* National Defense University.

References

Department of Defense, U.S. Army. *Individual
Military Education and Training.* Army Regulation
AR 350-1. Washington, DC: Headquarters,
Department of the Army, 1987.

—**ARMY COMPONENT COMMANDER (ACC)** is
the theater army commander, an army group
commander, an army commander, or, in some
cases, a corps commander. He and his chief
subordinates must maintain synchronization over
large areas. This always involves close cooperation with air forces and often requires joint
planning and operations with naval forces. In
addition to maintaining effective cooperation
with other armed forces of the United States, the
ACC and his staff must cooperate with allied air,
ground, or naval forces. In many cases, the forces
of allied nations are assigned to U.S. corps and
armies. The U.S. corps must also be prepared to
fight under command of allied commanders.

References

Department of Defense, U.S. Army. *Staff Organiza-
tion and Operations.* Field Manual FM 101-5.
Washington, DC: Headquarters, Department of the
Army, 1984.

—**ARMY COMPOSITION.** The Army consists of
the Regular Army, the Army National Guard of
the United States, the Army National Guard
while in the service of the United States, and the
U.S. Army Reserve, and all persons who are
appointed to or are enlisted in or are conscripted
into the Army without component. The organized peace establishment of the Army consists
of all military organizations of the Army with
their installation and supporting auxiliary elements, including combat, training, administrative, and logistic elements; and members of the
Army, including those not assigned to units
necessary to form the basis for a complete and
immediate mobilization for the national defense
in the event of a national emergency. *See also:*
United States Army.

References

Department of Defense, U.S. Army. *The Army*
(prepublication issue). Field Manual FM 100-1.
Washington, DC: Headquarters, Department of the
Army, 1986.

—**ARMY CORPS** is a tactical unit that is larger
than a division and smaller than a field army. A
corps usually consists of two or more divisions,
together with auxiliary arms and services. *See
also:* Corps.

References

Department of Defense, Joint Chiefs of Staff.
*Department of Defense Dictionary of Military and
Related Terms.* Washington, DC: GPO, 1986.

—**ARMY CORRESPONDENCE COURSE** is a formal course of instruction prepared by service
schools, centrally administered by the Army
Institute for Professional Development, and
completed through correspondence with the Institute. *See also:* Army Learning Center.

References

Department of Defense, U.S. Army. *Individual
Military Education and Training.* Army Regulation
AR 350-1. Washington, DC: Headquarters,
Department of the Army, 1984.

—**ARMY DEPOT,** located within the area of an
Army and designated by the Army commander,
is where supplies from the communications zone
or from local sources are received, classified,
stored, and distributed. *See also:* Depot.

References

Department of Defense, U.S. Army. *Dictionary of
United States Army Terms.* Army Regulation AR
310-25. Washington, DC: Headquarters, Department of the Army, 1986.

—**ARMY EXERCISE PROGRAM** includes joint,
combined, and unilateral exercises. Significant
joint and combined exercises are scheduled by
either the Joint Chiefs of Staff or unified commands and are centrally sponsored and coordinated through the Joint Chiefs of Staff exercise
program. Unilateral exercises are scheduled and
sponsored generally by a single service at corps
level or below. *See also:* Exercise.

References

Department of Defense, U.S. Army. *U.S. Army
Policy Statement, 1988.* Washington, DC:
Headquarters, Department of the Army, 1988.

—**ARMY FIELD COMMANDS** are all parts of the Department of the Army except the part that has been defined as Headquarters, Department of the Army. Army field commands include all field headquarters, forces, Reserve components, installations, activities, and functions that are under the control or supervision of the Secretary of the Army.

References

Department of Defense, U.S. Army. *Dictionary of United States Army Terms.* Army Regulation AR 310-25. Washington, DC: Headquarters, Department of the Army, 1986.

—**ARMY FINANCIAL MANAGEMENT** includes any action that formulates, establishes, directs, and controls Army financial operations with the ultimate objective of achieving optimum use of available financial resources in the pursuit of specified program goals. These management objectives are achieved by applying the established principles and procedures of programming, budgeting, accounting, auditing, analysis, and evaluation, conducted within the parameters of applicable statutory and regulatory constraints.

References

Department of Defense, U.S. Army. *Dictionary of United States Army Terms.* Army Regulation AR 310-25. Washington, DC: Headquarters, Department of the Army, 1986.

—**ARMY GENERAL STAFF** consists of a group of Army officers under the direction of the Chief of Staff, who render professional advice and assistance to the Secretary, the Under Secretary, and the Assistant Secretaries of the Army, in developing and providing broad basic policies, and plans and programs from the guidance of the Department of the Army. It specifically assists the Secretary of the Army in preparing and issuing directives and programs to implement such plans and policies, and in supervising the execution and implementation of these directives and programs.

References

Department of Defense, U.S. Army. *Dictionary of United States Army Terms.* Army Regulation AR 310-25. Washington, DC: Headquarters, Department of the Army, 1986.

—**ARMY GROUP.** In a theater of war where many forces are employed, theater army commanders, in coordination with the Commanders in Chief of unified or combined commands, may form army groups to control the operations of two to five field armies. Army groups have not been employed by the U.S. Army since World War II, but in a large conflict, they might be necessary again. As in the past, their main function would be to design and direct campaigns in a theater. In some cases, an army group commander might be designated the land component commander.

Army group commanders perform major missions for which they usually receive broad operational guidance. They control a variable number of field armies, depending on their mission, and should also control separate units necessary for their operations. Special operation forces units, psychological operations units, civil affairs organizations, and other support forces, including engineer, aviation, military intelligence, military police, signal, and combat service support units, are commonly needed to support the operations of army groups. Army groups also require the full range of air support for their operations.

Like field armies, army groups will be activated from existing army units. They will often be multinational forces and their headquarters will then be staffed by officers of participating allied forces.

References

Department of Defense, U.S. Army. *Low Intensity Conflict.* Field Manual FM 100-20. Washington, DC: Headquarters, Department of the Army, 1981.

—**ARMY IN THE FIELD** includes all types of military personnel and units used in, or intended for use in, a theater of operations.

References

Department of Defense, U.S. Army. *Dictionary of United States Army Terms.* Army Regulation AR 310-25. Washington, DC: Headquarters, Department of the Army, 1986.

—**ARMY IN THE FIELD LOGISTICS** is the portion of the Army Logistics System that pertains to functions internal to theaters of operations, units, and organizations deployed in overseas theaters, and Army in the field units in the continental United States. Army in the field logistic operations are sometimes referred to as consumer or retail logistic operations. *See also:* Army in the Field.

References

Department of Defense, U.S. Army. *Dictionary of United States Army Terms.* Army Regulation AR 310-25. Washington, DC: Headquarters, Department of the Army, 1986.

—**ARMY JOINT OPERATIONS PLANNING SYSTEM (AJOPS)** is the Army's interface with the JOPS and Joint Deployment Systems. The AJOPS is applicable to Army components of unified commands, the major Army commands, Military Traffic Management Command, and other supporting commands and agencies.

References
Department of Defense, U.S. Army. *Staff Organization and Operations.* Field Manual FM 101-5. Washington, DC: Headquarters, Department of the Army, 1984.

—**ARMY LANDING FORCE,** the Army component of an amphibious task force, is a task organization composing all Army units assigned for participation in an amphibious operation. The commander of the Army component of the amphibious task force is the Army landing force commander.

References
Department of Defense, U.S. Army. *Dictionary of United States Army Terms.* Army Regulation AR 310-25. Washington, DC: Headquarters, Department of the Army, 1986.

—**ARMY LEARNING CENTER** is a facility that provides education and learning support services. *See also:* Army Correspondence Course.

References
Department of Defense, U.S. Army. *Individual Military Education and Training.* Army Regulation AR 350-1. Washington, DC: Headquarters, Department of the Army, 1987.

—**(THE) ARMY MAINTENANCE MANAGEMENT SYSTEM (TAMMS)** establishes a chain of maintenance-related information on items in the Army inventory. This information is used by using unit commanders, as well as maintenance agencies and activities at the national level.

References
Department of Defense, U.S. Army. *Organizational Maintenance Operations.* Field Manual FM 29-2. Washington, DC: Headquarters, Department of the Army, 1984.

—**ARMY MANAGEMENT STRUCTURE** is a uniform classification of the nontactical activities of the Department of the Army for programming (except control programs), program performance data maintenance, budgeting program cost data maintenance, manpower utilization data maintenance, reviewing accomplishment in relation to the scheduling and use of resources, and for other prescribed management purposes.

References
Department of Defense, U.S. Army. *Dictionary of United States Army Terms.* Army Regulation AR 310-25. Washington, DC: Headquarters, Department of the Army, 1986.

—**ARMY MASTER DATA FILE** consists of the files required to record, maintain, and distribute supply management data between and from Army commands to requiring activities.

References
Department of Defense, U.S. Army. *Dictionary of United States Army Terms.* Army Regulation AR 310-25. Washington, DC: Headquarters, Department of the Army, 1986.

—**ARMY MEDICAL DEPARTMENT** is a term that encompasses the Army special branches that are under the supervision and management of the Surgeon General (i.e., the Medical Corps, the Dental Corps, the Veterinary Corps, the Medical Service Corps, the Army Medical Specialist Corps, and the Army Nurse Corps). *See also:* Medical Treatment.

References
Department of Defense, U.S. Army. *Dictionary of United States Army Terms.* Army Regulation AR 310-25. Washington, DC: Headquarters, Department of the Army, 1986.

—**ARMY MOBILIZATION AND OPERATIONS PLANNING SYSTEM (AMOPS)** is the vehicle by which all components of the Army plan and execute actions to provide and expand Army forces and resources to meet the requirements of Unified Commands. AMOPS serves as the Army supplement to the Joint Operations Planning System. *See also*: Unified Command.

References
Department of Defense, U.S. Army. *Operational Terms and Symbols.* Field Manual FM 101-5-1. Washington, DC: Headquarters, Department of the Army, 1985.

—**ARMY MODERNIZATION TRAINING** is the training required to support the Army's modernization process. This includes New Equipment Training, Displaced Equipment Training, Doctrine and Tactics Training, and Sustainment Training.

References
Department of Defense, U.S. Army. *Individual Military Education and Training.* Army Regulation AR 350-1. Washington, DC: Headquarters, Department of the Army, 1987.

—**ARMY NATIONAL GUARD** is the Army portion of the organized militia of the several states, Commonwealth of Puerto Rico, and District of Columbia whose units and members are federally recognized. *See also:* Army Composition, Regular Army, United States Army, United States Army Reserve.

References
Department of Defense, U.S. Army. *Dictionary of United States Army Terms.* Army Regulation AR 310-25. Washington, DC: Headquarters, Department of the Army, 1986.

—**ARMY NATIONAL GUARD OF THE UNITED STATES** is a Reserve component of the Army, all of whose members are members of the Army National Guard. *See also:* Army National Guard.

References
Department of Defense, U.S. Army. *Dictionary of United States Army Terms.* Army Regulation AR 310-25. Washington, DC: Headquarters, Department of the Army, 1986.

—**ARMY OF OCCUPATION** is an army in effective control of enemy territory for the purpose of maintaining law and order within the area to insure the carrying out of armistice or surrender terms.

References
Department of Defense, U.S. Army. *Dictionary of United States Army Terms.* Army Regulation AR 310-25. Washington, DC: Headquarters, Department of the Army, 1986.

—**ARMY OF THE UNITED STATES.** *See:* United States Army.

—**ARMY PERSONNEL CENTER** is an activity providing training, transient, and patient administrative control where two or more of the following processing activities are located at the same installation: (1) reception station, (2) overseas replacement station, (3) returnee-reassignment station, and (4) transfer station. *See also:* Army Personnel System.

References
Department of Defense, U.S. Army. *Dictionary of United States Army Terms.* Army Regulation AR 310-25. Washington, DC: Headquarters, Department of the Army, 1986.

—**ARMY PERSONNEL SYSTEM** is a broad system for effectively planning, organizing, directing, and supervising the procedures necessary to administer and operate personnel management. *See also*: Army Personnel Center.

References
Department of Defense, U.S. Army. *Dictionary of United States Army Terms.* Army Regulation AR 310-25. Washington, DC: Headquarters, Department of the Army, 1986.

—**ARMY POSTAL UNIT** is a table of organization and equipment organization established to operate an Army Post Office. *See also:* Postal Concentration Center, Postal Finance Officer, Postal Regulating Detachment, Terminal Post Officer.

References
Department of Defense, U.S. Army. *Dictionary of United States Army Terms.* Army Regulation AR 310-25. Washington, DC: Headquarters, Department of the Army, 1986.

—**ARMY** (PRIMARY ROLES). In general, the Army, within the Department of the Army includes land combat and service forces and aviation and water transport that are organic therein. It is organized, trained, and equipped primarily for prompt and sustained combat incident to operations on land. It is responsible for the preparation of land forces necessary for the effective prosecution of war except as otherwise assigned and, in accordance with integrated joint mobilization plans, for the expansion of the peacetime components of the Army to meet the needs of war. *See also:* United States Army.

References
Department of Defense, U.S. Army. *The Army* (prepublication issue). Field Manual FM 100-1. Washington, DC: Headquarters, Department of the Army, 1986.

—**ARMY PROGRAM FOR INDIVIDUAL TRAINING** defines the Army's requirements and capabilities for all individual training.

References
Department of Defense, U.S. Army. *Army Forces Training.* Army Regulation AR 350-41. Washington, DC: Headquarters, Department of the Army, 1986.

—**ARMY PROMOTION LIST (APL)** lists officers in all branches, except the medical and chaplain corps, who are being considered for promotion.

References
Department of Defense, U.S. Army. *Promotion of Officers on Active Duty.* Army Regulation AR 624-100. Washington, DC: Headquarters, Department of the Army, 1984.

—**ARMY READY MATERIEL PROGRAM** is an Army program to improve materiel readiness in terms of quantity, quality, and serviceability.

References

Department of Defense, U.S. Army. *Dictionary of United States Army Terms.* Army Regulation AR 310-25. Washington, DC: Headquarters, Department of the Army, 1986.

—**ARMY REMEDIAL ACTION PROJECT PROGRAM** implements, parallels, and complements the Joint Chiefs of Staff Remedial Action Program.

References

Department of Defense, U.S. Army. *Army Exercises.* Army Regulation AR 350-28. Washington, DC: Headquarters, Department of the Army, 1985.

—**ARMY SCHOOL** is an educational institution authorized by the Army to conduct formal courses, collective training (e.g., crew training), and training of National Guard and Reserve units. *See also:* Army College.

References

Department of Defense, U.S. Army. *Individual Military Education and Training.* Army Regulation AR 350-1. Washington, DC: Headquarters, Department of the Army, 1987.

—**ARMY SERVICE AREA** is the territory between the corps rear boundary and the combat zone rear boundary. Most of the Army administrative establishment and service troops are usually located in this area. *See also:* Rear Area.

References

Department of Defense, Joint Chiefs of Staff. *Department of Defense Dictionary of Military and Related Terms.* Washington, DC: GPO, 1986.

—**ARMY STAFF** is the staff of the Secretary of the Army at the seat of government that is presided over by the Chief of Staff. *See also:* Army Staff Proponent.

References

Department of Defense, U.S. Army. *Dictionary of United States Army Terms.* Army Regulation AR 310-25. Washington, DC: Headquarters, Department of the Army, 1986.

—**ARMY STAFF PROPONENT** is a single-action officer in each Army staff agency or directorate who is the contact for all matters pertaining to the Army remedial action project program.

References

Department of Defense, U.S. Army. *Army Exercises.* Army Regulation AR 350-28. Washington, DC: Headquarters, Department of the Army, 1985.

—**ARMY STRATEGIC CAPABILITIES PLAN** supports the Joint Strategic Capabilities Plan by further developing and expanding the guidance contained in the joint plan. *See also:* Joint Strategic Capabilities Plan.

References

Department of Defense, U.S. Army. *Dictionary of United States Army Terms.* Army Regulation AR 310-25. Washington, DC: Headquarters, Department of the Army, 1986.

—**ARMY SUBJECT SCHEDULE (ASUBJSCD)** is a Department of the Army publication that provides guidance to trainers for preparing and scheduling branch, general, or military occupational specialty training in a particular subject as outlined in the Army training publications.

References

Department of Defense, U.S. Army. *How to Prepare and Conduct Military Training.* Field Manual FM 21-6. Washington, DC: Headquarters, Department of the Army, 1975.

—**ARMY TERMINALS** are established by Department of the Army orders. They are primarily intended for embarking and debarking troops, and loading and discharging Army cargos to and from overseas destinations.

References

Department of Defense, U.S. Army. *Dictionary of United States Army Terms.* Army Regulation AR 310-25. Washington, DC: Headquarters, Department of the Army, 1986.

—**ARMY TRAINING AND EVALUATION PROGRAM (ARTEP)**, a Department of the Army publication, provides the training objectives and collective tasks that a unit must perform to accomplish its mission and survive on the battlefield. The ARTEP has training and evaluation outlines that contain the tasks, conditions, standards, and training support requirements that are used to conduct performance-oriented training. It is a fundamental tool for assigning training objectives, programming resources, and assessing unit proficiency. *See also:* Army Training Program.

References

Department of Defense, U.S. Army. *Army Exercises.* Army Regulation AR 350-28. Washington, DC: Headquarters, Department of the Army, 1985.

————. *Army Forces Training.* Army Regulation AR 350-41. Washington, DC: Headquarters, Department of the Army, 1986.

————. *Dictionary of United States Army Terms.* Army Regulation AR 310-25. Washington, DC: Headquarters, Department of the Army, 1986.

————. *Fire Support in Combined Arms Operations.* Field Manual FM 6-20. Washington, DC: Headquarters, Department of the Army, 1983.

————. *Unit Training Management.* Field Manual FM 25-2. Washington, DC: Headquarters, Department of the Army, 1984.

—**ARMY TRAINING PROGRAM (ATP)** is a Department of the Army publication that outlines the minimum essential training for individuals and units in the Active Army and in Reserve components who are undergoing a formal phase of training. ATPs are guides and references for units that are conducting Operational Readiness Training. ATPs prescribe the number of hours for training in specific subjects and they list the supporting Army Subject Schedules and related references and training aids. Because they are not written in performance terms, ATPs do not meet the peacetime training needs of the Active Army and Reserve components. ATPs are being replaced by the Army Training and Evaluation Program. *See also*: Army Training and Evaluation Program.

References

Department of Defense, U.S. Army. *Dictionary of United States Army Terms.* Army Regulation AR 310-25. Washington, DC: Headquarters, Department of the Army, 1986.

————. *How to Prepare and Conduct Military Training.* Field Manual FM 21-6. Washington, DC: Headquarters, Department of the Army, 1975.

—**ARMY TRAINING SYSTEM (ATS)** consists of the training base, training in units, and training support. These interrelated elements form a cohesive system for maintaining combat readiness in the Army. *See also:* Army Training Program.

References

Department of Defense, U.S. Army. *Army Exercises.* Army Regulation AR 350-28. Washington, DC: Headquarters, Department of the Army, 1985.

————. *Army Forces Training.* Army Regulation AR 350-41. Washington, DC: Headquarters, Department of the Army, 1986.

————. *Fire Support in Combined Arms Operations.* Field Manual FM 6-20. Washington, DC: Headquarters, Department of the Army, 1983.

————. *Unit Training Management.* Field Manual FM 25-2. Washington, DC: Headquarters, Department of the Army, 1984.

—**ARMY TRAINING TEST (ATT)** is a Department of the Army publication that provides guidance for testing, under simulated combat conditions, individuals and units up to and including battalions. ATTs are administered during and following the three formal phases of training: basic combat training, beginning unit training, and advanced unit training. In addition, ATTs are administered for writing an Operational Readiness Training Test. Because they are not written in performance terms and are not suited for Active Army and Reserve component training, ATTs are being replaced by the Army Training and Evaluation Program. *See also:* Army Training System.

References

Department of Defense, U.S. Army. *How to Prepare and Conduct Military Training.* Field Manual FM 21-6. Washington, DC: Headquarters, Department of the Army, 1975.

—**ARMY TROOPS** are troops allotted to an army that are not assigned to a division or a corps.

References

Department of Defense, U.S. Army. *Dictionary of United States Army Terms.* Army Regulation AR 310-25. Washington, DC: Headquarters, Department of the Army, 1986.

—**ARMY WAR ROOM** are facilities in the Pentagon that serve as the operational center for the Headquarters, Department of the Army. In emergencies, the center is augmented with operations personnel representing all major staff elements and becomes the Army Operations Center. Alternates are maintained at the emergency relocation sites for use under general war conditions. *See also:* National Military Command Center.

References

Department of Defense, U.S. Army. *Dictionary of United States Army Terms.* Army Regulation AR 310-25. Washington, DC: Headquarters, Department of the Army, 1986.

—**ARRIVAL TIME** is the time the head of a column reaches a designated point or line.

References

Department of Defense, U.S. Army. *The Infantry Battalion (Infantry, Airborne, Air Assault).* Field Manual FM 7-20. Washington, DC: Headquarters, Department of the Army, 1984.

—**ARTIFICIAL DAYLIGHT** is illumination of an intensity greater than the light of a full moon on a clear night. The optimum illumination is the equivalent of daylight. *See also:* Artificial Moonlight.

References

Department of Defense, Joint Chiefs of Staff. *Department of Defense Dictionary of Military and Related Terms.* Washington, DC: GPO, 1986.

—**ARTIFICIAL MOONLIGHT** is illumination of an intensity between that of starlight and that of a full moon on a clear night. *See also:* Battlefield Illumination.

References

Department of Defense, Joint Chiefs of Staff. *Department of Defense Dictionary of Military and Related Terms.* Washington, DC: GPO, 1986.

—**ARTILLERY BATTALION GROUP** is a tactical grouping of two or more artillery battalions for a specific mission, and is commanded by one of the battalion commanders.

References

Department of Defense, U.S. Army. *Dictionary of United States Army Terms.* Army Regulation AR 310-25. Washington, DC: Headquarters, Department of the Army, 1986.

—**ARTILLERY FIRING PLATFORM** for towed or self-propelled artillery weapons is necessary on soft ground to preclude weapon relaying after each round is fired. The pad distributes the load over a large area with no significant settlement and is flexible, level, and strong enough to withstand the turning and movement of self-propelled weapons. The pad allows firing in all directions. Trail logs are anchored outside the pad for towed weapons. For self-propelled weapons, the recoil spades are set in compacted soil material or in a layer of crushed rock around the pad. These positions provide limited protection with the use of a parapet.

References

Department of Defense, U.S. Army. *Survivability.* Field Manual FM 5-103. Washington, DC: Headquarters, Department of the Army, 1985.

—**ARTILLERY PREPARATION** is artillery fire delivered before an attack that is intended to disrupt communications and disorganize the enemy's defense.

References

Department of Defense, U.S. Army. *Operational Terms and Symbols.* Field Manual FM 101-5-1. Washington, DC: Headquarters, Department of the Army, 1985.

—**ASPECT** (ARMY AVIATION) is the range, direction, altitude, and closure rate of one aircraft in respect to another aircraft or to a formation.

References

Department of Defense, U.S. Army. *Air-to-Air Combat.* Field Manual FM 1-107. Washington, DC: Headquarters, Department of the Army, 1984.

—**ASSAILABLE FLANK** is an exposed enemy flank vulnerable to envelopment. For a flank to be assailable, there must be sufficient maneuver space to accommodate the attacking force.

References

Department of Defense, U.S. Army. *Operational Terms and Symbols.* Field Manual FM 101-5-1. Washington, DC: Headquarters, Department of the Army, 1985.

—**ASSAULT.** (1) An assault is the culmination of an attack that closes with the enemy. (2) In an amphibious operation, an assault is the period of time from the crossing of the line of departure by the first scheduled wave to the seizure of the initial objectives. (3) An assault is a phase of an airborne or air assault operation beginning with the delivery of the assault force into the objective area and extending through the attack of objectives and consolidation of the initial airhead. (4) In river crossings, an assault is the time from the launching of the first crossing effort until the initial bridgehead has been secured and responsibility has been passed to the crossing area commander. (5) To assault is to make a short, violent, but well-ordered attack against a local objective (e.g., a gun emplacement or fortified area). *See also:* Assault Breaching, Assault Course, Assault Echelon, Assault Fire, Assault Force, Assault Gun, Assault Objectives, Assault Phase, Assault Position, Assault Supplies, Landing Attack.

References

Department of Defense, U.S. Army. *Operational Terms and Symbols.* Field Manual FM 101-5-1. Washington, DC: Headquarters, Department of the Army, 1985.

—**ASSAULT BREACHING** is a tactical breach used when the momentum of the attack must be kept up. It is usually conducted under fire, therefore speed is extremely important. Combat engineers should be located with the lead elements of maneuver units to perform assault breaches. However, time and distance factors may require assault breaches by maneuver units without direct engineer participation.

References

Department of Defense, U.S. Army. *Engineer Combat Operations.* Field Manual FM 5-100. Washington, DC: Headquarters, Department of the Army, 1984.

—**ASSAULT COURSE** is an area of ground used to train soldiers in attacking an enemy in close combat.

References

Department of Defense, U.S. Army. *Dictionary of United States Army Terms.* Army Regulation AR 310-25. Washington, DC: Headquarters, Department of the Army, 1986.

—**ASSAULT ECHELON.** (1) An assault echelon is the element of a force scheduled for an initial assault on the objective area. (2) An assault echelon is the forces required in the initial stages of an airborne or air assault operation to secure the assault objectives. (3) An assault echelon is one or more units of an attacking force that is (are) used to begin and lead the attack. See *also:* Echelon.

References

Department of Defense, U.S. Army. *Operational Terms and Symbols.* Field Manual FM 101-5-1. Washington, DC : Headquarters, Department of the Army, 1985.

—**ASSAULT ELEMENT** is the part of the patrol that fires into (and when required, assaults) the kill zone. *See also:* Breaching Force, Security Element, Support Element.

References

Department of Defense, U.S. Army. *The Infantry Rifle Company (Infantry, Airborne, Air Assault, Ranger).* Field Manual FM 7-10. Washington, DC: Headquarters, Department of the Army, 1982.

—**ASSAULT ELEMENT** (AMBUSH) deploys close enough to the objective to permit immediate assault if it is detected by the enemy. As supporting fire is lifted or shifted, the element assaults, seizes, and secures the objective. It pro-

tects demolition teams, search teams, and other special teams while they work. On order or on signal, the assault element withdraws to the objective rally point. *See also:* Ambush Force, Security Element.

References

Department of Defense, U.S. Army. *The Infantry Rifle Company (Infantry, Airborne, Air Assault, Ranger).* Field Manual FM 7-10. Washington, DC: Headquarters, Department of the Army, 1982.

—**ASSAULT FIRE.** (1) Assault fire is fire delivered by attacking troops as they close with the enemy. (2) In artillery, assault fire is extremely accurate, short-range destruction fire at point targets.

References

Department of Defense, Joint Chiefs of Staff. *Department of Defense Dictionary of Military and Related Terms.* Washington, DC: GPO, 1986.

—**ASSAULT FORCE.** (1) In an amphibious, airborne, or air assault operation, assault force units are charged with seizing the lodgment area. (2) In offensive river crossing operations, the major subordinate units that are conducting the assault to, across, and beyond the water obstacle are the assault force. Assault forces lead, making the initial assault on the river, and continue the advance from the exit bank to the final objectives. (3) Assault forces are forces charged with passing through a breach in an enemy-fortified position or strongpoint and seizing an objective or completing the destruction of the enemy.

References

Department of Defense, U.S. Army. *Operational Terms and Symbols.* Field Manual FM 101-5-1. Washington, DC: Headquarters, Department of the Army, 1985.

—**ASSAULT GUN** is any of various sizes and types of guns that are self-propelled or mounted on tanks and are used for direct fire from close range against point targets.

References

Department of Defense, U.S. Army. *Dictionary of United States Army Terms.* Army Regulation AR 310-25. Washington, DC: Headquarters, Department of the Army, 1986.

—**ASSAULT OBJECTIVES** are key terrain features or installations whose seizure facilitates the overall accomplishment of an airborne or air assault operation.

References

Department of Defense, U.S. Army. *Operational Terms and Symbols.* Field Manual FM 101-5-1. Washington, DC: Headquarters, Department of the Army, 1985.

—**ASSAULT PHASE.** (1) The assault phase is the phase of an airborne, air assault, amphibious, or river crossing operation that begins with the delivery of the assault forces into the objective area and ends when all assault objectives have been seized. (2) The assault phase is the period during an attack that begins when the assault forces advance from their assault position and ends when the objective has been seized and consolidated. *See also:* Air Assault, Airborne Operation, Amphibious Operation, River Crossing.

References

Department of Defense, U.S. Army. *Operational Terms and Symbols.* Field Manual FM 101-5-1. Washington, DC: Headquarters, Department of the Army, 1985.

—**ASSAULT POSITION** is the position between the line of departure and the objective in an attack from which forces assault the objective. Ideally, it is the last recovered and concealed position before reaching the objective (primarily used by dismounted artillery).

References

Department of Defense, U.S. Army. *Operational Terms and Symbols.* Field Manual FM 101-5-1. Washington, DC: Headquarters, Department of the Army, 1985.

—**ASSAULT PROTECTIVE MINEFIELD** offers close-in temporary protection for a unit area. Mines are taken from basic load, are used overnight, and put back into basic load when the unit departs from the area. *See also:* Mine Warfare.

References

Department of Defense, U.S. Army. *Mine/Countermine Operations at the Company Level.* Field Manual FM 20-32. Washington, DC: Headquarters, Department of the Army, 1976.

—**ASSAULT SUPPLIES** are supplies of all classes that accompany the assault elements of a unit into the objective area.

References

Department of Defense, U.S. Army. *Dictionary of United States Army Terms.* Army Regulation AR 310-25. Washington, DC: Headquarters, Department of the Army, 1986.

—**ASSAULT WIRE** is very light, field telephone wire that is wound on reels small enough for one man to carry over difficult terrain under frontline conditions.

References

Department of Defense, U.S. Army. *Dictionary of United States Army Terms.* Army Regulation AR 310-25. Washington, DC: Headquarters, Department of the Army, 1986.

—**ASSEMBLY.** (1) Assembly is a signal given by drum or by bugle for units of troops to gather, usually in close formation. (2) An assembly is a grouping of units usually in close formation. (3) An assembly is a point in the air to which all units of an Air Force are assigned. (4) An assembly is a group of two or more physically connected or related parts that can be disassembed. (5) An assembly is an end-item completed to the condition in which it is normally issued, except for the installation of accessories that accommodate it for a specific use or location by a joining together, installation, or other association of components issued. (6) An assembly is the option or condemnation papers that form the basis for the acquisition of each tract of land. (7) An assembly is a meeting of Reservists at a previously designated place to participate in Reserve duty training. (8) An assembly is the designation of the program by which assemblages are constructed.

References

Department of Defense, U.S. Army. *Dictionary of United States Army Terms.* Army Regulation AR 310-25. Washington, DC: Headquarters, Department of the Army, 1986.

—**ASSESSMENT.** (1) An assessment is an analysis of the security, effectiveness, and potential of an existing or planned intelligence activity. (2) An assessment is a judgment of the motives, qualifications, and characteristics of present or prospective employees or "agents." (3) An assessment is an objective determination of the degree to which test results satisfy specified test objectives.

References

Department of Defense, Joint Chiefs of Staff. *Department of Defense Dictionary of Military and Related Terms.* Washington, DC: GPO, 1986.

Department of Defense, U.S. Army. *Dictionary of United States Army Terms.* Army Regulation AR 310-25. Washington, DC: Headquarters, Department of the Army, 1986.

—**ASSESSMENT AND RECOVERY PERSONNEL** are drawn from staffs and support elements at each echelon in the division to enable commanders to expedite reconstruction operations.

References

Department of Defense, U.S. Army. *Combat Service Support Operations-Division.* Field Manual FM 63-2. Washington, DC: Headquarters, Department of the Army, 1983.

—**ASSESSMENT AND RECOVERY TEAM** is a logistics team with all the aspects necessary to reconstitute a unit that has been depleted by military operations.

References

Department of Defense, U.S. Army. *NBC Decontamination.* Field Manual FM 3-5. Washington, DC: Headquarters, Department of the Army, 1985.

—**ASSET MANAGEMENT** is the planning, direction, and control of individual collection, counterintelligence, operations security support, and the electronic warfare resources necessary to accomplish a mission. Asset management generally is performed by the commander's units with assigned resources that are capable of performing any of the above missions. *See also*: Asset Tasking.

References

Department of Defense, U.S. Army. *Military Intelligence Battalion (CEWI) (Tactical Exploitation) (Corps): Counterintelligence, Interrogation, Electronic Warfare.* Field Manual FM 34-23. Washington, DC: Headquarters, Department of the Army, 1985.

————. *Military Intelligence Group (Combat Electronic Warfare and Intelligence) (Corps).* Field Manual FM 34-20. Washington, DC: Headquarters, Department of the Army, 1983.

—**ASSET TASKING** is the assignment of a mission to a specific subordinate element.

References

Department of Defense, Department of the Army. *Intelligence and Electronic Warfare Operations.* Field Manual FM 34-1. Washington, DC: Headquarters, Department of the Army, 1987.

—**ASSIGN.** (1) Assign is to place units or personnel in an organization when such placement is relatively permanent and where the organization controls, administers, and provides logistical support to units or personnel for the primary function, or greater portion of the functions, of the unit or personnel. (2) To assign is to detail individuals to specific duties or functions that are primarily or relatively permanent. *See also:* Assigned, Assignment, Attach, Operational Command, Operational Control, Organic.

References

Department of Defense, U.S. Army. *Operational Terms and Symbols.* Field Manual FM 101-5-1. Washington, DC: Headquarters, Department of the Army, 1985.

—**ASSIGNED** pertains to a unit that is permanently placed in an organization and is administered and controlled by the organization to which it is attached for its primary function or the greater portion of its functions.

References

Department of Defense, U.S. Army. *Operational Terms and Symbols.* Field Manual FM 101-5-1. Washington, DC: Headquarters, Department of the Army, 1985.

—**ASSIGNMENT** is the placing or sending of an individual to an approved billet to satisfy a validated need for manpower. Assignments are used to man the different components of the Army and to move or transfer personnel from one duty assignment to another.

References

Department of Defense, U.S. Army. *Dictionary of United States Army Terms.* Army Regulation AR 310-25. Washington, DC: Headquarters, Department of the Army, 1986.

—**ASSISTANT DIVISION OFFICER (ADE)** is the engineer point of contact at the division level. He provides day-to-day coordination with the division staff on matters of engineering concern and assists in planning engineering support for division operations. His normal day-to-day association is with G3 staff, yet he is available to the entire division staff.

References

Department of Defense, U.S. Army. *Engineer Combat Operations.* Field Manual FM 5-100. Washington, DC: Headquarters, Department of the Army, 1984.

—**ASSUMPTIONS** are suppositions on current or future events assumed to be true in the absence of positive proof. They enable the commander, while he is planning, to complete an estimate of the situation and make a decision on the course of action. *See also:* Estimate of the Situation.

References

Department of Defense, U.S. Army. *Staff Organization and Operations*. Field Manual FM 101-5. Washington, DC: Headquarters, Department of the Army, 1984.

—**AT MY COMMAND,** in artillery and naval gunfire support, is the command used to control the exact time of delivery of fire.

References

Department of Defense, Joint Chiefs of Staff. *Department of Defense Dictionary of Military and Related Terms*. Washington, DC: GPO, 1986.

—**AT PRIORITY CALL** is a precedence applied to the task of an artillery unit to provide fire to a formation or unit on a guaranteed basis. Normally, an observer and communications and liaison are not provided. An artillery unit in "direct support" may simultaneously be placed "at priority call" to another unit or agency for a particular task and a specific period of time.

References

Department of Defense, Joint Chiefs of Staff. *Department of Defense Dictionary of Military and Related Terms*. Washington, DC: GPO, 1986.

—**ATOMIC DEMOLITION MUNITION (ADM)** is a nuclear device designed to be detonated on or below the ground surface, or under water as a demolition munition against material-type targets to block, deny, or canalize the enemy. ADMs are used primarily for obstacle creation and denial operations and can be used only when the authority to use nuclear weapons has been granted. *See also:* Nuclear Warfare.

References

Department of Defense, U.S. Army. *Countermobility*. Field Manual FM 5-102. Washington, DC: Headquarters, Department of the Army, 1985.

—**ATROPINE** is a chemical substance prepared from plants and used to counteract the effects of nerve agent poisoning. *See also:* Chemical Warfare.

References

Department of Defense, U.S. Army. *Dictionary of United States Army Terms*. Army Regulation AR 310-25. Washington, DC: Headquarters, Department of the Army, 1986.

—**ATTACH.** (1) Attach is the placement of units or personnel in an organization where such placement is temporary. Subject to the limitations imposed by the attachment order, the commander of the formation, unit, or organization receiving the attachment exercises the same degree of command and control as he does over his own units and persons. However, the responsibility for transfer and promotion of personnel is normally retained by the parent formation unit or organization. (2) To attach is to detail individuals to specific functions where such functions are secondary or temporary (e.g., to attach for quarters and rations or attach for flying duty). *See also:* Assign, Operational Command , Operational Control, Organic.

References

Department of Defense, U.S. Army. *Air Defense Artillery Deployment: Chaparral/Vulcan/Stinger*. Field Manual FM 44-3. Washington, DC: Headquarters, Department of the Army, 1984.

————. *Operational Terms and Symbols*. Field Manual FM 101-5-1. Washington, DC: Headquarters, Department of the Army, 1985.

—**ATTACHED.** A unit placed in an organization on a temporary basis is attached. Although subject to the limitations specified in the attachment order, the commander to which the unit is attached exercises the same degree of command and control over, and responsibility for, the attached unit as he does over units organic to his command. However, responsibility for transfer, Uniform Code of Military Justice, and promotion of personnel normally is retained by the command to which the unit is assigned. The attachment order should state clearly the administrative and support responsibility variance of the gaining unit to the attached unit. *See also*: Attach.

References

Department of Defense, U.S. Army. *Staff Organization and Operations*. Field Manual FM 101-5. Washington, DC: Headquarters, Department of the Army, 1984.

—**ATTACHMENT** is an option that can be used to simplify logistic support or to accommodate temporary special command relationships. Subject to the limitations imposed by the attachment order, the command receiving the attachment order exercises the same command and control over the attached element as it does over organic elements. In short, attachment places an asset under the temporary control of a command or task force. Orders attaching an element usually specify limitations that are imposed upon the relationship. *See also:* Attach.

References

Department of Defense, U.S. Army. *Military Intelligence Battalion (CEWI) (Tactical Exploitation) (Corps): Counterintelligence, Interrogation, Electronic Warfare.* Field Manual FM 34-23. Washington, DC: Headquarters, Department of the Army, 1985.

—**ATTACHMENTS TO AN OPERATION PLAN OR ORDER** are separately identifiable amplifications of the basic plan or operation order. Attachments are annexes, appendixes, tabs, and inclosures. *See also:* Annex.

References

Department of Defense, U.S. Army. *Planning Logistics Support for Military Operations.* Field Manual FM 701-58. Washington, DC: Headquarters, Department of the Army, 1987.

—**ATTACK.** (1) An attack is an offensive action characterized by movement that is supported by fire. (2) An attack is an offensive action characterized by suppressive fire and movement with the intention of closing with and destroying enemy forces or seizing terrain. *See also:* Ambush, Deep Attack, Deliberate Attack, Hasty Attack, Main Attack, Raid, Spoiling Attack, Supporting Attack.

References

Department of Defense, U.S. Army. *Attack Helicopter Operations.* Field Manual FM 17-50. Washington, DC: Headquarters, Department of the Army, 1984.

—**ATTACK FORCE** is the element of the ambush force in a point ambush that fires and/or assaults into the kill zone to destroy the enemy. *See also:* Attack.

References

Department of Defense, U.S. Army. *The Rifle Squads (Mechanized and Light Infantry).* Training Circular TC 7-1. Washington, DC: Headquarters, Department of the Army, 1976.

—**ATTACK HELICOPTER** is a helicopter designed to search out, attack, and destroy enemy targets. *See also:* Attack Helicopter Liaison Officer, Attack Helicopter Team/Section (Army Aviation), Attack Helicopter Units, Attack Positions, Attack Route.

References

Department of Defense, Joint Chiefs of Staff. *Department of Defense Dictionary of Military and Related Terms.* Washington, DC: GPO, 1986.

—**ATTACK HELICOPTER LIAISON OFFICER (AHLO)** is an Army officer from an attack helicopter unit who conducts liaison with the ground maneuver force headquarters when a command relationship between the two units has been established. *See also:* Attack Helicopter.

References

Department of Defense, U.S. Army. *Attack Helicopter Operations.* Field Manual FM 17-50. Washington, DC: Headquarters, Department of the Army, 1984.

—**ATTACK HELICOPTER TEAM/SECTION** (ARMY AVIATION) consists of two or more attack helicopters under the control of a single leader (team or section leader). The team or section may be augmented by scout aircraft. *See also:* Attack Helicopter.

References

Department of Defense, U.S. Army. *Gunnery Training for Attack Helicopters.* Training Circular TC 17-17. Washington, DC: Headquarters, Department of the Army, 1975.

—**ATTACK HELICOPTER UNITS** are air maneuver units. They employ highly mobile, responsive aerial combat vehicles that operate as part of the combined arms team. They can destroy tanks and other armored vehicles with heavy antitank weapons, and they can destroy dismounted infantry and attack area targets with rockets. Attack helicopter units live in the ground environment. They maneuver like ground units to engage the enemy from the front, flanks, and rear. *See also:* Attack Helicopter.

References

Department of Defense, U.S. Army. *Armored and Mechanized Division Operations.* Field Manual FM 71-100. Washington, DC: Headquarters, Department of the Army, 1978.

—**ATTACK POSITION** is the last position occupied by the assault echelon before crossing the line of departure. *See also:* Forming Up Place.

References

Department of Defense, Joint Chiefs of Staff. *Department of Defense Dictionary of Military and Related Terms.* Washington, DC: GPO, 1986.

Department of Defense, U.S. Army. *Operational Terms and Symbols.* Field Manual FM 101-5-1. Washington, DC: Headquarters, Department of the Army, 1985.

—**ATTACK POSITIONS** (ARMY AVIATION) are the last covered and concealed positions used by attack helicopters to deploy and move into firing positions for target engagement. *See also:* Attack Helicopter.

References
Department of Defense, U.S. Army. *Gunnery Training for Attack Helicopters.* Training Circular TC 17-17. Washington, DC: Headquarters, Department of the Army, 1975.

—**ATTACK ROUTE** is the route used by attack helicopter teams to move to battle positions from a holding area, forward arming and refueling point, or assembly area. *See also:* Attack Helicopter.

References
Department of Defense, U.S. Army. *Attack Helicopter Operations.* Field Manual FM 17-50. Washington, DC: Headquarters, Department of the Army, 1984.

—**ATTACKS FROM A DEFENSIVE POSTURE** include spoiling attacks and counterattacks. Spoiling attacks are mounted to disrupt an expected enemy attack before it is launched. It is an attempt to strike the enemy while it is most vulnerable, during its preparations for the attack in assembly areas, in attack positions, or on the move prior to crossing the line of departure. In general, it is conducted like other attacks and may be hasty, when time is short, or deliberate, when adequate forewarning has been obtained. Frequently, the circumstances under which it is conducted preclude full exploitation, and the attacking force either halts on its objective or withdraws to its original position. When the situation permits, however, a spoiling attack should be exploited like any other attack.

References
Department of Defense, U.S. Army. *Staff Organization and Operations.* Field Manual FM 101-5. Washington, DC: Headquarters, Department of the Army, 1984.

—**ATTENTION.** (1) Attention is a prescribed erect position of readiness and alertness with eyes straight ahead, hands at the sides, heels together, and toes turned out at an angle of 45 degrees. Positions of attention are also prescribed for mounted individuals and for persons carrying weapons. Complete silence and immobility are required. (2) Attention is the command to take the position described in (1) above.

References
Department of Defense, U.S. Army. *Dictionary of United States Army Terms.* Army Regulation AR 310-25. Washington, DC: Headquarters, Department of the Army, 1986.

—**ATTENTION TO ORDERS** is a command given by the adjutant of a military organization to announce that he is about to issue orders.

References
Department of Defense, U.S. Army. *Dictionary of United States Army Terms.* Army Regulation AR 310-25. Washington, DC: Headquarters, Department of the Army, 1986.

—**ATTRITION** is the reduction of the effectiveness of a force caused by the loss of personnel or equipment. In air defense, attrition is a narrative mission assigned to the Air Force and certain high-to-medium altitude air defense units to inflict maximum damage to the enemy and prevent it from penetrating certain areas. This attrition mission is executed through area defenses and through a specialized application of area defenses called belt defenses. While short-range air defense weapons attrite enemy aircraft in accordance with established weapons control statuses and hostile criteria, attrition as a separate mission is not normally acceptable, due to the limited number of available short-range air defense systems and their limited air defense coverage. *See also:* Attrition Rate.

References
Department of Defense. Department of the Army. *Operational Terms and Symbols.* Field Manual FM 101-5-1. Washington, DC: Department of the Army, 1985.

———. *U.S. Army Air Defense Artillery Employment Hawk.* Field Manual FM 44-90. Washington, DC: Headquarters, Department of the Army, 1983.

—**ATTRITION RATE** is a factor normally expressed as a percentage. It reflects the degree of losses of personnel or materiel due to various causes within a specified period of time.

References
Department of Defense, Joint Chiefs of Staff. *Department of Defense Dictionary of Military and Related Terms.* Washington, DC: GPO, 1986.

—**AUGMENTATION** is the reinforcement of Unified or Specified Commands through deploying or redeploying forces assigned to other commands. *See also:* Augmentation Forces, Augmentation Teams.

References

Department of Defense, U.S. Army. *Dictionary of United States Army Terms.* Army Regulation AR 310-25. Washington, DC: Headquarters, Department of the Army, 1986.

—**AUGMENTATION FORCES** are forces to be transferred to the operational command of a supported commander during the execution of an operation plan that has been approved by the Joint Chiefs of Staff.

References

Department of Defense, U.S. Army. *Planning Logistics Support for Military Operations.* Field Manual FM 701-58. Washington, DC: Headquarters, Department of the Army, 1987.

—**AUGMENTATION TEAMS** are special teams provided by the table of organization and equipment to meet nonstandard requirements for command and control, liaison, maintenance supervision, fire coordination interface, and personnel and equipment for the operation of fire distribution systems.

References

Department of Defense, U.S. Army. *U.S. Army Air Defense Employment.* Field Manual FM 44-1. Washington, DC: Headquarters, Department of the Army, 1983.

—**AUTHENTICATION.** (1) Authentication is a communications security measure designed to protect against fraudulent or bogus transmissions and hostile imitative communications deception. It is done by establishing the validity of a transmission, message, station, or designator. (2) Authentication is a means or method for establishing the eligibility of a station, originator, or individual to receive specific information. Such eligibility can be based upon the receiver's security clearance, need to know, or other factors. *See also:* Authentication System.

References

Department of Defense, Defense Intelligence College. *Glossary of Intelligence Terms and Definitions.* Washington, DC: DIC, 1987.

—**AUTHENTICATION SYSTEM** is a cryptosystem or cryptographic process used for authentication.

References

Department of Defense, U.S. Army. *Dictionary of United States Army Terms.* Army Regulation AR 310-25. Washington, DC: Headquarters, Department of the Army, 1986.

—**AUTHORIZED ALLOWANCES OF SUPPLIES** is the quantity of supplies authorized in accordance with tables of allowances, tables of organization and equipment, or other appropriate authority.

References

Department of Defense, U.S. Army. *Dictionary of United States Army Terms.* Army Regulation AR 310-25. Washington, DC: Headquarters, Department of the Army, 1986.

—**AUTHORIZED ARMY NEWSPAPER** is a unit, command, or installation newspaper, theater newspaper, daily news summary, or news bulletin published by any command or agency of the Department of the Army.

References

Department of Defense, U.S. Army. *Dictionary of United States Army Terms.* Army Regulation AR 310-25. Washington, DC: Headquarters, Department of the Army, 1986.

—**AUTHORIZED LEVEL OF ORGANIZATION** of a unit is the ratio of authorized manpower spaces to the full tables of organization and equipment structure spaces, against which a unit is authorized to requisition personnel and equipment. It may be expressed in numerical- and letter-designated levels representing percentages of full tables of organization and equipment structure spaces, respectively. Equipment resources are specified for each level of organization. Inherent in the authorized level of organization for a unit approved by the Department of the Army is the stated distribution objective based upon a programmed capability of the Army to provide assets at the designated level of personnel and equipment.

References

Department of Defense, U.S. Army. *Dictionary of United States Army Terms.* Army Regulation AR 310-25. Washington, DC: Headquarters, Department of the Army, 1986.

—**AUTHORIZED MANPOWER** (STRENGTH) is the required manpower that can be supported by allocated manpower and that is reflected in the authorized columns of current or projected authorization documents. Because of budgetary constraints, authorized manpower may be less than required manpower; however, depending on missions and priorities, the authorized manpower (military or civilian) may be equal to, but never exceed, the required manpower in modification table of organization and equipment/tables of distribution and allowances.

References

Department of Defense, U.S. Army. *Dictionary of United States Army Terms.* Army Regulation AR 310-25. Washington, DC: Headquarters, Department of the Army, 1986.

—**AUTHORIZED PARTS LIST** is a list of authorized parts for units in each echelon of supply and maintenance as prescribed by appropriate authority.

References

Department of Defense, U.S. Army. *Dictionary of United States Army Terms.* Army Regulation AR 310-25. Washington, DC: Headquarters, Department of the Army, 1986.

—**AUTHORIZED STOCKAGE LIST (ASL).** (1) ASL is a list of items from all classes of supply that are authorized to be stocked at a specific echelon of supply. (2) ASL is a listing of repair parts, general supplies, common hardware, and special tools required by maintenance and supply units to perform their missions.

References

Department of Defense, U.S. Army. *Dictionary of United States Army Terms.* Army Regulation AR 310-25. Washington, DC: Headquarters, U.S. Army, 1986.

———. *Operational Terms and Symbols.* Field Manual FM 101-5-1. Washington, DC: Headquarters, Department of the Army, 1985.

———. *Planning Logistics Support for Military Operations.* Field Manual FM 701-58. Washington, DC: Headquarters, Department of the Army, 1987.

—**AUTHORIZED STRENGTH.** (1) Authorized strength is the total personnel spaces contained in current personnel authorization vouchers issued by a higher headquarters to a subordinate element. (2) Authorized strength is the total number of personnel that a U.S. Army Reserve troop program unit may have assigned in a paid drill status as prescribed by the Chief, Army Reserve.

References

Department of Defense, U.S. Army. *Dictionary of United States Army Terms.* Army Regulation AR 310-25. Washington, DC: Headquarters, Department of the Army, 1986.

—**AUTHORIZED STRENGTH OF A THEATER** is the sum of the table of organization strengths of authorized units, authorized overhead allotment (bulk), and authorized replacements in the pipeline.

References

Department of Defense, U.S. Army. *Dictionary of United States Army Terms.* Army Regulation AR 310-25. Washington, DC: Headquarters, Department of the Army, 1986.

—**AUXILIARY**, in unconventional warfare, is the element of the resistance force established to provide the organized civilian support of the resistance movement.

References

Department of Defense, U.S. Army. *Dictionary of United States Army Terms.* Army Regulation AR 310-25. Washington, DC: Headquarters, Department of the Army, 1986.

—**AUXILIARY EQUIPMENT** is equipment that supplements primary equipment or takes the place of primary equipment if such equipment becomes inoperative. This term includes equipment other than primary equipment but of greater importance than administrative support equipment. Examples of auxiliary equipment are maintenance support equipment at industrial/repair activities, vehicles, ordnance, communications, and engineer equipment other than that designated as primary equipment.

References

Department of Defense, U.S. Army. *Dictionary of United States Army Terms.* Army Regulation AR 310-25. Washington, DC: Headquarters, Department of the Army, 1986.

—**AUXILIARY TARGET** is a point at a known distance from the actual target. An auxiliary target is used as an adjusting point before firing on the actual target. Fire is delivered and adjusted on the auxiliary target. When the adjustment is complete, the necessary correction is put on the gun to shift its fire to the actual target. Auxiliary targets are used when fire on the actual targets is intended to surprise the enemy.

References

Department of Defense, U.S. Army. *Dictionary of United States Army Terms.* Army Regulation AR 310-25. Washington, DC: Headquarters, Department of the Army, 1986.

—**AVENUE OF APPROACH** is an air or ground route of an attacking force that leads to its objective or to key terrain in its path. *See also:* Key Terrain.

References
Department of Defense, U.S. Army. *Staff Organization and Operations.* Field Manual FM 101-5. Washington, DC: Headquarters, Department of the Army, 1984.

—**AVERAGE STRENGTH** is an arithmetic mean (average) of daily morning report strengths used in medical statistical reports for computing admission rates, incidence rates, mortality rates, and noneffective rates. It is also called mean strength, which was formerly the approved term.

References
Department of Defense, U.S. Army. *Dictionary of United States Army Terms.* Army Regulation AR 310-25. Washington, DC: Headquarters, Department of the Army, 1986.

—**AVIATION.** Three types of Army aviation units participate in combined arms operations: attack helicopters, air cavalry, and combat support aviation. Speed of movement, freedom from the effects of ground obstacles, and sensitivity to weather conditions characterize all aviation operations.

While aviation is relegated to supporting ground maneuver, it increasingly offers opportunities for actual maneuver by air. Thus, attack helicopter units provide highly maneuverable antiarmor firepower. They use natural cover and speed to compensate for their vulnerabilities. They are ideally suited for situations in which rapid reaction time is important or terrain restricts ground forces. Attack helicopters are best suited for attacking moving enemy armor formations. Attack helicopter units: overwatch ground maneuver forces with antitank fires; attack the flanks and rear of attacking or withdrawing enemy formations; counterattack enemy penetrations alone or in support of ground maneuver units; conduct raids in enemy-held territory; dominate key terrain by fire in support of ground maneuver forces; and engage enemy helicopters and close support aircraft.

References
Department of Defense, U.S. Army. *Staff Organization and Operations.* Field Manual FM 101-5. Washington, DC: Headquarters, Department of the Army, 1984.

—**AVIATION INTERMEDIATE MAINTENANCE (AVIM)** activities provide mobile maintenance support to aviation units. Maintenance repair tasks performed by AVIM activities are direct support and ground support functions. *See also:* Aviation Unit Maintenance.

References
Department of Defense, U.S. Army. *Repair Parts Supply for a Theater of Operations.* Field Manual FM 29-19. Washington, DC: Headquarters, Department of the Army, 1985.

—**AVIATION UNIT MAINTENANCE (AVUM)** are company-sized units or smaller. They are staffed and equipped to perform high frequency on-aircraft maintenance required to retain or return assigned aircraft to a serviceable condition (e.g., preventive maintenance, inspection, servicing, component replacement, and limited maintenance repair functions). *See also:* Aviation Intermediate Maintenance.

References
Department of Defense, U.S. Army. *Repair Parts Supply for a Theater of Operations.* Field Manual FM 29-19. Washington, DC: Headquarters, Department of the Army, 1985.

—**AWARD** is recognition given to individuals or units for certain acts or services, or badges, accolades, emblems, citations, commendations, streamers, and silver bands. *See also*: Awards.

References
Department of Defense, U.S. Army. *Dictionary of United States Army Terms.* Army Regulation AR 310-25. Washington, DC: Headquarters, Department of the Army, 1986.

—**AWARDS** is a term covering all decorations, medals, badges, ribbons, or appurtenances that are bestowed on an individual or unit for certain acts or services. *See also:* Appurtenances.

References
Department of Defense, U.S. Army. *Military Awards.* Army Regulation AR 672-5-1. Washington, DC: Headquarters, Department of the Army, 1984.

———. *Wear and Appearance of Army Uniforms and Insignia.* Army Regulation AR 670-1. Washington, DC: Headquarters, Department of the Army, 1986.

—**AXIAL ROUTE.** (1) An axial route is one running through the rear area into the forward area. (2) An axial route is part of a military road maneuver network that leads to and runs generally perpendicular to the forward edge of the battle area. It is identified by an odd number and is shown on military maps and overlays by a solid line. *See also:* Axis of Advance, Axis of Communication.

References

Department of Defense, U.S. Army. *Armored and Mechanized Division Operations.* Field Manual FM 71-100. Washington, DC: Headquarters, Department of the Army, 1978.

————. *Route Reconnaissance and Classification.* Field Manual FM 5-36. Washington, DC: Headquarters, Department of the Army, 1985.

—AXIS OF ADVANCE. (1) An axis of advance is a broadly defined route, from the line of departure to the objective, that indicates the general direction of the attack. (2) An axis of advance is a direction assigned for purposes of control. It is often a road or a group of roads, or a designated series of locations, extending in the direction of the enemy. (3) An axis of advance symbol graphically portrays a commander's intention, such as avoiding built-up areas or enveloping an enemy force. It follows terrain suitable for the size of the force assigned to the axis. A commander may maneuver his forces and supporting fires to either side of the axis, provided the unit remains oriented on the axis and the objective. Deviations from an assigned axis must not interfere with the maneuver of adjacent units without prior approval of the higher commander. Enemy forces that do not threaten security or jeopardize mission accomplishment may be bypassed. An axis of advance is not used to direct the control of terrain or the clearance of enemy forces from specific locations. Intermediate objectives are normally assigned for these purposes. *See also:* Axial Route, Axis of Communication, Direction of Attack.

References

Department of Defense, U.S. Army. *Armored and Mechanized Division Operations.* Field Manual FM 71-100. Washington, DC: Headquarters, Department of the Army, 1978.

————. *Operational Terms and Symbols.* Field Manual FM 101-5-1. Washington, DC: Headquarters, Department of the Army, 1985.

—AXIS OF COMMUNICATION is the line or route on which lie the starting position and probable future locations of the command post of a unit during a troop movement. It is the main route along which messages are relayed or sent to combat units in the field. *See also:* Axial Route, Axis of Advance.

References

Department of Defense, U.S. Army. *Tactical Single Channel Radio Communications Techniques.* Field Manual FM 24-18. Washington, DC: Headquarters, Department of the Army, 1984.

—AXIS OF TRUNNIONS is the axis about which a gun is rotated in elevation to increase or decrease the range of fire.

References

Department of Defense, U.S. Army. *Dictionary of United States Army Terms.* Army Regulation AR 310-25. Washington, DC: Headquarters, Department of the Army, 1986.

—AZIMUTH is the horizontal angle, measured clockwise, between a reference direction and the line to an observed or designated point. There are three base (reference) directions or azimuths: true, grid, and magnetic azimuth. *True azimuth* is an azimuth referenced to true north as defined by the axis of rotation of the earth. *Grid azimuth* is an azimuth referenced to grid north. It differs from true azimuth by the amount of grid convergence. *Magnetic azimuth* is an azimuth referenced to the local direction of the earth's magnetic field.

References

Department of Defense, U.S. Army. *Dictionary of United States Army Terms.* Army Regulation AR 310-25. Washington, DC: Headquarters, Department of the Army, 1986.

————. *Operational Terms and Symbols.* Field Manual FM 101-5-1. Washington, DC: Headquarters, Department of the Army, 1985.

—**BACK LOADING** is the act of loading outbound cargo on a semitrailer that delivered inbound cargo.

References
Department of Defense, U.S. Army. *Transportation Reference Data.* Field Manual FM 55-15. Washington, DC: Headquarters, Department of the Army, 1986.

—**BACK ORDER** is the portion of requested stock that was not immediately available for issue and that will be shipped at a later date. The record of the obligation to fill the order is also known as a back order or due-out.

References
Department of Defense, U.S. Army. *Repair Parts Supply for a Theater of Operations.* Field Manual FM 29-19. Washington, DC: Headquarters, Department of the Army, 1985.

—**BACK TELL** is the transfer of information from a higher to a lower echelon of command.

References
Department of Defense, U.S. Army. *Dictionary of United States Army Terms.* Army Regulation AR 310-25. Washington, DC: Headquarters, Department of the Army, 1986.

—**BACKGROUND COUNT** is the evidence or effect on a detector of radiation, other than that which it is desired to detect, caused by any agency. In connection with health protection, the background count usually includes radiations produced by naturally occurring radioactivity and cosmic rays. *See also:* Background Radiation.

References
Department of Defense, Joint Chiefs of Staff. *Department of Defense Dictionary of Military and Related Terms.* Washington, DC: GPO, 1986.

—**BACKGROUND INVESTIGATION (BI)** is a general intelligence term for an inquiry into the past life of a prospective intelligence agency employee and is required before the person can be given a security clearance. The investigation includes verifying the person's birth, citizenship, education, employment for the past five years, and travel information provided by the individual, a review of all federal agencies for derogatory information, a credit check, and a criminal records check. *See also:* Special Background Investigation.

References
Allen, Thomas B., and Polmar, Norman. *Merchants of Treason: America's Secrets for Sale.* New York: Delacorte Press, 1988.

Department of Defense, U.S. Army. *Counterintelligence.* Field Manual FM 34-60. Washington, DC: Headquarters, Department of the Army, 1985.

—**BACKGROUND RADIATION** consists of nuclear or ionizing radiations arising from within the body and from the surroundings to which individuals are always exposed. *See also:* Background Count.

References
Department of Defense, Joint Chiefs of Staff. *Department of Defense Dictionary of Military and Related Terms.* Washington, DC: GPO, 1986.

—**BACKHAUL** is a shipment of material to or through an area from which the material had previously been shipped.

References
Department of Defense, U.S. Army. *Transportation Reference Data.* Field Manual FM 55-15. Washington, DC: Headquarters, Department of the Army, 1986.

—**BADGE** is an award given to an individual for attaining a special skill or proficiency. Certain badges are available in full, miniature, and dress miniature sizes. *See also:* Accouterment.

References
Department of Defense, U.S. Army. *Wear and Appearance of Army Uniforms and Insignia.* Army Regulation AR 670-1. Washington, DC: Headquarters, Department of the Army, 1986.

—**BALANCED** defines a company team that has an equal number of tank and mechanized infantry platoons or a battalion task force that has an equal number of tank and mechanized companies.

References
Department of Defense, U.S. Army. *The Tank and Mechanized Infantry Battalion Task Force.* Field Manual FM 71-2. Washington, DC: Headquarters, Department of the Army, 1977.

—**BALANCED STOCK(S).** (1) Balanced stock is when the supply of and requirements for specific items are in equilibrium. (2) Balanced stock is an accumulation of supplies in quantities determined to be necessary to meet requirements for a fixed period.

References

Department of Defense, Joint Chiefs of Staff. *Department of Defense Dictionary of Military and Related Terms.* Washington, DC: GPO, 1986.

—**BASILAGE** is the marking of a route by a system of dim beacon lights that enable vehicles to travel at near day-time speed while under blackout conditions.

References

Department of Defense, Joint Chiefs of Staff. *Department of Defense Dictionary of Military and Related Terms.* Washington, DC: GPO, 1986.

—**BALL AND TRACER** rounds, a category of direct fire projectiles, are normally of a relatively small caliber (5.56 mm to 14.5 mm) and are fired from pistols, rifles, and machine guns. The round's projectile penetrates soft targets on impact at a high velocity. The penetration depends on the projectile's velocity, weight, and the angle at which it hits.

References

Department of Defense, U.S. Army. *Survivability.* Field Manual FM 5-103. Washington, DC: Headquarters, Department of the Army, 1985.

—**BALLISTIC METEOROLOGY** is the study of the effects of atmospheric phenomena on the motion of a projectile.

References

Department of Defense, U.S. Army. *Weather Support for Army Tactical Operations.* Field Manual FM 34-81. Washington, DC: Headquarters, U.S. Army, 1984.

—**BALLISTIC MISSILE** is a missile that does not rely on aerodynamic surfaces to produce lift and consequently follows a ballistic trajectory when thrust is terminated. *See also:* Guided Missile, Nuclear Warfare.

References

Department of Defense, Joint Chiefs of Staff. *Department of Defense Dictionary of Military and Related Terms.* Washington, DC: GPO, 1986.

—**BALLISTIC TABLE** is a compilation of ballistic data from which trajectory elements (e.g., angle of fall, range of vertex, time of flight, and ordinate at any time) can be obtained. *See also:* Ballistics.

References

Department of Defense, U.S. Army. *Dictionary of United States Army Terms.* Army Regulation AR 310-25. Washington, DC: Headquarters, Department of the Army, 1986.

—**BALLISTIC TRAJECTORY** is the trajectory traced after the positive propulsive force is terminated and the body is acted upon only by gravity and aerodynamic drag.

References

Department of Defense, Joint Chiefs of Staff. *Department of Defense Dictionary of Military and Related Terms.* Washington, DC: GPO, 1986.

—**BALLISTICS** is the science or art that deals with the motion, behavior, appearance, or modification of missiles or other vehicles that are acted upon by propellants, wind, gravity, temperature, or any other modifying substance, condition, or force.

References

Department of Defense, Joint Chiefs of Staff. *Department of Defense Dictionary of Military and Related Terms.* Washington, DC: GPO, 1986.

—**BALLISTICS OF PENETRATION** is the science that treats the motion of a projectile as it forces its way into targets of solid or semisolid substances (e.g., earth, concrete, or steel).

References

Department of Defense, U.S. Army. *Dictionary of United States Army Terms.* Army Regulation AR 310-25. Washington, DC: Headquarters, Department of the Army, 1986.

—**BALLISTITE** Is a smokeless powder used as a propelling charge in small arms and mortar ammunition.

References

Department of Defense, U.S. Army. *Dictionary of United States Army Terms.* Army Regulation AR 310-25. Washington, DC: Headquarters, Department of the Army, 1986.

—**BAND.** (1) A band is two or more line or wire entanglements or other obstacles, arranged one behind the other. Each line of obstacles is called a belt. (2) A band is a particular range of wave lengths in radio broadcasting.

References

Department of Defense, U.S. Army. *Dictionary of United States Army Terms.* Army Regulation AR 310-25. Washington, DC: Headquarters, Department of the Army, 1986.

—**BAND OF FIRE** is grazing fire, usually from one or more automatic guns, that gives a cone of dispersion so dense that a man trying to cross the line of fire would probably be hit. A final protection line uses a band of fire.

References

Department of Defense, U.S. Army. *Dictionary of United States Army Terms.* Army Regulation AR 310-25. Washington, DC: Headquarters, Department of the Army, 1986.

—**BANDIT** (ARMY AVIATION) is an aircraft that has been identified as a threat. *See also:* Bogey.

References

Department of Defense, U.S. Army. *Air-to-Air Combat.* Field Manual FM 1-107. Washington, DC: Headquarters, Department of the Army, 1984.

—**BANGALORE TORPEDO** is a metal tube or pipe packed with a high explosive charge. It is chiefly used to clear a path through barbed wire or mine fields.

References

Department of Defense, U.S. Army. *Dictionary of United States Army Terms.* Army Regulation AR 310-25. Washington, DC: Headquarters, Department of the Army, 1986.

—**BAR SIGHT** is the rear sight of a firearm, consisting of a moveable bar, usually with an open notch.

References

Department of Defense, U.S. Army. *Dictionary of United States Army Terms.* Army Regulation AR 310-25. Washington, DC: Headquarters, Department of the Army, 1986.

—**BARRAGE.** (1) A barrage is a prearranged barrier of fire delivered by small arms to protect friendly troops and installations by impeding enemy movements across defensive lines or areas. (2) A barrage is a protective screen of balloons moored to the ground and kept at given heights to prevent or hinder operations by enemy aircraft. This is also called a balloon barrage. (3) A barrage is a type of electronic countermeasure intended for simultaneous jamming over a wide area of the frequency spectrum. (4) A barrage is a method of fire employed against a fast opening or closing target, whereby a gun range or fuze setting is used that will place the initial shots ahead of the target in the direction of the target's anticipated advance. *See also:* Barrage Jamming, Electronic Warfare, Fire.

References

Department of Defense, U.S. Army. *Dictionary of United States Army Terms.* Army Regulation AR 310-25. Washington, DC: Headquarters, Department of the Army, 1986.

—**BARRAGE FIRE** is fire designed to fill a volume of space or area rather than fire aimed specifically at a given target. *See also:* Fire.

References

Department of Defense, Joint Chiefs of Staff. *Department of Defense Dictionary of Military and Related Terms.* Washington, DC: GPO, 1986.

—**BARRAGE JAMMING** is the simultaneous jamming of several adjacent channels or frequencies to prevent the enemy's reception of radio signals. *See also:* Jamming.

References

Department of Defense, Joint Chiefs of Staff. *Department of Defense Dictionary of Military and Related Terms.* Washington, DC: GPO, 1986.

—**BARREL.** (1) A barrel is a plastic or metal tube in which ammunition is fired and that controls the initial direction of the projectile. (2) A barrel is a standard unit of measurement of liquids in petroleum pipeline and storage operations, and equals 42 U.S. standard gallons.

References

Department of Defense, U.S. Army. *Dictionary of United States Army Terms.* Army Regulation AR 310-25. Washington, DC: Headquarters, Department of the Army, 1986.

—**BARREL EROSION** is the wearing away of the surface of the bore due to the combined effects of gas washing, scoring, and mechanical abrasion. Barrel erosion causes a reduction in muzzle velocity.

References

Department of Defense, U.S. Army. *Dictionary of United States Army Terms.* Army Regulation AR 310-25. Washington, DC: Headquarters, Department of the Army, 1986.

—**BARRICADE** is an intervening natural or artificial barrier sufficiently large and strong that it can limit the effect of an explosion on nearby buildings and exposures.

References

Department of Defense, U.S. Army. *Ammunition and Explosives Safety Standards.* Army Regulation AR 385-64. Washington, DC: Headquarters, Department of the Army, 1987.

—**BARRIER** is a coordinated series of obstacles employed to canalize, direct, restrict, delay, or stop the movement of an opposing force and to impose additional losses in personnel, time, and equipment on the opposing force.

References

Department of Defense, Joint Chiefs of Staff. *Department of Defense Dictionary of Military and Related Terms.* Washington, DC: GPO, 1986.

—**BARRIER FORCES** are air, surface, and submarine units and their supporting systems positioned across the likely courses of expected enemy transit for early detection and for providing warning, blocking, and destruction of the enemy.

References

Department of Defense, Joint Chiefs of Staff. *Department of Defense Dictionary of Military and Related Terms.* Washington, DC: GPO, 1986.

—**BARRIER INSPECTION** is a type of ordnance spot check inspection of vehicles in which an inspection team is posted near a road carrying heavy traffic, at a gasoline supply point, a ration supply point, or any similar location where vehicles of various units will be found. Vehicles are selected at random by the team and are inspected on the spot.

References

Department of Defense, U.S. Army. *Dictionary of United States Army Terms.* Army Regulation AR 310-25. Washington, DC: Headquarters, Department of the Army, 1986.

—**BARRIER LINE** is a traffic control boundary beyond which vehicles may not pass until other traffic with priority has passed.

References

Department of Defense, U.S. Army. *Dictionary of United States Army Terms.* Army Regulation AR 310-25. Washington, DC: Headquarters, Department of the Army, 1986.

—**BARRIER PLAN** is the part of an operation plan concerned with the use of obstacles to canalize, direct, restrict, delay, or stop the movement of an opposing force and the infliction of additional losses in personnel and equipment upon that opposing force. *See also:* Barrier, Barrier Tactics.

References

Department of Defense, U.S. Army. *Dictionary of United States Army Terms.* Army Regulation AR 310-25. Washington, DC: Headquarters, Department of the Army, 1986.

—**BARRIER TACTICS** are tactics based upon the use of fortified lines, both natural and artificial, that are supported by fire.

References

Department of Defense, U.S. Army. *Dictionary of United States Army Terms.* Army Regulation AR 310-25. Washington, DC: Headquarters, Department of the Army, 1986.

—**BASE.** (1) A base is a locality from which operations are projected or supported. (2) A base is an area or locality containing installations that provide logistic or other support. (3) A base is a unit or multiunit position that has a definite perimeter. Army, other services, or host nations may establish a base. A base defense operation center is established to coordinate rear battle functions. (4) A base is the element on which a movement is planned and regulated. (5) A base is a foundation or part upon which an object or instrument rests (e.g., a gun base). (6) A base is the part of a projectile below the rotating band. (7) A base is a line used in mapping, surveying, or controlling fire as a reference from which distance and angles are measured.

References

Department of Defense, U.S. Army. *Dictionary of United States Army Terms.* Army Regulation AR 310-25. Washington, DC: Headquarters, Department of the Army, 1986.

————. *Drills and Ceremonies.* Field Manual FM 22-5. Washington, DC: Headquarters, Department of the Army, 1986.

—**BASE CLUSTER.** Bases of combat, combat support, and combat service support units in the rear are grouped for rear battle or mission-related purposes. A base cluster has no clearly defined perimeter. A base cluster operations center is established to perform the coordination functions of the rear battle.

References

Department of Defense, U.S. Army. *Operational Terms and Symbols.* Field Manual FM 101-5-1. Washington, DC: Headquarters, Department of the Army, 1985.

————. *Rear Battle.* Field Manual FM 90-14. Washington, DC: Headquarters, Department of the Army, 1985.

—**BASE CLUSTER OPERATIONS** are measures taken among bases to coordinate mutual support. Base clusters are established due to the proximity of bases to one another and to meet the need for mutual support during rear battle operations and area damage control operations. *See also:* Base Cluster.

References

Department of Defense, U.S. Army. *Operational Terms and Symbols.* Field Manual FM 101-5-1. Washington, DC: Headquarters, Department of the Army, 1985.

—**BASE COMMAND** is an area containing a military base or group of such bases organized under one commander. *See also:* Command.

References

Department of Defense, Joint Chiefs of Staff. *Department of Defense Dictionary of Military and Related Terms.* Washington, DC: GPO, 1986.

—**BASE DEFENSE** is the local military measures, both normal and emergency, required to nullify or reduce the effectiveness of enemy attacks on, or sabotage of, a base, so as to insure that the maximum capacity of its facilities is available to U.S. forces. *See also:* Base Defense Force, Base Defense Operations, Base Defense Operations Center.

References

Department of Defense, Joint Chiefs of Staff. *Department of Defense Dictionary of Military and Related Terms.* Washington, DC: GPO, 1986.

—**BASE DEFENSE FORCE** is composed of the military personnel on a base who are tasked to organize and prepare a defense for the base against enemy attack. *See also:* Base Defense.

References

Department of Defense, U.S. Army. *Military Police Team, Squad, Platoon Combat Operations.* Field Manual FM 19-4. Washington, DC: Headquarters, Department of the Army, 1984.

—**BASE DEFENSE OPERATIONS** are defense measures taken by a base to provide internal and perimeter security. These measures include organizing and preparing personnel and equipment for defense of the base until military police or tactical combat forces can respond. *See also:* Base Defense.

References

Department of Defense, U.S. Army. *Operational Terms and Symbols.* Field Manual FM 101-5-1. Washington, DC: Department of the Army, 1985.

—**BASE DEFENSE OPERATIONS CENTER** is an area set up in a base to coordinate the defense of the base and air damage control operations. *See also:* Base Defense.

References

Department of Defense, U.S. Army. *Military Police Team, Squad, Platoon Combat Operations.* Field Manual FM 19-4. Washington, DC: Headquarters, Department of the Army, 1984.

—**BASE DEVELOPMENT** is the improvement or expansion of the resources and facilities of an area or a location to support military operations. *See also:* Base Development Plan.

References

Department of Defense, Joint Chiefs of Staff. *Department of Defense Dictionary of Military and Related Terms.* Washington, DC: GPO, 1986.

—**BASE DEVELOPMENT PLAN (BDP)** is a plan for facilities, installations, and bases required to support military operations. The BDP is a category of operations plan developed by an Army component command in support of employment and consolidated plans that identifies logistics and operational facility requirements and provides for acquiring or constructing and maintaining those facilities.

References

Department of Defense, U.S. Army. *Planning Logistics Support for Military Operations.* Field Manual FM 701-58. Washington, DC: Headquarters, Department of the Army, 1987.

—**BASE IGNITION** is a descriptive term applied to a signal or other ammunition or pyrotechnic item that ignites from the base, with a subsequent emission of smoke or chemicals.

References

Department of Defense, U.S. Army. *Dictionary of United States Army Terms.* Army Regulation AR 310-25. Washington, DC: Headquarters, Department of the Army, 1986.

—**BASE MAP.** (1) Base map is a map or chart showing certain fundamental information used as a base upon which additional specialized data are compiled or overprinted. (2) Base map is a map containing all the information from which maps showing specialized information can be prepared. *See also:* Map.

References

Department of Defense, Joint Chiefs of Staff. *Department of Defense Dictionary of Military and Related Terms.* Washington, DC: GPO, 1986.

—**BASE MAP SYMBOL** is a symbol used on a base map or chart (as opposed to one used on an overprint to the base map or chart). *See also:* Base Map, Map.

References

Department of Defense, Joint Chiefs of Staff. *Department of Defense Dictionary of Military and Related Terms.* Washington, DC: GPO, 1986.

—**BASE MORTAR** is mortar for which additional firing data are computed and with reference to which data for other mortars in the unit are computed.

References

Department of Defense, U.S. Army. *Dictionary of United States Army Terms.* Army Regulation AR 310-25. Washington, DC: Headquarters, Department of the Army, 1986.

—**BASE OF FIRE** is fire placed on an enemy or position to reduce or eliminate the enemy's capability to interfere by fire and/or movement of friendly maneuver element(s). It may be provided by a single weapon or a grouping of weapon systems.

References

Department of Defense, U.S. Army. *Dictionary of United States Army Terms.* Army Regulation AR 310-25. Washington, DC: Headquarters, Department of the Army, 1986.

———. *Operational Terms and Symbols.* Field Manual FM 101-5-1. Washington, DC: Headquarters, Department of the Army, 1985.

—**BASE OF OPERATIONS** is an area or facility from which a military force begins its offensive operations, to which it falls back in case of reverse, and in which supply facilities are organized.

References

Department of Defense, Joint Chiefs of Staff. *Department of Defense Dictionary of Military and Related Terms.* Washington, DC: GPO, 1986.

—**BASE OF TRAJECTORY** is a straight horizontal line from the center of a muzzle of a weapon to the point in the downward curve in the path of a projectile that is level with the muzzle.

References

Department of Defense, U.S. Army. *Dictionary of United States Army Terms.* Army Regulation AR 310-25. Washington, DC: Headquarters, Department of the Army, 1986.

—**BASE OPERATIONS SUPPORT** is the provision of administrative and logistical services. Base operations support includes, at the local level, supply operations, maintenance of materiel, personnel support, base services to include transportation and electronic (signal) communications, operation of utilities, maintenance of real property, minor construction, other engineering support, and administrative services (including automatic data processing support) rendered by or through activities of the supporting installation. The extent and financing of base operations support provided by a host installation to a tenant or satellite activity are documented in support agreements between the host and the tenant/satellite.

References

Department of Defense, U.S. Army. *Dictionary of United States Army Terms.* Army Regulation AR 310-25. Washington, DC: Headquarters, Department of the Army, 1986.

—**BASE PIECE.** (1) A base piece is the gun or howitzer in a battery for which the initial firing data may be calculated and with reference to which the firing data for other guns or howitzers may be computed. (2) A base piece may also mean the gun or howitzer nearest the battery center.

References

Department of Defense, U.S. Army. *Dictionary of United States Army Terms.* Army Regulation AR 310-25. Washington, DC: Headquarters, Department of the Army, 1986.

—**BASE RESERVES** are supplies stored in depots as a general reserve within a theater of operations.

References

Department of Defense, U.S. Army. *Dictionary of United States Army Terms.* Army Regulation AR 310-25. Washington, DC: Headquarters, Department of the Army, 1986.

—**BASE SECTION** is an area within the communications zone in the area of operations organized to provide logistic support to forward areas. *See also:* Communications Zone.

References

Department of Defense, Joint Chiefs of Staff. *Department of Defense Dictionary of Military and Related Terms.* Washington, DC: GPO, 1986.

—**BASE SPRAY** refers to fragments of a bursting shell thrown to the rear in the line of flight of a projectile. *See also:* Nose Spray, Side Spray.

References

Department of Defense, U.S. Army. *Dictionary of United States Army Terms.* Army Regulation AR 310-25. Washington, DC: Headquarters, Department of the Army, 1986.

—**BASE SURGE** is a cloud that rolls out from the bottom of the column produced by a subsurface burst of a nuclear weapon. For underwater bursts, the surge is, in effect, a cloud of liquid droplets that has the property of flowing almost as if it were a homogenous fluid. For subsurface land bursts, the surge is made up of small solid particles that behave like a fluid.

References

Department of Defense, Joint Chiefs of Staff. *Department of Defense Dictionary of Military and Related Terms.* Washington, DC: GPO, 1986.

—**BASE UNIT** is a unit of organization in a tactical operation around which a movement or maneuver is planned or performed. It is a base element.

References

Department of Defense, Joint Chiefs of Staff. *Department of Defense Dictionary of Military and Related Terms.* Washington, DC: GPO, 1986.

—**BASIC ALLOWANCE FOR QUARTERS (BAQ)** is a monetary allowance paid to all service personnel who are not furnished quarters in kind. *See also:* Military Pay and Allowances.

References

Department of Defense, U.S. Army. *Dictionary of United States Army Terms.* Army Regulation AR 310-25. Washington, DC: Headquarters, Department of the Army, 1986.

—**BASIC ALLOWANCE FOR SUBSISTENCE (BAS)** is a monetary allowance paid to all service personnel who are authorized to subsist by themselves. *See also:* Military Pay and Allowances.

References

Department of Defense, U.S. Army. *Dictionary of United States Army Terms.* Army Regulation AR 310-25. Washington, DC: Headquarters, Department of the Army, 1986.

—**BASIC BRANCH.** (1) Basic branch is the branch to which an officer is assigned upon commissioning or upon branch transfer (e.g., Infantry or Adjutant General's Corps), as differentiated from any detail. (2) Basic branch is a branch of the Army that is not a special branch. The special branches are currently the six corps of the Army Medical Department, the Judge Advocate General's Corps, and the Chaplains. *See also:* Branch.

References

Department of Defense, U.S. Army. *Dictionary of United States Army Terms.* Army Regulation AR 310-25. Washington, DC: Headquarters, Department of the Army, 1986.

—**BASIC COMBAT TRAINING (BCT)** is training in basic military subjects and fundamentals of basic infantry combat, given to newly inducted and enlisted Active Army and Reserve components personnel who have no prior military service.

References

Department of Defense, U.S. Army. *Dictionary of United States Army Terms.* Army Regulation AR 310-25. Washington, DC: Headquarters, Department of the Army, 1986.

—**BASIC COVER** (PHOTOGRAMMETRY) is an intelligence imagery and photoreconnaissance term for photographic and other aerial coverage of any permanent installation or area. Such imagery can be compared to that taken at a later time in order to determine the changes that have taken place. In this way, imagery can be used to monitor and report on the progress of such endeavors as ship building, military or civil construction, or other long-term intelligence-related enterprises. *See also:* Aerial Reconnaissance.

References

Department of Defense, Defense Intelligence College. *Glossary of Intelligence Terms and Definitions.* Washington, DC: DIC, 1987.

—**BASIC DAILY FOOD ALLOWANCE** is a prescribed quantity of food, defined by components and monetary value, required to provide a nutritionally adequate diet for one person for one day. The Department of Defense Food Cost Index is used to compute the basic daily food allowance.

References

Department of Defense, U.S. Army. *Dictionary of United States Army Terms.* Army Regulation AR 310-25. Washington, DC: Headquarters, Department of the Army, 1986.

—**BASIC ENLISTED SERVICE DATE** is the date that reflects the total of all periods of a person's enlisted service, active or inactive, as a member of the Regular and Reserve components of the U.S. Armed Forces.

References

Department of Defense, U.S. Army. *Enlisted Personnel Management System.* Army Regulation AR 600-200. Washington, DC: Headquarters, Department of the Army, 1984.

—**BASIC INTELLIGENCE.** (1) Basic intelligence is a general intelligence term for factual general reference material. It is assembled by collecting encyclopedic information concerning the geography and political, social, economic, and military structures, as well as biographic and cultural material and any information on the resources, capabilities, and vulnerabilities of a foreign nation or nations. This information is essential because it provides a foundation for planning, policymaking, and military operations. (2) Basic intelligence is fundamental intelligence concerning the general situation, resources, capabilities, and vulnerabilities of foreign countries or areas that may be used as reference material in planning operations at any level and in evaluating subsequent information relating to the same subject. *See also:* Intelligence.

References

Department of Defense, Defense Intelligence College. *Glossary of Intelligence Terms and Definitions.* Washington, DC: DIC, 1987.

U.S. Congress. Senate. *Final Report of the Senate Select Committee to Study Government Operations With Respect to Intelligence Activities. Report 94-755. Book I, Foreign and Military Intelligence* (Church Committee Report). Washington, DC: GPO, 1976.

—**BASIC ISSUE ITEMS** are the essential ancillary items required to operate the equipment and to enable it to perform the mission and function for which it was designed or intended.

References

Department of Defense, U.S. Army. *Dictionary of United States Army Terms.* Army Regulation AR 310-25. Washington, DC: Headquarters, Department of the Army, 1986.

—**BASIC LOAD.** For other than ammunition, basic loads are supplies kept by the using units for use in combat. The quantity of each item of supply in a basic load is related to the number of days in combat the unit may be sustained without supply. *See also:* Basic Load (Ammunition).

References

Department of Defense, Joint Chiefs of Staff. *Department of Defense Dictionary of Military and Related Terms.* Washington, DC: GPO, 1986.

Department of Defense, U.S. Army. *Operational Terms and Symbols.* Field Manual FM 101-5-1. Washington, DC: Headquarters, Department of the Army, 1985.

—**BASIC LOAD** (AMMUNITION) is the quantity of nonnuclear ammunition authorized and required to be on hand in a unit to meet combat needs until resupply can be accomplished. The basic load is specified by the theater army and is expressed in rounds, units, or units of weight, as appropriate.

References

Department of Defense, U.S. Army. *Air Defense Artillery Deployment: Chaparral/Vulcan/Stinger.* Field Manual FM 44-3. Washington, DC: Headquarters, Department of the Army, 1984.

———. *Operational Terms and Symbols.* Field Manual FM 101-5-1. Washington, DC: Headquarters, Department of the Army, 1985.

—**BASIC MILITARY NETWORK** consists of all routes designated in peacetime by the host nation to meet anticipated allied and national military movements and transportation requirements. A basic network has the facilities necessary to support normal military movements. *See also:* Basic Military Route Network.

References

Department of Defense, U.S. Army. *Route Reconnaissance and Classification.* Field Manual FM 5-36. Washington, DC: Headquarters, Department of the Army, 1985.

—**BASIC MILITARY ROUTE NETWORK** is composed of axial, lateral, and connecting routes that are designated in peacetime by the host nation to meet anticipated military movements and transport requirements, both allied and national.

References

Department of Defense, Joint Chiefs of Staff. *Department of Defense Dictionary of Military and Related Terms.* Washington, DC: GPO, 1986.

—**BASIC MILITARY TRAINING** is the training in military subjects a soldier receives in the first phase of basic training.

References

Department of Defense, U.S. Army. *Dictionary of United States Army Terms.* Army Regulation AR 310-25. Washington, DC: Headquarters, Department of the Army, 1986.

—**BASIC PAY** is pay (other than allowances) a member of the Army receives based upon grade and length of service. *See also:* Military Pay and Allowances.

References

Department of Defense, U.S. Army. *Dictionary of United States Army Terms.* Army Regulation AR 310-25. Washington, DC: Headquarters, Department of the Army, 1986.

—**BASIC PLAN** is the part of an operation plan that forms the base structure for annexes and appendices. It consists of general statements related to the situation, mission, execution, logistics, administration, and command and signal.

References

Department of Defense, U.S. Army. *Planning Logistics Support for Military Operations.* Field Manual FM 701-58. Washington, DC: Headquarters, Department of the Army, 1987.

—**BASIC PSYCHOLOGICAL OPERATIONS STUDY (BPS)** is a reference or detailed background document that describes the characteristics of a country, area, or region that are of greatest value for conducting psychological operations. These are psychological-operations-relevant vulnerabilities, characteristics, insights, and opportunities known about a specific country that are susceptible to exploitation. *See also:* Psychological Operations.

References

Department of Defense, U.S. Army. *Psychological Operations.* Field Manual FM 33-1. Washington, DC: Headquarters, Department of the Army, 1979.

Lowenthal, Mark M. *U.S. Intelligence: Evolution and Anatomy.* New York: Praeger, 1984.

—**BASIC SKILLS DECONTAMINATION** is the immediate neutralization or removal of contamination from exposed portions of the skin. Each individual must be able to perform this decon without supervision.

References

Department of Defense, U.S. Army. *NBC Operations.* Field Manual FM 3-100. Washington, DC: Headquarters, Department of the Army, 1985.

—**BASIC SKILLS EDUCATION PROGRAM (BSEP)** is the commander's primary on-duty education program. It provides soldiers with educational skills essential for progressing in Army careers. In coordination with the education services officer, commanders determine which soldiers should be enrolled in the program. The BSEP, which includes the Advanced Skills Education Program (ASEP), is implemented in three phases. BSEP I provides basic instruction in reading, writing, arithmetic, and language skills for soldiers in initial entry training. BSEP II improves educational skills needed to perform effectively through grade E5. ASEP, the third phase of this job-oriented instruction, enhances duty performance, military occupational specialty verification, and professional development. ASEP improves the educational skills required for duty performance and career development for grades E6 and above.

References

Department of Defense, U.S. Army. *Army Forces Training.* Army Regulation AR 350-41. Washington, DC: Headquarters, Department of the Army, 1986.

———. *Unit Training Management.* Field Manual FM 25-2. Washington, DC: Headquarters, Department of the Army, 1984.

—**BASIC STOPPING POWER** is the probability, expressed as a percentage, of a single vehicle being stopped by mines while attempting to cross a minefield.

References

Department of Defense, Joint Chiefs of Staff. *Department of Defense Dictionary of Military and Related Terms*. Washington, DC: GPO, 1986.

—**BASIC TACTICAL ORGANIZATION** is the conventional organization of landing force units for combat, involving combinations of infantry, supporting ground arms, and aviation for accomplishing missions ashore. This organizational form is employed as soon as possible following the landing of the various assault components of the landing force. *See also:* Basic Tactical Unit.

References

Department of Defense, Joint Chiefs of Staff. *Department of Defense Dictionary of Military and Related Terms*. Washington, DC: GPO, 1986.

—**BASIC TACTICAL UNIT** is a fundamental unit capable of carrying out an independent tactical mission in any branch of the Army (e.g., as a rifle company in the infantry or a battery in artillery).

References

Department of Defense, U.S. Army. *Dictionary of United States Army Terms*. Army Regulation AR 310-25. Washington, DC: Headquarters, Department of the Army, 1986.

—**BASIC TRAINING** is the initial training that provides new recruits with instruction in the basic skills that are common to all soldiers. It precedes advanced individual training. *See also:* Advanced Individual Training.

References

Department of Defense, U.S. Army. *Enlisted Personnel*. Army Regulation AR 635-200. Washington, DC: Headquarters, Department of the Army, 1984.

———. *Individual Military Education and Training*. Army Regulation AR 350-1. Washington, DC: Headquarters, Department of the Army, 1987.

—**BASIC UNDERTAKINGS** are the essential actions, expressed in broad terms, that must be done in order to implement the commander's concept successfully. These may include military, diplomatic, economic, psychological, and other measures. *See also:* Strategic Concept.

References

Department of Defense, Joint Chiefs of Staff. *Department of Defense Dictionary of Military and Related Terms*. Washington, DC: GPO, 1986.

—**BASIC UNIT TRAINING** is applicable training given during the final phase of basic training when soldiers, who are assigned to units, are first assembled and trained together in rehearsal of their role as an officially designated military organization. In some types of units, basic team training is given in place of basic unit training.

References

Department of Defense, U.S. Army. *Dictionary of United States Army Terms*. Army Regulation AR 310-25. Washington, DC: Headquarters, Department of the Army, 1986.

—**BASIS OF ISSUE** is the authority that prescribes the number of items to be issued to an individual, a unit, or a military organization, or for a unit piece of equipment.

References

Department of Defense, Joint Chiefs of Staff. *Department of Defense Dictionary of Military and Related Terms*. Washington, DC: GPO, 1986.

—**BATTALION** is a unit composed of a headquarters and two or more companies or batteries. It may be part of a regiment and be charged with only tactical functions, or it may be a separate unit and be charged with both administrative and tactical functions. *See also:* Brigades, Company, Corps, Division, Platoon, Regiment, Squad.

References

Department of Defense, U.S. Army. *Dictionary of United States Army Terms*. Army Regulation AR 310-25. Washington, DC: Headquarters, Department of the Army, 1986.

———. *The Infantry Battalion (Infantry, Airborne, Air Assault)*. Field Manual FM 7-20. Washington, DC: Headquarters, Department of the Army, 1984.

———. *Light Infantry Battalion Task Force*. Field Manual FM 7-72. Washington, DC: Headquarters, Department of the Army, 1987.

—**BATTALION ANTIARMOR DEFENSE PLAN** incorporates all means of defending against enemy armor. Tanks can initially engage personnel and other soft targets with their main guns at extended ranges. Enemy tanks are also attacked at extended range with missiles and with conventional munitions. As the enemy approaches to the forward edge of the battle area, other antiarmor weapons can be used to engage enemy armor as it comes within range of these weapons. *See also:* Forward Edge of the Battle Area.

References

Department of Defense, U.S. Army. *Tactics, Techniques, and Concepts of Antiarmor Warfare.* Field Manual FM 23-3. Washington, DC: Headquarters, Department of the Army, 1972.

—**BATTALION ASSESSMENT AND RECOVERY PERSONNEL** are personnel necessary for unit reconstruction. They come from the staff and technical personnel assigned to the battalion.

References

Department of Defense, U.S. Army. *Combat Service Support Operations-Division.* Field Manual FM 63-2. Washington, DC: Headquarters, Department of the Army, 1983.

—**BATTALION LANDING TEAM (BLT)** is found in an amphibious operation. It is an infantry battalion that is normally reinforced by the necessary combat and service elements. It is the basic unit for planning an assault landing and also known as a BLT. *See also:* Amphibious Operation.

References

Department of Defense, Joint Chiefs of Staff. *Department of Defense Dictionary of Military and Related Terms.* Washington, DC: GPO, 1986.

—**BATTALION SUPPORT AREA** is the portion of the battalion rear occupied by the battalion trains.

References

Department of Defense, U.S. Army. *Combat Service Support Operations-Division.* Field Manual FM 63-2. Washington, DC: Headquarters, Department of the Army, 1983.

—**BATTALION TASK FORCE (BTF)** is a combination of tank and mechanized infantry companies and other units grouped under the command of a tank or mechanized infantry battalion commander to conduct specific operations. A battalion task force may be tank-heavy, infantry-heavy, or balanced, depending on the concept and plan of operation. Frequently, attack helicopter units may operate with the BTF. The BTF fights as part of a brigade.

References

Department of Defense, U.S. Army. *Air Defense Artillery Deployment: Chaparral/Vulcan/Stinger.* Field Manual FM 44-3. Washington, DC: Headquarters, Department of the Army, 1984.

———. *The Infantry Battalion (Infantry, Airborne, Air Assault).* Field Manual FM 7-20. Washington, DC: Headquarters, Department of the Army, 1984.

———. *Light Infantry Battalion Task Force.* Field Manual FM 7-72. Washington, DC: Headquarters, Department of the Army, 1987.

———. *Operational Terms and Symbols.* Field Manual FM 101-5-1. Washington, DC: Headquarters, Department of the Army, 1985.

———. *The Tank and Mechanized Infantry Battalion Task Force.* Field Manual FM 71-2. Washington, DC: Headquarters, Department of the Army, 1977.

—**BATTALION TRAINS** are normally made up of battalion combat support service assets and the forward support elements of the forward area support team. Battalion trains can be deployed as a whole or echeloned into combat and field trains. *See also:* train.

References

Department of Defense, U.S. Army. *Combat Service Support Operations-Division.* Field Manual FM 63-2. Washington, DC: Headquarters, Department of the Army, 1983.

—**BATTALIONS/SQUADRONS** consist of two or more company-sized units and a headquarters. Most battalions are organized by branch, arm, or service and, in addition to their operational companies, contain a headquarters company that gives them the ability to perform some administrative and logistic services. Typically, battalions have three to five companies in addition to their headquarters.

Combat arms battalions are designed to perform single tactical missions as part of a brigade's tactical operations. Battalions attack, defend, delay, or move to assume new missions. Air and ground cavalry squadrons also perform reconnaissance and security missions. Field artillery battalions fire in support of any of these missions. Maneuver battalions can be reinforced with other combat and combat support companies to form task forces for special missions. Field artillery battalions can be reinforced with batteries of any kind to form artillery task forces.

Engineer, air defense artillery, and signal battalions assigned to or supporting divisions routinely operate throughout the division area of operations. Their commanders also perform the additional duties of division special staff officers.

Combat support and combat service support battalions vary widely in type and organization. They may be separate divisional or nondivisional battalions, but, in either case, they normally perform functional services for a larger supported unit within that unit's area of operations. All battalions are capable of at least limited, short-term self-defense.

References

Department of Defense, U.S. Army. *Operations.* Field Manual FM 100-5. Washington, DC: Headquarters, Department of the Army, 1986.

—**BATTERIES** (AIR DEFENSE ARTILLERY (ADA)) operate as the fighting elements of ADA battalions, or, if they are short-range air defense batteries, in direct support of maneuver brigades or battalions. Separate short-range air defense batteries exist in separate brigade-sized organizations.

References

Department of Defense, U.S. Army. *Staff Organization and Operations.* Field Manual FM 101-5. Washington, DC: Headquarters, Department of the Army, 1984.

—**BATTERIES** (FIELD ARTILLERY (FA)) are the basic firing units of FA battalions. They are organized with a firing battery, a headquarters, and limited support sections. They may fire and displace together or by platoons. Normally, batteries fight as a part of their parent battalion. Occasionally, they are attached to other batteries or FA battalions, and, in some cases, they respond directly to a maneuver battalion or company. More often, Multiple Launch Rocket, Lance, and Pershing batteries operate independently. Armored cavalry squadrons have organic howitzer batteries.

References

Department of Defense, U.S. Army. *Low Intensity Conflict.* Field Manual FM 100-20. Washington, DC: Headquarters, Department of the Army, 1981.

—**BATTERY** is a tactical and administrative artillery unit or subunit corresponding to a company or similar unit in other branches of the Army.

References

Department of Defense, Joint Chiefs of Staff. *Department of Defense Dictionary of Military and Related Terms.* Washington, DC: GPO, 1986.

—**BATTERY CENTER** is a point on the ground, the coordinates of which are used as a reference indicating the location of the battery in the production of firing data. It is also called the chart location of the battery.

References

Department of Defense, Joint Chiefs of Staff. *Department of Defense Dictionary of Military and Related Terms.* Washington, DC: GPO, 1986.

—**BATTERY FRONT** is the lateral distance between the flank guns of a battery.

References

Department of Defense, U.S. Army. *Dictionary of United States Army Terms.* Army Regulation AR 310-25. Washington, DC: Headquarters, Department of the Army, 1986.

—**BATTERY GROUND PATTERN** is the shape and dimensions of the pattern made by the location of the pieces of a battery emplaced for firing.

References

Department of Defense, U.S. Army. *Dictionary of United States Army Terms.* Army Regulation AR 310-25. Washington, DC: Headquarters, Department of the Army, 1986.

—**BATTERY OPERATIONS CENTER**, in field artillery operations, is a facility established to serve as an alternate fire direction center and as the battery command post.

References

Department of Defense, U.S. Army. *Dictionary of United States Army Terms.* Army Regulation AR 310-25. Washington, DC: Headquarters, Department of the Army, 1986.

———. *Fire Support in Combined Arms Operations.* Field Manual FM 6-20. Washington, DC: Headquarters, Department of the Army, 1983.

—**BATTERY** (TROOP) **LEFT** (RIGHT) is a method of fire in which weapons are discharged from the left (right), one after the other, at five-second intervals.

References

Department of Defense, Joint Chiefs of Staff. *Department of Defense Dictionary of Military and Related Terms.* Washington, DC: GPO, 1986.

—**BATTLE CASUALTY** is any casualty incurred in action. "In action" characterizes the casualty status as having been the direct result of hostile action, sustained in combat or relating thereto, or sustained going to or returning from a combat mission provided that the occurrence was directly related to hostile action. Included are persons killed or wounded mistakenly or accidentally by friendly fire directed at a hostile force or what is thought to be a hostile force. Not considered as sustained in action and thus not interpreted as battle casualties are injuries due to the elements, self-inflicted wounds, and, except in unusual cases, wounds or death inflicted by a friendly force while the individual is in absent-without-leave or dropped-from-rolls status or is voluntarily absent from a place of duty. *See also:* Nonbattle Casualty, Wounded in Action.

References

Department of Defense, Joint Chiefs of Staff. *Department of Defense Dictionary of Military and Related Terms.* Washington, DC: GPO, 1986.

Department of Defense, U.S. Army. *Planning for Health Service Support.* Field Manual FM 8-55. Washington, DC: Headquarters, Department of the Army, 1985.

—**BATTLE CLASP** is a metallic bar device denoting participation in a campaign in World War I. *See also:* Accouterment.

References

Department of Defense, U.S. Army. *Dictionary of United States Army Terms.* Army Regulation AR 310-25. Washington, DC: Headquarters, Department of the Army, 1986.

—**BATTLE COORDINATION ELEMENT** is an Army element operating at the Air Force's tactical air control center. It analyzes the land battle and provides air-land interface in either a single corps or multicorps situation.

References

Department of Defense, U.S. Army. *Fire Support in Combined Arms Operations.* Field Manual FM 6-20. Washington, DC: Headquarters, Department of the Army, 1983.

—**BATTLE DAMAGE ASSESSMENT (BDA).** (1) Battle damage assessment is a service provided by intermediate rear maintenance that evaluates combat damage to determine whether to repair, cannibalize, or evacuate. (2) Battle damage assessment is the use of ground or air observation forces to determine the damage inflicted on enemy forces by air strikes or other fire support systems.

References

Department of Defense, U.S. Army. *Operational Terms and Symbols.* Field Manual FM 101-5-1. Washington, DC: Headquarters, Department of the Army, 1985.

—**BATTLE DRILL** are the memorized actions of crews, squads, platoons, and companies that are executed the same way under every condition.

References

Department of Defense, U.S. Army. *Operational Terms and Symbols.* Field Manual FM 101-5-1. Washington, DC: Headquarters, Department of the Army, 1985.

—**BATTLE HONOR** is an award to a unit or individual denoting participation in a campaign. It is a streamer or band attached to the staff of the flag, color, or standard of a unit denoting battlefield participation or award of a unit decoration.

References

Department of Defense, U.S. Army. *Dictionary of United States Army Terms.* Army Regulation AR 310-25. Washington, DC: Headquarters, Department of the Army, 1986.

—**BATTLE INJURY AND WOUNDED IN ACTION.** For purposes of medical statistical reporting, a battle casualty patient (battle injury and wounded in action) is a patient who is admitted to a medical treatment facility for treatment of injuries or wounds either due directly to enemy action or received while in combat. A patient who is admitted as a battle casualty is reported as such as long as his hospitalization is continuous and uninterrupted. Discharge of a patient from a medical treatment facility ends his battle casualty status for medical reporting purposes. Killed in action cases are reported separately from injured or wounded in action cases. *See also:* Medical Treatment.

References

Department of Defense, U.S. Army. *Planning for Health Service Support.* Field Manual FM 8-55. Washington, DC: Headquarters, Department of the Army, 1985.

—**BATTLE MANAGEMENT** is the command and control personnel, equipment, and procedures needed to evaluate and direct military operations as situations develop so that the appropriate adjustments in force deployments and tactics proceed efficiently.

References
Collins, John M. *U.S.-Soviet Military Balance, 1980-1985*. Washington, DC: Congressional Research Service, 1985.

—**BATTLE MAP** is a map showing the ground features in sufficient detail for tactical use by all forces. It is usually at a scale of 1:25,000. *See also:* Map.

References
Department of Defense, Joint Chiefs of Staff. *Department of Defense Dictionary of Military and Related Terms*. Washington, DC: GPO, 1986.

—**BATTLE POSITION (BP)** is a defensive location oriented on the most likely enemy avenue of approach from which a unit may defend or attack. Such units can be as large as battalion task forces and as small as platoons. A unit assigned a BP is located within the general outline of the BP. Security, combat support, and combat service support forces may operate outside a BP to provide early enemy detection and all-around security.

References
Department of Defense, U.S. Army. *Operational Terms and Symbols*. Field Manual FM 101-5-1. Washington, DC: Headquarters, Department of the Army, 1985.

—**BATTLE RESERVES** are reserve supplies accumulated by an army, detached corps, or detached division in the vicinity of the battlefield, in addition to unit and individual reserves. *See also:* Reserve Supplies.

References
Department of Defense, Joint Chiefs of Staff. *Department of Defense Dictionary of Military and Related Terms*. Washington, DC: GPO, 1986.

—**BATTLE SIGHT** is a predetermined sight setting that, carried on a weapon, enables the firer to engage targets effectively at battle ranges when conditions do not permit exact sight settings.

References
Department of Defense, U.S. Army. *Dictionary of United States Army Terms*. Army Regulation AR 310-25. Washington, DC: Headquarters, Department of the Army, 1986.

—**BATTLE STAFF TRAINING** allows commanders and their staffs to fight air-land battles in diverse command post configurations under realistic combat conditions as smoothly functioning teams. This training is vital to the command and control of the units. It develops the proficiency of individual staff members and molds them into trained teams that can effectively manage and coordinate all systems to support the command's mission. Such training requires the individual staff members to know the unit's tactical standard operating procedures thoroughly. These procedures must be updated as appropriate to address changes in unit operations. Battle staff training relies heavily on simulations, since they are often the only way for a commander to present many air-land battle situations and tasks to his staff.

References
Department of Defense, U.S. Army. *How to Conduct Training Exercises*. Field Manual FM 25-4. Washington, DC: Headquarters, Department of the Army, 1984.

—**BATTLEFIELD AIR INTERDICTION (BAI)** is an air action against hostile surface targets that are in a position to directly affect friendly forces. BAI requires coordination in joint planning, but continuous coordination may not be required during the execution stage.

References
Department of Defense, U.S. Army. *Attack Helicopter Operations*. Field Manual FM 17-50. Washington, DC: Headquarters, Department of the Army, 1984.

———. *Fire Support in Combined Arms Operations*. Field Manual FM 6-20. Washington, DC: Headquarters, Department of the Army, 1983.

———. *Operational Terms and Symbols*. Field Manual FM 101-5-1. Washington, DC: Headquarters, Department of the Army, 1985.

———. *Operations*. Field Manual FM 100-5. Washington, DC: Headquarters, Department of the Army, 1986.

—**BATTLEFIELD CIRCULATION CONTROL (BCC)** is a military police mission involving route reconnaissance and surveillance, main supply route regulation enforcement, straggler and refugee control, and information dissemination.

References
Department of Defense, U.S. Army. *Operational Terms and Symbols*. Field Manual FM 101-5-1. Washington, DC: Headquarters, Department of the Army, 1985.

—**BATTLEFIELD EVACUATION** is the process of moving wounded, injured, or ill personnel from a battlefield and subsequently along the medical chain of evacuation. The zone of responsibility for battlefield evacuation normally lies to the front of medical units.

References

Department of Defense, U.S. Army. *Dictionary of United States Army Terms*. Army Regulation AR 310-25. Washington, DC: Headquarters, Department of the Army, 1986.

————. *Support Operations: Echelons Above Corps*. Field Manual FM 100-16. Washington, DC: Headquarters, Department of the Army, 1986.

—BATTLEFIELD ILLUMINATION

is the lighting of the battle area by artificial light that is either visible or invisible to the naked eye.

References

Department of Defense, Joint Chiefs of Staff. *Department of Defense Dictionary of Military and Related Terms*. Washington, DC: GPO, 1986.

—BATTLEFIELD PSYCHOLOGICAL ACTIVITIES

are planned psychological activities conducted as an integral part of combat operations and designed to put psychological pressure on enemy forces and civilians under enemy control in the battle area. *See also:* Psychological Operations.

References

Department of Defense, Joint Chiefs of Staff. *Department of Defense Dictionary of Military and Related Terms*. Washington, DC: GPO, 1986.

Department of Defense, U.S. Army. *Psychological Operations*. Field Manual FM 33-1. Washington, DC: Headquarters, Department of the Army, 1979.

—BATTLEFIELD RECOVERY

is to move disabled or abandoned materiel, either enemy or friendly, from the battlefield to a recovery collecting point or to a maintenance or supply establishment.

References

Department of Defense, U.S. Army. *Dictionary of United States Army Terms*. Army Regulation AR 310-25. Washington, DC: Headquarters, Department of the Army, 1986.

—BATTLEFIELD SURVEILLANCE,

an Army intelligence term, is the constant, systematic observation of a battle area to detect changes or events immediately in order to provide timely tactical intelligence information to the operational commander.

References

Department of Defense, U.S. Army. *Dictionary of United States Army Terms*. Army Regulation AR 310-25. Washington, DC: Headquarters, Department of the Army, 1986.

—BATTLES

consist of a series of related engagements. Battles last longer, involve larger forces, and often produce decisions that affect the subsequent course of the campaign. Battles occur when large forces (e.g., divisions, corps, and armies) commit themselves to fight for significant goals. They are often fought when the deliberate attack of one force meets determined resistance from the defender. Battles can also result from meeting engagements between forces contesting the initiative, which may be caused by the determination of the opposed commanders to impose their will on their enemy. Battles can also arise without strong direction when large forces meet and neither withdraws. Such actions might not even be recognized as battles until they have gone on for some time.

Battles may be short and intense and may be fought in a relatively small area (as on the Golan Heights in 1973), or they may vary in intensity over a period of days and weeks and extend over a wide area (as in the Battle of the Bulge). In either case, the battlesites of committed divisions, corps, or armies are surrounded by larger areas in which both combatants try to concentrate forces and support for the battle. Action in the surrounding areas can strongly affect the outcome of the battle.

Battles may not occur at all if the enemy can be rapidly overwhelmed in a series of minor engagements and prevented from mounting a coherent defense. Conversely, battles can also produce stalemates that favor neither side.

Battles or significant tactical gains made without battle determine the course of campaigns. Although battles often decided wars in the last century, subsequent experience suggests that battles between competent forces are more likely to decide phases of campaigns. They may be important enough to force an attacker to assume the defensive or allow the defender to take the operational offensive. Kursk, El Alamein, and the battle of the "Chinese Farm" in the Sinai are examples of such watershed battles. More commonly, tactical success by the attacker leads to a fluid operational interlude that lasts until the defender reestablishes a tenable resistance or the attacker overextends himself. Similarly, a tactical success by the defender is more likely to defer a decision or reduce the attacker's advantage than permit an immediate shift to the offensive.

References
Department of Defense, U.S. Army. *Operations.*
  Field Manual FM 100-5. Washington, DC:
  Headquarters, Department of the Army, 1986.

—**BATTLESIGHT AMMUNITION.** One round of ammunition that is designed to defeat the most probable threat target should be loaded into the chamber as the battlesight round. No one specific round will be adequate in every situation. For instance, if the tanks are the primary threat, armor piercing discarding sabot should be carried as the battlesight round. If massed troops pose the major threat, the antipersonnel round could be used.

References
Department of Defense, U.S. Army. *U.S. Army
  Policy Statement, 1988.* Washington, DC:
  Headquarters, Department of the Army, 1988.

—**BATTLESIGHT GUNNERY** is the most rapid method of engaging an enemy target and is preferred when quick target engagement is required and when the target is within battlesight range. The odds are four to one that the tank that fires first will be the victor in a tank duel. Battlesight gunnery combines the relatively flat trajectories of the main gun rounds with their superior target-defeating capability to reduce engagement times while maintaining a relatively high probability of first-round hits. Battlesight gunnery consists of a preloaded round in the gun, with either a range pre-indexed in the system or the gunner firing using a ballistic rectile that refers a specific portion of the rectile to the base of the visible target.

References
Department of Defense, U.S. Army. *U.S. Army
  Policy Statement, 1988.* Washington, DC:
  Headquarters, Department of the Army, 1988.

—**BEACHHEAD** is a designated area on a hostile shore that, when seized and held, insures the continuous landing of troops and material and provides the maneuvering space required for subsequent offensive operations ashore.

References
Department of Defense, U.S. Army. *Operational
  Terms and Symbols.* Field Manual FM 101-5-1.
  Washington, DC: Headquarters, Department of the
  Army, 1985.
Poyer, David. *The Med.* New York: St. Martin's
  Press, 1988.

—**BEDDOWN** is the provision of expedient facilities to meet the wartime needs of in-place and deployment forces.

References
Department of Defense, U.S. Army. *Support
  Operations: Echelons Above Corps.* Field Manual
  FM 100-16. Washington, DC: Headquarters,
  Department of the Army, 1986.

—**BEEHIVE** round is filled with many flechettes. A mechanical time fuze is added, which allows for effective target engagement to the maximum direct fire range of the gun.

References
Department of Defense, U.S. Army. *Dictionary of
  United States Army Terms.* Army Regulation AR
  310-25. Washington, DC: Headquarters, Department of the Army, 1986.

—**BEGINNING MORNING CIVIL TWILIGHT** is the instant that the center of the sun is six degrees below the horizon.

References
Department of Defense, U.S. Army. *Weather
  Support for Army Tactical Operations.* Field
  Manual FM 34-81. Washington, DC: Headquarters,
  Department of the Army, 1984.

—**BEGINNING MORNING NAUTICAL TWILIGHT (BMNT)** begins when the sun is twelve degrees below the horizon. It is the *start* of the period when, in good conditions and in the absence of other illumination, enough light is available to identify the general outlines of ground objects, conduct limited military operations, and engage in most types of ground movement without difficulty.

References
Department of Defense, U.S. Army. *Operational
  Terms and Symbols.* Field Manual FM 101-5-1.
  Washington, DC: Headquarters, Department of the
  Army, 1985.
————. *Weather Support for Army Tactical
  Operations.* Field Manual FM 34-81. Washington,
  DC: Headquarters, Department of the Army, 1984.

—**BELEAGUERED** is an organized element surrounded by a hostile force that prevents its members from escaping. *See also:* Besieged.

References
Department of Defense, U.S. Army. *Dictionary of
  United States Army Terms.* Army Regulation AR
  310-25. Washington, DC: Headquarters, Department of the Army, 1986.

—**BELOW THE ZONE** is a promotion eligibility category of the zone of commissioned or warrant officers who are being considered for promotion. Those below the zone have dates of rank that are junior to officers in the promotion zone. These are exceptional officers who are often called "front-runners." *See also:* Above the Zone.

References

Department of Defense, U.S. Army. *Promotion of Officers on Active Duty.* Army Regulation AR 624-100. Washington, DC: Headquarters, Department of the Army, 1984.

—**BELT DEFENSE** is a specialized application of area air defense where air defense artillery resources are deployed in a linear configuration to provide for early attrition of the enemy as it attempts to penetrate to rear areas.

References

Department of Defense, U.S. Army. *U.S. Army Air Defense Artillery Employment.* Field Manual FM 44-1. Washington, DC: Headquarters, Department of the Army, 1983.

—**BENCH STOCK SUPPLY.** Bench stock items are low-cost, consumable repair parts and supplies used at an unpredictable rate by maintenance shop repair personnel.

References

Department of Defense, U.S. Army. *Repair Parts Supply for a Theater of Operations.* Field Manual FM 29-19. Washington, DC: Headquarters, Department of the Army, 1985.

—**BESIEGED** is an organized element surrounded by a hostile force for the purpose of compelling it to surrender. *See also:* Beleaguered.

References

Department of Defense, U.S. Army. *Dictionary of United States Army Terms.* Army Regulation AR 310-25. Washington, DC: Headquarters, Department of the Army, 1986.

—**BETA PARTICLE** is a form of radiation referred to in skin burns as beta burns or beta. These particles have a range of approximately ten to fifteen meters in still air. Beta particles are emitted from the nucleus of an atom with a mass and charge equal in magnitude to that of an electron. The primary hazard from this radiation is through prolonged contact with the skin, resulting in beta burns. *See also:* Nuclear Warfare.

References

Department of Defense, U.S. Army. *NBC Operations.* Field Manual FM 3-100. Washington, DC: Headquarters, Department of the Army, 1985.

—**BIASES** cause errors when the tank gun is fired. Usually small, these errors have little effect on hit probability when firing at ranges within 1,200 meters, but become more significant as ranges to targets increase. Some biases can be compensated for the gunner by the tank fire control system. Biases include drift, cant, parallax, wind sensitivity, and droop and thermal bending.

References

Department of Defense, U.S. Army. *Tank Gunnery.* Field Manual FM 17-2-C2. Washington, DC: Headquarters, Department of the Army, 1980.

—**BILLET.** (1) A billet is a job. It is the way the federal government defines its workload and determines the number of people required. The justification of a billet is made in terms of man-hours and the responsibilities assigned. When a billet is approved, a person can be hired to do the job. (2) A billet is a shelter for troops. (3) To billet is to quarter troops. (4) A billet is a personnel position or assignment that may be filled by one person.

References

Department of Defense, Joint Chiefs of Staff. *Department of Defense Dictionary of Military and Related Terms.* Washington, DC: GPO, 1986.

—**BINARY CHEMICAL MUNITIONS.** National defense dictates that the United States reestablish a credible retaliatory chemical warfare capability. This policy is based upon the belief that such a capability is the most effective deterrent to the first use of chemicals by a potential enemy. The Army's current stockpile of conventional chemical munitions is very old, deteriorating, and becoming obsolete. The binary munition is a means of modernizing this stockpile in a manner that is both technologically feasible and environmentally acceptable. The binary concept is the basis for a process by which a lethal chemical agent is formed from nonlethal components by means of a chemical reaction during the flight of the weapon to a target. Significant advantages over current conventional chemical munitions are achieved in safety, security, surveillance, transportation, production, storage, handling, and final disposal. *See also:* Chemical Warfare.

—BIOLOGICAL AGENT is a microorganism that causes disease in humans, plants, or animals, or causes a deterioration of materiel. *See also:* Biological Operation, Biological Weapon.

References
Department of Defense, Joint Chiefs of Staff. *Department of Defense Dictionary of Military and Related Terms.* Washington, DC: GPO, 1986.

U.S. Congress. Senate. *Final Report of the Senate Select Committee to Study Government Operations With Respect to Intelligence Activities. Report 94-755. Book I, Foreign and Military Intelligence* (Church Committee Report). Washington, DC: GPO, 1976.

—BIOLOGICAL AMMUNITION is a type of ammunition, the filler of which is primarily a biological agent. *See also:* Biological Agent.

References
Department of Defense, Joint Chiefs of Staff. *Department of Defense Dictionary of Military and Related Terms.* Washington, DC: GPO, 1986.

—BIOLOGICAL DEFENSE includes the methods, plans, and procedures that are involved in establishing and executing defensive measures against an attack in which biological agents are used. *See also:* Biological Warfare.

References
Department of Defense, Joint Chiefs of Staff. *Department of Defense Dictionary of Military and Related Terms.* Washington, DC: GPO, 1986.

—BIOLOGICAL OPERATIONS are (1) the employment of biological agents to kill or injure humans or animals and to damage plants or materiel, or (2) a defense against such an attack. *See also:* Biological Agent, Biological Warfare, Biological Weapon.

References
Department of Defense, Joint Chiefs of Staff. *Department of Defense Dictionary of Military and Related Terms.* Washington, DC: GPO, 1986.

U.S. Congress. Senate. *Final Report of the Senate Select Committee to Study Government Operations With Respect to Intelligence Activities. Report 94-755. Book I, Foreign and Military Intelligence* (Church Committee Report). Washington, DC: GPO, 1976.

—BIOLOGICAL WARFARE is (1) the intentional use of organisms, toxic biological products, or plant growth regulators to kill or injure humans, animals, or plants, or (2) a defense against such action.

References
Department of Defense, Joint Chiefs of Staff. *Department of Defense Dictionary of Military and Related Terms.* Washington, DC: GPO, 1986.

U.S. Congress. Senate. *Final Report of the Senate Select Committee to Study Government Operations With Respect to Intelligence Activities. Report 94-755. Book I, Foreign and Military Intelligence* (Church Committee Report). Washington, DC: GPO, 1976.

—BIOLOGICAL WEAPON is a materiel that projects, disperses, or disseminates a biological agent, including anthropod vectors. *See also:* Biological Agent, Biological Operations, Biological Warfare.

References
Department of Defense, Joint Chiefs of Staff. *Department of Defense Dictionary of Military and Related Terms.* Washington, DC: GPO, 1986.

U.S. Congress. Senate. *Final Report of the Senate Select Committee to Study Government Operations With Respect to Intelligence Activities. Report 94-755. Book I, Foreign and Military Intelligence* (Church Committee Report). Washington, DC: GPO, 1976.

—BLACK, GRAY, AND WHITE LISTS, prepared at every level of command, identify persons who have been selected as counterintelligence targets. Each list represents a different category of people who are wanted for counterintelligence purposes. The categories range from people identified as hostile to the United States to those who seem to be favorably inclined to the United States. *See also:* Black Lists, Gray Lists, White Lists.

References
Department of Defense, U.S. Army. *Counterintelligence.* Field Manual FM 34-60. Washington, DC: Headquarters, Department of the Army, 1985.

—BLACK HAWK is the first utility helicopter that adds to the Army's division-level mobility; for example, it can reposition a 105-mm howitzer, its crew of six, and up to 30 rounds of ammunition in a single lift. Its critical components and systems are armored or redundant to enable it to withstand multiple small-arms hits, and its airframe is designed to progressively deform on impact to protect the crew in a crash. The use of advanced technology in the Black Hawk systems makes it the easiest helicopter to maintain in the field. Black Hawk is replacing the UH-1 "Huey" in air assault, air cavalry, and aeromedical evacuation missions. The UH-60A, Black Hawk, can carry more than twice the UH-1 payload and is capable of transporting an entire eleven-man, fully equipped squad faster than the Huey and in most weather conditions.

References

Department of Defense, U.S. Army. *Dictionary of United States Army Terms.* Army Regulation AR 310-25. Washington, DC: Headquarters, Department of the Army, 1986.

—**BLACK LISTS** are developed or compiled at all echelons and contain the identities and locations of individuals whose capture and detention are of prime importance to the U.S. Army. Black lists include the following:

- Known or suspected enemy or hostile espionage agents, saboteurs, political figures, and subversive individuals;
- Known or suspected leaders and members of hostile paramilitary, partisan, or guerilla groups;
- Political leaders known or suspected to be hostile to U.S. military and political objectives and/or to those of an allied nation;
- Known or suspected officials of enemy governments whose presence in the theater of operations poses a security threat to U.S. forces;
- Known or suspected enemy collaborators and sympathizers whose presence in the theater of operations poses a security threat to U.S. forces;
- Known enemy military or civilian personnel who have engaged in intelligence, counterintelligence, security, police, or political indoctrination activities among troops and civilians; and
- Other personalities indicated by the G2 as automatic arrestees (included in this category may be local political personalities, police chiefs, and heads of significant municipal and/or national departments or agencies).

See also: Gray Lists, White Lists.

References

Department of Defense, U.S. Army. *Counterintelligence.* Field Manual FM 34-60. Washington, DC: Headquarters, Department of the Army, 1985.

—**BLANKET** (SMOKE) is a dense, horizontal development of smoke. It is a heavy concentration used primarily over friendly areas to screen them from enemy ground and aerial observation. A smoke blanket may restrict movement and activity within the screen, thus hampering the operations of friendly troops. Smoke blankets are produced by smoke generators. *See also:* Smoke Screen.

References

Department of Defense, U.S. Army. *NBC Operations.* Field Manual FM 3-100. Washington, DC: Headquarters, Department of the Army, 1985.

—**BLAST** is the brief and rapid movement of air, vapor, or fluid away from a center of outward pressure (e.g., as in an explosion or in the combustion of rocket fuel, or the pressure accompanying this movement). This term is commonly used for "explosion," although the two terms may be distinguished. *See also:* Blast Impulse, Blast Line, Blast Overpressure, Blast Wave.

References

Department of Defense, Joint Chiefs of Staff. *Department of Defense Dictionary of Military and Related Terms.* Washington, DC: GPO, 1986.

—**BLAST EFFECT** is the destruction of or damage to structures and personnel by the force of an explosion on or above the surface of the ground. Blast effect may be contrasted with the cratering and ground-shock effects of a projectile or charge that goes off beneath the surface.

References

Department of Defense, Joint Chiefs of Staff. *Department of Defense Dictionary of Military and Related Terms.* Washington, DC: GPO, 1986.

—**BLAST IMPULSE** is the result of the overpressure from a blast wave of an explosion and the time during which it acts at a given point.

References

Department of Defense, U.S. Army. *Ammunition and Explosives Safety Standards.* Army Regulation AR 385-64. Washington, DC: Headquarters, Department of the Army, 1987.

—**BLAST LINE** is a horizontal radial line on the surface of the earth originating at ground zero on which measurements of blast from an explosion are taken.

References

Department of Defense, Joint Chiefs of Staff. *Department of Defense Dictionary of Military and Related Terms.* Washington, DC: GPO, 1986.

—**BLAST OVERPRESSURE** is the pressure over the normal pressure that is manifested in the shock wave of an explosion.

References

Department of Defense, U.S. Army. *Ammunition and Explosives Safety Standards*. Army Regulation AR 385-64. Washington, DC: Headquarters, Department of the Army, 1987.

—**BLAST WAVE** is a sharply defined wave of increased pressure that is rapidly propagated through a surrounding medium from a center of detonation or similar disturbance.

References

Department of Defense, Joint Chiefs of Staff. *Department of Defense Dictionary of Military and Related Terms*. Washington, DC: GPO, 1986.

—**BLISTER AGENT** is a chemical agent that injures the eyes and lungs, and burns or blisters the skin. It is also called a vesicant agent. *See also:* Blood Agent, Chemical Agent, Choking Agent, Nerve Agent, Vomiting Agent.

References

Department of Defense, Joint Chiefs of Staff. *Department of Defense Dictionary of Military and Related Terms*. Washington, DC: GPO, 1986.

—**BLOCK** is a mission assigned to a unit that requires it to deny the enemy access to a given area or to prevent enemy advance in a given direction. It may be for a specified time. Units assigned this mission may have to retain terrain and accept decisive engagement. *See also:* Contain, Fix.

References

Department of Defense, U.S. Army. *Operational Terms and Symbols*. Field Manual FM 101-5-1. Washington, DC: Headquarters, Department of the Army, 1985.

—**BLOCKED ROUTE** is a route that has become temporarily impassable because of material obstruction.

References

Department of Defense, U.S. Army. *Route Reconnaissance and Classification*. Field Manual FM 5-36. Washington, DC: Headquarters, Department of the Army, 1985.

—**BLOCKING POSITION** is a defensive position so sighted as to deny the enemy access to a given area or to prevent its advance in a given direction.

References

Department of Defense, U.S. Army. *Operational Terms and Symbols*. Field Manual FM 101-5-1. Washington, DC: Headquarters, Department of the Army, 1985.

—**BLOOD AGENT** is a chemical compound, including the cyanide group, that affects bodily functions by preventing the normal transfer of oxygen from the blood to body tissues. It is also called a cyanogen agent. *See also:* Blister Agent.

References

Department of Defense, U.S. Army. *Operational Terms and Symbols*. Field Manual FM 101-5-1. Washington, DC: Headquarters, Department of the Army, 1985.

—**BLOWBACK.** (1) Blowback is escape, to the rear and under pressure, of gases that were formed during the firing of a weapon. It may be caused by a defective breech mechanism, a ruptured cartridge case, or a faulty primer. (2) Blowback is a type of weapon operation in which the force of expanding gases acting to the rear against the face of the bolt furnishes all the energy required to initiate the complete cycle of operation. A weapon using this method of operation is characterized by the absence of any breech-lock or bolt-lock mechanism.

References

Department of Defense, Joint Chiefs of Staff. *Department of Defense Dictionary of Military and Related Terms*. Washington, DC: GPO, 1986.

—**BLUE BARK** is a term used to designate a report concerning the movement and treatment to be given family members of deceased military members and civilian employees of the Department of Defense when travel to or from the United States and between overseas areas is sponsored by a military department.

References

Department of Defense, U.S. Army. *Dictionary of United States Army Terms*. Army Regulation AR 310-25. Washington, DC: Headquarters, Department of the Army, 1986.

—**BLUE BELL** is a term used to designate a report concerning an incident involving suspected criminal conduct, wrongdoing, or mismanagement that may result in damaging public confidence in the Army.

References

Department of Defense, U.S. Army. *Dictionary of United States Army Terms.* Army Regulation AR 310-25. Washington, DC: Headquarters, Department of the Army, 1986.

—**BLUE COMMANDER** is the officer who has been designated to exercise operational control over blue forces during a specific period of an exercise. *See also:* Orange Commander.

References

Department of Defense, Joint Chiefs of Staff. *Department of Defense Dictionary of Military and Related Terms.* Washington, DC: GPO, 1986.

—**BLUE FORCES** are forces used in a friendly role during NATO exercises. *See also:* Orange Forces.

References

Department of Defense, Joint Chiefs of Staff. *Department of Defense Dictionary of Military and Related Terms.* Washington, DC: GPO, 1986.

—**BOARD** is a body of persons, military, civilian, or both, appointed to act as a fact-finding agency or as an advisory body to the appointing authority. A board may be authorized to recommend or to take final action on matters placed before it.

References

Department of Defense, U.S. Army. *Dictionary of United States Army Terms.* Army Regulation AR 310-25. Washington, DC: Headquarters, Department of the Army, 1986.

—**BOARD OF SURVEY** are officers appointed to investigate the circumstances of the loss or damage to, or destruction of, property and generally to fix the responsibility for the loss, damage, or destruction, and to take other action as required by law or regulations.

References

Department of Defense, U.S. Army. *Dictionary of United States Army Terms.* Army Regulation AR 310-25. Washington, DC: Headquarters, Department of the Army, 1986.

—**BOGEY** (ARMY AVIATION) is an aircraft that has been detected but not identified. *See also:* Bandit.

References

Department of Defense, U.S. Army. *Air-to-Air Combat.* Field Manual FM 1-107. Washington, DC: Headquarters, Department of the Army, 1984.

—**BOGEY DOPE** (ARMY AVIATION) is a request for information about an airborne target.

References

Department of Defense, U.S. Army. *Air-to-Air Combat.* Field Manual FM 1-107. Washington, DC: Headquarters, Department of the Army, 1984.

—**BOMB RELEASE LINE (BRL)** is an imaginary line around a defended area or objective over which an aircraft should release its bomb in order to obtain a hit or hits on an area or objective.

References

Department of Defense, U.S. Army. *Air Defense Artillery Deployment: Chaparral/Vulcan/Stinger.* Field Manual FM 44-3. Washington, DC: Headquarters, Department of the Army, 1984.

—**BOOBY TRAP.** (1) A booby trap is a device designed to kill or maim an unsuspecting person who disturbs an apparently harmless object or performs a normally safe act. (2) A booby trap is an explosive or nonexplosive device or other material deliberately placed to cause casualties when an apparently harmless object is disturbed or a normally safe act is performed.

References

Department of Defense, Joint Chiefs of Staff. *Department of Defense Dictionary of Military and Related Terms.* Washington, DC: GPO, 1986.

Department of Defense, U.S. Army. *Mine/Countermine Operations at the Company Level.* Field Manual FM 20-32. Washington, DC: Headquarters, Department of the Army, 1976.

————. *Operational Terms and Symbols.* Field Manual FM 101-5-1. Washington, DC: Headquarters, Department of the Army, 1985.

—**BORDER OPERATIONS** are designed to deny infiltration or exfiltration of insurgent personnel and materiel across international boundaries.

References

Department of Defense, U.S. Army. *Low Intensity Conflict.* Field Manual FM 100-20. Washington, DC: Headquarters, Department of the Army, 1981.

—**BORESIGHTING.** Boresighting establishes a convergent relationship between the axis of the tube or barrel of a weapon and the direct firesights. Boresighting is the basis for all sight adjustments. It is vital to accurate gunnery that the main gun be boresighted accurately and often. When the main gun has been properly boresighted, the extended axis of the tube and the lines of sight of the direct-fire sights will intercept at the boresight range (normally 1,200 meters). The relationship between the tube and the sights changes as the tube reacts to temperature changes.

References

Department of Defense, U.S. Army. *Air Cavalry Combat Brigade*. Field Manual FM 17-47. Washington, DC: Headquarters, Department of the Army, 1982.

—**BORROWED MILITARY MANPOWER** involves using manpower from a table of organization and equipment unit to perform duties within a table of distribution and analysis activity where a major-command-approved manpower requirement exists for which no manpower space has been authorized, or where manpower spaces have been authorized but the positions are vacant.

References

Department of Defense, U.S. Army. *Dictionary of United States Army Terms*. Army Regulation AR 310-25. Washington, DC: Headquarters, Department of the Army, 1986.

————. *Enlisted Personnel Management System*. Army Regulation AR 600-200. Washington, DC: Headquarters, Department of the Army, 1984.

—**BOUND.** (1) Bound is a single movement, usually from one covered and concealed position to another, by dismounted troops or combat vehicles. (2) Bound is the distance covered in one movement by a unit that is advancing in bounds. *See also:* Bounding Overwatch, Leapfrog.

References

Department of Defense, U.S. Army. *Operational Terms and Symbols*. Field Manual FM 101-5-1. Washington, DC: Headquarters, Department of the Army, 1985.

—**BOUNDARIES** mark sectors of responsibility. However, commanders must not allow boundaries to prevent fires on an enemy force simply because the enemy is on the other side of a boundary. *See also:* Boundary.

References

Department of Defense, U.S. Army. *Armored and Mechanized Division Operations*. Field Manual FM 71-100. Washington, DC: Headquarters, Department of the Army, 1978.

—**BOUNDARY** is a control measure normally drawn along identifiable terrain features and used to delineate areas of tactical responsibility for subordinate units. Within their boundaries, units may maneuver within the overall plan without close coordination with neighboring units unless they are otherwise restricted. Direct fire may be placed across boundaries on clearly identified enemy targets without prior coordination, provided that friendly forces are not endangered. Indirect fire also may be used after prior coordination. There are two types of boundaries: *lateral boundaries*, which are used to control combat operations of adjacent units; and *rear boundaries*, which are established to facilitate command and control.

References

Department of Defense, Joint Chiefs of Staff. *Department of Defense Dictionary of Military and Related Terms*. Washington, DC: GPO, 1986.

Department of Defense, U.S. Army. *Operational Terms and Symbols*. Field Manual FM 101-5-1. Washington, DC: Headquarters, Department of the Army, 1985.

—**BOUNDING MINE** is a type of antipersonnel mine, usually buried just below the surface of the ground. It has a small charge that throws the case up in the air; this explodes at a height of three or four feet, throwing shrapnel or fragments in all directions. *See also:* Mine Warfare.

References

Department of Defense, U.S. Army. *Dictionary of United States Army Terms*. Army Regulation AR 310-25. Washington, DC: Headquarters, Department of the Army, 1986.

—**BOUNDING OVERWATCH** is a movement technique used when contact with enemy forces is expected. The unit moves by bounds. One element is always halted to watch over another element while it moves. The overwatching element is positioned to support the moving unit by fire or fire and movement. *See also:* Bound.

References

Department of Defense, U.S. Army. *Operational Terms and Symbols*. Field Manual FM 101-5-1. Washington, DC: Headquarters, Department of the Army, 1985.

—**BRACKET.** (1) A bracket is the distance between two strikes or series of strikes, one of which is over the target and the other short of it, or one of which is to the right and the other to the left of the target. (2) Bracket means to deliver fire that places a bracket on the target. *See also:* Bracketing, Bracketing Elevation, Bracketing Method.

References

Department of Defense, U.S. Army. *Dictionary of United States Army Terms.* Army Regulation AR 310-25. Washington, DC: Headquarters, Department of the Army, 1986.

—**BRACKETING** is a method of adjusting fire in which a bracket is established by obtaining an over and a short along the firing line, and then successively splitting the bracket in half until a target hit or desired bracket is obtained.

References

Department of Defense, Joint Chiefs of Staff. *Department of Defense Dictionary of Military and Related Terms.* Washington, DC: GPO, 1986.

—**BRACKETING ELEVATION** is an elevation that gives both overs and shorts.

References

Department of Defense, U.S. Army. *Dictionary of United States Army Terms.* Army Regulation AR 310-25. Washington, DC: Headquarters, Department of the Army, 1986.

—**BRACKETING METHOD** is a method of adjusting artillery and mortar fire in which a bracket is established by obtaining an over and a short, with respect to the observer, then successfully splitting the bracket in half until a target hit is obtained or the smallest practicable range change has been made.

References

Department of Defense, U.S. Army. *Dictionary of United States Army Terms.* Army Regulation AR 310-25. Washington, DC: Headquarters, Department of the Army, 1986.

—**BRACKETING SALVO** is a group of shots in which the number of shots going over the target equals the number falling short of it. A bracketing salvo is also called bracketing volley.

References

Department of Defense, U.S. Army. *Dictionary of United States Army Terms.* Army Regulation AR 310-25. Washington, DC: Headquarters, Department of the Army, 1986.

—**BRADLEY FIGHTING VEHICLE SYSTEMS (BFVS), INFANTRY FIGHTING VEHICLE (IFV), AND CAVALRY FIGHTING VEHICLE (CFV)** provide the mechanized infantry with a full-track,

lightly armored fighting vehicle and the scout and armored cavalry units with a vehicle for their screening, reconnaissance, and security missions. Both IFV and CFV have a two-man turret that mounts the 25-mm automatic stabilized cannon, its primary armament, supported by the tube-launched, optically tracked, wire-guided antitank-guided missile system, and the 7.62-mm coaxial machinegun. The IFV has, in addition, six 5.56-mm firing port weapons positioned along the side and rear of the vehicle. The overall mobility of the vehicle is comparable to that of the M1 tank. The IFV carries a nine-man squad—commander, gunner, driver, and six squad members.

References

Department of Defense, U.S. Army. *Dictionary of United States Army Terms.* Army Regulation AR 310-25. Washington, DC: Headquarters, Department of the Army, 1986.

—**BRANCH.** (1) A branch is a subdivision of any organization. (2) A branch is a geographically separate unit of an activity that performs all or part of the primary functions of the parent activity on a smaller scale. Unlike an annex, a branch is not merely an overflow addition. (3) A branch is a grouping of officers that composes an arm or service of the Army in which an officer is commissioned or transferred, trained, developed, and promoted. All officers hold a single branch designation and may serve repetitive and progressive assignments associated with the branch. The branches of the Army are Adjutant General, Air Defense Artillery, Armor, Aviation, Civil Affairs (Reserve components only), Chemical, Engineer, Finance, Field Artillery, Infantry, Military Intelligence, Military Police, Ordnance, Quartermaster, Signal, and Transportation. *See also:* Basic Branch.

References

Department of Defense, Joint Chiefs of Staff. *Department of Defense Dictionary of Military and Related Terms.* Washington, DC: GPO, 1986.

Department of Defense, U.S. Army. *Officer Assignment Policies, Details, and Transfers.* Army Regulation AR 614-100. Washington, DC: Headquarters, Department of the Army, 1984.

—**BRANCH DETAIL** is a temporary assignment outside of one's branch to another branch for control and duty. The person's military status and branch are not changed as a result of this detail or assignment.

References

Department of Defense, U.S. Army. *Officer Assignment Policies, Details, and Transfers.* Army Regulation AR 614-100. Washington, DC: Headquarters, Department of the Army, 1984.

—**BRANCH IMMATERIAL POSITION** is a duty position that is not identified or limited to one specific branch of the Army, but indicates that any commissioned officer can fill the position.

References

Department of Defense, U.S. Army. *Dictionary of United States Army Terms.* Army Regulation AR 310-25. Washington, DC: Headquarters, Department of the Army, 1986.

————. *Officer Assignment Policies, Details, and Transfers.* Army Regulation AR 614-100. Washington, DC: Headquarters, Department of the Army, 1984.

—**BRANCH MANUAL** is a military occupational specialty manual that has been developed for officers who are being trained at the lieutenant or captain level.

References

Department of Defense, U.S. Army. *Individual Military Education and Training.* Army Regulation AR 350-1. Washington, DC: Headquarters, Department of the Army, 1987.

—**BRANCH MATERIAL** is used to describe any position, duty, or detail that requires an officer who has been qualified in a specific branch. *See also:* Branch Immaterial Position, Branch Material Position.

References

Department of Defense, U.S. Army. *Officer Assignment Policies, Details, and Transfers.* Army Regulation AR 614-100. Washington, DC: Headquarters, Department of the Army, 1984.

—**BRANCH MATERIAL POSITION** is a duty position identified with a particular branch of the Army in that the duties prescribed for the position require training and/or experience identified with the specific branch. *See also:* Branch Immaterial Position, Branch-Qualified Officer.

References

Department of Defense, U.S. Army. *Dictionary of United States Army Terms.* Army Regulation AR 310-25. Washington, DC: Headquarters, Department of the Army, 1986.

—**BRANCHES TO THE CAMPAIGN PLAN.** Good campaign plans provide for the operation underway and for the period following the coming battle. "Branches" to the plan—options for changing dispositions, orientation, or direction of movement and accepting or declining battle—preserve the commander's freedom to act. Such provisions for flexibility anticipate the enemy's likely actions and give the commander a means of dealing with them quickly. Expressed as contingency plans, such branches from the plan can be of decisive importance, since they shorten the friendly decision cycle and may allow the large unit commander to act faster than his opponent.

References

Department of Defense, U.S. Army. *Operations.* Field Manual FM 100-5. Washington, DC: Headquarters, Department of the Army, 1986.

—**BRANCH-QUALIFIED OFFICER** is an officer who must possess the following attributes or experience: (1) be technically qualified for a variety, but not necessarily all, the assignments in his branch; (2) be physically qualified to meet the demands of many, but not all, assignments normally expected of officers of his grade and branch; (3) have demonstrated either the ability or potential ability to command at an echelon appropriate with his present grade, with the indicated ability to command at the next higher echelon (if a specialist, have demonstrated his ability or potential to perform at the next higher echelon); (4) possess an ability to work for and/or with others; (5) evidence a desire for or have exhibited self-improvement; (6) have the ability to lead; and (7) have successfully completed or have sufficient branch assignments to receive equivalent credit for branch schools commensurate with grade and years of service. *See also:* Branch Immaterial Position, Branch Material Position.

References

Department of Defense, U.S. Army. *Dictionary of United States Army Terms.* Army Regulation AR 310-25. Washington, DC: Headquarters, Department of the Army, 1986.

—**BREACH** is the use of any means available to break through or secure a passage through an enemy defense, obstacle, minefield, or fortification. *See also:* Breaching.

References

Department of Defense, U.S. Army. *Operational Terms and Symbols*. Field Manual FM 101-5-1. Washington, DC: Headquarters, Department of the Army, 1985.

—**BREACHING** is the use of any available means to secure passage through an enemy minefield or fortification. The two methods of breaching are assault and deliberate. *See also:* Mine Warfare.

References

Department of Defense, Joint Chiefs of Staff. *Department of Defense Dictionary of Military and Related Terms*. Washington, DC: GPO, 1986.

—**BREACHING FORCE.** During an attack of an enemy-fortified position or strongpoint, the breaching forces are elements charged with breaching obstacles along an avenue of approach. Breaching forces clear enemy trenches, bunkers, and foxholes and create and hold open a breach in the enemy positions. *See also:* Assault Force.

References

Department of Defense, U.S. Army. *Operational Terms and Symbols*. Field Manual FM 101-5-1. Washington, DC: Headquarters, Department of the Army, 1985.

—**BREAK BULK POINT** is a transshipping activity to which multiple shipment units may be consigned for further distribution within the transportation system.

References

Department of Defense, U.S. Army. *Dictionary of United States Army Terms*. Army Regulation AR 310-25. Washington, DC: Headquarters, Department of the Army, 1986.

—**BREAK TURN** (ARMY AVIATION) is an immediate action, an emergency maneuver used when an enemy aircraft has successfully penetrated the section's lookout and is within firing range before being detected.

References

Department of Defense, U.S. Army. *Air-to-Air Combat*. Field Manual FM 1-107. Washington, DC: Headquarters, Department of the Army, 1984.

—**BREAKAWAY.** (1) Breakaway occurs when the shock front moves away from the exterior of the expanding fireball produced by the explosion of a nuclear weapon. (2) After the completion of an attack, breakaway means to turn to a heading as directed. *See also:* Nuclear Warfare.

References

Department of Defense, Joint Chiefs of Staff. *Department of Defense Dictionary of Military and Related Terms*. Washington, DC: GPO, 1986.

Department of Defense, U.S. Army. *Operational Terms and Symbols*. Field Manual FM 101-5-1. Washington, DC: Headquarters, Department of the Army, 1985.

—**BREAKOUT** is an offensive operation conducted by an encircled force. A breakout normally consists of an attack by a penetration force to open a gap through the enemy for the remainder of the force to pass.

References

Department of Defense, U.S. Army. *Operational Terms and Symbols*. Field Manual FM 101-5-1. Washington, DC: Headquarters, Department of the Army, 1985.

—**BREAKTHROUGH** is a rupturing of the enemy's forward defenses that occurs as a result of a penetration. A breakthrough permits the passage of an exploitation force.

References

Department of Defense, U.S. Army. *Operational Terms and Symbols*. Field Manual FM 101-5-1. Washington, DC: Headquarters, Department of the Army, 1985.

—**BREASTWORK** is earthwork that gives protection for defenders in a standing position, firing over the crest. Breastworks are constructed wholly or partly above the surface of the ground.

References

Department of Defense, U.S. Army. *Dictionary of United States Army Terms*. Army Regulation AR 310-25. Washington, DC: Headquarters, Department of the Army, 1986.

—**BREECHBLOCK** is a moveable steel block that closes the breech of a cannon.

References

Department of Defense, U.S. Army. *Dictionary of United States Army Terms*. Army Regulation AR 310-25. Washington, DC: Headquarters, Department of the Army, 1986.

—**BREVITY CODE/BREVITY LIST** is a code used solely to shorten the length of a message; it is not used to conceal the message's content. It provides no security to messages.

References

Department of Defense, Joint Chiefs of Staff. *Department of Defense Dictionary of Military and Related Terms.* Washington, DC: GPO, 1986.

Department of Defense, U.S. Army. *Communications Techniques: Electronics Countermeasures.* Field Manual FM 24-33. Washington, DC: Headquarters, Department of the Army, 1985.

—**BRIDGE DEMOLITION SCHEDULE NUMBER** is a code number or target number assigned by higher headquarters.

References

Department of Defense, U.S. Army. *Route Reconnaissance and Classification.* Field Manual FM 5-36. Washington, DC: Headquarters, Department of the Army, 1985.

—**BRIDGEHEAD.** (1) A bridgehead is an area of ground that is held or is to be gained on the enemy's side of an obstacle. (2) In river crossing operations, a bridgehead is an area on the enemy's side of the water obstacle large enough to accommodate the majority of the crossing force, has adequate terrain to permit the defense of the crossing sites, and provides a base for continuing the attack. At a minimum, ground must be secured that eliminates direct and observed indirect fires on the crossing sites. *See also:* Airhead, Beachhead, Bridgehead Line.

References

Department of Defense, U.S. Army. *Operational Terms and Symbols.* Field Manual FM 101-5-1. Washington, DC: Headquarters, Department of the Army, 1985.

—**BRIDGEHEAD LINE,** in offensive river crossing operations, is the limit of the objective area when developing a bridgehead.

References

Department of Defense, U.S. Army. *Operational Terms and Symbols.* Field Manual FM 101-5-1. Washington, DC: Headquarters, Department of the Army, 1985.

—**BRIEFING.** (1) A briefing is a lecture that informs an individual or individuals about the particulars concerning an event. (2) A briefing is a planned lecture that is delivered at scheduled intervals in order to inform an individual or individuals of the relevant events that have occurred since the last briefing. (3) Briefings are a means of presenting information to commanders, staffs, or other designated audiences. The techniques employed are determined by the purpose of the briefing, the desired response, and the role of the briefer. There are four types of military briefings: information, decision, mission, and staff briefings.

References

Department of Defense, U.S. Army. *Operations.* Field Manual FM 100-5. Washington, DC: Headquarters, Department of the Army, 1986.

—**BRIGADE ASSESSMENT AND RECOVERY PERSONNEL (BARP)** are personnel necessary for unit reconstruction. They come from staff and technical personnel who are assigned to the forward area support team.

References

Department of Defense, U.S. Army. *Combat Service Support Operations-Division.* Field Manual FM 63-2. Washington, DC: Headquarters, Department of the Army, 1983.

—**BRIGADE LANDING TEAM** is an assault landing team. It is a balanced task organization composed of a brigade headquarters, two or more battalion-level combat units, and the reinforcing combat and service elements required for combat and interim logistical support during the period it conducts independent tactical operations.

References

Department of Defense, U.S. Army. *Dictionary of United States Army Terms.* Army Regulation AR 310-25. Washington, DC: Headquarters, Department of the Army, 1986.

———. *Infantry, Airborne, and Air Assault Brigade Operations.* Field Manual FM 7-30. Washington, DC: Headquarters, Department of the Army, 1981.

—**BRIGADE SUPPORT AREA (BSA)** is the portion of the brigade occupied by the brigade trains. A designated area in which combat service support elements from division support command and corps support command provide logistic support to a brigade. The BSA normally is located from 20 to 25 kilometers behind the forward edge of the battle area.

References

Department of Defense, U.S. Army. *Combat Service Support Operations-Division.* Field Manual FM 63-2. Washington, DC: Headquarters, Department of the Army, 1983.

———. *Infantry, Airborne, and Air Assault Brigade Operations.* Field Manual FM 7-30. Washington, DC: Headquarters, Department of the Army, 1981.

———. *Operational Terms and Symbols.* Field Manual FM 101-5-1. Washington, DC: Headquarters, Department of the Army, 1985.

—BRIGADE TRAINS are normally made up of forward support units of the division support command and corps support command. Brigade trains are not echeloned into combat and field trains. *See also:* Train.

References

Department of Defense, U.S. Army. *Combat Service Support Operations-Division.* Field Manual FM 63-2. Washington, DC: Headquarters, Department of the Army, 1983.

—BRIGADES are units that control two or more battalions. Their capabilities for self-support and independent action vary considerably with the type of brigade. *See also:* Army, Battalion, Brigades (Maneuver), Brigades (Separate), Company, Corps, Division, Platoon, Regiment, Squad.

References

Department of Defense, U.S. Army. *Infantry, Airborne, and Air Assault Brigade Operations.* Field Manual FM 7-30. Washington, DC: Headquarters, Department of the Army, 1981.

———. *Operations.* Field Manual FM 100-5. Washington, DC: Headquarters, Department of the Army, 1986.

—BRIGADES (MANEUVER) are the major combat units of all types of divisions. They can also be organized as separate units. They can use any combination of maneuver battalions, and they are normally supported by field artillery battalions and aviation units and by smaller combat, combat support, and combat service support units. While separate brigades and armored cavalry regiments have a fixed organization, division commanders establish the organization of their brigades and change their organizations as frequently as necessary.

Brigades combine the efforts of their battalions and companies to fight engagements and to perform major tactical tasks in division battles. Their chief tactical responsibility is synchronizing the plans and actions of their subordinate units to accomplish a single task for the division or corps.

References

Department of Defense, U.S. Army. *Infantry, Airborne, and Air Assault Brigade Operations.* Field Manual FM 7-30. Washington, DC: Headquarters, Department of the Army, 1981.

———. *Operations.* Field Manual FM 100-5. Washington, DC: Headquarters, Department of the Army, 1986.

—BRIGADES (SEPARATE) of infantry, armor, air defense artillery, engineer, or aviation, and armored cavalry regiments can be used to reinforce corps or divisions and can be shifted from unit to unit to tailor forces for combat. Separate brigades and regiments are usually employed as units when attached to corps or divisions.

Other combat, combat support, and combat service support brigades and groups are organized to control nondivisional units for corps and larger units. Engineer, air defense artillery, signal, aviation, military police, and transportation brigades are typical of such units. They may also be the building blocks of large unit support structures (e.g., corps and theater army support commands) and of combat support commands (e.g., engineer commands). Divisions are supported by an organic brigade-sized support command of mixed combat service support battalions and companies.

References

Department of Defense, U.S. Army. *Infantry, Airborne, and Air Assault Brigade Operations.* Field Manual FM 7-30. Washington, DC: Headquarters, Department of the Army, 1981.

———. *Low Intensity Conflict.* Field Manual FM 100-20. Washington, DC: Headquarters, Department of the Army, 1981.

—BRUTE FORCE JAMMING is used in electronic warfare to describe jamming or blocking of radio signals with high power, either with a single high-powered transmitter or by cascading large numbers of jammers so that the enemy cannot receive radio signals. *See also:* Jamming.

References

Department of Defense, Joint Chiefs of Staff. *Department of Defense Dictionary of Military and Related Terms.* Washington, DC: GPO, 1986.

—BUDDY SYSTEM is a system that requires two or more persons to work or remain near each other in certain areas and on certain missions so that they can give each other mutual protection and assistance.

References

Department of Defense, U.S. Army. *Dictionary of United States Army Terms.* Army Regulation AR 310-25. Washington, DC: Headquarters, Department of the Army, 1986.

—**BUFFER DISTANCE** (NUCLEAR). (1) The buffer distance is the horizontal distance that, when added to the radius of safety, will give the desired assurance that the specified degree of risk will not be exceeded. It is normally expressed quantitatively in multiples of the delivery error. (2) The buffer distance is the vertical distance that is added to the fallout safe-height of a burst in order to determine the desired height of burst that will provide the desired assurance that militarily significant fallout will not occur. It is normally expressed quantitatively in multiples of the vertical error. *See also:* Nuclear Warfare.

References

Department of Defense, Joint Chiefs of Staff. *Department of Defense Dictionary of Military and Related Terms.* Washington, DC: GPO, 1986.

—**BUILDUP.** (1) Buildup is the process of attaining the prescribed strength of units and prescribed levels of vehicles, equipment, stores, and supplies. (2) Buildup is the means of accomplishing the process.

References

Department of Defense, Joint Chiefs of Staff. *Department of Defense Dictionary of Military and Related Terms.* Washington, DC: GPO, 1986.

—**BUILD-UP PHASE** is the second stage of smoke screen production, when the individual smoke streamers start to merge. *See also:* Smoke Screen.

References

Department of Defense, U.S. Army. *Deliberate Smoke Operations.* Field Manual FM 3-50. Washington, DC: Headquarters, Department of the Army, 1984.

—**BUILT-UP AREA** is a concentration of structures, facilities, and population.

References

Department of Defense, Joint Chiefs of Staff. *Department of Defense Dictionary of Military and Related Terms.* Washington, DC: GPO, 1986.

—**BULK REPLACEMENT STOCKAGE** is a bulk number of personnel authorized to be attached unassigned in the replacement system of an overseas theater and included in the authorized chargeable strength of a theater.

References

Department of Defense, U.S. Army. *Dictionary of United States Army Terms.* Army Regulation AR 310-25. Washington, DC: Headquarters, Department of the Army, 1986.

—**BULK STORAGE.** (1) Bulk storage is storage in a warehouse of supplies and equipment in large quantities, usually in the original containers, as distinguished from bin storage. (2) Bulk storage is storage of liquids (e.g., petroleum products in tanks), as distinguished from drum or packaged storage.

References

Department of Defense, Joint Chiefs of Staff. *Department of Defense Dictionary of Military and Related Terms.* Washington, DC: GPO, 1986.

Department of Defense, U.S. Army. *Operational Terms and Symbols.* Field Manual FM 101-5-1. Washington, DC: Headquarters, Department of the Army, 1985.

—**BULK SUPPLY** is any kind of military supply sent out in very large quantities (e.g., sand, gravel, paint, and gunpowder). Bulk supplies are measured by weight or volume rather than by number of units.

References

Department of Defense, U.S. Army. *Dictionary of United States Army Terms.* Army Regulation AR 310-25. Washington, DC: Headquarters, Department of the Army, 1986.

—**BUNKERS** are large fighting positions constructed for squad-size units that are required to remain in defensive positions for longer periods of time. They are built either above ground or below ground and are usually made of reinforced concrete. Because of the extensive engineering effort required to build bunkers, they are usually made during strongpoint concentration.

References

Department of Defense, U.S. Army. *Survivability.* Field Manual FM 5-103. Washington, DC: Headquarters, Department of the Army, 1985.

—**BURST.** (1) A burst is a series of shots fired by one pressure on the trigger of an automatic weapon. (2) Burst is an explosion of a projectile or bomb in the air or when it strikes the ground or target.

References

Department of Defense, U.S. Army. *Dictionary of United States Army Terms.* Army Regulation AR 310-25. Washington, DC: Headquarters, Department of the Army, 1986.

—**BURST ON TARGET (BOT),** if it can be employed, is the most rapid and accurate method of direct-fire adjustment. It is especially effective when engaging a target from a stationary position or when the firing vehicle is moving directly toward the target. After the gunner has made a precise lay and has fired to apply BOT: the gunner observes through his sight; relays after firing to maintain his correct initial sight picture; concentrates on the target, noting the point of the single rectile where the tracer or burst appears as it passes, strikes short of, or hits the target; announces his range sensing and BOT; using gun controls, immediately moves this point of the rectile, by the most direct route, to the center of the mass of the target; announces "ON THE WAY"; and fires again.

References

Department of Defense, U.S. Army. *Dictionary of United States Army Terms.* Army Regulation AR 310-25. Washington, DC: Headquarters, Department of the Army, 1986.

—**BURST RANGE** is the horizontal distance from the piece to the point of burst.

References

Department of Defense, U.S. Army. *Dictionary of United States Army Terms.* Army Regulation AR 310-25. Washington, DC: Headquarters, Department of the Army, 1986.

—**BUTT.** (1) A butt is a retaining wall at a target range, backed up with earth on the side next to the firing point, with a target pit on the opposite side. In this meaning, it is also called a target butt. (2) A butt is the rear end of the stock of a rifle or other small arm. *See also:* Butt Plate, Butt Stroke.

References

Department of Defense, U.S. Army. *Dictionary of United States Army Terms.* Army Regulation AR 310-25. Washington, DC: Headquarters, Department of the Army, 1986.

—**BUTT PLATE** is a metal or rubber covering of the end of the stock on small arms, particularly rifles.

References

Department of Defense, U.S. Army. *Dictionary of United States Army Terms.* Army Regulation AR 310-25. Washington, DC: Headquarters, Department of the Army, 1986.

—**BUTT STROKE** is a blow with the butt end of a rifle. A butt stroke is used in close combat, especially in bayonet fighting and bayonet drill.

References

Department of Defense, U.S. Army. *Dictionary of United States Army Terms.* Army Regulation AR 310-25. Washington, DC: Headquarters, Department of the Army, 1986.

—**BY THE NUMBERS** is a preparatory command given in close order drill to signify that the movement ordered is to be carried out step by step, at the command of the drill instructor.

References

Department of Defense, U.S. Army. *Dictionary of United States Army Terms.* Army Regulation AR 310-25. Washington, DC: Headquarters, Department of the Army, 1986.

—**BYPASS** is maneuvering around an obstacle, position, or enemy force in order to maintain the momentum of advance. Previously unreported obstacles and bypassed enemy forces are reported to higher headquarters.

References

Department of Defense, U.S. Army. *Operational Terms and Symbols.* Field Manual FM 105-5-1. Washington, DC: Headquarters, Department of the Army, 1985.

—**C-DAY** is the unnamed day on which a deployment operation commences or is to commence. The deployment may be movement of troops, cargo, weapon systems, or a combination of these elements using any or all types of transport. "C" is the only letter used to denote the above, with the highest command or headquarters responsible for coordinating the planning specifying the exact meaning of C-day. The command or headquarters directly responsible for the execution of the operation, if not the one coordinating the planning, does so withing the meaning specified by the highest command or headquarters coordinating the planning. *See also:* D-Day, H-Hour, M-Day, S-Day.

References

Department of Defense, U.S. Army. *Dictionary of United States Army Terms.* Army Regulation AR 310-25. Washington, DC: Headquarters, Department of the Army, 1986.

—**C-12 AIRPLANE** is a low-wing, twin-engine, pressurized cabin, passenger and cargo-carrying utility airplane. It can operate under instrument flight conditions day or night, in high-density air traffic control zones, and in known icing weather conditions. The C-12 contributes to the combat readiness and effectiveness of both active and reserve component units by providing priority transportation of cargo and personnel, intelligence gathering when equipped with special electronic equipment, medical evacuation, and command and control in peace, mobilization, and war.

References

Department of Defense, U.S. Army. *Dictionary of United States Army Terms.* Army Regulation AR 310-25. Washington, DC: Headquarters, Department of the Army, 1986.

—**CH-47 MODERNIZATION.** The CH-47 Chinook is the Army's medium-lift helicopter. Designed in the 1950s and fielded in 1962, its primary missions are movement of ammunition, repair parts, petroleum, and tactical movement of artillery, troops, and special weapons on the battlefield. In 1975, a modernization program was approved to upgrade the CH-47A, B, and C models into a new D model configuration. These improvements extend the usefulness of the fleet beyond the year 2000. They include new fiberglass rotor blades, a transmission and drive system, modularized hydraulics, an electrical system, advanced flight controls, a triple-hook cargo system, and an auxiliary power unit. These features greatly enhance the reliability, productivity, survivability, and safety of this fleet.

References

Department of Defense, U.S. Army. *Dictionary of United States Army Terms.* Army Regulation AR 310-25. Washington, DC: Headquarters, Department of the Army, 1986.

—**CADENCE** is the uniform rhythm in which a movement is executed, or the number of steps or counts per minute at which a movement is executed. Drill movements are normally executed at the cadence of quick time or double time. Quick time is the cadence of 120 counts or steps per minute; double time is the cadence of 180 counts or steps per minute.

References

Department of Defense, U.S. Army. *Drills and Ceremonies.* Field Manual FM 22-5. Washington, DC: Headquarters, Department of the Army, 1986.

—**CALL.** The President has the authority to call all or part of the Army National Guard into the active military service of the United States by unit whenever the country is invaded or is in danger of invasion from a foreign nation, when there is a rebellion or a danger of a rebellion against the authority of the government, or when the President is unable with the active forces at his command to execute the laws of the United States (10 U.S.C. § 3500). Pursuant to title 10, chapter 15 of the United States Code, the President may call the Army National Guard to suppress insurrection, rebellion, or interference with state or federal law.

References

Department of Defense, U.S. Army. *Dictionary of United States Army Terms.* Army Regulation AR 310-25. Washington, DC: Headquarters, Department of the Army, 1986.

—**CALL FIRE** is the fire delivered based upon a specific response to a request from the supported unit. *See also:* Fire.

References
Department of Defense, Joint Chiefs of Staff. *Department of Defense Dictionary of Military and Related Terms.* Washington, DC: GPO, 1986.

—**CALL FOR FIRE** is a request for fire containing the data necessary for obtaining the required fire on a target. *See also:* Call Fire.

References
Department of Defense, Joint Chiefs of Staff. *Department of Defense Dictionary of Military and Related Terms.* Washington, DC: GPO, 1986.

—**CALL OFF** is a command to the members of a unit to call out their titles or numbers in order.

References
Department of Defense, U.S. Army. *Dictionary of United States Army Terms.* Army Regulation AR 310-25. Washington, DC: Headquarters, Department of the Army, 1986.

—**CALL SIGN** is a combination of characters or pronounceable words that identifies a communications facility, command, authority, or unit. It is used primarily to establish and maintain communications. It is often the symbol used to identify a member of a communications net. *See also:* Indefinite Call Sign, Net Call Sign, Tactical Call Sign.

References
Department of Defense, Joint Chiefs of Staff. *Department of Defense Dictionary of Military and Related Terms.* Washington, DC: GPO, 1986.

—**CALL UP** is a set of signals used by a radio station to establish contact with another station.

References
Department of Defense, U.S. Army. *Dictionary of United States Army Terms.* Army Regulation AR 310-25. Washington, DC: Headquarters, Department of the Army, 1986.

—**CAMOUFLAGE** is the use of man-made concealment and disguise to hide troops, material, equipment, and installations in order to minimize the possibility of their detection or identification. It includes taking advantage of the natural environment and the use of natural and artificial materials.

References
Department of Defense, U.S. Army. *Operational Terms and Symbols.* Field Manual FM 101-5-1. Washington, DC: Headquarters, Department of the Army, 1985.

————. *The Rifle Squads (Mechanized) and Light Infantry.* Training Circular TC 7-1. Washington, DC: Headquarters, Department of the Army, 1976.

—**CAMP** is a group of tents, huts, or other shelter set up temporarily for troops and is more permanent than a bivouac. A military post, temporary or permanent, may be called a camp.

References
Department of Defense, Joint Chiefs of Staff. *Department of Defense Dictionary of Military and Related Terms.* Washington, DC: GPO, 1986.

—**CAMPAIGN** is a connected series of military operations that form a distinct phase of a war. It is waged to accomplish a long-range major strategic objective. *See also:* Campaign Plan.

References
Department of Defense, U.S. Army. *Operational Terms and Symbols.* Field Manual FM 101-5-1. Washington, DC: Headquarters, Department of the Army, 1985.

—**CAMPAIGN PLAN** is a plan for a series of related military operations aimed at accomplishing a common objective, normally within a specified time and space.

References
Department of Defense, Joint Chiefs of Staff. *Department of Defense Dictionary of Military and Related Terms.* Washington, DC: GPO, 1986.

Department of Defense, U.S. Army. *Staff Organization and Operations.* Field Manual FM 101-5. Washington, DC: Headquarters, Department of the Army, 1984.

—**CANALIZE** is to restrict operations to a narrow zone by use of existing or reinforcing obstacles or by direct or indirect fires in order to funnel or herd forces to their disadvantage.

References
Department of Defense, U.S. Army. *Dictionary of United States Army Terms.* Army Regulation AR 310-25. Washington, DC: Headquarters, Department of the Army, 1986.

————. *Mine/Countermine Operations at the Company Level.* Field Manual FM 20-32. Washington, DC: Headquarters, Department of the Army, 1976.

————. *Operational Terms and Symbols.* Field Manual FM 101-5-1. Washington, DC: Headquarters, Department of the Army, 1985.

—**CANCEL.** In artillery gunfire support, cancel, when coupled with a previous order other than an order for a quantity or type of ammunition, rescinds that order.

References

Department of Defense, Joint Chiefs of Staff. *Department of Defense Dictionary of Military and Related Terms.* Washington, DC: GPO, 1986.

—**CANNIBALIZATION.** (1) Cannibalization is the authorized removal of parts and assemblies from unserviceable, uneconomically repairable, or disposable items or components. The purpose of a cannibalization is to recover serviceable repair parts from scrap materiel to return them to the supply system. Cannibalization is an important source of supply, particularly when the need for the item is critical and the required delivery date cannot be met through routine supply channels. *See also:* Cannibalization Point, Cannibalize.

References

Department of Defense, U.S. Army. *Operational Terms and Symbols.* Field Manual FM 101-5-1. Washington, DC: Headquarters, Department of the Army, 1985.

———. *Organizational Maintenance Operations.* Field Manual FM 29-2. Washington, DC: Headquarters, Department of the Army, 1984.

———. *Repair Parts Supply for a Theater of Operations.* Field Manual FM 29-19. Washington, DC: Headquarters, Department of the Army, 1985.

—**CANNIBALIZATION POINT** is an area where uneconomically repairable or disposable end-items and components are collected and held for controlled cannibalization.

References

Department of Defense, U.S. Army. *Dictionary of United States Army Terms.* Army Regulation AR 310-25. Washington, DC: Headquarters, Department of the Army, 1986.

—**CANNIBALIZE** is to use personnel of one or more units to complete the authorized strength of another unit.

References

Department of Defense, U.S. Army. *Dictionary of United States Army Terms.* Army Regulation AR 310-25. Washington, DC: Headquarters, Department of the Army, 1986.

—**CANNON** is a complete assembly, consisting of an artillery tube and a breech mechanism, fire mechanism or base cap, that is a component of a gun, howitzer, or mortar. It may include muzzle appendages.

References

Department of Defense, U.S. Army. *Dictionary of United States Army Terms.* Army Regulation AR 310-25. Washington, DC: Headquarters, Department of the Army, 1986.

—**CANNONEER** is a member of a field artillery gun or howitzer crew whose primary duty is to service the piece.

References

Department of Defense, U.S. Army. *Dictionary of United States Army Terms.* Army Regulation AR 310-25. Washington, DC: Headquarters, Department of the Army, 1986.

—**CANNOT OBSERVE** is a type of fire control that indicates that the observer or spotter is unable to adjust fire, but believes a target exists at a given location and is of sufficient importance to justify firing upon it without adjustment or observation.

References

Department of Defense, Joint Chiefs of Staff. *Department of Defense Dictionary of Military and Related Terms.* Washington, DC: GPO, 1986.

—**CANT** is present in the fire control system whenever the gun trunnions are not horizontal. The M60A3 and the XM1 tank fire control systems correct for cant, but in other tanks cant causes an error in deflection in the direction in which the vehicle is canted and an elevation error that causes rounds to hit short. When possible, cant should be eliminated or minimized by the selection of level firing positions. When cant is unavoidable, the aiming point for the round being fired is slightly higher and in the opposite direction of the cant.

References

Department of Defense, U.S. Army. *Army Exercises.* Army Regulation AR 350-28. Washington, DC: Headquarters, Department of the Army, 1985.

—**CAPABILITY** is the ability to accomplish a specified course of action. A capability may or may not be accompanied by intention.

References

Department of Defense, Joint Chiefs of Staff. *Department of Defense Dictionary of Military and Related Terms.* Washington, DC: GPO, 1986.

—**CAPSTONE** is a program designed to align both radio-controlled and aircraft units into wartime configurations under a gaining command with the goal of training and planning in peacetime for wartime contingency plan missions.

References

Department of Defense, U.S. Army. *Army Exercises.* Army Regulation AR 350-28. Washington, DC: Headquarters, Department of the Army, 1985.

—**CAPTURE** is the taking into custody of a hostile force, equipment, or personnel as a result of military operations. *See also:* Captured.

References

Department of Defense, Joint Chiefs of Staff. *Department of Defense Dictionary of Military and Related Terms.* Washington, DC: GPO, 1986.

Department of Defense, U.S. Army. *Operational Terms and Symbols.* Field Manual FM 101-5-1. Washington, DC: Headquarters, Department of the Army, 1985.

—**CAPTURED.** (1) Captured means that it is definitely known that a hostile force has been taken into custody as a result of, and for reasons arising out of, any armed conflict in which the Armed Forces of the United States are engaged. (2) Captured describes all battle casualties who are known to have been taken into custody by a hostile force as a result of and for reasons arising out of any armed conflict in which the United States is engaged. Captured casualties are not usually included in medical statistical records or reports that are received by the Surgeon General, but they are reportable to the Adjutant General.

References

Department of Defense, U.S. Army. *Dictionary of United States Army Terms.* Army Regulation AR 310-25. Washington, DC: Headquarters, Department of the Army, 1986.

———. *Planning for Health Service Support.* Field Manual FM 8-55. Washington, DC: Headquarters, Department of the Army, 1985.

—**CAPTURED ENEMY DOCUMENT (CED)** is any piece of recorded information, regardless of form, obtained from the enemy that subsequently comes into the hands of a friendly force. A CED can be a U.S. or allied document that was once in the hands of the enemy. The types of CEDs are typed, handwritten, printed, painted, engraved, or drawn materials; sound or voice recordings; imagery (e.g., videotapes, movies, or photographs); computer storage media including, but not limited to, floppy disks; and reproductions of any of the items listed above.

References

Department of Defense, U.S. Army. *Intelligence Interrogation.* Field Manual FM 34-52. Washington, DC: Headquarters, Department of the Army, 1987.

—**CAREER FIELD** identifies the branch or functional area in which officers are assigned, developed, and promoted. *See also:* Career Management Field.

References

Department of Defense, U.S. Army. *Commissioned Officer Professional Development and Utilization.* Department of the Army Pamphlet 600-3. Washington, DC: Headquarters, Department of the Army, 1986.

———. *Officer Assignment Policies, Details, and Transfers.* Army Regulation AR 614-100. Washington, DC: Headquarters, Department of the Army, 1984.

—**CAREER MANAGEMENT FIELD** is a manageable grouping of related military operational specialties that guide soldiers' careers from skill level one through skill level five. It provides a logical progression to grade E9.

References

Department of Defense, U.S. Army. Enlisted *Personnel Management System.* Army Regulation AR 600-200. Washington, DC: Headquarters, Department of the Army, 1984.

———. *Individual Military Education and Training.* Army Regulation AR 350-1. Washington, DC: Headquarters, Department of the Army, 1986.

—**CAREER MANNING LEVEL** is a quantitative index, given in a percentage, that measures the extent to which qualified career personnel meet career requirements in the military occupational specialty.

References

Department of Defense, U.S. Army. *Enlisted Personnel Management System.* Army Regulation AR 600-200. Washington, DC: Headquarters, Department of the Army, 1984.

—**CAREER PERSONNEL** are enlisted members of the Regular Army who have completed three or more years of active federal military service. *See also:* Careerist, Enlisted Person, Member.

References
Department of Defense, U.S. Army. *Enlisted Personnel Management System.* Army Regulation AR 600-200. Washington, DC: Headquarters, Department of the Army, 1984.

—**CAREERIST.** (1) A careerist is a soldier who has more than 36 months of active federal service. This definition is used only within Headquarters, Department of the Army, and the Department of Defense for statistical purposes. A careerist should not be confused with "second or subsequent timer" as used in assignment or enlistment objectives. (2) A careerist is a category of reenlistment objective composed of soldiers on their second or subsequent enlistment who will have more than ten years of active federal service at the expiration term of service. *See also:* Enlisted Person, Member

References
Department of Defense, U.S. Army. Army Reenlistment *Program.* Army Regulation AR 601-28. Washington, DC: Headquarters, Department of the Army, 1984.

—**CARRY.** (1) Carry is the prescribed position for holding and carrying the color or guidon in a military formation. (2) Carry means to hold a color or guidon in this prescribed position.

References
Department of Defense, U.S. Army. *Dictionary of United States Army Terms.* Army Regulation AR 310-25. Washington, DC: Headquarters, Department of the Army, 1986.

—**CARTRIDGE.** (1) A cartridge is ammunition that is loaded into a weapon in one operation and contains in a unit assembly all of the components required to make the weapon function one time. (2) A cartridge is an explosive item designed to produce gaseous pressure for performing a mechanical operation other than the common one of expelling a projectile. This item, which is similar to a blank cartridge, is utilized by a device known as a cartridge actuated device. *See also:* Cartridge Case.

References
Department of Defense, U.S. Army. *Dictionary of United States Army Terms.* Army Regulation AR 310-25. Washington, DC: Headquarters, Department of the Army, 1986.

—**CARTRIDGE CASE** is a container that holds the primer and propellant and to which the projectile may be affixed.

References
Department of Defense, U.S. Army. *Dictionary of United States Army Terms.* Army Regulation AR 310-25. Washington, DC: Headquarters, Department of the Army, 1986.

—**CASUAL DETACHMENT** is a military unit consisting of officers or soldiers who have been separated from their units or are awaiting assignment.

References
Department of Defense, U.S. Army. *Dictionary of United States Army Terms.* Army Regulation AR 310-25. Washington, DC: Headquarters, Department of the Army, 1986.

—**CASUAL PAYMENT** is a payment made to a person temporarily separated from his organization and military pay record.

References
Department of Defense, U.S. Army. *Dictionary of United States Army Terms.* Army Regulation AR 310-25. Washington, DC: Headquarters, Department of the Army, 1986.

—**CASUALTY** is a person who is lost to the organization because of having been declared dead, wounded, injured, diseased, interned, captured, retained, missing, missing in action, beleaguered, besieged, or detained. *See also:* Battle Casualty, Nonbattle Casualty, Wounded in Action.

References
Department of Defense, Joint Chiefs of Staff. *Department of Defense Dictionary of Military and Related Terms.* Washington, DC: GPO, 1986.

Department of Defense, U.S. Army. *Wartime Casualty Reporting.* Field Manual FM 12-15. Washington, DC: Headquarters, Department of the Army, 1983.

—**CASUALTY AGENT** is an agent capable of producing serious injury or death when used in field concentrations. *See also:* Biological Warfare, Chemical Warfare.

References
Department of Defense, U.S. Army. *Dictionary of United States Army Terms.* Army Regulation AR 310-25. Washington, DC: Headquarters, Department of the Army, 1986.

—**CASUALTY ATTACK** is a surprise attack in which a high concentration of a toxic chemical agent is built up in a short time (two minutes or less) in an area occupied by personnel to obtain a maximum number of casualties. *See also:* Chemical Warfare.

References

Department of Defense, U.S. Army. *Dictionary of United States Army Terms.* Army Regulation AR 310-25. Washington, DC: Headquarters, Department of the Army, 1986.

—**CASUALTY DRILL** involves various methods or procedures intended to promote successful continuance of the mission or engagement even though the crew or team is reduced by casualties.

References

Department of Defense, U.S. Army. *Dictionary of United States Army Terms.* Army Regulation AR 310-25. Washington, DC: Headquarters, Department of the Army, 1986.

—**CASUALTY REPORTING.** When a soldier becomes a casualty, the next of kin must be notified as quickly as possible. In accordance with appropriate regulations and field guidance, prompt, factual, and accurate casualty reports are submitted by the first soldier having knowledge of the casualty. The report is forwarded through channels to Headquarters, Department of the Army, which notifies the next of kin.

References

Department of Defense, U.S. Army. *Combat Service Support Operations-Division.* Field Manual FM 63-2. Washington, DC: Headquarters, Department of the Army, 1983.

—**CAUSATIVE RESEARCH** is an investigation of variances in transactions. The investigation is a complete review of all transactions since the last inventory control point accountable records. The purpose of causative research is to assign a cause to a variance so that corrective action can be taken. Causative research ends when the cause of variance has been determined or when, after the review of transactions back to the last inventory or reconciliation, no conclusions could be drawn.

References

Department of Defense, U.S. Army. *Commander's Handbook for Property Accountability at the Unit Level.* Field Manual FM 10-14-1. Washington, DC: Headquarters, Department of the Army, 1984.

—**CAVALRY** is a combat maneuver force of combined arms that is mounted in ground and/or on aerial vehicles. It is uniquely organized, equipped, and trained to find the enemy in order to prevent the friendly main body from being engaged under adverse circumstances and to provide, within its capability, security for the main body.

The cavalry's organization and use exemplify two essential criteria of battle: (1) the need to find the enemy and develop the situation with the least force possible and (2) the need to provide reaction time and maneuver space with a force tailored to leave the largest possible residual of combat power in the main body available for use at the time and the place of decision. These criteria are based upon a principle of war—economy of force. Cavalry is an economy force.

It accomplishes its basic tasks—reconnaissance and security—through combined arms action at all levels from the scout team through the regiment.

References

Department of Defense, U.S. Army. *Cavalry.* Field Manual FM 17-95. Washington, DC: Headquarters, Department of the Army, 1977.

———. *Operations.* Field Manual FM 100-5. Washington, DC: Headquarters, Department of the Army, 1986.

———. *Staff Organization and Operations.* Field Manual FM 101-5. Washington, DC: Headquarters, Department of the Army, 1984.

—**CAVERN STORAGE SITE** is a natural cavern or former mining excavation that has been adapted for storing ammunition and explosives.

References

Department of Defense, U.S. Army. *Ammunition and Explosives Safety Standards.* Army Regulation AR 385-64. Washington, DC: Headquarters, Department of the Army, 1987.

—**CEASE FIRE** (AIR DEFENSE CONTROL ORDER) is a command given to air defense artillery units to refrain from firing on, but to continue to track, an airborne object. Missiles already in flight are permitted to continue to intercept.

References

Department of Defense, Joint Chiefs of Staff. *Department of Defense Dictionary of Military and Related Terms.* Washington, DC: GPO, 1986.

Department of Defense, U.S. Army. *Patriot Battalion Operations.* Field Manual FM 44-15. Washington, DC: Headquarters, Department of the Army, 1984.

—**CEILING VALUE** is the concentration of a chemical agent that may not be exceeded for any period of time. *See also:* Chemical Warfare.

References

Department of Defense, U.S. Army. *Ammunition and Explosives Safety Standards.* Army Regulation AR 385-64. Washington, DC: Headquarters, Department of the Army, 1987.

—**CENTER LINE** is a line on the ground representing the center of traverse of an artillery piece. It is used to facilitate emplacement of heavy field artillery to avoid subsequent shifting of the trails.

References

Department of Defense, U.S. Army. *Dictionary of United States Army Terms.* Army Regulation AR 310-25. Washington, DC: Headquarters, Department of the Army, 1986.

—**CENTER OF DISPERSION** is the theoretical center of hits or bursts that would have been made if an unlimited number of shots had been fired with the same data.

References

Department of Defense, U.S. Army. *Dictionary of United States Army Terms.* Army Regulation AR 310-25. Washington, DC: Headquarters, Department of the Army, 1986.

—**CENTER OF GRAVITY.** The concept of center of gravity is key to all operational design. It derives from the fact that an armed combatant—whether a warring nation or an alliance, an army in the field or one of its subordinate formations—is a complex organism whose effective operation depends on the performance of each of its component parts and on the smoothness with which they implement the will of the commander. As with any complex organism, some components are more vital than others to the smooth and reliable operation of the whole. If these are damaged or destroyed, their loss unbalances the entire structure, producing a cascading deterioration of cohesion and effectiveness, which may result in complete failure and will invariably leave the force vulnerable to further damage.

The center of gravity of an armed force refers to the sources of strength or balance. It is that characteristic, capability, or locality from which the force derives its freedom of action, physical strength, or will to fight. The great military strategist Karl von Clausewitz defined it as "the hub of all power and movement, on which everything depends." Its attack is—or should be—the focus of all operations.

Tactical formations can and frequently have centers of gravity (e.g., a key command post or a key piece of terrain on which the unit's operations are anchored). But the concept is usually and more usefully applied to larger forces at the operational level, where the size of the enemy force and scale of its operations make it difficult to decide where and how best to attack it.

Even at this level, the center of gravity may be a component of the field force—the mass of the enemy force, the boundary between two of its major combat formations, a vital command and control center, or perhaps its logistical base or lines of communication. During the Battle of the Bulge in 1944, St. Vith became a center of gravity for defending U.S. forces. A failure to retain it might have resulted in the complete collapse of the Allied center, with potentially disastrous consequences. But an operational center of gravity may also be more abstract (e.g., the cohesion among allied forces or the mental and psychological balance of a key commander).

At the strategic level, the center of gravity may be a key economic resource or locality, the strategic transport capabilities by which a nation maintains its armies in the field, or a vital part of the homeland itself.

References

Department of Defense, U.S. Army. *Operations.* Field Manual FM 100-5. Washington, DC: Headquarters, Department of the Army, 1986.

—**CENTER OF IMPACT** is the center of the dispersion pattern of impact bursts: in terms of range only, it is the range center; in terms of direction, it is the direction center.

References

Department of Defense, U.S. Army. *Dictionary of United States Army Terms.* Army Regulation AR 310-25. Washington, DC: Headquarters, Department of the Army, 1986.

—**CENTIGRAY** is the unit of measurement of the absorbed dose of ionizing radiation. "Centigray" has replaced "radiation absorbed dose" as a unit of measurement. *See also:* Nuclear Warfare.

References

Department of Defense, U.S. Army. *Operational Terms and Symbols.* Field Manual FM 101-5-1. Washington, DC: Headquarters, Department of the Army, 1985.

—**CENTRALIZED CONTROL** is the higher echelon air defense control that makes direct target assignments to fire units. *See also:* Decentralized Control.

References
Department of Defense, Joint Chiefs of Staff. *Department of Defense Dictionary of Military and Related Terms.* Washington, DC: GPO, 1986.

—**CENTRALLY MANAGED PERSONNEL** are soldiers in pay grades E6 through E9 for whom Headquarters of the Department of the Army exercises centralized management controls. These controls include assignment, promotion (with exceptions of grade E6), reclassification, education, qualification, and evaluation.

References
Department of Defense, U.S. Army. *Enlisted Personnel Management System.* Army Regulation AR 600-200. Washington, DC: Headquarters, Department of the Army, 1984.

—**CEREMONIES** are formations and movements in which troops execute movements in unison and with precision just as in a drill. The primary functions of ceremonies are to render honors, preserve tradition, and stimulate esprit de corps.

References
Department of Defense, U.S. Army. *Drills and Ceremonies.* Field Manual FM 22-5. Washington, DC: Headquarters, Department of the Army, 1986.

—**CERTIFICATE FOR DECORATION** is an embossed certificate denoting the award of a decoration.

References
Department of Defense, U.S. Army. *Dictionary of United States Army Terms.* Army Regulation AR 310-25. Washington, DC: Headquarters, Department of the Army, 1986.

—**CERTIFICATE OF ACHIEVEMENT** is a written testimonial denoting an act, achievement, or faithful service when a decoration is not warranted.

References
Department of Defense, U.S. Army. *Dictionary of United States Army Terms.* Army Regulation AR 310-25. Washington, DC: Headquarters, Department of the Army, 1986.

—**CERTIFICATE OF HONORABLE SERVICE** is a written statement to next of kin of personnel who die in active duty denoting recognition of his performance.

References
Department of Defense, U.S. Army. *Dictionary of United States Army Terms.* Army Regulation AR 310-25. Washington, DC: Headquarters, Department of the Army, 1986.

—**CERTIFICATE OF PROFICIENCY** is a written testimonial denoting completion of a prescribed course of instruction.

References
Department of Defense, U.S. Army. *Dictionary of United States Army Terms.* Army Regulation AR 310-25. Washington, DC: Headquarters, Department of the Army, 1986.

—**CERTIFICATE OF SERVICE** is a certificate stating that the person named has honorably competed the required period of active military service, or has been honorably separated or relieved from active military service prior to its completion. It also notes any special merit attained. *See also:* Enlisted Person, Member.

References
Department of Defense, U.S. Army. *Dictionary of United States Army Terms.* Army Regulation AR 310-25. Washington, DC: Headquarters, Department of the Army, 1986.

—**CHAFF** is composed of radar confusion reflectors, which are thin, narrow, metallic strips of various lengths and frequency responses that are used to reflect echoes and create confusion. *See also:* Chaff Element (DIPOLE).

References
Department of Defense, U.S. Army. *Air Defense Artillery Deployment: Chaparral/Vulcan/Stinger.* Field Manual FM 44-3. Washington, DC: Headquarters, Department of the Army, 1984.

—**CHAFF ELEMENT (DIPOLE)** is one resonant piece of chaff material.

References
Department of Defense, U.S. Army. *Air Defense Artillery Deployment: Chaparral/Vulcan/Stinger.* Field Manual FM 44-3. Washington, DC: Headquarters, Department of the Army, 1984.

—**CHAIN OF COMMAND** is the succession of commanding officers from a superior to a subordinate through which a command is exercised. It is also called a command channel.

References

Department of Defense, U.S. Army. *Operational Terms and Symbols*. Field Manual FM 101-5-1. Washington, DC: Headquarters, Department of the Army, 1985.

—**CHAIN OF EVACUATION.** (1) A chain of evacuation is a series of prisoner of war collecting points and cages, and routes by which prisoners of war, retained personnel, and civilian internees are collected and evacuated from the combat zone to rear areas. (2) Chain of evacuation is the series of medical treatment stations and facilities, and the evacuation routes along which they are positioned, where medical evacuation and treatment functions are performed. (3) Chain of evacuation is a series of points or installations indicating the direction of evacuating disabled or salvaged materiel.

References

Department of Defense, U.S. Army. *Dictionary of United States Army Terms*. Army Regulation AR 310-25. Washington, DC: Headquarters, Department of the Army, 1986.

—**CHAIRMAN, JOINT CHIEFS OF STAFF (CJCS)** is appointed by the President from the officers of the regular components of the Armed Forces. The CJCS serves at the pleasure of the President and may be appointed by the President for one additional term. He is the ranking officer in the Armed Forces, but he has no command authority over the JCS or any of the Armed Forces. Although the CJCS lacks command authority and his responsibilities are not precisely defined, his influence has grown over the years, especially as JCS spokesman and adviser to the Secretary of Defense, National Security Council, and the President.

References

Department of Defense, National Defense University. *Joint Staff Officer's Guide, 1986*. Washington, DC: GPO, 1986.

—**CHALK NUMBER** is a number assigned to an aircraft for identification purposes. It is used primarily to designate the position of aircraft being loaded or unloaded.

References

Department of Defense, U.S. Army. *USA/USAF Doctrine for Joint Airborne and Tactical Airlift Operations*. Field Manual FM 100-27. Washington, DC: Headquarters, Department of the Army, 1985.

—**CHALLENGE** is a process carried out to ascertain the friendly or hostile character or identity of another, using the command "Halt, who goes there?" If an additional challenge is used, it follows the original challenge and consists of a word or distinctive sound (e.g., a code word) that is disseminated only to friendly or authorized persons. *See also:* Challenge and Reply Communication, Guard.

References

Department of Defense, U.S. Army. *Guard Duty*. Field Manual FM 22-6. Washington, DC: Headquarters, Department of the Army, 1971.

—**CHALLENGE AND REPLY COMMUNICATION** is a prearranged procedure whereby one communicator requests authentication of another communicator, who establishes validity by a proper reply.

References

Department of Defense, U.S. Army. *Dictionary of United States Army Terms*. Army Regulation AR 310-25. Washington, DC: Headquarters, Department of the Army, 1986.

—**CHAMBER INTERVAL** is the distance between the natural walls of adjacent underground explosives storage sites. *See also:* Chamber Storage Site.

References

Department of Defense, U.S. Army. *Ammunition and Explosives Safety Standards*. Army Regulation AR 385-64. Washington, DC: Headquarters, Department of the Army, 1987.

—**CHAMBER STORAGE SITE** is an excavated chamber or series of excavated chambers especially suited for storing ammunition and explosives. A cavern may be subdivided or otherwise structurally modified for use as a chamber storage site.

References

Department of Defense, U.S. Army. *Ammunition and Explosives Safety Standards*. Army Regulation AR 385-64. Washington, DC: Headquarters, Department of the Army, 1987.

—**CHANGE OF STATION** is a detail, transfer, or assignment of a military member to duty at a new post. A change of station may be either a permanent change or a temporary change of station.

References
Department of Defense, U.S. Army. *Dictionary of United States Army Terms.* Army Regulation AR 310-25. Washington, DC: Headquarters, Department of the Army, 1986.

—**CHAPARRAL** is the Army's short-range air defense surface-to-air missile system. It is effective against all types of aircraft at low altitudes and protects forward deployed divisions and corps and theater rear areas. It is a self-contained, self-propelled system. Its tracked carrier provides excellent cross-country mobility. The launch station is self-contained and can be removed from the carrier and ground-emplaced. The missile is a lightweight, supersonic, fire-and-forget weapon, with an all-aspect infrared homing guidance system that is capable of engaging both approaching and receding targets. To reduce rocket motor smoke, current inventory missiles are retrofitted upon shelf-life expiration with smokeless motors. To assist the gunner in identifying targets as friendly, Chaparral has an identification friend-or-foe subsystem. It carries four ready missiles on launch rails and eight additional missiles in storage compartments. It was initially fielded in 1969 and will remain in the inventory through the 1990s.

References
Department of Defense, U.S. Army. *Air Defense Artillery Deployment: Chaparral/Vulcan/Stinger.* Field Manual FM 44-3. Washington, DC: Headquarters, Department of the Army, 1984.

———. *U.S. Army Air Defense Employment.* Field Manual FM 44-1. Washington, DC: Headquarters, Department of the Army, 1983.

—**CHAPLAIN** is a religious leader who contributes to the well-being of the soldier by providing religious support. He serves as a personal counsellor and as a leader in religious rites and worship. The chaplain also provides pastoral care and humanitarian services that maintain and strengthen the soldier's religious faith and moral character.

References
Department of Defense, U.S. Army. *The Chaplain and Chaplain Assistant in Combat Operations.* Field Manual FM 16-5. Washington, DC: Headquarters, Department of the Army, 1984.

—**CHARGE.** (1) A charge is the amount of propellant required for a fixed, semi-fixed, or separate loading projectile, round, or shell. (2) A charge is the quantity of explosive filling that is contained in a bomb, mine, and the like. (3) In combat engineering, a charge is a quantity of explosive prepared for demolition purposes.

References
Department of Defense, Joint Chiefs of Staff. *Department of Defense Dictionary of Military and Related Terms.* Washington, DC: GPO, 1986.

—**CHARGEABLE LEAVE** is an authorized absence deducted from a member's leave account. *See also:* Annual Leave.

References
Department of Defense, U.S. Army. *Leaves and Passes.* Army Regulation AR 630-5. Washington, DC: Headquarters, Department of the Army, 1984.

—**CHECK FIRE** is a command to cause a temporary halt in firing.

References
Department of Defense, Joint Chiefs of Staff. *Department of Defense Dictionary of Military and Related Terms.* Washington, DC: GPO, 1986.

—**CHECK LEFT OR CHECK RIGHT** (ARMY AVIATION) means to alter the heading by the requested number of degrees left or right and then return to the original heading.

References
Department of Defense, U.S. Army. *Air-to-Air Combat.* Field Manual FM 1-107. Washington, DC: Headquarters, Department of the Army, 1984.

—**CHECK TURN LEFT OR CHECK TURN RIGHT** (ARMY AVIATION) is an aircraft crossing maneuver that incorporates 30 to 60 degrees of heading change and repositions the wingman from left to right and vice versa.

References
Department of Defense, U.S. Army. *Air-to-Air Combat.* Field Manual FM 1-107. Washington, DC: Headquarters, Department of the Army, 1984.

—**CHECKPOINT.** (1) A checkpoint is a point on the ground designated to provide a reference for reportedly friendly locations and to control movement. Checkpoints should not be used to report enemy locations. (2) A checkpoint is a center of impact; a burst center. (3) A checkpoint is a geographical location on land or water above which the position of an aircraft in flight may be determined by observation or by electrical means. (4) A checkpoint is a place where military police check vehicular or pedestrian traffic in order to enforce circulation control measures and other laws, orders, and regulations. (5) A checkpoint is a reference point used to facilitate control. It may be selected throughout the zone of action or along an axis of advance or direction of attack.

References

Department of Defense, Joint Chiefs of Staff. *Department of Defense Dictionary of Military and Related Terms.* Washington, DC: GPO, 1986.

Department of Defense, U.S. Army. *Armored and Mechanized Division Operations.* Field Manual FM 71-100. Washington, DC: Headquarters, Department of the Army, 1978.

———. *Attack Helicopter Operations.* Field Manual FM 17-50. Washington, DC: Headquarters, Department of the Army, 1984.

———. *The Infantry Rifle Company (Infantry. Airborne, Air Assault, Ranger).* Field Manual FM 7-10. Washington, DC: Headquarters, Department of the Army, 1982.

———. *Operational Terms and Symbols.* Field Manual FM 101-5-1. Washington, DC: Headquarters, Department of the Army, 1985.

—**CHEMICAL AGENT** is a chemical compound that, when disseminated, causes incapacitating, lethal, or damaging effects on humans, animals or plants. Riot-control agents, herbicides, smoke, and flame are not consdiered chemical agents. Agents do not destroy material and structures, but make them unusable for periods of time because of chemical contamination absorption. *See also:* Chemical Warfare.

References

Department of Defense, U.S. Army. *Ammunition and Explosives Safety Standards.* Army Regulation AR 385-64. Washington, DC: Headquarters, Department of the Army, 1987.

———. *Survivability.* Field Manual FM 5-103. Washington, DC: Headquarters, Department of the Army, 1985.

U.S. Congress. Senate. *Final Report of the Senate Select Committee to Study Government Operations With Respect to Intelligence Activities. Report 94-755. Book I, Foreign and Military Intelligence* (Church Committee Report). Washington, DC: GPO, 1976.

—**CHEMICAL AGENT CUMULATIVE ACTION** is the building up of small ineffective doses of certain chemical agents within the human body to a point where the eventual effect is similar to one large dose. *See also:* Chemical Warfare.

References

Department of Defense, Joint Chiefs of Staff. *Department of Defense Dictionary of Military and Related Terms.* Washington, DC: GPO, 1986.

—**CHEMICAL AMMUNITION** is a type of ammunition, the filler of which is primarily a chemical agent. *See also:* Chemical Warfare.

References

Department of Defense, Joint Chiefs of Staff. *Department of Defense Dictionary of Military and Related Terms.* Washington, DC: GPO, 1986.

—**CHEMICAL AMMUNITION CARGO** is cargo composed of chemical compunds (e.g., white phosphorous shells and grenades). *See also:* Chemical Warfare.

References

Department of Defense, U.S. Army. *Dictionary of United States Army Terms.* Army Regulation AR 310-25. Washington, DC: Headquarters, Department of the Army, 1986.

—**CHEMICAL AMMUNITION STORAGE POINT** is where chemical munitions located in the communications zone or corps area are kept and distributed. These points in the corps area are normally located near division boundaries to facilitate stock issue. Chemical augmentation teams attached to conventional ammunition units or chemical ammunition units operate the chemical ammunition storage points. *See also:* Chemical Warfare.

References

Department of Defense, U.S. Army. *Support Operations: Echelons Above Corps.* Field Manual FM 100-16. Washington, DC: Headquarters, U.S. Army, 1986.

—**CHEMICAL, BIOLOGICAL, AND RADIO-LOGICAL (CBR) OPERATION** is a collective term used only to refer to a combined chemical, biological, and radiological operation. *See also:* Biological Warfare, Chemical Warfare, Nuclear Warfare.

References

Department of Defense, Joint Chiefs of Staff. *Department of Defense Dictionary of Military and Related Terms.* Washington, DC: GPO, 1986.

—**CHEMICAL DEFENSE** is the methods, plans, and procedures involved in establishing and executing defensive measures against using chemical agents. *See also:* Chemical Warfare.

References

Department of Defense, U.S. Army. *Dictionary of United States Army Terms.* Army Regulation AR 310-25. Washington, DC: Headquarters, Department of the Army, 1986.

—**CHEMICAL DOWNWIND MESSAGE (CDM)** is a weather forecast that is valid for three two-hour periods (six hours). The CDM forecasts wind direction, wind speed, air stability, humidity, air temperature, and any significant weather. *See also:* Chemical Warfare.

References

Department of Defense, U.S. Army. *Operational Terms and Symbols.* Field Manual FM 101-5-1. Washington, DC: Headquarters, Department of the Army, 1985.

—**CHEMICAL ENERGY ROUNDS** (A TYPE OF DIRECT FIRE PROJECTILE) use some form of chemical heat and blast to achieve penetration. They detonate either at impact or when maximum penetration is achieved. Such projectiles carry impact-detonated or delayed detonation high-explosive charges and are used mainly for direct fire from systems with high accuracy and consistently good target acquisition ability. Tanks, antitank weapons, and automatic cannons usually use these types of projectiles. The primary use of the projectile is to destroy all types of armored vehicles.

References

Department of Defense, U.S. Army. *Survivability.* Field Manual FM 5-103. Washington, DC: Headquarters, Department of the Army, 1985.

—**CHEMICAL FUZE** is a fuze that, when the shell hits the target, causes two or more chemicals that were previously separated to come together and cause a reaction. *See also:* Fuze (Specify Type).

References

Department of Defense, U.S. Army. *Mine/Countermine Operations at the Company Level.* Field Manual FM 20-32. Washington, DC: Headquarters, Department of the Army, 1976.

—**CHEMICAL HAND GRENADE** is a burning or bursting grenade that, depending on its filler, is used for casualty, incendiary, training, screening, or signaling. *See also:* Chemical Warfare.

References

Department of Defense, U.S. Army. *Dictionary of United States Army Terms.* Army Regulation AR 310-25. Washington, DC: Headquarters, Department of the Army, 1986.

—**CHEMICAL MINE** is a mine containing a chemical compound designed to kill, injure, or incapacitate personnel or to contaminate materiel or terrain. *See also:* Chemical Warfare.

References

Department of Defense, Joint Chiefs of Staff. *Department of Defense Dictionary of Military and Related Terms.* Washington, DC: GPO, 1986.

—**CHEMICAL OPERATIONS.** (1) Chemical opertaions are actions that involve using chemical agents (excluding riot control agents): to kill; to incapacitate humans or animals for a significant period; or to deny the use of facilities, materials, or areas. (2) Chemical operations are measures taken to defend against such operations. *See also:* Chemical Warfare.

References

Department of Defense, Joint Chiefs of Staff. *Department of Defense Dictionary of Military and Related Terms.* Washington, DC: GPO, 1986.

U.S. Congress. Senate. *Final Report of the Senate Select Committee to Study Government Operations With Respect to Intelligence Activities. Report 94-755. Book I, Foreign and Military Intelligence* (Church Committee Report). Washington, DC: GPO, 1976.

—**CHEMICAL PROJECTILE** is a bomb, rocket, or shell containing a chemical agent. *See also:* Chemical Warfare.

References

Department of Defense, U.S. Army. *Dictionary of United States Army Terms.* Army Regulation AR 310-25. Washington, DC: Headquarters, Department of the Army, 1986.

—**CHEMICAL RECONNAISSANCE** is a reconnaissance operation conducted to identify the type and the extent of chemical contamination. *See also:* Chemical Warfare.

References

Department of Defense, U.S. Army. *Military Police Team, Squad, Platoon Combat Operations.* Field Manual FM 19-4. Washington, DC: Headquarters, Department of the Army, 1984.

—**CHEMICAL STRIKE WARNING (CHEMWARN)** is a warning of impending friendly or suspected enemy chemical attack. *See also:* Chemical Warfare.

References

Department of Defense, U.S. Army. *NBC Operations.* Field Manual FM 3-100. Washington, DC: Headquarters, Department of the Army, 1985.

—**CHEMICAL SURVEY** is a directed effort to determine the nature and degree of chemical hazard in an area and to delineate the perimeter of the hazard area. *See also:* Chemical Warfare.

References

Department of Defense, Joint Chiefs of Staff. *Department of Defense Dictionary of Military and Related Terms.* Washington, DC: GPO, 1986.

—**CHEMICAL WARFARE (CW)** is the use of chemical agents: (1) to kill, injure, or incapacitate men or animals for a significant period of time and/or (2) to deny or hinder the use of areas, facilities, or materiel. *See also:* Biological Agent; Blister Agent; Blood Agent; Chemical Agent; Chemical Agent Cumulative Action; Chemical Ammunition; Chemical Ammunition Cargo; Chemical Ammunition Storage Point; Chemical, Biological, and Radiological Operation; Chemical Defense; Chemical Downwind Message; Chemical Fuze; Chemical Hand Grenade; Chemical Mine; Chemical Operations; Chemical Projectile; Chemical Reconnaissance; Chemical Strike Warning; Chemical Survey; Chemical Warfare; Chemical Weapon; Choking Agent; Nerve Agent; Vomiting Agent; V-series (Chemical Agents).

References

Department of Defense, U.S. Army. *Operational Terms and Symbols.* Field Manual FM 101-5-1. Washington, DC: Headquarters, Department of the Army, 1985.

—**CHEMICAL WEAPON** is an object that projects, disperses, or disseminates a chemical agent. *See also:* Chemical Warfare.

References

Department of Defense, U.S. Army. *Dictionary of United States Army Terms.* Army Regulation AR 310-25. Washington, DC: Headquarters, Department of the Army, 1986.

—**CHEVRON** is a cloth sewn on a uniform of varying design denoting grade, wound, enlisted service, or overseas service. *See also:* Accouterment.

References

Department of Defense, U.S. Army. *Dictionary of United States Army Terms.* Army Regulation AR 310-25. Washington, DC: Headquarters, Department of the Army, 1986.

—**CHIEF ARMY, NAVY, AIR FORCE, OR MARINE CORPS CENSOR** is an officer appointed by the commander of the Army, Navy, Air Force, or Marine Corps component of a unified command to supervise all censorship activities of that service.

References

Department of Defense, Joint Chiefs of Staff. *Department of Defense Dictionary of Military and Related Terms.* Washington, DC: GPO, 1986.

—**CHIEF OF STAFF (CoS)** is the senior or principal member or head of a staff, or the principal assistant in a staff capacity; the head or controlling member of a staff, for the purposes of coordination of work. It is a position without inherent power of command by reason of assignment, except for the power invested in it by the delegation to exercise command in another's name. The commander normally delegates authority to CoS that amounts to command of the staff. In the Army and Marine Corps, the title applies only to the staff on a brigade or division level or higher. In lower units, the corresponding title is executive officer. The CoS is usually responsible for executing staff tasks, coordinating the efforts of staff members, and insuring their efficient and prompt response.

References

Department of Defense, Joint Chiefs of Staff. *Department of Defense Dictionary of Military and Related Terms.* Washington, DC: GPO, 1986.

Department of Defense, U.S. Army. *Staff Organization and Operations.* Field Manual FM 101-5. Washington, DC: Headquarters, Department of the Army, 1984.

—**CHOKING AGENT** is a casualty agent that causes irritation and inflammation to the bronchial tubes and lungs (e.g., phosgene). *See also:* Chemical Warfare.

References

Department of Defense, U.S. Army. *Dictionary of United States Army Terms.* Army Regulation AR 310-25. Washington, DC: Headquarters, Department of the Army, 1986.

—**CHRONIC RADIATION DOSE** is a dose of ionizing radiation that is received either continuously or intermittently over a prolonged period of time. It may be high enough to cause radiation sickness and death, but if it is received at a low dose rate, a significant portion of the acute cellular damage will be repaired. *See also:* Acute Radiation Dose, Nuclear Warfare, Radiation Dose, Radiation Dose Rate.

References

Department of Defense, Joint Chiefs of Staff. *Department of Defense Dictionary of Military and Related Terms.* Washington, DC: GPO, 1986.

—**CIPHER** is any cryptographic system in which arbitrary symbols or groups of symbols represent units of plain text. The plain text is encoded in order to obscure or conceal its meaning. A cipher can be applied to plain textual material (e.g., letters, numbers, or polygraphs). The ciphered material either has no intrinsic meaning or has a meaning that is disregarded if the material produces one or more real words. *See also:* Cipher Group, Cipher System.

References

Clancy, Tom. *The Cardinal of the Kremlin.* New York: Putnam, 1988.

Department of Defense, Defense Intelligence College. *Glossary of Intelligence Terms and Definitions.* Washington, DC: DIC, 1987.

Kessler, Ronald. *Spy vs. Spy: Stalking Soviet Spies in America.* New York: Charles Scribner's Sons, 1988.

U.S. Congress. Senate. *Final Report of the Senate Select Committee to Study Government Operations With Respect to Intelligence Activities. Report 94-755. Book I, Foreign and Military Intelligence* (Church Committee Report). Washington, DC: GPO, 1976.

—**CIPHER GROUP** is a group of letters or numbers (usually five digits or characters) that is used to encrypt messages. The group is protected by off-line manual and machine cryptosystems to facilitate transmission or encryption/decryption. *See also:* Cipher.

References

Department of Defense, Defense Intelligence College. *Glossary of Intelligence Terms and Definitions.* Washington, DC: DIC, 1987.

—**CIPHER SYSTEM** is a cryptosystem in which a cryptographic treatment is applied to plain text elements of equal length. *See also:* Cipher.

References

Department of Defense, Defense Intelligence College. *Glossary of Intelligence Terms and Definitions.* Washington, DC: DIC, 1987.

—**CIPHER TEXT** is enciphered information. *See also:* Cipher.

References

Department of Defense, Defense Intelligence College. *Glossary of Intelligence Terms and Definitions.* Washington, DC: DIC, 1987.

—**CIRCULAR DISTRIBUTION 90** is the radius of a circle around the mean point of impact within which a single round of ammunition has a 90 percent probability of impacting or within which 90 percent of the rounds fired will impact.

References

Department of Defense, U.S. Army. *Nuclear Weapons Employment Doctrine and Procedures.* Field Manual FM 101-3-1. Washington, DC: Headquarters, Department of the Army, 1986.

—**CIRCULAR ERROR PROBABLE (CEP)** is an indicator of the delivery accuracy of a weapon system and used as a factor in determining the probable damage to a target. It is the radius of a circle within which half of the projectiles are expected to fall.

References

Department of Defense, U.S. Army. *Operational Terms and Symbols.* Field Manual FM 101-5-1. Washington, DC: Headquarters, Department of the Army, 1985.

—**CIRCULATION CONTROL** is the enforcement of measures to control the movement of persons and vehicles. *See also:* Circulation Control Point.

References

Department of Defense, U.S. Army. *Dictionary of United States Army Terms.* Army Regulation AR 310-25. Washington, DC: Headquarters, Department of the Army, 1986.

—**CIRCULATION CONTROL POINT** is a piece of terrain on the road net in a theater of operations that is secured and defended by military police. From here, the police control vehicle movements; control individual movement (including refugees and stragglers); insure route security; and perform intelligence gathering and reporting. The point may be composed of a variety of personnel and equipment, depending on the mission.

References

Department of Defense, U.S. Army. *Dictionary of United States Army Terms.* Army Regulation AR 310-25. Washington, DC: Headquarters, Department of the Army, 1986.

—CITATION is a written narrative statement of an act, deed, or meritorious performance of duty or service for which an award is made.

References

Department of Defense, U.S. Army. *Dictionary of United States Army Terms.* Army Regulation AR 310-25. Washington, DC: Headquarters, Department of the Army, 1986.

—CIVIL AFFAIRS (CA) are activities of a commander that embrace the relationship between the military forces and civil authorities and people in a friendly country or area or occupied country or area where military forces are present. Civil affairs usually involve the performance by the military forces of certain functions that are normally the responsibility of the local government. This relationship may occur prior to, during, or subsequent to military action in time of hostilities or other emergency and is normally covered by a treaty or other agreement, expressed or implied. Civil affairs also involve the military government in the form of administration by which an occupying power exercises executive, legislative, and judicial authority over occupied territory. *See also:* Civil Affairs Administration, Civil Affairs Agreement, Civil Affairs Command Support, Civil Affairs Foreign Internal Defense, Civil Affairs Officer, Civil Affairs Operations, Civil Affairs Unit, Civil Military Cooperation, Civil Military Operations, Civil Military Operations Estimate, Phases of Military Government.

References

Department of Defense, U.S. Army. *Operational Terms and Symbols.* Field Manual FM 101-5-1. Washington, DC: Headquarters, Department of the Army, 1985.

—CIVIL AFFAIRS (CA) ADMINISTRATION is the form of administration established in friendly territory whereby a foreign government, in accordance with an agreement that is either expressed or implied, exercises certain powers that are normally the functions of the local government. *See also:* Civil Affairs.

References

Department of Defense, U.S. Army. *Civil Affairs Operations.* Field Manual FM 41-10. Washington, DC: Headquarters, Department of the Army, 1985.

———. *Dictionary of United States Army Terms.* Army Regulation AR 310-25. Washington, DC: Headquarters, Department of the Army, 1986.

—CIVIL AFFAIRS (CA) AGREEMENT is an agreement that governs the relationship between allied armed forces in a friendly country and the civil authorities and people of that country. *See also:* Civil Affairs.

References

Department of Defense, U.S. Army. *Operational Terms and Symbols.* Field Manual FM 101-5-1. Washington, DC: Headquarters, Department of the Army, 1985.

—CIVIL AFFAIRS (CA) COMMAND SUPPORT is the mission support of general purpose forces in wartime to assist the commander coordinate HNS agreements and rear battle plans and minimize local population interference with U.S. military operations. *See also:* Civil Affairs.

References

Department of Defense, U.S. Army. *Civil Affairs Operations.* Field Manual FM 41-10. Washington, DC: Headquarters, Department of the Army, 1985.

—CIVIL AFFAIRS (CA) FOREIGN INTERNAL DEFENSE concerns actions that provide advice and assistance to special operations forces FID missions as a part of the U.S. security assistance program by assisting host national military forces conduct activities that mobilize and motivate its citizens to assist its government and military forces. *See also:* Civil Affairs.

References

Department of Defense, U.S. Army. *Civil Affairs Operations.* Field Manual FM 41-10. Washington, DC: Headquarters, Department of the Army, 1985.

—CIVIL AFFAIRS (CA) OFFICER is a military officer who, as a member of a civil affairs staff or unit, assists the commander plan and coordinate activities pertaining to the relationship between the military and the civil communities in an area where military forces are present. *See also:* Civil Affairs.

References

Department of Defense, U.S. Army. *Dictionary of United States Army Terms.* Army Regulation AR 310-25. Washington, DC: Headquarters, Department of the Army, 1986.

—**CIVIL AFFAIRS (CA) OPERATIONS** are activities conducted during peace and war to facilitate the relationships between U.S. military forces, civil authorities, and people of nations in which the military forces are operating. *See also:* Civil Affairs.

References
Department of Defense, U.S. Army. *Civil Affairs Operations.* Field Manual FM 41-10. Washington, DC: Headquarters, Department of the Army, 1985.

—**CIVIL AFFAIRS (CA) UNIT** is a military unit organized to perform the civil affairs activities of a commander. *See also:* Civil Affairs.

References
Department of Defense, U.S. Army. *Dictionary of United States Army Terms.* Army Regulation AR 310-25. Washington, DC: Headquarters, Department of the Army, 1986.

—**CIVIL MILITARY COOPERATION** encompasses all actions and measures undertaken between NATO commanders and national authorities, military or civil, in peace or in war, that concern the relationship between the allied armed forces and the government, civil population, or agencies in areas where such forces are stationed, supported, or employed. *See also:* Civil Affairs.

References
Department of Defense, U.S. Army. *Operational Terms and Symbols.* Field Manual FM 101-5-1. Washington, DC: Headquarters, Department of the Army, 1985.

—**CIVIL MILITARY OPERATIONS (CMO)** are activities that involve the interaction between the military force and the civilian authorities to foster favorable emotions, attitudes, and behavior in neutral, friendly, or hostile groups. *See also:* Civil Affairs.

References
Department of Defense, U.S. Army. *Civil Affairs Operations.* Field Manual FM 41-10. Washington, DC: Headquarters, Department of the Army, 1985.
———. *Staff Organization and Operations.* Field Manual FM 101-5. Washington, DC: Headquarters, Department of the Army, 1984.

—**CIVIL MILITARY OPERATIONS (CMO) ESTIMATE** analyzes the influence of CMO factors on the accomplishment of the mission. CMO estimates draw conclusions and make recommendations on the feasibility of various courses of action from the G5 or S5 perspective as well as on the effects of each course of action on CMO.

References
Department of Defense, U.S. Army. *Staff Organization and Operations.* Field Manual FM 101-5. Washington, DC: Headquarters, Department of the Army, 1984.

—**CIVIL TWILIGHT** is the interval between the instant the upper edge of the sun's disk appears on the horizon and the instant the center of the sun is six degrees below the horizon. In civil twilight, there is sufficient light to carry on normal daylight activities.

References
Department of Defense, U.S. Army. *Weather Support for Army Tactical Operations.* Field Manual FM 34-81. Washington, DC: Headquarters, Department of the Army, 1984.

—**CIVIL WAR** is an internal conflict that meets the following criteria:
- The insurgents occupy and control territory and have a functioning government;
- Other states offer some type of recognition to the insurgent government and define their attitude toward the conflict;
- The insurgents have armed forces that are commanded by someone who is responsible for their actions, carry their arms openly, wear a distinctive emblem, and conduct their operations in accordance with the laws of war; and
- A state of general hostilities accompanied by a military confrontation of major proportions is taking place.

References
Department of Defense, U.S. Army. *Dictionary of United States Army Terms.* Army Regulation AR 310-25. Washington, DC: Headquarters, Department of the Army, 1986.

—**CIVILIAN-SPONSORED UNIT** is one that, by mutual agreement between the Department of the Army and a civilian or governmental organization, is sponsored by that organization.

References
Department of Defense, U.S. Army. *Dictionary of United States Army Terms.* Army Regulation AR 310-25. Washington, DC: Headquarters, Department of the Army, 1986.

—**CLASP** is a metallic bar device attached to certain ribbons for information and identification.

References

Department of Defense, U.S. Army. *Dictionary of United States Army Terms.* Army Regulation AR 310-25. Washington, DC: Headquarters, Department of the Army, 1986.

—**CLASS A AGENT OFFICER** is a commissioned or warrant officer entrusted with public funds for the purpose of making payments specified in the appointment orders. *See also:* Class B Agent Officer.

References

Department of Defense, U.S. Army. *Dictionary of United States Army Terms.* Army Regulation AR 310-25. Washington, DC: Headquarters, Department of the Army, 1986.

—**CLASS B AGENT OFFICER** is a commissioned or warrant officer to whom public funds are entrusted by an accountable disbursing officer for the purpose of making payments or collections as an agent for the accountable officer. A class B agent officer is not restricted to specified payments or collections, but is given general authority to act for, and in the name of, the accountable officer. *See also:* Class A Agent Officer.

References

Department of Defense, U.S. Army. *Dictionary of United States Army Terms.* Army Regulation AR 310-25. Washington, DC: Headquarters, Department of the Army, 1986.

—**CLASSES OF SUPPLY** are the grouping of supplies, by type, into ten categories to ease supply management and planning. The following are the supply classes:

- **Class I**—Subsistence items and gratuitous-issue health and welfare items (e.g., meals ready to eat, T-rations, and fruits and vegetables).
- **Class II**—Items of equipment, other than principal items, that are prescribed in authorization/allowance tables (e.g., individual equipment, clothing items, tentage, tool sets, and administrative and housekeeping supplies).
- **Class III**—Petroleum, oils, and lubricants (e.g., petroleum fuels, hydraulic and insulating oils, chemical products, antifreeze compounds, compressed gases, and coal).
- **Class IV**—Construction and barrier materials (e.g., lumber, sand bags, and barbed wire).
- **Class V**—Ammunition (e.g., small arms ammunition, artillery rounds, hand grenades, explosives, mines, fuzes, detonators, missiles, bombs—includes special ammunition).
- **Class VI**—Personal demand items and items that would normally be sold through the exchange system (e.g., cigarettes, candy, and soap).
- **Class VII**—Major end-items (e.g., final combinations of items that are ready (assembled) for intended use; vehicles self-propelled artillery pieces; missile launchers; and major weapons systems).
- **Class VIII**—Medical material (e.g., medicine, stretchers, and surgical instruments).
- **Class IX**—Repair parts and components, including kits and assemblies, and items required for maintenance support of all equipment (e.g., batteries, spark plugs, and axles).
- **Class X**—Material required to support nonmilitary programs such as agricultural and economic development projects (e.g., commercial design tractors and farm tools).
- **MISC**—Miscellaneous items that do not fit into one of the ten classes above (e.g., water, maps, captured enemy material, and salvage material).

See also: Special Ammunition.

References

Department of Defense, U.S. Army. *Staff Organization and Operations.* Field Manual FM 101-5. Washington, DC: Headquarters, Department of the Army, 1984.

—**CLASSIFICATION** "reflects the fact that a determination has been made that the official information contained in the document requires, in the interests of national security, a degree of protection against unauthorized disclosure. The three security designations are CONFIDENTIAL, SECRET, and TOP SECRET, which are normally referred to as security classifications. The originator of the document usually assigns the security classification, along with downgrading instructions that indicate when the material might be reduced to a lower classification and when it will be declassified. The classification is clearly stamped on each page of the material and signifies that a determination has been made to classify the material at that level. In some cases, individual paragraphs of a document will be assigned classifications, so that it will be easier to downgrade the document to a lower security classification by removing the more highly classified material or even to sanitize the document to unclassified by removing all classified material."

References

Department of Defense, Defense Intelligence College. *Glossary of Intelligence Terms and Definitions.* Washington, DC: DIC, 1987.

Department of Defense, U.S. Army. *Operational Terms and Symbols.* Field Manual FM 101-5-1. Washington, DC: Headquarters, Department of the Army, 1985.

—**CLASSIFICATION AUTHORITY.** (1) Classification authority is an official within the Executive Branch of the government who has been authorized by an Executive Order to classify information or material. He delegates some of this authority to his subordinates, since the volume of classified material is enormous and beyond the capability of one person to process. (2) A classification authority is a commander who has custody of the soldier's Military Personnel Records Jacket. *See also:* Classification.

References

Department of Defense, Defense Intelligence College. *Glossary of Intelligence Terms and Definitions.* Washington, DC: DIC, 1987.

Department of Defense, U.S. Army. *Enlisted Personnel Management System.* Army Regulation AR 600-200. Washington, DC: Headquarters, Department of the Army, 1984.

—**CLASSIFIED INFORMATION** was defined by Congress in the Intelligence Identities Protection Act of 1982 as "information or material designated and clearly marked or clearly represented, pursuant to the provisions of a statute or Executive Order (or a regulation or order issued pursuant to a statute or Executive Order), as requiring a specific degree of protection against unauthorized disclosure for reasons of national security." An alternative official definition is "official information which has been determined to require protection against unauthorized disclosure in the interests of national security. Classified information is clearly designated as such by assigning a security classification to the information." *See also:* Classification.

References

Department of Defense, Defense Intelligence College. *Glossary of Intelligence Terms and Definitions.* Washington, DC: DIC, 1987.

Department of Defense, U.S. Army. *Operational Terms and Symbols.* Field Manual FM 101-5-1. Washington, DC: Headquarters, Department of the Army, 1985.

U.S. Congress. *Intelligence Identities Protection Act of 1982.* Public Law 97-200. Washington, DC: GPO, 1982.

—**CLASSIFIED MATTER** is official information that requires protection in the interests of national security. *See also:* Classification Authority.

References

Department of Defense, Joint Chiefs of Staff. *Department of Defense Dictionary of Military and Related Terms.* Washington, DC: GPO, 1986.

Department of Defense, U.S. Army. *Operational Terms and Symbols.* Field Manual FM 101-5-1. Washington, DC: Headquarters, Department of the Army, 1985.

—**CLAYMORE** is an antipersonnel mine designed to produce a vector fan-shaped pattern of fragments. *See also:* Mine Warfare.

References

Department of Defense, U.S. Army. *Dictionary of United States Army Terms.* Army Regulation AR 310-25. Washington, DC: Headquarters, Department of the Army, 1986.

—**CLEAR.** (1) To clear is to approve or authorize, or to obtain approval or authorization for: (a) a person or persons with regard to their actions, movements, and duties; (b) an object or group of objects (e.g., equipment or supplies) with regard to quality, quantity, purpose, movement, and disposition; or (c) a request, with regard to correctness of form or validity. (2) To clear is to give one or more aircraft a clearance. (3) To clear is to give a person a security clearance. (4) To clear is to fly over an obstacle without touching it. (5) To clear is to pass a designated point, line, or object. (6) To clear is to operate a gun so as to unload it or make certain that no ammunition remains, and to free a gun of stoppages. (7) To clear an engine is to open the throttle of an idling engine to free it from carbon. (8) To clear the air is to gain either temporary or permanent air superiority or control in a given sector.

References

Department of Defense, U.S. Army. *Operational Terms and Symbols.* Field Manual FM 101-5-1. Washington, DC: Headquarters, Department of the Army, 1985.

—**CLEAR ENEMY IN ZONE** is a requirement to eliminate organized resistance in an assigned zone by destroying, capturing, or forcing the withdrawal of enemy forces that could interfere with the unit's ability to accomplish its mission.

References

Department of Defense, U.S. Army. *Operational Terms and Symbols*. Field Manual FM 101-5-1. Washington, DC: Headquarters, Department of the Army, 1985.

—**CLEARANCE.** (1) A clearance is a determination that a person is eligible, under the standards of current Director of Central Intelligence directives and Department of Defense regulations, for access to classified information. However, clearance does not imply a need-to-know. (2) Clearance is removing all mines and devices from a field. *See also:* Mine Warfare.

References

Department of Defense, Defense Intelligence College. *Glossary of Intelligence Terms and Definitions*. Washington, DC: DIC, 1987.

Department of Defense, U.S. Army. *Mine/Countermine Operations at the Company Level*. Field Manual FM 20-32. Washington, DC: Headquarters, Department of the Army, 1976.

—**CLEARANCE TIME** is the time that the tail of a column passes a designated point or line.

References

Department of Defense, U.S. Army. *The Infantry Rifle Company (Infantry, Airborne, Air Assault, Ranger)*. Field Manual FM 7-10. Washington, DC: Headquarters, Department of the Army, 1982.

—**CLEARING OPERATION** is an operation designed to clear all mines from a route or area. *See also:* Mine Warfare.

References

Department of Defense, Joint Chiefs of Staff. *Department of Defense Dictionary of Military and Related Terms*. Washington, DC: GPO, 1986.

—**CLEARING STATION** is an operating field medical facility, established by a clearing company or medical company, that provides emergency or resuscitative treatment for patients until evacuated and definitive treatment for patients with minor illnesses, wounds, or injuries. *See also:* Medical Treatment.

References

Department of Defense, U.S. Army. *Dictionary of United States Army Terms*. Army Regulation AR 310-25. Washington, DC: Headquarters, Department of the Army, 1986.

—**CLIMATOLOGICAL INFORMATION** refers to data on average weather conditions and variations from the norm for a particular place or area for a specified period of the year.

References

Department of Defense, U.S. Army. *Weather Support for Army Tactical Operations*. Field Manual FM 34-81. Washington, DC: Headquarters, Department of the Army, 1984.

—**CLOCK CODE** (ARMY AVIATION) is used to indicate the angular position of an object with respect to the nose of the aircraft or axis of advance of the flight. A threat's location is expressed as a direction from twelve o'clock relative bearing in clock code and altitude in relation to the horizon (e.g., "Bogey, two o'clock high").

References

Department of Defense, U.S. Army. *Air-to-Air Combat*. Field Manual FM 1-107. Washington, DC: Headquarters, Department of the Army, 1984.

—**CLOCK METHOD** is a method of calling shots by reference to the figures on an imaginary clock dial assumed to have the target as its center. Thus, a shot directly above the target is at twelve o'clock. The same method is sometimes used to name the direction of the wind (e.g., a wind direction from the left is a nine o'clock wind).

References

Department of Defense, U.S. Army. *Dictionary of United States Army Terms*. Army Regulation AR 310-25. Washington, DC: Headquarters, Department of the Army, 1986.

—**CLOSE.** (1) Close is a preparatory command used to bring men marching at normal interval to close interval. (2) Close means to decrease distances between vehicles or units in a march column, or to bring the tail of a column into an area. (3) Close means to reduce the angle of divergence between artillery pieces of a battery to form a narrower sheaf. (4) Close is a term in a fire message to indicate that the target is near friendly forward elements. (5) Close means to discontinue operations in preparation for movement to another site.

References
Department of Defense, U.S. Army. Dictionary *of United States Army Terms.* Army Regulation AR 310-25. Washington, DC: Headquarters, Department of the Army, 1986.

—**CLOSE AIR SUPPORT** is air action against enemy targets that are located close to friendly forces. Thus, the detailed integration of each air mission with the fire and movement of the enemy forces is required. Close air support is requested and approved by the support unit commander, and is controlled by the forward air controller. *See also:* Air Interdiction, Air Support, Immediate Airlift Requests, Preplanned Mission Request.

References
Department of Defense, U.S. Army. *Air Defense Artillery Deployment: Chaparral/Vulcan/Stinger.* Field Manual FM 44-3. Washington, DC: Headquarters, Department of the Army, 1984.

———. *Attack Helicopter Operations.* Field Manual FM 17-50. Washington, DC: Headquarters, Department of the Army, 1984.

———. *Operational Terms and Symbols.* Field Manual FM 101-5-1. Washington, DC: Headquarters, Department of the Army, 1985.

———. *USA/USAF Doctrine for Joint Airborne and Tactical Airlift Operations.* Field Manual FM 100-27. Washington, DC: Headquarters, Department of the Army, 1985.

Poyer, David. *The Med.* New York: St. Martin's Press, 1988.

—**CLOSE AIR SUPPORT (CAS) MISSIONS** support land operations by attacking hostile targets in close proximity to friendly surface forces. Close air support can support offensive, counteroffensive, and defensive surface force operations with preplanned or immediate attacks. All preplanned and immediate close air support missions require access to the battlefield, timely intelligence information, and accurate weapons delivery.

Close air support enhances land force operations by providing the capability to deliver a wide range of weapons and massed firepower at decisive points. It can surprise the enemy, create opportunities for the maneuver or advance of friendly forces through shock action and concentrated attacks, protect the flanks of friendly forces, blunt enemy offensives, and protect the rear of land forces during retrograde operations. *See also:* Close Air Support.

References
Department of Defense, U.S. Army. *Operations.* Field Manual FM 100-5. Washington, DC: Headquarters, Department of the Army, 1986.

———. *USA/USAF Doctrine for Joint Airborne and Tactical Airlift Operations.* Field Manual FM 100-27. Washington, DC: Headquarters, Department of the Army, 1985.

—**CLOSE COLUMN** is a motor march formation in which the vehicles are spaced approximately twenty meters apart in daylight to increase the formation's density and reduce pass time. During limited visibility, the vehicles are spaced so that each driver can see the blackout markers of the vehicle to his front. This type column can be used when moving through towns to other congested areas or when moving over poorly marked routes.

References
Department of Defense, U.S. Army. *The Infantry Rifle Company (Infantry, Airborne, Air Assault, Ranger).* Field Manual FM 7-10. Washington, DC: Headquarters, Department of the Army, 1982.

—**CLOSE COMBAT** is fighting at close quarters with the enemy and using small arms, bayonets, and other hand weapons.

References
Department of Defense, U.S. Army. *Dictionary of United States Army Terms.* Army Regulation AR 310-25. Washington, DC: Headquarters, Department of the Army, 1986.

—**CLOSE CONFINEMENT** is the confinement of prisoners separate from the main prisoner group in quarters especially designated by the commanding officer for that purpose. The prisoners are under constant supervision. *See also:* Disciplinary Action.

References
Department of Defense, U.S. Army. *Dictionary of United States Army Terms.* Army Regulation AR 310-25. Washington, DC: Headquarters, Department of the Army, 1986.

—**CLOSE DEFENSIVE FIRES** are fires planned to destroy the integrity of the attacks by directing fire on the attacker before the assault to disrupt command, cover attack positions, neutralize observation, and weaken supporting fires. *See also:* Fire.

References

Department of Defense, U.S. Army. *Dictionary of United States Army Terms.* Army Regulation AR 310-25. Washington, DC: Headquarters, Department of the Army, 1986.

—**CLOSE IN SECURITY** is the use of cover camouflage, obstacles, antitank weapons, sentinels, and patrols to protect a unit against attack at close range.

References

Department of Defense, U.S. Army. *Dictionary of United States Army Terms.* Army Regulation AR 310-25. Washington, DC: Headquarters, Department of the Army, 1986.

—**CLOSE INTERVAL** (DRILLS AND CEREMONIES) is the lateral space between soldiers, measured from right to left by the soldier on the right placing the heel of his left hand on his hip, even with the top of the belt line, fingers and thumb joined and extended downward, with his elbow in line with the body and touching the arm of the soldier to his left. *See also:* Double Interval, (Drills and Ceremonies); Normal Interval.

References

Department of Defense, U.S. Army. *Training for Mobilization and War.* Field Manual FM 25-5. Washington, DC: Headquarters, Department of the Army, 1985.

—**CLOSE MARCH** is a command to take a close interval in marching. *See also:* Close Interval (Drills and Ceremonies).

References

Department of Defense, U.S. Army. *Dictionary of United States Army Terms.* Army Regulation AR 310-25. Washington, DC: Headquarters, Department of the Army, 1986.

—**CLOSE OPERATIONS** at any echelon are the current activities of major committed combat elements, together with their immediate combat support and combat service support. At the operational level, close operations comprise the efforts of large tactical formations—Corps and divisions—to win current battles. At the tactical level, close operations comprise the efforts of smaller tactical units to win current engagements.

At any echelon, close operations include the close, deep, and rear operations of subordinate elements. Thus, the close operations of a corps include the close, deep, and rear operations of

its committed divisions or separate brigades. Activities are part of close operations if they are designed to support the current fight. Among the activities typically composing close operations are maneuver (including deep maneuver); close combat (including close air support); indirect fire support (including counterfire); combat support and combat service support of committed units; and command and control.

Basic to close operations is the application of direct combat power with short-range weapons used by infantrymen. Close operations also rely heavily on the use of indirect fire support provided by conventional artillery.

References

Department of Defense, U.S. Army. *Department of the Army Policy Statement, 1988.* Washington, DC: Headquarters, Department of the Army, 1988.

———. *Operations.* Field Manual FM 100-5. Washington, DC: Headquarters, Department of the Army, 1986.

—**CLOSE OPERATIONS** (TACTICAL) involve the fight between the committed forces and the readily available tactical reserves of both combatants. Its principal elements are the coordinated plans for maneuver and fire support. These elements, however, rely on the integrated support of all other arms and services.

References

Department of Defense, U.S. Army. *Operations.* Field Manual FM 100-5. Washington, DC: Headquarters, Department of the Army, 1986.

—**CLOSE ORDER DRILL** is a drill formation and movements that are done at normal interval or at close interval. The formations and movements are those usually performed in drill marching, parades, and reviews, and those involving the manuals of the various hand weapons. *See also:* Combat Drill.

References

Department of Defense, U.S. Army. *Dictionary of United States Army Terms.* Army Regulation AR 310-25. Washington, DC: Headquarters, Department of the Army, 1986.

—**CLOSE RANKS.** (1) Close ranks is to lessen the distance between rows of men. It brings a unit from open ranks formation to normal interval. (2) Close ranks is a preparatory command to close ranks. *See also:* Open Ranks.

References
Department of Defense, U.S. Army. *Dictionary of United States Army Terms.* Army Regulation AR 310-25. Washington, DC: Headquarters, Department of the Army, 1986.

—**CLOSE STATION** is a command dismissing all personnel engaged in a drill, practice, or action at a given gun station.

References
Department of Defense, U.S. Army. *Dictionary of United States Army Terms.* Army Regulation AR 310-25. Washington, DC: Headquarters, Department of the Army, 1986.

—**CLOSE SUPPORT** is the action of the supporting force against targets or objectives that are sufficiently near the supported force as to require detailed integration or coordination of the supporting action with the fire, movement, or other actions of the supported force. *See also:* Close Support Mission.

References
Department of Defense, Joint Chiefs of Staff. *Department of Defense Dictionary of Military and Related Terms.* Washington, DC: GPO, 1986.

—**CLOSE SUPPORT MISSION** is a mission whose primary purpose is the close support of friendly ground forces to accomplish their immediate task and/or to prevent front-line enemy forces from accomplishing their missions. Close coordination of air, naval, and ground activities is required prior to and during the mission. This coordination may include ground-to-air control, air-to air-control, and the positive establishment of bombing, strafing, and no fire lines or zones prior to the mission. All available fire support means may be employed in close support missions.

References
Department of Defense, U.S. Army. *Dictionary of United States Army Terms.* Army Regulation AR 310-25. Washington, DC: Headquarters, Department of the Army, 1986.

—**CLOSE SUPPORTING FIRE** is fire that is placed on enemy troops, weapons, or positions that, because of their proximity, present the most immediate and serious threat to the supported staff. *See also:* Supporting Fire.

References
Department of Defense, Joint Chiefs of Staff. *Department of Defense Dictionary of Military and Related Terms.* Washington, DC: GPO, 1986.

—**CLOSED AREA** is a designated area in or over which passage of any kind is prohibited.

References
Department of Defense, Joint Chiefs of Staff. *Department of Defense Dictionary of Military and Related Terms.* Washington, DC: GPO, 1986.

—**CLOSING WITH THE ENEMY** refers to how the squad, platoon, or company gets from the point where contact is made with, to the positions occupied by, the enemy. It does not refer to a "charge" against enemy positions, although in rare cases that may be the best course of action.

References
Department of Defense, U.S. Army. *The Rifle Squads (Mechanized and Light Infantry).* Training Circular TC 7-1. Washington, DC: Headquarters, Department of the Army, 1976.

—**CLUSTER.** (1) A cluster is a fireworks signal in which a group of stars burns at the same time. (2) A cluster is a group of bombs that are released together and usually consists of fragmentation or incendiary bombs. (3) A cluster is two or more parachutes that are used for dropping light or heavy loads. (4) In land mine warfare, a cluster is a component of a pattern-laid minefield within a half-circle of a two-meter radius. It may be antitank, antipersonnel, or mixed. It consists of from one to five mines and no more than one antitank mine. (5) A cluster is two or more engines that are coupled together to function as one power unit. *See also:* Mine Warfare.

References
Department of Defense, U.S. Army. *Mine/Countermine Operations at the Company Level.* Field Manual FM 20-32. Washington, DC: Headquarters, Department of the Army, 1976.

—**CODE** is a cryptographic system in which arbitrary groups of signals or cryptographic equivalents, which are usually called code groups, are substituted for textual material (e.g., words, phrases, or sentences). The code groups typically consist of meaningless combinations of letters, numbers, or both. A code can be used for brevity (e.g., semaphore codes), or it can be used for security.

Codes have three distinctly different applications. In the broadest sense, coding is a means of converting information into a form suitable for communications or encryption (e.g., coded speech, morse code, or typewriter codes). In this case, no security is provided. The second application involves brevity lists. These are codes that are used to reduce the time required to transmit information (e.g., long, stereotypical sentences that can be reduced to a few characters). In this case, too, no security is provided. The final application is the cryptosystem. Here, cryptographic equivalents (usually called code groups) that typically consist of letters, digits, or both in otherwise meaningless combinations are substituted for information expressed in primary words, phrases, or sentences. Here, security is provided.

References

Clancy, Tom. *The Cardinal of the Kremlin.* New York: Putnam, 1988.

Department of Defense, Defense Intelligence College. *Glossary of Intelligence Terms and Definitions.* Washington, DC: DIC, 1987.

U.S. Congress. Senate. *Final Report of the Senate Select Committee to Study Government Operations With Respect to Intelligence Activities. Report 94-755. Book I, Foreign and Military Intelligence* (Church Committee Report). Washington, DC: GPO, 1976.

—**COHESION** is a bonding of soldiers with their leaders in a way that sustains their will and commitment to each other, their unit, and their mission. It is intertwined with discipline and is necessary for a unit to work as a smoothly functioning team.

References

Department of Defense, U.S. Army. *Army Forces Training.* Army Regulation AR 350-41. Washington, DC: Headquarters, Department of the Army, 1986.

———. *Military Leadership.* Field Manual FM 22-100. Washington, DC: Headquarters, Department of the Army, 1983.

—**COHESION OPERATIONAL READINESS TRAINING (COHORT) UNIT REPLACEMENT FOR THE ACTIVE ARMY.** Under COHORT, first-term soldiers and career soldiers in battalion-sized and smaller units stay together longer. The long-term relationship fosters greater horizontal (peer) and vertical (chain of command) bonding

within the unit. In addition, commanders have time to develop long-range training objectives, thereby obtaining higher performance standards than are attainable with an individual replacement system. It is one of the two subsystems of the new manning system and can be applied to company and battalion-sized units. *See also:* Regimental Affiliation.

References

Department of Defense, U.S. Army. *Army Forces Training.* Army Regulation AR 350-41. Washington, DC: Headquarters, Department of the Army, 1986.

———. *Department of the Army Policy Statement, 1988.* Washington, DC: Headquarters, Department of the Army, 1988.

—**COIL** is an arrangement of vehicles to form a circle.

References

Department of Defense, U.S. Army. *Operational Terms and Symbols.* Field Manual FM 101-5-1. Washington, DC: Headquarters, Department of the Army, 1985.

—**COIL UP** is the assembling of a march column, especially in armor, during a halt in a field or fields to minimize the distance from front to rear.

References

Department of Defense, U.S. Army. *Dictionary of United States Army Terms.* Army Regulation AR 310-25. Washington, DC: Headquarters, Department of the Army, 1986.

—**COLD DRY CLOTHING** is the cold wet clothing ensemble plus insulating layers to provide ample protection from very cold weather (minus 50 degrees Fahrenheit). *See also:* Cold Wet Clothing, Mukluk.

References

Department of Defense, U.S. Army. *Dictionary of United States Army Terms.* Army Regulation AR 310-25. Washington, DC: Headquarters, Department of the Army, 1986.

—**COLD WET CLOTHING** is water repellant, weather resistant outer layer plus inner layers of clothing with sufficient insulation to provide protection in moderately cold weather (above 14 degrees Fahrenheit). *See also:* Cold Dry Clothing, Mukluk.

References
Department of Defense, U.S. Army. *Dictionary of United States Army Terms.* Army Regulation AR 310-25. Washington, DC: Headquarters, Department of the Army, 1986.

—**COLLATERAL DAMAGE** (NUCLEAR) is undesirable civilian injuries or materiel damage that is caused by friendly nuclear weapons. *See also:* Nuclear Warfare.

References
Department of Defense, U.S. Army. *Dictionary of United States Army Terms.* Army Regulation AR 310-25. Washington, DC: Headquarters, Department of the Army, 1986.

————. *Fire Support in Combined Arms Operations.* Field Manual FM 6-20. Washington, DC: Headquarters, Department of the Army, 1983.

————. *Nuclear Weapons Employment Doctrine and Procedures.* Field Manual FM 101-3-1. Washington, DC: Headquarters, Department of the Army, 1986.

—**COLLATERAL DAMAGE DISTANCE** is the minimum distance in meters that a desired ground zero for a nuclear explosion must be separated from civilian personnel and materiel to ensure with a stated degree of assurance that injuries or property damage will not be exceeded. *See also:* Nuclear Warfare.

References
Department of Defense, U.S. Army. *Nuclear Weapons Employment Doctrine and Procedures.* Field Manual FM 101-3-1. Washington, DC: Headquarters, Department of the Army, 1986.

————. *Operational Terms and Symbols.* Field Manual FM 101-5-1. Washington, DC: Headquarters, Department of the Army, 1985.

—**COLLATERAL INFORMATION.** (1) Collateral information is all national security information that has been classified under the provisions of an Executive Order for which Intelligence Community special systems of compartmentation (sensitive compartmented information) are not formally established. Collateral information is less sensitive than sensitive compartment information and therefore requires less stringent security and storage procedures. (2) Collateral information is information that is classified CONFIDENTIAL, SECRET, or TOP SECRET in accordance with Department of Defense Regulation 5200.1. *See also:* Sensitive Compartmented Information.

References
Department of Defense, Defense Intelligence College. *Glossary of Intelligence Terms and Definitions.* Washington, DC: DIC, 1987.

—**COLLECTING POINT** is a facility within a corps or division. A general collecting point is a facility established to control civilians, prisoners, and stragglers. A maintenance collecting point is a point established to collect equipment awaiting repair, controlled exchange, cannibalization, or evacuation. The maintenance collecting point may be operated by the user or by intermediate maintenance units. *See also:* Collecting Station.

References
Department of Defense, U.S. Army. *Operational Terms and Symbols.* Field Manual FM 101-5-1. Washington, DC: Headquarters, Department of the Army, 1985.

—**COLLECTING STATION.** (1) A collecting station is a place in the forward area for collecting and sorting salvage materials. (2) A collecting station is a place designated for the grouping of refugees, expellees, and evacuees before they return to their homes or a designated location.

References
Department of Defense, U.S. Army. *Dictionary of United States Army Terms.* Army Regulation AR 310-25. Washington, DC: Headquarters, Department of the Army, 1986.

—**COLLECTION.** (1) Collection is the gathering of information and its delivery to the proper intelligence unit so that it can be made into intelligence. (2) Collection is the gathering, analyzing, and disseminating of nonpublic information, without the permission of the subject; and its delivery to the proper intelligence unit for processing. (3) In weapons systems, collection is the use of equipment or instruments to gather data concerning the testing and operation of foreign weapon systems. (4) In electronic intelligence, collection is the gathering of information from radars, navigation aids, countermeasures equipment, and other electronic devices of an enemy or a potential enemy, except for communications equipment. (5) Collection is an Army tactical intelligence term that means the acquisition of information to provide it to intelligence processing and/or production elements. *See also:* Intelligence.

References

Department of Defense. *Activities of DoD Intelligence Components that Affect U.S. Persons.* (Department of Defense Directive 5240.1.) Washington, DC: Department of Defense, 1982.

Department of Defense, Defense Intelligence College. *Glossary of Intelligence Terms and Definitions.* Washington, DC: DIC, 1987.

National Security Agency. *Limitations and Procedures in Signals Intelligence Operations of the USSS.* Washington, DC: GPO, 1976.

U.S. Congress. Senate. *Final Report of the Senate Select Committee to Study Government Operations With Respect to Intelligence Activities. Report 94-755. Book I, Foreign and Military Intelligence* (Church Committee Report). Washington, DC: GPO, 1976,

—**COLLECTION MANAGEMENT AND DISSEMINATION (CM&D) SECTION,** on the Army Corps level, works under the staff supervision of the G2, performs mission management for intelligence operations, and disseminates combat information and intelligence. Mission management provides for the direction and control of corps intelligence collection operations. It is based upon the requirements that have been identified in the Essential Elements of Information.

The CM&D section plans missions based upon identified requirements and available collection resources. Requirements for information are translated into specific collection missions by the section.

When mission planning is completed, the CM&D section prepares and transmits the mission tasking, and then monitors the status of the collection effort.

The CM&D section also provides rapid dissemination of information. It coordinates directly with the fire support element to provide an immediate exchange of target information. *See also:* Intelligence.

References

Department of Defense, U.S. Army. *Military Intelligence Group (Combat Electronic Warfare and Intelligence) (Corps).* Field Manual FM 34-20. Washington, DC: Headquarters, Department of the Army, 1983.

—**COLLECTION PLAN** is a scheme for collecting information from all sources to fulfill an intelligence requirement. Once the sources are identified, they are sent a written request asking them to submit the necessary information. *See also:* Collection Requirement, Intelligence.

References

Department of Defense, Joint Chiefs of Staff. *Department of Defense Dictionary of Military and Related Terms.* Washington, DC: GPO, 1986.

—**COLLECTION REQUIREMENT** is the way a need for intelligence information is officially expressed. It is a written description of the problem and an implicit authorization to use intelligence resources to get the required information. Collection requirements often originate with intelligence analysts, but they must be approved on at least the supervisory level. The procedure is designed to process the requirements rapidly, while permitting accountability of the resources spent on specific requirements. *See also:* Intelligence Requirement.

References

Department of Defense, Defense Intelligence College. *Glossary of Intelligence Terms and Definitions.* Washington, DC: DIC, 1987.

Department of Defense, U.S. Army. *Support Operations: Echelons Above Corps.* Field Manual FM 100-16. Washington, DC: Headquarters, Department of the Army, 1986.

—**COLLECTIVE PROTECTION** is a shelter, with filtered air, that provides a contamination-free working environment for selected personnel and allows relief from continuous wear of mission-oriented protective posture gear.

References

Department of Defense, U.S. Army. *NBC Operations.* Field Manual FM 3-100. Washington, DC: Headquarters, Department of the Army, 1985.

—**COLLECTIVE TRAINING,** either in institutions or in units, prepares a group of individuals (e.g., crews, teams, squads, or platoons) to accomplish the tasks that are required of the group. It is training to prepare teams and units to accomplish the mission of their combined arms and services on the battlefield.

References

Department of Defense, U.S. Army. *Army Forces Training.* Army Regulation AR 350-41. Washington, DC: Headquarters, Department of the Army, 1986.

———. *How to Prepare and Conduct Military Training.* Field Manual FM 21-6. Washington, DC: Headquarters, Department of the Army, 1975.

———. *Individual Military Education and Training.* Army Regulation AR 350-1. Washington, DC: Headquarters, Department of the Army, 1987.

————. *Training for Mobilization and War.* Field Manual FM 25-5. Washington, DC: Headquarters, Department of the Army, 1985.

—**COLOR** means a flag or flags of a dismounted unit. "To the color" is a bugle call sounded to salute the color, the President, Vice President, Ex-President, or a foreign chief magistrate. A color is also called the standard.

References
Department of Defense, U.S. Army. *Dictionary of United States Army Terms.* Army Regulation AR 310-25. Washington, DC: Headquarters, Department of the Army, 1986.

—**COLOR BEARER** is one who carries the color or standard at formal reviews and ceremonies. *See also:* Color Guard.

References
Department of Defense, U.S. Army. *Dictionary of United States Army Terms.* Army Regulation AR 310-25. Washington, DC: Headquarters, Department of the Army, 1986.

—**COLOR GUARD** is a guard of honor that carries and escorts the color or standard at formal reviews and ceremonies.

References
Department of Defense, U.S. Army. *Dictionary of United States Army Terms.* Army Regulation AR 310-25. Washington, DC: Headquarters, Department of the Army, 1986.

—**COLOR PATCHES** are pieces of material of various shapes and colors that can be temporarily applied to an object to camouflage it. *See also:* Camouflage.

References
Department of Defense, U.S. Army. *Dictionary of United States Army Terms.* Army Regulation AR 310-25. Washington, DC: Headquarters, Department of the Army, 1986.

—**COLOR SALUTE** is a salute made by dipping a color or standard. The national color is never dipped in salute.

References
Department of Defense, U.S. Army. *Dictionary of United States Army Terms.* Army Regulation AR 310-25. Washington, DC: Headquarters, Department of the Army, 1986.

—**COLUMN** is a formation in which the elements are one behind the other. In a platoon column, the members of each squad are one behind the other, with the squads abreast of each other. To change a line formation to a column formation, the command is "Right, face." To change a column formation to a line formation, the command is "Left, face." *See also:* Formation, Line, Vee, Wedge.

References
Department of Defense, U.S. Army. *Drills and Ceremonies.* Field Manual FM 22-5. Washington, DC: Headquarters, Department of the Army, 1986.

—**COLUMN FORMATION** is an arrangement of vehicles or dismounted troops that (1) provides good security and permits maximum fire to the flanks, (2) facilitates control, (3) facilitates rapid deployment into any other formation, and (4) is used in road marches, night movements, and when passing through defiles and dense woods.

References
Department of Defense, U.S. Army. *Operational Terms and Symbols.* Field Manual FM 101-5-1. Washington, DC: Headquarters, Department of the Army, 1985.

—**COLUMN GAP (TIME OR DISTANCE)** is the space between two consecutive elements following each other on the same route, stated in units of length (meters) or units of time (minutes). It is measured from the rear of one element to the front of the following element.

References
Department of Defense, U.S. Army. *The Infantry Rifle Company (Infantry, Airborne, Air Assault, Ranger).* Field Manual FM 7-10. Washington, DC: Headquarters, Department of the Army, 1982.

—**COLUMN HALF LEFT (RIGHT).** (1) Column half left (right) is a change of direction of a column of 45 degrees to the left (right). (2) Column half left (right) is a preparatory command to make such a change of direction.

References
Department of Defense, U.S. Army. *Dictionary of United States Army Terms.* Army Regulation AR 310-25. Washington, DC: Headquarters, Department of the Army, 1986.

—**COLUMN LEFT (RIGHT).** (1) Column left (right) is a change of direction of a column by a full 90 degrees turn to the left (right). (2) Column left (right) is a preparatory command to make such a turn.

References

Department of Defense, U.S. Army. *Dictionary of United States Army Terms*. Army Regulation AR 310-25. Washington, DC: Headquarters, Department of the Army, 1986.

—**COLUMN LENGTH** is the length of the roadway occupied by a column or a convoy in movement. It is also called the length of a column. *See also:* Road Space.

References

Department of Defense, Joint Chiefs of Staff. *Department of Defense Dictionary of Military and Related Terms*. Washington, DC: GPO, 1986.

—**COMBAT AIRCRAFT PARKING AREA** is an area that has been specifically designated for loading or unloading combat-configured munitions onto or from aircraft and parking aircraft that are loaded with combat-configured munitions.

References

Department of Defense, U.S. Army. *Ammunition and Explosives Safety Standards*. Army Regulation AR 385-64. Washington, DC: Headquarters, Department of the Army, 1987.

—**COMBAT AREA** is a restricted area (air, land, or sea) established to prevent or minimize mutual interference between friendly forces that are engaged in combat operations. *See also:* Combat Zone.

References

Department of Defense, Joint Chiefs of Staff. *Department of Defense Dictionary of Military and Related Terms*. Washington, DC: GPO, 1986.

—**COMBAT ARMS** branches are Air Defense Artillery, Armor, Aviation, Field Artillery, Infantry, and the Corps of Engineers.

References

Department of Defense, U.S. Army. *Officer Assignment Policies, Details, and Transfers*. Army Regulation AR 614-100. Washington, DC: Headquarters, Department of the Army, 1984.

—**COMBAT ARMS IMMATERIAL POSITION** is a duty position that is not identified with one specific branch of the Army but is limited to officers whose branches are Infantry, Armor, Field Artillery, Air Defense Artillery, Aviation, or Engineer.

References

Department of Defense, U.S. Army. *Commissioned Officer Professional Development and Utilization*. Department of the Army Pamphlet 600-3. Washington, DC: Headquarters, Department of the Army, 1986.

—**COMBAT ASL (AUTHORIZED STOCKAGE LIST)** is the portion of the ASL that a supply point must stock to support the customer's essential combat maintenance. This includes backup stocks to "umbrella" the mandatory parts list required at the prescribed load list level, plus any combat damage required to be stocked in the supply point.

References

Department of Defense, U.S. Army. *Organizational Maintenance Operations*. Field Manual FM 29-2. Washington, DC: Headquarters, Department of the Army, 1984.

—**COMBAT COMMANDER'S INSIGNIA** is assigned to enlisted personnel in grade E4 or above and to officers who occupy command positions in the chain of command of combat units. The insignia is a green cloth tab worn in the middle of the shoulder strap. *See also:* Insignia.

References

Department of Defense, U.S. Army. *Dictionary of United States Army Terms*. Army Regulation AR 310-25. Washington, DC: Headquarters, Department of the Army, 1986.

—**COMBAT CREW** is the flying crew of a combat aircraft or the operating crew of a combat vehicle.

References

Department of Defense, U.S. Army. *Dictionary of United States Army Terms*. Army Regulation AR 310-25. Washington, DC: Headquarters, Department of the Army, 1986.

—**COMBAT CRUISE** (ARMY AVIATION) is a tactical formation in which the wingman moves from ten degrees aft of abeam on the right to ten degrees abaft of abeam on the left.

References

Department of Defense, U.S. Army. *Air-to-Air Combat*. Field Manual FM 1-107. Washington, DC: Headquarters, Department of the Army, 1984.

—**COMBAT DEVELOPER** is the agency responsible for doctrine, concepts, requirements (both materiel and nonmateriel), and organization. *See also:* Combat Developments.

References

Department of Defense, U.S. Army. *Dictionary of United States Army Terms.* Army Regulation AR 310-25. Washington, DC: Headquarters, Department of the Army, 1986.

—**COMBAT DEVELOPMENTS** are a major component of force development that encompasses the formulation of concepts, doctrine, organizations, and materiel objectives and requirements for the employment of United States Army forces in a theater of operations and in the control of civil disturbances. It includes development of Army functional systems (logistics, personnel, administrative, and other as designated) that impact directly on or extend into a theater of operations. *See also:* Combat Developer.

References

Department of Defense, U.S. Army. *Dictionary of United States Army Terms.* Army Regulation AR 310-25. Washington, DC: Headquarters, Department of the Army, 1986.

—**COMBAT DRILL** is a drill conducted for the purpose of giving training in formations and movement designed for a small unit's use in battle. Combat drill is usually conducted at extended intervals and distances. *See also:* Close Order Drill.

References

Department of Defense, U.S. Army. *Dictionary of United States Army Terms.* Army Regulation AR 310-25. Washington, DC: Headquarters, Department of the Army, 1986.

—**COMBAT ECHELON** is part of an organization that engages in combat, as distinguished from troops engaged in supply or administration. *See also:* Echelon.

References

Department of Defense, U.S. Army. *Dictionary of United States Army Terms.* Army Regulation AR 310-25. Washington, DC: Headquarters, Department of the Army, 1986.

—**COMBAT EFFECTIVENESS** is the ability of a unit to perform its mission. Factors such as the status of fuel, ammunition, weapons systems, and personnel are assessed and rated from one to four (with one being the highest rating).

References

Department of Defense, U.S. Army. *Operational Terms and Symbols.* Field Manual FM 101-5-1. Washington, DC: Headquarters, Department of the Army, 1985.

—**COMBAT ELECTRONIC WARFARE INTELLIGENCE (CEWI).** In 1975, the U.S. Army Security Agency was broken up in a significant reorganization of Army Intelligence. On the tactical level, the Agency's assets were merged with other Army Intelligence resources to form multidisciplinary CEWI units. The goal was to provide better intelligence to field commanders by combining all the available intelligence and security resources into formations that would support the divisions and corps. *See also:* Electronic Warfare, Intelligence.

References

Finnegan, John P. *Military Intelligence: A Picture History.* Arlington, VA: U.S. Army Intelligence and Security Command, 1984.

—**COMBAT ELEMENT** means troops that take part in fighting, as distinguished from troops engaged in supply or administration.

References

Department of Defense, U.S. Army. *Dictionary of United States Army Terms.* Army Regulation AR 310-25. Washington, DC: Headquarters, Department of the Army, 1986.

—**COMBAT ENGINEER VEHICLE, FULL-TRACKED 165-MM GUN** is an armored, tracked vehicle that provides engineer support to other combat elements. The vehicle is equipped with a heavy-duty boom and winch, dozer blade, and a 165-mm demolition gun. It is also armed with 7.62-mm and 50-caliber machine guns.

References

Department of Defense, Joint Chiefs of Staff. *Department of Defense Dictionary of Military and Related Terms.* Washington, DC: GPO, 1986.

—**COMBAT ENGINEERS** contribute to the combined arms team by performing mobility, countermobility, and survivability missions. Mobility missions include breaching enemy minefields and obstacles, improving existing routes or building new ones, and providing bridge and raft support for crossing major water obstacles. Countermobility efforts limit the maneuver of enemy forces and enhance the effectiveness of U.S. fires. Engineers improve the survivability of the friendly force by hardening the command and control facilities and key logistic installations by fortifying battle positions in the defense. In addition, combat engineers are organized, equipped, and trained to fight as infantry in tactical emergencies.

References

Department of Defense, U.S. Army. *Operations.* Field Manual FM 100-5. Washington, DC: Headquarters, Department of the Army, 1986.

—**COMBAT ESSENTIAL END-ITEM** is equipment required by tactical units to close with and/or destroy the enemy.

References

Department of Defense, U.S. Army. *Dictionary of United States Army Terms.* Army Regulation AR 310-25. Washington, DC: Headquarters, Department of the Army, 1986.

—**COMBAT EXERCISE** means maneuvers or drill in fighting techniques. *See also:* Exercise.

References

Department of Defense, U.S. Army. *Dictionary of United States Army Terms.* Army Regulation AR 310-25. Washington, DC: Headquarters, Department of the Army, 1986.

—**COMBAT FIRING PRACTICE** is training whereby tactical units solve a problem involving a tactical situation in which ball ammunition is fired at targets representing the enemy.

References

Department of Defense, U.S. Army. *Dictionary of United States Army Terms.* Army Regulation AR 310-25. Washington, DC: Headquarters, Department of the Army, 1986.

—**COMBAT FORCES** are forces whose primary missions are to participate in combat. *See also:* Operating Forces.

References

Department of Defense, U.S. Army. *Dictionary of United States Army Terms.* Army Regulation AR 310-25. Washington, DC: Headquarters, Department of the Army, 1986.

—**COMBAT FORMATIONS** are extended formations, intended specifically for the rifle squad and platoon but adaptable to any type unit, that are designed to promote efficient control and tactical handling of small units in combat.

References

Department of Defense, U.S. Army. *Dictionary of United States Army Terms.* Army Regulation AR 310-25. Washington, DC: Headquarters, Department of the Army, 1986.

—**COMBAT HEROISM** is an act or acts by an individual engaged in actual conflict with the armed enemy, or in military operations that involve exposure to personal hazards due to direct enemy action or the imminence of such action. *See also:* Medal of Honor, Valor.

References

Department of Defense, U.S. Army. *Military Awards.* Army Regulation AR 672-5-1. Washington, DC: Headquarters, Department of the Army, 1984.

—**COMBAT INFORMATION** is raw data that can be passed directly to combat and combat support units for fire and maneuver, without interpretation, analysis, or integration with other data. *See also:* Combat Intelligence, Operational Intelligence.

References

Department of Defense, U.S. Army. *Intelligence and Electronic Warfare Operations.* Field Manual FM 34-1. Washington, DC: Headquarters, Department of the Army, 1984.

————. *Military Intelligence Battalion (CEWI) (Operations) (Corps).* Field Manual FM 34-21. Washington, DC: Headquarters, Department of the Army, 1982.

—**COMBAT INFORMATION AND INTELLIGENCE** is raw data that can be passed directly to combat and combat support units to be used for fire and maneuver, without interpretation, analysis, or integration with other data. Intelligence is data that requires some form of validation, integration, and comparison with other data, or analysis before it can be used or fully exploited. *See also:* Combat Information, Operational Intelligence.

References

Department of Defense, U.S. Army. *Intelligence and Electronic Warfare Operations.* Field Manual FM 34-1. Washington, DC: Headquarters, Department of the Army, 1984.

————. *Military Intelligence Battalion (CEWI) (Operations) (Corps).* Field Manual FM 34-21. Washington, DC: Headquarters, Department of the Army, 1982.

—**COMBAT INFORMATION CENTER** is the agency in a ship or aircraft manned and equipped to collect, display, evaluate, and disseminate tactical information for the use of the embarked flag officer, commanding officer, and certain control agencies.

References

Department of Defense, Joint Chiefs of Staff. *Department of Defense Dictionary of Military and Related Terms.* Washington, DC: GPO, 1986.

—**COMBAT INTELLIGENCE.** (1) Combat intelligence is unevaluated data. Because it is so highly perishable or because the tactical situation is so critical, the information must be provided immediately to a tactical commander. Combat information can be used for immediate fire and maneuver without processing. (2) Combat intelligence is knowledge of the enemy, weather, and the area's geographical features needed by a commander so that he can plan and conduct combat operations. *See also:* Combat Information, Tactical Intelligence.

References

Department of Defense, Defense Intelligence College. *Glossary of Intelligence Terms and Definitions.* Washington, DC: DIC, 1987.

Department of Defense, U.S. Army. *Military Intelligence Battalion (Combat Electronic Warfare Intelligence) (Division).* Field Manual FM 34-10. Washington, DC: Headquarters, Department of the Army, 1981.

————. *Military Intelligence Company (Combat Electronic Warfare and Intelligence) (Armored Cavalry Regiment/Separate Brigade).* Field Manual FM 34-30. Washington, DC: Headquarters, Department of the Army, 1983.

————. *Operational Terms and Symbols.* Field Manual FM 101-5-1. Washington, DC: Headquarters, Department of the Army, 1985.

—**COMBAT JUMP** is the act of leaving an aircraft in flight by parachute and landing in hostile territory.

References

Department of Defense, U.S. Army. *Dictionary of United States Army Terms.* Army Regulation AR 310-25. Washington, DC: Headquarters, Department of the Army, 1986.

—**COMBAT LIAISON** is a system of maintaining contact and communication between units during fighting in order to secure proper cooperation.

References

Department of Defense, U.S. Army. *Dictionary of United States Army Terms.* Army Regulation AR 310-25. Washington, DC: Headquarters, Department of the Army, 1986.

—**COMBAT MANEUVER FORCES** are forces that use fire and movement to engage the enemy with direct force weapon systems, as distinguished from forces that engage the enemy with indirect fires or otherwise provide combat support. These elements are primarily infantry, armor, cavalry (air and armored), and aviation.

References

Department of Defense, U.S. Army. *Operational Terms and Symbols.* Field Manual FM 101-5-1. Washington, DC: Headquarters, Department of the Army, 1985.

—**COMBAT MULTIPLIER** is the supporting and subsidiary means that significantly increase the relative combat strength of a force while actual force ratios remain constant (e.g., economizing in one area to mass in another, surprise, deception, camouflage, electronic warfare, psychological operations, and terrain reinforcement).

References

Department of Defense, U.S. Army. *Operational Terms and Symbols.* Field Manual FM 101-5-1. Washington, DC: Headquarters, Department of the Army, 1985.

—**COMBAT ORDERS** pertain to strategic or tactical operations and Combat Service Support of tactical operations. A combat order may be issued initially as a plan to become a future order. They include operation orders, administrative orders, and letters of instruction. *See also:* Combat Service Support, Operation Order.

References

Department of Defense, U.S. Army. *Dictionary of United States Army Terms.* Army Regulation AR 310-25. Washington, DC: Headquarters, Department of the Army, 1986.

————. *Staff Organization and Operations.* Field Manual FM 101-5. Washington, DC: Headquarters, Department of the Army, 1984.

—**COMBAT PATROL** is a tactical unit sent out from the main body of a force to engage in independent fighting. It may be used to provide security or to harass, destroy, or capture enemy troops, equipment, or installations. Operations include raids, ambushes, and security missions.

References
Department of Defense, U.S. Army. *The Infantry Rifle Company (Infantry, Airborne, Air Assault, Ranger)*. Field Manual FM 7-10. Washington, DC: Headquarters, Department of the Army, 1982.

———. *Operational Terms and Symbols*. Field Manual FM 101-5-1. Washington, DC: Headquarters, Department of the Army, 1985.

—**COMBAT PHASE** is the period during which the military force is actively engaged with the enemy.

References
Department of Defense, U.S. Army. *Dictionary of United States Army Terms*. Army Regulation AR 310-25. Washington, DC: Headquarters, Department of the Army, 1986.

—**COMBAT PLL (PRESCRIBED LOAD LIST)** is the portion of a unit's PLL needed to sustain essential maintenance operations under combat conditions. It includes all mandatory parts list items plus as much of the unit's essential demand-supported PLL as can be carried with organic equipment.

References
Department of Defense, Joint Chiefs of Staff. *Department of Defense Dictionary of Military and Related Terms*. Washington, DC: GPO, 1986.

Department of Defense, U.S. Army. *Organizational Maintenance Operations*. Field Manual FM 29-2. Washington, DC: Headquarters, Department of the Army, 1984.

—**COMBAT POWER.** (1) Combat power is a compilation of capabilities related to a specific military balance between countries or coalitions. The ingredients include the numbers and types of forces; technological attributes of weapons and equipment; discipline; morale; pride; confidence; hardiness; elan; loyalty; training; combat experience; command and control arrangements; staying power; and leadership. Combat power is illusory unless it is accompanied by the national will to use it as required. (2) Combat power is a complex combination of tangible and intangible factors that are transitory and reversible on the battlefield. Combat power is composed of the effects of maneuver, firepower, and protection, and the effectiveness of leadership. The skillful combination of these elements in a sound operational plan turns potential into actual power.

References
Department of Defense, U.S. Army. *Operational Terms and Symbols*. Field Manual FM 101-5-1. Washington, DC: Headquarters, Department of the Army, 1985.

—**COMBAT PRACTICE.** *See:* Combat Firing Practice.

—**COMBAT PRESCRIBED LIST.** The Army's Standardized Combat PLL/ASL Program makes the demand supported peacetime prescribed list and authorized stockage list more "combat ready." This program requires units to stock selected essential repair parts to sustain their equipment in combat. The selection is keyed to individual end-items. The parts selected are termed a mandatory parts list.

References
Department of Defense, U.S. Army. *Organizational Maintenance Operations*. Field Manual FM 29-2. Washington, DC: Headquarters, Department of the Army, 1984.

—**COMBAT PROFICIENCY TESTS** are tests given to a unit to determine its readiness for combat.

References
Department of Defense, U.S. Army. *Dictionary of United States Army Terms*. Army Regulation AR 310-25. Washington, DC: Headquarters, Department of the Army, 1986.

—**COMBAT READINESS** is synonymous with operational readiness with respect to missions or functions that are performed in combat. It is the unit's capability to perform its assigned missions as derived through its plans. The status of personnel, equipment, supplies, maintenance facilities, and training is considered when determining this capability. *See also:* Combat Ready.

References
Department of Defense, U.S. Army. *How to Prepare and Conduct Military Training*. Field Manual FM 21-6. Washington, DC: Headquarters, Department of the Army, 1975.

—**COMBAT READY** is synonymous with operationally ready with respect to missions or functions performed in combat.

References
Department of Defense, Joint Chiefs of Staff. *Department of Defense Dictionary of Military and Related Terms*. Washington, DC: GPO, 1986.

—**COMBAT RECONAISSANCE** is reconnaissance of the enemy in immediate contact with one's own forces, preliminary to or during combat.

References

Department of Defense, U.S. Army. *Dictionary of United States Army Terms*. Army Regulation AR 310-25. Washington, DC: Headquarters, Department of the Army, 1986.

—**COMBAT SERVICE SUPPORT (CSS)** is the assistance provided to operating forces in the fields in the form of administrative, chaplain, financial, legal, health, food, and personal services (e.g., laundry and dry cleaning); military police; supply; maintenance; transportation; construction; troop construction; acquisition and disposal of real property; facilities engineering; topographic and geodetic engineering functions; graves registration; property disposal; and other logistic services.

References

Department of Defense, Joint Chiefs of Staff. *Department of Defense Dictionary of Military and Related Terms*. Washington, DC: GPO, 1986.

Department of Defense, U.S. Army. *Air Defense Artillery Deployment: Chaparral/Vulcan/Stinger*. Field Manual FM 44-3. Washington, DC: Headquarters, Department of the Army, 1984.

————. *Combat Service Support*. Field Manual FM 100-10. Washington, DC: Headquarters, Department of the Army, 1983.

————. *Combat Service Support Operations-Corps*. Field Manual FM 63-3J. Washington, DC: Headquarters, Department of the Army, 1985.

————. *Dictionary of United States Army Terms*. Army Regulation AR 310-25. Washington, DC: Headquarters, Department of the Army, 1986.

————. *Operational Terms and Symbols*. Field Manual FM 101-5-1. Washington, DC: Headquarters, Department of the Army, 1985.

—**COMBAT SERVICE SUPPORT (CSS) AIR MOVEMENT** is the air transport of personnel and cargo, by strategic or theater airlift, that is not directly in support of combat operations.

References

Department of Defense, Joint Chiefs of Staff. *Department of Defense Dictionary of Military and Related Terms*. Washington, DC: GPO, 1986.

—**COMBAT SERVICE SUPPORT (CSS) BRANCHES** are the Adjutant General's Corps, the Finance Corps, the Ordnance Corps, the Transportation Corps, and the Quartermaster Corps. Engineer, Signal, and Military Police are both services and arms. *See also:* Combat Service Support.

References

Department of Defense, U.S. Army. *Combat Service Support*. Field Manual FM 100-10. Washington, DC: Headquarters, Department of the Army, 1983.

————. *Combat Service Support Operations-Corps*. Field Manual FM 63-3J. Washington, DC: Headquarters, Department of the Army, 1985.

————. *Officer Assignment Policies, Details, and Transfers*. Army Regulation AR 614-100. Washington, DC: Headquarters, Department of the Army, 1984.

—**COMBAT SERVICE SUPPORT (CSS) ELEMENTS** are elements whose primary missions are to provide service support to combat forces and that are a part, or are prepared to become a part, of a theater, command, or task force for combat operations. *See also:* Operating Forces, Service Troops, Troops.

References

Department of Defense, Joint Chiefs of Staff. *Department of Defense Dictionary of Military and Related Terms*. Washington, DC: GPO, 1986.

Department of Defense, U.S. Army. *Combat Service Support*. Field Manual FM 100-10. Washington, DC: Headquarters, Department of the Army, 1983.

————. *Combat Service Support Operations-Corps*. Field Manual FM 63-3J. Washington, DC: Headquarters, Department of the Army, 1985.

—**COMBAT SPREAD** (ARMY AVIATION) is a tactical formation in which the wingman flies ten degrees forward or aft of abeam on the right or left of the leader with a minimum lateral separation of 500 feet.

References

Department of Defense, U.S. Army. *Air-to-Air Combat*. Field Manual FM 1-107. Washington, DC: Headquarters, Department of the Army, 1984.

—**COMBAT SUPPORT (CS)** is fire support and operational assistance provided to combat elements. It includes artillery, air defense artillery, engineer, military police, signal, military intelligence, and chemical support. *See also:* Combat Service Support.

References

Department of Defense, U.S. Army. *Air Defense Artillery Deployment: Chaparral/Vulcan/Stinger*. Field Manual FM 44-3. Washington, DC: Headquarters, Department of the Army, 1984.

———. *Dictionary of United States Army Terms.* Army Regulation AR 310-25. Washington, DC: Headquarters, Department of the Army, 1986.

———. *Operational Terms and Symbols.* Field Manual FM 101-5-1. Washington, DC: Headquarters, Department of the Army, 1985.

—**COMBAT SUPPORT (CS) AIR MOVEMENT** is the air transport and delivery of combat personnel, equipment, and supplies that help a ground force to accomplish its mission. *See also:* Combat Support.

References

Department of Defense, U.S. Army. *USA/USAF Doctrine for Joint Airborne and Tactical Airlift Operations.* Field Manual FM 100-27. Washington, DC: Headquarters, Department of the Army, 1985.

—**COMBAT SUPPORT (CS) ARMS** are the Corps of Engineers, Chemical Corps, Military Intelligence, the Military Police Corps, and the Signal Corps. *See also:* Combat Support.

References

Department of Defense, U.S. Army. *Dictionary of United States Army Terms.* Army Regulation AR 310-25. Washington, DC: Headquarters, Department of the Army, 1986.

———. *Officer Assignment Policies, Details and Transfers.* Army Regulation AR 614-100. Washington, DC: Headquarters, Department of the Army, 1984.

—**COMBAT SUPPORT (CS) ELEMENTS** are elements whose primary missions are to provide service support to combat forces that are a part, or are prepared to become a part, of a theater, command, or task force formed for combat operations. *See also:* Operating Forces.

References

Department of Defense, Joint Chiefs of Staff. *Department of Defense Dictionary of Military and Related Terms.* Washington, DC: GPO, 1986.

—**COMBAT SUPPORT (CS) HOSPITAL** is a nonfixed medical treatment facility. *See also:* Medical Treatment.

References

Department of Defense, U.S. Army. *Dictionary of United States Army Terms.* Army Regulation AR 310-25. Washington, DC: Headquarters, Department of the Army, 1986.

—**COMBAT SUPPORT (CS) TRAINING** is advanced individual training conducted in U.S. Army training centers to include cooks, vehicle maintenance, clerical, supply, communications, and vehicle driver military occupational specialty qualification courses.

References

Department of Defense, U.S. Army. *Dictionary of United States Army Terms.* Army Regulation AR 310-25. Washington, DC: Headquarters, Department of the Army, 1986.

—**COMBAT SUPPORT (CS) TROOPS** are units or organizations whose primary mission is to furnish operational assistance for the combat elements. *See also:* Troops.

References

Department of Defense, Joint Chiefs of Staff. *Department of Defense Dictionary of Military and Related Terms.* Washington, DC: GPO, 1986.

—**COMBAT SURVEILLANCE** is a continuous, all-weather, day-and-night, systematic watch over the battle area to provide timely information for tactical combat operations.

References

Department of Defense, Joint Chiefs of Staff. *Department of Defense Dictionary of Military and Related Terms.* Washington, DC: GPO, 1986.

—**COMBAT SURVEILLANCE RADAR** is a radar used to maintain continuous watch over a combat area.

References

Department of Defense, Joint Chiefs of Staff. *Department of Defense Dictionary of Military and Related Terms.* Washington, DC: GPO, 1986.

—**COMBAT SURVIVAL** involves measures taken by service personnel when they are involuntarily separated from friendly forces in combat. It includes procedures relating to individual survival, evasion, escape, and conduct after capture.

References

Department of Defense, Joint Chiefs of Staff. *Department of Defense Dictionary of Military and Related Terms.* Washington, DC: GPO, 1986.

—**COMBAT (TACTICAL) LOADING (CROSS-LOADING)** is arranging personnel and storing equipment and supplies to conform and to facilitate the anticipated tactical operation of the organization that is embarked. Each individual item is stored so that it can be unloaded at the required time.

References

Department of Defense, Joint Chiefs of Staff. *Department of Defense Dictionary of Military and Related Terms.* Washington, DC: GPO, 1986.

Department of Defense, U.S. Army. *USA/USAF Doctrine for Joint Airborne and Tactical Airlift Operations.* Field Manual FM 100-27. Washington, DC: Headquarters, Department of the Army, 1985.

—**COMBAT TRAINS** are the portion of unit trains that provides the combat service support required for immediate response to the needs of forward tactical elements. At the company level, medical, recovery, and maintenance elements normally constitute the combat trains. At the battalion level, the combat trains normally consist of ammunition and petroleum, oil, and lubricants vehicles, maintenance/recovery vehicles and crews, and the battalion aid station. *See also:* Field Train, Unit Trains.

References

Department of Defense, U.S. Army. *Air Defense Artillery Deployment: Chaparral/Vulcan/Stinger.* Field Manual FM 44-3. Washington, DC: Headquarters, Department of the Army, 1984.

—**COMBAT TROOPS** are units or organizations whose primary mission is to destroy enemy forces and/or installations. *See also:* Troops.

References

Department of Defense, Joint Chiefs of Staff. *Department of Defense Dictionary of Military and Related Terms.* Washington, DC: GPO, 1986.

—**COMBAT UNIT** is a unit trained and equipped to fight as an independent tactical element.

References

Department of Defense, U.S. Army. *Dictionary of United States Army Terms.* Army Regulation AR 310-25. Washington, DC: Headquarters, Department of the Army, 1986.

—**COMBAT VEHICLE** is a vehicle, with or without armor, that is designed for a specific fighting function. Armor protection or armament that is mounted as supplemental equipment on noncombat vehicles does not change the classification of such vehicles to combat vehicles. *See also:* Vehicle.

References

Department of Defense, Joint Chiefs of Staff. *Department of Defense Dictionary of Military and Related Terms.* Washington, DC: GPO, 1986.

—**COMBAT ZONE.** (1) The combat zone is the area required by combat forces to conduct operations. (2) The combat area is the territory forward of the Army rear area boundary. It extends from the frontline to the front of the communications zone. *See also:* Communications Zone.

References

Department of Defense, U.S. Army. *Operational Terms and Symbols.* Field Manual FM 101-5-1. Washington, DC: Headquarters, Department of the Army, 1985.

—**COMBATANT.** (1) Combatants, in international law, are individual members of belligerent forces subject to the laws, rights, and duties of war. (2) A combatant is a soldier or unit assigned to duty as an active fighter or fighting unit, as distinguished from duty in the services (e.g., administrative, supply, or medical).

References

Department of Defense, U.S. Army. *Dictionary of United States Army Terms.* Army Regulation AR 310-25. Washington, DC: Headquarters, Department of the Army, 1986.

—**COMBINATION VEHICLE** is a towing vehicle (prime mover) and a towed load (trailer).

References

Department of Defense, U.S. Army. *Dictionary of United States Army Terms.* Army Regulation AR 310-25. Washington, DC: Headquarters, Department of the Army, 1986.

—**COMBINED** means between two or more forces or agencies of two or more allies. When all allies or services are not involved, the participating nations and services are identified (e.g., combined armies). *See also:* Joint.

References

Department of Defense, Joint Chiefs of Staff. *Department of Defense Dictionary of Military and Related Terms.* Washington, DC: GPO, 1986.

—**COMBINED ARMS** refers to the synchronized use of two or more separate units of different type weapons systems.

Combined arms tactics create a multiplier effect. The capability of the combined arms team is greater than the sum of the units operating independently. One example of this is using field artillery to make an attacking armored force button up and deploy. Once an armored vehicle is buttoned up, it becomes more vulnerable to attack by helicopters. After the enemy has been slowed or stopped by artillery and attack helicopters, friendly armored units can take the initiative and exploit this success.

Another example is the synchronized use of electronic means, direct and indirect fires, including tactical air support, to suppress enemy air defenses.

References

Department of Defense, U.S. Army. *Attack Helicopter Operations.* Field Manual FM 17-50. Washington, DC: Headquarters, Department of the Army, 1984.

—**COMBINED ARMS AND SERVICES STAFF SCHOOL (CAS³)** at Fort Leavenworth, Kansas, provides intensive staff training to officers during their sixth through ninth years of service. CAS³ insures that all officers—those who staff units that fight, support, and sustain the battle—receive appropriate training early enough in their careers to help them perform effectively. They learn to develop staff studies, staff estimates, operations plans and orders, and related staff products.

References

Department of Defense, U.S. Army. *Department of the Army Policy Statement, 1988.* Washington, DC: Headquarters, Department of the Army, 1988.

—**COMBINED ARMS AND SERVICES TRAINING (CAST).** Proficiency in combined arms and services training is required for units, staffs, and commanders to fight and win air-land battles. Examples of systems that must be integrated into training are fire support, intelligence, electronic warfare, airspace management, air defense artillery, ground maneuver, antiarmor, combat support, and combat service support.

References

Department of Defense, U.S. Army. *How to Conduct Training Exercises.* Field Manual FM 25-4. Washington, DC: Headquarters, Department of the Army, 1984.

—**COMBINED ARMS TEAM** is two or more arms mutually supporting each other. A team usually consists of tanks, infantry, cavalry, aviation, field artillery, air defense artillery, and engineers.

References

Department of Defense, U.S. Army. *Dictionary of United States Army Terms.* Army Regulation AR 310-25. Washington, DC: Headquarters, Department of the Army, 1986.

———. *Operational Terms and Symbols.* Field Manual FM 101-5-1. Washington, DC: Headquarters, Department of the Army, 1985.

—**COMBINED ATTACK** is a joint air attack team employment option in which, if the situation warrants, the elements of the team can attack targets at the same time using the same basic attack avenues. Timing is critical to a combined attack. The inbound call is used to sequence the individual attacks. The optimum situation is for the helicopters to attack as the close air action flight begins the approach to the target. As the close air action pilots pull up to begin their attack, the helicopters remask. The helicopters unmask to resume the attack as the close air action aircraft complete their escape maneuver and egress. This coordinated attack scheme can continue until the situation dictates a change or the battle is terminated.

References

Department of Defense, U.S. Army. *Air Defense Artillery Deployment: Chaparral/Vulcan/Stinger.* Field Manual FM 44-3. Washington, DC: Headquarters, Department of the Army, 1984.

———. *Army Exercises.* Army Regulation AR 350-28. Washington, DC: Headquarters, Department of the Army, 1985.

———. *Army Forces Training.* Army Regulation AR 350-41. Washington, DC: Headquarters, Department of the Army, 1986.

———. *Civil Affairs Operations.* Field Manual FM 41-10. Washington, DC: Headquarters, Department of the Army, 1985.

———. *Military Intelligence Group (Combat Electronic Warfare and Intelligence) (Corps).* Field Manual FM 34-20. Washington, DC: Headquarters, Department of the Army, 1983.

———. *Operational Terms and Symbols.* Field Manual FM 101-5-1. Washington, DC: Headquarters, Department of the Army, 1985.

—**COMBINED COMMAND** is the unification of two or more forces or agencies of two or more allies. When all allies or services are not involved, the participating nations and services are identified, as in combined armies.

References

Department of Defense, U.S. Army. *Civil Affairs Operations.* Field Manual FM 41-10. Washington, DC: Headquarters, Department of the Army, 1985.

—**COMBINED DOCTRINE** is the fundamental principles that guide the use of forces of two or more nations in a coordinated action toward a common objective. It is ratified by the participating nations. *See also:* Joint Doctrine, Multi-Service Doctrine.

References
Department of Defense, Joint Chiefs of Staff. *Department of Defense Dictionary of Military and Related Terms.* Washington, DC: GPO, 1986.

—**COMBINED EXERCISE** is an exercise that involves the military forces of more than one nation.

References
Department of Defense, U.S. Army. *Army Exercises.* Army Regulation AR 350-28. Washington, DC: Headquarters, Department of the Army, 1985.

—**COMBINED FORCE** is a military force composed of elements of two or more allied nations.

References
Department of Defense, Joint Chiefs of Staff. *Department of Defense Dictionary of Military and Related Terms.* Washington, DC: GPO, 1986.

—**COMBINED OBSTACLES OVERLAY** is an overlay for a map that depicts the most probable areas of passability and impassability to enemy forces as a result of terrain and weather conditions. The combined obstacles overlay file contains coordinate data describing boundaries of all impassable areas and descriptions of the types of obstacles that are present.

References
Department of Defense, U.S. Army. *Counter-Signals Intelligence (C-SIGINT) Operations.* Field Manual FM 34-62. Washington, DC: Headquarters, Department of the Army, 1986.

—**COMBINED OPERATION** is an operation conducted by forces of two or more allied nations that are acting together to accomplish a single mission. *See also:* Joint Operation.

References
Department of Defense, Joint Chiefs of Staff. *Department of Defense Dictionary of Military and Related Terms.* Washington, DC: GPO, 1986.

—**COMBINED STAFF** is a staff composed of personnel of two or more allied nations. *See also:* Integrated Staff, Joint Staff, Parallel Staff.

References
Department of Defense, Joint Chiefs of Staff. *Department of Defense Dictionary of Military and Related Terms.* Washington, DC: GPO, 1986.

—**COMBINED TRAINING.** (1) Combined training is training that involves elements of two or more forces of two or more nations. (2) Combined training is training a unit with the branch or branches with which it would normally operate.

References
Department of Defense, U.S. Army. *Army Forces Training.* Army Regulation AR 350-41. Washington, DC: Headquarters, Department of the Army, 1986.

———. *Dictionary of United States Army Terms.* Army Regulation AR 310-25. Washington, DC: Headquarters, Department of the Army, 1986.

—**COME-AS-YOU-ARE WAR** is a contingency serious enough to require Reserve component units to deploy in a peacetime configuration without the benefit of additional training or personnel and equipment fill.

References
Department of Defense, U.S. Army. *Dictionary of United States Army Terms.* Army Regulation AR 310-25. Washington, DC: Headquarters, Department of the Army, 1986.

—**COMMAND.** (1) A command is a unit or units, an organization, or an area under the direction of one individual. (2) Command is the authority that a military commander lawfully exercises over his subordinates by virtue of his rank or assignment. Command includes the responsibility and authority for planning, organizing, directing, coordinating, and controlling military forces in order to accomplish the missions that have been assigned to the commander. It includes responsibility for health, welfare, morale, and discipline of assigned personnel. (3) A command is an order that is given by the commander (i.e., it is the will of the commander that is expressed for the purpose of bringing about a particular action). (4) To command is to dominate by a field of weapon fire or by observation from a superior position. *See also:* Area Command, Base Command.

References
Department of Defense, Joint Chiefs of Staff. *Department of Defense Dictionary of Military and Related Terms.* Washington, DC: GPO, 1986.

—COMMAND AND CONTROL (C&C or C²). (1) Command and control is the exercising of authority and direction by a properly designated commander over the forces assigned to him as he accomplishes his mission. Command and control functions are fulfilled by organizing personnel, equipment, communications, and facilities and writing procedures so that a commander can plan, direct, and coordinate the forces assigned to him. (2) Command and control is an Army tactical intelligence term that means functions that are performed through the arrangement of personnel, equipment, communications, facilities, and procedures that provide for the direction of combat operations.

References
Department of Defense, U.S. Army. *Military Intelligence Battalion Combat Electronic Warfare and Intelligence (Aerial Exploitation) (Corps).* Field Manual FM 34-22. Washington, DC: Headquarters, Department of the Army, 1984.

———. *Military Intelligence Battalion (CEWI) (Tactical Exploitation) (Corps): Counterintelligence, Interrogation, Electronic Warfare.* Field Manual FM 34-23. Washington, DC: Headquarters, Department of the Army, 1985.

———. *Military Intelligence Company (Combat Electronic Warfare and Intelligence) (Armored Cavalry Regiment/Separate Brigade).* Field Manual FM 34-30. Washington, DC: Headquarters, Department of the Army, 1983.

———. *Operational Terms and Symbols.* Field Manual FM 101-5-1. Washington, DC: Headquarters, Department of the Army, 1985.

———. *Staff Organization and Operations.* Field Manual FM 101-5. Washington, DC: Headquarters, Department of the Army, 1984.

—COMMAND AND CONTROL (C & C) FACILITIES include command posts and supporting automation and communications systems. They provide processing and transmission of information and orders that are necessary for effective command and control.

References
Department of Defense, U.S. Army. *Staff Organization and Operations.* Field Manual FM 101-5. Washington, DC: Headquarters, Department of the Army, 1984.

—COMMAND AND CONTROL (C & C) ORGANIZATION, the organization of the headquarters for operations, is how the commander organizes his staff to accomplish his mission. The commander's organization includes the role and relationships of the staff, the authority and responsibilities of the staff, and the functional grouping of staff sections.

References
Department of Defense, U.S. Army. *Staff Organization and Operations.* Field Manual FM 101-5. Washington, DC: Headquarters, Department of the Army, 1984.

—COMMAND AND CONTROL (C & C) PROCESS, the decisionmaking procedures and techniques used by the headquarters, is how the commander and his staff accomplish the mission. It is used to find out what is going on, to decide what action to take, to issue instructions, and to supervise execution. These procedures and techniques include records, reporting systems, and briefings that support the decisionmaking process.

References
Department of Defense, U.S. Army. *Staff Organization and Operations.* Field Manual FM 101-5. Washington, DC: Headquarters, Department of the Army, 1984.

—COMMAND AND CONTROL (C & C) SKILLS TRAINING sustains skill proficiency for leaders, staffs, and individual soldiers. It reinforces common skills and those particular to duty positions. It trains each echelon to respond to the needs of higher, lower, adjacent, and attached combat, combat support, and combat service support units. Responding to subordinate units is particularly important. Inexperienced commanders and staffs tend to orient themselves to respond upward and overlook the needs of subordinate units. One prime purpose of training exercises is to teach leaders to focus on the needs of subordinate units in a sequence of timely troop-leading steps that allows units to execute the mission properly.

References
Department of Defense, U.S. Army. *How to Conduct Training Exercises.* Field Manual FM 25-4. Washington, DC: Headquarters, Department of the Army, 1984.

—COMMAND AND CONTROL (C & C) SYSTEM. (1) C & C system includes the equipment, procedures, communications, and personnel essential for a commander to plan, direct, and control operations of assigned forces pursuant to the missions assigned. (2) C & C system is the means by which a commander exercises command and control and integrates into operations the support provided by other Army elements and elements of other services. These tasks are accomplished through a system of three interrelated components: command and control organization, command and control process, and command and control facilities.

References

Department of Defense, Joint Chiefs of Staff. *Department of Defense Dictionary of Military and Related Terms.* Washington, DC: GPO, 1986.

Department of Defense, U.S. Army. *Staff Organization and Operations.* Field Manual FM 101-5. Washington, DC: Headquarters, Department of the Army, 1984.

—**COMMAND AND STAFF COMMUNICATIONS.** Communications between commands are accomplished through specified channels or links. The communications channel or link refers to the subject and to the function involved in the communication. Three types of channels or links of communications are the command channel, the staff channel, and the technical channel.

References

Department of Defense, U.S. Army. *Staff Organization and Operations.* Field Manual FM 101-5. Washington, DC: Headquarters, Department of the Army, 1984.

—**COMMAND AXIS** is a line along which a headquarters will move.

References

Department of Defense, Joint Chiefs of Staff. *Department of Defense Dictionary of Military and Related Terms.* Washington, DC: GPO, 1986.

—**COMMAND CENTER** is a facility from which a commander and his representatives direct operations and control forces. It is organized to gather, process, analyze, display, and disseminate planning and operational data and perform other related tasks.

References

Department of Defense, Joint Chiefs of Staff. *Department of Defense Dictionary of Military and Related Terms.* Washington, DC: GPO, 1986.

—**COMMAND CHANNEL** is the direct, official link between headquarters through which all orders and instructions are passed to subordinate units, except those that are passed on the technical channel. Command channels are from com-

mander to commander. Within the authority granted to them, staff officers use command channels when acting in the commander's name.

References

Department of Defense, U.S. Army. *Staff Organization and Operations.* Field Manual FM 101-5. Washington, DC: Headquarters, Department of the Army, 1984.

—**COMMAND CHANNELS** are the operational chain of command as defined by the Joint Chiefs of Staff.

References

Department of Defense, U.S. Army. *Dictionary of United States Army Terms.* Army Regulation AR 310-25. Washington, DC: Headquarters, Department of the Army, 1986.

—**COMMAND, CONTROL, AND COMMUNICATIONS (C³)** is an integrated system of doctrine, procedures, organizational structure, personnel, equipment, facilities, and communications that provides authorities at all levels with timely and adequate data to plan, direct, and control their activities. It is the process of directing and controlling the activities of military forces in order to attain an objective. It includes consideration of the physical means of its accomplishment: the communications, control centers, information-gathering systems, and the staffs and facilities necessary to gather and analyze information, plan for what is to be done, and supervise the execution of what has been ordered.

References

Department of Defense, Joint Chiefs of Staff. *Department of Defense Dictionary of Military and Related Terms.* Washington, DC: GPO, 1986.

Department of Defense, U.S. Army. *Combat Service Support Operations-Theater.* Field Manual FM 63-4. Washington, DC: Headquarters, Department of the Army, 1984.

———. *Support Operations: Echelons Above Corps.* Field Manual FM 100-16. Washington, DC: Headquarters, Department of the Army, 1986.

—**COMMAND, CONTROL, AND COMMUNICATIONS COUNTERMEASURES (C³CM)** are the combined use of operations security, military deception, jamming, and physical destruction supported by intelligence to deny information and to influence, damage, or destroy enemy C³ capabilities, while protecting one's own C³ capabilities from similar action by the enemy.

There are two divisions within C³CM *counter C³* involves measures taken to deny adversary commanders and other decisionmakers the ability to command and control their forces effectively. *C3 protection* involves measures taken to maintain the effectiveness of friendly C³ despite both adversary and friendly counter-C³ actions.

References

Department of Defense, Joint Chiefs of Staff. *Department of Defense Dictionary of Military and Related Terms.* Washington, DC: GPO, 1986.

Department of Defense, National Defense University. *Joint Staff Officer's Guide, 1986.* Washington, DC: GPO, 1986.

Department of Defense, U.S. Army. *Operational Terms and Symbols.* Field Manual FM 101-5-1. Washington, DC: Headquarters, Department of the Army, 1985.

—**COMMAND, CONTROL, AND COMMUNICATIONS NETWORK (C³Net)** are the different command and control entities and the systems that permit these entities to communicate with each other. In the modern era of computer and electronic systems, C³ nets are more secure, given the advances in electronics that have provided prevoiusly unachievable communications security. Conversely, these same systems are vulnerable, particularly in nuclear attacks, and may not function adequately under certain wartime conditions.

References

Department of Defense, U.S. Army. *Dictionary of United States Army Terms.* Army Regulation AR 310-25. Washington, DC: Headquarters, Department of the Army, 1986.

—**COMMAND, CONTROL, AND COMMUNICATIONS SYSTEMS (C³S)** are the individual communications and control systems that a commander and his staff need to direct operations. Such systems are grouped to form C³ networks.

References

Department of Defense, U.S. Army. *Dictionary of United States Army Terms.* Army Regulation AR 310-25. Washington, DC: Headquarters, Department of the Army, 1986.

—**COMMAND, CONTROL, AND INFORMATION SYSTEM** is an integrated system of doctrine, procedures, organizational structure, personnel, equipment, facilities, and communications that provides authorities at all levels with timely and adequate data to plan, direct, coordinate, and control their operations.

References

Department of Defense, Joint Chiefs of Staff. *Department of Defense Dictionary of Military and Related Terms.* Washington, DC: GPO, 1986.

Department of Defense, U.S. Army. *Air Defense Artillery Deployment: Chaparral/Vulcan/Stinger.* Field Manual FM 44-3. Washington, DC: Headquarters, Department of the Army, 1984.

———. *Support Operations: Echelons Above Corps.* Field Manual FM 100-16. Washington, DC: Headquarters, Department of the Army, 1986.

—**COMMAND, CONTROL, COMMUNICATIONS, AND INTELLIGENCE (C³I)** is relevant at both the tactical and strategic levels. It involves the entire system—all the people, properly organized, and all the equipment, intelligence, communications, facilities, and writing procedures—that a commander needs to plan, direct, and coordinate the forces that are assigned to him.

References

Department of Defense, U.S. Army. *Dictionary of United States Army Terms.* Army Regulation AR 310-25. Washington, DC: Headquarters, Department of the Army, 1986.

—**COMMAND CONTROLLED STOCKS** are stocks placed at the disposal of a designated NATO commander to provide him with a flexibility with which to influence the battle logistically. "Placed at the disposal of" implies responsibility for storage, maintenance, accounting, rotation or turnover, physical security, and subsequent transportation to a particular battle area.

References

Department of Defense, Joint Chiefs of Staff. *Department of Defense Dictionary of Military and Related Terms.* Washington, DC: GPO, 1986.

—**COMMAND DETONATED MINE** is a mine that is detonated by remotely controlled means. *See also:* Mine Warfare.

References

Department of Defense, U.S. Army. *Mine/Countermine Operations at the Company Level.* Field Manual FM 20-32. Washington, DC: Headquarters, Department of the Army, 1976.

—**COMMAND FIELD EXERCISE (CFX)** is a field training exercise with reduced combat unit and vehicle density, but with full command and control, combat support, and combat service support elements. It lies on a scale between command post exercises and field training exercises: available resources—money, time, personnel, and equipment—determine where CFXs fall on the scale. CFXs can also be used as backups for field training exercises if maneuver damage or other factors (e.g., changes in the weather) prohibit the planned field training exercise. *See also:* Field Training Exercise.

References

Department of Defense, U.S. Army. *Army Forces Training.* Army Regulation AR 350-41. Washington, DC: Headquarters, Department of the Army, 1986.

———. *How to Conduct Training Exercises.* Field Manual FM 25-4. Washington, DC: Headquarters, Department of the Army, 1984.

—**COMMAND GROUP** is a small party that accompanies the commander when he leaves the command post to be present at a critical action. The party is organized and equipped to suit the commander, and normally provides local security and other personal assistance for the commander as he requires.

References

Department of Defense, U.S. Army. *Dictionary of United States Army Terms.* Army Regulation AR 310-25. Washington, DC: Headquarters, Department of the Army, 1986.

———. *Operational Terms and Symbols.* Field Manual FM 101-5-1. Washington, DC: Headquarters, Department of the Army, 1985.

—**COMMAND INFORMATION** is information concerning military and civil events, conditions, policies, and actions provided to Army personnel by commanders.

References

Department of Defense, U.S. Army. *Dictionary of United States Army Terms.* Army Regulation AR 310-25. Washington, DC: Headquarters, Department of the Army, 1986.

—**COMMAND INFORMATION ACTIVITIES** are activities meant to improve the effectiveness of the Army by informing soldiers about military and civil events, conditions, policies, and actions to increase their understanding of their role in the Army and the Army's importance to the nation's defense.

References

Department of Defense, U.S. Army. *Dictionary of United States Army Terms.* Army Regulation AR 310-25. Washington, DC: Headquarters, Department of the Army, 1986.

—**COMMAND INSPECTIONS** insure proper use of equipment, maintain supply economy, insure compliance with established procedures, and evaluate operational readiness. Command inspections are made periodically by unit commanders and/or their supervisors.

References

Department of Defense, U.S. Army. *Organizational Maintenance Operations.* Field Manual FM 29-2. Washington, DC: Headquarters, Department of the Army, 1984.

—**COMMAND LIAISON** is close communications among commanders to share information and work together effectively.

References

Department of Defense, U.S. Army. *Dictionary of United States Army Terms.* Army Regulation AR 310-25. Washington, DC: Headquarters, Department of the Army, 1986.

—**COMMAND NET** is a communications network that connects an echelon of command with some or all of its subordinate echelons for the purpose of command control.

References

Department of Defense, Joint Chiefs of Staff. *Department of Defense Dictionary of Military and Related Terms.* Washington, DC: GPO, 1986.

—**COMMAND OF EXECUTION** is the second part of a command at which the order is carried out (e.g., in "forward, march," "forward" is the preparatory command, and "march" is the command of execution).

References

Department of Defense, U.S. Army. *Dictionary of United States Army Terms.* Army Regulation AR 310-25. Washington, DC: Headquarters, Department of the Army, 1986.

—**COMMAND POST (CP)** is the principal facility used by the commander for command and control combat operations. A CP consists of coordinating and special staff activities and representatives from supporting Army elements and other services that are necessary to carry out operations. Corps and division headquarters are particularly adaptable to organization by echelon into a tactical CP, a main CP, and a rear CP. *See also:* Main Command Post, Rear Command Post, Tactical Command Post.

References

Department of Defense, Joint Chiefs of Staff. *Department of Defense Dictionary of Military and Related Terms*. Washington, DC: GPO, 1986.

———. *Air Defense Artillery Deployment: Chaparral/Vulcan/Stinger*. Field Manual FM 44-3. Washington, DC: Headquarters, Department of the Army, 1984.

———. *Operational Terms and Symbols*. Field Manual FM 101-5-1. Washington, DC: Headquarters, Department of the Army, 1985.

———. *Staff Organizations and Operations*. Field Manual FM 101-5. Washington, DC: Headquarters, Department of the Army, 1984.

—**COMMAND POST EXERCISE (CPX)** is a military exercise involving commanders, their staffs, and communications elements within and between headquarters. It does not require the presence or participation of the soldiers in the unit. *See also:* Field Training Exercise.

References

Department of Defense, U.S. Army. *Army Exercises*. Army Regulation AR 350-28. Washington, DC: Headquarters, Department of the Army, 1985.

———. *Army Forces Training*. Army Regulation AR 350-41. Washington, DC: Headquarters, Department of the Army, 1986.

———. *How to Conduct Training Exercises*. Field Manual FM 25-4. Washington, DC: Headquarters, Department of the Army, 1984.

———. *How to Prepare and Conduct Military Training*. Field Manual FM 21-6. Washington, DC: Headquarters, Department of the Army, 1975.

—**COMMAND RELATIONSHIPS** are the methods by which command responsibility and authority are routinely established. *See also:* Assigned, Attached, Operational Command, Operational Control, Organic.

References

Department of Defense, U.S. Army. *Commander's Handbook for Property Accountability at the Unit Level*. Field Manual FM 10-14-1. Washington, DC: Headquarters, Department of the Army, 1984.

—**COMMAND REPORT** is a report used by commanders of designated headquarters and units to periodically submit information and evaluations on the combat operations of their commands, and to make recommendations based upon their experiences, including joint and combined operations and support activities, that are pertinent to doctrine, organization, equipment, training, administration, and tactics.

References

Department of Defense, U.S. Army. *Dictionary of United States Army Terms*. Army Regulation AR 310-25. Washington, DC: Headquarters, Department of the Army, 1986.

COMMAND RESPONSIBILITY is the obligation of a commander to insure the proper care, custody, and safekeeping of all government property within his command.

References

Department of Defense, U.S. Army. *Commander's Handbook for Property Accountability at the Unit Level*. Field Manual FM 10-14-1. Washington, DC: Headquarters, Department of the Army, 1984.

—**COMMAND-SPONSORED DEPENDENTS** are a soldier's dependents who are residing with him at a location outside of the continental United States. The accompanied-by-dependents tour must be authorized by Army Regulation AR 614-30 and the soldier must be authorized to serve the tour. The dependents must meet the following conditions: (1) they are entitled to travel to the soldier's duty station at government expense because of the soldier's permanent change of station orders; (2) they are authorized by appropriate authority to be at the soldier's duty station; and (3) their residency in the vicinity of the soldier's duty station must entitle the soldier to station allowances at the "with dependents" rate. *See also:* Tour of Duty.

References

Department of Defense, U.S. Army. *Leaves and Passes*. Army Regulation AR 630-5. Washington, DC: Headquarters, Department of the Army, 1984.

—**COMMAND STRENGTH** is strength chargeable to table of organization and equipment, to table of distribution units, and to allocations for nonpermanent party personnel activities that are indicated in the Troop Program and Troop List as organizations of, and are assigned to, the United States Army.

References

Department of Defense, U.S. Army. *Dictionary of United States Army Terms*. Army Regulation AR 310-25. Washington, DC: Headquarters, Department of the Army, 1986.

—**COMMANDER** (DRILL AND CEREMONIES). The commander is the person who is in charge of the drill or ceremony.

References

Department of Defense, U.S. Army. *Drills and Ceremonies*. Field Manual FM 22-5. Washington, DC: Headquarters, Department of the Army, 1986.

—**COMMANDER OF THE GUARD** is the senior officer or noncommissioned officer of the guard. He is the next senior person to the officer of the day. He is responsible for the instruction, discipline, and performance of duty of the guard. *See also:* Guard.

References

Department of Defense, U.S. Army. *Dictionary of United States Army Terms*. Army Regulation AR 310-25. Washington, DC: Headquarters, Department of the Army, 1986.

————. *Guard Duty*. Field Manual FM 22-6. Washington, DC: Headquarters, Department of the Army, 1971.

—**COMMANDER'S BASE ASSESSMENT** is a list, based on the commander's planning guidance, of the critical facilities, units, and supplies that the G3 provides to the rear area operations center. The rear area operation center, using the commander's guidance and the list, prioritizes the bases in the rear area.

References

Department of Defense, U.S. Army. *Military Police Team, Squad, Platoon Combat Operations*. Field Manual FM 19-4. Washington, DC: Headquarters, Department of the Army, 1984.

————. *Rear Battle*. Field Manual FM 90-14. Washington, DC: Headquarters, Department of the Army, 1985.

—**COMMANDERS' CONFERENCE** is a meeting of commanders or their representatives. Elements of the commanders' staffs may be present.

References

Department of Defense, U.S. Army. *Staff Organization and Operations*. Field Manual FM 101-5. Washington, DC: Headquarters, Department of the Army, 1984.

—**COMMANDER'S ESTIMATE** is the procedure whereby a commander decides how to best accomplish his assigned mission by considering the mission, enemy, terrain, and weather, troops available, and time and other relevant factors. The commander's estimate is based upon personal knowledge of the situation and on staff estimates. *See also:* Estimate of the Situation, Staff Estimates.

References

Department of Defense, Joint Chiefs of Staff. *Department of Defense Dictionary of Military and Related Terms*. Washington, DC: GPO, 1986.

Department of Defense, U.S. Army. *Operational Terms and Symbols*. Field Manual FM 101-5-1. Washington, DC: Headquarters, Department of the Army, 1985.

—**COMMANDER'S EVALUATION** is a local, hands-on test administered to an individual soldier by the unit's chain of command. It is used to indicate the soldier's ability to perform mission-critical tasks. It is one of the components of the Individual Training Evaluation Program.

References

Department of Defense, U.S. Army. *Army Forces Training*. Army Regulation AR 350-41. Washington, DC: Headquarters, Department of the Army, 1986.

————. *Training for Mobilization and War*. Field Manual FM 25-5. Washington, DC: Headquarters, Department of the Army, 1985.

—**COMMANDER'S INTENT** is the commander's vision of the battle (i.e., how he expects to fight and what he expects to accomplish).

References

Department of Defense, U.S. Army. *Operational Terms and Symbols*. Field Manual FM 101-5-1. Washington, DC: Headquarters, Department of the Army, 1985.

—**COMMANDER'S PLANNING GUIDANCE** is an essential element in the problem identification and analysis process. After familiarizing himself with the problem, the commander limits the area to be studied, provides appropriate information from his experience and knowledge, and assigns responsibility for the study. Adequate command guidance facilitates arriving at an appropriate solution and precludes wasted effort.

References

Department of Defense, U.S. Army. *Staff Organization and Operations*. Field Manual FM 101-5. Washington, DC: Headquarters, Department of the Army, 1984.

—**COMMANDER'S TRAINING GUIDANCE** is specific information provided by a commander to a trainer so that trainer can prepare and train properly. The guidance should include the commander's training objectives; to whom, when, and where the training is to be given; and the commander's reasons for the training. *See also:* Commander's Training Objective.

References

Department of Defense, U.S. Army. *How to Prepare and Conduct Military Training.* Field Manual FM 21-6. Washington, DC: Headquarters, Department of the Army, 1975.

—**COMMANDER'S TRAINING OBJECTIVE** is written in performance terms (i.e., task, condition, and training standards) developed or selected by a commander or training manager. It specifies the level of performance the soldiers undergoing training must meet or exceed.

References

Department of Defense, U.S. Army. *How to Prepare and Conduct Military Training.* Field Manual FM 21-6. Washington, DC: Headquarters, Department of the Army, 1975.

—**COMMANDING OFFICER** is the officer who commands an installation, organization, unit, garrison, or bivouac.

References

Department of Defense, U.S. Army. *Guard Duty.* Field Manual FM 22-6. Washington, DC: Headquarters, Department of the Army, 1971.

—**COMMISSARY STORE** is an activity that is usually located on an installation, that sells subsistence and household supplies to authorized individuals.

References

Department of Defense, U.S. Army. *Dictionary of United States Army Terms.* Army Regulation AR 310-25. Washington, DC: Headquarters, Department of the Army, 1986.

—**COMMISSION.** (1) A commission is a written order giving a person rank and authority as an officer in the armed forces. (2) Commission is the rank and the authority given by such an order.

References

Department of Defense, Joint Chiefs of Staff. *Department of Defense Dictionary of Military and Related Terms.* Washington, DC: GPO, 1986.

—**COMMISSIONED OFFICER** is an officer in any of the armed services who holds a grade and office under a commission that has been issued by the President. In the Army, a person who has been appointed to the grade of second lieutenant or higher is a commissioned officer.

References

Department of Defense, U.S. Army. *Dictionary of United States Army Terms.* Army Regulation AR 310-25. Washington, DC: Headquarters, Department of the Army, 1986.

—**COMMISSIONED OFFICER FORCE ALIGNMENT PLAN III (COFAPIII)** is a personnel strength management tool designed to align officer year groups by grade and branch, and to comply with the Defense Officer Personnel Management Act.

References

Department of Defense, U.S. Army. *Department of the Army Policy Statement, 1988.* Washington, DC: Headquarters, Department of the Army, 1988.

—**COMMITMENT.** (1) A commitment is the assignment of units and/or resources to specified action or uses. (2) A commitment is a promise or pledge that such resources or units will be assigned.

References

Department of Defense, U.S. Army. *Dictionary of United States Army Terms.* Army Regulation AR 310-25. Washington, DC: Headquarters, Department of the Army, 1986.

—**COMMITTED FORCE** is a force in contact with an enemy or deployed on a specific mission or course of action that precludes its employment elsewhere. Designation of enemy forces as committed forces depends primarily on their disposition, location at the time of the estimate, and the echelon at which the estimate is being prepared.

References

Department of Defense, U.S. Army. *Intelligence Analysis.* Field Manual FM 34-3. Washington, DC: Headquarters, Department of the Army, 1986.

———. *Operational Terms and Symbols.* Field Manual FM 101-5-1. Washington, DC: Headquarters, Department of the Army, 1985.

—**COMMITTEE** is a group of persons—military, civilian, or both—that has been appointed by appropriate authority as a permanent (standing committee) or temporary (ad hoc committee) advisory body to the appointing authority. It makes recommendations to the appropriate authority on matters placed before it. Membership on the committee is in addition to the individuals' primary duties, except that an individual may be assigned the primary duty of secretary or recorder, or as a member of an ad hoc committee during a specified time.

References

Department of Defense, U.S. Army. *Dictionary of United States Army Terms*. Army Regulation AR 310-25. Washington, DC: Headquarters, Department of the Army, 1986.

—**COMMODITY MANAGER** is an individual within the organization of an inventory control point or other such organization who is assigned management responsibility for the homogeneous grouping of materiel items.

References

Department of Defense, Joint Chiefs of Staff. *Department of Defense Dictionary of Military and Related Terms*. Washington, DC: GPO, 1986.

—**COMMON CONTROL** (ARTILLERY) refers to a horizontal and vertical major chart location of points in the target and position areas, tied in with the horizontal and vertical control in use by two or more units. It may be established by firing, surveying, or both, or by assumption. *See also:* Control Point.

References

Department of Defense, Joint Chiefs of Staff. *Department of Defense Dictionary of Military and Related Terms*. Washington, DC: GPO, 1986.

—**COMMON INFRASTRUCTURE** is the infrastructure essential to the training of NATO forces or to the implementation of NATO operational plans that, owing to its degree of common use or interest and its compliance with criteria laid down periodically by the North Atlantic Council, is commonly financed by NATO members. *See also:* Infrastructure.

References

Department of Defense, Joint Chiefs of Staff. *Department of Defense Dictionary of Military and Related Terms*. Washington, DC: GPO, 1986.

—**COMMON ITEM.** (1) A common item is any materiel required for use by more than one activity. (2) Common item is a term loosely used to denote any consumable item except repair parts or other technical items. (3) A common item is a materiel that is procured for, owned by (service stock), or used by any military department of the Department of Defense and that is required to be furnished to a recipient country under the grant-aid Military Assistance Program. (4) Common items are readily available commercial items. (5) Common items are items used by two or more services that are of similar manufacture or fabrication but may vary between the services as to color or shape (e.g., vehicles or clothing). (6) A common item is any part or component required in the assembly of two or more complete end-items.

References

Department of Defense, Joint Chiefs of Staff. *Department of Defense Dictionary of Military and Related Terms*. Washington, DC: GPO, 1986.

—**COMMON JOB** is a duty position that occurs in more than one military occupational specialty (e.g., radio-telephone operator).

References

Department of Defense, U.S. Army. *Individual Military Education and Training*. Army Regulation AR 350-1. Washington, DC: Headquarters, Department of the Army, 1987.

—**COMMON MILITARY EDUCATION AND TRAINING** is training directed by Headquarters, Department of the Army, that amplifies the broad mission training and provides a specific skill or knowledge for individuals, teams, or units. *See also:* Common Military Training.

References

Department of Defense, U.S. Army. *Individual Military Education and Training*. Army Regulation AR 350-1. Washington, DC: Headquarters, Department of the Army, 1987.

—**COMMON MILITARY TRAINING** is training that augments broad mission training to provide an individual with collective skills or knowledge. These subjects are not included in Soldier Training Publications or in Army Training and Evaluation Programs.

References

Department of Defense, U.S. Army. *Army Forces Training*. Army Regulation AR 350-41. Washington, DC: Headquarters, Department of the Army, 1986.

—**COMMON SERVICE OR COMMON SERVICING** is the support provided by one military service to another for which reimbursement is not required from the service that receives the support. *See also:* Servicing.

References

Department of Defense, Joint Chiefs of Staff. *Department of Defense Dictionary of Military and Related Terms*. Washington, DC: GPO, 1986.

Department of Defense, U.S. Army. *Transportation Reference Data*. Field Manual FM 55-15. Washington, DC: Headquarters, Department of the Army, 1986.

—**COMMON SUPPLIES** are supplies common to two or more services.

References
Department of Defense, Joint Chiefs of Staff. *Department of Defense Dictionary of Military and Related Terms*. Washington, DC: GPO, 1986.

—**COMMON TABLE OF ALLOWANCES** is an authorization document for items of materiel required for common use by individuals and/or by table of organization and equipment, table of distribution and allowances, or joint table of allowances units and activities Army-wide, including the Reserve components.

References
Department of Defense, U.S. Army. *Dictionary of United States Army Terms*. Army Regulation AR 310-25. Washington, DC: Headquarters, Department of the Army, 1986.

—**COMMON TASK** is an activity performed by every soldier at a specific skill level. *See also:* Common Task Test.

References
Department of Defense, U.S. Army. *Individual Military Education and Training*. Army Regulation AR 350-1. Washington, DC: Headquarters, Department of the Army, 1987.

—**COMMON TASK TEST (CTT)** is a hands-on test administered annually and used to evaluate proficiency on critical common tasks that are specified in the *Soldier's Manual of Common Task*. Alternate written tests are provided if the equipment required for hands-on testing is not available. The CTT is one of the three components of the Individual Training Evaluation Program.

References
Department of Defense, U.S. Army. *Army Forces Training*. Army Regulation AR 350-41. Washington, DC: Headquarters, Department of the Army, 1986.

———. *Training for Mobilization and War*. Field Manual FM 25-5. Washington, DC: Headquarters, Department of the Army, 1985.

—**COMMON-USER TRANSPORTATION** is a point-to-point transportation service managed by a single service to be used by two or more services or other authorized agencies for which reimbursement is normally required from the service or agency that is receiving the support.

References
Department of Defense, U.S. Army. *Transportation Reference Data*. Field Manual FM 55-15. Washington, DC: Headquarters, Department of the Army, 1986.

—**COMMONALITY** is a quality that applies to materiel or systems (1) that possess similar and interchangeable characteristics enabling each to be used, operated, or maintained without additional specialized training, by personnel trained on the others, and/or (2) that have interchangeable repair parts and/or components. Commonality also refers to consumable items that are interchangeably equivalent without adjustment.

References
Department of Defense, Joint Chiefs of Staff. *Department of Defense Dictionary of Military and Related Terms*. Washington, DC: GPO, 1986.

—**COMMUNICATIONS** are "the methods or means of conveying information from one person or place to another. This term does not include direct, unassisted conversation or correspondence through nonmilitary postal agencies." *See also:* Communications Security.

References
Department of Defense, U.S. Army. *Combat Communications*. Field Manual FM 24-1. Washington, DC: Headquarters, Department of the Army, 1976.

———. *Support Operations: Echelons Above Corps*. Field Manual FM 100-16. Washington, DC: Headquarters, Department of the Army, 1986.

U.S. Congress. Senate. *Final Report of the Senate Select Committee to Study Government Operations With Respect to Intelligence Activities. Report 94-755. Book I, Foreign and Military Intelligence* (Church Committee Report). Washington, DC: GPO, 1976.

—**COMMUNICATIONS CENTER** is "a facility that is responsible for receiving, transmitting, and delivering messages; it normally contains a message section, a cryptographic section, and a sending and receiving section, using electronic communications devices." *See also:* Communications Security.

References

Department of Defense, U.S. Army. *Tactical Single Channel Radio Communications Techniques.* Field Manual FM 24-18. Washington, DC: Headquarters, Department of the Army, 1984.

U.S. Congress. Senate. *Final Report of the Senate Select Committee to Study Government Operations With Respect to Intelligence Activities. Report 94-755. Book I, Foreign and Military Intelligence* (Church Committee Report). Washington, DC: GPO, 1976.

—**COMMUNICATIONS CHECKPOINT (CCP)** is an air control point that requires serial leaders to report either to the aviation mission commander or to the terminal control facility. *See also:* Air Control Point.

References

Department of Defense, U.S. Army. *Attack Helicopter Operations.* Field Manual FM 17-50. Washington, DC: Headquarters, Department of the Army, 1984.

————. *Operational Terms and Symbols.* Field Manual FM 101-5-1. Washington, DC: Headquarters, Department of the Army, 1985.

—**COMMUNICATIONS COUNTERMEASURES** are electronic activities directed specifically against enemy communications.

References

Department of Defense, U.S. Army. *Combat Communications.* Field Manual FM 24-1. Washington, DC: Headquarters, Department of the Army, 1976.

————. *Dictionary of United States Army Terms.* Army Regulation AR 310-25. Washington, DC: Headquarters, Department of the Army, 1986.

—**COMMUNICATIONS COVER** is a technique of concealing or altering communications so that unauthorized parties cannot collect information that would be of value.

References

Department of Defense, U.S. Army. *Dictionary of United States Army Terms.* Army Regulation AR 310-25. Washington, DC: Headquarters, Department of the Army, 1986.

—**COMMUNICATIONS DECEPTION** is the intentional transmitting, retransmitting, altering, absorbing, or manipulating telecommunications to cause a misinterpretation of the telecommunications. There are two types of communications deception. *Imitative communications deception* is intruding into foreign communications channels with signals or traffic that imitate the foreign communications in order to deceive the enemy. *Manipulative communications deception* is altering or simulating friendly communications in order to deceive the enemy.

References

Department of Defense, Defense Intelligence College. *Glossary of Intelligence Terms and Definitions.* Washington, DC: DIC, 1977.

—**COMMUNICATIONS-ELECTRONICS (C-E)** are all the equipment and gear needed for formal and informal secure electronic communications. The term refers to all design, development, installations, operations, and maintenance of electronics and electromechanical systems associated with collecting, transmitting, processing, storing, recording, and displaying data and information that is associated with all forms of military communications, excluding the information and data systems and equipment that have been otherwise assigned.

References

Department of Defense, U.S. Army. *Communications-Electronics Operation Instructions "The CEOI."* Training Circular TC 24-1. Washington, DC: Headquarters, Department of the Army, 1982.

————. *Communications Techniques: Electronics Countermeasures.* Field Manual FM 24-33. Washington, DC: Headquarters, Department of the Army, 1985.

————. *Dictionary of United States Army Terms.* Army Regulation AR 310-25. Washington, DC: Headquarters, Department of the Army, 1986.

—**COMMUNICATIONS-ELECTRONICS OPERATION INSTRUCTIONS (C-EOI)** are a series of orders issued for technically controlling and coordinating the signal activities of a command. The instructions contain frequencies, call signs, and other information to establish and maintain radio and other forms of communications.

References

Department of Defense, U.S. Army. *Communications Techniques: Electronics Countermeasures.* Field Manual FM 24-33. Washington, DC: Headquarters, Department of the Army, 1985.

—**COMMUNICATIONS INTELLIGENCE (COMINT).** The official definition of COMINT is intelligence and technical information that is derived from foreign communications by other than the intended recipients. It does not include monitoring foreign public media or communications intercepts that are obtained during counterintelligence investigations within the United States. The Senate Select Committee on Intelligence defined COMINT as:

Communications intelligence is technical and intelligence information derived from foreign communications by other than the intended recipients:

A. Foreign Communications are all communications except: (1) Those of the governments of the United States and the British Commonwealth, (2) Those exchanged among private organizations and nationals, acting in a private capacity of the United States and the British Commonwealth, and (3) Those of nationals of the United States and the British Commonwealth appointed or detailed by their governments to serve in the international organizations.

B. COMINT activities are those which produce COMINT by collecting and processing foreign communications passed by radio, wire, or other electromagnetic means, and by the processing of foreign encrypted communications. However transmitted, collection comprises search, intercept and direction finding. Processing comprises range estimation, transmitter/operator identification, signal analysis, traffic analysis, cryptanalysis, decryption, study of the plain text, the fusion of these processes, and the reporting of the results.

C. Exceptions to COMINT and COMINT activities. COMINT and COMINT activities defined here do not include (1) Intercept and processing of unencrypted written communications, except written plain text versions of communications which have been encrypted or are intended for subsequent encryption. (2) Intercept and processing of press, propaganda and other public broadcasts, except for encrypted or "hidden meaning" passages in such broadcasts. (3) Operations conducted by the United States, United Kingdom or Commonwealth security authorities. (4) Censorship. (5) The intercept and study of noncommunications transmissions (ELINT).

See also: Communications Security.

References

Allen, Thomas B., and Polmar, Norman. *Merchants of Treason: America's Secrets for Sale.* New York: Delacorte Press, 1988.

American Bar Association. *Oversight and Accountability of the U.S. Intelligence Agencies: An Evaluation.* Washington, DC: ABA, 1985.

Bamford, James. *The Puzzle Palace: A Report on America's Most Secret Agency.* New York: Penguin Books, 1983.

Corson, William R. *The Armies of Ignorance: The Rise of the American Intelligence Empire.* New York: Dial Press, 1977.

Department of Defense, Defense Intelligence College. *Glossary of Intelligence Terms and Definitions.* Washington, DC: DIC, 1987.

Department of Defense, U.S. Army. *Counter-Signals Intelligence (C-SIGINT) Operations.* Field Manual FM 34-62. Washington, DC: Headquarters, Department of the Army, 1986.

———. *Military Intelligence Battalion Combat Electronic Warfare and Intelligence (Aerial Exploitation) (Corps).* Field Manual FM 34-22. Washington, DC: Headquarters, Department of the Army, 1984.

———. *Military Intelligence Battalion (CEWI) (Tactical Exploitation) (Corps): Counterintelligence, Interrogation, Electronic Warfare.* Field Manual FM 34-23. Washington, DC: Headquarters, Department of the Army, 1985.

———. *Military Intelligence Battalion (Combat Electronic Warfare Intelligence) (Division).* Field Manual FM 34-10. Washington, DC: Headquarters, Department of the Army, 1981.

———. *Military Intelligence Company (Combat Electronic Warfare and Intelligence) (Armored Cavalry Regiment/Separate Brigade).* Field Manual FM 34-30. Washington, DC: Headquarters, Department of the Army, 1983.

Godson, Roy, ed. *Intelligence Problems for the 1980s, Number 1: Elements of Intelligence.* Rev. ed. Washington, DC: National Strategy Information Center, 1983.

———. *Intelligence Problems for the 1980s, Number 3: Counterintelligence.* Washington, DC: National Strategy Information Center, 1980.

———. *Intelligence Problems for the 1980s, Number 5: Clandestine Collection.* Washington, DC: National Strategy Information Center, 1982.

Kessler, Ronald. *Spy vs. Spy: Stalking Soviet Spies in America.* New York: Charles Scribner's Sons, 1988.

Laqueur, Walter. *A World of Secrets.* New York: Basic Books, 1985.

Maurer, Alfred C.; Turnstall, Marion D.; and Keagle, James M. *Intelligence Policy and Process.* Boulder, CO: Westview Press, 1985.

U.S. Congress. Senate. *Final Report of the Senate Select Committee to Study Government Operations With Respect to Intelligence Activities. Report 94-755. Book I, Foreign and Military Intelligence* (Church Committee Report). Washington, DC: GPO, 1976.

—**COMMUNICATIONS INTERCEPTION,** as defined by the Church Committee, is the raw data of communications intelligence. It is information taken from a communications system by someone other than the intended recipients. Communications intercepts, when received, are placed into the intelligence processing cycle in order to produce communications intelligence. *See also:* Communications Security.

References

Godson, Roy, ed. *Intelligence Problems for the 1980s, Number 1: Elements of Intelligence.* Rev. ed. Washington, DC: National Strategy Information Center, 1983.

————. *Intelligence Problems for the 1980s, Number 3: Counterintelligence.* Washington, DC: National Strategy Information Center, 1980.

Laqueur, Walter. *A World of Secrets.* New York: Basic Books, 1985.

U.S. Congress. Senate. *Final Report of the Senate Select Committee to Study Government Operations With Respect to Intelligence Activities. Report 94-755. Book I, Foreign and Military Intelligence* (Church Committee Report). Washington, DC: GPO, 1976.

—**COMMUNICATIONS JAMMING (COMJAM)** is electronic disruption of an enemy's communications system so that it cannot receive information. *See also:* Jamming.

References

Blackburn, N. Glenn. "Computers: A Counterintelligence Concern." Unpublished paper provided to the editors. Washington, DC, 1987.

Muzerall, Joseph V., and Carty, Thomas P. "COMSEC and Its Need for Key Management." *DP&CS* (Spring 1987).

—**COMMUNICATIONS NET** is an organization of stations capable of making direct communications on a common channel or frequency.

References

Department of Defense, U.S. Army. *Operational Terms and Symbols.* Field Manual FM 101-5-1. Washington, DC: Headquarters, Department of the Army, 1985.

—**COMMUNICATIONS PROFILE,** in communications security, is an analytic model of the communications associated with an organization or activity as they might appear to a hostile signals intelligence organization. The model is the result of a systematic examination of applied communications security measures, communications content and patterns, and the functions that they reflect. *See also:* Communications Security.

References

Department of Defense, U.S. Army. *Counter-Signals Intelligence (C-SIGINT) Operations.* Field Manual FM 34-62. Washington, DC: Headquarters, Department of the Army, 1986.

————. *Military Intelligence Battalion Combat Electronic Warfare and Intelligence (Aerial Exploitation) (Corps).* Field Manual FM 34-22. Washington, DC: Headquarters, Department of the Army, 1984.

————. *Military Intelligence Company (Combat Electronic Warfare and Intelligence) (Armored Cavalry Regiment/Separate Brigade).* Field Manual FM 34-30. Washington, DC: Headquarters, Department of the Army, 1983.

—**COMMUNICATIONS PROTECTION,** in communications security refers to the communications security measures applied to telecommunications (1) to deny unauthorized persons access to unclassified information that may be of value, (2) to prevent disruption, or (3) to ensure the authenticity of such telecommunications. *See also:* Communications Security.

References

Laqueur, Walter. *A World of Secrets.* New York: Basic Books, 1985.

—**COMMUNICATIONS SECURITY (COMSEC).** (1) COMSEC is the protection that results from all efforts to prevent unauthorized individuals from gaining access to and analyzing specific information of intelligence value. COMSEC involves misleading unauthorized persons when they analyze this information if they gain access to it, and it involves the authenticating of the information. Protecting U.S. telecommunications and other communications from exploitation by foreign intelligence services and from unauthorized disclosure is one of the responsibilities of the National Security Agency. Protective measures include cryptosecurity; emission security; and the physical security of classified communications security materials, equipment, and documents.

(2) COMSEC is an Army tactical intelligence term that refers to the protective measures taken to deny unauthorized persons access to information derived from national-security-related U.S. government telecommunications and to ensure the authenticity of such communications. Such protection results from the application of security measures (including cryptosecurity, transmissions security, and emissions security) to electrical systems generating, handling, pro-

cessing, or using national-security-related information. It also includes applying physical security measures to communications security information or materials.

As defined by the Church Committee, COMSEC "is the protection of United States telecommunications and other communications from exploitation by foreign intelligence services and from unauthorized disclosure. COMSEC is one of the missions of the National Security Agency. It includes cryptosecurity, transmission security, emission security, and physical security of classified equipment, material, and documents."

- **COMSEC account** is an administrative entity, identified by an account number, that is used to account for custody and control of COMSEC material.
- **COMSEC aids** are all COMSEC material, other than the equipment and devices, that perform or assist the user in performing cryptographic functions or that relate to associated functions or devices. COMSEC aids are often required in order to produce, operate, or maintain cryptosystems or cryptosystem components (e.g., COMSEC keying material, call sign/frequency systems, and supporting documentation, such as operating and maintenance manuals).
- **COMSEC assessment** is a determination of the significance of telecommunications vulnerabilities and the threats thereto.
- **COMSEC control program** refers to a set of instructions or routines for a computer that controls or affects externally performed functions of key generation, cryptovariable generation and distribution, message encryption/decryption, or authentication.
- **COMSEC custodian** is the individual designated by proper authority to be responsible for the receipt, transfer, accountability, safeguarding, and destruction of the COMSEC material issued to a COMSEC account.
- **COMSEC end-item** is a part or combination of component parts and/or material that is ready for its intended use in a COMSEC application.
- **COMSEC equipment** is an instrument or device (e.g., crypto-equipment, crypto-ancillary equipment, cryptoproduction equipment, and authentication equipment) designed to provide security to telecommunications by converting information to a form that is unintelli-

gible to an unauthorized interceptor and by reconverting such information to its original form for authorized recipients, as well as the equipment designed specifically to aid in, or is an essential element of, the conversion process.
- **COMSEC evaluation** is an assessment of the effectiveness of the COMSEC measures that have been applied to a particular telecommunications system and of the need, if any, for applying additional COMSEC measures.
- **COMSEC facility** is a facility that contains classified COMSEC material.
- **COMSEC firmware** is the program information contained in a programmable read-only memory, read-only memory, or a similar device that incorporates a COMSEC function.
- **COMSEC information** is all information concerning COMSEC and all COMSEC material.
- **COMSEC insecurity** is an occurrence that jeopardizes the security of COMSEC material or the secure electrical transmission of national security or national security-related information.
- **COMSEC material** includes COMSEC aids, equipments and components thereof, and devices that are identifiable by the Telecommunications Security nomenclature system or a similar system of a U.S. department or agency, foreign government, or international organization.
- **COMSEC Material Control System** is the logistic system through which accountable COMSEC material is distributed, controlled and safeguarded. It consists of all COMSEC Central Offices of Record, cryptologistic depots, and COMSEC accounts and subaccounts.
- **COMSEC measures** are all cryptographic, transmission security, emission security, and physical security techniques employed to protect telecommunications.
- **COMSEC monitoring** is the act of listening to, copying or recording transmissions of one's own official telecommunications to provide material for analysis in order to determine the degree of security being provided to those transmissions. It is one of the techniques of COMSEC surveillance.
- **COMSEC profile** is the identification of all COMSEC measures and materials that are available for a given operation,

system, or organization, and a determination of the amount and type of use of those measures and materials.

- **COMSEC signals acquisition and analysis** is the acquiring and analyzing of radio frequency propagation to determine empirically the vulnerability of the transmission media to interception by foreign intelligence services. This process includes cataloging the transmission spectrum and taking signal parametric measurements as required. It does not include acquiring information carried on the system. It is one of the techniques of COMSEC surveillance.
- **COMSEC software** consists of the computer or microprocessor instructions and/or routines that control or perform COMSEC and COMSEC-related functions and associated documentation.
- **COMSEC surveillance** is the systematic examination of telecommunications to determine the adequacy of COMSEC measures, to identify COMSEC deficiencies, to provide data from which to predict the effectiveness of proposed COMSEC measures, and to confirm the adequacy of such measures after they are implemented.
- **COMSEC survey** has two meanings. (1) It is the application of COMSEC analysis and assessment techniques to a specific operation, function, or program. (2) It is an examination and inspection of a physical location to determine whether alterations and modifications are necessary to make it acceptable for the installation and operation of COMSEC equipment.
- **COMSEC system** is the combination of all measures intended to provide communications security for a specific telecommunications system, including the associated cryptographic, transmission, emission, computer, and physical security measures, as well as the COMSEC support system (e.g., documentation, doctrine, keying material protection and distribution, and equipment engineering, production, distribution, modification, and maintenance).

References

Allen, Thomas B., and Polmar, Norman. *Merchants of Treason: America's Secrets for Sale.* New York: Delacorte Press, 1988.

Blackburn, N. Glenn. "Computers: A Counterintelligence Concern." Unpublished paper provided to the editors. Washington, DC, 1987.

Department of Defense. *Activities of DoD Intelligence Components that Affect U.S. Persons.* (Department of Defense Directive 5240.1). Washington, DC: Department of Defense, 1982.

Department of Defense, Joint Chiefs of Staff. *Department of Defense Dictionary of Military and Related Terms.* Washington, DC: GPO, 1986.

Department of Defense, U.S. Army. *Counterintelligence.* Field Manual FM 34-60. Washington, DC: Headquarters, Department of the Army, 1985.

———. *Counter-Signals Intelligence (C-SIGINT) Operations.* Field Manual FM 34-62. Washington, DC: Headquarters, Department of the Army, 1986.

———. *Military Intelligence Battalion Combat Electronic Warfare and Intelligence (Aerial Exploitation) (Corps).* Field Manual FM 34-22. Washington, DC: Headquarters, Department of the Army, 1984.

———. *Military Intelligence Battalion (CEWI) (Tactical Exploitation) (Corps): Counterintelligence, Interrogation, Electronic Warfare.* Field Manual FM 34-23. Washington, DC: Headquarters, Department of the Army, 1985.

———. *Military Intelligence Company (Combat Electronic Warfare and Intelligence) (Armored) Cavalry Regiment/Separate Brigade).* Field Manual FM 34-30. Washington, DC: Headquarters, Department of the Army, 1983.

Godson, Roy, ed. *Intelligence Problems for the 1980s, Number 1: Elements of Intelligence.* Rev. ed. Washington, DC: National Strategy Information Center, 1983.

Kessler, Ronald. *Spy vs. Spy: Stalking Soviet Spies in America.* New York: Charles Scribner's Sons, 1988.

Laqueur, Walter. *A World of Secrets.* New York: Basic Books, 1985.

Martin, Paul H. "Communications-Computer Security." *Journal of Electronic Defense* (June 1987).

Muzerall, Joseph V., and Carty, Thomas P. "COMSEC and Its Need for Key Management." *DP&CS* (Spring 1987).

Office of the President of the United States. *Executive Order 12036, U.S. Intelligence Activities.* Washington, DC, 1978.

U.S. Congress. Senate. *Final Report of the Senate Select Committee to Study Government Operations With Respect to Intelligence Activities. Report 94-755. Book I, Foreign and Military Intelligence* (Church Committee Report). Washington, DC: GPO, 1976.

Ware, Willis H. "Information Systems, Security, and Privacy." *EDUCOM Bulletin* (Summer 1984).

—COMMUNICATIONS ZONE (COMMZ) is the rear part of the theater of operations behind the corps area that contains the lines of communications, establishments for supply and evacuation, and other agencies required for maintaining field forces. The major functional and area commands of the theater army in the COMMZ provide combat support and combat service support to Army forces and other services and agencies as directed. Combat service support provided includes support to the COMMZ, rear area protection in conjunction with the host nation if viable within the COMMZ, and support to the combat zone as directed by theater army headquarters. *See also:* Combat Zone, Rear Area.

References

Department of Defense, U.S. Army. *Air Defense Artillery Deployment: Chaparral/Vulcan/Stinger.* Field Manual FM 44-3. Washington, DC: Headquarters, Department of the Army, 1984.

————. *Combat Service Support Operations-Theater.* Field Manual FM 63-4. Washington, DC: Headquarters, Department of the Army, 1984.

————. *Support Operations: Echelons Above Corps.* Field Manual FM 100-16. Washington, DC: Headquarters, Department of the Army, 1986.

—**COMPANIES** (CLOSE COMBAT). Company-sized units consist of two or more platoons, usually of the same type, with headquarters and, in some cases, a limited capacity for self-support. Companies are the basic elements for all battalions. They are also assigned as separate units of brigades and larger organizations.

All close combat companies can fight massed or by separate platoons. In infantry, armor, and attack helicopter battalions, companies normally fight as integral units. Cavalry troops and attack helicopter companies more frequently fight with their platoons in separate zones, sectors, or areas.

Company-sized combat units are capable of fighting without additional reinforcements. Ordinarily, however, companies or troops are augmented for operations with short-range air defense units and ground surveillance radar teams. They may also be reinforced with maneuver platoons of the same or a different type and with engineer squads or platoons to form teams. Company teams are formed to tailor forces for a particular mission. Such tailoring matches forces to missions with greater precision, but because it often disrupts teamwork within the company, company teams should be formed only after careful consideration and, whenever possible, should be trained together before they are committed.

References

Department of Defense, U.S. Army. *Operations.* Field Manual FM 100-5. Washington, DC: Headquarters, Department of the Army, 1986.

—**COMPANIES** (COMBAT ENGINEER) control three or four engineer platoons. They may be used by their own battalion in a variety of tasks or they may support maneuver brigades or battalions. Separate brigades and regiments usually have an assigned combat engineer company.

References

Department of Defense, U.S. Army. *Operations.* Field Manual FM 100-5. Washington, DC: Headquarters, Department of the Army, 1986.

—**COMPANY** is the basic administrative and tactical unit in most arms and services in the Army. A company is on a command level below the battalion and above the platoon and is equivalent to a battery of artillery. *See also:* Army, Battalion, Brigades, Corps, Division, Platoon, Regiment, Squad.

References

Department of Defense, U.S. Army. *Dictionary of United States Army Terms.* Army Regulation AR 310-25. Washington, DC: Headquarters, Department of the Army, 1986.

—**COMPANY COLUMN,** the company's primary movement formation, provides good lateral and in-depth dispersion. It is the easiest formation to control and allows for rapid movement. It also allows the company to deliver a limited volume of fire to the front and rear but a high volume to the flanks. The base platoon is the lead platoon.

References

Department of Defense, U.S. Army. *The Infantry Rifle Company (Infantry, Airborne, Air Assault, Ranger).* Field Manual FM 7-10. Washington, DC: Headquarters, Department of the Army, 1982.

—**COMPANY GRADE** is the classification of officers normally serving in a company. It is applied to lieutenants and captains. *See also:* Field Grade.

References

Department of Defense, U.S. Army. *Dictionary of United States Army Terms.* Army Regulation AR 310-25. Washington, DC: Headquarters, Department of the Army, 1986.

—**COMPANY LINE** is the company's basic assault formation. It provides for delivery of maximum fire to the front but little to the flanks. It is the most difficult formation to control. The company commander should designate a base platoon for the other platoons to guide on. The base platoon is normally the center platoon.

References

Department of Defense, U.S. Army. *The Infantry Rifle Company (Infantry, Airborne, Air Assault, Ranger)*. Field Manual FM 7-10. Washington, DC: Headquarters, Department of the Army, 1982.

—**COMPANY SUPPORT AREA** is the portion of the company rear occupied by the company trains.

References

Department of Defense, U.S. Army. *Combat Service Support Operations-Division*. Field Manual FM 63-2. Washington, DC: Headquarters, Department of the Army, 1983.

—**COMPANY TEAM** is a team formed by attaching one or more nonorganic tank, mechanized, or infantry platoons to a tank, mechanized, or infantry company either in exchange for or in addition to the organic platoons.

References

Department of Defense, U.S. Army. *Air Defense Artillery Deployment: Chaparral/Vulcan/Stinger*. Field Manual FM 44-3. Washington, DC: Headquarters, Department of the Army, 1984.

—**COMPANY TRAINS** are normally made up of combat service support assets and the forward support elements of the battalion trains (if required). Company trains can be echeloned into combat and field trains. *See also:* Train.

References

Department of Defense, U.S. Army. *Combat Service Support Operations-Division*. Field Manual FM 63-2. Washington, DC: Headquarters, Department of the Army, 1983.

—**COMPANY TRANSPORT** refers to the vehicles that form an organic part of company equipment and are directly available to the company commander for tactical use.

References

Department of Defense, U.S. Army. *Dictionary of United States Army Terms*. Army Regulation AR 310-25. Washington, DC: Headquarters, Department of the Army, 1986.

—**COMPANY V.** Company V is a formation used when the enemy's situation is vague but contact is expected to the front. The company com-

mander has two platoons up front to provide a heavy volume of fire on contact. He also has one platoon in the rear that can either overwatch or trail the others. If the company is hit from either flank, there are still two platoons to provide a heavy volume of fire, and one free to maneuver. However, this formation is difficult to control and moves very slowly. The base platoon is normally the right flank platoon.

References

Department of Defense, U.S. Army. *The Infantry Rifle Company (Infantry, Airborne, Air Assault, Ranger)*. Field Manual FM 7-10. Washington, DC: Headquarters, Department of the Army, 1982.

—**COMPANY WEDGE.** The company wedge formation is used when the enemy's situation is vague and contact is not expected. There are two platoons in the rear that can overwatch or trail the lead platoon. This formation provides a large volume of fire to the front or flanks. It allows the company commander to make contact with a small element (platoon) and still have one or two platoons to maneuver. If the company is hit from the flank, there is still one platoon free to maneuver. It is difficult to control, but it allows faster movement than the company V. The lead platoon is the base platoon. *See also:* Company V.

References

Department of Defense, U.S. Army. *The Infantry Rifle Company (Infantry, Airborne, Air Assault, Ranger)*. Field Manual FM 7-10. Washington, DC: Headquarters, Department of the Army, 1982.

—**COMPARTMENTATION,** in unconventional warfare, is the division of an organization or an activity into functional segments or cells to restrict communication among them and to prevent each segment from learning the identity or activities of other segments except on a need-to-know basis.

References

Department of Defense, U.S. Army. *Dictionary of United States Army Terms*. Army Regulation AR 310-25. Washington, DC: Headquarters, Department of the Army, 1986.

—**COMPATIBILITY.** Ammunition and explosives are considered compatible if they can be stored or transported together without increasing significantly either the probability of an accident or, for a given quantity, the magnitude of the effects of such an accident.

References
Department of Defense, U.S. Army. *Ammunition and Explosives Safety Standards.* Army Regulation AR 385-64. Washington, DC: Headquarters, Department of the Army, 1987.

—**COMPETITIVE CATEGORY** is a group of commissioned officers who compete among themselves for promotion and, if selected, are promoted in rank order as additional officers in the higher grade are needed in the competitive category. The Army competitive categories are (1) Army (includes officers in specialties 00 through 54 and 69 through 97); (2) Army Nurse Corps; (3) Medical Service Corps; (4) Veterinary Corps; (5) Army Medical Specialist Corps (combined with the Medical Corps for promotion above the grade of colonel); (6) Medical Corps; and (7) Dental Corps.

References
Department of Defense, U.S. Army. *Dictionary of United States Army Terms.* Army Regulation AR 310-25. Washington, DC: Headquarters, Department of the Army, 1986.

—**COMPLETE DECONTAMINATION** is the process of reducing the level of contamination hazard on a surface so that it will pose no threat.

References
Department of Defense, U.S. Army. *NBC Decontamination.* Field Manual FM 3-5. Washington, DC: Headquarters, Department of the Army, 1985.

—**COMPLETE PENETRATION** occurs when the projectile is in the target or when light can be seen from the rear of the target.

References
Department of Defense, U.S. Army. *Dictionary of United States Army Terms.* Army Regulation AR 310-25. Washington, DC: Headquarters, Department of the Army, 1986.

—**COMPLETE ROUND** applies to an assemblage of explosive and nonexplosive components designed to perform a specific function at the time and under the conditions desired. The following are examples of complete rounds of ammunition.
• **Separate loading**—Consists of a primer, propelling charge, and, except for blank ammunition, a projectile, and a fuze.
• **Fixed or semifixed**—Consists of a primer, propelling charge, cartridge case, a projectile, and, except when solid projectiles are used, a fuze.

• **Bomb**—Consists of all component parts required to drop and function the bomb at once.
• **Missile**—Consists of a complete warhead section and a missile body with its associated components and propellants.
• **Rocket**—Consists of all components necessary to function.

References
Department of Defense, Joint Chiefs of Staff. *Department of Defense Dictionary of Military and Related Terms.* Washington, DC: GPO, 1986.

—**COMPLETELY NONMETALLIC MINE** is a mine with no metal parts, even in the firing train. *See also:* Mine Warfare.

References
Department of Defense, U.S. Army. *Mine/Countermine Operations at the Company Level.* Field Manual FM 20-32. Washington, DC: Headquarters, Department of the Army, 1976.

—**COMPLETION TIME** is the time that the tail of a column passes the release point.

References
Department of Defense, U.S. Army. *The Infantry Rifle Company (Infantry, Airborne, Air Assault, Ranger).* Field Manual FM 7-10. Washington, DC: Headquarters, Department of the Army, 1982.

—**COMPONENT** is a generally expendable part or combination of parts that have a specified function and can be installed or replaced only as a whole.

References
Department of Defense, Joint Chiefs of Staff. *Department of Defense Dictionary of Military and Related Terms.* Washington, DC: GPO, 1986.

—**COMPONENT COMMAND** consists of the component commander and all individuals, units, detachments, organizations, or installations under his military command that have been assigned to the operational command of the Unified Command commander.

References
Department of Defense, U.S. Army. *Support Operations: Echelons Above Corps.* Field Manual FM 100-16. Washington, DC: Headquarters, Department of the Army, 1986.

—**COMPONENT FORCE** is a service element of a joint task force and is titled naval, land, or air component, as appropriate.

References
Department of Defense, U.S. Army. *Dictionary of United States Army Terms*. Army Regulation AR 310-25. Washington, DC: Headquarters, Department of the Army, 1986.

—**COMPONENT LIFE** is the period of acceptable usage after which the likelihood of failure sharply increases and before which the components are removed because of their operational unreliability.

References
Department of Defense, Joint Chiefs of Staff. *Department of Defense Dictionary of Military and Related Terms*. Washington, DC: GPO, 1986.

—**COMPONENT** (MATERIEL) is an assembly or a combination of parts, subassemblies, and assemblies that are mounted together in manufacture, assembly, maintenance, or rebuild. There are two types of components. *Components of end-items* are identified in technical publications (e.g., technical manuals) as part of an end-item. Troop-installed items, special tools, and test equipment are not components of end-items. *Components of assemblages* are identified in a supply catalog component listing as part of a set, kit, outfit, or other assemblage.

References
Department of Defense, Joint Chiefs of Staff. *Department of Defense Dictionary of Military and Related Terms*. Washington, DC: GPO, 1986.

Department of Defense, U.S. Army. *Repair Parts Supply for a Theater of Operations*. Field Manual FM 29-19. Washington, DC: Headquarters, Department of the Army, 1985.

—**COMPOSITE ARMOR** is a protective covering made of two or more materials, as distinguished from a single plate or piece or laminated structure made with all laminae of the same material. A composite armor structure can consist of laminae of different materials or a matrix of one material in which are imbedded pieces of particles of one or more different materials.

References
Department of Defense, U.S. Army. *Dictionary of United States Army Terms*. Army Regulation AR 310-25. Washington, DC: Headquarters, Department of the Army, 1986.

—**COMPOSITE DEFENSE**, in air defense artillery, is a defense that employs two or more types of fire units that are integrated into a single defense.

References
Department of Defense, U.S. Army. *Dictionary of United States Army Terms*. Army Regulation AR 310-25. Washington, DC: Headquarters, Department of the Army, 1986.

—**COMPOSITION C4** is a plastic explosive made of RDX and plasticizing materials. It is usually used in demolition blocks. It replaced composition C3, which is now a substitute standard.

References
Department of Defense, U.S. Army. *Dictionary of United States Army Terms*. Army Regulation AR 310-25. Washington, DC: Headquarters, Department of the Army, 1986.

—**COMPOSITION (ORDER-OF-BATTLE)** is the identification and organization of units. It applies to specific units or commands as opposed to type units.

Unit identification is often called the key to order-of-battle intelligence because it leads to the answers to many questions concerning the enemy. Unit identification consists of the complete designation of a specific unit by name or number, type, relative size or strength, and (usually) subordination. Through identification, the order-of-battle analyst is able to develop a history of the composition, training, tactics, and combat effectiveness of an enemy unit. Combined with organization, the identification of a specific unit alerts the analyst to the possible presence of other unidentified units of the same organization. *See also:* Order-of-Battle.

References
Department of Defense, U.S. Army. *Intelligence Analysis*. Field Manual FM 34-3. Washington, DC: Headquarters, Department of the Army, 1986.

—**COMPROMISING EMANATIONS** are unintentional data-related or intelligence-bearing signals that, if intercepted and analyzed, disclose classified information being transmitted, received, handled, or otherwise processed by information-processing equipment.

References
Department of Defense, U.S. Army. *Dictionary of United States Army Terms*. Army Regulation AR 310-25. Washington, DC: Headquarters, Department of the Army, 1986.

—**CONCEALMENT** is the provision of protection from observation or surveillance only. It can be natural or artificial, and disguises a soldier, carrier, position, equipment, or route. It includes camouflage, light, noise, movement, and odor discipline. *See also:* Camouflage, Cover, Surveillance.

References

Department of Defense, Joint Chiefs of Staff. *Department of Defense Dictionary of Military and Related Terms.* Washington, DC: GPO, 1986.

U.S. Congress. Senate. *Final Report of the Senate Select Committee to Study Government Operations With Respect to Intelligence Activities. Report 94-755. Book I, Foreign and Military Intelligence* (Church Committee Report). Washington, DC: GPO, 1976.

—**CONCENTRATION.** (1) A concentration is a weight of chemical agent present in a given volume of air. (2) A concentration is an assembly of troops in a given locality for purposes of training, attack, or defense. *See also:* Chemical Warfare.

References

Department of Defense, U.S. Army. *Dictionary of United States Army Terms.* Army Regulation AR 310-25. Washington, DC: Headquarters, Department of the Army, 1986.

—**CONCENTRATION AREA.** (1) A concentration area, usually in the theater of operations, is where troops are assembled before beginning active operations. (2) A concentration area is a limited area on which a volume of gunfire is placed within a limited time.

References

Department of Defense, Joint Chiefs of Staff. *Department of Defense Dictionary of Military and Related Terms.* Washington, DC: GPO, 1986.

—**CONCEPT** is a notion or statement of an idea, expressing how something might be done or accomplished, that may lead to an accepted procedure.

References

Department of Defense, Joint Chiefs of Staff. *Department of Defense Dictionary of Military and Related Terms.* Washington, DC: GPO, 1986.

—**CONCEPT OF OPERATIONS** is a broad verbal or graphic statement of a commander's assumptions or intent regarding an operation or a series of operations. The concept of operations frequently is embodied in campaign plans and in operation plans (particularly when the plans cover connected operations that are to be carried out simultaneously or in succession). The concept is designed to give an overall picture of the operation and is included primarily for additional clarity of purpose. Frequently, it is referred to as the commander's concept.

References

Department of Defense, Joint Chiefs of Staff. *Department of Defense Dictionary of Military and Related Terms.* Washington, DC: GPO, 1986.

—**CONDUCT OF FIRE AND MANEUVER** refers to actions conducted to close with and destroy the enemy, to learn more about its strength and disposition, or to move away from it. It is conducted by a fire element and a maneuver element. The actions of these two elements occur simultaneously. The fire element covers the move of the maneuver element by firing at the enemy. The maneuver element moves either to close with the enemy or to a better position from which to fire at it.

Depending on the distance to the enemy positions and the availability of cover, the fire element and the maneuver element switch roles as needed to keep moving. Before the maneuver element moves beyond supporting range of the fire element, it takes a position from which it can fire at the enemy. The fire element then becomes the maneuver element for the next move.

References

Department of Defense, U.S. Army. *The Infantry Rifle Company (Infantry, Airborne, Air Assault, Ranger).* Field Manual FM 7-10. Washington, DC: Headquarters, Department of the Army, 1982.

—**CONE OF DISPERSION.** A cone of dispersion is a cone-shaped pattern formed by the paths of a group of shots fired from a gun with the same sight setting. The shots follow different paths as a result of gun vibration, variations in ammunition, and other factors (e.g., changes in the wind's direction or velocity). It is also called a cone of fire or sheaf of fire.

References

Department of Defense, U.S. Army. *Dictionary of United States Army Terms.* Army Regulation AR 310-25. Washington, DC: Headquarters, Department of the Army, 1986.

—**CONFERENCE,** one of the principle presentation techniques used during Phase I of a training session, is designed to permit and encourage greater student participation. The conference method provides a vehicle for group problem solving and decisionmaking and can take advantage of the ideas and experiences of soldiers being trained.

References

Department of Defense, U.S. Army. *How to Prepare and Conduct Military Training.* Field Manual FM 21-6. Washington, DC: Headquarters, Department of the Army, 1975.

—**CONFIDENTIAL (C)** is the lowest of three U.S. security classifications. It is assigned to national security information that, if disclosed, could be expected to damage national security.

References

Allen, Thomas B., and Polmar, Norman. *Merchants of Treason: America's Secrets for Sale.* New York: Delacorte Press, 1988.

Department of Defense, Joint Chiefs of Staff. *Department of Defense Dictionary of Military and Related Terms.* Washington, DC: GPO, 1986.

—**CONFINEMENT FACILITY** is a complex for the incarceration of military prisoners. It applies to transient confinement facilities, installation confinement facilities, area confinement facilities, and hospitalized prisoner wards. *See also:* Disciplinary Action.

References

Department of Defense, U.S. Army. *Dictionary of United States Army Terms.* Army Regulation AR 310-25. Washington, DC: Headquarters, Department of the Army, 1986.

—**CONNECTED-CHAMBER STORAGE SITE** is an explosives storage site that consists of two or more chambers connected by ducts or passageways. Such chambers may be at the ends of branch tunnels off a main passageway.

References

Department of Defense, U.S. Army. *Ammunition and Explosives Safety Standards.* Army Regulation AR 385-64. Washington, DC: Headquarters, U.S. Army, 1987.

—**CONSIDERED LIST** is a list of soldiers considered by the Department of the Army's Promotion Selection Board. It is published after each board adjourns and contains the names of all soldiers who were considered (both selects and nonselects).

References

Department of Defense, U.S. Army. *Enlisted Personnel Management System.* Army Regulation AR 600-200. Washington, DC: Headquarters, Department of the Army, 1984.

—**CONSOLIDATED PLAN,** a category of the operations plan, is a plan developed jointly by a component command and the designated planning agent that incorporates the deployment and employment planning necessary to support a unified command's contingency plan.

References

Department of Defense, U.S. Army. *Dictionary of United States Army Terms.* Army Regulation AR 310-25. Washington, DC: Headquarters, Department of the Army, 1986.

—**CONSOLIDATION CAMPAIGN** is a campaign organized in priority areas as an interdepartmental civil-military effort. Normally conducted at the state level, this operation integrates programs that are designed to establish, maintain, or restore host country governmental control of the population and the area and to provide an environment within which the economic, political, and social activities of the population can be pursued and improved.

References

Department of Defense, U.S. Army. *Low Intensity Conflict.* Field Manual FM 100-20. Washington, DC: Headquarters, Department of the Army, 1981.

—**CONSOLIDATION OF POSITION** is the organizing and strengthening of a newly captured position so that it can be used against the enemy.

References

Department of Defense, Joint Chiefs of Staff. *Department of Defense Dictionary of Military and Related Terms.* Washington, DC: GPO, 1986.

—**CONSTITUTE** is to provide the legal authority for the existence of a new unit of the armed forces. The new unit is designated and listed, but it has no specific existence until it is activated. *See also:* Activate, Commission.

References

Department of Defense, Joint Chiefs of Staff. *Department of Defense Dictionary of Military and Related Terms.* Washington, DC: GPO, 1986.

—**CONSTRUCTED OBSTACLES** are reinforcing obstacles built by soldiers and machinery, generally without the use of explosives. They include a wide variety of obstacles ranging from tanglefoot to extensive concrete and steel obstacles. They fall into two broad categories: wire obstacles and antitank obstacles. Wire obstacles or entanglements are designed to impede the movement of foot troops and, in some cases, tracked and wheeled vehicles. Antitank obstacles (e.g., hurdles, cribs, posts, and abatis) include concrete and steel obstacles (e.g., tetrahedrons, hedgehogs, and falling block obstacles), and ditches.

References

Department of Defense, U.S. Army. *Countermobility.* Field Manual FM 5-102. Washington, DC: Head quarters, Department of the Army, 1985.

————. *Engineer Combat Operations.* Field Manual FM 5-100. Washington, DC: Headquarters, Department of the Army, 1984.

—**CONSUMABLE SUPPLIES** is a special classification for use in program expense accounting activities that encompasses nonexpendable supplies valued at less than $200 per item and all expendable supplies. This classification cannot be interpreted in a way that will allow existing requirements for maintenance of station property book records of nonexpendable supplies to be ignored.

References

Department of Defense, Joint Chiefs of Staff. *Department of Defense Dictionary of Military and Related Terms.* Washington, DC: GPO, 1986.

—**CONSUMPTION QUANTITY** is the anticipated consumption rate of a specific repair part based upon a specific equipment density and usage profile. *See also:* Consumption Rate.

References

Department of Defense, U.S. Army. *Maintenance and Repair Parts Consumption Planning Guide for Contingency Operations.* Field Manual FM 42-9-23. Washington, DC: Headquarters, Department of the Army, 1980.

—**CONSUMPTION RATE** is the average quantity of an item consumed or expended during a given time interval. It is expressed in quantities by the most appropriate unit of measurement.

References

Department of Defense, Joint Chiefs of Staff. *Department of Defense Dictionary of Military and Related Terms.* Washington, DC: GPO, 1986.

—**CONTACT PATROL** is a patrol detailed to maintain contact with adjoining units.

References

Department of Defense, U.S. Army. *Dictionary of United States Army Terms.* Army Regulation AR 310-25. Washington, DC: Headquarters, Department of the Army, 1986.

—**CONTACT POINT.** In land warfare, a contact point is an easily identifiable point on the terrain where two or more units are required to make contact.

References

Department of Defense, U.S. Army. *Armored and Mechanized Division Operations.* Field Manual FM 71-100. Washington, DC: Headquarters, Department of the Army, 1978.

————. *Attack Helicopter Operations.* Field Manual FM 17-50. Washington, DC: Headquarters, Department of the Army, 1984.

—**CONTACT REPORT** is a report indicating any detection of the enemy.

References

Department of Defense, Joint Chiefs of Staff. *Department of Defense Dictionary of Military and Related Terms.* Washington, DC: GPO, 1986.

—**CONTACT TEAM** is an element of a command organization or unit designated to visit another organization to provide service or intelligence (e.g., a detachment from a maintenance company sent forward to deliver supplies and/or make repairs on the ordnance materiel of units needing assistance).

References

Department of Defense, U.S. Army. *Dictionary of United States Army Terms.* Army Regulation AR 310-25. Washington, DC: Headquarters, Department of the Army, 1986.

—**CONTACT ZONE** is a six-meter area next to a crossing site. It is measured from the present water level and in the direction of the traveled route.

References

Department of Defense, U.S. Army. *Route Reconnaissance and Classification.* Field Manual FM 5-36. Washington, DC: Headquarters, Department of the Army, 1985.

—**CONTAIN** is to stop, hold, or surround the enemy or to cause it to center its activity on a given front, thus preventing it from withdrawing any of its forces for use elsewhere.

References

Department of Defense, Joint Chiefs of Staff. *Department of Defense Dictionary of Military and Related Terms.* Washington, DC: GPO, 1986.

—**CONTAMINATION.** (1) Contamination is the deposit and/or absorption of radioactive material or biological or chemical agents on or by structures, areas, personnel, or objects. (2) Contamination is food and/or water made unfit for human or animal consumption because of the presence of environmental chemicals, radioactive elements, bacteria, or organisms. (3) Contamination is the by-product of the growth of organisms or bacteria in decomposing material (including food substances) or waste in food or water. *See also:* Biological Warfare, Chemical Warfare, Nuclear Warfare.

References

Department of Defense, U.S. Army. *NBC Operations*. Field Manual FM 3-100. Washington, DC: Headquarters, Department of the Army, 1985.

—**CONTAMINATION AVOIDANCE** is the measures taken by an individual and/or unit to avoid or to minimize the effects of nuclear, biological, or chemical hazards. Passive contamination avoidance measures are concealment, dispersion, deception, and the use of cover to reduce the probability of the enemy's using nuclear, biological, or chemical weapons on U.S. units and to minimize the damage caused by these weapons if they are used. Active contamination avoidance measures are contamination control, detection, identification and marking contaminated areas, issuing contamination warnings, and relocating or rerouting to an uncontaminated area. *See also:* Biological Warfare, Chemical Warfare, Nuclear Warfare.

References

Department of Defense, U.S. Army. *NBC Operations*. Field Manual FM 3-100. Washington, DC: Headquarters, Department of the Army, 1985.

—**CONTAMINATION CONTROL** involves procedures to avoid, reduce, remove, or render harmless nuclear, biological, and chemical contamination in order to maintain or enhance the efficient conduct of military operations. *See also:* Biological Warfare, Chemical Warfare, Nuclear Warfare.

References

Department of Defense, U.S. Army. *NBC Operations*. Field Manual FM 3-100. Washington, DC: Headquarters, Department of the Army, 1985.

—**CONTAMINATION CONTROL POINT** is a specific location used by personnel to control entry to, and exit from, the contaminated area. *See also:* Biological Warfare, Chemical Warfare, Nuclear Warfare.

References

Department of Defense, U.S. Army. *NBC Operations*. Field Manual FM 3-100. Washington, DC: Headquarters, Department of the Army, 1985.

—**CONTAMINATION OBSTACLE,** which can be nuclear or chemical, is difficult to predict and control because it depends on winds for placement and is affected by weather and other environmental factors. The United States has renounced the first use of chemical weapons. Further, the most predictable source of nuclear contamination, atomic demolition munitions is subject to the same restrictions as all nuclear weapons and may not be available for use when needed. If an atomic demolition munition is used for cratering, there will be both close-in radiation and fallout, each effectively contaminating an area of reasonably predictable extent. *See also:* Chemical Warfare, Nuclear Warfare.

References

Department of Defense, U.S. Army. *Countermobility*. Field Manual FM 5-102. Washington, DC: Headquarters, Department of the Army, 1985.

—**CONTINENTAL UNITED STATES** refers to the forty-eight contiguous states and the District of Columbia.

References

Department of Defense, U.S. Army. *Leaves and Passes*. Army Regulation AR 630-5. Washington, DC: Headquarters, Department of the Army, 1984.

—**CONTINGENCY FORCE** is designed for rapidly deploying from bases that are normally located in the United States. It may operate independently of other Army combat forces. *See also:* Contingency Operations, Force

References

Department of Defense, U.S. Army. *Air Defense Artillery Deployment: Chaparral/Vulcan/Stinger*. Field Manual FM 44-3. Washington, DC: Headquarters, Department of the Army, 1984.

—**CONTINGENCY MAINTENANCE ALLOCATION CHART (CMAC)** is a maintenance allocation chart that identifies maintenance functions as essential, nonessential, or deferrable to guide repair of equipment during contingency operations.

References

Department of Defense, U.S. Army. *Maintenance and Repair Parts Consumption Planning Guide for Contingency Operations*. Field Manual FM 42-9-23. Washington, DC: Headquarters, Department of the Army, 1980.

—**CONTINGENCY OPERATIONS** are the Army's capability to respond to a short-duration (normally limited-objective) war in an area without an established U.S. base of operations. Such forces may fight jointly with other U.S. forces, with or without allied participation.

References

Department of Defense, U.S. Army. *Support Operations: Echelons Above Corps.* Field Manual FM 100-16. Washington, DC: Headquarters, Department of the Army, 1986.

—**CONTINGENCY OPERATIONS WITH ALLIES** occur where joint U.S. forces deploy and operate with allied forces. The situation assumes that limited technical expertise, a limited industrial base and transportation system, a semiskilled labor pool, and some host nation support agreements exist in or with the host nation.

References

Department of Defense, U.S. Army. *Civil Affairs Operations.* Field Manual FM 41-10. Washington, DC: Headquarters, Department of the Army, 1985.

—**CONTINGENCY PLAN** anticipates major occurrences that can reasonably be expected to occur in the principal geographic subareas of the command. As a category of the operations plan, a contingency plan is a plan for an emergency that may occur in a specific geographic subarea of a command. Its primary purpose here is to accelerate the actions that the command can take to react to the emergency.

References

Department of Defense, Joint Chiefs of Staff. *Department of Defense Dictionary of Military and Related Terms.* Washington, DC: GPO, 1986.

———. *Planning Logistics Support for Military Operations.* Field Manual FM 701-58. Washington, DC: Headquarters, Department of the Army, 1987.

—**CONTINGENCY SUPPORT STOCKS (COMSSTOCS)** are the general war reserves maintained in the continental United States for the initial supply of continental U.S. forces that are deployed for contingency operations. COMSSTOCS include Army-managed items and the Army-owned items managed by the Defense Logistics Agency and General Services Administration that meet established criteria.

References

Department of Defense, U.S. Army. Planning *Logistics Support for Military Operations.* Field Manual FM 701-58. Washington, DC: Headquarters, Department of the Army, 1987.

—**CONTINGENT EFFECTS** are the effects, both desirable and undesirable, that are in addition to the primary effects associated with a nuclear detonation. *See also:* Nuclear Warfare.

References

Department of Defense, Joint Chiefs of Staff. *Department of Defense Dictionary of Military and Related Terms.* Washington, DC: GPO, 1986.

—**CONTINGENT ZONE OF FIRE** is an area within which a designated ground unit or fire support ship may be called upon to deliver fire. *See also:* Zone of Fire.

References

Department of Defense, Joint Chiefs of Staff. *Department of Defense Dictionary of Military and Related Terms.* Washington, DC: GPO, 1986.

—**CONTINUITY OF COMMAND** is the degree or state of being continuous in the exercise of the authority vested in an individual of the armed forces for the direction, coordination, and control of military forces.

References

Department of Defense, Joint Chiefs of Staff. *Department of Defense Dictionary of Military and Related Terms.* Washington, DC: GPO, 1986.

—**CONTINUITY OF OPERATIONS** refers to a steady state of conduct in the functions, tasks, or duties necessary to accomplish a military action or mission when carrying out the national military strategy. It includes the functions and duties of the commander, as well as the supporting functions and duties performed by the staff and others acting under the authority and direction of the commander.

References

Department of Defense, Joint Chiefs of Staff. *Department of Defense Dictionary of Military and Related Terms.* Washington, DC: GPO, 1986.

—**CONTINUOUS ACTIVE DUTY** is active federal service in any of the Armed Forces of the United States, without a break in service of more than 90 days. It does not include active duty for training. *See also:* Retirement, Separation.

References

Department of Defense, U.S. Army. *Enlisted Personnel Management System.* Army Regulation AR 600-200. Washington, DC: Headquarters, Department of the Army, 1984.

—**CONTINUOUS FIRE.** (1) Continuous fire is fire conducted at a normal rate without interruption for any cause. (2) In field artillery and naval gunfire support, continuous fire is loading and firing at a specified rate or as rapidly as possible consistent with accuracy within the prescribed rate of fire for the weapon. Firing continues until it is terminated by the command "end of mission" or is temporarily suspended by the command "cease loading" or "check firing."

References
Department of Defense, Joint Chiefs of Staff. *Department of Defense Dictionary of Military and Related Terms.* Washington, DC: GPO, 1986.

—**CONTINUOUS ILLUMINATION FIRE** occurs when illuminating projectiles are fired at specified intervals to provide uninterrupted lighting on a target or a specified area.

References
Department of Defense, Joint Chiefs of Staff. *Department of Defense Dictionary of Military and Related Terms.* Washington, DC: GPO, 1986.

—**CONTINUOUS MONITORING** is surveillance for radiation in the unit area or along the unit route of march. It is initiated (1) when a nuclear detonation is observed, heard, or reported; (2) when a dose rate of one centigray (rad) per hour is read; or (3) when the unit is on the move. *See also:* Nuclear Warfare.

References
Department of Defense, U.S. Army. *NBC Operations.* Field Manual FM 3-100. Washington, DC: Headquarters, Department of the Army, 1985.

—**CONTOUR FLIGHT** (ARMY AVIATION) is a low altitude flight that conforms generally to the contour of the terrain. It is characterized by varying airspeed and altitude as dictated by vegetation, obstacles, and ambient light.

References
Department of Defense, U.S. Army. *Air Defense Artillery Deployment: Chaparral/Vulcan/Stinger.* Field Manual FM 44-3. Washington, DC: Headquarters, Department of the Army, 1984.

———. *Attack Helicopter Operations.* Field Manual FM 17-50. Washington, DC: Headquarters, Department of the Army, 1984.

———. *Gunnery Training for Attack Helicopters.* Training Circular TC 17-17. Washington, DC: Headquarters, Department of the Army, 1975.

—**CONTRACTUALLY OBLIGATED SOLDIER** is a soldier who is serving under an enlistment contract or extension (e.g., has completed statutory service obligation or has not acquired one). *See also:* Enlisted Person, Member.

References
Department of Defense, U.S. Army. *Enlisted Personnel.* Army Regulation AR 635-200. Washington, DC: Headquarters, Department of the Army, 1984.

—**CONTROL.** (1) Control is the authority that may be less than full command exercised by a commander over part of the activities of subordinate or other organizations. (2) In mapping, charting, and photogrammetry, control is a collective term for a system of marks or objects on the earth or on a map or photograph whose positions, elevations, or both have been or will be determined. (3) Control is the physical or psychological pressures exerted to assure that an agent or group will respond as directed. (4) Control is an indicator that governs the distribution and use of documents, information, or material. Such indicators are the subject of an Intelligence Community agreement and are specifically defined in the appropriate regulations. (5) In a geographical context, control is a system or network of points of fixed geodetic positions, with latitude, longitude, and evaluation determined by surveying instruments. (6) Concerning missiles in general, control means all processes concerning intelligence and maneuver that help the missile reach its intended destination. Within this context, control concerns the input of data either by the missile or from an external source that will force the missile to change direction. (7) Concerning an airframe, control is a device for effecting a change in motion. (8) In civil affairs, control is the degree of authority exercised by a military commander over a civil population, government, or economy in an area where U.S. armed forces are employed. *See also:* Administrative Control, Operational Command.

References
Department of Defense, Joint Chiefs of Staff. *Department of Defense Dictionary of Military and Related Terms.* Washington, DC: GPO, 1986.

Department of Defense, U.S. Army. *Dictionary of United States Army Terms.* Army Regulation AR 310-25. Washington, DC: Headquarters, Department of the Army, 1986.

—**CONTROL AND REPORTING CENTER (CRC)** is a subordinate air control element of the tactical air control center from which radar control and warning operations are conducted within its area of responsibility.

References

Department of Defense, U.S. Army. *U.S. Army Air Defense Artillery Employment.* Field Manual FM 44-1. Washington, DC: Headquarters, Department of the Army, 1983.

—**CONTROL BRANCH** is the branch to which an officer is assigned and accountable. It is responsible for his career management and reassignment. *See also:* Control Specialty.

References

Department of Defense, U.S. Army. *Dictionary of United States Army Terms.* Army Regulation AR 310-25. Washington, DC: Headquarters, Department of the Army, 1986.

———. *Officer Assignment Policies, Details and Transfers.* Army Regulation AR 614-100. Washington, DC: Headquarters, Department of the Army, 1984.

—**CONTROL POINT** is a position along a route of march where men are stationed to give information and instructions in order to regulate supply or traffic.

References

Department of Defense, Joint Chiefs of Staff. *Department of Defense Dictionary of Military and Related Terms.* Washington, DC: GPO, 1986.

Department of Defense, U.S. Army. *Dictionary of United States Army Terms.* Army Regulation AR 310-25. Washington, DC: Headquarters, Department of the Army, 1986.

—**CONTROL SPECIALTY** is the means whereby commissioned officers are accounted for by their area of expertise or knowledge. It represents the specialty under which the officer is charged or accounted for when determining the Army's commissioned officer inventory strength and when comparing strengths with authorizations. A control specialty is designated on a commissioned officer's assignment orders. *See also:* Control Branch.

References

Department of Defense, U.S. Army. *Dictionary of United States Army Terms.* Army Regulation AR 310-25. Washington, DC: Headquarters, Department of the Army, 1986.

—**CONTROLLED COMSEC (COMMUNICATIONS SECURITY) ITEM (CCI)** refers to a marking applied to unclassified end-items and assemblies that perform critical COMSEC functions and require access controls and physical security protection to assure their continued safety and integrity. *See also:* Communications Security.

References

Department of Defense, U.S. Army. *Dictionary of United States Army Terms.* Army Regulation AR 310-25. Washington, DC: Headquarters, Department of the Army, 1986.

—**CONTROLLED ENVIRONMENT TESTS AND ANALYSES (CETA)** are instrumented examinations of electronic equipment or systems that are or may be used to process classified information.

References

Department of Defense, U.S. Army. *Counterintelligence.* Field Manual FM 34-60. Washington, DC: Headquarters, Department of the Army, 1985.

—**CONTROLLED EXCHANGE** is the removal of serviceable parts from damaged or disabled unserviceable, but economically repairable, equipment so that they can be used in another that is to be returned to combat. *See also:* Cannibalization.

References

Department of Defense, U.S. Army. *Organizational Maintenance Operations.* Field Manual FM 29-2. Washington, DC: Headquarters, Department of the Army, 1984.

———. *Repair Parts Supply for a Theater of Operations.* Field Manual FM 29-19. Washington, DC: Headquarters, Department of the Army, 1985.

—**CONTROLLED FIRING AREA** is an area in which ordnance firing is conducted under controlled conditions to eliminate hazards to flying aircraft.

References

Department of Defense, Joint Chiefs of Staff. *Department of Defense Dictionary of Military and Related Terms.* Washington, DC: GPO, 1986.

—**CONTROLLED INVENTORY ITEMS** are designated as having characteristics that require them to be identified, accounted for, secured, or handled safely. Controlled inventory items are classified in order of degree of control normally exercised, as follows: classified item, pilferage item, and sensitive item.

References
Department of Defense, U.S. Army. *Dictionary of United States Army Terms.* Army Regulation AR 310-25. Washington, DC: Headquarters, Department of the Army, 1986.

—**CONTROLLED MINE** is a mine that, after laying, can be controlled by the user to make it safe and live or to fire it. *See also:* Mine.

References
Department of Defense, Joint Chiefs of Staff. *Department of Defense Dictionary of Military and Related Terms.* Washington, DC: GPO, 1986.

—**CONTROLLED NET** is a group of stations on a common channel of communication with one station designated as control and all other stations transmitting only when granted permission to do so.

References
Department of Defense, U.S. Army. *Dictionary of United States Army Terms.* Army Regulation AR 310-25. Washington, DC: Headquarters, Department of the Army, 1986.

—**CONTROLLED PASSING** is a traffic movement procedure that allows two lines of traffic traveling in opposite directions to alternately pass a point or section of route that can take only one lane of traffic at a time.

References
Department of Defense, Joint Chiefs of Staff. Department *of Defense Dictionary of Military and Related Terms.* Washington, DC: GPO, 1986.

—**CONTROLLED PATTERN** is a method of dropping parachuted supplies, weapons, and equipment from aircraft in flight and preventing their dispersal by connecting them in one group with webbing, rope, or another means.

References
Department of Defense, U.S. Army. *Dictionary of United States Army Terms.* Army Regulation AR 310-25. Washington, DC: Headquarters, Department of the Army, 1986.

—**CONTROLLED RESPONSE** is the selection, from a wide variety of feasible options, of the one that will provide the specific military response that is most advantageous under the circumstances.

References
Department of Defense, Joint Chiefs of Staff. *Department of Defense Dictionary of Military and Related Terms.* Washington, DC: GPO, 1986.

—**CONTROLLED ROUTE** is a route that is subject to supervised traffic or movement restrictions. Controlled routes include supervised routes, dispatched routes, and reserved routes.

References
Department of Defense, Joint Chiefs of Staff. *Department of Defense Dictionary of Military and Related Terms.* Washington, DC: GPO, 1986.

—**CONTROLLED SUPPLY RATE (CSR)** is the rate of ammunition use that can be sustained with available supplies. The CSR for weapon ammunition is expressed in rounds per unit, individual, or vehicle per day. The theater army announces the CSR for each item of ammunition, and, in turn, the commander of each subordinate tactical unit announces a CSR for his commanders at the next lower levels. The CSRs for individual items may vary from one command to the next and may be published in the operations plan, the fire support annex to the operations order, or a separate fragmentary order. The statement "the CSR is the required support rate" is used if there are no restrictions. A unit may not draw ammunition in excess of its CSR without authority from its next higher headquarters.

Sometimes corps or higher headquarters imposes a CSR on the division. It is less than the required supply rate and can be used when the corps cannot supply as much as the division believes it will need. When this is the case, the division commander, working with the G3 and G4, establishes priorities for distributing controlled ammunition. In the event that the CSR is considerably below anticipated requirements, some adjustment in the tactical plan may be necessary.

References
Department of Defense, U.S. Army. *Armored and Mechanized Division Operations.* Field Manual FM 71-100. Washington, DC: Headquarters, Department of the Army, 1978.

———. *Support Operations: Echelons Above Corps.* Field Manual FM 100-16. Washington, DC: Headquarters, Department of the Army, 1986.

—**CONTROLLING AUTHORITY** is a communications security term for the organization responsible for establishing and operating a cryptonet. *See also:* Communications Security.

References
Department of Defense, U.S. Army. *Dictionary of United States Army Terms.* Army Regulation AR 310-25. Washington, DC: Headquarters, Department of the Army, 1986.

—**CONVALESCENT LEAVE** is a period of authorized absence granted to a member who is under medical care for sickness or wounds and is not yet fully fit for duty. It is part of the treatment prescribed for recuperation and convalescence. *See also:* Medical Treatment.

References

Department of Defense, U.S. Army. *Leaves and Passes.* Army Regulation AR 630-5. Washington, DC: Headquarters, Department of the Army, 1984.

—**CONVENTIONAL FORCES** are forces capable of conducting operations using nonnuclear weapons. *See also:* Nuclear Warfare.

References

Department of Defense, Joint Chiefs of Staff. *Department of Defense Dictionary of Military and Related Terms.* Washington, DC: GPO, 1986.

—**CONVENTIONAL MAIN GUN AMMUNITION** is classified according to type and use.

Type

- *Service*—Combat ammunition.
- *Target practice*—ammunition that has flight characteristics similar to service ammunition, but no explosive in the projectile and is used for gunnery practice.
- *Blank*—has no projectile and is used only as a noisemaker.
- *Dummy*—has no propelling or explosive charge and is used only for loading practice.

Use

- *Armor defeating*—armor piercing discarding sabot, armor piercing, and high explosive anti-tank multipurpose are used against all tank and tank-like targets.
- *Antipersonnel*—antipersonnel is used against troops in the open.
- *Antimateriel*—high explosive plastic, high explosive, and high explosive antitank multipurpose are used against unarmored or lightly armored vehicles, troops in the open, buildings, and fortifications.
- *Special purpose*—includes (1) white phosphorus, which is used for marking and screening; (2) target practice, which is used to replace service ammunition in range firing; (3) blank, which is used in ceremonies and tactical field training (90-mm only); and (4) dummy, which is used only for instruction.

References

Department of Defense, U.S. Army. *Dictionary of United States Army Terms.* Army Regulation AR 310-25. Washington, DC: Headquarters, Department of the Army, 1986.

—**CONVENTIONAL MINES** are mines that are not designed to self-destruct. They are designed to be directly emplaced by hand or by mechanical mine planting equipment. They can be buried or self-laid, and can be emplaced in a classical pattern or without regard to pattern, depending on the tactical situation. As an industrially manufactured mine, it has a predictable design effect, a standard arming/disarming procedure, and a standard size and shape.

References

Department of Defense, U.S. Army. *Countermobility.* Field Manual FM 5-102. Washington, DC: Headquarters, Department of the Army, 1985.

———. *Mine/Countermine Operations at the Company Level.* Field Manual FM 20-32. Washington, DC: Headquarters, Department of the Army, 1976.

—**CONVENTIONAL, NUCLEAR, AND CHEMICAL FIRES.** Fire support includes mortars, field artillery, naval gunfire, army aviation, and air-delivered weapons. The long range and great flexibility of the fire support system make it possible to shift the focus and concentration of fire support rapidly over wide ranges. The commander can use it to support his scheme of maneuver, to mass firepower rapidly without shifting maneuver forces, and to delay, disrupt, or destroy enemy forces in depth. Commanders use the fire support system to destroy, neutralize, or suppress surface targets, including enemy weapons, formations, or facilities, and fires from the enemy rear. They also use it to suppress enemy air defense and, upon approval by National Command Authorities, to execute nuclear packages as indicated by higher headquarters. In a large-scale nuclear conflict, fire support could become the principal means of destroying enemy forces. The scheme of maneuver would then be designed specifically to exploit the effects of the fire support. *See also:* Chemical Warfare, Nuclear Warfare.

References

Department of Defense, U.S. Army. *Operations.* Field Manual FM 100-5. Washington, DC: Headquarters, Department of the Army, 1986.

—**CONVENTIONAL OBSTACLES** (A CATEGORY OF REINFORCING OBSTACLES) are normally planned and emplaced before the battle begins because of the on-site effort required for manpower/equipment, materials, and time. Emplacing obstacles continues during the battle but will be deeper in the main battle area and used to strengthen the defense. They could also be employed during the offense on flanks and in economy of force areas. Conventional obstacles include road craters, blown bridges, abatis, minefields, antitank ditches, and wire.

References
Department of Defense, U.S. Army. *Engineer Combat Operations.* Field Manual FM 5-100. Washington, DC: Headquarters, Department of the Army, 1984.

—**CONVENTIONAL TRAINING** is an instructor-oriented training approach that relies primarily on presentation techniques to teach skills and knowledge. It does not focus on a soldier's performance or on training to specified standards.

References
Department of Defense, U.S. Army. *How to Prepare and Conduct Military Training.* Field Manual FM 21-6. Washington, DC: Headquarters, Department of the Army, 1975.

—**CONVENTIONAL WAR** is an armed conflict without the use of nuclear weapons. *See also:* Nuclear Warfare.

References
Department of Defense, U.S. Army. *Support Operations: Echelons Above Corps.* Field Manual FM 100-16. Washington, DC: Headquarters, Department of the Army, 1986.

—**CONVENTIONAL WEAPON** is a weapon that is not nuclear, biological, or chemical. *See also:* Biological Warfare, Chemical Warfare, Nuclear Warfare.

References
Department of Defense, Joint Chiefs of Staff. *Department of Defense Dictionary of Military and Related Terms.* Washington, DC: GPO, 1986.

—**CONVERGE** is a request or command used in a call for fire to indicate that the observer or spotter desires a sheaf in which the planes of fire intersect at a point.

References
Department of Defense, Joint Chiefs of Staff. *Department of Defense Dictionary of Military and Related Terms.* Washington, DC: GPO, 1986.

—**CONVOY** is a group of vehicles organized for the purpose of control and orderly movement with or without escort protection.

References
Department of Defense, Joint Chiefs of Staff. *Department of Defense Dictionary of Military and Related Terms.* Washington, DC: GPO, 1986.

—**COOK OFF** is the functioning of a chambered round of ammunition that is initiated by the heat of the weapon.

References
Department of Defense, U.S. Army. *Dictionary of United States Army Terms.* Army Regulation AR 310-25. Washington, DC: Headquarters, Department of the Army, 1986.

—**COOPERATIVE LOGISTICS** is the support provided to a foreign government or agency through its participation in the U.S. Department of Defense supply system with reimbursement to the United States for the support that has been provided. *See also:* Cooperative Logistics Support Arrangements.

References
Department of Defense, Joint Chiefs of Staff. *Department of Defense Dictionary of Military and Related Terms.* Washington, DC: GPO, 1986.

—**COOPERATIVE LOGISTICS SUPPORT ARRANGEMENTS** refers to the procedural arrangements (cooperative logistics arrangements) and implementing procedures (supplementary procedures) that together support, define, or implement cooperative logistic understandings between the United States and a friendly foreign government during peacetime.

References
Department of Defense, Joint Chiefs of Staff. *Department of Defense Dictionary of Military and Related Terms.* Washington, DC: GPO, 1986.

—**COORDINATED ATTACK** is a carefully planned and executed offensive action in which the various elements of a command are employed so as to use their powers to the greatest advantage of the command as a whole.

References
Department of Defense, Joint Chiefs of Staff. *Department of Defense Dictionary of Military and Related Terms.* Washington, DC: GPO, 1986.

—**COORDINATED DEFENSE** is the air defense of two or more vulnerable areas that are too far apart to form an integrated defense, but are designed to effect economy of materiel and provide greater effectiveness with mutual support.

References

Department of Defense, U.S. Army. *Dictionary of United States Army Terms.* Army Regulation AR 310-25. Washington, DC: Headquarters, Department of the Army, 1986.

—**COORDINATED DRAFT PLAN** is a draft plan that has been circulated to and approved by the nations involved. It may be used for future planning and exercises and may be implemented during an emergency. *See also:* Draft Plan, Final Plan, Initial Draft Plan, Operation Plans.

References

Department of Defense, Joint Chiefs of Staff. *Department of Defense Dictionary of Military and Related Terms.* Washington, DC: GPO, 1986.

—**COORDINATED FIRE LINES (CFL)** delineate the area beyond which field artillery, mortars, and ships may fire at any time without additional coordination.

References

Department of Defense, U.S. Army. *Armored and Mechanized Division Operations.* Field Manual FM 71-100. Washington, DC: Headquarters, Department of the Army, 1978.

————. *Dictionary of United States Army Terms.* Army Regulation AR 310-25. Washington, DC: Headquarters, Department of the Army, 1986.

—**COORDINATING ALTITUDE.** (1) A coordinating altitude is a control measure designated to coordinate airspace use between high performance and rotary wing aircraft. (2) A coordinating altitude is an airspace that has been designated by the airspace authority below which Army facilities and above which Army activity must be coordinated with U.S. Air Force facilities.

References

Department of Defense, U.S. Army. *Airspace Management and Army Air Traffic in a Combat Zone.* Field Manual FM 1-60. Washington, DC: Headquarters, Department of the Army,

————. *Attack Helicopter Operations.* Field Manual FM 17-50. Washington, DC: Headquarters, Department of the Army, 1984.

————. *Operational Terms and Symbols.* Field Manual FM 101-5-1. Washington, DC: Headquarters, Department of the Army, 1985.

—**COORDINATING AUTHORITY** is a commander or an individual who has been assigned the responsibility for coordinating specific functions or activities that involve forces from two or more services or two or more forces from the same service. The commander or individual has the authority to require consultation between the agencies involved, but does not have the authority to compel agreement. If essential agreement cannot be obtained, the matter is referred to the appointing authority.

References

Department of Defense, Joint Chiefs of Staff. *Department of Defense Dictionary of Military and Related Terms.* Washington, DC: GPO, 1986.

—**COORDINATING POINT** is a control measure that refers to a specific location for the coordination of fires and maneuver between adjacent units. It is usually indicated whenever a boundary crosses the forward edge of the battle area and may be indicated when a boundary crosses report lines or phase lines that are used to control security forces. In NATO, physical contact between adjacent units is required.

References

Department of Defense, U.S. Army. *Armored and Mechanized Division Operations.* Field Manual FM 71-100. Washington, DC: Headquarters, Department of the Army, 1978.

————. *Operational Terms and Symbols.* Field Manual FM 101-5-1. Washington, DC: Headquarters, Department of the Army, 1985.

—**COORDINATING STAFF GROUP.** Coordinating staff officers are the commander's principal assistants, who are concerned with one (or a combination) of the broad fields of interest. They assist the commander by coordinating the plans, activities, and operations of the command. Collectively, they have responsibility for the commander's entire field of responsibilities, except for functional areas that the commander decides to control personally or areas that are reserved by law or regulation for specific staff officers. Although the special staff sections may not be an integral part of a particular coordinating staff section, each coordinating staff officer establishes procedures that ensure that all activities of special staff officers falling within his field of interest and responsibility are coordinated and integrated.

References

Department of Defense, U.S. Army. *Staff Organization and Operations*. Field Manual FM 101-5. Washington, DC: Headquarters, Department of the Army, 1984.

—**COORDINATION.** (1) In general, coordination is the act of obtaining concurrence from one or more groups, organizations, or agencies concerning a proposal or an activity over which they have some responsibility. In coordination, these bodies may concur, contribute, or not concur. In government parlance, it is often referred to as "staffing a paper." (2) In intelligence production, coordination is the act or process by which the person or body that wrote a draft of an estimate, assessment, or report gets the opinions of other producers on the quality of the product. Coordination is intended to make the product factually more accurate, to clarify the judgments made, to resolve disagreements on issues, or to sharpen the statements of disagreement on major unresolved issues. (3) Coordination is regulating and combining in harmonious action. *See also:* Intelligence Cycle.

References

Department of Defense, Defense Intelligence College. *Glossary of Intelligence Terms and Definitions*. Washington, DC: Defense Intelligence College, 1987.

Department of Defense, U.S. Army. *Military Leadership*. Field Manual FM 22-100. Washington, DC: Headquarters, Department of the Army, 1983.

—**COPPERHEAD,** a cannon-launched guided projectile, is a 155-mm projectile designed to destroy stationary or moving enemy tanks and other high-value targets. It can be fired from current or planned 155-mm howitzer. When the projectile reaches the general velocity of the target, it searches for and acquires the reflection of the laser beam projected on the target by a friendly forward observer. It then makes the necessary course corrections with its fins and homes in on the laser spot. Its accuracy is so high that it can drop down the open hatch of a moving tank at 16 kilometers. Copperhead is designed to complement rather than replace conventional 155-mm projectiles in artillery units.

References

Department of Defense, U.S. Army. *Department of the Army Policy Statement, 1988*. Washington, DC: Headquarters, Department of the Army, 1988.

—**CORDON (DRILL AND CEREMONIES)** is soldiers assembled in a line to honor a dignitary when he enters into or exits from a given place or vehicle.

References

Department of Defense, U.S. Army. *Drills and Ceremonies*. Field Manual FM 22-5. Washington, DC: Headquarters, Department of the Army, 1986.

—**CORPS** can be the highest Army operational headquarters in combat operations and as such has tactical, logistic, and administrative responsibilities. These duties are fulfilled by combat, combat support, and combat service support forces assigned to the corps. The corps has no fixed structure, but is organized based upon the forces that are available, the characteristics of the area of operations, the nature and duration of the assigned threat, and the enemy threat.

Generally, a U.S. corps is composed of two divisions, an armored cavalry regiment, and a separate brigade. The divisions and brigade can be any combination of armored, mechanized infantry, infantry, airborne, or airmobile forces. The corps is generally the first level of command where information from national and tactical intelligence systems are brought together. It uses this information to plan and allocate resources for operations up to 72 hours in the future. Defending corps commanders direct, coordinate, and support operations conducted by divisions against assaulting enemy divisions.

Corps are the Army's largest tactical units, the instruments with which higher echelons of command conduct maneuvers at the operational level. They are tailored for the theater and mission for which they are deployed. Once tailored, however, they contain all the necessary organic combat, combat support, and combat service support capabilities to sustain operations for a considerable period.

Corps plan and conduct major operations and battles. They synchronize tactical activities, including the maneuver of their divisions, the fires of their artillery units and supporting aerial forces, and the actions of their combat support and combat service support units. While corps normally fight as part of a larger land force—a field army or army group—they may also be used alone, either as an independent ground force or as the land component of a joint task force. When employed alone, they may exercise operational as well as tactical responsibilities.

Corps may be assigned divisions of any type that are required by the theater and the mission. They have organic support commands and are assigned combat and combat support organizations based upon their needs for a specific operation. Armored cavalry units, field artillery brigades, engineer brigades, air defense artillery brigades, and aviation brigades are the nondivisional units commonly available to the corps to bolster its main effort and to perform special combat functions. Separate infantry or armored brigades may also be assigned to corps. Signal brigades, military intelligence groups, and military police groups are the usual combat support organizations that are present in a corps. Other units (e.g., psychological operations battalions, special operating forces, and civil affairs units) may be assigned to corps when required. *See also:* Army, Battalion, Brigades, Company, Division, Platoon, Regiment, Squad.

References
Department of Defense, U.S. Army. *Dictionary of United States Army Terms.* Army Regulation AR 310-25. Washington, DC: Headquarters, Department of the Army, 1986.

————. *Low Intensity Conflict.* Field Manual FM 100-20. Washington, DC: Headquarters, Department of the Army, 1981.

————. *Military Intelligence Group (Combat Electronic Warfare and Intelligence) (Corps).* Field Manual FM 34-20. Washington, DC: Headquarters, Department of the Army, 1983.

—**CORPS OBSTACLE PLAN.** Centralized control of countermobility activities normally begins at the corps level with the corps obstacle plan. It is general in nature and is concerned with the use of obstacles as a part of a specific tactical operation. The plan supports the commander's concept of the operation and integrates the terrain aspects of the operation with the tactical plan.

References
Department of Defense, U.S. Army. *Countermobility.* Field Manual FM 5-102. Washington, DC: Headquarters, Department of the Army, 1985.

—**CORPS TROOPS** are troops assigned or attached to a corps, but not a part of one of the divisions that make up the corps (e.g., corps-level logistics units, corps artillery, and air defense and engineer brigades).

References
Department of Defense, Joint Chiefs of Staff. *Department of Defense Dictionary of Military and Related Terms.* Washington, DC: GPO, 1986.

—**CORRECTION.** (1) In fire control, a correction is any change in the firing data that will bring the mean point of contact or burst closer to the target. (2) Correction is a word used in communications procedure to indicate that an error in data has been announced and that the corrected data will follow.

References
Department of Defense, Joint Chiefs of Staff. *Department of Defense Dictionary of Military and Related Terms.* Washington, DC: GPO, 1986.

Department of Defense, U.S. Army. *The Rifle Squads (Mechanized and Light Infantry.* Training Circular TC 7-1. Washington, DC: Headquarters, Department of the Army, 1976.

—**CORRELATION,** in air defense, is the determination that an aircraft whose location is indicated on a radarscope, on a plotting board, or visually is the same aircraft for which information is being received from another source.

References
Department of Defense, Joint Chiefs of Staff. *Department of Defense Dictionary of Military and Related Terms.* Washington, DC: GPO, 1986.

—**CORTRAIN** is an alignment of major aircraft units within U.S. Armed Forces Command under assigned corps for purposes of training.

References
Department of Defense, U.S. Army. *Army Exercises.* Army Regulation AR 350-28. Washington, DC: Headquarters, Department of the Army, 1985.

—**COUNT OFF.** (1) Count off is the call out of one's numerical position in a line in successive order from a given starting point. (2) Count off is a command to count off.

References
Department of Defense, U.S. Army. *Dictionary of United States Army Terms.* Army Regulation AR 310-25. Washington, DC: Headquarters, Department of the Army, 1986.

—**COUNTERAIR** is air operations conducted to attain and maintain a desired degree of air superiority, thereby preventing enemy forces from effectively interfering with friendly surface and air operations. Counterair operations are generally classified as offensive or defensive. Offensive actions occur throughout enemy territory and are generally conducted at the initiative of friendly forces. Defensive actions are conducted near or over friendly territory and are generally in reaction to the initiative of the enemy. *See also:* Counterair Operations.

References

Department of Defense, U.S. Army. *Attack Helicopter Operations.* Field Manual FM 17-50. Washington, DC: Headquarters, Department of the Army, 1984.

———. *Operational Terms and Symbols.* Field Manual FM 101-5-1. Washington, DC: Headquarters, Department of the Army, 1985.

—**COUNTERAIR OPERATIONS.** The ultimate goal of counterair operations is to gain control of the air environment. Offensive counterair operations are conducted to seek out, neutralize, or destroy enemy forces at a time and place of one's choosing. Offensive counterair operations achieve this by seizing the offensive at the start of hostilities, conducting operations in the enemy's airspace, and neutralizing or destroying the enemy's air forces and the infrastructure supporting his air operations.

References

Department of Defense, U.S. Army. *Operations.* Field Manual FM 100-5. Washington, DC: Headquarters, Department of the Army, 1986.

—**COUNTERATTACK** is an attack, by part or all of a defending force against an enemy attacking force, to regain lost ground or to cut off or destroy enemy advance units. The general objective of a counterattack is to regain the initiative and to deny the enemy opportunity to succeed in its attack. In sustained defensive operations, it is undertaken to restore the battle position and is directed at limited objectives.

References

Department of Defense, U.S. Army. *Operational Terms and Symbols.* Field Manual FM 101-5-1. Washington, DC: Headquarters, Department of the Army, 1985.

—**COUNTERATTACKS AND SPOILING ATTACKS** are usually part of a defense or a delay. Counterattacks attempt to defeat an attacking enemy or regain key terrain; spoiling attacks preempt the attack before it gets underway. When the balance of power on the battlefield changes, the commander can exploit the situation by counterattacking to seize the initiative. Plans for all

necessary maneuver and support should be made in advance to assure timely execution and maximum possible impact.

References

Department of Defense, U.S. Army. *Operations.* Field Manual FM 100-5. Washington, DC: Headquarters, Department of the Army, 1986.

—**COUNTERBATTERY FIRE** is fire delivered to destroy or neutralize indirect fire weapon systems.

References

Department of Defense, Joint Chiefs of Staff. *Department of Defense Dictionary of Military and Related Terms.* Washington, DC: GPO, 1986.

—**COUNTERDECEPTION** is an attempt to negate or diminish the effects of a foreign deception operation.

References

Department of Defense, Joint Chiefs of Staff. *Department of Defense Dictionary of Military and Related Terms.* Washington, DC: GPO, 1986.

—**COUNTERESPIONAGE (CE)** is the aspect of counterintelligence concerned with aggressive operations against another intelligence service in order to reduce its effectiveness or to detect and neutralize foreign espionage. This is accomplished by identifying, penetrating, manipulating, deceiving, or repressing people, groups, or organizations conducting espionage in order to destroy, neutralize, exploit, or prevent further activity.

References

Allen, Thomas B., and Polmar, Norman. *Merchants of Treason: America's Secrets for Sale.* New York: Delacorte Press, 1988.

U.S. Congress. Senate. *Final Report of the Senate Select Committee to Study Government Operations With Respect to Intelligence Activities. Report 94-755. Book I, Foreign and Military Intelligence* (Church Committee Report). Washington, DC: GPO, 1976.

—**COUNTERFIRE** is fire intended to destroy, neutralize, or suppress the enemy's indirect fire systems.

References

Department of Defense, U.S. Army. *Fire Support in Combined Arms Operations.* Field Manual FM 6-20. Washington, DC: Headquarters, Department of the Army, 1983.

———. *Operational Terms and Symbols.* Field Manual FM 101-5-1. Washington, DC: Headquarters, Department of the Army, 1985.

—**COUNTERGUERRILLA WARFARE** refers to operations waged by a government's armed forces, paramilitary forces, or nonmilitary forces against guerrillas. *See also:* Guerrilla Warfare.

References

Becket, Henry S. A. *The Dictionary of Espionage: Spookspeak Into English.* New York: Stein and Day, 1986.

U.S. Congress. Senate. *Final Report of the Senate Select Committee to Study Government Operations With Respect to Intelligence Activities. Report 94-755. Book I, Foreign and Military Intelligence* (Church Committee Report). Washington, DC: GPO, 1976.

—**COUNTER-HUMAN INTELLIGENCE (C-HUMINT)** means the actions taken to determine enemy HUMINT collection capabilities and activities, the assessment of friendly vulnerabilities, and the subsequent development and recommendations or the implementation of countermeasures. It includes counterintelligence special operations, liaison, counterinterrogation, countervisual, counterolfactory, and counteracoustical means, security, and counterintelligence screening. *See also:* Intelligence.

References

Department of Defense, U.S. Army. *Counterintelligence.* Field Manual FM 34-60. Washington, DC: Headquarters, Department of the Army, 1985.

———. *Counter-Signals Intelligence (C-SIGINT) Operations.* Field Manual FM 34-62. Washington, DC: Headquarters, Department of the Army, 1986.

—**COUNTER-IMAGERY INTELLIGENCE** means the actions taken to determine the enemy's imagery intelligence capabilities and activities, which includes an assessment of its surveillance radar, photo, and infrared systems; and the assessment of friendly operations to identify patterns and signatures. The detected vulnerabilities are the targets for subsequent development and recommendations for countermeasures. Successful counter-IMINT operations rely heavily on pattern and movement analysis and evaluation and signature suppression actions. *See also:* Intelligence.

References

Department of Defense, U.S. Army. *Counterintelligence.* Field Manual FM 34-60. Washington, DC: Headquarters, Department of the Army, 1985.

———. *Counter-Signals Intelligence (C-SIGINT) Operations.* Field Manual FM 34-62. Washington, DC: Headquarters, Department of the Army, 1986.

—**COUNTERINSURGENCY (COIN)** is a term used to describe the military, paramilitary, political, economic, psychological, and civic actions government takes to defeat insurgency.

References

U.S. Congress. Senate. *Final Report of the Senate Select Committee to Study Government Operations With Respect to Intelligence Activities. Report 94-755. Book I, Foreign and Military Intelligence* (Church Committee Report). Washington, DC: GPO, 1976.

—**COUNTERINSURGENCY OPERATIONS** are military, paramilitary, political, economic, psychological, civic, and any other actions taken by a government to defeat rebellion and subversion within the nation. *See also:* Counterinsurgency.

References

U.S. Congress. Senate. *Final Report of the Senate Select Committee to Study Government Operations With Respect to Intelligence Activities. Report 94-755. Book I, Foreign and Military Intelligence* (Church Committee Report). Washington, DC: GPO, 1976.

—**COUNTERINTELLIGENCE (CI).** (1) Counterintelligence is gathering information and conducting activities to protect against espionage, other clandestine activities, sabotage, international terrorist activities, and assassinations conducted by or for foreign powers. It does not include personnel, physical, document, or communications security programs. (2) Counterintelligence is an Army tactical intelligence term that refers to activities intended to detect, evaluate, counteract, or prevent hostile intelligence collection, subversion, sabotage, international terrorism, or assassination that is conducted by or on behalf of any foreign power, organization, or person operating to the detriment of the U.S. Army. Counterintelligence includes the identification of the hostile multidiscipline intelligence collection threat, the determination of friendly vulnerabilities to that threat, and the recommendation and evaluation of security measures. (3) Counterintelligence, in an Army tactical intelligence context, also refers to activities concerned with identifying and countering the threat to security posed by hostile intelligence services or organizations or by individuals engaged in espionage, sabotage, or subversion. (4) Counterintelligence, as defined by the Church Committee, involves activities conducted to destroy the effectiveness of foreign intelligence operations and to protect information against espionage, individuals against subversion, and installations against sabotage. The term also refers to information developed by or used in counterintelligence operations. *See also:* Counterespionage, Countersabotage, Countersubversion, Foreign Counterintelligence.

Reference

Allen, Thomas B., and Polmar, Norman. *Merchants of Treason: America's Secrets for Sale.* New York: Delacorte Press, 1988.

Department of Defense, U.S. Army. *Counterintelligence.* Field Manual FM 34-60. Washington, DC: Headquarters, Department of the Army, 1985.

———. *Counter-Signals Intelligence (C-SIGINT) Operations.* Field Manual FM 34-62. Washington, DC: Headquarters, Department of the Army, 1986.

———. *Staff Organization and Operations.* Field Manual FM 101-5. Washington, DC: Headquarters, Department of the Army, 1984.

U.S. Congress. Senate. *Final Report of the Senate Select Committee to Study Government Operations With Respect to Intelligence Activities. Report 94-755. Book I, Foreign and Military Intelligence* (Church Committee Report). Washington, DC: GPO, 1976.

—**COUNTERINTELLIGENCE INFORMATION** is information, regardless of its source (e.g., human intelligence, communications intelligence, etc.) that is of value to counterintelligence forces. *See also:* Counterintelligence.

Reference

U.S. Congress. Senate. *Final Report of the Senate Select Committee to Study Government Operations With Respect to Intelligence Activities. Report 94-755. Book I, Foreign and Military Intelligence* (Church Committee Report). Washington, DC: GPO, 1976.

—**COUNTERINTERROGATION** includes measures taken to enable soldiers, if captured, to prolong resistance to enemy interrogation. It includes training in the provisions of the Geneva Convention, the Code of Conduct, and the techniques that are used by hostile interrogators.

Reference

Department of Defense, U.S. Army. *Counterintelligence.* Field Manual FM 34-60. Washington, DC: Headquarters, Department of the Army, 1985.

—**COUNTERMEASURES (CM)** are military activities in which devices or techniques are used to impair the enemy's operational effectiveness.

Reference

Department of Defense, U.S. Army. *Counter-Signals Intelligence (C-SIGINT) Operations.* Field Manual FM 34-62. Washington, DC: Headquarters, Department of the Army, 1986.

—**COUNTERMINE** encompasses the actions taken to counteract an enemy minefield by neutralizing or breaching it. *See also:* Mine Warfare.

Reference

Department of Defense, U.S. Army. *Counter-Signals Intelligence (C-SIGINT) Operations.* Field Manual FM 34-62. Washington, DC: Headquarters, Department of the Army, 1986.

———. *Mine/Countermine Operations at the Company Level.* Field Manual FM 20-32. Washington, DC: Headquarters, Department of the Army, 1985.

———. *Operational Terms and Symbols.* Field Manual FM 101-5-1. Washington, DC: Headquarters, Department of the Army, 1985.

—**COUNTERMINING,** in land mine warfare, is the tactics and techniques used to detect, avoid, breach, and/or neutralize enemy mines; and to deny the enemy the opportunity to use mines. *See also:* Mine Warfare.

Reference

Department of Defense, Joint Chiefs of Staff. *Department of Defense Dictionary of Military and Related Terms.* Washington, DC: GPO, 1986.

Department of Defense, U.S. Army. *Mine/Countermine Operations at the Company Level.* Field Manual FM 20-32. Washington, DC: Headquarters, Department of the Army, 1976.

———. *Operational Terms and Symbols.* Field Manual FM 101-5-1. Washington, DC: Headquarters, Department of the Army, 1985.

—**COUNTERMOBILITY OPERATIONS** involve the construction of obstacles and emplacement of minefields to delay, disrupt, and destroy the enemy by reinforcing the terrain. The primary purpose of countermobility operations is to slow or divert the enemy, to increase time for target acquisition, and to increase weapon effectiveness. *See also:* Mine Warfare.

Reference

Department of Defense, U.S. Army. *Operational Terms and Symbols.* Field Manual FM 101-5-1. Washington, DC: Headquarters, Department of the Army, 1985.

—**COUNTERMOBILITY SUPPORT** is divided into mine warfare and obstacle development, each with an ultimate goal of delaying, stopping, or channeling the enemy. Mine warfare includes mine categories, methods and systems of delivery, employment, reporting, recording, and marking. Obstacle development demonstrates innovative techniques and conventional improvements in planning and embracing obstacles other than minefields. *See also:* Mine Warfare.

Reference
Department of Defense, U.S. Army. *Countermobility.* Field Manual FM 5-102. Washington, DC: Headquarters, Department of the Army, 1985.

—**COUNTERMORTAR FIRE** is fire specifically directed against enemy mortars or rockets. *See also:* Fire.

Reference
Department of Defense, U.S. Army. *Dictionary of United States Army Terms.* Army Regulation AR 310-25. Washington, DC: Headquarters, Department of the Army, 1986.

—**COUNTERMOVE** is an operation undertaken in reaction to or in anticipation of a move by the enemy. *See also:* Counterattack.

Reference
Department of Defense, U.S. Army. *Operational Terms and Symbols.* Field Manual FM 101-5-1. Washington, DC: Headquarters, Department of the Army, 1985.

—**COUNTEROBSTACLE OPERATIONS** are actions that counteract an enemy obstacle system.

Reference
Department of Defense, U.S. Army. *Operational Terms and Symbols.* Field Manual FM 101-5-1. Washington, DC: Headquarters, Department of the Army, 1985.

—**COUNTEROFFENSIVE** is a large-scale offensive undertaken by a defending force in order to seize the initiative from the attacking force. *See also:* Counterattack.

Reference
Department of Defense, Joint Chiefs of Staff. *Department of Defense Dictionary of Military and Related Terms.* Washington, DC: GPO, 1986.

—**COUNTERPREPARATION FIRE** is intensive, prearranged fire delivered when the imminence of the enemy attack is discovered.

Reference
Department of Defense, Joint Chiefs of Staff. *Department of Defense Dictionary of Military and Related Terms.* Washington, DC: GPO, 1986.

—**COUNTERRECOIL** is the forward movement of a gun returning to firing position after recoil.

Reference
Department of Defense, U.S. Army. *Dictionary of United States Army Terms.* Army Regulation AR 310-25. Washington, DC: Headquarters, Department of the Army, 1986.

—**COUNTERRECONNAISSANCE** is the sum of all the efforts taken to prevent the enemy's observing a force, area, or place.

Reference
Department of Defense, Joint Chiefs of Staff. *Department of Defense Dictionary of Military and Related Terms.* Washington, DC: GPO, 1986.

—**COUNTERSABOTAGE (CS)** is the part of counterintelligence that detects, destroys, neutralizes, or prevents sabotage by identifying, penetrating, manipulating, deceiving, and repressing groups or organizations suspected of conducting it. *See also:* Sabotage.

Reference
U.S. Congress. Senate. *Final Report of the Senate Select Committee to Study Government Operations With Respect to Intelligence Activities. Report 94-755. Book I, Foreign and Military Intelligence* (Church Committee Report). Washington, DC: GPO, 1976.

—**COUNTER-SIGINT (SIGNALS INTELLIGENCE)** includes actions taken to determine enemy SIGINT and related electronic warfare capabilities and activities; to assess friendly operations to identify patterns, profiles, and signatures; to develop and recommend countermeasures; and to evaluate the effectiveness of applied countermeasures.

Reference
Department of Defense, U.S. Army. *Counterintelligence.* Field Manual FM 34-60. Washington, DC: Headquarters, Department of the Army, 1985.

—**COUNTERSIGN** is a secret challenge and its reply or password. The words composing the countersign are issued from the principal headquarters of a command to aid guards in their scrutiny of persons who apply to pass. These words are disseminated only to friendly personnel. A parole is a special password that is used to check on the countersign.

Reference
Department of Defense, Joint Chiefs of Staff. *Department of Defense Dictionary of Military and Related Terms.* Washington, DC: GPO, 1986.

Department of Defense, U.S. Army. *Guard Duty.* Field Manual FM 22-6. Washington, DC: Headquarters, Department of the Army, 1971.

—**COUNTERSUBVERSION**, as defined by the Church Committee, is "that part of counterintelligence that is designed to destroy the effectiveness of subversive activities through the detection, identification, exploitation, penetration, manipulation, deception, and repression of individuals, groups, or organizations conducting or capable of conducting such activities."

Reference
U.S. Congress. Senate. *Final Report of the Senate Select Committee to Study Government Operations With Respect to Intelligence Activities. Report 94-755. Book I, Foreign and Military Intelligence* (Church Committee Report). Washington, DC: GPO, 1976.

—**COUNTERTERRORISM** is offensive measures that respond to a terrorist act, or the documented threat of such an act. It includes the gathering of information and threat analyses in support of these measures.

Reference
Department of Defense, U.S. Army. *The Army Terrorism Counteraction Program.* Army Regulation AR 525-13. Washington, DC: Headquarters, Department of the Army, 1988.

—**COUNTER-VISUAL, -OLFACTORY, -ACOUSTICAL MEANS** are sights, odors, and sounds that are meant to deceive enemy scouts and forward-deployed reconnaissance and security elements who are trying to collect an extensive amount of intelligence information on the size or intention of friendly forces. These measures include the use of empty tents, bugle calls, and other configurations that imply that there are more forces than there are.

Reference
Department of Defense, U.S. Army. *Counterintelligence.* Field Manual FM 34-60. Washington, DC: Headquarters, Department of the Army, 1985.

—**COURIER** is a messenger (usually a commissioned or warrant officer) who is responsible for the secure physical transmission and delivery of documents or material. The courier hand carries the information to its destination. He is generally referred to as a command or local courier. *See also:* Armed Forces Courier Service.

Reference
U.S. Congress. Senate. *Final Report of the Senate Select Committee to Study Government Operations With Respect to Intelligence Activities. Report 94-755. Book I, Foreign and Military Intelligence* (Church Committee Report). Washington, DC: GPO, 1976.

—**COURSE OF ACTION.** (1) A course of action is any sequence of activities that an individual or a unit may follow. (2) A course of action is a possible plan open to an individual or a command that would accomplish or would be related to the accomplishment of the assigned mission. (3) A course of action is the scheme that has been adopted to accomplish a job or mission. (4) A course of action is a line of conduct in an engagement.

Reference
Department of Defense, U.S. Army. *Operational Terms and Symbols.* Field Manual FM 101-5-1. Washington, DC: Headquarters, Department of the Army, 1985.

—**COURT OF INQUIRY** is a board of three or more officers and a recorder appointed by the President, or other competent authority, to examine the nature of any transaction of, or accusation or imputation against, military personnel.

Reference
Department of Defense, U.S. Army. *Dictionary of United States Army Terms.* Army Regulation AR 310-25. Washington, DC: Headquarters, Department of the Army, 1986.

—**COURT OF MILITARY APPEALS** is a court composed of three civilian judges appointed by the President and confirmed by the Senate that exercises the appellate functions over the armed forces as to records of trial by courts-martial required by the Uniformed Code of Military Justice, articles 67 and 73. *See also:* Uniformed Code of Military Justice.

Reference
Department of Defense, U.S. Army. *Dictionary of United States Army Terms.* Army Regulation AR 310-25. Washington, DC: Headquarters, Department of the Army, 1986.

—**COVER.** (1) In clandestine and covert intelligence, cover is a disguise or role assumed by a person, organization, or installation to cover the fact that he, or it is engaged in clandestine operations. (2) Cover is an Army tactical intelligence term that means the measures necessary to protect a person, plan, operation, formation, or installation from the enemy intelligence effort and from the leakage of information. (3) Cover is to align oneself directly behind the man to one's immediate front while maintaining the correct distance. (4) Cover is protection from the fire of enemy weapons. This fire includes bullets, fragments, flame, nuclear effects, and biological and chemical agents. Cover also provides protection from enemy observation. It may be natural or artificial.

Reference

Department of Defense, Defense Intelligence College. *Glossary of Intelligence Terms and Definitions.* Washington, DC: DIC, 1987.

Department of Defense, U.S. Army. *Drills and Ceremonies.* Field Manual FM 22-5. Washington, DC: Headquarters, Department of the Army, 1986.

———. *Operational Terms and Symbols.* Field Manual FM 101-5-1. Washington, DC: Headquarters, Department of the Army, 1985.

———. *The Rifle Squads (Mechanized) and Light Infantry.* Training Circular TC 7-1. Washington, DC: Headquarters, Department of the Army, 1976.

U.S. Congress. Senate. *Final Report of the Senate Select Committee to Study Government Operations With Respect to Intelligence Activities. Report 94-755. Book I, Foreign and Military Intelligence* (Church Committee Report). Washington, DC: GPO, 1976.

—**COVER** (ARMY AVIATION) is an immediate climbing turn to a position from which fire support can be provided to lower flying aircraft.

Reference

Department of Defense, U.S. Army. *Dictionary of United States Army Terms.* Army Regulation AR 310-25. Washington, DC: Headquarters, Department of the Army, 1986.

—**COVER AND CONCEALMENT.** Terrain can protect a unit from observation and fire or it can hide forces. The cover afforded by slopes, folds, and depressions is critical because it preserves the strength of the force. Covered positions are as important to command posts, indirect fire units, reserves, combat support units, and combat service support units as they are to close combat units.

Concealment is protection from observation. Urban terrain, broken hills, high ground, and forested areas can be used to hide forces, but in operations against sophisticated forces, terrain alone cannot conceal a force or facility. Other measures that must be taken include limiting electronic and thermal emissions to conceal units and headquarters; camouflaging to conceal men and equipment; and limiting movement to help prevent the detection of hidden units. Even in fluid conditions, there will be opportunities to conceal forces for short periods.

Reference

Department of Defense, U.S. Army. *Operations.* Field Manual FM 100-5. Washington, DC: Headquarters, Department of the Army, 1986.

—**COVER OFF.** (1) Cover off means to take position directly behind the person in front, in close order drill. (2) Cover off means the command to straighten the files in a formation that is out of line.

Reference

Department of Defense, U.S. Army. *Dictionary of United States Army Terms.* Army Regulation AR 310-25. Washington, DC: Headquarters, Department of the Army, 1986.

—**COVERED APPROACH.** (1) A covered approach is any route that offers protection against enemy observation or fire. (2) A covered approach is an approach made under the protection that is furnished by forces, not natural cover.

Reference

Department of Defense, U.S. Army. *Dictionary of United States Army Terms.* Army Regulation AR 310-25. Washington, DC: Headquarters, Department of the Army, 1986.

———. *Operational Terms and Symbols.* Field Manual FM 101-5-1. Washington, DC: Headquarters, Department of the Army, 1985.

—**COVERED MOVEMENT** is a movement of troops when adequate security is provided by other friendly forces.

Reference

Department of Defense, U.S. Army. *Dictionary of United States Army Terms.* Army Regulation AR 310-25. Washington, DC: Headquarters, Department of the Army, 1986.

—**COVERING FIRE** is fire used to protect friendly troops from enemy direct fires.

Reference

Department of Defense, U.S. Army. *Operational Terms and Symbols.* Field Manual FM 101-5-1. Washington, DC: Headquarters, Department of the Army, 1985.

—**COVERING FORCE** accomplishes all the tasks of screening and guard forces. Additionally, a covering force operates apart from the main body in order to develop the situation early, and deceives, disorganizes, and destroys enemy forces. Unlike screening or guard forces, a covering force is a tactically self-contained force (i.e., it is organized with sufficient combat support and combat service support forces to operate independently of the main body). It operates at a considerable distance to the front, flank, or rear of a moving or stationary force. Its mission is to develop the situation early and defeat the enemy, if possible. If defeat is not possible, the covering force deceives, delays, and disorganizes the enemy and develops the situation so that the main body can effectively react.

In defensive situations, a covering force operating apart from the main body has four basic tasks. First, it tries to force the enemy into revealing the strength, location, and general direction of its main attack. Second, it attempts to deceive the enemy or prevent it from determining the strengths, dispositions, and locations of friendly forces, especially those in the main battle area. Third, it tries to strip away the enemy's air defense umbrella or force a displacement of the enemy's air defenses prior to attacking the main battle area. Finally, it tries to gain time for the main body to deploy, move, or prepare defenses within the main battle area.

In withdrawal operations, the covering force may cover the disengagement and withdrawal of the withdrawing force.

Reference
Department of Defense, Joint Chiefs of Staff. *Department of Defense Dictionary of Military and Related Terms.* Washington, DC: GPO, 1986.
Department of Defense, U.S. Army. *Air Defense Artillery Deployment: Chaparral/Vulcan/Stinger.* Field Manual FM 44-3. Washington, DC: Headquarters, Department of the Army, 1984.
———. *Operational Terms and Symbols.* Field Manual FM 101-5-1. Washington, DC: Headquarters, Department of the Army, 1985.

—**COVERING FORCE AREA (CFA),** in the defense, is the operational area between the forward edge of the battle area and the forward line of own troops. *See also:* Forward Edge of the Battle Area, Forward Line of Own Troops.

Reference
Department of Defense, U.S. Army. *Operational Terms and Symbols.* Field Manual FM 101-5-1. Washington, DC: Headquarters, Department of the Army, 1985.

—**CRATER** is a pit, depression, or cavity formed on the surface of the earth by an explosion. It may range from saucer shaped to conical, depending largely on the depth of the burst. In the case of a deep underground burst, no rupture of the surface may occur. The resulting cavity is termed a camouflet.

Reference
Department of Defense, Joint Chiefs of Staff. *Department of Defense Dictionary of Military and Related Terms.* Washington, DC: GPO, 1986.

—**CRAWL TRENCH** is a space dug in the ground, usually from two to two and one-half feet deep, as narrow as possible, and in a winding or zigzag pattern, which is used to conceal movement into or within a position. It provides only minimum protection.

Reference
Department of Defense, U.S. Army. *Survivability.* Field Manual FM 5-103. Washington, DC: Headquarters, Department of the Army, 1985.

—**CREDIBLE SERVICE** is all active or reserve active status service in the grade in which a person was ordered to active duty or higher that may be used to establish active duty date of ranks under this regulation. Service that is not credible for this purpose may be credible for other purposes.

Reference
Department of Defense, U.S. Army. *Promotion of Officers on Active Duty.* Army Regulation AR 624-100. Washington, DC: Headquarters, Department of the Army, 1984.

—**CREDIBLE THREAT** is a threat that the command or host nation authorities consider serious enough to change THREATCONs (Threat conditions) or implement additional antiterrorism measures.

Reference
Department of Defense, U.S. Army. *The Army Terrorism Counteraction Program.* Army Regulation AR 525-13. Washington, DC: Headquarters, Department of the Army, 1988.

—**CREEPING BARRAGE** is a barrage in which the fire of all units participating remains in the same relative position throughout and which advances in steps of one line at a time.

Reference
Department of Defense, Joint Chiefs of Staff. *Department of Defense Dictionary of Military and Related Terms.* Washington, DC: GPO, 1986.

—**CREST** is a terrain feature of such altitude that it restricts fire or observation in an area beyond, resulting in dead space, or limiting the minimum elevation, or both.

Reference
Department of Defense, Joint Chiefs of Staff. *Department of Defense Dictionary of Military and Related Terms.* Washington, DC: GPO, 1986.

—**CRESTED** is a verbal report indicating that the engagement of the target or observation of an area is not possible because of an obstacle or an intervening crest.

Reference
Department of Defense, Joint Chiefs of Staff. *Department of Defense Dictionary of Military and Related Terms.* Washington, DC: GPO, 1986.

—**CREW DRILL** relates to operating from the table of organization and equipment by more than one soldier, especially the operation of a crew-served weapon. Crew drills are practiced until a high level of proficiency and speed is achieved.

Reference
Department of Defense, U.S. Army. *Training for Mobilization and War.* Field Manual FM 25-5. Washington, DC: Headquarters, Department of the Army, 1985.

—**CRISIS MANAGEMENT TEAM (CMT)** is a team at a major Army command or installation level. It is concerned with plans, procedures, techniques, policies, and controls for dealing with terrorism, special threats, or other major disruptions occurring on government installations and facilities. A CMT considers all aspects of the incident and establishes contact with the area of concern.

Reference
Department of Defense, U.S. Army. *The Army Terrorism Counteraction Program.* Army Regulation AR 525-13. Washington, DC: Headquarters, Department of the Army, 1988.

—**CRITICAL CANCELLATION DATE** is the final date on which the President can cancel an exercise without having a severe impact on political, force, or financial commitments.

Reference
Department of Defense, U.S. Army. *Army Exercises.* Army Regulation AR 350-28. Washington, DC: Headquarters, Department of the Army, 1985.

—**CRITICAL INTELLIGENCE** is crucial data that requires the immediate attention of the commander. It is required to enable him to make decisions that will provide a timely and appropriate response to the actions of a potential or actual enemy. It includes but is not limited to the following: (1) strong indications that hostilities are about to break out; (2) indications that aggression is about to occur against a nation friendly to the United States; (3) indications of the impending use of nuclear, biological, or chemical weapons; and (4) the occurrence of significant events in potentially hostile nations that may lead to modifying U.S. nuclear strike plans. *See also:* Intelligence.

Reference
Department of Defense, Defense Intelligence College. *Glossary of Intelligence Terms and Definitions.* Washington, DC: DIC, 1987.

U.S. Congress. Senate. *Final Report of the Senate Select Committee to Study Government Operations With Respect to Intelligence Activities. Report 94-755. Book I, Foreign and Military Intelligence* (Church Committee Report). Washington, DC: GPO, 1976.

—**CRITICAL ITEM** is an essential item that is in short supply or is expected to be in short supply for an extended period. *See also:* Critical Supplies and Materials, Regulated Item.

Reference
Department of Defense, Joint Chiefs of Staff. *Department of Defense Dictionary of Military and Related Terms.* Washington, DC: GPO, 1986.

—**CRITICAL MOS (MILITARY OCCUPATIONAL SPECIALTY)** is a MOS that must meet the following criteria for assignment purposes. First, there would be an adverse impact on the planned operational missions of the Army if a shortage of soldiers with that MOS exists. Second, soldiers with other MOSs cannot perform the duties of the MOS without formal training. Third, training for the MOS must be formal and require special facilities, equipment, or instructors. Finally, the training input for the MOS is difficult to meet because of existing security, physical, mental, and educational requirements. *See also:* Military Operational Specialty.

Reference
Department of Defense, U.S. Army. *Enlisted Personnel Management System.* Army Regulation AR 600-200. Washington, DC: Headquarters, Department of the Army, 1984.

—**CRITICAL NODE** is an element, position, or communications entity whose disruption or destruction immediately downgrades the ability of a force to command, control, or effectively conduct combat operations.

Reference
Department of Defense, Joint Chiefs of Staff. *Department of Defense Dictionary of Military and Related Terms.* Washington, DC: GPO, 1986.

—**CRITICAL POINT.** (1) A critical point is a key geographical position that is important to the success of an operation. (2) In terms of time, a critical point is a crisis or turning point in an operation. (3) A critical point is a selected place along a line of march that is used as for reference when giving instructions. (4) A critical point is the location where there is a change of direction or change in slope in a ridge or stream. (5) A critical point is any location along a route of march where interference with a troop movement may occur.

Reference
Department of Defense, Joint Chiefs of Staff. *Department of Defense Dictionary of Military and Related Terms.* Washington, DC: GPO, 1986.

—**CRITICAL SUPPLIES** are items that are vital to supporting operations that, because of certain conditions, are in short supply or are expected to be in short supply.

Reference
Department of Defense, U.S. Army. Support *Operations: Echelons Above Corps.* Field Manual FM 100-16. Washington, DC: Headquarters, Department of the Army, 1986.

—**CRITICAL TASK** is an assignment that is essential for accomplishing a unit mission, successful individual performance, and/or survival in battle. It requires training and evaluation.

Reference
Department of Defense, U.S. Army. *Individual Military Education and Training.* Army Regulation AR 350-1. Washington, DC: Headquarters, Department of the Army, 1987.

———. *Training for Mobilization and War.* Field Manual FM 25-5. Washington, DC: Headquarters, Department of the Army, 1985.

—**CROSS TELL** is the transfer of information between facilities at the same operational level.

Reference
Department of Defense, Joint Chiefs of Staff. *Department of Defense Dictionary of Military and Related Terms.* Washington, DC: GPO, 1986.

—**CROSS-ATTACHMENT** is the exchange of subordinate units between units for a temporary period. For example, a tank battalion detaches a tank company that is subsequently attached to a mechanized infantry battalion, and the mechanized infantry battalion detaches a mechanized company that is then attached to the tank battalion.

Reference
Department of Defense, U.S. Army. *Air Defense Artillery Deployment: Chaparral/Vulcan/Stinger.* Field Manual FM 44-3. Washington, DC: Headquarters, Department of the Army, 1984.

———. *Operational Terms and Symbols.* Field Manual FM 101-5-1. Washington, DC: Headquarters, Department of the Army, 1985.

—**CROSS-COMPARTMENT** is a terrain compartment, the long axis of which is generally perpendicular to the direction of movement of a force.

Reference
Department of Defense, U.S. Army. *Operational Terms and Symbols.* Field Manual FM 101-5-1. Washington, DC: Headquarters, Department of the Army, 1985.

—**CROSS-COUNTRY MOVEMENT** is the movement of military vehicles (usually tactical) across terrain without using roads and bridges.

Reference
Department of Defense, U.S. Army. *Operational Terms and Symbols.* Field Manual FM 101-5-1. Washington, DC: Headquarters, Department of the Army, 1985.

—**CROSS-SERVICING.** (1) Cross-servicing is the function performed by one military service in support of another for which reimbursement is required from the service that receives the support. (2) Cross-servicing is the requirement to be able to service weapons systems, vehicles, planes, and other devices of allied forces, at one location or base by any allied force concerned. *See also:* Servicing.

Reference
Department of Defense, Joint Chiefs of Staff. *Department of Defense Dictionary of Military and Related Terms.* Washington, DC: GPO, 1986.

Department of Defense, U.S. Army. *Support Operations: Echelons Above Corps.* Field Manual FM 100-16. Washington, DC: Headquarters, Department of the Army, 1986.

—**CROSS-TRAINING** is training soldiers on other jobs and military occupational specialties within the unit to improve flexibility.

Reference
Department of Defense, U.S. Army. *Army Forces Training.* Army Regulation AR 350-41. Washington, DC: Headquarters, Department of the Army, 1986.

———. *Training for Mobilization and War.* Field Manual FM 25-5. Washington, DC: Headquarters, Department of the Army, 1985.

—**CROSS-TURN** (ARMY AVIATION) is a maneuver in which members of a flight reverse direction by turning toward each other.

Reference
Department of Defense, U.S. Army. *Dictionary of United States Army Terms.* Army Regulation AR 310-25. Washington, DC: Headquarters, Department of the Army, 1986.

—**CROSSING AREA** is a number of adjacent crossing sites under the control of one commander. *See also:* Crossing Area Commander.

Reference
Department of Defense, Joint Chiefs of Staff. *Department of Defense Dictionary of Military and Related Terms.* Washington, DC: GPO, 1986.

—**CROSSING AREA COMMANDER** is the officer who is responsible for the control of all crossing units and support forces while they are in the crossing area.

Reference
Department of Defense, U.S. Army. *Operational Terms and Symbols.* Field Manual FM 101-5-1. Washington, DC: Headquarters, Department of the Army, 1985.

—**CROSSING SITE** is the location along a water obstacle where the crossing can be made using amphibious vehicles, assault boats, rafts, bridges, or fording vehicles.

Reference
Department of Defense, U.S. Army. *Operational Terms and Symbols.* Field Manual FM 101-5-1. Washington, DC: Headquarters, Department of the Army, 1985.

—**CRYPTANALYSIS** is the steps and operations performed in converting encrypted messages into plain text without initial knowledge of the key that was used in the encryption. *See also:* CRYPTO.

Reference
Department of Defense, Joint Chiefs of Staff. *Department of Defense Dictionary of Military and Related Terms.* Washington, DC: GPO, 1986.

—**CRYPTO** is a designation applied to classified, cryptographic information that is so sensitive that it requires special rules for access and handling. *See also:* Communications Security, Cryptanalysis, Cryptocenter, Cryptochannel, Cryptographic, Cryptographic Information, Cryptographic Material, Cryptographic Security, Cryptographic System or Cryptosystem, Cryptography, Cryptoguard, Cryptologic Activities, Cryptology, Cryptomaterial, Cryptonet, Cryptonet Compartmentation, Cryptonet Controller, Cryptoperiod, Cryptoproduction Equipment, Cryptosecurity, Cryptoservice Message, Cryptosystem.

Reference
Department of Defense, Defense Intelligence College. *Glossary of Intelligence Terms and Definitions.* Washington, DC: DIC, 1987.

—**CRYPTOCENTER** is an establishment maintained for the encrypting and decrypting of messages. *See also:* CRYPTO.

Reference
Department of Defense, U.S. Army. *Tactical Single Channel Radio Communications Techniques.* Field Manual FM 24-18. Washington, DC: Headquarters, Department of the Army, 1984.

—**CRYPTOCHANNEL** is a complete system of crypto-communications between two or more entities. It is the basic unit in naval cryptographic communications and is analogous to a radio circuit. It includes (1) the cryptographic aids prescribed; (2) the holders thereof; (3) the indicators or other means of identification; (4) the area or areas in which they are effective; (5) the special purpose, if any, for which they are provided; and (6) pertinent notes as to distribution, usage, etc. A cryptochannel is analogous to a radio circuit. *See also:* Communications Security, CRYPTO.

Reference
Department of Defense, Joint Chiefs of Staff. *Department of Defense Dictionary of Military and Related Terms.* Washington, DC: GPO, 1986.

—**CRYPTOGRAPHIC** is a communications security term that means pertaining to, or concerning cryptography. *See also:* Communications Security, CRYPTO.

Reference
Department of Defense, U.S. Army. *Dictionary of United States Army Terms.* Army Regulation AR 310-25. Washington, DC: Headquarters, Department of the Army, 1986.

—**CRYPTOGRAPHIC INFORMATION** is detailed data of cryptographic techniques, processes, systems, equipment, functions, and capabilities, and all cryptomaterial. (Detailed means that disclosure of the information to unauthorized persons could reveal specific cryptographic features of classified crypto-equipment, or reveal weaknesses in equipment that could allow unauthorized decryption of encrypted traffic, or aid significantly in enemy cryptanalysis of a cryptosystem or of a specific message.) *See also:* Communications Security, CRYPTO.

Reference
Department of Defense, Defense Intelligence College. Glossary *of Intelligence Terms and Definitions.* Washington, DC: DIC, 1987.

—**CRYPTOGRAPHIC MATERIAL** are the documents, equipment, and devices used in signals intelligence or communications security. *See also:* Communications Security, CRYPTO.

Reference
U.S. Congress. Senate. *Final Report of the Senate Select Committee to Study Government Operations With Respect to Intelligence Activities. Report 94-755. Book I, Foreign and Military Intelligence* (Church Committee Report). Washington, DC: GPO, 1976.

—**CRYPTOGRAPHIC SECURITY** is the component of communications security that results from providing technically sound cryptographic systems and proper training in their use. *See also:* Communications Security, CRYPTO.

Reference
Department of Defense, Defense Intelligence College. *Glossary of Intelligence Terms and Definitions.* Washington, DC: DIC, 1987.

—**CRYPTOGRAPHIC SYSTEM or CRYPTOSYSTEM** is an entire system or unit that provides a single means of encrypting and decrypting material. It includes the equipment, their removable parts, the operating instructions, maintenance manuals, and any mechanical or electrical method or device that is used to disguise the system or its functions. *See also:* Communications Security, CRYPTO.

Reference
Department of Defense, Defense Intelligence College. *Glossary of Intelligence Terms and Definitions.* Washington, DC: DIC, 1987.

—**CRYPTOGRAPHY.** (1) Cryptography is a branch of cryptology that encompasses the vast variety of means and methods used to make plain text unintelligible so that it cannot be understood by unauthorized parties and the means and methods used to convert the same text back into intelligent text. (2) Cryptography is the application of such means and methods by means other than cryptanalysis. (3) Cryptography refers to the design and use of cryptosystems. (4) Cryptography, as defined by the Church Committee, is the enciphering of plain text so that it will be unintelligible to an unauthorized recipient. *See also:* Communications Security, CRYPTO.

Reference
Department of Defense, Defense Intelligence College. *Glossary of Intelligence Terms and Definitions.* Washington, DC: DIC, 1987.

U.S. Congress. Senate. *Final Report of the Senate Select Committee to Study Government Operations With Respect to Intelligence Activities. Report 94-755. Book I, Foreign and Military Intelligence* (Church Committee Report). Washington, DC: GPO, 1976.

—**CRYPTOGUARD** is a communications security term that has two meanings. (1) A cryptoguard is an activity responsible for decrypting, encrypting in another cryptosystem, and relaying telecommunications for other activities that do not hold compatible cryptosystems. (2) A cryptoguard is an activity that is responsible for providing secure communications services for other activities. *See also:* Communications Security, CRYPTO.

Reference
Department of Defense, U.S. Army. *Dictionary of United States Army Terms.* Army Regulation AR 310-25. Washington, DC: Headquarters, Department of the Army, 1986.

—**CRYPTOLOGIC ACTIVITIES** are the operations needed to produce signals intelligence and to maintain signals security. *See also:* Communications Security, CRYPTO.

Reference
Department of Defense, Defense Intelligence College. *Glossary of Intelligence Terms and Definitions.* Washington, DC: DIC, 1987.

—**CRYPTOLOGY.** (1) The Department of Defenses' official definition of cryptology is the science of secret communications. (2) Cryptology is a communications security term that means the science that deals with hidden, disguised, or encrypted communications. It embraces communications security and communications intelligence. (3) Cryptology, as defined by the Church Committee, is "the science that includes cryptoanalysis and cryptography, and embraces communications intelligence and communications security." *See also:* Communications Security, CRYPTO.

Reference

U.S. Congress. Senate. Final Re*port of the Senate Select Committee to Study Government Operations With Respect to Intelligence Activities. Report 94-755. Book I, Foreign and Military Intelligence* (Church Committee Report). Washington, DC: GPO, 1976.

—**CRYPTOMATERIAL** is all communications security material (including documents, devices, and equipment) that contains the cryptographic information needed to encrypt, decrypt, or authenticate communications. The material is marked "CRYPTO" or in another way to indicate that it has cryptographic information. *See also:* Communications Security, CRYPTO.

Reference

Department of Defense, Defense Intelligence College. *Glossary of Intelligence Terms and Definitions.* Washington, DC: DIC, 1987.

Department of Defense, Department of the Air Force. *Communications-Electronics Terminology.* Washington, DC: GPO, 1973.

—**CRYPTONET** is a communications security term that means two or more activities that hold the same keying material and can therefore communicate. *See also:* Communications Security, CRYPTO.

Reference

Department of Defense, U.S. Army. *Dictionary of United States Army Terms.* Army Regulation AR 310-25. Washington, DC: Headquarters, Department of the Army, 1986.

—**CRYPTONET COMPARTMENTATION** is a communications security term that means the limiting of the size of a cryptonet (i.e., the number of holders of a certain cryptovariable), as a means of controlling the volume of traffic protected by that cryptovariable or limiting the distribution of cryptovariables to specific user communities. *See also:* Communications Security, CRYPTO.

Reference

Department of Defense, U.S. Army. *Dictionary of United States Army Terms.* Army Regulation AR 310-25. Washington, DC: Headquarters, Department of the Army, 1986.

—**CRYPTONET CONTROLLER** is a communications security term that means the operator of a communications terminal who is responsible for generating and distributing cryptovariables in electrical form. *See also:* Communications Security, CRYPTO.

Reference

Department of Defense, U.S. Army. *Dictionary of United States Army Terms.* Army Regulation AR 310-25. Washington, DC: Headquarters, Department of the Army, 1986.

—**CRYPTOPERIOD** is a communications security term that means the time span during which a specific cryptovariable is authorized for use or in which the cryptovariables for a given system may remain in effect. *See also:* Communications Security, CRYPTO.

Reference

Department of Defense, U.S. Army. *Dictionary of United States Army Terms.* Army Regulation AR 310-25. Washington, DC: Headquarters, Department of the Army, 1986.

—**CRYPTOPRODUCTION EQUIPMENT** is a communications security term that means equipments and their components that are specifically designed for, and used in, manufacturing and the associated testing of keying material in hard-copy form. *See also:* Communications Security, CRYPTO.

Reference

Department of Defense, U.S. Army. *Dictionary of United States Army Terms.* Army Regulation AR 310-25. Washington, DC: Headquarters, Department of the Army, 1986.

—**CRYPTOSECURITY** is a component of communications security and is the result of providing technically sound cryptosystems and using them under proper security procedures. *See also:* Communications Security, CRYPTO.

Reference

Department of Defense, U.S. Army. *Support Operations: Echelons Above Corps.* Field Manual FM 100-16. Washington, DC: Headquarters, Department of the Army, 1986.

—**CRYPTOSERVICE MESSAGE** is a communications security term that means a message that is usually encrypted and transmitted between cryptocenters requesting or supplying information concerning the irregularities in message encryption or decryption. *See also:* Communications Security, CRYPTO.

Reference
Department of Defense, U.S. Army. *Dictionary of United States Army Terms.* Army Regulation AR 310-25. Washington, DC: Headquarters, Department of the Army, 1986.

—**CRYPTOSYSTEM** is a short term for cryptographic system. It is a communications security term that means the associated items of COMSEC equipment or materials that are used as a unit to provide a single means of encryption or decryption. *See also:* Communications Security, CRYPTO.

Reference
Department of Defense, Joint Chiefs of Staff. *Department of Defense Dictionary of Military and Related Terms.* Washington, DC: GPO, 1986.

—**CULMINATING POINTS.** Unless it is strategically decisive, every offensive operation will sooner or later reach a point where the strength of the attacker no longer significantly exceeds that of the defender, and beyond which continued offensive operations therefore risk overextension, counterattack, and defeat. In operational theory, this point is called the culminating point. The art of attack at all levels is to achieve the decisive objectives before the culminating point is reached. Conversely the art of defense is to hasten the culmination of the attack, recognize its advent, and be prepared to go over to the offense when it arrives.

Reference
Department of Defense, U.S. Army. *Operations.* Field Manual FM 100-5. Washington, DC: Headquarters, Department of the Army, 1986.

—**CURRENT FORCE** is the force that exists today. It represents the actual force structure or manning that is available to meet present contingencies. It is the basis for operations and security plans and orders. *See also:* Force, Intermediate Force Planning Level, Minimum Risk Force, Planning Force, Programmed Forces.

Reference
Department of Defense, Joint Chiefs of Staff. *Department of Defense Dictionary of Military and Related Terms.* Washington, DC: GPO, 1986.

—**CURRENT INTELLIGENCE** is a general intelligence term. (1) It is intelligence of all types and forms concerning events of immediate interest. Since it is often highly time-perishable, it is usually disseminated without evaluation and interpretation, since these processes could consume so much time that they would render the intelligence worthless. Although there is no time cutoff concerning current intelligence, such information rarely covers events that occurred more than 48 hours earlier. (2) Current intelligence, as defined by the Church Committee, are "summaries and analyses of recent events." *See also:* Intelligence.

Reference
Department of Defense, Joint Chiefs of Staff. *Department of Defense Dictionary of Military and Related Terms.* Washington, DC: GPO, 1986.
U.S. Congress. Senate. *Final Report of the Senate Select Committee to Study Government Operations With Respect to Intelligence Activities. Report 94-755. Book I, Foreign and Military Intelligence* (Church Comittee Report). Washington, DC: GPO, 1976.

—**CURRENT, RIVER STAGE, WATER DEPTH** is the speed of flow and the elevation of the water surface with reference to selected zero datum, and the depth of the streambed to the water's surface.

Reference
Department of Defense, U.S. Army. *Weather Support for Army Tactical Operations.* Field Manual FM 34-81. Washington, DC: Headquarters, Department of the Army, 1984.

—**CURTAIN (SMOKE)** is a dense vertical development of smoke placed between friendly and enemy positions. It prevents or restricts enemy ground observation of friendly positions and activities, but does not prevent enemy aerial observation of the same. *See also:* Smoke Screen.

Reference
Department of Defense, U.S. Army. *NBC Operations.* Field Manual FM 3-100. Washington, DC: Headquarters, Department of the Army, 1985.

—**CUSTODY** is the responsibility for the control of, transfer and movement of, and access to, weapons and components. Custody also includes the maintenance of accountability for weapons and components.

Reference
Department of Defense, Joint Chiefs of Staff. *Department of Defense Dictionary of Military and Related Terms.* Washington, DC: GPO, 1986.

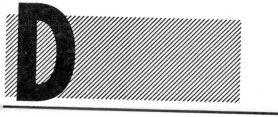

—DA (DEPARTMENT OF THE ARMY) RECOM-MENDED LIST is a list of soldiers recommended for promotion by a Department of the Army Promotion Selection Board and approved by the Headquarters, Department of the Army.

References

Department of Defense, U.S. Army. *Enlisted Personnel Management System.* Army Regulation AR 600-200. Washington, DC: Headquarters, Department of the Army, 1984.

—D-DAY. (1) The unnamed day on which a particular operation commences or is to commence. The highest command or headquarters responsible for coordinating the planning specifies the exact meaning of D-day. It can be the commencement of hostilities; the date of a major military effort; the execution date of an operation; or the date the operations phase is implemented, by land assault, air strike, naval bombardment, parachute assault, or amphibious assault. If more than one event is mentioned in a single plan, the secondary events are keyed to the primary event by adding or subtracting days as necessary. The letter "D" will be the only one used to denote the above. The command or headquarters directly responsible for executing the operation, if other than the one coordinating the planning, does so in light of the meanings specified by the highest planning headquarters. (2) Time in plans is indicated by a letter that shows the unit of time employed and figures, with a minus or plus sign, to indicate the time before or after the referenced event (e.g., if "D" is for a particular day and "H" for an hour, D+7 means seven days after D-day, and H-2 means two hours before "H" hour). *See also:* C-Day, M-Day, P-Day, H-Hour, P-Hour.

References

Department of Defense, Joint Chiefs of Staff. *Department of Defense Dictionary of Military and Related Terms.* Washington, DC: GPO, 1986.

—D-DAY CONSUMPTION/PRODUCTION DIF-FERENTIAL ASSETS, as applied to the D-to-P concept, are assets required to compensate for the inability of the production base to meet expenditure (consumption) requirements during the D-to-P period. *See also:* D-to-P Concept.

References

Department of Defense, Joint Chiefs of Staff. *Department of Defense Dictionary of Military and Related Terms.* Washington, DC: GPO, 1986.

—D-DAY MATERIEL READINESS GROSS CAPA-BILITY. As applied to the D-to-P concept, this term represents the sum of all assets on hand on D-day and the gross production capability (funded and unfunded) between D-day and P-day. When this capability equals the D-to-P materiel readiness gross requirement, requirements and capabilities are in balance. *See also:* D-to-P Concept, D-to-P Materiel Readiness Gross Requirement.

References

Department of Defense, Joint Chiefs of Staff. *Department of Defense Dictionary of Military and Related Terms.* Washington, DC: GPO, 1986.

—D-DAY PIPELINE ASSETS, as applied to the D-to-P concept, represent the sum of continental U.S. and overseas operating and safety levels of supply. *See also:* D-to-P Concept.

References

Department of Defense, Joint Chiefs of Staff. *Department of Defense Dictionary of Military and Related Terms.* Washington, DC: GPO, 1986.

—DAILY INTELLIGENCE SUMMARY (DISUM) is a daily analysis of crisis situations and a summation of relevant intelligence information that was produced during the previous 24 hours. The "as of" time for information, content, and submission time for the report is as specified by the joint force commander. *See also:* Intelligence.

References

Department of Defense, Joint Chiefs of Staff. *Department of Defense Dictionary of Military and Related Terms.* Washington, DC: GPO, 1986.

Von Hoene, John P.A. *Intelligence User's Guide.* Washington, DC: DIA, 1983.

—DAMAGE ASSESSMENT. (1) In a strategic context, a damage assessment is an appraisal of the effects of an attack on one or more elements of a nation's strength (e.g., military, economic, and political) to determine the residual capability for further operations. (2) In a tactical context, a damage assessment is a determination of the effect of attacks on targets.

References

Clancy, Tom. *The Cardinal of the Kremlin.* New York: Putnam, 1988.

Department of Defense, Defense Intelligence College. *Glossary of Intelligence Terms and Definitions.* Washington, DC: DIC, 1987.

Department of Defense, U.S. Army. *Operational Terms and Symbols.* Field Manual FM 101-5-1. Washington, DC: Headquarters, Department of the Army, 1985.

—**DAMAGE CRITERIA** are the critical levels of various effects (e.g., blast pressure and thermal radiation) required to achieve specified levels of damage.

References

Department of Defense, Joint Chiefs of Staff. *Department of Defense Dictionary of Military and Related Terms.* Washington, DC: GPO, 1986.

—**DAMAGE ESTIMATION** is an analysis of data to estimate the damage a specific weapon will cause to a target.

References

Department of Defense, U.S. Army. *Operational Terms and Symbols.* Field Manual FM 101-5-1. Washington, DC: Headquarters, Department of the Army, 1985.

—**DANGER** is information in a call for fire to indicate that friendly forces are within 1,500 meters of the target. *See also:* Danger Area.

References

Department of Defense, Joint Chiefs of Staff. *Department of Defense Dictionary of Military and Related Terms.* Washington, DC: GPO, 1986.

—**DANGER AREA.** (1) A danger area is a specified area above, below, or within which there may be potential danger. (2) In air traffic control, a danger area is an airspace of defined dimensions within which activities dangerous to the flight of aircraft may exist at specified times.

References

Department of Defense, Joint Chiefs of Staff. *Department of Defense Dictionary of Military and Related Terms.* Washington, DC: GPO, 1986.

—**DANGER CLOSE**, in artillery and naval gunfire support, is information in a call for fire to indicate that friendly forces are within 600 meters of the target.

References

Department of Defense, Joint Chiefs of Staff. *Department of Defense Dictionary of Military and Related Terms.* Washington, DC: GPO, 1986.

—**DANGER SPACE** is the space between the weapon and the target where the trajectory does not rise 1.8 meters (the average height of a standing human).

References

Department of Defense, Joint Chiefs of Staff. *Department of Defense Dictionary of Military and Related Terms.* Washington, DC: GPO, 1986.

—**DANGEROUS** is a target that can kill without seeing the victim. The target should be engaged as soon as possible after all most dangerous targets have been engaged. *See also:* Most Dangerous.

References

Department of Defense, U.S. Army. *Tank Gunnery.* Field Manual FM 17-2-C2. Washington, DC: Headquarters, Department of the Army, 1980.

—**DANGEROUS CARGO** refers to items that require special regulations for transport because of their dangerous properties.

References

Department of Defense, Joint Chiefs of Staff. *Department of Defense Dictionary of Military and Related Terms.* Washington, DC: GPO, 1986.

—**DATE ELIGIBLE TO RETURN FROM OVERSEAS (DEROS)** is the date an individual is eligible to return from overseas after having completed the prescribed overseas tour for the country in which he was serving. *See also:* Expiration Date of Term of Service, Permanent Change of Station.

References

Department of Defense, U.S. Army. *Overseas Service.* Army Regulation AR 614-30. Washington, DC: Headquarters, Department of the Army, 1984.

—**DATE OF RANK** is the date on which an officer was appointed in a particular grade. It is the date used to determine the relative seniority for officers holding the same grade.

References

Department of Defense, U.S. Army. *Promotion of Officers on Active Duty.* Army Regulation AR 624-100. Washington, DC: Headquarters, Department of the Army, 1984.

—DATE RETURNED FROM OVERSEAS (DROS) is the date an individual returned to the continental United States from his last overseas tour or an adjusted date. *See also:* Date Eligible to Return From Overseas.

References

Department of Defense, U.S. Army. *Overseas Service.* Army Regulation AR 614-30. Washington, DC: Headquarters, Department of the Army, 1984.

—DATE-TIME GROUP is the date and time, that a message was prepared for transmission. It is expressed as six digits followed by the zone suffix (e.g., 260733Z), with the first pair of digits denoting the date; the second pair, the hours; and the third pair, the minutes.

References

Department of Defense, Joint Chiefs of Staff. *Department of Defense Dictionary of Military and Related Terms.* Washington, DC: GPO, 1986.

—DAY OF ABSENCE is a day during which an officer or enlisted person is off duty status and away from the organization. It is used as a unit in figuring time or as a unit in figuring the time an officer or enlisted man is absent without leave. *See also:* Absent Without Leave.

References

Department of Defense, U.S. Army. *Dictionary of United States Army Terms.* Army Regulation AR 310-25. Washington, DC: Headquarters, Department of the Army, 1986.

—DAY OF DUTY is a day during which an officer or enlisted person is considered in duty status with his organization. It is used as a unit in figuring leave time. *See also:* Annual Leave.

References

Department of Defense, U.S. Army. *Dictionary of United States Army Terms.* Army Regulation AR 310-25. Washington, DC: Headquarters, Department of the Army, 1986.

—DEACTIVATE is the act of rendering an explosive device harmless or inert. *See also:* Inactivate.

References

Department of Defense, U.S. Army. *Dictionary of United States Army Terms.* Army Regulation AR 310-25. Washington, DC: Headquarters, Department of the Army, 1986.

—DEAD MINE is a mine that has been neutralized, sterilized, or rendered safe. *See also:* Mine Warfare.

References

Department of Defense, Joint Chiefs of Staff. *Department of Defense Dictionary of Military and Related Terms.* Washington, DC: GPO, 1986.

—DEAD SPACE. (1) Dead space is the volume of space above and around a gun or guided missile system into which it cannot fire because of mechanical or electronic limitations. (2) Dead space is an area within the maximum effective range of a weapon, surveillance device, or observer that cannot be covered by fire and observation from a given position because of intervening obstacles, the nature of the ground, the characteristics of the trajectory, or the limitations of the pointing capabilities of the systems.

References

Department of Defense, Joint Chiefs of Staff. *Department of Defense Dictionary of Military and Related Terms.* Washington, DC: GPO, 1986.

Department of Defense, U.S. Army. *Air Defense Artillery Deployment: Chaparral/Vulcan/Stinger.* Field Manual FM 44-3. Washington, DC: Headquarters, Department of the Army,1984.

———. *Operational Terms and Symbols.* Field Manual FM 101-5-1. Washington, DC: Headquarters, Department of the Army, 1985.

—DEAD STORAGE is storage of vehicles, equipment, or related materials for an indefinite time.

References

Department of Defense, U.S. Army. *Dictionary of United States Army Terms.* Army Regulation AR 310-25. Washington, DC: Headquarters, Department of the Army, 1986.

—DEADLINE is to remove a vehicle or piece of equipment from operation or use because: (1) it is inoperative due to damage, malfunctioning, or necessary repairs (this does not include items that are temporarily removed from use for routine maintenance or repairs that do not affect the combat capability); (2) it is unsafe; or (3) it would be damaged by further use. *See also:* Deadline Equipment.

References

Department of Defense, Joint Chiefs of Staff. *Department of Defense Dictionary of Military and Related Terms.* Washington, DC: GPO, 1986.

—**DEADLINE EQUIPMENT** is a major end-item of authorized equipment charged to a using unit or agency that has been removed from operation or immediate operational readiness because of actual or potential mechanical, electrical, or safety device failure. It does not include equipment scheduled for routine preventive maintenance or inspection.

References

Department of Defense, U.S. Army. *Dictionary of United States Army Terms.* Army Regulation AR 310-25. Washington, DC: Headquarters, Department of the Army, 1986.

—**DEADLY FORCE** is the effort required to curtail at once a dangerous situation. It is the physical force used by a person (e.g., firing a weapon) that causes or is likely to cause death or serious bodily harm.

References

Department of Defense, U.S. Army. *Technical Escort Operations.* Field Manual FM 3-20. Washington, DC: Headquarters, Department of the Army, 1981.

—**DEBARKATION** is the unloading of troops, equipment, or supplies from a ship or aircraft.

References

Department of Defense, Joint Chiefs of Staff. *Department of Defense Dictionary of Military and Related Terms.* Washington, DC: GPO, 1986.

—**DECAY RATE** is the rate of forgetting (knowledge or skills).

References

Department of Defense, U.S. Army. *Individual Military Education and Training.* Army Regulation AR 350-1. Washington, DC: Headquarters, Department of the Army, 1987.

—**DECENTRALIZED CONTROL**, in air defense, is the normal mode whereby a higher echelon monitors unit actions, making direct target assignments to units only when necessary to insure proper fire distribution or to prevent engagement of friendly aircraft. *See also:* Centralized Control.

References

Department of Defense, U.S. Army. *Civil Affairs Operations.* Field Manual FM 41-10. Washington, DC: Headquarters, Department of the Army, 1985.

—**DECENTRALIZED TRAINING.** (1) Decentralized training releases the authority and responsibility for the detailed planning, conduct, and internal evaluation of training to the battalion or separate company level. Brigade headquarters and above retain the responsibility for providing mission-type guidance to their subordinate units, allocating training resources, coordination, and the broad supervision/evaluation of training. (2) Decentralized training applies to how training may be conducted at the company, battery, or troop level.

References

Department of Defense, U.S. Army. *How to Prepare and Conduct Military Training.* Field Manual FM 21-6. Washington, DC: Headquarters, Department of the Army, 1975.

—**DECEPTION** is a general intelligence term that has different meanings in Army tactical intelligence; in counterintelligence, counterespionage, and counterinsurgency; and in signals intelligence, communications security, communications intelligence, operations security, and signals analysis. (1) Deception encompasses measures that mislead the enemy by manipulating, distorting, or falsifying information or evidence with the hope of prompting it to react in a manner that is prejudicial to its interests. (3) Deception is an Army tactical intelligence term that means the deliberate planning of interdependent activities in order to deny the enemy the ability to collect factual information and to provide it with misleading or false information in order to achieve tactical surprise. The term "deception" denotes manipulation, distortion, or falsification of the evidence given to the enemy concerning intentions and capabilities, while concurrently denying it true information. (3) Deception is a counterintelligence term that refers to a situation in which a penetrator of an automatic data processing system masquerades as a legitimate user. He must have access to the system procedural guides of the system he is penetrating to succeed if proper hardware and software security controls have been built into that system. *See also:* Communications Deception, Electronic Countermeasures, Manipulative Deception.

References

Department of Defense, U.S. Army. *Counter-Signals Intelligence (C-SIGINT) Operations.* Field Manual FM 34-62. Washington, DC: Headquarters, Department of the Army, 1986.

———. *Intelligence and Electronic Warfare Operations*. Field Manual FM 34-1. Washington, DC: Headquarters, Department of the Army, 1984.

———. *Military Intelligence Battalion (CEWI) (Operations) (Corps)*. Field Manual FM 34-21. Washington, DC: Headquarters, Department of the Army, 1982.

———. *Military Intelligence Group (Combat Electronic Warfare and Intelligence) (Corps)*. Field Manual FM 34-20. Washington, DC: Headquarters, Department of the Army, 1983.

———. *Operational Terms and Symbols*. Field Manual FM 101-5-1. Washington, DC: Headquarters, Department of the Army, 1985.

—**DECEPTION JAMMER** is a specialized type of radar jammer used primarily against weapons control radars and missile homing systems. It attempts to create a "more profitable target" for the weapon to home in on, rather than attempting to obliterate the target information. *See also:* Jamming.

References

Department of Defense, U.S. Army. *Counter-Signals Intelligence (C-SIGINT) Operations*. Field Manual FM 34-62. Washington, DC: Headquarters, Department of the Army, 1986.

———. *Military Intelligence Battalion (CEWI) (Operations) (Corps)*. Field Manual FM 34-21. Washington, DC: Headquarters, Department of the Army, 1982.

—**DECEPTION MEANS** are methods, resources, and techniques used to convey information to a foreign power. There are three categories of deception means.

- **Physical means** are activities and resources that convey or deny selected information to a foreign power (e.g., military operations, including exercises, reconnaissance, training activities, and movement of forces; dummy equipment and devices; tactics; bases, logistic actions, stockpiles, and repair activity; and test and evaluation activities).
- **Technical means** are military materiel resources and their associated operating techniques that convey or deny selected information to a foreign power through the deliberate radiation, reradiation, alteration absorption, or reflection of energy; emission or suppression of chemical or biological odors; or emission or suppression of nuclear particles.
- **Administrative means** are resources, methods, and techniques that convey or deny oral, pictorial, documentary, or other physical evidence to a foreign power.

See also: Deception.

References

Department of Defense, Joint Chiefs of Staff. *Department of Defense Dictionary of Military and Related Terms*. Washington, DC: GPO, 1986.

—**DECEPTION MEASURES.** Deception requires the provision of false indicators to the enemy. For example, if the supporting attack is a feint to be portrayed as a main attack, the unit conducting the feint must give the enemy evidence that it is the main attack. Information passes back and forth between opposing forces on a battlefield by what is seen, heard, smelled, and picked up by communications-electronics. Deception measures are, therefore, classed as visual, sonic, olfactory, and electronic. *See also:* Deception, Feint.

References

Department of Defense, U.S. Army. *Tactical Deception*. Field Manual FM 90-2. Washington, DC: Headquarters, Department of the Army, 1978.

—**DECEPTION OPERATION** is a military operation conducted to mislead the enemy. A unit conducting such an operation may or may not make contact with the enemy. The operation includes demonstrations, feints, displays, and ruses. *See also:* Deception.

References

Department of Defense, U.S. Army. *Operational Terms and Symbols*. Field Manual FM 101-5-1. Washington, DC: Headquarters, Department of the Army, 1985.

—**DECIPHER** means to convert enciphered text into plain text by using a cipher system. *See also:* Cipher, Code, Communications Security, Decode, Encipher, Encode.

References

Department of Defense, Defense Intelligence College. *Glossary of Intelligence Terms and Definitions*. Washington, DC: DIC, 1987.

—**DECISION.** In an estimate of the situation, a decision is a clear and concise statement of the line of action a commander intends to follow as the one most favorable to the successful accomplishment of his mission.

References

Department of Defense, Joint Chiefs of Staff. *Department of Defense Dictionary of Military and Related Terms*. Washington, DC: GPO, 1986.

—**DECISION BRIEFING** is intended to obtain an answer or a decision. It is the presentation of a staff officer's recommended solution resulting from analysis or study of a problem or problem area. *See also:* Briefing.

References

Department of Defense, U.S. Army. *Staff Organizations and Operations.* Field Manual FM 101-5. Washington, DC: Headquarters, Department of the Army, 1984.

—**DECISIVE ENGAGEMENT** occurs when a unit is considered fully committed and cannot maneuver or extricate itself. In the absence of outside assistance, the action must be fought to a conclusion and either won or lost with the forces at hand. *See also:* Engagement.

References

Department of Defense, U.S. Army. *Operational Terms and Symbols.* Field Manual FM 101-5-1. Washington, DC: Headquarters, Department of the Army, 1985.

—**DECISIVE TERRAIN.** Key terrain is decisive terrain if it has an extraordinary impact on the mission. To designate terrain as decisive is to recognize that the successful accomplishment of the mission, whether offensive or defensive, depends on seizing and retaining it. The commander designates decisive terrain, which is rare, to communicate its importance in his concept of operations, first to his staff, and later, to subordinate commanders. *See also:* Key Terrain.

References

Department of Defense, U.S. Army. *Operational Terms and Symbols.* Field Manual FM 101-5-1. Washington, DC: Headquarters, Department of the Army, 1985.

—**DECLASSIFICATION** is the removal of official information from the protective status that it had because of its security classification on the basis that its disclosure is no longer detrimental to national security. *See also:* Declassification and Downgrading Instructions.

References

Department of Defense, Defense Intelligence College. *Glossary of Intelligence Terms and Definitions.* Washington, DC: DIC, 1987.

Department of Defense, Information Security Oversight Office. *Directive No. 1: National Security Information.* Reprinted in *Federal Register,* 1982, pp. 27836-27841.

Department of Defense, Joint Chiefs of Staff. *Department of Defense Dictionary of Military and Related Terms.* Washington, DC: GPO, 1986.

—**DECLASSIFICATION AND DOWNGRADING INSTRUCTIONS** are notations on a classified document that indicate when the material may be downgraded to a lower classification and when it may be declassified. For sensitive information that cannot be automatically declassified, a notation indicates that the document is excluded or exempt from the general downgrading system and must be reviewed before it is downgraded or declared to be unclassified.

References

Department of Defense. Information Security Oversight Office. *Directive No. 1: National Security Information.* Reprinted in *Federal Register,* 1982, pp. 27836-27841.

—**DECODE** means to use a code system to convert an encoded message back into plain text. *See also:* Communications Security.

References

Clancy, Tom. *The Cardinal of the Kremlin.* New York: Putnam, 1988.

Department of Defense, Defense Intelligence College. *Glossary of Intelligence Terms and Definitions.* Washington, DC: DIC, 1987.

—**DECONFLICTION** are actions taken to prevent interference among the effects of two friendly nuclear weapons. *See also:* Nuclear Warfare.

References

Department of Defense, U.S. Army. *Fire Support in Combined Arms Operations.* Field Manual FM 6-20. Washington, DC: Headquarters, Department of the Army, 1983.

—**DECONTAMINANT** is any substance used to break down, neutralize, or remove chemical, biological, or radioactive material posing a threat to equipment or personnel. *See also:* Biological Warfare, Chemical Warfare, Nuclear Warfare.

References

Department of Defense, U.S. Army. *NBC Operations.* Field Manual FM 3-100. Washington, DC: Headquarters, Department of the Army, 1985.

—**DECONTAMINATION (DECON).** (1) Decontamination is the process of making any person, object, or area safe by absorbing, destroying, neutralizing, making harmless, or removing chemical or biological agents. (2) Decontamination is the removal of radioactive material clinging to or around a decontaminated person, object, or area. *See also:* Biological Warfare, Chemical Warfare, Nuclear Warfare.

References

Department of Defense, U.S. Army. *NBC Operations.* Field Manual FM 3-100. Washington, DC: Headquarters, Department of the Army, 1985.

————. *Operational Terms and Symbols.* Field Manual FM 101-5-1. Washington, DC: Headquarters, Department of the Army, 1985.

—**DECONTAMINATION STATION** is a building or location suitably equipped and organized to cleanse personnel and materiel of chemical, biological, or radiological contaminants. *See also:* Biological Warfare, Chemical Warfare, Nuclear Warfare.

References

Department of Defense, U.S. Army. *NBC Operations.* Field Manual FM 3-100. Washington, DC: Headquarters, Department of the Army, 1985.

—**DECORATION(S)** are distinctively designed marks of honor denoting heroism or meritorious/ outstanding service/achievement. U.S. Army personnel decorations are the Medal of Honor, Distinguished Service Cross, Distinguished Service Medal, Silver Star, Legion of Merit, Distinguished Flying Cross, Soldier's Medal, Bronze Star Medal, Purple Heart, Meritorious Service Medal, Air Medal, Army Commendation Medal, and the Army Achievement Medal. *See also:* Valor.

References

Department of Defense, U.S. Army. *Military Awards.* Army Regulation AR 672-5-1. Washington, DC: Headquarters, Department of the Army, 1984.

————. *Wear and Appearance of Army Uniforms and Insignia.* Army Regulation AR 670-1. Washington, DC: Headquarters, Department of the Army, 1986.

—**DECOY** is any imitation of a person, object, or phenomenon intended to deceive enemy surveillance devices or mislead an enemy evaluation. *See also:* Chaff.

References

Department of Defense, Joint Chiefs of Staff. *Department of Defense Dictionary of Military and Related Terms.* Washington, DC: GPO, 1986.

—**DECRYPT** means to use a cryptosystem to transform an encrypted communication into plain text. The term decrypt encompasses the terms decipher and decode. *See also:* Cipher, Code, Communications Security, Decipher, Decode.

References

Department of Defense, Defense Intelligence College. *Glossary of Intelligence Terms and Definitions.* Washington, DC: DIC, 1987.

—**DEDICATED BATTERY** is a cannon battery whose total firepower is immediately available to suppress enemy weapons that threaten a designated company or team during a movement to contact.

References

Department of Defense, U.S. Army. *Fire Support in Combined Arms Operations.* Field Manual FM 6-20. Washington, DC: Headquarters, Department of the Army, 1983.

————. *Operational Terms and Symbols.* Field Manual FM 101-5-1. Washington, DC: Headquarters, Department of the Army, 1985.

—**DEEP ATTACK** is a vital component of the AirLand Battle requiring an in-depth disruption of enemy forces in both offensive and defensive operations. Deep attack prevents the enemy from massing and creates opportunities for offensive actions to allow its defeat. Primary assets for the conduct of deep attack are air and artillery interdictions. *See also:* Deep Battle, Envelopment.

References

Department of Defense, U.S. Army. *Operational Terms and Symbols.* Field Manual FM 101-5-1. Washington, DC: Headquarters, Department of the Army, 1985.

————. *U.S. Army Air Defense Employment.* Field Manual FM 44-1. Washington, DC: Headquarters, Department of the Army, 1983.

—**DEEP BATTLE** encompasses all actions that support the friendly scheme of maneuver and that deny the enemy commander the ability to employ those of his forces that are not yet engaged at the time, place, or in the strength of his choice.

The deep battle component of the AirLand Battle is designed to support the commander's basic scheme of maneuver by an in-depth disruption of enemy forces. Its goal is to create opportunities for offensive action against committed enemy forces by delaying the arrival of enemy reserves or follow-on forces, or by destroying key enemy organizations. Surveillance operations are conducted to identify significant enemy forces in the area of interest while electronic warfare, long-range fire, and in-depth maneuver are used to attack enemy forces whose delay or disruption is important to the success of the commander's plan. In the defense, the deep battle aims to prevent the enemy from concentrating overwhelming combat power. The main objectives are to separate and disrupt attacking echelons, to protect friendly maneuvers and to degrade the enemy's fire support, command and control systems, and combat and combat service support. *See also:* AirLand Battle.

References

Department of Defense, U.S. Army.
Countermobility. Field Manual FM 5-102.
Washington, DC: Headquarters, Department of the Army, 1985.

————. *Operational Terms and Symbols.* Field Manual FM 101-5-1. Washington, DC: Headquarters, Department of the Army, 1985.

—**DEEP-CUT VEHICLE POSITION** is a position prepared to provide protection for support vehicles (e.g., cargo trucks; maintenance and computer vans; communications; decontamination equipment; petroleum, oils, and lubricants transporters; and earthmoving equipment). The position is usually open on each end for drive-in access/egress, or prepared with a rear wall and having only one entrance. The position is designed so that the tops of the vehicles are at least one foot below the top of the surrounding walls. *See also:* Position.

References

Department of Defense, U.S. Army. *Survivability.*
Field Manual FM 5-103. Washington, DC:
Headquarters, Department of the Army, 1985.

—**DEEP FORDING** is the capability of a self-propelled gun or ground vehicle equipped with built-in waterproofing and/or a special waterproofing kit to negotiate a water obstacle with its wheels or tracks in contact with the ground. *See also:* Shallow Fording.

References

Department of Defense, Joint Chiefs of Staff.
Department of Defense Dictionary of Military and Related Terms. Washington, DC: GPO, 1986.

—**DEEP FORDING CAPABILITY** is the characteristic of a self-propelled gun or ground vehicle equipped with built-in waterproofing and/or a special waterproofing kit to negotiate a water obstacle with its wheels or tracks in contact with the ground. *See also:* Shallow Fording.

References

Department of Defense, Joint Chiefs of Staff.
Department of Defense Dictionary of Military and Related Terms. Washington, DC: GPO, 1986.

—**DEEP OPERATIONS** are defense in depth operations in which the commander supports his basic scheme of maneuver against specific enemy forces that threaten his success. In either attack or defense, well-timed deep operations against enemy forces not yet in contact are necessary for success. Successful deep operations limit the enemy's freedom of action, alter the tempo of operations in favor of the friendly force, and advantageously isolate the close fight. Deep operations are an integral part of the overall plan; they selectively attack vulnerable enemy forces and facilities as a synchronized part of the unified tactical effort. Divisional brigades and smaller tactical units do not normally conduct separate deep operations, but their tactical training and operations must anticipate the arrival of enemy follow-on forces, prevent surprise through normal security measures forward, and deceive the enemy as to the best time and place to commit those follow-on forces. *See also:* Defense in Depth.

References

Department of Defense, U.S. Army. *Operations.*
Field Manual FM 100-5. Washington, DC:
Headquarters, Department of the Army, 1986.

—**DEEP SUPPORTING FIRE** is fire, directed at objectives not in the immediate vicinity of an army's own forces to neutralize and destroy enemy reserves and weapons and to interfere with enemy command, supply, communications, and observations. *See also:* Close Supporting Fire, Direct Supporting Fire, Supporting Fire.

References

Department of Defense, Joint Chiefs of Staff.
Department of Defense Dictionary of Military and Related Terms. Washington, DC: GPO, 1986.

—**DEFEND** is a mission assigned to a unit that requires it to destroy an attacking enemy force or to stop the enemy from penetrating the assigned sector or battle position. Subunits of the defending unit may have missions such as defend, delay, or counterattack. *See also:* Defense.

References

Department of Defense, U.S. Army. *Tank Platoon Division 86 (Test).* Field Manual FM 17-5. Washington, DC: Headquarters, Department of the Army, 1984.

—**DEFENSE.** A defense is a coordinated effort by a force to defeat the attackers and prevent them from achieving their objectives. Defensive operations take many forms, but traditional usage divides defensive arrangements into two broad categories.

- **Mobile defenses** focus on destroying the attacking force by permitting the enemy to advance into a position that exposes it to counterattack and envelopment by a mobile reserve.
- **Area defenses** focus on retaining terrain by maneuvering the enemy into positions from which it can be destroyed largely by fire.

There are three typical defense missions.

- **Defend in sector** is a mission that requires a defending unit to prevent enemy forces from passing beyond the rear boundary of the sector, while retaining flank security and insuring integrity of effort within the parent unit's scheme of maneuver. Initial positions generally are established as far forward as possible, but a commander may use any technique to accomplish the mission.
- **Defend a battle position** is a mission that places a unit in a battle position to concentrate its fires, to limit its maneuver, or to place it in an advantageous position to counterattack. The battle position is a general location on the ground. The commander positions his forces on the best terrain within and in the vicinity of the battle position and may position security forces forward of and about it. He can also locate combat support and combat service support elements outside the battle position. The commander can maneuver his forces freely within the battle position and seize the initiative to maneuver outside of it to attack enemy forces.
- **Defend a strongpoint** is a mission that implies retention of the position at all costs. Repeated assaults must be expected and repelled. Combat support and combat service support assets may be employed outside the strongpoint.

See also: Defense Area, Defense Design Requirements, Defense in Depth, Defense in Place, Defense Plan, Defense Planning, Defense Readiness Condition, Defense Counter Air, Defensive Fire, Defensive Operations, Defensive Zone.

References

Department of Defense, U.S. Army. *Operational Terms and Symbols.* Field Manual FM 101-5-1. Washington, DC: Headquarters, Department of the Army, 1985.

———. *Operations.* Field Manual FM 100-5. Washington, DC: Headquarters, Department of the Army, 1986.

—**DEFENSE AREA.** (1) A defense area, for a particular command, is the area from the forward edge of the battle area to its rear boundary, and where the decisive battle is fought. (2) A defense area is an area assigned to a given unit to be protected from, and held against, enemy attack. *See also:* Defense.

References

Department of Defense, Joint Chiefs of Staff. *Department of Defense Dictionary of Military and Related Terms.* Washington, DC: GPO, 1986.

Department of Defense, U.S. Army. *Dictionary of United States Army Terms.* Army Regulation AR 310-25. Washington, DC: Headquarters, Department of the Army, 1986.

—**DEFENSE DESIGN** is the process of considering air defense artillery employment principles, employment guidelines, and defense design requirements in conjunction with weapon system capabilities. It is one of the four phases of the defense planning sequence. *See also:* Defense Planning

References

Department of Defense, U.S. Army. *U.S. Army Air Defense Artillery Employment Hawk.* Field Manual FM 44-90. Washington, DC: Headquarters, Department of the Army, 1983.

———. *U.S. Army Air Defense Employment.* Field Manual FM 44-1. Washington, DC: Headquarters, Department of the Army, 1983.

—**DEFENSE DESIGN REQUIREMENTS** are required specifications based upon a consideration of METT-T (mission, enemy, terrain, troops, and time available) in conjunction with the specific characteristics of each type of air defense artillery weapon to be used in the defense. Defense design requirements are considered along with employment principles and employment guidelines in the defense design phase of the defense planning sequence. *See also:* Defense, Defense Planning.

References
Department of Defense, U.S. Army. *U.S. Army Air Defense Artillery Employment Hawk.* Field Manual FM 44-90. Washington, DC: Headquarters, Department of the Army, 1983.
————. *U.S. Army Air Defense Employment.* Field Manual FM 44-1. Washington, DC: Headquarters, Department of the Army, 1983.

—**DEFENSE EMERGENCY** is an emergency condition that exists when: (1) a major attack is made upon U.S. forces overseas or upon allied forces in any theater and is confirmed by either the commander of a command established by the Secretary of Defense or by higher authority; or (2) an overt attack of any type is made upon the United States and is confirmed either by the commander of a command established by the Secretary of Defense or by higher authority.

References
Department of Defense, Joint Chiefs of Staff. *Department of Defense Dictionary of Military and Related Terms.* Washington, DC: GPO, 1986.

—**DEFENSE IN DEPTH** is the establishing of mutually supporting defense positions that are designed to absorb and progressively weaken attack, prevent initial observations of the whole position by the enemy, and allow the commander to maneuver his reserve. *See also:* Defense.

References
Department of Defense, Joint Chiefs of Staff. *Department of Defense Dictionary of Military and Related Terms.* Washington, DC: GPO, 1986.

—**DEFENSE IN PLACE** is a system of defense based upon firm resistance without retreat, as opposed to delaying action in successive positions. *See also:* Defense.

References
Department of Defense, U.S. Army. *Dictionary of United States Army Terms.* Army Regulation AR 310-25. Washington, DC: Headquarters, Department of the Army, 1986.

—**DEFENSE INTELLIGENCE GROUND ORDER OF BATTLE (DIGOB)** is a part of the Defense Intelligence Order of Battle System of the Defense Intelligence Agency On-Line System that provides analysts access to detailed equipment inventories of ground forces. *See also:* Intelligence.

References
Von Hoene, John P. A. *Intelligence User's Guide.* Washington, DC: DIA, 1983.

—**DEFENSE PLAN** is a coordinated plan for preventing or defeating an enemy attack. It includes plans for elements of the defense (e.g., tactical organization, fire, air defense, security, air support, ground organizations, counterattack, communications, and supplies). *See also:* Defense.

References
Department of Defense, U.S. Army. *Dictionary of United States Army Terms.* Army Regulation AR 310-25. Washington, DC: Headquarters, Department of the Army, 1986.

—**DEFENSE PLANNING** is a command responsibility that begins with the establishment of air defense priorities and follows a sequential process of four complete phases: the analysis phase, the defense design phase, the evaluation of alternatives phase, and the implementation phase. *See also:* Defense.

References
Department of Defense, U.S. Army. *U.S. Army Air Defense Artillery Employment Hawk.* Field Manual FM 44-90. Washington, DC: Headquarters, Department of the Army, 1983.
————. *U.S. Army Air Defense Employment.* Field Manual FM 44-1. Washington, DC: Headquarters, Department of the Army, 1983.

—**DEFENSE READINESS CONDITION (DEFCON)** is a standard system of progressive alert postures for use between the Joint Chiefs of Staff and the Commanders of the Unified and Specified Commands and for use by the military services. The conditions match situations of varying degrees of severity and are identified by the short titles DEFCON 5, 4, 3, 2, or 1, with 5 being the lowest posture and 1 being at war. As each higher DEFCON is put into effect, military forces react accordingly. DEFCON 5 is a low condition, while DEFCON 4 is a normal state of peacetime preparedness. Troops in the field, aircraft aloft, and ships at sea would normally have watches and readiness conditions set that would conform to DEFCON 4. DEFCON 3 is a posture of heightened alert and was set, for example, in 1973, when the United States was unsure of Soviet intentions during the Yom Kippur War in October of that year. DEFCON 2 is a posture that is assumed when hostilities are imminent; DEFCON 1 is combat. *See also:* Defense.

References

Department of Defense, Joint Chiefs of Staff. *Department of Defense Dictionary of Military and Related Terms.* Washington, DC: GPO, 1986.

Department of Defense, National Defense University. *Joint Staff Officer's Guide, 1986.* Washington, DC: GPO, 1986.

—**DEFENSE SCHOOL COURSE** is a program of instruction used by two or more Services or agencies administered by a Service or agency that is designated as the executive agency. The curriculum is developed under policy guidance and approval authority of the Office of the Secretary of Defense.

References

Department of Defense, U.S. Army. *Individual Military Education and Training.* Army Regulation AR 350-1. Washington, DC: Headquarters, Department of the Army, 1986.

—**DEFENSIVE COASTAL AREA** is a coastal area and the air, land, and water area adjacent to the coastline within which defense operations may involve land, sea, and air forces.

References

Department of Defense, Joint Chiefs of Staff. *Department of Defense Dictionary of Military and Related Terms.* Washington, DC: GPO, 1986.

—**DEFENSIVE COUNTER AIR (DCA)** missions are conducted to detect, identify, intercept, and destroy enemy air forces that are attempting to attack friendly forces or penetrate friendly airspace. These missions defend friendly lines of communication, protect friendly bases, and support friendly land forces while denying the enemy the freedom to carry out offensive operations. *See also:* Defense.

References

Department of Defense, U.S. Army. *Operations.* Field Manual FM 100-5. Washington, DC: Headquarters, Department of the Army, 1986.

—**DEFENSIVE FIRE** is fire delivered by supporting units to assist and protect a unit engaged in defensive action. *See also:* Defense.

References

Department of Defense, Joint Chiefs of Staff. *Department of Defense Dictionary of Military and Related Terms.* Washington, DC: GPO, 1986.

—**DEFENSIVE MINE COUNTERMEASURES** are countermeasures intended to reduce the effects of enemy minelaying. *See also:* Countermeasures, Mine Warfare.

References

Department of Defense, Joint Chiefs of Staff. *Department of Defense Dictionary of Military and Related Terms.* Washington, DC: GPO, 1986.

—**DEFENSIVE MINEFIELD**, in land mine warfare, is a minefield laid according to an established plan in order to prevent a penetration between positions and to strengthen the defense of those positions. *See also:* Minefield.

References

Department of Defense, Joint Chiefs of Staff. *Department of Defense Dictionary of Military and Related Terms.* Washington, DC: GPO, 1986.

—**DEFENSIVE OPERATIONS** are operations conducted with the immediate purpose of causing an enemy attack to fail. Defensive operations may also achieve one or more of the following: gain time; concentrate forces elsewhere; wear down enemy forces as a prelude to offensive operations; and retain tactical, strategic, or political objectives. *See also:* Defense.

References

Department of Defense, U.S. Army. *Operational Terms and Symbols.* Field Manual FM 101-5-1. Washington, DC: Headquarters, Department of the Army, 1985.

—**DEFENSIVE SMOKE SCREEN** is a local smoke screen placed in front of (or on) tactically important objects or positions to neutralize enemy observation. Smoke pots and smoke generators are usually used to produce long-duration defensive screens. *See also:* Smoke Screen.

References

Department of Defense, U.S. Army. *Deliberate Smoke Operations.* Field Manual FM 3-50. Washington, DC: Headquarters, Department of the Army, 1984.

—**DEFENSIVE ZONE** is a strip of terrain, generally parallel to the front, that includes two or more organized, or partially organized, battle positions. *See also:* Defense.

References

Department of Defense, Joint Chiefs of Staff. *Department of Defense Dictionary of Military and Related Terms.* Washington, DC: GPO, 1986.

—**DEFERRABLE MAINTENANCE OPERATION** is a maintenance operation that can be deferred for approximately 120 days without causing degradation of the end-item to the extent that it cannot be used to perform its intended mission. Additionally, such deferral does not cause appreciable damage to other components of the end-item. However, the operation should be performed as soon as operational considerations and parts availability permit.

References

Department of Defense, U.S. Army. *Maintenance and Repair Parts Consumption Planning Guide for Contingency Operations.* Field Manual FM 42-9-23. Washington, DC: Headquarters, Department of the Army, 1980.

—**DEFERRED MAINTENANCE** is maintenance specifically intended to eliminate an existing fault, but not affect the continued successful operation, of the device or program. *See also:* Deferrable Maintenance Operation.

References

Department of Defense, Joint Chiefs of Staff. *Department of Defense Dictionary of Military and Related Terms.* Washington, DC: GPO, 1986.

—**DEFILADE.** (1) A defilade is protection from hostile observation and fire provided by an obstacle (e.g., a hill, ridge, or bank). (2) A defilade is a vertical distance by which a position is concealed from enemy observation. (3) Defilade is to shield from enemy fire by using natural or artificial obstacles.

References

Department of Defense, Joint Chiefs of Staff. *Department of Defense Dictionary of Military and Related Terms.* Washington, DC: GPO, 1986.

Department of Defense, U.S. Army. *Operational Terms and Symbols.* Field Manual FM 101-5-1. Washington, DC: Headquarters, Department of the Army, 1985.

—**DEFILE** is a narrow passage that tends to constrict the movement of troops.

References

Department of Defense, U.S. Army. *Operational Terms and Symbols.* Field Manual FM 101-5-1. Washington, DC: Headquarters, Department of the Army, 1985.

—**DEFLAGRATION** is a rapid chemical reaction that generates enough heat to enable it to continue and accelerate without input of heat from another source. Deflagration occurs on the surface with the reaction products flowing away from the unreacted material along with surface matter at subsonic velocity. The effect of a true deflagration under confinement is an explosion. Confining the reaction increases pressure, rate of reaction, and temperature, and may cause a detonation.

References

Department of Defense, U.S. Army. *Ammunition and Explosives Safety Standards.* Army Regulation AR 385-64. Washington, DC: Headquarters, Department of the Army, 1987.

—**DEFLECTION CHANGE** is a change in the azimuth setting applying to all guns in a battery when the target moves, or when a shift is made from one target to another. Deflection change does not include the deflection difference that allows for the difference in positions of the various guns firing at the same target. *See also:* Deflection Correction.

References

Department of Defense, U.S. Army. *Dictionary of United States Army Terms.* Army Regulation AR 310-25. Washington, DC: Headquarters, Department of the Army, 1986.

—**DEFLECTION CORRECTION** is a correction that must be applied to the azimuth or shift measured on a firing chart so that the line of fire will pass through the target.

References

Department of Defense, U.S. Army. *Dictionary of United States Army Terms.* Army Regulation AR 310-25. Washington, DC: Headquarters, Department of the Army, 1986.

—**DEFLECTION ERROR** is the distance to the right or to the left of the target between the point aimed at and the burst of a projectile or the mean point of impact of a salvo. *See also:* Salvo.

References

Department of Defense, U.S. Army. *Dictionary of United States Army Terms.* Army Regulation AR 310-25. Washington, DC: Headquarters, Department of the Army, 1986.

—**DEFLECTION SCALE** is the scale on a sight, marked in mils, for applying corrections in deflection or for laying the weapon in direction.

References
Department of Defense, U.S. Army. *Dictionary of United States Army Terms.* Army Regulation 310-25. Washington, DC: Headquarters, Department of the Army, 1986.

—**DEFOLIANT OPERATION** is the use of defoliating agents on vegetated areas in support of military operations. *See also:* Chemical Warfare.

References
Department of Defense, Joint Chiefs of Staff. *Department of Defense Dictionary of Military and Related Terms.* Washington, DC: GPO, 1986.

—**DEFOLIATING AGENT** is a chemical that causes trees, shrubs, and other plants to shed their leaves prematurely. *See also:* Chemical Warfare.

References
Department of Defense, Joint Chiefs of Staff. *Department of Defense Dictionary of Military and Related Terms.* Washington, DC: GPO, 1986.

—**DEFUZED MINE** is a mine from which the fuze has been removed. *See also:* Mine Warfare.

References
Department of Defense, U.S. Army. *Mine/Countermine Operations at the Company Level.* Field Manual FM 20-32. Washington, DC: Headquarters, Department of the Army, 1976.

—**DEFUZING** is removing a fuze from a mine. *See also:* Mine Warfare.

References
Department of Defense, Joint Chiefs of Staff. *Department of Defense Dictionary of Military and Related Terms.* Washington, DC: GPO, 1986.

—**DEGREE OF RISK** (NUCLEAR), as specified by the commander, is the risk to which friendly forces may be subjected to the effects of the detonation of a nuclear weapon that is used to attack close-in enemy targets. Acceptable degrees of risk under different tactical conditions are classified as emergency, moderate, and negligible. *See also:* Emergency Risk (Nuclear), Moderate Risk (Nuclear), Negligible Risk (Nuclear), Nuclear Warfare.

References
Department of Defense, U.S. Army. *Operational Terms and Symbols.* Field Manual FM 101-5-1. Washington, DC: Headquarters, Department of the Army, 1985.

—**DELAY** is conducted when forces are insufficient to attack or to defend or when the defensive plan calls for drawing the attacker into an area for counterattack. Delays gain time for friendly forces to: reestablish the defense; cover a defending or withdrawing unit; protect a friendly unit's flank; or economize a force effort. In a delay, a unit trades space for time. The intent is to slow the enemy, cause enemy casualties, and, if possible, stop it without becoming decisively engaged. This is done by defending, disengaging, moving, and defending again. Companies do not conduct delays independently but rather as part of their battalion.

References
Department of Defense, U.S. Army. *The Infantry Rifle Company (Infantry, Airborne, Air Assault, Ranger).* Field Manual FM 7-10. Washington, DC: Headquarters, Department of the Army, 1982.

———. *Operations.* Field Manual FM 100-5. Washington, DC: Headquarters, Department of the Army, 1986.

—**DELAY ACTION** is the predetermined delayed explosion of ammunition after its fuze has been activated. *See also:* Delay Firing Device.

References
Department of Defense, U.S. Army. *Dictionary of United States Army Terms.* Army Regulation AR 310-25. Washington, DC: Headquarters, Department of the Army, 1986.

—**DELAY FIRING DEVICE** is a device designed to actuate a firing circuit or train after a fixed or variable preset period of time.

References
Department of Defense, U.S. Army. *Mine/Countermine Operations at the Company Level.* Field Manual FM 20-32. Washington, DC: Headquarters, Department of the Army, 1976.

—**DELAY FROM ALTERNATE POSITIONS** is a technique involving two maneuver units in a single sector. While the first is fighting, the second occupies the next position in depth and prepares to assume responsibility for the operation. The first force disengages and passes through or around the second. It then prepares to resume the delay from a position in greater depth, while the second force takes up the fight. *See also:* Delay.

References

Department of Defense, U.S. Army. *Operational Terms and Symbols.* Field Manual FM 101-5-1. Washington, DC: Headquarters, Department of the Army, 1985.

—DELAY FROM DELAY (BATTLE) POSITIONS. The battalion commander normally assigns the company the mission to delay from delay positions when: the primary threat is armor or motorized units; the battalion is delaying in an armor restrictive area in which the enemy can be canalized into selected areas; the terrain is available that dominates armor avenues of approach; or the battalion sector is narrow. *See also:* Delay.

References

Department of Defense, U.S. Army. *The Infantry Rifle Company (Infantry, Airborne, Air Assault, Ranger).* Field Manual FM 7-10. Washington, DC: Headquarters, Department of the Army, 1982.

—DELAY FROM SUCCESSIVE POSITIONS is a technique that occurs when a sector is so wide that available forces cannot occupy more than a single tier of positions. Maneuver units delay continuously on and between positions throughout the sectors, fighting rearward from one position to another, each as long as possible or for a specified time. *See also:* Delay.

References

Department of Defense, U.S. Army. *Operational Terms and Symbols.* Field Manual FM 101-5-1. Washington, DC: Headquarters, Department of the Army, 1985.

—DELAY IN SECTOR. The battalion commander normally assigns the company the mission to delay in sector when: the primary threat is infantry; the battalion sector cannot be adequately covered from one position; there are multiple avenues of approach; there are limited fields of fire and observation; or the battalion sector is extremely wide. *See also:* Delay.

References

Department of Defense, U.S. Army. *The Infantry Rifle Company (Infantry, Airborne, Air Assault, Ranger).* Field Manual FM 7-10. Washington, DC: Headquarters, Department of the Army, 1982.

—DELAY OPERATIONS are normally conducted when there are insufficient forces to attack or defend, making it necessary to trade space for time. Delay operations are conducted much like the active defense, except that the purpose of the defense is to stop the enemy, while the purpose of the delay is to slow the enemy, often for a specified time. Thus, when a force is delaying, as in the active defense, some of its subordinate units may be attacking, some defending, and some disengaging to move to other positions. *See also:* Delay.

References

Department of Defense, U.S. Army. *Armored and Mechanized Division Operations.* Field Manual FM 71-100. Washington, DC: Headquarters, Department of the Army, 1978.

—DELAYED ACTION MINE is an explosive charge designed to go off some time after it has been planted. It is often left behind by a retreating enemy to harass or destroy pursuing forces. *See also:* Mine Warfare.

References

Department of Defense, U.S. Army. *Dictionary of United States Army Terms.* Army Regulation AR 310-25. Washington, DC: Headquarters, Department of the Army, 1986.

—DELAYED CONTACT FIRE is a firing system arranged to explode a mine at a set time after it has been touched or disturbed. *See also:* Fire.

References

Department of Defense, U.S. Army. *Dictionary of United States Army Terms.* Army Regulation AR 310-25. Washington, DC: Headquarters, Department of the Army, 1986.

—DELAYED OPENING. (1) A delayed opening is an accidental temporary failure of a parachute to function. (2) A delayed opening occurs when personnel or equipment are deliberately dropped from an aircraft and their descent is slowed by parachute when close to the ground.

References

Department of Defense, U.S. Army. *Dictionary of United States Army Terms.* Army Regulation AR 310-25. Washington, DC: Headquarters, Department of the Army, 1986.

—DELAYING ACTION is a retrograde operation in which space is traded for time and maximum punishment is inflicted on the army, without becoming decisively involved in combat. *See also:* Disengagement, Retirement, Retrograde Movement, Withdrawal.

References
Department of Defense, U.S. Army. *Dictionary of United States Army Terms.* Army Regulation AR 310-25. Washington, DC: Headquarters, Department of the Army, 1986.

—**DELAYING OPERATION** is usually conducted when the commander needs time to concentrate or withdraw forces, to establish defenses in greater depth, to economize an area, or to complete offensive actions elsewhere. In the delay, the destruction of the enemy force is secondary to slowing its advance to gain time.

A delay in sector is a low-risk mission that requires a unit to slow and defeat as much of the enemy as possible without sacrificing the tactical integrity of the unit. This mission can be given to forces in the covering force area or the main battle area.

A delay forward of a specified line for a specified time or specified event is a high-risk mission that requires a unit to prevent enemy forces from reaching the specified area earlier than the specified time or event, regardless of the cost. This mission can be given to units in either the covering force area or in the main battle area. *See also:* Disengagement, Retirement, Retrograde, Withdrawal.

References
Department of Defense, Joint Chiefs of Staff. *Department of Defense Dictionary of Military and Related Terms.* Washington, DC: GPO, 1986.

Department of Defense, U.S. Army. *Operational Terms and Symbols.* Field Manual FM 101-5-1. Washington, DC: Headquarters, Department of the Army, 1985.

—**DELAYING POSITION** is a position taken to slow the advance of the enemy without being decisively engaged. *See also:* Delaying Operation.

References
Department of Defense, U.S. Army. *Dictionary of United States Army Terms.* Army Regulation AR 310-25. Washington, DC: Headquarters, Department of the Army, 1986.

—**DELEGATION OF AUTHORITY.** When a superior in the chain of command assigns a mission to a subordinate, he also delegates the necessary authority for the subordinate to accomplish the mission. Command responsibility works in two directions. While the commander is responsible to his superiors for mission accomplishment, he also has a responsibility to his subordinates. Having delegated authority to his subordinates, the commander must provide them with the necessary guidance, resources (including time), and support to accomplish their mission. However, the superior retains overall responsibility for the accomplishment of the mission.

References
Department of Defense, Joint Chiefs of Staff. *Department of Defense Dictionary of Military and Related Terms.* Washington, DC: GPO, 1986.

Department of Defense, U.S. Army. *Operational Terms and Symbols.* Field Manual FM 101-5-1. Washington, DC: Headquarters, Department of the Army, 1985.

————. *Staff Organization and Operations.* Field Manual FM 101-54. Washington, DC: Headquarters, Department of the Army, 1984.

—**DELIBERATE AMBUSH** is an ambush planned against a specific target. Planning for it requires detailed information about the target (e.g., size, nature, organization, armament, equipment, route of movement, and projected times it will reach or pass certain points on its route). *See also:* Ambush, Hasty Ambush.

References
Department of Defense, U.S. Army. *The Rifle Squads (Mechanized and Light Infantry.* Training Circular TC 7-1. Washington, DC: Headquarters, Department of the Army, 1976.

—**DELIBERATE ATTACK** is an attack that has been planned and carefully coordinated with all concerned elements based upon thorough reconnaissance, evaluation of all intelligence and relative combat strength, analysis of various courses of action, and other factors affecting the situation. It generally is conducted against a well-organized defense when a hasty attack is not possible or has been conducted and failed. It replaces a coordinated attack. *See also:* Ambush, Attack, Coordinated Attack, Hasty Attack, Raid.

References
Department of Defense, Joint Chiefs of Staff. *Department of Defense Dictionary of Military and Related Terms.* Washington, DC: GPO, 1986.

Department of Defense, U.S. Army. *Operational Terms and Symbols.* Field Manual FM 101-5-1. Washington, DC: Headquarters, Department of the Army, 1985.

————. *Tank Gunnery.* Field Manual FM 17-12. Washington, DC: Headquarters, Department of the Army, 1984.

—**DELIBERATE BREACH** is conducted when it is not possible or necessary to cross an obstacle in stride or after a hasty breach has failed. A deliberate breach is characterized by detailed planning and preparation, and is executed with whatever resources are available. *See also:* Deliberate Breaching, Hasty Breach.

References

Department of Defense, Joint Chiefs of Staff. *Department of Defense Dictionary of Military and Related Terms.* Washington, DC: GPO, 1986.

Department of Defense, U.S. Army. *Operational Terms and Symbols.* Field Manual FM 101-5-1. Washington, DC: Headquarters, Department of the Army, 1985.

—**DELIBERATE BREACHING** is the creation by engineers of a lane through a minefield or of a clear route through a barrier or fortification. Deliberate breaching which is systematically planned and carried out, is done when speed and the protection of friendly troops are not vital. *See also:* Deliberate Breach.

References

Department of Defense, Joint Chiefs of Staff. *Department of Defense Dictionary of Military and Related Terms.* Washington, DC: GPO, 1986.

Department of Defense, U.S. Army. *Operations.* Field Manual FM 100-5. Washington, DC: Headquarters, Department of the Army, 1986.

—**DELIBERATE DECONTAMINATION** entails operations and techniques to decontaminate clothing and equipment so that operators and crew members can perform their mission with their individual and respiratory protection removed. *See also:* Biological Warfare, Chemical Warfare, Hasty Decontamination, Nuclear Warfare.

References

Department of Defense, U.S. Army. *NBC Operations.* Field Manual FM 3-100. Washington, DC: Headquarters, Department of the Army, 1985.

—**DELIBERATE DEFENSE** is a defense normally organized when time for organization is available because one's forces are not in contact with the enemy or contact with the enemy is not imminent. *See also:* Hasty Defense.

References

Department of Defense, U.S. Army. *Operational Terms and Symbols.* Field Manual FM 101-5-1. Washington, DC: Headquarters, Department of the Army, 1985.

—**DELIBERATE DEMOLITIONS** are used when enemy interference during preparations is unlikely and there is sufficient time for thorough reconnaissance and careful preparation. Deliberate preparation permits economical use of explosives, since there is time to accurately calculate the explosives needed and to place them so that the required effects are obtained. *See also:* Demolition.

References

Department of Defense, U.S. Army. *Engineer Combat Operations.* Field Manual FM 5-100. Washington, DC: Headquarters, U.S. Army, 1984.

—**DELIBERATE FIRE** is fire delivered at a rate intentionally less than normal to permit adjustment corrections, meet specific tactical requirements, or conserve ammunition. *See also:* Fire.

References

Department of Defense, U.S. Army. *Dictionary of United States Army Terms.* Army Regulation AR 310-25. Washington, DC: Headquarters, Department of the Army, 1986.

—**DELIBERATE POSITIONS** (INFANTRY) are modified hasty positions prepared during periods of relaxed enemy pressure. Improvements include adding overhead cover, digging trenches to adjacent positions, and maintaining camouflage. *See also:* Hasty Positions (Infantry).

References

Department of Defense, U.S. Army. *Survivability.* Field Manual FM 5-103. Washington, DC: Headquarters, Department of the Army, 1985.

—**DELIBERATE PROTECTIVE MINEFIELDS** are used to protect static installations (e.g., depots, airfields, and missile sites). Conventional mines are always used and are emplaced in standard patterns, usually by engineers. The field is always fenced, marked, and covered by fire. These minefields are usually emplaced for long periods, and when they are to be removed, they are cleared by engineers. *See also:* Mine Warfare.

References

Department of Defense, U.S. Army. *Countermobility.* Field Manual FM 5-102. Washington, DC: Headquarters, Department of the Army, 1985.

———. *Mine/Countermine Operations at the Company Level.* Field Manual FM 20-32. Washington, DC: Headquarters, Department of the Army, 1976.

—**DELIBERATE RIVER CROSSING** is a crossing of a water obstacle that requires extensive planning, detailed preparation, and centralized control. *See also:* Hasty River Crossing, River Crossing.

References

Department of Defense, U.S. Army. *Operational Terms and Symbols.* Field Manual FM 101-5-1. Washington, DC: Headquarters, Department of the Army, 1985.

—**DELIBERATE ROUTE RECONNAISSANCE** is a thorough survey, conducted when enough time and qualified personnel are available to analyze and classify the significant features of a route.

References

Department of Defense, U.S. Army. *Route Reconnaissance and Classification.* Field Manual FM 5-36. Washington, DC: Headquarters, Department of the Army, 1985.

—**DELIVERY ERROR** is the inaccuracy associated with a given weapon system that results in a dispersion of shots about, rather than at, the aiming point. *See also:* Circular Error Probable, Deviation, Dispersion, Dispersion Error, Horizontal Error.

References

Department of Defense, Joint Chiefs of Staff. *Department of Defense Dictionary of Military and Related Terms.* Washington, DC: GPO, 1986.

—**DEMAND** is a valid requirement for material placed on the supply system by an authorized customer. Demand is categorized as recurring or nonrecurring and is measured in terms of frequency and quantity.

References

Department of Defense, U.S. Army. *Dictionary of United States Army Terms.* Army Regulation AR 310-25. Washington, DC: Headquarters, Department of the Army, 1986.

—**DEMANDED SUPPLIES** are supplies that require a requisition in order to be obtained. Items in supply classes II, III (packaged), IV, VII, and IX are considered demanded supplies. *See also:* Supplies.

References

Department of Defense, U.S. Army. *Operational Terms and Symbols.* Field Manual FM 101-5-1. Washington, DC: Headquarters, Department of the Army, 1985.

—**DEMILITARIZATION** is the act of destroying the offensive and defensive characteristics inherent in certain types of equipment or material. It includes mutilation, dumping at sea, scrapping, burning, or alteration to prevent the further use of such equipment and material for its originally intended military or lethal purpose. *See also:* Demilitarized Zone.

References

Department of Defense, U.S. Army. *Dictionary of United States Army Terms.* Army Regulation AR 310-25. Washington, DC: Headquarters, Department of the Army, 1986.

—**DEMILITARIZED ZONE (DMZ)** is a defined area where stationing or concentrating any military forces or establishing any military facilities is prohibited. Perhaps the most famous is the DMZ that separates North and South Korea where numerous confrontations between North Korean and United Nations forces have occurred.

References

Department of Defense, Joint Chiefs of Staff. *Department of Defense Dictionary of Military and Related Terms.* Washington, DC: GPO, 1986.

Department of Defense, U.S. Army. *Dictionary of United States Army Terms.* Army Regulation AR 310-25. Washington, DC: Headquarters, Department of the Army, 1986.

—**DEMOLITION** is the destruction of structures, facilities, or material by use of fire, water, explosives, mechanical, or other means. *See also:* Demolition Belt, Demolition Chamber, Demolition Firing Party, Demolition Kit, Demolition Obstacles, Demolition Tool Kit.

References

Department of Defense, Joint Chiefs of Staff. *Department of Defense Dictionary of Military and Related Terms.* Washington, DC: GPO, 1986.

—**DEMOLITION BELT** is a land area selected by the division commander to be sown with explosive charges, mines, or other obstacles to deny its use to enemy operations and to protect friendly troops. The term also refers to a continuous series of obstacles that are set across the whole front. The demolition belt is normally prepared by the engineers.

References

Department of Defense, Joint Chiefs of Staff. *Department of Defense Dictionary of Military and Related Terms.* Washington, DC: GPO, 1986.

—**DEMOLITION CHAMBER** is a space intentionally provided in a structure for the emplacement of explosive charges.

References

Department of Defense, Joint Chiefs of Staff. *Department of Defense Dictionary of Military and Related Terms.* Washington, DC: GPO, 1986.

—**DEMOLITION FIRING PARTY** is the party at the site that is technically responsible for the demolition.

References

Department of Defense, Joint Chiefs of Staff. *Department of Defense Dictionary of Military and Related Terms.* Washington, DC: GPO, 1986.

—**DEMOLITION GUARD** is a local force positioned to insure that a target is not captured by the enemy before the orders given for its demolition have been successfully fulfilled. The commander of the demolition guard is responsible for the operational command of all troops at the demolition site, including the demolition firing party, and is responsible for transmitting the order to fire to the demolition party.

References

Department of Defense, Joint Chiefs of Staff. *Department of Defense Dictionary of Military and Related Terms.* Washington, DC: GPO, 1986.

—**DEMOLITION KIT** is a demolition tool kit, that includes explosives.

References

Department of Defense, Joint Chiefs of Staff. *Department of Defense Dictionary of Military and Related Terms.* Washington, DC: GPO, 1986.

—**DEMOLITION OBSTACLES** are created by detonating explosives, including nuclear explosives. Demolitions are commonly used to create reinforcing obstacles.

References

Department of Defense, U.S. Army. *Countermobility.* Field Manual FM 5-102. Washington, DC: Headquarters, Department of the Army, 1985.

—**DEMOLITION TOOL KIT** is composed of the tools, materials, and nonexplosive accessories that are necessary to prepare demolition charges.

References

Department of Defense, Joint Chiefs of Staff. *Department of Defense Dictionary of Military and Related Terms.* Washington, DC: GPO, 1986.

—**DEMONSTRATION.** (1) Demonstration is an attack or show of force on a front where a decision is not sought, and is made to deceive the enemy. It is similar to a feint except that no contact with the enemy is sought. Decoys, dummy positions, and inoperative equipment may be used in support of the operation. (2) A demonstration is a presentation technique designed to show soldiers what they are expected to do and how to do it (e.g., displays, field or troop demonstrations, training films, TV tapes, and skits). *See also:* Feints, Military Mission Options.

References

Department of Defense, U.S. Army. *Armored and Mechanized Division Operations.* Field Manual FM 71-100. Washington, DC: Headquarters, Department of the Army, 1978.

———. *How to Prepare and Conduct Military Training.* Field Manual FM 21-6. Washington, DC: Headquarters, Department of the Army, 1975.

———. *Operational Terms and Symbols.* Field Manual FM 101-5-1. Washington, DC: Headquarters, Department of the Army, 1985.

—**DENIAL MEASURE** is an action to hinder or deny the enemy the use of space, personnel, supplies, or facilities (e.g., by destroying, removing, contaminating, or erecting obstructions). *See also:* Denial Objects/Areas, Denial Operation, Denial Target.

References

Department of Defense, U.S. Army. *Operational Terms and Symbols.* Field Manual FM 101-5-1. Washington, DC: Headquarters, Department of the Army, 1985.

—**DENIAL OBJECTS/AREAS** are items or locations that are defined by the corps commander in the obstacle and denial plan as areas, facilities, or installations that subordinate units will prevent the enemy from seizing and controlling.

References

Department of Defense, U.S. Army. *Operational Terms and Symbols.* Field Manual FM 101-5-1. Washington, DC: Headquarters, Department of the Army, 1985.

—**DENIAL OPERATION** is an operation to prevent or hinder enemy occupation of, or benefit from, areas or objects having tactical or strategic value.

References

Department of Defense, U.S. Army. *Operational Terms and Symbols*. Field Manual FM 101-5-1. Washington, DC: Headquarters, Department of the Army, 1985.

—**DENIAL TARGET** concerns facilities, areas, or installations to be destroyed or denied to the enemy. Because of the political implications, denial targets are directed only at the corps or theater level; however, they are executed by the unit in whose sector the target is located. Examples of such targets are power plants, railroad facilities, and petroleum oil, and lubricant storage tanks.

References

Department of Defense, U.S. Army. *Operational Terms and Symbols*. Field Manual FM 101-5-1. Washington, DC: Headquarters, Department of the Army, 1985.

—**DENOMINATIONAL COVERAGE** is religious support provided by chaplains to members of their own faith (e.g., Roman Catholics, Jews, Orthodox Jews, and Protestants). *See also:* Chaplain.

References

Department of Defense, U.S. Army. *The Chaplain and Chaplain Assistant in Combat Operations*. Field Manual FM 16-5. Washington, DC: Headquarters, Department of the Army, 1984.

—**DENSITY** is the average number of mines per meter of minefield front. *See also:* Mine Warfare.

References

Department of Defense, Joint Chiefs of Staff. *Department of Defense Dictionary of Military and Related Terms*. Washington, DC: GPO, 1986.

—**DEPARTMENT OF THE ARMY (DA)** is the executive part of the Department of the Army at the seat of government and all field headquarters, forces, reserve components, installations, activities, and functions under the control or supervision of the Secretary of the Army.

References

Department of Defense, Joint Chiefs of Staff. *Department of Defense Dictionary of Military and Related Terms*. Washington, DC: GPO, 1986.

—**DEPARTMENTAL DETAIL** is a temporary assignment and duty in a soldier's service in which he is appointed to another service. His military status as a member of the service in which he is appointed is not affected.

References

Department of Defense, U.S. Army. *Officer Assignment Policies, Details and Transfers*. Army Regulation AR 614-100. Washington, DC: Headquarters, Department of the Army, 1984.

—**DEPARTURE AIRFIELD CONTROL GROUP/ ARRIVAL AIRFIELD CONTROL GROUP (DACG/AACG).** The major commander of the land component whose units are being supported by an Air Force airlift is responsible for providing a DACG. The mission of the DACG is to coordinate and control the loading of personnel, equipment, and supplies into Air Force aircraft. The DACG should be organized as a provisional unit. Personnel and equipment resources come from units or activities that are not immediately required to accompany the transported forces.

References

Department of Defense, U.S. Army. *USA/USAF Doctrine for Joint Airborne and Tactical Airlift Operations*. Field Manual FM 100-27. Washington, DC: Headquarters, Department of the Army, 1985.

—**DEPARTURE AREA** is the general area encompassing all base camps, bivouacs, and departure airfield facilities. *See also:* Marshalling Area.

References

Department of Defense, U.S. Army. *USA/USAF Doctrine for Joint Airborne and Tactical Airlift Operations*. Field Manual FM 100-27. Washington, DC: Headquarters, Department of the Army, 1985.

—**DEPARTURE SITE(S)** are individual airfield facilities used by airborne forces to launch an airborne operation. *See also:* Departure Area.

References

Department of Defense, U.S. Army. *USA/USAF Doctrine for Joint Airborne and Tactical Airlift Operations*. Field Manual FM 100-27. Washington, DC: Headquarters, Department of the Army, 1985.

—**DEPENDENT-RESTRICTED TOUR** is a location outside of the continental United States with an established overseas tour that does not permit command-sponsored dependents. It is also referred to as an unaccompanied hardship overseas tour or as a remote tour. *See also:* Tour of Duty.

References

Department of Defense, U.S. Army. *Overseas Service*. Army Regulation AR 614-30. Washington, DC: Headquarters, Department of the Army, 1984.

—**DEPLOYABILITY POSTURE** is the state or stage of a unit's preparedness to be relocated to participate in a military operation. *See also:* Deployment, Deployment Exercises, Deployment Plan, Deployment Planning.

References

Department of Defense, U.S. Army. *Planning Logistics Support for Military Operations*. Field Manual FM 701-58. Washington, DC: Headquarters, Department of the Army, 1987.

—**DEPLOYMENT.** (1) Deployment is the act of extending battalions and smaller units in width, depth, or both width and depth to increase readiness for contemplated action. (2) In a strategic sense, deployment is the relocation of forces to desired areas of operation. (3) Deployment is the designated location of troops and troop units as indicated in a troop schedule. (4) Deployment is the series of functions that occur from the time a packed parachute is placed in operation until it is fully opened and supporting its load.

References

Department of Defense, Joint Chiefs of Staff. *Department of Defense Dictionary of Military and Related Terms*. Washington, DC: GPO, 1986.

—**DEPLOYMENT EXERCISES (DEPEXs)** provide training for individual soldiers, units, and support agencies in the tasks and procedures involved in relocating from home stations or installations to areas of hostilities.

References

Department of Defense, U.S. Army. *How to Conduct Training Exercises*. Field Manual FM 25-4. Washington, DC: Headquarters, Department of the Army, 1984.

—**DEPLOYMENT PLAN,** a category of the operation plan, is a plan developed by an Army component command that provides for the relocation of assigned Army forces in support of a Unified Command supporting plan and in support of the Unified Command and Army component command operation plans.

References

Department of Defense, U.S. Army. *Planning Logistics Support for Military Operations*. Field Manual FM 701-58. Washington, DC: Headquarters, Department of the Army, 1987.

—**DEPLOYMENT PLANNING** is the part of operation planning that concerns the relocation of forces to the desired area of operations.

References

Department of Defense, U.S. Army. *Planning Logistics Support for Military Operations*. Field Manual FM 701-58. Washington, DC: Headquarters, Department of the Army, 1987.

—**DEPLOYMENT-QUALIFIED EQUIPMENT** is equipment that has been determined to be free of conditions that would limit its reliability in performing its primary mission under combat conditions for a period of 90 days of operations and has scored READY in accordance with applicable Equipment Serviceability Criteria.

References

Department of Defense, U.S. Army. *Planning Logistics Support for Military Operations*. Field Manual FM 701-58. Washington, DC: Headquarters, Department of the Army, 1987.

—**DEPOT.** (1) In supply, a depot is an activity for the receipt, classification, storage, accounting, issue, maintenance, procurement, manufacture, assembly, research, salvage, or disposal of material. (2) In personnel, a depot is an activity for receiving, processing, training, assigning, and forwarding personnel replacements. *See also:* Army Depot, Depot Maintenance, Depot Repair, Depot Supply, Depot Support, General Depot, Master Depot.

References

Department of Defense, Joint Chiefs of Staff. *Department of Defense Dictionary of Military and Related Terms*. Washington, DC: GPO, 1986.

—**DEPOT MAINTENANCE** is maintenance performed on materiel that requires major overhaul or a complete rebuilding of parts, assemblies, subassemblies, and end-items, including manufacturing parts, modifications, testing, and reclaiming as required. Depot maintenance supports lower levels of maintenance by providing technical assistance and by performing maintenance that is beyond their responsibility. It also provides stocks of serviceable equipment by using more extensive facilities for repair than are available in lower level maintenance activities. *See also:* Depot.

References

Department of Defense, Joint Chiefs of Staff. *Department of Defense Dictionary of Military and Related Terms.* Washington, DC: GPO, 1986.

Department of Defense, U.S. Army. *Dictionary of United States Army Terms.* Army Regulation 310-25. Washington, DC: Headquarters, Department of the Army, 1986.

—**DEPOT REPAIR** is repair work normally performed at a communications zone or zone of interior installation by maintenance personnel especially trained and equipped to make fifth-echelon repairs. *See also:* Depot.

References

Department of Defense, Joint Chiefs of Staff. *Department of Defense Dictionary of Military and Related Terms.* Washington, DC: GPO, 1986.

—**DEPOT SUPPLY** parallels depot maintenance. It is the service, authorized and prescribed, performed by specially trained and designated semimobile and fixed organizations and/or specially trained personnel of fixed installations to determine the requirements for acquisition, accounting for, and wholesale distribution of supplies and equipment to supported retail echelons of supply and to collateral depot maintenance activities. *See also:* Depot.

References

Department of Defense, U.S. Army. *Dictionary of United States Army Terms.* Army Regulation 310-25. Washington, DC: Headquarters, Department of the Army, 1986.

—**DEPOT SUPPORT** is the mission, maintenance, and supply support that provides the reserve and potential required to insure an uninterrupted flow of supplies into the combat zone or area of operations. This support mission is provided by fixed-type units operating in a communications zone or zone of interior. *See also:* Depot.

References

Department of Defense, U.S. Army. *Dictionary of United States Army Terms.* Army Regulation AR 310-25. Washington, DC: Headquarters, Department of the Army, 1986.

—**DEPTH** is the extension of operations in space, time, and resources. Through the use of depth, a commander obtains space to maneuver effec-

tively; time to plan, arrange, and execute operations; and resources to win. Momentum in the attack and elasticity in defense derive from depth.

References

Department of Defense, U.S. Army. *Operations.* Field Manual FM 100-5. Washington, DC: Headquarters, Department of the Army, 1986.

—**DEPTH** (DRILLS AND CEREMONIES) is the space from the front to the rear of a formation, including the front and rear elements.

References

Department of Defense, U.S. Army. *Drills and Ceremonies.* Field Manual FM 22-5. Washington, DC: Headquarters, Department of the Army, 1986.

—**DEPUTY CHIEF OF STAFF** is an officer who assists the Chief of Staff of corps or higher staffs by supervising various staff activities and acting for the Chief of Staff in his absence.

References

Department of Defense, U.S. Army. *Dictionary of United States Army Terms.* Army Regulation AR 310-25. Washington, DC: Headquarters, Department of the Army, 1986.

—**DESCENDING BRANCH** is the portion of the trajectory traced while the projectile is falling.

References

Department of Defense, U.S. Army. *Dictionary of United States Army Terms.* Army Regulation AR 310-25. Washington, DC: Headquarters, Department of the Army, 1986.

—**DESCRIPTION OF TARGET**, in artillery, is a step in the call for fire in which the observer or spotter describes the installation, personnel, equipment, or activity to be taken under fire.

References

Department of Defense, Joint Chiefs of Staff. *Department of Defense Dictionary of Military and Related Terms.* Washington, DC: GPO, 1986.

—**DESIGNATED BED CAPACITY** is the specified number of patients' beds in a table of organization and equipment, advanced base catalog. It specifies the number of beds a particular type of medical treatment facility is designated to provide. The figure is used in referring to the bed capacity of land-based, nonfixed medical treatment facilities providing inpatient care. *See also:* Medical Treatment.

References
Department of Defense, U.S. Army. *Dictionary of United States Army Terms.* Army Regulation AR 310-25. Washington, DC: Headquarters, Department of the Army, 1986.

—DESIGNATED OBSERVER, in nuclear warfare, is a unit or representative with special equipment (e.g., theodolites or radar instruments) that enables more precise measurements of the nuclear cloud than would normally be available from other units. *See also:* Nuclear Warfare.

References
Department of Defense, U.S. Army. *NBC Operations.* Field Manual FM 3-100. Washington, DC: Headquarters, Department of the Army, 1985.

—DESIGNATION OF DAYS AND HOURS. The following designations have the meaning shown:
- **D-day**—day on which an operation, a hostility or any other operation, commences or is scheduled to commence;
- **E-day**—day on which a NATO exercise commences;
- **K-day**—day on which a convoy system is introduced or is scheduled to be introduced on a particular convoy lane;
- **M-day**—day on which mobilization commences or is scheduled to commence; and
- **H-hour**—specific time at which an operation or exercise commences or is scheduled to commence.

These terms are also used as references for the designation of days/hours before or after the event. *See also:* C-Day, D-Day, S-Day.

References
Department of Defense, Joint Chiefs of Staff. *Department of Defense Dictionary of Military and Related Terms.* Washington, DC: GPO, 1986.

—DESIRED EFFECTS, in nuclear warfare, are the damage and casualties to the enemy or material that a commander desires to achieve from a nuclear weapon detonation. The damage effects on material are classified as light, moderate, or severe. Casualty effects on personnel may be immediate, prompt, or delayed. *See also:* Nuclear Warfare.

References
Department of Defense, Joint Chiefs of Staff. *Department of Defense Dictionary of Military and Related Terms.* Washington, DC: GPO, 1986.

—DESIRED GROUND ZERO (DGZ) is the point on the ground on, above, or below where a nuclear weapon is planned to be detonated. It is the aiming point for the weapon. *See also:* Nuclear Warfare.

References
Department of Defense, U.S. Army. *Nuclear Weapons Employment Doctrine and Procedures.* Field Manual FM 101-3-1. Washington, DC: Headquarters, Department of the Army, 1986.
———. *Operational Terms and Symbols.* Field Manual FM 101-5-1. Washington, DC: Headquarters, Department of the Army, 1985.

—DESTROYED is the condition of a target so damaged that it cannot function as intended or be restored to a usable condition. For a building, all vertical supports and spanning members are so damaged that nothing is salvageable. For bridges, all spans have dropped and all piers require replacement.

References
Department of Defense, Joint Chiefs of Staff. *Department of Defense Dictionary of Military and Related Terms.* Washington, DC: GPO, 1986.

—DESTRUCTION is a type of adjustment for destroying a given target. *See also:* Destroyed.

References
Department of Defense, Joint Chiefs of Staff. *Department of Defense Dictionary of Military and Related Terms.* Washington, DC: GPO, 1986.

—DESTRUCTION AREA is the area in which it is planned that the enemy airborne threat will be destroyed or defeated. The area may be further subdivided into air intercept, missile (long-, medium-, and short-range), or antiaircraft gun zones.

References
Department of Defense, Joint Chiefs of Staff. *Department of Defense Dictionary of Military and Related Terms.* Washington, DC: GPO, 1986.

—DESTRUCTION FIRE is fire delivered for the sole purpose of destroying material objects. *See also:* Destruction.

References
Department of Defense, Joint Chiefs of Staff. *Department of Defense Dictionary of Military and Related Terms.* Washington, DC: GPO, 1986.
Department of Defense, U.S. Army. *Fire Support in Combined Arms Operations.* Field Manual FM 6-20. Washington, DC: Headquarters, Department of the Army, 1983.

—**DESTRUCTION RADIUS**, in mine warfare, is the maximum distance that a minesweeping exploding charge will destroy a mine by causing the detonation of the mine's main charge. *See also:* Mine Warfare.

References

Department of Defense, Joint Chiefs of Staff. *Department of Defense Dictionary of Military and Related Terms.* Washington, DC: GPO, 1986.

—**DESTRUCTIVE FIRE MISSION**, in artillery, is fire delivered only for the purpose of destroying a point target.

References

Department of Defense, Joint Chiefs of Staff. *Department of Defense Dictionary of Military and Related Terms.* Washington, DC: GPO, 1986.

—**DETACHED UNIT** is a unit serving away from the organization to which it is organic and to which it remains assigned. A detached unit may function as an independent organization or it may be attached to or serve with or under another organization. *See also:* Assign, Attach, Operational Control.

References

Department of Defense, U.S. Army. *Operational Terms and Symbols.* Field Manual FM 101-5-1. Washington, DC: Headquarters, Department of the Army, 1985.

—**DETACHMENT (DET).** (1) A detachment is a part of a unit separated from its main organization for duty elsewhere. (2) A detachment is a temporary military unit formed from other units or parts of other units. *See also:* Detachment Left in Contact.

References

Department of Defense, Joint Chiefs of Staff. *Department of Defense Dictionary of Military and Related Terms.* Washington, DC: GPO, 1986.

—**DETACHMENT LEFT IN CONTACT (DLIC).** A DLIC is used in a withdrawal not under pressure. It is normally organized from platoons of forward companies and commanded by the battalion executive officer, although it may be a mission assigned to a single reinforced company. The DLIC may comprise as much as a one-third of the battalion's maneuver elements. The primary purpose of the DLIC is to deceive the enemy into believing the battalion is still in position as the majority of units withdraw. If the withdrawal

is discovered and the enemy attacks, the DLIC defends/delays within its capability. It disengages and withdraws after the main body has begun to move to the next mission.

References

Department of Defense, U.S. Army. *Operational Terms and Symbols.* Field Manual FM 101-5-1. Washington, DC: Headquarters, Department of the Army, 1985.

—**DETAIL** is a temporary removal from assignment in one's control branch and specialty and temporary assignment of duty in another branch, arm, service, or designated duty.

References

Department of Defense, U.S. Army. *Officer Assignment Policies, Details and Transfers.* Army Regulation AR 614-100. Washington, DC: Headquarters, Department of the Army, 1984.

—**DETAILED AIRCRAFT DECON** is the decontamination of an aircraft by the detailed equipment decon technique. *See also:* Detailed Equipment Decon.

References

Department of Defense, U.S. Army. *NBC Decontamination.* Field Manual FM 3-5. Washington, DC: Headquarters, Department of the Army, 1985.

—**DETAILED EQUIPMENT DECON** is the process of removing or neutralizing contamination on the interior and exterior surfaces of unit equipment to negligible risk levels to allow mission-oriented-protective-posture-level reduction for extended periods. *See also:* Biological Warfare, Chemical Warfare, Nuclear Warfare.

References

Department of Defense, U.S. Army. *Operational Terms and Symbols.* Field Manual FM 101-5-1. Washington, DC: Headquarters, Department of the Army, 1985.

—**DETAILED REPORT** (PHOTOGRAPHIC INTERPRETATION) is a written, comprehensive, analytical intelligence report based upon the interpretation of photography. Usually only one subject or target is discussed in detail in the report. *See also:* Aerial Reconnaissance.

References

Department of Defense, Joint Chiefs of Staff. *Department of Defense Dictionary of Military and Related Terms.* Washington, DC: GPO, 1986.

—**DETAILED TROOP DECON** is the process of decontaminating individual fighting equipment to negligible risk levels; removing contaminated mission-oriented-protective-posture gear, including protective masks; decontaminating protective masks; and monitoring personnel for decon effectiveness. This is done to remove mission-oriented-protective-posture levels for extended periods. *See also:* Biological Warfare, Chemical Warfare, Nuclear Warfare.

References
Department of Defense, U.S. Army. *NBC Decontamination.* Field Manual FM 3-5. Washington, DC: Headquarters, Department of the Army, 1985.

—**DETAINED** is a casualty, other than one captured or interned, who is known to have been taken into custody against his will while apparently alive and there is no conclusive evidence that he has died after he was taken into custody. *See also:* Detainee, Detainee Collecting Point, Detainee Processing Station.

References
Department of Defense, U.S. Army. *Dictionary of United States Army Terms.* Army Regulation AR 310-25. Washington, DC: Headquarters, Department of the Army, 1986.

—**DETAINEE** refers to any person who is captured or otherwise detained by an armed force. *See also:* Detained.

References
Department of Defense, Joint Chiefs of Staff. *Department of Defense Dictionary of Military and Related Terms.* Washington, DC: GPO, 1986.

—**DETAINEE COLLECTING POINT** is a facility or other location where detainees are assembled before being moved to a detainee processing station. *See also:* Detained, Detainee Processing Station.

References
Department of Defense, Joint Chiefs of Staff. *Department of Defense Dictionary of Military and Related Terms.* Washington, DC: GPO, 1986.

—**DETAINEE PROCESSING STATION** is a facility or other location where detainees are administratively processed and are provided custodial care, pending their disposition and subsequent release, transfer, or movement to a prisoner-of-war or civilian internee camp. *See also:* Detained.

References
Department of Defense, Joint Chiefs of Staff. *Department of Defense Dictionary of Military and Related Terms.* Washington, DC: GPO, 1986.

—**DETAINER** is a written notice to civil authorities that the person in their custody is a soldier of the Army. The notice states that military authorities desire to take custody when the person is released. *See also:* Disciplinary Action.

References
Department of Defense, U.S. Army. *Promotion of Officers on Active Duty.* Army Regulation AR 624-100. Washington, DC: Headquarters, Department of the Army, 1984.

—**DETECTION.** (1) Detection, in tactical operations, is the perception, but unconfirmed by recognition, of an object of possible military interest. (2) In surveillance, detection is the determination through the transmission by a surveillance system that an event has occurred. (3) In nuclear-biological-chemical operations, detection is the discovery, identification, and marking of contaminated areas. Detection is the act of finding out, through chemical detectors or radiological monitoring/survey teams, the location of nuclear-biological-chemical hazards that have been placed by the enemy. *See also:* Biological Warfare, Chemical Warfare, Nuclear Warfare.

References
Department of Defense, U.S. Army. *NBC Operations.* Field Manual FM 3-100. Washington, DC: Headquarters, Department of the Army, 1985.

———. *NBC Protection.* Field Manual FM 3-4. Washington, DC: Headquarters, Department of the Army, 1985.

—**DETECTOR PAPER** is either of two chemical-agent detector papers that detect liquid chemical agents under any weather conditions. *M9 detector paper* is dispensed from a roll two-inches wide and 30-feet long. The adhesive back allows it to be worn by individuals, attached to vehicles, or affixed to a piece of equipment. *ABC-M8 detector paper* detects the presence of liquid VGH chemical agents. ABC-M8 paper cannot detect chemical agents in water or aerosol agents in the air. When it contacts liquid nerve or blister agents, it produces specific color changes. Color codes are on the cover of the book containing the papers for comparison. *See also:* Chemical Warfare.

References
Department of Defense, U.S. Army. *NBC Protection.* Field Manual FM 3-4. Washington, DC: Headquarters, Department of the Army, 1985.

—**DETENTION FACILITIES** are field-expedient facilities that are set up or are built to temporarily detain U.S. military prisoners.

References
Department of Defense, U.S. Army. *Military Police Team, Squad, Platoon Combat Operations.* Field Manual FM 19-4. Washington, DC: Headquarters, Department of the Army, 1984.

—**DETERRENCE** refers to measures taken by the United States and its allies to prevent hostile action by any other state outside the alliance.

References
Department of Defense, U.S. Army. *NBC Operations.* Field Manual FM 3-100. Washington, DC: Headquarters, Department of the Army, 1985.

—**DETONATING NET** is a network of detonating cord interlaced in a mesh design. Detonating nets are used to clear paths through minefields by exploding the mines over which the nets are placed and detonated. *See also:* Mine Warfare.

References
Department of Defense, U.S. Army. *Dictionary of United States Army Terms.* Army Regulation AR 310-25. Washington, DC: Headquarters, Department of the Army, 1986.

—**DETONATION** is a violent chemical reaction within a chemical compound or mechanical mixture that produces heat and pressure. A detonation is a reaction that proceeds through the reacted material toward the unreacted material at a supersonic velocity. The result of the chemical reaction is exertion of extremely high pressure on the surrounding medium, forming a propagating shock wave that originally is of supersonic velocity. A detonation, when the material is located on or near the surface of the ground, is characterized normally by a crater.

References
Department of Defense, U.S. Army. *Ammunition and Explosives Safety Standards.* Army Regulation AR 385-64. Washington, DC: Headquarters, Department of the Army, 1987.

—**DETOUR** is the divergence from the intended route to a destination because movement has become difficult or impossible.

References
Department of Defense, Joint Chiefs of Staff. *Department of Defense Dictionary of Military and Related Terms.* Washington, DC: GPO, 1986.

—**DEVIATION** is the distance by which a point of impact or burst misses the target. *See also:* Circular Error Probable, Delivery Error, Dispersion Error, Horizontal Error.

References
Department of Defense, Joint Chiefs of Staff. *Department of Defense Dictionary of Military and Related Terms.* Washington, DC: GPO, 1986.

—**DEWARN** is notification by signals to permit users to remove mask, hood, and gloves without risk of exposure to primary chemical hazards. *See also:* Chemical Warfare.

References
Department of Defense, Joint Chiefs of Staff. *Department of Defense Dictionary of Military and Related Terms.* Washington, DC: GPO, 1986.

—**DIAMOND FORMATION.** (1) A diamond formation is a rhombus-shaped arrangement made up of four or five parts of a unit to permit maneuvering. The fifth part of a diamond formation is in the center when five are used. Such a formation is most often used by mechanized units. (2) A diamond formation is a squad formation often used when readiness for action in any direction is required.

References
Department of Defense, U.S. Army. *Dictionary of United States Army Terms.* Army Regulation AR 310-25. Washington, DC: Headquarters, Department of the Army, 1986.

—**DIED OF WOUNDS (DOW) RECEIVED IN ACTION** refers to battle casualties who die of wounds or other injuries received in action after having reached a medical facility. DOW casualties differ from battle casualties who are found dead or who die before reaching a medical treatment facility while still alive. All cases counted as DOW received in action are counted as wounded in action. *See also:* Killed in Action, Wounded in Action.

References
Department of Defense, Joint Chiefs of Staff. *Department of Defense Dictionary of Military and Related Terms.* Washington, DC: GPO, 1986.

Department of Defense, U.S. Army. *Planning for Health Service Support.* Field Manual FM 8-55. Washington, DC: Headquarters, Department of the Army, 1985.

—**DIRECT AIR SUPPORT CENTER (DASC)** is the operational component of the tactical air control system designed to coordinate and direct tactical air support operations. It is under the operational control of the tactical air control center. Its primary function is to react fast to immediate requests from surface forces for close air support, tactical air reconnaissance, and tactical airlift. The DASC also advises and assists the Army unit with which it operates concerning the employment of all U.S. Air Force resources.

References

Department of Defense, U.S. Army. *Attack Helicopter Operations.* Field Manual FM 17-50. Washington, DC: Headquarters, Department of the Army, 1984.

—**DIRECT COMBAT PROBABILITY CODING (DCPC)** is a method for determining the probability of participation in direct combat of each position using the criteria of unit mission, military occupational specialty duties, tactical doctrine, and battlefield location. DCPC policy recognizes that the modern battlefield is fluid lethal and that all soldiers may be exposed to some form of combat throughout the theater of operations. *See also:* Direct Combat Probability Coding Policy.

References

Department of Defense, U.S. Army. *Officer Assignment Policies, Details and Transfers.* Army Regulation AR 614-100. Washington, DC: Headquarters, Department of the Army, 1984.

—**DIRECT COMBAT PROBABILITY CODING POLICY (DCPCP).** DCPCP is the system the Army developed to define where women should serve on the battlefield. It identifies the risk of direct combat for every position in the Army, and excludes women from jobs that involve direct combat.

References

Department of Defense, U.S. Army. *U.S. Army Policy Statement,* 1988. Washington, DC: Headquarters, U.S. Army, 1988.

—**DIRECT DAMAGE ASSESSMENT** is an examination of an actual strike area by air observation, air photography, or direct observation.

References

Department of Defense, Joint Chiefs of Staff. *Department of Defense Dictionary of Military and Related Terms.* Washington, DC: GPO, 1986.

—**DIRECT DEPLOYING UNITS** are reserve component units that deploy directly from the home station to an overseas theater of operations.

References

Department of Defense, U.S. Army. *Training for Mobilization and War.* Field Manual FM 25-5. Washington, DC: Headquarters, Department of the Army, 1985.

—**DIRECT EXCHANGE** is a supply method of issuing serviceable materiel in exchange for unserviceable materiel on an item-for-item basis. This exchange requires minimal paperwork.

References

Department of Defense, U.S. Army. *Support Operations: Echelons Above Corps.* Field Manual FM 100-16. Washington, DC: Headquarters, Department of the Army, 1986.

———. *Repair Parts Supply for a Theater of Operations.* Field Manual FM 29-19. Washington, DC: Headquarters, Department of the Army, 1985.

—**DIRECT FIRE** is gunfire delivered on a target that can be seen by the aimer of the firing unit. *See also:* Direct Fire Sights.

References

Department of Defense, Joint Chiefs of Staff. *Department of Defense Dictionary of Military and Related Terms.* Washington, DC: GPO, 1986.

Department of Defense, U.S. Army. *Operational Terms and Symbols.* Field Manual FM 101-5-1. Washington, DC: Headquarters, Department of the Army, 1985.

—**DIRECT FIRE PROJECTILES** are primarily designed to strike a target at a speed fast enough to penetrate it. There are two types of direct fire projectiles: chemical and kinetic energy.

References

Department of Defense, U.S. Army. *Survivability.* Field Manual FM 5-103. Washington, DC: Headquarters, Department of the Army, 1985.

—**DIRECT FIRE SIGHTS.** (1) Direct fire sights permit laying fire directly on the target, as distinguished from those used to lay fire on an aiming point. (2) Direct fire sights are sights that are used in air defense guns when the director(s) is (are) not available.

References
Department of Defense, U.S. Army. *Dictionary of United States Army Terms.* Army Regulation AR 310-25. Washington, DC: Headquarters, Department of the Army, 1986.

—**DIRECT ILLUMINATION** is light provided by pyrotechnics or searchlights.
References
Department of Defense, Joint Chiefs of Staff. *Department of Defense Dictionary of Military and Related Terms.* Washington, DC: GPO, 1986.

—**DIRECT LAYING** is laying in which the sights of weapons are aligned directly on the target. *See also:* Direct Fire, Laying.
References
Department of Defense, Joint Chiefs of Staff. *Department of Defense Dictionary of Military and Related Terms.* Washington, DC: GPO, 1986.

—**DIRECT RESPONSIBLITY** is the obligation of a designated responsible officer for the care and safekeeping of government property specifically entrusted to his custody.
References
Department of Defense, U.S. Army. *Commander's Handbook for Property Accountability at the Unit Level.* Field Manual FM 10-14-1. Washington, DC: Headquarters, Department of the Army, 1984.

—**DIRECT SUPPORT (DS)** is a mission requiring one force to support another specific force and authorizing it to answer directly the supported force's request for assistance. A unit in DS of a specific unit or force is required to give priority of support to that unit or force. The supporting unit takes support requests directly from the supported unit or force, normally establishes liaison and communication, and advises the supported unit. A unit in DS has no command relationship with the supported force and therefore cannot be suballocated, reassigned, or reorganized by the supported force. *See also:* Direct Support Artillery, Direct Support Unit.
References
Department of Defense, Joint Chiefs of Staff. *Department of Defense Dictionary of Military and Related Terms.* Washington, DC: GPO, 1986.

Department of Defense, Department of the Army. *Intelligence and Electronic Warfare Operations.* Field Manual FM 34-1. Washington, DC: Headquarters, Department of the Army, 1984.

———. *Military Intelligence Battalion Combat Electronic Warfare and Intelligence (Aerial Exploitation) (Corps).* Field Manual FM 34-22. Washington, DC: Headquarters, Department of the Army, 1984.

———. *Military Intelligence Battalion (CEWI) (Tactical Exploitation) (Corps): Counterintelligence, Interrogation, Electronic Warfare.* Field Manual FM 34-23. Washington, DC: Headquarters, Department of the Army, 1985.

———. *Operational Terms and Symbols.* Field Manual FM 101-5-1. Washington, DC: Headquarters, Department of the Army, 1985.

———. *Staff Organizationsand Operations.* Field Manual FM 101-5. Washington, DC: Headquarters, Department of the Army, 1984.

—**DIRECT SUPPORT ARTILLERY** is artillery whose primary task is to provide fire requested by a small unit. *See also:* Artillery.
References
Department of Defense, Joint Chiefs of Staff. *Department of Defense Dictionary of Military and Related Terms.* Washington, DC: GPO, 1986.

—**DIRECT SUPPORT SUPPLY SYSTEM** is the computer software used on decentralized, automated, service support system hardware.
References
Department of Defense, U.S. Army. *Support Operations: Echelons Above Corps.* Field Manual FM 100-16. Washington, DC: Headquarters, Department of the Army, 1986.

—**DIRECT SUPPORT SYSTEM (DSS)** is the standard peacetime Army distribution system for supply classes II, III (packaged), IV, V (missile components only), VII, and IX. However, the DSS in wartime is restricted to airline of communications class IX and selected II items. *See also:* Supplies.
References
Department of Defense, U.S. Army. *Combat Service Support Operations-Division.* Field Manual FM 63-2. Washington, DC: Headquarters, Department of the Army, 1983.

—**DIRECT SUPPORT UNIT** is a unit that has a mission of supporting another unit of the command. It receives and executes missions directly on call from, and gives priority to, the supported unit, but remains under the command of its normal high commander. *See also:* Direct Support.

210 DIRECT SUPPORT UNIT

References

Department of Defense, U.S. Army. *Dictionary of United States Army Terms.* Army Regulation AR 310-25. Washington, DC: Headquarters, Department of the Army, 1986.

—**DIRECT SUPPORTING FIRE** is fire delivered in support of part of a force, as opposed to general supporting fire, which is delivered in support of the force as a whole. *See also:* Close Supporting Fire, Deep Supporting Fire, Supporting Fire.

References

Department of Defense, Joint Chiefs of Staff. *Department of Defense Dictionary of Military and Related Terms.* Washington, DC: GPO, 1986.

—**DIRECTING POINT** is a point of known location, normally at the geometric center of the gun of an air defense artillery battery, for which the firing data are computed.

References

Department of Defense, U.S. Army. *Dictionary of United States Army Terms.* Army Regulation AR 310-25. Washington, DC: Headquarters, Department of the Army, 1986.

—**DIRECTION.** (1) Direction, in artillery, is a term used by the spotter or observer in a call to fire to indicate the bearing to the spotting line. (2) Direction, in Army aviation, is the signal given as left or right with respect to the nose of the aircraft or flight path.

References

Department of Defense, U.S. Army. *Air-to-Air Combat.* Field Manual FM 1-107. Washington, DC: Headquarters, U.S. Army, 1984.

—**DIRECTION** (INTELLIGENCE CYCLE) is the process of (1) determining which intelligence requirements are most important and therefore should be satisfied, (2) preparing a collection plan to guide all concerned in fulfilling these requirements, (3) issuing orders and requests for information from intelligence collection agencies, and (4) continuously monitoring the progress of the collecting agencies in collecting the information. *See also:* Intelligence, Intelligence Cycle.

References

Von Hoene, John P.A. *Intelligence User's Guide.* Washington, DC: DIA, 1983.

—**DIRECTION FINDING (DF).** (1) Direction finding is a procedure using a directional antenna and a display unit on an intercept receiver or ancillary equipment to obtain bearings on radio transmitters. (2) Direction finding, in the Army tactical intelligence context, is a step in the signals intelligence process. *See also:* SIGINT Process.

References

Department of Defense, Defense Intelligence College. *Glossary of Intelligence Terms and Definitions.* Washington, DC: DIC, 1987.

Department of Defense, Joint Chiefs of Staff. *Department of Defense Dictionary of Military and Related Terms.* Washington, DC: GPO, 1986.

Department of Defense, U.S. Army. *Counter-Signals Intelligence (C-SIGINT) Operations.* Field Manual FM 34-62. Washington, DC: Headquarters, Department of the Army, 1986.

—**DIRECTION FINDING (DF) BASELINE** is the imaginary line or axis along which the DF equipment of a DF network (three or more DF sites) is deployed. Establishing either a ground-based strategic or tactical DF baseline involves placing the DF equipment so that good bearing angles for triangulation within the target area are possible. Triangulation is the intersection of bearings at the target area. *See also:* Direction Finding.

References

Department of Defense, U.S. Army. *Direction Finding Operations.* Field Manual FM 34-88. Washington, DC: Headquarters, Department of the Army, 1984.

—**DIRECTION OF ATTACK** is a specific direction or route that the main attack or the main body of the force will follow. If used, it is normally at battalion or lower levels. Direction of attack is a more restrictive control measure than axis of advance, and units are not free to maneuver off the assigned route. It is usually associated with infantry units conducting night attacks, units involved in limited visibility operations, or in counterattacks. *See also:* Axis of Advance.

References

Department of Defense, U.S. Army. *Attack Helicopter Operations.* Field Manual FM 17-50. Washington, DC: Headquarters, Department of the Army, 1984.

———. *Operational Terms and Symbols.* Field Manual FM 101-5-1. Washington, DC: Headquarters, Department of the Army, 1985.

—**DIRECTION OF FIRE** is the direction on which a cannon or missile is laid. It represents the direction to the most significant threat in the target area.

References

Department of Defense, U.S. Army. *Operational Terms and Symbols*. Field Manual FM 101-5-1. Washington, DC: Headquarters, Department of the Army, 1985.

—**DIRECTIONS OF ATTACK** can be assigned when objectives are not assigned. They may also be useful supplementary control measures. *See also:* Direction of Attack.

References

Department of Defense, U.S. Army. *Armored and Mechanized Division Operations*. Field Manual FM 71-100. Washington, DC: Headquarters, Department of the Army, 1978.

————. *Operational Terms and Symbols*. Field Manual FM 101-5-1. Washington, DC: Headquarters, Department of the Army, 1985.

—**DIRECTIVE.** (1) A directive is a military communication in which policy is established or a specific action is ordered. (2) A directive is a plan to be put into effect when so directed or if a stated contingency arises. (3) In general, a directive is a communication initiating or governing action, conduct, or procedure.

References

Department of Defense, Joint Chiefs of Staff. *Department of Defense Dictionary of Military and Related Terms*. Washington, DC: GPO, 1986.

—**DIRECTIVE** (DRILL AND CEREMONIES) is an oral order given by the commander to direct or cause a subordinate leader or lead element to take action.

References

Department of Defense, U.S. Army. *Drills and Ceremonies*. Field Manual FM 22-5. Washington, DC: Headquarters, Department of the Army, 1986.

—**DIRECTORATE** is an integral component of a Headquarters, Department of the Army Staff agency, major command headquarters staff office, or installation headquarters that has primary responsibility for staff coordination and management of assigned functions. Responsibilities, accompanied by commensurate authority to act for the activity head or commander, normally include policy development, staff coordination, establishment of controls, and review of effectiveness of operations. *See also:* Headquarters, Department of the Army.

References

Department of Defense, U.S. Army. *Dictionary of United States Army Terms*. Army Regulation AR 310-25. Washington, DC: Headquarters, Department of the Army, 1986.

—**DIRTY TRICK DEVICE** is a manufactured boobytrap that looks like a common item (e.g., a telephone, book, or cigarette lighter).

References

Department of Defense, U.S. Army. *Mine/ Countermine Operations at the Company Level*. Field Manual FM 20-32. Washington, DC: Headquarters, Department of the Army, 1976.

—**DISAPPEARING TARGET** is a target that is exposed to the firer's view for only a short time.

References

Department of Defense, U.S. Army. *Dictionary of United States Army Terms*. Army Regulation AR 310-25. Washington, DC: Headquarters, Department of the Army, 1986.

—**DISARM** is to remove the detonating device or fuze from a bomb, mine, missile, or other explosive ordnance, or to render an explosive device incapable of exploding in the usual manner. *See also:* Disarmed Mine.

References

Department of Defense, U.S. Army. *Dictionary of United States Army Terms*. Army Regulation AR 310-25. Washington, DC: Headquarters, Department of the Army, 1986.

—**DISARMED MINE** is a mine that has been rendered inoperative by breaking a link in the firing sequence. *See also:* Mine.

References

Department of Defense, Joint Chiefs of Staff. *Department of Defense Dictionary of Military and Related Terms*. Washington, DC: GPO, 1986.

—**DISBAND** is to withdraw the designation of a unit from current records of the Army by official order. The term "discontinued," in lieu of "disbanded," applies to units that are not constituted. Constituted units can be disbanded only by authority of the Secretary of the Army. *See also:* Inactivate.

References

Department of Defense, U.S. Army. *Dictionary of United States Army Terms.* Army Regulation AR 310-25. Washington, DC: Headquarters, Department of the Army, 1986.

—**DISCHARGE** is complete severance from all military status that had been gained by enlistment or induction. It applies (1) to military personnel who terminate their military service by means other than death; or (2) to termination of a specific status; or (3) to the discharge certificate (i.e., the document that effects the discharge). *See also:* Dishonorable Discharge, General Discharge, Honorable Discharge.

References

Department of Defense, U.S. Army. *Enlisted Personnel.* Army Regulation AR 635-200. Washington, DC: Headquarters, Department of the Army, 1984.

—**DISCIPLINARY ACTION** involves all the authorized measures, including court martial and nonjudicial punishment, taken to punish acts of misconduct by military personnel. *See also:* Close Confinement, Confinement Facility, Disciplinary Barracks, Disciplinary Training Center, Dishonorable Discharge, Dismissal, General Court-Martial, General Discharge, Military Prisoner, Mitigation of Sentence, Nonjudicial Punishment, Provost Court, Punishment Book, Punitive Articles, Reduced Diet, Rehabilitation Training Center, Retraining Brigade, Sentenced Prisoner, Special Court-Martial, Standard Detention Unit, Stockade, Summary Court-Martial, Transient Installation Confinement Facility, Uniform Code of Military Justice.

References

Department of Defense, U.S. Army. *Dictionary of United States Army Terms.* Army Regulation AR 310-25. Washington, DC: Headquarters, Department of the Army, 1986.

—**DISCIPLINARY BARRACKS** are the part of a military correctional treatment facility used to confine, and retain prisoners before restoring them to honorable duty status or permitting them to return to civilian life. *See also:* Disciplinary Action.

References

Department of Defense, U.S. Army. *Dictionary of United States Army Terms.* Army Regulation AR 310-25. Washington, DC: Headquarters, Department of the Army, 1986.

—**DISCIPLINARY TRAINING CENTER** is an Army correctional facility in an overseas territory used during a national emergency to rehabilitate prisoners. *See also:* Disciplinary Action.

References

Department of Defense, U.S. Army. *Dictionary of United States Army Terms.* Army Regulation AR 310-25. Washington, DC: Headquarters, Department of the Army, 1986.

—**DISCIPLINE** is the prompt and effective performance of duty in response to orders or the performance of the right action in the absence of orders. A disciplined unit forces itself to do its duty in any situation.

References

Department of Defense, U.S. Army. *Military Leadership.* Field Manual FM 22-100. Washington, DC: Headquarters, Department of the Army, 1983.

—**DISCIPLINE, LAW, AND ORDER** (A G-1 STAFF RESPONSIBILITY). The area of discipline, law and order involves collecting and analyzing data; developing assessments (positive and negative); and providing information and/or recommendations to the commander on matters of morale and discipline (e.g., the frequency of absence without leave, desertion, court-martial offenses, arrests, and large numbers of requests for transfer).

This area also involves planning and supervising activities of administration of discipline, law, and order. Specifically, the G1 is concerned with absence without leave, collection and disposition of stragglers, rewards and punishment, general instructions that especially concern individuals, preventive measures taken, disciplinary installations, military police support (law enforcement), military justice and courts-martial, operation of stockades, and establishment of measures for prisoner rehabilitation, control of civilians, and handling of enemy prisoners of war.

References

Department of Defense, U.S. Army. *Staff Organizations and Operations.* Field Manual FM 101-5. Washington, DC: Headquarters, Department of the Army, 1984.

—**DISEASE.** All patients—other than battle injury, wounded in action, and nonbattle injury cases— are classified as disease cases. Patients suffering from mental disorders developed under battle conditions are classified as disease patients, *not* as casualties. Patients readmitted as the result of an "old" traumatism are considered disease patients. An old traumatism is defined as a case readmitted for a condition that is a result of a previously recorded traumatism (battle or nonbattle) incurred in the military service. Patients suffering from reactions to medicine (other than acute poisoning) and patients admitted for the after-effect of an injury incurred prior to entering the military service are classified as disease cases. Food poisoning cases or food infection cases, except when due to food containing nonbacterial poisons, are classified as disease cases. A battle casualty patient who is dropped from medical reports as a disposition to absent without leave is, if readmitted, classified as a disease patient. *See also:* Medical Treatment.

References
Department of Defense, U.S. Army. *Planning for Health Service Support.* Field Manual FM 8-55. Washington, DC: Headquarters, Department of the Army, 1985.

—**DISENGAGEMENT**, in arms control, is a general term for proposals that would result in the geographic separation of opposing nonindigenous forces without directly affecting indigenous military forces.

References
Department of Defense, Joint Chiefs of Staff. *Department of Defense Dictionary of Military and Related Terms.* Washington, DC: GPO, 1986.

—**DISENGAGING BY SIMULTANEOUS MOVEMENT OF ALL FORCES.** At times, a unit may disengage from the enemy by moving simultaneously away from it, using no overwatching force. This may be done when facing light enemy forces, when a major obstacle is between the enemy and friendly forces, when mechanized forces are facing light enemy infantry, or when some other factor reduces the relative mobility of the enemy or slows its reaction time. When this happens, speed of execution rather than deception is the key to success. At a specified time, elements rapidly move to squad, platoon, and company assembly areas, and move from the area. The squad leader must have his element prepared to move at the designated time, but the preparations must be done so as not to alert the enemy of the disengagement. Often, on order of the platoon leader and just prior to withdrawing, units will fire a short, but heavy, volume of fire in front and to the flanks of their position to disrupt the enemy.

References
Department of Defense, U.S. Army. *The Rifle Squads (Mechanized and Light Infantry).* Training Circular TC 7-1. Washington, DC: Headquarters, Department of the Army, 1976.

—**DISENGAGING UNDER ENEMY PRESSURE.** Fire and maneuver are the basic methods for conducting a disengagement under pressure. One unit acts as an overwatching force and holds off the enemy while other units move back into overwatch positions. When the moving unit gets to the overwatch position, it in turn overwatches the movement of the forward unit. This leapfrogging process is repeated until contact with the enemy is broken or until the unit passes a higher level of overwatching force. *See also:* Disengaging When Not Under Enemy Pressure.

References
Department of Defense, U.S. Army. *The Rifle Squads (Mechanized and Light Infantry).* Training Circular TC 7-1. Washington, DC: Headquarters, Department of the Army, 1976.

—**DISENGAGING WHEN NOT UNDER ENEMY PRESSURE.** Disengagements "not under pressure" are conducted when the disengaging force commander thinks that he can disengage his unit by using deception and/or stealth before the enemy can react. The success of this type of disengagement depends primarily on secrecy and deception or speed of execution, because one tries to pull out before the enemy realizes one is moving and can react. This tactic is usually conducted at night or during periods of reduced visibility. A disengagement not under pressure can be conducted by stealth or by all units moving simultaneously. *See also:* Disengaging Under Enemy Pressure.

References
Department of Defense, U.S. Army. *The Rifle Squads (Mechanized and Light Infantry).* Training Circular TC 7-1. Washington, DC: Headquarters, Department of the Army, 1976.

—**DISHONORABLE DISCHARGE** is a formal release from military service, without honor. It can only be given to a soldier upon his conviction and sentence by a general court-martial. *See also:* Disciplinary Action, General Court Martial.

References
Department of Defense, U.S. Army. *Dictionary of United States Army Terms.* Army Regulation AR 310-25. Washington, DC: Headquarters, Department of the Army, 1986.

—**DISLOCATED CIVILIAN** is a term that means a refugee, a displaced person, or a war victim.

References
Department of Defense, U.S. Army. *Civil Affairs Operations.* Field Manual FM 41-10. Washington, DC: Headquarters, Department of the Army, 1985.

—**DISMISS** is an order to a unit to break ranks after a drill, ceremony, or formation of any kind.

References
Department of Defense, U.S. Army. *Dictionary of United States Army Terms.* Army Regulation AR 310-25. Washington, DC: Headquarters, Department of the Army, 1986.

—**DISMISSAL** is the release of an officer or cadet from the service without honor upon sentence of dismissal of a court-martial of military commission. *See also:* Disciplinary Action.

References
Department of Defense, U.S. Army. *Dictionary of United States Army Terms.* Army Regulation AR 310-25. Washington, DC: Headquarters, Department of the Army, 1986.

—**DISMOUNTED DEFILADE** is concealment sufficient to hide a dismounted man from observation.

References
Department of Defense, U.S. Army. *Dictionary of United States Army Terms.* Army Regulation AR 310-25. Washington, DC: Headquarters, Department of the Army, 1986.

—**DISMOUNTED TOW POSITION** is a fighting position for the tow antitank weapon. Primary consideration must be given to insuring that the position does not interfere with the launch or tracking operations of the missile and that the backblast will not cause casualties among friendly troops. *See also:* Towed Artillery.

References
Department of Defense, U.S. Army. *Survivability.* Field Manual FM 5-103. Washington, DC: Headquarters, Department of the Army, 1985.

—**DISPATCH ROUTE**, in road traffic, is a roadway over which full control, in terms of priorities of use and regulation of the movement of traffic in time and space, is exercised. A movement authorization is required, even for a single vehicle, to use it. *See also:* Route.

References
Department of Defense, Joint Chiefs of Staff. *Department of Defense Dictionary of Military and Related Terms.* Washington, DC: GPO, 1986.
Department of Defense, U.S. Army. *Route Reconnaissance and Classification.* Field Manual FM 5-36. Washington, DC: Headquarters, Department of the Army, 1985.

—**DISPERSAL** is the relocation of forces in order to increase survivability. *See also:* Dispersion.

References
Department of Defense, Joint Chiefs of Staff. *Department of Defense Dictionary of Military and Related Terms.* Washington, DC: GPO, 1986.

—**DISPERSION.** (1) Dispersion is a scattered pattern of hits around the mean point of impact of bombs and projectiles that are dropped under ideal conditions. (2) In antiaircraft gunnery, dispersion is the scattering of shots in range and deflection about the mean point of explosion. (3) Dispersion is the spreading or separating of troops, materiel, establishments, or activities that are usually concentrated in limited areas to reduce vulnerability. (4) In chemical and biological operations, dispersion is the dissemination of agents in liquid or aerosol form. (5) In airdrop operations, dispersion is the scatter of personnel or cargo on the drop zone. *See also:* Delivery Error, Deviation, Dispersion Error, Error Probable, Horizontal Error.

References
Department of Defense, Joint Chiefs of Staff. *Department of Defense Dictionary of Military and Related Terms.* Washington, DC: GPO, 1986.

—**DISPERSION ALLOWANCE** is the percentage of all hospital beds at a level of hospitalization required to remain empty to allow for necessary patient dispersion and hospital flexibility. A certain flexibility is needed to initiate hospital relocation using this uncommitted bed capacity or to absorb the sudden influx of patients generated by a mass casualty situation. Additionally, separating patients because of contagious disease, sex, treatment (medical or surgical), and psychiatric problems, among others, creates a certain number of empty beds within the various wards of a hospital. *See also:* Medical Treatment.

References
Department of Defense, U.S. Army. *Planning for Health Service Support.* Field Manual FM 8-55. Washington, DC: Headquarters, U.S. Army, 1985.

—**DISPERSION ERROR** is the distance from the point of impact or burst of a round to the mean point of impact or burst.

References

Department of Defense, Joint Chiefs of Staff. *Department of Defense Dictionary of Military and Related Terms.* Washington, DC: GPO, 1986.

—**DISPERSION FACTOR** is a number used in computing bed requirements and is mathematically derived from the dispersion allowance. It equals 100 percent divided by 100 percent minus the dispersion allowance. When multiplied by the calculated number of patients remaining, it yields the number of beds required to provide the necessary dispersion. In determining the dispersion allowance, the planner must be continually informed as to both the existing and possible future tactical situations. The normal dispersion factor is based on World War II and the Korean War figures and may have to be increased considerably in a future war. Due to increased exposure to deep penetrations and destruction of support areas by the enemy, medical facilities may have to be small and well-dispersed. These contingencies will reduce the efficient use of beds and require the application of a greater dispersion allowance/factor for planning purposes. Normally, 80 percent occupancy of available beds is the operational maximum, which equals a 20 percent dispersion allowance. *See also:* Medical Treatment.

References

Department of Defense, U.S. Army. *Planning for Health Service Support.* Field Manual FM 8-55. Washington, DC: Headquarters, Department of the Army, 1985.

—**DISPERSION PATTERN** is the distribution of a series of rounds fired from one weapon or a group of weapons under conditions as nearly identical as possible to the points of bursts or impact being dispersed about a point called the mean point of contact.

References

Department of Defense, Joint Chiefs of Staff. *Department of Defense Dictionary of Military and Related Terms.* Washington, DC: GPO, 1986.

—**DISPLACED EQUIPMENT TRAINING** is training provided to users and supporters on how to operate, maintain, and use equipment that is in the total Army inventory.

References

Department of Defense, U.S. Army. *Army Forces Training.* Army Regulation AR 350-41. Washington, DC: Headquarters, Department of the Army, 1986.

—**DISPOSAL** is the authorized act of getting rid of records, documents, and excess, obsolete, or surplus property. It may be accomplished by, but is not limited to, transfer, donation, sale, and abandonment, but does not include redistribution.

References

Department of Defense, U.S. Army. *Dictionary of United States Army Terms.* Army Regulation AR 310-25. Washington, DC: Headquarters, Department of the Army, 1986.

—**DISPOSITION.** (1) Disposition is the distribution of the elements of a command within an area. It is the location of the elements of a command and is usually depicted in terms of the exact location of each unit headquarters and the deployment of the forces subordinate to it. (2) Disposition is a prescribed arrangement of all the tactical units composing a flight or group of aircraft. (3) Disposition is the release of a patient from a medical facility because he is returning to duty, is transferring to another treatment facility, has died, or his medical case has been terminated.

References

Department of Defense, Joint Chiefs of Staff. *Department of Defense Dictionary of Military and Related Terms.* Washington, DC: GPO, 1986.

Department of Defense, U.S. Army. *Intelligence Analysis.* Field Manual FM 34-3. Washington, DC: Headquarters, Department of the Army, 1986.

Von Hoene, John P.A. *Intelligence User's Guide.* Washington, DC: DIA, 1983.

—**DISPOSITION FACTOR.** Assuming a constant rate of admission of one patient per day during a specific estimated period (and none thereafter), the disposition factor is the expected number of patients receiving a particular disposition from a particular level of hospitalization during each consecutive period. Types of disposition include return to duty, died in hospital, evacuated, or disability discharge (only in the continental United States). Disposition factors are also provided for each patient classification, for each disposition type, and for different evacuation policies. *See also:* Medical Treatment.

References

Department of Defense, U.S. Army. *Planning for Health Service Support.* Field Manual FM 8-55. Washington, DC: Headquarters, Department of the Army, 1985.

—**DISPOSITION IN DEPTH** contains a series of mutually supporting battle positions on armor-restrictive terrain, protected by infantry, and strengthened by obstacles. The closer the forward positions can take on linear characteristics, the better, since infiltration by dismounted infantry is a threat. Positions are arrayed in depth, and units remain in place except for local and internal movement to alternate and supplementary positions. If certain positions become untenable during the battle, the commander withdraws them according to previously prepared plans. The depth of the defense is derived from the initial positioning of the platoons and weapons, not from maneuver.

References

Department of Defense, U.S. Army. *The Infantry Rifle Company (Infantry, Airborne, Air Assault, Ranger).* Field Manual FM 7-10. Washington, DC: Headquarters, Department of the Army, 1982.

—**DISRUPTIVE PATTERN**, in surveillance, is an arrangement of suitably colored irregular shapes that is intended to enhance its camouflage when applied to the surface of an object. *See also:* Camouflage.

References

Department of Defense, Joint Chiefs of Staff. *Department of Defense Dictionary of Military and Related Terms.* Washington, DC: GPO, 1986.

—**DISSEMINATION.** (1) Dissemination is the timely delivery of intelligence in the appropriate oral, written, or graphic form and by suitable means to those who need it. (2) Dissemination is a step in the Army tactical intelligence signals intelligence process. *See also:* Intelligence Cycle, SIGINT Process.

References

Department of Defense, U.S. Army. *Counter-Signals Intelligence (C-SIGINT) Operations.* Field Manual FM 34-62. Washington, DC: Headquarters, Department of the Army, 1986.

———. *Military Intelligence Company (Combat Electronic Warfare and Intelligence) (Armored Cavalry Regiment/Separate Brigade).* Field Manual FM 34-30. Washington, DC: Headquarters, Department of the Army, 1983.

———. *Support Operations: Echelons Above Corps.* Field Manual FM 100-16. Washington, DC: Headquarters, Department of the Army, 1986.

—**DISTANCE.** (1) Distance is the space between elements when the elements are one behind the other. Between units, it varies with the size of the formation; between individuals, it is an arm's length to the front plus six inches, or about 36 inches, measured from the chest of one man to the back of the man immediately in front. (2) Distance is the space between adjacent men, animals, vehicles, or units in a formation measured from front to rear. (3) Distance is the space between known reference points or a ground observer and a target, measured in meters (artillery) or in units that are specified by the observer. *See also:* Interval.

References

Department of Defense, Joint Chiefs of Staff. *Department of Defense Dictionary of Military and Related Terms.* Washington, DC: GPO, 1986.

Department of Defense, U.S. Army. *Drills and Ceremonies.* Field Manual FM 22-5. Washington, DC: Headquarters, Department of the Army, 1986.

—**DISTILLED MUSTARD** is a virtually odorless pale yellow liquid that injures the eyes and lungs and blisters the skin. *See also:* Chemical Warfare.

References

Department of Defense, U.S. Army. *Dictionary of United States Army Terms.* Army Regulation AR310-25. Washington, DC: Headquarters, Department of the Army, 1986.

—**DISTINGUISHED HIMSELF BY.** For a person to have distinguished himself, he must, by praiseworthy accomplishment, be set apart from other persons in the same or similar circumstances. A determination of the distinction requires careful consideration of exactly what it is or was expected as the ordinary, routine, or customary behavior and accomplishment for individuals of like rank and experience for the circumstances involved. *See also:* Valor.

References

Department of Defense, U.S. Army. *Military Awards.* Army Regulation AR 672-5-1. Washington, DC: Headquarters, Department of the Army, 1984.

—**DISTRIBUTED FIRE** is fire dispersed so as to engage an area target most effectively. *See also:* Fire.

References

Department of Defense, Joint Chiefs of Staff. *Department of Defense Dictionary of Military and Related Terms.* Washington, DC: GPO, 1986.

—**DISTRIBUTION.** (1) Distribution is the arrangement of troops for any purpose (e.g., a battle, march, or maneuver). (2) Distribution is a planned pattern of projectiles about a point. (3) Distribution is a planned spread of fire to cover a desired frontage or depth. (4) Distribution is an official delivery of anything (e.g., orders or supplies). (5) Distribution is the functional phase of military logistics that embraces the act of dispensing materiel, facilities, or services. (6) Distribution is the process of assigning military personnel to activities, units, or billets. *See also:* Distribution Point, Distribution System.

References

Department of Defense, Joint Chiefs of Staff. *Department of Defense Dictionary of Military and Related Terms.* Washington, DC: GPO, 1986.

—**DISTRIBUTION POINT** is a point at which supplies and ammunition, obtained from supporting supply points by a division or other unit, are broken down for distribution to subordinate units. Distribution points usually carry no stocks, and items that are drawn are issued as soon as possible.

References

Department of Defense, Joint Chiefs of Staff. *Department of Defense Dictionary of Military and Related Terms.* Washington, DC: GPO, 1986.

—**DISTRIBUTION SYSTEM** is the complex of facilities, installations, methods, and procedures designed to receive, store, maintain, distribute, and control the flow of military materiel between the point of receipt into the military system and the point of issue to using activities and units.

References

Department of Defense, Joint Chiefs of Staff. *Department of Defense Dictionary of Military and Related Terms.* Washington, DC: GPO, 1986.

—**DIVERSION.** (1) A diversion is a deliberate, premeditated distraction intended to draw the enemy's attention away from another occurrence or operation. (2) A diversion is the rerouting of cargo or passengers to a new transshipment point or destination or to a different mode of transportation before arriving at the ultimate destination. (3) A diversion is a change that has been made in the prescribed route for operational or tactical reasons. A diversion order does not constitute a change in destination.

References

Clancy, Tom. *The Cardinal of the Kremlin.* New York: Putnam, 1988.

Department of Defense, Joint Chiefs of Staff. *Department of Defense Dictionary of Military and Related Terms.* Washington, DC: GPO, 1986.

Department of Defense, U.S. Army. *Transportation Reference Data.* Field Manual FM 55-15. Washington, DC: Headquarters, Department of the Army, 1986.

—**DIVERSIONARY ATTACK** is an attack whereby a force attacks, or threatens to attack, a target other than the main target to draw enemy defenses away from the main effort. *See also:* Demonstration.

References

Department of Defense, Joint Chiefs of Staff. *Department of Defense Dictionary of Military and Related Terms.* Washington, DC: GPO, 1986.

—**DIVERSIONARY LANDING** is an operation in which troops are landed to divert the enemy's reaction away from the main landing. *See also:* Diversionary Operations.

References

Department of Defense, Joint Chiefs of Staff. *Department of Defense Dictionary of Military and Related Terms.* Washington, DC: GPO, 1986.

—**DIVERSIONARY OPERATIONS** include feints and demonstrations. A feint is a supporting attack designed to divert the enemy's attention from the main effort. It is normally executed by brigades or smaller units. Feints are usually shallow, limited-objective attacks conducted before or during the main attack. A demonstration is a show of force in an area where a decision is not sought. A demonstration threatens attack, but does not actually make contact with the enemy intentionally. *See also:* Diversionary Landing.

References

Department of Defense, U.S. Army. *Operations.* Field Manual FM 100-5. Washington, DC: Headquarters, Department of the Army, 1986.

—**DIVING FIRE** (ARMY AVIATION) is fire delivered from an aircraft descending in forward flight.

References

Department of Defense, U.S. Army. *Gunnery Training for Attack Helicopters.* Training Circular TC 17-17. Washington, DC: Headquarters, Department of the Army, 1975.

—**DIVING WALL** is a wall designed to prevent, control, or delay propagation of an explosion between quantities of explosives on opposite sides of the wall.

References

Department of Defense, U.S. Army. *Ammunition and Explosives Safety Standards.* Army Regulation AR 385-64. Washington, DC: Headquarters, Department of the Army, 1987.

—**DIVISION (DIV)** is the largest U.S. Army organization that trains and fights as a team. A division is organized with varying numbers and types of combat, combat support, and combat service support units. It is a fixed combined arms organization, usually composed of from eight to eleven maneuver battalions, three to four field artillery battalions, and other combat, combat support, and combat service support units. Capable of performing any combat mission and designed to be largely self-sustaining, divisions are the basic units of maneuver at the tactical level. Infantry, armored, mechanized infantry, airborne, air assault, and motorized infantry divisions are all presently in the force.

Divisions possess great flexibility. They tailor their own brigades and attached forces for specific combat missions. Their combat support and combat service support battalions and separate companies may be attached to or placed in support of brigades to perform a particular mission.

Divisions perform major tactical operations for the corps and can conduct sustained battles and engagements. They almost never direct actions at the operations level (campaigns or major operations) but they may be used by corps or field armies to perform tasks of operational importance. These may include exploiting tactical advantages to seize objectives in depth, moving to gain contact with enemy forces, or moving by air to seize positions behind an enemy force. *See also:* Army, Battalion, Brigade, Company, Corps, Division Artillery, Division Assessment and Recovery Personnel, Division Engineer, Division Support Area, Division Support Command, Divisional Unit, Platoon, Regiment, Squad.

References

Department of Defense, U.S. Army. *Armored and Mechanized Division Operations.* Field Manual FM 71-100. Washington, DC: Headquarters, Department of the Army, 1978.

———. *Division Artillery, Field Artillery Brigade and Field Artillery Section (Corps).* Field Manual FM 6-20-2. Washington, DC: Headquarters, Department of the Army, 1981.

———. *Division Headquarters and Headquarters Detachments, Supply and Transport Battalions and Supply and Service Battalions.* Field Manual FM 29-7. Washington, DC: Headquarters, Department of the Army, 1984.

———. *Operations.* Field Manual FM 100-5. Washington, DC: Headquarters, Department of the Army, 1986.

—**DIVISION ARTILLERY** is artillery that is a permanent integral part of a division. For tactical purposes, all field artillery under the command of a division commander is considered division artillery.

References

Department of Defense, U.S. Army. *Division Artillery, Field Artillery Brigade and Field Artillery Section (Corps).* Field Manual FM 6-20-2. Washington, DC: Headquarters, Department of the Army, 1981.

———. *Fire Support in Combined Arms Operations.* Field Manual FM 6-20. Washington, DC: Headquarters, Department of the Army, 1983.

—**DIVISION ASSESSMENT AND RECOVERY PERSONNEL** are personnel who are necessary for unit reconstitution and come from staff and technical personnel assigned to direct support command.

References

Department of Defense, U.S. Army. *Combat Service Support Operations-Division.* Field Manual FM 63-2. Washington, DC: Headquarters, Department of the Army, 1983.

———. *Division Headquarters and Headquarters Detachments, Supply and Transport Battalions and Supply and Service Battalions.* Field Manual FM 29-7. Washington, DC: Headquarters, Department of the Army, 1984.

—**DIVISION ENGINEER.** (1) A division engineer is the officer in command of an engineer division who represents the Chief of Engineers and who has responsibility for construction work and civil works activities in his division. (2) The division engineer is a senior engineer officer in command of all engineer troops of a division, and is a member of the special staff of the division commander.

References

Department of Defense, U.S. Army. *Dictionary of United States Army Terms.* Army Regulation AR 310-25. Washington, DC: Headquarters, Department of the Army, 1986.

—**DIVISION SUPPORT AREA (DSA)** is the portion of the division rear occupied by the division support command command post and organic and attached units. This area may also contain combat support units and corps support command elements operating in support of the division.

References

Department of Defense, U.S. Army. *Combat Service Support Operations-Division.* Field Manual FM 63-2. Washington, DC: Headquarters, Department of the Army, 1983.

———. *Division Headquarters and Headquarters Detachments, Supply and Transport Battalions and Supply and Service Battalions.* Field Manual FM 29-7. Washington, DC: Headquarters, Department of the Army, 1984.

—**DIVISION SUPPORT COMMAND (DISCOM)** is an organic divisional unit responsible for providing division-level supply, transportation, maintenance, medical, and miscellaneous services for all assigned and attached elements of the division.

References

Department of Defense, U.S. Army. *Dictionary of United States Army Terms.* Army Regulation AR310-25. Washington, DC: Headquarters, Department of the Army, 1986.

—**DIVISIONAL UNIT** is a unit of the type that is organically assigned to a division.

References

Department of Defense, U.S. Army. *Dictionary of United States Army Terms.* Army Regulation AR 310-25. Washington, DC: Headquarters, Department of the Army, 1986.

—**DOCTRINE,** in Army tactical intelligence terminology, means the fundamental principles by which military forces or elements of military forces guide their actions in support of national objectives. Doctrine is authoritative, but requires judgment in its application.

An army's fundamental doctrine is the condensed expression of its approach to fighting campaigns, major operations, battles, and engagements. Tactics, techniques, procedures, organizations, support structures, equipment, and training must all derive from it. It must be rooted in time-tested theories and principles, yet forward-looking and adaptable to changing technologies, threats, and missions. It must be definitive enough to guide operations, yet versatile enough to accommodate a wide variety of worldwide situations. To be useful, doctrine must be uniformly known and understood. *See also:* Operational Art, Strategy, Tactics.

References

Department of Defense, U.S. Army. *U.S. Army Air Defense Artillery Employment.* Field Manual FM 44-1. Washington, DC: Headquarters, Department of the Army, 1983.

———. *Counter-Signals Intelligence (C-SIGINT) Operations.* Field Manual FM 34-62. Washington, DC: Headquarters, Department of the Army, 1986.

———. *Operations.* Field Manual FM 100-5. Washington, DC: Headquarters, Department of the Army, 1986.

—**DOCTRINE AND TACTICS TRAINING** is instruction on equipment, interoperability, and management of new or displaced equipment that considers the comparison of newer to older equipment and associated threats.

References

Department of Defense, U.S. Army. *Army Forces Training.* Army Regulation AR 350-41. Washington, DC: Headquarters, Department of the Army, 1986.

—**DOSE** is the total amount of ionizing radiation received by a specific area of the body or by the whole body. The unit of measure used in military training is the centigray. *See also:* Nuclear Warfare.

References

Department of Defense, U.S. Army. *Technical Escort Operations.* Field Manual FM 3-20. Washington, DC: Headquarters, Department of the Army, 1981.

—**DOSE RATE CONTOUR LINE** is a line on a map, diagram, or overlay joining all points at which the radiation dose rate at a given time is the same. *See also:* Nuclear Warfare.

References

Department of Defense, U.S. Army. *NBC Operations.* Field Manual FM 3-100. Washington, DC: Headquarters, Department of the Army, 1985.

—**DOSIMETRY** is the measurement of radiation doses. It applies to the devices (dosimeters) and to the techniques used. *See also:* Nuclear Warfare.

References

Department of Defense, U.S. Army. *NBC Operations.* Field Manual FM 3-100. Washington, DC: Headquarters, Department of the Army, 1985.

—**DOUBLE ENVELOPMENT** is a form of enveloping maneuver executed by three principal tactic groups: a secondary attack force that attacks the enemy position frontally, and two enveloping attack forces that move around the flanks of the enemy position to attack the flanks or objectives in the rear of the enemy front line. *See also:* Envelopment, Single Envelopment.

References

Department of Defense, U.S. Army. *Dictionary of United States Army Terms.* Army Regulation AR 310-25. Washington, DC: Headquarters, Department of the Army, 1986.

—**DOUBLE INTERVAL** (DRILLS CEREMONIES) is the lateral space between soldiers, measured from right to left by raising both arms shoulder height with the fingers extended and joined (palms down) so that the fingertips of the soldiers to the right and to the left are touching. *See also:* Close Interval (Drills and Ceremonies); Interval.

References

Department of Defense, U.S. Army. *Drills and Ceremonies.* Field Manual FM 22-5. Washington, DC: Headquarters, Department of the Army, 1986.

—**DOUBLE STAGGERED COLUMN** is a two-lane column of vehicles moving in the same direction, spaced so that the vehicles in one lane are opposite the space between the vehicles in the other lane.

References

Department of Defense, U.S. Army. *Dictionary of United States Army Terms.* Army Regulation AR 310-25. Washington, DC: Headquarters, Department of the Army, 1986.

—**DOWN TIME.** (1) Down time is the interval between the arrival of an empty ammunition train at an ammunition supply point and its departure with a load. (2) Down time is the interval between receipt of a request for supplies at a supply depot and their delivery to the troops. (3) Down time is the time during which any material is not available for use because of maintenance problems.

References

Department of Defense, U.S. Army. *Dictionary of United States Army Terms.* Army Regulation AR 310-25. Washington, DC: Headquarters, Department of the Army, 1986.

—**DOWNGRADE** is the process of changing a security classification from a higher to a lower classification. Some classified material is automatically downgraded after a period of time; other material is excluded from such an automatic procedure and must be reviewed and personally downgraded.

References

Department of Defense, Defense Intelligence College. *Glossary of Intelligence Terms and Definitions.* Washington, DC: DIC, 1987.

Department of Defense, Joint Chiefs of Staff. *Department of Defense Dictionary of Military and Related Terms.* Washington, DC: GPO, 1986.

—**DOWNWIND HAZARD PREDICTION** is a warning of a chemical downwind hazard message prepared by the corps or division. The chemical downwind message is not confined to the area directly attacked, but—because chemical vapor and aerosol travels with the wind—it can produce casualties among unprotected troops downwind of the initial point of attack. This gives units in the area time to avoid the hazard or (if the mission requires) minimize the effect of chemical attack on the unit while remaining in the contaminated area. *See also:* Chemical Warfare.

References

Department of Defense, U.S. Army. *NBC Operations.* Field Manual FM 3-100. Washington, DC: Headquarters, Department of the Army, 1985.

—**DRAFT PLAN** is a plan that has been coordinated and agreed upon by the involved military headquarters and is ready for coordination with the nations involved (i.e., the nations that would be required to take national actions to support it). It may be used for future planning and exercises and may form the basis for an operation order to be implemented in an emergency. *See also:* Initial Draft Plan, Coordinated Draft Plan, Operation Plan.

References

Department of Defense, Joint Chiefs of Staff. *Department of Defense Dictionary of Military and Related Terms.* Washington, DC: GPO, 1986.

—**DRAGON** is a medium-range, wire-guided antitank missile that replaced the 90-mm recoilless rifle. It is designed to provide an accurate man-portable antitank capability at the platoon level. It consists of a round (missile and launcher) and a tracker. *See also:* Dragon Position.

References

Department of Defense, Joint Chiefs of Staff. *Department of Defense Dictionary of Military and Related Terms.* Washington, DC: GPO, 1986.

—**DRAGON POSITION** is a hasty or deliberate crew-served fighting position from which the Dragon antitank weapon is employed. Special consideration must be given to the weapon's backblast and muzzleblast as well as to cleared fields of fire. *See also:* Dragon.

References

Department of Defense, U.S. Army. *Survivability.* Field Manual FM 5-103. Washington, DC: Headquarters, Department of the Army, 1985.

—**DRESS.** (1) Dress is to form a straight line in a drill formation. (2) Dress is the command to make this line. *See also:* Dress Left (Right).

References

Department of Defense, U.S. Army. *Dictionary of United States Army Terms.* Army Regulation 310-25. Washington, DC: Headquarters, Department of the Army, 1986.

—**DRESS LEFT (RIGHT)** is the preparatory command at which soldiers turn their heads and eyes to the left (right) and straighten a line. *See also:* Dress.

References

Department of Defense, U.S. Army. *Dictionary of United States Army Terms.* Army Regulation 310-25. Washington, DC: Headquarters, Department of the Army, 1986.

—**DRESS PARADE** is a ceremony at which soldiers in their dress uniforms take formation under arms. *See also:* Dress Uniforms.

References

Department of Defense, U.S. Army. *Dictionary of United States Army Terms.* Army Regulation AR 310-25. Washington, DC: Headquarters, Department of the Army, 1986.

—**DRESS UNIFORMS** are the uniforms worn as formal duty uniforms or at formal or informal social functions before or after retreat. These include the green dress uniform (for enlisted soldiers only) and the blue and white dress uniforms.

References

Department of Defense, U.S. Army. *Dictionary of United States Army Terms.* Army Regulation AR 310-25. Washington, DC: Headquarters, Department of the Army, 1986.

———. *Wear and Appearance of Army Uniforms and Insignia.* Army Regulation AR 670-1. Washington, DC: Headquarters, Department of the Army, 1986.

—**DRIFT** is the deviation of the projectile from the vertical plane of fire, which is due to gyroscopic action that results from gravitational and atmospherically induced torques on the spinning projectile. Clockwise rotation of the projectile forces spin stabilized rounds to drift to the right. Fin stabilized rounds, however, are not subject to drift.

References

Department of Defense, U.S. Army. *Tank Gunnery.* Field Manual FM 17-12. Washington, DC: Headquarters, Department of the Army, 1984.

—**DRILL.** (1) A drill is a collective task at the squad or platoon level that has been identified as one of the most vital tasks performed by that unit for success in combat. Drills are totally or largely METT-T (mission, enemy, terrain, troops, and time available) independent, require minimal leader actions to execute, and are standardized for execution throughout the Army. They are usually executed or initiated on a cue (e.g., a specified enemy action or a simple leader order). Drills are U.S. Army standard doctrine and may not be modified in training. (2) A drill is composed of certain movements by which a unit (or individuals) is moved in a uniform manner from one formation to another, or from one place to another. The movements are executed in unison and with precision. *See also:* Drill Call.

References

Department of Defense, U.S. Army. *Army Forces Training.* Army Regulation AR 350-41. Washington, DC: Headquarters, Department of the Army, 1986.

———. *Drills and Ceremonies.* Field Manual FM 22-5. Washington, DC: Headquarters, Department of the Army, 1986.

———. *Light Infantry Battalion Task Force.* Field Manual FM 7-72. Washington, DC: Headquarters, Department of the Army, 1987.

—**DRILL CALL** is a bugle call used as a warning to turn out for drill.

References
Department of Defense, U.S. Army. *Dictionary of United States Army Terms.* Army Regulation AR 310-25. Washington, DC: Headquarters, Department of the Army, 1986.

—**DRILL MINE** is an inexpensive representation of the same size, shape, and weight as a live mine, which is suitable to use in logistic and dispenser drills. *See also:* Mine Warfare.

References
Department of Defense, U.S. Army. *Dictionary of United States Army Terms.* Army Regulation AR 310-25. Washington, DC: Headquarters, Department of the Army, 1986.

—**DRILL SERGEANT** is a noncommissioned officer who has successfully completed the prescribed course of instruction in a U.S. Army Drill Sergeant School and is thereby qualified to instruct and supervise basic combat and advanced individual trainees.

References
Department of Defense, U.S. Army. *Dictionary of United States Army Terms.* Army Regulation AR 310-25. Washington, DC: Headquarters, Department of the Army, 1986.

—**DROOP AND THERMAL BENDING** are cause errors that can be compensated for by crew action. Droop is due to the length and weight of the gun tube, in which gravity pulls the tube down from the line of sight. By reestablishing an accurate gun-sight relationship, frequent reboresighting will reduce the effects of tube droop. Thermal bending is caused by uneven heating or cooling of the outside surface of the gun tube, for example, by the heat of the sun on the upper surface of the gun tube. This is particularly a problem with long barreled guns. Excessive thermal bending can cause the rounds to completely miss the target. Frequent reboresighting reduces the effects of thermal bending by reestablishing an accurate gun-sight relationship.

References
Department of Defense, U.S. Army. *Tank Gunnery.* Field Manual FM 17-12. Washington, DC: Headquarters, Department of the Army, 1984.

—**DROP** is (1) a parachute jump by one individual or a group of individuals; (2) a supply delivery by parachute from aircraft in flight; or (3) the act of making such a jump or delivery. *See also:* Drop Zone, Drop Zone Wind Profile.

References
Department of Defense, U.S. Army. *Dictionary of United States Army Terms.* Army Regulation AR 310-25. Washington, DC: Headquarters, Department of the Army, 1986.

—**DROP ZONE (DZ)** is a specific area upon which airborne troops, equipment, or supplies are airdropped.

References
Department of Defense, U.S. Army. *Long-Range Surveillance.* Field Manual FM 7-93. Washington, DC: Headquarters, Department of the Army, 1987.

———. *USA/USAF Doctrine for Joint Airborne and Tactical Airlift Operations.* Field Manual FM 100-27. Washington, DC: Headquarters, Department of the Army, 1985.

—**DROP ZONE WIND PROFILE** is a graphic depiction of wind speed and direction from the surface to a predetermined height within the area in which soldiers and/or supplies are to be dropped by air.

References
Department of Defense, U.S. Army. *Weather Support for Army Tactical Operations.* Field Manual FM 34-81. Washington, DC: Headquarters, Department of the Army, 1984.

—**DRY GAP BRIDGE** is a bridge, fixed or portable, used to span a gap that does not normally contain water (e.g., an antitank ditch or a road crater).

References
Department of Defense, Joint Chiefs of Staff. *Department of Defense Dictionary of Military and Related Terms.* Washington, DC: GPO, 1986.

—**D-TO-P ASSETS REQUIRED ON D-DAY.** As applied to the D-to-P concept, this asset requirement represents the stocks that must be physically available on D-day to meet initial allowance requirements, to fill the wartime pipeline between the producers and users (even if P-day and D-day occur simultaneously), and to provide any required D-to-P consumption/production differential stockage. The D-to-P assets required on D-day are also represented as the difference between D-to-P Materiel Readiness Gross Requirements and the cumulative sum of all production deliveries during the D-to-P period. *See also:* D-to-P Concept, D-to-P Materiel Readiness Gross Requirement.

References

Department of Defense, Joint Chiefs of Staff. *Department of Defense Dictionary of Military and Related Terms.* Washington, DC: GPO, 1986.

—**D-TO-P CONCEPT** is a logistic planning concept by which the gross materiel readiness requirement in support of approved forces at planned wartime rates for conflicts of indefinite duration will be satisfied by a balanced mix of assets on hand on D-day and assets to be gained from production through P-day when the planned rate of production deliveries to the users equals the planned wartime rate of expenditure (consumption). *See also:* D-to-P Assets Required on D-day, D-to-P Materiel Readiness Gross Requirement.

References

Department of Defense, Joint Chiefs of Staff. *Department of Defense Dictionary of Military and Related Terms.* Washington, DC: GPO, 1986.

—**D-TO-P MATERIEL READINESS GROSS REQUIREMENT,** as applied to the D-to-P concept, is the gross requirement for all supplies and materiel needed to meet all initial pipeline and anticipated expenditure (consumption) requirements between D-day and P-day. The requirement includes initial allowances, continental U.S. and overseas operating and safety levels, in transit levels of supply, and the cumulative sum of all items expended (consumed) during the D-to-P period. *See also:* D-to-P Concept.

References

Department of Defense, Joint Chiefs of Staff. *Department of Defense Dictionary of Military and Related Terms.* Washington, DC: GPO, 1986.

—**DUAL-CAPABLE FORCES** are forces that are capable of using dual-capable (nuclear or conventional) weapons. *See also:* Nuclear Warfare.

References

Department of Defense, Joint Chiefs of Staff. *Department of Defense Dictionary of Military and Related Terms.* Washington, DC: GPO, 1986.

—**DUAL CAPABLE UNIT** is a nuclear-certified delivery unit capable of executing both conventional and nuclear missions. *See also:* Nuclear Warfare.

References

Department of Defense, Joint Chiefs of Staff. *Department of Defense Dictionary of Military and Related Terms.* Washington, DC: GPO, 1986.

—**DUAL (MULTI)-CAPABLE WEAPONS.** (1) Dual (multi)-capable weapons are weapons, weapons systems, or vehicles capable of selective equipage with different types or mixes of firepower. (2) This term is sometimes restricted to weapons that are capable of handling both nuclear and nonnuclear munitions. *See also:* Nuclear Warfare.

References

Department of Defense, Joint Chiefs of Staff. *Department of Defense Dictionary of Military and Related Terms.* Washington, DC: GPO, 1986.

—**DUAL-PURPOSE WEAPON** is a weapon designed for delivering effective fire against air or surface targets. *See also:* Dual (Multi)-Purpose Weapons.

References

Department of Defense, Joint Chiefs of Staff. *Department of Defense Dictionary of Military and Related Terms.* Washington, DC: GPO, 1986.

—**DUAL (MULTI)-PURPOSE WEAPONS** are weapons that can be effectively used in two or more basically different military functions and/or levels of conflict.

References

Department of Defense, Joint Chiefs of Staff. *Department of Defense Dictionary of Military and Related Terms.* Washington, DC: GPO, 1986.

—**DUD** is explosive munition that has not been armed as intended or that has failed to explode after being armed. *See also:* Absolute Dud, Dud Probability, Flare Dud.

References

Department of Defense, Joint Chiefs of Staff. *Department of Defense Dictionary of Military and Related Terms.* Washington, DC: GPO, 1986.

—**DUD PROBABILITY** is the expected percentage of failures in a given number of firings.

References

Department of Defense, Joint Chiefs of Staff. *Department of Defense Dictionary of Military and Related Terms.* Washington, DC: GPO, 1986.

—**DUE IN** are quantities of materiel that are scheduled to be received by vendors, repair facilities, assembly operation, interdepot transfers, and other sources. *See also:* Due Out.

References
Department of Defense, Joint Chiefs of Staff. *Department of Defense Dictionary of Military and Related Terms.* Washington, DC: GPO, 1986.

—**DUE OUT** is the portion of requisitioned stock that is not immediately available for supply and that will not be referred to a secondary source of supply for supply action, but will be recorded as a commitment for future issue.

References
Department of Defense, U.S. Army. *Dictionary of United States Army Terms.* Army Regulation AR 310-25. Washington, DC: Headquarters, Department of the Army, 1986.

—**DUMMY MESSAGE** is a message sent for a purpose other than its content indicates, which may consist of dummy groups or meaningless text.

References
Department of Defense, Joint Chiefs of Staff. *Department of Defense Dictionary of Military and Related Terms.* Washington, DC: GPO, 1986.

—**DUMMY MINEFIELD** is a minefield containing no live mines and presents only a psychological threat. *See also:* Mine Warfare.

References
Department of Defense, Joint Chiefs of Staff. *Department of Defense Dictionary of Military and Related Terms.* Washington, DC: GPO, 1986.

—**DUMP** is a temporary storage area, usually in the open, for bombs, ammunition, equipment, or supplies.

References
Department of Defense, Joint Chiefs of Staff. *Department of Defense Dictionary of Military and Related Terms.* Washington, DC: GPO, 1986.

—**DURABLE ITEMS** are items that are not consumed in use, and that retain their original identity during use, but that are not classified nonexpendable or expendable.

References
Department of Defense, U.S. Army. *Commander's Handbook for Property Accountability at the Unit Level.* Field Manual FM 10-14-1. Washington, DC: Headquarters, Department of the Army, 1984.

—**DUSTER** (ANTIAIRCRAFT WEAPON) is a self-propelled, twin 40-mm antiaircraft weapon used against low-flying aircraft. It is designated the M42.

References
Department of Defense, Joint Chiefs of Staff. *Department of Defense Dictionary of Military and Related Terms.* Washington, DC: GPO, 1986.

—**DUTY** is a prescribed task to which military personnel are assigned. *See also:* Duty Assignment, Duty Branch, Duty Detail, Duty Military Occupational Specialty, Duty of Great Responsibility, Duty of Responsibility, Duty Officer, Duty Position, Duty Roster, Duty Specialty, Duty Station, Duty Status, Duty With Troops or Duty With Troop Units.

References
Department of Defense, U.S. Army. *Dictionary of United States Army Terms.* Army Regulation AR 310-25. Washington, DC: Headquarters, Department of the Army, 1986.

—**DUTY ASSIGNMENT** is a group of closely related tasks and responsibilities that are normally assumed by one individual who is assigned to a position in a military unit. A military occupational specialty usually qualifies a person for a variety of duty assignments. A duty assignment is also known as a duty position. *See also:* Duty.

References
Department of Defense, U.S. Army. *Dictionary of United States Army Terms.* Army Regulation AR 310-25. Washington, DC: Headquarters, Department of the Army, 1986.

—**DUTY BRANCH** is the branch in which an officer is serving as a result of appointment, assignment, or detail. *See also:* Duty.

References
Department of Defense, U.S. Army. *Dictionary of United States Army Terms.* Army Regulation AR 310-25. Washington, DC: Headquarters, Department of the Army, 1986.

—**DUTY DETAIL** is a unique duty assignment that does not affect one's control branch. Such military duties include assignment to Army general staff, defense agencies, general staff with troops, inspectors general, National Guard Bureau, aide-de-camp, and appointments to adjutant. *See also:* Duty.

References

Department of Defense, U.S. Army. *Officer Assignment Policies, Details and Transfers.* Army Regulation AR 614-100. Washington, DC: Headquarters, Department of the Army, 1984.

—**DUTY MOS** is a military occupational specialty that identifies authorized manning table positions that a soldier is assigned and in which he is performing duty; or the MOS of the duty he is performing if not assigned to an authorized manning table position. *See also:* Duty.

References

Department of Defense, U.S. Army. *Enlisted Personnel Management System.* Army Regulation AR 600-200. Washington, DC: Headquarters, Department of the Army, 1984.

—**DUTY OF GREAT RESPONSIBILITY** is duty that, by virtue of the position held, carries the ultimate responsibility for the successful operation of a major command, activity, agency, installation, or project. The discharge of such duty must involve the acceptance and fulfillment of the obligation so as to greatly benefit the interests of the United States. *See also:* Duty.

References

Department of Defense, U.S. Army. *Military Awards.* Army Regulation AR 672-5-1. Washington, DC: Headquarters, Department of the Army, 1984.

—**DUTY OF RESPONSIBILITY** is duty that, by virtue of the position held, carries a high degree of the responsibility for successful operation of a major command, activity, agency, installation, or project, or which requires the exercise of judgment and decision affecting plans, policies, operations, or the lives and well-being of others. *See also:* Duty.

References

Department of Defense, U.S. Army. *Military Awards.* Army Regulation AR 672-5-1. Washington, DC: Headquarters, Department of the Army, 1984.

—**DUTY OFFICER** is an officer detailed to be constantly available for call in emergencies during a specific period. The officer is also called the staff duty officer. *See also:* Duty.

References

Department of Defense, U.S. Army. *Dictionary of United States Army Terms.* Army Regulation AR 310-25. Washington, DC: Headquarters, Department of the Army, 1986.

—**DUTY POSITION.** *See:* Duty Assignment.

—**DUTY ROSTER** is a list of the personnel of a unit, showing the duties each man has performed (e.g., guard, fatigue, or kitchen police). It is kept to determine the date of the individual's next tour of duty and to insure a fair distribution of duties among the personnel of the unit. *See also:* Duty.

References

Department of Defense, U.S. Army. *Dictionary of United States Army Terms.* Army Regulation AR 310-25. Washington, DC: Headquarters, Department of the Army, 1986.

—**DUTY SPECIALTY** is the specialty of the position in which an officer is currently serving, as reflected in the authorization document. *See also:* Duty.

References

Department of Defense, U.S. Army. *Dictionary of United States Army Terms.* Army Regulation AR 310-25. Washington, DC: Headquarters, Department of the Army, 1986.

—**DUTY STATION** is a military establishment or post to which an officer or enlisted man has been assigned for duty. *See also:* Duty.

References

Department of Defense, U.S. Army. *Dictionary of United States Army Terms.* Army Regulation 310-25. Washington, DC: Headquarters, Department of the Army, 1986.

—**DUTY STATUS** is the standing of an officer or enlisted person who is considered to be performing his full military duty and is entitled to receive full pay. *See also:* Duty.

References

Department of Defense, U.S. Army. *Dictionary of United States Army Terms.* Army Regulation AR 310-25. Washington, DC: Headquarters, Department of the Army, 1986.

—**DUTY WITH TROOPS OR DUTY WITH TROOP UNITS** refers to the assignment of an officer on duty with a troop unit when assigned to, and performing, duty as follows:
- Any position with a unit under an approved table of organization;
- Any position with training units of service schools, unit training centers, and replacement training centers;
- Any position in which the officer exercises direct command over troops

organized for other than purely
administrative or disciplinary purposes.
See also: Duty.

References

Department of Defense, U.S. Army. *Dictionary of United States Army Terms.* Army Regulation AR 310-25. Washington, DC: Headquarters, Department of the Army, 1986.

—**DWARF DUD** is a nuclear weapon that, when launched at or emplaced on a target, fails to provide the yield that would be expected within a reasonable range and under normal operation of the weapon. This constitutes a dud only in the relative sense. *See also:* Nuclear Warfare.

References

Department of Defense, Joint Chiefs of Staff. *Department of Defense Dictionary of Military and Related Terms.* Washington, DC: GPO, 1986.

—**DWELL AT/ON.** In artillery, this term is used when fire is to continue for an indefinite period at specified time or on a particular target or targets.

References

Department of Defense, Joint Chiefs of Staff. *Department of Defense Dictionary of Military and Related Terms.* Washington, DC: GPO, 1986.

—**DYNAMIC OBSTACLES** (a category of reinforcing obstacles) are the family of scatterable mines. They have a specific active life before self-destruction; therefore scatterable mines do not present permanent obstacles that later can impede U.S. forces' mobility. They may be delivered by helicopter (M56 antitank/antivehicular mine) and artillery (artillery delivered antipersonnel mine).

References

Department of Defense, U.S. Army. *Engineer Combat Operations.* Field Manual FM 5-100. Washington, DC: Headquarters, Department of the Army, 1984.

—**DYNAMICS OF COMBAT POWER** decide the outcome of campaigns, major operations, battles, and engagements. Combat power is the ability to fight. It measures the effect by combining maneuver, firepower protection, and leadership in combat actions against an enemy in war. Leaders combine maneuver, firepower, and protection capabilities available to them in countless combinations that are appropriate to the situation. They also attempt to interfere with the enemy leader's ability to generate the greatest effect against them by interfering with the enemy's ability to effectively maneuver, apply firepower, or provide protection. Therefore, while quantitative measures of available capability are important, the quality of available capabilities, the ability of the leader to bring them to bear, and the ability of the leader to avoid the enemy's efforts to degrade his own capabilities before or during battle may be equally or more important. This explains why the larger or stronger force does not always win.

In the course of campaigns, major operations, battles, and engagements, the balance of combat power may shift back and forth between opponents. This is especially likely when engaged forces are roughly equal in capabilities. When physical strengths are nearly equal, the qualities of skill, courage, character, perseverance, innovativeness, and strength of will of both soldiers and leaders are always decisive. There are also many cases in history where forces inferior in physical quantitative or qualitative measures but superior in moral qualities achieved success. In such cases, the skill of the leaders in using the environment to their advantage, applying sound tactical or operational methods, and providing purpose, direction, and motivation to their soldiers and subordinate leaders was always critical.

At both the operational and tactical levels, the generation of combat power requires the conversion of the potential of forces, resources, and tactical opportunity into actual capability through violent and coordinated action concentrated at the decisive time and place. Superior combat power is generated through a commander's skillful combination of the elements of maneuver, firepower, protection, and leadership in a sound plan flexibly but forcefully executed.

In the final analysis and once the force is engaged, superior combat power derives from the courage and competence of soldiers, the excellence of their training, the capability of their equipment, the soundness of their combined arms doctrine, and, above all, the quality of their leadership.

References

Department of Defense, U.S. Army. *Operations.* Field Manual FM 100-5. Washington, DC: Headquarters, Department of the Army, 1986.

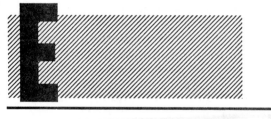

—**EARMARKED FOR ASSIGNMENT** is the status of forces that nations have agreed to assign to the operational command or operational control of a NATO commander at some future date. In designing such forces, nations should specify when they will be available in terms currently agreed upon.

References
Department of Defense, Joint Chiefs of Staff. *Department of Defense Dictionary of Military and Related Terms.* Washington, DC: GPO, 1986.

—**EARNED LEAVE** is an authorized absence earned by a member and credited to his leave account at any given date. *See also:* Annual Leave.

References
Department of Defense, U.S. Army. *Leaves and Passes.* Army Regulation AR 630-5. Washington, DC: Headquarters, Department of the Army, 1984.

—**ECHELON.** (1) An echelon is a subdivision of a headquarters (e.g., a forward echelon or a rear echelon). (2) An echelon is a separate level of command. Compared with a regiment, a division is a higher echelon, while a battalion is a lower echelon. (3) An echelon is a fraction of a command in the direction of depth, to which a principal combat mission is assigned (e.g., an attack echelon, reserve echelon, or support echelon). (4) An echelon is a formation whose subdivisions are placed one behind the another, with a lateral and even spacing to the same side. *See also:* Echeloned Displacement.

References
Department of Defense, Joint Chiefs of Staff. *Department of Defense Dictionary of Military and Related Terms.* Washington, DC: GPO, 1986.

—**ECHELONED DISPLACEMENT** is the movement of a unit from one position to another while continuing to perform its primary function. Normally, the unit divides into two functional elements (base and advance); and while the base continues to operate, the advance displaces to a new site where, after it becomes operational, it is joined by the base element.

References
Department of Defense, Joint Chiefs of Staff. *Department of Defense Dictionary of Military and Related Terms.* Washington, DC: GPO, 1986.

—**ECONOMIC INTELLIGENCE,** a component of strategic intelligence, is foreign intelligence concerning the production, distribution, and consumption of goods and services, labor, finance, taxation, and other aspects of a nation's economy or of the international economic system. The U.S. State Department is the primary producer of economic intelligence of the free world, while the Central Intelligence Agency has reporting responsibility for communist countries.

Economics is the science of production, distribution, and use of wealth—the material means of satisfying human desires. It analyzes factors of production and determines how they can be used to produce the items that satisfy these material wants. Thus, economics concerns the basic aspects of human living, the relations among people and nations, and the competition among people and nations for the world's resources. That competition has been, and continues to be, a major cause of war.

It can be said, then, that economic intelligence is intelligence that deals with the extent and use of the natural and human resources and the potential of nations. The position of the United States as a major economic power makes it inevitable that almost any economic development affects in some way its position in international affairs. For this reason, the study of the national economy of foreign nations is one of the most important tasks in strategic intelligence. Economic weapons can be among the most effective means of international conflict short of direct military action, and economic potential is perhaps the best single measure of a nation's strategic capabilities.

Economic intelligence serves three related purposes in the design of policies to preserve U.S. national security:

1. *To estimate the magnitude of possible present or future military or other threats to the United States and its allies.* A potential enemy can undertake and successfully carry out only operations— military or otherwise—that its economy is capable of mounting and sustaining. In the short run, national strength can be measured in terms of manpower that can be mobilized and stocks of weapons and military supplies that are

available. Today, however, it is recognized that military potential for anything but the briefest campaigns depends on the total resources of a nation—resources necessary to sustain the civilian economy and those necessary to produce and operate the weapons of war. An objective appraisal of the nature and magnitude of any actual or potential threats to U.S. interests is necessary if U.S. policy planners are to appreciate realistically the magnitude of the necessary defense effort that must be sustained to preserve U.S. freedom and defend U.S. national interests.

2. *To assist in estimating the intentions of a potential enemy.* This is difficult, despite the deceptive simplicity of the concept. The economic resources of a potential enemy and their disposition offer it a selection of possible or probable courses of action (e.g., efforts to achieve a state of military preparedness do not necessarily foretell the advent of military aggression). Military preparedness makes aggression possible, but not inevitable. Thus, while it is possible to establish the outside limits of the range of possibilities and even to develop estimates of probabilities based upon the existence of key indications, it would be foolhardy to assume that analysis of economic indications of the intentions of a government has reached a level at all close to an exact science.

3. *To assist in estimating the probable development of the relative strengths of the Soviet bloc and other foreign economies for the next few years.* These comparative estimates are needed to guide U.S. policymakers in developing the political policies that will offer the best chance of achieving the objectives without hostilities. Questions of relative economic strength are basic to the development of such a policy. There are equally grave dangers in a serious overestimation of future economic strength, because either may produce policies that are more likely to bring on war than would a more accurate estimate.

Economic Warfare

Economic warfare can take several forms: diplomatic and financial pressures to induce neutral countries to cease trading with the enemy; preclusive buying policy, such as the one the United States applied during World War II, to keep critical materials away from the enemy; or military action directed toward the seizure or destruction of the enemy's economic resources. For these purposes, it is necessary to know the strong and weak points of national economies and of international economic relations.

The intelligence officer gives the military operational planners accurate information on the location and character of steel plants, freight yards, oil refineries, power stations, chemical plants, and other industrial installations. This assessment of a particular country reveals industrial bottlenecks and the degree to which the military effort would be hampered by the loss of certain materials or specific facilities.

The answers to certain questions help in assessing the capabilities, vulnerabilities, and probable courses of action of a nation. Intelligence wants to know what raw materials are available, in what quantities, and from what sources. The Intelligence Community usually makes a distinction between basic foodstuffs and basic industrial materials. The list of industrial raw materials is divided into three groups: the metallic minerals (e.g., copper), the nonmetallic minerals (e.g., coal), and the organic substances (e.g., wood, rubber, and hides).

The most dependable supply of a raw material usually lies within a country's own boundaries. In peacetime a nation can usually get materials from abroad, but during a war transportation may be obstructed by a blockade, a lack of shipping, or congestion of railroads and ports. Since it is usually uncertain as to which side will control the sea lanes, estimates of a nation's raw material potential must take into account the possible disruption of lines of communications to foreign sources of supply.

It is also important to know what industrial capacity is available and its limitations from the perspective of war goods production. A nation's industrial capacity is a product of the skillful use of manpower, natural resources, and capital. But high industrial potential does not automatically result from possession of these elements. Some countries—China, for example—have abundant manpower and extensive deposits of minerals but lack sufficient mines and factories to benefit from these resources. On the other hand, countries like the Netherlands have important industries despite a lack of key raw materials.

The adaptability of a nation's productive capacity to meet the demands of war depends to a considerable degree on its peacetime economic policies. Sometimes competitive private enterprise has been relied on with relatively little governmental interference in order to achieve the maximum degree of industrial development. In the United States, this policy has resulted in a high degree of efficiency and an industrial establishment that is well adjusted to competition. A shortcoming of such an economic policy is the underdevelopment of production in some lines that are crucial in wartime.

In contrast to a policy of relying on private initiative, there are many degrees of government control. Through various degrees of control, including government ownership, a nation may achieve a close approximation to a war economy in peacetime. This situation prevailed in Germany prior to 1939. The Soviet Union has been on such an economic basis for decades.

Once a war has begun, even a country committed to the principle of free enterprise finds it necessary to impose controls. There are ways, however, in which such a country may prepare in advance for the adjustment of peacetime industry to wartime needs. Examples are stockpiling strategic materials and the peacetime placement of "educational" orders for minor quantities of military equipment to familiarize manufacturers with the problems that will be encountered in wartime. Advance planning for an industrial mobilization can help a nation avoid shortages of essential items in wartime.

The ability to produce goods depends on many considerations in addition to the availability of raw materials and a nation's industrial capacity. Among the most important are the availability of labor, especially skilled workers; an adequate transportation system; stability of the country's financial structure; and efficiency in executing the country's economic policies.

Economic Mobilization

The ability to recognize when a nation is mobilizing economically for war is significant indication of its probable course of action. The term "economic mobilization" means the changing of a nation's war potential into actual war energies. The aim of a war economy is to insure the maximum use of the nation's total resources, human and material, in the effort to defeat the enemy.

Economic mobilization for war requires at least four steps. First, available manpower must be used to provide adequate personnel for the armed forces and simultaneously to allot sufficient workers to produce war materials and essential civilian goods. Labor must be directed into the necessary channels through a system of freezes, priorities, and drafts. Second, to curtail civilian production and expand war production, the flow of raw materials must be controlled so that essential production is supplied adequately. Third, as an aid to financing the war and to smooth the operation of the economic system, it is necessary to establish a system of price controls. Fourth, the rationing of scarce civilian goods is imperative to insure the maximum efficiency and highest morale of the population.

For economic mobilization for war, the totalitarian countries with their controlled economic systems are better positioned technically than are the free enterprise economies. Even in peacetime, they have numerous controls operating to govern investments, production, foreign trade, prices, wages, and employment.

Sources of Economic Intelligence

Economic intelligence can be useful only to the extent that the information is both timely and reliable. This fundamental fact highlights the importance of collecting intelligence, making collection no less important to intelligence production than the analytical process.

The number one priority for U.S. intelligence today is the Soviet Union and its communist allies. These countries share a highly developed sense of security consciousness, with the result that information of all kinds, including economic data, is sharply curtailed.

This is not to say that the open Soviet publications that are available to the Intelligence Community are not useful; on the contrary, they provide a substantial portion of the information that is currently received. The point is that through the control of such public media as newspapers and trade journals the Soviet authorities have created wide gaps in U.S. knowledge. Information about certain fields of activity such as armaments is very tightly controlled, including information about industries that are only indirectly related to armaments. One of these, for example, is the extraction and manufacture of nonferrous metals.

The selective nature of published information that has been received about the Soviet bloc has placed a high premium on the capability of attachés and reporting officers who are stationed in the bloc countries, since their observations and insights offer the greatest chance of filling intelligence gaps. Other sources come into play (e.g., foreign broadcasts, defectors, commercial contacts, and clandestine sources). These are used differently and with varying effectiveness, depending on the opportunity and on the economic problem to be solved. The most reliable source of economic intelligence on the bloc, however, has undoubtedly been and probably will continue to be published information that is interpreted and supplemented by informed attachés and economic reporting officer reports. *See also:* Strategic Intelligence.

References

Clauser, Jerome K., and Weir, Sandra M. *Intelligence Research Methodology.* State College, PA: HRB-Singer, Inc. 1975.

Department of Defense, Defense Intelligence College. *Glossary of Intelligence Terms and Definitions.* Washington, DC: DIC, 1987.

Department of Defense, Joint Chiefs of Staff. *Department of Defense Dictionary of Military and Related Terms.* Washington, DC: GPO, 1986.

Godson, Roy, ed. *Intelligence Problems for the 1980s, Number 1: Elements of Intelligence.* Rev. ed. Washington, DC: National Strategy Information Center, 1983.

———. *Intelligence Problems for the 1980s, Number 4: Covert Action.* Washington, DC: National Strategy Information Center, 1981.

Kent, Sherman. *Strategic Intelligence for American World Policy.* Princeton, NJ: Princeton University Press, 1966.

Laqueur, Walter. *A World of Secrets.* New York: Basic Books, 1985.

Treverton, Gregory F. *Covert Action: The Limits of Intervention in the Postwar World.* New York: Basic Books, 1987.

Turner, Stansfield. *Secrecy and Democracy: The CIA in Transition.* Boston: Houghton Mifflin, 1985.

U.S. Congress. Senate. *Final Report of the Senate Select Committee to Study Government Operations With Respect to Intelligence Activities. Report 94-755. Book I, Foreign and Military Intelligence* (Church Committee Report). Washington, DC: GPO, 1976.

—**ECONOMY OF FORCE** (PRINCIPLE OF WAR) means to allocate minimum essential combat power to secondary efforts. As a reciprocal of the principle of mass, economy of force in the strategic dimension suggests that in the absence of unlimited resources, a nation may have to accept some risks in areas where vital national interests are not immediately at stake. This means that if a nation must focus predominant power toward a clearly defined primary threat, it cannot allow attainment of that objective to be compromised by necessary diversions to areas of lower priority. This choice involves risk, requires astute strategic planning and judgment by political and military leaders, and places a premium on the need for flexibility of thought and action.

At the operational and tactical levels, the principle of economy of force requires that minimum needs be employed in secondary areas. It requires, as at the strategic level, the acceptance of prudent risks in selected areas in order to achieve superiority in the area where decision is sought. Economy of force missions may require the forces employed to attack, to defend, to delay, or to conduct deception operations. *See also:* Principles of War.

References

Department of Defense, U.S. Army. *Operations.* Field Manual FM 100-5. Washington, DC: Headquarters, Department of the Army, 1986.

———. *The Army.* (Prepublication Issue.) Field Manual FM 100-1. Washington, DC: Headquarters, Department of the Army, 1986.

———. *The Tank and Mechanized Infantry Company Team.* Field Manual FM 71-1. Washington, DC: Headquarters, Department of the Army, 1977.

—**EFFECTIVE BEATEN ZONE** is the section of the target area in which a high percentage of shots fall, usually 82 percent of the hits. It is also called an effective pattern, or the 82 percent zone.

References

Department of Defense, U.S. Army. *Dictionary of United States Army Terms.* Army Regulation AR 310-25. Washington, DC: Headquarters, Department of the Army, 1986.

—**EFFECTIVE DAMAGE** is the damage necessary to render a target element inoperative, unserviceable, nonproductive, or uninhabitable.

References

Department of Defense, Joint Chiefs of Staff. *Department of Defense Dictionary of Military and Related Terms.* Washington, DC: GPO, 1986.

—**EFFECTIVE DOWNWIND MESSAGE** is a message that forecasts wind speed and direction at heights corresponding to preselected nuclear weapons yields. *See also:* Nuclear Warfare.

References

Department of Defense, Joint Chiefs of Staff. *Department of Defense Dictionary of Military and Related Terms.* Washington, DC: GPO, 1986.

Department of Defense, U.S. Army. *Survivability.* Field Manual FM 5-103. Washington, DC: Headquarters, Department of the Army, 1985.

—**EFFECTIVE RANGE** is the range at which a weapon or weapons system has a 50 percent probability of hitting the target.

References

Department of Defense, U.S. Army. *Operational Terms and Symbols.* Field Manual FM 101-5-1. Washington, DC: Headquarters, Department of the Army, 1985.

—**EFFECTIVE WIND** is a wind from the surface to 800 meters above the surface that influences sound-ranging operations.

References

Department of Defense, U.S. Army. *Weather Support for Army Tactical Operations.* Field Manual FM 34-81. Washington, DC: Headquarters, Department of the Army, 1984.

—**ELASTICITY IN THE DEFENSE** is achieved and maintained when resources and forces are deployed in depth, adequate reconnaissance is provided beyond areas of immediate concern, reserves are positioned in depth with adequate maneuver room to strike critical blows at exposed enemy forces, uncommitted enemy forces are delayed or prevented from interfering with the defense of forward deployed or counterattacking forces, adequate air protection is provided, the enemy's command and control system is disrupted, vulnerable rear area facilities are protected, and defending forces aggressively concentrate combat power in critical areas.

References

Department of Defense, U.S. Army. *The Army.* (Prepublication issue.) Field Manual FM 100-1. Washington, DC: Headquarters, Department of the Army, 1986.

—**ELECTRO-EXPLOSIVE DEVICE** is an electrically initiated device having an explosive or pyrotechnic output, or having a mechanical output resulting from an explosive or pyrotechnic action.

References

Department of Defense, Joint Chiefs of Staff. *Department of Defense Dictionary of Military and Related Terms.* Washington, DC: GPO, 1986.

—**ELECTROMAGNETIC COMPATIBILITY (EMC)** is the ability of different systems to function with each other electromagnetically. It is desirable

for different systems on a single platform to be compatible so that they do not damage each other. *See also:* Communications Security.

References

Department of Defense, Joint Chiefs of Staff. *Department of Defense Dictionary of Military and Related Terms.* Washington, DC: GPO, 1986.

Godson, Roy, ed. *Intelligence Problems for the 1980s, Number 1: Elements of Intelligence.* Rev. ed. Washington, DC: National Strategy Information Center, 1983.

—**ELECTROMAGNETIC EMISSIONS,** as defined by Army tactical intelligence, are fields of electric and magnetic energy that travel through space. Depending on their frequency and rate of oscillation, they are known as radio waves, gamma rays, X rays, ultraviolet rays, infrared light, or radar waves. *See also:* Communications Security.

References

Godson, Roy, ed. *Intelligence Problems for the 1980s, Number 1: Elements of Intelligence.* Rev. ed. Washington, DC: National Strategy Information Center, 1983.

Department of Defense, U.S. Army. *Counter-Signals Intelligence (C-SIGINT) Operations.* Field Manual FM 34-62. Washington, DC: Headquarters, Department of the Army, 1986.

————. *Military Intelligence Battalion Combat Electronic Warfare and Intelligence (Aerial Exploitation) (Corps).* Field Manual FM 34-22. Washington, DC: Headquarters, Department of the Army, 1984.

————. *Military Intelligence Company (Combat Electronic Warfare and Intelligence) (Armored Cavalry Regiment/Separate Brigade).* Field Manual FM 34-30. Washington, DC: Headquarters, Department of the Army, 1983.

—**ELECTROMAGNETIC PULSE (EMP)** is an electronic wave generated by a nuclear detonation that induces a current in any electrical conductor. An EMP can temporarily disrupt or overload and damage components of electronic equipment if they are not properly protected. *See also:* Communications Security.

References

Department of Defense, Joint Chiefs of Staff. *Department of Defense Dictionary of Military and Related Terms.* Washington, DC: GPO, 1986.

Department of Defense, U.S. Army. *U.S. Army Air Defense Artillery Employment.* Field Manual FM 44-1. Washington, DC: Headquarters, Department of the Army, 1983.

—ELECTROMAGNETIC RADIATION, in signals intelligence, communications security, operations security, and signals analysis, refers to radiation composed of oscillating electric and magnetic fields. Such waves, which include radar and radio waves, travel at the speed of light. *See also:* Communications Security.

References
Department of Defense, Joint Chiefs of Staff. *Department of Defense Dictionary of Military and Related Terms.* Washington, DC: GPO, 1986.

Godson, Roy, ed. *Intelligence Problems for the 1980s, Number 1: Elements of Intelligence.* Rev. ed. Washington, DC: National Strategy Information Center, 1983.

—ELECTROMAGNETIC RADIATION HAZARDS are hazards caused by a transmitter/antenna installation that (1) generates electromagnetic radiation in the vicinity of ordnance, personnel, or fueling operations in excess of established safe levels; or (2) increases the existing levels to a hazardous level. The term also refers to a personnel, fueling, or ordnance installation located in an area illuminated by electromagnetic radiation at a level that is hazardous to the planned operations or occupancy.

References
Department of Defense, U.S. Army. *NBC Operations.* Field Manual FM 3-100. Washington, DC: Headquarters, Department of the Army, 1985.

—ELECTROMAGNETIC SPECTRUM, in electronic warfare, signals intelligence, communications security, operations security, and signals analysis, refers to the frequencies (or wavelengths) present in a given electromagnetic radiation. A particular spectrum might include a single frequency or a range of frequencies. As defined by the Church Committee, electromagnetic spectrum means: "The frequencies (or wavelengths) present in a given electromagnetic radiation (radiation made up of oscillating electric and magnetic fields and propagated with the speed of light—such as radar or radio waves). A particular spectrum could include a single frequency, or a broad range of frequencies." *See also:* Communications Security.

References
Department of Defense, Joint Chiefs of Staff. *Department of Defense Dictionary of Military and Related Terms.* Washington, DC: GPO, 1986.

U.S. Congress. Senate. *Final Report of the Senate Select Committee to Study Government Operations With Respect to Intelligence Activities. Report 94-*

755. Book I, Foreign and Military Intelligence (Church Committee Report). Washington, DC: GPO, 1976.

—ELECTROMAGNETIC VULNERABILITY (EMV) are the characteristics of a system that cause it to suffer a definite degradation (i.e., incapability to perform the designated mission) as a result of having been subjected to a certain level of electromagnetic environmental effects.

References
Department of Defense, Joint Chiefs of Staff. *Department of Defense Dictionary of Military and Related Terms.* Washington, DC: GPO, 1986.

—ELECTRONIC CAMOUFLAGE, electronic warfare, is the use of radar-absorbent or reflecting materials to change the radar-echoing properties of a surface. The purpose is to prevent the detection of the surface if it is hit by a radar signal. *See also:* Electronic Warfare.

References
Godson, Roy, ed. *Intelligence Problems for the 1980s, Number 1: Elements of Intelligence.* Rev. ed. Washington, DC: National Strategy Information Center, 1983.

—ELECTRONIC COUNTER-COUNTERMEASURES (ECCM) is the division of electronic warfare involving actions taken to insure the effective use of the electromagnetic spectrum despite an adversary's use of electronic countermeasures. *See also:* Electronic Countermeasures.

References
Department of Defense, Joint Chiefs of Staff. *Department of Defense Dictionary of Military and Related Terms.* Washington, DC: GPO 1986.

—ELECTRONIC COUNTERMEASURES (ECM) are a division of electronic warfare that involve actions taken to prevent or reduce an enemy's use of the electromagnetic spectrum. ECM includes *electronic jamming,* which is the deliberate radiation, reradiation, or reflection of electromagnetic energy in order to impair the enemy's use of its electronic equipment. ECM also includes *electronic deception,* which is similar to electronic jamming but is meant to mislead the enemy so that it misinterprets the information it receives from its electronic systems. Three types of electronic deception are noteworthy:

1. *manipulative deception* involves

altering or simulating friendly electro-magnetic radiations in order to deceive an adversary;

2. *simulative electronic deception* involves actions that simulate real or fictional friendly capabilities in order to mislead the enemy;

3. *imitative deception* involves introducing radiations into enemy channels that imitate its own emissions.

See also: Communications Security, Electronic Warfare.

References

Deacon, Richard. *Spyclopedia: An Encyclopaedia of Spies, Secret Services, Operations, Jargon, and All Subjects Related to the World of Espionage.* London: Macdonald, 1987.

Department of Defense, Defense Intelligence College. *Glossary of Intelligence Terms and Definitions.* Washington, DC: DIC, 1987.

Department of Defense, Joint Chiefs of Staff. *Department of Defense Dictionary of Military and Related Terms.* Washington, DC: GPO, 1986.

Department of Defense, U.S. Army. *Counter-Signals Intelligence (C-SIGINT) Operations.* Field Manual FM 34-62. Washington, DC: Headquarters, Department of the Army, 1986.

———. *Intelligence and Electronic Warfare Operations.* Field Manual FM 34-1. Washington, DC: Headquarters, Department of the Army, 1984.

———. *Military Intelligence Battalion Combat Electronic Warfare and Intelligence (Aerial Exploitation) (Corps).* Field Manual FM 34-22. Washington, DC: Headquarters, Department of the Army, 1984.

———. *Military Intelligence Battalion (Combat Electronic Warfare Intelligence) (Division).* Field Manual FM 34-10. Washington, DC: Headquarters, Department of the Army, 1981.

———. *Military Intelligence Battalion (CEWI) (Operations) (Corps).* Field Manual FM 34-21. Washington, DC: Headquarters, Department of the Army, 1982.

———. *Military Intelligence Battalion (CEWI) (Tactical Exploitation) (Corps): Counterintelligence, Interrogation, Electronic Warfare.* Field Manual FM 34-23. Washington, DC: Headquarters, Department of the Army, 1985.

———. *Military Intelligence Company (Combat Electronic Warfare and Intelligence) (Armored Cavalry Regiment/Separate Brigade).* Field Manual FM 34-30. Washington, DC: Headquarters, Department of the Army, 1983.

———. *Military Intelligence Group (Combat Electronic Warfare and Intelligence) (Corps).* Field Manual FM 34-20. Washington, DC: Headquarters, Department of the Army, 1983.

Godson, Roy, ed. *Intelligence Problems for the 1980s, Number 1: Elements of Intelligence.* Rev. ed. Washington, DC: National Strategy Information Center, 1983.

—**ELECTRONIC DECEPTION,** an Army tactical intelligence term, means the deliberate radiation, reradiation, alteration, suppression, absorption, denial, enhancement, or reflection of electro-magnetic energy in a manner that is intended to convey misleading information or to deny the receipt of valid information by an enemy or by enemy electronics-dependent weapons. Electronic deception includes manipulative electronic deception, simulated electronic deception, and imitative deception. *See also:* Electronic Countermeasures.

—**ELECTRONIC EMISSION SECURITY** involves measures taken to protect all transmissions from interception and electronic analysis. *See also:* Communications Security.

References

Department of Defense, Defense Intelligence College. *Glossary of Intelligence Terms and Definitions.* Washington, DC: DIC, 1987.

Department of Defense, Joint Chiefs of Staff. *Department of Defense Dictionary of Military and Related Terms.* Washington, DC: GPO, 1986.

—**ELECTRONIC IMITATIVE DECEPTION** is introducing into the enemy's electronic systems radiations that imitate its own emissions.

References

Department of Defense, Joint Chiefs of Staff. *Department of Defense Dictionary of Military and Related Terms.* Washington, DC: GPO, 1986.

—**ELECTRONIC INTELLIGENCE (ELINT),** in general, is technical and intelligence information derived from foreign electromagnetic radiations other than those involving communications and those from atomic detonations and radioactive sources. ELINT is part of the National Security Agency/Central Security Service Signals Intelligence Mission. In Army tactical intelligence, the term is defined as the intercepting and processing of noncommunications signals in order to determine the intentions, capabilities, and locations, as well as the equipment characteristics and functions of the transmitters. *See also:* Communications Security.

References

Department of Defense, Defense Intelligence College. *Glossary of Intelligence Terms and Definitions.* Washington, DC: DIC, 1987.

Department of Defense, Joint Chiefs of Staff. *Department of Defense Dictionary of Military and Related Terms.* Washington, DC: GPO, 1986.

Department of Defense, U.S. Army. *Counter-Signals Intelligence (C-SIGINT) Operations.* Field Manual FM 34-62. Washington, DC: Headquarters, Department of the Army, 1986.

————. *Intelligence and Electronic Warfare Operations.* Field Manual FM 34-1. Washington, DC: Headquarters, Department of the Army, 1984.

————. *Military Intelligence Battalion Combat Electronic Warfare and Intelligence (Aerial Exploitation) (Corps).* Field Manual FM 34-22. Washington, DC: Headquarters, Department of the Army, 1984.

————. *Military Intelligence Battalion (Combat Electronic Warfare Intelligence) (Division).* Field Manual FM 34-10. Washington, DC: Headquarters, Department of the Army, 1981.

————. *Military Intelligence Battalion (CEWI) (Operations) (Corps).* Field Manual FM 34-21. Washington, DC: Headquarters, Department of the Army, 1982.

————. *Military Intelligence Company (Combat Electronic Warfare and Intelligence) (Armored Cavalry Regiment/Separate Brigade).* Field Manual FM 34-30. Washington, DC: Headquarters, Department of the Army, 1983.

————. *Military Intelligence Group (Combat Electronic Warfare and Intelligence) (Corps).* Field Manual FM 34-20. Washington, DC: Headquarters, Department of the Army, 1983.

Godson, Roy, ed. *Intelligence Problems for the 1980s, Number 1: Elements of Intelligence.* Rev. ed. Washington, DC: National Strategy Information Center, 1983.

—**ELECTRONIC JAMMING,** in electronic warfare, is the deliberate radiation, reradiation, or reflection of electromagnetic signals with the aim of impairing the enemy's use of its electronic devices. *See also:* Electronic Countermeasures, Jamming.

References

Department of Defense, Joint Chiefs of Staff. *Department of Defense Dictionary of Military and Related Terms.* Washington, DC: GPO, 1986.

U.S. Congress. Senate. *Final Report of the Senate Select Committee to Study Government Operations With Respect to Intelligence Activities. Report 94-755. Book I, Foreign and Military Intelligence* (Church Committee Report). Washington, DC: GPO, 1976.

—**ELECTRONIC MANIPULATIVE DECEPTION** is the alteration of friendly electromagnetic emission characteristics, patterns, or procedures to eliminate revealing, or convey misleading, telltale indicators that may be used by hostile forces. *See also:* Electronic Deception, Electronic Imitative Deception, Electronic Simulative Deception.

References

Department of Defense, Joint Chiefs of Staff. *Department of Defense Dictionary of Military and Related Terms.* Washington, DC: GPO, 1986.

—**ELECTRONIC ORDER OF BATTLE (EOB)** is a listing of a foreign nation's noncommunications electronic devices. The listing includes name or nomenclature of the emitter, its location, site designation, the function of the site, and any other information that has military significance. *See also:* Electronic Intelligence.

References

Department of Defense, Defense Intelligence College. *Glossary of Intelligence Terms and Definitions.* Washington, DC: DIC, 1987.

Godson, Roy, ed. *Intelligence Problems for the 1980s, Number 1: Elements of Intelligence.* Rev. ed. Washington, DC: National Strategy Information Center, 1983.

—**ELECTRONIC RECONNAISSANCE (ER)** in electronic warfare, means detecting, collecting, identifying, evaluating, and locating electromagnetic signals other than communications signals and radiation from nuclear detonations and radioactive sources. *See also:* Electronic Warfare.

References

Department of Defense, Joint Chiefs of Staff. *Department of Defense Dictionary of Military and Related Terms.* Washington, DC: GPO, 1986.

Laqueur, Walter. *A World of Secrets.* New York: Basic Books, 1985.

—**ELECTRONIC SECURITY (ELSEC)** is the protection that results from all the measures taken to deny unauthorized persons access to information of military value that might be derived from their intercepting and analyzing one's noncommunications electromagnetic radiations. *See also:* Communications Security.

References

Department of Defense, Defense Intelligence College. *Glossary of Intelligence Terms and Definitions.* Washington, DC: DIC, 1987.

Department of Defense, Joint Chiefs of Staff. *Department of Defense Dictionary of Military and Related Terms.* Washington, DC: GPO, 1986.

Department of Defense, U.S. Army. *Counterintelligence.* Field Manual FM 34-60. Washington, DC: Headquarters, Department of the Army, 1985.

Godson, Roy, ed. *Intelligence Problems for the 1980s, Number 1:Elements of Intelligence.* Rev. ed. Washington, DC: National Strategy Information Center, 1983.

U.S. Congress. Senate. *Final Report of the Senate Select Committee to Study Government Operations With Respect to Intelligence Activities. Report 94-755. Book I, Foreign and Military Intelligence* (Church Committee Report). Washington, DC: GPO, 1976.

—**ELECTRONIC SIMULATIVE DECEPTION** is the creation of electromagnetic emissions to represent friendly notional or actual capabilities to mislead hostile forces. *See also:* Electronic Deception.

References

Department of Defense, Joint Chiefs of Staff. *Department of Defense Dictionary of Military and Related Terms.* Washington, DC: GPO, 1986.

—**ELECTRONIC WARFARE (EW)** is a form of military action involving the use electromagnetic energy to determine, exploit, reduce, or prevent the enemy's use of the electromagnetic spectrum while insuring that friendly forces can still use the same spectrum. The three divisions of electronic warfare are electronic warfare support measures, electronic countermeasures, and electronic counter-countermeasures. *See also:* Communications Security, Electronic Countermeasures, Electronic Counter-Countermeasures, Electronic Warfare Support Measures.

References

Department of Defense, Defense Intelligence College. *Glossary of Intelligence Terms and Definitions.* Washington, DC: DIC, 1987.

Department of Defense, Joint Chiefs of Staff. *Department of Defense Dictionary of Military and Related Terms.* Washington, DC: GPO, 1986.

Department of Defense, U.S. Army. *Counter-Signals Intelligence (C-SIGINT) Operations.* Field Manual FM 34-62. Washington, DC: Headquarters, Department of the Army, 1986.

————. *Military Intelligence Battalion Combat Electronic Warfare and Intelligence (Aerial Exploitation) (Corps).* Field Manual FM 34-22. Washington, DC: Headquarters, Department of the Army, 1984.

————. *Military Intelligence Battalion (Combat Electronic Warfare Intelligence) (Division).* Field Manual FM 34-10. Washington, DC: Headquarters, Department of the Army, 1981.

————. *Military Intelligence Battalion (CEWI) (Operations) (Corps).* Field Manual FM 34-21. Washington, DC: Headquarters, Department of the Army, 1982.

—**ELECTRONIC WARFARE SUPPORT MEASURES (ESM)** are a part of electronic warfare involving actions taken to search for, intercept, locate, and immediately identify radiated electromagnetic energy for the purposes of immediate threat recognition. These measures provide information required for immediate action involving electronic countermeasures, electronic counter-countermeasures, avoidance, targeting, and other tactical endeavors. In Army tactical intelligence, direction finding of radios and radars is an ESM technique. *See also:* Communications Security, Electronic Warfare.

References

Department of Defense, Defense Intelligence College. *Glossary of Intelligence Terms and Definitions.* Washington, DC: DIC, 1987.

Department of Defense, Joint Chiefs of Staff. *Department of Defense Dictionary of Military and Related Terms.* Washington, DC: GPO, 1986.

Department of Defense, U.S. Army. *Counter-Signals Intelligence (C-SIGINT) Operations.* Field Manual FM 34-62. Washington, DC: Headquarters, Department of the Army, 1986.

————. *Military Intelligence Battalion Combat Electronic Warfare and Intelligence (Aerial Exploitation) (Corps).* Field Manual FM 34-22. Washington, DC: Headquarters, Department of the Army, 1984.

————. *Military Intelligence Battalion (Combat Electronic Warfare Intelligence) (Division).* Field Manual FM 34-10. Washington, DC: Headquarters, Department of the Army, 1981.

—**ELECTRO-OPTICAL INTELLIGENCE** (ELECTRO-OPTINT) is intelligence information derived from information collected by optically monitoring the electromagnetic spectrum from ultraviolet (0.01 micrometers) through far (long wavelength) infrared (1,000 micrometers). *See also:* Optical Intelligence.

References

Department of Defense, Defense Intelligence College. *Glossary of Intelligence Terms and Definitions.* Washington, DC: DIC, 1987.

—**ELEMENT.** (1) An element is a staff or operational organization (e.g., office, directorate, division, or branch) that forms the principal structure of, and is immediately subordinate to, the next larger organization. (2) An element is a portion of an airborne or air-landed unit that is described by its method of entry into the combat area (e.g., a parachute, airplane, seaborne, or overland element). *See also:* Echelon.

References

Department of Defense, U.S. Army. *Dictionary of United States Army Terms.* Army Regulation AR 310-25. Washington, DC: Headquarters, Department of the Army, 1986.

—**ELEMENT** (DRILLS AND CEREMONIES) is an individual, squad, section, platoon, company, or larger unit that forms as part of the next higher unit.

References

Department of Defense, U.S. Army. *Drills and Ceremonies.* Field Manual FM 22-5. Washington, DC: Headquarters, Department of the Army, 1986.

—**ELEMENT OF AN OPERATION PLAN ORDER** is an item listed in the table of contents. The term includes the attachments to the operation plan or order. *See also:* Operation Order.

References

Department of Defense, U.S. Army. *Planning Logistics Support for Military Operations.* Field Manual FM 701-58. Washington, DC: Headquarters, Department of the Army, 1987.

—**ELEVATION.** (1) Elevation is the vertical angle between the horizontal and the axis of the bore or rail of a weapon that is required for a projectile to reach a prescribed range. (2) In air defense artillery, the angular height is sometimes called elevation, and dials on some equipment, which indicate angular height, are marked "elevation."

References

Department of Defense, U.S. Army. *Dictionary of United States Army Terms.* Army Regulation AR 310-25. Washington, DC: Headquarters, Department of the Army, 1986.

—**EMANATIONS SECURITY (EMSEC)** is the protection that results from all the measures that are designed to deny unauthorized individuals access to information. The use of EMSEC implies that the conversations, if intercepted and analyzed, would be of intelligence value. EMSEC does not include measures regarding crypto-graphic equipment or telecommunications systems, which are protected under other programs. *See also:* Communications Security, Emission Security.

References

Department of Defense, Defense Intelligence College. *Glossary of Intelligence Terms and Definitions.* Washington, DC: DIC, 1987.

—**EMERGENCY AIRLIFT** is required when supplies are critical to the tactical mission or the survival of the unit. Requests are coordinated through the Air Force airlift advance notification/coordination net. *See also:* Emergency Airlift Mission.

References

Department of Defense, U.S. Army. *Repair Parts Supply for a Theater of Operations.* Field Manual FM 29-19. Washington, DC: Headquarters, Department of the Army, 1985.

—**EMERGENCY AIRLIFT MISSION** is the highest priority airlift mission available in the theater. This priority applies to both preplanned and immediate airlift requests submitted for validation. The land component commander will approve the use of this priority only when it is critical to the survival of a unit or to the accomplishment of the overall ground tactical plan. If the mission is validated after considering the risks involved, every effort will be made to provide airlift support, as requested.

References

Department of Defense, U.S. Army. *USA/USAF Doctrine for Joint Airborne and Tactical Airlift Operations.* Field Manual FM 100-27. Washington, DC: Headquarters, Department of the Army, 1985.

—**EMERGENCY BURIAL** is a burial, usually on the battlefield, when conditions do not permit either evacuation for interment in a cemetery or burial according to national or international regulations.

References

Department of Defense, U.S. Army. *Combat Service Support.* Field Manual FM 100-10. Washington, DC: Headquarters, Department of the Army, 1983.

—**EMERGENCY DEPLOYMENT READINESS EXERCISES** are minimum notice exercises to test unit deployment capabilities under contingency conditions. *See also:* Exercise.

References

Department of Defense, U.S. Army. *Army Exercises.* Army Regulation AR 350-28. Washington, DC: Headquarters, Department of the Army, 1985.

———. *Army Forces Training.* Army Regulation AR 350-41. Washington, DC: Headquarters, Department of the Army, 1986.

—**EMERGENCY DESTRUCTION OF NUCLEAR WEAPONS** is the destruction of nuclear munitions, components, and associated classified material, without significant nuclear yield, to render the weapon tactically useless, to prevent the disclosure of classified design information, and to prevent salvage of the weapon for reprocessing. *See also:* Nuclear Warfare.

References

Department of Defense, Joint Chiefs of Staff. *Department of Defense Dictionary of Military and Related Terms.* Washington, DC: GPO, 1986.

—**EMERGENCY IN WAR** is an operational contingency in a limited area caused by a critical aggravation of combat operations and requires special and immediate action by national and allied commanders. The existence of such an emergency is determined by the allied commander responsible for the limited area involved, in consultation with the national commander concerned.

References

Department of Defense, Joint Chiefs of Staff. *Department of Defense Dictionary of Military and Related Terms.* Washington, DC: GPO, 1986.

—**EMERGENCY LEAVE** is an authorized absence granted for a personal or family emergency requiring the member's presence. Leave that is granted from a post or station in the continental United States, even though it is prompted by an emergency, is ordinary leave. *See also:* Annual Leave.

References

Department of Defense, U.S. Army. *Dictionary of United States Army Terms.* Army Regulation AR 310-25. Washington, DC: Headquarters, Department of the Army, 1986.

———. *Leaves and Passes.* Army Regulation AR 630-5. Washington, DC: Headquarters, Department of the Army, 1984.

—**EMERGENCY LEVEL** is the number or amount of supplies required for certain mobilization reserve items. This level is authorized in lieu of a general mobilization reserve materiel requirement and the peacetime safety level of those items where the economic order principles are applied and result in an operating level of supply of two years or more.

References

Department of Defense, U.S. Army. *Dictionary of United States Army Terms.* Army Regulation AR 310-25. Washington, DC: Headquarters, Department of the Army, 1986.

—**EMERGENCY PRIORITY** is a category of immediate mission request that takes precedence over all other priorities (e.g., enemy breakthrough). *See also:* Immediate Mission Request.

References

Department of Defense, Joint Chiefs of Staff. *Department of Defense Dictionary of Military and Related Terms.* Washington, DC: GPO, 1986.

—**EMERGENCY REPAIR** is the immediate repair of a damaged facility to the minimum extent necessary to return it to an operational status.

References

Department of Defense, U.S. Army. *Support Operations: Echelons Above Corps.* Field Manual FM 100-16. Washington, DC: Headquarters, Department of the Army, 1986.

—**EMERGENCY RISK** (NUCLEAR) is a degree of risk where the anticipated effects may cause temporary shock and casualties and may significantly reduce the unit's combat efficiency. *See also:* Degree of Risk (Nuclear), Moderate Risk (Nuclear), Negligible Risk (Nuclear), Nuclear Warfare.

References

Department of Defense, Joint Chiefs of Staff. *Department of Defense Dictionary of Military and Related Terms.* Washington, DC: GPO, 1986.

—**EMERGENCY STAFF DESIGNEE** is an individual (or staff group) who, with minimal prior warning, can move to designated alternate or relocation sites, form an emergency staff, and conduct essential functions.

References

Department of Defense, U.S. Army. *Planning Logistics Support for Military Operations.* Field Manual FM 701-58. Washington, DC: Headquarters, Department of the Army, 1987.

—**EMISSION CONTROL (EMCON)** is an Army tactical intelligence term that means the selective and controlled use of electromagnetic, acoustic, or other emitters (1) to optimize command and control capabilities while minimizing, for operations security, detection by enemy sensors; (2) to minimize mutual interference among friendly systems; and/or (3) to execute a military deception plan. *See also:* Communications Security.

References

Department of Defense, Joint Chiefs of Staff. *Department of Defense Dictionary of Military and Related Terms.* Washington, DC: GPO, 1986.

Department of Defense, U.S. Army. *Counter-Signals Intelligence (C-SIGINT) Operations.* Field Manual FM 34-62. Washington, DC: Headquarters, Department of the Army, 1986.

————. *Military Intelligence Battalion Combat Electronic Warfare and Intelligence (Aerial Exploitation) (Corps).* Field Manual FM 34-22. Washington, DC: Headquarters, Department of the Army, 1984.

————. *Military Intelligence Company (Combat Electronic Warfare and Intelligence) (Armored Cavalry Regiment/Separate Brigade).* Field Manual FM 34-30. Washington, DC: Headquarters, Department of the Army, 1983.

—**EMISSION SECURITY (EMSEC)**, in communications security, means the measures taken to deny unauthorized parties access to information passed on cryptographic equipment and telecommunications systems. *See also:* Communications Security.

References

Department of Defense, Defense Intelligence College. *Glossary of Intelligence Terms and Definitions.* Washington, DC: DIC, 1987.

Department of Defense, Joint Chiefs of Staff. *Department of Defense Dictionary of Military and Related Terms.* Washington, DC: GPO, 1986.

Department of Defense, U.S. Army. *Counter-Signals Intelligence (C-SIGINT) Operations.* Field Manual FM 34-62. Washington, DC: Headquarters, Department of the Army, 1986.

—**EMPLACEMENT.** (1) Emplacement is a prepared position for one or more weapons or pieces of equipment, for protection against hostile bombardment, and from which personnel can execute their tasks. (2) Emplacement is the act of fixing a gun in a prepared position from which it may be fired.

References

Department of Defense, Joint Chiefs of Staff. *Department of Defense Dictionary of Military and Related Terms.* Washington, DC: GPO, 1986.

—**EMPLOYMENT GUIDELINES** are the guidelines considered in conjunction with employment principles and *defense design* requirements in the *defense phase* of the *defense planning* sequence. They are provided as aids to commanders for positioning individual fire units in designing an air defense and are incorporated in a proper mix that considers the availability of resources and the requirements of each tactical situation. *See also:* Defense Design, Defense Design Requirements, Defense Planning, Employment Principles.

References

Department of Defense, U.S. Army. *U.S. Army Air Defense Employment.* Field Manual FM 44-1. Washington, DC: Headquarters, Department of the Army, 1983.

—**EMPLOYMENT PLAN** (a category of the operating plan) is a plan developed by Army component commands or a designated/employment planning agent that provides for the employment of the Army component commands forces in support of the Unified Command. Additionally, joint employment plans are developed, as directed by a unified commander, that provide for the employment of joint forces in the area of operations. *See also:* Unified Command.

References

Department of Defense, U.S. Army. *Planning Logistics Support for Military Operations.* Field Manual FM 701-58. Washington, DC: Headquarters, Department of the Army, 1987.

—**EMPLOYMENT PRINCIPLES** are the four basic tenets that provide the doctrinal basis for air defense action design and underlie the effective employment of air defense weapons on the battlefield. They are mass, mix, mobility, and integration. These factors are considered in conjunction with employment guidelines and defense design requirements in the defense design phase of the defense planning sequence. *See also:* Defense Design, Employment Guidelines.

References

Department of Defense, U.S. Army. *U.S. Army Air Defense Artillery Employment Hawk.* Field Manual FM 44-90. Washington, DC: Headquarters, Department of the Army, 1983.

————. *U.S. Army Air Defense Employment.* Field Manual FM 44-1. Washington, DC: Headquarters, U.S. Department of the Army, 1983.

—**ENCIPHER** means to encrypt or convert a plain text into unintelligible form by using a cipher system. *See also:* Cipher, Communications Security.

References

Department of Defense, Joint Chiefs of Staff. *Department of Defense Dictionary of Military and Related Terms.* Washington, DC: GPO, 1986.

Department of Defense, Defense Intelligence College. *Glossary of Intelligence Terms and Definitions.* Washington, DC: DIC, 1987.

—**ENCODE** is the process of converting plain text into a different form (encoded text) by means of a code. *See also:* Encrypt.

References

Department of Defense, Defense Intelligence College. *Glossary of Intelligence Terms and Definitions.* Washington, DC: DIC, 1987.

—**ENCRYPT** means to convert plain text into a different, unintelligible form (encrypted form) in order to conceal its meaning. The term encrypt encompasses the terms "encipher" and "encode."

References

Department of Defense, Defense Intelligence College. *Glossary of Intelligence Terms and Definitions.* Washington, DC: DIC, 1987.

Department of Defense, Joint Chiefs of Staff. *Department of Defense Dictionary of Military and Related Terms.* Washington, DC: GPO, 1986.

Department of Defense, U.S. Army. *Communications Techniques: Electronics Countermeasures.* Field Manual FM 24-33. Washington, DC: Headquarters, Department of the Army, 1985.

—**END EVENING CIVIL TWILIGHT (EECT)** is the instant that the center of the sun is six degrees below the horizon. *See also:* End Evening Nautical Twilight.

References

Department of Defense, U.S. Army. *Weather Support for Army Tactical Operations.* Field Manual FM 34-81. Washington, DC: Headquarters, Department of the Army, 1984.

—**END EVENING NAUTICAL TWILIGHT (EENT)** occurs when the sun has dropped twelve degrees beneath the horizon and is the instant of last available daylight for the visual control of limited ground operations. At the EENT, there is no further sunlight.

References

Department of Defense, U.S. Army. *Operational Terms and Symbols.* Field Manual FM 101-5-1. Washington, DC: Headquarters, Department of the Army, 1985.

————. *Weather Support for Army Tactical Operations.* Field Manual FM 34-81. Washington, DC: Headquarters, Department of the Army, 1984.

—**END OF MISSION**, in artillery, is an order given to stop firing on a specific target.

References

Department of Defense, Joint Chiefs of Staff. *Department of Defense Dictionary of Military and Related Terms.* Washington, DC: GPO, 1986.

—**END POINT MARKER (EPM)** is a marker located at the beginning of a mine strip, mine row, or base line. *See also:* Mine Warfare.

References

Department of Defense, U.S. Army. *Mine/Countermine Operations at the Company Level.* Field Manual FM 20-32. Washington, DC: Headquarters, Department of the Army, 1976.

—**END STRENGTH** is the actual or authorized strength of the Army or a subdivision of it, at the end of a specific period (e.g., fiscal year, calendar year, month, or operation). *See also:* Initial Strength.

References

Department of Defense, U.S. Army. *Dictionary of United States Army Terms.* Army Regulation AR 310-25. Washington, DC: Headquarters, Department of the Army, 1986.

————. *Planning Logistics Support for Military Operations.* Field Manual FM 701-58. Washington, DC: Headquarters, Department of the Army, 1987.

—**END-ITEM** is a final combination of end-products, component parts, and/or materials that is ready for its intended use (e.g., combat, combat support, or combat service support). Examples of end-items are ships, tanks, mobile machine shops, or aircraft. *See also:* End-Item Density.

References

Department of Defense, Joint Chiefs of Staff. *Department of Defense Dictionary of Military and Related Terms.* Washington, DC: GPO, 1986.

Department of Defense, U.S. Army. *Repair Parts Supply for a Theater of Operations*. Field Manual FM 29-19. Washington, DC: Headquarters, Department of the Army, 1985.

—**END-ITEM DENSITY** is the quantity of end-items requiring maintenance and supply support in a command or geographical area.

References

Department of Defense, U.S. Army. *Army Reenlistment Program*. Army Regulation AR 601-28. Washington, DC: Headquarters, Department of the Army, 1984.

—**ENEMY CAPABLITIES** is a general intelligence term that has two meanings. (1) Enemy capabilities are the courses of action open to the enemy that, if adopted, will adversely affect the accomplishment of a friendly mission (e.g., attack, defense, or withdrawl). The term "capabilities" also includes all the options available to it under each course of action. "Enemy capabilities" are considered with due respect to all known factors that can affect military operations, including time, space, weather, terrain, and the strength and disposition of enemy forces. (2) On the strategic level, the capabilities of an enemy nation are the courses of action that are within that nation's power to accomplish its national objectives during peacetime and while at war. *See also:* Intelligence.

References

Department of Defense, Joint Chiefs of Staff. *Department of Defense Dictionary of Military and Related Terms*. Washington, DC: GPO, 1986.

Department of Defense, U.S. Army. *Dictionary of United States Army Terms*. Army Regulation AR 310-25. Washington, DC: Headquarters, Department of the Army, 1986.

—**ENEMY STATE** is a state, recognized or unrecognized, that is at war or is engaged in armed conflict with the United States.

References

Department of Defense, U.S. Army. *Code of Conduct/Survival, Evasion, Resistance and Escape (SERE) Training*. Army Regulation AR 350-30. Washington, DC: Headquarters, Department of the Army, 1985.

————. *Dictionary of United States Army Terms*. Army Regulation AR 310-25. Washington, DC: Headquarters, Department of the Army, 1986.

—**ENEMY STRENGTH COMPUTATIONS** provide a method for estimating the level of combat effectiveness of enemy forces. The computations are determined in terms of committed forces, reinforcing and supporting units, and the number of nuclear weapons and chemical and biological delivery systems suspected or identified as being deployed within the friendly commander's areas of operation, influence, and interest. *See also:* Intelligence.

References

Department of Defense, U.S. Army. *Intelligence Analysis*. Field Manual FM 34-3. Washington, DC: Headquarters, Department of the Army, 1986.

—**ENFILADE FIRE** is fire directed down the line of an enemy assault formation.

References

Department of Defense, U.S. Army. *The Rifle Squads (Mechanized and Light Infantry)*. Training Circular TC 7-1. Washington, DC: Headquarters, Department of the Army, 1976.

—**ENGAGE** (AIR DEFENSE FIRE CONTROL ORDER) is an order used to direct a unit to fire on a specific target. It cancels any previous fire control order that may have been issued on that track. Due to the intensity of future conflicts, the preferred engagement mode for Patriot is the automatic mode. Based upon the tactical situation, an alternate method of fire other than the one selected by the computer may be manually selected by the operator. *See also:* Patriot.

References

Department of Defense, U.S. Army. *Patriot Battalion Operations*. Field Manual FM 44-15. Washington, DC: Headquarters, Department of the Army, 1984.

—**ENGAGE HOLD** is an air defense fire control order. It is used to restrain the Patriot system from automatically engaging a specified target. Missiles in flight are allowed to continue to intercept. "Engage hold" may be used in lieu of "cease fire" in the automatic engagement mode, and is only used by Patriot units. *See also:* Patriot.

References

Department of Defense, U.S. Army. *Patriot Battalion Operations*. Field Manual FM 44-15. Washington, DC: Headquarters, Department of the Army, 1984.

—**ENGAGED** (ARMY AVIATION) is when a member of a flight is attacked by an enemy aircraft. The engaged aircraft will become the tactical leader of the flight. The role may change several times during a flight.

References

Department of Defense, U.S. Army. *Air-to-Air Combat.* Field Manual FM 1-107. Washington, DC: Headquarters, Department of the Army, 1984.

—**ENGAGEMENT**, in air defense, is an attack with guns or air-to-air missiles by an interceptor aircraft, or the launch of an air defense missile by air defense artillery and the missile's subsequent travel to intercept. *See also:* Engagement Control.

References

Department of Defense, Joint Chiefs of Staff. *Department of Defense Dictionary of Military and Related Terms.* Washington, DC: GPO, 1986.

—**ENGAGEMENT AREA** is an area in which the commander concentrates fire on an enemy force with the massed fires of all available weapons. Engagement areas are routinely identified by a target reference point in the center of the trap area or by prominent terrain features around the area. Although engagement areas can also be divided into sectors of fire, it is important to understand that defensive systems are not designed around engagement areas, but rather around avenues of approach. Engagement areas and sectors of fire are not intended to restrict fires or to cause operations to become static or fixed. Rather, they are used only as a tool to concentrate fires and to optimize their effects. They may also be called the killing areas, killing grounds, or kill zones.

References

Department of Defense, U.S. Army. *Attack Helicopter Operations.* Field Manual FM 17-50. Washington, DC: Headquarters, Department of the Army, 1984.

———. *Operational Terms and Symbols.* Field Manual FM 101-5-1. Washington, DC: Headquarters, Department of the Army, 1985.

—**ENGAGEMENT CONTROL,** in air defense, is the degree of control exercised over the operational functions of an air defense unit that are related to detection, identification, engagement and destruction of hostile targets.

References

Department of Defense, Joint Chiefs of Staff. *Department of Defense Dictionary of Military and Related Terms.* Washington, DC: GPO, 1986.

—**ENGAGEMENT SIMULATION** is a family of training techniques and products designed to realistically simulate the lethality and casualty-producing effects of modern weapons in two-sided, free-play tactical training exercises. The Army has two types of engagement simulations: realistic training (REALTRAIN) and multiple integrated laser engagement system (MILES). *See also:* MILES, REALTRAIN.

References

Department of Defense, U.S. Army. *How to Prepare and Conduct Military Training.* Field Manual FM 21-6. Washington, DC: Headquarters, Department of the Army, 1975.

———. *Unit Training Management.* Field Manual FM 25-2. Washington, DC: Department of the Army, 1984.

—**ENGINEER.** (1) An engineer is a soldier who is a member of the Corps of Engineers who performs engineer duties, including construction, demolition, surveying, road and bridge building, and camouflage. (2) An engineer is the senior officer of the engineer troops in a large unit. He is a staff officer, and advises the commander on engineering matters. *See also:* Engineer Reconnaissance, Engineer Support, Engineer System.

References

Department of Defense, U.S. Army. *Dictionary of United States Army Terms.* Army Regulation AR 310-25. Washington, DC: Headquarters, Department of the Army, 1986.

—**ENGINEER RECONNAISSANCE** is terrain reconnaissance—Either general or specific—that supports engineer activities. General engineer reconnaissance, which gathers engineer information of a broad nature, is conducted to locate and evaluate construction material, resources, and terrain features that have engineer implications. Special engineer reconnaissance obtains more detailed information regarding a specific engineer task or tasks.

References

Department of Defense, U.S. Army. *Route Reconnaissance and Classification.* Field Manual FM 5-36. Washington, DC: Headquarters, Department of the Army, 1985.

—ENGINEER SUPPORT. The engineer system has three basic purposes: it preserves the freedom of maneuver of friendly forces; it obstructs the maneuver of the enemy in areas where fire and maneuver can be used to destroy it; and it enhances the survivability of friendly forces with protective construction. Engineer plans must be fully coordinated with the scheme of maneuver and fire support plans. The commander must allocate funds and furnish a list of clearly identified mission priorities. Engineer operations are time and labor intensive. They must begin as early as possible and have enough flexibility to change as the battle develops.

References
Department of Defense, U.S. Army. *Operations.* Field Manual FM 100-5. Washington, DC: Headquarters, Department of the Army, 1986.

—ENGINEER SYSTEM consists of division and corps engineer assets located in the division area. The system contains the skills and equipment necessary to enhance friendly mobility and survivability, to counter mobility of opposing forces, and to accomplish the general engineering work.

References
Department of Defense, U.S. Army. *Engineer Combat Operations.* Field Manual FM 5-100. Washington, DC: Headquarters, Department of the Army, 1984.

—ENLISTED EVALUATION SYSTEM is used to rate a soldier's proficiency and duty performance.

References
Department of Defense, U.S. Army. *Dictionary of United States Army Terms.* Army Regulation AR 310-25. Washington, DC: Headquarters, Department of the Army, 1986.

———. *Enlisted Personnel Management System.* Army Regulation AR 600-200. Washington, DC: Headquarters, Department of the Army, 1984.

—ENLISTED GRADE STRUCTURE exists for enlisted personnel and consists of pay grades with titles that are indicated in the table of comparative grades.

References
Department of Defense, U.S. Army. *Dictionary of United States Army Terms.* Army Regulation AR 310-25. Washington, DC: Headquarters, Department of the Army, 1986.

—ENLISTED OCCUPATIONAL CLASSIFICATION SYSTEM involves the procedures and processes for identifying and correlating individual capabilities, limitations, and aptitudes with the requirements of specific military jobs. *See also:* Military Occupational Specialty.

References
Department of Defense, U.S. Army. *Enlisted Personnel Management System.* Army Regulation AR 600-200. Washington, DC: Headquarters, Department of the Army, 1984.

—ENLISTED PERSON is a term used to refer to both male and female members of the Army below the grade of an officer or warrant officer. *See also:* Enlisted Grade Structure, Enlisted Specialist, Enlistee, Enlistment, Enlistment Option.

References
Department of Defense, U.S. Army. *Dictionary of United States Army Terms.* Army Regulation AR 310-25. Washington, DC: Headquarters, Department of the Army, 1986.

—ENLISTED PERSONNEL MANAGEMENT SYSTEM is the process by which enlisted personnel are professionally developed to satisfy force structure authorizations (e.g., access recruiting, training, assigning, promoting, rotation, professional developing, transferring, discharging, reenlisting, and retiring military personnel). It is also referred to as force renewal.

References
Department of Defense, U.S. Army. *Enlisted Personnel Management System.* Army Regulation AR 600-200. Washington, DC: Headquarters, Department of the Army, 1984.

—ENLISTED SPECIALIST is an enlisted person, E-4 or higher, who performs specific administrative or technical duties in which the administrative or technical requirements of the position are more important than the leadership requirements.

References
Department of Defense, U.S. Army. *Dictionary of United States Army Terms.* Army Regulation AR 310-25. Washington, DC: Headquarters, Department of the Army, 1986.

—ENLISTEE is an individual who voluntarily enrolls as a member of one of the Armed Forces for a period of enlistment.

References

Department of Defense, U.S. Army. *Dictionary of United States Army Terms*. Army Regulation AR 310-25. Washington, DC: Headquarters, Department of the Army, 1986.

—**ENLISTMENT** is voluntary enrollment in the Army, as contrasted with induction into it.

References

Department of Defense, U.S. Army. *Dictionary of United States Army Terms*. Army Regulation AR 310-25. Washington, DC: Headquarters, Department of the Army, 1986.

—**ENLISTMENT OPTION** is the opportunity prospective enlistees have to choose the duty or geographical area that they will be trained in or assigned to upon their enlistment.

References

Department of Defense, U.S. Army. *Dictionary of United States Army Terms*. Army Regulation AR 310-25. Washington, DC: Headquarters, Department of the Army, 1986.

—**ENTRY SKILLS** are specific measurable behaviors that have been determined after an analysis of the particular learning requirements of the subject, to be basic to subsequent knowledge or skill in the course. They are knowledge and skills that are necessary to begin subsequent instruction. *See also:* Entry-Level Training.

References

Department of Defense, U.S. Army. *Individual Military Education and Training*. Army Regulation AR 350-1. Washington, DC: Headquarters, Department of the Army, 1987.

—**ENTRY-LEVEL TRAINING** is training personnel receive on their initial entry into the Army. It provides an orderly transition from civilian to military life and includes (1) for enlisted soldiers, the traditional basic training and other individual training needed to prepare them for initial duty assignments; (2) for warrant officers, the Warrant Officer Entry Course, plus functional courses that prepare them for their first duty assignment or for effective integration into the Army; (3) for commissioned officers, the officer basic course that prepares them for their first duty assignment. *See also:* Basic Training.

References

Department of Defense, U.S. Army. *Individual Military Education and Training*. Army Regulation AR 350-1. Washington, DC: Headquarters, Department of the Army, 1987.

—**ENVELOPMENT** is the basic form of maneuver in any doctrine that seeks to apply strength against weakness. Envelopment avoids the enemy's front, where its forces are most protected and its fires most easily concentrated. Instead, while fixing the enemy's attention forward by supporting or diversionary attacks, the attacker maneuvers its main effort around or over the enemy's defenses to strike at the enemy's flanks and rear. Flank attacks are a variant of the envelopment, in which access to the enemy's flank and rear is furnished by the enemy's own forward movement. Single envelopments are directed against only one flank of the defending forces, while double envelopments attack both flanks. Either variant can develop into an encirclement if the attacking force is able to sever the defender's lines of communications and prevent it from receiving reinforcements or escaping. *See also:* Double Envelopment, Single Envelopment, Turning Movement.

References

Department of Defense, Joint Chiefs of Staff. *Department of Defense Dictionary of Military and Related Terms*. Washington, DC: GPO, 1986.

Department of Defense, U.S. Army. *The Army*. (Prepublication Issue.) Field Manual FM 100-1. Washington, DC: Headquarters, Department of the Army, 1986.

———. *Dictionary of United States Army Terms*. Army Regulation AR 310-25. Washington, DC: Headquarters, Department of the Army, 1986.

———. *The Tank and Mechanized Infantry Company Team*. Field Manual FM 71-1. Washington, DC: Headquarters, Department of the Army, 1977.

—**ENVIRONMENTAL AND MORALE LEAVE (EML)** is leave granted in conjunction with an environmental and morale leave program established at overseas installations. EML programs are established where adverse environmental conditions exist that offset the full benefit of annual leave programs. *See also:* Annual Leave.

References

Department of Defense, U.S. Army. *Leaves and Passes*. Army Regulation AR 630-5. Washington, DC: Headquarters, Department of the Army, 1984.

—**EQUIPMENT** is all nonexpendable items needed to outfit/equip an individual or organization. *See also:* Supplies.

References
Department of Defense, Joint Chiefs of Staff.
*Department of Defense Dictionary of Military and
Related Terms.* Washington, DC: GPO, 1986.

—**EQUIPMENT CONCENTRATION SITE** is an
equipment storage area established by a commander to support U.S. Army Reserve units
during operations and mobilization.

References
Department of Defense, Joint Chiefs of Staff.
*Department of Defense Dictionary of Military and
Related Terms.* Washington, DC: GPO, 1986.

—**EQUIPMENT HISTORICAL RECORDS** are permanent records of factual and up-to-date information on the receipt, operation, maintenance,
modification, transfer, and disposal of equipment.

References
Department of Defense, U.S. Army. *Organizational
Maintenance Operations.* Field Manual FM 29-2,
Washington, DC: Headquarters, Department of the
Army, 1984.

—**EQUIPMENT OPERATIONALLY READY** is the
status of equipment in the possession of an operating unit that indicates that the equipment
can fulfill its intended mission in a system configuration that offers a high assurance of an effective, reliable, and safe performance.

References
Department of Defense, Joint Chiefs of Staff.
*Department of Defense Dictionary of Military and
Related Terms.* Washington, DC: GPO, 1986.

—**EQUIPMENT REQUIREMENTS DATA/EQUIP-
MENT DENSITY DATA (ERD/EDD)** is a listing
of all equipment authorized by the table of organization and equipment/table of allowance,
modification table of organization and equipment /modification table of allowance and
modification table of distribution and allowances, equipment assets reported by units, and
equipment assets contained in approved operational projects, by a six-digit alphanumeric line
item number, national stock number, nomenclature, make and model, and quantity for each
unit/organization or part of it. ERD/EDD is used
as a basis for computing supply in support of
contingency operations.

References
Department of Defense, U.S. Army. *Planning
Logistics Support for Military Operations.* Field
Manual FM 701-58. Washington, DC: Headquar-
ters, Department of the Army, 1987.

—**EQUIPMENT RESERVE** are supplies that must
be procured and stored in advance to meet anticipated issue demand or other unforeseen
operational needs.

References
Department of Defense, U.S. Army. *Dictionary of
United States Army Terms.* Army Regulation AR
310-25. Washington, DC: Headquarters, Department of the Army, 1986.

—**EQUIPMENT-ORIENTED COLLECTIVE TRAIN-
ING** is collective training designed to prepare
crews, teams, and units to use crew-served
equipment (e.g., a tank, artillery piece, or mortar).

References
Department of Defense, U.S. Army. *How to Prepare
and Conduct Military Training.* Field Manual FM
21-6. Washington, DC: Headquarters, Department
of the Army, 1975.

—**EQUIVALENT TRAINING** is training, instructions, or appropriate duty for individual members of a unit in lieu of regular scheduled unit
training or regularly scheduled unit training assemblies, and for which pay and retirement credit
are authorized.

References
Department of Defense, U.S. Army. *Enlisted
Personnel Management System.* Army Regulation
AR 600-200. Washington, DC: Headquarters,
Department of the Army, 1984.

—**ESCALATION** is a deliberate or unpremeditated
increase in scope or violence of a conflict.

References
Department of Defense, Joint Chiefs of Staff.
*Department of Defense Dictionary of Military and
Related Terms.* Washington, DC: GPO, 1986.

—**ESCAPE** is the act of removing oneself from enemy control after having been captured. It includes escaping from an enemy prisoner of war
compound or temporary holding facility, or escaping during transit. Once the escapee has been
removed from enemy control, he is back in an
evasion situation. *See also:* Escape Chit, Escape
Line, Evasion and Escape.

References

Department of Defense, U.S. Army. *Code of Conduct/Survival, Evasion, Resistance and Escape (SERE) Training.* Army Regulation AR 350-30. Washington, DC: Headquarters, Department of the Army, 1985.

—**ESCAPE CHIT** is identification carried by an individual that is normally made of cloth upon which is printed, in the language of the area, a message promising a reward for assisting the bearer to safety. Replicas of the U.S. and allied flags are sometimes superimposed on the escape chit as well. It is also known as a blood chit.

References

Department of Defense, U.S. Army. *Dictionary of United States Army Terms.* Army Regulation AR 310-25. Washington, DC: Headquarters, Department of the Army, 1986.

—**ESCAPEE** is any person who has been physically captured by the enemy and succeeds in getting free. *See also:* Evasion and Escape.

References

Department of Defense, Joint Chiefs of Staff. *Department of Defense Dictionary of Military and Related Terms.* Washington, DC: GPO, 1986.

Department of Defense, U.S. Army. *Code of Conduct/Survival, Evasion, Resistance and Escape (SERE) Training.* Army Regulation AR 350-30. Washington, DC: Headquarters, Department of the Army, 1985.

—**ESCAPE LINE** is a planned route to allow personnel engaged in clandestine activity to depart from a site or area when the possibility of apprehension exists.

References

Department of Defense, Joint Chiefs of Staff. *Department of Defense Dictionary of Military and Related Terms.* Washington, DC: GPO, 1986.

—**ESCORT.** (1) In intelligence, an escort is a individual who accompanies an uncleared visitor (one who either does not have a security clearance or one whose security clearance cannot be confirmed) through the security area of the agency. An escort is assigned when it is necessary to grant the visitor access to the area. The escort must assure that the visitor sees no classified material and is not given the opportunity to steal documents or materials. Such visitors are usually maintenance, repair, or cleaning personnel. (2) An escort is an armed guard who accompanies a person as a mark of honor. (3) To escort is to convoy. (4) An escort is a member of the Armed Forces who is assigned to accompany, assist, or guide an individual or group (e.g., an escort officer). *See also:* Escort Forces, Escort Guard.

References

Department of Defense, Joint Chiefs of Staff. *Department of Defense Dictionary of Military and Related Terms.* Washington, DC: GPO, 1986.

Department of Defense, U.S. Army. *Dictionary of United States Army Terms.* Army Regulation AR 310-25. Washington, DC: Headquarters, Department of the Army, 1986.

—**ESCORT FORCES** are combat forces of various types that protect other forces against enemy attack.

References

Department of Defense, Joint Chiefs of Staff. *Department of Defense Dictionary of Military and Related Terms.* Washington, DC: GPO, 1986.

—**ESCORT GUARD** supervises and guards prisoners of war in camps, in enclosures, on work details, during interrogation, and during evacuation or transfer.

References

Department of Defense, U.S. Army. *Dictionary of United States Army Terms.* Army Regulation AR 310-25. Washington, DC: Headquarters, Department of the Army, 1986.

—**ESCORT JAMMING,** in electronic warfare, is jamming that is performed by an aircraft carrying sophisticated electronic gear in order to protect accompanying aircraft that it is protecting. *See also:* Jamming.

References

Department of Defense, U.S. Army. *Dictionary of United States Army Terms.* Army Regulation AR 310-25. Washington, DC: Headquarters, Department of the Army, 1986.

—**ESCORT OF THE COLOR** is a ceremony of escorting the color with a color guard. *See also:* Color, Color Guard.

References

Department of Defense, U.S. Army. *Dictionary of United States Army Terms.* Army Regulation AR 310-25. Washington, DC: Headquarters, Department of the Army, 1986.

—**ESPIONAGE.** (1) The Army's official definition of espionage is "activity that is conducted with the goal of secretly acquiring information of intelligence value. Espionage activity is considered unlawful by the country against which it is committed." (2) Espionage, as defined by the Church Committee, is "clandestine intelligence collection activity. This term is often interchanged with 'clandestine collection'." (3) The Defense Investigative Review Council defined espionage as "overt, covert, or clandestine activity that is designed to obtain information relating to the national defense with the intent or reason to believe that it will be used to the injury of the United States or to the advantage of a foreign nation."

References
Department of Defense, Defense Intelligence College. *Glossary of Intelligence Terms and Definitions.* Washington, DC: DIC, 1987.

U.S. Congress. Senate. *Final Report of the Senate Select Committee to Study Government Operations With Respect to Intelligence Activities. Report 94-735. Book I; Foreign and Military Intelligence* (Church Committee Report). Washington, DC: GPO, 1976.

—**ESPRIT** is the spirit, the soul, the state of mind of the unit. It is the overall consciousness of the unit that the soldier identifies with and feels a part of. *See also:* Morale.

References
Department of Defense, U.S. Army. *Military Leadership.* Field Manual FM 22-100. Washington, DC: Headquarters, Department of the Army, 1983.

—**ESSENTIAL COMMUNICATIONS TRAFFIC** are the transmissions (record/voice) that must be sent electrically in order for the command or activity concerned to avoid a serious impact on mission accomplishment, safety, or life.

References
Department of Defense, Joint Chiefs of Staff. *Department of Defense Dictionary of Military and Related Terms.* Washington, DC: GPO, 1986.

—**ESSENTIAL ELEMENTS OF FRIENDLY INFORMATION (EEFI)** are the key questions concerning friendly intentions and military capabilities that are likely to be asked by enemy planners and decisionmakers. *See also:* Essential Elements of Information.

References
Department of Defense, Joint Chiefs of Staff. *Department of Defense Dictionary of Military and Related Terms.* Washington, DC: GPO, 1986.

Department of Defense, U.S. Army. *Counter-Signals Intelligence (C-SIGINT) Operations.* Field Manual FM 34-62. Washington, DC: Headquarters, Department of the Army, 1986.

—**ESSENTIAL ELEMENTS OF INFORMATION (EEI)** are the items of intelligence information that concern a foreign power, forces, targets, or the foreign physical environment that are absolutely vital for timely and accurate decisionmaking. *See also:* Information Requirements.

References
Department of Defense, Defense Intelligence College. *Glossary of Intelligence Terms and Definitions.* Washington, DC: DIC, 1987.

Department of Defense, Joint Chiefs of Staff. *Department of Defense Dictionary of Military and Related Terms.* Washington, DC: GPO, 1986.

Department of Defense, U.S. Army. *Military Intelligence Battalion (CEWI) (Tactical Exploitation) (Corps): Counterintelligence, Interrogation, Electronic Warfare.* Field Manual FM 34-23. Washington, DC: Headquarters, Department of the Army, 1985.

—**ESSENTIAL REPAIR PARTS STOCKAGE LIST (ERPSL)** is a list of support items computed and stocked in prescribed quantities for supporting systems that have been approved by Headquarters, Department of the Army. ERPSL items are necessary to enable a mission-essential system to perform its intended function at the prescribed operational availability rate that has been established in Army regulations.

References
Department of Defense, U.S. Army. *Repair Parts Supply for a Theater of Operations.* Field Manual FM 29-19. Washington, DC: Headquarters, Department of the Army, 1985.

—**ESTABLISHMENT** is an installation, together with its personnel and equipment, organized into an operating entity. *See also:* Installation.

References
Department of Defense, Joint Chiefs of Staff. *Department of Defense Dictionary of Military and Related Terms.* Washington, DC: GPO, 1986.

—**ESTIMATE.** (1) An estimate is an analysis of a foreign situation, development, or trend that identifies its major elements, interprets its significance, and appraises the future possibilities and the possible results of the various actions that might be taken. (2) An estimate is an appraisal of the capabilities, vulnerabilities, and potential courses of action of a foreign nation or group of nations that result from a specific national plan, policy, decision, or contemplated course of action. (3) An estimate is an analysis of an actual or contemplated clandestine operation in relation to the situation in which it is or would be conducted in order to identify and appraise such factors as available and needed assets and potential obstacles, accomplishments, and consequences. (4) In air intercept, estimate is a code meaning, "Provide a quick estimate of the height/range/size of designated contact," or "I estimate height/depth/range/size of designated contact is _____." *See also:* Intelligence Cycle, Intelligence Estimate.

References

Department of Defense, Joint Chiefs of Staff. *Department of Defense Dictionary of Military and Related Terms.* Washington, DC: GPO, 1986.

—**ESTIMATE OF THE SITUATION** is the process of reasoning in which a commander considers all the factors affecting a military situation and decides on a course of action to accomplish his mission.

References

Department of Defense, Joint Chiefs of Staff. *Department of Defense Dictionary of Military and Related Terms.* Washington, DC: GPO, 1986.

Department of Defense, U.S. Army. *Dictionary of United States Army Terms.* Army Regulation AR 310-25. Washington, DC: Headquarters, Department of the Army, 1986.

—**ESTIMATED EXPENDITURE OF AMMUNITION** is the expected number of projectiles that will be fired in a given period. It is used to determine the firepower potential of an area fire weapon.

References

Department of Defense, U.S. Army. *Dictionary of United States Army Terms.* Army Regulation AR 310-25. Washington, DC: Headquarters, Department of the Army, 1986.

—**ESTIMATIVE INTELLIGENCE** is a type of intelligence that projects or forecasts probable future foreign courses of action and developments and discusses their implications for the United States or U.S. interests. Estimative intelligence may or may not be coordinated within the Intelligence Community and may be either national or departmental intelligence. *See also:* Intelligence.

References

Department of Defense, Defense Intelligence College. *Glossary of Intelligence Terms and Definitions.* Washington, DC: DIC, 1987.

—**EVACUATION.** (1) Evacuation is the process of moving any person who is wounded, injured, or ill to or between medical treatment facilities. (2) Evacuation is the clearance of personnel, animals, or materiel from a given locality. (3) Evacuation is the controlled process of collecting, classifying, and shipping unserviceable or abandoned U.S. or foreign materiel, to appropriate reclamation, maintenance, technical intelligence, or disposal facilities. *See also:* Evacuation Policy.

References

Department of Defense, Joint Chiefs of Staff. *Department of Defense Dictionary of Military and Related Terms.* Washington, DC: GPO, 1986.

Department of Defense, U.S. Army. *Operational Terms and Symbols.* Field Manual FM 101-5-1. Washington, DC: Headquarters, Department of the Army, 1985.

—**EVACUATION POLICY.** (1) Evacuation policy is a command decision indicating the number of days that patients may be held within the command for treatment. Patients who, in the opinion of responsible medical officers, cannot be returned to full duty status within the prescribed period are evacuated to the next level of care by the first available means, provided that the travel involved will not aggravate their disabilities. (2) Evacuation policy is a command decision concerning the movement of civilians from the area of military operations for security and safety reasons. It involves the need to arrange for movement, reception, care, and control of such individuals. (3) Evacuation policy is a command policy concerning the evacuation of unserviceable or abandoned materiel, the establishment of controls and procedures, and the dissemination of condition standards and disposition instructions. *See also:* Medical Treatment.

References

Department of Defense, Joint Chiefs of Staff. *Department of Defense Dictionary of Military and Related Terms.* Washington, DC: GPO, 1986.

Department of Defense, U.S. Army. *Health Service Support in a Communications Zone (Test)*. Field Manual FM 8-21. Washington, DC: Headquarters, Department of the Army, 1981.

—**EVACUEE** is a civilian who is removed from a place of residence by military direction for personal security reasons or because of the requirements of the military situation. *See also:* Displaced Person, Expellee, Refugee.

References

Department of Defense, Joint Chiefs of Staff. *Department of Defense Dictionary of Military and Related Terms*. Washington, DC: GPO, 1986.

—**EVADER** is any person who is isolated in hostile or unfriendly territory and eludes capture. *See also:* Evasion and Escape.

References

Department of Defense, Joint Chiefs of Staff. *Department of Defense Dictionary of Military and Related Terms*. Washington, DC: GPO, 1986.

Department of Defense, U.S. Army. *Code of Conduct/Survival, Evasion, Resistance and Escape (SERE) Training*. Army Regulation AR 350-30. Washington, DC: Headquarters, Department of the Army, 1985.

—**EVALUATION**, as defined in the Church Committee Report, is "the process of appraising or assessing the value of an intelligence activity or product in terms of its contribution to the achievement of a specific goal, or the credibility, reliability, pertinency, accuracy, or usefulness of a piece of information or performance of an intelligence system in terms of intelligence need." An evaluation may be done with or without reference to cost or risk. *See also:* Intelligence Cycle.

References

Department of Defense, Defense Intelligence College. *Glossary of Intelligence Terms and Definitions*. Washington, DC: DIC, 1987.

Department of Defense, Joint Chiefs of Staff. *Department of Defense Dictionary of Military and Related Terms*. Washington, DC: GPO, 1986.

U.S. Congress. Senate. *Final Report of the Senate Select Committee to Study Government Operations With Respect to Intelligence Activities. Report 94-755. Book I, Foreign and Military Intelligence* (Church Committee Report). Washington, DC: GPO, 1976.

—**EVALUATION OF TRAINING** is the process of determining by objective and subjective means the extent of the learning of individuals and units. The purpose is to determine if a training objective has been attained and how well the available resources have been used to provide the training manager with the information that he needs to modify or update the training program. It also is used to provide feedback to trainers and soldiers who are being trained.

References

Department of Defense, U.S. Army. *How to Prepare and Conduct Military Training*. Field Manual FM 21-6. Washington, DC: Headquarters, Department of the Army, 1975.

—**EVASION** is the act of returning to friendly control (moving through enemy controlled terrain) after one has been separated from a friendly unit or after one has escaped from enemy control. *See also:* Evasion and Escape.

References

Department of Defense, U.S. Army. *Code of Conduct/Survival, Evasion, Resistance and Escape (SERE) Training*. Army Regulation AR 350-30. Washington, DC: Headquarters, Department of the Army, 1985.

—**EVASION AND ESCAPE (E&E)** are the means by which military personnel and selected individuals can pass from enemy-held or hostile areas to friendly areas. *See also:* Evader, Evasion and Escape Intelligence.

References

Department of Defense, Joint Chiefs of Staff. *Department of Defense Dictionary of Military and Related Terms*. Washington, DC: GPO, 1986.

Department of Defense, Defense Intelligence College. *Glossary of Intelligence Terms and Definitions*. Washington, DC: DIC, 1987.

Department of Defense, U.S. Army. *Dictionary of United States Army Terms*. Army Regulation AR 310-25. Washington, DC: Headquarters, Department of the Army, 1986.

—**EVASION AND ESCAPE (E&E) INTELLIGENCE** is intelligence information that has been prepared to help people avoid capture if they are lost in enemy-held territory or to escape from the enemy if they are captured. *See also:* Evader, Evasion and Escape.

References

Department of Defense, Joint Chiefs of Staff. *Department of Defense Dictionary of Military and Related Terms*. Washington, DC: GPO, 1986.

Department of Defense, Defense Intelligence College. *Glossary of Intelligence Terms and Definitions.* Washington, DC: DIC, 1987.

Department of Defense, U.S. Army. *Long-Range Surveillance.* Field Manual FM 7-93. Washington, DC: Headquarters, U.S. Army, 1987.

—**EVASION AND ESCAPE (E&E) MECHANISM** is a system composed of individuals or groups of individuals or organizations, together with material and facilities, that are either in position or can be placed in position by appropriate allied or U.S. agencies to accomplish or support E&E operations. *See also:* Evasion and Escape.

References

Department of Defense, U.S. Army. *Code of Conduct/Survival, Evasion, Resistance and Escape (SERE) Training.* Army Regulation AR 350-30. Washington, DC: Headquarters, Department of the Army, 1985.

—**EVASION AND ESCAPE (E&E) NET** is the organization within enemy-held or hostile areas that receives, moves, and exfiltrates military personnel or selected individuals to friendly control. *See also:* Exfiltration, Unconventional Warfare.

References

Department of Defense, Joint Chiefs of Staff. *Department of Defense Dictionary of Military and Related Terms.* Washington, DC: GPO, 1986.

—**EVASION AND ESCAPE (E&E) ROUTE** is a course of travel, preplanned or not, that an escapee or evader uses in an attempt to leave enemy territory and return to friendly lines. *See also:* Evasion and Escape.

References

Department of Defense, Joint Chiefs of Staff. *Department of Defense Dictionary of Military and Related Terms.* Washington, DC: GPO, 1986.

—**EVENT TEMPLATE** is a model against which enemy activity can be recorded and compared. It represents a sequential projection of events that relate to space and time on the battlefield, and indicates the enemy's ability to adopt a particular course of action. Event templates differ from doctrinal/situational templates in that they are not graphics inscribed on plastic or drawings of force dispositions, but rather lists of enemy action in chronological sequence. *See also:* Situational Template.

References

Department of Defense, U.S. Army. *Operational Terms and Symbols.* Field Manual FM 101-5-1. Washington, DC: Headquarters, Department of the Army, 1985.

—**EXCESS LEAVE** is an absence that exceeds the time that has been accrued or advanced. The member is not entitled to pay and allowances for such leave. Generally, a minus leave balance at the time of release from active duty, discharge, first extension of enlistment, desertion, or death is excess leave. *See also:* Annual Leave.

References

Department of Defense, U.S. Army. *Leaves and Passes.* Army Regulation AR 630-5. Washington, DC: Headquarters, Department of the Army, 1984.

—**EXCESS PROPERTY** is the quantity of property in possession of any component of the Department of Defense that exceeds the amount authorized for retention by that component.

References

Department of Defense, Joint Chiefs of Staff. *Department of Defense Dictionary of Military and Related Terms.* Washington, DC: GPO, 1986.

—**EXECUTING COMMANDER** (NUCLEAR WEAPONS) is a commander to whom nuclear weapons are released for delivery against specific targets or in accordance with approved plans. *See also:* Releasing Commander (Nuclear Weapons).

References

Department of Defense, Joint Chiefs of Staff. *Department of Defense Dictionary of Military and Related Terms.* Washington, DC: GPO, 1986.

—**EXECUTION PLANNING** is the part of operation planning in which a plan or concept is translated into an operation order. It includes adapting the plan or concept to the prevailing circumstances, the designation of units to satisfy force requirements, the establishment of appropriate deployability posture, the scheduling of necessary transportation resources, and the dissemination of movement tables to regulate the deployment of forces requiring common-user transportation. *See also:* Operation Order.

References

Department of Defense, U.S. Army. *Planning Logistics Support for Military Operations.* Field Manual FM 701-58. Washington, DC: Headquarters, Department of the Army, 1987.

—**EXERCISE** is a military maneuver or simulated wartime operation that involves planning, preparation, and execution. It is carried out for training and evaluation purposes. It may be a combined, joint, or single-service exercise, depending on the participating organizations. *See also:* Command Post Exercise, Field Exercise.

References

Department of Defense, Joint Chiefs of Staff. *Department of Defense Dictionary of Military and Related Terms.* Washington, DC: GPO, 1986.

—**EXERCISE COMMANDER** is a commander taking part in the exercise who issues appropriate operation orders to the forces under his control. He may also be given responsibility for controlling, conducting, and/or directing the exercise. *See also:* Exercise.

References

Department of Defense, Joint Chiefs of Staff. *Department of Defense Dictionary of Military and Related Terms.* Washington, DC: GPO, 1986.

—**EXERCISE DIRECTING STAFF** refers to a group of officers who, because of their experience, qualifications, and a through knowledge of the exercise instructions, are selected to direct or control an exercise. *See also:* Exercise.

References

Department of Defense, Joint Chiefs of Staff. *Department of Defense Dictionary of Military and Related Terms.* Washington, DC: GPO, 1986.

—**EXERCISE PLANNING DIRECTIVE** is a specification from the officer scheduling the exercise that provides further guidance about it to its planners. *See also:* Exercise.

References

Department of Defense, Joint Chiefs of Staff. *Department of Defense Dictionary of Military and Related Terms.* Washington, DC: GPO, 1986.

—**EXERCISE PROGRAM** refers to the specifications of the exercises programmed by a NATO commander for a particular calendar year. *See also:* Exercise.

References

Department of Defense, Joint Chiefs of Staff. *Department of Defense Dictionary of Military and Related Terms.* Washington, DC: GPO, 1986.

—**EXERCISE SPECIFICATION** refers to the fundamental requirements for the exercise. It provides in advance an outline of the concept, form, scope, setting, aim, objectives, force requirements, political implications, analysis arrangements, and costs of the exercise. *See also:* Exercise.

References

Department of Defense, Joint Chiefs of Staff. *Department of Defense Dictionary of Military and Related Terms.* Washington, DC: GPO, 1986.

—**EXERCISE SPONSOR** is the commander who conceives a particular exercise and orders that it be planned and executed, either by his staff or by a subordinate headquarters. *See also:* Exercise.

References

Department of Defense, Joint Chiefs of Staff. *Department of Defense Dictionary of Military and Related Terms.* Washington, DC: GPO, 1986.

—**EXERCISE STUDY** is an activity that may take the form of a map exercise, a war game, a series of lectures, a discussion group, or an operational analysis. *See also:* Exercise.

References

Department of Defense, Joint Chiefs of Staff. *Department of Defense Dictionary of Military and Related Terms.* Washington, DC: GPO, 1986.

—**EXERCISE TERM** is a combination of two words, normally unclassified, which are used exclusively to designate a test, drill, or exercise. An exercise term is used to preclude the possibility of confusing exercise directives with actual operations directives. *See also:* Exercise.

References

Department of Defense, Joint Chiefs of Staff. *Department of Defense Dictionary of Military and Related Terms.* Washington, DC: GPO, 1986.

—**EXFILTRATION** is smuggling an agent out of an unfriendly country. *See also:* Evasion and Escape, Evasion and Escape Intelligence.

References

Becket, Henry S.A. *The Dictionary of Espionage: Spookspeak Into English.* New York: Stein and Day, 1986.

Deacon, Richard. *Spyclopedia: An Encyclopedia of Spies, Secret Services, Operations, Jargon, and All Subjects Related to the World of Espionage.* London: Macdonald, 1987.

Department of Defense, Joint Chiefs of Staff. *Department of Defense Dictionary of Military and Related Terms.* Washington, DC: GPO, 1986.

—**EXISTENCE LOAD** consists of items other than those in the fighting load that are required to sustain or protect the combat soldier, that may be necessary for increased personnel and environmental protection, and that are not normally carried by the individual. *See also:* Fighting Load.

References
Department of Defense, Joint Chiefs of Staff. *Department of Defense Dictionary of Military and Related Terms.* Washington, DC: GPO, 1986.

—**EXISTING OBSTACLES** are obstructions present on the battlefield that were not placed there through military effort. They may be natural (e.g., lakes and mountains), or cultural (e.g., towns or railroad embankments). *See also:* Expedient Obstacles.

References
Department of Defense, U.S. Army. *Countermobility.* Field Manual FM 5-102. Washington, DC: Headquarters, Department of the Army, 1985.

—**EXPEDIENT OBSTACLES** are obstructions that offer an almost unlimited potential for use (e.g., roadblocks made from cars and trucks that have been loaded with rocks or other heavy materials; pushing trees, large rocks, and other material onto a climbable slope to further slow or to stop the enemy; and flooding areas to make the soil untrafficable to armored vehicles). The logistic burden associated with other reinforcing obstacles places a great premium on the imagination and ingenuity in the use of available resources.

References
Department of Defense, U.S. Army. *Engineer Combat Operations.* Field Manual FM 5-100. Washington, DC: Headquarters, Department of the Army, 1984.

—**EXPEDITIONARY FORCE** is an armed force organized to accomplish a specific objective in a foreign country.

References
Department of Defense, Joint Chiefs of Staff. *Department of Defense Dictionary of Military and Related Terms.* Washington, DC: GPO, 1986.

—**EXPEDITIONARY TROOPS,** in amphibious operations, are all the troops of all services that are assigned to a joint expeditionary force for all operations ashore. *See also:* Amphibious Operations.

References
Department of Defense, U.S. Army. *Dictionary of United States Army Terms.* Army Regulation AR 310-25. Washington, DC: Headquarters, Department of the Army, 1986.

—**EXPENDABLE PROPERTY** is property that may be consumed in use or loses its identity in use and may be dropped from stock record accounts when it is issued or used.

References
Department of Defense, Joint Chiefs of Staff. *Department of Defense Dictionary of Military and Related Terms.* Washington, DC: GPO, 1986.

—**EXPENDABLE SUPPLIES AND MATERIAL** are supplies consumed in use (e.g., ammunition, paint, fuel, cleaning and preserving materials, surgical dressing, drugs, and medicines), or supplies that lose their identity, (e.g., spare parts). These are sometimes referred to as consumable supplies and material. *See also:* Expendable Property.

References
Department of Defense, Joint Chiefs of Staff. *Department of Defense Dictionary of Military and Related Terms.* Washington, DC: GPO, 1986.

—**EXPENDITURE** is the amount of ammunition used by a unit. During combat, corps ammunition is considered expended when it is issued to the user by the ammunition supply point.

References
Department of Defense, U.S. Army. *Support Operations: Echelons Above Corps.* Field Manual FM 100-16. Washington, DC: Headquarters, Department of the Army, 1986.

—**EXPIRATION TERM OF SERVICE (ETS)** is the scheduled date on which an individual's statutory or contractual (whichever is later) term of military service ends. *See also:* Date Eligible to Return From Overseas, Permanent Change of Station.

References
Department of Defense, U.S. Army. *Processing Personnel for Separation.* Army Regulation AR 635-10. Washington, DC: Headquarters, Department of the Army, 1984.

—**EXPLODER** is a device designed to generate an electric current in a firing circuit after the user has deliberately acted to initiate an explosive charge or charges.

References

Department of Defense, Joint Chiefs of Staff. *Department of Defense Dictionary of Military and Related Terms.* Washington, DC: GPO, 1986.

—**EXPLOITATION.** (1) Exploitation, in intelligence, is the process of obtaining intelligence information from any source and taking advantage of it for tactical or strategic purposes. In signals intelligence, exploitation is producing information from encrypted messages where the encryption system is unknown. It includes decryption, translation, and solution of specific controls (e.g., indicators and specific keys). (2) Exploitation is taking full advantage of success in battle and following up initial gains. (3) Exploitation is an offensive operation that usually follows a successful attack and is designed to disorganize the enemy in depth. *See also:* Intelligence Cycle, Pursuit, Signals Intelligence.

References

Department of Defense, Defense Intelligence College. *Glossary of Intelligence Terms and Definitions.* Washington, DC: DIC, 1987.

Department of Defense, Joint Chiefs of Staff. *Department of Defense Dictionary of Military and Related Terms.* Washington, DC: GPO, 1986.

Department of Defense, U.S. Army. *Low Intensity Conflict.* Field Manual FM 100-20. Washington, DC: Headquarters, Department of the Army, 1981.

U.S. Congress. Senate. *Final Report of the Senate Select Committee to Study Government Operations With Respect to Intelligence Activities. Report 94-755. Book I, Foreign and Military Intelligence* (Church Committee Report). Washington, DC: GPO, 1976.

—**EXPLOSION.** (1) An explosion is a chemical reaction of any chemical compound or mechanical mixture that, when initiated, undergoes a very rapid combustion or decomposition, thereby releasing large volumes of highly heated gases that exert pressure on the surrounding medium. (2) An explosion is a mechanical reaction in which failure of the container causes the sudden release of pressure from within a pressure vessel (e.g., the pressure rupture of a steam boiler). Depending on the rate of energy release, an explosion can be categorized as a deflagration, a detonation, or a pressure rupture.

References

Department of Defense, U.S. Army. *Ammunition and Explosives Safety Standards.* Army Regulation AR 385-64. Washington, DC: Headquarters, Department of the Army, 1987.

—**EXPLOSIVE CHARGE** is the explosive used in firing a gun (whether it is a propelling charge that throws the projectile or a bursting charge that breaks the casing of a projectile) to produce demolition, fragmentation, or chemical action.

References

Department of Defense, Joint Chiefs of Staff. *Department of Defense Dictionary of Military and Related Terms.* Washington, DC: GPO, 1986.

—**EXPLOSIVE FILLED MINE**, in mine warfare, is a mine containing an explosive charge but not necessarily the firing train that is needed to detonate it. *See also:* Exercise Filled Mine, Fitted Mine.

References

Department of Defense, Joint Chiefs of Staff. *Department of Defense Dictionary of Military and Related Terms.* Washington, DC: GPO, 1986.

—**EXPLOSIVE ORDNANCE** are all the munitions containing explosives, nuclear fission or fusion materials, and biological and chemical agents. This includes bombs and warheads; guided and ballistic missiles; artillery, mortar, rocket and small arms ammunition; all mines, torpedoes, and depth charges; demolition charges; pyrotechnics; clusters and dispensers; cartridge and propellent actuated devices; electro-explosive devices; clandestine and improvised explosive devices; and all similar or related items or components that are explosive in nature.

References

Department of Defense, Joint Chiefs of Staff. *Department of Defense Dictionary of Military and Related Terms.* Washington, DC: GPO, 1986.

—**EXPLOSIVE ORDNANCE DISPOSAL (EOD)** is the detection, identification, field evaluation, rendering-safe, recovery, and final disposal of unexploded explosive ordnance. It may also include the rendering safe and/or disposal of explosive ordnance that has become hazardous by damage or deterioration when the disposal of such ordnance is beyond the capabilities of personnel normally assigned the responsibility for routine disposal. *See also:* Explosive Ordnance Disposal Incident, Explosive Ordnance Disposal Procedures, Explosive Ordnance Disposal Unit.

References

Department of Defense, Joint Chiefs of Staff. *Department of Defense Dictionary of Military and Related Terms.* Washington, DC: GPO, 1986.

—**EXPLOSIVE ORDNANCE DISPOSAL (EOD) INCIDENT** is the suspected or detected presence of unexploded explosive ordnance, or damaged explosive ordnance, that constitutes a hazard to operations, installations, personnel, or material. Not included in this definition are the accidental arming or other conditions that develop during the manufacture of high explosive material, technical service assembly operations, or the laying of mines or demolition charges.

References
Department of Defense, Joint Chiefs of Staff. *Department of Defense Dictionary of Military and Related Terms*. Washington, DC: GPO, 1986.

—**EXPLOSIVE ORDNANCE DISPOSAL (EOD) PROCEDURES** are the particular courses or modes of action that are taken by explosive ordnance disposal personnel for access to, diagnosis, rendering safe, recovery, and final disposal of explosive ordnance or any hazardous material that is associated with an explosive ordnance disposal incident. There are five types of procedures.

- **Access procedures** are actions taken to locate exactly, and to gain access to, unexploded explosive ordnance.
- **Diagnostic procedures** are actions taken to identify and evaluate unexploded explosive ordnance.
- **Render safe procedures** are procedures involving special explosive ordnance disposal methods and tools that prevent an unacceptable detonation by interrupting functions or separating essential components of unexploded explosive ordnance.
- **Recovery procedures** are actions taken to recover unexploded explosive ordnance.
- **Final disposal procedures** are actions that involve the final disposal of explosive ordnance and may include demolition or burning in place, removal to a disposal area, or other appropriate means.

References
Department of Defense, Joint Chiefs of Staff. *Department of Defense Dictionary of Military and Related Terms*. Washington, DC: GPO, 1986.

—**EXPLOSIVE ORDNANCE DISPOSAL (EOD) UNIT** is composed of personnel with special training and equipment who render explosive ordnance (e.g., bombs, mines, projectiles, and booby traps) safe, make intelligence reports on such ordnance, and supervise the ordnance's safe removal of the same.

References
Department of Defense, Joint Chiefs of Staff. *Department of Defense Dictionary of Military and Related Terms*. Washington, DC: GPO, 1986.

—**EXPLOSIVE ORDNANCE RECONNAISSANCE** involves investigating, detecting, locating, marking, initially identifying, and reporting suspected unexploded explosive ordnance by explosive ordnance reconnaissance agents in order to determine what action needs to be taken to deactivate the ordnance.

References
Department of Defense, Joint Chiefs of Staff. *Department of Defense Dictionary of Military and Related Terms*. Washington, DC: GPO, 1986.

—**EXPLOSIVES FACILITY** is any structure or location containing ammunition and explosives. Combat aircraft parking areas or ammunition and explosives aircraft cargo areas are not included in this term.

References
Department of Defense, U.S. Army. *Ammunition and Explosives Safety Standards*. Army Regulation AR 385-64. Washington, DC: Headquarters, Department of the Army, 1987.

—**EXPLOSIVE TRAIN** is a succession of initiating and igniting elements that are arranged to cause a charge to function.

References
Department of Defense, Joint Chiefs of Staff. *Department of Defense Dictionary of Military and Related Terms*. Washington, DC: GPO, 1986.

—**EXPOSED AREA** is a geographic area in danger of being overrun by hostile forces, or where the local political or military situation poses a real threat to the security of sensitive compartmented information located there or the sensitive compartmented activities conducted there.

References
Department of Defense, U.S. Army. *Dictionary of United States Army Terms*. Army Regulation AR 310-25. Washington, DC: Headquarters, Department of the Army, 1986.

—**EXPOSED SITE (ES)** is a location exposed to the potential hazardous effects (e.g., blast, fragments, debris, and heat flux) from an explosion at a potential explosion site (PES). The distance to a PES and the level of protection required for an ES determine the quantity of ammunition or explosives permitted in a PES.

References
Department of Defense, U.S. Army. *Ammunition and Explosives Safety Standards.* Army Regulation AR 385-64. Washington, DC: Headquarters, Department of the Army, 1987.

—**EXPOSURE DOSE** is a measurement of radiation in relation to its ability to produce ionization. The unit of measurement of the exposure dose is the roentgen. *See also:* Nuclear Warfare.

References
Department of Defense, Joint Chiefs of Staff. *Department of Defense Dictionary of Military and Related Terms.* Washington, DC: GPO, 1986.

—**EXTENDED DEFENSE** is a form of position defense employed on a wide front. It is characterized by limited mutual support, great depth of position, and withholding of a strong reserve.

References
Department of Defense, U.S. Army. *Dictionary of United States Army Terms.* Army Regulation AR 310-25. Washington, DC: Headquarters, Department of the Army, 1986.

—**EXTENDED EFFECT ANTIPERSONNEL MINE** is a mine designed to kill or incapacitate personnel without cover within a radius of several meters from the mine. *See also:* Mine Warfare.

References
Department of Defense, U.S. Army. *Mine/ Countermine Operations at the Company Level.* Field Manual FM 20-32. Washington, DC: Headquarters, Department of the Army, 1976.

—**EXTENSION** (ARMY AVIATION) is maneuver by a fighter to reverse direction without a significant gain in altitude.

References
Department of Defense, U.S. Army. *Air-to-Air Combat.* Field Manual FM 1-107. Washington, DC: Headquarters, Department of the Army, 1984.

—**EXTENSION COURSE** is a training or instruction developed by a service school as part of the program but conducted in locations other than service schools or Army training centers.

References
Department of Defense, U.S. Army. *Individual Military Education and Training.* Army Regulation AR 350-1. Washington, DC: Headquarters, Department of the Army, 1987.

—**EXTENSION TRAINING MATERIALS** are the items or instruction used to train personnel to do tasks that cannot be learned by using only the technical manual as a job aid. This includes training extension courses, graphic training aids, training devices, and resident training materials exported to units.

References
Department of Defense, U.S. Army. *Individual Military Education and Training.* Army Regulation AR 350-1. Washington, DC: Headquarters, Department of the Army, 1987.

—**EXTENSION TRAINING MATERIALS (ETM) CATALOGS** list ETM that support training units (e.g., graphic training aids, training devices, lessons, field manuals, motion pictures, and videotapes). *See also:* Extension Training Materials.

References
Department of Defense, U.S. Army. *Unit Training Management.* Field Manual FM 25-2. Washington, DC: Headquarters, Department of the Army, 1984.

—**EXTENT OF DAMAGE** is the visible plan area of damage to a target element, and is usually expressed in units of 1,000 square feet, in a detailed damage analysis, or in an approximate percentage in immediate-type damage assessment reports (e.g., 50 percent structural damage).

References
Department of Defense, Joint Chiefs of Staff. *Department of Defense Dictionary of Military and Related Terms.* Washington, DC: GPO, 1986.

—**EXTERIOR GUARDS** include lookouts, listening posts, outposts, specifically designated patrols and other guards in combat zones, and guards outside the limits of a military installation. Exterior guards perform their duties as prescribed by special orders and instructions. *See also:* Interior Guard.

References
Department of Defense, U.S. Army. *Guard Duty.* Field Manual FM 22-6. Washington, DC: Headquarters, Department of the Army, 1971.

—**EXTERIOR LINES.** A force is said to be operating on exterior lines when its operations converge on the enemy. Successful operations on exterior lines require a stronger force, but in return offer the opportunity to encircle and annihilate a weaker opponent. The partial encirclement and destruction of German armies in the Argentan pocket following the Allied breakout in Normandy resulted from effective operations on exterior lines. *See also:* Interior Lines.

References
Department of Defense, U.S. Army. *Operations.* Field Manual FM 100-5. Washington, DC: Headquarters, Department of the Army, 1986.

—**EXTERNAL REINFORCING FORCE** is a reinforcing force principally stationed in peacetime outside its major NATO command area of operations.

References
Department of Defense, Joint Chiefs of Staff. *Department of Defense Dictionary of Military and Related Terms.* Washington, DC: GPO, 1986.

—**EXTRACTION ZONE (EZ)** is a specified ground area upon which equipment or supplies are delivered by means of a jointly approved extraction technique from an aircraft in flight in close proximity to the ground.

References
Department of Defense, Joint Chiefs of Staff. *Department of Defense Dictionary of Military and Related Terms.* Washington, DC: GPO, 1986.

Department of Defense, U.S. Army. *USA/USAF Doctrine for Joint Airborne and Tactical Airlift Operations.* Field Manual FM 100-27. Washington, DC: Headquarters, Department of the Army, 1985.

—**EXTRA REGIMENTAL ASSIGNMENT** is assigned duty outside of a soldier's regiment that is consistent with regimental affiliation. Assignments "consistent with regimental affiliation" are assignments in table of distribution and allowance units, above battalion in the soldier's branch, or to any unit position in another branch. *See also:* Regimental Affiliation.

References
Department of Defense, U.S. Army. *Officer Assignment Policies, Details and Transfers.* Army Regulation AR 614-100. Washington, DC: Headquarters, Department of the Army, 1984.

—**EXTREME COMMUNITY HARDSHIP** is a situation that may, because a reservist is mobilized, have a substantially adverse effect on the health, safety, or welfare of the community. Any request for a determination of such hardship shall be made by the reservist and must be supported by documentation as required by the Secretary of the Army.

References
Department of Defense, U.S. Army. *Dictionary of United States Army Terms.* Army Regulation AR 310-25. Washington, DC: Headquarters, Department of the Army, 1986.

—**EXTREME PERSONAL HARDSHIP** is an adverse impact on a reservist's dependents resulting from his mobilization. Any request for a determination of such hardship shall be made by the reservist and must be supported by documentation as required by the Secretary of the Army. *See also:* Extreme Community Hardship.

References
Department of Defense, U.S. Army. *Dictionary of United States Army Terms.* Army Regulation AR 310-25. Washington, DC: Headquarters, Department of the Army, 1986.

—**EYES LEFT (RIGHT)** is a command given to troops in march formation to turn their heads and eyes to the left (right). The movement constitutes a salute to the reviewing party.

References
Department of Defense, U.S. Army. *Dictionary of United States Army Terms.* Army Regulation AR 310-25. Washington, DC: Headquarters, Department of the Army, 1986.

—**FABRICATION,** the making of a part locally, is done when a critical part is not available.

References

Department of Defense, U.S. Army. *Organizational Maintenance Operations.* Field Manual FM 29-2. Washington, DC: Headquarters, Department of the Army, 1984.

—**FACILITY.** (1) A facility is a real property entity that consists of one or more of the following: a building, a utility system, pavement, and underlying land. (2) A facility is any part of or adjunct to a physical plant, or any item of equipment that is an operating entity or that contributes or can contribute to the execution of a function by providing a specific type of physical assistance. *See also:* Installation.

References

Department of Defense, Joint Chiefs of Staff. *Department of Defense Dictionary of Military and Related Terms.* Washington, DC: GPO, 1986.

Department of Defense, U.S. Army. *Dictionary of United States Army Terms.* Army Regulation AR 310-25. Washington, DC: Headquarters, Department of the Army, 1986.

—**FADED** (ARMY AVIATION) refers to a contact that has disappeared from radar. *See also:* Bogey.

References

Department of Defense, U.S. Army. *Air-to-Air Combat.* Field Manual FM 1-107. Washington, DC: Headquarters, Department of the Army, 1984.

—**FAILED SELECTION FOR PROMOTION** is an officer below the grade of colonel who was eligible for promotion but was not promoted. He is in or above the promotion zone, was considered for promotion, and was not recommended for promotion by a Department of the Army promotion selection board, or an Army special selection board considering an officer who was not considered by an appropriate Department of the Army selection board.

References

Department of Defense, U.S. Army. *Promotion of Officers on Active Duty.* Army Regulation AR 624-100. Washington, DC: Headquarters, Department of the Army, 1984.

—**FAIR WEAR AND TEAR** is the loss or impairment of the appearance, effectiveness, worth, or utility of an item that has occurred solely because of the normal and customary use of the item for its intended purpose.

References

Department of Defense, U.S. Army. *Commander's Handbook for Property Accountability at the Unit Level.* Field Manual FM 10-14-1. Washington, DC: Headquarters, Department of the Army, 1984.

—**FALLOUT.** (1) Fallout is the precipitation to the earth of radioactive particulate matter from a nuclear cloud. The term is also applied to the particulate matter itself. (2) Fallout is to leave a place in formation or to leave one's position in a formation but remain in the immediate vicinity. (3) Fallout is a command permitting soldiers to leave their places in ranks but keeping them in the immediate vicinity. *See also:* Nuclear Warfare.

References

Department of Defense, Joint Chiefs of Staff. *Department of Defense Dictionary of Military and Related Terms.* Washington, DC: GPO, 1986.

Department of Defense, U.S. Army. *Dictionary of United States Army Terms.* Army Regulation AR 310-25. Washington, DC: Headquarters, Department of the Army, 1986.

—**FALLOUT CONTOURS** are lines that join points having the same radiation intensity, thereby defining a fallout pattern. The radiation is represented in terms of roentgens per hour. *See also:* Fallout, Nuclear Warfare.

References

Department of Defense, U.S. Army. *NBC Operations.* Field Manual FM 3-100. Washington, DC: Headquarters, Department of the Army, 1985.

—**FALLOUT PATTERN** is the distribution of fallout as portrayed by fallout contours. *See also:* Fallout, Nuclear Warfare.

References

Department of Defense, U.S. Army. *NBC Operations.* Field Manual FM 3-100. Washington, DC: Headquarters, Department of the Army, 1985.

—**FALLOUT PREDICTION** is an estimate of the location and intensity of militarily significant quantities of radioactive fallout. It is made before and immediately after a nuclear detonation. *See also:* Fallout, nuclear warfare.

References

Department of Defense, U.S. Army. *NBC Operations.* Field Manual FM 3-100. Washington, DC: Headquarters, Department of the Army, 1985.

—**FALLOUT WINDS** are tropospheric winds that carry radioactive fallout materials. These winds are observed by standard winds-aloft observation techniques. *See also:* Nuclear Warfare.

References

Department of Defense, U.S. Army. *NBC Operations.* Field Manual FM 3-100. Washington, DC: Headquarters, Department of the Army, 1985.

—**FAN CAMERA PHOTOGRAPHY,** in photoreconnaissance, is photography that is taken simultaneously by an assembly of three or more cameras, systematically installed at fixed angles relative to each other so that they provide wide lateral coverage with overlapping images. *See also:* Aerial Reconnaissance.

References

Von Hoene, John P. A. *Intelligence User's Guide.* Washington, DC: DIA, 1983.

—**FAR AMBUSH** is an ambush in which the attack force does not assault into the killing zone. This may be appropriate in open terrain offering good fields of fire, or when attack is by fire only (e.g., an armor ambush). *See also:* Ambush.

References

Department of Defense, U.S. Army. *The Rifle Squads (Mechanized and Light Infantry).* Training Circular TC 7-1. Washington, DC: Headquarters, Department of the Army, 1976.

—**FEINT.** (1) A feint is a show of force intended to mislead the enemy. It normally consists of a shallow, limited objective attack executed by a small portion of the total force. Its purpose is to draw the enemy's attention and, if possible, forces away from the division's main attack. Units conducting a feint deploy and fight as though their operation is the main effort. If the force penetrates the enemy defensive system, the commander conducting the feint does not exploit the opportunity unless he is directed to do so. (2) A feint is to make a pretended blow or attack. (3) In riverine crossing operations, a feint is a show of force by a small proportion of the assault force with a limited objective attack on the far side of the river that is intended to deceive the enemy as to the exact location of the actual crossing sites. *See also:* Demonstration, Ruses.

References

Department of Defense, U.S. Army. *Armored and Mechanized Division Operations.* Field Manual FM 71-100. Washington, DC: Headquarters, Department of the Army, 1978.

———. *Dictionary of United States Army Terms.* Army Regulation AR 310-25. Washington, DC: Headquarters, Department of the Army, 1986.

———. *Engineer Combat Operations.* Field Manual FM 5-100. Washington, DC: Headquarters, Department of the Army, 1984.

———. *Operational Terms and Symbols.* Field Manual FM 101-5-1. Washington, DC: Headquarters, Department of the Army, 1985.

—**FIELD ARMY.** Field armies may be formed by theater Army commanders in coordination with the commanders in chief of the Unified Commands to control and direct the operations of assigned corps. They will normally be constituted from existing army assets and structured to meet specific operational requirements. In joint and combined operations, the subordinate units of field armies may include units of other services or of allied forces. When the field army is the largest land formation in a theater of war, its commander may serve as the land component commander, and he may design and direct the land campaign for the entire theater.

Field armies exercise major operational responsibilities. When subordinated to an army group, they become the primary units of operational maneuver, conducting the decisive operations of the land campaign. When operating independently or as the land component of a joint force, field armies may be charged with planning and conducting the land campaign in a theater of war or a theater of operations. In either case, field army commanders employ subordinate corps to concentrate combat power, to accept or decline battle, and to exploit the outcome of tactical actions.

Field armies and equivalent organizations are primarily operational headquarters. They may establish priorities for combat service support among their subordinate forces, but combat service support is normally provided by a theater army, service component command, or national support organization. In contingency operations, the field army may assume responsibility for the logistic support of army forces in the field. In such an operation, it would require the assignment of support organizations from the theater army or Unified Command.

References

Department of Defense, U.S. Army. *Low Intensity Conflict*. Field Manual FM 100-20. Washington, DC: Headquarters, Department of the Army, 1981.

—**FIELD ARTILLERY.** (1) Field artillery is a basic branch and arm of the Army. The branch name identifies personnel and units that use cannons, rockets, and missile systems, with target acquisition means to assist in land combat operations. (2) Field artillery are artillery weapons that are sufficiently mobile to accompany and support infantry, mechanized, armored, airborne, and airmobile units in the field. The primary mission is to engage ground targets with nuclear or nonnuclear fire. It is the principal fire support element in fire and maneuver, and not only provides conventional, nuclear, and chemical fires with cannon, rocket, and missile systems, but also integrates all means of fire support available to the commander. It is capable of suppressing enemy direct fire forces, attacking enemy artillery and mortars, and delivering scatterable mines to isolate and interdict enemy forces or to protect friendly operations. It contributes to deep operations by delaying or disrupting enemy forces in depth and by suppressing enemy air defense systems to facilitate Army and Air Force air operations. The artillery can also screen operations with smoke or illuminate the battlefield. Field artillery cannons are classified according to caliber as: light (120-mm or less); medium (121-160-mm); heavy (161-210-mm); or very heavy (greater than 210-mm). *See also:* Direct Support Artillery, General Support Artillery.

References

Department of Defense, Joint Chiefs of Staff. *Department of Defense Dictionary of Military and Related Terms*. Washington, DC: GPO, 1986.

Department of Defense, U.S. Army. *Dictionary of United States Army Terms*. Army Regulation AR 310-25. Washington, DC: Headquarters, Department of the Army, 1986.

———. *Operations*. Field Manual FM 100-5. Washington, DC: Headquarters, Department of the Army, 1986.

—**FIELD ARTILLERY AMMUNITION SUPPORT VEHICLE (FAASV),** designated M992, is designed to provide ballistic protection for am-

munition, and powered ammunition handling, for the Army's M109 and M110 self-propelled field artillery battalions in Europe. The FAASV is equipped with hydraulically powered ammunition handling equipment consisting of an X-Y stacker and conveyor to allow transfer of ammunition to the supported howitzer. An armored door on the FAASV swings up to provide overhead protection during ammunition transfer to the howitzer. FAASV shares a common chassis with the M109A2 howitzer, and retains the ballistic protection, cross country mobility, and road speed of that vehicle.

References

Weapons Systems: U.S. Army, Navy and Air Force Directory, 1986-1988. Washington, DC: DCP, 1986.

—**FIELD ARTILLERY CANNON CALIBRATION** is the comparison of the muzzle velocity of a given artillery piece with an accepted standard of performance. That standard may be accepted arbitrarily from the performance of a group of weapons being calibrated together, as in comparative calibration, or it may be the standard defined in the firing tables, as in absolute calibration.

References

Department of Defense, U.S. Army. *Dictionary of United States Army Terms*. Army Regulation AR 310-25. Washington, DC: Headquarters, Department of the Army, 1986.

—**FIELD ARTILLERY OBSERVER** is a person who watches the effects of artillery fire, adjusts the center of impact of that fire onto a target, and reports the results to the firing agency. *See also:* Spotter.

References

Department of Defense, Joint Chiefs of Staff. *Department of Defense Dictionary of Military and Related Terms*. Washington, DC: GPO, 1986.

—**FIELD ARTILLERY SURVEY** is a survey consisting of the topographic operations necessary to construct a firing chart from unobserved fires. The main object of the survey is to determine, with sufficient exactness, the relative locations of pieces and targets both horizontally and vertically.

References

Department of Defense, U.S. Army. *Dictionary of United States Army Terms*. Army Regulation AR 310-25. Washington, DC: Headquarters, Department of the Army, 1986.

—**FIELD ARTILLERY TACTICAL OPERATIONS CENTER** is a facility within which are merged targeting, operations, and fire control for field artillery support operations. *See also:* Field Artillery Observer, Field Artillery Survey, General Staff.

References

Department of Defense, U.S. Army. *Dictionary of United States Army Terms.* Army Regulation AR 310-25. Washington, DC: Headquarters, Department of the Army, 1986.

————. *Fire Support in Combined Arms Operations.* Field Manual FM 6-20. Washington, DC: Headquarters, Department of the Army, 1983.

—**FIELD (TROOP) DEMONSTRATION** is a form of display used widely in tactical training to demonstrate concepts, operations, and procedures.

References

Department of Defense, U.S. Army. *How to Prepare and Conduct Military Training.* Field Manual FM 21-6. Washington, DC: Headquarters, Department of the Army, 1985.

—**FIELD EXERCISE (FX)** is an exercise conducted in the field under simulated combat conditions in which the troops and armament of one side are actually present while those of the other side may be imaginary, or partially or fully represented by a second force. *See also:* Command Post Exercise.

References

Department of Defense, U.S. Army. *How to Prepare and Conduct Military Training.* Field Manual FM 21-6. Washington, DC: Headquarters, Department of the Army, 1985.

————. *Operational Terms and Symbols.* Field Manual FM 101-5-1. Washington, DC: Headquarters, Department of the Army, 1985.

—**FIELD FORTIFICATIONS** are temporary emplacements or shelters that are reasonably easy to construct by units with minor engineer supervisory and equipment participation.

References

Department of Defense, Joint Chiefs of Staff. *Department of Defense Dictionary of Military and Related Terms.* Washington, DC: GPO, 1986.

—**FIELD GRADE** is a classification of officers ranking above a captain and below a brigadier general. Field grade includes colonels, lieutenant colonels, and majors. *See also:* Company Grade.

References

Department of Defense, U.S. Army. *Dictionary of United States Army Terms.* Army Regulation AR 310-25. Washington, DC: Headquarters, Department of the Army, 1986.

—**FIELD HOSPITAL** is a nonfixed medical treatment facility. *See also:* Hospital.

References

Department of Defense, U.S. Army. *Dictionary of United States Army Terms.* Army Regulation AR 310-25. Washington, DC: Headquarters, Department of the Army, 1986.

—**FIELD KITCHEN** is a mobile or temporary kitchen in the field or at a temporary installation.

References

Department of Defense, U.S. Army. *Dictionary of United States Army Terms.* Army Regulation AR 310-25. Washington, DC: Headquarters, Department of the Army, 1986.

—**FIELD MANUALS (FMs)**, other than "how to fight" manuals, are written by the Department of the Army to cover specific subjects that are essential to successful operations. They contain instructional, informational, and reference material relative to military training and operations. They are the primary means of promulgating military doctrine, tactics, and techniques. *See also:* Field Service Regulations, Technical Manual.

References

Department of Defense, U.S. Army. *Dictionary of United States Army Terms.* Army Regulation AR 310-25. Washington, DC: Headquarters, Department of the Army, 1986.

————. *The Rifle Squads (Mechanized and Light Infantry).* Training Circular TC 7-1. Washington, DC: Headquarters, Department of the Army, 1976.

—**FIELD OF FIRE** is the area that a weapon or group of weapons may effectively cover with fire from a given position.

References

Department of Defense, U.S. Army. *Air Defense Artillery Deployment: Chaparral/Vulcan/Stinger.* Field Manual FM 44-3. Washington, DC: Headquarters, Department of the Army, 1984.

———. *Operational Terms and Symbols.* Field Manual FM 101-5-1. Washington, DC: Headquarters, Department of the Army, 1985.

—**FIELD OF VISION** is the total solid angle of sight available to a gunner from his normal position.

References

Department of Defense, Joint Chiefs of Staff. *Department of Defense Dictionary of Military and Related Terms.* Washington, DC: GPO, 1986.

—**FIELD OFFICER OF THE DAY** is a field grade officer who is detailed as the personal representative of the commanding officer. During his tour of duty, he is responsible to the commanding officer for the security of the installation or activity and for other duties as may be assigned, depending on the local directives.

References

Department of Defense, U.S. Army. *Guard Duty.* Field Manual FM 22-6. Washington, DC: Headquarters, Department of the Army, 1971.

—**FIELD PRESS CENSORSHIP** is the security review of news material subject to the jurisdiction of the Armed Forces of the United States, including all information or material intended for dissemination to the public. *See also:* Military Censorship.

References

Department of Defense, Joint Chiefs of Staff. *Department of Defense Dictionary of Military and Related Terms.* Washington, DC: GPO, 1986.

—**FIELD PROMOTION AUTHORITY** is a commander who may promote an officer to the grade of First Lieutenant or temporary CW2.

References

Department of Defense, U.S. Army. *Promotion of Officers on Active Duty.* Army Regulation AR 624-100. Washington, DC: Headquarters, Department of the Army, 1984.

—**FIELD RATION** is food issued, not money for food issued to, and authorized for, troops in the field. The field ration includes the type A ration, type B ration, and packaged operational rations. *See also:* Field Ration, Type A, Rations.

References

Department of Defense, U.S. Army. *Dictionary of United States Army Terms.* Army Regulation AR 310-25. Washington, DC: Headquarters, Department of the Army, 1986.

—**FIELD RATION, TYPE A** is made up of nonperishable and perishable items and is not used in a theater until the theater commander determines that the logistics system can support a perishable ration and the Department of the Army approves its use. Usually, this occurs only when the situation requires the presence of U.S. forces for more than six months. Even when perishable rations are available, the tactical situation in parts of the theater may still require the use of nonperishable and operational rations.

References

Department of Defense, U.S. Army. *Support Operations: Echelons Above Corps.* Field Manual FM 100-16. Washington, DC: Headquarters, Department of the Army, 1986.

—**FIELD SERVICE REGULATIONS** are the 100-series of Department of the Army field manuals that are published to present the official fundamental doctrines and broad policies for use as a basis for conducting operations by division and larger unit commanders and staffs. *See also:* Field Manual, Technical Manuals.

References

Department of Defense, U.S. Army. *Dictionary of United States Army Terms.* Army Regulation AR 310-25. Washington, DC: Headquarters, Department of the Army, 1986.

—**FIELD SERVICES** include graves registration; airdrop; clothing exchange and bath; laundry and renovation; bakery services; and salvage. Because some of these services are provided only during wartime, a large portion of the Army's field services are provided by reserve component units that are brought into the theater. Field services are required for health, sanitation, welfare, and morale purposes. Provisions must be made at the outset for their performance by Army or other resources. *See also:* Field Services for the Division.

References

Department of Defense, U.S. Army. *Combat Service Support Operations-Theater.* Field Manual FM. 63-4. Washington, DC: Headquarters, Department of the Army, 1984.

—**FIELD SERVICES FOR THE DIVISION** are the logistics support functions that include graves registration, airdrop, clothing exchange and bath, laundry and renovation, bread baking, and salvage.

References
Department of Defense, U.S. Army. *Combat Service Support Operations-Theater*. Field Manual FM 63-4. Washington, DC: Headquarters, Department of the Army, 1984.

—**FIELD TRAIN** is a unit train not required for immediate support of combat elements. Field trains may include kitchen and baggage trains, administrative trains, heavy maintenance, water, and the ammunition, fuel, and lubricants trucks that are not required for direct support of troops in the immediate engagement. They are located rearward to prevent interference with the tactical operation. *See also:* Train.

References
Department of Defense, U.S. Army. *Air Defense Artillery Deployment: Chaparral/Vulcan/Stinger*. Field Manual FM 44- 3. Washington, DC: Headquarters, Department of the Army, 1984.

———. *Dictionary of United States Army Terms*. Army Regulation AR 310-25. Washington, DC: Headquarters, Department of the Army, 1986.

———. *Operational Terms and Symbols*. Field Manual FM 101-5-1. Washington, DC: Headquarters, Department of the Army, 1985.

—**FIELD TRAINING EXERCISE (FTX)** is an exercise conducted in the field under simulated wartime conditions. High-cost, high-overhead exercises, they require command and control of all echelons in battle functions—intelligence, combat support, combat service support, maneuver, and communications—against an actual or simulated opposing force. They are conducted in a realistic environment using the full combined arms teams. They provide both intersystems and intrasystems training to fight air-land battles, using all unit personnel and equipment. FTXs must include all attached units.

FTXs provide the most realistic environment of all training exercises. They allow participants to appreciate real time and distance factors, involve several tactical situations in which one or more units must participate, and may require movement and communications over long distances. *See also:* Command Post Exercise (CPX).

References
Department of Defense, U.S. Army. *Army Forces Training*. Army Regulation AR 350-41. Washington, DC: Headquarters, Department of the Army, 1986.

———. *How to Conduct Training Exercises*. Field Manual FM 25-4. Washington, DC: Headquarters, Department of the Army, 1984.

—**FIELD TYPE** is a term that describes equipment, troops, or units used primarily to carry out a combat mission.

References
Department of Defense, U.S. Army. *Dictionary of United States Army Terms*. Army Regulation AR 310-25. Washington, DC: Headquarters, Department of the Army, 1986.

—**FIELD UNIFORMS** are utility uniforms and organizational uniforms (excluding the hospital duty and food service uniforms) that are worn in a field, training, or combat environments. *See also:* Service Uniform.

References
Department of Defense, U.S. Army. *Wear and Appearance of Army Uniforms and Insignia*. Army Regulation AR 670-1. Washington, DC: Headquarters, Department of the Army, 1986.

—**FIGHTER ENGAGEMENT ZONE (FEZ)** is normally an area where no effective surface-to-air capability is deployed.

References
Department of Defense, U.S. Army. *Patriot Battalion Operations*. Field Manual FM 44-15. Washington, DC: Headquarters, Department of the Army, 1984.

—**FIGHTER LIAISON OFFICER (FLO)** is a member of the tactical air control party who meets all of the prerequisites of a forward air controller and is qualified to control air strikes. He advises the air liaison officer and ground commander's staff on the capabilities, limitations, and use of close air support resources. He also assists and advises in the development of close air support requests and coordinates close air support missions with the fire support element. *See also:* Tactical Air Control Party.

References
Department of Defense, U.S. Army. *Operational Terms and Symbols*. Field Manual FM 101-5-1. Washington, DC: Headquarters, Department of the Army, 1985.

—**FIGHTING LOAD** consists of items of individual clothing, equipment, and weapons.

References
Department of Defense, Joint Chiefs of Staff. *Department of Defense Dictionary of Military and Related Terms*. Washington, DC: GPO, 1986.

—**FIGHTING POSITION** is a place on the battle-field from which troops engage the enemy with direct and indirect fire weapons. The positions provide necessary protection for personnel, yet allow for fields of fire and maneuver.

References

Department of Defense, U.S. Army. *Survivability.* Field Manual FM 5-103. Washington, DC: Headquarters, Department of the Army, 1985.

—**FILE** is a column that has a front of one element. *See also:* Column, Element.

References

Department of Defense, U.S. Army. *Drills and Ceremonies.* Field Manual FM 22-5. Washington, DC: Headquarters, Department of the Army, 1986.

—**FILLER** is a substance carried in an ammunition container (e.g., a projectile, mine, bomb, or grenade). A filler may be an explosive, a chemical, or an inert substance.

References

Department of Defense, Joint Chiefs of Staff. *Department of Defense Dictionary of Military and Related Terms.* Washington, DC: GPO, 1986.

—**FILLER PERSONNEL** are individuals of suitable grade and skill whose presence is initially required to bring a unit or organization to its authorized strength.

References

Department of Defense, Joint Chiefs of Staff. *Department of Defense Dictionary of Military and Related Terms.* Washington, DC: GPO, 1986.

—**FINAL COORDINATION LINE (FCL)** is a phase line often used by battalions and companies to coordinate lifting and shifting of support fire and/or to coordinate the deployment of attacking units before an assault. The line should be recognizable on the ground and is not a fire support coordination measure.

References

Department of Defense, U.S. Army. *The Infantry Rifle Company (Infantry, Airborne, Air Assault, Ranger).* Field Manual FM 7-10. Washington, DC: Headquarters, Department of the Army, 1982.

———. *Operational Terms and Symbols.* Field Manual FM 101-5-1. Washington, DC: Headquarters, Department of the Army, 1985.

—**FINAL OR INTERMEDIATE DISPOSITIONS** are returns to duty, died in hospital, and disability discharge (continental U.S. level only). An intermediate disposition is a patient evacuation to the next level of hospitalization (or in some cases, another hospital at the same level). *See also:* Medical Treatment.

References

Department of Defense, U.S. Army. *Planning for Health Service Support.* Field Manual FM 8-55. Washington, DC: Headquarters, Department of the Army, 1985.

—**FINAL PLAN** is a plan, of which drafts have been coordinated and approved, that has been signed by or on behalf of a competent authority. *See also:* Operation Plan.

References

Department of Defense, Joint Chiefs of Staff. *Department of Defense Dictionary of Military and Related Terms.* Washington, DC: GPO, 1986.

—**FINAL PROTECTIVE FIRE (FPF)** is an immediately available preplanned barrier of direct and indirect fire designed to provide close protection to friendly positions and installations by impeding enemy movement into defensive areas.

References

Department of Defense, U.S. Army. *Operational Terms and Symbols.* Field Manual FM 101-5-1. Washington, DC: Headquarters, Department of the Army, 1985.

—**FINAL PROTECTIVE LINE (FPL)** is a line of grazing fire across the unit's front and where an enemy assault is to be checked by interlocking fire from all available weapons. *See also:* Final Protective Fire.

References

Department of Defense, U.S. Army. *Dictionary of United States Army Terms.* Army Regulation AR 310-25. Washington, DC: Headquarters, Department of the Army, 1986.

———. *Operational Terms and Symbols.* Field Manual FM 101-5-1. Washington, DC: Headquarters, Department of the Army, 1985.

———. *The Rifle Squads (Mechanized and Light Infantry).* Training Circular TC 7-1. Washington, DC: Headquarters, Department of the Army, 1976.

—**FINANCE OFFICER** is the accountable disbursing officer for a tactical organization or other organization not operating under the integrated accounting system.

References

Department of Defense, U.S. Army. *Dictionary of United States Army Terms.* Army Regulation AR 310-25. Washington, DC: Headquarters, Department of the Army, 1986.

—**FINANCIAL PROPERTY ACCOUNTING** is the establishment and maintenance of property accounts in monetary terms, and the rendition of property reports in monetary terms.

References

Department of Defense, Joint Chiefs of Staff. *Department of Defense Dictionary of Military and Related Terms.* Washington, DC: GPO, 1986.

—**FIRE.** (1) Fire is the command that is given to discharge a weapon. (2) To fire is to detonate the main explosive charge by means of a firing system. *See also:* Barrage Fire, Call Fire, Close Supporting Fire, Counterfire, Counter-Preparation Fire, Covering Fire, Deep Supporting Fire, Destruction Fire, Distributed Fire, Grazing Fire, Harassing Fire, Indirect Fire, Interdiction Fire, Neutralization Fire, Observed Fire, Preparation Fire, Radar Fire, Registration Fire, Scheduled Fire, Supporting Fire, Suppressive Fire, Unobserved Fire, Zone Fire.

References

Department of Defense, Joint Chiefs of Staff. *Department of Defense Dictionary of Military and Related Terms.* Washington, DC: GPO, 1986.

—**FIRE AND MANEUVER** is a tactical technique, usually an extension of a bounding overwatch, that is used once contact is made with the enemy. In it, one element moves while the other provides base fire. *See also:* Fire and Movement, Fire Barrage.

References

Department of Defense, U.S. Army. *Air Defense Artillery Deployment: Chaparral/Vulcan/Stinger.* Field Manual FM 44-3. Washington, DC: Headquarters, Department of the Army, 1984.

—**FIRE AND MOVEMENT** is the simultaneous moving and firing by men and/or vehicles. This technique is primarily used during the assault of enemy positions.

References

Department of Defense, U.S. Army. *Operational Terms and Symbols.* Field Manual FM 101-5-1. Washington, DC: Headquarters, Department of the Army, 1985.

—**FIRE BARRAGE** is an order to deliver a prearranged barrier of fire. Specification of the particular barrage may be made by code name, numbering system, unit assignment, or other designated means.

References

Department of Defense, Joint Chiefs of Staff. *Department of Defense Dictionary of Military and Related Terms.* Washington, DC: GPO, 1986.

—**FIRE CAPABILITIES CHART** is a chart, usually in the form of an overlay, showing the areas that can be reached by the fire of the bulk of the weapons of a unit.

References

Department of Defense, Joint Chiefs of Staff. *Department of Defense Dictionary of Military and Related Terms.* Washington, DC: GPO, 1986.

—**FIRE CONTROL (FC)** is the control of all operations in connection with the application of fire on a target. *See also:* Control, Fire Control Equipment, Fire Control Orders, Fire Control Radar, Fire Control System.

References

Department of Defense, Joint Chiefs of Staff. *Department of Defense Dictionary of Military and Related Terms.* Washington, DC: GPO, 1986.

—**FIRE CONTROL (FC) EQUIPMENT** is equipment required to directly aim guns or controlled missiles at a target. It includes all instruments used in calculating and adjusting the proper elevation and deflection of guns in flight (e.g., radars, telescopes, range finders, predictors, directors, other computers, power plants, and the communication control systems connecting these elements).

References

Department of Defense, U.S. Army. *Dictionary of United States Army Terms.* Army Regulation 310-25. Washington, DC: Headquarters, Department of the Army, 1986.

—**FIRE CONTROL (FC) ORDERS** are commands used to control air defense engagements on a case-by-case basis, regardless of the prevailing weapons control status. These commands are most often used by higher control echelons when monitoring the decentralized operations of subordinate units. They can be transmitted electronically or verbally. Patriot fire control orders are engage, hold fire, cease fire, engage hold, and stop fire. *See also:* Patriot.

References

Department of Defense, U.S. Army. *Patriot Battalion Operations.* Field Manual FM 44-15. Washington, DC: Headquarters, Department of the Army, 1984.

————. *U.S. Army Air Defense Artillery Employment.* Field Manual FM 44-1. Washington, DC: Headquarters, Department of the Army, 1983.

————. *U.S. Army Air Defense Artillery Employment Hawk.* Field Manual FM 44-90. Washington, DC: Headquarters, Department of the Army, 1983.

—**FIRE CONTROL (FC) RADAR** is a radar that provides target information to a weapon fire control system.

References

Department of Defense, Joint Chiefs of Staff. *Department of Defense Dictionary of Military and Related Terms.* Washington, DC: GPO, 1986.

—**FIRE CONTROL (FC) SYSTEM** is a group of interrelated fire control equipments and/or instruments designed for use with a weapon or a group of weapons.

References

Department of Defense, Joint Chiefs of Staff. *Department of Defense Dictionary of Military and Related Terms.* Washington, DC: GPO, 1986.

—**FIRE COORDINATION AREA** is an area that has been given specified restraints and into which fire in excess of those restraints cannot be delivered without the approval of the authority that established the restraints.

References

Department of Defense, Joint Chiefs of Staff. *Department of Defense Dictionary of Military and Related Terms.* Washington, DC: GPO, 1986.

—**FIRE COORDINATION EXERCISE (FCX)** is a scaled down live-fire exercise wherein entire command and control systems are fielded with nominal weapon systems. It can be conducted at the platoon, company/team, and battalion/task force levels. The purpose of the FCX is to exercise the command and control skills of the leadership of the unit through the integration of all organic weapon systems, as well as indirect and supporting fires. Subcaliber devices are substituted for service ammunition to permit fire planning and simulated employment of all weapon systems available to support the commander in the execution of his assigned mission. An FCX stresses target acquisition. It presents target displays and target arrays to player units, placing commanders and leaders in realistic battlefield situations. Targets controlled electronically and mechanically appear at the ap-

propriate places and times according to the scenario. Commanders use FCXs to train subordinate leaders to integrate and distribute direct and indirect fire systems so that the optimum weapons engage the targets at optimum ranges as they become vulnerable to engagement.

References

Department of Defense, U.S. Army. *How to Prepare and Conduct Military Training.* Field Manual FM 21-6. Washington, DC: Headquarters, Department of the Army, 1985.

————. *Individual Military Education and Training.* Army Regulation AR 350-1. Washington, DC: Headquarters, Department of the Army, 1987.

————. *Training for Mobilization and War.* Field Manual FM 25-5. Washington, DC: Headquarters, Department of the Army, 1985.

—**FIRE DEFENSE GUN** is a machine gun placed where it can cover the enemy from the time it starts the attack until it breaks through the front lines of the battle position.

References

Department of Defense, U.S. Army. *Dictionary of United States Army Terms.* Army Regulation AR 310-25. Washington, DC: Headquarters, Department of the Army, 1986.

—**FIRE DIRECTION** is the tactical use of firepower: the exercise of tactical command of one or more units in selecting targets, concentrating or distributing fire, and allocating fire for each mission. It also includes the methods and techniques that are used in fire direction centers to convert target information into appropriate fire commands. *See also:* Fire Direction Center, Fire Direction Net.

References

Department of Defense, U.S. Army. *Dictionary of United States Army Terms.* Army Regulation AR 310-25. Washington, DC: Headquarters, Department of the Army, 1986.

—**FIRE DIRECTION CENTER (FDC)** is the gunnery and communications personnel and equipment of a command post through which and whom the commander exercises fire direction and/or fire control. The center receives target intelligence and requests for fire, and translates them into appropriate fire direction.

References

Department of Defense, Joint Chiefs of Staff. *Department of Defense Dictionary of Military and Related Terms.* Washington, DC: GPO, 1986.

Department of Defense, U.S. Army. *U.S. Army Air Defense Artillery Employment Hawk.* Field Manual FM 44-90. Washington, DC: Headquarters, Department of the Army, 1983.

—**FIRE DIRECTION NET** is a communication system linking observers, liaison officers, air observers, and the firing batteries with the fire direction center for the purpose of fire control.

References

Department of Defense, U.S. Army. *Dictionary of United States Army Terms.* Army Regulation AR 310-25. Washington, DC: Headquarters, Department of the Army, 1986.

—**FIRE FIGHT** is the delivery of fire between opposing units. It is a phase of attack that usually follows the approach march and deployment, and comes before the assault.

References

Department of Defense, U.S. Army. *Dictionary of United States Army Terms.* Army Regulation AR 310-25. Washington, DC: Headquarters, Department of the Army, 1986.

—**FIRE FOR EFFECT.** (1) Fire for effect is fire delivered after the mean point of impact or burst is within the desired distance of the target or adjusting/ranging point. (2) Fire for effect is a term in a call for fire to indicate the adjustment/ranging is satisfactory and fire for effect is desired.

References

Department of Defense, Joint Chiefs of Staff. *Department of Defense Dictionary of Military and Related Terms.* Washington, DC: GPO, 1986.

—**FIRE MISSION.** (1) Fire mission is a specific assignment given to a fire unit as part of a definite plan. (2) A fire mission is an order used to alert the weapon/battery area and indicate that the message following is a call for fire. *See also:* Fire Plan.

References

Department of Defense, Joint Chiefs of Staff. *Department of Defense Dictionary of Military and Related Terms.* Washington, DC: GPO, 1986.

—**FIRE PLAN** is a tactical plan for using the weapons of a unit or formation so that their fire will be coordinated.

References

Department of Defense, Joint Chiefs of Staff. *Department of Defense Dictionary of Military and Related Terms.* Washington, DC: GPO, 1986.

—**FIRE STORM** is stationary mass fire, generally in built-up urban areas, generating strong, inrushing winds from all sides. The winds keep the fires from spreading while adding oxygen to increase their intensity.

References

Department of Defense, Joint Chiefs of Staff. *Department of Defense Dictionary of Military and Related Terms.* Washington, DC: GPO, 1986.

—**FIRE SUPPORT** is assistance to the elements of the ground forces that close with the enemy (e.g., infantry and armor units), and is rendered by delivering field artillery fire, naval gun fire, and close air support. Fire support may also be provided by tanks, air defense artillery, and Army aviation. *See also:* Fire Support Area, Fire Support Coordination, Fire Support Coordination Center, Fire Support Coordinator, Fire Support Element, Fire Support Mission Area, Fire Support Officer, Fire Support Plan, Fire Support Team, Fire Support Team Vehicle, General Staff.

References

Department of Defense, U.S. Army. *Dictionary of United States Army Terms.* Army Regulation 310-25. Washington, DC: Headquarters, Department of the Army, 1986.

—**FIRE SUPPORT AREA** is a maneuver area assigned to fire support ships from which they can provide gunfire support to an amphibious operation.

References

Department of Defense, Joint Chiefs of Staff. *Department of Defense Dictionary of Military and Related Terms.* Washington, DC: GPO, 1986.

—**FIRE SUPPORT COORDINATION** is the planning and executing of fire support so that targets are adequately covered by a suitable weapon or group of weapons.

References

Department of Defense, U.S. Army. *Fire Support in Combined Arms Operations.* Field Manual FM 6-20. Washington, DC: Headquarters, Department of the Army, 1983.

—**FIRE SUPPORT COORDINATION CENTER** is a location in which communications facilities and personnel necessary for the coordination of all forms of fire support are centralized. *See also:* Supporting Arms Coordinator.

References

Department of Defense, Joint Chiefs of Staff. *Department of Defense Dictionary of Military and Related Terms*. Washington, DC: GPO, 1986.

—**FIRE SUPPORT COORDINATION LINE (FSCL)** is a line established by the appropriate ground commander to insure coordination of fire that is not under his control but which may affect current tactical operations. The FSCL is used to coordinate fires of air, ground, or sea weapons systems using any type of ammunition against surface targets. The FSCL should follow well-defined terrain features. Its establishment must be coordinated with the appropriate tactical air commander and other supporting elements. Supporting elements may attack targets forward of the FSCL, without prior coordination with the ground force commander, provided the attack will not produce adverse surface effects on, or to the rear of, the line. Attacks against surface targets behind this line must be coordinated with the appropriate ground force commander. *See also:* Coordinated Fire Line.

References

Department of Defense, U.S. Army. *Armored and Mechanized Division Operations*. Field Manual FM 71-100. Washington, DC: Headquarters, Department of the Army, 1978.

————. *Operational Terms and Symbols*. Field Manual FM 101-5-1. Washington, DC: Headquarters, Department of the Army, 1985.

—**FIRE SUPPORT COORDINATOR (FSCOORD)** is the senior field artillery officer at each echelon above maneuver platoon level who serves as the principal adviser to the commander for the planning and coordination of all available fire support.

References

Department of Defense, U.S. Army. *Operational Terms and Symbols*. Field Manual FM 101-5-1. Washington, DC: Headquarters, Department of the Army, 1985.

—**FIRE SUPPORT ELEMENT (FSE)** is a functional portion of a force tactical operations center that provides centralized targeting, coordination, and integration of fires, delivered by fire support means under the control of, or in support of, the force on surface targets. This element is staffed by personnel from the field artillery headquarters or from the field artillery staff section of the force and representatives of other fire support means.

References

Department of Defense, U.S. Army. *Dictionary of United States Army Terms*. Army Regulation 310-25. Washington, DC: Headquarters, Department of the Army, 1986.

————. *Operational Terms and Symbols*. Field Manual FM 101-5-1. Washington, DC: Headquarters, Department of the Army, 1985.

—**FIRE SUPPORT MISSION AREA (FSMA)** includes the systems directly related to the generation of *indirect* firepower. This mission area includes not only conventional, nuclear, and chemical fire support provided by cannons, rockets, and missile systems, but also the target acquisition and communications systems that are integral to field artillery operations.

References

Weapons Systems: U.S. Army, Navy and Air Force Directory, 1986-1988. Washington, DC: DCP, 1986.

—**FIRE SUPPORT OFFICER (FSO),** in fire support operations, is the officer who is the full-time coordinator of all fire support and is the field artillery commander's representative at the supported headquarters.

References

Department of Defense, U.S. Army. *Dictionary of United States Army Terms*. Army Regulation AR 310-25. Washington, DC: Headquarters, Department of the Army, 1986.

————. *Fire Support in Combined Arms Operations*. Field Manual FM 6-20. Washington, DC: Headquarters, Department of the Army, 1983.

—**FIRE SUPPORT PLAN** is a plan on how fire support will be used to support an operation. It should include a portion for each means of fire support involved.

References

Department of Defense, U.S. Army. *Operational Terms and Symbols*. Field Manual FM 101-5-1. Washington, DC: Headquarters, Department of the Army, 1985.

—**FIRE SUPPORT TEAM (FIST),** in fire support operations, is composed of a team chief (field artillery lieutenant) and all necessary additional personnel and equipment required to request, coordinate, and direct fire support efforts at the company or troop level.

References

Department of Defense, U.S. Army. *Dictionary of United States Army Terms.* Army Regulation AR 310-25. Washington, DC: Headquarters, Department of the Army, 1986.

————. *Fire Support in Combined Arms Operations.* Field Manual FM 6-20. Washington, DC: Headquarters, Department of the Army, 1983.

————. *Operational Terms and Symbols.* Field Manual FM 101-5-1. Washington, DC: Headquarters, Department of the Army, 1985.

—**FIRE SUPPORT TEAM VEHICLE (FISTV).** The M981, or FISTV, is a modified M113A2 armored personnel carrier that gives the field artillery's fire support teams the capability to rapidly direct mortar, artillery, and air-delivered fire support using any of its four radios to designate targets for laser-guided munitions such as Copperhead and HELLFIRE. To perform these functions, this vehicle is equipped with a ground/vehicle laser locator designator, a north-seeking gyrocompass, and a position locating and reporting system. These electronic components enable rapid generation of very accurate target location data, which are transmitted to the artillery battalion's fire direction center by an on-board four-channel digital message device. The FISTV also protects the crew against small arms fire and fragmenting artillery. Tactical missions it performs include surveillance, target acquisition, location, and communications.

References

Weapons Systems: U.S. Army, Navy and Air Force Directory, 1986-1988. Washington, DC: DCP, 1986.

—**FIRE TRENCH** is a trench from which soldiers can fire their rifles or other small arms and in which they are relatively protected.

References

Department of Defense, U.S. Army. *Dictionary of United States Army Terms.* Army Regulation AR 310-25. Washington, DC: Headquarters, Department of the Army, 1986.

—**FIRE UNIT** is a unit whose fire in battle is under the immediate and effective control of one leader.

References

Department of Defense, U.S. Army. *Dictionary of United States Army Terms.* Army Regulation AR 310-25. Washington, DC: Headquarters, Department of the Army, 1986.

—**FIREBALL** is the luminous sphere of hot gases that forms a few millionths of a second after detonation of a nuclear weapon and immediately starts expanding and cooling. *See also:* Nuclear Warfare.

References

Department of Defense, Joint Chiefs of Staff. *Department of Defense Dictionary of Military and Related Terms.* Washington, DC: GPO, 1986.

—**FIREBRAND** is a projected burning or hot fragment whose thermal energy is transferred to a receptor.

References

Department of Defense, U.S. Army. *Ammunition and Explosives Safety Standards.* Army Regulation AR 385-64. Washington, DC: Headquarters, Department of the Army, 1987.

—**FIREFINDER RADARS**, the artillery locating radar, AN/TPQ-37; and the mortar-locating radar, AN/TPQ-36, enable friendly forces to locate and bring immediate fire upon enemy mortar, artillery, and rocket-launching positions, silencing them before they can adjust their fires on friendly units and positions. The world's first automatic hostile-weapon-locating-systems, FIREFINDER radars, use advanced phased array antenna techniques and computer-controlled signal processing. They function by spotting enemy projectiles in flight and mathematically backplotting their trajectory. The position of the weapon is reported in grid coordinates, which can be fed automatically into an artillery fire direction center, enabling it to target the enemy weapons with guns, rockets, or other ordnance. In tests, both radars, in combination with fire control devices, enabled an artillery unit to have accurate counterfire on the way before the first enemy projectile struck the ground. In actual combat action in Lebanon (1984), the AN/TPQ-36 performed equally well or better than the test results. Each Army division is to be equipped with two artillery-locating radars and three mortar locating radars.

References

Weapons Systems: U.S. Army, Navy and Air Force Directory, 1986-1988. Washington, DC: DCP, 1986.

—**FIREPOWER.** Firepower provides the destructive force essential to defeat the enemy's ability and will to fight. It facilitates maneuver by suppressing the enemy's fires and disrupting the movement of its forces. It exploits maneuver by neutralizing the enemy's tactical forces and destroying its ability and will to fight. Firepower may also be used independently of maneuver to destroy, delay, or disrupt uncommitted enemy forces. Current weapons and means of massing fires make firepower devastatingly effective against troops, materiel, and facilities in greater depth and accuracy and with more flexibility than ever before. Tactical leaders must understand the techniques of controlling and integrating fire, maneuver, and protection, coordinating direct and indirect fires, using air and naval fires, and substituting massed fires for massed troops. Commanders must understand the techniques of integrating Air Force, Naval, and Army firepower effectively when conducting campaigns and major operations.

Firepower supports friendly operational maneuver by damaging key enemy forces or facilities, creating delays in enemy movement, complicating the enemy's command and control, and degrading its artillery, air defense, and air support. At the operational level, firepower can also disrupt the movement, fire support, command and control, and sustainment of enemy forces.

Maximum effective firepower against the enemy requires that many functions be coordinated and performed well: Systems and procedures for allocating priorities must be effective; targets must be efficiently located and identified; gunnery must be rapid and accurate; firing systems and supporting equipment must be mobile and moved to advantageous positions; there must be a steady supply of the proper munitions in adequate quantities; hardware must be maintained and replaced as necessary; and the various components of the firing system must be protected from enemy action. Finally, and most importantly, effective firepower depends on well-trained crews, observers, and fire direction personnel.

References

Department of Defense, Joint Chiefs of Staff. *Department of Defense Dictionary of Military and Related Terms.* Washington, DC: GPO, 1986.

Department of Defense, U.S. Army. *Operations.* Field Manual FM 100-5. Washington, DC: Headquarters, Department of the Army, 1986.

—**FIRING BATTERY.** (1) A firing battery is the part of a battery actually at the firing position when a battery is prepared for action. It includes the pieces, personnel, and equipment necessary for its operation. (2) A firing battery is organized and equipped to fire artillery weapons, as differentiated from a headquarters or service battery. (3) A firing battery is an element of a field artillery cannon battery. *See also:* Battery.

References

Department of Defense, U.S. Army. *Dictionary of United States Army Terms.* Army Regulation AR 310-25. Washington, DC: Headquarters, Department of the Army, 1986.

—**FIRING POSITIONS** (ARMY AVIATION) are occupied by individual attack helicopters in order to engage targets. They may or may not be located on the attack position. *See also:* Attack Helicopter.

References

Department of Defense, U.S. Army. *Gunnery Training for Attack Helicopters.* Training Circular TC 17-17. Washington, DC: Headquarters, Department of the Army, 1975.

—**FIRING SYSTEM,** in demolition, is a system composed of elements that are designed to fire the main charge or charges.

References

Department of Defense, Joint Chiefs of Staff. *Department of Defense Dictionary of Military and Related Terms.* Washington, DC: GPO, 1986.

—**FIRST CLASS GUNNER.** (1) First class gunner is a classification, given for skill in the use of cannon and machine guns, that ranks next above the grade of second class gunner and next below that of expert. The grade of first class gunner corresponds to that of sharpshooter. (2) A first class gunner is a soldier having that classification.

References

Department of Defense, U.S. Army. *Dictionary of United States Army Terms.* Army Regulation AR 310-25. Washington, DC: Headquarters, Department of the Army, 1986.

—**FIRST ENLISTMENT** (INITIAL ENLISTMENT) is a voluntary enrollment in the Regular Army as an enlisted member for the first time by a person with no prior Regular Army service or with prior service only in other branches of the Armed Forces. *See also:* First Timer.

References

Department of Defense, U.S. Army. *Army Reenlistment Program.* Army Regulation AR 601-28. Washington, DC: Headquarters, Department of the Army, 1984.

—**FIRST LIGHT** is the beginning of nautical twilight (i.e., when the center of the morning sun is twelve degrees below the horizon).

References

Department of Defense, Joint Chiefs of Staff. *Department of Defense Dictionary of Military and Related Terms*. Washington, DC: GPO, 1986.

—**FIRST SERGEANT** is the occupational title for the chief noncommissioned officer of a company, battery, or similar unit.

References

Department of Defense, U.S. Army. *Dictionary of United States Army Terms*. Army Regulation AR 310-25. Washington, DC: Headquarters, Department of the Army, 1986.

—**FIRST STRIKE** is the first offensive move of a war. It is usually associated with nuclear weapons. *See also:* Nuclear Warfare.

References

Department of Defense, Joint Chiefs of Staff. *Department of Defense Dictionary of Military and Related Terms*. Washington, DC: GPO, 1986.

—**FIRST TIMER** is a term used only within Headquarters, Department of the Army, and the Department of Defense for statistical purposes to indicate a person with 36 months or less of active federal military service.

References

Department of Defense, U.S. Army. *Army Reenlistment Program*. Army Regulation AR 601-28. Washington, DC: Headquarters, Department of the Army, 1984.

———. *Enlisted Personnel Management System*. Army Regulation AR 600-200. Washington, DC: Headquarters, Department of the Army, 1984.

—**FISCAL YEAR** is a term used in budgeting. It is the twelve-month period that begins on October 1 of one calendar year and ends on September 30 of the next calendar year.

References

Department of Defense, U.S. Army. *Dictionary of United States Army Terms*. Army Regulation AR 310-25. Washington, DC: Headquarters, Department of the Army, 1986.

—**FIVE S's** are the initials for five prisoner of war handling procedures: search, segregate, silence, speed, and safeguard. *See also:* Prisoner of War.

References

Department of Defense, U.S. Army. *Military Police Team, Squad, Platoon Combat Operations*. Field Manual FM 19-4. Washington, DC: Headquarters, Department of the Army, 1984.

—**FIX.** (1) Fix are the actions taken to prevent the enemy from moving any part of its forces from a specific location and/or for a specific period by holding or surrounding them to prevent their withdrawal for use elsewhere. (2) A fix is a position determined from terrestrial, electronic, or astronomical data. *See also:* Fix and Surpass.

References

Department of Defense, Joint Chiefs of Staff. *Department of Defense Dictionary of Military and Related Terms*. Washington, DC: GPO, 1986.

Department of Defense, U.S. Army. *Operational Terms and Symbols*. Field Manual FM 101-5-1. Washington, DC: Headquarters, Department of the Army, 1985.

—**FIX AND SUPPRESS.** When the enemy cannot be bypassed and a hasty attack would be too costly, the attacking unit fixes and suppresses the enemy. This insures that the enemy does not have the capability to fire and/or maneuver against the main body of the battalion while it moves to attack or bypass the enemy. When the company has sufficiently suppressed the enemy, the battalion commander orders it to either break contact and rejoin the battalion or hand off the enemy to a following unit.

References

Department of Defense, U.S. Army. *The Infantry Rifle Company (Infantry, Airborne, Air Assault, Ranger)*. Field Manual FM 7-10. Washington, DC: Headquarters, Department of the Army, 1982.

—**FIXED AMMUNITION** is a type of ammunition in which the cartridge case is permanently attached to the projectile. *See also:* Ammunition.

References

Department of Defense, U.S. Army. *The Infantry Rifle Company (Infantry. Airborne, Air Assault, Ranger)*. Field Manual FM 7-10. Washington, DC: Headquarters, Department of the Army, 1982.

—**FIXED CAPITAL PROPERTY.** (1) Fixed capital property are assets of a permanent character having a continuing value. (2) As used in military establishments, fixed capital property includes real estate and equipment installed or in use, either in productive plants or in field operations. The term is synonymous with fixed assets.

References

Department of Defense, Joint Chiefs of Staff. *Department of Defense Dictionary of Military and Related Terms.* Washington, DC: GPO, 1986.

—**FIXED MEDICAL TREATMENT FACILITY** is a medical treatment facility designed to operate for an extended period of time at a specific site. *See also:* Hospital.

References

Department of Defense, Joint Chiefs of Staff. *Department of Defense Dictionary of Military and Related Terms.* Washington, DC: GPO, 1986.

—**FIXED POST SYSTEM** is the process of assigning sentinels to guard duty at fixed posts, where they will remain until relieved.

References

Department of Defense, U.S. Army. *Guard Duty.* Field Manual FM 22-6. Washington, DC: Headquarters, Department of the Army, 1971.

—**FIXED SHELTER** is collective protection, usually in a rear area in a permanent location (e.g., a building basement), a bunker, or an expandable rigid wall, tactical shelter. It is used for field hospitals, operating rooms, maintenance shops, data processing centers, field kitchens, fire control centers, and supply storage areas.

References

Department of Defense, U.S. Army. *NBC Operations.* Field Manual FM 3-100. Washington, DC: Headquarters, Department of the Army, 1985.

———. *NBC Protection.* Field Manual FM 3-4. Washington, DC: Headquarters, Department of the Army, 1985.

—**FLAG** is a cloth with a distinguishing color or design that has a special meaning or serves as a signal (e.g., the U.S. flag, the white flag of truce, and weather flags). In the military service, the color is a flag of a dismounted unit; an ensign is the national flag; a pennant is a small triangular flag usually flown for identification of the unit; and a guidon is a flag carried by Army units for identification, especially in drills and ceremonies. *See also:* Garrison Flag.

References

Department of Defense, U.S. Army. *Dictionary of United States Army Terms.* Army Regulation AR 310-25. Washington, DC: Headquarters, Department of the Army, 1986.

—**FLAG OFFICER** is a term applied to an officer holding the rank of general; lieutenant general; major general; or brigadier general in the U.S. Army, Air Force, or Marine Corps; or admiral, vice admiral, or rear admiral in the U.S. Navy or Coast Guard.

References

Department of Defense, Joint Chiefs of Staff. *Department of Defense Dictionary of Military and Related Terms.* Washington, DC: GPO, 1986.

—**FLAIL TANK** is a specially constructed tank equipped with a flailing device made of chains attached to a roller powered by the tank engine. It is used to detonate antitank mines. *See also:* Mine Warfare.

References

Department of Defense, U.S. Army. *Dictionary of United States Army Terms.* Army Regulation AR 310-25. Washington, DC: Headquarters, Department of the Army, 1986.

—**FLAME** is thickened fuel (by adding oil or gel to gasoline) used to kill, dislodge, or demoralize personnel, neutralize fortifications, and destroy flammable material.

References

Department of Defense, U.S. Army. *NBC Operations.* Field Manual FM 3-100. Washington, DC: Headquarters, Department of the Army, 1985.

—**FLAME FIELD EXPEDIENT** is a handmade weapon used by soldiers to extend their combat power. Sometimes the weapon is constructed hastily for use in repelling an attacking force. It can be used to explode and produce casualties, to light up an area, or to signal between ground troops and friendly tactical aircraft (e.g., flame mines, flame fougasses, and illuminators).

References

Department of Defense, U.S. Army. *NBC Operations.* Field Manual FM 3-100. Washington, DC: Headquarters, Department of the Army, 1985.

—**FLAME THROWER** is a weapon that projects and can ignite incendiary fuel. *See also:* Chemical Warfare.

References

Department of Defense, Joint Chiefs of Staff. *Department of Defense Dictionary of Military and Related Terms.* Washington, DC: GPO, 1986.

—**FLANK** (DRILLS AND CEREMONIES) is the right or left of any side formation as observed by an element within that formation.

References

Department of Defense, U.S. Army. *Guard Duty.* Field Manual FM 22-6. Washington, DC: Headquarters, Department of the Army, 1971.

—**FLANK GUARD** is a security element operating to the flank of a moving or stationary force to protect it from enemy ground observation, direct fire, and surprise attack. A flank guard for a stationary force deploys to the flank and defends; a flank guard for a moving force establishes a series of troop-size battle positions generally parallel to the main body's axis of advance and occupies new positions as the main body advances.

References

Department of Defense, Joint Chiefs of Staff. *Department of Defense Dictionary of Military and Related Terms.* Washington, DC: GPO, 1986.

Department of Defense, U.S. Army. *Cavalry.* Field Manual FM 17-95. Washington, DC: Headquarters, Department of the Army, 1977.

———. *Operational Terms and Symbols.* Field Manual FM 101-5-1. Washington, DC: Headquarters, Department of the Army, 1985.

—**FLANK WIND** is wind that blows across the smoke objective and smoke source. *See also:* Smoke Screen.

References

Department of Defense, U.S. Army. *Deliberate Smoke Operations.* Field Manual FM 3-50. Washington, DC: Headquarters, Department of the Army, 1984.

—**FLANKING ATTACK** is an offensive maneuver aimed at the flank of an enemy. *See also:* Frontal Attack.

References

Department of Defense, U.S. Army. *The Army* (Prepublication Issue). Field Manual FM 100-1. Washington, DC: Headquarters, Department of the Army, 1986.

———. *Operations.* Field Manual FM 100-5. Washington, DC: Headquarters, Department of the Army, 1986.

—**FLARE DUD** is a nuclear weapon that when launched at a target, detonates with anticipated yield but at an altitude appreciably greater than intended. It is not a dud in terms of yield, but rather in terms of the effects on the target and the normal operation of the weapon. *See also:* Nuclear Warfare.

References

Department of Defense, Joint Chiefs of Staff. *Department of Defense Dictionary of Military and Related Terms.* Washington, DC: GPO, 1986.

—**FLASH BLINDNESS** (DAZZLE) is an impairment of vision resulting from an intense flash of light. It includes temporary or permanent loss of vision and may be associated with retinal burns. Flash blindness from a nuclear burst during daylight hours persists for about two minutes for personnel who are facing directly toward the burst or a reflective surface. At night, flash blindness affects almost all personnel in the target area. A similar effect may be induced by the intense illumination of image intensification devices.

References

Department of Defense, Joint Chiefs of Staff. *Department of Defense Dictionary of Military and Related Terms.* Washington, DC: GPO, 1986.

Department of Defense, U.S. Army. *Nuclear Weapons Employment Doctrine and Procedures.* Field Manual FM 101-3-1. Washington, DC: Headquarters, Department of the Army, 1986.

—**FLASH BURN** is a burn caused by excessive exposure of the bare skin to thermal radiation.

References

Department of Defense, Joint Chiefs of Staff. *Department of Defense Dictionary of Military and Related Terms.* Washington, DC: GPO, 1986.

—**FLASH DEFILADE.** (1) A flash defilade is a condition in which the flash of firing at a gun position is concealed from enemy observation by an intervening obstacle (e.g., a hill or the side of a ravine). (2) A flash defilade is the vertical distance by which the flash of a gun is concealed from enemy observation.

References

Department of Defense, U.S. Army. *Dictionary of United States Army Terms.* Army Regulation AR 310-25. Washington, DC: Headquarters, Department of the Army, 1986.

—**FLASH MESSAGE** is a category of precedence reserved for initial enemy contact messages or operational combat messages of extreme emergency. Brevity is mandatory. *See also:* Precedence (Communications).

References
Department of Defense, Joint Chiefs of Staff.
*Department of Defense Dictionary of Military and
Related Terms*. Washington, DC: GPO, 1986.

—**FLASH TO BANG TIME** is the interval between
when the flash of a weapon being fired is seen
and the sound of that discharge is heard.

References
Department of Defense, U.S. Army. *Dictionary of
United States Army Terms*. Army Regulation AR
310-25. Washington, DC: Headquarters, Department of the Army, 1986.

—**FLECHETTE** is a small fin-stabilized missile used
in antipersonnel ammunition. *See also:* Beehive.

References
Department of Defense, U.S. Army. *Dictionary of
United States Army Terms*. Army Regulation AR
310-25. Washington, DC: Headquarters, Department of the Army, 1986.

—**FLEETING TARGET** is a moving target (e.g.,
aircraft, vehicles, and marching troops) that remains within observing distance for such a short
period that it affords little time for deliberate
adjustment and fire against it.

References
Department of Defense, U.S. Army. *Dictionary of
United States Army Terms*. Army Regulation AR
310-25. Washington, DC: Headquarters, Department of the Army, 1986.

—**FLEXIBILITY.** When the United States and its
allies are faced with aggression, or the threat of
aggression, the nation must be able to call upon
its military establishment for forces suited in type
and degree to appropriate levels of conflict. The
Army must be able to operate effectively with a
wide variety of weapons, organizations, and
tactics so that decisions on the use of forces
may be based upon broad national and allied
interests and values rather than limited by the
force structure. Flexibility also requires that, with
some exceptions, no major unit be limited by
organization, training, or equipment to operate
in a specific area or under special conditions.
The division, the basic tactical maneuver unit,
is a combined arms integrated maneuver element of a fighting corps. For reasons of flexibility, the Army consists of a mix of heavy and
light divisions and separate brigades. Support
forces at echelons above division are tailored to
meet the peculiar requirements of specific division missions and areas of conflict. Proper task
organization of all elements within divisions,
and concentration of the full range of capabilities at echelons above division are essential to
maintaining requisite flexibility for worldwide
contingencies. *See also:* Principles of War.

References
Department of Defense, U.S. Army. *The Army*.
(Prepublication Issue.) Field Manual FM 100-1.
Washington, DC: Headquarters, Department of the
Army, 1986.

—**FLIGHT ROUTE** is a predetermined plotted route
between points. Crew members use ground reference points and pilotage navigation techniques
to identify and follow a flight route.

References
Department of Defense, U.S. Army. *Attack
Helicopter Operations*. Field Manual FM 17-50.
Washington, DC: Headquarters, Department of the
Army, 1984.

—**FLIGHT TRAINING** is training that supports the
Army's Aviation Pilot Training Program, and is
normally categorized as undergraduate helicopter pilot training and other flight training (i.e.,
advanced, graduate, and familiarization).

References
Department of Defense, U.S. Army. *Individual
Military Education and Training*. Army Regulation
AR 350-1. Washington, DC: Headquarters,
Department of the Army, 1987.

—**FOG OIL** is a group of petroleum compounds of
selected molecular weight and composition that
are used to facilitate smoke formation by at-
omization or combustion. The resulting smoke
is white. *See also:* Smoke Screen.

References
Department of Defense, U.S. Army. *Deliberate
Smoke Operations*. Field Manual FM 3-50.
Washington, DC: Headquarters, Department of the
Army, 1984.

—**FOLLOW AND SUPPORT FORCE** is a committed force that follows a force conducting an offensive operation, and normally conducts exploitation or pursuit operations. Such a force is
not a reserve but is committed to accomplishing
any or all of these tasks: destroy bypassed units;
relieve in place any direct pressure or encircling
force that has halted to contain the enemy; block
movement of reinforcements; secure lines of
communications; guard prisoners, key areas, and
installations; secure key terrain; and control
refugees.

References
Department of Defense, U.S. Army. *Operational Terms and Symbols*. Field Manual FM 101-5-1. Washington, DC: Headquarters, Department of the Army, 1985.

———. *The Tank and Mechanized Infantry Battalion Task Force*. Field Manual FM 71-2. Washington, DC: Headquarters, Department of the Army, 1977.

—**FOLLOW-ON CONSTRUCTION** is an upgrade of an expedient facility, and is normally accomplished from 30 to 90 days after a project is completed.

References
Department of Defense, U.S. Army. *Support Operations: Echelons Above Corps*. Field Manual FM 100-16. Washington, DC: Headquarters, Department of the Army, 1986.

—**FOLLOW-ON RESTORATION** is the upgrade of emergency repairs that normally restore the facility to its original condition.

References
Department of Defense, Joint Chiefs of Staff. *Department of Defense Dictionary of Military and Related Terms*. Washington, DC: GPO, 1986.

—**FOLLOW-UP** is an inquiry about the action being taken on a previously submitted document or requirement.

References
Department of Defense, U.S. Army. *Dictionary of United States Army Terms*. Army Regulation AR 310-25. Washington, DC: Headquarters, Department of the Army, 1986.

—**FOLLOW-UP ECHELON** are forces that are moved into the objective area after the assault echelon of an airborne, airmobile, air assault, or amphibious operation to sustain the defense and to conduct offensive operations as part of the larger force after linkup. Normally it includes follow-up elements of the assault units, maintenance unit headquarters, and elements of the supply and service battalion. *See also:* Assault Echelon, Rear Echelon.

References
Department of Defense, U.S. Army. *Dictionary of United States Army Terms*. Army Regulation 310-25. Washington, DC: Headquarters, Department of the Army, 1986.

———. *Operational Terms and Symbols*. Field Manual FM 101-5-1. Washington, DC: Headquarters, Department of the Army, 1985.

—**FOLLOW-UP ELEMENTS** are elements following a march column. The elements may be for cleanup, for prevention of straggling, for maintenance and recovery of equipment, or for other purposes.

References
Department of Defense, U.S. Army. *Dictionary of United States Army Terms*. Army Regulation AR 310-25. Washington, DC: Headquarters, Department of the Army, 1986.

—**FOLLOW-UP SUPPLY** is the initial resupply delivered directly to forces in the airhead by air. It is prepackaged on a unit basis for automatic or on-call delivery.

References
Department of Defense, U.S. Army. *Dictionary of United States Army Terms*. Army Regulation AR 310-25. Washington, DC: Headquarters, Department of the Army, 1986.

———. *USA/USAF Doctrine for Joint Airborne and Tactical Airlift Operations*. Field Manual FM 100-27. Washington, DC: Headquarters, Department of the Army, 1985.

—**FOOT LANE** is a lane normally two meters wide and marked with white marking tape along its centerline. At least one foot lane is needed for each assault company if a mounted assault is not feasible.

References
Department of Defense, U.S. Army. *Engineer Combat Operations*. Field Manual FM 5-100. Washington, DC: Headquarters, Department of the Army, 1984.

—**FOOT MARCH** is the movement of an infantry unit by foot.

References
Department of Defense, U.S. Army. *The Infantry Rifle Company (Infantry, Airborne, Air Assault, Ranger)*. Field Manual FM 7-10. Washington, DC: Headquarters, Department of the Army, 1982.

—**FORCE** is an aggregation or combination of military personnel, weapon systems, vehicles, and necessary support.

References
Department of Defense, Joint Chiefs of Staff. *Department of Defense Dictionary of Military and Related Terms*. Washington, DC: GPO, 1986.

—**FORCE AUGMENTATION** are high priority reserve component units (division forces and nondivisional units to round out the Active

Army), Army of the United States units, and individual reinforcements necessary to bring these units to full table of organization and equipment strength to achieve a specified division force objective.

References

Department of Defense, U.S. Army. *Dictionary of United States Army Terms.* Army Regulation AR 310-25. Washington, DC: Headquarters, Department of the Army, 1986.

—**FORCE DEVELOPMENT TESTING AND EX-PERIMENTATION** consists of tests, ranging from small-scope, highly instrumented, high resolution field experiments, to the broader in scope, less instrumented, low resolution, and highly subjective field tests that are performed to support the force development process by examining the impact, potential, and effectiveness of selected concepts, tactics, doctrine, organization, and materiel. Force development testing and experimentation assesses the interdependence among doctrine, tactics, organization, and materiel, and may support the materiel acquisition process by providing data to assist in establishing a required operational capability, to develop fundamental data necessary for a full understanding of a materiel system, or to assist in validating doctrine and/or tactics to counter a possible threat response to a system once it is deployed.

References

Department of Defense, U.S. Army. *Dictionary of United States Army Terms.* Army Regulation AR 310-25. Washington, DC: Headquarters, Department of the Army, 1986.

—**FORCE LIST** is a total list of forces required by an operation plan, including assigned forces, augmentation forces, and other forces to be employed in support of the plan.

References

Department of Defense, Joint Chiefs of Staff. *Department of Defense Dictionary of Military and Related Terms.* Washington, DC: GPO, 1986.

—**FORCE MODERNIZATION TRAINING** is the training of active and reserve component individuals, crews, and units in how to operate, maintain (organization, direct support/general support, and depot), shoot, and use new and displaced equipment.

References

Department of Defense, U.S. Army. *Dictionary of United States Army Terms.* Army Regulation AR 310-25. Washington, DC: Headquarters, Department of the Army, 1986.

—**FORCE PLANNING.** As part of the Department of Defense Planning, Programming, and Budgeting System, force planning is an integral part of preparation for war. It stems from requirements derived from national military objectives; combat operations doctrine; resource availability; the mechanics of force structuring and manning; and the research, development, and acquisition of arms and equipment. Successful force planning involves an appreciation of the art of war. Using the principles of war as a frame of reference, the force planner can better appreciate the usefulness of the designed force on the battlefield.

References

Department of Defense, U.S. Army. *The Army* (Prepublication Issue). Field Manual FM 100-1. Washington, DC: Headquarters, Department of the Army, 1986.

—**FORCE PROTECTION** is a security program designed to protect soldiers, civilian employees, family members, facilities, and equipment, in all locations and situations. It is accomplished through the planned and integrated application of terrorism counteraction, physical security, and personal protective services, and supported by counterintelligence and other security services.

References

Department of Defense, U.S. Army. *The Army Terrorism Counteraction Program.* Army Regulation AR 525-13. Washington, DC: Headquarters, Department of the Army, 1988.

—**FORCE READINESS** is a continuing capability to fulfill the Army's mission and includes mobility, flexibility, and staying power.

References

Department of Defense, U.S. Army. *The Army.* (Prepublication Issue.) Field Manual FM 100-1. Washington, DC: Headquarters, Department of the Army, 1986.

———. *Dictionary of United States Army Terms.* Army Regulation AR 310-25. Washington, DC: Headquarters, Department of the Army, 1986.

—**FORCE REQUIREMENTS NUMBER (FRN)** is an alphanumeric code used to uniquely identify force entries in a given operation plan time-phased force and deployment data. *See also:* Operation Plan.

References

Department of Defense, Joint Chiefs of Staff. *Department of Defense Dictionary of Military and Related Terms.* Washington, DC: GPO, 1986.

Department of Defense, U.S. Army. *Planning Logistics Support for Military Operations.* Field Manual FM 701-58. Washington, DC: Headquarters, Department of the Army, 1987.

—**FORCE SHORTFALL** is a deficiency in the number or type of units available for planning, within the time required for the performance of the assigned task.

References

Department of Defense, U.S. Army. *Planning Logistics Support for Military Operations.* Field Manual FM 701-58. Washington, DC: Headquarters, Department of the Army, 1987.

—**FORCE SOURCING** is the identification of actual units, their origins, ports of embarkation, and movement characteristics to satisfy the time-phased force requirements of a supported commander.

References

Department of Defense, Joint Chiefs of Staff. *Department of Defense Dictionary of Military and Related Terms.* Washington, DC: GPO, 1986.

—**FORCE TABS,** with reference to war plans, are the statement of the time-phased deployments of major combat units by major commands and geographical areas.

References

Department of Defense, Joint Chiefs of Staff. *Department of Defense Dictionary of Military and Related Terms.* Washington, DC: GPO, 1986.

—**FORCED CROSSING** is going across a stream in the face of enemy opposition.

References

Department of Defense, U.S. Army. *Dictionary of United States Army Terms.* Army Regulation AR 310-25. Washington, DC: Headquarters, Department of the Army, 1986.

—**FORCES ALLOTTED TO NATO** are the forces made available to NATO by a nation under the categories of: (1) NATO command forces; (2) NATO assigned forces; (3) NATO earmarked forces; and (4) other forces for NATO.

References

Department of Defense, Joint Chiefs of Staff. *Department of Defense Dictionary of Military and Related Terms.* Washington, DC: GPO, 1986.

—**FORCES IN BEING** are forces classified as being in state of readiness "A" or "B" as prescribed in the appropriate military document.

References

Department of Defense, Joint Chiefs of Staff. *Department of Defense Dictionary of Military and Related Terms.* Washington, DC: GPO, 1986.

—**FORD** is a shallow part of a body of water that can be crossed without using bridging or rafts. It is a location in a water barrier where the physical characteristics of current, bottom, and approaches permit personnel and/or vehicles and other equipment to cross the water barrier while remaining in contact with the bottom.

References

Department of Defense, U.S. Army. *Operational Terms and Symbols.* Field Manual FM 101-5-1. Washington, DC: Headquarters, Department of the Army, 1985.

—**FOREIGN COUNTERINTELLIGENCE (FCI)** is a general intelligence term that includes both the intelligence activity and the finished intelligence that is produced as a result of these operations. Foreign counterintelligence is intended to detect, counteract, and prevent espionage and other clandestine intelligence activities, sabotage, international terrorist activities, or assassinations conducted on behalf of foreign powers, organizations, or persons. Foreign counterintelligence does not include personnel, physical, document, or communications security programs. *See also:* Counterintelligence, Communications Security.

References

Department of Defense, Defense Intelligence College. *Glossary of Intelligence Terms and Definitions.* Washington, DC: DIC, 1987.

—**FOREIGN INSTRUMENTATION SIGNALS (FIS)** is a technical intelligence term for electromagnetic signals associated with testing and operationally deploying non-U.S. aerospace, surface, and subsurface systems that may have either military or civilian application. It includes but is not limited to telemetry, beaconry, electronic interrogation, tracking/fusing/arming command system, and video data link signals. *See also:* Foreign Instrumentation Signals Intelligence.

References

Department of Defense, Defense Intelligence College. *Glossary of Intelligence Terms and Definitions.* Washington, DC: DIC, 1987.

Department of Defense, U.S. Army. *Counterintelligence.* Field Manual FM 34-60. Washington, DC: Headquarters, Department of the Army, 1985.

—**FOREIGN INSTRUMENTATION SIGNALS INTELLIGENCE** is the technical and intelligence information derived from processing intercepted foreign instrumentation signals. *See also:* Foreign Instrumentation Signals Intelligence Information Reporting, Foreign Instrumentation Signals Internals.

References

Department of Defense, Defense Intelligence College. *Glossary of Intelligence Terms and Definitions.* Washington, DC: DIC, 1987.

—**FOREIGN INSTRUMENTATION SIGNALS INTELLIGENCE (FISINT) INFORMATION REPORTING** is all foreign instrumentation signals raw data and products, including original and duplicate analog and digital recordings; data displays and listings; field reports; intercept listings; results of signals analysis, data manipulation, and data analysis; and product reports.

References

Department of Defense, U.S. Army. *Dictionary of United States Army Terms.* Army Regulation AR 310-25. Washington, DC: Headquarters, Department of the Army, 1986.

—**FOREIGN INSTRUMENTATION SIGNALS (FIS) INTERNALS** are preselected measurements from onboard engineering sensors or guidance computer calculations that are superimposed (or "modulated") on a radio carrier and are transmitted to specially configured instrumentation sites on the ground. The measurement data are separated (or "demodulated") from the radio signal and are displayed for study by test and evaluation engineers.

References

U.S. Congress. *Central Intelligence Information Act. Public Law 98-477, 1984.* Washington, DC: GPO, 1984.

—**FOREIGN INTELLIGENCE (FI)** is a general intelligence term. (1) It is the product that results from collecting, evaluating, analyzing, integrating, and interpreting intelligence information about a foreign power that is of value to U.S. national security, foreign relations, or economic interests and that is provided by a government intelligence agency. (2) The U.S. Army defines foreign intelligence differently. Foreign intelligence includes all evaluated information concerning one or more aspects of foreign nations, foreign materiel, or areas of operations of immediate or potential significance to the accomplishment of the Army mission, and is obtained and disseminated through intelligence channels. (3) The Church Committee defined foreign intelligence as "intelligence concerning areas outside the United States." (4) A more complete definition that also infers greater latitude for intelligence operations is given by the U.S. Army. It defines foreign intelligence in the following manner. Foreign intelligence is:

"a. Information concerning the capabilities, intentions, and activities of any foreign power, or of any non-U.S. person, whether within or outside the United States or concerning areas outside the United States.

b. Information relating to the ability of the United States to protect itself against actual or potential attack or other hostile acts of a foreign power or its agents.

c. Information with respect to foreign powers or non-U.S. persons which because of its importance is deemed essential to the security of the United States or the conduct of its foreign affairs.

d. Information relating to the ability of the United States to defend itself against the activities of foreign intelligence services."

(5) An alternative definition resulted from Presidential Executive Order 12333, "United States Intelligence Activities," dated December 4, 1981. It defined foreign intelligence as "information relating to the capabilities, intentions, and activities of foreign powers, organizations or persons, but not including counterintelligence except for information on international terrorist activities." *See also:* Intelligence Cycle.

References

Department of Defense. *Activities of DoD Intelligence Components that Affect U.S. Persons.* (Department of Defense Directive 5240.1.) Washington, DC: Department of Defense, 1982.

Department of Defense, Defense Intelligence College. *Glossary of Intelligence Terms and Definitions.* Washington, DC: DIC, 1987.

Department of Defense, U.S. Army. *RDTGE Managers Intelligence and Threat Support Guide.* Alexandria, VA: Headquarters, Army Materiel Development and Readiness Command, 1983.

U.S. Congress. Senate. *Final Report of the Senate Select Committee to Study Government Operations With Respect to Intelligence Activities. Report 94-755. Book I, Foreign and Military Intelligence* (Church Committee Report). Washington, DC: GPO, 1976.

—**FOREIGN INTERNAL DEFENSE** is the participation by civilian and military agencies of a government in any of the action programs taken over by another government to free and protect its society from subversion, lawlessness, and insurgency. Such defense consists of economic and technical development assistance; welfare and emergency relief humanitarian assistance; and military and economic security assistance. Security assistance programs include military assistance, education, and training; foreign military sales financing; economic support fund; peacekeeping operations; and commercial export sales. U.S. security assistance forces can include airborne, special forces, civil affairs, psychological operations, combat arms, combat support, and combat service support units. U.S. Army forces can conduct advisory, intelligence, civil-military, population and resource control, and tactical operations in a foreign internal defense role. *See also:* Civil Affairs, Civil Military Cooperation.

References

Department of Defense, U.S. Army. *Civil Affairs Operations*. Field Manual FM 41-10. Washington, DC: Headquarters, Department of the Army, 1985.

———. *Low Intensity Conflict*. Field Manual FM 100-20. Washington, DC: Headquarters, Department of the Army, 1981.

———. *U.S. Army Policy Statement, 1988*. Washington, DC: Headquarters, Department of the Army, 1988.

—**FOREIGN SERVICE.** For those stationed in the continental United States, foreign service is military service performed outside U.S. continental limits. For those stationed outside the continental United States, it is military service performed outside the limits of the overseas area of residence, but excludes service within the continental United States.

References

Department of Defense, U.S. Army. *Dictionary of United States Army Terms*. Army Regulation AR 310-25. Washington, DC: Headquarters, Department of the Army, 1986.

—**FORK** is a change in elevation of artillery required to shift the center of impact in range.

References

Department of Defense, U.S. Army. *Dictionary of United States Army Terms*. Army Regulation AR 310-25. Washington, DC: Headquarters, Department of the Army, 1986.

—**FORMAL COMMAND INSPECTION** applies to all units and activities. The unit that is to be inspected is usually notified in advance. *See also:* Annual General Inspections.

References

Department of Defense, U.S. Army. *Organizational Maintenance Operations*. Field Manual FM 29-2. Washington, DC: Headquarters, Department of the Army, 1984.

—**FORMATION** is the arrangement of elements of a unit in a prescribed manner. *See also:* Column, Line.

References

Department of Defense, Joint Chiefs of Staff. *Department of Defense Dictionary of Military and Related Terms*. Washington, DC: GPO, 1986.

Department of Defense, U.S. Army. *Drills and Ceremonies*. Field Manual FM 22-5. Washington, DC: Headquarters, Department of the Army, 1986.

—**FORMING UP PLACE** is the last position occupied by an assault echelon before it crosses the start line or line of departure. It is also called the attack position. *See also:* Line of Departure.

References

Department of Defense, Joint Chiefs of Staff. *Department of Defense Dictionary of Military and Related Terms*. Washington, DC: GPO, 1986.

—**FORMS OF MANEUVER** refers to the general orientation of a force approaching the enemy. The three basic forms of maneuver are the frontal attack, penetration, and envelopment. *See also:* Attack, Envelopment, Penetration.

References

Department of Defense, U.S. Army. *Operational Terms and Symbols*. Field Manual FM 101-5-1. Washington, DC: Headquarters, Department of the Army, 1985.

—**FORT.** (1) A fort is a permanent post (as opposed to a camp, which is a temporary installation). (2) A fort is a land area within which harbor defense units are located. (3) A fort is a strong, fortified building or place that can be defended against an enemy.

References

Department of Defense, U.S. Army. *Dictionary of United States Army Terms*. Army Regulation AR 310-25. Washington, DC: Headquarters, Department of the Army, 1986.

—FORWARD AEROMEDICAL EVACUATION is the phase of evacuation that provides airlift for patients between points within the battlefield, from the battlefield to the initial point of treatment, and to subsequent points of treatment within the combat zone. *See also:* Medical Treatment.

References

Department of Defense, Joint Chiefs of Staff. *Department of Defense Dictionary of Military and Related Terms*. Washington, DC: GPO, 1986.

—FORWARD AIR CONTROLLER (FAC) is a member of the tactical air control party who, from a ground or airborne position, controls aircraft engaged in close air support of ground positions. *See also:* Air Liaison Officer.

References

Department of Defense, Joint Chiefs of Staff. *Department of Defense Dictionary of Military and Related Terms*. Washington, DC: GPO, 1986.

Department of Defense, U.S. Army. *Attack Helicopter Operations*. Field Manual FM 17-50. Washington, DC: Headquarters, Department of the Army, 1984.

———. *Operational Terms and Symbols*. Field Manual FM 101-5-1. Washington, DC: Headquarters, Department of the Army, 1985.

—FORWARD AREA is an area that is near combat.

References

Department of Defense, Joint Chiefs of Staff. *Department of Defense Dictionary of Military and Related Terms*. Washington, DC: GPO, 1986.

—FORWARD ARMING AND REFUELING POINT (FARP) is a temporary facility organized, equipped, and deployed by an aviation unit commander and located closer to the area of operations than the aviation unit's combat service support area to provide the fuel and ammunition to helicopter units in combat.

References

Department of Defense, Joint Chiefs of Staff. *Department of Defense Dictionary of Military and Related Terms*. Washington, DC: GPO, 1986.

Department of Defense, U.S. Army. *Air Defense Artillery Deployment: Chaparral/Vulcan/Stinger*. Field Manual FM 44-3. Washington, DC: Headquarters, Department of the Army, 1984.

———. *Attack Helicopter Operations*. Field Manual FM 17-50. Washington, DC: Headquarters, Department of the Army, 1984.

———. *Combat Service Support*. Field Manual FM 100-10. Washington, DC: Headquarters, Department of the Army, 1983.

———. *Operational Terms and Symbols*. Field Manual FM 101-5-1. Washington, DC: Headquarters, Department of the Army, 1985.

—FORWARD ASSEMBLY AREA is an area where attack helicopters can move forward and shut down for extended periods while awaiting orders to go into battle. This location should be situated at or near the supported unit's tactical operations center for more rapid response times. Considerations for forward assembly areas are the same as those for assembly areas. *See also:* Attack Helicopter.

References

Department of Defense, U.S. Army. *Attack Helicopter Operations*. Field Manual FM 17-50. Washington, DC: Headquarters, Department of the Army, 1984.

—FORWARD COMBAT ZONE (FCZ) is the area forward of the corps rear boundaries. *See also:* Forward Area, Forward Defense, Forward Defense Area.

References

Department of Defense, U.S. Army. *Rear Battle*. Field Manual FM 90-14. Washington, DC: Headquarters, Department of the Army, 1985.

—FORWARD DEFENSE is a strategic concept that calls for retaining or repulsing military aggression as close to the original line of contact as possible in order to protect important areas further to the rear.

References

Collins, John M. *U.S.-Soviet Military Balance, 1980-1985*. Washington, DC: Congressional Research Service, 1985.

—FORWARD DEFENSE AREA is the area in which the forward defense positions are located in a mobile defense. *See also:* Forward Defense Position.

References

Department of Defense, U.S. Army. *Dictionary of United States Army Terms.* Army Regulation 310-25. Washington, DC: Headquarters, Department of the Army, 1986.

—**FORWARD DEFENSE POSITION,** in the mobile defense, is any combination of islands of resistance, strong points, and observation posts used by the defender to warn of an impending attack, canalize the attackers into less favorable terrain, and block or impede the attacking force. Forward defense positions are occupied by the minimum forces necessary, while the bulk of the defending force is used in offensive action. *See also:* Forward Defense Area.

References

Department of Defense, U.S. Army. *Dictionary of United States Army Terms.* Army Regulation AR 310-25. Washington, DC: Headquarters, Department of the Army, 1986.

—**FORWARD DEPLOYED FORCES** are U.S. forces located in a foreign country to operate with allied forces in an established theater. This situation assumes that the host nation has the technical expertise and that an extensive industrial base, a well-developed transportation system, a skilled labor pool, and some formal agreements exist.

References

Department of Defense, U.S. Army. *Civil Affairs Operations.* Field Manual FM 41-10. Washington, DC: Headquarters, Department of the Army, 1985.

—**FORWARD ECHELON** is the part of a headquarters principally concerned with the tactical control of the battle. *See also:* Rear Echelon.

References

Department of Defense, U.S. Army. *Dictionary of United States Army Terms.* Army Regulation AR 310-25. Washington, DC: Headquarters, Department of the Army, 1986.

—**FORWARD EDGE OF THE BATTLE AREA (FEBA)** is the forward limit of the main battle area. It is composed of the foremost limits of a series of areas in which ground combat units are deployed, excluding the areas in which the covering or screening forces are operating. It is designated to coordinate fire support, the positioning of forces, or the maneuver of units. *See also:* Forward Line of Own Troops.

References

Department of Defense, Joint Chiefs of Staff. *Department of Defense Dictionary of Military and Related Terms.* Washington, DC: GPO, 1986.

Department of Defense, U.S. Army. *Operational Terms and Symbols.* Field Manual FM 101-5-1. Washington, DC: Headquarters, Department of the Army, 1985.

—**FORWARD LINE OF OWN TROOPS (FLOT)** is a line that indicates the most forward positions of friendly forces in any kind of military operation at a specific time. It may include the forward elements of the covering force or the advance guard. The FLOT may be at, beyond, or short of the forward edge of the battle area, depicting the nonlinear battlefield. *See also:* Forward Command Post, Forward Edge of the Battle Area.

References

Department of Defense, U.S. Army. *Intelligence and Electronic Warfare Operations.* Field Manual FM 34-1. Washington, DC: Headquarters, Department of the Army, 1987.

———. *Long-Range Surveillance.* Field Manual FM 7-93. Washington, DC: Headquarters, Department of the Army, 1987.

———. *Operational Terms and Symbols.* Field Manual FM 101-5-1. Washington, DC: Headquarters, Department of the Army, 1985.

—**FORWARD OBSERVER (FO)** is an observer operating with front line troops and trained to adjust ground or naval gunfire and pass back battlefield information. In the absence of a forward air controller, the observer may control close air support strikes. *See also:* Spotter.

References

Department of Defense, Joint Chiefs of Staff. *Department of Defense Dictionary of Military and Related Terms.* Washington, DC: GPO, 1986.

Department of Defense, U.S. Army. *Operational Terms and Symbols.* Field Manual FM 101-5-1. Washington, DC: Headquarters, Department of the Army, 1985.

—**FORWARD OPERATIONAL BASE (FOB)** is a command, control, and support element established by a special forces operational base (SFOB). It normally is established for specific missions requiring a separate command and control headquarters reporting directly to a joint unconventional warfare command/joint unconventional warfare task force. The organization, mission, and functions parallel those of a SFOB, but on a reduced scale. An FOB also is established to extend the span of control when distances involved preclude effective command or support of deployed operational elements. The organization and functions of the FOB vary with the mission; duration and scope of operations; and security, communications, administrative, and logistical support requirements. *See also:* Special Forces Operational Base.

References

Department of Defense, U.S. Army. *Operational Terms and Symbols.* Field Manual FM 101-5-1. Washington, DC: Headquarters, Department of the Army, 1985.

—**FORWARD SLOPE** is any slope that descends toward the enemy.

References

Department of Defense, Joint Chiefs of Staff. *Department of Defense Dictionary of Military and Related Terms.* Washington, DC: GPO, 1986.

—**FORWARD TELL** is the transfer of information to a higher level of command.

References

Department of Defense, Joint Chiefs of Staff. *Department of Defense Dictionary of Military and Related Terms.* Washington, DC: GPO, 1986.

—**FORWARD THRUST** is the Chaplain doctrine that emphasizes providing moral and spiritual support to smaller, more exposed forward groups of troops. *See also:* Chaplain.

References

Department of Defense, U.S. Army. *The Chaplain and Chaplain Assistant in Combat Operations.* Field Manual FM 16-5. Washington, DC: Headquarters, Department of the Army, 1984.

—**FOUGASSE** is a mine that is constructed so that when its charge is exploded, pieces of metal, rock, gasoline, or other substances are blown in a predetermined direction. *See also:* Mine Warfare.

References

Department of Defense, U.S. Army. *Dictionary of United States Army Terms.* Army Regulation AR 310-25. Washington, DC: Headquarters, Department of the Army, 1986.

—**FOULING** is the deposit that remains in the bore of a gun after it has been fired.

References

Department of Defense, U.S. Army. *Dictionary of United States Army Terms.* Army Regulation AR 310-25. Washington, DC: Headquarters, Department of the Army, 1986.

—**FOUR-MAN TEAM** is a group of four trainees who are formed into a team during their advanced individual training. They complete their training together and, insofar as requirements permit, are assigned to the same station or unit as a team. *See also:* Regimental Affiliation.

References

Department of Defense, U.S. Army. *Dictionary of United States Army Terms.* Army Regulation AR 310-25. Washington, DC: Headquarters, Department of the Army, 1986.

—**FOUR-ROUND ILLUMINATION DIAMOND is** a method of distributing the fire of illumination shells that, by a combination of lateral spread, provides illumination to a large area.

References

Department of Defense, Joint Chiefs of Staff. *Department of Defense Dictionary of Military and Related Terms.* Washington, DC: GPO, 1986.

—**FOX I** (ARMY AVIATION) is the actual or simulated launch of wire-guided weapons.

References

Department of Defense, U.S. Army. *Air-to-Air Combat.* Field Manual FM 1-107. Washington, DC: Headquarters, Department of the Army, 1984.

—**FOX II** (ARMY AVIATION) is the actual or simulated launch of infrared-guided weapons.

References

Department of Defense, U.S. Army. *Air-to-Air Combat.* Field Manual FM 1-107. Washington, DC: Headquarters, Department of the Army, 1984.

—**FOX III** (ARMY AVIATION) is the actual or simulated launch of 2.75-inch FFAFs or firing of guns.

References

Department of Defense, U.S. Army. *Air-to-Air Combat.* Field Manual FM 1-107. Washington, DC: Headquarters, Department of the Army, 1984.

—**FOXHOLE** is a small pit used for cover. It is usually for one or two men, and is constructed so that the occupant(s) can fire effectively from it.

References

Department of Defense, U.S. Army. *Dictionary of United States Army Terms.* Army Regulation AR 310-25. Washington, DC: Headquarters, Department of the Army, 1986.

—**FRACTIONAL DAMAGE** is a fraction or percentage of the elements of a target that may be damaged or become casualties from a nuclear attack.

References

Department of Defense, U.S. Army. *Dictionary of United States Army Terms.* Army Regulation AR 310-25. Washington, DC: Headquarters, Department of the Army, 1986.

—**FRAGMENTARY ORDER (FRAGO)** is an abbreviated operations order often issued daily and is used to make changes in missions assigned to units and to inform them of changes in the tactical situation. *See also:* Operations Order.

References

Department of Defense, Joint Chiefs of Staff. *Department of Defense Dictionary of Military and Related Terms.* Washington, DC: GPO, 1986.

Department of Defense, U.S. Army. *Air Defense Artillery Deployment: Chaparral/Vulcan/Stinger.* Field Manual FM 44-3. Washington, DC: Headquarters, Department of the Army, 1984.

———. *Light Infantry Battalion Task Force.* Field Manual FM 7-72. Washington, DC: Headquarters, Department of the Army, 1987.

———. *Long-Range Surveillance.* Field Manual FM 7-93. Washington, DC: Headquarters, Department of the Army, 1987.

———. *Operational Terms and Symbols.* Field Manual FM 101-5-1. Washington, DC: Headquarters, Department of the Army, 1985.

———. *Staff Organization and Operations.* Field Manual FM 101-5. Washington, DC: Headquarters, Department of the Army, 1984.

—**FRAGMENTATION** is the breaking up of the confining material of a chemical compound or mechanical mixture when an explosion takes place. Fragments may be complete items, subassemblies, pieces thereof, or pieces of equipment or buildings containing the items. *See also:* Fragmentation (Artillery Projectile).

References

Department of Defense, U.S. Army. *Ammunition and Explosives Safety Standards.* Army Regulation AR 385-64. Washington, DC: Headquarters, Department of the Army, 1987.

—**FRAGMENTATION** (ARTILLERY PROJECTILE) occurs when the projectile disintegrates, producing a mass of high-speed steel fragments that can perforate and become imbedded in fighting and protective positions. The pattern or distribution of fragments greatly affects the design of fighting and protective positions. Airburst of artillery shells provides the greatest unrestricted distribution of fragments. Fragments created by surface and delay bursts are restricted by obstructions on the ground.

References

Department of Defense, U.S. Army. *Ammunition and Explosives Safety Standards.* Army Regulation AR 385-64. Washington, DC: Headquarters, Department of the Army, 1987.

———. *Survivability.* Field Manual FM 5-103. Washington, DC: Headquarters, Department of the Army, 1985.

—**FRAGMENTED UNIT** is a unit that does not enter a specific objective area complete. A unit is considered fragmented if portions of it are deployed to the objective area at different times, by different modes of transport, or to different objective areas, or if a portion of the unit is not deployed. Lettered companies and unnumbered table of organization and equipment detachments and teams organic to battalions or companies are not fragmented units unless one or more of the above conditions exist.

References

Department of Defense, U.S. Army. *Planning Logistics Support for Military Operations.* Field Manual FM 701-58. Washington, DC: Headquarters, Department of the Army, 1987.

—**FRANGIBLE BULLET** is a brittle plastic or other nonmetallic bullet for firing practice that, breaks into powder or small fragments upon striking a target without penetrating it.

References

Department of Defense, U.S. Army. *Dictionary of United States Army Terms.* Army Regulation AR 310-25. Washington, DC: Headquarters, Department of the Army, 1986.

—**FREE** (ARMY AVIATION) refers to an aircraft of a flight not directly engaged by an enemy in a two-versus-two or two-versus-many engagement. The free aircraft always maneuvers to support the engaged aircraft visually or with fire.

References

Department of Defense, U.S. Army. *Air-to-Air Combat.* Field Manual FM 1-107. Washington, DC: Headquarters, Department of the Army, 1984.

—**FREE DROP** is the dropping of equipment or supplies from an aircraft without the use of parachutes. Energy-dissipating material may be placed around the load to lessen the shock when it hits the ground. The load descends at a rate of 130 to 150 feet per second. Fortification or barrier material, clothing in bales, and other such items may be free dropped. *See also:* Airdrop, Air Movement, Free Fall, High Velocity Drop, Low Velocity Drop.

References

Department of Defense, Joint Chiefs of Staff. *Department of Defense Dictionary of Military and Related Terms.* Washington, DC: GPO, 1986.

Department of Defense, U.S. Army. *USA/USAF Doctrine for Joint Airborne and Tactical Airlift Operations.* Field Manual FM 100-27. Washington, DC: Headquarters, Department of the Army, 1985.

—**FREE FALL** is a parachute maneuver in which the parachute is manually activated at the discretion of the jumper or automatically at a preset altitude. *See also:* Airdrop, Free Drop, High Velocity Air Drop.

References

Department of Defense, Joint Chiefs of Staff. *Department of Defense Dictionary of Military and Related Terms.* Washington, DC: GPO, 1986.

—**FREE FIRE AREA (FFA),** in fire support operations, is an area into which any fire support may fire without overall coordination.

References

Department of Defense, U.S. Army. *Dictionary of United States Army Terms.* Army Regulation AR 310-25. Washington, DC: Headquarters, Department of the Army, 1986.

———. *Fire Support in Combined Arms Operations.* Field Manual FM 6-20. Washington, DC: Headquarters, Department of the Army, 1983.

———. *Operational Terms and Symbols.* Field Manual FM 101-5-1. Washington, DC: Headquarters, Department of the Army, 1985.

—**FREE FLIGHT** is the portion of a missile's trajectory that is without thrust. The term can apply to both guided missiles and free flight rockets.

References

Department of Defense, U.S. Army. *Dictionary of United States Army Terms.* Army Regulation AR 310-25. Washington, DC: Headquarters, Department of the Army, 1986.

—**FREE ISSUE** is materiel provided for use or consumption without charge to the fund or fund subdivision that finances the activity to which it is issued.

References

Department of Defense, Joint Chiefs of Staff. *Department of Defense Dictionary of Military and Related Terms.* Washington, DC: GPO, 1986.

—**FREE MANEUVER** is a practice maneuver in which each force acts as it chooses. It is limited only by the field orders received, by restrictions of area and time, and by the actions of the opposing force.

References

Department of Defense, U.S. Army. *Dictionary of United States Army Terms.* Army Regulation AR 310-25. Washington, DC: Headquarters, Department of the Army, 1986.

—**FREE NET** is a radio net in which any station may communicate with any other station in the same net without first obtaining permission from the net control station to do so.

References

Department of Defense, U.S. Army. *Dictionary of United States Army Terms.* Army Regulation AR 310-25. Washington, DC: Headquarters, Department of the Army, 1986.

—**FREE PLAY EXERCISE** tests the capabilities of forces under simulated contingency and/or wartime conditions. It is limited only by the artificialities or restrictions required by peacetime safety regulations. *See also:* Exercise.

References

Department of Defense, Joint Chiefs of Staff. *Department of Defense Dictionary of Military and Related Terms.* Washington, DC: GPO, 1986.

—**FREE ROCKET** is a rocket that is not subject to guidance or control in flight.

References

Department of Defense, Joint Chiefs of Staff. *Department of Defense Dictionary of Military and Related Terms.* Washington, DC: GPO, 1986.

—**FREEZE OR THAW DEPTH** is the level to which ground will either freeze or thaw, depending on its geographical location.

References

Department of Defense, U.S. Army. *Weather Support for Army Tactical Operations.* Field Manual FM 34-81. Washington, DC: Headquarters, Department of the Army, 1984.

—**FREIGHT CONSOLIDATING ACTIVITY** is a transportation activity that receives less than carload or truckload shipments of materiel in order to assemble them into carload or truckload lots for movement to the consignee, a freight distributing activity, or another break bulk point. *See also:* Freight Distributing Activity.

References

Department of Defense, Joint Chiefs of Staff. *Department of Defense Dictionary of Military and Related Terms.* Washington, DC: GPO, 1986.

—**FREIGHT DISTRIBUTING ACTIVITY** is a transportation activity that receives and unloads consolidated carloads or truckloads of less than carload or truckload shipments of material and forwards the individual shipments to the designees.

References

Department of Defense, Joint Chiefs of Staff. *Department of Defense Dictionary of Military and Related Terms.* Washington, DC: GPO, 1986.

—**FREQUENCY OF OCCURRENCE** is the number of times the listed mission-essential maintenance operation is expected to be performed on equipment within the conditions stated in the usage profile.

References

Department of Defense, U.S. Army. *Maintenance and Repair Parts Consumption Planning Guide for Contingency Operations.* Field Manual FM 42-9-23. Washington, DC: Headquarters, Department of the Army, 1980.

—**FREQUENCY PER 100 OPERATIONS** is the estimated need for a specific repair part when a mission-essential maintenance operation is performed 100 times. This number is expressed as a percentage of use. *See also:* Frequency of Occurrence.

References

Department of Defense, U.S. Army. *Maintenance and Repair Parts Consumption Planning Guide for Contingency Operations.* Field Manual FM 42-9-23. Washington, DC: Headquarters, Department of the Army, 1980.

—**FREQUENCY SPECTRUM DESIGNATION (FSD)** is as follows: VLF (very low frequency) is below 30 kHz (0.03 MHz); LF (low frequency) is from 30 to 300 kHz (0.03-0.3 MHz); MF (medium frequency) is from 300 to 3,000 kHz (0.3-3 MHz); HF (high frequency) is from 3 to 30 MHz; VHF (very high frequency) is from 30 to 300 MHz; UHF (ultra high frequency) is from 300 to 3,000 MHz; SHF (super high frequency) is from 3,000 to 30,000 MHz (3-30 GHz); and EHF (extremely high frequency) is from 30 to 300 GHz.

References

Department of Defense, U.S. Army. *Tactical Single Channel Radio Communications Techniques.* Field Manual FM 24-18. Washington, DC: Headquarters, Department of the Army, 1984.

—**FROCKING** is a personnel action in which a soldier is allowed to wear the insignia of a higher grade so that his grade title is commensurate with his duty position, although no pay or allowances are authorized in the higher grade until the person is actually promoted. *See also:* Promotion.

References

Department of Defense, U.S. Army. *Enlisted Personnel Management System.* Army Regulation AR 600-200. Washington, DC: Headquarters, Department of the Army, 1984.

—**FRONT.** (1) A front is the lateral space occupied by an element measured from the extremity of one flank to the extremity of the other flank. (2) The front is the direction of the enemy. (3) A front is a line of contact of two opposing forces. (4) When a combat situation does not exist or is not assumed, the front is the direction toward which the command is faced. *See also:* Frontage.

References

Department of Defense, Joint Chiefs of Staff. *Department of Defense Dictionary of Military and Related Terms.* Washington, DC: GPO, 1986.

Department of Defense, U.S. Army. *Operational Terms and Symbols.* Field Manual FM 101-5-1. Washington, DC: Headquarters, Department of the Army, 1985.

—**FRONT** (DRILL AND CEREMONIES) is the space between individuals or elements from side to side.

References

Department of Defense, U.S. Army. *Drills and Ceremonies.* Field Manual FM 22-5. Washington, DC: Headquarters, Department of the Army, 1986.

—**FRONTAGE** is the width of the front plus the distance beyond the flanks covered by observation and fire by a unit in combat. *See also:* Front.

References

Department of Defense, U.S. Army. *Dictionary of United States Army Terms.* Army Regulation AR 310-25. Washington, DC: Headquarters, Department of the Army, 1986.

————. *Operational Terms and Symbols.* Field Manual FM 101-5-1. Washington, DC: Headquarters, Department of the Army, 1985.

—**FRONTAL ATTACK.** (1) A frontal attack is an offensive maneuver in which the main action is directed against the front of the enemy forces and over the most direct approaches. (2) In air intercept, a frontal attack is an attack by an interceptor aircraft that terminates with a heading crossing angle greater than 135 degrees. *See also:* Frontal Fire.

References

Department of Defense, Joint Chiefs of Staff. *Department of Defense Dictionary of Military and Related Terms.* Washington, DC: GPO, 1986.

Department of Defense, U.S. Army. *Operational Terms and Symbols.* Field Manual FM 101-5-1. Washington, DC: Headquarters, Department of the Army, 1985.

————. *The Tank and Mechanized Infantry Company Team.* Field Manual FM 71-1. Washington, DC: Headquarters, Department of the Army, 1977.

—**FRONTAL FIRE** is fire delivered at right angles to the front of a target.

References

Department of Defense, U.S. Army. *Dictionary of United States Army Terms.* Army Regulation AR 310-25. Washington, DC: Headquarters, Department of the Army, 1986.

—**FRUSTRATED CARGO** is any shipment of supplies and/or equipment that is stopped before reaching its destination and for which further shipping instructions must be obtained.

References

Department of Defense, Joint Chiefs of Staff. *Department of Defense Dictionary of Military and Related Terms.* Washington, DC: GPO, 1986.

—**FUELING** is the process of refilling the fuel tanks of vehicles.

References

Department of Defense, U.S. Army. *Dictionary of United States Army Terms.* Army Regulation AR 310-25. Washington, DC: Headquarters, Department of the Army, 1986.

—**FULL COMMAND** is the military authority and responsibility of a superior officer to issue orders to subordinates. It covers every aspect of military operations and administration and exists only within national exercises. The term "command", as used internationally, implies a lesser degree of authority than when it is used in a purely national sense. It follows that no NATO commander has full command over the forces that are assigned to him. This is because nations, in assigning forces to NATO, assign only operational command or operational control. *See also:* Command.

References

Department of Defense, Joint Chiefs of Staff. *Department of Defense Dictionary of Military and Related Terms.* Washington, DC: GPO, 1986.

—**FULL MOBILIZATION** is the expansion of the active Armed Forces because an action by Congress and the President has called for all reserve component units in the existing approved force structure, all individual reservists, retired military personnel, and the resources needed for their support to meet the requirements of a war or other national emergency involving an external threat to the national security.

References

Department of Defense, Joint Chiefs of Staff. *Department of Defense Dictionary of Military and Related Terms.* Washington, DC: GPO, 1986.

—**FULL STEP** is a 30-inch step taken in walking or marching.

References

Department of Defense, U.S. Army. *Dictionary of United States Army Terms.* Army Regulation AR 310-25. Washington, DC: Headquarters, Department of the Army, 1986.

—**FULL-TIME SUPPORT (FTS) OF RESERVE COMPONENTS.** The Army National Guard and the U.S. Army Reserve require full-time personnel to improve readiness through training, recruiting, administration, maintenance support, and mobilization for troop program units. These personnel help insure the state of readiness that is needed to perform the assigned missions effectively.

References

Department of Defense, U.S. Army. *U.S. Army Policy Statement, 1988.* Washington, DC: Headquarters, Department of the Army, 1988.

—**FUNCTIONAL AREA** is a grouping of officers by career field, other than arm, service, or branch that is characterized by interrelated tasks or skills, which usually require significant education, training, and experience.

References
Department of Defense, U.S. Army. *Commissioned Officer Professional Development and Utilization.* Department of the Army Pamphlet 600-3. Washington, DC: Headquarters, Department of the Army, 1986.

———. *Officer Assignment Policies, Details and Transfers.* Army Regulation AR 614-100. Washington, DC: Headquarters, Department of the Army, 1984.

—**FUNCTIONAL COURSE** is a training course that trains soldiers in the specific critical skills they need to perform in certain areas within an military occupational specialty or specialty skills identifier. This training may be either an extension course or service school training.

References
Department of Defense, U.S. Army. *Individual Military Education and Training.* Army Regulation AR 350-1. Washington, DC: Headquarters, Department of the Army, 1987.

—**FUNCTIONS** are the appropriate duties, responsibilities, missions, or tasks assigned to an individual, office, or organization. As defined in the National Security Act of 1947, as amended, the term "function" includes functions, powers, and duties.

References
Department of Defense, Joint Chiefs of Staff. *Department of Defense Dictionary of Military and Related Terms.* Washington, DC: GPO, 1986.

—**FUZE** (SPECIFY TYPE), in artillery and gunfire support, is a command or request to indicate the type of fuze action desired (e.g., delay, quick, time, or proximity fuze).

References
Department of Defense, Joint Chiefs of Staff. *Department of Defense Dictionary of Military and Related Terms.* Washington, DC: GPO, 1986.

—**FUZE RANGE** is the range at which a projectile will burst when the fuze is set for a given time. *See also:* Fuze (Specify Type).

References
Department of Defense, U.S. Army. *Dictionary of United States Army Terms.* Army Regulation AR 310-25. Washington, DC: Headquarters, Department of the Army, 1986.

—**FUZE WELL** is a cavity in the mine that holds the primary fuze. *See also:* Mine Warfare.

References
Department of Defense, U.S. Army. *Mine/Countermine Operations at the Company Level.* Field Manual FM 20-32. Washington, DC: Headquarters, Department of the Army, 1976.

—**FUZE WITH DELAYED ARMING** is a fuze that activates only at a predetermined period after the action of "commit to arm." *See also:* Fuze (Specify Type).

References
Department of Defense, U.S. Army. *Mine/Countermine Operations at the Company Level.* Field Manual FM 20-32. Washington, DC: Headquarters, Department of the Army, 1976.

—**FUZED MINE** is a mine whose firing train is complete, but whose safety devices prevent it from functioning. *See also:* Mine Warfare.

References
Department of Defense, U.S. Army. *Mine/Countermine Operations at the Company Level.* Field Manual FM 20-32. Washington, DC: Headquarters, Department of the Army, 1976.

—G1, ASSISTANT CHIEF OF STAFF, PERSONNEL,

is the principal staff officer for the commander on all matters concerning human resources. The G1, who is concerned with soldier personal readiness, monitors and assesses the elements of personnel administration and management that provide policies, services, and facilities affecting a soldier's human potential and commitment. The principal activities of the G1 are receiving information for coordinating, advising, and planning to assist the commander in accomplishing the organizational mission. *See also:* General Staff.

References

Department of Defense, U.S. Army. *Dictionary of United States Army Terms.* Army Regulation 310-25. Washington, DC: Headquarters, Department of the Army, 1986.

————. *Staff Organizations and Operations.* Field Manual FM 101-5. Washington, DC: Headquarters, Department of the Army, 1984.

—G2, ASSISTANT CHIEF OF STAFF, INTELLIGENCE,

is the principal staff officer for the commander on all military intelligence matters. The G2 acquires, analyzes, and evaluates intelligence information and data, and presents the assessment evaluation and recommendation to the commander. *See also:* General staff, Intelligence.

References

Department of Defense, U.S. Army. *Dictionary of United States Army Terms.* Army Regulation AR 310-25. Washington, DC: Headquarters, Department of the Army, 1986.

————. *Staff Organization and Operations.* Field Manual FM 101-5. Washington, DC: Headquarters, Department of the Army, 1984.

—G2 AND G3 AIR OPERATIONS SECTIONS

are staff sections under the G3 at the division level, and are subsections of both the G2 and the G3 at the corps and higher levels. The sections are composed of personnel who have been trained in air/ground operations.

References

Department of Defense, U.S. Army. *Dictionary of United States Army Terms.* Army Regulation AR 310-25. Washington, DC: Headquarters, Department of the Army, 1986.

—G3, ASSISTANT CHIEF OF STAFF, OPERATIONS,

is the principal staff officer for the commander in matters concerning operations, plans, organization, and training. The operations officer's responsibilities require a high degree of coordination with other staff members. *See also:* General Staff.

References

Department of Defense, U.S. Army. *Dictionary of United States Army Terms.* Army Regulation 310-25. Washington, DC: Headquarters, Department of the Army, 1986.

————. *Staff Organization and Operations.* Field Manual FM 101-5. Washington, DC: Headquarters, Department of the Army, 1984.

—G3 AIR

is an assistant G3 of the staff of each division, corps, army, army group, and theater headquarters, who is especially trained in the methods and use of air power.

References

Department of Defense, U.S. Army. *Dictionary of United States Army Terms.* Army Regulation AR 310-25. Washington, DC: Headquarters, Department of the Army, 1986.

—G4, ASSISTANT CHIEF OF STAFF, LOGISTICS,

is the principal staff officer for the commander in matters of supply, maintenance, transportation, and services. *See also:* General Staff.

References

Department of Defense, U.S. Army. *Dictionary of United States Army Terms.* Army Regulation AR 310-25. Washington, DC: Headquarters, Department of the Army, 1986.

————. *Staff Organization and Operations.* Field Manual FM 101-5. Washington, DC: Headquarters, Department of the Army, 1984.

—G5, ASSISTANT CHIEF OF STAFF, CIVIL-MILITARY OPERATIONS,

is the principal staff officer for the commander in all matters concerning the civilian impact on military operations and the political, economic, and social effects of military operations on civilian personnel. He has staff responsibility for the activities embracing the relationships among the military forces, the civil authorities, and the people in the area of operations. Civil-military operatons in NATO are primarily conducted with and through the host nation territorial army (or equivalent organization). *See also:* Civil-Military Operations, General Staff.

References

Department of Defense, U.S. Army. *Dictionary of United States Army Terms.* Army Regulation AR 310-25. Washington, DC: Headquarters, Department of the Army, 1986.

————. *Staff Organization and Operations.* Field Manual FM 101-5. Washington, DC: Headquarters, Department of the Army, 1984.

—**GADGET.** (1) A gadget pertains to radar equipment. (The type of equipment may be indicated by a letter listed in the operation orders.) It may be followed by a color to indicate the state of jamming. The following colors are used:
- Green—clear of jamming
- Amber—sector is partially jammed
- Red—sector is completely jammed
- Blue—completely jammed

(2) In Army Aviation, the term "gadgets" is used as follows to indicate the status of the onboard electronic countermeasures equipment:
- Gadgets well—equipment is working
- Gadgets sick—equipment is downgraded
- Gadgets bent—equipment is inoperative

See also: Jammer.

References

Department of Defense, Joint Chiefs of Staff. *Department of Defense Dictionary of Military and Related Terms.* Washington, DC: GPO, 1986.

Department of Defense, U.S. Army. *Air-to-Air Combat.* Field Manual FM 1-107. Washington, DC: Headquarters, Department of the Army, 1984.

—**GAMMA RADIATION** is primarily an internal hazard, although it originates from an external source. Gamma rays, the primary radiation for soldiers on the battlefield, are short wavelength electromagnetic radiations of nuclear origin that are emitted from the nucleus of the atom. *See also:* Nuclear Warfare.

References

Department of Defense, U.S. Army. *NBC Operations.* Field Manual FM 3-100. Washington, DC: Headquarters, Department of the Army, 1985.

—**GAP.** (1) A gap is any break or breach in the continuity of tactical dispositions or formations beyond effective small arms coverage. (2) A gap is a portion of a minefield of specified width in which no mines have been laid so that friendly forces can pass through the minefield in a tactical formation. *See also:* Gap Crossing, Lane.

References

Department of Defense, U.S. Army. *Staff Organizations and Operations.* Field Manual FM 101-5. Washington, DC: Headquarters, Department of the Army, 1984.

—**GAP CROSSING** is the negotiation of natural and manmade gaps. *See also:* Gap.

References

Department of Defense, U.S. Army. *Support Operations: Echelons Above Corps.* Field Manual FM 100-16. Washington, DC: Headquarters, Department of the Army, 1986.

—**GAP FILLER RADAR** is a radar used to supplement the coverage of the principal radar in areas where its coverage is inadequate.

References

Department of Defense, Joint Chiefs of Staff. *Department of Defense Dictionary of Military and Related Terms.* Washington, DC: GPO, 1986.

—**GARBLE** is an unintentional error in transmission, reception, encryption, or decryption that changes the text of a message or any portion of it in such a manner that it is incorrect or undecipherable.

References

Department of Defense, Joint Chiefs of Staff. *Department of Defense Dictionary of Military and Related Terms.* Washington, DC: GPO, 1986.

—**GARNISHING,** in surveillance, is natural or artificial material applied to an object to achieve or assist in camouflaging it. *See also:* Camouflage.

References

Department of Defense, Joint Chiefs of Staff. *Department of Defense Dictionary of Military and Related Terms.* Washington, DC: GPO, 1986.

—**GARRISON FLAG** is the largest U.S. flag. It is flown on posts only on holidays and important occasions as required by Army regulations.

References

Department of Defense, U.S. Army. *Dictionary of United States Army Terms.* Army Regulation AR 310-25. Washington, DC: Headquarters, Department of the Army, 1986.

—**GARRISON FORCE** is all units assigned to a base or area for defense, development, operation, and maintenance facilities.

References

Department of Defense, Joint Chiefs of Staff. *Department of Defense Dictionary of Military and Related Terms.* Washington, DC: GPO, 1986.

—**GENERAL CARGO** is cargo that can be loaded in general, nonspecialized loading areas (e.g., boxes, barrels, bales, crates, packages, bundles, and pallets).

References

Department of Defense, Joint Chiefs of Staff. *Department of Defense Dictionary of Military and Related Terms.* Washington, DC: GPO, 1986.

—**GENERAL COURT-MARTIAL** is the highest type of court-martial. Its board consists of at least five members, not including the military judge. A general court-martial board has the power to try any offense punishable by the Uniform Code of Military Justice. *See also:* Special Court-Martial, Summary Court-Martial.

References

Department of Defense, U.S. Army. *Dictionary of United States Army Terms.* Army Regulation AR 310-25. Washington, DC: Headquarters, Department of the Army, 1986.

—**GENERAL DECLASSIFICATION SCHEDULE (GDS).** When collateral material (i.e., material that is not within sensitive compartmented information channels) is classified, it comes under a general declassification schedule. This means that its classification will be lowered at specific time intervals and that it will be declassified after a certain date. If the originator believes that the information is sufficiently sensitive that it should not be downgraded and declassified automatically, he can request that it be exempted from the GDS. In this case, the classification cannot be changed without a specific review and assessment of the document.

References

Department of Defense, Joint Chiefs of Staff. *Department of Defense Dictionary of Military and Related Terms.* Washington, DC: GPO, 1986.

Department of Defense, U.S. Army. *Dictionary of United States Army Terms.* Army Regulation AR 310-25. Washington, DC: Headquarters, Department of the Army, 1986.

—**GENERAL DEPOT** is a supply establishment for the receipt, storage, and issue of two or more commodities or types of supplies. *See also:* Depot.

References

Department of Defense, U.S. Army. *Dictionary of United States Army Terms.* Army Regulation 310-25. Washington, DC: Headquarters, Department of the Army, 1986.

—**GENERAL DISCHARGE** is a form of severing service from the Army. It is under honorable conditions for satisfactory service, and is given to a soldier who does not qualify for an honorable discharge. *See also:* Disciplinary Action, Dishonorable Discharge, Honorable Discharge.

References

Department of Defense, U.S. Army. *Dictionary of United States Army Terms.* Army Regulation AR 310-25. Washington, DC: Headquarters, Department of the Army, 1986.

—**GENERAL ENGINEERING** are missions that do not contribute directly to mobility, countermobility, and survivability of the committed maneuver units, but that are essential for firepower and logistical support.

References

Department of Defense, U.S. Army. *Support Operations: Echelons Above Corps.* Field Manual FM 100-16. Washington, DC: Headquarters, Department of the Army, 1986.

—**GENERAL HOSPITAL.** (1) A general hospital is a fixed numbered medical treatment facility organized and operated by a table of organization and equipment unit in a theater of operations. It provides defined and specialized medical and surgical treatment. (2) A general hospital is a named, fixed medical treatment facility, under the command of the Commander, United States Army Health Services Command, or the major overseas commander, especially staffed and equipped to provide facilities for observation, definitive treatment, and final disposition of patients who require relatively long periods of hospitalization or highly specialized treatment. *See also:* Medical Treatment.

References

Department of Defense, U.S. Army. *Dictionary of United States Army Terms.* Army Regulation 310-25. Washington, DC: Headquarters, Department of the Army, 1986.

—**GENERAL INTELLIGENCE** is military intelligence covering: (1) military capabilities, including orders of battle, organization, training, tactics, and all other factors bearing on military strength and effectiveness; (2) area and terrain intelligence, including urban areas, coasts, and landing beaches, and medical/environmental, meteorological, and geological intelligence; (3) transportation in all modes; (4) materiel production and support industries, telecommunications, and military economics; (5) location and identification of military-related installations; (6) government control; (7) evasion and escape; (8) threats and forecasts; and (9) indications. *See also:* Intelligence.

References
Department of Defense, U.S. Army. *RDTGE Managers Intelligence and Threat Support Guide.* Alexandria, VA: Headquarters, Army Materiel Development and Readiness Command, 1983.

—**GENERAL MAP** is a small-scale map used for general planning. *See also:* Map.

References
Department of Defense, Joint Chiefs of Staff. *Department of Defense Dictionary of Military and Related Terms.* Washington, DC: GPO, 1986.

—**GENERAL ORDERS.** (1) General orders are permanent instructions, issued in order form, that apply to all members of a command, as compared with special orders, which affect only individuals or small groups. General orders are usually concerned with matters of policy or administration. (2) General orders are a series of permanent guard orders that govern the duties of a sentry on a post.

References
Department of Defense, Joint Chiefs of Staff. *Department of Defense Dictionary of Military and Related Terms.* Washington, DC: GPO, 1986.

—**GENERAL PLANS** are a category of the operation plan developed by Army component commands in support of unified commands' general plans, directives, or other documents. General plans establish broad guidance and data bases necessary for developing other types of plans within the planning system. *See also:* Operation Plan.

References
Department of Defense, U.S. Army. *Planning Logistics Support for Military Operations.* Field Manual FM 701-58. Washington, DC: Headquarters, Department of the Army, 1987.

—**GENERAL PURCHASING AGENTS** are agents who have been appointed in the principal overseas areas of operations to supervise, control, coordinate, negotiate, and develop the local procurement of supplies, services, and facilities by U.S. Armed Forces, so that local resources and production can be used most effectively.

References
Department of Defense, Joint Chiefs of Staff. *Department of Defense Dictionary of Military and Related Terms.* Washington, DC: GPO, 1986.

—**GENERAL RESERVE** are extra troops under the control of the overall commander. *See also:* Floating Reserve.

References
Department of Defense, Joint Chiefs of Staff. *Department of Defense Dictionary of Military and Related Terms.* Washington, DC: GPO, 1986.

—**GENERAL SKILL TRAINING** is individual training that provides commissioned officers, warrant officers, and enlisted personnel with the skills and knowledge they need to perform specified duties and tasks that are related to a specialty or duty position.

References
Department of Defense, U.S. Army. *Individual Military Education and Training.* Army Regulation AR 350-1. Washington, DC: Headquarters, Department of the Army, 1987.

—**GENERAL STAFF (GS)** is a group of officers in the headquarters of Army or Marine divisions, Marine brigades and aircraft wings, or similar or larger units that assist their commanders in planning, coordinating, and supervising operations. A general staff may consist of four or more principal sections: personnel (G1), military intelligence (G2), operations (G3), logistics (G4), and, in Army organizations, civil affairs-military government (G5). A particular section may be added or eliminated by the commander, depending on the need that has been demonstrated. In Army brigades, units smaller than a brigade are designated S1, S2, etc., with corresponding duties, and are referred to as a unit staff. *See also:* Staff.

References
Department of Defense, Joint Chiefs of Staff. *Department of Defense Dictionary of Military and Related Terms.* Washington, DC: GPO, 1986.

—**GENERAL SUPPLY SUPPORT BASE (GSSB)** is the supply of stocks maintained at the corps and theater area Army command levels. These stocks consist of pre-positioned war reserve materiel to include end-items and repair parts to support peacetime readiness with high priority fill and to support war-time sustainment. *See also:* Pre-Positioned War Materiel Stocks.

References
Department of Defense, U.S. Army. *Support Operations: Echelons Above Corps.* Field Manual FM 100-16. Washington, DC: Headquarters, Department of the Army, 1986.

—**GENERAL SUPPORT (GS).** (1) General support is an Army tactical intelligence term that refers to the support provided to the combat force as a whole as directed by the combat force commander and task-organized by the Military Intelligence team leader. General support provides the Military Intelligence support that is responsive to the force commander. It is the most standardized of the standard tactical missions. (2) General support is support that is given to the supported force as a whole, rather than to a specific subdivision. Subdivisions and subordinate units may request support through the supported force headquarters, but only the supported force headquarters can determine priorities and assign missions to GS units. *See also:* General Support Artillery, General Support Reinforcing.

References
Department of Defense, Department of the Army. *Intelligence and Electronic Warfare Operations.* Field Manual FM 34-1. Washington, DC: Headquarters, Department of the Army, 1984.

———. *Military Intelligence Company (Combat Electronic Warfare and Intelligence) (Armored Cavalry Regiment/Separate Brigade).* Field Manual FM 34-30. Washington, DC: Headquarters, Department of the Army, 1983.

———. *Military Intelligence Battalion (Combat Electronic Warfare Intelligence) (Division).* Field Manual FM 34-10. Washington, DC: Headquarters, Department of the Army, 1981.

———. *Operational Terms and Symbols.* Field Manual FM 101-5-1. Washington, DC: Headquarters, Department of the Army, 1985.

———. *Staff Organization and Operations.* Field Manual FM 101-5. Washington, DC: Headquarters, Department of the Army, 1984.

—**GENERAL SUPPORT (GS) ARTILLERY** is artillery that executes the fire as directed by the commander of the unit to which it organically belongs or is attached. It fires in support of the operation as a whole rather than in support of a specific subordinate unit. *See also:* Direct Support Artillery, General Support Reinforcing, Reinforcing (Artillery).

References
Department of Defense, U.S. Army. *Operational Terms and Symbols.* Field Manual FM 101-5-1. Washington, DC: Headquarters, Department of the Army, 1985.

—**GENERAL SUPPORT REINFORCING (GSR).** (1) General support reinforcing is a tactical artillery mission. GSR artillery is assigned the mission to support the force as a whole and to provide reinforcing fires for another artillery unit. (2) In tactical intelligence, GSR means providing support to the combat force as a whole, with secondary emphasis on supporting another Military Intelligence unit or element. A Military Intelligence unit with an assigned GSR mission responds to the needs of the combat force commander and is task-organized by the Military Intelligence commander, responding to requests from the reinforced Military Intelligence unit or element as a secondary priority. The GSR Military Intelligence unit remains under the operational control of the Military Intelligence Commander. *See also:* General Support Artillery.

References
Department of Defense, Department of the Army. *Intelligence and Electronic Warfare Operations.* Field Manual FM 34-1. Washington, DC: Headquarters, Department of the Army, 1984.

———. *Military Intelligence Company (Combat Electronic Warfare and Intelligence) (Armored Cavalry Regiment/Separate Brigade).* Field Manual FM 34-30. Washington, DC: Headquarters, Department of the Army, 1983.

———. *Military Intelligence Battalion (Combat Electronic Warfare Intelligence) (Division).* Field Manual FM 34-10. Washington, DC: Headquarters, Department of the Army, 1981.

———. *Operational Terms and Symbols.* Field Manual FM 101-5-1. Washington, DC: Headquarters, Department of the Army, 1985.

———. *Staff Organization and Operations.* Field Manual FM 101-5. Washington, DC: Headquarters, Department of the Army, 1984.

—**GENERAL SUPPORT ROCKET SYSTEM** is a multiple rocket launcher system that supplements cannon artillery by delivering large quantities of firepower in a short time against critical, time-sensitive targets.

References

Department of Defense, Joint Chiefs of Staff. *Department of Defense Dictionary of Military and Related Terms.* Washington, DC: GPO, 1986.

—**GENERAL WAR** is an armed conflict between major powers in which the total reserves of the parties involved are used and the national survival of each is endangered. *See also:* High Intensity Conflict, Low Intensity Conflict.

References

Department of Defense, Joint Chiefs of Staff. *Department of Defense Dictionary of Military and Related Terms.* Washington, DC: GPO, 1986.

Department of Defense, U.S. Army. *Support Operations: Echelons Above Corps.* Field Manual FM 100-16. Washington, DC: Headquarters, Department of the Army, 1986.

—**GEOGRAPHIC(AL) INTELLIGENCE,** a component of strategic intelligence, is foreign intelligence dealing with the location, description, and analysis and cultural factors of the world, including terrain, climate, natural resources, transportation, boundaries, and population distribution, and their changes over time. The agency primarily responsible for the production of geographic(al) intelligence is the Defense Intelligence Agency.

The Intelligence Community defines geography as the science of describing the land, sea, air, and the distribution of plant and animal life, including humans and their industries. To the Intelligence Community, geography is a synthetic science that relies on the results of specialized sciences (e.g., astronomy, physics, geology, oceanography, meteorology, biology, and bacteriology) for its data.

In this context, military geographic intelligence is the military evaluation of all geographic factors that influence military operations. Military geography, as the term is used in strategic intelligence, embraces all natural and artificial aspects of the physical environment. It is concerned not only with the factors of position, size, shape, boundaries, weather, climate, land forms, drainage, vegetation and surface materials, but also with the cultural factors that have altered the landscape or terrain. Military geographic

intelligence in its broadest terms is practically synonymous with strategic intelligence. Both have the same objective: to estimate and predict the strategic capabilities, vulnerabilities, and probable courses of action of nations and their peoples. In arriving at an estimate, both consider all elements of the human environment, including the relatively abstract factors as well as the more obvious elements of the natural and cultural landscape.

The principal function of the military geographer is to evaluate the effect of the physical landscape on military operations. Strategic intelligence on economic, political, and sociological factors is produced largely by specialists in those fields. A geographic interpretation of the work of these specialists, however, contributes to the selection of strategic areas as military objectives and enters into the determination of the routes to them. The vulnerability or defensibility of military objectives is interpreted by the military geographer after a thorough analysis and evaluation of any or all of the factors discussed below.

Location

The location of an area relative to the historical centers of gravity has shaped the destiny of individual nations and of whole regions. The location of a nation on a world trade route, for example, influences its political policies, economic development, and human technology. Militarily, location may limit the land accessibility of an area but not its accessibility by air or water.

Size

The importance of an area's size is affected by the destiny of the transportation net and the dispersion of vital centers. Militarily, these factors may determine whether space can be exchanged for time by the defenders in ground operations. (Perhaps the greatest example of this is the way the Russians and later the Soviets used their land so effectively in war. By withdrawing and burning the land, they forced the French under Napoleon and the Germans under Hitler to continually extend their supply lines, which became ever more vulnerable to interdiction.) However, a vast expanse of land alone does not provide great military strength, because modern power is based to a large extent on productive facilities that are not necessarily a corollary of size. Perhaps the greatest example of this factor is Saudi Arabia, a huge area rich in oil but has potential problems defending it. Air power has changed the effect of this factor, and the use of other new weapons will probably do likewise.

Shape of Boundaries

The shape of an area, either alone or in combination with other geographic factors, significantly influences basic military plans. There are offensive and defensive advantages to a compact shape, as opposed to a long, narrow one. For example, the Norwegians and Chileans must consider the huge length and narrow width of their nations as major factors in their defensive strategic calculations. Almost as important is the shape of a vital part of a given country, since it may provide the key to the control of the entire nation.

Whether a boundary follows a river, the crest of a mountain range, or a straight line across a plain, its chief military significance pertains to ground operations. But, the military importance of immediately and easily identifying boundaries is also crucial in air operations, where enemy and nonenemy territories join and national interests can be gravely damaged through bombing error.

Coasts and Landing Beaches

Intelligence on the physical characteristics of coasts and landing beaches is an integral part of military geographic intelligence, and of key importance to strategic planners in selecting the type of operations to be undertaken and in evaluating the risks involved.

Accurate data on coasts and landing beaches are vital for planning amphibious operations because of their role in permitting access to enemy-held areas. Also, they substitute for or complement ports in the initial phase of a campaign. In defensive planning, certain characteristics of coasts and landing beaches affect the disposition and capabilities of the defender.

The data required for a beach primarily concern its physical characteristics: location, nearshore approaches, tidal patterns, length and width, gradient and underwater slope, materials and trafficability, and type of obstructions. The terrain flanking and backing the beach determines its exits.

A coastal description also concerns cultural features (e.g., road nets, railroads, airfields, towns, harbors, and anchorages). A coastal de-

scription of the entire area must be included in order to relate the beaches to the surrounding terrain.

Weather and Climate

Weather and climate, in relation to strategic planning, are extremely significant factors of military geographic intelligence. Weather refers to the meteorological conditions (e.g., wind, temperature, rain, and snow) affecting an area at a specific time or for a short period of time. Climate refers to the frequency and range of meteorological conditions affecting an area over a long period of time.

Data on temperature, precipitation, clouds, fog, humidity, winds, and their effects on air, airborne, and amphibious operations, transportation facilities, physical condition of troops, equipment performance, storage and supply of equipment, clothing and shelter for personnel, disease, morale, reconnaissance, and other operations are the chief components of climate and weather intelligence. Data on special weather phenomena (e.g., typhoons, monsoons, hurricanes, tornadoes, and sand-storms) are also important.

Climate and weather influence strategic planning indirectly through their effect on the economic, sociological, and political character of an area. Although these factors are considered in economic, sociological, and political intelligence, military geographical intelligence considers the significance of their interrelationships. Complete strategic planning depends, therefore, on knowledge of both the indirect and direct military implications of weather and climate.

Topography

The topography aspects of geographic intelligence emphasize the military significance of such factors as relief, drainage, vegetation, and soil trafficability.

Relief, landforms, and drainage patterns. Among the environmental factors of major significance to military operations are the size, configuration, and operational implications of landforms and the arrangement of drainage features. Not only do relief features confine or facilitate military operations, but they may also affect such other militarily significant geographic factors as climate. A major element in military geographic analysis is the evaluation of information regarding the shape, height, degree of slope, and trends of relief and drainage features in relation to such problems as determining locations for airheads and beachheads, bivouac areas, specific obstacles to ground movement, and the logical directions for the advance or withdrawal of enemy forces.

Drainage characteristics. The significance of lakes, streams, canals, and swamps as barriers or as navigable waterways reflect such conditions as seasonal depths, currents, widths, bottom characteristics, ice conditions, banks, shorelines, and vegetation in relation to military operations.

Water resources. Data on water resources involve quantitative and qualitative values of such factors as potability, contamination, turbidity, mineral content, and seasonability of supply.

Soil and rocks. Scientific soil and geological surveys from which military interpretation can be derived exist in few countries. Hence, descriptions and samples of soils and rocks together with evaluations in terms of their militarily significant properties are best derived from field observations and collection. Important data of intelligence interest are as follows: rapidity of soil drainage and thickness and character of surface materials as they affect or would affect the construction of roads, airstrips, emplacements, trenches, foxholes and minefields; availability of sand or gravel for road building, emplacement repair, and construction; and the precise nature of the soil as to its effects on the rates of wear of tires, shoes, moving parts, and other types of equipment.

Vegetation. Accurate information on the vegetation of an area is essential for anticipating such military problems as the degree of ease or difficulty of moving men and equipment, the ability to effect strategic and tactical surprise, the availability of concealment from ground and air observation, the extent to which mechanized and motorized equipment may be employed, and the suitability for air landings and air drops. Characteristics such as heights, density of sand, stem diameters, coloration, rooting strength, and cultivation practices evaluated in terms of military significance are essential data. For example, much of this data would be crucial for estimates of the construction difficulties to be anticipated, the ease or difficulty that should be anticipated in moving trucks and vehicles, the problems that will occur concerning concealment of men and equipment, and the potential fire hazard existing in the area.

Cultural features. Such features as mines, quarries, tombs, burial mounds, ditches, hedge rows, terraces, and roads, which occur in sufficient concentration to be of importance in the planning of military operations, are seldom described in terms that bring out their military significance—if data on them are available at all.

Special physical phenomena. Information concerning such factors as seismic disturbances, volcanic phenomena, permafrost, and other factors peculiar to an area assumes military significance in many instances in relation to the extent and frequency of such phenomena.

Urban Areas

The heterogeneity of this subject necessitates close attention. The military significance of such factors as the distribution and pattern of cities and towns, the general characteristics of urban and rural settlement, and the main types of towns is obvious.

Main types of towns. Towns are classified according to function and physical vulnerability, and defensibility characteristics. The purpose of this classification is to determine the key strategic towns or cities and their relative importance. Factors considered include use (industrial, commercial, administrative, political, or combination); pattern (radial, rectangular, etc.); construction (frame, masonry, etc.); utilities (water, power, sanitation, etc.); and population (districted, scattered, etc.).

Strategic towns. The principal militarily significant towns can be defined on the basis of the above information. The defining of key towns is, in effect, a culmination of geographic intelligence and is indispensable to the military planner for determining the defensibility of the town, its political and industrial relationship to the nation, and the effect of its expansion or destruction on the economy or war effort of the nation concerned.

Military Geographic Regions

The military geographic region is conceived as an area in which the combination of environmental conditions is sufficiently uniform to permit or require throughout its extent the use of the same general mode of military operations or kinds of warfare and of the same general types of equipment and personnel. The delineation of such regions requires a full understanding of the environmental and military factors involved. Although the size of a country is not necessarily a factor in determining the number of military geographic regions that it may include, the large countries are more likely than the small countries to include more than one such region. Research analysts can distinguish between areas having different environmental complexes, but the delimitation of such regions and the validity of the military characterization can be appreciably refined through the field observation of intelligence personnel who assess the areas in terms of their military aspects. In preparing an analysis of each military region, all aspects of military intelligence must be considered. The description of a region in terms of well-known regions greatly enhances the value of the intelligence produced.

Strategic Areas, Approaches, Internal Routes.

The efforts of geographic intelligence to assess a country's capabilities and vulnerabilities focus on the areas to which strategic significance attaches for any particular reason. An adjunct to such an assessment includes an evaluation of the external approaches and internal routes directed against it, and particularly against its strategic areas. This aspect of geographic intelligence is subject to change and must be continuously reviewed to insure that the assessments of areas and the approaches thereto correctly reflect current conditions. See also: Strategic Intelligence.

References
Clauser, Jerome K., and Weir, Sandra M. Intelligence Research Methodology. State College, PA: HRB-Singer, Inc., 1975.

Department of Defense, Defense Intelligence College. Glossary of Intelligence Terms and Definitions. Washington, DC: DIC, 1987.

Godson, Roy, ed. Intelligence Problems for the 1980s, Number 1: Elements of Intelligence. Rev. ed. Washington, DC: National Strategy Information Center, 1983.

Kent, Sherman. Strategic Intelligence for American World Policy. Princeton, NJ: Princeton University Press, 1966.

—**GO** (ARMY AVIATION) is a command to execute a tactical maneuver.

References
Department of Defense, U.S. Army. Air-to-Air Combat. Field Manual FM 1-107. Washington, DC: Headquarters, Department of the Army, 1984.

—**GO NO-GO** is the condition or state of a component or system to operate: "go" functioning properly; or "no-go," not functioning properly.

References
Department of Defense, Joint Chiefs of Staff. Department of Defense Dictionary of Military and Related Terms. Washington, DC: GPO, 1986.

—**GRADE** is a step or degree, in a graduated scale of office or military rank, established and designated as a grade by law or regulation. See also: Grade Conversion.

References
Department of Defense, U.S. Army. Promotion of Officers on Active Duty. Army Regulation AR 624-100. Washington, DC: Headquarters, Department of the Army, 1984.

—**GRADE CONVERSION** is a change from non-commissioned officer to a specialist status within the same pay grade.

References
Department of Defense, U.S. Army. Enlisted Personnel Management System. Army Regulation AR 600-200. Washington, DC: Headquarters, Department of the Army, 1984.

—**GRADUATION LEAVE** is a period of nonchargeable absence to the graduates of the U.S. Military Academy who are appointed as commissioned officers in the Armed Forces. This leave must be used or taken by these individuals before they report to the first permanent duty station.

References
Department of Defense, U.S. Army. Leaves and Passes. Army Regulation AR 630-5. Washington, DC: Headquarters, Department of the Army, 1984.

—**GRAY LISTS** contain the identities and locations of individuals whose inclinations and attitudes toward the political and military objectives of the United States are obscure. Regardless of their political inclinations or attitudes, personalities may be listed on gray lists when they are known to possess information or particular skills that are required by U.S. forces. They may be individuals whose political motivations require further exploration before they can be used effectively by U.S. forces. Examples of individuals who may be included in this category are the following:

- Potential or actual defectors from the hostile cause whose bona fides have not been established;

- Individuals who have resisted, or are believed to have resisted, the enemy government and who may be willing to cooperate with U.S. forces, but whose bona fides have not been established; and
- Scientists and technicians who are suspected of having been engaged against their will in enemy research projects or high technology programs.

See also: Black Lists, White Lists.

References

Department of Defense, U.S. Army. *Counterintelligence.* Field Manual FM 34-60. Washington, DC: Headquarters, Department of the Army, 1985.

—**GRAZING FIRE** is fire approximately parallel to the ground where the center of the cone of fire does not rise above one meter from the ground.

References

Department of Defense, U.S. Army. *Operational Terms and Symbols.* Field Manual FM 101-5-1. Washington, DC: Headquarters, Department of the Army, 1985.

—**GRENADE SUMPS** are holes usually dug at the bottom of a position's front wall where the water collects. The sump is about three feet long, one half foot wide, and is dug at a 30 degree angle. The slant of the floor channels excess water and grenades into the sump. *See also:* Position.

References

Department of Defense, U.S. Army. *Survivability.* Field Manual FM 5-103. Washington, DC: Headquarters, Department of the Army, 1985.

—**GRID COORDINATES** are the easting and northing values of a grid that designate the location of a point in respect to the grid. Coordinates are usually expressed in the nearest 100, 10, or 1 meter, with the easting and northing values combined into a single expression (e.g., 329378 (nearest 100 meters), 32943785 (nearest 10 meters), 3294837853 (nearest 1 meter)).

References

Department of Defense, U.S. Army. *Operational Terms and Symbols.* Field Manual FM 101-5-1. Washington, DC: Headquarters, Department of the Army, 1985.

—**GROUND CONTROL INTERCEPTION** is a technique that permits the control of friendly aircraft or missiles for the purposes of insuring interception.

References

Department of Defense, Joint Chiefs of Staff. *Department of Defense Dictionary of Military and Related Terms.* Washington, DC: GPO, 1986.

—**GROUND CONTROLLED INTERCEPT (GCI) (ARMY AVIATION)** are vectors (usually radar) given to an air crew to intercept a target. *See also:* Ground Control Interception.

References

Department of Defense, U.S. Army. *Air-to-Air Combat.* Field Manual FM 1-107. Washington, DC: Headquarters, Department of the Army, 1984.

—**GROUND FIRE** is small arms ground-to-air fire directed against aircraft.

References

Department of Defense, Joint Chiefs of Staff. *Department of Defense Dictionary of Military and Related Terms.* Washington, DC: GPO, 1986.

—**GROUND FORCES INTELLIGENCE STUDY (GROFIS)** provides a good summary of ground forces' compositions, identifications, and strengths. These studies are categorized by regions and by countries of the world. Published annually or biennially, they cover the missions, tasks, organization, capabilities, policies, and military trends of the subject nation or region. *See also:* Ground Order of Battle.

References

Von Hoene, John P.A. *Intelligence User's Guide.* Washington, DC: DIA, 1983.

—**GROUND LIAISON OFFICER (GLO)** is an officer trained in offensive air support activities. Ground liaison officers are normally organized into parties under the control of the appropriate Army commander in order to provide liaison with Air Force and naval units engaged in training and combat operations. *See also:* Ground Liaison Party, Ground Liaison Section.

References

Department of Defense, Joint Chiefs of Staff. *Department of Defense Dictionary of Military and Related Terms.* Washington, DC: GPO, 1986.

—**GROUND LIAISON PARTY** is an Army unit that consists of a variable number of personnel who are responsible for liaison with a tactical air support agency.

References

Department of Defense, Joint Chiefs of Staff. *Department of Defense Dictionary of Military and Related Terms*. Washington, DC: GPO, 1986.

—**GROUND LIAISON SECTION** is an Army unit that consists of a varying number of Army officers, other ranks, and vehicles that are responsible for army/air liaison, under the control of the Army headquarters.

References

Department of Defense, Joint Chiefs of Staff. *Department of Defense Dictionary of Military and Related Terms*. Washington, DC: GPO, 1986.

—**GROUND OBSERVER CENTER** is a center to which ground observer teams report and that, in turn, pass information to the appropriate control and/or reporting agency. *See also:* Ground Observer Organization, Ground Observer Team.

References

Department of Defense, Joint Chiefs of Staff. *Department of Defense Dictionary of Military and Related Terms*. Washington, DC: GPO, 1986.

—**GROUND OBSERVER ORGANIZATION** is a corps of ground watchers deployed at suitable points throughout an air defense system in order to provide visual and aural information on aircraft movements.

References

Department of Defense, Joint Chiefs of Staff. *Department of Defense Dictionary of Military and Related Terms*. Washington, DC: GPO, 1986.

—**GROUND OBSERVER TEAM** consists of small units or detachments deployed to provide information, obtained by oral or visual means, on aircraft movements over a defended area.

References

Department of Defense, Joint Chiefs of Staff. *Department of Defense Dictionary of Military and Related Terms*. Washington, DC: GPO, 1986.

—**GROUND ORDER OF BATTLE (GOB)** is a Defense Intelligence Agency publication. It is published by country or region and provides detailed information on a nation's army forces, the army's command structure, its territorial and tactical organization, and the distribution of its units.

References

Department of Defense, Defense Intelligence College. *Glossary of Intelligence Terms and Definitions*. Washington, DC: DIC, 1987.

—**GROUND RESOLUTION,** in photoreconnaissance, is a measurement of the smallest detail that can be distinguished on the ground by a sensor system under specific conditions. *See also:* Aerial Photograph.

References

Reeves, Robert; Anson, Abraham; and Landen, David. *Manual of Remote Sensing*. Falls Church, VA: American Society of Photogrammetry, 1975.

—**GROUND RETURN,** in radar intelligence, refers to radar echoes reflected from the ground or terrain. The radio echoes are also called ground clutter. *See also:* Radar Intelligence.

References

Department of Defense, Joint Chiefs of Staff. *Department of Defense Dictionary of Military and Related Terms*. Washington, DC: GPO, 1986.

—**GROUND TACTICAL PLAN** is an airborne or air assault operational plan that covers the conduct of operations in the objective area. *See also:* Air Movement Plan, Landing Plan, Marshaling Plan.

References

Department of Defense, U.S. Army. *Operational Terms and Symbols*. Field Manual FM 101-5-1. Washington, DC: Headquarters, Department of the Army, 1985.

—**GROUND ZERO** is the center of the actual impact of a bomb, missile, or other projectile. The term is most often used in respect to the detonation of nuclear weapons.

References

Department of Defense, Joint Chiefs of Staff. *Department of Defense Dictionary of Military and Related Terms*. Washington, DC: GPO, 1986.

—**GROUP** is a flexible administrative and tactical unit composed of either two or more battalions or two or more squadrons. The term also applies to combat support and service support units.

References
Department of Defense, Joint Chiefs of Staff. *Department of Defense Dictionary of Military and Related Terms.* Washington, DC: GPO, 1986.

—**GROUP BURIAL** is a burial in a common grave of two or more individually unidentified remains. *See also:* Burial.

References
Department of Defense, Joint Chiefs of Staff. *Department of Defense Dictionary of Military and Related Terms.* Washington, DC: GPO, 1986.

—**GROUP OF TARGETS** refers to two or more targets on which are to be fired at simultaneously. A group of targets is designated by a letter/number combination or a nickname.

References
Department of Defense, Joint Chiefs of Staff. *Department of Defense Dictionary of Military and Related Terms.* Washington, DC: GPO, 1986.

—**GROUP RENDEZVOUS** is a checkpoint at which formations of the same type join before proceeding. *See also:* Force Rendezvous.

References
Department of Defense, Joint Chiefs of Staff. *Department of Defense Dictionary of Military and Related Terms.* Washington, DC: GPO, 1986.

—**GUARD (GD).** (1) A guard is a security element whose primary task is to protect the main force by fighting to gain time, while also observing and reporting information. (2) A guard is a term used to refer to a special unit that is responsible to the officer of the day for the protection and security of an installation or area. This unit includes a commander of the guard, a sergeant of the guard, commanders of the relief, and the guards; The term is also used to refer to an individual who is responsible to keep watch over, protect, shield, defend, warn, or perform any duties prescribed by general orders and/or special orders. He is also referred to as a sentinel, sentry, or lookout. *See also:* Guard Force, Guard Operations, Guardhouse.

References
Department of Defense, Joint Chiefs of Staff. *Department of Defense Dictionary of Military and Related Terms.* Washington, DC: GPO, 1986.
Department of Defense, U.S. Army. *Guard Duty.* Field Manual FM 22-6. Washington, DC: Headquarters, Department of the Army, 1971.

—**GUARD FORCE** accomplishes all the tasks of a screening force, and prevents enemy ground observation of, and direct fire against, the main body. A guard force reconnoiters, attacks, defends, and delays as necessary to accomplish its mission. It normally operates within the range of the main body's indirect fire weapons.

References
Department of Defense, U.S. Army. *Operational Terms and Symbols.* Field Manual FM 101-5-1. Washington, DC: Headquarters, Department of the Army, 1985.

—**GUARD OPERATIONS.** The purpose of a guard operation is to obtain early warning, reaction time, and maneuver space to the front, flank, or rear of a moving or stationary force. A guard operation is usually conducted within range of artillery with the main body. There are three types of guard formations: advance guard, flank guard, and rear guard. A guard force reconnoiters, screens, attacks, and defends as required for mission accomplishment. Guard operations may be conducted by cavalry units to the front, flank, or rear of a stationary or moving force. Air cavalry conducts screening operations as part of armored cavalry guard operations. *See also:* Advance Guard, Flank Guard, Rear Guard.

References
Department of Defense, U.S. Army. *Cavalry.* Field Manual FM 17-95. Washington, DC: Headquarters, Department of the Army, 1977.

—**GUARDHOUSE** is a building, tent, or other location occupied by individuals who have been detailed for interior guard duty. It is the headquarters for the guard.

References
Department of Defense, U.S. Army. *Guard Duty.* Field Manual FM 22-6. Washington, DC: Headquarters, Department of the Army, 1971.

—**GUARDRAIL** aircraft is an Army tactical intelligence aircraft that provides collection and emitter location information for enemy communications systems. It intercepts enemy high frequency, very high frequency, and ultra high frequency communications emitters and locates high frequency and very high frequency communications emitters. It processes the information and reports it to users over secure, direct communications in near real time. The system consists of: a remotely controlled collection and data transmitting system aboard an RU-21 or

RC-12 aircraft; ground support and maintenance equipment; an integrated processing facility; and a tactical commander's terminal.

References

Department of Defense, U.S. Army. *Military Intelligence Battalion Combat Electronic Warfare and Intelligence (Aerial Exploitation) (Corps)*. Field Manual FM 34-22. Washington, DC: Headquarters, Department of the Army, 1984.

—**GUERRILLA** is a combat participant in guerrilla warfare. *See also:* Guerrilla Operations, Guerrilla Warfare.

References

Department of Defense, Joint Chiefs of Staff. *Department of Defense Dictionary of Military and Related Terms*. Washington, DC: GPO, 1986.

U.S. Congress. Senate. *Final Report of the Senate Select Committee to Study Government Operations With Respect to Intelligence Activities. Report 94-755. Book I, Foreign and Military Intelligence* (Church Committee Report). Washington, DC: GPO, 1976.

—**GUERRILLA OPERATIONS** are the covert activities conducted by lightly armed indigenous forces operating in an area controlled by a hostile central government or an occupying foreign power. *See also:* Guerrilla, Guerrilla Warfare.

References

Oseth, John M. *Regulating U.S. Intelligence Operations: A Study in the Definition of the National Interest*. Frankfurt: University of Kentucky Press, 1985.

—**GUERRILLA WARFARE** refers to the hostilities conducted by lightly armed indigenous forces operating in an area controlled by a hostile central government or an occupying foreign power. It is conducted to complement, support, or extend conventional military operations. The guerilla is fundamentally an offensive weapon of war whose superior knowledge of the terrain and ability to surprise the enemy allow him to mount hit-and-run operations with great effectiveness. *See also:* Guerrilla, Guerrilla Operations, Unconventional Warfare.

References

Department of Defense, U.S. Army. *Operational Terms and Symbols*. Field Manual FM 101-5-1. Washington, DC: Headquarters, Department of the Army, 1985.

U.S. Congress. Senate. *Final Report of the Senate Select Committee to Study Government Operations With Respect to Intelligence Activities. Report 94-755. Book I, Foreign and Military Intelligence* (Church Committee Report). Washington, DC: GPO, 1976.

—**GUIDANCE.** (1) Guidance is advice that identifies, interprets, clarifies, or expands on an information need. In collection, it also means the general direction of the intelligence effort. (2) Guidance is policy, direction, decision, or instruction having the effect of an order when it is promulgated by a higher echelon. (3) Guidance is the entire process by which target intelligence information received by the guided missile is used to effect proper flight control in order to cause timely direction changes for effective target interception. *See also:* Intelligence.

References

Department of Defense, Defense Intelligence College. *Glossary of Intelligence Terms and Definitions*. Washington, DC: DIC, 1987.

Department of Defense, Joint Chiefs of Staff. *Department of Defense Dictionary of Military and Related Terms*. Washington, DC: GPO, 1986.

U.S. Congress. Senate. *Final Report of the Senate Select Committee to Study Government Operations With Respect to Intelligence Activities. Report 94-755. Book I, Foreign and Military Intelligence* (Church Committee Report). Washington, DC: GPO, 1976.

—**GUIDE** (DRILL AND CEREMONIES) is the person responsible for maintaining the prescribed direction and rate of march.

References

Department of Defense, U.S. Army. *Drills and Ceremonies*. Field Manual FM 22-5. Washington, DC: Headquarters, Department of the Army, 1986.

—**GUIDE SIGNS** are signs used to indicate locations, distances, directions, routes, and similar information.

References

Department of Defense, Joint Chiefs of Staff. *Department of Defense Dictionary of Military and Related Terms*. Washington, DC: GPO, 1986.

—**GUIDED MISSILE (GM)** is an unmanned vehicle moving above the earth's surface and whose trajectory and flight path can be altered by an external or an internal mechanism. *See also:* Aerodynamic Missile, Ballistic Missile.

References

Department of Defense, Joint Chiefs of Staff. *Department of Defense Dictionary of Military and Related Terms*. Washington, DC: GPO, 1986.

—**GUIDED MISSILE (GM) (SURFACE-TO-AIR)** is a surface-launched guided missile used against air targets.

References
Department of Defense, Joint Chiefs of Staff. *Department of Defense Dictionary of Military and Related Terms.* Washington, DC: GPO, 1986.

—**GUIDED MISSILE (GM) (SURFACE-TO-SUR-FACE)** is a surface-launched guided missile used against surface targets.

References
Department of Defense, Joint Chiefs of Staff. *Department of Defense Dictionary of Military and Related Terms.* Washington, DC: GPO, 1986.

—**GUIDED ROUTE** is a route upon which a unit has placed personnel, on its own initiative and under conditions prescribed by the commander or maneuver regulations, to direct only personnel and vehicles of their unit.

References
Department of Defense, U.S. Army. *Route Reconnaissance and Classification.* Field Manual FM 5-36. Washington, DC: Headquarters, Department of the Army, 1985.

—**GUN.** (1) A gun is a cannon with a relatively long barrel, operating with a relatively low angle of fire, and having a high muzzle velocity. (2) A gun is a cannon with a tube length of 30 calibers or more. *See also:* Howitzer, Mortar.

References
Department of Defense, Joint Chiefs of Staff. *Department of Defense Dictionary of Military and Related Terms.* Washington, DC: GPO, 1986.

—**GUN, ANTIAIRCRAFT ARTILLERY SP, TWIN 40-MM, M42A1 (DUSTER)** is a self-propelled full-tracked armored vehicle used with maneuver forces in forward combat areas in order to defend against low-altitude air attack.

References
Department of Defense, U.S. Army. *U.S. Army Air Defense Artillery Employment.* Field Manual FM 44-1. Washington, DC: Headquarters, Department of the Army, 1983.

—**GUN CARRIAGE** is a mobile or fixed support for a gun. It sometimes includes the elevating and traversing mechanisms, and is sometimes called a carriage.

References
Department of Defense, Joint Chiefs of Staff. *Department of Defense Dictionary of Military and Related Terms.* Washington, DC: GPO, 1986.

—**GUN-TARGET LINE** is an imaginary straight line from the gun to the target.

References
Department of Defense, U.S. Army. *Operational Terms and Symbols.* Field Manual FM 101-5-1. Washington, DC: Headquarters, Department of the Army, 1985.

—**GUN-TYPE WEAPON** is a device in which two or more pieces of fissionable material, each less than a critical mass, are brought together very rapidly to form a supercritical mass that can explode as the result of a rapidly expanding fission chain.

References
Department of Defense, Joint Chiefs of Staff. *Department of Defense Dictionary of Military and Related Terms.* Washington, DC: GPO, 1986.

—**GUNS (ARMY AVIATION)** is a report that indicates that friendly aircraft are either too close to threaten aircraft or are out of parameters to engage with infrared weapons.

References
Department of Defense, U.S. Army. *Air-to-Air Combat.* Field Manual FM 1-107. Washington, DC: Headquarters, Department of the Army, 1984.

—H-HOUR is the specific hour on D-day at which a particular operation commences. It may be the commencement of hostilities; the hour at which an operation plan is executed or is to be executed (as distinguished from the hour that the order to execute is issued); or the hour that the operation phase is implemented, either by land assault, amphibious assault, parachute assault, or naval bombardment. The highest command or headquarters coordinating the planning specifies the meaning of H-hour within the above definition. If several operations or phases of an operation are to be conducted in the same area on D-day and confusion could arise over the use of the same hour designation, the letters F, L, S, W, and Y may be used. If this occurs the letters used and their meaning must be stated in the plan or order. Reference to hours preceding or following H-hour are referred to by using a plus or minus and an Arabic numeral following the letter H (e.g., H-3 is 3 hours prior to H-hour; and H+7 is 7 hours after H-hour). If a time element other than hours is expressed, it must be spelled out (e.g., H+30 minutes). *See also:* D-Day.

References
Department of Defense, U.S. Army. *Operational Terms and Symbols.* Field Manual FM 101-5-1. Washington, DC: Headquarters, Department of the Army, 1985.

—HABITUAL ASSOCIATION is the close and continuous relationship established between support elements and the combat units that they support, or between combat units that are frequently cross-attached to insure a mutual understanding of operating procedures and techniques and to increase overall responsiveness. *See also:* Regimental Affiliation.

References
Department of Defense, U.S. Army. *Operational Terms and Symbols.* Field Manual FM 101-5-1. Washington, DC: Headquarters, Department of the Army, 1985.

—HALF LEFT (RIGHT) is a direction, 45 degrees to the left (right) of the original front in which a soldier faces in executing the command. It is also the preparatory command to face in a direction 45 degrees to the left (right) of the original front.

References
Department of Defense, U.S. Army. *Dictionary of United States Army Terms.* Army Regulation AR 310-25. Washington, DC: Headquarters, Department of the Army, 1986.

—HALF THICKNESS is the thickness of absorbing material necessary to reduce by half the intensity of radiation that passes through it. *See also:* Nuclear Warfare.

References
Department of Defense, U.S. Army. *NBC Operations.* Field Manual FM 3-100. Washington, DC: Headquarters, Department of the Army, 1985.

—HALF-LOADED, in automatic arms, is a belt or magazine inserted and received charged, but without the first cartridge in the chamber.

References
Department of Defense, U.S. Army. *Dictionary of United States Army Terms.* Army Regulation AR 310-25. Washington, DC: Headquarters, Department of the Army, 1986.

—HALF-TRACK VEHICLE is a combination wheeled and track-laying motor vehicle in which the rear end is supported on, and propelled by, complete band tracks and the front end is supported on, and steered by, wheels.

References
Department of Defense, U.S. Army. *Dictionary of United States Army Terms.* Army Regulation 310-25. Washington, DC: Headquarters, Department of the Army, 1986.

—HALO is a type of airdrop used to drop supplies and equipment from high altitudes because the aircraft must fly above the threat umbrella. The rigged load is pulled from the aircraft by a stabilizing parachute and free falls to a low altitude where a cargo parachute opens to allow a low velocity landing. *See also:* Free Fall.

References
Department of Defense, U.S. Army. *USA/USAF Doctrine for Joint Airborne and Tactical Airlift Operations.* Field Manual FM 100-27. Washington, DC: Headquarters, Department of the Army, 1985.

—**HALVING** is a division of the field of view, observed from a coincidence-type rangefinder, into two equal portions, one the mirror image of the other. *See also:* Halving Adjustment, Halving Line.

References
Department of Defense, U.S. Army. *Dictionary of United States Army Terms.* Army Regulation 310-25. Washington, DC: Headquarters, Department of the Army, 1986.

—**HALVING ADJUSTMENT** is an adjustment of a coincidence-type rangefinder so that the two sections of the field of view, divided by the halving line, are mirror images of each other.

References
Department of Defense, U.S. Army. *Dictionary of United States Army Terms.* Army Regulation AR 310-25. Washington, DC: Headquarters, Department of the Army, 1986.

—**HALVING LINE** is a line that divides the two parts of the field of view of a coincidence-type rangefinder so that the two sections of the field of view, divided by the halving line, are mirror images of each other.

References
Department of Defense, U.S. Army. *Dictionary of United States Army Terms.* Army Regulation AR 310-25. Washington, DC: Headquarters, Department of the Army, 1986.

—**HAND RECEIPT** is a document used by an individual to record his acceptance of, and responsibility for, material. *See also:* Accountable Officer.

References
Department of Defense, U.S. Army. *Dictionary of United States Army Terms.* Army Regulation AR 310-25. Washington, DC: Headquarters, Department of the Army, 1986.

—**HANDOFF.** (1) Handoff is the passing of responsibility for the battle from one commander to another (e.g., the passage of responsibility from the covering force commander to the main battle area commander during an active defense). The time and assistance required for passage depend on the terrain, the ability of field artillery positioned in the main battle area to support, and the capability of main battle area forces and commanders to assume control. (2) Handoff is the passage or handoff of the battle that occurs between units at all echelons of command during passage of lines and relief operations. (3) Handoff is the handover of targets between individual weapon systems (e.g., it may occur between two tanks when one is repositioning or is between scout helicopters and attack helicopters, or it may occur between fighter aircraft during the engagement of enemy armor).

References
Department of Defense, U.S. Army. *Attack Helicopter Operations.* Field Manual FM 17-50. Washington, DC: Headquarters, Department of the Army, 1984.

—**HANDOVER,** in attack helicopter operations, means the same as handoff. *See also:* Attack Helicopter.

References
Department of Defense, U.S. Army. *Attack Helicopter Operations.* Field Manual FM 17-50. Washington, DC: Headquarters, Department of the Army, 1984.

—**HANDOVER LINE** is a control measure, usually a phase line, preferably following easily defined terrain features, at which responsibility for the conduct of combat operations is passed from one force to another. *See also:* Phase Line.

References
Department of Defense, U.S. Army. *Dictionary of United States Army Terms.* Army Regulation AR 310-25. Washington, DC: Headquarters, Department of the Army, 1986.

—**HANG FIRE** is an undesired delay in the functioning of a firing system.

References
Department of Defense, Joint Chiefs of Staff. *Department of Defense Dictionary of Military and Related Terms.* Washington, DC: GPO, 1986.

—**HARASSING** is the attack of any target within the area of a land battle that is not connected with interdiction or close air support. *See also:* Harassing Fire, Harassment.

References
Department of Defense, U.S. Army. *Dictionary of United States Army Terms.* Army Regulation AR 310-25. Washington, DC: Headquarters, Department of the Army, 1986.

—**HARASSING FIRE** is fire designed to disturb the rest of the enemy's troops, to curtail enemy movement, and, by threat of losses, to lower enemy morale. *See also:* Fire.

References
Department of Defense, Joint Chiefs of Staff.
*Department of Defense Dictionary of Military and
Related Terms.* Washington, DC: GPO, 1986.

—**HARASSMENT** is an incident whose primary
objective is to disrupt the activities of a unit or
installation, rather than to inflict serious casualties or damage. *See also:* Harassing Fire.

References
Department of Defense, Joint Chiefs of Staff.
*Department of Defense Dictionary of Military and
Related Terms.* Washington, DC: GPO, 1986.

—**HARDENED SITE** is constructed to protect
against the effects of conventional and nuclear
explosions. The site may also be equipped to
provide protection against a chemical or biological attack. *See also:* Nuclear Warfare.

References
Department of Defense, Joint Chiefs of Staff.
*Department of Defense Dictionary of Military and
Related Terms.* Washington, DC: GPO, 1986.

—**HARDSTAND.** (1) A hardstand is a paved or
stabilized area where vehicles are parked. (2) A
hardstand is an open ground area with a prepared
surface that is used for storing materiel.

References
Department of Defense, Joint Chiefs of Staff.
*Department of Defense Dictionary of Military and
Related Terms.* Washington, DC: GPO, 1986.

—**HARMONIZE** is to align rocket launchers, guns,
or cameras to produce the desired pattern or
point of fire at a specified range, followed by
the alignment of the gunsight so that its line of
sight passes through the aim point of the desired
strike pattern.

References
Department of Defense, U.S. Army. *Dictionary of
United States Army Terms.* Army Regulation AR
310-25. Washington, DC: Headquarters, Department of the Army, 1986.

—**HASTY AMBUSH** is an immediate action drill
in response to an unexpected meeting at close
range with an enemy force. It is not normally
carried out at the company level. *See also:* Deliberate Ambush.

References
Department of Defense, U.S. Army. *The Infantry
Rifle Company (Infantry, Airborne, Air Assault,
Ranger).* Field Manual FM 7-10. Washington, DC:
Headquarters, Department of the Army, 1982.

————. *The Rifle Squads (Mechanized and Light
Infantry).* Training Circular TC 7-1. Washington,
DC: Headquarters, Department of the Army, 1976.

—**HASTY ATTACK** result from meeting engagements with the enemy or successful defenses. In
a hasty attack, the commander attacks quickly
from his existing dispositions to gain the upper
hand or to keep the enemy from organizing resistance. In moving to contact, the commander
must employ formations that permit him to attack
effectively on short notice. When defending, he
must foresee offensive opportunities and dispose
his forces in ways that facilitate the launching of
hasty attacks. Such attacks are not planned in
detail, but commanders should anticipate them
and plan their dispositions and fires to facilitate
them. Speed of attack can offset a lack of thorough preparation, but, from the early moments
of the meeting engagement or decision to attack,
every available element of combat support must
be committed to the attack as rapidly as possible. *See also:* Deliberate Attack.

References
Department of Defense, U.S. Army. *Operational
Terms and Symbols.* Field Manual FM 101-5-1.
Washington, DC: Headquarters, Department of the
Army, 1985.

————. *Operations.* Field Manual FM 100-5.
Washington, DC: Headquarters, Department of the
Army, 1986.

—**HASTY BREACH** is the breach of an obstacle or
obstacles conducted to maintain the momentum
of an attack by attempting to breach "in stride"
as obstacles are encountered. It can be conducted by a unit of any size, but is best accomplished with the assets of a task force. It is
normally conducted by combat elements. *See
also:* Deliberate Breach.

References
Department of Defense, U.S. Army. *Operational
Terms and Symbols.* Field Manual FM 101-5-1.
Washington, DC: Headquarters, Department of the
Army, 1985.

—**HASTY BREACHING** is the rapid creation of a
route through a minefield, barrier, or fortification by an expedient method. *See also:* Mine
Warfare.

References
Department of Defense, Joint Chiefs of Staff.
*Department of Defense Dictionary of Military and
Related Terms.* Washington, DC: GPO, 1986.

—**HASTY DECON** are actions performed by teams or squads using equipment found within battalion-sized units to reduce the spread of nuclear, chemical, or biological contamination on people or equipment and to allow temporary relief from MOPP4. *See also:* Deliberate Decontamination, MOPP4.

References

Department of Defense, U.S. Army. *NBC Operations.* Field Manual FM 3-100. Washington, DC: Headquarters, Department of the Army, 1985.

—**HASTY DECON OPERATION** is a decon operation that consists of two techniques, the MOPP gear exchange and the vehicle washdown. *See also:* Biological Warfare, Chemical Warfare, MOPP, Nuclear Warfare.

References

Department of Defense, U.S. Army. *NBC Decontamination.* Field Manual FM 3-5. Washington, DC: Headquarters, Department of the Army, 1985.

—**HASTY DEFENSE** is organized while in contact with the enemy or when contact is imminent and the time to organize is limited. It is characterized by improving the natural defensive strength of the terrain by using foxholes, emplacements, and obstacles. *See also:* Deliberate Defense.

References

Department of Defense, U.S. Army. *Operational Terms and Symbols.* Field Manual FM 101-5-1. Washington, DC: Headquarters, Department of the Army, 1985.

—**HASTY DEMOLITIONS** are explosives used when time is limited and the economy of explosives is secondary to speed.

References

Department of Defense, U.S. Army. *Operations.* Field Manual FM 100-5. Washington, DC: Headquarters, Department of the Army, 1986.

—**HASTY MINEFIELD BREACH.** (1) A hasty minefield breach is a combat breach of an enemy field covered by enemy fire. (2) A hasty minefield breach is a rapid breach that maintains the momentum of the assault. *See also:* Mine Warfare.

References

Department of Defense, U.S. Army. *Mine/ Countermine Operations at the Company Level.* Field Manual FM 20-32. Washington, DC: Headquarters, Department of the Army, 1976.

—**HASTY POSITIONS** (COMBAT VEHICLE). Hasty fighting positions for combat vehicles, including armored personnel carriers, combat engineering vehicles, and mortar carriers, take advantage of natural terrain features or are prepared with a minimum of construction effort. A frontal parapet, as high as practical without interfering with the vehicles' weapon systems, shields them from frontal attack and provides limited concealment for them if they are properly camouflaged. Protection is improved if the position is made deeper and the parapet is extended around the vehicles' sides. Because of the false sense of security provided by parapets against kinetic energy and hypervelocity projectiles, hasty vehicle fighting positions with parapets are not recommended for tanks, infantry fighting vehicles, and improved tube-bunched, optically tracked, wire-guided vehicles. Hasty fighting positions offer protection from high-explosive antitank projectiles. As the tactical situation permits, hasty positions are improved to deliberate positions. *See also:* Deliberate Positions, Hasty Positions (Infantry).

References

Department of Defense, U.S. Army. *Survivability.* Field Manual FM 5-103. Washington, DC: Headquarters, Department of the Army, 1985.

—**HASTY POSITIONS** (INFANTRY). When time and materials are limited, troops in contact with the enemy use a hasty fighting position located behind whatever cover is available. The cover should provide frontal protection from direct fire while allowing fire to the front and oblique. For protection from indirect fire, a hasty fighting position is located in a depression or hole at least eighteen inches deep. *See also:* Deliberate Positions (Infantry).

References

Department of Defense, U.S. Army. *Survivability.* Field Manual FM 5-103. Washington, DC: Headquarters, Department of the Army, 1985.

—**HASTY PROTECTIVE MINEFIELDS** are used as part of a unit's defensive perimeter. They are usually laid by units using conventional or scatterable mines from their basic loads. *See also:* Mine Warfare.

References

Department of Defense, U.S. Army. *Countermobility.* Field Manual FM 5-102. Washington, DC: Headquarters, Department of the Army, 1985.

—**HASTY RIVER CROSSING** is the crossing of a river or stream by using any means readily available, without pausing to make elaborate preparations. This is also called a hasty crossing. *See also:* Deliberate River Crossing.

References

Department of Defense, U.S. Army. *Operational Terms and Symbols.* Field Manual FM 101-5-1. Washington, DC: Headquarters, Department of the Army, 1985.

—**HASTY ROUTE RECONNAISSANCE** is a limited reconnaissance, conducted to determine the immediate military trafficability of a specified route.

References

Department of Defense, U.S. Army. *Route Reconnaissance and Classification.* Field Manual FM 5-36. Washington, DC: Headquarters, Department of the Army, 1985.

—**HAWK MISSILE SYSTEM** is a mobile, medium-range air defense guided missile system designed to provide nonnuclear air defense coverage against low-to-medium altitude air attacks.

References

Department of Defense, U.S. Army. *U.S. Army Air Defense Employment.* Field Manual FM 44-1. Washington, DC: Headquarters, Department of the Army, 1983.

—**HAZARD** is any real or potential condition that can cause injury, illness, or death to personnel, or can cause damage to, or loss of, equipment or property. *See also:* Hazard Analysis, Hazard Level.

References

Department of Defense, U.S. Army. *Dictionary of United States Army Terms.* Army Regulation AR 310-25. Washington, DC: Headquarters, Department of the Army, 1986.

—**HAZARD ANALYSIS** is the logical, systematic examination of an item, process, facility, or system to identify the probability, causes, and consequences of potential or real hazards.

References

Department of Defense, U.S. Army. *Dictionary of United States Army Terms.* Army Regulation AR 310-25. Washington, DC: Headquarters, Department of the Army, 1986.

—**HAZARD LEVEL** is a quantitative description of the potential severity of a systems hazard, stated in relative terms.

References

Department of Defense, U.S. Army. *Dictionary of United States Army Terms.* Army Regulation AR 310-25. Washington, DC: Headquarters, Department of the Army, 1986.

—**HAZARD SIGN** (ROAD TRANSPORT) is used to indicate traffic hazards. Military hazard signs should be used in communications zone areas only in accordance with existing agreements with the national authorities.

References

Department of Defense, Joint Chiefs of Staff. *Department of Defense Dictionary of Military and Related Terms.* Washington, DC: GPO, 1986.

—**HAZARDOUS AND/OR DANGEROUS MATERIALS** consist of explosives; flammable substances; toxic chemicals; sources of ionizing radiation or radiant energy; oxidizing material; and corrosive material, compressed gases, and any compound, mixture, element, or material that, because of its nature, is hazardous to store and/or handle. Dangerous materials are any materials that, under conditions incident to transportation, are likely to cause fires, create serious damage by chemical action, or create a serious transportation hazard. They include explosives, flammables, corrosives, combustibles, oxidizing materials, poisons, compressed gases, toxics, unduly magnetic materials, defensive biological/etiological agents, and radiologicals. *See also:* Hazardous Fragment.

References

Department of Defense, U.S. Army. *Dictionary of United States Army Terms.* Army Regulation AR 310-25. Washington, DC: Headquarters, Department of the Army, 1986.

—**HAZARDOUS FRAGMENT** is an object or material having an impact energy of 58 ft-lbs or greater. *See also:* Hazardous Fragment Density.

References

Department of Defense, U.S. Army. *Ammunition and Explosives Safety Standards.* Army Regulation AR 385-64. Washington, DC: Headquarters, Department of the Army, 1987.

—**HAZARDOUS FRAGMENT DENSITY** is a density of hazardous fragments exceeding one per 600 square feet.

References

Department of Defense, U.S. Army. *Ammunition and Explosives Safety Standards*. Army Regulation AR 385-64. Washington, DC: Headquarters, Department of the Army, 1987.

—**HAZE** (SMOKE) is a light concentration of smoke placed over friendly areas to restrict accurate enemy observation and fire. Hazy smoke is not dense enough to disrupt friendly operations; however, it can hinder aerial and ground observation of friendly units by the enemy. *See also:* Smoke Screen.

References

Department of Defense, U.S. Army. *NBC Operations*. Field Manual FM 3-100. Washington, DC: Headquarters, Department of the Army, 1985.

—**HEAD** (DRILL AND CEREMONIES) is the leading element of a column.

References

Department of Defense, U.S. Army. *Drills and Ceremonies*. Field Manual FM 22-5. Washington, DC: Headquarters, Department of the Army, 1986.

—**HEAD SPACE** is the distance between the face of a bolt (fully closed) and the cartridge seating shoulder of the chamber, or the distance between the face of the bolt (fully closed) and the datum diameter in the sealing cone of the chamber.

References

Department of Defense, U.S. Army. *Dictionary of United States Army Terms*. Army Regulation AR 310-25. Washington, DC: Headquarters, Department of the Army, 1986.

—**HEADQUARTERS** (HQ) is the executive and/or administrative elements of a command unit. *See also:* Headquarters Company (Battery) (Troop), Headquarters Detachment.

References

Department of Defense, U.S. Army. *Dictionary of United States Army Terms*. Army Regulation AR 310-25. Washington, DC: Headquarters, Department of the Army, 1986.

—**HEADQUARTERS COMPANY** (BATTERY) (TROOP) is an administrative and tactical element of a battalion or larger unit that has personnel who are used for administrative, intelligence, communications, and other necessary activities.

References

Department of Defense, U.S. Army. *Dictionary of United States Army Terms*. Army Regulation AR 310-25. Washington, DC: Headquarters, Department of the Army, 1986.

—**HEADQUARTERS, DEPARTMENT OF THE ARMY, (HQDA),** is the executive part of the Department of the Army at the seat of the government. It is the highest level headquarters in the Department of the Army, and is composed of the Army Secretariat, the Army General and Special Staffs, and specifically designated support agencies. Headquarters, Department of the Army, exercises directive and supervisory controls within the Department of the Army.

References

Department of Defense, U.S. Army. *Dictionary of United States Army Terms*. Army Regulation AR 310-25. Washington, DC: Headquarters, Department of the Army, 1986.

—**HEADQUARTERS DETACHMENT** is an administrative and tactical element of a battalion or larger unit. In this meaning, a headquarters detachment usually differs from a headquarters company in that it has fewer personnel assigned to it.

References

Department of Defense, U.S. Army. *Dictionary of United States Army Terms*. Army Regulation AR 310-25. Washington, DC: Headquarters, Department of the Army, 1986.

—**HEADWIND** is a wind blowing away from the smoke objective and directly toward the smoke source. *See also:* Smoke Screen.

References

Department of Defense, U.S. Army. *Deliberate Smoke Operations*. Field Manual FM 3-50. Washington, DC: Headquarters, Department of the Army, 1984.

—**HEALTH CLINIC** is a medical treatment facility designed, equipped, and staffed to provide ambulatory health services to eligible beneficiaries, to include active duty and retired military personnel and their families, and the family members of deceased military personnel. It normally has general radiology, laboratory, and pharmacy capabilities, and offers special medical care in one or more subspecialties of medicine or dentistry in accordance with the availability of space and facilities and the capabilities of the professional staff assigned. It also provides medical, administrative, and logistical functions, as directed by the Medical Department Activity or General Hospital to which it is subordinate. It may be equipped with beds (normally less than 25) for observing patients awaiting transfers to hospitals, and for care of less than 72 hours for patients who cannot be cared for on an outpatient status, but do not require hospitalization. *See also:* Hospital.

References

Department of Defense, U.S. Army. *Dictionary of United States Army Terms.* Army Regulation AR 310-25. Washington, DC: Headquarters, Department of the Army, 1986.

—**HEALTH SERVICE SUPPORT IN A THEATER OF OPERATIONS.** The health service support system represents a continuum of care beginning at the forward line of own troops and ending in the continental U.S. base. The system's effectiveness is measured by its ability to return to duty soldiers who are wounded, sick, or injured, since it is functionally aligned to prevent, collect, assess, treat, evacuate, and rehabilitate sick and injured soldiers. *See also:* Medical Treatment.

References

Department of Defense, U.S. Army. *Health Service Support in the Theater of Operations.* Field Manual FM 8-10. Washington, DC: Headquarters, Department of the Army, 1978.

———. *Planning for Health Service Support.* Field Manual FM 8-55. Washington, DC: Headquarters, Department of the Army, 1985.

—**HEALTH SERVICES** are all the medical services performed, provided, or arranged to promote, improve, conserve, or restore the mental or physical well-being of personnel in the Army and, as directed, in other services, agencies, and organizations. These services include, but are not limited to, the management of health services resources (e.g., manpower, funds, and facilities); preventive and curative health measures; the health service doctrine; evacuation of the sick (physically and mentally), injured, and wounded; selection of the medically fit and disposition of the medically unfit; medical supply, equipment, and their maintenance; and medical, dental, veterinary, laboratory, optometric, medical food, and medical intelligence services. *See also:* Medical Treatment.

References

Department of Defense, U.S. Army. *Health Service Support in a Communications Zone (Test).* Field Manual FM 8-21. Washington, DC: Headquarters, Department of the Army, 1981.

———. *Health Service Support in the Theater of Operations.* Field Manual FM 8-10. Washington, DC: Headquarters, Department of the Army, 1978.

—**HEALTH STANDARDS** are all the measures or bases of comparison that have been developed or obtained concerning personal and environmental health services to determine the content, extent, value, quantity, method of measurement, and other characteristics of health services or the state of health of an individual or community. The standards include, but are not limited to, establishing physical and mental fitness standards for military duty; collecting and evaluating epidemiological, social, demographic, and related data; and establishing normative base lines for comparative purposes. *See also:* Medical Treatment.

References

Department of Defense, U.S. Army. *Dictionary of United States Army Terms.* Army Regulation AR 310-25. Washington, DC: Headquarters, Department of the Army, 1986.

—**HEAVY ANTITANK WEAPON** is a weapon that can be operated from the ground or on a vehicle, and is used to defeat armor and other material targets.

References

Department of Defense, Joint Chiefs of Staff. *Department of Defense Dictionary of Military and Related Terms.* Washington, DC: GPO, 1986.

—**HEAVY DROP** is a system of delivering heavy supplies and equipment by parachute. Either a conveyor system alone or a combination of an extraction parachute and a conveyor system can be used to discharge the load from the aircraft while it is in flight.

References

Department of Defense, U.S. Army. *Dictionary of United States Army Terms.* Army Regulation AR 310-25. Washington, DC: Headquarters, Department of the Army, 1986.

—**HEAVY LEVEL OF OPERATIONS** refers to operations whereby more than 60 percent of all force maneuver echelons and all fire support means are engaged in all-out combat over a period of time. These operations could, if necessary, include the use of resources from the next higher echelon in order to assure that the force's mission is accomplished.

References

Department of Defense, U.S. Army. *Dictionary of United States Army Terms.* Army Regulation AR 310-25. Washington, DC: Headquarters, Department of the Army, 1986.

—**HEAVY MACHINE GUN** is a classification of machine guns that include the .30 caliber water-cooled machine gun, and all larger caliber machine guns.

References

Department of Defense, U.S. Army. *Dictionary of United States Army Terms.* Army Regulation 310-25. Washington, DC: Headquarters, Department of the Army, 1986.

—**HEAVY SHELLPROOF SHELTER** is a sturdy protective shelter that protects against a continuous bombardment by shells of eight-inch or larger caliber.

References

Department of Defense, U.S. Army. *Dictionary of United States Army Terms.* Army Regulation 310-25. Washington, DC: Headquarters, Department of the Army, 1986.

—**HEIGHT** is the vertical distance of an object, point, or level above the ground or another established reference plane. The height may be indicated as follows:

- **Very low**—less than 500 feet;
- **Low**—500 to 2,000 feet (above ground level);
- **Medium**—2,000 to 25,000 feet;
- **High**—25,000 to 50,000 feet; and
- **Very high**—more than 50,000 feet.

References

Department of Defense, Joint Chiefs of Staff. *Department of Defense Dictionary of Military and Related Terms.* Washington, DC: GPO, 1986.

—**HEIGHT OF BURST (HOB)** is the vertical distance from the earth's surface or target to the point of a nuclear burst. *See also:* Desired Ground Zero, Optimum Height of Burst, Safe Burst Height.

References

Department of Defense, U.S. Army. *Nuclear Weapons Employment Doctrine and Procedures.* Field Manual FM 101-3-1. Washington, DC: Headquarters, Department of the Army, 1986.

————. *Operational Terms and Symbols.* Field Manual FM 101-5-1. Washington, DC: Headquarters, Department of the Army, 1985.

—**HELD FOR TREATMENT** is a status for a patient held at a medical facility other than a hospital or convalescent center. *See also:* Medical Treatment.

References

Department of Defense, U.S. Army. *Health Service Support in a Communications Zone (Test).* Field Manual FM 8-21. Washington, DC: Headquarters, Department of the Army, 1981.

————. *Health Service Support in the Theater of Operations.* Field Manual FM 8-10. Washington, DC: Headquarters, Department of the Army, 1978.

—**HELICAL SCANNING** is the scanning motion of a radar antenna in which a point on the axis of the transmitted beam describes a distorted helix. The antenna rotates continuously about the vertical axis while the elevation angle changes slowly from the horizontal to the vertical.

References

Department of Defense, U.S. Army. *Dictionary of United States Army Terms.* Army Regulation AR 310-25. Washington, DC: Headquarters, Department of the Army, 1986.

—**HELICOPTER APPROACH ROUTE** is the track or series of tracks along which helicopters move to a specific landing site or landing zone. *See also:* Helicopter Lane, Helicopter Retirement Route.

References

Department of Defense, Joint Chiefs of Staff. *Department of Defense Dictionary of Military and Related Terms.* Washington, DC: GPO, 1986.

—**HELICOPTER ASSAULT FORCE** is a task organization that combines helicopters, supporting units, and helicopter-borne troop units for use in helicopter-borne assault operations.

References

Department of Defense, Joint Chiefs of Staff. *Department of Defense Dictionary of Military and Related Terms.* Washington, DC: GPO, 1986.

—**HELICOPTER BREAK-UP POINT** is a control point at which helicopters returning from a landing zone break formation and either are released to return to base or are dispatched for other use. *See also:* Helicopter Retirement Route.

References

Department of Defense, Joint Chiefs of Staff. *Department of Defense Dictionary of Military and Related Terms.* Washington, DC: GPO, 1986.

—**HELICOPTER DIRECTION CENTER** is an air operations installation under the overall control of the Tactical Air Control Center, the Tactical Air Direction Center, or the Direct Air Support Center, as appropriate, from which the helicopter operations are controlled and directed. *See also:* Helicopter Flight.

References

Department of Defense, U.S. Army. *Dictionary of United States Army Terms.* Army Regulation AR 310-25. Washington, DC: Headquarters, Department of the Army, 1986.

—**HELICOPTER DROP POINT** is a designated point within a landing zone where helicopters are unable to land because of terrain, but in which they can discharge cargo or troops while hovering.

References

Department of Defense, Joint Chiefs of Staff. *Department of Defense Dictionary of Military and Related Terms.* Washington, DC: GPO, 1986.

—**HELICOPTER FLIGHT** is an individual helicopter or two (or more) helicopters grouped under a flight leader. The helicopters of the flight have been launched from a single helicopter transport or base at approximately the same time.

References

Department of Defense, U.S. Army. *Dictionary of United States Army Terms.* Army Regulation AR 310-25. Washington, DC: Headquarters, Department of the Army, 1986.

—**HELICOPTER FLIGHT RENDEZVOUS** is an air control point in the vicinity of a helicopter transport or base where helicopters are assembled into flights prior to proceeding to the wave rendezvous. It is designated by a code name.

References

Department of Defense, U.S. Army. *Dictionary of United States Army Terms.* Army Regulation AR 310-25. Washington, DC: Headquarters, Department of the Army, 1986.

—**HELICOPTER LANDING DIAGRAM** is a diagram that graphically portrays the routes to and from the landing zones and the helicopter transports. *See also:* Helicopter Drop Point, Helicopter Flight Rendezvous.

References

Department of Defense, U.S. Army. *Dictionary of United States Army Terms.* Army Regulation AR 310-25. Washington, DC: Headquarters, Department of the Army, 1986.

—**HELICOPTER LANDING SITE** is a designated subdivision of a helicopter landing zone in which a single flight or wave of assault helicopters land to embark or disembark troops or cargo. *See also:* Helicopter Landing Zone.

References

Department of Defense, Joint Chiefs of Staff. *Department of Defense Dictionary of Military and Related Terms.* Washington, DC: GPO, 1986.

—**HELICOPTER LANDING ZONE (HLZ)** is a specified ground area for landing assault helicopters to embark or disembark troops or cargo. A landing zone may contain one or more landing sites. *See also:* Helicopter Landing Site.

References

Department of Defense, Joint Chiefs of Staff. *Department of Defense Dictionary of Military and Related Terms.* Washington, DC: GPO, 1986.

—**HELICOPTER LANE** is a safety air corridor in which helicopters fly to or from their destination during helicopter operations. *See also:* Helicopter Approach Route, Helicopter Retirement Route.

References

Department of Defense, Joint Chiefs of Staff. *Department of Defense Dictionary of Military and Related Terms.* Washington, DC: GPO, 1986.

—**HELICOPTER RETIREMENT ROUTE** is the track or series of tracks along which helicopters move from a specific landing site or landing zone. *See also:* Helicopter Approach Route, Helicopter Lane.

References

Department of Defense, Joint Chiefs of Staff. *Department of Defense Dictionary of Military and Related Terms.* Washington, DC: GPO, 1986.

—**HELICOPTER SUPPORT TEAM** is a task organization formed and equipped for use in a landing and movement of helicopter-borne troops, equipment, and supplies and to evacuate selected casualties and prisoners of war. *See also:* Helicopter Team.

References
Department of Defense, Joint Chiefs of Staff. *Department of Defense Dictionary of Military and Related Terms.* Washington, DC: GPO, 1986.

—**HELICOPTER TEAM** consists of the combat-equipped troops lifted in one helicopter at one time.

References
Department of Defense, Joint Chiefs of Staff. *Department of Defense Dictionary of Military and Related Terms.* Washington, DC: GPO, 1986.

—**HELICOPTER TRANSPORT AREA** is an area seaward and on the flanks of the outer transport and landing ship areas, but preferably inside the area screen, to which helicopter transports proceed for launching or recovering helicopters.

References
Department of Defense, Joint Chiefs of Staff. *Department of Defense Dictionary of Military and Related Terms.* Washington, DC: GPO, 1986.

—**HELICOPTER WAVE RENDEZVOUS** is an air control point where helicopter flights are assembled into helicopter waves prior to executing a mission. It is designated by a code name. *See also:* Helicopter Flight.

References
Department of Defense, U.S. Army. *Dictionary of United States Army Terms.* Army Regulation AR 310-25. Washington, DC: Headquarters, Department of the Army, 1986.

—**HELIPAD** is a prepared area designated and used for helicopter takeoffs and landings. It includes the touchdown or hover point.

References
Department of Defense, Joint Chiefs of Staff. *Department of Defense Dictionary of Military and Related Terms.* Washington, DC: GPO, 1986.

—**HELIPORT** is a facility designed for operating, basing, servicing, and maintaining helicopters.

References
Department of Defense, Joint Chiefs of Staff. *Department of Defense Dictionary of Military and Related Terms.* Washington, DC: GPO, 1986.

—**HELLFIRE MODULAR MISSILE SYSTEM** is the main antiarmor armament of the Apache AH-64 helicopter. Hellfire is a laser-guided missile that has greater lethality, increased firing rates, a greater stand-off range, greater versatility, and a shorter flight time than the tube-launched, optically-tracked, wire-guided missile system. A third-generation airborne antiarmor weapon, Hellfire homes in on a laser spot that can be projected from ground observers, other aircraft, or the launching craft itself. This allows the Apache to launch its missiles indirectly, and in some situations, without seeing its target. The Apache can carry sixteen Hellfire missiles, and Hellfire is being considered for adaptation on Air force, Marine Corps, and other Army aircraft. *See also:* Apache AH-64 Helicopter.

References
Department of Defense, U.S. Army. *U.S. Army Policy Statement, 1988.* Washington, DC: Headquarters, Department of the Army, 1988.
———. *Weapons Systems: U.S. Army, Navy, and Air Force Directory, 1986–1988.* Washington, DC: DCP, 1986.

—**HERBICIDE** is a chemical compound that can kill or damage plants. *See also:* Chemical Warfare.

References
Department of Defense, Joint Chiefs of Staff. *Department of Defense Dictionary of Military and Related Terms.* Washington, DC: GPO, 1986.

—**HERBICIDE OPERATION** is the use of herbicides in a military operation. *See also:* Chemical Warfare.

References
Department of Defense, U.S. Army. *Dictionary of United States Army Terms.* Army Regulation AR 310-25. Washington, DC: Headquarters, Department of the Army, 1986.

—**HERCULES** is a medium-range troop and cargo transport designed for air-drop or air-land delivery into a combat zone as well as for conventional airlift. It is equipped with four turbo-prop engines and an integral ramp and cargo door. The D model is ski equipped; the E variant has additional fuel capacity for extended range and is designated the C-130. The in-flight refueling tanker, which is also used for aerial rescue missions, is designated the HC-130, the gunship version is the AC-130, and the drone control version is the DC-130.

References
Department of Defense, Joint Chiefs of Staff.
*Department of Defense Dictionary of Military and
Related Terms.* Washington, DC: GPO, 1986.

—**HEROISM** involves specific acts of bravery or
outstanding courage, or a closely related series
of heroic acts that are performed within a short
period of time. *See also:* Valor.

References
Department of Defense, U.S. Army. *Military Awards.*
Army Regulation AR 672-5-1. Washington, DC:
Headquarters, Department of the Army, 1984.

—**HERRINGBONE** is an arrangement of vehicles
at left and right angles to the line of march. This
arrangement is used to establish security during
an unscheduled halt.

References
Department of Defense, U.S. Army. *Operational
Terms and Symbols.* Field Manual FM 101-5-1.
Washington, DC: Headquarters, Department of the
Army, 1985.

—**HIDE** is the positioning of a vehicle, individual,
or unit so that no part is exposed to observation
or direct fire. *See also:* Defilade, Hull-Down
Position, Turret-Down Position.

References
Department of Defense, U.S. Army. *Operational
Terms and Symbols.* Field Manual FM 101-5-1.
Washington, DC: Headquarters, Department of the
Army, 1985.

—**HIGH AIRBURST (HAB)** is the fallout safe height
for a nuclear weapon that increases the damage
to, or the casualties on, soft targets, or reduces
the induced radiation contamination at the actual point of impact. *See also:* Ground Zero,
Nuclear Warfare, Soft Target.

References
Department of Defense, U.S. Army. *Nuclear
Weapons Employment Doctrine and Procedures.*
Field Manual FM 101-3-1. Washington, DC:
Headquarters, Department of the Army, 1986.

—**HIGH ALTITUDE,** conventionally, is an altitude
above 10,000 meters (33,000 feet). *See also:*
Altitude (Army Aviation).

References
Department of Defense, Joint Chiefs of Staff.
*Department of Defense Dictionary of Military and
Related Terms.* Washington, DC: GPO, 1986.

—**HIGH ALTITUDE BOMBING (HAB)** is horizontal bombing with a release height of over
15,000 feet. *See also:* Altitude (Army Aviation),
High Altitude.

References
Department of Defense, Joint Chiefs of Staff.
*Department of Defense Dictionary of Military and
Related Terms.* Washington, DC: GPO, 1986.

—**HIGH ALTITUDE BURST (HAB)** is the explosion of a nuclear weapon that takes place at a
height in excess of 100,000 feet (30,000 meters).
See also: Nuclear Warfare.

References
Department of Defense, Joint Chiefs of Staff.
*Department of Defense Dictionary of Military and
Related Terms.* Washington, DC: GPO, 1986.

—**HIGH ALTITUDE LOW OPENING (HALO)** is a
method of delivering equipment and supplies
from airlift aircraft that must fly at altitudes above
the threat umbrella.

References
Department of Defense, U.S. Army. *USA/USAF
Doctrine for Joint Airborne and Tactical Airlift
Operations.* Field Manual FM 100-27. Washington,
DC: Headquarters, Department of the Army, 1985.

—**HIGH-ANGLE,** in artillery, is an order or request to obtain high-angle fire. *See also:* High-
Angle Fire.

References
Department of Defense, Joint Chiefs of Staff.
*Department of Defense Dictionary of Military and
Related Terms.* Washington, DC: GPO, 1986.

—**HIGH-ANGLE FIRE.** (1) High-angle fire is fire
delivered at angles of elevation that are greater
than the elevation that corresponds to the
maximum range of the gun and ammunition
concerned. (2) High-angle fire is fire whose range
decreases as the angle of elevation increases.
See also: High-Angle.

References
Department of Defense, U.S. Army. *Operational
Terms and Symbols.* Field Manual FM 101-5-1.
Washington, DC: Headquarters, Department of the
Army, 1985.

—**HIGH BURST RANGING** is an adjustment of
gunfire by observing the airbursts. It is also called
airburst ranging.

References
Department of Defense, U.S. Army. *Dictionary of United States Army Terms.* Army Regulation AR 310-25. Washington, DC: Headquarters, Department of the Army, 1986.

—**HIGH-COST, LOW-DENSITY MISSILE SYSTEMS** are normally assigned to the corps and theater army in relatively low densities. These systems include Hawk, Nike Hercules, Pershing IA, Pershing II, and Patriot.

References
Department of Defense, U.S. Army. *Combat Service Support Operations-Division.* Field Manual FM 63-2. Washington, DC: Headquarters, Department of the Army, 1983.

—**HIGH DENSITY AIRSPACE CONTROL ZONE (HIDACZ)** is an airspace of defined dimensions, designated by the airspace control authority, in which there is a concentrated employment of numerous and varied users (e.g., aircraft, artillery, mortars, naval gunfire, local air defense weapons, and surface-to-surface missiles). A HIDACZ is established by the area air defense commander in his capacity as the airspace control authority, upon request of the ground force commanders. When a request for a HIDACZ is approved, the requesting commander is normally given authority for short-range air defense within the HIDACZ area. *See also:* Area Air Defense Commander, SHORAD.

References
Department of Defense, U.S. Army. *Airspace Management and Army Air Traffic in a Combat Zone.* Field Manual FM 1-60. Washington, DC: Headquarters, Department of the Army, 1977.

————. *Operational Terms and Symbols.* Field Manual FM 101-5-1. Washington, DC: Headquarters, Department of the Army, 1985.

————. *Patriot Battalion Operations.* Field Manual FM 44-15. Washington, DC: Headquarters, Department of the Army, 1984.

—**HIGH DOLLAR SPARE PARTS BREAKOUT** is the process of screening spare and repair parts to determine the procurement method. It is also called the Department of Defense High Dollar Spare Parts Breakout Program, and is commonly referred to as "Breakout."

References
Department of Defense, U.S. Army. *Dictionary of United States Army Terms.* Army Regulation 310-25. Washington, DC: Headquarters, Department of the Army, 1986.

—**HIGH EXPLOSIVE (HE)** is generally applied to the bursting charges for bombs, projectiles, grenades, mines, and demolition charges. HE is defined by the Department of Transportation as materials that are susceptible to detonation by a blasting cap. *See also:* High Explosive Cargo, High Explosive (Category of Direct Fire Projectile), High Explosive Equivalent, High Explosive Projectile.

References
Department of Defense, U.S. Army. *Dictionary of United States Army Terms.* Army Regulation AR 310-25. Washington, DC: Headquarters, Department of the Army, 1986.

—**HIGH EXPLOSIVE CARGO** is cargo such as artillery ammunition, bombs, depth charges, demolition material, rockets, and missiles.

References
Department of Defense, Joint Chiefs of Staff. *Department of Defense Dictionary of Military and Related Terms.* Washington, DC: GPO, 1986.

—**HIGH EXPLOSIVE (HE)** (CATEGORY OF DIRECT FIRE PROJECTILE). HE rounds include high explosive antitank rounds, recoilless rifle rounds, and antitank rockets. They are designed to detonate a shaped charge on impact. At detonation, an extremely high velocity molten jet is formed. This jet perforates large thicknesses of high-density material, continues along its path, and sets fuel and ammunition on fire. The high explosive antitank rounds generally range in size from 60 to 120 millimeters.

References
Department of Defense, U.S. Army. *Survivability.* Field Manual FM 5-103. Washington, DC: Headquarters, Department of the Army, 1985.

—**HIGH EXPLOSIVE EQUIVALENT OR EXPLOSIVE EQUIVALENT** is the amount of a standard explosive that, when detonated, will produce a blast effect comparable to that which results at the same distance from the detonation or explosion of a given amount of the material for which performance is being evaluated. It is usually expressed as a percentage of the total net weight of all reactive materials contained in the item or system. For the purpose of these standards, TNT is used for comparison.

References
Department of Defense, U.S. Army. *Ammunition and Explosives Safety Standards*. Army Regulation AR 385-64. Washington, DC: Headquarters, Department of the Army, 1987.

—**HIGH EXPLOSIVE PROJECTILE** is a projectile with a bursting charge of high explosive. It is used against personnel and materiel.

References
Department of Defense, U.S. Army. *Dictionary of United States Army Terms*. Army Regulation AR 310-25. Washington, DC: Headquarters, Department of the Army, 1986.

—**HIGH FREQUENCY/DIRECTION FINDING (HF/DF)** is exploring the high frequency spectrum for emitter signals in order to determine their directions and locations. HF/DF is used extensively in reconnaissance to determine the approximate direction or bearing of a transmitting antenna. When a DF station obtains a line of bearing, it provides an approximate direction, but not the distance, to the emitter. However, when two or more stations are located at significantly different directions from the emitter, the line of bearing from each can provide an accurate location. *See also:* Intelligence Collection.

References
Department of Defense, U.S. Army. *Counter-Signals Intelligence (C-SIGINT) Operations*. Field Manual FM 34-62. Washington, DC: Headquarters, Department of the Army, 1986.

—**HIGH GRADE CRYPTOSYSTEM** is a cryptosystem designed to provide lasting security by resisting solution for a long or an indefinite period of time. *See also:* CRYPTO.

References
Department of Defense, U.S. Army. *Dictionary of United States Army Terms*. Army Regulation AR 310-25. Washington, DC: Headquarters, Department of the Army, 1986.

—**HIGH INTENSITY CONFLICT** is the unlimited use of force by one or more nations to gain or protect territory. This form of conflict includes the use of nuclear weapons and may include some or all of the techniques and characteristics of low and mid-intensity conflict. *See also:* Low Intensity Conflict.

References
Department of Defense, U.S. Army. *Psychological Operations*. Field Manual FM 33-1. Washington, DC: Headquarters, Department of the Army, 1979.

—**HIGH MOBILITY MULTIPURPOSE WHEELED VEHICLE (HMMWV)** is a successor to the M274 (one-half-ton MULES), all one-and-one-quarter-ton trucks and selected M151 one-quarter-ton jeeps. HMMWVs are used by airborne, airmobile, and light infantry divisions as the weapons carrier for the tube-launched, optically-tracked, wire-guided missile. It can also fulfill reconnaissance, fire support, communications, personnel transport, and command and control roles, and it can be used as ambulances for various other Army units. This high mobility four by four diesel-powered vehicle uses a common chassis with various body configurations to meet the above requirements. The tri-service HMMWV program also provides vehicles to respond to U.S. Marine Corps and U.S. Air Force requirements. It is a complementary program to the nondevelopmental commercial utility and cargo vehicle.

References
Weapons Systems: U.S. Army, Navy and Air Force Directory, 1986-1988. Washington, DC: DCP, 1986.

—**HIGH-MOBILITY SHELTER** is collective protection (protection for several people) that can be removed easily.

References
Department of Defense, U.S. Army. *NBC Protection*. Field Manual FM 3-4. Washington, DC: Headquarters, Department of the Army, 1985.

—**HIGH ORDER DENOTATION** is a complete and instantaneous explosion.

References
Department of Defense, U.S. Army. *Dictionary of United States Army Terms*. Army Regulation AR 310-25. Washington, DC: Headquarters, Department of the Army, 1986.

—**HIGH PAYOFF TARGET (HPT)** are high value targets which, if successfully attacked, would contribute substantially to the success of the commander's plans. *See also:* High Value Target (HVT).

References

Department of Defense, U.S. Army. *Operational Terms and Symbols.* Field Manual FM 101-5-1. Washington, DC: Headquarters, Department of the Army, 1985.

—**HIGH PORT** is a position in which the rifle is carried while a soldier is charging or jumping. The rifle is carried diagonally across the body with the left wrist in front of the left shoulder and the right wrist near the right hip.

References

Department of Defense, U.S. Army. *Dictionary of United States Army Terms.* Army Regulation AR 310-25. Washington, DC: Headquarters, Department of the Army, 1986.

—**HIGH PRESSURE TEST AMMUNITION** is ammunition with an especially powerful propelling charge. *See also:* Service Ammunition.

References

Department of Defense, U.S. Army. *Dictionary of United States Army Terms.* Army Regulation AR 310-25. Washington, DC: Headquarters, Department of the Army, 1986.

—**HIGH RISK PERSONNEL** are people who, by their grade, assignment, symbolic value, location, or specific threat, are more likely to be attractive or accessible terrorist targets. *See also:* High Threat Area for Travel Security.

References

Department of Defense, U.S. Army. *The Army Terrorism Counteraction Program.* Army Regulation AR 525-13. Washington, DC: Headquarters, Department of the Army, 1988.

—**HIGH THREAT AREA FOR TRAVEL SECURITY** are the terrorist-threatened areas that have been identified either by a Principal Deputy Assistant Secretary of Defense for International Security Affairs memorandum (subject: Travel Security), by the International Threat Analysis Center Monthly Intelligence Summary, or by the commander who is responsible for the area concerned. *See also:* High Risk Personnel.

References

Department of Defense, U.S. Army. *The Army Terrorism Counteraction Program.* Army Regulation AR 525-13. Washington, DC: Headquarters, Department of the Army, 1988.

—**HIGH-TO-MEDIUM ALTITUDE AIR DEFENSE (HIMAD)** refers to generally long-range missile systems that provide overall medium- and high-altitude coverage for Army field forces. HIMAD weapons are normally positioned behind the forward line of own troops and out of enemy artillery range. HIMAD systems include Hawk and Patriot. *See also:* HIMAD.

References

Department of Defense, U.S. Army. *Air Defense Artillery Deployment: Chaparral/Vulcan/Stinger.* Field Manual FM 44-3. Washington, DC: Headquarters, Department of the Army, 1984.

—**HIGH VALUE ASSET CONTROL SYSTEM** are supply items identified for intensive management control under approved inventory management techniques designed to maintain an optimum inventory level of high investment items. They are also known as hi-value asset control items.

References

Department of Defense, Joint Chiefs of Staff. *Department of Defense Dictionary of Military and Related Terms.* Washington, DC: GPO, 1986.

—**HIGH VALUE TARGET (HVT)** is a target whose loss to the enemy is expected to cause a substantial degradation of an important battlefield function. *See also:* Targeting.

References

Department of Defense, U.S. Army. *Operational Terms and Symbols.* Field Manual FM 101-5-1. Washington, DC: Headquarters, Department of the Army, 1985.

—**HIGH VELOCITY.** (1) High velocity is a muzzle velocity of an artillery projectile of from 3,000 feet per second to, but not including, 3,500 feet per second. (2) High velocity of small arms ammunition is between 3,500 and 5,000 feet per second. (3) In tank cannon projectiles, high velocity is between 1,550 and 3,350 feet per second.

References

Department of Defense, U.S. Army. *Dictionary of United States Army Terms.* Army Regulation AR 310-25. Washington, DC: Headquarters, Department of the Army, 1986.

—**HIGH-VELOCITY AIRDROP** is a type of airdrop. Ring-slot cargo, cargo-extraction, and pilot parachutes are used to stabilize loads for a high-velocity airdrop. The parachute has enough drag to hold the load upright during its descent at from 70 to 90 feet per second. The items to be airdropped are placed on energy-dissipating material and are then rigged in an airdrop container. Subsistence, packaged petroleum, oil, and lubricant products, ammunition, and other such items can be high-velocity airdropped.

References

Department of Defense, U.S. Army. *USA/USAF Doctrine for Joint Airborne and Tactical Airlift Operations.* Field Manual FM 100-27. Washington, DC: Headquarters, Department of the Army, 1985.

—**HIGHEST MORAL GOOD** is the moral outcome that best helps the Army serve the ideals of the nation.

References

Department of Defense, U.S. Army. *Military Leadership.* Field Manual FM 22-100. Washington, DC: Headquarters, Department of the Army, 1983.

—**HIGHWAY CAPABILITY** is the number of vehicles (highway vehicle capability) or the number of short tons payload (highway tonnage capability) that can be moved over a highway with proper consideration of the type of roadway, maintenance, hills, curves, weather, other traffic, and the types of vehicles that are to be used. *See also:* Highway Capacity.

References

Department of Defense, U.S. Army. *Planning Logistics Support for Military Operations.* Field Manual FM 701-58. Washington, DC: Headquarters, Department of the Army, 1987.

—**HIGHWAY CAPACITY** is the maximum traffic obtainable on a given roadway when using all available lanes. *See also:* Highway Capability.

References

Department of Defense, U.S. Army. *Planning Logistics Support for Military Operations.* Field Manual FM 701-58. Washington, DC: Headquarters, Department of the Army, 1987.

—**HIGHWAY INFORMATION POST** is a post that has been established by the military police in order to furnish information to facilitate efficient traffic management. It may be used to supplement highway regulation points and highway traffic control posts.

References

Department of Defense, U.S. Army. *Dictionary of United States Army Terms.* Army Regulation AR 310-25. Washington, DC: Headquarters, Department of the Army, 1986.

—**HIGHWAY REGULATION** is the planning, routing, and scheduling of the actual use of highways by vehicles, pedestrians (including troops, refugees, and civilians), and animals so that the highway transportation facilities and equipment are used most efficiently in meeting operational requirements. *See also:* Highway Information Post, Highway Traffic Control, Highway Traffic Headquarters.

References

Department of Defense, U.S. Army. *Dictionary of United States Army Terms.* Army Regulation AR 310-25. Washington, DC: Headquarters, Department of the Army, 1986.

—**HIGHWAY REGULATION POINT** is a point on the highway at which the highway transport service records and reports the arrival and departure of, and regulates elements of, highway movement by issuing instructions for the continuance of the march, detours, diversions, schedules, and related matters.

References

Department of Defense, U.S. Army. *Dictionary of United States Army Terms.* Army Regulation AR 310-25. Washington, DC: Headquarters, Department of the Army, 1986.

—**HIGHWAY TRAFFIC CONTROL** is the enforcement of the rules of the road, traffic regulations, and road discipline, including spot direction. It is a function of the provost marshal and military police.

References

Department of Defense, U.S. Army. *Dictionary of United States Army Terms.* Army Regulation AR 310-25. Washington, DC: Headquarters, Department of the Army, 1986.

—**HIGHWAY TRAFFIC HEADQUARTERS** exercises established highway regulations in order to use the highway transportation facilities and equipment most effectively so that a maximum response is made to the assigned tasks. The regulations provide for planning, routing, scheduling, and directing the actual use of the highways by vehicles, and pedestrians, including troops, refugees, and other civilians, and animals.

References

Department of Defense, U.S. Army. *Transportation Reference Data.* Field Manual FM 55-15. Washington, DC: Headquarters, Department of the Army, 1986.

—**HIGHWAY TRANSPORT LIFT** is the payload tonnage of personnel that can be transported by a vehicle or by a truck unit in one trip.

References

Department of Defense, U.S. Army. *Dictionary of United States Army Terms.* Army Regulation AR 310-25. Washington, DC: Headquarters, Department of the Army, 1986.

—**HIMAD** is a high-to-medium-altitude air defense system, that currently includes the Hawk, Patriot, and Nike Hercules weapons systems. *See also:* SHORAD Systems.

References

Department of Defense, U.S. Army. *U.S. Army Air Defense Employment.* Field Manual FM 44-1. Washington, DC: Headquarters, Department of the Army, 1983.

———. *U.S. Army Air Defense Artillery Employment Hawk.* Field Manual FM 44-90. Washington, DC: Headquarters, Department of the Army, 1983.

—**HIP POCKET ORDERS** are orders by which Army retirees are recalled to active duty in the event of mobilization.

References

Department of Defense, U.S. Army. *U.S. Army Policy Statement, 1988.* Washington, DC: Headquarters, Department of the Army, 1988.

—**HISTORICAL COST** is the actual expenditure for a weapon system, other items of materiel, or any objective in terms of historical dollars or an equivalent outlay that is ascertained after the fact. Historical dollars may be converted to current year or constant dollars by using appropriate indices.

References

Department of Defense, U.S. Army. *Dictionary of United States Army Terms.* Army Regulation AR 310-25. Washington, DC: Headquarters, Department of the Army, 1986.

—**HIT** (ARMY AVIATION) indicates that a friendly aircraft has been hit by weapons fire.

References

Department of Defense, U.S. Army. *Air-to-Air Combat.* Field Manual FM 1-107. Washington, DC: Headquarters, Department of the Army, 1984.

—**HOLD.** (1) To hold is to maintain or retain possession of an area or a position by force. (2) In an attack, to hold is to exert sufficient pressure to prevent the movement or redistribution of enemy forces. (3) In air traffic, to hold is to keep an aircraft within a specified space or location that is identified by visual or other means in accordance with air control traffic instructions.

References

Department of Defense, Joint Chiefs of Staff. *Department of Defense Dictionary of Military and Related Terms.* Washington, DC: GPO, 1986.

—**HOLD FIRE**, an air defense emergency fire control order, is used to stop firing and to protect friendly aircraft. It includes the command destruction of any missiles already launched.

References

Department of Defense, Joint Chiefs of Staff. *Department of Defense Dictionary of Military and Related Terms.* Washington, DC: GPO, 1986.

Department of Defense, U.S. Army. *Patriot Battalion Operations.* Field Manual FM 44-15. Washington, DC: Headquarters, Department of the Army, 1984.

—**HOLDING AREA.** (1) A holding area is the nearest covered and concealed position to the pickup zone or crossing site where troops are held until it is time for them to move forward. (2) In attack helicopter operations, a holding area is a covered or concealed position between the assembly area and the battle positions that helicopters may occupy while aeroscouts coordinate their movement into battle positions. It should provide good cover and concealment and should have an area for the aircraft to hover or land. (3) In airmobile and river crossing operations, a holding area is the nearest covered and concealed position to the pickup zone or crossing site, where troops are held until it is time for them to move forward. *See also:* Pickup Zone.

References

Department of Defense, U.S. Army. *Attack Helicopter Operations.* Field Manual FM 17-50. Washington, DC: Headquarters, Department of the Army, 1984.

———. *Dictionary of United States Army Terms.* Army Regulation AR 310-25. Washington, DC: Headquarters, Department of the Army, 1986.

———. *Gunnery Training for Attack Helicopters.* Training Circular TC 17-17. Washington, DC: Headquarters, Department of the Army, 1975.

———. *Operational Terms and Symbols.* Field Manual FM 101-5-1. Washington, DC: Headquarters, Department of the Army, 1985.

—**HOLDING ATTACK** is an attack designed to hold the enemy in position, to deceive it as to where the main attack is being made, to prevent it from reinforcing the elements opposing the main attack, or to cause it to commit its reserves prematurely at an indecisive location. *See also:* Holding Force.

References

Department of Defense, Joint Chiefs of Staff. *Department of Defense Dictionary of Military and Related Terms.* Washington, DC: GPO, 1986.

—**HOLDING FORCE** is a force assigned to hold a place or position.

References

Department of Defense, U.S. Army. *Dictionary of United States Army Terms.* Army Regulation AR 310-25. Washington, DC: Headquarters, Department of the Army, 1986.

—**HOLDING LINE,** in retrograde river crossing operations, is the outer limit of the area established between the enemy and the water obstacle to preclude direct and observed indirect fires into crossing areas. *See also:* Bridgehead Line.

References

Department of Defense, U.S. Army. *Dictionary of United States Army Terms.* Army Regulation AR 310-25. Washington, DC: Headquarters, Department of the Army, 1986.

—**HOLDING STATION** is a medical treatment facility established by a medical unit at a railhead, airhead, or port to provide temporary shelter and emergency treatment for patients who are awaiting further transportation. *See also:* Medical Treatment.

References

Department of Defense, U.S. Army. *Dictionary of United States Army Terms.* Army Regulation AR 310-25. Washington, DC: Headquarters, Department of the Army, 1986.

—**HOLDING YARD** is a location of groups of rail cars, trucks, or trailers used to hold ammunition, explosives, and dangerous materials for interim periods before the materials are stored or shipped.

References

Department of Defense, U.S. Army. *Ammunition and Explosives Safety Standards.* Army Regulation AR 385-64. Washington, DC: Headquarters, Department of the Army, 1987.

—**HOLLOW CHARGE** is a shaped charge that produces a deep cylindrical hole of relatively small diameter in the direction of axis of rotation.

References

Department of Defense, Joint Chiefs of Staff. *Department of Defense Dictionary of Military and Related Terms.* Washington, DC: GPO, 1986.

—**HOME OF RECORD** is the place that is recorded in an individual's current personnel records as the home of the member when he was commissioned, reinstated, appointed, enlisted, re-enlisted, or ordered to active duty.

References

Department of Defense, U.S. Army. *Processing Personnel for Separation.* Army Regulation AR 635-10. Washington, DC: Headquarters, Department of the Army, 1984.

—**HOMING GUIDANCE** is a system by which a missile steers itself toward a target by means of a self-contained mechanism that is activated by distinguishing characteristics of the target. *See also:* Active Homing Guidance, Guidance, Passive Homing Guidance.

References

Department of Defense, Joint Chiefs of Staff. *Department of Defense Dictionary of Military and Related Terms.* Washington, DC: GPO, 1986.

—**HOMING STATION** is a radio aid to navigation that incorporates direction-finding facilities.

References

Department of Defense, U.S. Army. *Dictionary of United States Army Terms.* Army Regulation AR 310-25. Washington, DC: Headquarters, Department of the Army, 1986.

—**HONORABLE DISCHARGE** is a form of discharge given to a soldier whose service has been honest and faithful, and who has been given conduct ratings of at least Good; has been given efficiency ratings of at least Fair; has not been convicted by a general court-martial; and has not been convicted more than once by a special court-martial. *See also:* Discharge, Dishonorable Discharge, General Discharge.

References

Department of Defense, U.S. Army. *Dictionary of United States Army Terms.* Army Regulation AR 310-25. Washington, DC: Headquarters, Department of the Army, 1986.

—**HORIZON** is the apparent or visible junction between the earth and the sky. It is also called the apparent, visible, or local horizon. It is a horizontal plane passing through a point of vision or perspective center. The apparent or visible horizon approximates the true horizon only when the point of vision is very close to sea level.

References
Department of Defense, Joint Chiefs of Staff. *Department of Defense Dictionary of Military and Related Terms*. Washington, DC: GPO, 1986.

Reeves, Robert; Anson, Abraham; and Landen, David. *Manual of Remote Sensing*. Falls Church, VA: American Society of Photogrammetry, 1975.

—**HORIZONTAL ACCURACY** is a statement of the relative and/or absolute positional accuracy of a point computed in a plane. It is usually expressed in circular error (in percent).

References
Department of Defense, U.S. Army. *Dictionary of United States Army Terms*. Army Regulation AR 310-25. Washington, DC: Headquarters, Department of the Army, 1986.

—**HORIZONTAL ACTION MINE,** in land mine warfare, is a mine designed to produce a destructive effect in a plane approximately parallel to the ground. *See also:* Mine Warfare.

References
Department of Defense, Joint Chiefs of Staff. *Department of Defense Dictionary of Military and Related Terms*. Washington, DC: GPO, 1986.

—**HORIZONTAL CLOCK SYSTEM** is a system used to describe the direction of the wind by reference to the figures of an imaginary clock dial. The firing point is considered the center of the clock and the target is at twelve o'clock. At three o'clock, the wind comes directly from the right, and at nine o'clock, it comes directly from the left.

References
Department of Defense, U.S. Army. *Dictionary of United States Army Terms*. Army Regulation AR 310-25. Washington, DC: Headquarters, Department of the Army, 1986.

—**HORIZONTAL ERROR** is the error in range, in deflection, or in radius, that a weapon may be expected to exceed as often as not. Horizontal error of weapons making a nearly vertical ap-

proach to the target is described in terms of circular error probable. Horizontal error of weapons producing an elliptical dispersion pattern is expressed in terms of probable error. *See also:* Circular Error Probable, Delivery Error, Deviation, Dispersion Error.

References
Department of Defense, Joint Chiefs of Staff. *Department of Defense Dictionary of Military and Related Terms*. Washington, DC: GPO, 1986.

—**HORNED SCULLY** is an underwater obstacle designed to tear holes in the bottoms of boats. It consists of a tapered block of concrete with steel rails. It is usually pointed and has projecting angles from the top and bottom.

References
Department of Defense, U.S. Army. *Dictionary of United States Army Terms*. Army Regulation AR 310-25. Washington, DC: Headquarters, Department of the Army, 1986.

—**HOSPITAL** is a medical treatment facility capable of providing inpatient care. It is appropriately staffed and equipped to provide diagnostic and therapeutic services, as well as the necessary supporting services that are required to perform its assigned mission and functions. A hospital, in addition, may also function as a clinic. *See also:* Medical Support.

References
Department of Defense, Joint Chiefs of Staff. *Department of Defense Dictionary of Military and Related Terms*. Washington, DC: GPO, 1986.

—**HOSPITAL ADMISSION** is the initial entry point of an individual as an inpatient into a hospital for a single episode of illness or injury anywhere in the theater of operations. If the same inpatient is discharged from a hospital and is later readmitted for a different illness or injury, or a recurrence of the same ailment or injury, the individual is counted as another separate admission. *See also:* Medical Support.

References
Department of Defense, U.S. Army. *Planning for Health Service Support*. Field Manual FM 8-55. Washington, DC: Headquarters, Department of the Army, 1985.

—**HOSPITAL BEDS** are beds used for inpatient care at a military medical treatment facility functioning as a hospital. *See also:* Medical Support.

References

Department of Defense, U.S. Army. *Dictionary of United States Army Terms*. Army Regulation AR 310-25. Washington, DC: Headquarters, Department of the Army, 1986.

————. *Health Service Support in a Communications Zone (Test)*. Field Manual FM 8-21. Washington, DC: Headquarters, Department of the Army, 1981.

—**HOSPITAL CENTER** is a command and control unit to which hospitals and other medical units can be assigned or attached for administrative control. *See also:* Medical Support.

References

Department of Defense, U.S. Army. *Dictionary of United States Army Terms*. Army Regulation AR 310-25. Washington, DC: Headquarters, Department of the Army, 1986.

—**HOSPITALIZATION** is the status of being admitted as an inpatient to a hospital facility that is appropriately staffed and equipped to provide diagnostic and therapeutic services as well as the necessary supporting services to perform its mission. *See also:* Medical Support.

References

Department of Defense, U.S. Army. *Dictionary of United States Army Terms*. Army Regulation AR 310-25. Washington, DC: Headquarters, Department of the Army, 1986.

—**HOSPITALIZATION UNIT** is one of three identical subunits (or elements) that make up a field hospital. *See also:* Field Hospital, Medical Support.

References

Department of Defense, U.S. Army. *Dictionary of United States Army Terms*. Army Regulation AR 310-25. Washington, DC: Headquarters, Department of the Army, 1986.

—**HOSPITALIZED PRISONERS WARD** is the hospital ward in which prisoners who require hospital treatment are confined pending completion of such treatment. *See also:* Medical Support.

References

Department of Defense, U.S. Army. *Dictionary of United States Army Terms*. Army Regulation AR 310-25. Washington, DC: Headquarters, Department of the Army, 1986.

—**HOST COUNTRY** is a nation in which representatives or organizations of another nation are present because of government invitation or international agreement.

References

Department of Defense, Joint Chiefs of Staff. *Department of Defense Dictionary of Military and Related Terms*. Washington, DC: GPO, 1986.

—**HOST INSTALLATION/ACTIVITY** has management control of facilities and/or administrative and logistical support (including base operations support) needed by another activity or unit. The second, tenant unit is dependent on the host for all or a portion of its administrative and logistical support requirements. *See also:* Tenant, Tenant Activity.

References

Department of Defense, U.S. Army. *Dictionary of United States Army Terms*. Army Regulation AR 310-25. Washington, DC: Headquarters, Department of the Army, 1986.

—**HOST NATION (HN)** is a nation that receives the forces or supplies of allied nations or allows NATO organizations to be located on, operate in, or travel through, its territory. *See also:* Host Country, Host Nation Post, Host Nation Support.

References

Department of Defense, Joint Chiefs of Staff. *Department of Defense Dictionary of Military and Related Terms*. Washington, DC: GPO, 1986.

Department of Defense, U.S. Army. *Support Operations: Echelons Above Corps*. Field Manual FM 100-16. Washington, DC: Headquarters, Department of the Army, 1986.

—**HOST NATION POST** is a post that has been agreed on by the local national authorities and should be permanently filled by them in view of its administrative/national nature.

References

Department of Defense, Joint Chiefs of Staff. *Department of Defense Dictionary of Military and Related Terms*. Washington, DC: GPO, 1986.

—**HOST NATION SUPPORT (HNS)** is civil and military assistance rendered in peace and war by a host nation to allied forces and NATO organizations that are located on or in transit through the host nation's territory. The basis of such assistance is commitments arising from the NATO Alliance or from bilateral or multilateral agreements concluded between the host nation, NATO organizations, and the nation(s) having forces operating on the host nation's territory.

References

Department of Defense, Joint Chiefs of Staff. *Department of Defense Dictionary of Military and Related Terms.* Washington, DC: GPO, 1986.

Department of Defense, U.S. Army. *Dictionary of United States Army Terms.* Army Regulation AR 310-25. Washington, DC: Headquarters, Department of the Army, 1986.

———. *Support Operations: Echelons Above Corps.* Field Manual FM 100-16. Washington, DC: Headquarters, Department of the Army, 1986.

—**HOSTAGE** is a person who is held against his will as security for the performance or nonperformance of specific actions. *See also:* Terrorism Counteraction.

References

Department of Defense, U.S. Army. *The Army Terrorism Counteraction Program.* Army Regulation AR 525-13. Washington, DC: Headquarters, Department of the Army, 1988.

—**HOSTILE** is a contact that has been positively identified as the enemy's. *See also:* Bogey.

References

Department of Defense, U.S. Army. *U.S. Army Policy Statement, 1988.* Washington, DC: Headquarters, Department of the Army, 1988.

—**HOSTILE ACTS** are basic rules that have been established for defining and recognizing hostile acts by aircraft, submarines, surface units, and ground forces. They are promulgated by the commanders of Unified or Specified Commands, and by other appropriate commanders when authorized to do so.

References

Department of Defense, Joint Chiefs of Staff. *Department of Defense Dictionary of Military and Related Terms.* Washington, DC: GPO, 1986.

—**HOSTILE CRITERIA** is a description of the conditions under which an aircraft or vehicle may be identified as hostile for engagement purposes. *See also:* Bogey.

References

Department of Defense, U.S. Army. *Air Defense Artillery Deployment: Chaparral/Vulcan/Stinger.* Field Manual FM 44-3. Washington, DC: Headquarters, Department of the Army, 1984.

———. *Operational Terms and Symbols.* Field Manual FM 101-5-1. Washington, DC: Headquarters, Department of the Army, 1985.

—**HOSTILE TRACK** (AIR DEFENSE) is the classification assigned to a track that, based upon established criteria, is determined to be an enemy airborne, ballistic, or orbiting threat. *See also:* Bogey.

References

Department of Defense, Joint Chiefs of Staff. *Department of Defense Dictionary of Military and Related Terms.* Washington, DC: GPO, 1986.

—**HOT** refers to a person, place, or thing considered contaminated. *See also:* Nuclear Warfare.

References

Department of Defense, U.S. Army. *Technical Escort Operations.* Field Manual FM 3-20. Washington, DC: Headquarters, Department of the Army, 1981.

—**HOT LINE** is a real or imaginary line that separates contaminated from uncontaminated areas. *See also:* Nuclear Warfare.

References

Department of Defense, U.S. Army. *NBC Decontamination.* Field Manual FM 3-5. Washington, DC: Headquarters, Department of the Army, 1985.

—**HOT PHOTOGRAPHIC INTERPRETATION REPORT (HOTPHOTOREP)** is a preliminary unformatted report of significant information from tactical reconnaissance imagery that is dispatched prior to the compilation of the initial photo interpretation report. It should pertain to a single objective, event, or activity of significant interest to justify immediate reporting. *See also:* Aerial Reconnaissance.

References

Department of Defense, Defense Intelligence College. *Glossary of Intelligence Terms and Definitions.* Washington, DC: DIC, 1987.

Department of Defense, Joint Chiefs of Staff. *Department of Defense Dictionary of Military and Related Terms.* Washington, DC: GPO, 1986.

—**HOT PHOTOGRAPHIC REPORT** is a standardized imagery interpretation report providing priority intelligence information that has been obtained from the interpretation of sensor imagery that has not previously been included in a mission report or is included to update information that was originally provided in a mission report. *See also:* Aerial Reconnaissance.

References
Department of Defense, U.S. Army. *Dictionary of United States Army Terms*. Army Regulation AR 310-25. Washington, DC: Headquarters, Department of the Army, 1986.

—**HOT SPOT** is a region in a contaminated area in which the radiation level is considerably greater than that in neighboring regions in the area. *See also:* Nuclear Warfare.

References
Department of Defense, Joint Chiefs of Staff. *Department of Defense Dictionary of Military and Related Terms*. Washington, DC: GPO, 1986.

—**HOUSEKEEPING SUPPLIES** are items listed in tables of allowances and tables of distribution and allowances that are required for shelter, health, welfare, and administration of personnel.

References
Department of Defense, U.S. Army. *Dictionary of United States Army Terms*. Army Regulation AR 310-25. Washington, DC: Headquarters, Department of the Army, 1986.

—**HOVERING** is a self-sustaining maneuver whereby a fixed, or nearly fixed, position is maintained relative to a spot on the surface of the earth or underwater. *See also:* Hovering Ceiling.

References
Department of Defense, Joint Chiefs of Staff. *Department of Defense Dictionary of Military and Related Terms*. Washington, DC: GPO, 1986.

—**HOVERING CEILING** is the highest altitude at which the helicopter is capable of hovering in standard atmosphere.

References
Department of Defense, Joint Chiefs of Staff. *Department of Defense Dictionary of Military and Related Terms*. Washington, DC: GPO, 1986.

—**HOW TO FIGHT MANUALS** are special technical manuals that tell leaders how to fight.

References
Department of Defense, U.S. Army. *The Rifle Squads (Mechanized and Light Infantry)*. Training Circular TC 7-1. Washington, DC: Headquarters, Department of the Army, 1976.

—**HOWITZER.** (1) A howitzer is a cannon that combines certain characteristics of guns and mortars. It delivers projectiles with medium velocities, either by low or high trajectories. (2) A howitzer is normally a cannon with a tube length of 20 to 30 caliber; however, the tube length can exceed 30 caliber and still be considered a howitzer when the high angle fire zoning solution permits range overlap between charges. *See also:* Gun, Mortar.

References
Department of Defense, Joint Chiefs of Staff. *Department of Defense Dictionary of Military and Related Terms*. Washington, DC: GPO, 1986.

—**HOWLER** is an electrical device similar to an automobile horn and placed at gun positions as a firing signal in a time interval system of tracking a moving target.

References
Department of Defense, U.S. Army. *Dictionary of United States Army Terms*. Army Regulation AR 310-25. Washington, DC: Headquarters, Department of the Army, 1986.

—**HULL** is the massive armored body of a tank, exclusive of the tracks, motor, turret, and armament.

References
Department of Defense, U.S. Army. *Dictionary of United States Army Terms*. Army Regulation AR 310-25. Washington, DC: Headquarters, Department of the Army, 1986.

—**HULL-DOWN POSTION** is the positioning of an armored vehicle so that the muzzle of the gun or launcher is the lowest part of the vehicle that is exposed to the front. The best firing position is one that provides cover, concealment, maximum fields of fire, and covered routes into and out of the position. This position should be level and dry. A hull-down position conceals and protects the tank hull but permits main gun direct fire, and should be used for all direct-fire tank gun engagements.

References
Department of Defense, U.S. Army. *Operational Terms and Symbols*. Field Manual FM 101-5-1. Washington, DC: Headquarters, Department of the Army, 1985.

———. *Tank Gunnery*. Field Manual FM 17-12. Washington, DC: Headquarters, Department of the Army, 1984.

—**HUMAN COLLECTION.** *See:* Human Intelligence.

—**HUMAN FACTORS RESEARCH** is concerned with the discovery and development of principles and techniques for the more effective use of personnel and increasing the efficiency with which Army personnel perform their duties, operate, and maintain their equipment and weapons, give and accept commands, adapt to environmental and psychological stresses, and perform in combat. *See also:* Human Resources Development.

References
Department of Defense, U.S. Army. *Dictionary of United States Army Terms.* Army Regulation AR 310-25. Washington, DC: Headquarters, Department of the Army, 1986.

—**HUMAN RESOURCES COLLECTION** is a general intelligence term for all the activity associated with collecting information from human sources. *See also:* Human Intelligence.

References
Department of Defense, Defense Intelligence College. *Glossary of Intelligence Terms and Definitions.* Washington, DC: DIC, 1987.

—**HUMAN RESOURCES DEVELOPMENT** is personnel management that involves planning, organizing, directing, coordinating, and controlling activities primarily designed for their effect on individual morale and organizational esprit. It also involves the development of individual potential and of an organizational climate that enhances the attitudes, motivation, commitment, and sense of well-being of soldiers and their families. It includes activities that are related to leadership and discipline, job and career satisfaction, human relations, alcohol and drug abuse prevention, spiritual guidance and counseling, physical and mental well-being, community services, and maintenance of law and order. *See also:* Human Factors Research.

References
Department of Defense, U.S. Army. *Dictionary of United States Army Terms.* Army Regulation AR 310-25. Washington, DC: Headquarters, Department of the Army, 1986.

—**HUMAN RESOURCES INTELLIGENCE** is intelligence information derived from the intelligence collection discipline that uses human beings as both sources and collectors, and where the human being is the primary collection instrument.

References
Department of Defense, Joint Chiefs of Staff. *Department of Defense Dictionary of Military and Related Terms.* Washington, DC: GPO, 1986.

—**HUMAN SOURCE** is a general intelligence term for a person who knowingly or unknowingly provides information of potential intelligence value to an intelligence agency or activity.

References
Department of Defense, Defense Intelligence College. *Glossary of Intelligence Terms and Definitions.* Washington, DC: DIC, 1987.

—**HUNG BOMB** is a bomb that accidentally remains attached to the aircraft after it is released from the bomb rack.

References
Department of Defense, U.S. Army. *Dictionary of United States Army Terms.* Army Regulation AR 310-25. Washington, DC: Headquarters, Department of the Army, 1986.

—**HUNG STRIKER** is a defective striker of a grenade fuze that failed to strike the primer and explode the grenade.

References
Department of Defense, U.S. Army. *Dictionary of United States Army Terms.* Army Regulation AR 310-25. Washington, DC: Headquarters, Department of the Army, 1986.

—**HUNTING.** (1) Hunting is the action of a radar antenna in which it oscillates about, rather than stopping smoothly at, the point determined by the setting of the control. (2) Hunting is the rapid up and down movement of a tank gun tube that is caused by an oversensitized gyrostabilizer control unit.

References
Department of Defense, U.S. Army. *Dictionary of United States Army Terms.* Army Regulation AR 310-25. Washington, DC: Headquarters, Department of the Army, 1986.

—**HYBRID COLLECTIVE PROTECTION** is a combination of overpressure and ventilated-facepiece systems. *See also:* Nuclear Warfare.

References
Department of Defense, U.S. Army. *NBC Protection.* Field Manual FM 3-4. Washington, DC: Headquarters, Department of the Army, 1985.

—**HYDROPNEUMATIC** is pertaining to, or operated by means of, a liquid or gas. The term is ordinally used in connection with certain artillery recoil and equilibrator mechanisms that provide variable absorption of energy or thrust. *See also:* Recoil Cylinder.

References

Department of Defense, U.S. Army. *Dictionary of United States Army Terms.* Army Regulation AR 310-25. Washington, DC: Headquarters, Department of the Army, 1986.

—**HYPERVELOCITY.** (1) Hypervelocity is the muzzle velocity of an artillery projectile of 3,500 feet per second or more. (2) Hypervelocity in small arms is a muzzle velocity of 5,000 feet per second or more. (3) In tank cannon projectiles, hypervelocity is a muzzle velocity in excess of 3,350 feet per second. *See also:* High Velocity.

References

Department of Defense, U.S. Army. *Dictionary of United States Army Terms.* Army Regulation AR 310-25. Washington, DC: Headquarters, Department of the Army, 1986.

—**I METHOD** is a way to transmit a message from one station to another so that other stations for which it is intended can receive it without having to acknowledge they received it. The station called is responsible for the correct reception of the message at that station.

References

Department of Defense, U.S. Army. *Dictionary of United States Army Terms.* Army Regulation AR 310-25. Washington, DC: Headquarters, Department of the Army, 1986.

—**I SAY AGAIN** is a radiotelephone procedure proword that means "I am repeating my transmission or the portion indicated." *See also:* Proword.

References

Department of Defense, U.S. Army. *The Rifle Squads (Mechanized and Light Infantry).* Training Circular TC 7-1. Washington, DC: Headquarters, Department of the Army, 1976.

—**ICE MINE** is a waterproof mine placed in or under the ice. It is detonated by a pressure device on the surface or is exploded deliberately to break river or lake ice. *See also:* Mine Warfare.

References

Department of Defense, U.S. Army. *Dictionary of United States Army Terms.* Army Regulation 310-25. Washington, DC: Headquarters, Department of the Army, 1986.

—**ICE MINING** is the breaking up of river or lake ice using antitank or antipersonnel mines in order to deny passage to the enemy. Causing the mines to explode may be effected by control, passage of time, or enemy initiation. *See also:* Mine Warfare.

References

Department of Defense, U.S. Army. *Dictionary of United States Army Terms.* Army Regulation AR 310-25. Washington, DC: Headquarters, Department of the Army, 1986.

—**ICING** is a mass of surface ice formed by successive freezing of sheets of water that seep from the ground, a river, or a spring. Ice that is thick or localized is called an icing mound; ice that survives the summer is called a taryn.

References

Department of Defense, U.S. Army. *Dictionary of United States Army Terms.* Army Regulation AR 310-25. Washington, DC: Headquarters, Department of the Army, 1986.

—**IDEAL BOMB** is an imaginary bomb that incurs no air resistance as it falls toward the target.

References

Department of Defense, U.S. Army. *Dictionary of United States Army Terms.* Army Regulation AR 310-25. Washington, DC: Headquarters, Department of the Army, 1986.

—**IDENTIFICATION.** (1) Identification is the process of determining the friendly or hostile character of an unknown detected contact. (2) In ground combat operations, identification is discrimination between recognizable objects as being friendly or enemy, or the name that belongs to the object as a member of a class. (3) Identification, the identification of the presence of chemical or biological agents or nuclear radiation, involves positively identifying field concentrations of blood, blister, and nerve agents by using the M256 or M256A1 detector kit. Biological agents require a laboratory facility for identification, while nuclear radiation is measured by the unit's radiac instruments. (4) In arms control, identification is the process of determining which nation is responsible for the detected violations of any arms control measure. *See also:* Biological Warfare; Chemical Warfare; Identification, Friend or Foe; Nuclear Warfare.

References

Department of Defense, Joint Chiefs of Staff. *Department of Defense Dictionary of Military and Related Terms.* Washington, DC: GPO, 1986.

Department of Defense, U.S. Army. *Dictionary of United States Army Terms.* Army Regulation AR 310-25. Washington, DC: Headquarters, Department of the Army, 1986.

———. *NBC Protection.* Field Manual FM 3-4. Washington, DC: Headquarters, Department of the Army, 1985.

—**IDENTIFICATION, FRIEND OR FOE (IFF)** is a method that uses electronic detection and associated identification equipment to determine the friendly or unfriendly character of aircraft, vehicles, or ships by other aircraft, vehicles, weapons, or ships. It is a system that emits electromagnetic transmissions, to which equipment carried by friendly forces automatically respond allowing each to distinguish themselves from enemy forces.

References

Department of Defense, U.S. Army. *Air Defense Artillery Deployment: Chaparral/Vulcan/Stinger.* Field Manual FM 44-3. Washington, DC: Headquarters, Department of the Army, 1984.

————. *Operational Terms and Symbols.* Field Manual FM 101-5-1. Washington, DC: Headquarters, Department of the Army, 1985.

—**IDENTIFICATION SMOKE** is smoke used to identify targets, supply, and evacuation points, and friendly unit perimeters. It is also used for prearranged battlefield communications.

References

Department of Defense, U.S. Army. *Operational Terms and Symbols.* Field Manual FM 101-5-1. Washington, DC: Headquarters, Department of the Army, 1985.

—**IDENTIFY** is a code meaning, "Identify the contact designated by any means at your disposal." *See also:* Identification, Recognition.

References

Department of Defense, Joint Chiefs of Staff. *Department of Defense Dictionary of Military and Related Terms.* Washington, DC: GPO, 1986.

—**IGNITER.** (1) An igniter is a device containing an extremely burnable substance, usually a form of black powder, that is used to amplify the initiation of a primer in the functioning of a fuze. An igniter may be used to assist in the initiation of a propelling charge and in some types of projectile bursting charges. (2) An igniter is a device containing a spontaneously combustible material (e.g., white phosphorus) that is used to ignite the fillings of incendiary bombs at the time the bomb casing ruptures. (3) An igniter is a device used to initiate the burning of the fuel mixture in a ramjet or rocket combustion chamber. *See also:* Igniter Pad, Igniter Train, Igniting Fuze, Igniting Mixture, Ignition.

References

Department of Defense, U.S. Army. *Dictionary of United States Army Terms.* Army Regulation AR 310-25. Washington, DC: Headquarters, Department of the Army, 1986.

—**IGNITER PAD** is a black powder charge attached to the base increment of separate loading propelling charges to provide for a complete and uniform ignition.

References

Department of Defense, U.S. Army. *Dictionary of United States Army Terms.* Army Regulation AR 310-25. Washington, DC: Headquarters, Department of the Army, 1986.

—**IGNITER TRAIN** is a step-by-step arrangement of charges in pyrotechnic bombs and shells by which the initial fire from the primer is transmitted and intensified until it reaches and sets off the main charge. An explosive bomb or projectile uses a similar series, called an explosive train.

References

Department of Defense, U.S. Army. *Dictionary of United States Army Terms.* Army Regulation AR 310-25. Washington, DC: Headquarters, Department of the Army, 1986.

—**IGNITING FUZE** is a type of grenade fuze that ignites the filler through the medium of a small quantity of black powder.

References

Department of Defense, U.S. Army. *Dictionary of United States Army Terms.* Army Regulation AR 310-25. Washington, DC: Headquarters, Department of the Army, 1986.

—**IGNITING MIXTURE** is an explosive mixture used as a fuze in pyrotechnic signals.

References

Department of Defense, U.S. Army. *Dictionary of United States Army Terms.* Army Regulation AR 310-25. Washington, DC: Headquarters, Department of the Army, 1986.

—**IGNITING POWDER.** *See:* Igniter.

—**IGNITION** is the action of a device used as the first element of an explosive train that, upon receiving the proper impulse, causes the rapid burning of a propellent or pyrotechnic item. *See also:* Ignition Cartridge.

References

Department of Defense, U.S. Army. *Dictionary of United States Army Terms.* Army Regulation AR 310-25. Washington, DC: Headquarters, Department of the Army, 1986.

—**IGNITION CARTRIDGE.** (1) An ignition cartridge is an igniter in cartridge form that may be used alone or with additional propellent increments as a propelling charge for certain mortar ammunition. (2) An ignition cartridge is an assembly consisting of a primer and an igniter that is used to provide an impulse sufficient to start certain types of diesel engines.

References

Department of Defense, U.S. Army. *Dictionary of United States Army Terms.* Army Regulation AR 310-25. Washington, DC: Headquarters, Department of the Army, 1986.

—**ILLUMINANT COMPOSITION** is a mixture of materials used in pyrotechnic devices to produce high intensity light.

References

Department of Defense, U.S. Army. *Dictionary of United States Army Terms.* Army Regulation AR 310-25. Washington, DC: Headquarters, Department of the Army, 1986.

—**ILLUMINATION FIRE** is fire designed to light an area. *See also:* Illuminant Composition.

References

Department of Defense, Joint Chiefs of Staff. *Department of Defense Dictionary of Military and Related Terms.* Washington, DC: GPO, 1986.

—**ILLUMINATOR RADAR** is an integral part of a guided missile weapon system used to track and illuminate a target. The illuminating energy is reflected by the target, detected by the missile, and used by the missile to home in on the target. In an active homing guidance system, the illuminator radar is on board the missile; in a semiactive homing system, the radar may be aboard a ship or an aircraft, or on land.

References

Department of Defense, U.S. Army. *Dictionary of United States Army Terms.* Army Regulation AR 310-25. Washington, DC: Headquarters, Department of the Army, 1986.

—**IMAGE** is a representation of an object by electronic or optical means on film, electronic display devices, or other media. *See also:* Aerial Reconnaissance.

References

Department of Defense, Defense Intelligence College. *Glossary of Intelligence Terms and Definitions.* Washington, DC: DIC, 1987.

Department of Defense. U.S. Army. *Dictionary of United States Army Terms.* Army Regulation AR 310-25. Washington, DC: Headquarters, Department of the Army, 1986.

―――. *Intelligence Imagery.* Field Manual FM 34-55. Washington, DC: Headquarters, Department of the Army, 1985.

Reeves, Robert; Anson, Abraham; and Landen, David. *Manual of Remote Sensing.* Falls Church, VA: American Society of Photogrammetry, 1975.

—**IMAGE INTERPRETER** is a military intelligence specialist who is qualified to recognize, identify, locate, describe, and analyze objects, activities, and terrain that are represented on imagery, and to extract intelligence information from the imagery. *See also:* Aerial Reconnaissance.

References

Department of Defense, U.S. Army. *Dictionary of United States Army Terms.* Army Regulation AR 310-25. Washington, DC: Headquarters, Department of the Army, 1986.

—**IMAGERY** are representations of objects reproduced electronically or optically on film, electronic display devices, or other media. *See also:* Aerial Reconnaissance.

References

Department of Defense, Defense Intelligence College. *Glossary of Intelligence Terms and Definitions.* Washington, DC: DIC, 1987.

Department of Defense. U.S. Army. *Intelligence Imagery.* Field Manual FM 34-55. Washington, DC: Headquarters, Department of the Army, 1985.

―――. *Support Operations: Echelons Above Corps.* Field Manual FM 100-16. Washington, DC: Headquarters, Department of the Army, 1986.

—**IMAGERY ANNOTATION,** in photoreconnaissance, is material or information written on the imagery that is often used to amplify the written report. The following annotations are required on imagery produced by the U.S. Army:
- A titling strip, which includes a grid reference or the geographic coordinates of the target or object;
- A reference point to illustrate the geographical reference that is quoted in the titling strip;
- The target category and description;
- An orientation aid in the form of an arrowhead; and
- Interpretation annotations that indicate the individual target category item.

See also: Aerial Reconnaissance.

References

Department of Defense, Defense Intelligence College. *Glossary of Intelligence Terms and Definitions.* Washington, DC: DIC, 1987.

Department of Defense. U.S. Army. *Intelligence Imagery.* Field Manual FM 34-55. Washington, DC: Headquarters, Department of the Army, 1985.

—**IMAGERY EXPLOITATION** is the processing and printing of imagery; assembling it into imagery packs; identifying, interpreting, measuring, and extracting information; preparing reports; and disseminating the information to the customer. *See also:* Aerial Reconnaissance.

References

Department of Defense. U.S. Army. *Intelligence Imagery.* Field Manual FM 34-55. Washington, DC: Headquarters, Department of the Army, 1985.

Reeves, Robert; Anson, Abraham; and Landen, David. *Manual of Remote Sensing.* Falls Church, VA: American Society of Photogrammetry, 1975.

—**IMAGERY INTELLIGENCE (IMINT)** refers to the products of imagery interpretation derived from exploiting the visual photography, infrared sensors, lasers, electro-optics, and radar sensors of the images of objects that have been reproduced optically or electronically on film, electronic display devices, or other media, and that have been processed for intelligence use by an imagery interpreter or imagery analyst. *See also:* Aerial Reconnaissance.

References

Department of Defense, Defense Intelligence College. *Glossary of Intelligence Terms and Definitions.* Washington, DC: DIC, 1987.

Department of Defense, U.S. Army. *Dictionary of United States Army Terms.* Army Regulation AR 310-25. Washington, DC: Headquarters, Department of the Army, 1986.

———. *Intelligence Imagery.* Field Manual FM 34-55. Washington, DC: Headquarters, Department of the Army, 1985.

———. *Operational Terms and Symbols.* Field Manual FM 101-5-1. Washington, DC: Headquarters, Department of the Army, 1985.

———. *Support Operations: Echelons Above Corps.* Field Manual FM 100-16. Washington, DC: Headquarters, Department of the Army, 1986.

Reeves, Robert; Anson, Abraham; and Landen, David. *Manual of Remote Sensing.* Falls Church, VA: American Society of Photogrammetry, 1975.

—**IMAGERY INTERPRETATION (II)** is the process of locating, recognizing, identifying, and describing objects, activities, and terrain that appear on imagery. *See also:* Aerial Reconnaissance.

References

Department of Defense, Defense Intelligence College. *Glossary of Intelligence Terms and Definitions.* Washington, DC: DIC, 1987.

Department of Defense, U.S. Army. *Intelligence Imagery.* Field Manual FM 34-55. Washington, DC: Headquarters, Department of the Army, 1985.

———. *Support Operations: Echelons Above Corps.* Field Manual FM 100-16. Washington, DC: Headquarters, Department of the Army, 1986.

—**IMAGERY INTERPRETER (II)** is an individual who has been trained to examine photography and other imagery in order to locate, recognize, identify, and describe objects, activities, and terrain that is of intelligence interest. *See also:* Aerial Reconnaissance.

References

Department of Defense, Defense Intelligence College. *Glossary of Intelligence Terms and Definitions.* Washington, DC: DIC, 1987.

Department of Defense, U.S. Army. *Intelligence Imagery.* Field Manual FM 34-55. Washington, DC: Headquarters, Department of the Army, 1985.

—**IMITATIVE COMMUNICATIONS DECEPTION (ICD),** in electronic warfare, is intruding on communications channels for deceptive purposes by introducing signals or traffic that imitate other communications. *See also:* Communications Deception, Electronic Warfare.

References

Department of Defense, Defense Intelligence College. *Glossary of Intelligence Terms and Definitions.* Washington, DC: DIC, 1987.

—**IMITATIVE DECEPTION,** in electronic warfare, is introducing electromagnetic radiations that imitate enemy emissions into enemy channels. *See also:* Electronic Warfare.

References

Department of Defense, Defense Intelligence College. *Glossary of Intelligence Terms and Definitions.* Washington, DC: DIC, 1987.

—**IMITATIVE ELECTRONIC DECEPTION (IED)** is imitating enemy electromagnetic radiations (predominately communications) after intruding into its electromagnetic channels in order to deceive it or to disrupt its operations. *See also:* Electronic Deception, Manipulative Electronic Deception.

References

Department of Defense, U.S. Army. *Operational Terms and Symbols.* Field Manual FM 101-5-1. Washington, DC: Headquarters, Department of the Army, 1985.

—**IMMEDIATE ACTION** is a procedure applied to reduce any delay or stoppage in operations without attempting to determine its cause.

References

Department of Defense, U.S. Army. *Dictionary of United States Army Terms.* Army Regulation AR 310-25. Washington, DC: Headquarters, Department of the Army, 1986.

—**IMMEDIATE AIR SUPPORT** meets specific requests that arise during a battle that, by their nature, cannot be planned for in advance. *See also:* Air Support.

References

Department of Defense, Joint Chiefs of Staff. *Department of Defense Dictionary of Military and Related Terms.* Washington, DC: GPO, 1986.

—**IMMEDIATE AIRLIFT** responds to unanticipated, urgent requirements. The airlift control center can provide aircraft quickly at designated locations, or it can decide to cancel preplanned missions and make standby arrangements for the special service.

References

Department of Defense, U.S. Army. *Repair Parts Supply for a Theater of Operations.* Field Manual FM 29-19. Washington, DC: Headquarters, Department of the Army, 1985.

—**IMMEDIATE AIRLIFT REQUESTS** are requests that cannot be filled by a preplanned mission due to their time critical nature. *See also:* Immediate Airlift.

References

Department of Defense, U.S. Army. *USA/USAF Doctrine for Joint Airborne and Tactical Airlift Operations.* Field Manual FM 100-27. Washington, DC: Headquarters, Department of the Army, 1985.

—**IMMEDIATE MESSAGE** is a precedence category reserved for messages relating to situations that gravely affect the security of national or allied forces or people and that require immediate delivery to the addressees. *See also:* Precedence.

References

Department of Defense, Joint Chiefs of Staff. *Department of Defense Dictionary of Military and Related Terms.* Washington, DC: GPO, 1986.

—**IMMEDIATE MISSION REQUEST** is a request for an air strike on a target that, by its nature, could not be identified sufficiently in advance to permit detailed mission coordination and planning. *See also:* Preplanned Mission Request.

References

Department of Defense, U.S. Army. *Operational Terms and Symbols.* Field Manual FM 101-5-1. Washington, DC: Headquarters, Department of the Army, 1985.

—**IMMEDIATE NUCLEAR SUPPORT** is nuclear support to meet specific requests that arise during the course of battle, and that, by their nature, cannot be planned for in advance. *See also:* Nuclear Warfare.

References

Department of Defense, Joint Chiefs of Staff. *Department of Defense Dictionary of Military and Related Terms.* Washington, DC: GPO, 1986.

—**IMMEDIATE OPERATIONAL READINESS** refers to the actions directly related to the assumption of an alert or quick-reaction posture. Typical readiness operations include strip alert, airborne alert/indoctrination, no-notice launch of an alert force, and maintaining missiles in an alert configuration. *See also:* Nuclear Weapon Exercise, Nuclear Weapon Maneuver.

References

Department of Defense, Joint Chiefs of Staff. *Department of Defense Dictionary of Military and Related Terms.* Washington, DC: GPO, 1986.

—**IMMEDIATE PERMANENT INEFFECTIVENESS, 8,000 cGy (RADS).** If exposed to radiation of this intensity, personnel become ineffective within three minutes of exposure and remain ineffective for any task until death. Death occurs within one day. *See also:* Nuclear Warfare.

References

Department of Defense, U.S. Army. *Operational Terms and Symbols.* Field Manual FM 101-5-1. Washington, DC: Headquarters, Department of the Army, 1985.

—**IMMEDIATE REENLISTMENT** is a voluntary second or subsequent enrollment in the Regular Army as an enlisted member immediately upon separation from active military service in the Army. This term represents a concurrent action in which the separation documents are not given to the person until he has reenlisted in the Regular Army. *See also:* Reenlistment.

References
Department of Defense, U.S. Army. *Army Reenlistment Program.* Army Regulation AR 601-280. Washington, DC: Headquarters, Department of the Army, 1984.

—**IMMEDIATE SUPPRESSIVE FIRE,** in combined arms operations, occurs when direct fire weapons and supporting field artillery units respond immediately after the enemy has fired from, or has been seen and can fire from, a given location.

References
Department of Defense, U.S. Army. *Fire Support in Combined Arms Operations.* Field Manual FM 6-20. Washington, DC: Headquarters, Department of the Army, 1983.

—**IMMEDIATE TRANSIENT INEFFECTIVENESS.** Personnel become ineffective for any task within three minutes of exposure to nuclear radiation and remain so for approximately seven minutes, regardless of the physical demands of the task. They recover to greater than 75 percent of their preexposure level and remain so for about 30 minutes. At about 40 minutes postexposure, they become performance degraded and remain so for about five hours for undemanding tasks (two hours for demanding tasks), at which time radiation sickness symptoms are likely to be present in sufficient severity to render them ineffective for all tasks. They remain ineffective until their death, which occurs in five to six days. *See also:* Nuclear Warfare.

References
Department of Defense, U.S. Army. *Operational Terms and Symbols.* Field Manual FM 101-5-1. Washington, DC: Headquarters, Department of the Army, 1985.

—**IMMERSION PROOF,** unless otherwise specified, means that an item of equipment, when it is ready for field transport, can be submerged for two hours in salt water or freshwater to a covering depth of three feet and still operate normally immediately after being removed from the water.

References
Department of Defense, U.S. Army. *Dictionary of United States Army Terms.* Army Regulation AR 310-25. Washington, DC: Headquarters, Department of the Army, 1986.

—**IMPACT ACTION FUZE** is set in action by the striking of a projectile or bomb against an object. Percussion fuzes and contact fuzes are impact action fuzes. The term is synonymous with direct action fuze. *See also:* Fuze.

References
Department of Defense, Joint Chiefs of Staff. *Department of Defense Dictionary of Military and Related Terms.* Washington, DC: GPO, 1986.

—**IMPACT AREA** is an area having designated boundaries within the limits of which all ordnance will detonate on impact.

References
Department of Defense, Joint Chiefs of Staff. *Department of Defense Dictionary of Military and Related Terms.* Washington, DC: GPO, 1986.

—**IMPACT (CONTACT SURFACE) BURST** is a nuclear burst used to cause blast, ground shock, and cratering. It may be used against hard underground targets located relatively near the surface. Fallout is produced from such a burst. *See also:* Nuclear Warfare.

References
Department of Defense, U.S. Army. *Nuclear Weapons Employment Doctrine and Procedures.* Field Manual FM 101-3-1. Washington, DC: Headquarters, Department of the Army, 1986.

—**IMPERMEABLE PROTECTIVE CLOTHING** is clothing made of material that prevents the passage of toxic chemical agents in any physical form. It can be worn for only a short time because of the excessive heat that it causes. *See also:* Chemical Warfare.

References
Department of Defense, U.S. Army. *Dictionary of United States Army Terms.* Army Regulation AR 310-25. Washington, DC: Headquarters, Department of the Army, 1986.

—**IMPLOSION WEAPON** is a weapon in which the volume of its fissionable material, less than a critical mass at ordinary pressure, can be suddenly reduced by compression caused by using chemical explosives, so that the weapon becomes supercritical and produces a nuclear explosion. *See also:* Nuclear Warfare.

References
Department of Defense, Joint Chiefs of Staff.
Department of Defense Dictionary of Military and Related Terms. Washington, DC: GPO, 1986.

—IMPROVED CONVENTIONAL MUNITIONS

are characterized by the delivery of two or more antipersonnel or antimateriel and/or antiarmor submunitions by an artillery warhead or projectile.

References
Department of Defense, Joint Chiefs of Staff.
Department of Defense Dictionary of Military and Related Terms. Washington, DC: GPO, 1986.

—IMPROVED HAWK

is a medium-range air defense guided missile system designed to provide air defense coverage against low- to medium-altitude air attacks. It is a mobile all-weather, day and night operational missile system providing vital air defense against enemy air attack. HAWK has superior fire control, lethality, range, reliability, and effectiveness in an electronic countermeasures environment. In the basic HAWK configuration, over twenty high performance aircraft were destroyed in the Middle East War of 1973. Currently, HAWK is being reorganized into a more streamlined and efficient fighting organization. Each platoon contains a platoon command post, which controls the platoon's equipment and fights the air battle; an acquisition and a tracking radar; an optical tracking system; an identification friend or foe system; and three to four launchers containing nine to twelve ready missiles. The HAWK missile carries a large proximity fuze, and a high-explosive warhead, which can destroy a target by passing near it.

References
Weapons Systems: U.S. Army, Navy, and Air Force Directory, 1986–1988. Washington, DC: DCP, 1986.

—IMPROVED TOW VEHICLE (ITV)

is an antitank vehicle designed to enhance the Army's antitank capability in response to the significant numerical superiority in armor of the Soviet and Warsaw Pact Ground Forces. ITV combines two existing weapons systems: the tube launched, optically tracked, wire-guided (TOW) missile system and the M113 armored personnel carrier. The TOW components are mounted in a launcher platform that is attached to a M27 cupola. An elevating mechanism positions the launcher platform from and into the stow, reload, and elevated positions. An optical image transfer assembly allows the gunner to stay within the M113 and still use the TOW's day and night optical sights. The vehicle carries twelve TOW rounds. The system can fire two TOW missiles from its launcher while the crew remains under armor, and reloading can be accomplished from inside the vehicle. The elevated hammerhead launcher allows the vehicle to remain behind cover, even while it is firing its missiles. If it becomes disabled, the TOW components can be removed and used in a ground-mounted mode. A periscope has been provided to the commander for target acquisition. A 7.62-mm, M60 machine gun is pintle-mounted and attached to a monorail on the cupola.

References
Weapons Systems: U.S. Army, Navy, and Air Force Directory, 1986–1988. Washington, DC: DCP, 1986.

—IMPROVISED EXPLOSIVE DEVICES

are devices that are placed or fabricated and incorporate destructive, lethal, noxious, pyrotechnic, or incendiary chemicals designed to destroy, disfigure, distract, or harass. They may use military stores, but are normally devised from nonmilitary components. *See also:* Chemical Warfare.

References
Department of Defense, Joint Chiefs of Staff.
Department of Defense Dictionary of Military and Related Terms. Washington, DC: GPO, 1986.

—IMPROVISED MINE

is a mine fabricated from available materials at or near its point of use. *See also:* Mine Warfare.

References
Department of Defense, Joint Chiefs of Staff.
Department of Defense Dictionary of Military and Related Terms. Washington, DC: GPO, 1986.

—IN CONNECTION WITH MILITARY OPERATIONS AGAINST AN ARMED ENEMY.

This phrase covers all military operations, including combat, support, and supply, that have a direct bearing on the outcome of an engagement or engagements against armed opposition. To perform such duty, or to accomplish an act or achievement in connection with military operations against an armed enemy, the individual must have been subjected to either personal hazard as a result of direct enemy action, or the imminence of such action, or must have had the conditions under which his duty or accomplishment took place complicated by enemy action or the imminence of enemy action.

References
Department of Defense, U.S. Army. *Military Awards.* Army Regulation AR 672-5-1. Washington, DC: Headquarters, Department of the Army, 1984.

—**IN SUPPORT OF.** (1) In support of is assisting or protecting another formation, unit, or organization while remaining under original control. (2) In support of is a term that describes the mission when a health service unit has to provide priority effort to a specific supported unit or group of units. The health service unit is not attached to the supported unit but remains under the command of the medical command and control headquarters. "In support of " differs from "direct support " in that a health service unit normally does not provide support exclusively to a supported unit and may not receive and execute missions directly on call from a supported unit. This term is normally used in regard to the mission of medical treatment and evacuation of units. *See also:* Medical Treatment.

References
Department of Defense, U.S. Army. *Health Service Support in a Communications Zone (Test).* Field Manual FM 8-21. Washington, DC: Headquarters, Department of the Army, 1981.

—**IN TRANSIT INVENTORY** is the materiel in the military distribution system that is in the process of being moved from the point of receipt from procurement and production (either the contractor's plant or the first destination, depending on the point of delivery) to a storage or distribution point.

References
Department of Defense, Joint Chiefs of Staff. *Department of Defense Dictionary of Military and Related Terms.* Washington, DC: GPO, 1986.

—**IN-HOUSE WORK** includes all work performed by Department of Defense personnel, including monitoring of contractor efforts. The cost of in-house work includes both the direct and the indirect costs associated with the performance of Department of Defense personnel. This includes the materials and supplies that are obtained through the supply system, but excludes contracts and grants that are directly financed by research, development, test, and evaluation.

References
Department of Defense, U.S. Army. *Dictionary of United States Army Terms.* Army Regulation AR 310-25. Washington, DC: Headquarters, Department of the Army, 1986.

—**IN-PLACE FORCE** is a NATO-assigned force that, in peacetime, is principally stationed in the designated combat zone of the NATO Command to which it is committed. *See also:* NATO Command Forces.

References
Department of Defense, Joint Chiefs of Staff. *Department of Defense Dictionary of Military and Related Terms.* Washington, DC: GPO, 1986.

—**IN PLACE RIGHT OR IN PLACE LEFT** (ARMY AVIATION) is a maneuver in which the formation turns a designated number of degrees while each aircraft maintains its position in the flight.

References
Department of Defense, U.S. Army. *Air-to-Air Combat.* Field Manual FM 1-107. Washington, DC: Headquarters, Department of the Army, 1984.

—**IN-PROCESS REVIEW** is a review of a nonmajor development program conducted at critical points in the life cycle to evaluate the military utility, including costs, to accomplish effective coordination and to facilitate proper and timely decisions bearing on the future course of the program. The primary function of the in-process review is to review programs and recommend appropriate course(s) of action, and to provide supporting rationale as the basis for materiel acquisition decisions by the appropriate level of authority.

References
Department of Defense, U.S. Army. *Dictionary of United States Army Terms.* Army Regulation AR 310-25. Washington, DC: Headquarters, Department of the Army, 1986.

—**IN-SERVICE COUPLES WITH FAMILY MEMBERS** are service members of the regular and reserve components of any service who are married to each other, either or both of whom have physical custody of one or more children under the age of 18 or have family members who are incapable of self-care regardless of their age.

References

Department of Defense, U.S. Army. *Dictionary of United States Army Terms.* Army Regulation AR 310-25. Washington, DC: Headquarters, Department of the Army, 1986.

—**IN SUPPORT** is an expression used to denote the task of providing artillery supporting fire to a formation or unit. Liaison and observation are not normally provided. *See also:* At Priority Call, Direct Support.

References

Department of Defense, Joint Chiefs of Staff. *Department of Defense Dictionary of Military and Related Terms.* Washington, DC: GPO, 1986.

—**INACTIVATE** is to remove a unit from the active list of the Army. *See also:* Disband.

References

Department of Defense, U.S. Army. *Dictionary of United States Army Terms.* Army Regulation AR 310-25. Washington, DC: Headquarters, Department of the Army, 1986.

—**INACTIVE BEDS** are the medical treatment facility bed spaces with beds, not necessarily set up, for which equipment and fixtures are on hand and installed, but for which an operating staff has not been provided. *See also:* Medical Treatment.

References

Department of Defense, U.S. Army. *Dictionary of United States Army Terms.* Army Regulation AR 310-25. Washington, DC: Headquarters, Department of the Army, 1986.

—**INACTIVE DUTY TRAINING (IDT)** consists of four-hour drill periods with or without pay, and is usually associated with unit training assemblies, additional training assemblies, multiple unit training assemblies, periods of appropriate duty or equivalent duty or equivalent training, and any special additional duties that are authorized for reserve component personnel by an authority designated by the Secretary concerned, and performed by them in connection with the prescribed activities of the organization in which they are assigned. *See also:* Active Duty for Training, Annual Training.

References

Department of Defense, U.S. Army. *Army Forces Training.* Army Regulation AR 350-41. Washington, DC: Headquarters, Department of the Army, 1986.

————. *Training for Mobilization and War.* Field Manual FM 25-5. Washington, DC: Headquarters, Department of the Army, 1985.

————. *Unit Training Management.* Field Manual FM 25-2. Washington, DC: Headquarters, Department of the Army, 1984.

—**INACTIVE INSTALLATION** is an installation not in use, either intermittently or otherwise, by Active Army or Army Reserve component organizations, except for caretaking detachments. Inactive installations are retained on a nonuse status in support of mobilization requirements, or are pending disposal or transfer to another federal agency. *See also:* Installation.

References

Department of Defense, U.S. Army. *Dictionary of United States Army Terms.* Army Regulation AR 310-25. Washington, DC: Headquarters, Department of the Army, 1986.

—**INACTIVE NATIONAL GUARD** is a continuing military status for the qualified officers, warrant officers, and enlisted persons who are temporarily prevented from participating in National Guard training. The individuals who are assigned to the Inactive National Guard continue to be in the Ready Reserve and are subject to order to active duty in time of war or national emergency as members of the Army National Guard of the United States.

References

Department of Defense, U.S. Army. *Dictionary of United States Army Terms.* Army Regulation AR310-25. Washington, DC: Headquarters, Department of the Army, 1986.

—**INACTIVE STATUS** is the state of being officially connected with the military service, but not actively serving in it. *See also:* Inactive Status List.

References

Department of Defense, U.S. Army. *Dictionary of United States Army Terms.* Army Regulation AR 310-25. Washington, DC: Headquarters, Department of the Army, 1986.

—**INACTIVE STATUS LIST** is a segment of the Standby Reserve made up of eligible members who are unable to participate in training, but whose retention in the Army Reserve is desirable.

References

Department of Defense, U.S. Army. *Dictionary of United States Army Terms.* Army Regulation AR 310-25. Washington, DC: Headquarters, Department of the Army, 1986.

—**INBOUND CALL** is a communication initiated by the close air support flight to the tactical air coordinator, airborne, to begin the exchange of battle information before an engagement.

References

Department of Defense, U.S. Army. *Attack Helicopter Operations.* Field Manual FM 17-50. Washington, DC: Headquarters, Department of the Army, 1984.

—**INCAPACITATING AGENT** is an agent that produces temporary physiological or mental effects, or both, that render individuals incapable of performing their assigned duties. *See also:* Chemical Warfare.

References

Department of Defense, Joint Chiefs of Staff. *Department of Defense Dictionary of Military and Related Terms.* Washington, DC: GPO, 1986.

—**INCENDIARY** is ammunition with flammable filling.

References

Department of Defense, U.S. Army. *Dictionary of United States Army Terms.* Army Regulation AR 310-25. Washington, DC: Headquarters, Department of the Army, 1986.

—**INCIDENCE RATE** is the ratio of the number of new cases of a disease or injury, or a group of diseases or injuries (all new cases, both inpatient and outpatient), during a given period of time, to the total average strength during the period. It is usually expressed as the number of new cases per 1,000 average strength per year. *See also:* Medical Treatment.

References

Department of Defense, U.S. Army. *Dictionary of United States Army Terms.* Army Regulation AR 310-25. Washington, DC: Headquarters, Department of the Army, 1986.

—**INCIDENTS** are brief clashes or other military disturbances, usually of a transitory nature, that do not involve protracted hostilities. *See also:* Low Intensity Conflict.

References

Department of Defense, Joint Chiefs of Staff. *Department of Defense Dictionary of Military and Related Terms.* Washington, DC: GPO, 1986.

—**INCREMENT** is an amount of propellent added to, or taken away from, a propelling charge of semifixed or separate-loading ammunition. Such adjustments are made to allow for desired differences in range.

References

Department of Defense, U.S. Army. *Dictionary of United States Army Terms.* Army Regulation AR 310-25. Washington, DC: Headquarters, Department of the Army, 1986.

—**INDEFINITE CALL SIGN** is a call sign that does not represent a specific facility, command, authority, activity, or unit, but that may represent any one or any group of these. *See also:* Call Sign.

References

Department of Defense, Joint Chiefs of Staff. *Department of Defense Dictionary of Military and Related Terms.* Washington, DC: GPO, 1986.

—**INDETERMINATE CHANGE OF STATION** is an assignment to temporary duty away from one's permanent station on orders that state that the individual or unit will not return to the former permanent station, but will be ordered to a new one, which will be determined at a later date. *See also:* Permanent Change of Station.

References

Department of Defense, U.S. Army. *Dictionary of United States Army Terms.* Army Regulation AR 310-25. Washington, DC: Headquarters, Department of the Army, 1986.

—**INDICATION,** an indications and warning term, is a specific action that has been observed or that can be inferred from intelligence sources and is related to the preparation for or the rejection of hostile activity. There is a relationship between indication and indicator. In indications and warning terminology, an *indicator* is an act one expects the enemy to perform and therefore watches for. An *indication* is an indicator that has actually occurred. *See also:* Indicator.

References

Department of Defense, Defense Intelligence College. *Glossary of Intelligence Terms and Definitions.* Washington, DC: DIC, 1987.

—**INDICATIONS** (INTELLIGENCE), in intelligence and warning refers to the specialized form of current and estimative intelligence that seeks to discern, in advance, the intent of a foreign country to initiate hostilities, or to cause a crisis that leads to hostilities or to action by U.S. forces. *See also:* Indications and Warning.

References

Department of Defense, Defense Intelligence College. *Glossary of Intelligence Terms and Definitions.* Washington, DC: DIC, 1987.

—**INDICATIONS AND WARNING (I&W)** refers to intelligence activities performed to detect and report time-sensitive intelligence on foreign events that could threaten U.S. or allied military, economic, or political interests, or U.S. citizens abroad. It includes the timely warning of hostile enemy actions or intentions; imminent hostilities; serious insurgency; nuclear or nonnuclear attack on the United States, overseas U.S. forces or allies; hostile reactions to U.S. reconnaissance activities; terrorist attacks; and other similar activities. *See also:* Indications.

References

Department of Defense, Defense Intelligence College. *Glossary of Intelligence Terms and Definitions.* Washington, DC: DIC, 1987.

Department of Defense, U.S. Army. *Support Operations: Echelons Above Corps.* Field Manual FM 100-16. Washington, DC: Headquarters, Department of the Army, 1986.

—**INDICATIONS AND WARNING (I&W) IN-TELLIGENCE** is information that alerts or warns of an impending course of action by a foreign power that is detrimental to U.S. interests. This information is the product of a recognition and correlation of threat indications and the synthesis of a threat posture. *See also:* Indications, Indications and Warning.

References

Department of Defense, Defense Intelligence College. *Glossary of Intelligence Terms and Definitions.* Washington, DC: DIC, 1987.

—**INDICATIONS AND WARNING (I&W) SYS-TEM** is a network of intelligence-production facilities with analytical resources that are capable of contributing to or developing I&W intelligence, and disseminating this product within their own command and to all other facilities, organizations, or commands within the Department of Defense network. *See also:* Indications, Indications and Warning.

References

Department of Defense, Joint Chiefs of Staff. *Department of Defense Dictionary of Military and Related Terms.* Washington, DC: GPO, 1986.

—**INDICATIONS CENTER** is an intelligence situation room or plot, distinguished by continuous around-the-clock operations, highly qualified personnel, comprehensive communications, concentration on all aspects of possible enemy attack or other situations that might require action by U.S. forces, and adherence to procedures established for operation of the Department of Defense Indications System. The indications center is the focal point for performing the operational intelligence functions of a command. *See also:* Watch Center.

References

Department of Defense, Defense Intelligence College. *Glossary of Intelligence Terms and Definitions.* Washington, DC: DIC, 1987.

—**INDICATIONS WATCH OFFICER** is an intelligence watch officer or duty officer who serves in an indications center. The senior indications officer is the command's intelligence duty officer and the duty representative of the commander in intelligence matters. An indications officer is trained to identify signs of hostilities and cope with other intelligence that requires immediate attention. *See also:* Watch Center.

References

Department of Defense, Joint Chiefs of Staff. *Department of Defense Dictionary of Military and Related Terms.* Washington, DC: GPO, 1986.

—**INDICATOR,** in general intelligence usage, is an item of information that reflects upon the intention or capability of a potential enemy to adopt or reject a course of action. (2) In Army tactical intelligence, the term has the above meaning and can also mean activities that can contribute to the determination of a friendly course of action. (3) In indications and warning, an indicator is an action—specific, generalized, or theoretical—that an enemy might be expected to take in preparation for an aggressive act. It is a hypothetical event or action that may be necessary to establish a threat. For any potential threat, various indicators may be necessary. For one case, certain indicators may be observed, yet in another situation, different indicators may be expected. These potential actions are referred to as indicators, and lists of indicators have been developed to aid warning analysts perform their job. When an indicator is observed while it is occurring, it is referred to as an indication (e.g., an indicator may be the deployment of artillery to forward areas, when this action is observed, it is an indication). *See also:* Indication.

References
Department of Defense, Defense Intelligence
College. *Glossary of Intelligence Terms and
Definitions.* Washington, DC: DIC, 1987.

—INDIRECT AIR SUPPORT includes all forms of
air support provided to land or naval forces that
do not immediately assist the forces in the tactical battle.

References
Department of Defense, Joint Chiefs of Staff.
*Department of Defense Dictionary of Military and
Related Terms.* Washington, DC: GPO, 1986.

—INDIRECT FIRE is fire delivered from a weapon
at a target that cannot be seen by the person
aiming the weapon.

References
Department of Defense, U.S. Army. *Air Defense
Artillery Deployment: Chaparral/Vulcan/Stinger.*
Field Manual FM 44-3. Washington, DC: Headquarters, Department of the Army, 1984.

———. *Operational Terms and Symbols.* Field
Manual FM 101-5-1. Washington, DC: Headquarters, Department of the Army, 1985.

—INDIRECT ILLUMINATION is battlefield illumination provided by using searchlight or pyrotechnic illuminants that use diffusion or reflection. Illumination by diffusion is illuminating
an area beneath and to the flanks of a slightly
elevated searchlight or pyrotechnic illuminant,
in which the area is lit by the light scattered
from atmospheric particles. Illumination by reflection is illuminating an area by reflecting light
from a low cloud. Either or both of the effects
are present when a searchlight is used in defilade
or with its beam spread to maximum width.

References
Department of Defense, Joint Chiefs of Staff.
*Department of Defense Dictionary of Military and
Related Terms.* Washington, DC: GPO, 1986.

—INDIRECT LAYING is aiming a gun either by
sighting at a fixed object instead of the target or
by using a means of pointing other than a sight
(e.g., a gun director) when the target cannot be
seen from the gun position. *See also:* Indirect
Laying Position.

References
Department of Defense, Joint Chiefs of Staff.
*Department of Defense Dictionary of Military and
Related Terms.* Washington, DC: GPO, 1986.

—INDIRECT LAYING POSITION is a gun position masked by some feature of the ground surface that hides the enemy target from direct view.

References
Department of Defense, U.S. Army. *Dictionary of
United States Army Terms.* Army Regulation AR
310-25. Washington, DC: Headquarters, Department of the Army, 1986.

**—INDIVIDUAL AND COLLECTIVE TRAINING
PLAN** is a plan developed to reflect how training on new and improved equipment will be
incorporated into continental U.S. schools,
training centers, and units worldwide. It details
all the training support required for weapon and
equipment systems and describes the individual
and collective training required for each military
operational specialty and table of organization
and equipment associated with a weapon system
or equipment system.

References
Department of Defense, U.S. Army. *Individual
Military Education and Training.* Army Regulation
AR 350-1. Washington, DC: Headquarters,
Department of the Army, 1987.

———. *Training for Mobilization and War.* Field
Manual FM 25-5. Washington, DC: Headquarters,
Department of the Army, 1985.

———. *Unit Training Management.* Field Manual
FM 25-2. Washington, DC: Headquarters,
Department of the Army, 1984.

—INDIVIDUAL EQUIPMENT is personal clothing and equipment issued for an individual's
exclusive personal use. *See also:* Equipment.

References
Department of Defense, U.S. Army. *Commander's
Handbook for Property Accountability at the Unit
Level.* Field Manual FM 10-14-1. Washington, DC:
Headquarters, Department of the Army, 1984.

**—INDIVIDUAL MOBILIZATION AUGMENTEE
(IMA) DETACHMENT** is a functional unit that
consists of at least five Army mobilization designees providing inactive duty training for soldiers in a nonpay status. *See also:* Individual
Mobilization Augmentee Proponent, Individual
Mobilization Augmentee Training.

References
Department of Defense, U.S. Army. *Training for
Mobilization and War.* Field Manual FM 25-5.
Washington, DC: Headquarters, Department of the
Army, 1985.

————. *Unit Training Management*. Field Manual FM 25-2. Washington, DC: Headquarters, Department of the Army, 1984.

—**INDIVIDUAL MOBILIZATION AUGMENTEE (IMA) PROPONENT** is any Department of Defense, Department of the Army, or other federal agency whose mobilization table of distribution and allowances and table of organization and equipment provides positions to be filled by preselected U.S. Army Reserve soldiers.

References

Department of Defense, U.S. Army. *Training for Mobilization and War*. Field Manual FM 25-5. Washington, DC: Headquarters, Department of the Army, 1985.

————. *Unit Training Management*. Field Manual FM 25-2. Washington, DC: Headquarters, Department of the Army, 1984.

—**INDIVIDUAL MOBILIZATION AUGMENTEE (IMA) TRAINING.** The IMA program preassigns individual reservists to positions required upon mobilization in Active Army units, Department of the Army, or Department of Defense staffs. IMA program members train for two weeks each year with their units or staff agencies.

References

Department of Defense, U.S. Army. *Training for Mobilization and War*. Field Manual FM 25-5. Washington, DC: Headquarters, Department of the Army, 1985.

————. *Unit Training Management*. Field Manual FM 25-2. Washington, DC: Headquarters, Department of the Army, 1984.

————. *U.S. Army Policy Statement, 1988*. Washington, DC: Headquarters, Department of the Army, 1988.

—**INDIVIDUAL NUCLEAR, BIOLOGICAL, AND CHEMICAL PROTECTION** is protection provided by protective clothing or personal equipment to an individual who is in a nuclear, biological, and chemical environment. *See also:* Biological Warfare, Chemical Warfare, Nuclear Warfare.

References

Department of Defense, Joint Chiefs of Staff. *Department of Defense Dictionary of Military and Related Terms*. Washington, DC: GPO, 1986.

—**INDIVIDUAL READY RESERVIST** is a member of the Ready Reserve who is not assigned to the Selected Reserve and is not on active duty. *See also:* Ready Reserve.

References

Department of Defense, Joint Chiefs of Staff. *Department of Defense Dictionary of Military and Related Terms*. Washington, DC: GPO, 1986.

—**INDIVIDUAL REPLECEMENT SYSTEM** is the personnel management system currently used to fill Army-wide requirements, defined at the grade and military occupational specialty level of detail, by individually selected soldiers from the Army.

References

Department of Defense, U.S. Army. *Army Forces Training*. Army Regulation AR 350-41. Washington, DC: Headquarters, Department of the Army, 1986.

—**INDIVIDUAL RESERVES** are the supplies carried on a soldier, animal, or vehicle for individual use in an emergency. *See also:* Reserve Supplies.

References

Department of Defense, Joint Chiefs of Staff. *Department of Defense Dictionary of Military and Related Terms*. Washington, DC: GPO, 1986.

—**INDIVIDUAL STREAMER** is the initial phase of a smoke screen (i.e., before the several smoke streamers merge to form a complete screen). *See also:* Smoke Screen.

References

Department of Defense, U.S. Army. *Deliberate Smoke Operations*. Field Manual FM 3-50. Washington, DC: Headquarters, Department of the Army, 1984.

—**INDIVIDUAL TRAINING** is training that the individual officer, noncommissioned officer, or enlisted person receives, either in institutions or in units, to prepare him to perform specified duties and tasks that are related to an assigned military occupational specialty and duty position. The majority of individual training is contained in soldier's manuals for enlisted personnel and military occupational specialty manuals for officers. *See also:* Individual Training Evaluation Program, Individual Training Plan, Individual Training Plan Proposal.

References

Department of Defense, U.S. Army. *Army Forces Training*. Army Regulation AR 350-41. Washington, DC: Headquarters, Department of the Army, 1986.

————. *How to Prepare and Conduct Military Training.* Field Manual FM 21-6. Washington, DC: Headquarters, Department of the Army, 1975.

—**INDIVIDUAL TRAINING EVALUATION PROGRAM (ITEP)** formalizes the evaluation of the individual soldier's task proficiency in units. The three components are the commander's evaluation, the common task test, and the skill qualification test. The components are used to evaluate the soldier's ability to perform the critical tasks required by his military occupational specialty, and to assess tasks for competency for training feedback. They are also used for personnel management purposes.

References
Department of Defense, U.S. Army. *Army Forces Training.* Army Regulation AR 350-41. Washington, DC: Headquarters, Department of the Army, 1986.

————. *Training for Mobilization and War.* Field Manual FM 25-5. Washington, DC: Headquarters, Department of the Army, 1985.

————. *Unit Training Management.* Field Manual FM 25-2. Washington, DC: Headquarters, Department of the Army, 1984.

—**INDIVIDUAL TRAINING PLAN (ITP)** is a collection of documents that guide the development, implementation, and evaluation of the life-cycle training program for an enlisted or warrant officer military occupational specialty, commissioned officer branch, or functional training requirement. Key elements are the individual training plan proposals for the resident courses involved.

References
Department of Defense, U.S. Army. *Individual Military Education and Training.* Army Regulation AR 350-1. Washington, DC: Headquarters, Department of the Army, 1987.

————. *Training for Mobilization and War.* Field Manual FM 25-5. Washington, DC: Headquarters, Department of the Army, 1985.

————. *Unit Training Management.* Field Manual FM 25-2. Washington, DC: Headquarters, Department of the Army, 1984.

—**INDIVIDUAL TRAINING PLAN PROPOSAL (ITPP)** is a document that initiates the individual training plan by identifying new or revised training requirements that outline the proponent's training strategy, establish a schedule for development and implementation, and identify the required resources. The ITPP is kept current as the training program is developed and implemented.

References
Department of Defense, U.S. Army. *Individual Military Education and Training.* Army Regulation AR 350-1. Washington, DC: Headquarters, Department of the Army, 1987.

————. *Training for Mobilization and War.* Field Manual FM 25-5. Washington, DC: Headquarters, Department of the Army, 1985.

————. *Unit Training Management.* Field Manual FM 25-2. Washington, DC: Headquarters, Department of the Army, 1984.

—**INDUCED RADIATION** is radiation produced as a result of foil elements and/or materiel being exposed to a strong neutron force.

References
Department of Defense, U.S. Army. *Nuclear Weapons Employment Doctrine and Procedures.* Field Manual FM 101-3-1. Washington, DC: Headquarters, Department of the Army, 1986.

————. *Operational Terms and Symbols.* Field Manual FM 101-5-1. Washington, DC: Headquarters, Department of the Army, 1985.

—**INDUCTEE** is a person who has been inducted into military service under the provisions of the Universal Military Training and Service Act.

References
Department of Defense, U.S. Army. *Dictionary of United States Army Terms.* Army Regulation AR 310-25. Washington, DC: Headquarters, Department of the Army, 1986.

—**INDUSTRIAL COLLEGE OF THE ARMED FORCES (ICAF)** is the senior service college dedicated to the study of the management of resources for national security. As a division of the National Defense University, the Industrial College is chartered to conduct senior-level courses of study and research in the management of resources in support of national security in order to enhance the preparation of selected military officers and senior career civilian officials for positions of high trust in the federal government. Curricula of the Resident Program range over the entire field of national security affairs, but emphasize the management of resources in dealing with problems of national security. The courses stress the study of the national economy (especially the industrial sector), the management of human and natural resources, and aspects of management in both government and business. The Department of Defense—particularly its management philosophy, systems, and practices—receives major attention. Concurrent with these broader aspects, courses are conducted in economics, management, and analytical techniques for decisionmaking. The program can be regarded as an application of these disciplines to the field of national security affairs. *See also:* National Defense University, National War College.

References
Department of Defense, U.S. Army. *Dictionary of United States Army Terms.* Army Regulation AR 310-25. Washington, DC: Headquarters, Department of the Army, 1986.

—**INDUSTRIAL DEFENSE** refers to all nonmilitary measures in effect to assure the uninterrupted productive capability of vital facilities and attendant resources that are essential for mobilization. These measures are designed to prevent and minimize the loss or disruption of the productive capability from any cause or hazard and to provide for the rapid restoration of production after any damage occurs.

References
Department of Defense, U.S. Army. *Dictionary of United States Army Terms.* Army Regulation AR 310-25. Washington, DC: Headquarters, Department of the Army, 1986.

—**INERT AMMUNITION** refers to the condition of a munition, or component thereof, that contains an inactive filler in lieu of the service ammunition filler, whether it is an explosive, pyrotechnic, or chemical filler. *See also:* Inert Filling.

References
Department of Defense, U.S. Army. *Dictionary of United States Army Terms.* Army Regulation AR 310-25. Washington, DC: Headquarters, Department of the Army, 1986.

—**INERT FILLING** ia a prepared nonexplosive filling of the same weight as the explosive filling.

References
Department of Defense, Joint Chiefs of Staff. *Department of Defense Dictionary of Military and Related Terms.* Washington, DC: GPO, 1986.

—**INERT MINE** is an exact replica of a live mine, but does not contain explosive or pyrotechnic elements. Inert mines are mines that are removed from the assembly line just prior to being loaded with explosives. *See also:* Mine Warfare.

References
Department of Defense, U.S. Army. *Mine/ Countermine Operations at the Company Level.* Field Manual FM 20-32. Washington, DC: Headquarters, Department of the Army, 1976.

—**INERTIAL GUIDANCE** is a guidance system designed to project a missile over a predetermined path, wherein the path of the missile is adjusted after launching by devices wholly within the missile and independent of outside information.

References
Department of Defense, Joint Chiefs of Staff. *Department of Defense Dictionary of Military and Related Terms.* Washington, DC: GPO, 1986.

—**INFANTRY** is a basic branch and arm of the Army. The branch name identifies the personnel and units that close with the enemy by fire and maneuver to destroy or capture it, or to repel its assault by fire, close combat, and/or counterattack. Personnel and units so identified fight dismounted or mounted according to the mobility means that are provided.

References
Department of Defense, U.S. Army. *Dictionary of United States Army Terms.* Army Regulation AR 310-25. Washington, DC: Headquarters, Department of the Army, 1986.

—**INFILTRATION.** (1) Infiltration is a means of reaching the enemy's rear without fighting through prepared defenses. It is the covert movement of all or part of the attacking force through enemy lines to a favorable position in their rear. Successful infiltration requires above all the avoidance of detection and engagement. Since that requirement limits the size and strength of the infiltrating force, infiltration alone can rarely defeat the defense but rather is normally used in conjunction with some other form of maneuver. Infiltration is most feasible in rough areas that are poorly covered by observation and fire. It may be used to attack lightly defended positions or stronger positions from the flank. (2) Infiltration, when used in conjunction with a tactical vehicular march, means that the vehicles are dispatched individually or in small groups at irregular intervals to reduce the density and prevent an undue massing of vehicles. *See also:* Infiltration Line.

References

Department of Defense, U.S. Army. *Operational Terms and Symbols.* Field Manual FM 101-5-1. Washington, DC: Headquarters, Department of the Army, 1985.

————. *Operations.* Field Manual FM 100-5. Washington, DC: Headquarters, Department of the Army, 1986.

—**INFILTRATION LANE** is a lane through which the company moves by stealth in order to pass through enemy lines without being detected. The company must stay within the limits of the line.

References

Department of Defense, U.S. Army. *The Infantry Rifle Company (Infantry, Airborne, Air Assault, Ranger).* Field Manual FM 7-10. Washington, DC: Headquarters, Department of the Army, 1982.

—**INFINITY METHOD** is a method of adjusting two lines of sighting to make them parallel.

References

Department of Defense, U.S. Army. *Dictionary of United States Army Terms.* Army Regulation AR 310-25. Washington, DC: Headquarters, Department of the Army, 1986.

—**INFLIGHT RELIABILITY** is the percentage of the total number of tactical missiles that have been launched that deliver the warhead (or payload) armed for detonation (or simulated warhead functioning) within four circular error probables of the assigned aiming point in the target area.

References

Department of Defense, U.S. Army. *Dictionary of United States Army Terms.* Army Regulation AR 310-25. Washington, DC: Headquarters, Department of the Army, 1986.

—**INFLUENCE FUZE** is a fuze designed to actuate without physical contact with a target. *See also:* Fuze (Specify Type).

References

Department of Defense, U.S. Army. *Mine/Countermine Operations at the Company Level.* Field Manual FM 20-32. Washington, DC: Headquarters, Department of the Army, 1976.

—**INFORMAL COMMAND INSPECTION** may be made at any time. No advance notice is given and no set procedure is required. This type of inspection provides a better picture of the true conditions within a unit. The commander sees the unit as it is operating, and improper practices and malfunctions are more easily detected. *See also:* Inspection.

References

Department of Defense, U.S. Army. *Organizational Maintenance Operations.* Field Manual FM 29-2. Washington, DC: Headquarters, Department of the Army, 1984.

—**INFORMATION.** Information is a general intelligence term for all types of unevaluated material at all levels of reliability from any source of potential intelligence information. *See also:* Intelligence Cycle, Intelligence Information.

References

Department of Defense, Defense Intelligence College. *Glossary of Intelligence Terms and Definitions.* Washington, DC: DIC, 1987.

Department of Defense, U.S. Army. *Support Operations: Echelons Above Corps.* Field Manual FM 100-16. Washington, DC: Headquarters, Department of the Army, 1986.

—**INFORMATION AND TRAVEL OFFICE** is an activity that assists the military community in meeting its leisure travel needs. The services provided include leisure counseling, planning itineraries, information services, tickets to a range of activities (e.g., cultural programs, dinner theaters, and sporting events), and one-day and overnight package tours.

References

Department of Defense, U.S. Army. *Dictionary of United States Army Terms.* Army Regulation AR 310-25. Washington, DC: Headquarters, Department of the Army, 1986.

—**INFORMATION BRIEFING** is a lecture intended to inform the listeners and to gain their understanding. The briefing does not include conclusions, recommendations, or require decisions. It deals primarily with facts.

References

Department of Defense, U.S. Army. *Staff Organization and Operations.* Field Manual FM 101-5. Washington, DC: Headquarters, Department of the Army, 1984.

—**INFORMATION DISPLAY,** automated or manual, may be required to supplement the details contained on a situation map or to make information available that is not suitable for posting on the situation map.

References

Department of Defense, U.S. Army. *Staff Organization and Operations.* Field Manual FM 101-5. Washington, DC: Headquarters, Department of the Army, 1984.

—**INFORMATION REPORT** is a report used to forward raw information that has been collected in order to fulfill intelligence requirements. *See also:* Intelligence.

References

Department of Defense, Joint Chiefs of Staff. *Department of Defense Dictionary of Military and Related Terms.* Washington, DC: GPO, 1986.

—**INFORMATION REQUIREMENTS** are items of information regarding the enemy and its environment that need to be collected and processed in order to meet the intelligence requirements of the commander. *See also:* Priority Intelligence Requirements.

References

Department of Defense, U.S. Army. *Operational Terms and Symbols.* Field Manual FM 101-5-1. Washington, DC: Headquarters, Department of the Army, 1985.

—**INFORMATION RESOURCE MANAGEMENT** is the planning, budgeting, organizing, directing, training, promoting, controlling, and other managerial activities involved in the collection, use, and dissemination of information.

References

Department of Defense, U.S. Army. *Dictionary of United States Army Terms.* Army Regulation AR 310-25. Washington, DC: Headquarters, Department of the Army, 1986.

—**INFORMATION SECURITY.** (1) On the joint intelligence level, information security is "the process of safeguarding knowledge against unauthorized disclosure; or the result of any system of administrative policies and procedures for identifying, controlling, and protecting from unauthorized disclosure or release to the public, information that is authorized protection by executive order or statute." (2) Information security is an Army tactical intelligence term that means the prevention of disclosures of operational information through written, verbal, or graphic communications. Restrictions are placed on personnel and the release of operational information to safeguard against the unintentional disclosure of data to the enemy.

References

Department of Defense, U.S. Army. *Military Intelligence Group (Combat Electronic Warfare and Intelligence) (Corps).* Field Manual FM 34-20. Washington, DC: Headquarters, Department of the Army, 1983.

—**INFRARED (IR)** pertains to or designates the invisible rays of light just beyond the red end of the visible spectrum that are emitted by a hot body. They are detected by their thermal and photographic effects. Their wavelengths are longer than those of visible light and shorter than those of radio waves. *See also:* Infrared Intelligence.

References

Department of Defense, Defense Intelligence College. *Glossary of Intelligence Terms and Definitions.* Washington, DC: DIC, 1987.

Reeves, Robert; Anson, Abraham; and Landen, David. *Manual of Remote Sensing.* Falls Church, VA: American Society of Photogrammetry, 1975.

—**INFRARED COUNTERMEASURES (IRCM)** are countermeasures used specifically against threats operating in the infrared spectrum.

References

Department of Defense. U.S. Army. *Intelligence Imagery.* Field Manual FM 34-55. Washington, DC: Headquarters, Department of the Army, 1985.

Reeves, Robert; Anson, Abraham; and Landen, David. *Manual of Remote Sensing.* Falls Church, VA: American Society of Photogrammetry, 1975.

—**INFRARED IMAGERY** is the imagery produced as a result of sensing electromagnetic radiations emitted or reflected from a target surface in the infrared portion of the electromagnetic spectrum (approximately 0.72 to 1,000 microns). *See also:* Infrared Intelligence.

References

Department of Defense. U.S. Army. *Intelligence Imagery.* Field Manual FM 34-55. Washington, DC: Headquarters, Department of the Army, 1985.

Reeves, Robert; Anson, Abraham; and Landen, David. *Manual of Remote Sensing.* Falls Church, VA: American Society of Photogrammetry, 1975.

—**INFRARED IMAGING** is the remote sensing of radiant temperatures. An electronic sensor is used to produce detailed or general intelligence coverage of an area or target by sensing the apparent temperature differences between the terrain features and the military or cultural features of the terrain.

Infrared imagery sensors are passive; they do not generate their own illumination like radar. This reduces their vulnerability to detection by the enemy, but lower natural energy levels in the thermal region generally require that missions be flown at low altitude over enemy targets. Some types of infrared sensors have a limited standoff capability.

Infrared systems can be operated by day or night and have the capability to see through light atmospheric conditions. *See also:* Infrared Intelligence.

References

Department of Defense. U.S. Army. *Intelligence Imagery*. Field Manual FM 34-55. Washington, DC: Headquarters, Department of the Army, 1985.

—**INFRARED INTELLIGENCE (IRINT)** is the intelligence information gleaned from the detection of infrared energy that is radiated, reradiated, or reflected from the surface of the earth. By comparing the minute differences between the amounts of energy radiated by an object and its background, an image of the object can be projected for recording on film or for a television-like display. Since virtually every object and terrain feature radiates a different level of energy, high resolution images can be produced. The quality of the imagery nearly equals that of photography, but infrared imagery systems have far greater capabilities than photographic systems, since they are immune to many conditions (e.g., smoke, darkness, clouds, fog, and vegetation) that can block photography.

References

Department of Defense, U.S. Army. *Intelligence Imagery*. Field Manual FM 34-55. Washington, DC: Headquarters, Department of the Army, 1985.

———. *Military Intelligence Battalion Combat Electronic Warfare and Intelligence (Aerial Exploitation) (Corps)*. Field Manual FM 34-22. Washington, DC: Headquarters, Department of the Army, 1984.

Reeves, Robert; Anson, Abraham; and Landen, David. *Manual of Remote Sensing*. Falls Church, VA: American Society of Photogrammetry, 1975.

—**INFRARED RADIATION.** (1) Infrared radiation is electromagnetic radiation lying in the wavelength interval from about 0.8 microns to an indefinite upper boundary, which is sometimes arbitrarily set at 1,000 microns (0.01 cm). At the lower limit of this interval, the infrared radiation spectrum is bounded by visible radiation, while on its upper limit it is bounded by microwave radiation of the type important in radar technology. Infrared radiation is also called long-wave radiation. (2) Infrared radiation is the radiation emitted from a given target surface in the infrared portion of the electromagnetic spectrum. *See also:* Infrared Intelligence.

References

Department of Defense, U.S. Army. *Dictionary of United States Army Terms*. Army Regulation AR 310-25. Washington, DC: Headquarters, Department of the Army, 1986.

—**INFRARED RESOLUTION** is the finest (minimum size) target detail that can be identified and distinguished in the imagery being examined. *See also:* Infrared Intelligence.

References

Department of Defense, U.S. Army. *Dictionary of United States Army Terms*. Army Regulation AR 310-25. Washington, DC: Headquarters, Department of the Army, 1986.

—**INFRASTRUCTURE** generally refers to all fixed and permanent installations, fabrications, or facilities for supporting and controlling military forces. *See also:* National Infrastructure.

References

Department of Defense, Joint Chiefs of Staff. *Department of Defense Dictionary of Military and Related Terms*. Washington, DC: GPO, 1986.

—**INHABITED BUILDING DISTANCE** is the minimum distance that may be expected to protect buildings or structures from substantial damage from a blast effect. *See also:* Blast.

References

Department of Defense, U.S. Army. *Dictionary of United States Army Terms*. Army Regulation AR 310-25. Washington, DC: Headquarters, Department of the Army, 1986.

—**INHERENT DISTORTION** is the distortion of the display of a received radar signal caused by the design characteristics of a particular set.

References

Department of Defense, U.S. Army. *Dictionary of United States Army Terms.* Army Regulation AR 310-25. Washington, DC: Headquarters, Department of the Army, 1986.

—**INHIBITOR** is an inert material surrounding a propellent rocket grain to control the burning surface.

References

Department of Defense, U.S. Army. *Dictionary of United States Army Terms.* Army Regulation AR 310-25. Washington, DC: Headquarters, Department of the Army, 1986.

—**INITIAL ACTIVE DUTY TRAINING** is the first period of active duty for training prescribed by law or regulation for non-prior-service enlistees that, when satisfactorily completed, produces a trained member in a military specialty. It is also training designed to provide basic combat survival skills to reserve component personnel during basic training, advanced individual training, or one-station unit training.

References

Department of Defense, U.S. Army. *Army Forces Training.* Army Regulation AR 350-41. Washington, DC: Headquarters, Department of the Army, 1986.

————. *Operational Terms and Symbols.* Field Manual FM 101-5-1. Washington, DC: Headquarters, Department of the Army, 1985.

—**INITIAL BULK STOCK AREA DEPOT** refers to station stocks supplied during the period necessary to accumulate issue experience and to determine the proper stock levels on the basis of specific usage.

References

Department of Defense, U.S. Army. *Dictionary of United States Army Terms.* Army Regulation AR 310-25. Washington, DC: Headquarters, Department of the Army, 1986.

—**INITIAL DEMAND** is a request made for the initial issue of supplies that have not previously been furnished.

References

Department of Defense, U.S. Army. *Dictionary of United States Army Terms.* Army Regulation AR 310-25. Washington, DC: Headquarters, Department of the Army, 1986.

—**INITIAL DRAFT PLAN** is a plan that has been drafted and coordinated by the originating headquarters and is ready for external coordination with other military headquarters. It cannot be directly implemented by the issuing commander, but it may form the basis for an operation order issued by the commander in the event of an emergency. *See also:* Coordinated Draft Plan, Draft Plan, Final Plan, Operation Plan.

References

Department of Defense, Joint Chiefs of Staff. *Department of Defense Dictionary of Military and Related Terms.* Washington, DC: GPO, 1986.

—**INITIAL ENTRY INTO MILITARY SERVICE** is entry for the first time into military status (active duty or reserve) by induction, enlistment, or appointment in any Service of the Armed Forces of the United States. Appointment may be as a commissioned or warrant officer; as a cadet or midshipman at the Service academy of one of the armed forces; or as a midshipman, U.S. Naval Reserve, or U.S. Naval Reserve Officers' Training Corps training at a civilian institution. *See also:* Initial Entry Training.

References

Department of Defense, Joint Chiefs of Staff. *Department of Defense Dictionary of Military and Related Terms.* Washington, DC: GPO, 1986.

—**INITIAL ENTRY TRAINING (IET)** is the time a first-term soldier spends in enlisted entry-level training at the U.S. Army Training and Doctrine Command training base producing an initial military occupational specialty. For combat arms soldiers, this training time is usually spent in one-station unit training. For combat support and combat service support soldiers, the training time is usually spent between basic training and advanced individual training, or with a one-station unit. IET trains soldiers in basic Skill Level 1 tasks of their military occupational specialties. The tasks taught in the institution are identified in the trainer's guide and in the soldiers' individual training records that are transferred from the training unit. Once assigned to their units, soldiers complete their Skill Level 1 training. Unit personnel train them in their new assignments and also on Skill Level 1 tasks that were not taught in the institution. *See also:* Inactive Duty Training.

References

Department of Defense, U.S. Army. *Army Forces Training.* Army Regulation AR 350-41. Washington, DC: Headquarters, Department of the Army, 1986.

————. *Unit Training Management.* Field Manual FM 25-2. Washington, DC: Headquarters, Department of the Army, 1984.

—**INITIAL HEADING** is the heading at the start of a rating period while using the astrogyro system of steering.

References

Department of Defense, U.S. Army. *Dictionary of United States Army Terms.* Army Regulation AR 310-25. Washington, DC: Headquarters, Department of the Army, 1986.

—**INITIAL HOSPITAL ADMISSION** is the first admission to a hospital facility for an episode of medical treatment. *See also:* Medical Treatment.

References

Department of Defense, U.S. Army. *Dictionary of United States Army Terms.* Army Regulation AR 310-25. Washington, DC: Headquarters, Department of the Army, 1986.

—**INITIAL ISSUE** is the issue of materiel not previously furnished to an individual or an organization (including new inductees and newly activated organizations) and the issue of newly authorized items of materiel.

References

Department of Defense, Joint Chiefs of Staff. *Department of Defense Dictionary of Military and Related Terms.* Washington, DC: GPO, 1986.

—**INITIAL NUCLEAR EFFECTS** are all the initial effects, including nuclear radiation, blast, and thermal and electromagnetic pulse. *See also:* Nuclear Warfare.

References

Department of Defense, U.S. Army. *Operational Terms and Symbols.* Field Manual FM 101-5-1. Washington, DC: Headquarters, Department of the Army, 1985.

—**INITIAL NUCLEAR RADIATION** is all the radiation (essentially neutrons and gamma rays) that occur within the first minute after a nuclear detonation. *See also:* Nuclear Warfare.

References

Department of Defense, U.S. Army. *Nuclear Weapons Employment Doctrine and Procedures.* Field Manual FM 101-3-1. Washington, DC: Headquarters, Department of the Army, 1986.

—**INITIAL OPERATING CAPABILITY (IOC).** IOC is the first attainment of the capability to effectively employ a weapon, item of equipment, or system of approved specific characteristics that is manned or operated by an adequately trained, equipped, and supported military unit or force.

References

Department of Defense, Joint Chiefs of Staff. *Department of Defense Dictionary of Military and Related Terms.* Washington, DC: GPO, 1986.

—**INITIAL PHOTO INTERPRETATION REPORT,** in intelligence imagery and photoreconnaissance, is a first-phase interpretation report. It presents the results of the initial reading of new imagery to answer the specific requirements for which the mission was requested. *See also:* Initial Programmed Interpretation Report.

References

Department of Defense. U.S. Army. *Intelligence Imagery.* Field Manual FM 34-55. Washington, DC: Headquarters, Department of the Army, 1985.

—**INITIAL POINT.** (1) The initial point is the first point at which a moving target is located on a plotting board. (2) An initial point is a well-defined point, easily distinguishable visually and/or electronically, that is used as a starting point for a bomb run to the target. (3) In airborne operations, the initial point is a point that is close to the landing area where serials (troop carrier air formations) make final alterations in course to pass over individual drop or landing zones. (4) In helicopter operations, the initial point is an air control point in the vicinity of the landing zone from which individual flights of helicopters are directed to their prescribed landing sites. (5) An initial point is any designated place at which a column or element thereof is formed by the successive arrival of its various subdivisions, and comes under the control of the commander ordering the move.

References

Department of Defense, Joint Chiefs of Staff. *Department of Defense Dictionary of Military and Related Terms.* Washington, DC: GPO, 1986.

—**INITIAL POINT** (ARMY AVIATION) is the point for beginning an attack, the point from which close air support aircraft begin their final attack run-in. It should be identifiable from the air at U.S. Air Force operating altitude. It is selected by the forward-forward air controller or tactical air controller airborne. *See also:* Initial Point.

References

Department of Defense, U.S. Army. *Air-to-Air Combat.* Field Manual FM 1-107. Washington, DC: Headquarters, Department of the Army, 1984.

———. *Attack Helicopter Operations.* Field Manual FM 17-50. Washington, DC: Headquarters, Department of the Army, 1985.

—**INITIAL PROGRAMMED INTEPRETATION RE-PORT (IPIR),** in intelligence imagery and photoreconnaissance, is a report that provides information on mission objectives not mentioned in other reports. An IPIR is requested when extensive or detailed data from a systematic review of sensor imagery are needed and the rapid response required by the reconnaissance exploitation report would be hindered by the format, size, or quantity of the imagery involved. *See also:* Image, Radar Exploitation Report, Reconnaissance Exploitation Report, Supplemental Programmed Interpretation Report.

References

Department of Defense. U.S. Army. *Intelligence Imagery.* Field Manual FM 34-55. Washington, DC: Headquarters, Department of the Army, 1985.

—**INITIAL RADIATION** is the radiation, essentially neutrons and gamma rays, resulting from a nuclear burst and emitted from the fireball within one minute after the burst. *See also:* Induced Radiation, Nuclear Warfare.

References

Department of Defense, Joint Chiefs of Staff. *Department of Defense Dictionary of Military and Related Terms.* Washington, DC: GPO, 1986.

—**INITIAL REQUIREMENTS** are all the supplies needed to equip soldiers or organizations when they are put on active duty.

References

Department of Defense, U.S. Army. *Dictionary of United States Army Terms.* Army Regulation AR 310-25. Washington, DC: Headquarters, Department of the Army, 1986.

—**INITIAL SERVICE SUPPORT REQUIREMENTS** are the requirements for the initial outfitting of operational and maintenance allowances and additional quantities for the initial positioning of retail and pipeline stocks.

References

Department of Defense, U.S. Army. *Dictionary of United States Army Terms.* Army Regulation AR 310-25. Washington, DC: Headquarters, Department of the Army, 1986.

—**INITIAL SKILL TRAINING** is formal training normally given immediately after basic training for enlisted personnel and upon commissioning for officer personnel. It provides the skills and knowledge needed for an individual's first duty assignment, including the enlisted advanced individual training, one-station unit training, the officer basic course, and certain warrant officer training. *See also:* Advanced Individual Training.

References

Department of Defense, U.S. Army. *Individual Military Education and Training.* Army Regulation AR 350-1. Washington, DC: Headquarters, Department of the Army, 1987.

—**INITIAL SOURCE OF SUPPLY** is the point to which requisitions are sent by requisitioners for supply or approval and necessary action. This point may be an Army depot, inventory control point, head of a procuring agency, or a procurement office, depending on the circumstances.

References

Department of Defense, U.S. Army. *Dictionary of United States Army Terms.* Army Regulation AR 310-25. Washington, DC: Headquarters, Department of the Army, 1986.

—**INITIAL STRENGTH** is the actual or authorized strength of the Army, or a subdivision thereof, at the beginning of a specific time period (e.g., a fiscal year, calendar year, or month of operation).

References

Department of Defense, U.S. Army. *Planning Logistics Support for Military Operations.* Field Manual FM 701-58. Washington, DC: Headquarters, Department of the Army, 1987.

—**INITIAL TIMER** is a person serving an initial term of active federal military service. Persons who have served on active duty solely under the Reserve Forces Act of 1955 and the Reserve

Enlisted Program of 1963 or have less than 180 days of prior active federal service are considered initial timers. Those with more than 180 days of prior service as a member of one of the Armed Forces other than the Army are not considered initial timers. *See also:* First Timer.

References
Department of Defense, U.S. Army. *Army Reenlistment Program.* Army Regulation AR 601-280. Washington, DC: Headquarters, Department of the Army, 1984.

—**INITIAL UTILIZATION ASSIGNMENT** is the assignment of graduates from military and civilian schools immediately following the completion of their training to positions requiring such training.

References
Department of Defense, U.S. Army. *Dictionary of United States Army Terms.* Army Regulation AR 310-25. Washington, DC: Headquarters, Department of the Army, 1986.

—**INITIATING DIRECTIVE** initiates an amphibious operation. It is issued by a commander of a command that has been established by the Joint Chiefs of Staff or by other commanders so authorized by the Joint Chiefs of Staff or by higher authority. *See also:* Amphibious Operation.

References
Department of Defense, U.S. Army. *Dictionary of United States Army Terms.* Army Regulation AR 310-25. Washington, DC: Headquarters, Department of the Army, 1986.

—**INITIATIVE** is setting or changing the terms of battle by action. It implies an offensive spirit in the conduct of all operations. Applied to the force as a whole, initiative requires a constant effort to force the enemy to conform to one's operational purpose and tempo while retaining one's freedom of action. Applied to individual soldiers and leaders, it requires a willingness and ability to act independently within the framework of the higher commander's intent. In both cases, initiative requires audacity that may involve risk-taking and an atmosphere that supports it. In the attack, initiative implies never allowing the enemy to recover from the initial shock of the attack. In the defense, initiative implies quickly turning the table on the attacker.

References
Department of Defense, U.S. Army. *Operations.* Field Manual FM 100-5. Washington, DC: Headquarters, Department of the Army, 1986.

—**INITIATOR** is a small quantity of very sensitive and powerful explosives used to start the detonation of another, less sensitive explosive.

References
Department of Defense, U.S. Army. *Dictionary of United States Army Terms.* Army Regulation AR 310-25. Washington, DC: Headquarters, Department of the Army, 1986.

—**INJURY** is a term comprising such conditions as fractures, wounds, sprains, strains, dislocations, concussions, and compressions. It also includes conditions resulting from extremes of temperature or prolonged exposure. Acute poisonings, except those due to contaminated food, resulting from exposure to a toxic or poisonous substance are also injuries. *See also:* Battle Casualty, Casualty, Non-Battle Casualty.

References
Department of Defense, Joint Chiefs of Staff. *Department of Defense Dictionary of Military and Related Terms.* Washington, DC: GPO, 1986.

—**INOPERABLE EQUIPMENT** is an item of equipment that has an outstanding urgent modification work order or is an item that has a deficiency. The category does not include equipment undergoing routine or scheduled preventive maintenance services or routine inspection at the organizational maintenance level.

References
Department of Defense, U.S. Army. *Dictionary of United States Army Terms.* Army Regulation AR 310-25. Washington, DC: Headquarters, Department of the Army, 1986.

—**INOPERATIVE TIME** is any period of time during which a prisoner is not entitled to be credited with serving his sentence of confinement.

References
Department of Defense, U.S. Army. *Dictionary of United States Army Terms.* Army Regulation AR 310-25. Washington, DC: Headquarters, Department of the Army, 1986.

—**INSERTION.** (1) Insertion is the placing of troops and equipment into an operational area in air assault operations. (2) Insertion is the placing of observation posts, patrols, or raiding parties either by helicopter or parachute.

References
Department of Defense, U.S. Army. *Air Defense Artillery Deployment: Chaparral/Vulcan/Stinger.* Field Manual FM 44-3. Washington, DC: Headquarters, Department of the Army, 1984.

————. *Operational Terms and Symbols.* Field Manual FM 101-5-1. Washington, DC: Headquarters, Department of the Army, 1985.

—**INSIGNIA** are distinctive devices that are worn on the uniform to show grade, organization, rating, and service. *See also:* Accouterment.

References

Department of Defense, U.S. Army. *Dictionary of United States Army Terms.* Army Regulation AR 310-25. Washington, DC: Headquarters, Department of the Army, 1986.

—**INSPECTION** is an examination and testing of supplies and services (including, when appropriate, raw materials, components, and intermediate assemblies) to determine whether the supplies and services conform to the contract requirements.

References

Department of Defense, U.S. Army. *Dictionary of United States Army Terms.* Army Regulation AR 310-25. Washington, DC: Headquarters, Department of the Army, 1986.

—**INSPECTION DATE** is a date by which all shelf-life items should be inspected during the period of storage and prior to issue or use.

References

Department of Defense, U.S. Army. *Dictionary of United States Army Terms.* Army Regulation AR 310-25. Washington, DC: Headquarters, Department of the Army, 1986.

—**INSPECTION STATION** is a designated location at which trucks and rail cars containing ammunition and explosives are inspected.

References

Department of Defense, U.S. Army. *Ammunition and Explosives Safety Standards.* Army Regulation AR 385-64. Washington, DC: Headquarters, Department of the Army, 1987.

—**INSTALLATION.** (1) Installation is a target intelligence term that pertains to the target that is to be destroyed. An installation is a grouping of facilities, located in the same vicinity, that supports particular functions. Installations may be elements of a base. In another sense, installations are fixed and consist of a single function or group of functions that are collocated at the same coordinates or are located in geographic proximity. (2) An installation is the land and the improvements permanently affixed to the land that are under the control of the Department of the Army and are used by Army organizations. Where installations are located contiguously, the combined property is designated as one installation and the separate functions as activities of that installation. In addition to those used primarily by troops, "installation" applies to such real properties as depots, arsenals, ammunition plants (both contractor and government operated), hospitals, terminals, and other special mission installations. (3) Installation denotes an installation primarily used for or is primarily useful in the production of materiel or of research and development. Such installations may be government-owned and government-operated; government-owned and privately operated; or privately owned and privately operated. *See also:* Target Intelligence.

References

Department of Defense, U.S. Army. *Intelligence Imagery.* Field Manual FM 34-55. Washington, DC: Headquarters, Department of the Army, 1985.

————. Support *Operations: Echelons Above Corps.* Field Manual FM 100-16. Washington, DC: Headquarters, Department of the Army, 1986.

—**INSTALLATION ALLOWANCES** are allowances of expendable and nonexpendable items contained in published authorizations (e.g., tables of organization and equipment, tables of distribution and allowances, supply or technical manuals, circulars, supply bulletins, approved projects, and letters of special authority that are applicable to specific installations and units). *See also:* Installation.

References

Department of Defense, U.S. Army. *Dictionary of United States Army Terms.* Army Regulation AR 310-25. Washington, DC: Headquarters, Department of the Army, 1986.

—**INSTALLATION CONFINEMENT FACILITY** is a facility that provides pretrial confinement services for prisoners awaiting courts-martial at the installation and acting as a transfer point for other prisoners pending their movement to an area confinement facility or correctional facility.

References

Department of Defense, U.S. Army. *Dictionary of United States Army Terms.* Army Regulation AR 310-25. Washington, DC: Headquarters, Department of the Army, 1986.

—**INSTALLATION FOOD SERVICE MANAGEMENT PLAN** is an integration of documents that presents in graphic and tabular form a continuous inventory of the installation's dining facilities, the proposed plan for the conversion or modernization of existing permanent dining facilities, and the construction of new dining facilities.

References

Department of Defense, U.S. Army. *Dictionary of United States Army Terms.* Army Regulation AR 310-25. Washington, DC: Headquarters, Department of the Army, 1986.

—**INSTALLATION HANDBOOKS** contain complete information concerning every military installation in every U.S. city or area of interest. They are useful, particularly during peacetime, for establishing that forces are already in place. Two particularly useful handbooks are the *Automated Installation Intelligence File* and the *Contingency Facilities Planning List.*

References

Department of Defense, U.S. Army. *Intelligence Analysis.* Field Manual FM 34-3. Washington, DC: Headquarters, Department of the Army, 1986.

—**INSTALLATION PROPERTY** is the equipment and supplies, except organizational property, authorized in published authorization media for use by units, organizations, and personnel while they are stationed at an installation. *See also:* Installation Property Book.

References

Department of Defense, U.S. Army. *Commander's Handbook for Property Accountability at the Unit Level.* Field Manual FM 10-14-1. Washington, DC: Headquarters, Department of the Army, 1984.

—**INSTALLATION PROPERTY BOOK** is a record maintained to account for property at continental U.S. stations.

References

Department of Defense, U.S. Army. *Dictionary of United States Army Terms.* Army Regulation AR 310-25. Washington, DC: Headquarters, Department of the Army, 1986

—**INSTALLATION TYPE** is the designation of a continental U.S. installation that provides management services to support the major units that are assigned. There are four types of installations: *Type A* is an installation where any Army Corps headquarters is located as its permanent continental U.S. station. *Type B* is an installation where an Army division is located

as its permanent continental U.S. station and the division commander is the senior officer permanently assigned. *Type C* is an installation where a training center, service school, or similar size activity is located and assigned to the same major command as the installation. *Type D* is an installation where a continental U.S. Army or higher headquarters is located and that Headquarters, Department of the Army, has specifically excluded staff dual role assignment from the requirement for installation or an installation on which a variety of activities and units are located, none of which classify the installation as Type A, B, or C. *See also:* Installation.

References

Department of Defense, U.S. Army. *Dictionary of United States Army Terms.* Army Regulation AR 310-25. Washington, DC: Headquarters, Department of the Army, 1986.

—**INSTALLED BUILDING EQUIPMENT** are items of equipment and furnishings, including materials for installation thereof, required to make the facility usable. They are affixed as a permanent part of the structure (e.g., plumbing fixtures and equipment; fixed heating, ventilating, cooling, and air-conditioning; electrical and fixed fire protection systems; elevators and escalators; overhead-crane runways; and laboratory counters, cabinets, and similar fixed equipment). Excluded are machine tools, production and research equipment, and their foundations.

References

Department of Defense, U.S. Army. *Dictionary of United States Army Terms.* Army Regulation AR 310-25. Washington, DC: Headquarters, Department of the Army, 1986.

—**INSTITUTIONAL TRAINING** is training conducted in schools (i.e., Army service schools, U.S. Army Reserve schools, and the noncommissioned officer academy) or training centers. The institutions that conduct this type of training are commonly referred to as being part of the training base.

References

Department of Defense, U.S. Army. *Army Forces Training.* Army Regulation AR 350-41. Washington, DC: Headquarters, Department of the Army, 1986.

———. *How to Prepare and Conduct Military Training.* Field Manual FM 21-6. Washington, DC: Headquarters, Department of the Army, 1975.

————. *Training for Mobilization and War.* Field Manual FM 25-5. Washington, DC: Headquarters, Department of the Army, 1985.

—INSTRUCTION. Instruction is a statement that specifies an operation and the values and locations of its operands. In this context, "instruction" is preferable to "command" or "order", which are sometimes used synonymously. "Command" should be reserved for electronic signals; "order" should be reserved for sequence, interpolation, or related usage.

References

Department of Defense, U.S. Army. *Dictionary of United States Army Terms.* Army Regulation AR 310-25. Washington, DC: Headquarters, Department of the Army, 1986.

—INSTRUMENT DIRECTION, in artillery, is the recorded reference direction of a high airburst, as indicated on an instrument at the battery position, that enables the executive subsequently to check and correct computed or scale deflection settings.

References

Department of Defense, U.S. Army. *Dictionary of United States Army Terms.* Army Regulation AR 310-25. Washington, DC: Headquarters, Department of the Army, 1986.

—INSTRUMENT METEOROLOGICAL CONDITIONS (IMC) are meteorological conditions expressed in terms of visibility, distance from clouds, and ceiling, less the minimal specified for visual meteorological conditions.

References

Department of Defense, U.S. Army. *Airspace Management and Army Air Traffic in a Combat Zone.* Field Manual FM 1-60. Washington, DC: Headquarters, Department of the Army, 1977.

—INSTRUMENTATION is the scientific or technical equipment used to measure, sense, record, transmit, process, or display data during tests or examinations of materiel.

References

Department of Defense, U.S. Army. *Dictionary of United States Army Terms.* Army Regulation AR 310-25. Washington, DC: Headquarters, Department of the Army, 1986.

—INSURANCE STOCKAGE OBJECTIVE is a fixed quantity of materiel that may be required only occasionally or intermittently. It is not computed on a recurring demand basis, and is stocked because the item is essential or it requires procurement lead time. An item having an insurance stockage objective does not have any other type of stockage objective (including the protectable mobilization, reserve materiel objective). *See also:* Insurance-Type Items, Insurance-Type Parts.

References

Department of Defense, U.S. Army. *Dictionary of United States Army Terms.* Army Regulation AR 310-25. Washington, DC: Headquarters, Department of the Army, 1986.

—INSURANCE-TYPE ITEMS are items that have no computed demand and are stocked on the basis of predetermined specific quantities. They tend to become dead assets. These are items for which no failure is predicted through normal usage, but, if a failure is experienced or loss occurs through accident, the lack of a replacement item would seriously hamper the operational capability of a weapon or weapons system. Allowances are generally low and replacements are made on the basis of usage, which is nominal. *See also:* Insurance Stockage Objective.

References

Department of Defense, U.S. Army. *Dictionary of United States Army Terms.* Army Regulation AR 310-25. Washington, DC: Headquarters, Department of the Army, 1986.

—INSURANCE-TYPE PARTS are very low mortality, infrequently used parts. They are usually heavy and bulky, and are normally utilized only at depot maintenance level.

References

Department of Defense, U.S. Army. *Dictionary of United States Army Terms.* Army Regulation AR 310-25. Washington, DC: Headquarters, Department of the Army, 1986.

—INSURGENCY. (1) Insurgency is an organized movement aimed at the overthrow of a constituted government through the use of subversion or armed conflict. (2) Insurgency is a condition resulting from a revolt or insurrection against a constituted government that falls short of a civil war. *See also:* Counterinsurgency.

References

Department of Defense, U.S. Army. *Civil Affairs Operations.* Field Manual FM 41-10. Washington, DC: Headquarters, Department of the Army, 1985.

————. *Low Intensity Conflict.* Field Manual FM 100-20. Washington, DC: Headquarters, Department of the Army, 1981.

—**INSURGENT WAR** is a struggle between a constituted government and organized insurgents who are frequently supported from without, but acting violently from within their country. The insurgents exploit the political, social, economic, military, and civil vulnerabilities of the government to cause its internal destruction or overthrow. Such wars are distinguished from lesser insurgencies by the gravity of the threat to the government and the insurgent object of eventual regional and national control. *See also:* Insurgency.

References
Department of Defense, U.S. Army. *Low Intensity Conflict.* Field Manual FM 100-20. Washington, DC: Headquarters, Department of the Army, 1981.

—**INTEGRATED DEFENSE** is air defense in which two or more vital areas are defended with a single overall defense.

References
Department of Defense, U.S. Army. *Dictionary of United States Army Terms.* Army Regulation AR 310-25. Washington, DC: Headquarters, Department of the Army, 1986.

—**INTEGRATED EQUIPMENT** is equipment in which is embodied both a communications capability and a crypto capability. *See also:* CRYPTO.

References
Department of Defense, U.S. Army. *Dictionary of United States Army Terms.* Army Regulation AR 310-25. Washington, DC: Headquarters, Department of the Army, 1986.

—**INTEGRATED LOGISTIC SUPPORT** is a composite of the elements necessary to assure the effective and economical sustaining of a system or equipment, at all levels of maintenance, throughout its programmed life cycle. It is characterized by the harmony and coherence of its elements and levels of maintenance and is an integral part of all other aspects of system acquisition and operation.

References
Department of Defense, U.S. Army. *Support Operations: Echelons Above Corps.* Field Manual FM 100-16. Washington, DC: Headquarters, Department of the Army, 1986.

—**INTEGRATED MATERIEL INVENTORY MANAGEMENT** is the management, by a designated commodity manager, of the following related logistical missions:

- **Cataloging Direction**—the initiation of actions requiring the timely identification of items and preparation of prescribed Department of the Army manuals, leading to the cataloging of the items.
- **Requirements Computation**—the computation of quantitative requirements, subject to the review and approval of higher authority, when prescribed.
- **Budgeting Direction**—the development of budget estimates and apportionment requests, subject to review and approval.
- **Procurement Direction**—the authority, within limitation of approved programs or as otherwise directed by higher authority, to require procurement to be accomplished.
- **Distribution Management**—The control of stocks in, due into, or planned for the distribution system on a quantitative and monetary basis.
- **Overhaul Direction**—The authority to require overhaul to be accomplished.
- **Disposal Direction**—The authority to require disposal to be accomplished.

References
Department of Defense, U.S. Army. *Dictionary of United States Army Terms.* Army Regulation 310-25. Washington, DC: Headquarters, Department of the Army, 1986.

—**INTEGRATED NBC (NUCLEAR/BIOLOGICAL/CHEMICAL) TRAINING** is training that requires the accomplishment of individual and unit missions under actual or simulated NBC conditions. *See also:* Biological Warfare, Chemical Warfare, Nuclear Warfare.

References
Department of Defense, U.S. Army. *Army Forces Training.* Army Regulation AR 350-41. Washington, DC: Headquarters, Department of the Army, 1986.

—**INTEGRATED STAFF** refers to people who are assigned to staff posts regardless of their nationality or service. Only one officer is appointed to each post on the headquarters staff, irrespective of the officer's nationality and Service area. *See also:* Combined Staff, Joint Staff, Parallel Staff, Staff.

References
Department of Defense, Joint Chiefs of Staff. *Department of Defense Dictionary of Military and Related Terms.* Washington, DC: GPO, 1986.

—**INTEGRATED WARFARE** occurs when the opposing forces employ both conventional and unconventional weapons in combat.

References

Department of Defense, Joint Chiefs of Staff. *Department of Defense Dictionary of Military and Related Terms*. Washington, DC: GPO, 1986.

—**INTEGRATING CENTER** is an activity specifically authorized and designated to formulate, develop, and integrate concepts, doctrine, organization, materiel requirements, systems, and training in broad functional areas. *See also:* Integration Training.

References

Department of Defense, U.S. Army. *Dictionary of United States Army Terms*. Army Regulation 310-25. Washington, DC: Headquarters, Department of the Army, 1986.

—**INTEGRATION.** (1) Integration is a stage in the intelligence cycle in which a pattern is formed through selecting and combining evaluated information. (2) In photography, integration is the combining of several photographic images into a single image, or the process by which the average radar picture seen on several scans of the time base is obtained on a print. *See also:* Image, Intelligence Cycle.

References

Department of Defense, Joint Chiefs of Staff. *Department of Defense Dictionary of Military and Related Terms*. Washington, DC: GPO, 1986.

—**INTEGRATION TRAINING** is the completion of initial entry training in Skill Level 1 tasks for an individual who is newly arrived in a unit. The training is limited specifically to the tasks associated with the mission, organization, and equipment of the unit to which the individual is assigned. It may be conducted by the unit using training materials supplied by U.S. Army Training and Doctrine Command, by troop schools, or by in-service or contract-mobile training teams. In all cases, this training is supported by the U.S. Army Training and Docrtine Command school proponent.

References

Department of Defense, U.S. Army. *Unit Training Management*. Field Manual FM 25-2. Washington, DC: Headquarters, Department of the Army, 1984.

—**INTELLIGENCE (INTEL).** Intelligence should be differentiated from information and intelligence information. *Information* is unevaluated material of every type. *Intelligence information* is information that has not been processed into intelligence, but may be of intelligence value. Intelligence is the product that results or the knowledge that is derived from the cyclical processing of information. Sherman Kent maintains that intelligence has three definitional subsets: knowledge (the knowledge that a nation must have for proper decisionmaking); institution (the physical organization of people who are pursuing a certain type of knowledge); and activity (the actions of collection, evaluation, research, analysis, study, presentation, and more).

On the strategic level, intelligence is the product resulting from collecting, processing, integrating, analyzing, evaluating, and interpreting information concerning foreign countries or areas, hostile or potentially hostile forces or elements, and areas of actual or potential operations. The term is also applied to the activity that results from the product and the organizations that are engaged in such activity.

On the Army tactical intelligence level, the term is similarly defined, but also includes information on weather and terrain. In this context, intelligence is considered immediately or potentially significant to military planning and operations.

The Church Committee defined intelligence as "the product resulting from the collection, collation, evaluation, analysis, integration, and interpretation of all collected information."

The many types of intelligence include the following, many of which are discussed fully under their own headings: acoustic(al) intelligence, actionable intelligence, basic intelligence, biographical intelligence, cartographic intelligence, combat intelligence, communications intelligence, counterintelligence, critical intelligence, current intelligence, departmental intelligence, domestic intelligence, economic intelligence, electronic intelligence, electro-optical intelligence, energy intelligence, estimative intelligence, evasion and escape intelligence, finished intelligence, foreign counterintelligence, foreign instrumentation and signals intelligence, foreign intelligence, foreign material intelligence, geographic(al) intelligence, human intelligence, imagery intelligence, joint intelligence, laser intelligence, literature intelligence, measurement and signature intelligence , medical intelligence, military intelligence, national intelligence, nuclear intelligence, nuclear proliferation intelligence, operational intelligence, optical intelligence, photographic intelligence, political intelligence, positive intelligence, radar intelligence, radiation intelligence, raw intelligence, scientific and technical intelligence, signals intelligence, sociological intelligence, special intelligence, strategic intelligence, tactical intelligence, target intelligence, technical intelligence, telemetry intelligence. *See also:* Intelligence Cycle.

References

American Bar Association. *Oversight and Accountability of the U.S. Intelligence Agencies: An Evaluation.* Washington, DC: ABA, 1985.

Corson, William R. *The Armies of Ignorance: The Rise of the American Intelligence Empire.* New York: Dial Press, 1977.

Department of Defense, Defense Intelligence Agency. *Defense Intelligence Agency Manual.* Washington, DC: DIA, 1987.

Department of Defense, Defense Intelligence College. *Glossary of Intelligence Terms and Definitions.* Washington, DC: DIC, 1987.

Department of Defense, Joint Chiefs of Staff. *Department of Defense Dictionary of Military and Related Terms.* Washington, DC: GPO, 1986.

Kent, Sherman. *Strategic Intelligence for American World Policy.* Princeton, NJ: Princeton University Press, 1966.

Laqueur, Walter. *A World of Secrets.* New York: Basic Books, 1985.

Treverton, Gregory F. *Covert Action: The Limits of Intervention in the Postwar World.* New York: Basic Books, 1987.

Turner, Stansfield. *Secrecy and Democracy: The CIA in Transition.* Boston: Houghton Mifflin, 1985.

U.S. Congress. Senate. *Final Report of the Senate Select Committee to Study Government Operations With Respect to Intelligence Activities. Report 94-755. Book I, Foreign and Military Intelligence* (Church Committee Report). Washington, DC: GPO, 1976.

—INTELLIGENCE ACTIVITIES. (1) Intelligence activities are any or all of the activities accomplished by intelligence organizations. In June 1977, U.S. Senate Resolution 400 defined intelligence activities as: "(A) the collection, analysis, production, dissemination or use of information which relates to any foreign country, or any government, political group, party, military force, movement, or other association in such foreign country, and which relates to the defense, foreign policy, national security, or related policies of the United States, and other activity which is in support of these activities; (B) activities taken to counter similar activities directed against the United States; (C) covert or clandestine activities affecting the relations of the United States with any foreign government, political group, parity, military force, movement or other association; (D) the collection, analysis, production, dissemination or use of information about the activities of persons within the United States, its territories and possessions, or nationals of the United States abroad whose political and related activities pose, or may be considered by any department, agency, bureau, office, division, instrumentality or employee of the United States to pose, a threat to the internal security of the United States, and covert or clandestine activities directed against such persons. Such term does not include tactical foreign military intelligence serving no national policymaking function." (2) Intelligence activities are the activities of Department of Defense intelligence components that are authorized under Presidential Executive Order 12333, of December 4, 1981. *See also:* Intelligence.

References

American Bar Association. *Oversight and Accountability of the U.S. Intelligence Agencies: An Evaluation.* Washington, DC: ABA, 1985.

Department of Defense. *Activities of DoD Intelligence Components that Affect U.S. Persons.* (Department of Defense Directive 52401.) Washington, DC: DoD, 1982.

Department of Defense, Defense Intelligence College. *Glossary of Intelligence Terms and Definitions.* Washington, DC: DIC, 1987.

Kent, Sherman. *Strategic Intelligence for American World Policy.* Princeton, NJ: Princeton University Press, 1966.

Laqueur, Walter. *A World of Secrets.* New York: Basic Books, 1985.

Treverton, Gregory F. *Covert Action: The Limits of Intervention in the Postwar World.* New York: Basic Books, 1987.

Turner, Stansfield. *Secrecy and Democracy: The CIA in Transition.* Boston: Houghton Mifflin, 1985.

—INTELLIGENCE ANALYSIS SYSTEM is a single, integrated system that extends from the battalion level to the national agencies. The all-source intelligence system includes the directors, coordinators, producers, and executors. All are linked together both laterally and vertically to insure a coordinated and effective effort. The elements of the analysis system include intelligence officers and their staff sections, echelons above corps intelligence centers, tactical operations center support elements, technical control and analysis elements, and battlefield information coordination centers. *See also:* Intelligence.

References

Department of Defense, U.S. Army. *Intelligence Analysis*. Field Manual FM 34-3. Washington, DC: Headquarters, Department of the Army, 1986.

—**INTELLIGENCE ANNEX** is a supporting document of an operation plan or order that provides detailed information on the enemy situation, assignment of intelligence tasks, and intelligence administrative procedures. *See also:* Intelligence.

References

American Bar Association. *Oversight and Accountability of the U.S. Intelligence Agencies: An Evaluation*. Washington, DC: ABA, 1985.

Maurer, Alfred C.; Turnstall, Marion D.; and Keagle, James M. *Intelligence Policy and Process*. Boulder, CO: Westview Press, 1985.

U.S. Congress. Senate. *Final Report of the Senate Select Committee to Study Government Operations With Respect to Intelligence Activities. Report 94-755. Book I, Foreign and Military Intelligence* (Church Committee Report). Washington, DC: GPO, 1976.

—**INTELLIGENCE ASSESSMENT** is a category of intelligence production that is found in most analytical studies dealing with subjects that have policy significance. It is based upon a thorough analysis of the subject, but, unlike intelligence assessments, does not attempt to project future developments and their implications. It is usually coordinated within the producing intelligence organization but may not be coordinated with other intelligence agencies. *See also:* Estimative Intelligence.

References

American Bar Association. *Oversight and Accountability of the U.S. Intelligence Agencies: An Evaluation*. Washington, DC: ABA, 1985.

Department of Defense, Defense Intelligence College. *Glossary of Intelligence Terms and Definitions*. Washington, DC: DIC, 1987.

Kent, Sherman. *Strategic Intelligence for American World Policy*. Princeton, NJ: Princeton University Press, 1966.

Laqueur, Walter. *A World of Secrets*. New York: Basic Books, 1985.

Maurer, Alfred C.; Turnstall, Marion D.; and Keagle, James M. *Intelligence Policy and Process*. Boulder, CO: Westview Press, 1985.

Treverton, Gregory F. *Covert Action: The Limits of Intervention in the Postwar World*. New York: Basic Books, 1987.

Turner, Stansfield. *Secrecy and Democracy: The CIA in Transition*. Boston: Houghton Mifflin, 1985.

—**INTELLIGENCE ASSET** is any resource (e.g., a person, group, instrument, installation, or technical system) that can be used by an intelligence organization. *See also:* Intelligence.

References

American Bar Association. *Oversight and Accountability of the U.S. Intelligence Agencies: An Evaluation*. Washington, DC: ABA, 1985.

Department of Defense, Defense Intelligence College. *Glossary of Intelligence Terms and Definitions*. Washington, DC: DIC, 1987.

Department of Defense, Joint Chiefs of Staff. *Department of Defense Dictionary of Military and Related Terms*. Washington, DC: GPO, 1986.

Kent, Sherman. *Strategic Intelligence for American World Policy*. Princeton, NJ: Princeton University Press, 1966.

Laqueur, Walter. *A World of Secrets*. New York: Basic Books, 1985.

Maurer, Alfred C.; Turnstall, Marion D.; and Keagle, James M. *Intelligence Policy and Process*. Boulder, CO: Westview Press, 1985.

Treverton, Gregory F. *Covert Action: The Limits of Intervention in the Postwar World*. New York: Basic Books, 1987.

Turner, Stansfield. *Secrecy and Democracy: The CIA in Transition*. Boston: Houghton Mifflin, 1985.

—**INTELLIGENCE COLLECTION (IC)** is the gathering of information by all means (signals intelligenc, human intelligence, photographic, etc.) and from all sources (ranging from unclassified or open sources to the most highly classified sources available) that pertains to a given intelligence problem and the delivery of that information to the appropriate office or facility for processing and production. *See also:* Intelligence, Intelligence Cycle.

References

American Bar Association. *Oversight and Accountability of the U.S. Intelligence Agencies: An Evaluation*. Washington, DC: ABA, 1985.

Department of Defense, Defense Intelligence College. *Glossary of Intelligence Terms and Definitions.* Washington, DC: DIC, 1987.

Kent, Sherman. *Strategic Intelligence for American World Policy.* Princeton, NJ: Princeton University Press, 1966.

Laqueur, Walter. *A World of Secrets.* New York: Basic Books, 1985.

Maurer, Alfred C.; Turnstall, Marion D.; and Keagle, James M. *Intelligence Policy and Process.* Boulder, CO: Westview Press, 1985.

Treverton, Gregory F. *Covert Action: The Limits of Intervention in the Postwar World.* New York: Basic Books, 1987.

Turner, Stansfield. *Secrecy and Democracy: The CIA in Transition.* Boston: Houghton Mifflin, 1985.

—**INTELLIGENCE COLLECTION PLAN** is a plan for gathering information from all sources to satisfy an intelligence requirement. Specifically, it is a logical plan for transforming the essential elements of information into orders or requests to sources for information within a required time limit. *See also:* Intelligence, Intelligence Cycle.

References

American Bar Association. *Oversight and Accountability of the U.S. Intelligence Agencies: An Evaluation.* Washington, DC: ABA, 1985.

Kent, Sherman. *Strategic Intelligence for American World Policy.* Princeton, NJ: Princeton University Press, 1966.

Laqueur, Walter. *A World of Secrets.* New York: Basic Books, 1985.

Maurer, Alfred C.; Turnstall, Marion D.; and Keagle, James M. *Intelligence Policy and Process.* Boulder, CO: Westview Press, 1985.

—**INTELLIGENCE COLLECTION REQUIREMENT** (ICR) is the means by which an intelligence analyst expresses an intelligence need to the intelligence collector. The ICR discusses the specific information shortfall, addresses the precise information needed in detail, and provides a time frame of when the information is needed. The analyst also provides any other information that might assist the collector in fulfilling the requirement. The ICR has replaced the Specific Intelligence Collection Requirement, which fulfilled a similar role. *See also:* Intelligence, Intelligence Cycle.

References

American Bar Association. *Oversight and Accountability of the U.S. Intelligence Agencies: An Evaluation.* Washington, DC: ABA, 1985.

Kent, Sherman. *Strategic Intelligence for American World Policy.* Princeton, NJ: Princeton University Press, 1966.

Maurer, Alfred C.; Turnstall, Marion D.; and Keagle, James M. *Intelligence Policy and Process.* Boulder, CO: Westview Press, 1985.

U.S. Congress. Senate. *Final Report of the Senate Select Committee to Study Government Operations With Respect to Intelligence Activities. Report 94-755. Book I, Foreign and Military Intelligence* (Church Committee Report). Washington, DC: GPO, 1976.

—**INTELLIGENCE CYCLE** is the process by which information is gathered, converted into intelligence, and delivered to the customer. There are usually five steps in the cycle:

- **Planning and direction.** An intelligence agency first determines that there is a need for intelligence information. Its people prepare a collection plan that defines the needs, suggests information-collection measures, and provides other advice and guidelines. Funding is approved, orders are issued, and requests are sent to the collection entities asking them to gather information. The collection entities' progress is continuously monitered.
- **Collection.** Information or intelligence information is gathered and delivered to the production or processing activity.
- **Processing.** The collected information is converted into a form suitable for intelligince production.
- **Production.** The information is converted into finished intelligence through integrating, analyzing, evaluating, and interpreting all available information. Intelligence products are prepared in response to known or anticipated customer requirements.
- **Dissemination.** The finished intelligence products (in oral, written, or graphic form) are distributed to departmental and agency intelligence consumers.

See also: Information, Intelligence, Intelligence Information.

References

Department of Defense, Defense Intelligence College. *Glossary of Intelligence Terms and Definitions.* Washington, DC: DIC, 1987.

Maurer, Alfred C.; Turnstall, Marion D.; and Keagle, James M. *Intelligence Policy and Process.* Boulder, CO: Westview Press, 1985.

U.S. Congress. Senate. *Final Report of the Senate Select Committee to Study Government Operations With Respect to Intelligence Activities. Report 94-*

755. Book I, Foreign and Military Intelligence (Church Committee Report). Washington, DC: GPO, 1976.

—**INTELLIGENCE DATA BASE** is all intelligence data and finished intelligence products at a given organization. *See also:* Intelligence.

References

Maurer, Alfred C.; Turnstall, Marion D.; and Keagle, James M. *Intelligence Policy and Process.* Boulder, CO: Westview Press, 1985.

U.S. Congress. Senate. *Final Report of the Senate Select Committee to Study Government Operations With Respect to Intelligence Activities. Report 94-755. Book I, Foreign and Military Intelligence.* (Church Committee Report). Washington, DC: GPO, 1976.

—**INTELLIGENCE ESTIMATE (IE)** is the product of estimative intelligence. It is prepared by appraising the elements of intelligence relating to a specific situation or condition in order to determine the courses of action that are open to an enemy or probable enemy, as well as their probable order of adoption. In other words, it is intelligence that predicts the degree of likelihood of possible future events, developments or courses of action, and their implications and consequences. *See also:* Estimate, Estimative Intelligence.

References

Department of Defense, Defense Intelligence College. *Glossary of Intelligence Terms and Definitions.* Washington, DC: DIC, 1987.

Kent, Sherman. *Strategic Intelligence for American World Policy.* Princeton, NJ: Princeton University Press, 1966.

Laqueur, Walter. *A World of Secrets.* New York: Basic Books, 1985.

Maurer, Alfred C.; Turnstall, Marion D.; and Keagle, James M. *Intelligence Policy and Process.* Boulder, CO: Westview Press, 1985.

Turner, Stansfield. *Secrecy and Democracy: The CIA in Transition.* Boston: Houghton Mifflin, 1985.

U.S. Congress. Senate. *Final Report of the Senate Select Committee to Study Government Operations With Respect to Intelligence Activities. Report 94-755. Book I, Foreign and Military Intelligence* (Church Committee Report). Washington, DC: GPO, 1976.

—**INTELLIGENCE INFORMATION REPORT (IIR)** is the final product resulting from the collection step of the intelligence cycle. It is used to forward the raw information that has been collected to fulfill intelligence requirements. *See also:* Intelligence Report.

References

Department of Defense, Defense Intelligence Agency. *Defense Intelligence Agency Manual.* Washington, DC: DIA, 1987.

Department of Defense, Defense Intelligence College. *Glossary of Intelligence Terms and Definitions.* Washington, DC: DIC, 1987.

Maurer, Alfred C.; Turnstall, Marion D.; and Keagle, James M. *Intelligence Policy and Process.* Boulder, CO: Westview Press, 1985.

—**INTELLIGENCE JOURNAL** is a chronological log of intelligence activities that covers a specific period (usually 24 hours). It is an index of reports and messages that have been received and transmitted, important events that have occurred, and actions that have been taken. The journal is a permanent and official record. *See also:* Journal.

References

Department of Defense, U.S. Army. *Intelligence and Electronic Warfare Operations.* Field Manual FM 34-1. Washington, DC: Headquarters, Department of the Army, 1984.

—**INTELLIGENCE OFFICER (IO)** is a professional (vice clerical) employee of an intelligence organization who is engaged in intelligence activities. *See also:* Intelligence.

References

Department of Defense, Defense Intelligence College. *Glossary of Intelligence Terms and Definitions.* Washington, DC: DIC, 1987.

Maurer, Alfred C.; Turnstall, Marion D.; and Keagle, James M. *Intelligence Policy and Process.* Boulder, CO: Westview Press, 1985.

—**INTELLIGENCE OPERATIONS** are the organized efforts of a commander to gather information on terrain, weather, and the enemy. Obtaining useful information prior to the initiation of operations is vital. Assembling an accurate picture for simultaneous action at all levels of command and timely distribution of information throughout the command are crucial aspects of intelligence operations. Intelligence operations normally begin before a tactical operation and continue as the battle develops. Such operations may employ any of the unit's resources—units in contact with the enemy, cavalry units, patrols, electronic warfare units, and field artillery radars—and they routinely rely on higher levels of command for intelligence support. Local population and government agencies also add to the intelligence picture. *See also:* Intelligence.

References

Department of Defense, U.S. Army. *Operations.* Field Manual FM 100-5. Washington, DC: Headquarters, U.S. Army, 1986.

—**INTELLIGENCE ORGANIZATION** is any organization, agency, group, or other entity involved in intelligence activity. *See also:* Foreign Intelligence Service, Intelligence Agency.

References

Department of Defense, Defense Intelligence College. *Glossary of Intelligence Terms and Definitions.* Washington, DC: DIC, 1987.

Maurer, Alfred C.; Turnstall, Marion D.; and Keagle, James M. *Intelligence Policy and Process.* Boulder, CO: Westview Press, 1985.

—**INTELLIGENCE PREPARATION OF THE BATTLEFIELD (IPB)** is an Army tactical intelligence term that means the detailed analysis of enemy, weather, and terrain in specific geographic areas. It provides an analytical tool for relating changes in enemy doctrine and capabilities to specific terrain and weather scenarios. *See also:* Intelligence.

References

Department of Defense, U.S. Army. *Intelligence and Electronic Warfare Operations.* Field Manual FM 34-1. Washington, DC: Headquarters, Department of the Army, 1987.

————. *Military Intelligence Battalion (Combat Electronic Warfare Intelligence) (Division).* Field Manual FM 34-10. Washington, DC: Headquarters, Department of the Army, 1981.

————. *Military Intelligence Battalion (CEWI) (Operations) (Corps).* Field Manual FM 34-21. Washington, DC: Headquarters, Department of the Army, 1982.

————. *Military Intelligence Battalion (CEWI) (Tactical Exploitation) (Corps): Counterintelligence, Interrogation, Electronic Warfare.* Field Manual FM 34-23. Washington, DC: Headquarters, Department of the Army, 1985.

————. *Military Intelligence Company (Combat Electronic Warfare and Intelligence) (Armored Cavalry Regiment/Separate Brigade).* Field Manual FM 34-30. Washington, DC: Headquarters, Department of the Army, 1983.

————. *Military Intelligence Group (Combat Electronic Warfare and Intelligence) (Corps).* Field Manual FM 34-20. Washington, DC: Headquarters, Department of the Army, 1983.

—**INTELLIGENCE PRODUCT** is the result of intelligence analysis. It is finished intelligence that is ready for presentation to the customer. *See also:* Intelligence Cycle, Intelligence Production.

References

Maurer, Alfred C.; Turnstall, Marion D.; and Keagle, James M. *Intelligence Policy and Process.* Boulder, CO: Westview Press, 1985.

—**INTELLIGENCE PRODUCTION REQUIREMENT (IPR)** is a form printed by the Department of Defense and completed by the intelligence customers. It is the means by which customers describe their requirement to the Defense Intelligence Agency. This requirement is a stated need for the production of intelligence on a general or specific subject, program, system, or weapon. The requirement is then approved and processed by the Defense Intelligence Agency. The IPR is the preferred way to establish a long-term requirement (i.e., requirement sufficiently important to warrant the scheduling of products in the appropriate general or scientific and technical intelligence production program and to necessitate the use of considerable analytical resources to satisfy it). *See also:* Intelligence.

References

Department of Defense, Defense Intelligence College. *Glossary of Intelligence Terms and Definitions.* Washington, DC: DIC, 1987.

—**INTELLIGENCE REPORT (IR)** is a product of the production step of the intelligence cycle. On the tactical level, an intelligence report, called an INTREP, is a specific report of information, usually on a single item, that is made at any level of command in tactical operations and is disseminated as rapidly as possible in keeping with the timeliness of the information. *See also:* Intelligence Information Report.

References

Department of Defense, Defense Intelligence College. *Glossary of Intelligence Terms and Definitions.* Washington, DC: DIC, 1987.

Maurer, Alfred C.; Turnstall, Marion D.; and Keagle, James M. *Intelligence Policy and Process.* Boulder, CO: Westview Press, 1985.

—**INTELLIGENCE REPORTING** is preparing and sending information by any means. In general, the term is limited to reports that are prepared by an intelligence collector and transmitted by him to headquarters, and by this component of the intelligence structure to one or more intelligence-producing centers or facilities. Even in this limited sense, reporting embraces both collection and dissemination. The term is applied to normal and specialist intelligence reports. *See also:* Normal Intelligence Reports, Specialist Intelligence Reports.

References

American Bar Association. *Oversight and Accountability of the U.S. Intelligence Agencies: An Evaluation.* Washington, DC: ABA, 1985.

Kent, Sherman. *Strategic Intelligence for American World Policy.* Princeton, NJ: Princeton University Press, 1966.

Maurer, Alfred C.; Turnstall, Marion D.; and Keagle, James M. *Intelligence Policy and Process.* Boulder, CO: Westview Press, 1985.

Treverton, Gregory F. *Covert Action: The Limits of Intervention in the Postwar World.* New York: Basic Books, 1987.

—**INTELLIGENCE REQUIREMENT (IR)** is any subject for which there is a need to collect intelligence information and produce intelligence. It may appear as a consumer statement of intelligence need for which information is not readily available. *See also:* Essential Elements of Information.

References

Department of Defense, Defense Intelligence College. *Glossary of Intelligence Terms and Definitions.* Washington, DC: DIC, 1987.

Department of Defense, U.S. Army. *Support Operations: Echelons Above Corps.* Field Manual FM 100-16. Washington, DC: Headquarters, Department of the Army, 1986.

—**INTELLIGENCE SUMMARY (INTSUM)** is a specific report that provides a summary of intelligence items at frequent intervals. *See also:* Intelligence.

References

Department of Defense, Joint Chiefs of Staff. *Department of Defense Dictionary of Military and Related Terms.* Washington, DC: GPO, 1986.

—**INTELLIGENCE-RELATED ACTIVITIES (IRA)** are endeavors that are specifically excluded from the National Foreign Intelligence Program that respond to departmental or agency tasking for time-sensitive information on foreign activities and that respond to national Intelligence Community advisory tasking of collection capabilities. IRA have a primary mission of supporting departmental or agency missions or operational forces, of training personnel for intelligence duties, and of being devoted to research and development for intelligence and related capabilities. Specifically excluded from these activities are programs that are so closely integrated with a weapon system that their primary function is to provide targeting data for immediate use.

In 1974-76, the House Appropriations Committee, in an attempt to get the Department of Defense to report on intelligence systems (e.g., the SR-71 Blackbird) that were not reported in the intelligence budget, created a budget category called IRA. Also included in IRA were the Navy's surveillance systems that tracked Soviet submarines and the warning systems that were used by the Department of Defense to monitor bombers, missiles, and satellites. Between 1976 and 1980, more systems were added to IRA, and by 1980 the Department of Defense had embraced IRA as a management tool to coordinate and control a wide range of service intelligence activities. *See also:* Intelligence.

References

American Bar Association. *Oversight and Accountability of the U.S. Intelligence Agencies: An Evaluation.* Washington, DC: ABA, 1985.

Laqueur, Walter. *A World of Secrets.* New York: Basic Books, 1985.

Maurer, Alfred C.; Turnstall, Marion D.; and Keagle, James M. *Intelligence Policy and Process.* Boulder, CO: Westview Press, 1985.

Treverton, Gregory F. *Covert Action: The Limits of Intervention in the Postwar World.* New York: Basic Books, 1987.

—**INTENSITY FACTOR** is a multiplying factor used in planning activities to evaluate the foreseeable intensity or the specific nature of an operation in a given area for a given period. It is applied to the standard day of supply in order to calculate the combat day of supply.

References

Department of Defense, Joint Chiefs of Staff. *Department of Defense Dictionary of Military and Related Terms.* Washington, DC: GPO, 1986.

—**INTENSIVELY MANAGED ITEM** is an item of supply, usually expensive, that has been designated by the proper national inventory control point as an item that must be closely accounted for in both the supply system and in all command echelons. Items to be intensively managed are (1) of high unit cost and/or high annual demand or (2) highly essential to a particular mission or weapons system. The overall supply status must be reviewed frequently because of the item's high cost or importance.

References
Department of Defense, U.S. Army. *Dictionary of United States Army Terms*. Army Regulation AR 310-25. Washington, DC: Headquarters, Department of the Army, 1986.

—**INTENTION** is an aim or design (as distinct from capability) to execute a specified course of action.

References
Department of Defense, Joint Chiefs of Staff. *Department of Defense Dictionary of Military and Related Terms*. Washington, DC: GPO, 1986.

—**INTERCARDINAL POINTS** are the directions of northeast, southeast, southwest, and northwest.

References
Department of Defense, U.S. Army. *Dictionary of United States Army Terms*. Army Regulation AR 310-25. Washington, DC: Headquarters, Department of the Army, 1986.

—**INTERCEPT(ION).** (1) In a general sense, interception is acquiring electromagnetic signals (e.g., radio signals) with electronic collection equipment for intelligence purposes and without the consent of the signaller. (2) Interception is an Army tactical intelligence term that means the act of listening, copying, or recording emissions by someone other than the intended party. The goals of interception are to: collect emissions for information content; determine the locations and characteristics of the emitters; determine the parameters, structure and functions of the emissions; and determine the organizational or individual identities of communications or noncommunications emitters. (3) In the context of definition (2), interception is a step in the Army tactical intelligence signals intelligence process. *See also:* SIGINT Process.

References
Department of Defense, U.S. Army. *Counter-Signals Intelligence (C-SIGINT) Operations*. Field Manual FM 34-62. Washington, DC: Headquarters, Department of the Army, 1986.

—**INTERCHANGE** is the transfer of a shipment, when moving on a through bill of lading, from one carrier to another whose lines constitute all or part of a joint route.

References
Department of Defense, U.S. Army. *Dictionary of United States Army Terms*. Army Regulation AR 310-25. Washington, DC: Headquarters, Department of the Army, 1986.

—**INTERCHANGEABILITY** is a condition that exists when two or more items possess such functional and physical characteristics as to be equivalent in performance and durability. These items can be exchanged one for the other without alteration of the items themselves, or of adjoining items, except for adjustment, and without selection for fit and performance. *See also:* Compatibility, Interchangeability Lists.

References
Department of Defense, Joint Chiefs of Staff. *Department of Defense Dictionary of Military and Related Terms*. Washington, DC: GPO, 1986.

—**INTERCHANGEABILITY LISTS** are lists of parts that are common to, and interchangeable among, various types of general purpose and combat vehicles.

References
Department of Defense, U.S. Army. *Dictionary of United States Army Terms*. Army Regulation AR 310-25. Washington, DC: Headquarters, Department of the Army, 1986.

—**INTERDICT.** (1) To interdict is to isolate or seal off an area by any means (e.g., deny the use of a route or approach). (2) To interdict is to prevent, hinder, or delay the use of an area or route by enemy forces. *See also:* Interdiction, Interdiction Fire, Interdiction Minefields.

References
Department of Defense, U.S. Army. *Operational Terms and Symbols*. Field Manual FM 101-5-1. Washington, DC: Headquarters, Department of the Army, 1985.

—**INTERDICTION** is isolating or sealing off an area by any means to deny its use as a route or approach.

References
Department of Defense, U.S. Army. *Attack Helicopter Operations*. Field Manual FM 17-50. Washington, DC: Headquarters, Department of the Army, 1984.

—**INTERDICTION FIRE** is fire that is placed on an area or point to prevent the enemy from using it.

References

Department of Defense, U.S. Army. *Attack Helicopter Operations.* Field Manual FM 17-50. Washington, DC: Headquarters, Department of the Army, 1984.

————. *Operational Terms and Symbols.* Field Manual FM 101-5-1. Washington, DC: Headquarters, Department of the Army, 1985.

—**INTERDICTION MINEFIELDS** are placed on the enemy or in its rear areas to kill, disorganize, and disrupt lines of communication and command and control facilities. They are usually used by the corps or division to separate enemy forces and delay or destroy enemy follow-on echelons. They are emplaced by using air-delivered or fire-support-delivered scatterable mines. *See also:* Mine Warfare.

References

Department of Defense, U.S. Army. *Countermobility.* Field Manual FM 5-102. Washington, DC: Headquarters, Department of the Army, 1985.

————. *Engineer Combat Operations.* Field Manual FM 5-100. Washington, DC: Headquarters, Department of the Army, 1984.

—**INTERFACE** is a boundary of point common to two or more similar or dissimilar command and control systems, subsystems, or other entities against which or at which necessary information exchange occurs.

References

Department of Defense, U.S. Army. *Air Defense Artillery Deployment: Chaparral/Vulcan/Stinger.* Field Manual FM 44- 3. Washington, DC: Headquarters, Department of the Army, 1984.

—**INTERFERENCE** is any electrical disturbance that causes undesirable responses in electrical equipment, resulting in difficulty in receiving signals.

References

Department of Defense, U.S. Army. *Communications Techniques: Electronics Countermeasures.* Field Manual FM 24-33. Washington, DC: Headquarters, Department of the Army, 1985.

————. *Operational Terms and Symbols.* Field Manual FM 101-5-1. Washington, DC: Headquarters, Department of the Army, 1985.

—**INTERIOR BALLISTICS** is a subdivision of ballistics that deals with the phenomena associated with imparting kinetic energy to missiles.

References

Department of Defense, U.S. Army. *Dictionary of United States Army Terms.* Army Regulation AR 310-25. Washington, DC: Headquarters, Department of the Army, 1986.

—**INTERIOR GUARD** is detailed by commanders of military installations to protect property and enforce specific military regulations. The elements of an interior guard are classified according to their purpose and include the main guard and special guards. The main guard consists of a combination of patrols and fixed posts. Special guards protect parks, trains, boats, and aircraft and perform other duties. *See also:* Captain of the Guard, Guard.

References

Department of Defense, U.S. Army. *Guard Duty.* Field Manual FM 22-6. Washington, DC: Headquarters, Department of the Army, 1971.

—**INTERIOR LINES.** Classical theory makes special note of the relationship between opposing lines of operations. A force is said to be operating on interior lines when its operations diverge from a central point and it is therefore closer to separate enemy forces than the latter are to each other. Interior lines benefit a weaker force by allowing it to shift the main effort laterally more rapidly than the enemy. Germany's decisive victory at Tannenberg was a classic example of the use of interior lines. *See also:* Exterior Lines.

References

Department of Defense, U.S. Army. *Operations.* Field Manual FM 100-5. Washington, DC: Headquarters, Department of the Army, 1986.

—**INTERMEDIATE AREA ILLUMINATION** is illumination in the area, extending in depth from the far boundary of the close-in (about 2,000 meters) to the maximum effective range of the bulk of division artillery weapons (about 10,000 meters).

References

Department of Defense, Joint Chiefs of Staff. *Department of Defense Dictionary of Military and Related Terms.* Washington, DC: GPO, 1986.

—**INTERMEDIATE FORCE PLANNING LEVEL** is the level established during planning force development to depict the buildup from the current force to the planning force. The intermediate force planning level is insufficient to carry out strategy with a reasonable assurance of success and consequently cannot be referred to as the Planning Force. *See also:* Current Force, Force, Minimum Risk Force, Planning Force, Programmed Forces.

References

Department of Defense, Joint Chiefs of Staff. *Department of Defense Dictionary of Military and Related Terms.* Washington, DC: GPO, 1986.

—**INTERMEDIATE MAINTENANCE.** Intermediate maintenance is a maintenance level organized into intermediate (direct support) and intermediate (general support) maintenance. The mission of intermediate direct support maintenance is to repair end-items of equipment on a return-to-user basis and repair selected/designated unserviceable components/modules in support of the direct exchange system. Intermediate direct support maintenance is performed by designated table of organization and equipment or table of distribution and allowances maintenance units, regardless of their geographic location in the theater or in the continental United States. The mission of intermediate general support maintenance is to provide support to the theater supply system through repair of components, end-items, and associated items.

References

Department of Defense, U.S. Army. *Combat Service Support Operations-Theater.* Field Manual FM 63-4. Washington, DC: Headquarters, Department of the Army, 1984.

————. *Repair Parts Supply for a Theater of Operations.* Field Manual FM 29-19. Washington, DC: Headquarters, Department of the Army, 1985.

—**INTERMEDIATE MARKER** is a marker (natural, artificial, or specially installed) that is used as a point of reference between a landmark and the minefield. *See also:* Mine Warfare.

References

Department of Defense, U.S. Army. *Mine/ Countermine Operations at the Company Level.* Field Manual FM 20-32. Washington, DC: Headquarters, Department of the Army, 1976.

—**INTERMEDIATE OBJECTIVES.** The commander may designate intermediate objectives if he believes that this will help in accomplishing his mission. They are normally key terrain features between the line of departure and the final objective.

References

Department of Defense, U.S. Army. *The Infantry Rifle Company (Infantry, Airborne, Air Assault, Ranger).* Field Manual FM 7-10. Washington, DC: Headquarters, Department of the Army, 1982.

—**INTERMEDIATE TRAINING OBJECTIVE** is a goal written in performance terms (e.g., tasks, conditions, and training standards) that supports a commander's specific training objective and helps make training in that objective logical and progressive.

References

Department of Defense, U.S. Army. *How to Prepare and Conduct Military Training.* Field Manual FM 21-6. Washington, DC: Headquarters, Department of the Army, 1975.

—**INTERMENT FLAG** is a national flag that is draped over the casket of the honored dead in a military funeral. It is 9.5 feet by 5 feet in dimensions.

References

Department of Defense, U.S. Army. *Dictionary of United States Army Terms.* Army Regulation AR 310-25. Washington, DC: Headquarters, Department of the Army, 1986.

—**INTERNAL ATTACK** is the full range of measures taken by organized insurgents to bring about the internal destruction and overthrow of a constituted government. *See also:* Guerrilla Operations.

References

Department of Defense, U.S. Army. *Dictionary of United States Army Terms.* Army Regulation AR 310-25. Washington, DC: Headquarters, Department of the Army, 1986.

—**INTERNAL CONTROL.** (1) Internal control is the organization plan and all of the coordination methods and measures adopted within an entity to safeguard its assets, check the accuracy and reliability of its accounting data, promote operational efficiency, and encourage adherence to prescribed managerial policies. (2) Internal control is the control exercised over the movement and discipline of a convoy, serial, or march unit, by its own officers and noncommissioned officers.

References

Department of Defense, U.S. Army. *Dictionary of United States Army Terms.* Army Regulation AR 310-25. Washington, DC: Headquarters, Department of the Army, 1986.

—**INTERNAL DEFENSE** is the full range of measures taken by a government to free and protect its society from subversion, lawlessness, and insurgency. *See also:* Terrorist Counteraction.

References

Department of Defense, U.S. Army. *Low Intensity Conflict.* Field Manual FM 100-20. Washington, DC: Headquarters, Department of the Army, 1981.

—**INTERNAL DEFENSE AND DEVELOPMENT (IDAD)** is the combining of the terms "internal defense" and "internal development" and is not otherwise defined.

References

Department of Defense, U.S. Army. *Civil Affairs Operations.* Field Manual FM 41-10. Washington, DC: Headquarters, Department of the Army, 1985.

—**INTERNAL DEFENSE ASSISTANCE OPERATION** is any operation undertaken by the military, paramilitary, police, or other security agencies of an outside power to strengthen the host government politically, economically, psychosocially, or militarily. *See also:* Terrorist Counteraction.

References

Department of Defense, U.S. Army. *Dictionary of United States Army Terms.* Army Regulation AR 310-25. Washington, DC: Headquarters, Department of the Army, 1986.

—**INTERNAL DEVELOPMENT** is action taken by a nation to promote its growth by building viable political, economic, military, and social institutions that respond to the needs of its society. *See also:* Terrorist Counteraction.

References

Department of Defense, U.S. Army. *Civil Affairs Operations.* Field Manual FM 41-10. Washington, DC: Headquarters, Department of the Army, 1985.

—**INTERNAL REVIEW** is a function that provides assurance of the effectiveness of internal controls that are associated with the procedural aspects of all areas of operations, including administration.

References

Department of Defense, U.S. Army. *Dictionary of United States Army Terms.* Army Regulation AR 310-25. Washington, DC: Headquarters, Department of the Army, 1986.

—**INTERNAL SECURITY.** (1) Internal security is the prevention of action against U.S. resources, industries, and institutions and the protection of life and property in the event of a domestic emergency by the use of all measures, in peace and war, other than military defense. (2) Internal security is a condition resulting from the measures taken within a command to safeguard the defense information it becomes aware of or possesses including the physical security of documents and materials. *See also:* Terrorist Counteraction.

References

Department of Defense, U.S. Army. *Dictionary of United States Army Terms.* Army Regulation 310-25. Washington, DC: Headquarters, Department of the Army, 1986.

—**INTERNATIONAL LOADING GAUGE (GIC)** is the loading gauge on which the international railway agreements are based. A load whose dimensions fall within the limits of this gauge may move without restriction on most of the railways of continental Western Europe. GIC is an abbreviation for "gabarit international de chargement," formerly called pulse position indicator.

References

Department of Defense, Joint Chiefs of Staff. *Department of Defense Dictionary of Military and Related Terms.* Washington, DC: GPO, 1986.

—**INTERNATIONAL LOGISTIC SUPPORT** is the provision of military logistic support by one participating nation to one or more participating nations, either with or without reimbursement. *See also:* International Logistics, Inter-Service Support, Support.

References

Department of Defense, U.S. Army. *Dictionary of United States Army Terms.* Army Regulation AR 310-25. Washington, DC: Headquarters, Department of the Army, 1986.

—**INTERNATIONAL LOGISTICS** is the negotiating, planning, and implementation of supporting logistics arrangements between nations, their forces, and agencies. It includes furnishing logistic support (major end-items, materiel, and/or services) to, or receiving logistic support from, one or more friendly governments, international organizations, or military forces, with or without reimbursement. It also includes the planning and actions that are related to the intermeshing of a significant element, component or activity of the military logistics systems or procedures of the United States with those of one or more foreign governments, international organizations, or military forces on a temporary or permanent basis. It includes the planning and actions that are related to the utilization of U.S. logistics policies, systems, and/or procedures to meet the requirements of one or more foreign governments, international organizations or forces.

References

Department of Defense, Joint Chiefs of Staff. *Department of Defense Dictionary of Military and Related Terms.* Washington, DC: GPO, 1986.

—**INTERNATIONAL OR TRANSNATIONAL TERRORISM** is terrorism that transcends national boundaries in carrying out its acts. In defining international terrorism, the purpose of the act, the nationalities of the victims, or the resolution of the incident are considered. These acts are usually designed to attract wide publicity in order to focus attention on the existence, cause, or demands of the terrorists. *See also:* Terrorist Counteraction.

References

Department of Defense, U.S. Army. *The Army Terrorism Counteraction Program.* Army Regulation AR 525-13. Washington, DC: Headquarters, Department of the Army, 1988.

—**INTERNED** describes all battle casualties who are known to have been taken into custody by a nonbelligerent foreign power as a result of and for reasons arising out of any armed conflict in which the U.S. Armed Forces are engaged. Interned casualties are not usually included in the medical statistical records or reports received by The Surgeon General, but they are reportable to the Adjutant General. *See also:* Internee, Internment Installation Procedures, Internment Serial Number.

References

Department of Defense, U.S. Army. *Planning for Health Service Support.* Field Manual FM 8-55. Washington, DC: Headquarters, Department of the Army, 1985.

—**INTERNEE** is a person who, during war, is kept within a particular country or is forced to stay in a certain place. Protected persons, as defined in the Geneva Convention of 1949, may only be made internees in accordance with the requirements therein stated.

References

Department of Defense, U.S. Army. *Dictionary of United States Army Terms.* Army Regulation AR 310-25. Washington, DC: Headquarters, Department of the Army, 1986.

—**INTERNMENT INSTALLATION PROCEDURES** are local regulations, standard operating procedures, or other instructions governing prisoner-of-war camp or civilian internee camp activities or those persons interned in such camps.

References

Department of Defense, U.S. Army. *Dictionary of United States Army Terms.* Army Regulation AR 310-25. Washington, DC: Headquarters, Department of the Army, 1986.

—**INTERNMENT SERIAL NUMBER** is the identification number assigned by a military police prisoner-of-war processing company to a prisoner-of-war, civilian internee, or retained person.

References

Department of Defense, U.S. Army. *Dictionary of United States Army Terms.* Army Regulation AR 310-25. Washington, DC: Headquarters, Department of the Army, 1986.

—**INTEROPERABILITY.** (1) Interoperability is the ability of systems, units, or forces to provide services to and accept services from other systems, units, or forces and to use the services exchanged to enable them to operate effectively together. (2) Interoperability is the condition achieved among communications-electronic systems or items of communications-electronic equipment when information or services can be exchanged directly and satisfactorily between them and/or their users. The degree of interoperability should be defined when referring to specific cases. (3) Interoperability is the capability of two or more items or components of equipment to perform essentially the same function or to complement each other in a system, regardless of the differences in technical characteristics and with negligible additional training of personnel. *See also:* Interoperation.

References

Department of Defense, U.S. Army. *Dictionary of United States Army Terms.* Army Regulation AR 310-25. Washington, DC: Headquarters, Department of the Army, 1986.

—**INTEROPERATION** is the use of interoperable systems, units, or forces.

References

Department of Defense, Joint Chiefs of Staff. *Department of Defense Dictionary of Military and Related Terms.* Washington, DC: GPO, 1986.

—**INTERPRETABILITY,** in intelligence imagery and photoreconnaissance, is the suitability of imagery for interpretation with respect to answering adequately the requirements of the customer. Interpretability is assessed in terms of quality and scale, according to the following criteria:

- **Poor**—denotes imagery that is unsuitable for interpretation to adaquately answer the customer's requirements concerning a given type of target.
- **Fair**—denotes imagery that is suitable for interpretation to answer customer requirements concerning a target but with only average detail.
- **Good**—denotes imagery that is suitable for interpretation to answer customer requirements concerning a target in considerable detail.
- **Excellent**—denotes imagery that is suitable for interpretation to answer customer requirements concerning a target in complete detail.

See also: Image.

References

Department of Defense, Joint Chiefs of Staff. *Department of Defense Dictionary of Military and Related Terms.* Washington, DC: GPO, 1986.

—**INTERPRETATION** is a general intelligence term for a process in the production step of the intelligence cycle in which the significance of information or intelligence information is weighted relative to the available body of knowledge. *See also:* Intelligence Cycle.

References

Department of Defense, Defense Intelligence College. *Glossary of Intelligence Terms and Definitions.* Washington, DC: DIC, 1987.

—**INTERROGATION** is the art of questioning and examining a source to obtain the maximum amount of usable information. The goal of any interrogation is to obtain usable and reliable information that meets the intelligence requirements of any echelon of command lawfully and quickly. The sources may be civilian internees, insurgents, enemy prisoners of war, defectors, refugees, displaced persons, and agents or sus-pected agents. Types of interrogations include the interview, the debriefing, and elicitation. A successful interrogation produces needed information that is timely, complete, clear, and accurate. It involves the interaction of two personalities, the source and the interrogator. Each contact between these two differs to some degree because of their individual characteristics and capabilities, and because the circumstances of each contact and the physical environment vary. *See also:* Intelligence.

References

Department of Defense, Joint Chiefs of Staff. *Department of Defense Dictionary of Military and Related Terms.* Washington, DC: GPO, 1986.

—**INTERROGATOR RESPONDER** are the components of identification, friend or foe, equipment that challenge and receive replies. *See also:* Identification, Friend or Foe.

References

Department of Defense, U.S. Army. *Dictionary of United States Army Terms.* Army Regulation AR 310-25. Washington, DC: Headquarters, Department of the Army, 1986.

—**INTERRUPTER** is a safety device in a fuze that prevents it from acting until the projectile has left the muzzle of the gun. *See also:* Fuze (Specify Type).

References

Department of Defense, U.S. Army. *Dictionary of United States Army Terms.* Army Regulation AR 310-25. Washington, DC: Headquarters, Department of the Army, 1986.

—**INTERSECTION** is a method of locating a point by plotting the azimuth to that point from two or more known fixed points. The intersection of these azimuths indicates the location of the point.

References

Department of Defense, U.S. Army. *Dictionary of United States Army Terms.* Army Regulation AR 310-25. Washington, DC: Headquarters, Department of the Army, 1986.

—**INTERSECTIONAL SERVICE** is a communications zone combat service support organization assigned the full responsibility within the communications zone for the performance of a designated function or service. It must operate across military boundaries, usually over long distances, and may extend its operations into the combat zone.

References
Department of Defense, U.S. Army. *Dictionary of United States Army Terms.* Army Regulation AR 310-25. Washington, DC: Headquarters, Department of the Army, 1986.

—**INTER-SERVICE EDUCATION** is military education provided by one Service to members of another Service. *See also:* Military Education, Military Training.

References
Department of Defense, Joint Chiefs of Staff. *Department of Defense Dictionary of Military and Related Terms.* Washington, DC: GPO, 1986.

—**INTER-SERVICE SCHOOL OR COURSE** is a school or course used by two or more Services or agencies and is administered by a coordinating Service or agency. It presents a curriculum developed in coordination with the participating (using) Services.

References
Department of Defense, U.S. Army. *Individual Military Education and Training.* Army Regulation AR 350-1. Washington, DC: Headquarters, Department of the Army, 1987.

—**INTER-SERVICE SUPPORT** is action by one military service or an element thereof to provide logistic and/or administrative support to another military service or an element thereof. Such action can be either recurring or nonrecurring, and on an installation, area, or worldwide basis. *See also:* International Logistic Support, Interservice Support Agreement, Support.

References
Department of Defense, U.S. Army. *The Infantry Rifle Company (Infantry, Airborne, Air Assault, Ranger).* Field Manual FM 7-10. Washington, DC: Headquarters, Department of the Army, 1982.

—**INTER-SERVICE SUPPORT AGREEMENT** is a document wherein the participants, to preclude any misunderstanding, state clearly in writing, the agreement for the provision of inter-service support that has been arrived at between the two activities involved, especially the obligations assumed by each and the rights granted to each.

References
Department of Defense, U.S. Army. *Dictionary of United States Army Terms.* Army Regulation AR 310-25. Washington, DC: Headquarters, Department of the Army, 1986.

—**INTER-SERVICE TRAINING** is military training provided by one service to members of another service. *See also:* Military Education and Military Training.

References
Department of Defense, Joint Chiefs of Staff. *Department of Defense Dictionary of Military and Related Terms.* Washington, DC: GPO, 1986.

—**INTER-SERVICE TRANSFER** is a transfer between uniformed services by a commissioned officer.

References
Department of Defense, U.S. Army. *Promotion of Officers on Active Duty.* Army Regulation AR 624-100. Washington, DC: Headquarters, Department of the Army, 1984.

—**INTERSERVICEABLE ITEM** is an item of materiel that has been identified for use by more than one military service.

References
Department of Defense, U.S. Army. *Dictionary of United States Army Terms.* Army Regulation AR 310-25. Washington, DC: Headquarters, Department of the Army, 1986.

—**INTERTHEATER SHIPMENTS** are shipments that move into or out of the theater through water or air terminals.

References
Department of Defense, U.S. Army. *Transportation Reference Data.* Field Manual FM 55-15. Washington, DC: Headquarters, Department of the Army, 1986.

—**INTERVAL.** (1) An interval is the space between adjacent individuals, ground vehicles, or units in a formation that are placed side by side, measured abreast. (2) An interval is the time lapse between photographic exposures. (3) At battery right or left, in artillery, an interval is the time between one gun firing and the next gun firing. Five seconds is the standard interval. (4) At rounds of fire for effect, in artillery, the interval is the time in seconds between successive rounds from each gun.

References
Department of Defense, U.S. Army. *Dictionary of United States Army Terms.* Army Regulation AR 310-25. Washington, DC: Headquarters, Department of the Army, 1986.

—**INTERVIEW-ORIENTED BACKGROUND IN-VESTIGATION (IBI)** is an investigation conducted by the Defense Investigative Service. It is the principal type of investigation conducted when a person requires a background investigation. In addition to an in-depth subject interview, an IBI includes a national agency check, the interview of three developed character references, three employment references with employment records checks, plus selective follow-up as required to verify unfavorable or resolve questionable information. *See also:* Background Investigation, National Agency Check.

References
Department of Defense, U.S. Army. *Counterintelligence.* Field Manual FM 34-60. Washington, DC: Headquarters, Department of the Army, 1985.

—**INTRALINE DISTANCE** is the minimum distance permitted between any two buildings within an explosives operating line.

References
Department of Defense, U.S. Army. *Dictionary of United States Army Terms.* Army Regulation AR 310-25. Washington, DC: Headquarters, Department of the Army, 1986.

—**INTRANSIT STRENGTH** applies to personnel who are accountable to the reporting organization and who are en route to or from the organization in a permanent change of station status.

References
Department of Defense, U.S. Army. *Dictionary of United States Army Terms.* Army Regulation AR 310-25. Washington, DC: Headquarters, Department of the Army, 1986.

—**INTRASERVICE SUPPORT** is an action on the part of one Department of the Army activity to provide logistic, medical, and/or administrative support to another Department of the Army activity on: (1) a recurring or nonrecurring basis; (2) an installation within the continental U.S. Army area, continental U.S.-wide, or worldwide basis; and (3) either a reimbursable or nonreimbursable basis. *See also:* Intraservice Support Agreement.

References
Department of Defense, U.S. Army. *Dictionary of United States Army Terms.* Army Regulation AR 310-25. Washington, DC: Headquarters, Department of the Army, 1986.

—**INTRASERVICE SUPPORT AGREEMENT** is a document wherein the participants to an intraservice support transaction, to preclude any misunderstanding, state clearly in writing, the arrangements that have been arrived at between the two activities involved, especially the obligations assumed by each and the rights granted to each.

References
Department of Defense, U.S. Army. *Dictionary of United States Army Terms.* Army Regulation AR 310-25. Washington, DC: Headquarters, Department of the Army, 1986.

—**INTRATHEATER SHIPMENTS** are movements of supplies or equipment originating and terminating within the same theater.

References
Department of Defense, U.S. Army. *Transportation Reference Data.* Field Manual FM 55-15. Washington, DC: Headquarters, Department of the Army, 1986.

—**INTRUSION** is the intentional insertion of radio signals into friendly transmissions to deceive or confuse the system operator.

References
Department of Defense, U.S. Army. *Operational Terms and Symbols.* Field Manual FM 101-5-1. Washington, DC: Headquarters, Department of the Army, 1985.

—**INTRUSION RESISTANT COMMUNICATIONS CABLE** is a cable designed to provide substantial physical protection and electrical isolation for the wire lines making up the information-carrying core. The protective measures used are devices that detect slight changes in the physical or electrical state of the cable and that provide visible or audible indications at a central control point of attempted intrusion. These are also known as alarmed cables.

References
Department of Defense, U.S. Army. *Dictionary of United States Army Terms.* Army Regulation AR 310-25. Washington, DC: Headquarters, Department of the Army, 1986.

—**INVENTORY CONTROL** is the phase of military logistics that includes managing, cataloging, requirements determinations, procurement, distribution, overhaul, and disposal of materiel. It is synonymous with materiel control, materiel management, inventory management, and supply management. *See also:* Inventory Control Point.

References
Department of Defense, Joint Chiefs of Staff. *Department of Defense Dictionary of Military and Related Terms.* Washington, DC: GPO, 1986.

—**INVENTORY CONTROL POINT** is an organizational unit or activity within the Department of Defense supply system assigned the primary responsibility for the materiel management of a group of items either for a particular Service or for the Defense Department as a whole. Materiel inventory management includes cataloging direction, requirements computation, procurement direction, distribution management, disposal direction, and, generally, rebuild direction.

References
Department of Defense, Joint Chiefs of Staff. *Department of Defense Dictionary of Military and Related Terms.* Washington, DC: GPO, 1986.

—**INVENTORY LOT** is a subgrouping of the total items in storage for the purpose of physical inventory. The lot is generally by federal supply class, a range of numbers within a federal supply class, or controlled inventory numbers.

References
Department of Defense, U.S. Army. *Dictionary of United States Army Terms.* Army Regulation AR 310-25. Washington, DC: Headquarters, Department of the Army, 1986.

—**INVENTORY RECONCILIATION** is a match between depot counts/custodial records and the accountable records to identify and adjust accountable records when they disagree with the physical count documents or custodial records.

References
Department of Defense, U.S. Army. *Dictionary of United States Army Terms.* Army Regulation AR 310-25. Washington, DC: Headquarters, Department of the Army, 1986.

—**INVENTORY TEMPORARILY IN USE** accounts for nonexpendable items of stock-fund-financed materiel (including materiel that has been obtained from the defense stock fund or a division of the army stock fund as consigned inventory) that is authorized for issue on a loan basis for short periods of time, after which the materiel will be returned to the supply source from which it was acquired.

References
Department of Defense, U.S. Army. *Dictionary of United States Army Terms.* Army Regulation AR 310-25. Washington, DC: Headquarters, Department of the Army, 1986.

—**INVERSION** is an increase of air temperature with an increase in height, with the ground being colder than the surrounding air. This condition usually occurs on clear or partially clear nights and early mornings until about one hour after sunrise, but can last longer. When stable conditions exist, there are no convection currents and, with wind speeds below five knots, little mechanical turbulence. Therefore stable conditions are the most favorable for ground release smoke. The upper extreme of this condition is termed the stable or inversion cap.

References
Department of Defense, U.S. Army. *Deliberate Smoke Operations.* Field Manual FM 3-50. Washington, DC: Headquarters, Department of the Army, 1984.

—**INVOLUNTARY ORDER OR RECALL TO ACTIVE DUTY** is the ordering or calling of individual members of the Army Reserve or retired Army personnel for full-time duty in the active military service of the United States without the members' consent.

References
Department of Defense, U.S. Army. *Dictionary of United States Army Terms.* Army Regulation 310-25. Washington, DC: Headquarters, Department of the Army, 1986.

—**IROQUOIS** is a light single-rotor helicopter used for cargo/personnel transport and attack helicopter support. Some versions are armed with machine guns and light air-to-ground rockets. Iroquois is designated UH-1. *See also:* Attack Helicopter.

References
Department of Defense, Joint Chiefs of Staff. *Department of Defense Dictionary of Military and Related Terms.* Washington, DC: GPO, 1986.

—**IRREGULAR FORCES** are armed individuals or groups who are not members of the regular armed forces, police, or other internal security forces.

References
Department of Defense, Joint Chiefs of Staff. *Department of Defense Dictionary of Military and Related Terms.* Washington, DC: GPO, 1986.

—**IRREGULAR OUTER EDGE** (LAND MINE WARFARE) consists of short mine strips laid in an irregular manner in front of a minefield facing the enemy to deceive it as to the type or extent of the minefield. Generally, the irregular outer edge is only used in minefields with buried mines. *See also:* Mine Warfare.

References

Department of Defense, Joint Chiefs of Staff. *Department of Defense Dictionary of Military and Related Terms.* Washington, DC: GPO, 1986.

—**IRREGULARITY** is a failure to comply with the letter or spirit of regulations, laws, and orders, or an improper exercise of authority beyond that which has been granted.

References

Department of Defense, U.S. Army. *Dictionary of United States Army Terms.* Army Regulation AR 310-25. Washington, DC: Headquarters, Department of the Army, 1986.

—**IRRITANT GAS CHAMBER** is a reasonably airtight room or enclosed space of sufficient size to conduct the protective mask exercises.

References

Department of Defense, U.S. Army. *Dictionary of United States Army Terms.* Army Regulation AR 310-25. Washington, DC: Headquarters, Department of the Army, 1986.

—**ISLOLEAD CURVE** is a curved line, on a chart or diagram, used to show how far ahead of a moving target a gun must be aimed to allow for the time that the projectile will take to reach the target. The isolead curve connects points of equal lead on a chart or diagram.

References

Department of Defense, U.S. Army. *Dictionary of United States Army Terms.* Army Regulation AR 310-25. Washington, DC: Headquarters, Department of the Army, 1986.

—**ISSUE COMMISSARY.** The official definition of an issue commissary is "the element of an installation that is responsible for acquiring, storing, issuing, selling, and accounting for subsistence supplies that are used for subsisting personnel who are authorized to subsist at government expense, and by activities and organizations authorized to purchase therefrom." Commissaries are found on many military bases. Similar to supermarkets, they are stocked with food and household supplies that are sold to military personnel and their families. They are subsidized by the government and the prices are therefore less than in commercial stores. Control is maintained by checking the customers' military identification card as they enter the commissary. In commissaries located in countries where there is an active black market, certain items (e.g., cigarettes and coffee) may be rationed. Under this procedure, the individual is issued a ration card, usually monthly, and is permitted to buy only a certain amount of a rationed item.

References

Department of Defense, U.S. Army. *Dictionary of United States Army Terms.* Army Regulation AR 310-25. Washington, DC: Headquarters, Department of the Army, 1986.

—**ISSUE PRIORITY GROUP** is a relative sequential grouping of priority designators used for assigning priority delivery dates and processing times.

References

Department of Defense, U.S. Army. *Dictionary of United States Terms.* Army Regulation AR 310-25. Washington, DC: Headquarters, Department of the Army, 1986.

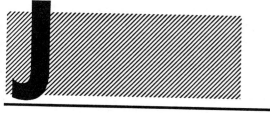

—**JAMMER** is an electronic device that intentionally introduces unwanted signals into a radio or receiver for the purpose of denying information. *See also:* Jammer Band (Width), Jamming, Jamming Effectiveness, Jamming Platform, Jamming Signal, Jamming Target.

References

Department of Defense, U.S. Army. *Intelligence and Electronic Warfare Operations.* Field Manual FM 34-1. Washington, DC: Headquarters, Department of the Army, 1987.

———. *Military Intelligence Battalion (Combat Electronic Warfare Intelligence) (Division).* Field Manual FM 34-10. Washington, DC: Headquarters, Department of the Army, 1981.

———. *Military Intelligence Battalion (CEWI) (Operations) (Corps).* Field Manual FM 34-21. Washington, DC: Headquarters, Department of the Army, 1982.

———. *Military Intelligence Company (Combat Electronic Warfare and Intelligence) (Armored Cavalry Regiment/Separate Brigade).* Field Manual FM 34-30. Washington, DC: Headquarters, Department of the Army, 1983.

———. *Military Intelligence Group (Combat Electronic Warfare and Intelligence) (Corps).* Field Manual FM 34-20. Washington, DC: Headquarters, Department of the Army, 1983.

—**JAMMER BAND** (WIDTH) is a band of frequency in which the output of the jammer is concentrated. *See also:* Jammer.

References

Department of Defense, U.S. Army. *Military Intelligence Battalion (Combat Electronic Warfare Intelligence) (Division).* Field Manual FM 34-10. Washington, DC: Headquarters, Department of the Army, 1981.

———. *Military Intelligence Battalion (CEWI) (Operations) (Corps).* Field Manual FM 34-21. Washington, DC: Headquarters, Department of the Army, 1982.

———. *Military Intelligence Company (Combat Electronic Warfare and Intelligence) (Armored Cavalry Regiment/Separate Brigade).* Field Manual FM 34-30. Washington, DC: Headquarters, Department of the Army, 1983.

—**JAMMING,** as defined by the Army, means "the deliberate radiation, reradiation, or reflection of electromagnetic energy with the object of impairing the use of electronic devices by the enemy." Jamming is an electronic countermeasure. *See also:* Jammer.

References

Department of Defense, U.S. Army. *Intelligence and Electronic Warfare Operations.* Field Manual FM 34-1. Washington, DC: Headquarters, Department of the Army, 1987.

———. *Military Intelligence Company (Combat Electronic Warfare and Intelligence) (Armored Cavalry Regiment/Separate Brigade).* Field Manual FM 34-30. Washington, DC: Headquarters, Department of the Army, 1983.

———. *Military Intelligence Battalion (Combat Electronic Warfare Intelligence) (Division).* Field Manual FM 34-10. Washington, DC: Headquarters, Department of the Army, 1981.

———. *Military Intelligence Battalion (CEWI) (Operations) (Corps).* Field Manual FM 34-21. Washington, DC: Headquarters, Department of the Army, 1982.

———. *Military Intelligence Group (Combat Electronic Warfare and Intelligence) (Corps).* Field Manual FM 34-20. Washington, DC: Headquarters, Department of the Army, 1983.

———. *Operational Terms and Symbols.* Field Manual FM 101-5-1. Washington, DC: Headquarters, Department of the Army, 1985.

—**JAMMING EFFECTIVENESS** is the percentage of information in a text message that is incorrectly received. *See also:* Jammer.

References

Department of Defense, U.S. Army. *Operational Terms and Symbols.* Field Manual FM 101-5-1. Washington, DC: Headquarters, Department of the Army, 1985.

—**JAMMING PLATFORM** is the vehicle or other source from which jamming emanates. *See also:* Jammer.

References

Department of Defense, U.S. Army. *Operational Terms and Symbols.* Field Manual FM 101-5-1. Washington, DC: Headquarters, Department of the Army, 1985.

—**JAMMING SIGNAL** is the electromagnetic wave that is propagated by a jammer to transmit energy to a communications or noncommunications receiver for interference purposes. *See also:* Jammer.

References
Department of Defense, U.S. Army. *Operational Terms and Symbols.* Field Manual FM 101-5-1. Washington, DC: Headquarters, Department of the Army, 1985.

—**JAMMING TARGET** is any receiving system or set of receiving systems that are intended for interference or jamming. *See also:* Jammer.

References
Department of Defense, U.S. Army. *Operational Terms and Symbols.* Field Manual FM 101-5-1. Washington, DC: Headquarters, Department of the Army, 1985.

—**JAN (JOINT ARMY, NAVY) GRID** is a joint Army-Navy grid system that covers the entire surface of the earth and has been adopted to afford security in referring to geographical positions. It is set up by prescribing the location of the origin and size of the grid squares, both in terms of latitude and longitude. There are twelve master areas, and special JAN grids that are based upon the above principle may be issued by the local authorities. JAN grids are usually used on Mercator projections.

References
Department of Defense, U.S. Army. *Dictionary of United States Army Terms.* Army Regulation AR 310-25. Washington, DC: Headquarters, Department of the Army, 1986.

—**JATO (JET-ASSISTED TAKEOFF) UNIT** is a takeoff in which a rocket motor unit is normally used to assist the initial action of the main propulsion plant.

References
Department of Defense, U.S. Army. *Dictionary of United States Army Terms.* Army Regulation AR 310-25. Washington, DC: Headquarters, Department of the Army, 1986.

—**JAZZ (ARMY AVIATION)** is an oral report which indicates that all members of a flight must monitor for important information that will follow and will not be repeated.

References
Department of Defense, U.S. Army. *Air-to-Air Combat.* Field Manual FM 1-107. Washington, DC: Headquarters, Department of the Army, 1984.

—**JCS (JOINT CHIEFS OF STAFF) EXERCISE PRO-GRAM** provides valuable wartime mission training to Army units. To the maximum extent possible, exercise force lists integrate active and reserve units according to CAPSTONE alignments. The participation of high priority reserve units is planned in conjunction with the Overseas Deployment for Training Program. *See also:* Exercise.

References
Department of Defense, National Defense University. *Joint Staff Officer's Guide, 1986.* Washington, DC: GPO, 1986.

Department of Defense, U.S. Army. *U.S. Army Policy Statement, 1988.* Washington, DC: Headquarters, Department of the Army, 1988.

—**JCS (JOINT CHIEFS OF STAFF)-COORDIN-ATED EXERCISE** is a minor exercise whose scheduling requires coordination by the Joint Chiefs of Staff because it involves the units or forces of more than one commander-in-chief, or agency. *See also:* Exercise.

References
Department of Defense, National Defense University. *Joint Staff Officer's Guide, 1986.* Washington, DC: GPO, 1986.

—**JCS (JOINT CHIEFS OF STAFF)-DIRECTED EXERCISE** is an exercise directed by a strategic mobility commander or major commander-in-chief and is of major interest to the Joint Chiefs of Staff. *See also:* Exercise.

References
Department of Defense, National Defense University. *Joint Staff Officer's Guide, 1986.* Washington, DC: GPO, 1986.

—**JINK (ARMY AVIATION)** is a maneuver, usually a series of S-turns, conducted by a pilot in order to break a lock-on or engagement by the enemy.

References
Department of Defense, U.S. Army. *Air-to-Air Combat.* Field Manual FM 1-107. Washington, DC: Headquarters, Department of the Army, 1984.

—**JOB ANALYSIS** is the collection analysis and organization of occupational data. It includes the separation of the work performed in a specific position into its duties and tasks to determine what the duties are, how and why they are performed, the skills that are required, and the physical and mental demands that the position requires.

References
Department of Defense, U.S. Army. *Dictionary of United States Army Terms*. Army Regulation AR 310-25. Washington, DC: Headquarters, Department of the Army, 1986.

—**JOB BOOK** is a book in which a noncommissioned officer supervisor records a soldier's ability to perform the tasks of a duty position as prescribed in the soldier's manual. The noncommissioned officer then can identify and plan for training needs to improve the soldier's performance.

References
Department of Defense, U.S. Army. *Army Forces Training*. Army Regulation AR 350-41. Washington, DC: Headquarters, Department of the Army, 1986.

————. *Organizational Maintenance Operations*. Field Manual FM 29-2. Washington, DC: Headquarters, Department of the Army, 1984.

—**JOB PERFORMANCE AID** is a package integrating various training products necessary to train to a level of competency in a particular job or duty position. Components are a Training Management Instruction Packet, training products appropriate to tasks of the duty positions, and materials and equipment needed to train in the tasks.

References
Department of Defense, U.S. Army. *Individual Military Education and Training*. Army Regulation AR 350-1. Washington, DC: Headquarters, U.S. Army, 1987.

—**JOINT** connotes activities, operations, or organizations, in which elements of more than one service of the same nation participate. When all services are not involved, the participating services are identified (e.g., Joint Army-Navy). *See also:* Combined.

References
Department of Defense, National Defense University. *Joint Staff Officer's Guide, 1986*. Washington, DC: GPO, 1986.

—**JOINT AIR ATTACK TEAM (JAAT)** is a combination of U.S. Army helicopters and U.S. Air Force close air support aircraft operating together to destroy enemy armored and mechanized forces. *See also:* Attack Helicopter.

References
Department of Defense, U.S. Army. *Attack Helicopter Operations*. Field Manual FM 17-50. Washington, DC: Headquarters, Department of the Army, 1984.

————. *Operational Terms and Symbols*. Field Manual FM 101-5-1. Washington, DC: Headquarters, Department of the Army, 1985.

—**JOINT AIRBORNE TRAINING** is training operations and exercises involving airborne and appropriate troop carrier units. This training includes (1) air delivery of personnel and equipment; (2) assault operations by airborne troops and/or air transportable units; (3) loading exercises and local orientation flights of short duration; and (4) maneuvers and exercises as agreed upon by the services concerned or as authorized by the Joint Chiefs of Staff.

References
Department of Defense, National Defense University. *Joint Staff Officer's Guide, 1986*. Washington, DC: GPO, 1986.

—**JOINT AMPHIBIOUS OPERATION** is an amphibious operation conducted by significant elements of two or more services. *See also:* Amphibious Operation, Joint Amphibious Task Force.

References
Department of Defense, National Defense University. *Joint Staff Officer's Guide, 1986*. Washington, DC: GPO, 1986.

—**JOINT AMPHIBIOUS TASK FORCE (JATF),** in amphibious warfare, means a temporary grouping of units of two or more military services under a single commander. The task force is organized to accomplish an amphibious landing assault on enemy shores.

References
Department of Defense, National Defense University. *Joint Staff Officer's Guide, 1986*. Washington, DC: GPO, 1986.

—**JOINT AREA PETROLEUM OFFICE** is a component staff agency that has been established to assist the Joint Petroleum Office in compiling requirements for fuels and lubricants. *See also:* Joint Petroleum Office.

References
Department of Defense, U.S. Army. *Dictionary of United States Army Terms*. Army Regulation AR 310-25. Washington, DC: Headquarters, Department of the Army, 1986.

—**JOINT ARMY-NAVY-AIR FORCE PUBLICA-TIONS (JANAPs)** are a series of publications produced by supporting agencies of the Joint Chiefs of Staff and are intended for distribution within the Army, Navy, and Air Force.

References

Department of Defense, National Defense University. *Joint Staff Officer's Guide, 1986.* Washington, DC: GPO, 1986.

—**JOINT BUS MILITARY AGREEMENT** is similar to the Joint Military Passenger Agreement and provides for a percentage reduction in bus fares and special services for official travel by members of the Department of Defense. This agreement is negotiated annually. *See also:* Joint Military Passenger Agreement.

References

Department of Defense, U.S. Army. *Dictionary of United States Army Terms.* Army Regulation AR 310-25. Washington, DC: Headquarters, Department of the Army, 1986.

—**JOINT CHIEFS OF STAFF (JCS)** is a staff within the Department of Defense that consists of the Chairman, who is the presiding officer of the staff but has no vote; the Chief of Staff, United States Army; the Chief of Naval Operations; and the Chief of Staff, United States Air Force. The Joint Chiefs of Staff are the principal military advisers to the President, the National Security Council, and the Secretary of Defense. *See also:* Joint Deployment Agency, Joint Deployment Community, Joint Deployment System, Joint Doctrine, Joint Force Memorandum, Joint Intelligence, Joint Operational Intelligence Agency, Joint Operations Center, Joint Staff, Joint Strategic Capabilities Plan, Joint Strategic Objectives Plan, Joint Strategic Planning Document, Joint Strategic Planning System, Joint Task Force, JOPS Publications.

References

Department of Defense, National Defense University. *Joint Staff Officer's Guide, 1986.* Washington, DC: GPO, 1986.

—**JOINT COMMON USER ITEM** is an item of an interchangeable nature that is in common use by two or more services of a nation.

References

Department of Defense, Joint Chiefs of Staff. *Department of Defense Dictionary of Military and Related Terms.* Washington, DC: GPO, 1986.

—**JOINT COMMUNICATIONS NETWORK** is the aggregation of all the joint communications systems in a theater. It includes the joint multichannel trunking and switching system and the joint command and control communications systems.

References

Department of Defense, Joint Chiefs of Staff. *Department of Defense Dictionary of Military and Related Terms.* Washington, DC: GPO, 1986.

—**JOINT DEPLOYMENT AGENCY (JDA)** is the activity that supports the Joint Chiefs of Staff and supported commanders in planning for and executing deployments. *See also:* Joint Chiefs of Staff.

References

Department of Defense, National Defense University. *Joint Staff Officer's Guide, 1986.* Washington, DC: GPO, 1986.

—**JOINT DEPLOYMENT COMMUNITY (JDC)** consists of the headquarters, commands, and agencies involved in training, preparing, moving, receiving, employing, supporting, and sustaining military forces that are assigned or committed to a theater of operations or an objective area. It usually consists of the Organization of the Joint Chiefs of Staff, the services, certain service major commands, Unified and Specified Commands (and their service component commands), transportation operating agencies, the Joint Deployment Agency, joint task forces (as applicable), the Defense Logistics Agency, and other defense agencies (e.g., the Defense Intelligence Agency) that may be appropriate to a given scenario. *See also:* Joint Chiefs of Staff.

References

Department of Defense, National Defense University. *Joint Staff Officer's Guide, 1986.* Washington, DC: GPO, 1986.

—**JOINT DEPLOYMENT SYSTEM (JDS)** is a system that consists of personnel, procedures, directives, communications systems, and electronic data processing systems needed to directly support time-sensitive planning and execution and to complement peacetime deliberate planning. The JDS is specifically coordinated for time-sensitive deployment planning and execution, and provides senior decision makers at the National Command Authority, Joint Chiefs of Staff, Commanders-in-Chief, and services with a single source for deployment management information during periods of crisis. *See also:* Joint Chiefs of Staff.

References

Department of Defense, National Defense University. *Joint Staff Officer's Guide, 1986.* Washington, DC: GPO, 1986.

Department of Defense, U.S. Army. *U.S. Army Policy Statement, 1988.* Washington, DC: Headquarters, U.S. Army, 1988.

—**JOINT DOCTRINE** consists of the fundamental principles that guide the use of forces of two or more services of the same nation in a coordinated action toward a common objective. It is ratified by all four services and may be promulgated by the Joint Chiefs of Staff. *See also:* Combined Doctrine, Joint Chiefs of Staff, Multi-Service Doctrine.

References

Department of Defense, National Defense University. *Joint Staff Officer's Guide, 1986.* Washington, DC: GPO, 1986.

—**JOINT EXERCISE** is an exercise involving the forces of more than one service. *See also:* Exercise.

References

Department of Defense, National Defense University. *Joint Staff Officer's Guide, 1986.* Washington, DC: GPO, 1986.

Department of Defense, U.S. Army. *Army Exercises.* Army Regulation AR 350-28. Washington, DC: Headquarters, Department of the Army, 1985.

—**JOINT FORCE** is a generic term applied to a force composed of significant elements of the Army, Navy, Marine Corps, or Air Force, or any two of these services. The joint force operates under a single commander who is authorized to exercise united command or operational control.

References

Department of Defense, National Defense University. *Joint Staff Officer's Guide, 1986.* Washington, DC: GPO, 1986.

—**JOINT FORCE MEMORANDUM (JFM)** is a document prepared annually by the Joint Chiefs of Staff and submitted to the Secretary of Defense. It provides recommendations concerning the Joint Force Program within the fiscal guidance that has been provided by the Secretary of Defense. *See also:* Joint Chiefs of Staff.

References

Department of Defense, National Defense University. *Joint Staff Officer's Guide, 1986.* Washington, DC: GPO, 1986.

—**JOINT INTELLIGENCE** is a general intelligence term that has two meanings. (1) In the military context, joint intelligence is intelligence produced by more than one military service of the same nation. (2) In the context of the Intelligence Community, joint intelligence is intelligence produced by intelligence organizations of more than one country. *See also:* Joint Chiefs of Staff.

References

Department of Defense, Defense Intelligence College. *Glossary of Intelligence Terms and Definitions.* Washington, DC: DIC, 1987.

Department of Defense, National Defense University. *Joint Staff Officer's Guide, 1986.* Washington, DC: GPO, 1986.

—**JOINT MANPOWER PROGRAM (JMP)** is the document that reflects an activity's mission, functions, organization, current and projected manpower needs, and, when applicable, its required mobilization augmentation. A recommended joint manpower program also identifies and justifies any changes proposed by the commander or director of a joint activity for the next five fiscal years.

References

Department of Defense, National Defense University. *Joint Staff Officer's Guide, 1986.* Washington, DC: GPO, 1986.

—**JOINT MEDICAL REGULATING OFFICE** is the unified command office that regulates control over the movement of patients between various Armed Forces medical treatment facilities. *See also:* Medical Treatment.

References

Department of Defense, U.S. Army. *Support Operations: Echelons Above Corps.* Field Manual FM 100-16. Washington, DC: Headquarters, Department of the Army, 1986.

—**JOINT MILITARY AIR TRANSPORTATION AGREEMENT** is similar to the Joint Military Passenger Agreement and provides for a percentage reduction in air fares and for special services for the official travel of members of the Department of Defense. This agreement is negotiated annually. *See also:* Joint Military Passenger Agreement.

References

Department of Defense, U.S. Army. *Dictionary of United States Army Terms.* Army Regulation AR 310-25. Washington, DC: Headquarters, Department of the Army, 1986.

—JOINT MILITARY PASSENGER AGREEMENT is negotiated annually between the railroads and the Department of Defense and makes provisions for a percentage reduction in rail fares and special services for the official travel of members of the Department of Defense.

References

Department of Defense, U.S. Army. *Dictionary of United States Army Terms.* Army Regulation AR 310-25. Washington, DC: Headquarters, Department of the Army, 1986.

—JOINT OPERATION is an operation carried out by two or more armed forces of the United States. *See also:* Combined Operation, Joint Operations Area, Joint Operations Graphic (Air), Joint Operations Graphic (Ground), Joint Operations Graphics.

References

Department of Defense, National Defense University. *Joint Staff Officer's Guide, 1986.* Washington, DC: GPO, 1986.

Department of Defense, U.S. Army. *Operational Terms and Symbols.* Field Manual FM 101-5-1. Washington, DC: Headquarters, Department of the Army, 1985.

—JOINT OPERATIONAL INTELLIGENCE AGENCY (JOIA) is an intelligence agency in which two or more services are integrated to furnish the operational intelligence that is essential to a commander of a joint force and to supplement the intelligence available from the subordinate forces of the command. *See also:* Joint Chiefs of Staff.

References

Department of Defense, National Defense University. *Joint Staff Officer's Guide, 1986.* Washington, DC: GPO, 1986.

—JOINT OPERATIONS AREA (JOA) is the portion of an area of conflict in which a joint force commander conducts military operations pursuant to an assigned mission and the administration that is incident to such military operations.

References

Department of Defense, National Defense University. *Joint Staff Officer's Guide, 1986.* Washington, DC: GPO, 1986.

—JOINT OPERATIONS CENTER (JOC) is a facility manned by personnel from more than one armed service and is a component of a joint force commander's headquarters. It is established for planning, monitoring, and guiding the execution of the commander's decisions. *See also:* Joint Chiefs of Staff.

References

Department of Defense, National Defense University. *Joint Staff Officer's Guide, 1986.* Washington, DC: GPO, 1986.

—JOINT OPERATIONS GRAPHIC (JOG) (AIR) series is prepared for air use and contains detailed information on air facilities (e.g., radio ranges, runway lengths, and landing surfaces). Elevations and contours on the JOG (air) are given in feet.

References

Department of Defense, U.S. Army. *Map Reading.* Field Manual FM 21-26. Washington, DC: Headquarters, Department of the Army, 1969.

—JOINT OPERATIONS GRAPHIC (GROUND) series is prepared for use by ground units, and only stable or permanent air facilities are identified. Elevations and contours are located in the same positions as on the air version, but are given in meters.

References

Department of Defense, U.S. Army. *Map Reading.* Field Manual FM 21-26. Washington, DC: Headquarters, Department of the Army, 1969.

—JOINT OPERATIONS GRAPHICS (JOGs) are based upon the format of the standard 1:250,000 scale of military topographic maps and contain additional information that is needed in today's joint air-ground operational environment.

References

Department of Defense, U.S. Army. *Map Reading.* Field Manual FM 21-26. Washington, DC: Headquarters, Department of the Army, 1969.

—JOINT OPERATIONAL PLANNING SYSTEM (JOPS). Operation plans for possible deployment and use of U.S. military forces overseas are normally prepared in peacetime using a deliberate planning process. When situations become sufficiently grave for the United States to consider using military force, existing plans are adjusted or new courses of action are considered to meet time-sensitive requirements. The Military Planning System that is used to support joint military operation planning and crisis management is the JOPS. The objective is the timely development of adequate, suitable, and feasible operation plans and orders by the Joint Chiefs of Staff, the Commanders of the Unified and Specified Commands, and the Joint Task Force Commanders.

To meet this objective, JOPS accomplishes the following: (1) it establishes the joint planning process; (2) it prescribes standard formats and minimum content; (3) it provides standard data files and common functional programs; (4) it provides for the effective refinement and review of operation plans, and review of noncombatant evacuation operation plans, continuity of operations plans, and disaster relief plans that are submitted to fulfill the assigned planning tasks that have been assigned or approved by the Joint Chiefs of Staff; (5) it provides for testing the transportation feasibility of operation plans; (6) it provides for reporting and processing shortfalls and limiting factors; and (7) it provides procedures for the timely conversion of operation plans into operation orders, when applicable, in a time of national crisis.

Planning is a continuous process. It begins when a task is assigned and ends only when the requirements for the plan are cancelled or when the plan is implemented. Planning is accomplished by following a deliberate series of steps that lead a commander and his planning staff step-by-step through the planning process. Using the deliberate planning process, the staff will either produce an operational plan in concept format or an operation plan in complete format, depending on the level of planning detail that is required by the Joint Chiefs of Staff.

When an operation plan is conceived, it is based upon an existing or an expected situation and, as the plan is being developed, it is built with forces that are designated for the operation. A plan remains current only as long as the conditions at the time of planning remain the same. Consequently, a plan cannot be "put on the shelf" to gather dust after it has been produced. It must be reexamined periodically to insure that the information it contains is still current and that it still satisfies the original need. Maintaining the currency of the plan is the responsibility of the commander who prepared it, but new or revised intelligence is submitted by various members of the planning community. Plan maintenance is coordinated by the Joint Deployment Agency. The Joint Chiefs of Staff require an annual review of all plans under their

direction, and they can direct the revision of any plan on an ad hoc basis. Maintenance and review of existing plans is normally the most time-consuming task of the staff officer. Even though an existing concept plan or operation plan is current, it must be modified at the time of implementation. At this time, the plan is transformed into an operation order using the crisis action system, a time-sensitive planning process that tailors, expands, and further develops an existing plan.

Deliberate planning begins when a commander receives joint strategic capabilities plan tasking, and it ends when the plan and its supporting plans have been completed and approved. The joint strategic capabilities plan initiates the planning process, which normally consists of five phases:

- **Phase I—Initiating Phase.** Planning tasks are assigned and major combat forces and strategic transportation forces are identified for planning purposes.
- **Phase II—Concept Development Phase.** Planning guidance is issued, courses of military action are proposed and tested, information and intelligence on factors that could affect the mission are collected and analyzed, and a concept of operations is developed, reviewed, approved, and distributed.
- **Phase III—Plan Development Phase.** All forces are selected and time-phased, support requirements are determined, and strategic transportation capabilities are tested. All data produced and collected are entered into the plan's time-phased force and deployment data computer file. This computer file and the written portions of the plan, which are documented during this phase, make up the operation plan in complete format.
- **Phase IV—Plan Review Phase.** Plans are submitted to the tasking authority, formally reviewed, and approved for implementation.
- **Phase V—Supporting Plans Phase.** All required supporting plans are completed, documented in the appropriate format, and submitted to and approved by the reviewing authority.

See also: Joint Chiefs of Staff.

References
Department of Defense, National Defense University. *Joint Staff Officer's Guide, 1986.* Washington, DC: GPO, 1986.

Department of Defense, U.S. Army. *Planning Logistics Support for Military Operations.* Field Manual FM 701-58. Washington, DC: Headquarters, Department of the Army, 1987.

————. *Staff Organization and Operations.* Field Manual FM 101-5. Washington, DC: Headquarters, Department of the Army, 1984.

—**JOINT PETROLEUM OFFICE** is a theater staff agency that has been established in major geographic areas or theaters of operations to compile the requirements of fuels and lubricants for all services located in those areas.

References
Department of Defense, U.S. Army. *Dictionary of United States Army Terms.* Army Regulation AR 310-25. Washington, DC: Headquarters, Department of the Army, 1986.

—**JOINT PURCHASE** is a method of purchasing in which purchases of the same item by two or more departments are made by an activity that has been jointly established, staffed, and financed by them for that purpose. *See also:* Joint Common User Item.

References
Department of Defense, Joint Chiefs of Staff. *Department of Defense Dictionary of Military and Related Terms.* Washington, DC: GPO, 1986.

—**JOINT RESCUE COORDINATION CENTER** is an installation staffed by supervisory personnel from all participating services and that possesses sufficient facilities to direct and coordinate all available search and rescue facilities within a specified area.

References
Department of Defense, Joint Chiefs of Staff. *Department of Defense Dictionary of Military and Related Terms.* Washington, DC: GPO, 1986.

—**JOINT SCHOOL OR COURSE** is organized training or instruction used by two or more services and has a joint faculty.

References
Department of Defense, National Defense University. *Joint Staff Officer's Guide, 1986.* Washington, DC: GPO, 1986.

Department of Defense, U.S. Army. *Individual Military Education and Training.* Army Regulation AR 350-1. Washington, DC: Headquarters, Department of the Army, 1983.

—**JOINT SERVICING** is the function performed by a jointly staffed and financed activity in support of two or more military services. *See also:* Servicing.

References
Department of Defense, Joint Chiefs of Staff. *Department of Defense Dictionary of Military and Related Terms.* Washington, DC: GPO, 1986.

—**JOINT STAFF.** (1) A joint staff is the staff of a commander of a unified or specified command, or of a joint task force, that includes members from the several services that make up the force. These members should be assigned in a way that allows the commander to understand the tactics, techniques, capabilities, needs, and limitations of the component parts of the force. The positions on the staff should be divided so that service representation and influence generally reflect the service composition of the force. (2) The Joint Staff is the staff of the Joint Chiefs of Staff that was provided for under the National Security Act of 1947, as amended. *See also:* Joint Chiefs of Staff.

References
Department of Defense, National Defense University. *Joint Staff Officer's Guide, 1986.* Washington, DC: GPO, 1986.

—**JOINT STRATEGIC CAPABILITIES PLAN (JSCP)** is a plan that provides Joint Chiefs of Staff guidance to the commanders of the Unified and Specified Commands and the chiefs of the military services. It is a short-range plan prepared by the J-5, Joint Chiefs of Staff and based upon the joint intelligence estimate for planning, projected forces available, and subsequent Secretary of Defense guidance. It is divided into two volumes. Volume I is entitled *Concepts, Tasks, and Planning Guidance,* and Volume II is *Forces.* It also has fourteen supporting annexes:

Annex	Title
A	Intelligence
B	Logistics
C	Nuclear
D	Psychological Operations
E	Unconventional Warfare
F	Chemical Warfare; Nuclear, Biological and Chemical Defense; Riot Control Agents; and Herbicides
G	Mapping, Charting, and Geodesy
H	Nuclear Weapons Damage Considerations; Civil Defense; Recovery; and Reconstitution of CONUS

I	Communications and
	Electronics
J	Mobility
K	Military Deception
L	Civil Affairs
M	Electronic Warfare
N	Mobilization

The JSCP, which is reviewed and published annually in March, is a document that is critical to the commanders of the Unified and Specified Commands and to the services because it describes the major forces that will be available for planning purposes. Additionally, it assigns tasks, provides planning guidance for the development of operation plans to accomplish those tasks, and gives planning guidance to the services for support of the Unified and Specified Commands in the execution of their assigned tasks. The JSCP also includes a section that presents the military objectives, the strategic concepts, and the national strategy for employing current forces.

The JSCP tasking is based upon the capabilities of available forces, intelligence reports, and guidance by the Secretary of Defense. It directs the development of operational plans to support national security objectives by assigning tasks to the Unified and Specified Commanders. This document initiates the Joint Operational Planning System. *See also:* Joint Chiefs of Staff, Joint Operational Planning System.

References

Department of Defense, National Defense University. *Joint Staff Officer's Guide, 1986.* Washington, DC: GPO, 1986.

—**JOINT STRATEGIC OPERATIONS PLAN (JSOP),** is a plan that is prepared annually and provides the advice of the Joint Chiefs of Staff to the President and the Secretary of Defense on the military strategy and force objectives that are necessary for attaining the national security objectives of the United States. In addition to recommendations on major forces, it includes the rationale supporting the forces and assessment of associated risks, costs and manpower estimates, and other supporting data. The JSOP is published in two volumes: *Strategy* (Volume I); *Analysis and Force Tabulations* (Volume II). *See also:* Joint Chiefs of Staff.

References

Department of Defense, National Defense University. *Joint Staff Officer's Guide, 1986.* Washington, DC: GPO, 1986.

—**JOINT STRATEGIC PLANNING DOCUMENT (JSPD)** is one of seven documents listed under joint strategic planning system, that make up the system. The JSPD conveys to the President, the National Security Council, and the Secretary of Defense the Joint Chiefs of Staff position on the military strategy and force structure that are required to support the national security objectives. It is the basis of major policy discussion with the Secretary of Defense and is timed to precede the publication of the Defense Guidance. It is published in two volumes: JPSDA I, *Strategy and Force Planning Guidance*, provides Joint Chiefs of Staff views on national defense objectives, policies, strategy, and planning for the mid-range period. It addresses previous versions of the defense guidance, provides Joint Chiefs of Staff advice on national defense matters, and contains a recommended national military strategy. Volume I consists of (1) military objectives; (2) Joint Chiefs of Staff threat appraisal; (3) military strategy; and (4) force planning guidance to the commanders-in-chief and the services.

The second volume is JPSDA II, *Analysis and Force Requirements*. It is force-oriented and contains Joint Chiefs of Staff views on the military requirements that must be met to support national objectives and to execute the stated national strategy with a reasonable degree of success. It is derived from commander-in-chief and service inputs, and assesses the capabilities and associated risks of the programmed force against the planning force and makes appropriate planning recommendations to the Secretary of Defense. The volume also contains risk-reduction measures, since the resources needed to achieve the planning force are usually not available and the programmed force therefore has less capability to execute the national military strategy. The volume also supports the planning, programming and budgeting system with Joint Chiefs of Staff advice. In addition to the basic volume, there are annexes that provide military assessments and advice in the following functional areas:

Annex	Title
A	Intelligence
B	Nuclear
C	Command, Control and
	Communications
D	Research and Development
E	Mapping, Charting and
	Geodesy
F	Manpower and Personnel

The JSPD is noteworthy for several reasons. First, it provides the Secretary of Defense, the National Security Council, and the President with Joint Chiefs of Staff advice on U.S. policy, national military strategy, and force recommendations. Second, it establishes a Joint Chiefs of Staff position as a reference for Presidential and National Security Council-directed actions. Third, it provides Joint Chiefs of Staff recommendations to the Office of the Secretary of Defense that influences the development of the Defense Guidance. Fourth, it includes recommendations for risk-reduction measures in respect to which mission or program areas should receive emphasis if additional funds become available. Finally, it requires commander-in-chief and service involvement in its development. *See also:* Joint Chiefs of Staff.

References

Department of Defense, National Defense University. *Joint Staff Officer's Guide, 1986*. Washington, DC: GPO, 1986.

—JOINT STRATEGIC PLANNING SYSTEM (JSPS)

is the means by which the Joint Chiefs of Staff give military advice to the President and the Secretary of Defense; establish the strategic basis for the Secretary of Defense's guidance; develop the guidance and allot forces for contingency planning and operations in the near term; and develop the continuity necessary for the preparation of the next Joint Chiefs of Staff cycle. Many of the system's estimates are produced by the Directorate for Estimates, Defense Intelligence Agency.

The Joint Chiefs of Staff are charged by the National Security Act of 1947 with preparing strategic plans and for providing for the strategic direction of U.S. Armed Forces. The Joint Chiefs of Staff use a series of documents that make up the JSPS in order to accomplish their strategic planning responsibilities. The combination of all these documents and their interrelationships constitute the framework for the JSPS.

The JSPS consists of seven documents:
- The Joint Long-Range Strategic Appraisal;
- The Joint Intelligence Estimate for Planning;
- The Intelligence Priorities for Strategic Planning;
- The Joint Strategic Planning Document;
- The Joint Strategic Planning Document Supporting Analysis;
- The Joint Program Assessment Memo-

randum; and
- The Joint Security Assistance Memorandum.

The publication dates are contingent on the program/budget review schedule, which is published annually by the Office of the Secretary of Defense. *See also:* Joint Chiefs of Staff.

References

Department of Defense, National Defense University. *Joint Staff Officer's Guide, 1986*. Washington, DC: GPO, 1986.

Department of Defense, U.S. Army. *Planning Logistics Support for Military Operations*. Field Manual FM 701-58. Washington, DC: Headquarters, Department of the Army, 1987.

—JOINT SUPPRESSION OF ENEMY AIR DEFENSES (J-SEAD)

increases the overall effectiveness of friendly air-land operations. The two types of J-SEAD are campaign and localized.

The theater air commander conducts the theaterwide J-SEAD operation against specific surface-to-air defense systems. The locations of most campaign targets dictate this. However, Army surface-to-air weapons complement these efforts. More than one J-SEAD operation may be necessary during a campaign.

Localized J-SEAD operations attack specific targets or support airborne, air-mobile, or other air operations. Battalions and larger Army units plan localized J-SEAD operations to protect friendly aircraft and to maximize the effect of air support. Such operations normally involve jammers. suppressive fires, and passive measures (e.g., camouflage or deception) to degrade the effects of enemy air defenses. Localized J-SEAD operations can use field artillery, attack helicopters, direct fire weapons, and electronic warfare.

References

Department of Defense, U.S. Army. *Attack Helicopter Operations*. Field Manual FM 17-50. Washington, DC: Headquarters, Department of the Army, 1984.

———. *Operations*. Field Manual FM 100-5. Washington, DC: Headquarters, Department of the Army, 1986.

—JOINT SURVEILLANCE AND TARGET ATTACK RADAR SYSTEM (Joint STARS)

is a radar system that locates and tracks moving targets at extended ranges on the battlefield. It can provide target location updates for indirect fire artillery and in-flight guidance that is required for the longer range missiles. It provides the ground commander with real-time moving target data from Air Force platforms in a common secure data link format.

References

Weapons Systems: U.S. Army, Navy, and Air Force Directory, 1986- 1988. Washington, DC: DCP, 1986.

—**JOINT TABLE OF ALLOWANCES (JTA)** is a document that authorizes end-items of materiel for units that are operated jointly by two or more military assistance advisory groups or missions.

References

Department of Defense, National Defense University. *Joint Staff Officer's Guide, 1986.* Washington, DC: GPO, 1986.

—**JOINT TABLE OF DISTRIBUTION (JTD)** is a manpower document that identifies the positions and enumerates the spaces that have been approved for each organizational element for a specific fiscal year (authorization year), and the spaces that have been accepted for planning and programming purposes for the four subsequent fiscal years (program years). *See also:* Joint Manpower Program.

References

Department of Defense, Joint Chiefs of Staff. *Department of Defense Dictionary of Military and Related Terms.* Washington, DC: GPO, 1986.

—**JOINT TACTICAL INFORMATION DISTRIBUTION SYSTEM (JTIDS)** is an intelligence term used on the joint intelligence and national level to describe a tri-service (Army, Navy, and Air Force) system that provides jam resistance and communication, navigation, and identification capabilities in the tactical intelligence environment. To enhance military operations, the JTIDS capabilities include pseudo-noise, nodeless information distribution, high data rate, frequency hopping, and crypto-secure communications.

References

Department of Defense, National Defense University. *Joint Staff Officer's Guide, 1986.* Washington, DC: GPO, 1986.

—**JOINT TARGET LIST (JTL)** is a consolidated list of selected targets considered to have a military significance in the joint operations area.

References

Department of Defense, Joint Chiefs of Staff. *Department of Defense Dictionary of Military and Related Terms.* Washington, DC: GPO, 1986.

—**JOINT TASK FORCE (JTF)** is an intelligence term used on the joint intelligence and national level to describe a force composed of personnel from the Army, Navy, Air Force, or Marine Corps (at least two services) that has been designated as such by the Secretary of Defense or a commander of a Unified Command, a Specified Command, or an existing task force. *See also:* Joint Chiefs of Staff.

References

Department of Defense, National Defense University. *Joint Staff Officer's Guide, 1986.* Washington, DC: GPO, 1986.

Department of Defense, U.S. Army. *Operations.* Field Manual FM 100-5. Washington, DC: Headquarters, Department of the Army, 1986.

———. *Operational Terms and Symbols.* Field Manual FM 101-5-1. Washington, DC: Headquarters, Department of the Army, 1985.

—**JOINT TRAINING** is training in which elements of more than one service of the same nation participate. *See also:* Joint Training Exercises, Joint Training Procedures.

References

Department of Defense, U.S. Army. *Army Forces Training.* Army Regulation AR 350-41. Washington, DC: Headquarters, Department of the Army, 1986.

—**JOINT TRAINING EXERCISES (JTXs)** involve two or more services of the U.S. Armed Forces. *See also:* Joint Training.

References

Department of Defense, U.S. Army. *How to Conduct Training Exercises.* Field Manual FM 25-4. Washington, DC: Headquarters, Department of the Army, 1984.

—**JOINT TRAINING PROCEDURES** are measures that have been agreed upon jointly by the service agencies charged with developing doctrine involving more than one service. Such procedures may provide the basis for joint doctrine.

References

Department of Defense, U.S. Army. *Dictionary of United States Army Terms.* Army Regulation AR 310-25. Washington, DC: Headquarters, Department of the Army, 1986.

—**JOINT UNCONVENTIONAL WARFARE COMMAND/JOINT UNCONVENTIONAL WARFARE TASK FORCE (JUWC/JUWTF)** is a force composed of commando-like forces from two or more services that is constituted by the Secretary of Defense or by the commander of a Unified or Specified Command, or an existing joint task force.

References

Department of Defense, U.S. Army. *Operational Terms and Symbols.* Field Manual FM 101-5-1. Washington, DC: Headquarters, Department of the Army, 1985.

—**JOINT U.S. CONTINGENCY OPERATIONS** occur when a joint U.S. force deploys without allies. This situation assumes that no agreements exist, support for the industrial base and transportation system is unknown or questionable, technical expertise is limited, and an unskilled labor pool may be available in the host nation. Effective agreements can reduce the support that is required to be deployed to support U.S. forces for the first 60 days.

References

Department of Defense, U.S. Army. *Civil Affairs Operations.* Field Manual FM 41-10. Washington, DC: Headquarters, Department of the Army, 1985.

—**JOINT USER TESTING** is testing in which the Army participates with another service. These tests are conducted to evaluate Army systems or concepts having an interface with or requiring a test environment of another service, or concepts of another service that require testing in an Army environment.

References

Department of Defense, U.S. Army. *Dictionary of United States Army Terms.* Army Regulation AR 310-25. Washington, DC: Headquarters, Department of the Army, 1986.

—**JOINT ZONE** (AIR, LAND OR SEA) is an area that has been established for the purpose of permitting friendly surface, air, and subsurface forces to operate simultaneously.

References

Department of Defense, Joint Chiefs of Staff. *Department of Defense Dictionary of Military and Related Terms.* Washington, DC: GPO, 1986.

—**JOPS (JOINT OPERATIONAL PLANNING SYSTEM) PUBLICATIONS.** The JOPS is published in four volumes: Volume I is unclassified and provides guidance and administrative procedures for developing, coordinating, disseminating, reviewing, and approving joint plans for conducting military operations; Volume II is classified and provides planning guidance for functional areas; Volume III is unclassified and describes the worldwide military command and control system (referred to as JOPS III, it supports the planning of joint operations); and Volume IV is unclassified and describes the crisis action system that provides guidance and procedures for evaluating operations plans or other courses of action involving the use of military force and for executing planning for the selected course of action during emergency and time-sensitive situations. *See also:* Joint Chiefs of Staff.

References

Department of Defense, U.S. Army. *Operations.* Field Manual FM 100-5. Washington, DC: Headquarters, Department of the Army, 1986.

—**JOURNAL.** (1) A journal, in the Army tactical intelligence context, is a permanent, chronological record of each message and document that enters a counter-signals intelligence section. It provides a complete compilation of all incoming reports for the purpose of future recovery, which can be used for cross-referencing. It covers a specified time (i.e., usually a 24-hour period). (2) A journal is a chronological record of events about a unit or staff action during a given period. It is an important aid to the efficient conduct of operations. It provides a ready reference for the commander and staff and serves as a permanent record for training matters, operational reviews, and historical research. *See also:* Intelligence Journal.

References

Department of Defense, U.S. Army. *Counter-Signals Intelligence (C-SIGINT) Operations.* Field Manual FM 34-62. Washington, DC: Headquarters, Department of the Army, 1986.

———. *Operations.* Field Manual FM 100-5. Washington, DC: Headquarters, Department of the Army, 1986.

———. *Staff Organization and Operations.* Field Manual FM 101-5. Washington, DC: Headquarters, Department of the Army, 1984.

—**JUMP** (ARMY AVIATION) is a surprise attack on the blind or weak side of a formation.

References

Department of Defense, U.S. Army. *Air-to-Air Combat.* Field Manual FM 1-107. Washington, DC: Headquarters, Department of the Army, 1984.

—**JUMP SPEED** is the airspeed at which parachute jumps can be made from an aircraft in relative safety. *See also:* Jump Attitude, Jumpmaster.

References

Department of Defense, Joint Chiefs of Staff. *Department of Defense Dictionary of Military and Related Terms.* Washington, DC: GPO, 1986.

—**JUMPING ATTITUDE** is the steady, level flight of a troop carrier aircraft at reduced speed, which is necessary to permit parachutists to jump safely.

References

Department of Defense, U.S. Army. *Dictionary of United States Army Terms.* Army Regulation AR 310-25. Washington, DC: Headquarters, Department of the Army, 1986.

—**JUMPMASTER** is an individual who has been designated by the airborne commander to control parachutists from the time they enter the aircraft until the time they exit during parachute operations.

References

Department of Defense, U.S. Army. *USA/USAF Doctrine for Joint Airborne and Tactical Airlift Operations.* Field Manual FM 100-27. Washington, DC: Headquarters, Department of the Army, 1985.

—**JUNIOR RESERVE OFFICERS TRAINING CORPS** is composed of organized units, at public and private secondary schools, that host a unit and meet the standards that are required by the Department of Defense.

References

Department of Defense, U.S. Army. *Dictionary of United States Army Terms.* Army Regulation AR 310-25. Washington, DC: Headquarters, Department of the Army, 1986.

—**K TRANSFER,** in field artillery ground fire, is the shifting of fire from one point to another in the transfer limits of the piece, with the actual range being corrected by the application of the K.

References
Department of Defense, U.S. Army. *Dictionary of United States Army Terms.* Army Regulation AR 310-25. Washington, DC: Headquarters, Department of the Army, 1986.

—**KEY,** in cryptography, is a symbol or a sequence of signals (or electrical or mechanical correlates of symbols) that control the operations of encryption and decryption. *See also:* CRYPTO.

References
Department of Defense, U.S. Army. *Dictionary of United States Army Terms.* Army Regulation AR 310-25. Washington, DC: Headquarters, Department of the Army, 1986.

—**KEY AREA** is an area of paramount importance in a military operation.

References
Department of Defense, Joint Chiefs of Staff. *Department of Defense Dictionary of Military and Related Terms.* Washington, DC: GPO, 1986.

—**KEY BILLET** is an overseas position of unusual responsibility, and is designated as such in order to provide an extended tour for continuity.

References
Department of Defense, U.S. Army. *Overseas Service.* Army Regulation AR 614-30. Washington, DC: Headquarters, Department of the Army, 1984.

—**KEY CARD** is a card that contains a pattern of punched holes that establishes the key for a cryptosystem in a given cryptoperiod. *See also:* CRYPTO.

References
Department of Defense, U.S. Army. *Dictionary of United States Army Terms.* Army Regulation AR 310-25. Washington, DC: Headquarters, Department of the Army, 1986.

—**KEY EMPLOYEE** is a civilian employee of a federal government agency who occupies a key position. *See also:* Key Individual.

References
Department of Defense, U.S. Army. *Dictionary of United States Army Terms.* Army Regulation AR 310-25. Washington, DC: Headquarters, Department of the Army, 1986.

—**KEY INDIVIDUAL** is a person who is occupying a position indispensable to an organization, activity, or project.

References
Department of Defense, U.S. Army. *Military Awards.* Army Regulation AR 672-5-1. Washington, DC: Headquarters, Department of the Army, 1984.

—**KEY ITEM** is an item that, because of an official determination, is not stored at multiple points.

References
Department of Defense, U.S. Army. *Dictionary of United States Army Terms.* Army Regulation AR 310-25. Washington, DC: Headquarters, Department of the Army, 1986.

—**KEY POINT** is a site or installation, the destruction or capture of which would seriously affect the war effort or the success of an operation. *See also:* Key Area.

References
Department of Defense, Joint Chiefs of Staff. *Department of Defense Dictionary of Military and Related Terms.* Washington, DC: GPO, 1986.

—**KEY POSITION** is a billet in a federal government agency designated to be of crucial importance by the agency head and approved as such by the Secretary of the Army. An agency head may nominate a position as key when: (1) no qualified and immediate replacement exists for the incumbent or the duties of the position cannot be reassigned to other employees and (2) the incumbent's immediate recall to active duty during an emergency would seriously impair production and research that are vital to the national military effort; activities necessary to maintain the national or community health, safety, or welfare; or the effective functioning and continuity of a government agency. *See also:* Key Employee.

References
Department of Defense, U.S. Army. *Dictionary of United States Army Terms.* Army Regulation AR 310-25. Washington, DC: Headquarters, Department of the Army, 1986.

—**KEY SYMBOL,** in psychological operations, is a simple, suggestive, repetitive element (e.g., a rhythm, sign, or color) that has an immediate impact on a target audience and creates a favorable environment for the acceptance of a psychological theme.

References
Department of Defense, Joint Chiefs of Staff. *Department of Defense Dictionary of Military and Related Terms.* Washington, DC: GPO, 1986.

—**KEY TERRAIN** is any location or area, whose seizure or retention affords a marked advantage to either combatant. Since this advantage is situational, the commander designates key terrain only after he has analyzed his mission. He may designate certain key terrain as decisive terrain if accomplishing his mission depends on seizing and retaining it. He designates it as such in his concept of operation in order to communicate its importance to his staff and subordinate commanders. Many battlefields have decisive terrain. *See also:* Key Area, Key Point.

References
Department of Defense, U.S. Army. *Operations.* Field Manual FM 100-5. Washington, DC: Headquarters, Department of the Army, 1986.

—**KEYHOLING** is the tumbling of a bullet in flight that occurs because the bullet failed to receive enough spin from the rifling in the barrel that fired it.

References
Department of Defense, U.S. Army. *Dictionary of United States Army Terms.* Army Regulation AR 310-25. Washington, DC: Headquarters, Department of the Army, 1986.

—**KEYING** is the breaking or interrupting, either manually or automatically, of a radio carrier wave.

References
Department of Defense, U.S. Army. *Dictionary of United States Army Terms.* Army Regulation AR 310-25. Washington, DC: Headquarters, Department of the Army, 1986.

—**KEYING MATERIAL** is cryptomaterial that supplies the cryptoequipment arrangements and setting, or that is used directly in the encryption and decryption process. It is also cryptomaterial that supplies sequences or messages used for command, control, or authentication of a command, or can be used directly in their transmissions. *See also:* CRYPTO.

References
Department of Defense, U.S. Army. *Dictionary of United States Army Terms.* Army Regulation AR 310-25. Washington, DC: Headquarters, Department of the Army, 1986.

—**KILL,** as applied to air defense, denotes that a hostile airborne, ballistic, or orbiting object has been destroyed or has been rendered non-effective. "Kill" is further defined as:

- **Carrier**—the immediate structural breakup of the target aircraft.
- **Weapon**—the destruction or damage of a nuclear weapon so as to preclude its detonation or to considerably degrade its yield.
- **Track**—the destruction of all target aircraft within a given flight (track).

References
Department of Defense, U.S. Army. *Dictionary of United States Army Terms.* Army Regulation AR 310-25. Washington, DC: Headquarters, Department of the Army, 1986.

—**KILL PROBABILITY** is a measure of the probability of destroying a target.

References
Department of Defense, Joint Chiefs of Staff. *Department of Defense Dictionary of Military and Related Terms.* Washington, DC: GPO, 1986.

—**KILL ZONE** is the part of an ambush site where fire is concentrated in order to isolate, trap, and destroy a target.

References
Department of Defense, Joint Chiefs of Staff. *Department of Defense Dictionary of Military and Related Terms.* Washington, DC: GPO, 1986.

Department of Defense, U.S. Army. *The Infantry Rifle Company (Infantry. Airborne, Air Assault, Ranger).* Field Manual FM 7-10. Washington, DC: Headquarters, Department of the Army, 1982.

———. *The Rifle Squads (Mechanized and Light Infantry).* Training Circular TC 7-1. Washington, DC: Headquarters, Department of the Army, 1976.

—**KILLED IN ACTION (KIA)** is a battle casualty who is killed on the battlefield or who dies as a result of wounds or injuries before reaching a medical treatment facility. *See also:* Blue Bark, Casualty Reporting, Died of Wounds Received in Action, Missing in Action, National Cemetery, Post Cemetery, Wounded in Action.

References
Department of Defense, U.S. Army. *Planning for Health Service Support*. Field Manual FM 8-55. Washington, DC: Headquarters, Department of the Army, 1985.

—**KILLING ZONE** is the area where the commander plans to force the enemy to concentrate in order to destroy it. *See also:* Kill Zone.

References
Department of Defense, U.S. Army. *Dictionary of United States Army Terms*. Army Regulation AR 310-25. Washington, DC: Headquarters, Department of the Army, 1986.

—**KILOTON WEAPON** is a nuclear weapon, whose yield is measured in terms of thousands of tons of trinitroluene explosive equivalents, producing yields from 1 to 999 kilotons. *See also:* Megaton Weapon.

References
Department of Defense, Joint Chiefs of Staff. *Department of Defense Dictionary of Military and Related Terms*. Washington, DC: GPO, 1986.

—**KINETIC ENERGY AMMUNITION** is designed to damage fortifications, armor, or ships through the kinetic energy that the missile has on impact with the target. *See also:* Kinetic Energy Projectile.

References
Department of Defense, U.S. Army. *Dictionary of United States Army Terms*. Army Regulation AR 310-25. Washington, DC: Headquarters, Department of the Army, 1986.

—**KINETIC ENERGY PROJECTILE,** a type of direct fire projectile, uses high velocity and mass (momentum) to penetrate its target. Currently, the hypervelocity projectile causes the most concern for the survivability of a position. The materials used in the position must dissipate the projectile's energy and thus prevent its total penetration. Shielding against direct fire projectiles should initially stop or deform them in order to prevent or limit their penetration. Armor piercing discarding sabot, and armor piercing are both kinetic energy rounds. Such rounds are often used against tanks and heavily armored vehicles.

References
Department of Defense, U.S. Army. *Survivability*. Field Manual FM 5-103. Washington, DC: Headquarters, Department of the Army, 1985.

———. *Tank Gunnery*. Field Manual FM. 17-2-C2. Washington, DC: Headquarters, Department of the Army, 1980.

—**KINETIC LEAD** is the correction of allowance made for the relative motion of a target when computing the lead angle in gunnery.

References
Department of Defense, U.S. Army. *Dictionary of United States Army Terms*. Army Regulation AR 310-25. Washington, DC: Headquarters, Department of the Army, 1986.

—**KITCHEN POLICE (KP)** are military or civilian personnel who are detailed or hired to perform kitchen duties other than cooking. Their duties involve the preliminary preparation of fruits and vegetables, and the sanitation and cleaning of the dining facility building and equipment.

References
Department of Defense, U.S. Army. *Dictionary of United States Army Terms*. Army Regulation AR 310-25. Washington, DC: Headquarters, Department of the Army, 1986.

—**KNIFE REST,** a portable metal or wooden frame strung with barbed wire, is used as a barricade on roads or wherever a readily removable barrier is needed. With a metal frame, it can be used as an underwater obstacle in beach defenses.

References
Department of Defense, U.S. Army. *Dictionary of United States Army Terms*. Army Regulation AR 310-25. Washington, DC: Headquarters, Department of the Army, 1986.

—**KNOCK IT OFF** (ARMY AVIATION) is a call made to end an engagement or a maneuver. During training, it is used when the learning objective is met or exceeded.

References
Department of Defense, U.S. Army. *Air-to-Air Combat*. Field Manual FM 1-107. Washington, DC: Headquarters, U.S. Army, 1984.

—**KNOT** is a speed of one nautical mile per hour.

References
Department of Defense, U.S. Army. *Dictionary of United States Army Terms*. Army Regulation AR 310-25. Washington, DC: Headquarters, Department of the Army, 1986.

—**L-SHAPED AMBUSH FORMATION** is a variation of the line formation. The long leg of the "L" (assault element) is parallel to the kill zone to allow for flanking fire. The short leg (support element direct fire weapons) is at the end of, and at right angles to, the kill zone. This allows enfilade fire that interlocks with flanking fire from the other leg. The support element mortars, when available, are positioned to the flank or rear. This formation can be used either on a straight stretch of road, a trail, or a stream, or at a sharp bend in these terrain features. *See also:* Kill Zone, Line (Ambush Formation).

References
Department of Defense, U.S. Army. *The Infantry Rifle Company (Infantry, Airborne, Air Assault, Ranger).* Field Manual FM 7-10. Washington, DC: Headquarters, Department of the Army, 1982.

—**LABELED CARGO** is cargo of a dangerous nature (e.g., explosives, flammable or corrosive liquids), that is designated by different colored labels to indicate the requirement for special handling and storage. Examples of such colored labels are the following:

- **Green**—required on shipments of nonflammable gases.
- **Red**—required on shipments of articles of flammable character.
- **White**—required on shipments of acids or corrosive liquids.
- **Yellow**—required on shipments of flammable solids and oxidizing materials.

References
Department of Defense, U.S. Army. *Dictionary of United States Army Terms.* Army Regulation AR 310-25. Washington, DC: Headquarters, Department of the Army, 1986.

—**LAG RATE,** in manpower control usage, is a percentage that indicates the ratio of the shortage between the actual and the authorized manpower strengths. *See also:* Manpower Requirements.

References
Department of Defense, U.S. Army. *Dictionary of United States Army Terms.* Army Regulation AR 310-25. Washington, DC: Headquarters, Department of the Army, 1986.

—**LAND COMBAT SUPPORT SYSTEM** is a maintenance set consisting primarily of a digital computer that is used to isolate faults in electronic circuits and to determine the repairs that are needed. It may be used to support a variety of missile systems, particularly those that are used in land combat.

References
Department of Defense, U.S. Army. *Dictionary of United States Army Terms.* Army Regulation AR 310-25. Washington, DC: Headquarters, Department of the Army, 1986.

—**LAND CONTROL OPERATIONS** involve the use of ground forces, supported by naval and air forces, as appropriate, to achieve military objectives in vital land areas. Such operations include destruction of opposing ground forces, securing key terrain, protection of vital lines of communication, and establishment of local military superiority in areas of land operations. *See also:* AirLand Battle, Land Forces.

References
Department of Defense, Joint Chiefs of Staff. *Department of Defense Dictionary of Military and Related Terms.* Washington, DC: GPO, 1986.

—**LAND FORCES.** The basic objective of land forces is to defeat the enemy's forces. The Army conducts combat operations on land that defeat the enemy, and seize, occupy, and defend land areas. The Marine Corps seizes or defends advanced naval bases and conducts land operations that are essential to the naval campaign.

References
Department of Defense, U.S. Army. *The Army.* (Prepublication Issue.) Field Manual FM 100-1. Washington, DC: Headquarters, Department of the Army, 1986.

—**LAND MINES** are reinforcing obstacles other than minefields that are primarily designed to enhance the fires and kill ratio of antitank weapons. Mines and minefields perform this function, as well as kill or destroy enemy vehicles and personnel. There are two categories of land mines: conventional and scatterable. *See also:* Conventional Mines, Mine Warfare, Scatterable Mines.

References
Department of Defense, U.S. Army.
Countermobility. Field Manual FM 5-102.
Washington, DC: Headquarters, Department of the
Army, 1985.

—**LAND, SEA, OR AEROSPACE PROJECTION
OPERATIONS** is the use of land, sea, or air
forces, or appropriate combinations thereof, to
project U.S. military power into areas controlled
or threatened by enemy forces. These operations
may include the penetration of such areas by
amphibious, airborne, or land-transported
means, as well as air combat operations by land-
based or carrier-based air power, or both.

References
Department of Defense, Joint Chiefs of Staff.
*Department of Defense Dictionary of Military and
Related Terms.* Washington, DC: GPO, 1986.

—**LAND SEARCH** is the search of terrain by earth-
bound personnel, rather than those in aircraft.

References
Department of Defense, Joint Chiefs of Staff.
*Department of Defense Dictionary of Military and
Related Terms.* Washington, DC: GPO, 1986.

—**LAND SPECIAL SECURITY FORCE** consists of
the reserve component units designated to protect critical continental U.S. installations and
activities during the initial phase of an emergency. *See also:* Emergency in War.

References
Department of Defense, U.S. Army. *Dictionary of
United States Army Terms.* Army Regulation AR
310-25. Washington, DC: Headquarters, Department of the Army, 1986.

—**LAND TAIL** is the portion of an airborne or air-
transported unit that is not committed to combat
by air and joins its organization by land movement.

References
Department of Defense, U.S. Army. *Dictionary of
United States Army Terms.* Army Regulation AR
310-25. Washington, DC: Headquarters, Department of the Army, 1986.

—**LANDING AREA.** (1) A landing area is the part
of the objective area within which the landing
operations of an amphibious force are conducted. It includes the beach, the approaches to
the beach, the transport areas, the fire support
areas, the air occupied by close supporting air-

craft, and the land included in the advance inland to the initial objective. (2) In airborne operations, the landing area is the general area
that is used for landing troops and materiel either
by airdrop or air landing. This area includes one
or more drop zones or landing strips. *See also:*
Amphibious Operation.

References
Department of Defense, Joint Chiefs of Staff.
*Department of Defense Dictionary of Military and
Related Terms.* Washington, DC: GPO, 1986.

—**LANDING ATTACK** is an attack against enemy
defenses by troops landed from ships, aircraft,
boats, or amphibious vehicles. *See also:* Assault.

References
Department of Defense, Joint Chiefs of Staff.
*Department of Defense Dictionary of Military and
Related Terms.* Washington, DC: GPO, 1986.

—**LANDING BEACH** is the portion of usable
coastline usually required for the assault landing
of a battalion landing team or similar unit. *See
also:* Amphibious Operation, Landing Craft.

References
Department of Defense, U.S. Army. *Operational
Terms and Symbols.* Field Manual FM 101-5-1.
Washington, DC: Headquarters, Department of the
Army, 1985.

—**LANDING CRAFT** is a craft used in amphibious
operations. It is specifically designed for carrying troops and equipment and for beaching,
unloading, and retracting. It is also used for logistic cargo resupply operations. *See also:* Amphibious Operation.

References
Department of Defense, Joint Chiefs of Staff.
*Department of Defense Dictionary of Military and
Related Terms.* Washington, DC: GPO, 1986.

—**LANDING DIAGRAM** is a graphic means of il-
lustrating the plan for the ship-to-shore movement. *See also:* Amphibious Operation.

References
Department of Defense, Joint Chiefs of Staff.
*Department of Defense Dictionary of Military and
Related Terms.* Washington, DC: GPO, 1986.

—**LANDING FORCE** is a task organization of troop
units, and aviation and ground forces, that are
assigned to an amphibious assault. It is the
highest troop echelon in the amphibious operation. *See also:* Amphibious Force.

References
Department of Defense, Joint Chiefs of Staff.
*Department of Defense Dictionary of Military and
Related Terms.* Washington, DC: GPO, 1986.

—**LANDING FORCE COMMANDER** is the officer
in the initiating directive who is designated to
command the landing force. *See also:* Amphibious Operation.

References
Department of Defense, Joint Chiefs of Staff.
*Department of Defense Dictionary of Military and
Related Terms.* Washington, DC: GPO, 1986.

—**LANDING GROUP,** a subordinate task organization of the landing force, is capable of conducting landing operations under a single tactical command, and against a position or group of positions. *See also:* Amphibious Operation, Landing Force.

References
Department of Defense, Joint Chiefs of Staff.
*Department of Defense Dictionary of Military and
Related Terms.* Washington, DC: GPO, 1986.

—**LANDING PLAN** is an airborne, air assault, or
air movement plan prescribing the sequence,
the place of arrival, and the method of entry of
military forces into the objective area. The
purpose of the plan is to get the correct units to
the correct place in the correct order so that the
ground tactical plan can be executed properly.
See also: Air Movement Plan, Ground Tactical
Plan, Marshalling Plan.

References
Department of Defense, U.S. Army. *Operational
Terms and Symbols.* Field Manual FM 101-5-1.
Washington, DC: Headquarters, Department of the
Army, 1985.

—**LANDING POINT** is a point within a landing
site where one helicopter or vertical take-off
and landing aircraft can land. *See also:* Airfield.

References
Department of Defense, Joint Chiefs of Staff.
*Department of Defense Dictionary of Military and
Related Terms.* Washington, DC: GPO, 1986.

—**LANDING SCHEDULE,** in an amphibious operation, is a schedule that shows the beach, hour,
and priorities of landing assault units. It is used
to coordinate the movements of landing craft
from the transports to the beach in order to
maneuver ashore properly. *See also:* Amphibious Operation.

References
Department of Defense, Joint Chiefs of Staff.
*Department of Defense Dictionary of Military and
Related Terms.* Washington, DC: GPO, 1986.

—**LANDING SHIP** is an assault ship designed for
long sea voyages and for the rapid unloading of
forces and equipment over and onto a beach.
See also: Amphibious Operation, Landing Ship
Dock.

References
Department of Defense, Joint Chiefs of Staff.
*Department of Defense Dictionary of Military and
Related Terms.* Washington, DC: GPO, 1986.

—**LANDING SHIP DOCK (LSD)** is a ship designed to transport and launch loaded amphibious craft or amphibian vehicles with their
crews and embarked personnel and equipment
and to provide limited docking and repair services to small ships and craft.

References
Department of Defense, Joint Chiefs of Staff.
*Department of Defense Dictionary of Military and
Related Terms.* Washington, DC: GPO, 1986.

—**LANDING SITE.** (1) A landing site is a continuous segment of coastline over which troops,
equipment, and supplies can be landed by surface means. The minimum length of the site
must allow for at least one landing beach; the
site is restricted in maximum length only by the
extent of usable, uninterrupted coastline. (2) A
landing site is a location where aircraft take off
and land. *See also:* Airfield.

References
Department of Defense, U.S. Army. *Operational
Terms and Symbols.* Field Manual FM 101-5-1.
Washington, DC: Headquarters, Department of the
Army, 1985.

—**LANDING VEHICLE, TRACKED, ENGINEER,
MODEL 1 (LVTE-1)** is a lightly armored amphibious vehicle designed for minefield and
obstacle clearance in amphibious assaults and
inland operations. For protection, it is equipped
with line charges in front of the vehicle and a
bull-dozer-type blade with scarifier teeth.

References
Department of Defense, Joint Chiefs of Staff.
*Department of Defense Dictionary of Military and
Related Terms.* Washington, DC: GPO, 1986.

—**LANDING ZONE** is any specified zone used for landing aircraft.

References
Department of Defense, U.S. Army. *USA/USAF Doctrine for Joint Airborne and Tactical Airlift Operations*. Field Manual FM 100-27. Washington, DC: Headquarters, Department of the Army, 1985.

—**LANDING ZONE CONTROL PARTY** is a group of personnel who are specially trained and equipped to establish and operate communications and signal devices from the ground for traffic control of aircraft and helicopters for a specific landing zone. *See also:* Pathfinders.

References
Department of Defense, U.S. Army. *Operational Terms and Symbols*. Field Manual FM 101-5-1. Washington, DC: Headquarters, Department of the Army, 1985.

—**LANDMARK** is a feature, either natural or artificial, that can be accurately determined on the ground from a grid reference.

References
Department of Defense, Joint Chiefs of Staff. *Department of Defense Dictionary of Military and Related Terms*. Washington, DC: GPO, 1986.

—**LANDS** are the raised portions between the grooves in a gun. They are spiral channels that are cut into the bore of the gun and are also called grooves.

References
Department of Defense, U.S. Army. *Dictionary of United States Army Terms*. Army Regulation AR 310-25. Washington, DC: Headquarters, Department of the Army, 1986.

—**LANE** is a clear route through an obstacle. A lane for foot troops is a minimum of one meter wide, but may be wider. A foot lane is marked with tracing tape along its center line. A single lane for vehicles is a minimum of eight meters wide, a double lane is at least fifteen meters wide. Vehicle lanes are marked by any means available. *See also:* Gap.

References
Department of Defense, U.S. Army. *Operational Terms and Symbols*. Field Manual FM 101-5-1. Washington, DC: Headquarters, Department of the Army, 1985.

—**LANE MARKER,** in land mine warfare, is a sign used to mark a minefield lane. Lane markers, at the entrance to and exit from the lane, may be referenced to a landmark or intermediate marker. *See also:* Minefield Lane.

References
Department of Defense, Joint Chiefs of Staff. *Department of Defense Dictionary of Military and Related Terms*. Washington, DC: GPO, 1986.

—**LANGUAGE IDENTIFIER CODE** is an identification of a foreign language. In job descriptions it notes the requirement for a language, and on personnel records it reflects that the person can speak a designated foreign language.

References
Department of Defense, U.S. Army. *Dictionary of United States Army Terms*. Army Regulation AR 310-25. Washington, DC: Headquarters, Department of the Army, 1986.

—**LAPEL BUTTON** is a miniature enameled replica of an award. It is worn only on civilian clothing.

References
Department of Defense, U.S. Army. *Wear and Appearance of Army Uniforms and Insignia*. Army Regulation AR 670-1. Washington, DC: Headquarters, Department of the Army, 1986.

—**LAPSE** is a marked decrease of air temperature with increasing altitude, with the ground being warmer than the surrounding air. This condition is usually encountered between 11 a.m. and 3 p.m. (1100 and 1500 hours) when the skies are clear. During unstable or lapse conditions, strong convection currents are found, and for smoke operations, the state is defined as unstable. This condition is normally the most unfavorable for the release of smoke. *See also:* Smoke Screen.

References
Department of Defense, U.S. Army. *Deliberate Smoke Operations*. Field Manual FM 3-50. Washington, DC: Headquarters, Department of the Army, 1984.

—**LARGE-LOT STORAGE** is a quantity of material that will require four or more pallet columns stored to the maximum height. It is usually accepted as stock stored in carload or greater quantities.

References
Department of Defense, Joint Chiefs of Staff. *Department of Defense Dictionary of Military and Related Terms*. Washington, DC: GPO, 1986.

—**LARGE-SCALE MAP** is a map having a scale of 1:75,000 or larger. *See also:* Map.

References

Department of Defense, Joint Chiefs of Staff. *Department of Defense Dictionary of Military and Related Terms.* Washington, DC: GPO, 1986.

—**LASER** is light amplification by the stimulated emission of radiation. *See also:* Laser Designator, Laser Guidance Unit, Laser Guided Weapon, Laser Illuminator, Laser Linescan, Laser Rangefinder, Laser Ranging, Laser Target Designating System.

References

Department of Defense, U.S. Army. *Dictionary of United States Army Terms.* Army Regulation AR 310-25. Washington, DC: Headquarters, Department of the Army, 1986.

—**LASER DESIGNATOR** is a device that emits a beam of laser energy that is used to mark a specific place or object.

References

Department of Defense, Joint Chiefs of Staff. *Department of Defense Dictionary of Military and Related Terms.* Washington, DC: GPO, 1986.

—**LASER GUIDANCE UNIT** is a device that incorporates a laser seeker to provide guidance commands to the control system of a missile, projectile, or bomb.

References

Department of Defense, Joint Chiefs of Staff. *Department of Defense Dictionary of Military and Related Terms.* Washington, DC: GPO, 1986.

—**LASER GUIDED WEAPON** uses a seeker to detect laser energy reflected from a laser-marked or designated target. Through signal processing guidance commands are provided to a control system that guides the weapon to the point where the laser energy is being reflected.

References

Department of Defense, Joint Chiefs of Staff. *Department of Defense Dictionary of Military and Related Terms.* Washington, DC: GPO, 1986.

—**LASER ILLUMINATOR** is a device for enhancing the light in a zone of action by irradiating or lighting the area with a laser beam.

References

Department of Defense, Joint Chiefs of Staff. *Department of Defense Dictionary of Military and Related Terms.* Washington, DC: GPO, 1986.

—**LASER INTELLIGENCE (LASINT)** in signals intelligence, is the technical and intelligence information that is derived from laser systems. It is a subcategory of electro-optical intelligence. *See also:* Signals Intelligence.

References

Department of Defense, Defense Intelligence College. *Glossary of Intelligence Terms and Definitions.* Washington, DC: DIC, 1987.

Department of Defense, Joint Chiefs of Staff. *Department of Defense Dictionary of Military and Related Terms.* Washington, DC: GPO, 1986.

—**LASER LINESCAN** is a linescan system that is designed to operate by using a laser as the primary source of illumination.

References

Department of Defense, U.S. Army. *Dictionary of United States Army Terms.* Army Regulation AR 310-25. Washington, DC: Headquarters, Department of the Army, 1986.

—**LASER RANGEFINDER** is a device that uses laser energy to determine the distance from the device to a place, object, or other target.

References

Department of Defense, Joint Chiefs of Staff. *Department of Defense Dictionary of Military and Related Terms.* Washington, DC: GPO, 1986.

—**LASER RANGING** is the use of laser transmissions to determine the range to the target. The data it provides are normally input into a weapon delivery computer.

References

Department of Defense, U.S. Army. *Dictionary of United States Army Terms.* Army Regulation AR 310-25. Washington, DC: Headquarters, Department of the Army, 1986.

—**LASER TARGET DESIGNATING SYSTEM** is used to direct (aim or point) laser energy at a target. The system consists of the laser designator or laser target marker with the display and control components necessary to acquire the target and to direct the beam of laser energy.

References

Department of Defense, U.S. Army. *Dictionary of United States Army Terms.* Army Regulation AR 310-25. Washington, DC: Headquarters, Department of the Army, 1986.

—**LASHING POINT** is a ring, shackle, loop, or other fitting on vehicles, stores, or equipment. It is used with lashings. *See also:* Lashings.

References
Department of Defense, U.S. Army. *Dictionary of United States Army Terms*. Army Regulation AR 310-25. Washington, DC: Headquarters, Department of the Army, 1986.

—**LASHINGS** are the equipment that fasten or secure a load to its carrier to prevent it from shifting during transit. *See also:* Lashing Point.

References
Department of Defense, U.S. Army. *Dictionary of United States Army Terms*. Army Regulation AR 310-25. Washington, DC: Headquarters, Department of the Army, 1986.

—**LAST LIGHT**, in intelligence imagery and photoreconnaissance, is the end of evening nautical twilight (i.e., when the center of the evening sun is twelve degrees below the horizon). *See also:* Aerial Photograph.

References
Department of Defense, Joint Chiefs of Staff. *Department of Defense Dictionary of Military and Related Terms*. Washington, DC: GPO, 1986.

—**LATE,** in artillery, is a report made to the observer or spotter, whenever there is a delay in reporting "shot." A time in seconds is given with the report. *See also:* Shot.

References
Department of Defense, Joint Chiefs of Staff. *Department of Defense Dictionary of Military and Related Terms*. Washington, DC: GPO, 1986.

—**LATENT LETHALITY (LL) 650 cGy (RADS)** is an established level of exposure to radiation. (1) *Physically undemanding tasks.* At 650 cGy (rads), the individual's ability to perform physically undemanding tasks becomes degraded within three hours of exposure and remains so until approximately two days after exposure, at which time the individual will experience a six-day recovery period. At eight days after exposure, the individual relapses into degraded performance and remains so until four weeks after exposure. At this time he begins to exhibit radiation sickness symptoms of sufficient severity that he becomes ineffective. He remains ineffective until death, which is approximately six weeks after exposure. (2) *Physically demanding tasks.* At 650 cGy (rads), the individual's performance suffers within two hours of exposure and remains so for three weeks, at which time radiation sickness symptoms are so severe that the individual is ineffective. The individual remains ineffective until death, which occurs approximately six weeks after exposure. *See also:* Nuclear Warfare.

References
Department of Defense, U.S. Army. *Operational Terms and Symbols*. Field Manual FM 101-5-1. Washington, DC: Headquarters, Department of the Army, 1985.

—**LATENT RESERVE BEDS** are medical treatment facility bed spaces for which both the required medical and nursing staff and some or all of the medical equipment and fixtures necessary to convert them into operating beds are missing. *See also:* Medical Treatment.

References
Department of Defense, U.S. Army. *Dictionary of United States Army Terms*. Army Regulation AR 310-25. Washington, DC: Headquarters, Department of the Army, 1986.

—**LATERAL.** (1) A lateral is an underground gallery constructed parallel to the front line, and from which other parallel galleries for attack, defense, and listening are projected toward the enemy. A lateral differs from a fishbone, which is a series of independent galleries that are cut in the direction of the enemy. (2) Lateral is to one side of a line (e.g., the observer target line in control of fire).

References
Department of Defense, U.S. Army. *Dictionary of United States Army Terms*. Army Regulation AR 310-25. Washington, DC: Headquarters, Department of the Army, 1986.

—**LATERAL EMPLOYMENT** is a change from specialist to noncommissioned officer within the same pay grade.

References
Department of Defense, U.S. Army. *Enlisted Personnel Management System*. Army Regulation AR 600-200. Washington, DC: Headquarters, Department of the Army, 1984.

—**LATERAL ROUTE** is generally parallel to the forward edge of the battle area. It crosses, or feeds into, axial routes. *See also:* Route.

References
Department of Defense, Joint Chiefs of Staff. *Department of Defense Dictionary of Military and Related Terms*. Washington, DC: GPO, 1986.

LAY **393**

—**LATERAL SPREAD** is a technique used to place the mean point of impact of two or more units 100 meters apart on a line perpendicular to the gun-target line.

References

Department of Defense, Joint Chiefs of Staff. *Department of Defense Dictionary of Military and Related Terms.* Washington, DC: GPO, 1986.

—**LATEST ARRIVAL DATE** is the latest date that a unit should arrive "in-theater" in order to support a specific operations plan.

References

Department of Defense, U.S. Army. *Dictionary of United States Army Terms.* Army Regulation AR 310-25. Washington, DC: Headquarters, Department of the Army, 1986.

—**LAUNCH** is the transition that occurs to project a missile into flight. *See also:* Launch Pad, Launch Time, Launcher, Launching Area, Launching Site.

References

Department of Defense, Joint Chiefs of Staff. *Department of Defense Dictionary of Military and Related Terms.* Washington, DC: GPO, 1986.

—**LAUNCH PAD** is a concrete or other hard surface area on which a missile launcher is positioned.

References

Department of Defense, Joint Chiefs of Staff. *Department of Defense Dictionary of Military and Related Terms.* Washington, DC: GPO, 1986.

—**LAUNCH TIME** is the time at which an aircraft or missile is scheduled to be airborne.

References

Department of Defense, Joint Chiefs of Staff. *Department of Defense Dictionary of Military and Related Terms.* Washington, DC: GPO, 1986.

—**LAUNCHER** is a structural device designed to support and hold a missile in position for firing.

References

Department of Defense, Joint Chiefs of Staff. *Department of Defense Dictionary of Military and Related Terms.* Washington, DC: GPO, 1986.

—**LAUNCHING AREA,** in a guided missile fire unit, is an area from which missiles are launched.

References

Department of Defense, U.S. Army. *Dictionary of United States Army Terms.* Army Regulation AR 310-25. Washington, DC: Headquarters, Department of the Army, 1986.

—**LAUNCHING SITE** is an area or installation capable of launching missiles from the surface to the air or from the surface to the surface.

References

Department of Defense, Joint Chiefs of Staff. *Department of Defense Dictionary of Military and Related Terms.* Washington, DC: GPO, 1986.

—**LAW AND ORDER (LO) OPERATIONS** are military police missions that include law enforcement, criminal investigation, and the confinement of U.S. military prisoners.

References

Department of Defense, U.S. Army. *Operational Terms and Symbols.* Field Manual FM 101-5-1. Washington, DC: Headquarters, Department of the Army, 1985.

—**LAW OF WAR** is the part of international law that regulates the conduct of armed hostilities. It is often termed the law of armed conflict. *See also:* Rules of Engagement.

References

Department of Defense, Joint Chiefs of Staff. *Department of Defense Dictionary of Military and Related Terms.* Washington, DC: GPO, 1986.

—**LAW (LIGHT ANTITANK WEAPON) POSITION** is a hasty or deliberate fighting position from which the LAW is fired. Special care must be taken to insure that the LAW's backblast does not injure friendly troops or is not deflected by obstructions.

References

Department of Defense, U.S. Army. *Survivability.* Field Manual FM 5-103. Washington, DC: Headquarters, Department of the Army, 1985.

—**LAY.** (1) To lay is to direct or adjust the aim of a weapon. (2) Laying is the setting of a weapon for a given range, or for a given direction, or both. (3) To lay is to drop one or more aerial bombs or aerial mines onto the surface from an aircraft. (4) To lay is to spread a smoke screen on the ground from an aircraft. (5) To lay (or to lay out) is to calculate or project a course. *See also:* Smoke Screen.

References
Department of Defense, Joint Chiefs of Staff.
*Department of Defense Dictionary of Military and
Related Terms.* Washington, DC: GPO, 1986.

—**LEAD.** (1) Lead is the distance ahead of a moving target that a gun must be aimed in order to compensate for the target's movement so that the bullet will hit the target, rather than falling behind it. (2) Lead is the vertical and lateral angles between the gun target line and the axis of the bore at the moment of firing at a moving target. (3) To lead is to aim a gun ahead of a moving target. (4) A lead is one target length, as it appears to the gunner. (5) In highway operations, a lead is the linear spacing between the heads of successive vehicles, serials, march units, or columns. (6) A lead is an ice crack, wider than three to five feet that is too wide for men, sledges, and dogs to cross easily. *See also:* Lead Curve, Leader's Rule.

References
Department of Defense, U.S. Army. *Dictionary of
United States Army Terms.* Army Regulation AR
310-25. Washington, DC: Headquarters, Department of the Army, 1986.

—**LEAD AZODE.** *See:* Mercuric Fulminate.

—**LEAD CURVE** is a line on a chart that records in graphic form the lead that is involved in aiming a gun at a moving target. *See also:* Lead.

References
Department of Defense, U.S. Army. *Dictionary of
United States Army Terms.* Army Regulation AR
310-25. Washington, DC: Headquarters, Department of the Army, 1986.

—**LEAD STYPHNATE** is a primary high explosive that consists of reddish-brown rhombic crystals. It is used extensively in some explosive trains.

References
Department of Defense, U.S. Army. *Dictionary of
United States Army Terms.* Army Regulation AR
310-25. Washington, DC: Headquarters, Department of the Army, 1986.

—**LEADER'S RULE** is a method of determining the safe range for machine guns firing over the heads of friendly troops when the range to the target is more than 900 meters.

References
Department of Defense, U.S. Army. *Dictionary of
United States Army Terms.* Army Regulation AR
310-25. Washington, DC: Headquarters, Department of the Army, 1986.

—**LEADERSHIP** is the most essential element of combat power. It provides purpose, motivation, and direction in combat. It is the leader who determines the degree to which maneuver, firepower, and protection are maximized; who ensures that these elements are effectively balanced; and who decides how to bring them to bear against the enemy. *See also:* Leadership, Authoritarian; Leadership, Delagative; Leadership, Military; Leadership That Motivates.

References
Department of Defense, U.S. Army. *Management of
Stress in Army Operations.* Field Manual FM 26-2.
Washington, DC: Headquarters, Department of the Army, 1986.
———. *Operations.* Field Manual FM 100-5.
Washington, DC: Headquarters, Department of the Army, 1986.

—**LEADERSHIP AND COMMAND AT SENIOR LEVELS,** as officially defined by the U.S. Army, is "the art of direct and indirect influence and the skill of creating conditions for sustained organizational success to achieve the desired result. Its purpose is to produce decisive results at the large-unit level. Leadership and command at senior levels is the wellspring from which all sustained unit actions flow. Only the coordinated action of many units combined over time ensures success in battles and campaigns."

References
Department of Defense, U.S. Army. *Leadership and
Command at Senior Levels.* Field Manual FM 22-103. Washington, DC: Headquarters, Department of the Army, 1987.
———. *Management of Stress in Army Operations.*
Field Manual FM 26-2. Washington, DC: Headquarters, Department of the Army, 1986.

—**LEADERSHIP, AUTHORITARIAN,** is a style of leadership in which the leader tells his subordinates what he wants done and how he wants it done without asking for their advice or ideas.

References
Department of Defense, U.S. Army. *Military
Leadership.* Field Manual FM 22-100. Washington, DC: Headquarters, Department of the Army, 1983.

—**LEADERSHIP, DELEGATIVE,** is a style of leadership in which the leader entrusts decision-making authority to a subordinate or a group of subordinates, yet remains responsible for their decisions.

References

Department of Defense, U.S. Army. *Military Leadership*. Field Manual FM 22-100. Washington, DC: Headquarters, Department of the Army, 1983.

—**LEADERSHIP, MILITARY,** is the process by which a soldier influences others to accomplish the mission. He carries out this process by applying his leadership attributes (e.g., his beliefs, values, ethics, character, knowledge, and skills).

References

Department of Defense, U.S. Army. *Military Leadership*. Field Manual FM 22-100. Washington, DC: Headquarters, Department of the Army, 1983.

—**LEADERSHIP THAT MOTIVATES** is the result of applying the principles of motivation, teaching, coaching, and counseling.

References

Department of Defense, U.S. Army. *Military Leadership*. Field Manual FM 22-100. Washington, DC: Headquarters, Department of the Army, 1983.

—**LEAD-IN** is an explosive train that conducts a detonating impulse into an explosive-filled cavity.

References

Department of Defense, U.S. Army. *Dictionary of United States Army Terms*. Army Regulation AR 310-25. Washington, DC: Headquarters, Department of the Army, 1986.

—**LEADING LINE** is a position line, through or advanced to pass through the destination, that is used as the required track for advancing forces.

References

Department of Defense, U.S. Army. *Dictionary of United States Army Terms*. Army Regulation AR 310-25. Washington, DC: Headquarters, Department of the Army, 1986.

—**LEAFLET BOMB** is a device used for dropping large quantities of propaganda leaflets from high flying aircraft. It insures that the leaflets will reach their targets with a minimum of drift from air currents. *See also:* Leaflet Projectile.

References

Department of Defense, U.S. Army. *Dictionary of United States Army Terms*. Army Regulation AR 310-25. Washington, DC: Headquarters, Department of the Army, 1986.

—**LEAFLET PROJECTILE** is a standard base ejection projectile especially designed for leaflet dissemination. When it is loaded with propaganda leaflets, the projectile matches the ballistic characteristics of a high explosive projectile.

References

Department of Defense, U.S. Army. *Dictionary of United States Army Terms*. Army Regulation AR 310-25. Washington, DC: Headquarters, Department of the Army, 1986.

—**LEAPFROG.** (1) Leapfrog is a form of movement in which supporting elements are moved successively through or by one another along the axis of movement of supported forces. (2) Leapfrog is a technique in medical tactics for maintaining continuous medical support for maneuvering forces and forces in combat by alternately displacing medical units that are performing the same or similar functions along a common axis of movement. *See also:* Bound, Bounding Overwatch, Traveling Overwatch.

References

Department of Defense, U.S. Army. *Dictionary of United States Army Terms*. Army Regulation AR 310-25. Washington, DC: Headquarters, Department of the Army, 1986.

—**LEARNING CENTER** is a facility dedicated primarily as a delivery point for individualized or small group multi-media-based instruction. Learning centers contain the equipment and instructional materials to meet training and educational needs. *See also:* Army Learning Center.

References

Department of Defense, U.S. Army. *Army Forces Training*. Army Regulation AR 350-41. Washington, DC: Headquarters, Department of the Army, 1986.

—**LEAST DANGEROUS** is a classification for a target. A least dangerous target is one that does not have the immediate capability of killing but can report on targets that can. The soldier should engage this type of target as soon as possible after all the dangerous targets are destroyed.

References

Department of Defense, U.S. Army. *Tank Gunnery*. Field Manual FM 17-2-C2. Washington, DC: Headquarters, Department of the Army, 1980.

—**LEAST SEPARATION DISTANCE (LSD)** is the minimum distance in meters that a desired ground zero must be separated from an object to preclude damage or preclude obstacles with 90 percent assurance. *See also:* Desired Ground Zero, Minimum Safe Distance, Preclusion of Damage, Preclusion of Obstacles, Preclusion Oriented Analysis, Target Oriented Analysis.

References
Department of Defense, U.S. Army. *Nuclear Weapons Employment Doctrine and Procedures.* Field Manual FM 101-3-1. Washington, DC: Headquarters, Department of the Army, 1986.
————. *Operational Terms and Symbols.* Field Manual FM 101-5-1. Washington, DC: Headquarters, Department of the Army, 1985.

—**LEAVE** is authorized absence from one's place of duty and is chargeable against the member's leave account. It is earned at the rate of two and one-half days per month for those on active duty for 30 days or more, except for those in a nonpay status. *See also:* Absent Without Leave, Annual Leave, Emergency Leave, Leave Area, Leave Awaiting Orders, Leave En Route, Leave Year.

References
Department of Defense, U.S. Army. *Leaves and Passes.* Army Regulation AR 630-5. Washington, DC: Headquarters, Department of the Army, 1984.

—**LEAVE AREA** is an area established, usually in the large cities or resorts of the communications zone, to provide the opportunity for rest and relaxation for Army personnel who are on leave or on pass.

References
Department of Defense, U.S. Army. *Dictionary of United States Army Terms.* Army Regulation AR 310-25. Washington, DC: Headquarters, Department of the Army, 1986.

—**LEAVE AWAITING ORDERS** is an authorized absence from duty while awaiting further orders and disposition in connection with disability separation proceedings.

References
Department of Defense, U.S. Army. *Leaves and Passes.* Army Regulation AR 630-5. Washington, DC: Headquarters, Department of the Army, 1984.

—**LEAVE EN ROUTE** is a delay chargeable to leave that is granted to a member when he is traveling to a new duty station in connection with temporary duty or a permanent change in station.

References
Department of Defense, U.S. Army. *Leaves and Passes.* Army Regulation AR 630-5. Washington, DC: Headquarters, Department of the Army, 1984.

—**LEAVE YEAR** is a year from October 1 to the following September 30, that is used in calculating leaves of absence for military personnel. Military personnel earn 30 days of leave per year.

References
Department of Defense, U.S. Army. *Dictionary of United States Army Terms.* Army Regulation AR 310-25. Washington, DC: Headquarters, Department of the Army, 1986.

—**LEFT (OR RIGHT).** (1) Left and right are terms used to establish the relative position of a body of troops. The person using the terms is assumed to be facing in the direction of the enemy regardless of whether the troops are advancing toward or are withdrawing from the enemy. (2) Left (or right), in artillery, is a correction that is used in adjusting fire to indicate that a lateral shift of the mean point of impact perpendicular to the reference line or spotting line is desired.

References
Department of Defense, U.S. Army. *Operational Terms and Symbols.* Field Manual FM 101-5-1. Washington, DC: Headquarters, Department of the Army, 1985.

—**LEFT (RIGHT) BANK** is that bank of a stream or river on the left (right) of the observer when he is facing in the direction of flow or downstream.

References
Department of Defense, Joint Chiefs of Staff. *Department of Defense Dictionary of Military and Related Terms.* Washington, DC: GPO, 1986.

—**LEFT FACE.** (1) In a dismounted drill, left face is the movement from the position of attention by which a person turns on the heel of the left foot and the ball of the right foot so as to face 90 degrees to the left of the original position. (2) Left face is the command to exercise this movement.

References
Department of Defense, U.S. Army. *Dictionary of United States Army Terms.* Army Regulation AR 310-25. Washington, DC: Headquarters, Department of the Army, 1986.

—**LEGAL ASSISTANCE OFFICER** is a commissioned officer of the Judge Advocate General's Corps who is designated to assist military personnel and their families with their personal legal (noncriminal) problems. *See also:* Legal Assistance Program.

References

Department of Defense, U.S. Army. *Dictionary of United States Army Terms.* Army Regulation AR 310-25. Washington, DC: Headquarters, Department of the Army, 1986.

—**LEGAL ASSISTANCE PROGRAM** is a program cosponsored by the Military Service and the American Bar Association through which legal assistance and advice is provided to military personnel and their families to help them solve their personal legal (noncriminal) problems.

References

Department of Defense, U.S. Army. *Dictionary of United States Army Terms.* Army Regulation AR 310-25. Washington, DC: Headquarters, Department of the Army, 1986.

—**LEGEND** is an explanation of symbols used on a map, chart, or sketch. It is commonly printed in tabular form at the side of the figure. *See also:* Map.

References

Department of Defense, Joint Chiefs of Staff. *Department of Defense Dictionary of Military and Related Terms.* Washington, DC: GPO, 1986.

—**LENGTH OF A COLUMN** is the length of roadway occupied by a column, including the gaps in the column. It is measured from the front to the rear of the column.

References

Department of Defense, U.S. Army. *The Infantry Rifle Company (Infantry, Airborne, Air Assault, Ranger).* Field Manual FM 7-10. Washington, DC: Headquarters, Department of the Army, 1982.

—**LESS THAN A TRUCKLOAD** is a quantity of freight less than that which qualifies for a truckload rate.

References

Department of Defense, U.S. Army. *Dictionary of United States Army Terms.* Army Regulation AR 310-25. Washington, DC: Headquarters, Department of the Army, 1986.

—**LESS THAN RELEASE UNIT** is a shipment unit that can be placed in the transportation system without being offered for positive clearance to a movement control authority.

References

Department of Defense, U.S. Army. *Dictionary of United States Army Terms.* Army Regulation AR 310-25. Washington, DC: Headquarters, Department of the Army, 1986.

—**LESSON PLAN** is a practical, economical aid to: (1) prepare training; (2) provide a record of the specific training conducted; and (3) assist future trainers. Lesson plans are not designed to record every word of a trainer's presentation, but rather to specify the minimum information needed to conduct the training. *See also:* Army Learning Center.

References

Department of Defense, U.S. Army. *How to Prepare and Conduct Military Training.* Field Manual FM 21-6. Washington, DC: Headquarters, Department of the Army, 1975.

—**LETTER CONTRACT,** as defined by the U.S. Army, is "a written preliminary contractual instrument that authorizes the immediate commencement of manufacture of supplies or performance of services including, but not limited to, preproduction planning and procurement of necessary materials."

References

Department of Defense, U.S. Army. *Dictionary of United States Army Terms.* Army Regulation AR 310-25. Washington, DC: Headquarters, Department of the Army, 1986.

—**LETTER OF INSTRUCTIONS** is a form of order by which superior commanders give information as to broad aims, policies, and strategic plans for operations in large areas over a considerable period of time. It is issued to large units of a command and has the same authority as an operation order. A letter of instruction is intended to guide and control the operations of a large command.

References

Department of Defense, U.S. Army. *Dictionary of United States Army Terms.* Army Regulation AR 310-25. Washington, DC: Headquarters, Department of the Army, 1986.

—LEVEL OF EFFORT-ORIENTED ITEMS concerns items for which requirements computations are based on such factors as equipment and personnel density and time and rate of use. *See also:* Mission-Oriented Items.

References
Department of Defense, Joint Chiefs of Staff. *Department of Defense Dictionary of Military and Related Terms.* Washington, DC: GPO, 1986.

—LEVEL OF PROTECTION is the extent of preservation, packaging, and packing required to protect a supply item against specific storage, shipping, and handling hazards. The levels of protection are: Level A, Military Protection; Level B, Limited Military Protection; and Level C, Minimum Military Protection.

References
Department of Defense, U.S. Army. *Dictionary of United States Army Terms.* Army Regulation AR 310-25. Washington, DC: Headquarters, Department of the Army, 1986.

—LEVEL OF SUPPLY is the quantity of supplies or materiel authorized or directed to be held in anticipation of future demands. *See also:* Requisitioning Objective, Safety Level of Supply, Stockage Objective, Strategic Reserve.

References
Department of Defense, Joint Chiefs of Staff. *Department of Defense Dictionary of Military and Related Terms.* Washington, DC: GPO, 1986.

—LEVEL POINT is a point on the descending branch of the trajectory that is at the same altitude as the origin. It is the point where the trajectory cuts the base, and is sometimes referred to as the point of fall.

References
Department of Defense, U.S. Army. *Dictionary of United States Army Terms.* Army Regulation AR 310-25. Washington, DC: Headquarters, Department of the Army, 1986.

—LEVELS OF ENEMY ATTACK. Enemy forces and their activities in the rear areas are divided into three categories:
- **Level I** is characterized by enemy controlled agent activity, sabotage by enemy sympathizers, and terrorist activity.
- **Level II** is characterized by diversionary and sabotage operations, by unconventional forces, and by sabotage and reconnaissance missions conducted by

tactical units of less than battalion size.
- **Level III** is characterized by air mobile and assault operations, by airborne operations, by ground forces deliberate operations, by amphibious operations, and by infiltration operations.

In addition to the above enemy force levels, other disruptions exist, such as fires, and conventional, chemical, and nuclear shelling and bombing.

References
Department of Defense, U.S. Army. *Support Operations: Echelons Above Corps.* Field Manual FM 100-16. Washington, DC: Headquarters, Department of the Army, 1986.

—LEVELS OF HOSPITALIZATION include the combat zone, the communications zone, and the continental United States. The combat zone and communications zone levels of hospitalization may be considered, in combination, as the theater level. Likewise, all theaters of operations combined with the continental United States constitute the total (worldwide) hospitalization system. *See also:* Medical Treatment.

References
Department of Defense, U.S. Army. *Planning for Health Service Support.* Field Manual FM 8-55. Washington, DC: Headquarters, Department of the Army, 1985.

—LEVELS OF MAINTENANCE. The U.S. Army's maintenance system is being redesigned to provide a more responsive maintenance system, improved operational readiness, and increased battlefield mobility and flexibility. The system provides a direct link to the ultimate user from the Department of the Army through the commodity management chain. The Army's maintenance structure concept has three levels: unit, intermediate, and depot. *See also:* Depot Maintenance, Intermediate Maintenance, Unit Maintenance.

References
Department of Defense, U.S. Army. *Combat Service Support Operations-Theater.* Field Manual FM 63-4. Washington, DC: Headquarters, Department of the Army, 1984.

—LEVY is an imposition made on Army commands by Headquarters, Department of the Army, for the mandatory reassignment of enlisted personnel in specified military occupational specialties, grades, and, if necessary, special qualifications to meet Army requirements as they exist worldwide.

References

Department of Defense, U.S. Army. *Dictionary of United States Army Terms*. Army Regulation AR 310-25. Washington, DC: Headquarters, Department of the Army, 1986.

—**LIAISON** is the contact or communication maintained between elements of military forces to insure: mutual understanding and unity of purpose and action; cooperation and understanding between commanders and staffs of headquarters or units working together; tactical unity and mutual support by adjacent units; and coordination. *See also:* Liaison Officers.

References

Department of Defense, U.S. Army. *Air Defense Artillery Deployment: Chaparral/Vulcan/Stinger*. Field Manual FM 44-3. Washington, DC: Headquarters, Department of the Army, 1984.

———. *Operational Terms and Symbols*. Field Manual FM 101-5-1. Washington, DC: Headquarters, Department of the Army, 1985.

———. *Staff Organization and Operations*. Field Manual FM 101-5. Washington, DC: Headquarters, Department of the Army, 1984.

—**LIAISON OFFICERS** are representatives of the commander. They work under the direction of the chief of staff, the G3, or another designated individual. The commander may also designate an officer or noncommissioned officer to perform liaison duties for specific purposes or periods of time.

References

Department of Defense, U.S. Army. *Staff Organization and Operations*. Field Manual FM 101-5. Washington, DC: Headquarters, Department of the Army, 1984.

—**LIBERATED TERRITORY** is any area, domestic, neutral or friendly, that, having been occupied by an enemy, is retaken by friendly forces.

References

Department of Defense, Joint Chiefs of Staff. *Department of Defense Dictionary of Military and Related Terms*. Washington, DC: GPO, 1986.

—**LIFE CYCLE** encompasses all of the phases through which an item passes from the time it is initially developed until the time it is either consumed in use or is disposed.

References

Department of Defense, Joint Chiefs of Staff. *Department of Defense Dictionary of Military and Related Terms*. Washington, DC: GPO, 1986.

—**LIFT** consists of all helicopters assigned to a particular mission to move troops and equipment.

References

Department of Defense, U.S. Army. *Operational Terms and Symbols*. Field Manual FM 101-5-1. Washington, DC: Headquarters, Department of the Army, 1985.

—**LIGHT ELEPHANT STEEL SHELTER** is a shelter for personnel and materiel made from steel arch sections of medium size and weight. This shelter is larger and stronger than the two-man steel shelter, but is smaller than the elephant steel shelter. It serves as a splinter-proof cover. *See also:* Shelter.

References

Department of Defense, U.S. Army. *Dictionary of United States Army Terms*. Army Regulation AR 310-25. Washington, DC: Headquarters, Department of the Army, 1986.

—**LIGHT INFANTRY** includes rifle, airborne, ranger, and air assault infantry forces. It is hallmarked by its great flexibility and can operate effectively in most terrain and weather. It may be the dominant arm in low-intensity conflicts, particularly given its rapid strategic deployability. In such cases, it can take the initiative from light regular forces and insurgents by fighting them on equal terms. Heavier or more mobile units can support light infantry in large battles or engagements. In operations where armored forces predominate, light infantry units can:

- Capitalize on natural obstacles (e.g., wetlands, forests, and mountains) and occupy strongpoints in close terrain as pivots for operational and tactical level maneuver;
- Make initial penetrations in difficult terrain for exploitations by armor and mechanized infantry;
- Attack over approaches that are not feasible for heavy forces;
- Capture or defend forested and built-up areas;
- Control restrictive routes for use by other forces;
- Follow and support exploiting heavy forces when augmented with transportation; and
- Conduct rear area operations, capitalizing on air mobility.

In operations in which light forces predominate, airborne, airmobile, or other light infantry forces lead the combined arms attack, and all other arms support the infantry.

References

Department of Defense, U.S. Army. *Operations.* Field Manual FM 100-5. Washington, DC: Headquarters, Department of the Army, 1986.

———. *The Rifle Squads (Mechanized and Light Infantry).* Training Circular TC 7-1. Washington, DC: Headquarters, Department of the Army, 1976.

—**LIGHT LEVEL OF OPERATIONS** reflects operations involving less than 30 percent of all force maneuver echelons and less than 50 percent of fire support means. The forces involved are engaged in sporadic combat over a period of time during which employment of next higher echelon resources, to assure accomplishment of the mission, will not be required. *See also:* Heavy Level of Operations.

References

Department of Defense, U.S. Army. *Dictionary of United States Army Terms.* Army Regulation AR 310-25. Washington, DC: Headquarters, Department of the Army, 1986.

—**LIGHT LINE (LL)** is a designated line forward of which vehicles are required to use black-out lights at night.

References

Department of Defense, U.S. Army. *Operational Terms and Symbols.* Field Manual FM 101-5-1. Washington, DC: Headquarters, Department of the Army, 1985.

—**LIGHT SHELTER** is a shelter that can protect against the continuous bombardment from eight-inch shells. It is not to be confused with a light shell proof shelter, which is built to withstand six-inch shells. *See also:* Heavy Shellproof Shelter.

References

Department of Defense, U.S. Army. *Dictionary of United States Army Terms.* Army Regulation AR 310-25. Washington, DC: Headquarters, Department of the Army, 1986.

—**LIGHT TANK** is a tank that weighs less than 40 tons. The United States no longer uses the classifications of heavy, medium, and light tank. *See also:* Medium Tank.

References

Collins, John M. *U.S.-Soviet Military Balance, 1980-1985.* Washington, DC: Congressional Research Service, 1985.

—**LIMIT OF ADVANCE** is a recognizable terrain feature beyond which attacking troops will not advance. One limit of advance is selected beyond each platoon objective if the platoons are to seize separate objectives. A limit of advance helps insure that supporting fire from friendly units is not fired on friendly troops. It should be far enough beyond and to the flanks of an objective to give security elements space in which to do their job.

References

Department of Defense, U.S. Army. *The Infantry Rifle Company (Infantry, Airborne, Air Assault, Ranger).* Field Manual FM 7-10. Washington, DC: Headquarters, Department of the Army, 1982.

———. *Operational Terms and Symbols.* Field Manual FM 101-5-1. Washington, DC: Headquarters, Department of the Army, 1985.

—**LIMIT OF FIRE.** (1) A limit of fire is the boundary marking off an area on which gunfire can be delivered. (2) A limit of fire consists of the safe angular limits for firing at aerial targets.

References

Department of Defense, Joint Chiefs of Staff. *Department of Defense Dictionary of Military and Related Terms.* Washington, DC: GPO, 1986.

—**LIMIT VELOCITY** is the lowest possible velocity at which any one of the projectiles completely penetrates the target. Since the limit velocity is difficult to obtain, a more easily obtainable value is usually used. The limit velocity is designated as the ballistic limit.

References

Department of Defense, U.S. Army. *Dictionary of United States Army Terms.* Army Regulation AR 310-25. Washington, DC: Headquarters, Department of the Army, 1986.

—**LIMITED ACCESS AUTHORIZATION (LAA)** is the formal authority granted to a non-U.S. citizen to have access to specifically prescribed and limited U.S. classified defense information and materials. In each case, a background investigation, which covers the last fifteen years of the person's life, is conducted and the results must be favorable. An LAA may remain in effect for a maximum of five years before a reinvestigation is required. *See also:* Background Investigation.

References

Department of Defense, U.S. Army. *Counterintelligence.* Field Manual FM 34-60. Washington, DC: Headquarters, Department of the Army, 1985.

—**LIMITED ACCESS ROUTE** is a one-way route with one or more restrictions that preclude its use by the full range of military traffic. *See also:* Single Flow Route.

References
Department of Defense, Joint Chiefs of Staff. *Department of Defense Dictionary of Military and Related Terms.* Washington, DC: GPO, 1986.

—**LIMITED DISTRIBUTION MESSAGES** are messages that must receive limited distribution but may be handled by regular communications personnel using the required handling precautions for the messages based on their security classification.

References
Department of Defense, U.S. Army. *Dictionary of United States Army Terms.* Army Regulation AR 310-25. Washington, DC: Headquarters, Department of the Army, 1986.

—**LIMITED STANDARD ARTICLE** is an item that is not satisfactory as a standard type, but is a usable substitute, and is either in use or is available for issue to meet an existing supply demand.

References
Department of Defense, U.S. Army. *Dictionary of United States Army Terms.* Army Regulation AR 310-25. Washington, DC: Headquarters, Department of the Army, 1986.

—**LIMITED STANDARD TYPE** are items that are not acceptable for U.S. Army operational requirements and will not, therefore, be counted as assets against operational requirements. This category is limited to: (1) items that are not acceptable to meet operational requirements but are useful for training and (2) items that are not acceptable to meet operational requirements of the U.S. Army, but are being retained to meet peculiar or unique requirements other than the training requirement that was discussed in the category above.

References
Department of Defense, U.S. Army. *Dictionary of United States Army Terms.* Army Regulation AR 310-25. Washington, DC: Headquarters, Department of the Army, 1986.

—**LIMITED STORAGE** is a storage classification for supplies intended for withdrawal within 90 days, allowing for the possibility of the least protected storage condition that is authorized for a specific material.

References
Department of Defense, U.S. Army. *Dictionary of United States Army Terms.* Army Regulation AR 310-25. Washington, DC: Headquarters, Department of the Army, 1986.

—**LIMITED VISIBILTY OPERATIONS** are operations conducted at night or other periods of reduced visibility.

References
Department of Defense, U.S. Army. *Operational Terms and Symbols.* Field Manual FM 101-5-1. Washington, DC: Headquarters, Department of the Army, 1985.

—**LIMITED WAR** is an armed conflict that falls short of general war, exclusive of incidents, involving the overt engagement of military forces of two or more nations. *See also:* Incidents, Low-Intensity Conflict.

References
Department of Defense, U.S. Army. *Support Operations: Echelons Above Corps.* Field Manual FM 100-16. Washington, DC: Headquarters, Department of the Army, 1986.

—**LIMITING FACTOR** is a deficiency in the resources (e.g., movement capabilities, personnel, logistics, or facilities) that are required to support an operation.

References
Department of Defense, U.S. Army. *Planning Logistics Support for Military Operations.* Field Manual FM 701-58. Washington, DC: Headquarters, Department of the Army, 1987.

—**LINE.** (1) A line is an arrangement of vehicles or personnel that permits maximum fire to the flanks; is difficult to control; does not provide as much depth as a column formation; permits closure of an objective in the least amount of time; and is used when emerging from creeks, smoke, and wooded areas and for the assault of objectives. (2) A line, in artillery, is a spotting or an observation that is used by a spotter or observer to indicate that a burst or bursts occurred on the spotting line. (3) In ballistic meteorological messages, a line is the vertical height of the trajectory of which the associated ballistic or meteorological elements are applicable. Information for a line is derived from meteorological data from the surface to a height defined by the line number. *See also:* Column, Vee, Wedge.

References
Department of Defense, U.S. Army. *Operational Terms and Symbols.* Field Manual FM 101-5-1. Washington, DC: Headquarters, Department of the Army, 1985

—**LINE** (AMBUSH FORMATION). In the ambush formation, the assault element and the direct fire weapons of the support element are deployed generally parallel to the target's route of movement (e.g., a road, trail, or stream). This positions these elements parallel to the long axis of the kill zone and subjects the target to flanking fire.

References
Department of Defense, U.S. Army. *The Infantry Rifle Company (Infantry. Airborne, Air Assault, Ranger).* Field Manual FM 7-10. Washington, DC: Headquarters, Department of the Army, 1982.

—**LINE** (MARCHING FORMATION) is a formation in which the elements are side by side and abreast of each other. In a platoon line, the members of each squad are abreast of each other while the squads are one behind the other. *See also:* Column, Formation

References
Department of Defense, U.S. Army. *Drills and Ceremonies.* Field Manual FM 22-5. Washington, DC: Headquarters, Department of the Army, 1986.

—**LINE HAUL,** in highway transportation, is a type of haul involving long trips over the road wherein the proportion of running time is high in relation to the time consumed in loading and unloading. Line hauls usually are evaluated on the basis of ton miles forward per day. In rail transportation, line haul applies to the movement or carriage of material over tracks of a carrier from one point to another, but excludes switching service.

References
Department of Defense, U.S. Army. *Dictionary of United States Army Terms.* Army Regulation AR 310-25. Washington, DC: Headquarters, Department of the Army, 1986.

—**LINE ITEM NUMBER** is a number assigned to a generic nomenclature by a U.S. Army technical committee action for the purpose of identifying the line on which the official generic nomenclature is listed. The line item number is used as a tool for sorting items into a sequence. It is also used in supply management for consolidating assets, requirements, and other data for all federally stock-numbered items to which it is related.

References
Department of Defense, U.S. Army. *Dictionary of United States Army Terms.* Army Regulation AR 310-25. Washington, DC: Headquarters, Department of the Army, 1986.

—**LINE MAP.** *See:* Lined Photomap.

—**LINE OF AIM** is a line from the weapon delivery sight to the aiming point.

References
Department of Defense, U.S. Army. *Dictionary of United States Army Terms.* Army Regulation AR 310-25. Washington, DC: Headquarters, Department of the Army, 1986.

—**LINE OF CONTACT (LC)** is a general trace delineating the location where two opposing forces are engaged. *See also:* Line of Departure, Line of Departure/Line of Contact, Forward Edge of the Battle Area, Forward Edge of Own Troops.

References
Department of Defense, U.S. Army. *Attack Helicopter Operations.* Field Manual FM 17-50. Washington, DC: Headquarters, Department of the Army, 1984.

———. *Operational Terms and Symbols.* Field Manual FM 101-5-1. Washington, DC: Headquarters, Department of the Army, 1985.

—**LINE OF DEPARTURE (LD).** (1) A line of departure is a line designated to coordinate the commitment of attacking units or scouting elements at a specified time of attack. It is a jumpoff line and should be easily identifiable on the ground and on a map, and should generally be perpendicular to the direction of the attack. (2) A line of departure, in ground operations, is a line, ordinarily located on or behind the last available terrain mask, that can be reached without exposure to hostile observation and small arms fire. Suitable, clearly defined features (e.g., roads, the edge of a forest, and friendly front lines) can be used. (3) A line of departure is a line that is tangent to the trajectory at the instant of the projectile's departure from its origin. It is displaced vertically from the line of elevation by the amount of the vertical jump. *See also:* Line of Contact, Line of Departure/Line of Contact.

References
Department of Defense, U.S. Army. *Armored and Mechanized Division Operations.* Field Manual FM 71-100. Washington, DC: Headquarters, Department of the Army, 1978.

———. *Attack Helicopter Operations.* Field Manual FM 17-50. Washington, DC: Headquarters, Department of the Army, 1984.

———. *Operational Terms and Symbols.* Field Manual FM 101-5-1. Washington, DC: Headquarters, Department of the Army, 1985.

—**LINE OF DEPARTURE/LINE OF CONTACT (LD/ LC)** is the designation of forward friendly positions as the LD when opposing forces are in contact with friendly forces.

References

Department of Defense, U.S. Army. *Attack Helicopter Operations.* Field Manual FM 17-50. Washington, DC: Headquarters, Department of the Army, 1984.

———. *Operational Terms and Symbols.* Field Manual FM 101-5-1. Washington, DC: Headquarters, Department of the Army, 1985.

—**LINE OF DRIFT.** (1) Line of drift is a natural route along which wounded men may be expected to go back from a combat position for medical aid. (2) A line of drift is a route along which stragglers may be expected to go from the zone of action to the rear areas.

References

Department of Defense, U.S. Army. *Dictionary of United States Army Terms.* Army Regulation AR 310-25. Washington, DC: Headquarters, Department of the Army, 1986.

—**LINE OF DUTY.** (1) Line of duty is authorized duty in service. (2) Line of duty is a classification of all sickness, injury, or death that is suffered by personnel in the active military service of the United States, unless caused by fault or neglect, and unless the disease, injury, or condition existed prior to military service and was not aggravated by that service.

References

Department of Defense, U.S. Army. *Dictionary of United States Army Terms.* Army Regulation AR 310-25. Washington, DC: Headquarters, Department of the Army, 1986.

—**LINE OF FALL** is a line tangent to the trajectory at the level point.

References

Department of Defense, U.S. Army. *Dictionary of United States Army Terms.* Army Regulation AR 310-25. Washington, DC: Headquarters, Department of the Army, 1986.

—**LINE OF IMPACT** is a line tangent to the trajectory at the point of impact or burst.

References

Department of Defense, Joint Chiefs of Staff. *Department of Defense Dictionary of Military and Related Terms.* Washington, DC: GPO, 1986.

—**LINE OF POSITION** is a line indicating a series of positions on which the observer is estimated to be at the time of the observation.

References

Department of Defense, U.S. Army. *Dictionary of United States Army Terms.* Army Regulation AR 310-25. Washington, DC: Headquarters, Department of the Army, 1986.

—**LINE OF SIGHT.** (1) A line of sight is the line between the target and the aiming reference. (2) A line of sight is the straight line between two points. This line is in the plane of the great circle, but does not follow the curvature of the earth.

References

Department of Defense, U.S. Army. *Dictionary of United States Army Terms.* Army Regulation AR 310-25. Washington, DC: Headquarters, Department of the Army, 1986.

—**LINE OF SITE** is a straight line joining the origin and a point, usually a target.

References

Department of Defense, U.S. Army. *Dictionary of United States Army Terms.* Army Regulation AR 310-25. Washington, DC: Headquarters, Department of the Army, 1986.

—**LINE OF SKIRMISHERS** is a line of dismounted men who are in staggered formation and are at extended intervals.

References

Department of Defense, U.S. Army. *Dictionary of United States Army Terms.* Army Regulation AR 310-25. Washington, DC: Headquarters, Department of the Army, 1986.

—**LINE OFFICER** is an officer belonging to a combatant branch of the Army; an officer of the line.

References

Department of Defense, U.S. Army. *Dictionary of United States Army Terms.* Army Regulation AR 310-25. Washington, DC: Headquarters, Department of the Army, 1986.

—**LINE OFFSET METHOD** is a method by which a curved line can be surveyed. From a known starting point, a straight line is laid out that will cut the curve at two points, at equal distances, from the starting point. At set distances along this line in each direction from the starting point, perpendiculars of known length are set up. By joining their ends, the curve is established.

References

Department of Defense, U.S. Army. *Dictionary of United States Army Terms.* Army Regulation AR 310-25. Washington, DC: Headquarters, Department of the Army, 1986.

—**LINE REPLACEABLE UNIT** is a composite group of modules or subassemblies performing one or more discrete functions in a communications-electronics system. They are constructed as an independently packaged unit and are intended for direct installation in a communications-electronic equipment.

References

Department of Defense, U.S. Army. *Dictionary of United States Army Terms.* Army Regulation AR 310-25. Washington, DC: Headquarters, Department of the Army, 1986.

—**LINE SHOT.** (1) A line shot is a projectile that strikes on the line from the observer to the target. (2) A line shot is a projectile that passes through any part of the cone of sight that is formed by an air target.

References

Department of Defense, U.S. Army. *Dictionary of United States Army Terms.* Army Regulation AR 310-25. Washington, DC: Headquarters, Department of the Army, 1986.

—**LINEAR** (ARMY AVIATION) is a point during formation maneuvering when all aircraft are aligned. A linear alignment allows the attacker to engage more than one attacker during a single attack run.

References

Department of Defense, U.S. Army. *Air-to-Air Combat.* Field Manual FM 1-107. Washington, DC: Headquarters, Department of the Army, 1984.

—**LINEAR DISPOSITION (LD)** allows interlocking and overlapping observation and fields of fire along the company sector. The bulk of the company's combat power is well forward. The commander relies on fighting from well-arranged and well-prepared fighting positions. Since he plans to use a high volume of direct and indirect fire to stop the attacker, the reserve is usually small, perhaps only a squad.

References

Department of Defense, U.S. Army. *The Infantry Rifle Company (Infantry, Airborne, Air Assault, Ranger).* Field Manual FM 7-10. Washington, DC: Headquarters, Department of the Army, 1982.

—**LINEAR DISPOSITION WITH DEPTH** is a modification of the linear disposition. It allows interlocking and overlapping observation and fields of fire, while also allowing a large reserve and depth in defense. It may be used when the enemy has both infantry and armor or when there is an armor avenue of approach through the company sector.

References

Department of Defense, U.S. Army. *The Infantry Rifle Company (Infantry, Airborne, Air Assault, Ranger).* Field Manual FM 7-10. Washington, DC: Headquarters, Department of the Army, 1982.

—**LINEAR ERROR (LE).** (1) LE is a one-dimensional error (e.g., an error in elevation) derived by the normal distribution function. (2) LE is the difference between the true or known value and the measured or derived value, and is normally expressed in terms of a percentage probability level. For example, LE 90 percent is the term used to express the linear error at 90 percent probability (i.e., the Map Accuracy Standard).

References

Department of Defense, U.S. Army. *Dictionary of United States Army Terms.* Army Regulation AR 310-25. Washington, DC: Headquarters, Department of the Army, 1986.

—**LINEAR FEATURE** is a feature portrayed by a line that does not represent an area. It is also called a line feature.

References

Department of Defense, U.S. Army. *Dictionary of United States Army Terms.* Army Regulation AR 310-25. Washington, DC: Headquarters, Department of the Army, 1986.

—**LINEAR OBSTACLE SPACING** is the distance between obstacles that cross the entire terrain unit and have a regular pattern (e.g., a row of crops or ricefield dikes).

References
Department of Defense, U.S. Army. *Dictionary of United States Army Terms.* Army Regulation AR 310-25. Washington, DC: Headquarters, Department of the Army, 1986.

—**LINEAR SPEED METHOD** is a method of calculating firing data in which the future position of a moving target is determined by finding the direction of flight and the ground speed of the target. By multiplying the ground speed by the time of flight of the projectile, the future position is determined. Linear speed method and angular travel method are two methods of computing targeting data.

References
Department of Defense, U.S. Army. *Dictionary of United States Army Terms.* Army Regulation AR 310-25. Washington, DC: Headquarters, Department of the Army, 1986.

—**LINED PHOTOMAP** is a photomap that omits the unnecessary detail. It is usually made by tracing from or bleaching an air photograph. *See also:* Aerial Reconnaissance.

References
Department of Defense, U.S. Army. *Dictionary of United States Army Terms.* Army Regulation AR 310-25. Washington, DC: Headquarters, Department of the Army, 1986.

—**LINES OF COMMUNICATION (LOCs)** (LOGISTIC ROUTES) are all the routes (land, water, and air) that connect an operating military force with a base of operations and along which supplies and military forces move.

References
Department of Defense, U.S. Army. *Route Reconnaissance and Classification.* Field Manual FM 5-36. Washington, DC: Headquarters, Department of the Army, 1985.

————. *Support Operations: Echelons Above Corps.* Field Manual FM 100-16. Washington, DC: Headquarters, Department of the Army, 1986.

—**LINES OF COMMUNICATION (LOCS) STUDIES** are produced by the Defense Intelligence Agency. They are comprehensive studies of all types of communications within and between countries. They include data on ports, railways, highways, inland waterways, air transportation, beaches, and telecommunications. *See also:* Lines of Communication (Logistic Routes).

References
Von Hoene, John P. A. *Intelligence User's Guide.* Washington, DC: DIA, 1983.

—**LINES OF OPERATION** define the directional orientation of a force in relation to the enemy. Lines of operation connect the force with the base (or bases) of operation on the one hand, and its operational objective on the other. Normally, a campaign or major operation will have a single line of operation, although multiple lines of operation in a single campaign are not uncommon. Often, such situations produce difficulties, as in the Allied campaign in northern France and the Low Countries, where Field Marshal Montgomery and General Patton competed for resources that might better have been concentrated in support of one or the other commander.

References
Department of Defense, U.S. Army. *Operations.* Field Manual FM 100-5. Washington, DC: Headquarters, Department of the Army, 1986.

—**LINES OF SUPPORT.** Maintaining uninterrupted sustaining support throughout all phases of the operation or campaign is the central challenge of operational sustainment. Such continuity is provided in large part by establishing lines of communication linking the theater base or bases to the forward tactical formations. Depending on the geography of the theater, the availability of transportation assets, and the threat, ground lines of communication may be supplemented by air lines of communication and sea lines of communication.

References
Department of Defense, U.S. Army. *Operations.* Field Manual FM 100-5. Washington, DC: Headquarters, Department of the Army, 1986.

—**LINK.** (1) A link, in communications, is a general term used to indicate the existence of communications facilities between two points. (2) A link is a metal unit that connects the cartridges for an automatic weapon and, with them, forms a feed belt.

References
Department of Defense, Joint Chiefs of Staff. *Department of Defense Dictionary of Military and Related Terms.* Washington, DC: GPO, 1986.

—**LINK-LIFT VEHICLE** is the conveyance, together with its operating personnel, used to satisfy a movement requirement between nodes. *See also:* Nodes.

References

Department of Defense, Joint Chiefs of Staff. *Department of Defense Dictionary of Military and Related Terms.* Washington, DC: GPO, 1986.

—**LINK-ROUTE SEGMENTS** are route segments that connect nodes wherein link-lift vehicles perform the movement function. *See also:* Link-Lift Vehicle, Node.

References

Department of Defense, Joint Chiefs of Staff. *Department of Defense Dictionary of Military and Related Terms.* Washington, DC: GPO, 1986.

—**LINKUP.** (1) Linkup is the process of joining a ready-for-issue weapon with a trained crew that results in a ready-to-fight weapon system. (2) A linkup is a meeting of friendly ground forces, such as when an advancing force reaches an objective area that was previously seized by an airborne or air assault force, or when an encircled element breaks out to rejoin friendly forces, or when converging maneuver forces meet. *See also:* Linkup Operations, Linkup Point.

References

Department of Defense, U.S. Army. *Combat Service Support Operations-Division.* Field Manual FM 63-2. Washington, DC: Headquarters, Department of the Army, 1983.

————. *Operational Terms and Symbols.* Field Manual FM 101-5-1. Washington, DC: Headquarters, Department of the Army, 1985.

—**LINKUP OPERATIONS** are conducted to join two friendly forces. Both forces may be moving toward each other, or one may be stationary while the other is moving. Linkup operations may be conducted in a variety of circumstances. They are most often conducted to complete the encirclement of an enemy force, assist the breakout of a friendly force, or to join an attacking force with a force that has been inserted in the enemy rear (e.g., an airborne or air assault force). *See also:* Linkup, Linkup Point.

References

Department of Defense, U.S. Army. *Armored and Mechanized Division Operations.* Field Manual FM 71-100. Washington, DC: Headquarters, Department of the Army, 1978.

—**LINKUP POINT** is an easily identifiable point on the ground where two forces conducting a linkup meet. When one force is stationary, linkup points normally are established where the moving force's routes of advance intersect the stationary force's security elements. Linkup points for two moving forces are established on boundaries where the two forces are expected to converge. *See also:* Linkup, Linkup Operations.

References

Department of Defense, U.S. Army. *Operational Terms and Symbols.* Field Manual FM 101-5-1. Washington, DC: Headquarters, Department of the Army, 1985.

—**LIQUID EXPLOSIVE** is an explosive that is fluid at normal temperatures.

References

Department of Defense, Joint Chiefs of Staff. *Department of Defense Dictionary of Military and Related Terms.* Washington, DC: GPO, 1986.

—**LIQUID PROPELLENTS** are liquid or gaseous substances (e.g., fuels, oxidizers, or monopropellents) that are used for the propulsion or operation of missiles, rockets, and other related devices.

References

Department of Defense, U.S. Army. *Ammunition and Explosives Safety Standards.* Army Regulation AR 385-64. Washington, DC: Headquarters, Department of the Army, 1987.

—**LIST OF TARGETS/TARGET LIST** is a tabulation of confirmed or suspected targets maintained by any echelon for information and fire support planning purposes. *See also:* Targeting.

References

Department of Defense, Joint Chiefs of Staff. *Department of Defense Dictionary of Military and Related Terms.* Washington, DC: GPO, 1986.

Department of Defense, U.S. Army. *Fire Support in Combined Arms Operations.* Field Manual FM 6-20. Washington, DC: Headquarters, Department of the Army, 1983.

—**LISTENING POSTS (LP)** are positions from which one listens and observes during periods of reduced visibility (e.g., in darkness, smoke, or bad weather).

References
Department of Defense, U.S. Army. *The Rifle Squads (Mechanized and Light Infantry)*. Training Circular TC 7-1. Washington, DC: Headquarters, Department of the Army, 1976.

—**LISTENING SILENCE** is a period of time specified by a commander during which the transmitters of all radio sets that are used for signal communications within the command are completely shut down and are not operated except during emergencies that are specifically described in the orders. All receivers remain in operation on net frequencies unless special orders are issued to the contrary.

References
Department of Defense, U.S. Army. *Dictionary of United States Army Terms*. Army Regulation AR 310-25. Washington, DC: Headquarters, Department of the Army, 1986.

—**LISTENING WATCH** is a continuous receiver watch established for the reception of traffic addressed to, or of interest to, the unit maintaining the watch.

References
Department of Defense, Joint Chiefs of Staff. *Department of Defense Dictionary of Military and Related Terms*. Washington, DC: GPO, 1986.

—**LITERAL KEY** is a key composed of a sequence of letters.

References
Department of Defense, U.S. Army. *Dictionary of United States Army Terms*. Army Regulation AR 310-25. Washington, DC: Headquarters, Department of the Army, 1986.

—**LITTER** is a basket or frame used to transport injured persons.

References
Department of Defense, Joint Chiefs of Staff. *Department of Defense Dictionary of Military and Related Terms*. Washington, DC: GPO, 1986.

—**LITTER PATIENT** is a sick or injured person who must be transported by a litter.

References
Department of Defense, Joint Chiefs of Staff. *Department of Defense Dictionary of Military and Related Terms*. Washington, DC: GPO, 1986.

—**LITTER RELAY POINT** is a point where a new litter team takes over the further movement of a casualty, and the first team returns for another casualty. The object is to provide short litter hauls for the litter bearers. The casualty may or may not be placed on a wheeled litter at the relay point.

References
Department of Defense, U.S. Army. *Dictionary of United States Army Terms*. Army Regulation AR 310-25. Washington, DC: Headquarters, Department of the Army, 1986.

—**LIVE EXERCISE** is an exercise using real forces and units.

References
Department of Defense, Joint Chiefs of Staff. *Department of Defense Dictionary of Military and Related Terms*. Washington, DC: GPO, 1986.

—**LIVE FIRE EXERCISES (LFXs)** are high-cost, resource-intensive exercises in which player units move or maneuver and employ organic and supporting weapon systems using full-service ammunition with an attendant integration of all combat, combat support, and combat service support units.

The extensive range and ammunition requirements for LFXs usually limit them to platoon and company team levels. Consequently, unit and weapon systems integration at the company team level is the principal focus of the exercise.

References
Department of Defense, U.S. Army. *How to Conduct Training Exercises*. Field Manual FM 25-4. Washington, DC: Headquarters, Department of the Army, 1984.
———. *Training for Mobilization and War*. Field Manual FM 25-5. Washington, DC: Headquarters, Department of the Army, 1985.

—**LOAD CONTROL GROUP** consists of the personnel concerned with the organization and control of loading within a pick-up zone.

References
Department of Defense, Joint Chiefs of Staff. *Department of Defense Dictionary of Military and Related Terms*. Washington, DC: GPO, 1986.

—**LOADING** is the process of putting troops, equipment, and supplies into ships, aircraft, trains, road transport, or other means of conveyance. *See also:* Administrative Loading, Unit Loading.

References
Department of Defense, Joint Chiefs of Staff. *Department of Defense Dictionary of Military and Related Terms*. Washington, DC: GPO, 1986.

—**LOADING PLAN** is the sum of all the individually prepared documents that, taken together, present in detail all instructions for the arrangement of personnel, and the loading of equipment for one or more units or other special grouping of personnel or material. The plan is used by forces that are moving by highway, water, rail, or air transportation. *See also:* Ocean Manifest.

References
Department of Defense, Joint Chiefs of Staff. *Department of Defense Dictionary of Military and Related Terms.* Washington, DC: GPO, 1986.

—**LOADING TIME** is a specified time, established jointly by the aircraft and airborne commanders concerned, when the aircraft and loads are available and the loading is to begin.

References
Department of Defense, U.S. Army. *USA/USAF Doctrine for Joint Airborne and Tactical Airlift Operations.* Field Manual FM 100-27. Washington, DC: Headquarters, Department of the Army, 1985.

—**LOADING TRAY.** (1) A loading tray is a trough-shaped carrier on which heavy projectiles are placed so that they can be more easily and safely slipped into the breech of a gun. (2) A loading tray is the hollowed slide that guides the shells into the breech of some types of automatic weapons.

References
Department of Defense, U.S. Army. *Dictionary of United States Army Terms.* Army Regulation AR 310-25. Washington, DC: Headquarters, Department of the Army, 1986.

—**LOADMASTER** is an Air Force technician qualified to plan loads, to operate auxiliary equipment, and to supervise the loading and unloading of aircraft.

References
Department of Defense, U.S. Army. *USA/USAF Doctrine for Joint Airborne and Tactical Airlift Operations.* Field Manual FM 100-27. Washington, DC: Headquarters, Department of the Army, 1985.

—**LOCAL ADMINISTRATION** is an administration controlled by a local commander and is related specifically to the troops or the operations in his area. It involves discipline and the interior economy and covers such matters as quartering and accommodations; provision of light, water, and power; the care an well-being of personnel

(including rationing); hygiene and sanitation; fire protection; maintenance of barracks and camps; supervision of stores accounting and internal checking; allocation of ranges, training areas, and recreation facilities; local movement of personnel and materiel; local road traffic control and movement; security (including preventive measures against vandalism and theft); relations with local civilian authorities and population; allocation of any local pool of labor and unit transport; and allocation of local duties.

References
Department of Defense, U.S. Army. *Dictionary of United States Army Terms.* Army Regulation AR 310-25. Washington, DC: Headquarters, Department of the Army, 1986.

—**LOCAL EFFECT ANTIPERSONNEL MINE** is designed to incapacitate a person and is set off by a limited action, such as a person stepping on it.

References
Department of Defense, U.S. Army. *Mine/Countermine Operations at the Company Level.* Field Manual FM 20-32. Washington, DC: Headquarters, Department of the Army, 1976.

—**LOCAL MEAN TIME** is the time interval that has elapsed since the mean sun's transit of the observer's anti-meridian.

References
Department of Defense, Joint Chiefs of Staff. *Department of Defense Dictionary of Military and Related Terms.* Washington, DC: GPO, 1986.

—**LOCAL NATIONAL** is a non-U.S. citizen who is normally a resident in, but not necessarily a citizen of, the country in which he is employed, and who is employed and paid under the conditions of employment and wage scales that are prescribed by the country in which he resides.

References
Department of Defense, U.S. Army. *Dictionary of United States Army Terms.* Army Regulation AR 310-25. Washington, DC: Headquarters, Department of the Army, 1986.

—**LOCAL PROCUREMENT** is the process of obtaining personnel, services, supplies, and equipment from local or indigenous sources. When a needed item is not readily available through the supply system but is available on the local economy, the Army may be able to purchase it locally. Local procurement may also be used to purchase selected maintenance services.

References

Department of Defense, U.S. Army. *Organizational Maintenance Operations*. Field Manual FM 29-2. Washington, DC: Headquarters, Department of the Army, 1984.

—**LOCAL PURCHASE** is the function of acquiring a decentralized item of supply from sources outside the Department of Defense. *See also:* Local Procurement.

References

Department of Defense, Joint Chiefs of Staff. *Department of Defense Dictionary of Military and Related Terms*. Washington, DC: GPO, 1986.

—**LOCAL RECORD AUDIT** is a match between valid location records, excluding quantity, to identify and correct situations where items are in physical storage but are not recorded on accountable records, or on record but not in storage, or when storage item data (i.e., the National Stock Number, unit of issue, condition code, ownership code, security/pilferage code, or shelf life code) do not match. The audit includes research of mismatches and the scheduling of special inventories, if required.

References

Department of Defense, U.S. Army. *Dictionary of United States Army Terms*. Army Regulation AR 310-25. Washington, DC: Headquarters, Department of the Army, 1986.

—**LOCAL SECURITY** consists of the security elements established in proximity to a unit to prevent surprise by the enemy.

References

Department of Defense, U.S. Army. *Operational Terms and Symbols*. Field Manual FM 101-5-1. Washington, DC: Headquarters, Department of the Army, 1985.

—**LOCATE** is to establish a broad operating area for the use of air defense artillery fire units.

References

Department of Defense, U.S. Army. *Air Defense Employment*. Field Manual FM. 44-1. Washington, DC: Headquarters, Department of the Army, 1983.

———. *U.S. Army Air Defense Artillery Employment Hawk*. Field Manual FM 44-90. Washington, DC: Headquarters, Department of the Army, 1983.

—**LOCK ON** is an electronics term that signifies that a tracking or target-seeking system is continuously and automatically tracking a target in one or more coordinates (i.e., range, azimuth, elevation, or altitude). *See also:* Electronic Warfare.

References

Department of Defense, U.S. Army. *Air Defense Artillery Employment Hawk*. Field Manual FM 44-90. Washington, DC: Headquarters, Department of the Army, 1983.

———. *Air Defense Employment*. Field Manual FM 44-1. Washington, DC: Headquarters, Department of the Army, 1983.

—**LODGMENT AREA** is a foothold gained in territory held by the enemy.

References

Department of Defense, U.S. Army. *Support Operations: Echelons Above Corps*. Field Manual FM 100-16. Washington, DC: Headquarters, Department of the Army, 1986.

—**LOGISTIC ASSESSMENT** is an evaluation of (1) the logistic support that is required to support military operations in a theater of operations, country or area and (2) the actual and/or potential logistics support that is available for conducting military operations either within the theater, country, or area, or elsewhere.

References

Department of Defense, Joint Chiefs of Staff. *Department of Defense Dictionary of Military and Related Terms*. Washington, DC: GPO, 1986.

—**LOGISTIC ASSISTANCE** is a generic term used to denote the types of assistance between and within military commands in both peacetime and wartime. *See also:* Integrated Logistic Support.

References

Department of Defense, Joint Chiefs of Staff. *Department of Defense Dictionary of Military and Related Terms*. Washington, DC: GPO, 1986.

—**LOGISTIC CONSTRAINT.** (1) A logistic constraint is an inhibitor in terms of the numbers of standard obstacles by type, as defined by the unit's standing operating procedure, that is given to all tactical commanders who are developing obstacle plans. Materials, transportation, and construction effort availability in specific sectors dictate the constraint. Its purpose is to keep obstacle plans within limits that can be reasonably accomplished. (2) A logistic constraint is any logistic shortage that impacts on tactical operations. *See also:* Obstacle Plan.

References

Department of Defense, U.S. Army. *Operational Terms and Symbols.* Field Manual FM 101-5-1. Washington, DC: Headquarters, Department of the Army, 1985.

—LOGISTIC ESTIMATE OF THE SITUATION (STAFF ESTIMATE) is an appraisal resulting from an orderly examination of the logistic factors influencing the contemplated courses of action. The purpose is to provide conclusions concerning the logistic feasibility of various courses of action and the effects of each course on logistic operations. *See also:* Estimate of the Situation.

References

Department of Defense, Joint Chiefs of Staff. *Department of Defense Dictionary of Military and Related Terms.* Washington, DC: GPO, 1986.

—LOGISTIC IMPLICATIONS TEST is an analysis of the major aspects of a joint strategic war plan and the consideration of the logistic implications resulting from it as they may limit the acceptability of the plan. The logistic analysis and consideration are conducted concurrently with the development of the strategic plan. The objective is to establish whether the logistic requirements generated by the plan balance with availabilities, and to set forth the logistic implications that should be weighed by the Joint Chiefs of Staff in their consideration of the plan. *See also:* Joint Chiefs of Staff.

References

Department of Defense, Joint Chiefs of Staff. *Department of Defense Dictionary of Military and Related Terms.* Washington, DC: GPO, 1986.

—LOGISTIC SUPPORT (MEDICAL) is medical care, treatment, hospitalization, and evacuation, and the furnishing of medical services, supplies, and materiel. *See also:* Medical Treatment.

References

Department of Defense, Joint Chiefs of Staff. *Department of Defense Dictionary of Military and Related Terms.* Washington, DC: GPO, 1986.

—LOGISTICS is the science of planning and carrying out the movement and maintenance of forces. In its most comprehensive sense, it is the aspects of military actions that deal with (1) the design, development, acquisition, storage, movement, distribution, maintenance, evacuation, and disposition of materiel; (2) the movement, evacuation, and hospitalization of personnel; (3) the acquisition or construction, maintenance, operation, and disposition of facilities; and (4) the acquisition or furnishing of services. *See also:* Logistics Immaterial Position, Logistics Over-the-Shore Operations, Logistics Readiness Center, Logistics Sourcing, Logistics System Manager.

References

Department of Defense, Joint Chiefs of Staff. *Department of Defense Dictionary of Military and Related Terms.* Washington, DC: GPO, 1986.

———. *Operational Terms and Symbols.* Field Manual FM 101-5-1. Washington, DC: Headquarters, Department of the Army, 1985.

—LOGISTICS IMMATERIAL POSITION is a duty position that is not identified with one specific branch of the Army but is limited to officers whose branches are Ordnance, Quartermaster, and Transportation.

References

Department of Defense, U.S. Army. *Commissioned Officer Professional Development and Utilization.* Department of the Army Pamphlet 600-3. Washington, DC: Headquarters, Department of the Army, 1986.

—LOGISTICS OVER-THE-SHORE OPERATIONS (LOTs) is the loading and unloading of ships without the benefit of fixed-port facilities in friendly or nondefended territory; and, in time of war, during phases of theater development in which there is no opposition from the enemy.

References

Department of Defense, U.S. Army. *Planning Logistics Support for Military Operations.* Field Manual FM 701-58. Washington, DC: Headquarters, Department of the Army, 1987.

—LOGISTICS READINESS CENTER is an agency located with the theater army headquarters. It interfaces with the Theater Army Materiel Management Center to keep the theater army commander and staff informed of the essential needs of the using units and the status of selected critical on-hand stocks. It also provides to the Theater Army Materiel Management Center the theater army commander's direction and guidance concerning priorities and quantities to be issued to best logistically support the battle.

References

Department of Defense, U.S. Army. *Support Operations: Echelons Above Corps.* Field Manual FM 100-16. Washington, DC: Headquarters, Department of the Army, 1986.

—**LOGISTICS SOURCING** is the identification of the origin and determination of the availability of the time-phased force and deployment data nonunit logistics requirements.

References
Department of Defense, Joint Chiefs of Staff. *Department of Defense Dictionary of Military and Related Terms*. Washington, DC: GPO, 1986.

—**LOGISTICS SYSTEM MANAGER** is a theater army-level designated manager for critical logistical functions. He is located at the theater army headquarters logistics readiness center and is responsible for the total system management of critical supplies, equipment, and services as directed by the theater army commander.

References
Department of Defense, U.S. Army. *Support Operations: Echelons Above Corps*. Field Manual FM 100-16. Washington, DC: Headquarters, Department of the Army, 1986.

—**LONG RECOIL.** *See:* Recoil Operated.

—**LONG SUPPLY** is the situation wherein the total quantity of an item of materiel on hand within a military service exceeds the service's M-day materiel requirement for the item. This situation, when it occurs, requires a further determination as to that portion of the quantity in long supply that is to be retained as either economic retention stock or contingency retention stock, and that portion, called excess stock, that is not to be retained. *See also:* M-Day Force Materiel Requirement.

References
Department of Defense, U.S. Army. *Dictionary of United States Army Terms*. Army Regulation AR 310-25. Washington, DC: Headquarters, Department of the Army, 1986.

—**LONG TOUR AREA** is an overseas area in which the prescribed tour length is 36 months or longer for personnel who are accompanied by their families, and 24 months or longer for personnel who are unaccompanied by their dependents. *See also:* Tour of Duty.

References
Department of Defense, U.S. Army. *Dictionary of United States Army Terms*. Army Regulation AR 310-25. Washington, DC: Headquarters, Department of the Army, 1986.

—**LONG-LIFE ITEM** is an item with an average service life of over twenty years. *See also:* Consumption Rate.

References
Department of Defense, U.S. Army. *Dictionary of United States Army Terms*. Army Regulation AR 310-25. Washington, DC: Headquarters, Department of the Army, 1986.

—**LONG-RANGE DEVELOPMENT FORECAST** is guidance for long-range developments in respect to military policies, objectives, plans, and programs.

References
Department of Defense, U.S. Army. *Dictionary of United States Army Terms*. Army Regulation AR 310-25. Washington, DC: Headquarters, Department of the Army, 1986.

—**LONG-RANGE PROGRAM** provides a logical and consistent framework for developing the future Army and for fielding the requisite warfighting capabilities. It considers the threats to national security, the national military strategy, the requirements of the Unified and Specified Commands, the Army's AirLand Battle Doctrine, and the long-range vision of the Army's leadership.

References
Department of Defense, U.S. Army. *U.S. Army Policy Statement, 1988*. Washington, DC: Headquarters, Department of the Army, 1988.

—**LONG-RANGE RADAR.** (1) A long-range radar is equipment whose maximum range on a reflecting target of one square meter normal to the signal path exceeds 300 miles but is less than 800 miles, provided that a line of sight exists between the target and the radar. *See also:* Very Long-Range Radar.

References
Department of Defense, U.S. Army. *Dictionary of United States Army Terms*. Army Regulation AR 310-25. Washington, DC: Headquarters, Department of the Army, 1986.

—**LONG-RANGE RECONNAISSANCE PATROL (LRRP)** is a military unit specially organized, equipped, and trained to function as an information-gathering agency that is responsive to the intelligence requirements of the tactical commander. The LRRP consists of people who are qualified to perform reconnaissance, surveillance, and target acquisition within the dispatching unit's area of interest. The LRRP should not duplicate organic unit reconnaissance patrols that proceed to an objective area to acquire certain information and then return when the specific mission has been accomplished. The LRRP is employed to maintain surveillance over enemy routes, areas, or specific locations that are beyond the capability of organic reconnaissance units for extended periods, reporting all sightings of enemy activity within the area of observation. This can be done from a fixed position or by reconnaissance while moving. *See also:* Long-Range Reconnaissance Patrol Company.

References
Department of Defense, U.S. Army. *Long-Range Reconnaissance Patrol Company.* Field Manual FM 31-18. Washington, DC: Headquarters, Department of the Army, 1968.

—**LONG-RANGE RECONNAISSANCE PATROL (LRRP) COMPANY** is a military unit specifically organized, equipped, and trained to perform LRRP missions. Located at the corps and field army (when authorized by Headquarters, Department of the Army), the LRRP company consists of a company headquarters and three patrol platoons.

References
Department of Defense, U.S. Army. *Long-Range Reconnaissance Patrol Company.* Field Manual FM 31-18. Washington, DC: Headquarters, Department of the Army, 1968.

—**LONG-TERM PSYOP CAMPAIGN** consists of propaganda and psychological actions conducted to support strategic objectives and are directed at large target audiences to achieve long-range psychological objectives when no specific response time is required. *See also:* Psychological Operations.

References
Department of Defense, U.S. Army. *Psychological Operations.* Field Manual FM 33-1. Washington, DC: Headquarters, Department of the Army, 1979.

—**LOOP SLING** is an adjustment of the sling strap of a rifle for firing in which the left arm is passed through the loop in the strap that is then tightened and adjusted for the firer. This adjustment provides a steadier grip than does the hasty sling, but it requires more time to make.

References
Department of Defense, U.S. Army. *Dictionary of United States Army Terms.* Army Regulation AR 310-25. Washington, DC: Headquarters, Department of the Army, 1986.

—**LOOSE ISSUE STOCK** are supplies that have been removed from their initial containers for issue in small quantities.

References
Department of Defense, U.S. Army. *Dictionary of United States Army Terms.* Army Regulation AR 310-25. Washington, DC: Headquarters, Department of the Army, 1986.

—**LOSS REPLACEMENT** is an individual who is added to a unit in order to fill a vacancy that has occurred due to loss. *See also:* Replacement.

References
Department of Defense, U.S. Army. *Dictionary of United States Army Terms.* Army Regulation AR 310-25. Washington, DC: Headquarters, Department of the Army, 1986.

—**LOST,** in artillery, is a spotting or an observation that is used by a spotter or an observer to indicate that rounds fired by a gun or mortar were not observed.

References
Department of Defense, Joint Chiefs of Staff. *Department of Defense Dictionary of Military and Related Terms.* Washington, DC: GPO, 1986.

—**LOST SHIPMENT** is a shipment reported to be lost that is never found.

References
Department of Defense, U.S. Army. *Dictionary of United States Army Terms.* Army Regulation AR 310-25. Washington, DC: Headquarters, Department of the Army, 1986.

—**LOT** is a quantity of supplies of the same general classification (e.g., a substance, clothing, or equipage) that is received and stored at any one time. *See also:* Lot Number.

References
Department of Defense, U.S. Army. *Dictionary of United States Army Terms.* Army Regulation AR 310-25. Washington, DC: Headquarters, Department of the Army, 1986.

—**LOT INTEGRITY** is the perpetual segregation of ammunition by lot number, whether in a storage environment or at the firing site, throughout its life cycle.

References
Department of Defense, U.S. Army. *Dictionary of United States Army Terms*. Army Regulation AR 310-25. Washington, DC: Headquarters, Department of the Army, 1986.

—**LOT NUMBER** is the identification number assigned to a particular quantity or lot of materiel (e.g., ammunition) that has come from a single manufacturer.

References
Department of Defense, U.S. Army. *Dictionary of United States Army Terms*. Army Regulation AR 310-25. Washington, DC: Headquarters, Department of the Army, 1986.

—**LOW AIRBURST** is the fallout safe height of burst for a nuclear weapon that maximizes the damage to or casualties on surface targets, while still giving a 99 percent assurance of precluding militarily significant fallout. *See also:* Nuclear Warfare.

References
Department of Defense, U.S. Army. *Nuclear Weapons Employment Doctrine and Procedures*. Field Manual FM 101-31-1. Washington, DC: Headquarters, Department of the Army, 1986.

—**LOW ALTITUDE BOMBING SYSTEM** is a low-level bombing technique wherein the attacker approaches the target at a very low altitude, makes a definite pull-up at a given point, releases the bomb at a predetermined point during the pull-up, and tosses the bomb into the target area.

References
Department of Defense, U.S. Army. *Dictionary of United States Army Terms*. Army Regulation AR 310-25. Washington, DC: Headquarters, Department of the Army, 1986.

—**LOW ALTITUDE PARACHUTE EXTRACTION SYSTEM (LAPES)** is a variation of airdrop by parachute in which the parachute is used to pull the load from the rear ramp of an aircraft flying at a reduced speed just a few feet off the ground. It is a low level self-contained system that is capable of delivering heavy loads into an area where it is not feasible to deliver loads from an altitude of five to ten feet. One or more platforms may be dropped.

References
Department of Defense, U.S. Army. *Jungle Operations*. Field Manual FM 90-5. Washington, DC: Headquarters, Department of the Army, 1982.

————. *USA/USAF Doctrine for Joint Airborne and Tactical Airlift Operations*. Field Manual FM 100-27. Washington, DC: Headquarters, Department of the Army, 1985.

—**LOW ANGLE**, in artillery, is an order or request to obtain low-angle fire. *See also:* Low-Angle Fire.

References
Department of Defense, Joint Chiefs of Staff. *Department of Defense Dictionary of Military and Related Terms*. Washington, DC: GPO, 1986.

—**LOW-ANGLE FIRE** is fire delivered at angles of elevation that are below the elevation that corresponds to the maximum range of the gun and ammunition concerned.

References
Department of Defense, Joint Chiefs of Staff. *Department of Defense Dictionary of Military and Related Terms*. Washington, DC: GPO, 1986.

—**LOW EXPLOSIVE** is an explosive that undergoes a relatively slow chemical transformation, thereby producing a deflagration or auto-combustion at rates that vary from a few centimeters per minute to approximately 400 meters per second. It is suitable for use in igniter trains and certain types of propellants. *See also:* High Explosive.

References
Department of Defense, U.S. Army. *Dictionary of United States Army Terms*. Army Regulation AR 310-25. Washington, DC: Headquarters, Department of the Army, 1986.

—**LOW LEVEL KEYING** is the use of low-level voltage and current on keying contacts (e.g., keying at positive or negative 2 volts at 70 microamperes or less).

References
Department of Defense, U.S. Army. *Dictionary of United States Army Terms*. Army Regulation AR 310-25. Washington, DC: Headquarters, Department of the Army, 1986.

—**LOW VELOCITY.** (1) Low velocity is a type of airdrop. Cargo parachutes are used, and the items to be dropped are rigged on an airdrop platform or in an airdrop container. Energy-dissipating material is placed beneath the load to lessen the shock when it hits the ground. Cargo parachutes are attached to the load to reduce the rate of descent to no more than 28 feet per second.

Fragile material, vehicles, and artillery may be low-velocity dropped. (2) In artillery, low velocity is a muzzle velocity of an artillery projectile of 2,499 feet per second or less. *See also:* High-Velocity Airdrop.

References
Department of Defense, U.S. Army. *Dictionary of United States Army Terms.* Army Regulation AR 310-25. Washington, DC: Headquarters, Department of the Army, 1986.

—**LOW-GRADE CRYPTOSYSTEM** is a cryptosystem that has been designed to provide temporary security. Combat or operational codes are examples of low grade cryptosystems. *See also:* CRYPTO.

References
Department of Defense, U.S. Army. *Dictionary of United States Army Terms.* Army Regulation AR 310-25. Washington, DC: Headquarters, Department of the Army, 1986.

—**LOW-INTENSITY CONFLICT (LIC)** is a limited politico-military struggle to achieve political, social, economic, and psychological objectives. It is often protracted and ranges from diplomatic, economic, and psycho-social pressures through terrorism and insurgency. It is generally confined to a geographic area and is often characterized by constraints on the weaponry, tactics, and level of violence. Based on national objectives and strategy, the U.S. Army's missions in LIC fall into four general categories: foreign internal defense; terrorism counteraction; peacekeeping operations; and peacetime contingency operations. LIC is further divided into LIC Type A and LIC Type B. *See also:* Low-Intensity Conflict (Type A), Low-Intensity Conflict (Type B).

References
Department of Defense, U.S. Army. *Civil Affairs Operations.* Field Manual FM 41-10. Washington, DC: Headquarters, Department of the Army, 1985.

————. *U.S. Army Policy Statement, 1988.* Washington, DC: Headquarters, Department of the Army, 1988.

Oseth, John M. "Intelligence and Low Intensity Conflict." *Naval War College Review* (Nov.-Dec. 1984): 19-36.

—**LOW-INTENSITY CONFLICT (LIC)** (TYPE A) involves internal defense and development assistance operations involving actions by U.S. combat forces to establish, regain, or maintain control of specific land areas that are threatened by guerrilla warfare, revolution, subversion, or other tactics that are aimed at an internal seizure of power.

References
Department of Defense, U.S. Army. *Low Intensity Conflict.* Field Manual FM 100-20. Washington, DC: Headquarters, Department of the Army, 1981.

—**LOW-INTENSITY CONFLICT (LIC)** (TYPE B) involves internal defense and development assistance operations involving U.S. advice, combat support and combat service support for indigenous or allied forces that are engaged in establishing, regaining, or maintaining control of specific land areas that are threatened by guerrilla warfare, revolution, subversion, or other tactics that are aimed at an internal seizure of power.

References
Department of Defense, U.S. Army. *Low Intensity Conflict.* Field Manual FM 100-20. Washington, DC: Headquarters, Department of the Army, 1981.

—**LOW-LEVEL FLIGHT** (ARMY AVIATION) is a flight that is generally carried out above obstacles but at an altitude where detection by an enemy force is avoided or minimized. It is performed at a constant indicated altitude and airspeed. *See also:* Low-Level Flight Operations.

References
Department of Defense, U.S. Army. *Air Defense Artillery Deployment: Chaparral/Vulcan/ Stinger.* Field Manual FM 44-3. Washington, DC: Headquarters, Department of the Army, 1984.

————. *Attack Helicopter Operations.* Field Manual FM. 17-50. Washington, DC: Headquarters, Department of the Army, 1984.

————. *Gunnery Training for Attack Helicopters.* Training Circular TC 17-17. Washington, DC: Headquarters, Department of the Army, 1975.

—**LOW-LEVEL FLIGHT OPERATIONS** involve flying Army aircraft at altitudes that afford cover and concealment from ground visual and electronic detection in order to fully exploit surprise.

References
Department of Defense, U.S. Army. *Dictionary of United States Army Terms.* Army Regulation AR 310-25. Washington, DC: Headquarters, Department of the Army, 1986.

—**LOW-LEVEL NAVIGATION** is the technique of directing an aircraft along a desired course at low altitudes (generally below 500 feet absolute altitude) by using pilotage, dead reckoning, and electronic navigational aides in such a manner that the position of the aircraft is known at any time.

References

Department of Defense, U.S. Army. *Dictionary of United States Army Terms.* Army Regulation AR 310-25. Washington, DC: Headquarters, Department of the Army, 1986.

—**LOW-LEVEL SIGNALING** is the use of low levels of voltage and current on signal lines (e.g., at the rate of 6 volts at 1 milliampere or less).

References

Department of Defense, U.S. Army. *Dictionary of United States Army Terms.* Army Regulation AR 310-25. Washington, DC: Headquarters, Department of the Army, 1986.

—**LOW-LEVEL TRANSIT ROUTE** is a temporary corridor of defined dimensions that facilitates the low-level passage of friendly aircraft through friendly air defenses and controlled or restricted airspace.

References

Department of Defense, U.S. Army. *Operational Terms and Symbols.* Field Manual FM 101-5-1. Washington, DC: Headquarters, Department of the Army, 1985.

—**LOW-ORDER BURST** is the breaking of a projectile into a few large fragments instead of a large number of smaller fragments as a result of a low-order detonation. *See also:* Low-Order Detonation.

References

Department of Defense, U.S. Army. *Dictionary of United States Army Terms.* Army Regulation AR 310-25. Washington, DC: Headquarters, Department of the Army, 1986.

—**LOW-ORDER DETONATION** is an incomplete detonation of the explosive charge in a bomb, projectile, or other similar high explosive.

References

Department of Defense, U.S. Army. *Dictionary of United States Army Terms.* Army Regulation AR 310-25. Washington, DC: Headquarters, Department of the Army, 1986.

—**LOW-VISIBILITY OPERATIONS** are sensitive operations wherein the political/military restrictions inherent in covert and clandestine operations are either not necessary or not feasible. These operations are taken as required either to limit the exposure of those involved or to conceal their activities.

References

Department of Defense, Joint Chiefs of Staff. *Department of Defense Dictionary of Military and Related Terms.* Washington, DC: GPO, 1986.

—**LUBRICATION ORDER** is the primary approved medium for the publication of mandatory lubricating instructions on all equipment that requires lubrication by organizational maintenance.

References

Department of Defense, U.S. Army. *Dictionary of United States Army Terms.* Army Regulation AR 310-25. Washington, DC: Headquarters, Department of the Army, 1986.

—**LUNG DAMAGING AGENT** is a potentially lethal chemical agent causing extensive damage to the respiratory tract. *See also:* Chemical Warfare.

References

Department of Defense, U.S. Army. *Dictionary of United States Army Terms.* Army Regulation AR 310-25. Washington, DC: Headquarters, Department of the Army, 1986.

—**LYDDITE**, also called melnite, is a powerful explosive containing picric acid and is used in shells.

References

Department of Defense, U.S. Army. *Dictionary of United States Army Terms.* Army Regulation AR 310-25. Washington, DC: Headquarters, Department of the Army, 1986.

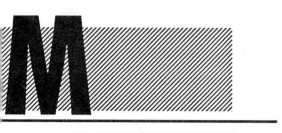

—**M-DAY** is the day the Secretary of Defense directs a mobilization (i.e., partial, full, or total) based upon a decision by the President, Congress, or both. All mobilization planning (e.g., alert, movement, transportation, and deployment) or employment planning is based upon this date. *See also:* C-Day, D-Day, H-Hour, M-Day Force, M-Day Force Materiel Requirements, S-Day.

References

Department of Defense, U.S. Army. *Army Forces Training.* Army Regulation AR 350-41. Washington, DC: Headquarters, Department of the Army, 1986.

————. *Training for Mobilization and War.* Field Manual FM 25-5. Washington, DC: Headquarters, Department of the Army, 1985.

—**M-DAY FORCE** is the total strength in units and/or individuals that is required, planned, or can be mobilized on M-day. *See also:* M-Day.

References

Department of Defense, U.S. Army. *Dictionary of United States Army Terms.* Army Regulation AR 310-25. Washington, DC: Headquarters, Department of the Army, 1986.

—**M-DAY FORCE MATERIEL REQUIREMENT** is the quantity of an item required to be on hand and on order on M-day minus one day in order to equip and provide a materiel pipeline for the approved peacetime U.S. active and reserve force structure.

References

Department of Defense, Joint Chiefs of Staff. *Department of Defense Dictionary of Military and Related Terms.* Washington, DC: GPO, 1986.

—**M1/M1A1 ABRAMS TANK** is the Army's primary ground combat weapon system for closing with and destroying enemy forces using firepower, mobility, and shock action. This is accomplished in coordination with other ground and air systems under all battlefield conditions and levels of combat intensity. The Abrams' special armor and the compartmentation of fuel and main gun ammunition that is stored away from the crew, together with an automatic fire detection and suppression system, make it a less vulnerable and more survivable tank on the modern battlefield. Its improved day-night fire control and shoot-on-the-move capability assure its ability to deliver highly accurate and lethal fires on both armored and unprotected targets. The 1500-horsepower engine and improved suspension system enable the tank to move quickly across the battlefield, while reducing its exposure to threat weapons.

References

Weapons Systems: U.S. Army, Navy and Air Force Directory, 1986–1988. Washington, DC: DCP, 1986.

—**M2/M3 BRADLEY FIGHTING VEHICLE (BFV)** is a full-tracked, armored vehicle equipped with tube-launched, optically tracked; wire-guided antitank missiles, a 25-mm cannon and a 7.62-mm coaxial machine gun. The BFV has the cross country mobility to operate at high speeds in tandem with the M1 Abrams tank in a combined arms team. Bradley allows the U.S. Army's mechanized forces to maneuver and fight during day and night, and to provide overwatching fires while on the move. *See also:* M1/M1A1 Abrams Tank.

References

Department of Defense, U.S. Army. *U.S. Army Policy Statement, 1988.* Washington, DC: Headquarters, Department of the Army, 1988.

—**M9 ARMORED COMBAT EARTHMOVER (ACE)** is a tracked, armored earth-moving machine designed to provide needed engineering support to forward deployed fighting forces. Its mobility, 30 mph speed, and survivability, including small arms, fragmentation, and operator nuclear/biological/chemical protection, enable the ACE to move with the flow of the battle, providing fighting positions, clearing and creating obstacles, and performing other combat engineering functions to enhance and multiply the combat power of U.S. ground forces when and where needed.

References

Department of Defense, U.S. Army. *Survivability.* Field Manual FM 5-103. Washington, DC: Headquarters, Department of the Army, 1985.

Weapons Systems: U.S. Army, Navy, and Air Force Directory, 1986–1988. Washington, DC: DCP, 1986.

—**M16A2 RIFLE** incorporates improvements in the sights, pistol grip, stock, and overall combat effectiveness of the M16A1. In addition, its maximum effective range is 550 meters, 90 meters longer than the 460-meter range of the M16A1, and its heavier barrel is designed to fire standard NATO ammunition.

References

Department of Defense, U.S. Army. *M16A1 Rifle and Rifle Marksmanship.* Field Manual FM 23-9. Washington, DC: Headquarters, Department of the Army, 1974.

————. *U.S. Army Policy Statement, 1988.* Washington, DC: Headquarters, Department of the Army, 1988.

—**M60A3 TANK** is an improved version of the Army's M60 series tank, which has been in operation since 1961. The most significant improvements include gun stabilization, a laser rangefinder, a solid-state computer, and a thermal shroud, which have enhanced the tank's first-round hit capability. The addition of a tank thermal imaging sight that extends the unit's capabilities during reduced visibility has also improved the tank's fighting capability.

References

Weapons Systems: U.S. Army, Navy, and Air Force Directory, 1986- 1988. Washington, DC: DCP, 1986.

—**M88A1 MEDIUM RECOVERY VEHICLE (MRV)** is a full-tracked, armored vehicle designed for hoisting, winching, and towing operations to accomplish the battlefield recovery and evacuation of tanks and other tracked combat vehicles. The M88A1 is the Army's primary recovery vehicle for the M1 Abrams tank, M2/M3 Bradley Fighting Vehicles, M60 series tanks, the SGT YORK Air Defense Gun, and for heavy self-propelled artillery.

References

Weapons Systems: U.S. Army, Navy, and Air Force Directory, 1986-1988. Washington, DC: DCP, 1986.

—**M109A2/A3 SELF-PROPELLED HOWITZER** is an improved version of the M109 self-propelled howitzer that was fielded in the early 1960s. Improvements have been made in the howitzer's reliability, maintainability, and safety. Ammunition storage has been improved by the addition of a larger storage rack that holds 22 rounds and has accommodations for guided projectiles. The

M109A2/A3 is designed to provide support to armored and mechanized infantry units. As a "tracked" vehicle, it can accompany armored units in any terrain. The unit can be air-transported in a C5 aircraft and can fire any 155-mm nuclear or the conventional howitzer ammunition in the Army's current inventory. (M109A3 is a modified M109A1 with the same performance capabilities as the M109A2.)

References

Weapons Systems: U.S. Army, Navy, and Air Force Directory, 1986-1988. Washington, DC: DCP, 1986.

—**M110A2 SELF-PROPELLED EIGHT-INCH HOWITZER** is an improved version of the Army's heaviest cannon artillery weapon. It is employed in division artillery general support battalions and separate Corps and Army battalions. Its missions, aside from general support of friendly units, include counterartillery and air defense suppression. It has both a conventional and a nuclear capability.

References

Weapons Systems: U.S. Army, Navy, and Air Force Directory, 1986-1988. Washington, DC: DCP, 1986.

—**M113A2, ARMORED PERSONNEL CARRIER (APC),** an upgraded version of the M113 first built in 1960, is an aluminum armored amphibious vehicle designed to transport troops, equipment, and cargo during combat operations. It is used as an infantry and engineer squad carrier, a mortar carrier, a missile carrier, a command post, a medical evacuation carrier, a maintenance support vehicle, and other special roles. Because of its mobility, firepower, and armor protection limitations, it cannot fulfill the role of a fighting vehicle and is being replaced as a squad carrier and scout vehicle by Bradley fighting vehicles.

References

Weapons Systems: U.S. Army, Navy, and Air Force Directory, 1986-1988. Washington, DC: DCP, 1986.

—**M119 LIGHT HOWITZER.** The British Light Gun M119 fulfills the light infantry division requirement for an extended-range, lightweight 105-mm howitzer. The M119 is towable behind the high mobility multipurpose wheeled vehicle and can be air-transported by the Black Hawk helicopter. The M119 fires standard U.S. 105-mm projectiles to a range of fourteen kilometers and has the potential to fire rocket-assisted projectiles to a range of 19.5 kilometers.

References

Department of Defense, U.S. Army. *U.S. Army Policy Statement, 1988*. Washington, DC: Headquarters, Department of the Army, 1988.

—**M198 155-MM MEDIUM TOWED HOWITZER** has replaced the World War II-vintage 155-mm towed howitzer. It is used by the active and reserve Army to provide direct support to the field artillery battalions of infantry divisions and separate brigades and in corps battalions in support of airborne and air assault divisions. It has much greater reliability and range than earlier howitzers, and can be delivered by parachute or carried by cargo aircraft and medium helicopters.

References

Weapons Systems: U.S. Army, Navy, and Air Force Directory, 1986-1988. Washington, DC: DCP, 1986.

—**MK-19, MOD 3 GRENADE LAUNCHER** is a self-powered, air-cooled, blow-back, 40-mm automatic grenade launcher capable of a cyclic rate of fire of from 325 to 375 rounds per minute. It provides more accurate, longer range fire power against enemy personnel and lightly armored vehicles than the weapons that it replaces (i.e., the M2 machine gun and the vehicle-mounted M60 machine gun). It can engage point targets up to 1,600 meters and can provide area suppressive fires up to 2,200 meters.

References

Department of Defense, U.S. Army. *40-MM Grenade Launchers M203 and M79*. Field Manual FM 23-31. Washington, DC: Headquarters, Department of the Army, 1972.

———. *U.S. Army Policy Statement, 1988*. Washington, DC: Headquarters, Department of the Army, 1988.

—**MAC (MILITARY AIRLIFT COMMAND) MISSION COMMANDER** is designated when MAC aircraft are participating in deployment, redeployment, or employment operations during exercises, contingencies, and other airlift operations that are specified in the implementing directive. The MAC mission commander is responsible to the appointing authority for the successful accomplishment of the MAC portion of the mission. *See also:* Military Airlift Command.

References

Department of Defense, U.S. Army. *USA/USAF Doctrine for Joint Airborne and Tactical Airlift Operations*. Field Manual FM 100-27. Washington, DC: Headquarters, Department of the Army, 1985.

—**MACHINE GUN POSITION.** Fighting positions for machine guns are built so that the gun can fire to the front or to the oblique. However, the primary sector of fire is usually oblique so that the gun fires across the unit's front. Since two soldiers are needed to fire the machine gun, the hole that is dug is shaped so that both soldiers, the gunner and the assistant gunner, can fire it to either side of the frontal protection.

References

Department of Defense, U.S. Army. *Machine gun 7.62-MM, M60*. Field Manual FM 23-67. Washington, DC: Headquarters, Department of the Army, 1964.

———. *Survivability*. Field Manual FM 5-103. Washington, DC: Headquarters, Department of the Army, 1985.

—**MAGAZINE** is any building or structure, except an operating building, that is used for storing ammunition and explosives. *See also:* Magazine, Earth-Covered, Nonstandard.

References

Department of Defense, U.S. Army. *Ammunition and Explosives Safety Standards*. Army Regulation AR 385-64. Washington, DC: Headquarters, Department of the Army, 1987.

—**MAGAZINE, EARTH-COVERED, NONSTANDARD** refers to all earth-covered magazines except those with earth coverings that are equal to or greater than that which is required by standard magazines.

References

Department of Defense, U.S. Army. *Ammunition and Explosives Safety Standards*. Army Regulation AR 385-64. Washington, DC: Headquarters, Department of the Army, 1987.

—**MAIN ATTACK** is the principal attack or effort into which the commander places the bulk of his offensive capability. It is an attack that is directed against the chief objective of the campaign or battle. *See also:* Main Battle Area.

References

Department of Defense, U.S. Army. *Operational Terms and Symbols*. Field Manual FM 101-5-1. Washington, DC: Headquarters, Department of the Army, 1985.

—**MAIN BATTLE AREA (MBA)** is the portion of the battlefield that extends rearward from the forward edge of the battle area and in which the decisive battle is fought to defeat the enemy. The MBA may include lateral and rear boundaries. For any particular command, this area extends from the forward edge of the battle area to the rear boundaries of the units comprising its main defensive forces. *See also:* Forward Edge of the Battle Area.

References

Department of Defense, U.S. Army. *Military Intelligence Group (Combat Electronic Warfare and Intelligence) (Corps)*. Field Manual FM 34-20. Washington, DC: Headquarters, Department of the Army, 1983.

———. *Operational Terms and Symbols*. Field Manual FM 101-5-1. Washington, DC: Headquarters, Department of the Army, 1985.

———. *Air Defense Artillery Employment*. Field Manual FM 44-1. Washington, DC: Headquarters, Department of the Army, 1983.

—**MAIN BODY.** (1) The main body is the principal part of a tactical command or formation. It does not include detached elements of the command (e.g., advance guards, flank guards, or covering forces). (2) In a motor column, the main body includes all the vehicles except for the column head, trail, and control vehicles. The main body consists primarily of the vehicles carrying the bulk of the cargo or troops within the column.

References

Department of Defense, U.S. Army. *Operational Terms and Symbols*. Field Manual FM 101-5-1. Washington, DC: Headquarters, Department of the Army, 1985.

—**MAIN COMMAND POST (CP)** consists of the staff activities involved in controlling and sustaining current, and in planning future, operations. The main CP, which normally operates under the control of the chief of staff, consists of G1, G2, G3, and G4 elements, fire support and chemical elements, a tactical air control party element, and an Army airspace command and control element consisting of air defense artillery and Army aviation staff elements. The main CP exercises command and control of the current operation where a tactical CP is not employed. It is located well to the rear of the forward deployed forces. At division level, this means out of range of most enemy artillery. *See also:* Command Post, Rear Command Post, Tactical Command Post.

References

Department of Defense, U.S. Army. *Operational Terms and Symbols*. Field Manual FM 101-5-1. Washington, DC: Headquarters, Department of the Army, 1985.

———. *Staff Organization and Operations*. Field Manual FM 101-5. Washington, DC: Headquarters, Department of the Army, 1984.

—**MAIN DETONATING,** in demolition, is a line of detonating cord used to transmit the detonation wave to two or more mine branches.

References

Department of Defense, Joint Chiefs of Staff. *Department of Defense Dictionary of Military and Related Terms*. Washington, DC: GPO, 1986.

—**MAIN GUARD** is the regular interior guard of a post or unit whose principal duties are to patrol the area and to protect the personnel, buildings, and equipment. A main guard is a subdivision of the interior guard of a command. Other subdivisions include the escort guard and the honor guards. *See also:* Escort Guard, Interior Guard.

References

Department of Defense, U.S. Army. *Guard Duty*. Field Manual FM 22-6. Washington, DC: Headquarters, Department of the Army, 1971.

—**MAIN LINE OF RESISTANCE (MLR)** is a line at the forward edge of the battle position, designated for the purpose of coordinating the fire of all units and supporting weapons, including air and naval gunfire. It defines the forward limits of a series of mutually supporting defensive areas, but it does not include the areas occupied or used by covering or screening forces. *See also:* Forward Edge of the Battle Area.

References

Department of Defense, Joint Chiefs of Staff. *Department of Defense Dictionary of Military and Related Terms*. Washington, DC: GPO, 1986.

—**MAIN ROAD** is a road that can be used as the principal ground line of communication to an area or locality. Usually, it can accommodate two-way, all-weather, high-speed traffic. *See also:* Main Supply Route.

References

Department of Defense, Joint Chiefs of Staff. *Department of Defense Dictionary of Military and Related Terms.* Washington, DC: GPO, 1986.

—**MAIN SUPPLY ROUTE (MSR)** is a route within an area of operations on which most traffic in support of military operations flows.

References

Department of Defense, Joint Chiefs of Staff. *Department of Defense Dictionary of Military and Related Terms.* Washington, DC: GPO, 1986.

Department of Defense, U.S. Army. *Operational Terms and Symbols.* Field Manual FM 101-5-1. Washington, DC: Headquarters, Department of the Army, 1985.

—**MAINTAIN CONTACT WITH THE ENEMY** involves actions that prevent the enemy from disengaging.

References

Department of Defense, U.S. Army. *Operational Terms and Symbols.* Field Manual FM 101-5-1. Washington, DC: Headquarters, Department of the Army, 1985.

—**MAINTAINABILITY.** (1) Maintainability is the inherent characteristics of a design or installation that determine the ease, economy, safety, and accuracy with which it can be maintained. (2) Maintainability is the ability to restore a product to service or to perform preventive maintenance within the required limits. *See also:* Maintenance (Materiel).

References

Department of Defense, U.S. Army. *Support Operations: Echelons Above Corps.* Field Manual FM 100-16. Washington, DC: Headquarters, Department of the Army, 1986.

—**MAINTENANCE (MAINT) (MATERIEL).** (1) Maintenance includes all the actions taken to retain materiel in a serviceable condition or to restore it to serviceability. It includes inspection, testing, servicing, and a classification as to serviceability, repair, rebuilding, and reclamation. (2) Maintenance is all the supply and repair actions taken to keep a force in a condition to carry out its mission. (3) Maintenance is the routine recurring work required to keep a facility (e.g., a plant, building, structure, ground facility, utility system, or other real property) in a condition that allows it to be continuously used, at

its original or designed capacity and efficiency, and for its intended purpose. *See also:* the Maintenance entries that follow.

References

Department of Defense, Joint Chiefs of Staff. *Department of Defense Dictionary of Military and Related Terms.* Washington, DC: GPO, 1986.

—**MAINTENANCE (MAINT) AREA** consists of maintenance activities that retain or restore materiel to a serviceable condition.

References

Department of Defense, Joint Chiefs of Staff. *Department of Defense Dictionary of Military and Related Terms.* Washington, DC: GPO, 1986.

—**MAINTENANCE (MAINT) ASSISTANCE AND INSTRUCTION TEAM** provides technical expertise to individual unit commanders to help them identify and solve the equipment maintenance problems that are contributing to the inability of their units to meet materiel readiness standards.

References

Department of Defense, U.S. Army. *Dictionary of United States Army Terms.* Army Regulation AR 310-25. Washington, DC: Headquarters, Department of the Army, 1986.

—**MAINTENANCE (MAINT) CALIBRATION** is a procedure performed using calibrated test and measuring equipment to detect and adjust any variation in other test and measuring equipment.

References

Department of Defense, U.S. Army. *Dictionary of United States Army Terms.* Army Regulation AR 310-25. Washington, DC: Headquarters, Department of the Army, 1986.

—**MAINTENANCE (MAINT) CATEGORIES** is a materiel maintenance system designation based upon the extent of the capabilities, facilities, and skills required for a given operation. *See also:* Maintenance Concept.

References

Department of Defense, U.S. Army. *Dictionary of United States Army Terms.* Army Regulation AR 310-25. Washington, DC: Headquarters, Department of the Army, 1986.

—**MAINTENANCE (MAINT) CHAIN OF COMMAND** follows the normal chain of command down to and including the equipment operator. It includes heads of staff sections and other supervisors who are responsible for equipment or operators.

References
Department of Defense, U.S. Army. *Organizational Maintenance Operations.* Field Manual FM 29-2. Washington, DC: Headquarters, Department of the Army, 1984.

—**MAINTENANCE (MAINT) CHECK** is performed to insure that a function or component performs correctly or is correctly assembled or locked.

References
Department of Defense, U.S. Army. *Dictionary of United States Army Terms.* Army Regulation AR 310-25. Washington, DC: Headquarters, Department of the Army, 1986.

—**MAINTENANCE (MAINT) CONCEPT** refers to the manner in which an end-item is maintained and supported. It indicates the maintenance capabilities required of both the using and supporting units, and provides information concerning its tactical employment, the maintenance environment, mobility considerations, allowable downtime, and other operational considerations. Technical information is included that describes the military and civilian occupational series codes that must be developed to support the item and information on how to recognize new or changed skill requirements.

References
Department of Defense, U.S. Army. *Dictionary of United States Army Terms.* Army Regulation AR 310-25. Washington, DC: Headquarters, Department of the Army, 1986.

—**MAINTENANCE (MAINT) ENGINEERING** is the organized application of techniques, engineering skills, and effort to insure that weapons systems and equipment are designed and developed so that they can be effectively and economically maintained.

References
Department of Defense, Joint Chiefs of Staff. *Department of Defense Dictionary of Military and Related Terms.* Washington, DC: GPO, 1986.

—**MAINTENANCE (MAINT) EXPENDITURE LIMIT** is the maximum expenditure permitted for a one-time repair of an item at the organizational, direct, general, or depot categories of maintenance. It includes the cost of repair parts and labor

service. Items with a repair cost that exceeds the maintenance expenditure limit are classified as economically unrepairable.

References
Department of Defense, U.S. Army. *Dictionary of United States Army Terms.* Army Regulation AR 310-25. Washington, DC: Headquarters, Department of the Army, 1986.

—**MAINTENANCE (MAINT) FLOAT** are end-items of equipment authorized for stockage at installations or activities to be used as replacements for unserviceable equipment that cannot be timely repaired by the support maintenance activity. A maintenance float includes both the operational readiness float and the repair cycle float. An operational *readiness float* refers to mission-essential, maintenance-significant equipment that is authorized for stockage by maintenance support units or activities to replace unserviceable repairable equipment to meet operational commitments. *A repair cycle float* refers to mission-essential, maintenance-significant equipment, specified by Headquarters, Department of the Army, for stockage in the supply system so that equipment from organizations can be removed for scheduled overhaul and crash damaged aircraft can be depot repaired without detracting from a unit's readiness condition.

References
Department of Defense, U.S. Army. Di*ctionary of United States Army Terms.* Army Regulation AR 310-25. Washington, DC: Headquarters, Department of the Army, 1986.

—**MAINTENANCE (MAINT) OPERATION** is a maintenance task identified as a separate line number in the supply system (e.g., service, repair, or replace).

References
Department of Defense, U.S. Army. *Maintenance and Repair Parts Consumption Planning Guide for Contingency Operations.* Field Manual FM 42-9-23. Washington, DC: Headquarters, Department of the Army, 1980.

—**MAINTENANCE (MAINT) PERIOD** is any time allotted to maintenance on the battalion, company, platoon, or section training schedule. There are four types of maintenance periods: unit equipment maintenance; before-, during-, and after-operation maintenance as an integral part of any equipment operation for training, administration, and support; individual maintenance skills training (including on-the-job training); and motor stables maintenance.

References
Department of Defense, U.S. Army. *Organizational Maintenance Operations.* Field Manual FM 29-2. Washington, DC: Headquarters, Department of the Army, 1984.

—MAINTENANCE (MAINT) PLAN, an annual plan developed with the annual training program, is designed to support all unit activities involving training, readiness, or equipment operation. *See also:* Annual Training.

References
Department of Defense, U.S. Army. *Organizational Maintenance Operations.* Field Manual FM 29-2. Washington, DC: Headquarters, Department of the Army, 1984.

—MAINTENANCE (MAINT) PROGRAM contains the written procedures developed to meet unit organizational maintenance requirements. *See also:* Maintenance Plan.

References
Department of Defense, U.S. Army. *Organizational Maintenance Operations.* Field Manual FM 29-2. Washington, DC: Headquarters, Department of the Army, 1984.

—MAINTENANCE (MAINT) RECORDS control scheduling, inspection procedures, and repair work loads. They provide a uniform method for recording the corrective action that has been taken by the maintenance elements involved.

References
Department of Defense, U.S. Army. *Organizational Maintenance Operations.* Field Manual FM 29-2. Washington, DC: Headquarters, Department of the Army, 1984.

—MAINTENANCE (MAINT) SERVICEABILITY STANDARDS are established by the Commanding General, United States Army Materiel Command, Commanding General, United States Army Communications Command, The Surgeon General; and the Chief of Engineers. These standards must be met to assure that end-items, components, or assemblies function properly and are capable of accomplishing their intended missions.

References
Department of Defense, U.S. Army. *Dictionary of United States Army Terms.* Army Regulation AR 310-25. Washington, DC: Headquarters, Department of the Army, 1986.

—MAINTENANCE (MAINT) SHOP STOCKS are inexpensive, expendable, and quickly consumed items and repair parts at general and direct support maintenance activities. They are used to support assigned maintenance missions, and their stocks are in addition to shop supplies.

References
Department of Defense, U.S. Army. *Dictionary of United States Army Terms.* Army Regulation AR 310-25. Washington, DC: Headquarters, Department of the Army, 1986.

—MAINTENANCE (MAINT) STATUS is a deliberately imposed nonoperating condition, with adequate personnel, to maintain and preserve installations, materiel, and facilities so that they may be quickly restored to operable condition.

References
Department of Defense, Joint Chiefs of Staff. *Department of Defense Dictionary of Military and Related Terms.* Washington, DC: GPO, 1986.

—MAINTENANCE (MAINT) SUPPORT PLAN is a plan initiated at the beginning of the development phase for a military item or at the beginning of the procurement phase for a commercial item, which is continually updated. (commercial items that are modified to meet military requirements are considered military items.) The plan contains data describing how the item is to be used and a time-phased schedule of actions required for the maintenance support of the item while it is in the field. *See also:* Maintenance Plan.

References
Department of Defense, U.S. Army. *Dictionary of United States Army Terms.* Army Regulation AR 310-25. Washington, DC: Headquarters, Department of the Army, 1986.

—MAINTENANCE SUPPORT TEAM (MST) refers to repairers sent forward by an intermediate maintenance unit to assist forward units perform maintenance on disabled equipment. It was formerly called a contact team.

References
Department of Defense, U.S. Army. *Operational Terms and Symbols.* Field Manual FM 101-5-1. Washington, DC: Headquarters, Department of the Army, 1985.

—**MAINTENANCE (MAINT) TEAM** consists of personnel from a maintenance activity, organization, or unit who provide organizational level maintenance support to a designated unit or operation for specific tasks.

References

Department of Defense, U.S. Army. *Repair Parts Supply for a Theater of Operations.* Field Manual FM 29-19. Washington, DC: Headquarters, Department of the Army, 1985.

—**MAINTENANCE (MAINT) TIME GUIDELINES** are the time constraints established by the commander based upon the tactical situation, tools, skills, and repair parts available to guide the repair, recovery, or evacuation decision.

References

Department of Defense, U.S. Army. *Operational Terms and Symbols.* Field Manual FM 101-5-1. Washington, DC: Headquarters, Department of the Army, 1985.

—**MAINTENANCE (MAINT) TRAINING PLAN** is an annual plan, developed with the annual training program and maintenance plan, that provides or requests school, on-the-job training, and unit training at all levels to insure the presence of qualified maintenance personnel.

References

Department of Defense, U.S. Army. *Organizational Maintenance Operations.* Field Manual FM 29-2. Washington, DC: Headquarters, Department of the Army, 1984.

—**MAJOR ACTIVITY** is a principal functional subdivision of the Army management structure. Each major activity conforms with a separate Army appropriation or with one of the major subdivisions (i.e., budget programs or budget projects) of the Operations and Maintenance Appropriation. *See also:* Major Army Command, Major Army Subcommand.

References

Department of Defense, U.S. Army. *Dictionary of United States Army Terms.* Army Regulation AR 310-25. Washington, DC: Headquarters, Department of the Army, 1986.

—**MAJOR ARMY COMMAND (MACOM)** is a specifically designated Army field command directly subordinate to Headquarters, Department of the Army. Army component commands of unified and specified commands are major Army commands.

References

Department of Defense, U.S. Army. *Army Exercises.* Army Regulation AR 350-28. Washington, DC: Headquarters, Department of the Army, 1985.

————. *Planning Logistics Support for Military Operations.* Field Manual FM 701-58. Washington, DC: Headquarters, Department of the Army, 1987.

—**MAJOR ARMY SUBCOMMAND** is a command directly subordinate to, and constituting a major mission element of, a major Army command.

References

Department of Defense, U.S. Army. *Dictionary of United States Army Terms.* Army Regulation AR 310-25. Washington, DC: Headquarters, Department of the Army, 1986.

—**MAJOR ASSEMBLY** is a self-contained unit that has an individual identity. It is a completed assembly of component parts, such as a motor, and is ready for operation, but is used as a portion of, and is intended for, further installation in an end-item or major item. *See also:* Major Combination.

References

Department of Defense, U.S. Army. *Dictionary of United States Army Terms.* Army Regulation AR 310-25. Washington, DC: Headquarters, Department of the Army, 1986.

—**MAJOR COMBINATION,** a composite unit of materiel of two or more major items, is inherently complete intended for independent use.

References

Department of Defense, U.S. Army. *Dictionary of United States Army Terms.* Army Regulation AR 310-25. Washington, DC: Headquarters, Department of the Army, 1986.

—**MAJOR DISRUPTIONS ON INSTALLATIONS, UNITS, AND FACILITIES** include acts, threats, or attempts to kidnap, extort, bomb, hijack, ambush, or steal major weapons, etc. Such acts, which can create widespread publicity, require special response, tactics, and management. *See also:* Terrorism Counteraction.

References

Department of Defense, U.S. Army. *The Army Terrorism Counteraction Program.* Army Regulation AR 525-13. Washington, DC: Headquarters, Department of the Army, 1988.

—**MAJOR INVENTORY VARIANCE** occurs when the total dollar value for the stock number of the item overage or shortage exceeds $200.

References
Department of Defense, U.S. Army. *Dictionary of United States Army Terms.* Army Regulation AR 310-25. Washington, DC: Headquarters, Department of the Army, 1986.

—**MAJOR MATERIEL CATEGORY** is the broadest materiel classification that consolidates, for management and accounting purposes, all items of supply in various groups and/or classes of the Federal Supply Classification, on the basis of their application, cognizant inventory control points, or other significant relationships in supply management.

References
Department of Defense, U.S. Army. *Dictionary of United States Army Terms.* Army Regulation AR 310-25. Washington, DC: Headquarters, Department of the Army, 1986.

—**MAJOR MEDICAL ASSEMBLAGE** is a grouping or collection of medical supplies and allied items as identified by a Federal Stock Number. *See also:* Medical Treatment.

References
Department of Defense, U.S. Army. *Dictionary of United States Army Terms.* Army Regulation AR 310-25. Washington, DC: Headquarters, Department of the Army, 1986.

—**MAJOR NATO COMMANDERS** are the Supreme Allied Commander Atlantic, Supreme Allied Commander Europe, and Allied Commander-in-Chief Channel. *See also:* Commander(s), Major Subordinate Commanders, Principal Subordinate Commanders, Subordinate Area Commanders.

References
Department of Defense, Joint Chiefs of Staff. *Department of Defense Dictionary of Military and Related Terms.* Washington, DC: GPO, 1986.

—**MAJOR PROGRAMS** are projects or tasks designated as such by the Headquarters, Department of the Army. All programs selected for Defense Systems Acquisition Review Council and/or Army Systems Acquisition Review Council review are designated as major Army programs. The Secretary of Defense designates Army programs for Defense Systems Acquisition Review Council review. The Headquarters, Department of the Army, may designate additional programs for Army Systems Acquisition Review Council review only. The designation of a major program considers the following: Office of the Secretary of Defense designation of Decision Coordinating Paper/Defense Systems Acquisition Review Council systems; the significance of the added operational capability; the level of interest expressed or anticipated (e.g., congressional, Office of the Secretary of Defense, Secretary of the Army, or Chief of Staff, Army); the overall resource impact; the relationships to other programs and materiel developers; the requirements for cooperation with other Department of Defense components and allied governments; and the development risks and system complexity.

References
Department of Defense, U.S. Army. *Dictionary of United States Army Terms.* Army Regulation AR 310-25. Washington, DC: Headquarters, Department of the Army, 1986.

—**MAJOR REPAIR** is work done on materiel or equipment that need complete overhaul or substantial replacement of parts, or that require special tools.

References
Department of Defense, U.S. Army. *Dictionary of United States Army Terms.* Army Regulation AR 310-25. Washington, DC: Headquarters, Department of the Army, 1986.

—**MAJOR SUBORDINATE COMMANDERS.** (1) The major subordinate commanders are the NATO commanders responsible to the Supreme Allied Commander for an allocated geographical area or function. (2) In the U.S. context, the major subordinate commanders are the continental U.S. Army and Military District Washington commanders and other commanders designated by a major Army commander. *See also:* Commander(s), Major NATO Commanders, Principal Subordinate Commanders, Subordinate Area Commanders.

References
Department of Defense, Joint Chiefs of Staff. *Department of Defense Dictionary of Military and Related Terms.* Washington, DC: GPO, 1986.

Department of Defense, U.S. Army. *Dictionary of United States Army Terms.* Army Regulation AR 310-25. Washington, DC: Headquarters, Department of the Army, 1986.

—**MAJOR WEAPON SYSTEM** is one of a limited number of systems or subsystems that, for reasons of military urgency, criticality, or resource requirements, is determined to be vital to the national interest by the Department of Defense.

References

Department of Defense, Joint Chiefs of Staff. *Department of Defense Dictionary of Military and Related Terms.* Washington, DC: GPO, 1986.

—**MAKE SAFE** synonymous with disarm, or disable, refers to the action(s) necessary to prevent or interrupt the complete function of an explosive system. Necessary actions include: installing safety devices (e.g., pins or locks); disconnecting components (e.g., hoses, linkages, or batteries); bleeding components (e.g., accumulators or reservoirs; removing explosive devices (e.g., initiators, fuzes, or detonators), and intervening, as in welding or lockwiring. *See also:* Disarm.

References

Department of Defense, Joint Chiefs of Staff. *Department of Defense Dictionary of Military and Related Terms.* Washington, DC: GPO, 1986.

—**MAN PORTABLE** refers to an item that can be carried by one man. (1) It qualifies items carried as an integral part of the individual, crew served, or team equipment of the dismounted soldier in conjunction with his assigned duties (upper weight limit is approximately 14 kilograms, or 31 pounds. (2) In land warfare, man portable refers to equipment that can be carried by one man over a long distance without seriously degrading his performance of his normal duties. *See also:* Man Portable Air Defense, Man Transportable.

References

Department of Defense, Joint Chiefs of Staff. *Department of Defense Dictionary of Military and Related Terms.* Washington, DC: GPO, 1986.

—**MAN PORTABLE AIR DEFENSE SYSTEM** (MANPADS) consists of man-portable, shoulder-fired, heat seeking air defense guided missile systems designed to counter high-speed, low-level, attack aircraft. MANPADS include Redeye and Stinger. *See also:* Redeye, Stinger Missile System.

References

Department of Defense, U.S. Army. *Air Defense Artillery Deployment: Chaparral/Vulcan/Stinger.* Field Manual FM 44-3. Washington, DC: Headquarters, Department of the Army, 1984.

—**MAN SPACE** is the space and weight factor used to determine the combat capacity of vehicles, craft, and transport aircraft, based upon the requirements of one person with individual equipment. The person is assumed to weigh between 222 and 250 pounds and to occupy 13.5 cubic feet of space.

References

Department of Defense, Joint Chiefs of Staff. *Department of Defense Dictionary of Military and Related Terms.* Washington, DC: GPO, 1986.

—**MAN TRANSPORTABLE** refers to items, usually transported on wheeled, tracked, or air vehicles, but can be transported by one or more individuals for limited distances (i.e., 100 to 500 meters).

References

Department of Defense, Joint Chiefs of Staff. *Department of Defense Dictionary of Military and Related Terms.* Washington, DC: GPO, 1986.

—**MANAGEMENT** is a process of establishing and attaining objectives to carry out responsibilities. It consists of continuing actions of planning, organizing, directing, coordinating, controlling, and evaluating the use of men, money, materials, and facilities to accomplish missions and tasks. Management is inherent in command, but it does not include as extensive authority and responsibility as does command. *See also:* Management and Control System (Mobility), Management Control Number, Management Headquarters, Management System.

References

Department of Defense, Joint Chiefs of Staff. *Department of Defense Dictionary of Military and Related Terms.* Washington, DC: GPO, 1986.

—**MANAGEMENT AND CONTROL SYSTEM** (MOBILITY) are elements of organizations and/or activities that are a part of, or are closely related to, the mobility system, and that authorize requirements to be moved, to obtain and allocate lift resources, or to direct the operation of linklift vehicles.

References

Department of Defense, Joint Chiefs of Staff. *Department of Defense Dictionary of Military and Related Terms.* Washington, DC: GPO, 1986.

—**MANAGEMENT CONTROL NUMBER** is a number similar to a Federal Stock Number and is assigned by the National Inventory Control Points under certain specific conditions for identification and accounting purposes. It consists of an applicable four-digit class code number from the Federal Supply Classification and a letter to designate the assigning agency, followed by a six-digit number.

References

Department of Defense, U.S. Army. *Dictionary of United States Army Terms.* Army Regulation AR 310-25. Washington, DC: Headquarters, Department of the Army, 1986.

—**MANAGEMENT HEADQUARTERS** is a headquarters primarily concerned with the long-range planning, programming, and budgeting of resources; the development of policies and procedures; and the coordination of effort and evaluation (as opposed to the planning for and direct control of operations).

References

Department of Defense, U.S. Army. *Dictionary of United States Army Terms.* Army Regulation AR 310-25. Washington, DC: Headquarters, Department of the Army, 1986.

—**MANAGEMENT SYSTEM** is the integrated procedures, methods, policies, practices, and personnel used by a commander or other supervisor to plan, organize, direct, coordinate, and control an organization.

References

Department of Defense, U.S. Army. *Dictionary of United States Army Terms.* Army Regulation AR 310-25. Washington, DC: Headquarters, Department of the Army, 1986.

—**MANDATORY PARTS LIST (MPL)** is a listing of repair parts essential for combat equipment to perform, approved by Headquarters, Department of the Army.

References

Department of Defense, U.S. Army. *Repair Parts Supply for a Theater of Operations.* Field Manual FM 29-19. Washington, DC: Headquarters, Department of the Army, 1985.

—**MANDATORY RELEASE DATE** is the date a soldier reaches a reenlistment ineligibility point, or attains age 55, whichever occurs first. If the soldier is granted a waiver or an exception to policy for either of these criteria, the mandatory release date is adjusted.

References

Department of Defense, U.S. Army. *Enlisted Personnel Management System.* Army Regulation AR 600-200. Washington, DC: Headquarters, Department of the Army, 1984.

—**MANEUVER** (PRINCIPLE OF WAR). Strategically, this principle has three interrelated dimensions: flexibility, mobility, and maneuverability. The first involves the need for flexibility in thought, plans, and operations. Such flexibility enhances the ability to react rapidly to unforeseen circumstances. Given the global nature of U.S. interests and the dynamic character of the international scene, such flexibility is crucial. The second dimension involves strategic mobility, which is especially critical for an insular power such as the United States. To react promptly and to concentrate and to project power on the primary objective, strategic airlift and sealift are essential. The final strategic dimension involves maneuverability within the theater of operations so as to focus maximum strength against the enemy's weakest point and thereby gain the strategic advantage.

Tactically and operationally, maneuver is an essential element of combat power. It contributes significantly to sustaining the initiative, to exploiting success, to preserving freedom of action, and to reducing vulnerability. The object of maneuver is to concentrate or to disperse forces so as to place the enemy at a disadvantage, thus achieving results that would otherwise be more costly in men and materiel. At all levels, the successful application of this principle requires fire, movement, and flexibility of thought, plans, and operations, and the considered application of the principles of mass and economy of force. At the operational level, maneuver is how the commander sets the terms of battle, declines battle, or takes advantage of tactical actions.

Alternatively, maneuver and firepower are inseparable and complementary elements of combat. Although one might dominate a phase of the battle, the coordinated use of both characterizes all operations. Their joint use makes the destruction of larger enemy forces feasible and enhances the protection of a friendly force. When nuclear weapons are available for use, maneuver may mainly exploit the effects of fire.

Maneuver is, overall, the movement of forces in relation to the enemy to secure or retain a positional advantage. It is the dynamic element of combat (i.e., the means of concentrating forces at the critical point to achieve the surprise, psychological shock, physical momentum, or moral dominance to enable smaller forces to defeat larger ones). The effects of maneuver may also be achieved without movement by allowing the enemy to move into a disadvantageous position (e.g., an ambush or with stay-behind forces; in either case, maneuver is rarely possible without firepower and protection). Operational maneuver requires protection from enemy air power; tactical maneuver may require suppressive fires and covering terrain. Effective maneuver keeps the enemy off balance and thus protects the force. It continually poses new problems for the enemy, rendering its reactions ineffective and eventually leading to its defeat.

Maneuver occurs at both the operational and the tactical levels. *Operational maneuver* seeks a decisive impact on the conduct of a campaign, attempting to gain the advantage of a position before battle and to exploit tactical successes to achieve operational results. *Tactical maneuver* seeks to set the terms of combat in a battle or engagement. It is the means of gaining and sustaining the initiative, exploiting success, preserving freedom of action, and reducing the vulnerability of friendly forces. At both levels, effective maneuver is vital to achieving superior combat power.

At all levels, effective maneuver demands air and ground mobility, knowledge of the enemy and terrain, effective command and control, flexible operational practices, sound organization, and reliable logistic support. Successful tactical maneuver depends on skillful movement along indirect approaches supported by direct and indirect fires. It may also use deception and concealment to cause an enemy to move. It requires imaginative, bold, competent, independent commanders, discipline, coordination, and speed; well-trained troops; and logistically ready units. Effective operational maneuver requires the anticipation of friendly and enemy actions beyond the current battle, the careful coordination of tactical and logistical activities, and the movement of large formations to great depths. *See also:* Principles of War.

References

Department of Defense, U.S. Army. *Air Defense Artillery Employment Hawk.* Field Manual FM 44-90. Washington, DC: Headquarters, Department of the Army, 1983.

————. *Air Defense Employment.* Field Manual FM 44-1. Washington, DC: Headquarters, U.S. Army, 1983.

————. *Operational Terms and Symbols.* Field Manual FM 101-5-1. Washington, DC: Headquarters, Department of the Army, 1985.

————. *Operations.* Field Manual FM 100-5. Washington, DC: Headquarters, Department of the Army, 1986.

—MANEUVER AMONG COMBAT VEHICLE FIGHTING POSITIONS. Success on the battlefield requires maneuver among fighting positions between main gun firings. Maximum use of reversed slope hills, and natural concealment is required to conceal the fighting vehicles that are maneuvering among fighting positions. After a major weapon system fires its main gun, the vehicle and gun usually must maneuver while concealed to another position before firing again. If a major weapon system immediately reappears in the old position, the enemy will know where to fire its next round.

References

Department of Defense, U.S. Army. *Survivability.* Field Manual FM 5-103. Washington, DC: Headquarters, Department of the Army, 1985.

—MANEUVERING FORCE is an element of a combat unit that seeks to seize an attack objective through movement to a more advantageous position with respect to the enemy.

References

Department of Defense, U.S. Army. *Dictionary of United States Army Terms.* Army Regulation AR 310-25. Washington, DC: Headquarters, Department of the Army, 1986.

—MANIPULATIVE COMMUNICATIONS COVER consists of measures taken to alter or conceal the characteristics of communications to prevent the enemy from identifying them. Manipulative communications cover is also known as communications cover. *See also:* Communications Security.

References

Department of Defense, Defense Intelligence College. *Glossary of Intelligence Terms and Definitions.* Washington, DC: DIC, 1987.

—MANIPULATIVE DECEPTION, in communications security, means altering or simulating friendly signals to deceive the enemy. It is also referred to as manipulative communications deception. *See also:* Communications Security.

References

Department of Defense, Defense Intelligence College. *Glossary of Intelligence Terms and Definitions.* Washington, DC: DIC, 1987.

—MANIPULATIVE ELECTRONIC DECEPTION (MED) is the manipulation of friendly electromagnetic radiations (e.g., by traffic leveling, providing false traffic peaks, and padding traffic) to deceive the enemy as to the intentions of friendly units. *See also:* Electronic Warfare, Imitative Electronic Deception.

References
Department of Defense, U.S. Army. *Operational Terms and Symbols.* Field Manual FM 101-5-1. Washington, DC: Headquarters, Department of the Army, 1985.

—**MANNING,** is the first challenge of sustainment, assures the uninterrupted flow of fighting men to the battle area and provides the necessary personnel services during operations.

References
Department of Defense, U.S. Army. *Operations.* Field Manual FM 100-5. Washington, DC: Headquarters, Department of the Army, 1986. *See also:* Manning Level, Manning Table.

—**MANNING LEVEL** is a personnel ceiling imposed against normally approved troop strengths because of a shortage of personnel due to limited procurement, funds, or other factors.

References
Department of Defense, U.S. Army. *Dictionary of United States Army Terms.* Army Regulation AR 310-25. Washington, DC: Headquarters, Department of the Army, 1986.

—**MANNING TABLE** is a chart of the personnel in an organization that shows the duties to which each is assigned.

References
Department of Defense, U.S. Army. *Dictionary of United States Army Terms.* Army Regulation AR 310-25. Washington, DC: Headquarters, Department of the Army, 1986.

—**MANPOWER CONTROL** is the determination of the minimum manpower requirements necessary to accomplish a mission and to allocate and use manpower within the constraints imposed by manpower ceilings and fund limitations. *See also:* Manpower Management.

References
Department of Defense, U.S. Army. *Dictionary of United States Army Terms.* Army Regulation AR 310-25. Washington, DC: Headquarters, Department of the Army, 1986.

—**MANPOWER MANAGEMENT** refers to the control necessary to ensure the most efficient and economical use of available manpower. *See also:* Manpower Management Survey.

References
Department of Defense, Joint Chiefs of Staff. *Department of Defense Dictionary of Military and Related Terms.* Washington, DC: GPO, 1986.

—**MANPOWER MANAGEMENT SURVEY** is a systematic evaluation of a functional area, using expert knowledge, manpower scaling guides, experience, and other practical considerations, to determine the validity and managerial efficiency of the function's present or proposed manpower establishment.

References
Department of Defense, Joint Chiefs of Staff. *Department of Defense Dictionary of Military and Related Terms.* Washington, DC: GPO, 1986.

—**MANPOWER REQUIREMENTS** are the human resources needed to accomplish the specified work loads of organizations. *See also:* Manpower Resources.

References
Department of Defense, Joint Chiefs of Staff. *Department of Defense Dictionary of Military and Related Terms.* Washington, DC: GPO, 1986.

—**MANPOWER RESOURCES** are the human resources that can be applied to fulfill manpower requirements. *See also:* Manpower Requirements.

References
Department of Defense, Joint Chiefs of Staff. *Department of Defense Dictionary of Military and Related Terms.* Washington, DC: GPO, 1986.

—**MANPOWER VOUCHER** is a quarterly directive of the Department of the Army that provides an employment limitation on the number of direct-hire civilian personnel working full-time in permanent positions, on the total number of foreign employees (including indirect hire employees) regardless of type of positions that they fill, and on the number of military personnel used by a command to fulfill the organization of units.

References
Department of Defense, U.S. Army. *Dictionary of United States Army Terms.* Army Regulation AR 310-25. Washington, DC: Headquarters, Department of the Army, 1986.

—**MANUAL CRYPTOSYSTEM,** in communications security, means a cryptosystem in which the cryptographic processes are performed manually without the use of cryptoequipment, limited protection equipment, or auto-manual devices. *See also:* Communications Security.

References

Department of Defense, Defense Intelligence College. *Glossary of Intelligence Terms and Definitions.* Washington, DC: DIC, 1987.

—**MAP** is a graphic representation of the earth's surface, at an established scale. It has natural or artificial physical features and a means of orientation.

References

Department of Defense, U.S. Army. *Military Symbols.* Field Manual FM 21-30. Washington, DC: Headquarters, Department of the Army, 1970.

Reeves, Robert; Anson, Abraham; and Landen, David. *Manual of Remote Sensing.* Falls Church, VA: American Society of Photogrammetry, 1975.

—**MAP K** is a proportional correction for the discrepancy between the scale of a firing chart and that of the plotting scale that is being used.

References

Department of Defense, U.S. Army. *Dictionary of United States Army Terms.* Army Regulation AR 310-25. Washington, DC: Headquarters, Department of the Army, 1986.

—**MAP MANEUVER** refers to exercises in which military operations with opposing sides are conducted on a map, with military troops represented by markers, or symbols, which are moved to represent the maneuvering of troops on the ground. *See also:* Exercise.

References

Department of Defense, U.S. Army. *How to Prepare and Conduct Military Training.* Field Manual FM 21-6. Washington, DC: Headquarters, Department of the Army, 1975.

—**MAP ORIENTATION** is the act of placing a map so that its north lines point to the corresponding north. *See also:* Map.

References

Department of Defense, U.S. Army. *Military Symbols.* Field Manual FM 21-30. Washington, DC: Headquarters, Department of the Army, 1970.

—**MAP RECONNAISSANCE** is the study of the ground features on a map (e.g., roads, woods, and waterways) to obtain the information needed to prepare a tactical plan or maneuver. *See also:* Map.

References

Department of Defense, U.S. Army. *Dictionary of United States Army Terms.* Army Regulation AR 310-25. Washington, DC: Headquarters, Department of the Army, 1986.

—**MAP SCALE** is the relationship between the distance on a map and the distance on the ground expressed as a ratio (e.g., 1:25,000, or 1/25,000, means that one inch on the map equals 25,000 inches on the ground). A large scale map covers a smaller area (e.g., a 1/25,000 map is a larger scale map than a 1/100,000 map). *See also:* Map.

References

Department of Defense, U.S. Army. *Dictionary of United States Army Terms.* Army Regulation AR 310-25. Washington, DC: Headquarters, Department of the Army, 1986.

—**MAP TEMPLET** is a thin transparent sheet divided into grid squares of a definite size and used in point designation. *See also:* Map.

References

Department of Defense, U.S. Army. *Dictionary of United States Army Terms.* Army Regulation AR 310-25. Washington, DC: Headquarters, Department of the Army, 1986.

—**MARCH COLUMN** refers to all elements of a force using the same route for a single movement under the control of a single commander. When possible, a force marches over multiple routes to reduce closing time. A large column may consist of subdivisions, each under the control of a subordinate commander. March columns, regardless of size, consist of three elements: a head, a main body, and a trail party. The *head* refers to the first vehicles of the column that normally set the pace. The *main body* consists of the major elements of column serials and march units (a serial, a major subdivision of a march column, is organized as a single unit under one commander for planning, regulation, and control. A battalion task force usually forms into a serial. A march unit, a subdivision of a serial and normally a squad, section, platoon, company, troop, or battery, moves and halts under the control of a single commander using voice, visual signals, or radio when no other means of communication can be used). The *trail party,* which follows the march column, includes the personnel and equipment necessary for the emergency repair and recovery of vehicles, medical aid and evacuation, and unscheduled refueling. *See also:* Column.

References

Department of Defense, U.S. Army. *Operational Terms and Symbols*. Field Manual FM 101-5-1. Washington, DC: Headquarters, Department of the Army, 1985.

—**MARCH OBJECTIVE** is the goal assigned to a lead unit in a movement to contact. It is designated on terrain likely to be occupied by enemy troops and at a depth expected to insure contact with the enemy. Thus, march objectives help the lead element to orient the movement. *See also:* Movement to Contact.

References

Department of Defense, U.S. Army. *The Infantry Rifle Company (Infantry, Airborne, Air Assault, Ranger)*. Field Manual FM 7-10. Washington, DC: Headquarters, Department of the Army, 1982.

—**MARCH OUTPOST** refers to observation posts and patrols established to protect a command during a halt in the march.

References

Department of Defense, U.S. Army. *Dictionary of United States Army Terms*. Army Regulation AR 310-25. Washington, DC: Headquarters, Department of the Army, 1986.

—**MARCH SECURITY** is protection against air and ground threats conducted by a unit in march formation.

References

Department of Defense, U.S. Army. *The Infantry Rifle Company (Infantry, Airborne, Air Assault, Ranger)*. Field Manual FM 7-10. Washington, DC: Headquarters, Department of the Army, 1982.

—**MARCH SERIAL.** *See:* Serial.

—**MARCH UNIT** is a unit that moves and halts at the command of a single commander. It is normally a squad, section, platoon, company, or battery.

References

Department of Defense, U.S. Army. *The Infantry Rifle Company (Infantry, Airborne, Air Assault, Ranger)*. Field Manual FM 7-10. Washington, DC: Headquarters, Department of the Army, 1982.

—**MARK.** (1) In artillery and naval gunfire support, mark means a call for fire on a specified location to orient the observer/spotter or to indicate targets; or a report made by the observer or spotter in firing illumination shells to indicate the instant of optimum light on the target. (2)

Mark, in close air support and air interdiction, means the point of weapon release. It is usually preceded by the preparatory command "standby." *See also:* Mark Target, Marking Fire.

References

Department of Defense, Joint Chiefs of Staff. *Department of Defense Dictionary of Military and Related Terms*. Washington, DC: GPO, 1986.

—**MARK TARGET** is an order to a marker, in target practice, to mark the shot on a target.

References

Department of Defense, U.S. Army. *Dictionary of United States Army Terms*. Army Regulation AR 310-25. Washington, DC: Headquarters, Department of the Army, 1986.

—**MARK TIME** is a command that requires the soldiers' feet to move as they do in marching, but without advancing.

References

Department of Defense, U.S. Army. *Dictionary of United States Army Terms*. Army Regulation AR 310-25. Washington, DC: Headquarters, Department of the Army, 1986.

—**MARKET CENTER** is an agency established for the procurement of perishable subsistence items.

References

Department of Defense, U.S. Army. *Dictionary of United States Army Terms*. Army Regulation AR 310-25. Washington, DC: Headquarters, Department of the Army, 1986.

—**MARKING** is the application of numbers, letters, labels, tags, symbols, or colors for handling or identification during the shipment or storage of items.

References

Department of Defense, U.S. Army. *Dictionary of United States Army Terms*. Army Regulation AR 310-25. Washington, DC: Headquarters, Department of the Army, 1986.

—**MARKING FIRE,** in fire support operations, consists of fires placed on, above, or in the vicinity of a surface target for the purpose of identification.

References

Department of Defense, Joint Chiefs of Staff. *Department of Defense Dictionary of Military and Related Terms*. Washington, DC: GPO, 1986.

Department of Defense, U.S. Army. *Fire Support in Combined Arms Operations*. Field Manual FM 6-20. Washington, DC: Headquarters, Department of the Army, 1983.

—**MARKING PANEL** is a sheet of material displayed for visual communication, usually between friendly units. *See also:* Panel Code.

References
Department of Defense, Joint Chiefs of Staff. *Department of Defense Dictionary of Military and Related Terms.* Washington, DC: GPO, 1986.

—**MARSHALLING.** (1) Marshalling is the process by which units participating in an amphibious, airborne, or air assault operation assemble or move to temporary camps in the vicinity of embarkation points to complete preparations for combat or to prepare for loading. (2) Marshalling is the process of assembling, holding, and organizing supplies and/or equipment, especially transport vehicles, for onward movement. *See also:* Staging Area.

References
Department of Defense, U.S. Army. *Operational Terms and Symbols.* Field Manual FM 101-5-1. Washington, DC: Headquarters, Department of the Army, 1985.

—**MARSHALLING AREA.** (1) A marshalling area is the area in which unit camps and departure airfields are located and from which the air movement is initiated. (2) In amphibious operations, a marshalling area is the designated area in which, as part of the mounting process, units are reorganized for embarkation, vehicles and equipment are prepared to move directly to embarkation areas, and housekeeping facilities are provided for troops by other units. *See also:* Mounting.

References
Department of Defense, U.S. Army. *Operational Terms and Symbols.* Field Manual FM 101-5-1. Washington, DC: Headquarters, Department of the Army, 1985.
———. *USA/USAF Doctrine for Joint Airborne and Tactical Airlift Operations.* Field Manual FM 100-27. Washington, DC: Headquarters, Department of the Army, 1985.

—**MARSHALLING PLAN** is an airborne operational plan by which units of a force complete final preparations for combat, move to departure airfields, and load for takeoff. It begins when the elements of the force are literally "sealed" in marshalling areas and it terminates at the loading. *See also:* Air Movement Plan, Ground Tactical Plan, Landing Plan.

References
Department of Defense, U.S. Army. *Operational Terms and Symbols.* Field Manual FM 101-5-1. Washington, DC: Headquarters, Department of the Army, 1985.
———. *USA/USAF Doctrine for Joint Airborne and Tactical Airlift Operations.* Field Manual FM 100-27. Washington, DC: Headquarters, Department of the Army, 1985.

—**MARTIAL LAW,** or martial rule, is the public necessity for partial or complete military control over domestic territory in times of emergency. In the United States, it is usually authorized by the President, but it may be imposed by a military commander in the interests of public safety.

References
Department of Defense, U.S. Army. *Dictionary of United States Army Terms.* Army Regulation AR 310-25. Washington, DC: Headquarters, Department of the Army, 1986.

—**MASINT.** *See:* Measurement and Signature Intelligence.

—**MASK CLEARANCE.** (1) Mask clearance is the absence of an obstruction in the path of a trajectory. (2) Mask clearance is the distance by which a projectile passes over an object between the weapon and its target.

References
Department of Defense, U.S. Army. *Air Defense Artillery Deployment: Chaparral/Vulcan/Stinger.* Field Manual FM 44-3. Washington, DC: Headquarters, Department of the Army, 1984.

—**MASKING,** in electronic warfare, is the use of additional transmitters to hide the location of the source or purpose of a particular electromagnetic radiation. *See also:* Electronic Warfare.

References
Department of Defense, Joint Chiefs of Staff. *Department of Defense Dictionary of Military and Related Terms.* Washington, DC: GPO, 1986.

—**MASK-ONLY** is a protective measure that provides relief through the use of MOPP gear for personnel who work in a contaminated environment. Personnel must be within protective shelters (e.g., vans, tanks, or buildings where the danger of transfer hazards is minimal). A soldier in mask-only posture can tolerate exposure to vapor hazards. Mask-only permits longer work periods, but personnel must assume the full MOPP level before exiting the sheltered area. *See also:* MOPP Gear.

References

Department of Defense, U.S. Army. *NBC Operations.* Field Manual FM 3-100. Washington, DC: Headquarters, Department of the Army, 1985.

————. *NBC Protection.* Field Manual FM 3-4. Washington, DC: Headquarters, Department of the Army, 1985.

—MASS means to concentrate combat power at the decisive place and time. (1) In the strategic context, this principle suggests that the nation should commit, or be prepared to commit, most of its national power to the areas worldwide where the threat to its vital security interests is greatest. For nations, such as the United States, that have global security interests in terms of politico-military alliances and commitments and resource dependencies, the accurate and timely determination of where the threat to vital national interests is greatest is becoming increasingly more difficult to ascertain. It is therefore incumbent upon military strategists to anticipate the most likely areas of concern and to develop suitable contingency plans. Since every possible contingency or trouble spot cannot be anticipated or planned for, it is essential for Army planners and forces to be flexibile in thought and action.

In terms of operations and tactics, this principle suggests that superior combat power must be concentrated at the decisive place and time in order to achieve decisive results. This superiority results from the commander's choice of the proper elements of the combat power to retain the initiative. The massing of forces, together with the proper application of other principles of war, may enable smaller forces to achieve decisive campaign and battle outcomes. (2) Mass is the concentration of combat power. (3) In military formations, mass exists when units are spaced at less than the normal distances and intervals.

References

Department of Defense, U.S. Army. *Staff Organization and Operations.* Field Manual FM 101-5. Washington, DC: Headquarters, Department of the Army, 1984.

—MASS CASUALTIES. (1) Mass casualties refer to large numbers of casualties that occur in a relatively short ime and far exceed local logistical support capabilities. (2) Mass casualties are the unreplaced soldiers who are killed, wounded, or ill, and, because of their numbers or duties, reduce the unit strength and effectiveness to the point where mission success is doubtful.

References

Department of Defense, Joint Chiefs of Staff. *Department of Defense Dictionary of Military and Related Terms.* Washington, DC: GPO, 1986.

—MASS FORMATION is the formation of a company or any larger unit in which the squads in a column are abreast one another.

References

Department of Defense, U.S. Army. *Dictionary of United States Army Terms.* Army Regulation AR 310-25. Washington, DC: Headquarters, Department of the Army, 1986.

—MASS-DETONATING EXPLOSIVES include high explosives, black powder, certain propellants, certain pyrotechnics, and other similar explosives. Alone or in combination, or loaded into ammunition or containers, most of these explosives explode instantaneously when a small portion is subjected to fire, to severe concussion or impact, to the impulse of an initiating agent, or to the effect of a considerable discharge of outside energy. Such an explosion normally causes severe structural damage to adjacent objects, which may explode immediately if they are stored sufficiently close to and not adequately protected from the initially exploding pile with a time interval short enough so that two or more quantities must be considered as one for Q-D purposes. *See also:* High Explosive, Q-D.

References

Department of Defense, U.S. Army. *Ammunition and Explosives Safety Standards.* Army Regulation AR 385-64. Washington, DC: Headquarters, Department of the Army, 1987.

—MASSED FIRES are many elements that are accurately and simultaneously attacking the same target or a small area. *See also:* Kill Zone, Killing Zone.

References

Department of Defense, U.S. Army. *Fire Support in Combined Arms Operations.* Field Manual FM 6-20. Washington, DC: Headquarters, Department of the Army, 1983.

————. *Operational Terms and Symbols.* Field Manual FM 101-5-1. Washington, DC: Headquarters, Department of the Army, 1985.

—**MASTER DEPOT** is a base depot that has responsibility for accounting for, and controlling the distribution of, all supplies of the class or type assigned to it for the entire theater or a major section of the theater. It becomes the theater stock control point for the designated items. *See also:* Depot.

References

Department of Defense, U.S. Army. *Dictionary of United States Army Terms.* Army Regulation AR 310-25. Washington, DC: Headquarters, Department of the Army, 1986.

—**MASTER FORCE LIST (MFL)** is a file that contains the current status of each requirement for a given operation plan. The list is made available for file transfer service transfer to other worldwide military command and control system activities from a file produced from the joint deployment system data base. *See also:* Operation Plan, Worldwide Military Command and Control System.

References

Department of Defense, Joint Chiefs of Staff. *Department of Defense Dictionary of Military and Related Terms.* Washington, DC: GPO, 1986.

—**MASTER STATION** is the station in a given system of transmitting stations that controls the transmissions of the other stations (i.e., the slave stations).

References

Department of Defense, U.S. Army. *Dictionary of United States Army Terms.* Army Regulation AR 310-25. Washington, DC: Headquarters, Department of the Army, 1986.

—**MASTER WARNING SIGNAL** is an alert used to indicate that any one of a number of warning signals has been activated.

References

Department of Defense, U.S. Army. *Dictionary of United States Army Terms.* Army Regulation AR 310-25. Washington, DC: Headquarters, Department of the Army, 1986.

—**MATERIAL SHORTAGE REPORT** is an Army shortage report of the items that are not available to meet the continental U.S. terminal arrival date expressed in the operation plan. *See also:* Operation Plan.

References

Department of Defense, U.S. Army. *Dictionary of United States Army Terms.* Army Regulation AR 310-25. Washington, DC: Headquarters, Department of the Army, 1986.

—**MATERIALS HANDLING** is the movement of materials (e.g., raw, scrap, semi-finished, and finished materials) to, through, and from productive processes; in warehouses and storage; and in receiving and shipping areas. *See also:* Materials Handling Equipment.

References

Department of Defense, Joint Chiefs of Staff. *Department of Defense Dictionary of Military and Related Terms.* Washington, DC: GPO, 1986.

—**MATERIALS HANDLING EQUIPMENT** are mechanical devices (e.g., fork lifts, roller conveyors, or straddle trucks) that are used to handle supplies.

References

Department of Defense, Joint Chiefs of Staff. *Department of Defense Dictionary of Military and Related Terms.* Washington, DC: GPO, 1986.

Department of Defense, U.S. Army. *Dictionary of United States Army Terms.* Army Regulation AR 310-25. Washington, DC: Headquarters, Department of the Army, 1986.

—**MATERIEL** are all items (including ships, tanks, self-propelled weapons, aircraft, related spares, repair parts, and support equipment, but excluding real property, installations, and utilities) necessary to equip, support, maintain, and operate military activities. *See also:* Equipment, Personal Property.

References

Department of Defense, Joint Chiefs of Staff. *Department of Defense Dictionary of Military and Related Terms.* Washington, DC: GPO, 1986.

—**MATERIEL AND POWDER REPORT** is a report on the performance of weapons and ammunition.

References

Department of Defense, U.S. Army. *Dictionary of United States Army Terms.* Army Regulation AR 310-25. Washington, DC: Headquarters, Department of the Army, 1986.

—**MATERIEL COGNIZANCE** denotes responsibility for exercising supply management over items or categories of materiel. *See also:* Materiel.

MATERIEL RELEASE CONFIRMATION **435**

References

Department of Defense, Joint Chiefs of Staff. *Department of Defense Dictionary of Military and Related Terms.* Washington, DC: GPO, 1986.

—**MATERIEL DEVELOPER** is the agency responsible for the research, development, and production validation of an item, including the systems needed for its logistic support, that responds to the Department of the Army's objectives and requirements.

References

Department of Defense, U.S. Army. *Dictionary of United States Army Terms.* Army Regulation AR 310-25. Washington, DC: Headquarters, Department of the Army, 1986.

—**MATERIEL INSPECTION AND RECEIVING REPORT** is a shipping document used for shipping supplies from vendors in the continental United States to installations of the three military departments. *See also:* Materiel.

References

Department of Defense, U.S. Army. *Dictionary of United States Army Terms.* Army Regulation AR 310-25. Washington, DC: Headquarters, Department of the Army, 1986.

—**MATERIEL INVENTORY OBJECTIVE** is the quantity of an item required to be on hand and on order on M-day in order to equip, provide a materiel pipeline, and sustain the approved U.S. force structure (active and reserve) and the Allied forces designated for U.S. materiel support, through the period prescribed for war materiel planning purposes. It is the quantity by which the war materiel requirement exceeds the war materiel procurement capability and the war materiel requirement adjustment. It includes the M-day force materiel requirement and the war reserve materiel requirement. *See also:* M-day, Materiel.

References

Department of Defense, Joint Chiefs of Staff. *Department of Defense Dictionary of Military and Related Terms.* Washington, DC: GPO, 1986.

—**MATERIEL MANAGEMENT CENTER (MMC)** is an activity that has formal accountability for property, except medical and commissary supplies, in a division, corps, or theater army. An MMC is responsible for the phases of military logistics that include managing, cataloging, requirements determination, acquisition, distri-

bution, overhaul, disposal, and action taken to retain equipment in a serviceable condition. It incorporates the functions of quality control, supply control, stock control, and maintenance management. *See also:* Materiel, Materiel Inventory Objective, Materiel Pipeline, Materiel Requirements..

References

Department of Defense, U.S. Army. *Planning Logistics Support for Military Operations.* Field Manual FM 701-58. Washington, DC: Headquarters, Department of the Army, 1987.

———. *Repair Parts Supply for a Theater of Operations.* Field Manual FM 29-19. Washington, DC: Headquarters, Department of the Army, 1985.

—**MATERIEL MODERNIZATION** is improvement, qualitatively or quantitatively, of equipment of the active Army and reserve components with items of materiel that reflect the optimum application of current technology and industrial capability, and results in a combat capability that equals or excels that of other nations.

References

Department of Defense, U.S. Army. *Dictionary of United States Army Terms.* Army Regulation AR 310-25. Washington, DC: Headquarters, Department of the Army, 1986.

—**MATERIEL PIPELINE** is the quantity of an item required to maintain an uninterrupted flow of replacements for it in the worldwide supply system. *See also:* Materiel, Materiel Management Center.

References

Department of Defense, Joint Chiefs of Staff. *Department of Defense Dictionary of Military and Related Terms.* Washington, DC: GPO, 1986.

—**MATERIEL READINESS** is the availability of materiel required by a military organization to support its wartime activities or contingencies, disaster relief, or emergencies.

References

Department of Defense, Joint Chiefs of Staff. *Department of Defense Dictionary of Military and Related Terms.* Washington, DC: GPO, 1986.

—**MATERIEL RELEASE CONFIRMATION** is a notification from a shipping or storage activity informing the originator of a materiel release order of the action taken on the order. It is also used with an appropriate shipment status document identifier code as a reply to a followup that has been initiated by the inventory control point. *See also:* Materiel, Materiel Release Order.

References

Department of Defense, Joint Chiefs of Staff. *Department of Defense Dictionary of Military and Related Terms.* Washington, DC: GPO, 1986.

—**MATERIEL RELEASE ORDER** is an order issued by an accountable supply system manager, usually an inventory control point or accountable depot or stock point, directing a nonaccountable activity, usually a storage site or materiel drop point, that is within the same supply distribution complex to release and ship materiel. *See also:* Materiel, Materiel Release Confirmation.

References

Department of Defense, Joint Chiefs of Staff. *Department of Defense Dictionary of Military and Related Terms.* Washington, DC: GPO, 1986.

—**MATERIEL REQUIREMENTS** are the quantities of items of equipment and supplies necessary to equip, provide a materiel pipeline, and sustain a service, formation, organization, or unit in fulfilling its purposes or tasks during a specified period. *See also:* Materiel, Materiel Pipeline.

References

Department of Defense, Joint Chiefs of Staff. *Department of Defense Dictionary of Military and Related Terms.* Washington, DC: GPO, 1986.

—**MAXI MART** is a simplified troop issue procedure wherein authorized facilities and customers "self-shop" for perishable, nonperishable, and condiment subsistence items that are stocked by the troop subsistence activity.

References

Department of Defense, U.S. Army. *Dictionary of United States Army Terms.* Army Regulation AR 310-25. Washington, DC: Headquarters, Department of the Army, 1986.

—**MAXIMUM CREDIBLE EVENT (MCE).** (1) In hazards evaluation, the MCE from a hypothetical accidental explosion, fire, or agent release is the worst single event that is likely to occur from a given quantity and disposition of ammunition and explosives. The event must be realistic and reasonably likely to occur considering the explosion propagation, burning characteristics, and physical protection given to the items involved. The MCE evaluated on this ba-

sis is then used as a basis for calculating effects and making casualty predictions. (2) An MCE for a chemical agent is the hypothetical maximum quantity of an agent that could be released from an ammunition dump, bulk container, or process as a result of a single unintended, unplanned, or accidental occurrence. It must be realistic and reasonably likely to occur.

References

Department of Defense, U.S. Army. *Ammunition and Explosives Safety Standards.* Army Regulation AR 385-64. Washington, DC: Headquarters, Department of the Army, 1987.

—**MAXIMUM EFFECTIVE RANGE (MER)** is the maximum distance at which a weapon may be expected to be accurate and achieve the desired result. *See also:* Maximum Range.

References

Department of Defense, Joint Chiefs of Staff. *Department of Defense Dictionary of Military and Related Terms.* Washington, DC: GPO, 1986.

—**MAXIMUM GRADEABILITY** is the steepest slope that a vehicle can negotiate in low gear. It is usually expressed in percentage of slope (i.e., the ratio between the vertical rise and the horizontal distance travelled). It is sometimes expressed by the degree of angle between the slope and the horizontal.

References

Department of Defense, U.S. Army. *Dictionary of United States Army Terms.* Army Regulation AR 310-25. Washington, DC: Headquarters, Department of the Army, 1986.

—**MAXIMUM HOSPITAL BENEFIT** is the point during hospitalization when the patient's recovery appears to have stabilized and additional hospitalization will not directly contribute to any further substantial recovery. *See also:* Medical Treatment.

References

Department of Defense, U.S. Army. *Dictionary of United States Army Terms.* Army Regulation AR 310-25. Washington, DC: Headquarters, Department of the Army, 1986.

—**MAXIMUM ISSUE QUANTITY** is the largest number (or amount) of an item that is authorized for issue per requisition. Quantities above this limit must be reviewed by supply personnel before they are issued.

References

Department of Defense, U.S. Army. *Dictionary of United States Army Terms*. Army Regulation AR 310-25. Washington, DC: Headquarters, Department of the Army, 1986.

—**MAXIMUM OBSTACLE ELEVATION FIGURE** is a figure shown in designated areas on aeronautical charts to indicate the minimum altitude necessary to clear any possible vertical obstructions.

References

Department of Defense, U.S. Army. *Dictionary of United States Army Terms*. Army Regulation AR 310-25. Washington, DC: Headquarters, Department of the Army, 1986.

—**MAXIMUM ORDINATE,** in artillery, is (1) the highest point along the trajectory of a projectile or (2) the difference in altitude between the origin and the summit of the projectile's trajectory.

References

Department of Defense, Joint Chiefs of Staff. *Department of Defense Dictionary of Military and Related Terms*. Washington, DC: GPO, 1986.

—**MAXIMUM PERMISSIBLE DOSE (MPD)** is the radiation dose that a military commander or other appropriate authority may prescribe as the limiting cumulative radiation dose to be received over a specific period of time by members of his command, consistent with current operational military considerations. *See also:* Nuclear Warfare.

References

Department of Defense, Joint Chiefs of Staff. *Department of Defense Dictionary of Military and Related Terms*. Washington, DC: GPO, 1986.

—**MAXIMUM RANGE** is the greatest distance a weapon can fire without consideration of dispersion. *See also:* Maximum Effective Range.

References

Department of Defense, Joint Chiefs of Staff. *Department of Defense Dictionary of Military and Related Terms*. Washington, DC: GPO, 1986.

—**MAXIMUM SECURITY INSTITUTION** is a designation given to a disciplinary barracks in which one or more serious offenders are usually confined. It is constructed to reduce the possibility of escape, and may be enclosed by walls. The prisoners are normally quartered in cells, and most of their activities are conducted within the enclosure. *See also:* Disciplinary Action.

References

Department of Defense, U.S. Army. *Dictionary of United States Army Terms*. Army Regulation AR 310-25. Washington, DC: Headquarters, Department of the Army, 1986.

—**MAXIMUM SUSTAINED SPEED** is the highest speed at which a vehicle, with its rated payload, can be driven for an extended period on a level first-class highway without sustaining damage.

References

Department of Defense, Joint Chiefs of Staff. *Department of Defense Dictionary of Military and Related Terms*. Washington, DC: GPO, 1986.

—**MAYDAY** is a distress call.

References

Department of Defense, Joint Chiefs of Staff. *Department of Defense Dictionary of Military and Related Terms*. Washington, DC: GPO, 1986.

—**MEACONING,** in electronic warfare, is a system of receiving beacon signals and then rebroadcasting them on the same frequency to confuse navigation efforts. Meaconing stations cause inaccurate bearings to be obtained by aircraft and ground stations. *See also:* Jamming.

References

Department of Defense, Defense Intelligence College. *Glossary of Intelligence Terms and Definitions*. Washington, DC: DIC, 1987.

Department of Defense, U.S. Army. *Communications Techniques: Electronics Countermeasures*. Field Manual FM 24-33. Washington, DC: Headquarters, Department of the Army, 1985.

———. *Operational Terms and Symbols*. Field Manual FM 101-5-1. Washington, DC: Headquarters, Department of the Army, 1985.

—**MEACONING, INTRUSION, JAMMING, AND INTERFERENCE (MIJI)** is a form of electronic warfare used to disrupt hostile navigational or communications equipment. *See also:* Meaconing, Intrusion, Jamming, and Interference Report.

References

Department of Defense, Defense Intelligence College. *Glossary of Intelligence Terms and Definitions*. Washington, DC: DIC, 1987.

—**MEACONING, INTRUSION, JAMMING, AND INTERFERENCE (MIJI) REPORT** is a report that records and describes interference experienced with communications that was determined not to be caused by locally generated spurious signals or technical difficulties. The report is prepared based upon an interference report that has been forwarded from the unit or element that initially experienced the interference. The unit-level interference report is transmitted by the fastest and most secure means available.

References
Department of Defense, U.S. Army. *Operational Terms and Symbols.* Field Manual FM 101-5-1. Washington, DC: Headquarters, Department of the Army, 1985.

—**MEAL BASIS OF ISSUE** refers to subsistence articles and food issued for a given day and for the number of individuals who are expected to consume each meal during that time. *See also:* Meal Ready to Eat, Individual.

References
Department of Defense, U.S. Army. *Dictionary of United States Army Terms.* Army Regulation AR 310-25. Washington, DC: Headquarters, Department of the Army, 1986.

—**MEAL READY TO EAT, INDIVIDUAL (MRE)** is the basic individual meal consumed during combat operations. Twelve different meals are available.

References
Department of Defense, U.S. Army. *Support Operations: Echelons Above Corps.* Field Manual FM 100-16. Washington, DC: Headquarters, Department of the Army, 1986.

—**MEAL SURCHARGE** is money collected from certain people who are eating in an appropriated fund dining facility to cover the operating expenses over and above the basic reimbursement rate for food costs. It is credited to the appropriated fund dining facility funds.

References
Department of Defense, U.S. Army. *Dictionary of United States Army Terms.* Army Regulation AR 310-25. Washington, DC: Headquarters, Department of the Army, 1986.

—**MEAL TICKET** is a government voucher that authorizes a public eating place to furnish meals within a certain price limit to the person or persons named, and to charge the cost to the government.

References
Department of Defense, U.S. Army. *Dictionary of United States Army Terms.* Army Regulation AR 310-25. Washington, DC: Headquarters, Department of the Army, 1986.

—**MEANS OF COMMUNICATION** is a medium (e.g., radios of all types, wire lines, messengers, mail and visual or sound signal devices) by which a message is conveyed from one person or place to another. *See also:* Means of Signal Communication.

References
Department of Defense, U.S. Army. *Dictionary of United States Army Terms.* Army Regulation AR 310-25. Washington, DC: Headquarters, Department of the Army, 1986.

—**MEANS OF SIGNAL COMMUNICATION** is a medium by which a message is conveyed from one person or place to another.

References
Department of Defense, U.S. Army. *Tactical Single Channel Radio Communications Techniques.* Field Manual FM 24-18. Washington, DC: Headquarters, Department of the Army, 1984.

—**MEASUREMENT AND SIGNATURE INTELLIGENCE (MASINT)** is scientific and technical intelligence information obtained by the quantitative and qualitative analysis of metric, angle, spatial, wavelength, modulation, plasma, hydromagnetic, and other data derived from specific technical sensors in order to identify and measure any distinctive features associated with the source, emitter or sender. MASINT includes but is not limited to radar intelligence; nuclear intelligence; radiation intelligence; acoustic intelligence; electro-optic intelligence; event-related dynamic measurements photography; and debris collection. *See also:* Scientific and Technical Intelligence.

References
Department of Defense, Defense Intelligence College. *Glossary of Intelligence Terms and Definitions.* Washington, DC: DIC, 1987.

Department of Defense, U.S. Army. *Military Intelligence Battalion (CEWI) (Tactical Exploitation) (Corps): Counterintelligence, Interrogation, Electronic Warfare.* Field Manual FM 34-23. Washington, DC: Headquarters, Department of the Army, 1985.

———. *Support Operations: Echelons Above Corps.* Field Manual FM 100-16. Washington, DC: Headquarters, Department of the Army, 1986.

Laqueur, Walter. *A World of Secrets.* New York: Basic Books, 1985.

—**MEASUREMENT CARGO** is cargo that stores more than 40 cubic feet to the ton of 2,240 pounds or weighs less than 55 pounds per cubic foot on which transportation and stevedoring charges are assessed on the basis of measurement. *See also:* Measurement Ton.

References

Department of Defense, U.S. Army. *Dictionary of United States Army Terms.* Army Regulation AR 310-25. Washington, DC: Headquarters, Department of the Army, 1986.

—**MEASUREMENT TON,** or ship ton, is a measure of cubic volume of cargo, and is expressed in units of 40 cubic feet. It is also used to indicate the cubic capacity of a ship that is available for cargo. *See also:* Measurement Cargo.

References

Department of Defense, U.S. Army. *Dictionary of United States Army Terms.* Army Regulation AR 310-25. Washington, DC: Headquarters, Department of the Army, 1986.

—**MECH HEAVY** is a company team that has more mechanized infantry platoons than tank platoons or a battalion task force that has more mechanized infantry companies than tank companies.

References

Department of Defense, U.S. Army. *The Tank and Mechanized Infantry Battalion Task Force.* Field Manual FM 71-2. Washington, DC: Headquarters, Department of the Army, 1977.

—**MECHANICAL MINELAYING EQUIPMENT** is a machine designed to lay mines in or on the ground. *See also:* Mine Warfare.

References

Department of Defense, U.S. Army. *Mine/ Countermine Operations at the Company Level.* Field Manual FM 20-32. Washington, DC: Headquarters, Department of the Army, 1976.

—**MECHANICAL TIME FUZE** is a fuze with a clock-like mechanism that controls the time when it will go off.

References

Department of Defense, U.S. Army. *Dictionary of United States Army Terms.* Army Regulation AR 310-25. Washington, DC: Headquarters, Department of the Army, 1986.

—**MECHANIZED INFANTRY (MI)** is organized and equipped for armored warfare. Both its offensive and defensive operations are characterized by rapid changes in location and by rapid changes from mounted to dismounted combat. The armored personnel carrier is the heart of the

mechanized infantry squad and must be exploited whenever possible if the squad is to be successful on a fast-moving armor battlefield. Its carrier gives the squad the mobility, protection, and firepower it needs to operate as an equal partner in the tank-infantry team. This team is ideally suited for the modern battlefield. The tanks destroy enemy armor while the mechanized infantry destroys the enemy's infantry and antitank defenses. Antitank guided missiles also give the infantry the ability to add to the fire of tanks against enemy armor.

Mechanized infantry complements armor through its ability to seize and hold ground. It suppresses enemy infantry and antitank guided missile elements. Infantrymen can dismount to patrol difficult terrain, to clear or emplace obstacles and minefields, to infiltrate and attack enemy positions, or to protect tanks in urban and wooded areas and in limited-visibility conditions.

Mechanized infantrymen have the same mobility as tankers but less firepower and protection than tankers have. Armor and mechanized infantry must perform as a team to defeat enemy armored forces. When equipped with infantry-fighting vehicles, the mechanized infantry can accompany tanks in mounted assault, although care must be taken in determining when and where the infantry must dismount to accomplish the mission; in the attack, such infantrymen can act as fixing forces; in the defense, they act as pivot points for maneuvering tank-heavy forces.

References

Department of Defense, U.S. Army. *Operations.* Field Manual FM 100-5. Washington, DC: Headquarters, Department of the Army, 1986.

———. *The Rifle Squads (Mechanized and Light Infantry).* Training Circular TC 7-1. Washington, DC: Headquarters, Department of the Army, 1976.

—**MEDAL** is an award issued to an individual for performing certain duties, acts, or services. It consists of a suspension ribbon made in distinctive colors from which hangs a medallion. The term is used in the context of the three categories of awards (i.e., decorations, Good Conduct Medal, and service medals) or to refer to the item that is tangible evidence of the award. *See also:* Valor.

References

Department of Defense, U.S. Army. *Military Awards.* Army Regulation AR 672-5-1. Washington, DC: Headquarters, Department of the Army, 1984.

————. *Wear and Appearance of Army Uniforms and Insignia.* Army Regulation AR 670-1. Washington, DC: Headquarters, Department of the Army, 1986.

—**MEDAL OF HONOR** is the nation's highest decoration. It is awarded in the name of Congress for conspicuous heroism in combat at the risk of one's life. The heroic act must be such that, if the individual had not done it, he would not be censured for failing to perform his duty. It is often incorrectly referred to as the Congressional Medal of Honor, and is first in decoration precedence. Those awarded the Medal of Honor deserve a salute from all persons in uniform, regardless of rank. *See also:* Valor.

References
Department of Defense, U.S. Army. *Dictionary of United States Army Terms.* Army Regulation AR 310-25. Washington, DC: Headquarters, Department of the Army, 1986.

—**MEDIAN INCAPACITATING DOSE** is the amount or quantity of a chemical agent that, when introduced into the body, will incapacitate 50 percent of exposed, unprotected personnel. *See also:* Chemical Warfare.

References
Department of Defense, Joint Chiefs of Staff. *Department of Defense Dictionary of Military and Related Terms.* Washington, DC: GPO, 1986.

—**MEDICAL DEPARTMENT ACTIVITY** is an organization encompassing a U.S. Army Community Hospital or designated U.S. Army Health Clinic and the associated activities that are responsible for providing health services within an assigned geographical area. It normally has control over Army Medical Department facilities, activities, or units (except for their tables of equipment and organization) that are located within the area. *See also:* Medical Treatment.

References
Department of Defense, U.S. Army. *Dictionary of United States Army Terms.* Army Regulation AR 310-25. Washington, DC: Headquarters, Department of the Army, 1986.

—**MEDICAL EVACUEES** are personnel who are wounded, injured, or ill and must be moved to or between medical facilities. *See also:* Medical Treatment.

References
Department of Defense, Joint Chiefs of Staff. *Department of Defense Dictionary of Military and Related Terms.* Washington, DC: GPO, 1986.

—**MEDICAL EXAMINATION** is a mental and physical examination performed to determine an individual's physical status. A final examination consists of a complete physical and neuropsychiatric examination, which includes a detailed medical history, chest X-ray, serological test for syphilis, urinalysis (including microscopic), and other tests, and a pelvic examination for women examinees. A preliminary physical examination is a final-type examination performed to provide advanced information regarding the physical status of an individual. Approval of the individual's physical status based upon a preliminary examination is not binding. A screening physical examination includes a brief medical history and a physical examination and the appropriate X-ray or other laboratory procedures of any system of the body that is suspected or found to be abnormal or defective. A supplemental physical examination consists of a physical reexamination of any part of a final type, special tests, or special examination of any particular system of the body. When required, it is usually performed by a medical or surgical specialist. *See also:* Screening.

References
Department of Defense, U.S. Army. *Dictionary of United States Army Terms.* Army Regulation AR 310-25. Washington, DC: Headquarters, Department of the Army, 1986.

—**MEDICAL FIELD FEEDING** is the preparation and distribution of regular and modified diets to patients and assigned personnel at all levels of medical care in the field environment. *See also:* Medical Treatment.

References
Department of Defense, U.S. Army. *Dictionary of United States Army Terms.* Army Regulation AR 310-25. Washington, DC: Headquarters, Department of the Army, 1986.

—**MEDICAL INTELLIGENCE (MEDINT)** is foreign intelligence concerning foreign, natural, and man-made environments that could affect the health of military forces. It includes general medical intelligence, which is concerned with foreign biological and medical capabilities and health situations, and medical scientific and technical intelligence, which assesses and predicts the technological advances that have medical significance, including defense against chemical, biological, and radiological warfare. Medical intelligence applies to both tactical and strategic planning and operations, including military and humanitarian efforts. *See also:* Intelligence.

References
Department of Defense, Defense Intelligence College. *Glossary of Intelligence Terms and Definitions.* Washington, DC: DIC, 1987.

—**MEDICAL LABORATORY** is a mobile or fixed unit established to provide immediately available facilities for epidemiological and sanitary investigations, laboratory examinations to supplement those of other laboratories, and provision of certain laboratory supplies. *See also:* Medical Treatment.

References
Department of Defense, U.S. Army. *Dictionary of United States Army Terms.* Army Regulation AR 310-25. Washington, DC: Headquarters, Department of the Army, 1986.

—**MEDICAL LOGISTICS CONTROL GROUP** is a subordinate agency of the medical command that coordinates all medical logistics activities within a theater. It commands and controls the operations of all communications zone medical supply maintenance and, through automated systems, provides the medical logistics link between the theater and continental U.S.-based medical supply facilities. *See also:* Medical Treatment.

References
Department of Defense, U.S. Army. *Support Operations: Echelons Above Corps.* Field Manual FM 100-16. Washington, DC: Headquarters, Department of the Army, 1986.

—**MEDICAL OFFICER** is a physician with officer rank. *See also:* Medical Treatment.

References
Department of Defense, Joint Chiefs of Staff. *Department of Defense Dictionary of Military and Related Terms.* Washington, DC: GPO, 1986.

—**MEDICAL REGULATING** is the function of coordinating and controlling the movement of patients to, from, and between medical treatment facilities. *See also:* Medical Treatment.

References
Department of Defense, U.S. Army. *Dictionary of United States Army Terms.* Army Regulation AR 310-25. Washington, DC: Headquarters, Department of the Army, 1986.

—**MEDICAL REGULATOR** is the officer of the medical component of one of the armed services who exercises regulatory control over the movement of patients between medical treatment facilities. Using timely information on bed availability and existing patient work loads by specialized category in various treatment facilities, he directs the flow of evacuees to the proper medical treatment facilities. *See also:* Medical Treatment.

References
Department of Defense, U.S. Army. *Dictionary of United States Army Terms.* Army Regulation AR 310-25. Washington, DC: Headquarters, Department of the Army, 1986.

—**MEDICAL SERVICE** differentiates the medical service as a branch within Army medicine from other branches (e.g., the dental service and veterinary service). It is also a title of a hospital subdivision that provides general medical services (rather than e.g., surgical or orthopedic services). *See also:* Medical Treatment.

References
Department of Defense, U.S. Army. *Dictionary of United States Army Terms.* Army Regulation AR 310-25. Washington, DC: Headquarters, Department of the Army, 1986.
———. *Health Service Support in a Communications Zone (Test).* Field Manual FM 8-21. Washington, DC: Headquarters, Department of the Army, 1981.

—**MEDICAL SUPPORT** is broadly synonymous with health services, and the two terms may be used interchangeably. *See also:* Medical Treatment.

References
Department of Defense, U.S. Army. *Health Service Support in a Communications Zone (Test).* Field Manual FM 8-21. Washington, DC: Headquarters, Department of the Army, 1981.

—**MEDICAL TREATMENT** is the application of medical procedures by trained professional and technical personnel, and the management of patients under such procedures, to relieve pain and suffering, to save lives, and to cure disease, injury, or other disorders. *See also:* Aid Man, Aid Station, Hospital, Medical Department Activity, Medical Evacuees, Medical Examination, Medical Field Feeding, Medical Laboratory, Medical Logistics Control Group, Medical Officer, Medical Regulating, Medical Regulator, Medical Service, Medical Support, Medical Treatment Facility, Medical Warning Tag.

References
Department of Defense, U.S. Army. *Dictionary of United States Army Terms.* Army Regulation AR 310-25. Washington, DC: Headquarters, Department of the Army, 1986.

—**MEDICAL TREATMENT FACILITY (MTF)** is any facility established to provide (or capabile of providing) medical treatment. This includes hospitals, clearing stations, clinics, aid stations, dispensaries, and convalescent centers. *See also:* Medical Treatment.

References
Department of Defense, U.S. Army. *Health Service Support in a Communications Zone (Test).* Field Manual FM 8-21. Washington, DC: Headquarters, Department of the Army, 1981.

—**MEDICAL WARNING TAG** allows rapid recognition of selected health problems when records are not immediately available and the individual requiring treatment is unable to give his medical history. *See also:* Medical Treatment.

References
Department of Defense, U.S. Army. *Dictionary of United States Army Terms.* Army Regulation AR 310-25. Washington, DC: Headquarters, Department of the Army, 1986.

—**MEDIUM ATOMIC DEMOLITION MUNITION** is a low-yield, team-portable, atomic demolition munition that can be detonated either by remote control or by a timer device.

References
Department of Defense, Joint Chiefs of Staff. *Department of Defense Dictionary of Military and Related Terms.* Washington, DC: GPO, 1986.

—**MEDIUM DOLLAR VALUE ITEM** is an end-item or repair part whose value of total demand at continental U.S. depots is between $2,500 and $25,000.

References
Department of Defense, U.S. Army. *Dictionary of United States Army Terms.* Army Regulation AR 310-25. Washington, DC: Headquarters, Department of the Army, 1986.

—**MEDIUM SECURITY INSTITUTION** is the designation given to disciplinary barracks or rehabilitation centers in which less serious offenders may be committed for confinement. It is usually enclosed with a fence rather than a wall, and its prisoners are normally housed in barracks or dormitories. *See also:* Maximum Security Institution.

References
Department of Defense, U.S. Army. *Dictionary of United States Army Terms.* Army Regulation AR 310-25. Washington, DC: Headquarters, Department of the Army, 1986.

—**MEDIUM TANK** is a tank weighing between 40 and 60 tons. (The United States no longer officially uses the heavy, medium, and light tank designations.) *See also:* Light Tank.

References
Collins, John M. *U.S.-Soviet Military Balance, 1980-1985.* Washington, DC: Congressional Research Service, 1985.

—**MEDIUM-COST, HIGH-DENSITY MISSILE SYSTEMS** are assigned in relatively high densities to combat and combat support units in the theater of operations. This class is sometimes referred to as small missile systems and includes air defense guns and night sights. All antitank missiles, night sights, and Lance are frequently referred to as land combat systems, and all air defense items are frequently referred to as SHORADS (short-range air defense systems). Small missile systems include Shillelagh, TOW, Dragon, Chaparral/Vulcan, Lance, Bradley fighting vehicle system TOW subsystem, multiple rocket launcher system, Roland, forward area alerting radar, and night sights.

References
Department of Defense, U.S. Army. *Combat Service Support Operations-Division.* Field Manual FM 63-2. Washington, DC: Headquarters, Department of the Army, 1983.

—**MEDIUM-LOT STORAGE** is generally defined as a quantity of material that requires one to three pallet stacks to store.

References
Department of Defense, Joint Chiefs of Staff. *Department of Defense Dictionary of Military and Related Terms.* Washington, DC: GPO, 1986.

—**MEDIUM-RANGE BALLISTIC MISSILE** is a ballistic missile with a range of from 600 to 1,500 nautical miles. *See also:* Short-Range Ballistic Missile.

References

Department of Defense, Joint Chiefs of Staff. *Department of Defense Dictionary of Military and Related Terms.* Washington, DC: GPO, 1986.

—**MEDIUM-RANGE RADAR** is equipment whose maximum range on a reflecting target of one square meter within the signal path exceeds 240 kilometers but is less than 480 kilometers, provided that a line of sight exists between the target and the radar. *See also:* Long-Range Radar, Short-Range Radar.

References

Department of Defense, U.S. Army. *Dictionary of United States Army Terms.* Army Regulation AR 310-25. Washington, DC: Headquarters, Department of the Army, 1986.

—**MEETING ENGAGEMENTS.** A movement to contact often results in a meeting engagement. Such encounters often occur by chance in small unit operations and when reconnaissance has been ineffective in brigade or larger unit operations. A meeting engagement may also occur when each opponent is aware of the other and both decide to attack without delay to obtain positional advantage, to gain a decisive terrain feature, or to assert moral dominance. A meeting engagement may also occur when one force deploys hastily for defense while the other attempts to prevent it. *See also:* Movement to Contact.

References

Department of Defense, U.S. Army. *Operational Terms and Symbols.* Field Manual FM 101-5-1. Washington, DC: Headquarters, Department of the Army, 1985.

_____. *Operations.* Field Manual FM 100-5. Washington, DC: Headquarters, Department of the Army, 1986.

—**MEGATON** is a unit of measurement for nuclear energy yield. It equals the energy released from the detonation of one million tons of trinitroluene (TNT). *See also:* Nuclear Warfare.

References

Department of Defense, U.S. Army. *Dictionary of United States Army Terms.* Army Regulation AR 310-25. Washington, DC: Headquarters, Department of the Army, 1986.

—**MEGATON WEAPON** is a nuclear weapon whose yield is measured in millions of tons of trinitroluene (TNT) explosive equivalents. *See also:* Kiloton Weapon.

References

Department of Defense, Joint Chiefs of Staff. *Department of Defense Dictionary of Military and Related Terms.* Washington, DC: GPO, 1986.

—**MELINITE,** a powerful explosive similar to lyddite, is made by combining picric acid with guncotton. *See also:* Lyddite.

References

Department of Defense, U.S. Army. *Dictionary of United States Army Terms.* Army Regulation AR 310-25. Washington, DC: Headquarters, Department of the Army, 1986.

—**MEMBER, ENLISTED PERSON** is an enlisted man or woman of the Army, including all persons enlisted in a component of the Army. *See also:* Basic Enlisted Service Date; Certificate of Service; Contractually Obligated Soldier; Noncommissioned Officer; Nonprior Service Personnel; Prior Service Personnel; Service Record; Soldier, Enlisted Person.

References

Department of Defense, U.S. Army. *Army Reenlistment Program.* Army Regulation AR 601-28. Washington, DC: Headquarters, Department of the Army, 1984.

_____. *Enlisted Personnel.* Army Regulation AR 635-200. Washington, DC: Headquarters, Department of the Army, 1984.

_____. *Enlisted Personnel Management System.* Army Regulation AR 600-200. Washington, DC: Headquarters, Department of the Army, 1984.

_____. *Selection of Enlisted Soldiers for Training and Assignment.* Army Regulation AR 614-200. Washington, DC: Headquarters, Department of the Army, 1984.

—**MEMORANDUM OF AGREEMENT (MOA)** is a written agreement between military units that explains how they will support each other. Tenant commands (i.e., those located on the property or in the facilities of a parent command) have an MOA regarding the use of the parent command's facilities. *See also:* Memorandum of Understanding.

References

Department of Defense, Joint Chiefs of Staff. *Department of Defense Dictionary of Military and Related Terms.* Washington, DC: GPO, 1986.

Department of Defense, U.S. Army. *Support Operations: Echelons Above Corps.* Field Manual FM 100-16. Washington, DC: Headquarters, Department of the Army, 1986.

—**MEMORANDUM OF UNDERSTANDING (MOU)** is the documentation of mutually agreed to statements of facts, intentions, procedures, and parameters for future actions and matters of coordination. Such documentation is not a substitute for formal interservice, interdepartmental/agency, or intraservice support agreements. MOUs are used to document mutually agreed parameters within which interservice, intradepartmental/agency, and/or intraservice support agreements will be developed. *See also:* Memorandum of Agreement.

References
Department of Defense, U.S. Army. *Dictionary of United States Army Terms.* Army Regulation AR 310-25. Washington, DC: Headquarters, Department of the Army, 1986.

—**MERCURIC FULMINATE** (FULMINATE OF MERCURY) is an initiating high explosive that is detonated by heat, impact, or friction. Overall, it is being replaced by lead azide. *See also:* Lead Azide.

References
Department of Defense, U.S. Army. *Dictionary of United States Army Terms.* Army Regulation AR 310-25. Washington, DC: Headquarters, Department of the Army, 1986.

—**MERGER TRAINING** is training that prepares a noncommissioned officer to supervise one or more different military occupational specialties at skill levels that are lower than his own.

References
Department of Defense, U.S. Army. *Training for Mobilization and War.* Field Manual FM 25-5. Washington, DC: Headquarters, Department of the Army, 1985.

—**MERITORIOUS ACHIEVEMENT** is an act well above the expected performance of duty. Although the act should be an exceptional accomplishment with definite beginning and ending dates, the length of time is not a primary consideration. However, speed of accomplishment of an important task can be a factor in determining the value of the act. *See also:* Meritorious Service.

References
Department of Defense, U.S. Army. *Military Awards.* Army Regulation AR 672-5-1. Washington, DC: Headquarters, Department of the Army, 1984.

—**MERITORIOUS SERVICE** is service distinguished by a succession of outstanding acts of achievement over a sustained period of time. *See also:* Meritorious Achievement.

References
Department of Defense, U.S. Army. *Military Awards.* Army Regulation AR 672-5-1. Washington, DC: Headquarters, Department of the Army, 1984.

—**MESS KIT**, or mess gear, is eating equipment the soldier uses in the field. It includes a knife, fork, spoon, cup, and a meat can.

References
Department of Defense, U.S. Army. *Dictionary of United States Army Terms.* Army Regulation AR 310-25. Washington, DC: Headquarters, Department of the Army, 1986.

—**MESS UNIFORMS** are uniforms worn for formal social occasions when prescribed by the host. They include the blue and white mess uniforms for men, and the black, blue, white, and all-white mess uniforms for women. *See also:* Service Uniform.

References
Department of Defense, U.S. Army. *Wear and Appearance of Army Uniforms and Insignia.* Army Regulation AR 670-1. Washington, DC: Headquarters, Department of the Army, 1986.

—**MESSAGE** is a thought or idea expressed briefly in plain, coded, or secret language and prepared in any form suitable for transmission by any means of communication. *See also:* Communications Security.

References
Department of Defense, Joint Chiefs of Staff. *Department of Defense Dictionary of Military and Related Terms.* Washington, DC: GPO, 1986.

—**MESSAGE** (TELECOMMUNICATIONS) is information expressed in plain or encrypted language and prepared in a format specified for transmission by a telecommunications system. *See also:* Message.

References
Department of Defense, Joint Chiefs of Staff. *Department of Defense Dictionary of Military and Related Terms.* Washington, DC: GPO, 1986.

—**MESSAGE BOOK.** (1) A message book is a record or log of all messages sent from a message center, radio station, or similar facility. (2) A message book is a book of blank forms used to write messages. *See also:* Message.

References

Department of Defense, U.S. Army. *Dictionary of United States Army Terms.* Army Regulation AR 310-25. Washington, DC: Headquarters, Department of the Army, 1986.

—**MESSAGE INDICATOR** is a group of symbols usually at the beginning of the text of an encrypted message or transmission. It identifies or governs the arrangement of the cryptovariables applicable to the message or transmission, and establishes the starting point of the key cycle. *See also:* Communications Security.

References

Department of Defense, U.S. Army. *Dictionary of United States Army Terms.* Army Regulation AR 310-25. Washington, DC: Headquarters, Department of the Army, 1986.

—**MESSAGE KEYING ELEMENT** is the part of the specific key that changes with every message. *See also:* Communications Security.

References

Department of Defense, U.S. Army. *Dictionary of United States Army Terms.* Army Regulation AR 310-25. Washington, DC: Headquarters, Department of the Army, 1986.

—**MESSAGE PARTS** are the result of dividing a long message into shorter messages of different lengths to enhance transmission security or to comply with communications requirements. Message parts must be prepared so that they appear to be unrelated; statements identifying the parts are encrypted in the texts. *See also:* Message.

References

Department of Defense, U.S. Army. *Dictionary of United States Army Terms.* Army Regulation AR 310-25. Washington, DC: Headquarters, Department of the Army, 1986.

—**METHOD OF RESUPPLY** is how a unit makes its supply requirements known to the issuing installation (e.g., include requisition, automatic resupply, on-call resupply, status report, and expenditure report).

References

Department of Defense, U.S. Army. *Dictionary of United States Army Terms.* Army Regulation AR 310-25. Washington, DC: Headquarters, Department of the Army, 1986.

—**MEZZANINE SPACE** is room provided by the construction of an intermediate or partial story between the floor and ceiling of a building. It is used for storage.

References

Department of Defense, U.S. Army. *Dictionary of United States Army Terms.* Army Regulation AR 310-25. Washington, DC: Headquarters, Department of the Army, 1986.

—**MIDPOINT,** in gunnery, is the point on an air target's course that is at a minimum slant range from the gun position.

References

Department of Defense, U.S. Army. *Dictionary of United States Army Terms.* Army Regulation AR 310-25. Washington, DC: Headquarters, Department of the Army, 1986.

—**MID-RANGE ESTIMATE** is a projected estimation of information to be included in the joint strategic objectives plan. It is prepared before the annual development of the joint strategic objectives plan and provides a coordinated Army position to be used by the Army planners preparing the joint strategic objectives plan. *See also:* Joint Strategic Objectives Plan.

References

Department of Defense, U.S. Army. *Dictionary of United States Army Terms.* Army Regulation AR 310-25. Washington, DC: Headquarters, Department of the Army, 1986.

—**MID-TERM PSYOP (PSYCHOLOGICAL OPERATIONS) CAMPAIGN** consists of propaganda and psychological actions conducted to support operational objectives. It is directed at intermediate target audiences to achieve mid-range psychological objectives within a specified time. *See also:* Psychological Operations.

References

Department of Defense, U.S. Army. *Psychological Operations.* Field Manual FM 33-1. Washington, DC: Headquarters, Department of the Army, 1979.

—**MILES (MULTIPLE INTEGRATED LASER ENGAGEMENT SYSTEM)** is similar to REALTRAIN, except that adapters on the weapons fire eye-safe laser beams, which are picked up by sensors attached to field gear and vehicles. A continuous alarm goes off immediately when a soldier is "killed" or the equipment is "destroyed." The soldier hears an intermittent alarm when there is a near-miss. MILES is the more realistic of the two engagement simulations. *See also:* REALTRAIN.

References
Department of Defense, U.S. Army. *Unit Training Management.* Field Manual FM 25-2. Washington, DC: Headquarters, Department of the Army, 1984.

—**MILITARILY SIGNIFICANT FALLOUT** is radioactive contamination that can inflict radiation doses on personnel and cause them to be less effective in combat. *See also:* Nuclear Warfare.

References
Department of Defense, Joint Chiefs of Staff. *Department of Defense Dictionary of Military and Related Terms.* Washington, DC: GPO, 1986.

—**MILITARY.** (1) In general, military is a term meaning of, or pertaining, to war or to the affairs of war, whether they are Army, Navy, or Air Force matters. (2) Military means, of or pertaining only to the Army.

References
Department of Defense, U.S. Army. *Dictionary of United States Army Terms.* Army Regulation AR 310-25. Washington, DC: Headquarters, Department of the Army, 1986.

—**MILITARY AFFILIATE RADIO SYSTEM (MARS)** is a program conducted by the Departments of the Army, Navy, and Air Force in which amateur radio stations and operators participate in and contribute to the mission of providing auxiliary and emergency communications on a local, national, or international basis as an adjunct to normal military communications.

References
Department of Defense, Joint Chiefs of Staff. *Department of Defense Dictionary of Military and Related Terms.* Washington, DC: GPO, 1986.

—**MILITARY AIR MOVEMENT NUMBER** is a symbol assigned for identification, record, secrecy, and administrative handling purposes. It is used when fifteen or more Department of the Army personnel travel within the continental limits of the United States by military aircraft.

References
Department of Defense, U.S. Army. *Dictionary of United States Army Terms.* Army Regulation AR 310-25. Washington, DC: Headquarters, Department of the Army, 1986.

—**MILITARY AIRLIFT COMMAND (MAC)** is the single-manager operating agency for a designated airlift service.

References
Department of Defense, U.S. Army. *Transportation Reference Data.* Field Manual FM 55-15. Washington, DC: Headquarters, Department of the Army, 1986.

—**MILITARY AREA** is a specific geographical area in which an overriding military mission exists and which has specifically been declared as such by the President, the Secretary of Defense, or a person delegated the authority to do so.

References
Department of Defense, U.S. Army. *Dictionary of United States Army Terms.* Army Regulation AR 310-25. Washington, DC: Headquarters, Department of the Army, 1986.

—**MILITARY ASSISTANCE** refers collectively to three major military security assistance programs: the Military Assistance Grant Aid Program, the Foreign Military Sales Program, and the Excess Defense Articles Program.

References
Department of Defense, U.S. Army. *Civil Affairs Operations.* Field Manual FM 41-10. Washington, DC: Headquarters, Department of the Army, 1985.
———. *Low Intensity Conflict.* Field Manual FM 100-20. Washington, DC: Headquarters, Department of the Army, 1981.

—**MILITARY ASSISTANCE AND ADVISORY GROUP (MAAG)** encompasses joint U.S. military advisory groups, military missions, military advisory groups, U.S. military groups, and U.S. military representatives exercising responsibility at the government level for security assistance and other Department of Defense matters with the host countries to which they are accredited. Defense attachés are included when they are specifically designated. In general, the MAAG is a joint service group, normally under the military command of a commander of a unified command and representing the Secretary of Defense, that primarily administers the U.S. military assistance planning and programming in the host country.

References

Department of Defense, U.S. Army. *Low Intensity Conflict*. Field Manual FM 100-20. Washington, DC: Headquarters, Department of the Army, 1981.

—**MILITARY ASSISTANCE ARTICLES AND SERVICES LIST** is a Department of Defense publication that lists the source, availability, and price of items and services that can be used by the unified commands and military departments in preparing their military assistance plans and programs.

References

Department of Defense, Joint Chiefs of Staff. *Department of Defense Dictionary of Military and Related Terms*. Washington, DC: GPO, 1986.

—**MILITARY ASSISTANCE PROGRAM (MAP)** is the portion of the U.S. security assistance authorized by the Foreign Assistance Act of 1961, as amended. It provides defense articles and services to recipients on a nonreimbursable (grant) basis.

References

Department of Defense, Joint Chiefs of Staff. *Department of Defense Dictionary of Military and Related Terms*. Washington, DC: GPO, 1986.

—**MILITARY AUTHORIZATION IDENTIFICATION NUMBER** is a symbol and number assigned to a group of fifteen or more persons, who are "moving with or without organizational equipment or impedimenta, in commercial railway or passenger or mixed train service, between points within continental United States and points in contiguous countries." It is not assigned to movements where the authority to route and arrange for movements has been delegated to a field agency.

References

Department of Defense, U.S. Army. *Dictionary of United States Army Terms*. Army Regulation AR 310-25. Washington, DC: Headquarters, Department of the Army, 1986.

—**MILITARY BALANCE** is the comparative combat powers of two competing countries or coalitions.

References

Collins, John M. *U.S.-Soviet Military Balance, 1980-1985*. Washington, DC: Congressional Research Service, 1985.

—**MILITARY BEHAVIOR** is the conduct of an individual while serving as a soldier in the Army.

References

Department of Defense, U.S. Army. *Enlisted Personnel*. Army Regulation AR 635-200. Washington, DC: Headquarters, U.S. Army, 1984.

—**MILITARY CENSORSHIP** encompasses censorship conducted by personnel of the U.S. Armed Forces (e.g., armed forces censorship, civil censorship, prisoner of war censorship, and field press censorship).

References

Department of Defense, Joint Chiefs of Staff. *Department of Defense Dictionary of Military and Related Terms*. Washington, DC: GPO, 1986.

—**MILITARY CHARACTERISTICS** are the aspects of equipment that govern its ability to perform the desired military functions. These include physical and operational characteristics but not technical characteristics.

References

Department of Defense, Joint Chiefs of Staff. *Department of Defense Dictionary of Military and Related Terms*. Washington, DC: GPO, 1986.

—**MILITARY CIVIC ACTION** is the use of preponderantly indigenous military forces on projects that are useful to the local population. Such action can be in education, training, public works, agriculture, transportation, communications, health, sanitation, and other fields that contribute to economic and social development. One goal of such action is to serve to improve the standing of the military forces with the population. (U.S. forces may at times advise or engage in military civic actions in overseas areas.) *See also:* Civil Affairs.

References

Department of Defense, U.S. Army. *Low Intensity Conflict*. Field Manual FM 100-20. Washington, DC: Headquarters, Department of the Army, 1981.

—**MILITARY CLIMB CORRIDOR** is a controlled airspace of defined vertical and horizontal dimensions that extends outward from a military airfield.

References

Department of Defense, U.S. Army. *Dictionary of United States Army Terms*. Army Regulation AR 310-25. Washington, DC: Headquarters, Department of the Army, 1986.

—**MILITARY COMMISSION** is a court convened by military authority to try persons not usually subject to military law and who are charged with violating the laws of war. It is convened in areas subject to military government or martial law and is intended to try persons charged with violations of proclamations, ordinances, and valid domestic civil and criminal laws of the territory concerned.

References
Department of Defense, U.S. Army. *Dictionary of United States Army Terms.* Army Regulation AR 310-25. Washington, DC: Headquarters, Department of the Army, 1986.

—**MILITARY CONVOY** is a land or maritime convoy controlled and reported as a military unit.

References
Department of Defense, Joint Chiefs of Staff. *Department of Defense Dictionary of Military and Related Terms.* Washington, DC: GPO, 1986.

Department of Defense, U.S. Army. *Military Convoy Operations in the Continental United States.* Field Manual FM 55-312. Washington, DC: Headquarters, Department of the Army, 1981.

—**MILITARY COURTESY** refers to the rules of conduct that are required, either by regulation or tradition, for military personnel.

References
Department of Defense, U.S. Army. *Dictionary of United States Army Terms.* Army Regulation AR 310-25. Washington, DC: Headquarters, Department of the Army, 1986.

—**MILITARY CREST** is an area on the forward slope of a hill or ridge from which the most amount of the slope down to the base of the hill or ridge can be observed.

References
Department of Defense, U.S. Army. *Operational Terms and Symbols.* Field Manual FM 101-5-1. Washington, DC: Headquarters, Department of the Army, 1985.

—**MILITARY CURRENCY** is currency prepared by a power and declared by its military commander to be the legal tender for use by civilian and military personnel as prescribed in the areas occupied by its forces. It is distinctively designed to distinguish it from the official currency of both countries concerned, but it may be denominated in the monetary unit of either.

References
Department of Defense, Joint Chiefs of Staff. *Department of Defense Dictionary of Military and Related Terms.* Washington, DC: GPO, 1986.

—**MILITARY DAMAGE ASSESSMENT** is an appraisal of the effects of an attack on a nation's military forces to determine the residual capability and to support planning for military recovery and reconstitution. *See also:* Damage Assessment.

References
Department of Defense, Joint Chiefs of Staff. *Department of Defense Dictionary of Military and Related Terms.* Washington, DC: GPO, 1986.

—**MILITARY DECEPTION** is an Army tactical intelligence term referring to actions executed to mislead foreign decisionmakers causing them to make and accept certain estimates of their opponent's military capabilities, intentions, operations, or other activities that prompt them to react in a manner that contributes to the achievement of their opponent's objectives. There are three categories of military deception:

(1) **Strategic military deception** is planned and executed to result in foreign national policies and actions that support the originator's national objectives, policies, and strategic military plans.

(2) **Tactical military deception** is planned and executed by and in support of operational commanders against the pertinent threat, to result in opposing operational actions favorable to the originator's plans and operations.

(3) **Department/Service military deception** is planned and executed by the Military Services about military systems, doctrine, tactics, techniques, personnel or service operations, or other activities to result in foreign actions that increase or maintain the originator's capabilities relative to adversaries.

See also: Deception.

References
Department of Defense, U.S. Army. *Military Intelligence Battalion (Combat Electronic Warfare Intelligence) (Division).* Field Manual FM 34-10. Washington, DC: Headquarters, Department of the Army, 1981.

———. *Military Intelligence Battalion Combat Electronic Warfare and Intelligence (Aerial Exploitation) (Corps).* Field Manual FM 34-22. Washington, DC: Headquarters, Department of the Army, 1984.

—**MILITARY DEFENSE** pertains to the activities and measures that are designed, in whole or in part, to prevent the successful completion of any organized enemy military action physically directed at any part of the continental United States, its territories, or possessions.

References

Department of Defense, U.S. Army. *Dictionary of United States Army Terms.* Army Regulation AR 310-25. Washington, DC: Headquarters, Department of the Army, 1986.

—**MILITARY DEPARTMENT** is one of the departments within the Department of Defense that were created by the National Security Act of 1947, as amended.

References

Department of Defense, Joint Chiefs of Staff. *Department of Defense Dictionary of Military and Related Terms.* Washington, DC: GPO, 1986.

—**MILITARY DESIGNED VEHICLE** is one having military characteristics resulting from military research and development processes. It is designed primarily for use by forces in the field in direct connection with, or support of, combat or tactical operations.

References

Department of Defense, Joint Chiefs of Staff. *Department of Defense Dictionary of Military and Related Terms.* Washington, DC: GPO, 1986.

—**MILITARY DYNAMITE** is a blasting explosive in cartridges especially suited for use in military construction, quarrying, and service demolition work. It is less sensitive than commercial dynamite and has good storage characteristics.

References

Department of Defense, U.S. Army. *Dictionary of United States Army Terms.* Army Regulation AR 310-25. Washington, DC: Headquarters, Department of the Army, 1986.

—**MILITARY EDUCATION** is the systematic instruction of individuals in the science and art of war. It is designed to prepare soldiers for military careers. *See also:* Military Training.

References

Department of Defense, U.S. Army. *Individual Military Education and Training.* Army Regulation AR 350-1. Washington, DC: Headquarters, Department of the Army, 1987.

—**MILITARY EQUIPMENT POOL** is a group of weapons, special munitions, and special equipment that may be assigned at the battalion, company, platoon, or squad level for use as required by the tactical situation and the unit's mission. The term is preceded by the appropriate organizational designation whenever a specific level of organization is intended (e.g., battalion mobile equipment pool).

References

Department of Defense, U.S. Army. *Dictionary of United States Army Terms.* Army Regulation AR 310-25. Washington, DC: Headquarters, Department of the Army, 1986.

—**MILITARY GEOGRAPHIC DOCUMENTATION** is military geographic information that can be evaluated, processed, summarized, and published. *See also:* Geographic Intelligence.

References

Department of Defense, Joint Chiefs of Staff. *Department of Defense Dictionary of Military and Related Terms.* Washington, DC: GPO, 1986.

—**MILITARY GEOGRAPHIC INFORMATION** comprises information concerning the physical aspects, resources, and artificial features that is necessary for military planning and operations. *See also:* Geographic Intelligence.

References

Department of Defense, Joint Chiefs of Staff. *Department of Defense Dictionary of Military and Related Terms.* Washington, DC: GPO, 1986.

—**MILITARY GEOGRAPHY** is a specialized field of geography dealing with natural and man-made features that may affect the planning and conduct of military operations. *See also:* Geographic Intelligence.

References

Department of Defense, Joint Chiefs of Staff. *Department of Defense Dictionary of Military and Related Terms.* Washington, DC: GPO, 1986.

—**MILITARY GOVERNMENT COURT** is a court established by a commander who has military government responsibility. The court has jurisdiction over cases arising under enactments of military government or indigenous law and concerns all persons in an occupied territory, except members of the occupying and allied military forces who are subject to military law. *See also:* Military Governor.

References

Department of Defense, U.S. Army. *Dictionary of United States Army Terms.* Army Regulation AR 310-25. Washington, DC: Headquarters, Department of the Army, 1986.

—**MILITARY GOVERNMENT ORDINANCE** is an enactment, on the authority of a military governor, that promulgates laws and rules regulating the occupied territory under his control. *See also:* Military Governor.

References

Department of Defense, Joint Chiefs of Staff. *Department of Defense Dictionary of Military and Related Terms.* Washington, DC: GPO, 1986.

—**MILITARY GOVERNOR** is the military commander or other designated person who, in an occupied territory, exercises supreme authority over the civil population subject to the laws and usages of war and to any directive received from his government or his superior. *See also:* Military Commission, Military Government Court, Military Government Ordinance.

References

Department of Defense, Joint Chiefs of Staff. *Department of Defense Dictionary of Military and Related Terms.* Washington, DC: GPO, 1986.

—**MILITARY GRID** is composed of two sets of parallel lines intersecting at right angles and forming squares. It is superimposed on maps and charts, and permits identification of ground locations with respect to other locations and the computation of direction and distance to other points. *See also:* Military Grid Reference System.

References

Department of Defense, Joint Chiefs of Staff. *Department of Defense Dictionary of Military and Related Terms.* Washington, DC: GPO, 1986.

—**MILITARY GRID REFERENCE SYSTEM** is a system that uses a standard-scaled grid square, based upon a point of origin on a map. It permits either position referencing or the computation of direction and distance between grid positions. *See also:* Military Grid.

References

Department of Defense, Joint Chiefs of Staff. *Department of Defense Dictionary of Military and Related Terms.* Washington, DC: GPO, 1986.

—**MILITARY IMPEDIMENTA NUMBER** is a number assigned by the Association of American Railroads for purposes of identification, record, secrecy, and administrative handling of movements of military property in the domestic freight train service.

References

Department of Defense, U.S. Army. *Dictionary of United States Army Terms.* Army Regulation AR 310-25. Washington, DC: Headquarters, Department of the Army, 1986.

—**MILITARY INTELLIGENCE (MI)** is basic, current, or estimative intelligence on any foreign military or military-related situation or activity that is significant to military policymaking or to the planning and conduct of military operations and activities. In the indications and warning context, military intelligence means analyzed, evaluated, and interpreted information on foreign nations that (1) describes and defines the military forces of the country and their offensive and defensive capabilities, assesses the military strategy, tactics, and doctrine of a nation, and estimates its probable use of military force; and (2) provides decisionmakers, planners, and commanders with the data needed to choose courses of action required to counter foreign military threats, and to conduct operations with U.S. forces, if necessary.

References

Corson, William R. *The Armies of Ignorance: The Rise of the American Intelligence Empire.* New York: Dial Press, 1977.

Department of Defense, Defense Intelligence College. *Glossary of Intelligence Terms and Definitions.* Washington, DC: DIC, 1987.

Department of Defense, U.S. Army. *Counter-Signals Intelligence (C-SIGINT) Operations.* Field Manual FM 34-62. Washington, DC: Headquarters, Department of the Army, 1986.

—**MILITARY INTERVENTION** is a deliberate act by a nation or group of nations to introduce military forces into an existing controversy. *See also:* Military Mission Options.

References

Department of Defense, Joint Chiefs of Staff. *Department of Defense Dictionary of Military and Related Terms.* Washington, DC: GPO, 1986.

—**MILITARY JURISDICTION** is the power and authority to impose military law. It includes the administration of military law and is usually exercised by military courts. *See also:* Uniform Code of Military Justice.

References

Department of Defense, U.S. Army. *Dictionary of United States Army Terms.* Army Regulation AR 310-25. Washington, DC: Headquarters, Department of the Army, 1986.

—**MILITARY JUSTICE** is the application of military law to persons who are subject to it and are accused of committing offenses under the Uniform Code of Military Justice. *See also:* Uniform Code of Military Justice.

References

Department of Defense, U.S. Army. *Dictionary of United States Army Terms.* Army Regulation AR 310-25. Washington, DC: Headquarters, Department of the Army, 1986.

—**MILITARY LOAD CLASSIFICATION** is a standard system in which a route, bridge, or raft is assigned class number(s) representing the load it can carry. Vehicles are also assigned number(s) indicating the minimum class of route, bridge, or raft that they are authorized to use. *See also:* Route Classification.

References

Department of Defense, Joint Chiefs of Staff. *Department of Defense Dictionary of Military and Related Terms.* Washington, DC: GPO, 1986.

—**MILITARY MAIL** is domestic and international mail bearing a military address or return address and which, at some stage in transmission, comes into the custody of a military department. *See also:* Military Mail Terminal.

References

Department of Defense, U.S. Army. *Dictionary of United States Army Terms.* Army Regulation AR 310-25. Washington, DC: Headquarters, Department of the Army, 1986.

—**MILITARY MAIL TERMINAL.** (1) Within the continental United States, a military mail terminal is an Army postal activity that operates in conjunction with a postal concentration center and that monitors the intransit processing, dispatch, and transportation of military mail addressed to overseas Army and Air Force post offices. It provides unit locator service for mail that is undeliverable as addressed. (2) Overseas,

a military mail terminal is an Army mail processing activity that provides for the receipt, separation, distribution, routing, and dispatch of mails to and from organizations and activities that are served on a general support basis. *See also:* Military Mail.

References

Department of Defense, U.S. Army. *Dictionary of United States Army Terms.* Army Regulation AR 310-25. Washington, DC: Headquarters, Department of the Army, 1986.

—**MILITARY MANUFACTURER** is a military arsenal, factory, manufacturing depot, or fabricating activity that produces items of a purely military nature.

References

Department of Defense, U.S. Army. *Dictionary of United States Army Terms.* Army Regulation AR 310-25. Washington, DC: Headquarters, Department of the Army, 1986.

—**MILITARY MISSION OPTIONS.** The Department of Defense has organized the U.S. warfighting capability so that the Unified and Specified Commanders (commanders-in-Chief or CINCs) are the agents of the National Command Authority who are responsible for implementing military action. The military options that are available to the CINC and the National Command Authority as a possible solution to a problem cover a range of force options. The specific option that is chosen for a given situation represents a finite description (a snapshot) of what is on the continuum of force possibilities. When faced with a problem, the CINC would look at his overall military capability as well as what would be the most appropriate action for the circumstances. The CINC's regional view of the problem could be balanced by the global view of the National Command Authority and Joint Chiefs of Staff. The National Command Authority perspective is most sensitive to the political, diplomatic, and economic factors that would influence the solution finally chosen to satisfy national objectives. The military factor may not determine the solution to a particular problem, but it may be a part of many solutions. If the use of military force were contemplated, the National Command Authority could provide the CINC with guidance as to the level of military force that is envisioned. Whether the CINC is involved with regional or global planning, within his area of responsibility he would most likely want to prepare for the "worst case" conditions that are envisioned in a scenario, even if a lesser application of force may be applied. As the CINC develops his mission statement, from the spectrum of force possibilities he might consider the following types of force options.

Presence. Presence is best visualized in connection with the current unified command structure. With its established unified commands, the U.S. government shows resolve on a global basis. The size or permanence of the force can vary according to the situation. Presence could be a large number of forward-deployed forces as are currently deployed in Europe, or it could be one ship making a port call to a certain port at a critical time. The timeliness of the force may have more to do with the success of this option than the size of the force. The presence of the Military Assistance Advisory Groups, missions, and security assistance operations around the world relates to the U.S. level of interest and assessment of the threat. Forward-deployed forces provide an added dimension to the U.S. global influence and represent a U.S. initiative in maintaining that influence. Presence has much to do with "showing the flag." U.S. military presence, when properly executed, is a significant source of international goodwill as well.

Show of force. A show of force is an extension of presence that stops short of bringing opposing forces together in conflict. It has been referred to as "muscle flexing" or "saber-rattling." Properly applied and timed correctly, a show of force may provide just the deterrent that is required to prevent any further escalation of hostilities. To be properly applied, the show of force must be credible in the eyes of the party that the United States is trying to influence.

Demonstration. A show of force and a demonstration are similar, but they differ in the degree of the implied threat. The purpose of a demonstration is not to seek a decision. However, the demonstration actually employs force, but it does so in a manner that is designed to warn or threaten the opposition rather than to engage in combat. A demonstration can warn the potential aggressor that the United States has the capability and the will to get as tough as necessary for the situation. A demonstration can also be staged to deceive the enemy as to true U.S. actions. Feints of "cover and deception"

movements are a form of demonstration. Normally, deception operations are used in conjunction with another action (e.g., an invasion).

Quarantine. This term was used during the 1962 Cuban Missile Crisis to mean, a collective, peaceful process involving limited coercive measures interdicting the unreasonable movement of certain types of offensive military weapons and associated material by one state into the territory of another. Quarantine, in the classic sense, means a period during which a ship is detained in isolation until it is free of a contagious disease. When both definitions are combined, the meaning becomes an act short of war designed to exclude specific items from movement into or from a state.

Blockade. Of the different degrees of blockade, one type is absolute, and its objective is to cut off enemy communications and commerce. It attempts to isolate a place or region, and it could apply to all means of transportation regardless of whether the nation of registry is participating in the conflict. The target nation may consider such a total blockade as an "act of war." A lesser degree of blockade has been called a "pacific blockade." This type may or may not be perceived as an act of war. It is often limited to carriers flying the flag of the state against which retaliatory measures are taken. A blockade is a method of bringing pressure to bear on the opposition.

Force entry. This option can involve the actual use of military forces in an objective area. It is the most extreme mission option available to the CINC. In this option, U.S. forces are moved forward with the intention of engaging in combat if necessary to accomplish their mission. Whether armed conflict occurs will depend on the resistance that is met. Combat operations could range from an administrative landing to conduct police-type operations to an outright invasion under a state of war. With an invasion, a combat assault is made against armed forces to gain entry into a hostile area. The point of armed conflict takes place at the point of entry. However, many U.S. plans result in administrative landings that are intended to support a friendly government. If armed conflict were to result in this case, the point of armed conflict would not be coincident with the point of entry. This option could employ some or all of the less drastic force options previously discussed.

Psychological operations/unconventional warfare/civil affairs. The joint force commander may plan for these options along with and as a part of his major operations plans. In some situations, he may use these options independently. Psychological operations try to create attitudes and behavior favorable to achieving plan objectives. Unconventional warfare can be military or paramilitary operations. Psychological operations and unconventional warfare operations may range from clandestine to overt actions. Civil affairs operations are activities that embrace the relationship between U.S. military forces and the civilian authorities and people in the objective area. Civil affairs activities normally are in support of other operations. *See also:* Specified Command, Unified Command.

References
Department of Defense, Defense Intelligence Agency. *Defense Intelligence Agency Manual.* Washington, DC: DIA, 1987.

Kent, Sherman. *Strategic Intelligence for American World Policy.* Princeton, NJ: Princeton University Press, 1966.

Laqueur, Walter. *A World of Secrets.* New York: Basic Books, 1985.

—**MILITARY NECESSITY** is the principle whereby a belligerent has the right to apply any measures not forbidden by laws of war to successfully conclude a military operation.

References
Department of Defense, Joint Chiefs of Staff. *Department of Defense Dictionary of Military and Related Terms.* Washington, DC: GPO, 1986.

—**MILITARY NUCLEAR POWER** is a nation that has nuclear weapons and the capability to use them. *See also:* Nuclear Power.

References
Department of Defense, Joint Chiefs of Staff. *Department of Defense Dictionary of Military and Related Terms.* Washington, DC: GPO, 1986.

—**MILITARY OCCUPATION** is a condition in which a territory is under the effective control of a foreign armed force. *See also:* Occupied Territory, Phases of Military Government.

References
Department of Defense, Joint Chiefs of Staff. *Department of Defense Dictionary of Military and Related Terms.* Washington, DC: GPO, 1986.

—**MILITARY OCCUPATIONAL SPECIALTY (MOS)** is a term used to identify similar duty positions that require similarly qualified people and serve a valid military mission-related purpose. The duties are so closely related that most people at a given skill level can perform them. There are five levels:

- **Advanced** refers to specialized occupational qualifications above the entry military occupational specialty level required for the journeyman, supervisory, or leadership levels of skill.
- **Duty** is the military occupational specialty level in which the soldier is actually performing his duty.
- **Entry** is the level that reflects the occupational qualifications that are required to perform in the duty positions that represent the lowest level of skill within an entry group.
- **Primary** is the military occupational specialty that represents the highest or most significant job skill that the individual can best perform.
- **Secondary** is any military occupational specialty, other than the soldier's primary one, that has been awarded.

See also: the following entries under Military Occupational Specialty.

References
Department of Defense, U.S. Army. *Army Forces Training.* Army Regulation AR 350-41. Washington, DC: Headquarters, Department of the Army, 1986.

———. *Personnel Selection and Classification, Warrant Officer Occupational Specialties.* Army Regulation AR 611-112. Washington, DC: Headquarters, Department of the Army, 1987.

—**MILITARY OCCUPATIONAL SPECIALTY (MOS) CODE** is a fixed number that indicates a given MOS. It is also known as an MOS number or a specification serial number. *See also:* Military Occupational Specialty.

References
Department of Defense, U.S. Army. *Dictionary of United States Army Terms.* Army Regulation AR 310-25. Washington, DC: Headquarters, Department of the Army, 1986.

—**MILITARY OCCUPATIONAL SPECIALTY (MOS) DATA REPORT** is a printed report that contains identifying information, the military occupational specialty evaluation score attained by the individual, and a profile of the examinee's standing in each subject area in the military occupational specialty evaluation test. *See also:* Military Occupational Specialty.

References

Department of Defense, U.S. Army. *Dictionary of United States Army Terms.* Army Regulation AR 310-25. Washington, DC: Headquarters, Department of the Army, 1986.

—**MILITARY OCCUPATIONAL SPECIALTY (MOS) EVALUATION SCORE** denotes the individual's knowledge, skills, and ability to perform the duties in a particular MOS. Two types of MOS evaluation scores are used. The first, the primary MOS evaluation score, is a composite score computed from the individual's Military Occupational Specialty Evaluation Test Commander's Evaluation Report and a performance test, when applicable. In some MOSs, the primary MOS scores may be computed solely on the score achieved on the Commander's Evaluation Report. The second type is the secondary MOS evaluation score. It is determined from testing in a secondary MOS that has been transformed to the military occupation evaluation score scale. In some MOSs, the secondary MOS evaluation score may be a composite score that has been computed from the scores achieved on the performance test and the applicable MOS evaluation test. *See also:* Military Occupational Specialty.

References

Department of Defense, U.S. Army. *Dictionary of United States Army Terms.* Army Regulation AR 310-25. Washington, DC: Headquarters, Department of the Army, 1986.

—**MILITARY OCCUPATIONAL SPECIALTY (MOS) EVALUATION TEST** is an examination designed to evaluate the individual's knowledge and skills in a particular MOS and skill level. The MOS evaluation test is a major component of the Army's Enlisted Evaluation System. *See also:* Military Occupational Specialty.

References

Department of Defense, U.S. Army. *Dictionary of United States Army Terms.* Army Regulation AR 310-25. Washington, DC: Headquarters, Department of the Army, 1986.

—**MILITARY OCCUPATIONAL SPECIALTY (MOS) EVALUATION TEST AID** is a Department of the Army pamphlet that addresses a specific MOS and contains information about the Enlisted

Evaluation System, the technical requirements of the MOS, and a list of study references pertaining to the MOS. The aid is designed to assist enlisted personnel in preparing for the MOS evaluation test. *See also:* Military Occupational Specialty.

References

Department of Defense, U.S. Army. *Dictionary of United States Army Terms.* Army Regulation AR 310-25. Washington, DC: Headquarters, Department of the Army, 1986.

—**MILITARY OCCUPATIONAL SPECIALTY (MOS) IMBALANCE** is a condition where the number of soldiers with a particular primary MOS differs from the approved worldwide authorization for that primary MOS: (1) by +/-5% for an MOS that is authorized 200 or more spaces; and (2) by ten soldiers or less for an MOS that is authorized less than 200 spaces. *See also:* Military Occupational Specialty.

References

Department of Defense, U.S. Army. *Dictionary of United States Army Terms.* Army Regulation AR 310-25. Washington, DC: Headquarters, Department of the Army, 1986.

—**MILITARY OCCUPATIONAL SPECIALTY (MOS) MISMATCH** exists when a soldier's duty MOS does not equal his primary MOS, secondary MOS, or an additionally awarded MOS. It also exists when the soldier's duty MOS does not follow the normal career progression of the primary MOS or secondary MOS, or cannot be substituted for the primary MOS. *See also:* Military Occupational Specialty.

References

Department of Defense, U.S. Army. *Dictionary of United States Army Terms.* Army Regulation AR 310-25. Washington, DC: Headquarters, Department of the Army, 1986.

—**MILITARY OCCUPATIONAL SPECIALTY (MOS) NUMBER.** *See:* Military Occupational Specialty Code.

—**MILITARY OCCUPATIONAL SPECIALTY (MOS) PREFIX** is a number or letter that is added to the four-digit officer MOS code to identify additional requirements of certain positions and the additional qualifications of personnel who are capable of filling such positions. *See also:* Military Occupational Specialty.

References

Department of Defense, U.S. Army. *Dictionary of United States Army Terms*. Army Regulation AR 310-25. Washington, DC: Headquarters, Department of the Army, 1986.

—**MILITARY OCCUPATIONAL SPECIALTY (MOS) QUALIFICATION SCORE** is an MOS evaluation score of at least 70, the minimum qualification considered necessary to perform a duty satisfactorily in the MOS and skill level in which the person has been evaluated under the Enlisted Evaluation System. *See also:* Military Occupational Specialty.

References

Department of Defense, U.S. Army. *Dictionary of United States Army Terms*. Army Regulation AR 310-25. Washington, DC: Headquarters, Department of the Army, 1986.

—**MILITARY OCCUPATIONAL SPECIALTY (MOS) SUFFIX** is a number added to the basic characters of a warrant officer MOS code to identify additional requirements of certain positions and the additional qualifications of personnel who are capable of filling such positions. *See also:* Military Occupational Specialty.

References

Department of Defense, U.S. Army. *Dictionary of United States Army Terms*. Army Regulation AR 310-25. Washington, DC: Headquarters, Department of the Army, 1986.

—**MILITARY OPERATIONS ON URBANIZED TERRAIN (MOUT)** include all military actions planned and conducted on terrain where manmade construction affects the tactical options that are available to the commander. *See also:* Military Operations on Urbanized Terrain Facilities.

References

Department of Defense, U.S. Army. *Military Operations on Urbanized Terrain (MOUT)*. Field Manual FM 90-10. Washington, DC: Headquarters, Department of the Army, 1979.

—**MILITARY OPERATIONS ON URBANIZED TERRAIN (MOUT) FACILITIES** are designed to train soldiers in the techniques that are necessary to fight in built-up areas. *See also:* Military Operations on Urbanized Terrain.

References

Department of Defense, U.S. Army. *U.S. Army Policy Statement, 1988*. Washington, DC: Headquarters, Department of the Army, 1988.

—**MILITARY PACKAGING** describes the materials and methods or procedures prescribed in federal and military specifications, standards, drawings, or other authorized documents that provide the packaging protection necessary to prevent damage or deterioration of materiel during the worldwide distribution.

References

Department of Defense, U.S. Army. *Dictionary of United States Army Terms*. Army Regulation AR 310-25. Washington, DC: Headquarters, Department of the Army, 1986.

—**MILITARY PAY AND ALLOWANCES.** *See:* Basic Allowance for Quarters, Basic Allowance for Subsistence, Basic Daily Food Allowance, Basic Pay, Severance Allowance.

—**MILITARY PAY ORDER** is a form used to change the pay status of an individual in the military service whose pay account is maintained on a military pay record.

References

Department of Defense, U.S. Army. *Dictionary of United States Army Terms*. Army Regulation AR 310-25. Washington, DC: Headquarters, Department of the Army, 1986.

—**MILITARY PAY RECORD** is a form used by finance and accounting officers to maintain the pay account of an Army member. *See also:* Military Pay Order, Military Pay Voucher.

References

Department of Defense, U.S. Army. *Dictionary of United States Army Terms*. Army Regulation AR 310-25. Washington, DC: Headquarters, Department of the Army, 1986.

—**MILITARY PAY VOUCHER** is a form used by finance and accounting officers to effect payment of pay and allowances to an Army member.

References

Department of Defense, U.S. Army. *Dictionary of United States Army Terms*. Army Regulation AR 310-25. Washington, DC: Headquarters, Department of the Army, 1986.

—**MILITARY PERSONNEL MANAGEMENT** is the process of planning, organizing, directing, coordinating, and controlling the procurement, training, education, utilization, separation, retirement, development, and motivation of military personnel to assist in the successful accomplishment of the organizational mission. It includes all procedures related to military job analysis and evaluation; position and personnel classification, assignment, and utilization; maintenance of adequate records and reports required for the successful operation of the Army personnel system; Human Resources Development activities to include development of individual potential; and development of an organizational climate that enhances the attitude, motivation, commitment, and sense of well-being of soldiers and their families.

References

Department of Defense, U.S. Army. *Dictionary of United States Army Terms.* Army Regulation AR 310-25. Washington, DC: Headquarters, Department of the Army, 1986.

—**MILITARY PERSONNEL RECORDS JACKET** is the individual military personnel records maintained in Department of the Army Form 201, the Military Personnel Records Jacket, U.S. Army. It is normally kept in the Military Personnel Office serving the member's unit. *See also:* Military Personnel Management.

References

Department of Defense, U.S. Army. *Enlisted Personnel.* Army Regulation AR 635-200. Washington, DC: Headquarters, Department of the Army, 1984.

———. *Enlisted Personnel Management System.* Army Regulation AR 600-200. Washington, DC: Headquarters, Department of the Army, 1984.

———. *Processing Personnel for Separation.* Army Regulation AR 635-10. Washington, DC: Headquarters, Department of the Army, 1984.

———. *Promotion of Officers on Active Duty.* Army Regulation AR 624-100. Washington, DC: Headquarters, Department of the Army, 1984.

———. *Selection of Enlisted Soldiers for Training and Assignment.* Army Regulation AR 614-200. Washington, DC: Headquarters, Department of the Army, 1984.

—**MILITARY PLATFORM** is a side-loading platform generally at least 300 meters (1,000 feet long) that is used to load and unload military trains.

References

Department of Defense, Joint Chiefs of Staff. *Department of Defense Dictionary of Military and Related Terms.* Washington, DC: GPO, 1986.

—**MILITARY POLICE (MP)** are officers and enlisted members of the Military Police Corps who are charged with controlling the conduct of service personnel by enforcing military law, orders, and regulations; controlling traffic; exercising crime prevention, investigation, and reporting procedures; apprehending military absentees and escaped military prisoners; and providing security for military supplies, equipment, and materiel. Their jurisdiction is limited to individuals who are subject to the Uniform Code of Military Justice and to others as required to obey military law when it is proclaimed by the President or another competent civilian authority. The military police provide support to combat zones, exercise prescribed control over prisoners of war and indigenous civilians, and fight as infantry when necessary. *See also:* Military Police Response Forces.

References

Department of Defense, U.S. Army. *Dictionary of United States Army Terms.* Army Regulation AR 310-25. Washington, DC: Headquarters, Department of the Army, 1986.

———. *Military Police Support for the Airland Battle.* Field Manual FM 19-1. Washington, DC: Headquarters, Department of the Army, 1983.

—**MILITARY POLICE (MP) RESPONSE FORCES** are the MP forces assigned by the commander to respond or to conduct operations that involve closing with and destroying the attacking enemy forces that the base defenses are unable to repel.

References

Department of Defense, U.S. Army. *Rear Battle.* Field Manual FM 90-14. Washington, DC: Headquarters, Department of the Army, 1985.

—**MILITARY POSTAL CLERK** is a person of the Armed Forces who has been officially designated by the Postal Service and is authorized by public law to perform postal finance functions and other postal duties. The term includes Army, Navy, Air Force, Marine Corps, and Coast Guard postal clerks. *See also:* Military Mail.

References

Department of Defense, U.S. Army. *Dictionary of United States Army Terms.* Army Regulation AR 310-25. Washington, DC: Headquarters, Department of the Army, 1986.

—**MILITARY POSTURE** is the military strength, disposition, and readiness of armed forces to accomplish missions against specific opposition. *See also:* Military Mission Options.

References

Collins, John M. *U.S.-Soviet Military Balance, 1980-1985*. Washington, DC: Congressional Research Service, 1985.

—**MILITARY PRISONER** is a person who is subject to the Uniform Code of Military Justice and has been ordered into confinement by a proper authority. *See also:* Disciplinary Action.

References

Department of Defense, U.S. Army. *Dictionary of United States Army Terms*. Army Regulation AR 310-25. Washington, DC: Headquarters, Department of the Army, 1986.

—**MILITARY QUALIFICATION STANDARDS** are "the framework of the officer education and training program that provides officer candidates, cadets, lieutenants, and captains with career development goals in the attainment of military skills and professional military knowledge."

References

Department of Defense, U.S. Army. *Training for Mobilization and War*. Field Manual FM 25-5. Washington, DC: Headquarters, Department of the Army, 1985.

—**MILITARY RECORD** is an account of a soldier's behavior while in military service. This includes both his personal conduct and his performance of duty. *See also:* Military Personnel Records Jacket.

References

Department of Defense, U.S. Army. *Enlisted Personnel*. Army Regulation AR 635-200. Washington, DC: Headquarters, Department of the Army, 1984.

—**MILITARY REQUIREMENT** is an established need that justifies the prompt allocation of resources to accomplish approved military objectives, missions, or tasks. *See also:* Objective Force Level.

References

Department of Defense, Joint Chiefs of Staff. *Department of Defense Dictionary of Military and Related Terms*. Washington, DC: GPO, 1986.

—**MILITARY RESOURCES** are the military and civilian personnel, facilities, equipment, and supplies under the control of a Department of Defense component.

References

Department of Defense, Joint Chiefs of Staff. *Department of Defense Dictionary of Military and Related Terms*. Washington, DC: GPO, 1986.

—**MILITARY ROAD MANEUVER NETWORK (MRMN)** is the road system required by the commander to conduct and to receive the required logistical support for a specific operation. It is defined and controlled (through the allotment of maneuver credits) by the national or allied military authorities, according to the delineation of responsibilities in the theater of operations. If required, it may be modified to meet the military situation. The network is designated and controlled by the military commander who is exercising local territorial responsibility. *See also:* Military Road Network.

References

Department of Defense, U.S. Army. *Route Reconnaissance and Classification*. Field Manual FM 5-36. Washington, DC: Headquarters, Department of the Army, 1985.

———. *Transportation Reference Data*. Field Manual FM 55-15. Washington, DC: Headquarters, Department of the Army, 1986.

—**MILITARY ROAD NETWORK (MRN)** includes all the routes designated in peacetime by the host nations to meet anticipated allied and national military movements and transport movements.

References

Department of Defense, U.S. Army. *Transportation Reference Data*. Field Manual FM 55-15. Washington, DC: Headquarters, Department of the Army, 1986.

—**MILITARY SCIENCE** is a Reserve Officers' Training Corps course of instruction conducted at colleges and universities.

References

Department of Defense, U.S. Army. *Dictionary of United States Army Terms*. Army Regulation AR 310-25. Washington, DC: Headquarters, Department of the Army, 1986.

—**MILITARY SEALIFT COMMAND (MSC)** is the manager of ocean transportation that, under one authority, provides for the control, operation, and administration of sea transportation for Department of Defense personnel, mail, and cargo. This command was formerly designated the Military Sea Transportation Service.

References
Department of Defense, U.S. Army. *Transportation Reference Data.* Field Manual FM 55-15. Washington, DC: Headquarters, Department of the Army, 1986.

—**MILITARY SERVICE** is a branch of the U.S. Armed Forces, established by an act of Congress, in which persons are appointed, enlisted, or inducted for military service, and that operates and is administered within a military or executive department. The military services are the United States Army, the United States Navy, the United States Air Force, the United States Marine Corps, and the United States Coast Guard.

References
Department of Defense, Joint Chiefs of Staff. *Department of Defense Dictionary of Military and Related Terms.* Washington, DC: GPO, 1986.

—**MILITARY SPECIALIST** is an enlisted person who has been rated, based upon training and experience, as qualified to perform a specified military duty.

References
Department of Defense, U.S. Army. *Dictionary of United States Army Terms.* Army Regulation AR 310-25. Washington, DC: Headquarters, Department of the Army, 1986.

—**MILITARY SPECIFICATION** is a procurement specification in the military series promulgated by one or more of the military agencies that is used to procure military supplies, equipment, or services.

References
Department of Defense, U.S. Army. *Dictionary of United States Army Terms.* Army Regulation AR 310-25. Washington, DC: Headquarters, Department of the Army, 1986.

—**MILITARY STANDARD REQUISITIONING AND ISSUE PROCEDURE (MILSTRIP)** is a uniform procedure that has been established by the Department of Defense to govern the requisitioning and issuing of materiel within standardized priorities. *See also:* Military Standard Transportation and Movement Procedures.

References
Department of Defense, Joint Chiefs of Staff. *Department of Defense Dictionary of Military and Related Terms.* Washington, DC: GPO, 1986.

—**MILITARY STANDARD TRANSPORTATION AND MOVEMENT PROCEDURES (MILSTAMP)** are the uniform and standard transportation data, documentation, and control procedures applicable to all cargo movements in the Department of Defense transportation system. *See also:* Military Standard Requisitioning and Issue Procedure.

References
Department of Defense, Joint Chiefs of Staff. *Department of Defense Dictionary of Military and Related Terms.* Washington, DC: GPO, 1986.

—**MILITARY STRATEGIST** is an individual whose aptitude, experience, and education qualify him for strategy formulation and articulation. The military strategist understands the interrelationships of the international environment, national power, national resources, national security, and military and national strategies. He is knowledgeable in the role of military forces in supporting national objectives and policies, and understands the process of strategy formulation that is used by both the United States and its potential adversaries. *See also:* Military Strategy.

References
Department of Defense, U.S. Army. *Dictionary of United States Army Terms.* Army Regulation AR 310-25. Washington, DC: Headquarters, Department of the Army, 1986.

—**MILITARY STRATEGY** is the component of national strategy concerned with using the armed forces to secure national policy objectives through the use or threatened use of force. *See also:* Strategy.

References
Department of Defense, U.S. Army. *The Army.* (Prepublication Issue.) Field Manual FM 100-1. Washington, DC: Headquarters, Department of the Army, 1986.

———. *Operations.* Field Manual FM 100-5. Washington, DC: Headquarters, Department of the Army, 1986.

—**MILITARY STRENGTH OF THE ARMY** includes all military personnel in the active service of the United States Army who are assigned to table of organization and equipment units, or who are in the personnel pipeline. Personnel of the civilian components who are on active duty for training are not included.

References
Department of Defense, U.S. Army. *Dictionary of United States Army Terms.* Army Regulation AR 310-25. Washington, DC: Headquarters, Department of the Army, 1986.

—**MILITARY SYMBOLS** are graphic signs that are usually used on maps, displays, or diagrams to represent military units, installations, activities, and other items of military interest. Normally, military symbols are not printed on maps because the features or units they represent are constantly moving and changing, and because of security considerations. Instead, they are usually plotted on overlays with a grease pencil or marker, so that they can be erased and replotted as necessary.

References
Department of Defense, U.S. Army. *Map Reading.* Field Manual FM 21-26. Washington, DC: Headquarters, Department of the Army, 1969.

—**MILITARY TERMINAL** is any water or aerial port of embarkation operated by or for a military department as a terminal facility for receiving, loading, unloading, and forwarding military personnel and property. This term includes commercial terminals where activities are conducted under the military guidance.

References
Department of Defense, U.S. Army. *Transportation Reference Data.* Field Manual FM 55-15. Washington, DC: Headquarters, Department of the Army, 1986.

—**MILITARY TRAFFIC** is Department of Defense personnel, mail, and cargo that are to be or are being transported. *See also:* Military Traffic Management Command, Military Traffic Management Command Area, Military Traffic Management Command Area Office.

References
Department of Defense, Joint Chiefs of Staff. *Department of Defense Dictionary of Military and Related Terms.* Washington, DC: GPO, 1986.

—**MILITARY TRAFFIC MANAGEMENT COMMAND (MTMC)** is the jointly staffed, industrially funded major Army command that serves as the Department of Defense single-manager operating agency managing military traffic, land traffic, and common-user ocean terminals.

References
Department of Defense, U.S. Army. *Transportation Reference Data.* Field Manual FM 55-15. Washington, DC: Headquarters, Department of the Army, 1986.

—**MILITARY TRAFFIC MANAGEMENT COMMAND (MTMC) AREA** is a specified area within the continental United States that is established to facilitate certain traffic management functions.

References
Department of Defense, U.S. Army. *Dictionary of United States Army Terms.* Army Regulation AR 310-25. Washington, DC: Headquarters, Department of the Army, 1986.

—**MILITARY TRAFFIC MANAGEMENT COMMAND (MTMC) AREA OFFICE** is an activity of the MTMC that performs traffic management functions.

References
Department of Defense, U.S. Army. *Dictionary of United States Army Terms.* Army Regulation AR 310-25. Washington, DC: Headquarters, Department of the Army, 1986.

—**MILITARY TRAINING** is instructing personnel in order to improve their ability to perform specific military functions and tasks. It is also the exercising of one or more military units in order to enhance their combat readiness. *See also:* Military Education.

References
Department of Defense, U.S. Army. *The Army Terrorism Counteraction Program.* Army Regulation AR 525-13. Washington, DC: Headquarters, Department of the Army, 1988.

————. *Individual Military Education and Training.* Army Regulation AR 350-1. Washington, DC: Headquarters, Department of the Army, 1987.

—**MILITARY TRAINING COMPANY** is a unit established at disciplinary barracks to train and rehabilitate prisoners so that they can be restored to honorable duty status.

References
Department of Defense, U.S. Army. *Dictionary of United States Army Terms.* Army Regulation AR 310-25. Washington, DC: Headquarters, Department of the Army, 1986.

—**MILITARY UNIT RAILWAY** includes all railway and railway facilities, standard gauge or otherwise, that are operated, maintained, or constructed for a designated military installation by military personnel or by civilian personnel who are under military jurisdiction.

References
Department of Defense, U.S. Army. *Dictionary of United States Army Terms.* Army Regulation AR 310-25. Washington, DC: Headquarters, Department of the Army, 1986.

—**MILVAN** is a military-owned, dismountable container, conforming to U.S. and international standards, that is operated in a centrally controlled fleet that moves military cargo. *See also:* MILVAN Chassis.

References
Department of Defense, Joint Chiefs of Staff. *Department of Defense Dictionary of Military and Related Terms.* Washington, DC: GPO, 1986.

—**MILVAN CHASSIS** is the compatible chassis to which the MILVAN is attached by coupling the lower four standard corner fittings of the container to compatible mounting blocks in the chassis so that it can be transported by truck. *See also:* MILVAN.

References
Department of Defense, Joint Chiefs of Staff. *Department of Defense Dictionary of Military and Related Terms.* Washington, DC: GPO, 1986.

—**MINE,** in land mine warfare, is an explosive or other material, normally encased, that is designed to destroy or damage ground vehicles, boats, or aircraft, or designed to wound, kill, or otherwise incapacitate personnel. It may be detonated by its victim, the passage of time, a preset timer, or a controlled means. *See also:* Mine Clearance, Mine-Clearing Equipment, Mine Consumption, Mine Countermeasures, Mine Defense, Mine Detector, Mine Disposal, Mine Fuze, Mine Row, Mine Strip, Mine Warfare, Mine Weapons, Mined Area, Minefield, Minefield Gap, Minefield Lane, Minefield Marking, Minefield Record, Minefield Report, Minefield Trace.

References
Department of Defense, U.S. Army. *Mine/Countermine Operations at the Company Level.* Field Manual FM 20-32. Washington, DC: Headquarters, Department of the Army, 1976.

—**MINE CLEARANCE** is the process of detecting and removing land mines by manual or mechanical means. *See also:* Mine.

References
Department of Defense, U.S. Army. *Mine/Countermine Operations at the Company Level.* Field Manual FM 20-32. Washington, DC: Headquarters, Department of the Army, 1976.

—**MINE CLEARING EQUIPMENT** is a device designed to clear both mines that have been buried and that have been laid on the surface. *See also:* Mine.

References
Department of Defense, U.S. Army. *Mine/Countermine Operations at the Company Level.* Field Manual FM 20-32. Washington, DC: Headquarters, Department of the Army, 1976.

—**MINE CONSUMPTION** is a method of checking the use and employment of land mines. Here, mine consumption and stocks on hand are compared in units with similar missions. A large difference between units may reflect improper mine employment procedures. *See also:* Mine.

References
Department of Defense, U.S. Army. *Mine/Countermine Operations at the Company Level.* Field Manual FM 20-32. Washington, DC: Headquarters, Department of the Army, 1976.

—**MINE COUNTERMEASURES** are all the methods used to prevent or reduce the damage and danger from mines. *See also:* Mine.

References
Department of Defense, U.S. Army. *Mine/Countermine Operations at the Company Level.* Field Manual FM 20-32. Washington, DC: Headquarters, Department of the Army, 1976.

—**MINE DEFENSE** is the defense of a position or area by land and underwater mines. A mine defense system includes the personnel and equipment needed to plant, operate, maintain, and protect the minefields that are laid. *See also:* Mine.

References
Department of Defense, U.S. Army. *Mine/Countermine Operations at the Company Level.* Field Manual FM 20-32. Washington, DC: Headquarters, Department of the Army, 1976.

—**MINE DETECTOR** is a device capable of revealing the presence of mines that are on the surface or are slightly buried. A metallic mine detector detects mines that contain metal; a metallic/nonmetallic mine detector detects mines regardless of whether they contain metal. *See also:* Mine.

References

Department of Defense, U.S. Army. *Mine/ Countermine Operations at the Company Level.* Field Manual FM 20-32. Washington, DC: Headquarters, Department of the Army, 1976.

—**MINE DISPOSAL** entails the operations trained personnel conduct to render safe, neutralize, recover, remove, or destroy mines. *See also:* Mine.

References

Department of Defense, U.S. Army. *Mine/ Countermine Operations at the Company Level.* Field Manual FM 20-32. Washington, DC: Headquarters, Department of the Army, 1976.

—**MINE FUZE** is a device containing an explosive train that will detonate a mine when it is triggered by the target. *See also:* Mine.

References

Department of Defense, U.S. Army. *Mine/ Countermine Operations at the Company Level.* Field Manual FM 20-32. Washington, DC: Headquarters, Department of the Army, 1976.

—**MINE ROW** is a single row of mines or clusters. *See also:* Mine.

References

Department of Defense, U.S. Army. *Mine/ Countermine Operations at the Company Level.* Field Manual FM 20-32. Washington, DC: Headquarters, Department of the Army, 1976.

—**MINE STRIP**, in land mine warfare, is composed of two parallel mine rows laid simultaneously six meters or six paces apart. *See also:* Mine.

References

Department of Defense, U.S. Army. *Mine/ Countermine Operations at the Company Level.* Field Manual FM 20-32. Washington, DC: Headquarters, Department of the Army, 1976.

—**MINE WARFARE** is the strategic and tactical use of mines and their countermeasures. *See also:* Mine, Mine Weapons, Minefield.

References

Department of Defense, U.S. Army. *Mine/ Countermine Operations at the Company Level.* Field Manual FM 20-32. Washington, DC: Headquarters, Department of the Army, 1976.

—**MINE WEAPONS** is the collective term for all weapons used in mine warfare. *See also:* Mine.

References

Department of Defense, U.S. Army. *Mine/ Countermine Operations at the Company Level.* Field Manual FM 20-32. Washington, DC: Headquarters, Department of the Army, 1976.

—**MINED AREA** is an area declared to be dangerous due to the presence or suspected presence of mines. *See also:* Mine.

References

Department of Defense, U.S. Army. *Mine/ Countermine Operations at the Company Level.* Field Manual FM 20-32. Washington, DC: Headquarters, Department of the Army, 1976.

—**MINEFIELD,** in land warfare, is an area of ground containing mines that have been laid with or without a pattern. There are five types of minefields: protective, point, tactical, interdiction, and phony. *See also:* Defensive Minefield, Mine, Nuisance Minefield, Phony Minefields, Protective Minefields.

References

Department of Defense, U.S. Army. *Engineer Combat Operations.* Field Manual FM 5-100. Washington, DC: Headquarters, Department of the Army, 1984.

———. *Mine/Countermine Operations at the Company Level.* Field Manual FM 20-32. Washington, DC: Headquarters, Department of the Army, 1976.

———. *Operational Terms and Symbols.* Field Manual FM 101-5-1. Washington, DC: Headquarters, Department of the Army, 1985.

—**MINEFIELD GAP** is a portion of a minefield in which no mines have been laid and designed to enable a friendly force to pass through the minefield in tactical formation. It is seldom less than 100 meters wide. *See also:* Mine.

References

Department of Defense, U.S. Army. *Mine/ Countermine Operations at the Company Level.* Field Manual FM 20-32. Washington, DC: Headquarters, Department of the Army, 1976.

—**MINEFIELD LANE** is an unmined or neutralized marked route through any minefield. Normally lanes are two meters wide for the safe passage of foot troops, eight meters wide for one-way vehicular traffic, and sixteen meters wide for two-way traffic. The widths of the lanes through enemy minefields depend on the method of breaching and the purpose for which they are required. *See also:* Mine.

References

Department of Defense, U.S. Army. *Mine/ Countermine Operations at the Company Level.* Field Manual FM 20-32. Washington, DC: Headquarters, Department of the Army, 1976.

—**MINEFIELD MARKING** is the visible marking of all points required in laying a minefield and indicating the extent of such minefields. *See also:* Mine.

References

Department of Defense, U.S. Army. *Mine/ Countermine Operations at the Company Level.* Field Manual FM 20-32. Washington, DC: Headquarters, Department of the Army, 1976.

—**MINEFIELD RECORD** is a complete written record of all pertinent information concerning a minefield. It is submitted on a standard form by the officer in charge of the laying operations. *See also:* Mine.

References

Department of Defense, Joint Chiefs of Staff. *Department of Defense Dictionary of Military and Related Terms.* Washington, DC: GPO, 1986.

—**MINEFIELD REPORT.** Prior to laying a minefield, the company must report its intention to, and request permission of, the battalion to do so. After receiving permission, the company must report the initiation of minelaying. There are no standard formats for these reports. The unit's standing operations procedures, however, should specify the formats. *See also:* Mine.

References

Department of Defense, U.S. Army. *The Infantry Rifle Company (Infantry, Airborne, Air Assault, Ranger).* Field Manual FM 7-10. Washington, DC: Headquarters, Department of the Army, 1982.

—**MINEFIELD TRACE** is a real or imaginary line that is parallel to the longitudinal direction of a minefield. *See also:* Mine.

References

Department of Defense, U.S. Army. *Mine/ Countermine Operations at the Company Level.* Field Manual FM 20-32. Washington, DC: Headquarters, Department of the Army, 1976.

—**MINIATURE METAL** is a replica of a regular size medal, made to a scale one half that of the original. The Medal of Honor is not worn in miniature.

References

Department of Defense, U.S. Army. *Wear and Appearance of Army Uniforms and Insignia.* Army Regulation AR 670-1. Washington, DC: Headquarters, Department of the Army, 1986.

—**MINIMIZE** is a condition wherein normal telephone and message traffic is drastically reduced so that messages associated with a real or simulated emergency are not delayed.

References

Department of Defense, Joint Chiefs of Staff. *Department of Defense Dictionary of Military and Related Terms.* Washington, DC: GPO, 1986.

—**MINIMUM CLEARANCE** is the vertical distance by which one cone of fire must clear friendly troops when delivering overhead fire.

References

Department of Defense, U.S. Army. *Dictionary of United States Army Terms.* Army Regulation AR 310-25. Washington, DC: Headquarters, Department of the Army, 1986.

—**MINIMUM ESSENTIAL EQUIPMENT** is the part of authorized allowances of Army equipment, clothing, and supplies needed to preserve the integrity of a unit during movement, regardless of whether its mission is combat or service. Items in this category are normally carried by the troops or accompany them to the port and are placed on the same ships they board. In movement directives, minimum essential equipment refers to specific items of both organizational and individual clothing and equipment.

References

Department of Defense, Joint Chiefs of Staff. *Department of Defense Dictionary of Military and Related Terms.* Washington, DC: GPO, 1986.

—**MINIMUM NORMAL BURST ALTITUDE** is the distance above the terrain below which air defense nuclear warheads are not normally detonated. *See also:* Nuclear Warfare.

References

Department of Defense, Joint Chiefs of Staff. *Department of Defense Dictionary of Military and Related Terms.* Washington, DC: GPO, 1986.

—**MINIMUM QUADRANT ELEVATION** is the lowest quadrant elevation of a weapon at which the projectile will safely clear an obstacle between the weapon and the target.

References

Department of Defense, U.S. Army. *Dictionary of United States Army Terms.* Army Regulation AR 310-25. Washington, DC: Headquarters, Department of the Army, 1986.

—**MINIMUM RANGE.** (1) Minimum range is the least range setting of a gun at which a projectile will clear an obstacle or friendly troops located between the gun and the target. (2) Minimum range is the shortest distance to which a gun can fire from a given position. (3) The minimum range is the range at which a projectile or fuse will be armed.

References

Department of Defense, Joint Chiefs of Staff. *Department of Defense Dictionary of Military and Related Terms.* Washington, DC: GPO, 1986.

—**MINIMUM RESIDUAL RADIOACTIVITY WEAPON** is a nuclear weapon designed to have the least amount of the unwanted effects from fallout, rainout, and burst site radioactivity. *See also:* Nuclear Warfare.

References

Department of Defense, Joint Chiefs of Staff. *Department of Defense Dictionary of Military and Related Terms.* Washington, DC: GPO, 1986.

—**MINIMUM RISK FORCE (MRF)** is the force developed in Part II of the Joint Strategic Planning Document Supporting Analysis, that can achieve the national objectives with minimum risk. The Minimum risk force level represents the collective judgment of the Joint Chiefs of Staff and is not constrained by fiscal, manpower, logistic, mobility, basing, or other limitations. It can be described as "the forces to which, if you were to add additional forces, you would not realize a measurable decrease in risk." *See also:* Current Force, Force, Intermediate Force Planning Level, Planning Force, Programmed Force.

References

Department of Defense, Joint Chiefs of Staff. *Department of Defense Dictionary of Military and Related Terms.* Washington, DC: GPO, 1986.

—**MINIMUM RISK ROUTES (MRR)** are temporary flight paths recommended for use by the Air Force because they present the minimum known hazards to low-flying aircraft flying in the tactical operations area.

References

Department of Defense, U.S. Army. *Air Defense Artillery Deployment: Chaparral/Vulcan/Stinger.* Field Manual FM 44-3. Washington, DC: Headquarters, Department of the Army, 1984.

————. *Airspace Management and Army Air Traffic in a Combat Zone.* Field Manual FM 1-60. Washington, DC: Headquarters, Department of the Army, 1977.

—**MINIMUM RISK ROUTES/LOW-LEVEL TRANSIT ROUTES (MRR/LLTR)** are temporary corridors of defined dimensions through antiair defenses, a high density airspace control zone, or a restricted operations area. They are designed to reduce the risk to friendly high speed aircraft flying in the tactical operations area at very low or medium altitudes. The routes are normally confined to the airspace in which the antiair defenses must be maintained at Weapons Tight. Such circumstances exist where there is an inadequate timely control capability to permit a more flexible method of air defense. *See also:* Minimum Risk Routes, Weapons Tight.

References

Department of Defense, U.S. Army. *Patriot Battalion Operations.* Field Manual FM 44-15. Washington, DC: Headquarters, Department of the Army, 1984.

—**MINIMUM SAFE DISTANCE (MSD)** is the sum of the radius of safety and the buffer distance. It is the minimum distance in meters from the desired ground zero at which a specific degree of risk and vulnerability will not be exceeded with a 99 percent assurance. *See also:* Desired Ground Zero, Least Separation Distance, Troop Safety.

References

Department of Defense, U.S. Army. *Operational Terms and Symbols.* Field Manual FM 101-5-1. Washington, DC: Headquarters, Department of the Army, 1985.

—**MINIMUM SANITARY REQUIREMENTS** are the minimum factors to be considered when determining the hygienic qualifications of a subsistence establishment.

References
Department of Defense, U.S. Army. *Dictionary of United States Army Terms.* Army Regulation AR 310-25. Washington, DC: Headquarters, Department of the Army, 1986.

—**MINIMUM WARNING TIME** (NUCLEAR) is the sum of the system reaction time and the personnel reaction time. *See also:* Personnel Reaction Time (Nuclear).

References
Department of Defense, Joint Chiefs of Staff. *Department of Defense Dictionary of Military and Related Terms.* Washington, DC: GPO, 1986.

—**MINING EFFECT** is the destruction or damage caused by the force of an explosion that occurs below the surface of the ground or water. *See also:* Mine Warfare.

References
Department of Defense, U.S. Army. *Dictionary of United States Army Terms.* Army Regulation AR 310-25. Washington, DC: Headquarters, Department of the Army, 1986.

—**MINING SYSTEM** is a series of underground passages through enemy fortified positions that can be reached secretly by friendly forces in order to blow up the enemy.

References
Department of Defense, U.S. Army. *Dictionary of United States Army Terms.* Army Regulation AR 310-25. Washington, DC: Headquarters, Department of the Army, 1986.

—**MINOR MEDICAL ASSEMBLAGE** refers to medical supplies and equipment that are not assigned consignee combinations (e.g., kits and chests). *See also:* Medical Treatment.

References
Department of Defense, U.S. Army. *Dictionary of United States Army Terms.* Army Regulation AR 310-25. Washington, DC: Headquarters, Department of the Army, 1986.

—**MINOR NONEXPENDABLE SUPPLIES** are nonexpendable supplies, whose unit standard price is $25 or less.

References
Department of Defense, U.S. Army. *Dictionary of United States Army Terms.* Army Regulation AR 310-25. Washington, DC: Headquarters, Department of the Army, 1986.

—**MINOR REPAIR** is repair that, in general, permits an item to be quickly returned to service. It can be accomplished with few tools and little or no equipment, and normally does not require the evacuation of the system to a rear echelon.

References
Department of Defense, U.S. Army. *Dictionary of United States Army Terms.* Army Regulation AR 310-25. Washington, DC: Headquarters, Department of the Army, 1986.

—**MINUTE GUN** is a gun fired at regular intervals as a signal or mark of respect to a deceased individual. When fired as a mark of respect, the rounds are fired in one-minute intervals and the number of rounds fired is in strict accordance with regulations on personal salutes.

References
Department of Defense, U.S. Army. *Dictionary of United States Army Terms.* Army Regulation AR 310-25. Washington, DC: Headquarters, Department of the Army, 1986.

—**MIOSIS** is the excessive contraction of the pupils of the eyes caused by exposure to minute quantities of chemical agents. Since the pupils are unable to dilate and remain contracted, the performance of tasks (e.g., walking, identifying or engaging targets, or driving vehicles) is practically impossible. Miosis is often accompanied by pain, a headache, and a pinpointing of the pupils. *See also:* Chemical Warfare.

References
Department of Defense, U.S. Army. *NBC Operations.* Field Manual FM 3-100. Washington, DC: Headquarters, Department of the Army, 1985.

—**MIRV(MULTIPLE INDEPENDENTLY TARGETABLE REENTRY VEHICLE) ICBM (INTERCONTINENTAL BALLISTIC MISSILE)** is a ballistic missile with a multiple independently targetable reentry vehicle capability.

References
Lowenthal, Mark M. *U.S. Intelligence: Evolution and Anatomy.* New York: Praeger, 1984.

—**MISCELLANEOUS INSTALLATION** is a command installation that is not classified as an air, ground, or storage and shipping installation. Fortifications (e.g., seacoast batteries), and aircraft warning stations are examples of miscellaneous installations.

References
Department of Defense, U.S. Army. *Dictionary of United States Army Terms*. Army Regulation AR 310-25. Washington, DC: Headquarters, Department of the Army, 1986.

—**MISCELLANEOUS RECEIPT** is a collection required by law to be deposited in the general fund of the Treasury and cannot be spent until appropriated by Congress.

References
Department of Defense, U.S. Army. *Dictionary of United States Army Terms*. Army Regulation AR 310-25. Washington, DC: Headquarters, Department of the Army, 1986.

—**MISFIRE.** (1) A misfire is the failure of a projectile or system to fire or explode properly. (2) Misfire is the failure of a primer or propelling charge of a round or projectile to function wholly or in part.

References
Department of Defense, Joint Chiefs of Staff. *Department of Defense Dictionary of Military and Related Terms*. Washington, DC: GPO, 1986.

—**MISSILE (MSL)** is a weapon or object to which propulsive energy is applied or continues to be applied after launch.

References
Department of Defense, U.S. Army. *Dictionary of United States Army Terms*. Army Regulation AR 310-25. Washington, DC: Headquarters, Department of the Army, 1986.

—**MISSILE AND ROCKET SUPPORT MAINTENANCE** includes repairing and modifying missiles (except for the warheads and adaption kits), missile and gun control, launching, test, and handling equipment, and trainers. This support also includes the maintenance calibration of missile-peculiar test and handling equipment.

References
Department of Defense, U.S. Army. *Combat Service Support Operations-Division*. Field Manual FM 63-2. Washington, DC: Headquarters, Department of the Army, 1983.

—**MISSILE AND SPACE INTELLIGENCE CENTER** (HUNTSVILLE, ALABAMA), is a component of the Army Intelligence Agency. The Center provides detailed, all-source analysis on foreign strategic air defense, tactical air defense, short-range ballistic and antitank guided missiles, and related technologies. The Center also manages the Army's development and acquisition of threat simulators.

References
Department of Defense, U.S. Army. *AIA: Threat Analysis*. Falls Church, VA: U.S. Army Intelligence Agency, 1987.

—**MISSILE DISTANCE** is how far that a considerable number of missiles from quantity distance classes three, four, five, and six ammunition can be projected in the event of fire or explosion.

References
Department of Defense, U.S. Army. *Dictionary of United States Army Terms*. Army Regulation AR 310-25. Washington, DC: Headquarters, Department of the Army, 1986.

—**MISSILE EFFECTIVE RATE** is the percentage of tactical missiles that are either prepared missiles or ready missiles.

References
Department of Defense, U.S. Army. *Dictionary of United States Army Terms*. Army Regulation AR 310-25. Washington, DC: Headquarters, Department of the Army, 1986.

—**MISSILE ENGAGEMENT ZONE (MEZ)** normally applies to medium- and long-range surface-to-air missiles. An MEZ limits the volume of airspace within which these weapons can conduct engagements without specific direction from the authority that established the MEZ. The MEZ is tailored to the capabilities and characteristics of the weapon systems that are operating in the zone. It may be divided into separate areas of responsibility between two different high-to-medium altitude air defense systems.

References
Department of Defense, U.S. Army. *Patriot Battalion Operations*. Field Manual FM 44-15. Washington, DC: Headquarters, Department of the Army, 1984.

—**MISSILE INTERCEPT ZONE** is the geographical division of the destruction area where surface-to-air missiles are the primary means of destroying airborne objects. *See also:* Destruction Area.

References
Department of Defense, Joint Chiefs of Staff. *Department of Defense Dictionary of Military and Related Terms*. Washington, DC: GPO, 1986.

—**MISSILE LAUNCHER EFFECTIVE RATE** is the percentage of tactical missile launchers that are either prepared or ready missile launchers.

References

Department of Defense, U.S. Army. *Dictionary of United States Army Terms.* Army Regulation AR 310-25. Washington, DC: Headquarters, Department of the Army, 1986.

—**MISSILE MASTER** is a complete electronic fire distribution system that is designed for use in the continental United States in order to coordinate all air defense elements from target detection to target destruction. By using electronic computers, memory devices, communications, and display equipment, it automatically collects, displays, and disseminates all information describing the tactical air situation almost instantaneously to the battery commanders in the defense to enable them to employ their weapons effectively.

References

Department of Defense, U.S. Army. *Dictionary of United States Army Terms.* Army Regulation AR 310-25. Washington, DC: Headquarters, Department of the Army, 1986.

—**MISSILE MONITOR** is a mobile, electronic, air defense fire-distribution system for use at the Army air defense group, battalion, and battery levels. It employs digital data to exchange information within the system and provides the means for the Army air defense commander to monitor the actions of his units and take corrective action when necessary. It automatically exchanges information with adjacent missile monitor systems, since it is connected to them by data links.

References

Department of Defense, Joint Chiefs of Staff. *Department of Defense Dictionary of Military and Related Terms.* Washington, DC: GPO, 1986.

—**MISSILE ROUND** is a missile warhead that is completely assembled for launching. *See also:* Missile Section.

References

Department of Defense, U.S. Army. *Dictionary of United States Army Terms.* Army Regulation AR 310-25. Washington, DC: Headquarters, Department of the Army, 1986.

—**MISSILE SECTION** is a portion of a missile, individually packaged, that, when assembled with other portions, constitutes an entire missile. An entire missile is composed of the fore section, nose section, warhead section, guidance section, and propulsion section.

References

Department of Defense, U.S. Army. *Dictionary of United States Army Terms.* Army Regulation AR 310-25. Washington, DC: Headquarters, Department of the Army, 1986.

—**MISSILE SUPPORT ELEMENT** is a support activity that provides missile items to missile units.

References

Department of Defense, U.S. Army. *Dictionary of United States Army Terms.* Army Regulation AR 310-25. Washington, DC: Headquarters, Department of the Army, 1986.

—**MISSILE TRACKING RADAR** is a precision tracking radar that is an integral part of a guided missile system that is used to track a missile. In command guidance systems, it may provide the command link for transmitting steering orders and the burst command from the computer.

References

Department of Defense, U.S. Army. *Dictionary of United States Army Terms.* Army Regulation AR 310-25. Washington, DC: Headquarters, Department of the Army, 1986.

—**MISSING** is a nonbattle casualty whose whereabouts and status are unknown, whose absence appears to be involuntary, and who is not known to be in an unauthorized absence status. *See also:* Missing in Action.

References

Department of Defense, U.S. Army. *Dictionary of United States Army Terms.* Army Regulation AR 310-25. Washington, DC: Headquarters, Department of the Army, 1986.

—**MISSING IN ACTION (MIA)** is a battle casualty whose whereabouts and status are unknown, whose absence appears to be involuntary, and who is not known to be in an unauthorized absence status. *See also:* Died of Wounds Received in Action, Killed in Action, Wounded in Action.

References

Department of Defense, U.S. Army. *Dictionary of United States Army Terms.* Army Regulation AR 310-25. Washington, DC: Headquarters, Department of the Army, 1986.

—**MISSING MOVEMENT** is an intentional or unintentional act whereby a person who is subject to the Uniform Code of Military Justice misses the departure of a ship, aircraft, or unit with which he was required by duty to depart.

References

Department of Defense, U.S. Army. *Dictionary of United States Army Terms*. Army Regulation AR 310-25. Washington, DC: Headquarters, Department of the Army, 1986.

—**MISSION (MSN)** is an Army tactical intelligence term. (1) A mission is a task and its purpose that clearly indicate the action to be taken and the reason for it. (2) In general, especially when applied to lower military units, a mission is a duty or task assigned to an individual or a unit. *See also:* Mission Analysis; Mission Briefing; Mission Capable; Mission, Enemy, Terrain, Troops, and Time Available; Mission-Essential Maintenance Only; Mission-Essential Maintenance Operation; Mission-Essential Materiel; Mission-Essential Repair Parts List; Mission-Essential Support System; Mission-Essential Task List; Mission Item; Mission Load; Mission Management; Mission-Oriented Items; Mission-Oriented Protective Posture; Mission Property; Mission-Related Training; Mission Report; Mission Review Report (Photographic Interpretation); Mission Support Site; Mission Tasking; Mission Type Order.

References

Department of Defense, U.S. Army. *Counter-Signals Intelligence (C-SIGINT) Operations*. Field Manual FM 34-62. Washington, DC: Headquarters, Department of the Army, 1986.

———. *Military Intelligence Battalion Combat Electronic Warfare and Intelligence (Aerial Exploitation) (Corps)*. Field Manual FM 34-22. Washington, DC: Headquarters, Department of the Army, 1984.

———. *Military Intelligence Battalion (CEWI) (Tactical Exploitation) (Corps): Counterintelligence, Interrogation, Electronic Warfare*. Field Manual FM 34-23. Washington, DC: Headquarters, Department of the Army, 1985.

—**MISSION ANALYSIS** is how the commander obtains an understanding of the mission. It involves identifying the tasks to be performed, the purpose for them, and the constraints on the units' actions. *See also:* Mission.

References

Department of Defense, U.S. Army. *Staff Organization and Operations*. Field Manual FM 101-5. Washington, DC: Headquarters, Department of the Army, 1984.

—**MISSION BRIEFING** is used under operational conditions to provide information, to give specific instructions, or to instill an appreciation of a mission. *See also:* Briefing, Mission.

References

Department of Defense, U.S. Army. *Staff Organization and Operations*. Field Manual FM 101-5. Washington, DC: Headquarters, Department of the Army, 1984.

—**MISSION CAPABLE** is a condition status of an item of equipment or system that means the item or system is either fully or partially able to perform its functions. *See also:* Mission.

References

Department of Defense, U.S. Army. *Dictionary of United States Army Terms*. Army Regulation AR 310-25. Washington, DC: Headquarters, Department of the Army, 1986.

—**MISSION, ENEMY, TERRAIN, TROOPS, AND TIME AVAILABLE (METT-T)** refers to factors involved in planning and executing a military operation. Factors include the following:

- **Mission:** the who, what, when, where, and why of what is to be accomplished.
- **Enemy:** current information about the enemy's strength, location, disposition, activity, equipment, capability, and probable course of action.
- **Terrain** (includes weather): information about vegetation, soil type, hydrology, climate, and light data, which is analyzed to determine how the environment could affect current and future enemy and friendly operations.
- **Troops:** the quantity, level of training, and psychological state of friendly forces, to include the availability of weapons systems and critical equipment.
- **Time available:** the time available for both enemy and friendly forces to plan, prepare, and execute operations.

See also: Mission.

References

Department of Defense, U.S. Army. *Air Defense Artillery Employment Hawk*. Field Manual FM 44-90. Washington, DC: Headquarters, Department of the Army, 1983.

————. *Air Defense Employment*. Field Manual FM 44-1. Washington, DC: Headquarters, Department of the Army, 1983.

————. *Operational Terms and Symbols*. Field Manual FM 101-5-1. Washington, DC: Headquarters, Department of the Army, 1985.

—**MISSION-ESSENTIAL MAINTENANCE ONLY (MEMO)** occurs in combat when equipment must be kept operational on the battlefield and returned to service as quickly as possible. Nonessential maintenance is postponed until after the battle. When the need for a certain item becomes critical, the user may accept a downgraded capability rather than lose the entire item. *See also:* Mission.

References

Department of Defense, U.S. Army. *Organizational Maintenance Operations*. Field Manual FM 29-2. Washington, DC: Headquarters, Department of the Army, 1984.

—**MISSION-ESSENTIAL MAINTENANCE OPERATION (MEMO)** is a required maintenance operation that insures the end-item will continue to perform its intended mission. Preventive maintenance functions and services are included as MEMO. *See also:* Mission.

References

Department of Defense, U.S. Army. *Maintenance and Repair Parts Consumption Planning Guide for Contingency Operations*. Field Manual FM 42-9-23. Washington, DC: Headquarters, Department of the Army, 1980.

—**MISSION-ESSENTIAL MATERIEL.** (1) Mission-essential materiel is equipment authorized and available to combat, combat support, combat service support, and combat readiness training forces to accomplish their assigned missions. (2) For the purpose of organic industrial facilities, mission-essential materiel is Service-designated materiel that is authorized for combat, combat support, combat service support, and combat readiness training forces and activities that is required to support approved emergency or war plans, and where the materiel is used to destroy the enemy or its capacity to continue war, to provide battlefield protection of personnel, to communicate under war conditions, to detect, locate, or maintain surveillance over the enemy, to provide combat transportation and support of men and materiel, or to support training

functions, but is suitable under emergency plans to meet the purposes discussed above. *See also:* Mission.

References

Department of Defense, Joint Chiefs of Staff. *Department of Defense Dictionary of Military and Related Terms*. Washington, DC: GPO, 1986.

—**MISSION-ESSENTIAL REPAIR-PARTS LIST (MERPL)** is a listing of repair parts required to perform mission-essential maintenance only operations. This list is not used for requisitioning or retail stockage purposes. *See also:* Mission.

References

Department of Defense, U.S. Army. *Maintenance and Repair Parts Consumption Planning Guide for Contingency Operations*. Field Manual FM 42-9-23. Washington, DC: Headquarters, Department of the Army, 1980.

—**MISSION-ESSENTIAL SUPPORT SYSTEM** is a secondary item, that is not authorized for stockage but is required to insure the continued operation of an essential major item, system, or facility that is vital to an essential defense mission. The unserviceability or failure of the system would jeopardize a basic defense assignment or objective. *See also:* Mission.

References

Department of Defense, U.S. Army. *Dictionary of United States Army Terms*. Army Regulation AR 310-25. Washington, DC: Headquarters, Department of the Army, 1986.

—**MISSION ESSENTIAL TASK LIST (METL)** is a prioritized list of combat, combat support, and combat service support tasks that are derived from the unit's assigned mission or missions and are essential for mission accomplishment. The list is command-level-dependent and is the basis for the annual training plan. *See also:* Mission.

References

Department of Defense, U.S. Army. *Army Forces Training*. Army Regulation AR 350-41. Washington, DC: Headquarters, Department of the Army, 1986.

—**MISSION ITEM** is an item authorized to be stocked by a depot and for which a stock level has been established. *See also:* Mission.

References

Department of Defense, U.S. Army. *Dictionary of United States Army Terms.* Army Regulation AR 310-25. Washington, DC: Headquarters, Department of the Army, 1986.

—**MISSION LOAD** is the quantity of Class II, IV, and IX supplies authorized to be on hand or stored in depots so that support units can accomplish their peacetime and combat role support missions until they are resupplied. The mission load is related to direct support/general support maintenance, as well as the resupply of prescribed and mission loads of support units. A unit's mission load is normally transportable on unit vehicles and computed in fifteen-day increments that are designed to satisfy combat requirements. *See also:* Mission.

References

Department of Defense, U.S. Army. *Planning Logistics Support for Military Operations.* Field Manual FM 701-58. Washington, DC: Headquarters, Department of the Army, 1987.

—**MISSION MANAGEMENT.** (1) Mission management is the planning, direction, and control of operations needed to satisfy the commander's needs for intelligence, electronic warfare, counterintelligence, and operations security support. (2) Mission management is the translation of general requirements into specific needs and the identification and tasking of the organization or organizations that best satisfy those needs. *See also:* Mission.

References

Department of Defense, U.S. Army. *Military Intelligence Battalion (Combat Electronic Warfare Intelligence) (Division).* Field Manual FM 34-10. Washington, DC: Headquarters, Department of the Army, 1981.

———. *Military Intelligence Battalion Combat Electronic Warfare and Intelligence (Aerial Exploitation) (Corps).* Field Manual FM 34-22. Washington, DC: Headquarters, Department of the Army, 1984.

———. *Military Intelligence Battalion (CEWI) (Tactical Exploitation) (Corps): Counterintelligence, Interrogation, Electronic Warfare.* Field Manual FM 34-23. Washington, DC: Headquarters, Department of the Army, 1985.

———. *Military Intelligence Company (Combat Electronic Warfare and Intelligence) (Armored Cavalry Regiment/Separate Brigade).* Field Manual FM 34-30. Washington, DC: Headquarters, Department of the Army, 1983.

———. *Military Intelligence Group (Combat Electronic Warfare and Intelligence) (Corps).* Field Manual FM 34-20. Washington, DC: Headquarters, Department of the Army, 1983.

—**MISSION-ORIENTED ITEMS** are items for which requirements computations are based upon the assessment of enemy capabilities expressed as a known or estimated quantity of the total targets to be destroyed. *See also:* Level of Effort Oriented Items.

References

Department of Defense, Joint Chiefs of Staff. *Department of Defense Dictionary of Military and Related Terms.* Washington, DC: GPO, 1986.

—**MISSION-ORIENTED PROTECTIVE POSTURE (MOPP)** is a flexible system of chemical protection for operations in a toxic chemical environment. It requires personnel to wear individual protective clothing and equipment consistent with the chemical threat, the work rate imposed by the mission, the temperature, and the humidity, without unacceptably degrading their efficiency from the effects of heat stress, psychological stress, and other factors affecting the senses. There are five MOPP levels. *See also:* MOPP Zero, MOPP1, MOPP2, MOPP3, MOPP4.

References

Department of Defense, U.S. Army. *Air Defense Employment.* Field Manual FM 44-1. Washington, DC: Headquarters, Department of the Army, 1983.

———. *Nuclear Weapons Employment Doctrine and Procedures.* Field Manual FM 101-31-1. Washington, DC: Headquarters, Department of the Army, 1986.

———. *Operational Terms and Symbols.* Field Manual FM 101-5-1. Washington, DC: Headquarters, Department of the Army, 1985.

—**MISSION PROPERTY** is property stocked and issued primarily for special research, production, or maintenance missions at installations and activities. *See also:* Mission.

References

Department of Defense, U.S. Army. *Dictionary of United States Army Terms.* Army Regulation AR 310-25. Washington, DC: Headquarters, Department of the Army, 1986.

—**MISSION-RELATED TRAINING** is individual or collective training that contributes directly to the accomplishment of the unit's mission. It includes a variety of activities and excludes certain diversionary activities (e.g., special duty, administrative appointments, general educational classes, honor guards, fatigue details, and routine medical care). *See also:* Mission.

References
Department of Defense, U.S. Army. *How to Prepare and Conduct Military Training.* Field Manual FM 21-6. Washington, DC: Headquarters, Department of the Army, 1975.

—**MISSION REPORT** is a standard report containing the results of a mission and significant sightings along the flight route. *See also:* Mission.

References
Department of Defense, Joint Chiefs of Staff. *Department of Defense Dictionary of Military and Related Terms.* Washington, DC: GPO, 1986.

—**MISSION REVIEW REPORT** (PHOTOGRAPHIC INTERPRETATION) is an intelligence report on all targets covered by one photographic sortie. *See also:* Aerial Reconnaissance, Mission.

References
Department of Defense, Joint Chiefs of Staff. *Department of Defense Dictionary of Military and Related Terms.* Washington, DC: GPO, 1986.

—**MISSION-SUPPORT SITE,** in unconventional warfare, is a relatively secure location, used by a force as a temporary storage site or stopover point during operations. *See also:* Mission.

References
Department of Defense, U.S. Army. *Dictionary of United States Army Terms.* Army Regulation AR 310-25. Washington, DC: Headquarters, Department of the Army, 1986.

—**MISSION TASKING** is the assignment of a mission to an organization. *See also:* Mission.

References
Department of Defense, U.S. Army. *Military Intelligence Battalion (CEWI) (Operations) (Corps).* Field Manual FM 34-21. Washington, DC: Headquarters, Department of the Army, 1982.

—**MISSION-TYPE ORDER.** (1) A mission-type order is an order issued to a lower unit that will contribute to the accomplishment of the total mission that has been assigned to the higher headquarters. (2) A mission-type order is an order issued to a unit to perform a mission without specifying how the mission is to be accomplished. *See also:* Mission.

References
Department of Defense, Joint Chiefs of Staff. *Department of Defense Dictionary of Military and Related Terms.* Washington, DC: GPO, 1986.

—**MITIGATION OF SENTENCE** is to reduce in length or in severity, a punishment, imposed by a court-martial or other military tribunal. Overall, the general nature of the punishment remains the same. *See also:* Disciplinary Action.

References
Department of Defense, U.S. Army. *Dictionary of United States Army Terms.* Army Regulation AR 310-25. Washington, DC: Headquarters, Department of the Army, 1986.

—**MIXED,** in artillery, is the report of an observer or spotter indicating that the rounds fired resulted in an equal number of air and impact bursts. *See also:* Mixed Air, Mixed Graze.

References
Department of Defense, Joint Chiefs of Staff. *Department of Defense Dictionary of Military and Related Terms.* Washington, DC: GPO, 1986.

—**MIXED AIR,** in artillery, is the report of an observer or spotter indicating that the rounds fired resulted in both air and impact bursts, with the majority of bursts being air bursts.

References
Department of Defense, Joint Chiefs of Staff. *Department of Defense Dictionary of Military and Related Terms.* Washington, DC: GPO, 1986.

—**MIXED FORCE** is a military force that includes several different branches or services.

References
Department of Defense, U.S. Army. *Dictionary of United States Army Terms.* Army Regulation AR 310-25. Washington, DC: Headquarters, Department of the Army, 1986.

—**MIXED GRAZE,** in artillery, is a report by a spotter or an observer to indicate that the rounds fired resulted in both air and impact bursts, with the majority of bursts being impact bursts.

References
Department of Defense, Joint Chiefs of Staff. *Department of Defense Dictionary of Military and Related Terms.* Washington, DC: GPO, 1986.

—**MIXED MEDICAL COMMISSION** is a group of three doctors who examine sick and wounded prisoners of war. One doctor is appointed by the country who holds the prisoners and two are appointed from neutral nations. *See also:* Medical Treatment.

References

Department of Defense, U.S. Army. *Dictionary of United States Army Terms.* Army Regulation AR 310-25. Washington, DC: Headquarters, Department of the Army, 1986.

—**MIXED MINEFIELD** is a minefield that contains both antitank and antipersonnel mines. *See also:* Minefield.

References

Department of Defense, U.S. Army. *Mine/Countermine Operations at the Company Level.* Field Manual FM 20-32. Washington, DC: Headquarters, Department of the Army, 1976.

—**MIXED SALVO** is a series of shots in which some fall short of the target and some hit beyond it. A mixed salvo differs from a bracketing salvo in that the number of shots going over the target equals the number of shots falling short of it.

References

Department of Defense, U.S. Army. *Dictionary of United States Army Terms.* Army Regulation AR 310-25. Washington, DC: Headquarters, Department of the Army, 1986.

—**MOBILE ARMY SURGICAL HOSPITAL (MASH)** is a nonfixed medical treatment facility. *See also:* Hospital, Medical Treatment Facility.

References

Department of Defense, U.S. Army. *Dictionary of United States Army Terms.* Army Regulation AR 310-25. Washington, DC: Headquarters, Department of the Army, 1986.

—**MOBILE COMSEC (COMMUNICATIONS SECURITY) FACILITY** refers to a facility that contains classified COMSEC material and can operate while it is in motion. *See also:* Communications Security.

References

Department of Defense, Joint Chiefs of Staff. *Department of Defense Dictionary of Military and Related Terms.* Washington, DC: GPO, 1986.

—**MOBILE DEFENSE** is the defense of an area or position in which maneuver is used with organization of fire and use of terrain to seize the initiative from the enemy. Mobile defenses employ a combination of offensive, defensive, and delaying action to defeat the enemy attack. Their

exact design varies from case to case and must be described in detail in each instance. Commanders conducting a mobile defense deploy relatively small forces forward and use maneuver supported by fire and obstacles to wrest the initiative from the attacker after he has entered the defended area.

A force conducting a mobile defense must have mobility that equals to or is greater than that of the enemy. It must also be able to form the large reserve that will conduct the decisive counterattack. Since doing so almost always require thinning committed forces, a mobile defense cannot be conducted unless the temporary loss of some terrain is acceptable.

Because of the requirement to form a large reserve, mobile defenses are normally conducted by divisions and larger formations. However, large brigades and cavalry regiments may be able to conduct this form of defense in some circumstances. In any case, heavy forces are required for the reserve, and may also be used as security forces or to contain anticipated penetrations. Light forces in mobile defense are usually employed to hold the strongpoints in suitable terrain within or adjacent to the area of the enemy's penetration, or in some cases, to stop the enemy during a counterattack. *See also:* Area Defense, Point Defense.

References

Department of Defense, U.S. Army. *Operations.* Field Manual FM 100-5. Washington, DC: Headquarters, Department of the Army, 1986.

—**MOBILE EMPLOYMENT** is the use of air defense artillery to defend ground combat forces while they are moving. *See also:* Static Employment.

References

Department of Defense, U.S. Army. *Dictionary of United States Army Terms.* Army Regulation AR 310-25. Washington, DC: Headquarters, Department of the Army, 1986.

—**MOBILE PORT** is a temporary port established by orders from Department of the Army or from another competent authority. When the port is no longer needed, the organizations involved may be transferred intact with their equipment and supplies to establish another mobile port.

References

Department of Defense, U.S. Army. *Dictionary of United States Army Terms.* Army Regulation AR 310-25. Washington, DC: Headquarters, Department of the Army, 1986.

—**MOBILE RESERVES.** (1) Mobile reserves are troops held ready and in favorable positions for a probable reinforcement or counterattack. (2) Mobile reserves are reserve supplies loaded on trucks or cars for prompt movement to the front.

References

Department of Defense, U.S. Army. *Dictionary of United States Army Terms.* Army Regulation AR 310-25. Washington, DC: Headquarters, Department of the Army, 1986.

—**MOBILE STRIKING FORCE** is the portion of the general reserve, including combat and support elements from all components, that is available for immediate employment in any area on, or immediately after, D-day. *See also:* D-Day.

References

Department of Defense, U.S. Army. *Dictionary of United States Army Terms.* Army Regulation AR 310-25. Washington, DC: Headquarters, Department of the Army, 1986.

—**MOBILE SUPPLY POINT** consists of the equipment, supplies, and ammunition that have been placed on motor vehicles or on railcars and are readily available for rapid displacement in support of a designated combat force. It is usually established to support a fast moving situation.

References

Department of Defense, U.S. Army. *Dictionary of United States Army Terms.* Army Regulation AR 310-25. Washington, DC: Headquarters, Department of the Army, 1986.

—**MOBILE TRAINING TEAM** consists of one or more U.S. personnel who are drawn from Service resources and are sent on temporary duty to a foreign nation to give instruction. The mission of the team is to provide, by training instructor personnel, a military service to the foreign nation so that the nation has a self-training capability in a particular skill.

References

Department of Defense, Joint Chiefs of Staff. *Department of Defense Dictionary of Military and Related Terms.* Washington, DC: GPO, 1986.

—**MOBILE UNIT** is a unit equipped with enough vehicles that it can simultaneously transport all of its assigned personnel and equipment from one location to another.

References

Department of Defense, U.S. Army. *Dictionary of United States Army Terms.* Army Regulation AR 310-25. Washington, DC: Headquarters, Department of the Army, 1986.

—**MOBILE WARFARE,** or warfare of movement, occurs when opposing sides seek to seize and hold the initiative by the use of maneuver, organization of fire, and use of terrain.

References

Department of Defense, U.S. Army. *Dictionary of United States Army Terms.* Army Regulation AR 310-25. Washington, DC: Headquarters, Department of the Army, 1986.

—**MOBILITY.** (1) Mobility is negating or reducing the effects of obstacles in order to improve movement of weapon systems and critical supplies. It includes countermine, counterobstacle, and gap-crossing functions. (2) Mobility is a quality or capability of military forces that permits them to move from place to place while retaining the ability to fulfill their primary function.

References

Department of Defense, U.S. Army. *The Army.* (Prepublication Issue.) Field Manual FM 100-1. Washington, DC: Headquarters, U.S. Army, 1986.

———. *Support Operations: Echelons Above Corps.* Field Manual FM 100-16. Washington, DC: Headquarters, Department of the Army, 1986.

—**MOBILITY** (AN ELEMENT OF FORCE READINESS). Mobility implies readiness to move rapidly to the scene of action and to anticipate the requirement for forward deployment in critical areas, as well as the capability to move tactically on the battlefield. The tactical dimension of mobility requires that weapons, their carriers or platforms, personnel, supporting missions, and materiel be capable of rapid and responsive movement. This movement must be accomplished under any conditions of visibility and weather, over any type of terrain, on or above the surface of the earth, in order to apply force on the enemy at decisive times and places and to avoid, confuse, or counter the enemy's efforts. *See also:* Mobility.

References

Department of Defense, U.S. Army. *The Army* (Prepublication Issue.) Field Manual FM 100-1. Washington, DC: Headquarters, Department of the Army, 1986.

—**MOBILITY ECHELON** is a subordinate element of a type unit that is scheduled for deployment separately from the parent unit. Mobility echelons may be used in the Time-Phased Transportation Requirements List, but normally do not appear in it. *See also:* Time-Phased Transportation Requirements List.

References
Department of Defense, U.S. Army. *Planning Logistics Support for Military Operations.* Field Manual FM 701-58. Washington, DC: Headquarters, Department of the Army, 1987.

—**MOBILITY OPERATIONS** accomplish obstacle reduction by maneuver and engineer units to reduce or negate the effects of existing or reinforcing obstacles. The objectives are to maintain freedom of movement for maneuver units, weapon systems, and critical supplies. *See also:* Breach, Countermobility Operations, Survivability Operations, Terrain Reinforcement.

References
Department of Defense, U.S. Army. *Operational Terms and Symbols.* Field Manual FM 101-5-1. Washington, DC: Headquarters, Department of the Army, 1985.

—**MOBILIZATION.** (1) Mobilization is the act of assembling and organizing national resources to support national objectives in wartime or during other emergencies. (2) Mobilization is the process by which all or part of the Armed Forces are brought to a state of readiness for war or other national emergency. This includes activating all or part of the reserve components as well as assembling and organizing personnel, supplies, and materiel. Mobilization of the Armed Forces includes but is not limited to the following categories: selective, partial, full, and total.

References
Department of Defense, Joint Chiefs of Staff. *Department of Defense Dictionary of Military and Related Terms.* Washington, DC: GPO, 1986.

—**MOBILIZATION AND TRAINING EQUIPMENT SITE** is a location where a portion of an Army National Guard unit's authorized equipment is located by direction of the Chief, National Guard Bureau, and is maintained to support the unit's mobilization and training. *See also:* Army National Guard.

References
Department of Defense, U.S. Army. *Dictionary of United States Army Terms.* Army Regulation AR 310-25. Washington, DC: Headquarters, Department of the Army, 1986.

—**MOBILIZATION AUGMENTEE** is a member of the Individual Ready Reserve who is preselected, pretrained, and assigned to occupy an authorized active duty position that is not usually filled by active duty personnel, in a Military Department or a position in the Federal Emergency Management Agency, as required, during the early days of a mobilization. *See also:* Individual Ready Reservist.

References
Department of Defense, Joint Chiefs of Staff. *Department of Defense Dictionary of Military and Related Terms.* Washington, DC: GPO, 1986.

—**MOBILIZATION BASE** is all of the the resources available, or that can be made available, to meet foreseeable wartime needs. Such resources include the manpower and material resources and services required to support essential military, civilian, and survival activities, as well as the elements affecting their state of readiness. These elements include (but are not limited to) manning levels, state of training, modernization of equipment, mobilization, materiel reserves and facilities, continuity of government, civil defense plans and preparedness of the people, international agreements, planning with industry, dispersion, and standby legislation and controls.

References
Department of Defense, Joint Chiefs of Staff. *Department of Defense Dictionary of Military and Related Terms.* Washington, DC: GPO, 1986.

—**MOBILIZATION BASE UNITS** are certain reserve component units that have been selected to expand the mobilization and training base of the Army upon mobilization. *See also:* Mobilization Base.

References
Department of Defense, U.S. Army. *Dictionary of United States Army Terms.* Army Regulation AR 310-25. Washington, DC: Headquarters, Department of the Army, 1986.

—**MOBILIZATION DESIGNATION** is a position in a mobilization table of distribution that requires the premobilization selection and training of an officer from the Ready Reserve whose entry on active duty will be required between M-day and M plus three months, as specified in the table of distribution. *See also:* M-Day

References

Department of Defense, U.S. Army. *Dictionary of United States Army Terms.* Army Regulation AR 310-25. Washington, DC: Headquarters, Department of the Army, 1986.

—**MOBILIZATION EXERCISE** is an exercise involving all or part of the implementation of mobilization plans. *See also:* Mobilization Plan.

References

Department of Defense, Joint Chiefs of Staff. *Department of Defense Dictionary of Military and Related Terms.* Washington, DC: GPO, 1986.

—**MOBILIZATION ITEM** is an item that qualifies for selection as a mobilization reserve item in accordance with specific criteria.

References

Department of Defense, U.S. Army. *Dictionary of United States Army Terms.* Army Regulation AR 310-25. Washington, DC: Headquarters, Department of the Army, 1986.

—**MOBILIZATION PLAN** prescribes the actions required to mobilize, organize, and expand a force to meet wartime or emergency requirements that are directed by the Department of the Army and appropriate Joint Chiefs of Staff unified and specified commands. In a broader context, a mobilization plan is a plan for assembling and placing, in a state of readiness for war, the manpower and material resources of a nation.

References

Department of Defense, U.S. Army. *Staff Organization and Operations.* Field Manual FM 101-5. Washington, DC: Headquarters, Department of the Army, 1984.

—**MOBILIZATION PROGRAMS OF INSTRUCTION (MOBPOI)** are the portion of a program of instruction that establish the content and training support for individual training during mobilization. The MOBPOI document describes peacetime and mobilization requirements, with the major difference being integration training in the unit environment. *See also:* Mobilization.

References

Department of Defense, U.S. Army. *Training for Mobilization and War.* Field Manual FM 25-5. Washington, DC: Headquarters, Department of the Army, 1985.

—**MOBILIZATION TABLE OF DISTRIBUTION** is a table that reflects the planned mobilization mission, organizational structure, and personnel requirements for the units authorized under the tables of distribution in Army-wide mobilization operating programs.

References

Department of Defense, U.S. Army. *Dictionary of United States Army Terms.* Army Regulation AR 310-25. Washington, DC: Headquarters, Department of the Army, 1986.

—**MOBILIZATION TABLE OF DISTRIBUTION AND ALLOWANCES (MOBTDA)** reflects the planned, full-mobilization mission, organization, structure, and personnel equipment requirements for specific units. The MOBTDA is used at the Department of the Army level in making plans to change the training base and the civilian work force. *See also:* Mobilization Table of Distribution.

References

Department of Defense, U.S. Army. *Organizational Maintenance Operations.* Field Manual FM 29-2. Washington, DC: Headquarters, Department of the Army, 1984.

—**MOBILIZATION TRAINING CONSUMPTION** is a quantity of materiel required for replacement of consumption by forces from D-day through the month preceding the month of planned commitment to combat. Mobilization training consumption is also computed for nondeployable forces and certain other miscellaneous forces in the post D-day period. Mobilization training consumption plus combat consumption equals post D-day consumption. *See also:* D-Day.

References

Department of Defense, U.S. Army. *Dictionary of United States Army Terms.* Army Regulation AR 310-25. Washington, DC: Headquarters, Department of the Army, 1986.

—**MOCK-UP** is a model, built to scale, of a machine, apparatus, or weapon that is used to study the construction of or to test a new development or to teach personnel how to operate the actual machine, apparatus, or weapon.

References

Department of Defense, Joint Chiefs of Staff. *Department of Defense Dictionary of Military and Related Terms.* Washington, DC: GPO, 1986.

—**MODE** (IDENTIFICATION FRIEND OR FOE) is the number or letter referring to the specific pulse spacing of the signals that are transmitted by an interrogator. *See also:* Identification, Friend or Foe.

References

Department of Defense, Joint Chiefs of Staff. *Department of Defense Dictionary of Military and Related Terms.* Washington, DC: GPO, 1986.

—**MODE OF TRANSPORT** relates to how movement occurs. For each mode, there are several means of transport: inland surface transportation (i.e., rail, road, and inland waterway); sea transportation (i.e., coastal and ocean); air transportation; and pipelines.

References

Department of Defense, Joint Chiefs of Staff. *Department of Defense Dictionary of Military and Related Terms.* Washington, DC: GPO, 1986.

—**MODERATE LEVEL OF OPERATIONS** are operations that involve from 30 to 60 percent of all force maneuver echelons and over 50 percent of all fire support means in continuous combat over a considerable period of time. At this level of operations, the need to use the resources from the next higher echelon to accomplish the force mission is not anticipated.

References

Department of Defense, U.S. Army. *Dictionary of United States Army Terms.* Army Regulation AR 310-25. Washington, DC: Headquarters, Department of the Army, 1986.

—**MODERATE RISK** (NUCLEAR) is a degree of risk where the anticipated effects are tolerable, or at worst, a nuisance. *See also:* Degree of Risk; Emergency Risk (Nuclear); Negligible Risk (Nuclear); Unwarned, Exposed; Warned, Exposed; Warned, Protected Personnel.

References

Department of Defense, U.S. Army. *Operational Terms and Symbols.* Field Manual FM 101-5-1. Washington, DC: Headquarters, Department of the Army, 1985.

—**MODIFICATION KIT** is an assemblage of the materiel needed to make or perform a desired modification.

References

Department of Defense, U.S. Army. *Dictionary of United States Army Terms.* Army Regulation AR 310-25. Washington, DC: Headquarters, Department of the Army, 1986.

—**MODIFICATION TABLE OF ORGANIZATION AND EQUIPMENT (MTOE)** applies to specific units and modifies the table of organization and equipment to meet the unit's specific needs. It prescribes personnel and equipment authorizations and is based upon a unit's combat mission and unique circumstances. For example, an infantry battalion in the Pacific and one in Europe may have the same table of organization and equipment requirement but different authorizations as tailored by the MTOE. *See also:* Table of Organization and Equipment.

References

Department of Defense, U.S. Army. *Organizational Maintenance Operations.* Field Manual FM 29-2. Washington, DC: Headquarters, Department of the Army, 1984.

—**MODIFICATION WORK ORDER** is a Department of the Army publication that provides the authority and instructions necessary for modifying Army materiel. *See also:* Work Order.

References

Department of Defense, U.S. Army. *Dictionary of United States Army Terms.* Army Regulation AR 310-25. Washington, DC: Headquarters, Department of the Army, 1986.

—**MODIFY** in artillery, is an order by a person who is authorized to change a fire plan.

References

Department of Defense, Joint Chiefs of Staff. *Department of Defense Dictionary of Military and Related Terms.* Washington, DC: GPO, 1986.

—**MOMENTUM IN THE ATTACK** is achieved and maintained when resources and forces are concentrated to sustain operations over extended periods. In this situation, adequate reconnaissance is provided beyond areas of immediate concern, committed enemy forces are adequately fixed, uncommitted enemy forces are interdicted or otherwise prevented from interfering, adequate air protection is provided, the enemy's command and control system is disrupted, adequate reserves and follow and support forces are provided, vulnerable rear area facilities are protected, logistic resources are moved forward, and combat forces project tactical operations deep into the enemy's vulnerable areas.

References

Department of Defense, U.S. Army. *Operations.* Field Manual FM 100-5. Washington, DC: Headquarters, Department of the Army, 1986.

—**MONEY ACCOUNTS** are the statement of accountability and the supporting documents rendered by the finance and accounting officer at prescribed accounting periods.

References

Department of Defense, U.S. Army. *Dictionary of United States Army Terms.* Army Regulation AR 310-25. Washington, DC: Headquarters, Department of the Army, 1986.

—**MONEY LIST** is a form used by the finance and accounting officers to list the names of Army personnel who have been paid and the amounts of pay and allowances they have received.

References

Department of Defense, U.S. Army. *Dictionary of United States Army Terms.* Army Regulation AR 310-25. Washington, DC: Headquarters, Department of the Army, 1986.

—**MONITORING AND SURVEY.** Each unit is required to conduct monitoring, survey, and reconnaissance. The monitoring and survey report is a standardized report in the nuclear, biological, chemical warning and reporting system. *See also:* Biological Warfare, Chemical Warfare, Nuclear Warfare.

References

Department of Defense, U.S. Army. *NBC Operations.* Field Manual FM 3-100. Washington, DC: Headquarters, Department of the Army, 1985.

—**MONTHLY FLIGHT PAY** is incentive pay authorized to commissioned and warrant officer aviators while they are serving in operational flying positions and do not otherwise qualify for continuous flight pay.

References

Department of Defense, U.S. Army. *Dictionary of United States Army Terms.* Army Regulation AR 310-25. Washington, DC: Headquarters, Department of the Army, 1986.

—**MOPP** is an acronym for mission-oriented protective posture. It is a flexible system that provides maximum nuclear, biological, chemical protection for the individual with the lowest risk possible and still allows for mission accomplishment. The postures require personnel to wear individual protective clothing and equipment that is consistent with the chemical threat, the work rate imposed by the mission, the temperature, and the humidity without unacceptably degrading the efficiency from the effects of heat stress. *See also:* MOPP Gear, MOPP Gear Exchange, MOPP Levels, MOPP Zero, MOPP1, MOPP2, MOPP3, MOPP4.

References

Department of Defense, U.S. Army. *NBC Operations.* Field Manual FM 3-100. Washington, DC: Headquarters, Department of the Army, 1985.

—**MOPP GEAR** is a combination of all individual protective equipment including the suit, boots, gloves, mask with hood, first aid treatment, and decon kits. *See also:* MOPP.

References

Department of Defense, U.S. Army. *NBC Operations.* Field Manual FM 3-100. Washington, DC: Headquarters, Department of the Army, 1985.

—**MOPP GEAR EXCHANGE.** MOPP gear is exchanged to remove gross contamination from soldiers. The mask and hood are wiped down, and individual gear is brushed with decontaminants *See also:* MOPP.

References

Department of Defense, U.S. Army. *NBC Operations.* Field Manual FM 3-100. Washington, DC: Headquarters, Department of the Army, 1985.

—**MOPP LEVELS** The need to balance protection with the threat, temperature, and urgency of the mission led to the concept of MOPP. Commanders can raise or lower the amount of protection through five levels of MOPP—MOPP zero through MOPP4. In addition, commanders have a mask-only option. Protection increases with progression from MOPP zero to MOPP4, but efficiency decreases correspondingly, so, selecting the MOPP level that provides the best balance requires judgment. *See also:* MOPP.

References

Department of Defense, U.S. Army. *NBC Protection.* Field Manual FM 3-4, October 1985. Washington, DC: Headquarters, U.S. Army, 1985.

—**MOPP ZERO.** In MOPP zero, soldiers carry the protective mask. They have their MOPP gear readily available (i.e., within the work area, vehicle, fighting position, or the like). MOPP zero is appropriate when the enemy has an nuclear, biological, chemical employment capability but chemical warfare has not begun or when troops are first deployed outside the theater of operation. MOPP zero allows soldiers to be free of the burden of wearing the overgarment and mask and yet have them readily available when needed. The battle dress overgarment should remain sealed in the vapor-barrier bag until needed. Soldiers should also carry their M258A1 decontamination kit, M8/M9 detector paper, and NAAK. *See also:* MOPP.

References

Department of Defense, U.S. Army. *NBC Protection.* Field Manual FM 3-4. Washington, DC: Headquarters, Department of the Army, 1985.

—**MOPP1.** Soldiers in MOPP1 wear the battle dress overgarment. In hot weather, they can wear it directly over their underwear and may leave the jacket open for ventilation, but they must keep the trousers closed. They attach the M9 paper to the overgarment and wear the protective helmet cover. For soldiers in MOPP1, the reaction time needed to adopt MOPP4 protection against an attack is cut in half—from eight minutes to four. *See also:* MOPP.

References

Department of Defense, U.S. Army. *NBC Protection.* Field Manual FM 3-4. Washington, DC: Headquarters, Department of the Army, 1985.

—**MOPP2.** Soldiers add their chemical-protective overboots. These take about three to four minutes to put on, so, once troops are in MOPP2, they can go to higher MOPP levels in seconds. In hot weather, soldiers can leave the overgarment jacket open for ventilation, but they must keep the trousers closed. *See also:* MOPP.

References

Department of Defense, U.S. Army. *NBC Protection.* Field Manual FM 3-4. Washington, DC: Headquarters, Department of the Army, 1985.

—**MOPP3.** Soldiers wear the protective mask and hood in MOPP3, which make protection almost complete but significantly interferes with their ability to work. The mask and hood restrict vision; heat stress becomes a major factor; and a greater risk of heat exhaustion exists. In hot weather, soldiers may open the overgarment jacket and roll the protective-mask hood for ventilation, but must leave their trousers closed. *See also:* MOPP.

References

Department of Defense, U.S. Army. *NBC Protection.* Field Manual FM 3-4. Washington, DC: Headquarters, Department of the Army, 1985.

—**MOPP4.** At MOPP4, soldiers protect their hands with a pair of cotton-lined nuclear, biological, chemical rubber gloves. They close the overgarment and pull down and adjust the hood, making protection complete. Of all MOPP levels, MOPP4 has the most negative impact on individual efficiency and effectiveness. *See also:* MOPP.

References

Department of Defense, U.S. Army. *NBC Protection.* Field Manual FM 3-4. Washington, DC: Headquarters, Department of the Army, 1985.

—**MOPPING UP** is the removal of remaining enemy resistance in an area that has been surrounded or isolated, or through which other units have passed without eliminating all active resistance.

References

Department of Defense, Joint Chiefs of Staff. *Department of Defense Dictionary of Military and Related Terms.* Washington, DC: GPO, 1986.

—**MORALE** is the mental, emotional, and spiritual state of an individual. It is how the soldier feels (e.g., happy, hopeful, confident, appreciated, or worthless, sad, unrecognized, and depressed). High morale strengthens courage, energy, and the will to fight. *See also:* Morale Support Activities, Morale Support Company, Morale Support Officer.

References

Department of Defense, U.S. Army. *Military Leadership.* Field Manual FM 22-100. Washington, DC: Headquarters, Department of the Army, 1983.

—**MORALE SUPPORT ACTIVITIES** refers to morale support services that normally include arts, crafts, recreation centers, automotive repair, music, theater, youth activities, information, tour and travel, sports, outdoor recreation, and libraries.

References

Department of Defense, U.S. Army. *Military Leadership.* Field Manual FM 22-100. Washington, DC: Headquarters, Department of the Army, 1983.

—**MORALE SUPPORT COMPANY** refers to the technical troops who are provided for special services operations. The companies are separate, semimobile organizations that are trained and equipped to produce and provide entertainment and recreational facilities and activities for troops, including motion pictures, libraries, sports, live entertainment shows and novelty acts, musical entertainment, and crafts.

References

Department of Defense, U.S. Army. *Military Leadership.* Field Manual FM 22-100. Washington, DC: Headquarters, Department of the Army, 1983.

—**MORALE SUPPORT OFFICER** is a commissioned officer trained in military recreation and responsible for developing and operating voluntary free-time activities for military personnel. These activities include crafts, libraries, soldier music, soldier shows, service clubs, sports, and motion pictures. *See also:* Morale.

References

Department of Defense, U.S. Army. *Military Leadership.* Field Manual FM 22-100. Washington, DC: Headquarters, Department of the Army, 1983.

—**MORBIDITY** is the incidence and prevalence of specified morbid conditions (i.e., disease, injury, or other excused-from-duty conditions) in a given area or unit. *See also:* Medical Treatment.

References

Department of Defense, U.S. Army. *Health Service Support in a Communications Zone (Test).* Field Manual FM 8-21. Washington, DC: Headquarters, Department of the Army, 1981.

—**MORTALITY FACTOR** is a number used to determine the quantity of replacement parts that are to be allowed to any echelon of maintenance. It is based upon the durability of any given part relative to the durability of the entire unit. *See also:* Medical Treatment.

References

Department of Defense, U.S. Army. *Dictionary of United States Army Terms.* Army Regulation AR 310-25. Washington, DC: Headquarters, Department of the Army, 1986.

—**MORTALITY RATE** is the number of deaths that occur during a given time period per 1,000 men. The rate is calculated by dividing the number of deaths in the time period by the average strength during the same period, and multiplying the result by 1,000. The time period must be expressed and is usually one year. *See also:* Medical Treatment.

References

Department of Defense, U.S. Army. *Dictionary of United States Army Terms.* Army Regulation AR 310-25. Washington, DC: Headquarters, Department of the Army, 1986.

—**MORTAR** ia a muzzle-loading, indirect fire weapon with either a rifled or smooth bore. It usually has a shorter range than a howitzer, employs a higher angle of fire, and has a tube length of ten to twenty calibers. *See also:* Gun, Howitzer, Mortar Deflection Board, Mortar Position, Mortar Report.

References

Department of Defense, Joint Chiefs of Staff. *Department of Defense Dictionary of Military and Related Terms.* Washington, DC: GPO, 1986.

—**MORTAR DEFLECTION BOARD** is a control instrument used to find the corrections for wind, drift, and other factors, and the resultant adjustment that must be applied to the azimuth settings of a mortar.

References

Department of Defense, U.S. Army. *Dictionary of United States Army Terms.* Army Regulation AR 310-25. Washington, DC: Headquarters, Department of the Army, 1986.

—**MORTAR POSITION** is a circular-shaped hole. The position is dug enough to shield the weapon and crew, but not so deep as to restrict the weapon's operation.

References

Department of Defense, U.S. Army. *Survivability.* Field Manual FM 5-103. Washington, DC: Headquarters, Department of the Army, 1985.

—**MORTAR REPORT** is any report of enemy mortar fire that contains information on the caliber, direction, and time density of the mortar, and the area that has been shelled.

References

Department of Defense, U.S. Army. *Dictionary of United States Army Terms.* Army Regulation AR 310-25. Washington, DC: Headquarters, Department of the Army, 1986.

—**MOSAIC** is an intelligence imagery and photoreconnaissance term for an assembly of overlapping photographs that have been matched to form a continuous photographic representation. *See also:* Aerial Reconnaissance, Imagery.

References
Department of Defense. U.S. Army. *Intelligence Imagery*. Army Field Manual FM 34-55. Washington, DC: Headquarters, Department of the Army, 1985.

————. *Operational Terms and Symbols*. Field Manual FM 101-5-1. Washington, DC: Headquarters, Department of the Army, 1985.

—**MOST DANGEROUS** is a target that sees its victims, has the capability to kill it, and appears to be preparing to engage it. This target is the greatest threat and must be engaged quickly. If there is more than one most dangerous target, the closest should be engaged first. *See also:* Dangerous.

References
Department of Defense, U.S. Army. *Tank Gunnery*. Field Manual FM 17-12. Washington, DC: Headquarters, Department of the Army, 1984.

—**MOTOR CONVOY** consists of two or more vehicles that are under a single control. They may be with or without escort and are used to transport military personnel or materiel.

References
Department of Defense, U.S. Army. *Tank Gunnery*. Field Manual FM 17-12. Washington, DC: Headquarters, Department of the Army, 1984.

—**MOTOR MARCH** is the movement of a unit by truck transport. The formations used in a motor march are close column, open column, and infiltration.

References
Department of Defense, U.S. Army. *The Infantry Rifle Company (Infantry. Airborne, Air Assault, Ranger)*. Field Manual FM 7-10. Washington, DC: Headquarters, Department of the Army, 1982.

————. *Tank Gunnery*. Field Manual FM 17-12. Washington, DC: Headquarters, Department of the Army, 1984.

—**MOTOR MOVEMENT BY ECHELON.** *See:* Shuttling.

—**MOTOR POOL** is a group of motor vehicles available for use as needed by different organizations or individuals.

References
Department of Defense, U.S. Army. *Dictionary of United States Army Terms*. Army Regulation AR 310-25. Washington, DC: Headquarters, Department of the Army, 1986.

—**MOTOR ROUTE ORDER NUMBER** is a symbol assigned by the National Bus Military Bureau for purposes of identification, record, secrecy, and administrative handling of the movement of groups of more than fifteen military personnel by bus within the continental United States.

References
Department of Defense, U.S. Army. *Dictionary of United States Army Terms*. Army Regulation AR 310-25. Washington, DC: Headquarters, Department of the Army, 1986.

—**MOTOR TRANSPORT** consists of motor vehicles used for transporting military personnel, weapons, equipment, and supplies. This category excludes combat vehicles such as tanks, scout cars, and armored cars.

References
Department of Defense, U.S. Army. *Dictionary of United States Army Terms*. Army Regulation AR 310-25. Washington, DC: Headquarters, Department of the Army, 1986.

—**MOTOR TRANSPORT OFFICER** is a staff officer and the adviser to the commander on matters concerning motor transportation. *See also:* Motor Transport.

References
Department of Defense, U.S. Army. *Dictionary of United States Army Terms*. Army Regulation AR 310-25. Washington, DC: Headquarters, Department of the Army, 1986.

—**MOTOR TRANSPORT POOL.** *See:* Motor Pool.

—**MOTOR VEHICLE DRIVER BADGE** is a metallic badge denoting the completion of the prescribed tests and the performance of driver duty for one year by a motor vehicle driver.

References
Department of Defense, U.S. Army. *Dictionary of United States Army Terms*. Army Regulation AR 310-25. Washington, DC: Headquarters, Department of the Army, 1986.

—**MOTOR VEHICLE MECHANIC BADGE** is a metallic badge denoting the completion of the prescribed tests and the performance of mechanic duty for one year by a motor vehicle mechanic.

References
Department of Defense, U.S. Army. *Dictionary of United States Army Terms*. Army Regulation AR 310-25. Washington, DC: Headquarters, Department of the Army, 1986.

—**MOTORIZED INFANTRY (MTZ)** is more rapidly deployable than mechanized infantry, but more capable than light infantry of meeting and defeating heavy forces in open terrain. Motorized infantry derives its combat power from rapid ground mobility, heavy firepower, and superior command and control. It lacks the armor protection to survive against heavy forces in conditions where the terrain precludes rapid maneuver and affords little cover and concealment. In conditions that favor its employment, motorized infantry can attack and destroy enemy forces in open terrain, envelop or infiltrate weakly held enemy positions and attack vital assets in their rear, exploit penetrations of stronger positions by heavier forces, pursue and destroy retreating enemy forces, react rapidly to locate and destroy enemy forces operating in friendly rear areas, and dismount and fight as light infantry, if necessary.

References
Department of Defense, U.S. Army. *Operations.*
Field Manual FM 100-5. Washington, DC:
Headquarters, Department of the Army, 1986.

—**MOTORIZED UNIT** is a unit equipped with complete motor transportation that enables all of its personnel, weapons, and equipment to be moved at the same time without assistance from other sources.

References
Department of Defense, Joint Chiefs of Staff.
Department of Defense Dictionary of Military and Related Terms. Washington, DC: GPO, 1986.

—**MOUNT ADAPTER** is a device used to make a gun fit properly into a mount. *See also:* Mounting.

References
Department of Defense, U.S. Army. *Dictionary of United States Army Terms.* Army Regulation AR 310-25. Washington, DC: Headquarters, Department of the Army, 1986.

—**MOUNTAIN TROOPS** are soldiers equipped and trained in mountain warfare, including in skiing and mountain climbing.

References
Department of Defense, U.S. Army. *Dictionary of United States Army Terms.* Army Regulation AR 310-25. Washington, DC: Headquarters, Department of the Army, 1986.

—**MOUNTING.** (1) Mounting includes all the preparations made in areas that are designated for the purpose, in anticipation of an operation. It includes the assembly in the mounting area, preparation and maintenance within the mounting area, movement to loading points, and the subsequent embarkation into ships, craft, or aircraft, if applicable. (2) A mounting is a carriage or stand upon which a weapon is placed. *See also:* Mounting Area.

References
Department of Defense, Joint Chiefs of Staff.
Department of Defense Dictionary of Military and Related Terms. Washington, DC: GPO, 1986.

—**MOUNTING AREA** is a general locality where assigned forces of an amphibious or airborne operation, with their equipment, are assembled, prepared, and loaded in shipping and/or aircraft in preparation for an assault. *See also:* Mounting.

References
Department of Defense, Joint Chiefs of Staff.
Department of Defense Dictionary of Military and Related Terms. Washington, DC: GPO, 1986.

—**MOUNTING PHASE** is the period between the receipt of the warning order or planning directive and the time aircraft take off or ships depart. During this period, joint tactical and support planning is accomplished; the troops, equipment, and supplies are assembled and readied; and the briefings are conducted. The marshalling takes place during the last part of the mounting phase and includes the movement of participating personnel, supplies, and all equipment to the departure areas, and their loading into aircraft or ships. *See also:* Air Movement Phase, Assault Phase, Mounting, Move Out, Subsequent Operations Phase.

References
Department of Defense, U.S. Army. *Operational Terms and Symbols.* Field Manual FM 101-5-1. Washington, DC: Headquarters, Department of the Army, 1985.

—**MOVE OUT** is a command that follows instructions in spoken field orders. It indicates that the men addressed are to leave and carry out their orders.

References
Department of Defense, U.S. Army. *Dictionary of United States Army Terms.* Army Regulation AR 310-25. Washington, DC: Headquarters, Department of the Army, 1986.

————. *Transportation Reference Data*. Field Manual FM 55-15. Washington, DC: Headquarters, Department of the Army, 1986.

—MOVEMENT CONTROL TEAMS coordinate all movements and insure they are made effectively and economically. These teams vary in size and assignment. *See also:* Movement Control.

References
Department of Defense, U.S. Army. *Planning Logistics Support for Military Operations*. Field Manual FM 701-58. Washington, DC: Headquarters, Department of the Army, 1987.

————. *Transportation Reference Data*. Field Manual FM 55-15. Washington, DC: Headquarters, Department of the Army, 1986.

—MOVEMENT CREDIT is the allocation granted to one or more vehicles in order to move over a controlled route in a fixed time according to movement instructions. *See also:* Movement Control.

References
Department of Defense, U.S. Army. *Planning Logistics Support for Military Operations*. Field Manual FM 701-58. Washington, DC: Headquarters, Department of the Army, 1987.

————. *Transportation Reference Data*. Field Manual FM 55-15. Washington, DC: Headquarters, Department of the Army, 1986.

—MOVEMENT DIRECTIVE is the basic document published by the Department of the Army or the Department Air Force, or jointly, that authorizes a command to take action to move a designated unit from one location to another. *See also:* Movement Control.

References
Department of Defense, U.S. Army. *Planning Logistics Support for Military Operations*. Field Manual FM 701-58. Washington, DC: Headquarters, Department of the Army, 1987.

————. *Transportation Reference Data*. Field Manual FM 55-15. Washington, DC: Headquarters, Department of the Army, 1986.

—MOVEMENT INSTRUCTIONS are detailed instructions for the execution of a movement. They are issued by a transportation officer as an implementation of the movement programs, and they represent the accepted procedure that is to be followed by the shipper or the receiver of the transportation services. *See also:* Movement Control.

References
Department of Defense, U.S. Army. *Transportation Reference Data*. Field Manual FM 55-15. Washington, DC: Headquarters, Department of the Army, 1986.

—MOVEMENT ORDER is an order issued by a commander that covers the details of a move by his command. *See also:* Movement Control.

References
Department of Defense, U.S. Army. *Planning Logistics Support for Military Operations*. Field Manual FM 701-58. Washington, DC: Headquarters, Department of the Army, 1987.

————. *Transportation Reference Data*. Field Manual FM 55-15. Washington, DC: Headquarters, Department of the Army, 1986.

—MOVEMENT PLAN. (1) A movement plan is based upon up-to-date logistics data and presents a summary of the transportation requirements, priorities, and limiting factors that are incident to the movement of one or more units or another special grouping of personnel by highway, marine, rail, or air transportation. (2) A movement plan is a naval plan providing for the movement of the amphibious task force to the objective area. It includes information and instructions concerning the departure of ships, loading points, the passage at sea, and the approach to, arrival in, and assigned positions in the objective landing area. *See also:* Movement Control.

References
Department of Defense, U.S. Army. *Dictionary of United States Army Terms*. Army Regulation AR 310-25. Washington, DC: Headquarters, Department of the Army, 1986.

—MOVEMENT PRIORITY DESIGNATOR is a priority assigned to the movement of materiel by the Army logistic supply system. The principal determinant in such a movement of materiel is the importance of inventory in the overall distribution system so that the required delivery dates designated by the materiel manager are met. *See also:* Movement Control.

References
Department of Defense, U.S. Army. *Planning Logistics Support for Military Operations*. Field Manual FM 701-58. Washington, DC: Headquarters, Department of the Army, 1987.

—**MOVEMENT PROGRAM** is a plan prepared by a transportation movements section and issued in the name of the commander. Its purpose is to accomplish successfully the required movements by using the available transportation facilities for a given period. *See also:* Movement Control.

References

Department of Defense, U.S. Army. *Transportation Reference Data.* Field Manual FM 55-15. Washington, DC: Headquarters, Department of the Army, 1986.

—**MOVEMENT REPORT CONTROL CENTER** is the controlling agency for the entire movement report system. It has available all information relative to the movements of naval ships and other ships under naval control. *See also:* Movement Control.

References

Department of Defense, U.S. Army. *Planning Logistics Support for Military Operations.* Field Manual FM 701-58. Washington, DC: Headquarters, Department of the Army, 1987.

————. *Transportation Reference Data.* Field Manual FM 55-15. Washington, DC: Headquarters, Department of the Army, 1986.

—**MOVEMENT REPORT SYSTEM** is a system established to collect and make available to certain commands vital information on the status, location, and movement of flag commands, commissioned fleet units, and ships under operational control of the Navy. *See also:* Movement Control.

References

Department of Defense, U.S. Army. *Planning Logistics Support for Military Operations.* Field Manual FM 701-58. Washington, DC: Headquarters, Department of the Army, 1987.

————. *Transportation Reference Data.* Field Manual FM 55-15. Washington, DC: Headquarters, Department of the Army, 1986.

—**MOVEMENT REQUIREMENT** is a stated movement mode and time-phased need for the transport of units, personnel, and materiel from a specified origin to a specified destination. *See also:* Movement Control.

References

Department of Defense, U.S. Army. *Planning Logistics Support for Military Operations.* Field Manual FM 701-58. Washington, DC: Headquarters, Department of the Army, 1987.

————. *Transportation Reference Data.* Field Manual FM 55-15. Washington, DC: Headquarters, Department of the Army, 1986.

—**MOVEMENT RESTRICTION** is a restriction temporarily placed on traffic into and out of areas in order to permit the clearance of, or the prevention of, congestion. *See also:* Movement Control.

References

Department of Defense, U.S. Army. *Planning Logistics Support for Military Operations.* Field Manual FM 701-58. Washington, DC: Headquarters, Department of the Army, 1987.

————. *Transportation Reference Data.* Field Manual FM 55-15. Washington, DC: Headquarters, Department of the Army, 1986.

—**MOVEMENT SCHEDULE** is a schedule developed to monitor or track a separate entity, whether it is a force requirement or lift asset. The schedule reflects the assignment of specific lift resources (e.g., an aircraft or ship) that will be used to move the personnel and cargo included in a specific movement increment. Arrival and departure times at ports of embarkation are detailed to show a flow and work load at each location. Movement schedules are detailed enough to support plan implementation. *See also:* Movement Control.

References

Department of Defense, U.S. Army. *Planning Logistics Support for Military Operations.* Field Manual FM 701-58. Washington, DC: Headquarters, Department of the Army, 1987.

————. *Transportation Reference Data.* Field Manual FM 55-15. Washington, DC: Headquarters, Department of the Army, 1986.

—**MOVEMENT TABLE** provides detailed instructions and data concerning a move. When necessary, it is qualified by the words "road, " "rail," "air," or "sea" to signify the type of movement. It is normally issued as an annex to a movement order or instruction. *See also:* Movement Control.

References

Department of Defense, U.S. Army. *Planning Logistics Support for Military Operations.* Field Manual FM 701-58. Washington, DC: Headquarters, Department of the Army, 1987.

————. *Transportation Reference Data.* Field Manual FM 55-15. Washington, DC: Headquarters, Department of the Army, 1986.

—**MOVEMENT TECHNIQUES.** There are three techniques for moving when forces are not in contact with the enemy. *Travelling*, is used when speed is necessary and contact with the enemy is unlikely. All elements of the unit move simultaneously, with the unit leader located where he can best control his forces. *Travelling overwatch* is used when contact with the enemy is possible. The lead element and trail element are separated by a short distance that varies with the terrain. The trailing element moves at variable speeds and may pause for short periods to overwatch the lead element. It keys its movement to the terrain and to the lead element. It overwatches at a distance so that the enemy's engagement of the lead element will not prevent the trailing element from firing or moving to support the lead element. *Bounding overwatch* is used when contact with the enemy is expected. The unit moves by bounds, and one element is always halted and in position to overwatch another element while it moves. The overwatching element is positioned to support the moving unit by fire or fire and maneuver. The commander decides which movement technique is appropriate, basing his decision upon the likelihood of contact with the enemy, the need for speed, and the terrain and visibility. Movement techniques are not fixed formations. The distances between men and units vary and are based upon the mission, enemy, terrain, visibility, and other factors that affect control. *See also:* Movement Control.

References

Department of Defense, U.S. Army. *The Infantry Rifle Company (Infantry. Airborne, Air Assault, Ranger).* Field Manual FM 7-10. Washington, DC: Headquarters, Department of the Army, 1982.

———. *Operational Terms and Symbols.* Field Manual FM 101-5-1. Washington, DC: Headquarters, Department of the Army, 1985.

———. *U.S. Army Air Defense Employment.* Field Manual FM 44-1. Washington, DC: Headquarters, Department of the Army, 1983.

—**MOVEMENT TO CONTACT** is an offensive operation designed to gain initial ground contact with the enemy or to regain lost contact. When U.S. forces conducting an offensive operation are moving and are not in contact with the enemy, they are said to be moving to contact. The purpose of movement to contact is to gain or regain contact with the enemy in a way that risks the smallest part of the force while the remainder is available to immediately respond when contact is made. Movement to contact is usually made in three phases: contact remote, contact improbable, and contact imminent.

References

Department of Defense, U.S. Army. *Air Defense Artillery Deployment: Chaparral/Vulcan/Stinger.* Field Manual FM 44-3. Washington, DC: Headquarters, Department of the Army, 1984.

———. *Armored and Mechanized Division Operations.* Field Manual FM 71-100. Washington, DC: Headquarters, Department of the Army, 1978.

———. *Operational Terms and Symbols.* Field Manual FM 101-5-1. Washington, DC: Headquarters, Department of the Army, 1985.

———. *The Tank and Mechanized Infantry Battalion Task Force.* Field Manual FM 71-2. Washington, DC: Headquarters, Department of the Army, 1977.

—**MOVING PIVOT.** (1) A moving pivot is a person who acts as the turning point or pivot for a line of troops when they change their direction of march. (2) A moving pivot is the arc of a circle about which a column turns when it changes its direction of march.

References

Department of Defense, U.S. Army. *Dictionary of United States Army Terms.* Army Regulation AR 310-25. Washington, DC: Headquarters, Department of the Army, 1986.

—**MOVING SCREEN** is composed of patrols that are often motorized or mechanized detachments, which are used to keep enemy scouting parties at a distance and to deny enemy observation of one's troop movements.

References

Department of Defense, U.S. Army. *Dictionary of United States Army Terms.* Army Regulation AR 310-25. Washington, DC: Headquarters, Department of the Army, 1986.

—**MP (MILITARY POLICE) RESPONSE FORCE** is an MP force tasked to respond to and to close with and destroy attacking enemy forces that are beyond the capabilities of a base or a base cluster. *See also:* Military Police.

References

Department of Defense, U.S. Army. *Military Police Team, Squad, Platoon Combat Operations.* Field Manual FM 19-4. Washington, DC: Headquarters, Department of the Army, 1984.

—**MUDCAPPING** is a method of breaking up large rocks without drilling: a charge of high explosive is laid on a rock, covered with a shovelful of mud, and detonated.

References

Department of Defense, U.S. Army. *Dictionary of United States Army Terms.* Army Regulation AR 310-25. Washington, DC: Headquarters, Department of the Army, 1986.

—**MUKLUK** is a seal or caribou skin boot that is commonly worn by Eskimos. The mukluk boots used by the Army are the Eskimo "Kamik" and have dry tan leather or rubber soles, and canvas uppers extending up to just below the knees.

References

Department of Defense, U.S. Army. *Dictionary of United States Army Terms.* Army Regulation AR 310-25. Washington, DC: Headquarters, Department of the Army, 1986.

—**MULTI-ECHELON TRAINING** is a unit approach to individual and collective training designed to simultaneously prepare different elements of a battalion or a separate company. The tasks that are trained are individual, collective, or both, and are not necessarily related. For example, soldiers may receive individual training on soldiers manual tasks from noncommissioned officers, while other noncommisioned officers and officers exercise their skills in a command post exercise.

References

Department of Defense, U.S. Army. *How to Prepare and Conduct Military Training.* Field Manual FM 21-6. Washington, DC: Headquarters, Department of the Army, 1975.

———. *Training for Mobilization and War.* Field Manual FM 25-5. Washington, DC: Headquarters, Department of the Army, 1985.

—**MULTIGAUGE EQUIPMENT** is railway equipment constructed so that it can be used on more than one gauge of track.

References

Department of Defense, U.S. Army. *How to Prepare and Conduct Military Training.* Field Manual FM 21-6. Washington, DC: Headquarters, Department of the Army, 1975.

—**MULTI-IMPULSE FUZE** is a fuze designed to actuate after a given sequence of impulses of the same nature is applied to it. *See also:* Fuze (Specify Type).

References

Department of Defense, U.S. Army. *Mine/ Countermine Operations at the Company Level.* Field Manual FM 20-32. Washington, DC: Headquarters, Department of the Army, 1976.

—**MULTI-INFLUENCE FUZE** is an influence fuze that uses a combination of influences that are exerted by the target. *See also:* Fuze (Specify Type).

References

Department of Defense, U.S. Army. *Mine/ Countermine Operations at the Company Level.* Field Manual FM 20-32. Washington, DC: Headquarters, Department of the Army, 1976.

—**MULTIPURPOSE RANGE COMPLEX (MPRC)** is the key range facility. It provides challenging gunnery experiences for tank and mechanized infantry units up to the platoon level and can be used to enhance dismounted infantry and helicopter live-fire exercises.

References

Department of Defense, U.S. Army. *U.S. Army Policy Statement, 1988.* Washington, DC: Headquarters, Department of the Army, 1988.

—**MULTISECTION CHARGE** involves the separate loading of a propelling charge for semifixed ammunition. The charge is loaded into a number of powder bags, and range adjustments can be made by increasing or reducing the number of bags used. This contrasts with the single section charge, in which the size of the charge cannot be changed. The three types of multisection charges are the equal section charge, the base and increment charge, and the unequal section charge.

References

Department of Defense, U.S. Army. *Dictionary of United States Army Terms.* Army Regulation AR 310-25. Washington, DC: Headquarters, Department of the Army, 1986.

—**MULTISERVICE DOCTRINE** is the fundamental principles that guide the use of forces of the participating services of the same nation in coordinated action toward a common objective. It is ratified by the participating services and is normally promulgated in joint service publications that identify the services participating (e.g., Army-Navy doctrine). *See also:* Combined Doctrine, Joint Doctrine.

References

Department of Defense, Joint Chiefs of Staff. *Department of Defense Dictionary of Military and Related Terms.* Washington, DC: GPO, 1986.

—**MULTITARGET JAMMING,** in electronic warfare, refers to jamming that is meant to simultaneously, or on a time-sharing basis, present interference to two or more receiving systems or families of receiving systems. *See also:* Barrage Jamming, Jamming.

References

Department of Defense, U.S. Army. *Intelligence and Electronic Warfare Operations.* Field Manual FM 34-1. Washington, DC: Headquarters, Department of the Army, 1984.

———. *Military Intelligence Battalion (Combat Electronic Warfare Intelligence) (Division).* Field Manual FM 34-10. Washington, DC: Headquarters, Department of the Army, 1981.

———. *Military Intelligence Battalion (CEWI) (Operations) (Corps).* Field Manual FM 34-21. Washington, DC: Headquarters, Department of the Army, 1982.

———. *Military Intelligence Company (Combat Electronic Warfare and Intelligence) (Armored Cavalry Regiment/Separate Brigade).* Field Manual FM 34-30. Washington, DC: Headquarters, Department of the Army, 1983.

———. *Military Intelligence Group (Combat Electronic Warfare and Intelligence) (Corps).* Field Manual FM 34-20. Washington, DC: Headquarters, Department of the Army, 1983.

—**MULTIPLE EMPLOYMENT** is the concept whereby an attack helicopter unit, because of its mobility, can be assigned more than one mission during a single operation. For example, when employed in reserve, an attack helicopter battalion can simultaneously reinforce ground units with some or all of its companies in one or more locations for a limited time or for specific missions. It can be easily reconstituted to execute a contingency mission elsewhere in the battle. *See also:* Attack Helicopter.

References

Department of Defense, U.S. Army. *Attack Helicopter Operations.* Field Manual FM 17-50. Washington, DC: Headquarters, Department of the Army, 1984.

———. *Operational Terms and Symbols.* Field Manual FM 101-5-1. Washington, DC: Headquarters, Department of the Army, 1985.

—**MULTIPLE-IMPULSE FUZE** is a fuze designed to actuate after a given sequence of impulses of the same nature is applied to it. *See also:* Fuze (Specify Type).

References

Department of Defense, U.S. Army. *Mine/Countermine Operations at the Company Level.* Field Manual FM 20-32. Washington, DC: Headquarters, Department of the Army, 1976.

—**MULTIPLE INTEGRATED LASER SYSTEM** is a family of direct fire simulators, consisting of weapon-mounted laser transmitters and target-mounted receivers, that permits units and weapon systems to maneuver against each other, deliver simulated fires, and receive real-time hit and near-miss assessments.

References

Department of Defense, U.S. Army. *Army Forces Training.* Army Regulation AR 350-41. Washington, DC: Headquarters, Department of the Army, 1986.

—**MULTIPLE LAUNCH ROCKET SYSTEM (MLRS)** is a free-flight, area fire, artillery rocket system. The primary missions of the MLRS are counterfire and suppression of enemy air defenses. It supplements cannon artillery fires by developing large volumes of firepower in a short time against critical, time-sensitive targets. The basic warhead carries improved conventional submunitions. Germany, one of five partners in an international development program, is developing a scatterable mine warhead. In the future, a terminal guidance warhead to defeat armor, or a chemical warhead could be developed.

References

Department of Defense, U.S. Army. *U.S. Army Policy Statement, 1988.* Washington, DC: Headquarters, Department of the Army, 1988.

———. *Weapons Systems: U.S. Army, Navy, and Air Force Directory, 1986-1988.* Washington, DC: DCP, 1986.

—**MULTIPLE UNIT-TRAINING ASSEMBLY (MUTA)** is two or more unit-training assemblies executed during one day or more than one consecutive days. No more than two unit-training assemblies may be performed in one calendar day. The purpose of MUTAs is to consolidate unit-training assemblies in reserve component units to provide instruction of sufficient duration to accomplish the desired training. *See also:* United States Army Reserve.

References

Department of Defense, U.S. Army. *Army Forces Training*. Army Regulation AR 350-41. Washington, DC: Headquarters, Department of the Army, 1986.

—**MUNITIONS** are supplies and equipment needed by military forces for direct military purposes.

References

Department of Defense, U.S. Army. *Dictionary of United States Army Terms*. Army Regulation AR 310-25. Washington, DC: Headquarters, Department of the Army, 1986.

—**MUSTARD H** is a dark, oily, liquid chemical agent that injures the eyes and lungs and blisters the skin. It gives off a garlic or horseradish odor. *See also:* Distilled Mustard.

References

Department of Defense, U.S. Army. *Dictionary of United States Army Terms*. Army Regulation AR 310-25. Washington, DC: Headquarters, Department of the Army, 1986.

—**MUTUAL SUPPORT.** (1) Mutual support is the support that units render to each other against an enemy because of their assigned tasks, relative positions (with respect to each other and the enemy), and their inherent capabilities. It is normally associated with support rendered through fire and movement. (2) Mutual support is a condition that exists when positions are able to support each other by direct fire, thus preventing the enemy from attacking one position without being subjected to direct fire from one or more adjacent positions. In this situation, individual fire units are positioned so that effective fires can be delivered into the dead zone surrounding an adjacent fire unit that results from weapon system characteristics. *See also:* Cross-Servicing, Support.

References

Department of Defense, U.S. Army. *Air Defense Artillery Deployment: Chaparral/Vulcan/ Stinger*. Field Manual FM 44-3. Washington, DC: Headquarters, Department of the Army, 1984.

————. *Air Defense Employment*. Field Manual FM 44-1. Washington, DC: Headquarters, Department of the Army, 1983.

————. *Operational Terms and Symbols*. Field Manual FM 101-5-1. Washington, DC: Headquarters, Department of the Army, 1985.

—**MUZZLE BELL** is a bell-shaped, built-up section at the muzzle of some types of cannon.

References

Department of Defense, U.S. Army. *Dictionary of United States Army Terms*. Army Regulation AR 310-25. Washington, DC: Headquarters, Department of the Army, 1986.

—**MUZZLE BORESIGHT** is a disk with crosshairs, or some other marking, that is fitted into a gun at the muzzle. The crosshairs show the exact center of the bore, along which a soldier sights through another disk that is set into the breech recess of the gun. This allows him to line the bore of the gun on the fixed aiming point in order to make the axis of the bore correspond to the axis of the gun sights. The attachment at the breech is called the breech boresight.

References

Department of Defense, U.S. Army. *Dictionary of United States Army Terms*. Army Regulation AR 310-25. Washington, DC: Headquarters, Department of the Army, 1986.

—**MUZZLE BREAK** is a device attached to the muzzle of a weapon that uses escaping gas to reduce recoil.

References

Department of Defense, Joint Chiefs of Staff. *Department of Defense Dictionary of Military and Related Terms*. Washington, DC: GPO, 1986.

—**MUZZLE BURST** is an explosion, usually premature, of a projectile as it leaves the muzzle of a weapon, or at a very short distance from the weapon.

References

Department of Defense, U.S. Army. *Dictionary of United States Army Terms*. Army Regulation AR 310-25. Washington, DC: Headquarters, Department of the Army, 1986.

—**MUZZLE COMPENSATOR** is a device attached to the muzzle of a weapon that uses escaping gas to control muzzle movement.

References

Department of Defense, Joint Chiefs of Staff. *Department of Defense Dictionary of Military and Related Terms*. Washington, DC: GPO, 1986.

—**MUZZLE VELOCITY** is the velocity of a projectile with respect to the muzzle at the instant the projectile leaves the weapon.

References

Department of Defense, Joint Chiefs of Staff. *Department of Defense Dictionary of Military and Related Terms.* Washington, DC: GPO, 1986.

—**MUZZLE VELOCITY ERROR** is the numerical difference between the corrections that are determined by the application of meteorological data and other known variations and those that are determined at approximately the same time by registration. The error is expressed in meters per second and is assumed to represent the difference between the firing table muzzle velocity and the developed muzzle velocity. *See also:* Muzzle Velocity.

References

Department of Defense, U.S. Army. *Dictionary of United States Army Terms.* Army Regulation AR 310-25. Washington, DC: Headquarters, Department of the Army, 1986.

—**MUZZLE WAVE** is a compression wave or reaction of the air in front of the muzzle of a weapon immediately after it is fired.

References

Department of Defense, U.S. Army. *Dictionary of United States Army Terms.* Army Regulation AR 310-25. Washington, DC: Headquarters, Department of the Army, 1986.

—**NADIR,** in imagery and photoreconnaissance, is the point on the earth that is vertically below or beneath the observer. *See also:* Aerial Reconnaissance; Nadir, Ground; Nadir, Map; Nadir, Photograph.

References

Reeves, Robert; Anson, Abraham; and Landen, David. *Manual of Remote Sensing.* Falls Church, VA: American Society of Photogrammetry, 1975.

—**NADIR, GROUND,** in imagery and photoreconnaissance, is the point on the ground that is vertically beneath the center of the camera lens. *See also:* Nadir.

References

Reeves, Robert; Anson, Abraham; and Landen, David. *Manual of Remote Sensing.* Falls Church, VA: American Society of Photogrammetry, 1975.

—**NADIR, MAP,** in imagery and photoreconnaissance, is the map position for the ground nadir. *See also:* Nadir.

References

Reeves, Robert; Anson, Abraham; and Landen, David. *Manual of Remote Sensing.* Falls Church, VA: American Society of Photogrammetry, 1975.

—**NADIR, PHOTOGRAPH,** in imagery and photoreconnaissance, is the point at which a vertical line through the perspective center of the camera lens pierces the plane of the photograph. This is also referred to as the nadir point. *See also:* Nadir.

References

Reeves, Robert; Anson, Abraham; and Landen, David. *Manual of Remote Sensing.* Falls Church, VA: American Society of Photogrammetry, 1975.

—**NAMED AREAS OF INTEREST (NAI)** are points or areas on the ground, along a particular avenue of approach, through which enemy activity is expected to occur. Activity or lack of activity through an NAI helps to confirm or deny a particular enemy course of action.

References

Department of Defense, U.S. Army. *Operational Terms and Symbols.* Field Manual FM 101-5-1. Washington, DC: Headquarters, Department of the Army, 1985.

—**NAP-OF-THE-EARTH FLIGHT** (ARMY AVIATION) is a flight as close to the earth's surface as vegetation or obstacles will permit, and it generally follows the contours of the earth. The flight's airspeed and altitude vary according to the terrain, weather, and enemy situation.

References

Department of Defense, U.S. Army. *Air Defense Artillery Deployment: Chaparral/Vulcan/Stinger.* Field Manual FM 44.3. Washington, DC: Headquarters, Department of the Army, 1984.

———. *Attack Helicopter Operations.* Field Manual FM 17-50. Washington, DC: Headquarters, Department of the Army, 1984.

———. *Gunnery Training for Attack Helicopters.* Training Circular TC 17-17. Washington, DC: Headquarters, Department of the Army, 1975.

—**NAPALM.** (1) Napalm is powered aluminum soap or a similar compound that is used to gelatinize oil or gasoline for use in napalm bombs or flame throwers. (2) Napalm is the resultant gelatinized substance. *See also:* Chemical Warfare.

References

Department of Defense, Joint Chiefs of Staff. *Department of Defense Dictionary of Military and Related Terms.* Washington, DC: GPO, 1986.

—**NATIONAL AGENCY CHECK (NAC)** is the part of a background investigation that involves a review of the files of government agencies (i.e., the State Department, the Central Intelligence Agency, other military services, and the Immigration and Naturalization Service) and a fingerprint search of Federal Bureau Investigation files for derogatory information about an individual. *See also:* Access, Access Authorization.

References

Allen, Thomas B., and Polmar, Norman. *Merchants of Treason: America's Secrets for Sale.* New York: Delacorte Press, 1988.

Department of Defense, U.S. Army. *Counterintelligence.* Field Manual FM 34-60. Washington, DC: Headquarters, Department of the Army, 1985.

—**NATIONAL CAPTIAL REGION** is the area, including the District of Columbia, within the outer limits of Fairfax, Loudon, and Prince William Counties in Virginia, and Montgomery and Prince George's Counties in Maryland.

References
Department of Defense, U.S. Army. *Dictionary of United States Army Terms*. Army Regulation AR 310-25. Washington, DC: Headquarters, Department of the Army, 1986.

—**NATIONAL CEMETERY** is a burial place for members of the Armed Forces of the United States whose last active service terminated under honorable conditions and for members of their immediate families as authorized by law.

References
Department of Defense, U.S. Army. *Dictionary of United States Army Terms*. Army Regulation AR 310-25. Washington, DC: Headquarters, Department of the Army, 1986.

—**NATIONAL COMMAND** is a command organized by, and functions under the authority of, a specific nation. It may or may not be placed under a NATO commander. *See also:* National Commander.

References
Department of Defense, U.S. Army. *Operational Terms and Symbols*. Field Manual FM 101-5-1. Washington, DC: Headquarters, Department of the Army, 1985.

—**NATIONAL COMMAND AUTHORITY (NCA)** refers to the President and Secretary of Defense or their duly deputized alternates or successors.

References
Department of Defense, Joint Chiefs of Staff. *Department of Defense Dictionary of Military and Related Terms*. Washington, DC: GPO, 1986.

—**NATIONAL COMMANDER** is a commander, territorial or functional, who is not normally in the allied chain of command.

References
Department of Defense, Joint Chiefs of Staff. *Department of Defense Dictionary of Military and Related Terms*. Washington, DC: GPO, 1986.

—**NATIONAL COMPONENT** is composed of any national forces of one or more services that are under the command of a single national commander and are assigned to any NATO commander. *See also:* NATO Command Forces.

References
Department of Defense, Joint Chiefs of Staff. *Department of Defense Dictionary of Military and Related Terms*. Washington, DC: GPO, 1986.

—**NATIONAL COORDINATION CENTER** (AREA COORDINATION CENTER) is a composite organization that includes representatives of local military, paramilitary, and other governmental agencies that are responsible for planning and coordinating internal defense and development operations.

References
Department of Defense, U.S. Army. *Low Intensity Conflict*. Field Manual FM 100-20. Washington, DC: Headquarters, Department of the Army, 1981.

—**NATIONAL DEFENSE** encompasses measures taken by a country or coalition of countries to safeguard their interests and objectives against military attacks by foreign powers. *See also:* Deterrence, National Security.

References
Collins, John M. *U.S.-Soviet Military Balance, 1980-1985*. Washington, DC: Congressional Research Service, 1985.

—**NATIONAL DEFENSE ACT** is an act of Congress that was approved on June 3, 1916, as amended, that provided for the various components of the United States Army and its organization or maintenance.

References
Department of Defense, U.S. Army. *Dictionary of United States Army Terms*. Army Regulation AR 310-25. Washington, DC: Headquarters, Department of the Army, 1986.

—**NATIONAL DEFENSE AREA (NDA)** is an area established on nonfederal lands located within the United States or its possessions or territories for the purpose of safeguarding classified defense information or protecting Department of Defense equipment and/or material. The establishment of a national defense area temporarily places such nonfederal lands under the effective control of the Department of Defense and results only from an emergency event. The senior Department of Defense representative at the scene defines the boundary, marks it with a physical barrier, and posts warning signs. The landowner's consent and cooperation are obtained whenever possible; however, military necessity dictates the final decision regarding the location, shape, and size of the national defense area.

References

Department of Defense, Joint Chiefs of Staff. *Department of Defense Dictionary of Military and Related Terms.* Washington, DC: GPO, 1986.

—**NATIONAL DEFENSE CADET CORPS** is a program of instruction, under the provisions of 10 U.S.C. § 4651, at secondary schools that do not have Reserve Officers' Training Corps training to provide military training that will benefit the student and be of value to the Army if the student becomes a member.

References

Department of Defense, U.S. Army. *Dictionary of United States Army Terms.* Army Regulation AR 310-25. Washington, DC: Headquarters, Department of the Army, 1986.

—**NATIONAL DEFENSE UNIVERSITY (NDU)** is a joint-service, educational institution that was established by the Department of Defense on January 16, 1976. It is composed of two divisions, the National War College and the Industrial College of the Armed Forces, and is located at Fort Leslie J. McNair, Washington, D.C. The university's mission is to insure excellence in professional security (and interrelationships) and to develop executive skills for enhancing the preparation of selected personnel of the Department of Defense, the Department of State, and other government agencies to perform their senior policy, command, and staff functions involving the planning and implementation of national strategy and the management of resources for national security. The university also has three other resident programs. The Defense Strategy Seminar, a compactly structured, parallel two-week resident course, is conducted each summer for about 400 senior officers. The two-week Reserve Component National Security Seminar is presented to selected reserve-component officers at various military installations. A correspondence course on national security management is offered to regular and reserve officers and civilians who hold key positions in the government or in industry, or who may be expected to fill such positions in times of emergency mobilization. *See also:* Industrial College of the Armed Forces, National War College.

References

Department of Defense, U.S. Army. *Dictionary of United States Army Terms.* Army Regulation AR 310-25. Washington, DC: Headquarters, Department of the Army, 1986.

—**NATIONAL EMERGENCY** is a condition that is declared by the President or Congress by virtue of powers vested in them. Such a declaration authorizes certain emergency actions to be taken in the national interest. Such actions may include, partial, full, or total mobilization of the national resources. *See also:* Mobilization.

References

Department of Defense, Joint Chiefs of Staff. *Department of Defense Dictionary of Military and Related Terms.* Washington, DC: GPO, 1986.

—**NATIONAL ENSIGN** is the flag of the United States that is flown from the staff at the stern of ships. *See also:* Garrison Flag.

References

Department of Defense, U.S. Army. *Dictionary of United States Army Terms.* Army Regulation AR 310-25. Washington, DC: Headquarters, Department of the Army, 1986.

—**NATIONAL FORCES FOR THE DEFENSE OF THE NATO AREA** are nonallocated forces whose mission involves the defense of an area within the NATO area of responsibility. *See also:* NATO Command Forces.

References

Department of Defense, Joint Chiefs of Staff. *Department of Defense Dictionary of Military and Related Terms.* Washington, DC: GPO, 1986.

—**NATIONAL GUARD (NG).** *See:* Active National Guard.

—**NATIONAL GUARD OF THE UNITED STATES.** *See:* Army National Guard of the United States.

—**NATIONAL INFRASTRUCTURE** is an infrastructure that is provided and financed by a NATO member in its own territory solely for its own forces (including the forces assigned to or designated for NATO). *See also:* Infrastructure.

References

Department of Defense, Joint Chiefs of Staff. *Department of Defense Dictionary of Military and Related Terms.* Washington, DC: GPO, 1986.

—**NATIONAL INTELLIGENCE** is integrated departmental intelligence that covers the broad aspects of national policy and national security. *See also:* Intelligence.

References

Department of Defense, Joint Chiefs of Staff. *Department of Defense Dictionary of Military and Related Terms.* Washington, DC: GPO, 1986.

—**NATIONAL INTELLIGENCE ASSET** is funded in the National Foreign Intelligence Program. Its primary purpose is to collect or process intelligence information or to produce national intelligence. *See also:* Intelligence.

References

Department of Defense, Defense Intelligence College. *Glossary of Intelligence Terms and Definitions.* Washington, DC: DIC, 1987.

Department of Defense, U.S. Army. *Support Operations: Echelons Above Corps.* Field Manual FM 100-16. Washington, DC: Headquarters, Department of the Army, 1986.

—**NATIONAL INTELLIGENCE ESTIMATE** is a strategic estimate of the capabilities, vulnerabilities, and probable courses of action of foreign nations that is produced at the national level as a composite of the views of the Intelligence Community. *See also:* Intelligence.

References

Department of Defense, Joint Chiefs of Staff. *Department of Defense Dictionary of Military and Related Terms.* Washington, DC: GPO, 1986.

—**NATIONAL INTELLIGENCE SURVEYS** were basic intelligence studies that were produced on a coordinated interdepartmental basis and were concerned with the characteristics, basic resources, and relatively unchanging natural features of a foreign country or other area. *See also:* Intelligence.

References

Department of Defense, Joint Chiefs of Staff. *Department of Defense Dictionary of Military and Related Terms.* Washington, DC: GPO, 1986.

—**NATIONAL INVENTORY CONTROL POINT (NICP)** is an agency of the U.S. Army Materiel Command or the Defense Logistics Agency that is responsible for the worldwide inventory management of certain commodities that have been assigned to that point. The management responsibilities include cataloging, requirements computations, acquisition direction, distribution management, overhaul direction, and disposal direction.

References

Department of Defense, U.S. Army. *Planning Logistics Support for Military Operations.* Field Manual FM 701-58. Washington, DC: Headquarters, Department of the Army, 1987.

—**NATIONAL ITEM IDENTIFICATION NUMBER** is a nine-digit number assigned serially without regard to name, description, or federal supply classification group or class, but denoting the country of origin, to each supply item that is assigned an approved national item identification. It is also the second part of the two-part national/NATO stock number. *See also:* NATO Command Forces.

References

Department of Defense, U.S. Army. *Dictionary of United States Army Terms.* Army Regulation AR 310-25. Washington, DC: Headquarters, Department of the Army, 1986.

—**NATIONAL MAINTENANCE POINT (NMP)** is an organization that provides maintenance guidance to equipment users worldwide. The major functions of an NMP are maintenance engineering, preparing technical publications, providing logistics assistance, and performing maintenance management.

References

Department of Defense, U.S. Army. *Planning Logistics Support for Military Operations.* Field Manual FM 701-58. Washington, DC: Headquarters, Department of the Army, 1987.

—**NATIONAL MILITARY AUTHORITY** is the government agency (e.g., Ministry of Defense or Service Ministry) empowered to make decisions on military matters on behalf of its country. This authority may be delegated to a military or civilian group or to an individual at any level appropriate for dealing with allied commanders or their subordinates.

References

Department of Defense, Joint Chiefs of Staff. *Department of Defense Dictionary of Military and Related Terms.* Washington, DC: GPO, 1986.

—**NATIONAL MILITARY COMMAND CENTER (NMCC).** Located in the Pentagon, the NMCC is the Joint Chiefs of Staff's watch center. Manned around the clock, its watch teams provide the capability to react immediately to unforeseen events. Intelligence support for the NMCC is provided by the Defense Intelligence Agency's Directorate for NMIC Operations. Defense Intelligence Agency mans the National Military Intelligence Center, which is located next to the NMCC so that it can provide the maximum degree of intelligence support to the NMCC team.

The NMCC is the result of years of search to find the appropriate system to provide adequate intelligence and operational response to both the President and other national-level personages and to the operational commanders. Today, it is linked to the watch centers of the services, of the National Security Agency, and of other Intelligence Community members through the National Operations and Intelligence Watch Officers' Net. This allows all watch officers to converse immediately on events as they occur. In addition, the NMCC has the collection assets of the entire Intelligence Community at its disposal, and communications systems that allow it to converse with and support fully the operational commanders. *See also:* Intelligence.

References

Von Hoene, John P. A. *Intelligence User's Guide.* Washington, DC: DIA, 1983.

—**NATIONAL MILITARY COMMAND SYSTEM (NMCS)** is a primary component of the Worldwide Military Command and Control System designed to support the National Command Authorities and the Joint Chiefs of Staff exercise their responsibilities. *See also:* Intelligence.

References

Department of Defense, U.S. Army. *Planning Logistics Support for Military Operations.* Field Manual FM 701-58. Washington, DC: Headquarters, Department of the Army, 1987.

—**NATIONAL OBJECTIVES** are the fundamental aims, goals, or purposes of a nation—as opposed to the means for seeking these ends—toward which a policy is directed and efforts and resources of a country are applied. National objectives are usually articulated by the national leadership. *See also:* National Policy.

References

Department of Defense, Joint Chiefs of Staff. *Department of Defense Dictionary of Military and Related Terms.* Washington, DC: GPO, 1986.

—**NATIONAL POLICY** is a broad course of action or statements of guidance adopted by the government at the national level in pursuit of national objectives. *See also:* National Objectives.

References

Department of Defense, Joint Chiefs of Staff. *Department of Defense Dictionary of Military and Related Terms.* Washington, DC: GPO, 1986.

—**NATIONAL SALUTE.** (1) A national salute is a salute of 21 guns in honor of a national flag, the ruler of a foreign country, and under certain circumstances, the present or former President of the United States. (2) A national salute is a salute of 50 guns, one for each state, that is fired at noon on July 4th, to commemorate the signing of the Declaration of Independence. In this meaning, it is usually called the Salute to the Union.

References

Department of Defense, U.S. Army. *Dictionary of United States Army Terms.* Army Regulation AR 310-25. Washington, DC: Headquarters, Department of the Army, 1986.

—**NATIONAL SECURITY.** (1) National security is the territorial integrity, sovereignty, and international freedom of action of the United States. Intelligence activities relating to national security encompass all the military, economic, political, scientific and technological, and other aspects of foreign governments that pose actual or potential threats to U.S. interests. (2) The Joint Chiefs of Staff define national security as a collective term that encompasses both national defense and the foreign relations of the United States. Specifically, it is a condition provided by a military or defense advantage over any foreign nation or group of nations, a favorable foreign relations position, or a defense posture capable of successfully resisting hostile or destructive action from within or without, overt or covert.

References

Department of Defense, Defense Intelligence College. *Glossary of Intelligence Terms and Definitions.* Washington, DC: DIC, 1987.

Department of Defense, Joint Chiefs of Staff. *Department of Defense Dictionary of Military and Related Terms.* Washington, DC: GPO, 1986.

—**NATIONAL SERVICE LIFE INSURANCE** is government life insurance that is available upon application to all persons in active military service between October 8, 1940, and April 25, 1951. Also, prior to April 25, 1951, this insurance was available to people after separation from service if they had service between October 8, 1940, and September 2, 1945. After April 25, 1951, new insurance was available only to the following groups of individuals meeting specific requirements: (1) persons released from active service under other than dishonorable conditions with a service-connected disability; (2) individuals separated prior to January 1, 1957, who were ordered to active duty for 31 days or more (this insurance was available only within 120 days after separation); (3) individuals who surrendered permanent plans of National Service Life Insurance for cash while on active duty between April 25, 1951, and January 1, 1957; and (4) individuals who had term National Service Life Insurance and the term period expired prior to January 1, 1957, while the person was on active duty or within 120 days after separation. *See also:* United States Government Life Insurance.

References

Department of Defense, U.S. Army. *Dictionary of United States Army Terms.* Army Regulation AR 310-25. Washington, DC: Headquarters, Department of the Army, 1986.

—**NATIONAL STRATEGY** is the art and science of developing and using the political, economic, and psychological powers of a nation, together with its armed forces, during peace and war, to secure the achievement of national objectives. *See also:* Strategy.

References

Department of Defense, Joint Chiefs of Staff. *Department of Defense Dictionary of Military and Related Terms.* Washington, DC: GPO, 1986.

—**NATIONAL/TACTICAL INTERFACE** is the relationship between national and tactical intelligence activities and encompasses the full range of fiscal, technical, operational, and programmatic matters. *See also:* Intelligence, Strategic Intelligence.

References

Department of Defense, Defense Intelligence College. *Glossary of Intelligence Terms and Definitions.* Washington, DC: DIC, 1987.

Department of Defense, U.S. Army. *Support Operations: Echelons Above Corps.* Field Manual FM 100-16. Washington, DC: Headquarters, Department of the Army, 1986.

—**NATIONAL TECHNICAL MEANS (NTM)** was the term used in the SALT I agreement to refer to U.S. and Soviet reconnaissance and other satellites that could be used to monitor compliance with the agreement. The term is still used and means reconnaissance and other surveillance satellites. *See also:* Intelligence.

References

Lowenthal, Mark M. *U.S. Intelligence: Evolution and Anatomy.* New York: Praeger, 1984.

—**NATIONAL TRAINING CENTER (NTC),** located at Fort Irwin, California, is the Army's key facility for training mechanized and armored battalion task forces. It provides two weeks of advanced, intensive combat training on a rotational basis in a general environment that is comparable to Europe, North Africa, or the Middle East.

References

Department of Defense, U.S. Army. *Army Exercises.* Army Regulation AR 350-28. Washington, DC: Headquarters, Department of the Army, 1985.

————. *Army Forces Training.* Army Regulation AR 350-41. Washington, DC: Headquarters, Department of the Army, 1986.

————. *U.S. Army Policy Statement, 1988.* Washington, DC: Headquarters, Department of the Army, 1988.

—**NATIONAL WAR COLLEGE (NWC),** located on Fort Leslie J. McNair, Washington, D.C., is a part of the National Defense University. The college offers a ten-month curriculum to O5-O6 military officers (lieutenant colonel-colonel) and to civilians in equivalent grades. It is the only U.S. government program of study dedicated to national security policy formulation and the planning and implementation of national strategy. It is a senior service college course of study jointly sponsored by the Department of State and the Department of Defense. It is designed to promote excellence in the formulation of national security policy and strategy and to enhance the preparation of selected personnel in the Armed forces, the Department of State, and other U.S. departments and agencies to perform the high-level command and staff policy functions that are associated with national strategy formulation and implementation. The curriculum includes study and research in national security policy formulation, strategic planning and decisionmaking, trends in the international environment, security implications of major state and regional foreign and defense policies, and the role of joint and combined use of military power. *See also:* Industrial College of the Armed Forces, National Defense University.

References
Defense Intelligence Agency. *Training Compendium for General Defense Career Development Program (IDCP) Personnel DOD 1430.10M3-TNG.* Washington, DC: DIA, 1986.

Turner, Stansfield. *Secrecy and Democracy: The CIA in Transition.* Boston: Houghton Mifflin, 1985.

—**NATO COMMAND FORCES** are forces in being that nations have placed under the operational command or operational control of a NATO commander at a specified stage, state, or measure in the NATO alert system or as prescribed in special agreements. *See also:* Force, National Component, National Forces for the Defense of the NATO Area, National Item Identification Number, NATO Commander, NATO Military Authority, NATO Preparation Time, NATO Warning Time, NATO-Wide Exercise.

References
Department of Defense, Joint Chiefs of Staff. *Department of Defense Dictionary of Military and Related Terms.* Washington, DC: GPO, 1986.

Department of Defense, U.S. Army. *U.S. Army Policy Statement, 1988.* Washington, DC: Headquarters, Department of the Army, 1988.

—**NATO COMMANDER**, or allied commander, is a military commander in the NATO chain of command. *See also:* NATO Command Forces.

References
Department of Defense, Joint Chiefs of Staff. *Department of Defense Dictionary of Military and Related Terms.* Washington, DC: GPO, 1986.

—**NATO-EARMARKED FORCES** are forces that nations agree to place under the operational command or operational control of a NATO commander at some future time. *See also:* Force.

References
Department of Defense, Joint Chiefs of Staff. *Department of Defense Dictionary of Military and Related Terms.* Washington, DC: GPO, 1986.

—**NATO MILITARY AUTHORITY** is any international military headquarters or organization covered by the Protocol on the Status of International Military Headquarters set up pursuant to the North Atlantic Treaty (called the Paris Protocol) or any other military authority to which the NATO Council has applied the provisions of the Agreement on the Status of the North Atlantic Treaty Organization, National Representatives and International Staff (called the Ottawa Agreement) by virtue of the agreement. *See also:* NATO Command Forces.

References
Department of Defense, Joint Chiefs of Staff. *Department of Defense Dictionary of Military and Related Terms.* Washington, DC: GPO, 1986.

—**NATO PREPARATION TIME** is the time between the receipt of authorization from NATO political authorities for major NATO commanders to implement military measures to counter an impending attack and the start of the attack. *See also:* NATO Warning Time.

References
Department of Defense, Joint Chiefs of Staff. *Department of Defense Dictionary of Military and Related Terms.* Washington, DC: GPO, 1986.

—**NATO WARNING TIME** is the time between the recognition by a major NATO commander or higher NATO authority that an attack is impending and the start of the attack. *See also:* NATO Preparation Time.

References
Department of Defense, Joint Chiefs of Staff. *Department of Defense Dictionary of Military and Related Terms.* Washington, DC: GPO, 1986.

—**NAUTICAL TWILIGHT** is the time between the instant that the center of the sun's disk is six degrees below the horizon and the instant that the center of the sun is twelve degrees below the horizon. Nautical twilight provides enough illumination to carry on most ground movement activities without difficulty and approaches conditions expected under full daylight.

References
Department of Defense, U.S. Army. *Weather Support for Army Tactical Operations.* Field Manual FM 34-81. Washington, DC: Headquarters, Department of the Army, 1984.

—**NBC DEFENSE** is nuclear defense, biological defense, and chemical defense, collectively. The term is not used in the context of U.S. offensive operations. *See also:* Biological Warfare, Chemical Warfare, Nuclear Warfare.

References
Department of Defense, Joint Chiefs of Staff. *Department of Defense Dictionary of Military and Related Terms.* Washington, DC: GPO, 1986.

—**NEAR AMBUSH** is an ambush in which the attack force assaults into the killing zone. *See also:* Ambush, Killing Zone.

References
Department of Defense, U.S. Army. *The Rifle Squads (Mechanized and Light Infantry).* Training Circular TC 7-1. Washington, DC: Headquarters, Department of the Army, 1976.

—**NEAR SURFACE BURST** is a nuclear burst occurring low enough in the atmosphere for the fireball to contact the earth's surface. It causes fallout. *See also:* Nuclear Warfare.

References
Department of Defense, U.S. Army. *Nuclear Weapons Employment Doctrine and Procedures.* Field Manual FM 101-31-1. Washington, DC: Headquarters, Department of the Army, 1986.

—**NEED-TO-KNOW** means that an individual is not authorized access to classified material based solely upon his rank, office, position, or level of security clearance. Rather, access to such material is granted by the custodian of the classified information only when a valid need for the information exists. The custodian must also verify that the recipient has the appropriate clearance to have access to the information. *See also:* Access, Need-to-Know Principle.

References
Clancy, Tom. *The Cardinal of the Kremlin.* New York: Putnam, 1988.

—**NEED-TO-KNOW PRINCIPLE** is a general intelligence term. It is a determination by an authorized holder of classified information that access to specific classified material in his possession is required by one or more persons so that they can perform a specific and authorized function that is essential to accomplish a national security task or as required by federal statute, Executive Order, or other directly applicable regulation. In addition to an established "need to know," a person must have an appropriate security clearance and access approval prior to receiving the classified material. *See also:* Access, Need-to-Know.

References
Department of Defense, Joint Chiefs of Staff. *Department of Defense Dictionary of Military and Related Terms.* Washington, DC: GPO, 1986.

—**NEGLECT,** in naval gunfire support, is a report to the observer or spotter indicating that the last round was fired with incorrect data and that the next round or rounds will be fired using correct data.

References
Department of Defense, Joint Chiefs of Staff. *Department of Defense Dictionary of Military and Related Terms.* Washington, DC: GPO, 1986.

—**NEGLIGIBLE RISK** (NUCLEAR) is the measure of troop safety that provides the least risk to friendly troops. It is used to compute the minimum safe distance from a nuclear detonation. It is associated with a maximum of one percent incidence of casualties or 2.5 percent incidence of nuisance effects. Negligible risk should not be exceeded unless there is a significant tactical advantage to be gained. It is expressed in terms of risk to unwarned, exposed personnel; warned, exposed personnel; and warned, protected personnel. *See also:* Degree of Risk (Nuclear), Emergency Risk (Nuclear), Moderate Risk (Nuclear), Troop Safety.

References
Department of Defense, U.S. Army. *NBC Decontamination.* Field Manual FM 3-5. Washington, DC: Headquarters, Department of the Army, 1985.

———. *Operational Terms and Symbols.* Field Manual FM 101-5-1. Washington, DC: Headquarters, Department of the Army, 1985.

—**NERVE AGENT** is a lethal agent that causes paralysis by interfering with the transmission of nerve impulses. *See also:* Chemical Warfare.

References
Department of Defense, Joint Chiefs of Staff. *Department of Defense Dictionary of Military and Related Terms.* Washington, DC: GPO, 1986.

—**NET** (COMMUNICATIONS) is an organization of stations that is capable of direct communications on a common channel or frequency. *See also:* Net Authentication, Net Call Sign, Net Control Station.

References
Department of Defense, Joint Chiefs of Staff. *Department of Defense Dictionary of Military and Related Terms.* Washington, DC: GPO, 1986.

—**NET AUTHENTICATION** is an authentication procedure by which a net control station authenticates itself, and all other stations in the net systematically establish their validity.

References

Department of Defense, U.S. Army. *Dictionary of United States Army Terms*. Army Regulation AR 310-25. Washington, DC: Headquarters, Department of the Army, 1986.

—**NET CALL SIGN** is a call sign that represents all stations within the net. *See also:* Call Sign, Net Authentication.

References

Department of Defense, Joint Chiefs of Staff. *Department of Defense Dictionary of Military and Related Terms*. Washington, DC: GPO, 1986.

—**NET CONTROL STATION (NCS)** is a communications station that is designated to control traffic and enforce circuit discipline within a given net.

References

Department of Defense, U.S. Army. *Communications Techniques: Electronics Countermeasures*. Field Manual FM 24-33. Washington, DC: Headquarters, Department of the Army, 1985.

—**NET INVENTORY ASSETS** are the portion of the total materiel assets designated to meet the materiel inventory objective (i.e., the total materiel assets less the peacetime materiel consumption and losses through normal appropriation and procurement lead-time periods).

References

Department of Defense, Joint Chiefs of Staff. *Department of Defense Dictionary of Military and Related Terms*. Washington, DC: GPO, 1986.

—**NET WEIGHT** is the weight of a ground vehicle without fuel, engine oil, coolant, on-vehicle materiel, cargo, or operating personnel.

References

Department of Defense, Joint Chiefs of Staff. *Department of Defense Dictionary of Military and Related Terms*. Washington, DC: GPO, 1986.

—**NEUTRAL** is a meteorological condition that exists when conditions are between lapse and inversion. Neutral conditions tending toward lapse favor production of smoke curtains, while neutral conditions tending toward inversion favor smoke-blanket screens. *See also:* Lapse, Smoke Blanket, Smoke Screen.

References

Department of Defense, U.S. Army. *Deliberate Smoke Operations*. Field Manual FM 3-50. Washington, DC: Headquarters, Department of the Army, 1984.

—**NEUTRAL BURNING** is the burning of a single grain of propellant in two opposing directions. The initial diameter of the perforation is controlled so that the total burning surface changes little during the burning.

References

Department of Defense, U.S. Army. *Dictionary of United States Army Terms*. Army Regulation AR 310-25. Washington, DC: Headquarters, Department of the Army, 1986.

—**NEUTRALITY,** in international law, is the attitude of impartiality, during periods of war, adopted by third states toward belligerents and is recognized by the belligerents. In a U.S. enforcement action, the rules of neutrality apply to impartial members of the United Nations except insofar as they are excluded under the United Nations Charter.

References

Department of Defense, Joint Chiefs of Staff. *Department of Defense Dictionary of Military and Related Terms*. Washington, DC: GPO, 1986.

Department of Defense, U.S. Army. *Dictionary of United States Army Terms*. Army Regulation AR 310-25. Washington, DC: Headquarters, Department of the Army, 1986.

—**NEUTRALIZATION,** in mine warfare, occurs when a mine has been rendered, by external means, incapable of detonation as a target passes, but may remain dangerous to handle. *See also:* Mine Warfare.

References

Department of Defense, Joint Chiefs of Staff. *Department of Defense Dictionary of Military and Related Terms*. Washington, DC: GPO, 1986.

—**NEUTRALIZATION FIRE** is fire delivered to hamper and interrupt enemy movement or enemy weapons fire.

References

Department of Defense, U.S. Army. *Fire Support in Combined Arms Operations*. Field Manual FM 6-20. Washington, DC: Headquarters, Department of the Army, 1983.

————. *Operational Terms and Symbols*. Field Manual FM 101-5-1. Washington, DC: Headquarters, Department of the Army, 1985.

—**NEUTRALIZE.** (1) To neutralize is to render ineffective or unusable. (2) To neutralize is to render enemy equipment or personnel incapable of interfering with a particular operation. (3) To neutralize is to make harmless anything contaminated with a chemical agent. *See also:* Chemical Warfare.

References

Department of Defense, U.S. Army. *Operational Terms and Symbols.* Field Manual FM 101-5-1. Washington, DC: Headquarters, Department of the Army, 1985.

—**NEUTRALIZED AREA** is an area whose independence and integrity (inviolability) have been conferred and guaranteed by a treaty.

References

Department of Defense, U.S. Army. *Dictionary of United States Army Terms.* Army Regulation AR 310-25. Washington, DC: Headquarters, Department of the Army, 1986.

—**NEUTRON-INDUCED ACTIVITY** is radioactivity induced in the ground or in an object as a result of its direct irradiation by neutrons.

References

Department of Defense, Joint Chiefs of Staff. *Department of Defense Dictionary of Military and Related Terms.* Washington, DC: GPO, 1986.

—**NEW EQUIPMENT QUALIFICATION TRAINING** includes service school courses and on-the-job training. It is directed by a major commander or higher authority, and concerns a change in unit's mission or equipment.

References

Department of Defense, U.S. Army. *Enlisted Personnel Management System.* Army Regulation AR 600-200. Washington, DC: Headquarters, Department of the Army, 1984.

—**NEW EQUIPMENT TRAINING** concerns the identification and training of teachers, the development of training aids, and the teaching of soldiers concerning new equipment. *See also:* New Equipment Qualification Training.

References

Department of Defense, U.S. Army. *Army Forces Training.* Army Regulation AR 350-41. Washington, DC: Headquarters, Department of the Army, 1986.

—**NEW MANNING SYSTEM (NMS)** is a personnel management system that is designed to increase the combat effectiveness of the Army by stabilizing individuals in a unit. The goal is to reduce personnel turbulence in combat arms

(in both the company and the battalion) and to develop a greater sense of esprit among all soldiers. Coupled with the stabilization of the units is the movement of these units overseas within designated regimental pairings. The NMS is composed of two subsystems: the COHORT Unit Movement System and the U.S. Army Regional System. *See also:* Cohesion Operational Readiness Training Unit Replacement for the Active Army, Regimental Affiliation.

References

Department of Defense, U.S. Army. *Army Forces Training.* Army Regulation AR 350-41. Washington, DC: Headquarters, Department of the Army, 1986.

—**NEW WORK,** in repairs and utilities operations, encompasses the additions, alterations, and deletions required by changed conditions; the restorations necessitated by disasters; and minor new construction to real property.

References

Department of Defense, U.S. Army. *Dictionary of United States Army Terms.* Army Regulation AR 310-25. Washington, DC: Headquarters, Department of the Army, 1986.

—**NIGHT INTERCEPTION** is an air interception occurring in darkness. Night interceptions are normally controlled interceptions.

References

Department of Defense, U.S. Army. *Dictionary of United States Army Terms.* Army Regulation AR 310-25. Washington, DC: Headquarters, Department of the Army, 1986.

—**NIGHT LANDING** is a landing in which the troops being transported are scheduled to reach their first objective under the cover of darkness.

References

Department of Defense, U.S. Army. *Dictionary of United States Army Terms.* Army Regulation AR 310-25. Washington, DC: Headquarters, Department of the Army, 1986.

—**NIGHT TRAFFIC LINE** is a line beyond which wheeled vehicles are not permitted to pass during darkness.

References

Department of Defense, U.S. Army. *Dictionary of United States Army Terms.* Army Regulation AR 310-25. Washington, DC: Headquarters, Department of the Army, 1986.

—**NIGHT VISION DEVICE**, or night observation device, is a viewer that allows an operator to see in the dark.

References

Department of Defense, U.S. Army. *Deliberate Smoke Operations*. Field Manual FM 3-50. Washington, DC: Headquarters, Department of the Army, 1984.

—**NIKE HERCULES MISSILE SYSTEM** is an Army long-range, surface-to-air, air defense guided missile system provides nuclear or conventional defense against manned bombers and air-breathing missiles. The system is designed to operate in either a mobile or fixed-site configuration and has a capability of performing surface-to-surface missions. It is designated as the MIM-14.

References

Department of Defense, Joint Chiefs of Staff. *Department of Defense Dictionary of Military and Related Terms*. Washington, DC: GPO, 1986.

Department of Defense, U.S. Army. *Air Defense Employment*. Field Manual FM 44-1. Washington, DC: Headquarters, Department of the Army, 1983.

—**9-MM PERSONAL DEFENSE WEAPON** is replacing the .45M1911A1 caliber pistol and various .38 caliber revolvers that are currently used by the services. The 9-mm, a semiautomatic pistol that fires 9-mm NATO ammunition, has greater firepower and a better safety mechanism than .38 caliber revolver, and has double action.

References

Department of Defense, U.S. Army. *U.S. Army Policy Statement, 1988*. Washington, DC: Headquarters, Department of the Army, 1988.

—**NITROCELLULOSE** is a chemical substance formed by the action of a mixture of nitric and sulfuric acids on cotton or some other form of cellulose. Guncotton, an explosive, is a nitrocellulose that has a very high nitrogen content.

References

Department of Defense, U.S. Army. *Dictionary of United States Army Terms*. Army Regulation AR 310-25. Washington, DC: Headquarters, Department of the Army, 1986.

—**NO-FIRE AREA (NFA)**, in fire support operations, is a designated area into which no fires or effects from fire are allowed. The exceptions are when the establishing headquarters approves fires temporarily within the NFA on a mission basis and when the enemy force within the NFA engages a friendly force. The commander may engage the enemy to defend his force. *See also:* No-Fire Line.

References

Department of Defense, U.S. Army. *Fire Support in Combined Arms Operations*. Field Manual FM 6-20. Washington, DC: Headquarters, Department of the Army, 1983.

————. *Operational Terms and Symbols*. Field Manual FM 101-5-1. Washington, DC: Headquarters, Department of the Army, 1985.

—**NO-FIRE LINE** is a line in front of which artillery does not fire except on request or approval of the supported commander. Artillery may fire beyond the line at any time without endangering friendly forces. *See also:* No-Fire Area.

References

Department of Defense, Joint Chiefs of Staff. *Department of Defense Dictionary of Military and Related Terms*. Washington, DC: GPO, 1986.

—**NO-STRIKE TARGET LIST** is a list designated by a commander of the targets not to be destroyed. The destruction of targets on the list would interfere with or unduly hamper projected friendly military operations or friendly relations with indigenous personnel or governments.

References

Department of Defense, Joint Chiefs of Staff. *Department of Defense Dictionary of Military and Related Terms*. Washington, DC: GPO, 1986.

—**NO-YEAR APPROPRIATION** is an appropriation account available for incurring obligations until it is exhausted or until the purpose for which it was designated is accomplished. There is no fixed time restriction on the account.

References

Department of Defense, U.S. Army. *Dictionary of United States Army Terms*. Army Regulation AR 310-25. Washington, DC: Headquarters, Department of the Army, 1986.

—**NODE.** (1) A node is a location in a mobility system where a movement requirement is originated, processed for onward movement, or terminated. (2) A node is a point in a standing or stationary wave at which the amplitude is minimum. (3) In a switched communications network, nodes are the switching points, which may also include the patching and control facilities.

References

Department of Defense, Joint Chiefs of Staff. *Department of Defense Dictionary of Military and Related Terms.* Washington, DC: GPO, 1986.

Department of Defense, U.S. Army. *Dictionary of United States Army Terms.* Army Regulation AR 310-25. Washington, DC: Headquarters, Department of the Army, 1986.

—**NOISE,** in electronic warfare, is any unwanted receiver response other than another signal (i.e., interference). *See also:* Electronic Warfare.

References

Department of Defense, Joint Chiefs of Staff. *Department of Defense Dictionary of Military and Related Terms.* Washington, DC: GPO, 1986.

—**NOISE JAMMING,** in electronic warfare, is deliberate interference by using jamming signals that are random and essentially unsynchronized with the target radar. *See also:* Electronic Warfare, Jamming.

References

Department of Defense, Joint Chiefs of Staff. *Department of Defense Dictionary of Military and Related Terms.* Washington, DC: GPO, 1986.

—**NOISE-MODULATED JAMMING,** in electronic warfare, is random electronic noise that appears as background noise and tends to mask the desired signal. *See also:* Electronic Warfare, Jamming.

References

Department of Defense, Joint Chiefs of Staff. *Department of Defense Dictionary of Military and Related Terms.* Washington, DC: GPO, 1986.

—**NON-ALOC (AIR LINE OF COMMUNICATIONS) ITEMS** are supply items that are oversized or so heavy that they are not normally airlifted to an operating military force. This includes all classes of supply except ALOC class IX and selected items of class II. *See also:* Supplies.

References

Department of Defense, U.S. Army. *Support Operations: Echelons Above Corps.* Field Manual FM 100-16. Washington, DC: Headquarters, Department of the Army, 1986.

—**NONAPPROPRIATED FUND ACTIVITY (NAFA)** is an entity established by the Secretary of the Army for the purpose of administering monies that are not appropriated by the Congress for the benefit of the Army's military personnel or civilian employees and not incorporated under the laws of any state or the District of Columbia. Nonappropriated fund activities are instrumentalities of the United States. *See also:* Nonappropriated Funds.

References

Department of Defense, U.S. Army. *Dictionary of United States Army Terms.* Army Regulation AR 310-25. Washington, DC: Headquarters, Department of the Army, 1986.

—**NONAPPROPRIATE FUNDS** are funds generated by the Department of Defense military and civilian personnel and their dependents and are used to augment funds that have been appropriated by Congress. Their purpose is to provide a comprehensive, morale-building welfare, religious, educational, and recreational program that is designed to enhance the well-being of military and civilian personnel and their dependents.

References

Department of Defense, Joint Chiefs of Staff. *Department of Defense Dictionary of Military and Related Terms.* Washington, DC: GPO, 1986.

—**NONBATTLE CASUALTY** is a person who is not a battle casualty, but is lost to his organization because of disease or injury (which includes dying from disease or injury) or because he is missing and his absence does not appear to be voluntary or due to enemy action or to being interned. *See also:* Medical Treatment.

References

Department of Defense, Joint Chiefs of Staff. *Department of Defense Dictionary of Military and Related Terms.* Washington, DC: GPO, 1986.

—**NONBATTLE INJURY** is a category for all traumatisms except old traumatisms or battle injuries and wounds. "Traumatism" refers to a condition of ill health caused by an external agent. It includes conditions resulting from acute poisonings (even though taken internally) and from exposure to heat, cold, or light. Food poisonings and food infections due to food containing nonbacterial poisons are classified as nonbattle injuries. Injuries due to the elements (e.g., frostbite and immersion injury) are considered nonbattle injuries even when they are incurred in combat areas. *See also:* Medical Treatment.

References

Department of Defense, U.S. Army. *Planning for Health Service Support*. Field Manual FM 8-55. Washington, DC: Headquarters, Department of the Army, 1985.

—**NONBORESAFE FUZE** is a fuze that does not have a safety device to prevent the premature explosion of the main charge of a projectile while it is still in the bore of a gun.

References

Department of Defense, U.S. Army. *Dictionary of United States Army Terms*. Army Regulation AR 310-25. Washington, DC: Headquarters, Department of the Army, 1986.

—**NONCOMMISSIONED OFFICER (NCO)** is an enlisted man excluding a specialist, who has been appointed in paygrade E-4 or higher. Such personnel normally fill positions where leadership qualities are required. *See also:* Member, Enlisted Person.

References

Department of Defense, U.S. Army. *Dictionary of United States Army Terms*. Army Regulation AR 310-25. Washington, DC: Headquarters, Department of the Army, 1986.

—**NONCOMMISSIONED OFFICER EDUCATION SYSTEM (NCOES)** is a system of resident training (service school and NCO academy), supervised on-the-job training, self-study, and on-the-job experience. It provides job-related training for NCOs and specialists throughout their careers. The leaders instruct and develop their NCOs through formal NCO training and job experiences that complement the NCOES.

References

Department of Defense, U.S. Army. *Unit Training Management*. Field Manual FM 25-2. Washington, DC: Headquarters, Department of the Army, 1984.

—**NONCONTIGUOUS FACILITY** is a facility for which a Service has operational responsibility, but that is not located on, or in the vicinity of, a base complex of that Service. Its area includes only the facility occupied, and the minimum surrounding area necessary for close-in security.

References

Department of Defense, Joint Chiefs of Staff. *Department of Defense Dictionary of Military and Related Terms*. Washington, DC: GPO, 1986.

—**NONDELAY FUZE** is a fuze that functions as a result of the inertia of the firing pin (or primer) that results from the missile's retardation as it penetrates the target. The inertia causes the firing pin to strike the primer (or causes the primer to strike the pin), initiating the fuze action. This type of fuze is inherently slower in action than the super-quick or instantaneous fuze, since its action depends on the deceleration (retardation) of the missile during its penetration of the target. *See also:* Fuze (Specify Type).

References

Department of Defense, U.S. Army. *Dictionary of United States Army Terms*. Army Regulation AR 310-25. Washington, DC: Headquarters, Department of the Army, 1986.

—**NONDETERIORATING SUPPLIES** are items expected to be useful for a long period of time, which is usually specified.

References

Department of Defense, U.S. Army. *Dictionary of United States Army Terms*. Army Regulation AR 310-25. Washington, DC: Headquarters, Department of the Army, 1986.

—**NONDUTY STATUS** is the status of an officer or enlisted person who, for any reason (e.g., arrest, leave, sickness, confinement, or absence without leave) is not available for duty with the organization to which he belongs. This category does not apply to an individual who has been granted an authorized absence.

References

Department of Defense, U.S. Army. *Dictionary of United States Army Terms*. Army Regulation AR 310-25. Washington, DC: Headquarters, Department of the Army, 1986.

—**NONEFFECTIVE RATE** is the measure of the effect on the strength of the command of personnel who are excused from duty expressed as a ratio of the number of patients (noneffectives) at a given period to the strength over the period in thousands. The noneffective rate may be based upon all patients who are excused from duty or it may be specifically due to a particular disease or injury group or entity. The rate may be computed for a particular area, command, or for the entire Army.

References

Department of Defense, U.S. Army. *Dictionary of United States Army Terms*. Army Regulation AR 310-25. Washington, DC: Headquarters, Department of the Army, 1986.

—**NONESSENTIAL MAINTENANCE OPERATION** is a maintenance operation that may be deferred indefinitely under conditions set forth in the usage profile without appreciably degrading the end-item's performance.

References

Department of Defense, U.S. Army. *Maintenance and Repair Parts Consumption Planning Guide for Contingency Operations.* Field Manual FM 42-9-23. Washington, DC: Headquarters, Department of the Army, 1980.

—**NONEXPENDABLE PROPERTY** include items that are not consumed in use and that keep their original identity. Such items must be accounted for during their entire usage lives. *See also:* Nonexpendable Supplies and Materiel.

References

Department of Defense, U.S. Army. *Commander's Handbook for Property Accountability at the Unit Level.* Field Manual FM 10-14-1. Washington, DC: Headquarters, Department of the Army, 1984.

—**NONEXPENDABLE SUPPLIES AND MATERIEL** are supplies that are not consumed in use and that retain their original identity while being used (e.g., weapons, machines, tools, and equipment). *See also:* Nonexpendable Property.

References

Department of Defense, Joint Chiefs of Staff. *Department of Defense Dictionary of Military and Related Terms.* Washington, DC: GPO, 1986.

—**NONFIXED MEDICAL TREATMENT FACILITY** is a mobile medical treatment facility that can be moved from place to place. *See also:* Medical Treatment.

References

Department of Defense, Joint Chiefs of Staff. *Department of Defense Dictionary of Military and Related Terms.* Washington, DC: GPO, 1986.

—**NONJUDICIAL PUNISHMENT** entails light punishments and other corrective measures imposed by a commanding officer on any military person who does not demand a trial by court-martial. *See also:* Uniform Code of Military Justice.

References

Department of Defense, U.S. Army. *Dictionary of United States Army Terms.* Army Regulation AR 310-25. Washington, DC: Headquarters, Department of the Army, 1986.

—**NONMETALLIC MINE** is a mine whose casing is not made of metal and contains only small quantities of metal. *See also:* Mine Warfare.

References

Department of Defense, U.S. Army. *Mine/Countermine Operations at the Company Level.* Field Manual FM 20-32. Washington, DC: Headquarters, Department of the Army, 1976.

—**NONOPERATING STRENGTH** applies to the present and the absent strength of an organization classified under "personnel status" of the morning report heading as trainees, students, patients, or other categories on nonpermanent party personnel. It does not include individuals who are in transit to or from the command.

References

Department of Defense, U.S. Army. *Dictionary of United States Army Terms.* Army Regulation AR 310-25. Washington, DC: Headquarters, Department of the Army, 1986.

—**NONPAY STATUS** is the status of an officer or enlisted person who is not entitled to receive pay while in a nonduty status (e.g., when he is not available for duty with his unit because of neglect or causes that are his own fault). Absence without leave and time lost from duty because of illness due to the soldier's fault are cases in which a soldier is placed in a nonpay status. *See also:* Disciplinary Action.

References

Department of Defense, U.S. Army. *Dictionary of United States Army Terms.* Army Regulation AR 310-25. Washington, DC: Headquarters, Department of the Army, 1986.

—**NONPERISHABLE ITEM** is food that does not require refrigeration during its shipment or storage.

References

Department of Defense, U.S. Army. *Dictionary of United States Army Terms.* Army Regulation AR 310-25. Washington, DC: Headquarters, Department of the Army, 1986.

—**NONPERSISTENT** characterizes fielded chemicals that are expected to remain not long at the point of dissemination. *See also:* Chemical Warfare.

References

Department of Defense, U.S. Army. *Technical Escort Operations.* Field Manual FM 3-20. Washington, DC: Headquarters, Department of the Army, 1981.

—**NONPERSISTENT AGENT** is a chemical agent that, when released, dissipates or loses its ability to cause casualties after ten to fifteen minutes. *See also:* Chemical Warfare.

References

Department of Defense, Joint Chiefs of Staff. *Department of Defense Dictionary of Military and Related Terms.* Washington, DC: GPO, 1986.

—**NONPRIOR SERVICE PERSONNEL** are individuals who have no prior military service and receive a commission in or enlist directly into an Armed Force of the United States. *See also:* Member, Enlisted Person; Officer.

References

Department of Defense, Joint Chiefs of Staff. *Department of Defense Dictionary of Military and Related Terms.* Washington, DC: GPO, 1986.

—**NONPROCUREMENT FUNDS** are funds for operating and administrative supplies and expenses that do not involve the acquisition of materiel. Normal maintenance charges (e.g., repairs) are included, but spare parts and replacements are not.

References

Department of Defense, U.S. Army. *Dictionary of United States Army Terms.* Army Regulation AR 310-25. Washington, DC: Headquarters, Department of the Army, 1986.

—**NONPRODUCTIVE TIME,** in statistical work measurement, is time spent not working. It includes annual and sick leave. *See also:* Annual Leave.

References

Department of Defense, U.S. Army. *Dictionary of United States Army Terms.* Army Regulation AR 310-25. Washington, DC: Headquarters, Department of the Army, 1986.

—**NONRECOVERABLE ITEM** is an end-item or repair part normally consumed in use and not subject to repair or reuse.

References

Department of Defense, U.S. Army. *Dictionary of United States Army Terms.* Army Regulation AR 310-25. Washington, DC: Headquarters, Department of the Army, 1986.

—**NONRECURRING COSTS.** A nonrecurring cost is a one-time expense that is periodically incurred for the same organization. Such costs include expenses for the following: (1) preliminary design effort; (2) design engineering; (3) tests, spare parts, and mock-ups; (4) all partially completed reporting elements manufactured for tests (e.g., status, fatigue, dummy missile, ground integration missile components, or inert missiles); (5) costs of all tooling, manufacturing, and procurement efforts that were specifically incurred during development or testing; (6) the initial set of tools and all duplicate tools that are produced to permit attaining of a specific rate of production for a program; (7) training of service instructor personnel; and (8) the initial preparation of technical data and manuals.

References

Department of Defense, U.S. Army. *Dictionary of United States Army Terms.* Army Regulation AR 310-25. Washington, DC: Headquarters, Department of the Army, 1986.

—**NONRECURRING DEMAND** is a request by an authorized requisitioner to satisfy a one-time materiel requirement (e.g., to provide initial stockage allowances, to meet planned program requirements, or to satisfy a one-time project or maintenance requirement). Nonrecurring demands are normally not considered by the supporting supply system when determining demand-based requirements.

References

Department of Defense, U.S. Army. *Dictionary of United States Army Terms.* Army Regulation AR 310-25. Washington, DC: Headquarters, Department of the Army, 1986.

—**NONSPARKING TOOLS** refers to nonferrous tools used in ammunition maintenance and explosive disposal operations.

References

Department of Defense, U.S. Army. *Dictionary of United States Army Terms.* Army Regulation AR 310-25. Washington, DC: Headquarters, Department of the Army, 1986.

—**NONSTANDARD COMMERCIAL PROPERTY** is property used by civilians or commercially, but has never been processed for overall use by an Army technical committee.

References

Department of Defense, U.S. Army. *Dictionary of United States Army Terms.* Army Regulation AR 310-25. Washington, DC: Headquarters, Department of the Army, 1986.

—**NONSTANDARD ITEM** is an item of supply that has been determined by standardization action as not authorized for procurement.

References

Department of Defense, Joint Chiefs of Staff. *Department of Defense Dictionary of Military and Related Terms.* Washington, DC: GPO, 1986.

—**NONSTANDARD MILITARY PROPERTY** is property restricted in design and utility to the military service, but has never been processed for standardization by an Army technical committee.

References

Department of Defense, U.S. Army. *Dictionary of United States Army Terms.* Army Regulation AR 310-25. Washington, DC: Headquarters, Department of the Army, 1986.

—**NONSTOCKAGE LIST ITEM** is an item that is authorized for issue, but not authorized for stockage by a using unit or a stockage activity (a direct support unit or a general support unit) unless it meets the current Department of the Army stockage criteria promulgated in current Army Regulations.

References

Department of Defense, U.S. Army. *Dictionary of United States Army Terms.* Army Regulation AR 310-25. Washington, DC: Headquarters, Department of the Army, 1986.

—**NONSTOCKED ITEM** is an item for which a commodity commander has supply responsibility but that is not normally stocked in the depot system.

References

Department of Defense, Joint Chiefs of Staff. *Department of Defense Dictionary of Military and Related Terms.* Washington, DC: GPO, 1986.

Department of Defense, U.S. Army. *Support Operations: Echelons Above Corps.* Field Manual FM 100-16. Washington, DC: Headquarters, Department of the Army, 1986.

—**NONSTORAGE SPACE** is an area within a larger space that is not used for storage because of structural losses or designation for other that storage purposes (e.g., transit shed space when it is used or reserved for that purpose).

References

Department of Defense, U.S. Army. *Dictionary of United States Army Terms.* Army Regulation AR 310-25. Washington, DC: Headquarters, Department of the Army, 1986.

—**NONTACTICAL MISSILE** is a production missile produced and allocated for nontactical use (e.g., training, engineering, or development test and evaluation, or target work) or for modification to other programs. It may be inert (without propellent or explosive components).

References

Department of Defense, U.S. Army. *Dictionary of United States Army Terms.* Army Regulation AR 310-25. Washington, DC: Headquarters, Department of the Army, 1986.

—**NONTACTICAL TELECOMMUNICATIONS** are all communications systems, networks, facilities, services, and equipment not normally authorized by tables of organization and equipment and tables of allowances.

References

Department of Defense, U.S. Army. *Dictionary of United States Army Terms.* Army Regulation AR 310-25. Washington, DC: Headquarters, Department of the Army, 1986.

—**NONTACTICAL WHEELED VEHICLE FLEET** consists of motor vehicles that support general transportation services and the facility and equipment maintenance functions that are not directly connected to combat or tactical operations. The nontactical wheeled vehicle fleet is primarily of commercial design and is one of two categories of the wheeled vehicle fleet. The other is the tactical wheeled vehicle fleet. *See also:* Tactical Wheeled Vehicle Fleet.

References

Department of Defense, U.S. Army. *Dictionary of United States Army Terms.* Army Regulation AR 310-25. Washington, DC: Headquarters, Department of the Army, 1986.

—**NONTRANSPORTABLE PATIENT** is a person whose physical condition is so poor that his life would be threatened if he were evacuated before receiving proper medical treatment. *See also:* Medical Treatment.

References

Department of Defense, U.S. Army. *Dictionary of United States Army Terms.* Army Regulation AR 310-25. Washington, DC: Headquarters, Department of the Army, 1986.

—**NON-UNIT-RELATED CARGO** is all equipment and supplies transported to an area of operations, other than the equipment or accompanying supplies of a specific unit (e.g., resupply items, military support for allies, and support for non-military programs, such as civil relief). *See also:* Non-Unit-Related Personnel.

References

Department of Defense, U.S. Army. *Planning Logistics Support for Military Operations.* Field Manual FM 701-58. Washington, DC: Headquarters, Department of the Army, 1987.

—**NON-UNIT-RELATED PERSONNEL** are persons requiring transportation to an area of operations, other than those assigned to a specific unit (e.g., fillers, replacements, temporary duty/ temporary additional duty personnel, and civilians).

References

Department of Defense, U.S. Army. *Planning Logistics Support for Military Operations.* Field Manual FM 701-58. Washington, DC: Headquarters, Department of the Army, 1987.

—**NONVISIBLE PATH SEGMENT** is a portion of the moving target's flight path that is not visible to the sensor. *See also:* Nonvisible Time Segment.

References

Department of Defense, U.S. Army. *Dictionary of United States Army Terms.* Army Regulation AR 310-25. Washington, DC: Headquarters, Department of the Army, 1986.

—**NONVISIBLE TIME SEGMENT** is the length of time that a target is on a nonvisible path segment.

References

Department of Defense, U.S. Army. *Dictionary of United States Army Terms.* Army Regulation AR 310-25. Washington, DC: Headquarters, Department of the Army, 1986.

—**NORMAL BED CAPACITY** is the number of beds that can be set up in hospital wards and rooms designed for patients' beds, with a spacing of eight feet between centers and approximately 100 square feet per bed. These measurements are based upon normal peacetime needs. *See also:* Medical Treatment.

References

Department of Defense, U.S. Army. *Dictionary of United States Army Terms.* Army Regulation AR 310-25. Washington, DC: Headquarters, Department of the Army, 1986.

—**NORMAL CHARGE** is a charge using a standard amount of propellent to fire a gun under ordinary conditions, as compared with a reduced charge. *See also:* Reduced Charge.

References

Department of Defense, Joint Chiefs of Staff. *Department of Defense Dictionary of Military and Related Terms.* Washington, DC: GPO, 1986.

—**NORMAL IMPACT** is the striking of a projectile against a surface perpendicular to the missile's line of flight.

References

Department of Defense, U.S. Army. *Dictionary of United States Army Terms.* Army Regulation AR 310-25. Washington, DC: Headquarters, Department of the Army, 1986.

—**NORMAL INTELLIGENCE REPORTS** is a category of reports usually used to immediately disseminate individual items of intelligence. *See also:* Intelligence Reporting, Specialist Intelligence Report.

References

Department of Defense, Joint Chiefs of Staff. *Department of Defense Dictionary of Military and Related Terms.* Washington, DC: GPO, 1986.

—**NORMAL INTERVAL** is the lateral space between soldiers. It is measured from right to left by the soldier on the right holding his left arm shoulder height, fingers and thumb extended and joined, with the tip of his middle finger touching the right shoulder of the soldier to his left. *See also:* Close Interval, Double Interval.

References

Department of Defense, U.S. Army. *Drills and Ceremonies.* Field Manual FM 22-5. Washington, DC: Headquarters, Department of the Army, 1986.

—**NORMAL OPERATIONS,** generally and collectively, are the functions that the commander of a unified combatant command undertakes when he is assigned responsibility for a given geographic or functional area. Except as otherwise qualified in certain unified command plan paragraphs that relate to particular commands, "normal operations" of a unified command commander include planning and executing operations in contingencies, limited war, and general war; planning and conducting cold war activities; planning and administrating military assistance; and maintaining the relationships and exercising the directive or coordinating authority as prescribed by the Joint Chiefs of Staff. *See also:* Unified Command.

References
Department of Defense, Joint Chiefs of Staff. *Department of Defense Dictionary of Military and Related Terms.* Washington, DC: GPO, 1986.

—**NORTHERN OPERATIONS** include arctic and subarctic conditions. "Cold weather operations," "operations in the subarctic," arctic operations," "operations in the far north," "cold region operations," "operations in northern latitudes," and "northern operations," are synonyms for "northern operations."

References
Department of Defense, U.S. Army. *Dictionary of United States Army Terms.* Army Regulation AR 310-25. Washington, DC: Headquarters, Department of the Army, 1986.

—**NOSE SPRAY** are fragments of a bursting shell thrown forward in the line of flight.

References
Department of Defense, U.S. Army. *Dictionary of United States Army Terms.* Army Regulation AR 310-25. Washington, DC: Headquarters, Department of the Army, 1986.

—**NOT AUTHORIZED FOR POMCUS (PREPOSITIONED ORGANIZATIONAL MATERIEL CONFIGURED IN UNIT SETS)** are items designated by Headquarters, Department of the Army, normally excluded from POMCUS (e.g., aircraft and aircraft subsystems, band and musical equipment, radio equipment, protective masks, individual weapons, organizational clothing and equipment, communications security and equipment, binoculars, and selected night-vision material).

References
Department of Defense, U.S. Army. *Support Operations: Echelons Above Corps.* Field Manual FM 100-16. Washington, DC: Headquarters, Department of the Army, 1986.

—**NOT MISSION CAPABLE MAINTENANCE (NMCM).** Equipment is NMCM when it cannot perform its combat mission because it requires maintenance work. *See also:* Not Mission Capable Supply.

References
Department of Defense, U.S. Army. *Repair Parts Supply for a Theater of Operations.* Field Manual FM 29-19. Washington, DC: Headquarters, Department of the Army, 1985.

—**NOT MISSION CAPABLE SUPPLY (NMCS).** NMCS equipment cannot perform its combat mission because of a shortage of repair parts. *See also:* Not Mission Capable Maintenance.

References
Department of Defense, U.S. Army. *Repair Parts Supply for a Theater of Operations.* Field Manual FM 29-19. Washington, DC: Headquarters, Department of the Army, 1985.

—**NOT OPERATIONALLY READY, MAINTENANCE (NORM)** is a condition status of an operational unit's equipment or system, indicating that it cannot be operated because it needs maintenance work. *See also:* Not Operationally Ready, Supply.

References
Department of Defense, Joint Chiefs of Staff. *Department of Defense Dictionary of Military and Related Terms.* Washington, DC: GPO, 1986.

—**NOT OPERATIONALLY READY, SUPPLY** is a condition status of an operational unit's equipment or a system, indicating that it cannot be operated nor can maintenance work be performed. *See also:* Not Operationally Ready, Maintenance.

References
Department of Defense, Joint Chiefs of Staff. *Department of Defense Dictionary of Military and Related Terms.* Washington, DC: GPO, 1986.

—**NOTIONAL MOVES** are used to deceive. For example, by combining sonic, visual, and electronic measures, a small element of tracked vehicles, with proper communications equipment and careful spacing and timing, can convince the enemy that a company or battalion is, or was, moving from one location to another.

References
Department of Defense, U.S. Army. *Tactical Deception.* Field Manual FM 90-2. Washington, DC: Headquarters, Department of the Army, 1978.

—**NOTIONAL ORDER OF BATTLE** is the overall structure of a plan to deceive the enemy. It is constructed when a deception is planned and explains how the enemy must be deceived if it is to react in accordance with the deception objective.

References

Department of Defense, U.S. Army. *Tactical Deception*. Field Manual FM 90-2. Washington, DC: Headquarters, Department of the Army, 1978.

—NOTIONAL UNIT is a unit that is not defined in terms of a numerical or other actual designation (e.g, an infantry division, an artillery battalion, or a supply and service battalion).

References

Department of Defense, U.S. Army. *Planning Logistics Support for Military Operations*. Field Manual FM 701-58. Washington, DC: Headquarters, Department of the Army, 1987.

———. *Tactical Deception*. Field Manual FM 90-2. Washington, DC: Headquarters, Department of the Army, 1978.

—NOTIONAL UNIT/ACTIVITY is a measure to support the deception of the enemy, making it obtain a false appreciation of friendly strength, composition, and intentions. The concept is based upon the premise that a unit can be organized and used to display the characteristics of a larger unit or another type of unit.

References

Department of Defense, U.S. Army. *Tactical Deception*. Field Manual FM 90-2. Washington, DC: Headquarters, Department of the Army, 1978.

—NUCLEAR AIRBURST is the explosion of a nuclear weapon in the air, at a height greater than the maximum radius of the fireball. *See also:* Nuclear Warfare.

References

Department of Defense, Joint Chiefs of Staff. *Department of Defense Dictionary of Military and Related Terms*. Washington, DC: GPO, 1986.

Department of Defense, U.S. Army. *Glossary of Terms—Nuclear Weapon Phenomena and Effects*. DASIAC-SR-208. Washington, DC: Headquarters, Department of the Army, 1985.

—NUCLEAR, BIOLOGICAL, AND CHEMICAL (NBC) ELEMENT is the part of an operations center that coordinates chemical operations and biological defensive actions with other support operations. It also predicts the fallout resulting from the use of nuclear weapons by friendly and enemy forces, and evaluates chemical,

biological, and radiological contamination. *See also:* Biological Warfare, Chemical Warfare, Nuclear Warfare.

References

Department of Defense, U.S. Army. *Dictionary of United States Army Terms*. Army Regulation AR 310-25. Washington, DC: Headquarters, Department of the Army, 1986.

———. *Glossary of Terms—Nuclear Weapon Phenomena and Effects*. DASIAC-SR-208. Washington, DC: Headquarters, Department of the Army, 1985.

—NUCLEAR, BIOLOGICAL, CHEMICAL (NBC) AREA OF OBSERVATION is a geographical area consisting of several nuclear, biological, and chemical zones of observation. It can be compared to the area of responsibility of an Army or Army Group or an Allied Tactical Air Force. *See also:* Biological Warfare, Chemical Warfare, Nuclear Warfare.

References

Department of Defense, Joint Chiefs of Staff. *Department of Defense Dictionary of Military and Related Terms*. Washington, DC: GPO, 1986.

—NUCLEAR, BIOLOGICAL, CHEMICAL (NBC) COLLECTION CENTER is an agency responsible for the receipt, collation, and evaluation of reports of nuclear detonations, biological and chemical attacks, and the resultant contamination within the zone of observation and for the production and dissemination of appropriate reports and warnings. *See also:* Biological Warfare, Chemical Warfare, Nuclear Warfare.

References

Department of Defense, Joint Chiefs of Staff. *Department of Defense Dictionary of Military and Related Terms*. Washington, DC: GPO, 1986.

—NUCLEAR, BIOLOGICAL, CHEMICAL (NBC) CONTROL CENTER is the agency responsible for coordinating activities of all the nuclear, biological, and chemical collection centers in a given area of observation. This agency may also be a collection center for the area in which it is located. *See also:* Biological Warfare, Chemical Warfare, Nuclear Warfare.

References

Department of Defense, Joint Chiefs of Staff. *Department of Defense Dictionary of Military and Related Terms*. Washington, DC: GPO, 1986.

—**NUCLEAR, BIOLOGICAL, CHEMICAL (NBC) DEFENSE** are the methods, plans, procedures, and training required to establish defense measures against the effects of an attack by nuclear, biological, or chemical weapons. *See also:* Biological Warfare, Chemical Warfare, Nuclear Warfare.

References
Department of Defense, Joint Chiefs of Staff. *Department of Defense Dictionary of Military and Related Terms.* Washington, DC: GPO, 1986.

—**NUCLEAR, BIOLOGICAL, CHEMICAL (NBC) ZONE OF OBSERVATION** is a geographical area that defines the responsibility for collecting and reporting information on enemy and unidentified nuclear detonations, biological, and chemical attacks, and the resultant contamination. The boundaries of nuclear, biological, and chemical zones of observation, which may overlap, are determined by the organization of the forces concerned. *See also:* Biological Warfare, Chemical Warfare, Nuclear Warfare.

References
Department of Defense, Joint Chiefs of Staff. *Department of Defense Dictionary of Military and Related Terms.* Washington, DC: GPO, 1986.

—**NUCLEAR BONUS EFFECTS** are the desirable damage or casualties produced by the effects from friendly nuclear weapons that cannot be accurately calculated in targeting because the uncertainties involved preclude accurately predicting the number of casualties. *See also:* Nuclear Warfare.

References
Department of Defense, Joint Chiefs of Staff. *Department of Defense Dictionary of Military and Related Terms.* Washington, DC: GPO, 1986.

—**NUCLEAR BURST REPORT** is a standard report form used for transmitting information on nuclear explosions and their effects. *See also:* Nuclear Warfare.

References
Department of Defense, U.S. Army. *Dictionary of United States Army Terms.* Army Regulation AR 310-25. Washington, DC: Headquarters, Department of the Army, 1986.

—**NUCLEAR CLOUD** is an all-inclusive term for the volume of hot gases, smoke, dust, and other particulate matter from a nuclear bomb and its environment that is carried aloft when the fireball produced by the detonation of the nuclear weapon rises. *See also:* Nuclear Warfare.

References
Department of Defense, Joint Chiefs of Staff. *Department of Defense Dictionary of Military and Related Terms.* Washington, DC: GPO, 1986.

—**NUCLEAR COLLATERAL DAMAGE** is undesired damage or casualties produced by the effects from friendly nuclear weapons. *See also:* Nuclear Warfare.

References
Department of Defense, Joint Chiefs of Staff. *Department of Defense Dictionary of Military and Related Terms.* Washington, DC: GPO, 1986.

—**NUCLEAR COMMITMENT** is a statement by a NATO member that specific forces have been committed or will be committed to NATO in a nuclear only or in a dual capable role. *See also:* Nuclear Warfare.

References
Department of Defense, Joint Chiefs of Staff. *Department of Defense Dictionary of Military and Related Terms.* Washington, DC: GPO, 1986.

—**NUCLEAR COORDINATION** encompasses all actions involved in planning nuclear strikes, including liaison between nuclear commanders, to satisfy support requirements or because of the extension of weapons effects into the territory of another. *See also:* Nuclear Warfare.

References
Department of Defense, Joint Chiefs of Staff. *Department of Defense Dictionary of Military and Related Terms.* Washington, DC: GPO, 1986.

—**NUCLEAR DAMAGE** (LAND WARFARE). Nuclear damage is assessed according to three categories:
- **Light damage** does not prevent the immediate use of equipment or installations for which it was intended. Some repair by the user may be required to make full use of the equipment or the installations.
- **Moderate damage** precludes the use of equipment or installations until extensive repairs are made.
- **Severe damage** prevents the use of equipment or installations permanently.

See also: Nuclear Warfare.

References

Department of Defense, Joint Chiefs of Staff. *Department of Defense Dictionary of Military and Related Terms.* Washington, DC: GPO, 1986.

—**NUCLEAR DAMAGE ASSESSMENT** is an estimation of the damage to the population, forces, and resources resulting from a nuclear attack. It is performed during and after an attack and does not include the function of evaluating the operational significance of nuclear damage. *See also:* Nuclear Warfare.

References

Department of Defense, U.S. Army. *Operational Terms and Symbols.* Field Manual FM 101-5-1. Washington, DC: Headquarters, Department of the Army, 1985.

—**NUCLEAR DEFENSE** includes the methods, plans, and procedures involved in establishing and exercising defensive measures against the effects of an attack by nuclear weapons or radiological warfare agents. It encompasses both the training for, and the implementation of, these methods, plans, and procedures. *See also:* NBC Defense, Radiological Defense.

References

Department of Defense, Joint Chiefs of Staff. *Department of Defense Dictionary of Military and Related Terms.* Washington, DC: GPO, 1986.

—**NUCLEAR DELIVERY UNIT** is any level of organization capable of employing a nuclear weapon system or systems when the weapon or weapons have been released by proper authority. *See also:* Nuclear Warfare.

References

Department of Defense, Joint Chiefs of Staff. *Department of Defense Dictionary of Military and Related Terms.* Washington, DC: GPO, 1986.

—**NUCLEAR DELIVERY VEHICLE** is the portion of the weapon system that provides the means of delivery of a nuclear weapon to the target. *See also:* Nuclear Warfare.

References

Department of Defense, Joint Chiefs of Staff. *Department of Defense Dictionary of Military and Related Terms.* Washington, DC: GPO, 1986.

—**NUCLEAR DETONATION (NUDET)** is an explosion resulting from the fission and/or fusion reactions in nuclear materials (e.g., from a nuclear weapon). *See also:* Nuclear Warfare.

References

Department of Defense, U.S. Army. *Dictionary of United States Army Terms.* Army Regulation AR 310-25. Washington, DC: Headquarters, Department of the Army, 1986.

—**NUCLEAR DETONATION (NUDET) DETECTION AND REPORTING SYSTEM** is a system deployed to provide surveillance coverage of critical friendly target areas and to indicate the place, height of burst, yield, and ground zero of each nuclear detonation. *See also:* Nuclear Warfare.

References

Department of Defense, Joint Chiefs of Staff. *Department of Defense Dictionary of Military and Related Terms.* Washington, DC: GPO, 1986.

—**NUCLEAR INCIDENT** is an unexpected event involving a nuclear weapon, facility, or component that results in any of the following that do constitute a nuclear weapons accident: (1) an increase in the possibility of an explosion or radioactive contamination; (2) errors committed in assembling, testing, loading, or transporting equipment (also, the malfunctioning of equipment and materiel that could lead to an unintentional operation of all or part of the weapon arming and/or firing sequence, or that could lead to a substantial change in yield or increased dud probability); (3) an act of God, unfavorable environment, or condition resulting in damage to the weapon, facility, or component. *See also:* Nuclear Warfare.

References

Department of Defense, U.S. Army. *NBC Operations.* Field Manual FM 3-100. Washington, DC: Headquarters, Department of the Army, 1985.

—**NUCLEAR INTELLIGENCE (NUCINT)** is intelligence information derived from collecting and analyzing radiation and other effects from radioactive sources. *See also:* Intelligence.

References

Department of Defense, Defense Intelligence College. *Glossary of Intelligence Terms and Definitions.* Washington, DC: DIC, 1987.

Department of Defense, U.S. Army. *Counterintelligence.* Field Manual FM 34-60. Washington, DC: Headquarters, Department of the Army, 1985.

—**NUCLEAR ORDNANCE ITEMS** are assemblies, equipment, components, and parts peculiar in design to nuclear weapon programs. *See also:* Nuclear Warfare.

References
Department of Defense, U.S. Army. *Dictionary of United States Army Terms*. Army Regulation AR 310-25. Washington, DC: Headquarters, Department of the Army, 1986.

—**NUCLEAR PROLIFERATION INTELLIGENCE** is foreign intelligence relating to (1) the scientific, technical, and economic capabilities and programs and the political plans and intentions of nations or foreign organizations that do not have nuclear weapons, the means to acquire nuclear weapons, or the research, development, and manufacturing capabilities to produce nuclear weapons or (2) the attitudes, policies, and actions of foreign nations or organizations that have nuclear weapons to supply the technology, facilities, or special nuclear materials that could assist a nation or foreign organization that does not have nuclear weapons to acquire them. *See also:* Intelligence.

References
Department of Defense, Defense Intelligence College. *Glossary of Intelligence Terms and Definitions*. Washington, DC: DIC, 1987.

—**NUCLEAR RADIATION** is particulate and electromagnetic radiation emitted from atomic nuclei in various processes. The important nuclear radiations from the weapons standpoint are alpha and beta particles, gamma rays, and neutrons. *See also:* Nuclear Warfare.

References
Department of Defense, U.S. Army. *NBC Operations*. Field Manual FM 3-100. Washington, DC: Headquarters, Department of the Army, 1985.

—**NUCLEAR SAFETY** are the design features, procedures, and actions that protect against intentional and unintentional acts that could lead to a nuclear incident or accident. *See also:* Nuclear Warfare.

References
Department of Defense, U.S. Army. *Dictionary of United States Army Terms*. Army Regulation AR 310-25. Washington, DC: Headquarters, Department of the Army, 1986.

—**NUCLEAR STALEMATE** is a concept that postulates a situation wherein the relative strength of opposing nuclear forces results in mutual deterrence against the use of nuclear forces. *See also:* Nuclear Warfare.

References
Department of Defense, Joint Chiefs of Staff. *Department of Defense Dictionary of Military and Related Terms*. Washington, DC: GPO, 1986.

—**NUCLEAR STRIKE WARNING** is a warning of impending or suspected enemy nuclear attack. *See also:* Nuclear Warfare.

References
Department of Defense, Joint Chiefs of Staff. *Department of Defense Dictionary of Military and Related Terms*. Washington, DC: GPO, 1986.

—**NUCLEAR SURFACE BURST** is an explosion of a nuclear weapon at the surface of land or water; or above the surface, at a height less that the maximum radius of the fireball. *See also:* Nuclear Warfare.

References
Department of Defense, Joint Chiefs of Staff. *Department of Defense Dictionary of Military and Related Terms*. Washington, DC: GPO, 1986.

—**NUCLEAR VULNERABILITY ASSESSMENT** is an estimate of the probable effect on the population, forces, and resources from a nuclear attack. The assessment is performed predominantly for the preattack period; however, it may be extended to the transattack or postattack periods. *See also:* Nuclear Warfare.

References
Department of Defense, Joint Chiefs of Staff. *Department of Defense Dictionary of Military and Related Terms*. Washington, DC: GPO, 1986.

—**NUCLEAR WARFARE (NW)** is warfare involving the use of nuclear weapons. *See also:* Absolute Dud; Absorbed Dose; Access; Active Ballistic Missile Defense; Actual Ground Zero; Acute Radiation Dose; Airburst; Area of Militarily Significant Fallout; Atomic Demolition Munition; Ballistic Missile; Beta Particle; Collateral Damage Distance; Collateral Damage (Nuclear); Contamination; Contamination Avoidance; Contamination Control; Contamination Control Point; Contamination Obstacle; Conventional Forces; Conventional War; Conventional Weapon; Degree of Risk (Nuclear); Deliberate Decontamination; Desired Effects; Desired Ground Zero, Dose; Dose Rate Contour Line; Dosimetry; Effective Downwind Message; Emergency Destruction of Nuclear Weapons; Emergency Risk (Nuclear); Executing Commander (Nuclear Weapons); First Strike; Half Thickness; Hasty Decon; Height of Burst; High Airburst; High Altitude Burst; Immediate Nuclear Support; Initial Nuclear Effects; Initial Nuclear Radiation; Initial Radiation; Maximum Permissible Dose; Medium Atomic Demolition Munition; Megaton; Megaton Weapon; Minimum Residual Radioactivity Weapon; Moderate Risk (Nuclear); NBC Defense; Nuclear, Biological, and Chemical Element; Nuclear, Biological, Chemical Area of Observation; Nuclear, Biological, Chemical Collection Center; Nuclear, Biological, Chemical Control Center; Nuclear, Biological, Chemical Defense; Nuclear, Biological, Chemical Zone of Observation; Nuclear Bonus Effects; Nuclear Burst Report; Nuclear Cloud; Nuclear Collateral Damage; Nuclear Commitment; Nuclear Coordination; Nuclear Damage (Land Warfare); Nuclear Damage Assessment; Nuclear Defense; Nuclear Delivery Unit; Nuclear Delivery Vehicle; Nuclear Detonation; Nuclear Detonation, Detection, and Reporting System; Nuclear Incident; Nuclear Intelligence; Nuclear Ordnance Items; Nuclear Proliferation Intelligence; Nuclear Radiation; Nuclear Safety; Nuclear Stalemate; Nuclear Strike Warning; Nuclear Surface Burst; Nuclear Vulnerability Assessment; Nuclear Warfare; Nuclear Warning Message; Nuclear Weapon; Nuclear Weapon(s) Accident; Nuclear Weapon Degradation; Nuclear Weapon Employment Time; Nuclear Weapon Exercise; Nuclear Weapon Logistic Elements; Nuclear Weapon Maneuver; Nuclear Weapons Package; Nuclear Weapons Subpackage; Nuclear Weapons Surety; Nuclear Yield; Optimum Height of Burst; Passive Ballistic Missile Defense; Prescribed Nuclear Load; Prescribed Nuclear Stockage; Radiation Dose; Radiation Dose Rate; Radiation Exposure State; Radiation Sickness; Radioactivity; Scheduled Target (Nuclear); Theater Nuclear Forces, Weapons, Operations; Toxic Chemical, Biological, or Radiological Attack; Transattack Period; Weathering; Zone I (Nuclear); Zone II (Nuclear); Zone III (Nuclear).

References

Department of Defense, Joint Chiefs of Staff. *Department of Defense Dictionary of Military and Related Terms.* Washington, DC: GPO, 1986.

Department of Defense, U.S. Army. *Glossary of Terms—Nuclear Weapon Phenomena and Effects.* DASIAC-SR-208. Washington, DC: Headquarters, Department of the Army, 1985.

—**NUCLEAR WARNING MESSAGE** is a warning message that must be disseminated to all affected friendly forces any time nuclear weapon is to be detonated if its effects will have an impact on those forces.

References

Department of Defense, Joint Chiefs of Staff. *Department of Defense Dictionary of Military and Related Terms.* Washington, DC: GPO, 1986.

—**NUCLEAR WEAPON** is a complete assembly (e.g., implosion type, gun type, or thermonuclear type) in its intended ultimate configuration which, upon completion of the prescribed arming, fusing, and firing sequence, is capable of producing the intended nuclear reaction and release of energy.

References

Department of Defense, Joint Chiefs of Staff. *Department of Defense Dictionary of Military and Related Terms.* Washington, DC: GPO, 1986.

Department of Defense, U.S. Army. *Glossary of Terms—Nuclear Weapon Phenomena and Effects.* DASIAC-SR-208. Washington, DC: Headquarters, Department of the Army, 1985.

—**NUCLEAR WEAPON(S) ACCIDENT** is an unexpected event involving nuclear weapons or radiological nuclear weapon components that results in: (1) an accidental or unauthorized launching, firing, or use by U.S. forces or U.S.-supported allied forces, of a nuclear-capable weapon system that could cause a war; (2) a nuclear detonation; (3) a nonnuclear detonation or burning of a nuclear weapon or radiological nuclear weapon component; (4) radioactive contamination; (5) the seizure, theft, loss, or destruction of a nuclear weapon or radiological nuclear weapon component, including jettisoning; or (6) a public hazard, actual or implied.

References

Department of Defense, Joint Chiefs of Staff. *Department of Defense Dictionary of Military and Related Terms.* Washington, DC: GPO, 1986.

Department of Defense, U.S. Army. *Glossary of Terms—Nuclear Weapon Phenomena and Effects.* DASIAC-SR-208. Washington, DC: Headquarters, Department of the Army, 1985.

—**NUCLEAR WEAPON DEGRADATION** is the denigration of a nuclear warhead to such an extent that the anticipated nuclear yield is lessened.

References
Department of Defense, Joint Chiefs of Staff. *Department of Defense Dictionary of Military and Related Terms.* Washington, DC: GPO, 1986.

—**NUCLEAR WEAPON EMPLOYMENT TIME** is the time required to deliver a nuclear weapon after the decision to fire it has been made.

References
Department of Defense, Joint Chiefs of Staff. *Department of Defense Dictionary of Military and Related Terms.* Washington, DC: GPO, 1986.

—**NUCLEAR WEAPON EXERCISE** is an operation not directly related to immediate operational readiness. It includes removal of a weapon from its normal storage location, preparing it for use, delivering it to an employment unit, and its movement in a ground training exercise that includes loading it aboard an aircraft or missile and returning it to storage. It may include any or all of these operations, but it does not include launching or flying operations. Typical exercises include aircraft generation exercises, ground readiness exercises, ground tactical exercises, and various categories of inspections that are designed to evaluate the unit's capability to perform its prescribed mission. *See also:* Immediate Operational Readiness, Nuclear Weapon Maneuver.

References
Department of Defense, Joint Chiefs of Staff. *Department of Defense Dictionary of Military and Related Terms.* Washington, DC: GPO, 1986.

—**NUCLEAR WEAPONS LOGISTIC ELEMENT (NWLE)** refers to small liaison detachments provided to U.S. corps and combined commands. They provide the command link between the special ammunition logistics command and the supported elements. Specifically, the nuclear weapons logistic element coordinates the resupply and the movement control of nuclear and missile special ammunition at the corps and theater tactical operation centers. The mission of NWLEs is to expedite the flow of directives concerning the supply of nuclear weapons from the tactical operations center to materiel management center to storage locations. Stockage levels of nuclear weapons are established by command decisions that are based upon the tactical situation. Ordnance activities must keep supported firing and demolition units informed of the location of special ammunition supply points and, if possible, provide one-stop service for the issue of complete nuclear rounds.

References
Department of Defense, U.S. Army. *Operations for Nuclear-Capable Units.* Field Manual FM 100-50. Washington, DC: Headquarters, Department of the Army, 1980.

———. *Support Operations: Echelons Above Corps.* Field Manual FM 100-16. Washington, DC: Headquarters, Department of the Army, 1986.

—**NUCLEAR WEAPON MANEUVER** is an operation not related to immediate operational readiness. It may consist of all those operations listed for a nuclear weapon exercise and is intended to include flyaway in combat aircraft. It does not include the expenditure of the weapon. Typical maneuvers include nuclear operational readiness maneuvers and tactical air operations. *See also:* Immediate Operational Readiness, Nuclear Weapon Exercise.

References
Department of Defense, Joint Chiefs of Staff. *Department of Defense Dictionary of Military and Related Terms.* Washington, DC: GPO, 1986.

Department of Defense, U.S. Army. *Glossary of Terms—Nuclear Weapon Phenomena and Effects.* DASIAC-SR-208. Washington, DC: Headquarters, Department of the Army, 1985.

—**NUCLEAR WEAPONS PACKAGE** is a discrete grouping of nuclear weapons by specific yields that are planned for use in a specified area during a short period of time. *See also:* Nuclear Weapon Subpackage, Prescribed Nuclear Load.

References
Department of Defense, U.S. Army. *Nuclear Weapons Employment Doctrine and Procedures.* Field Manual FM 101-3-1. Washington, DC: Headquarters, Department of the Army, 1986.

———. *Operational Terms and Symbols.* Field Manual FM 101-5-1. Washington, DC: Headquarters, Department of the Army, 1985.

—**NUCLEAR WEAPONS SUBPACKAGE** is a division sub-element of a corps nuclear weapon package. It is only to be executed as part of a corps package. *See also:* Nuclear Weapon Package, Prescribed Nuclear Load.

References
Department of Defense, Joint Chiefs of Staff. *Department of Defense Dictionary of Military and Related Terms.* Washington, DC: GPO, 1986.

—**NUCLEAR WEAPONS SURETY** refers to the materiel, personnel, and procedures that contribute to the security, safety, and reliability of nuclear weapons and to the assurance that there will be no nuclear weapon accidents, incidents, unauthorized weapon detonations, or degradation in weapon performance at the target.

References

Department of Defense, Joint Chiefs of Staff. *Department of Defense Dictionary of Military and Related Terms.* Washington, DC: GPO, 1986.

—**NUCLEAR YIELD** is the energy released in a detonation of a nuclear weapon. It is usually measured in kilotons or megatons of TNT that would be required to produce the same energy release. The yields are categorized as *very low*: less than 1 kiloton; *low*: 1 to 10 kilotons; *medium*: 10 to 50 kilotons; *high*: 50 to 500 kilotons; *very high*: over 500 kilotons.

References

Department of Defense, U.S. Army. *Operational Terms and Symbols.* Field Manual FM 101-5-1. Washington, DC: Headquarters, Department of the Army, 1985.

—**NUISANCE MINEFIELD** is a minefield laid to delay and disorganize the enemy and to hinder its use of an area or route. *See also:* Minefield.

References

Department of Defense, Joint Chiefs of Staff. *Department of Defense Dictionary of Military and Related Terms.* Washington, DC: GPO, 1986.

—**NUMBER . . . IN (OUT)** in artillery, is used to indicate a change in the status of weapon number.

References

Department of Defense, Joint Chiefs of Staff. *Department of Defense Dictionary of Military and Related Terms.* Washington, DC: GPO, 1986.

—**(NUMBER OF) ROUNDS,** in artillery, is a command or request to indicate the number of projectiles per tube to be fired on a specific target.

References

Department of Defense, Joint Chiefs of Staff. *Department of Defense Dictionary of Military and Related Terms.* Washington, DC: GPO, 1986.

—**O-O LINE** is a line for coordinating field artillery observation. It is designated by the corps or force artillery commander and divides the primary responsibility for observing between the corps or force artillery and the division artillery.

References

Department of Defense, Joint Chiefs of Staff. *Department of Defense Dictionary of Military and Related Terms.* Washington, DC: GPO, 1986.

—**OV-1D MOHAWK SURVEILLANCE SYSTEM** is a two-passenger, twin turbo-prop combat aircraft equipped with side-looking airborne radar, and photographic or infrared sensors capable of monitoring enemy operations in daylight, darkness, and inclement weather. The primary sensor is the AN/APS-94F airborne radar surveillance system.

References

Weapons Systems: U.S. Army, Navy, and Air Force Directory, 1986-1988. Washington, DC: DCP, 1986.

—**OBJECTIVE.** An objective is an end or goal that is to be attained through the use of military force. *See also:* Objective Area.

References

Department of Defense, U.S. Army. *Dictionary of United States Army Terms.* Army Regulation AR 310-25. Washington, DC: Headquarters, Department of the Army, 1986.

—**OBJECTIVE** (PRINCIPLE OF WAR). The objective is to direct every military operation toward a clearly defined, decisive, and attainable goal.

A nation at war must apply the force necessary to attain the political purpose for which the war is being fought. When the purpose is to totally defeat the enemy, the strategic military objective will be the destruction of the enemy's will to resist, including the unconditional surrender of its armed forces. Strategic objectives cannot be clearly identified and developed, however, un-

til the political purpose has been determined by the President. Once developed, these objectives must be constantly analyzed and reviewed to insure that they accurately reflect the ultimate political purpose and any political constraints imposed on the application of military force.

Operational efforts must also be directed toward clearly defined, decisive, and attainable objectives that will achieve the strategic aims. Tactical objectives must achieve operational aims. The selection of objectives is based upon the overall mission of the command, the commander's assigned mission, the enemy forces, the means available, and the military characteristics of the operational area. Every commander must understand the overall mission of the higher command, his own mission, and the tasks he must perform. Then he must clearly communicate the intent of the operation to his subordinate commanders. *See also:* Principles of War.

References

Department of Defense, U.S. Army. *The Army.* (Prepublication Issue.) Field Manual FM 100-1. Washington, DC: Headquarters, Department of the Army, 1986.

———. *Operational Terms and Symbols.* Field Manual FM 101-5-1. Washington, DC: Headquarters, Department of the Army, 1985.

———. *Operations.* Field Manual FM 100-5. Washington, DC: Headquarters, Department of the Army, 1986.

—**OBJECTIVE AREA.** (1) An objective area is a defined geographical area that encompasses an objective that is to be captured or reached by military forces. This area is defined by competent authority for purposes of command and control. (2) An objective area is a city or other location where a civil disturbance is occurring or is anticipated, and where federal armed forces are, or may be, employed. (3) An objective area is the proposed area of airborne operations and includes the airhead.

References

Department of Defense, Joint Chiefs of Staff. *Department of Defense Dictionary of Military and Related Terms.* Washington, DC: GPO, 1986.

Department of Defense, U.S. Army. *Dictionary of United States Army Terms.* Army Regulation AR 310-25. Washington, DC: Headquarters, Department of the Army, 1986.

—**OBJECTIVE FORCE** is the force that can meet the projected threat and carry out the national strategy at a level of prudent risk and in consideration of reasonable attainability. *See also:* Objective Force Level.

References
Department of Defense, U.S. Army. *Dictionary of United States Army Terms.* Army Regulation AR 310-25. Washington, DC: Headquarters, Department of the Army, 1986.

—**OBJECTIVE FORCE LEVEL** is the level of military forces that must be reached within a definite time frame and resource level to accomplish approved military objectives, missions, or tasks. *See also:* Military Requirement.

References
Department of Defense, Joint Chiefs of Staff. *Department of Defense Dictionary of Military and Related Terms.* Washington, DC: GPO, 1986.

—**OBJECTIVE PLANE** is a plane that is tangent to the ground or coincides with the surface of the target, particularly the plane at the point of impact of a bomb or missile.

References
Department of Defense, U.S. Army. *Dictionary of United States Army Terms.* Army Regulation AR 310-25. Washington, DC: Headquarters, Department of the Army, 1986.

—**OBJECTIVE RALLY POINT (ORP)** is a place where the company temporarily halts to prepare for an objective and returns to after action at the objective. It is used primarily by patrols. *See also:* Objective.

References
Department of Defense, U.S. Army. *The Infantry Rifle Company (Infantry, Airborne, Air Assault, Ranger).* Field Manual FM 7-10. Washington, DC: Headquarters, Department of the Army, 1982.

—**OBJECTIVES** are normally assigned in an attack. They may be the only control measures assigned and are used to focus the efforts of the attacking units. *See also:* Objective, Objective (Principle of War).

References
Department of Defense, U.S. Army. *Armored and Mechanized Division Operations.* Field Manual FM 71-100. Washington, DC: Headquarters, Department of the Army, 1978.

—**OBLIGATED RESERVIST** is an individual who has a statutory requirement under the Military Selective Service Act of 1967 or Section 651, United States Code to serve on active duty in the U.S. armed forces or to serve while not on active duty in a reserve component for a period not to exceed that prescribed by the applicable statute.

References
Department of Defense, Joint Chiefs of Staff. *Department of Defense Dictionary of Military and Related Terms.* Washington, DC: GPO, 1986.

—**OBLIGATED STOCKS** are specified quantities of certain items that are issued only for a specifically designated purpose (e.g., a special project or a mobilization).

References
Department of Defense, U.S. Army. *Dictionary of United States Army Terms.* Army Regulation AR 310-25. Washington, DC: Headquarters, Department of the Army, 1986.

—**OBLIGATED TOUR** is the initial tour of active duty that is served by other than Regular Army officers. *See also:* Tour of Duty.

References
Department of Defense, U.S. Army. *Dictionary of United States Army Terms.* Army Regulation AR 310-25. Washington, DC: Headquarters, Department of the Army, 1986.

—**OBLIGATED VOLUNTEER OFFICER** is a commissioned or warrant officer serving an initial tour with a given expiration date or a limited extension of an initial tour of active duty with a given expiration date. *See also:* Initial Tour.

References
Department of Defense, U.S. Army. *Promotion of Officers on Active Duty.* Army Regulation AR 624-100. Washington, DC: Headquarters, Department of the Army, 1984.

—**OBLIGATION** is the dollar amount specifically reserved against an appropriation or fund to pay for an outstanding order, a contract, or a service that has been performed.

References
Department of Defense, U.S. Army. *Dictionary of United States Army Terms.* Army Regulation AR 310-25. Washington, DC: Headquarters, Department of the Army, 1986.

—**OBLIGATION AUTHORITY.** (1) An obligation authority is any congressional or administrative authorization to incur obligations, although it may not be permitted to pay for obligations. (2) Obligation authority is a specific form of authority known as citation-of-funds, which is used within the Department of the Army and Department of the Air Force. *See also:* Allocation, Suballotment.

References

Department of Defense, U.S. Army. *Dictionary of United States Army Terms.* Army Regulation AR 310-25. Washington, DC: Headquarters, Department of the Army, 1986.

—**OBLIGATION OF FUNDS** is the cost of an order placed, a contract awarded, a service received, or other transaction that legally reserves an appropriation or fund for expenditure.

References

Department of Defense, U.S. Army. *Dictionary of United States Army Terms.* Army Regulation AR 310-25. Washington, DC: Headquarters, Department of the Army, 1986.

—**OBLIGATIONS INCURRED** are the total cost of obligations that have been established against an appropriation or fund during a given time period.

References

Department of Defense, U.S. Army. *Dictionary of United States Army Terms.* Army Regulation AR 310-25. Washington, DC: Headquarters, Department of the Army, 1986.

—**OBLIQUE AIR PHOTOGRAPH** is a photograph taken with the camera axis directed between the horizontal and vertical planes. *See also:* Aerial Reconnaissance.

References

Reeves, Robert; Anson, Abraham; and Landen, David. *Manual of Remote Sensing.* Falls Church, VA: American Society of Photogrammetry, 1975.

—**OBLIQUE COMPARTMENT** is a compartment of terrain whose long axis is diagonal to the direction of march or to the front.

References

Department of Defense, U.S. Army. *Dictionary of United States Army Terms.* Army Regulation AR 310-25. Washington, DC: Headquarters, Department of the Army, 1986.

—**OBLIQUE LINE OVERLAP** is a succession of overlapping oblique photographs that have been taken in a straight line. They cannot be pieced together (as can a vertical line overlap); but they give a series of useful perspective views. The overlap between successive photographs is usually 50 percent. *See also:* Aerial Reconnaissance.

References

Reeves, Robert; Anson, Abraham; and Landen, David. *Manual of Remote Sensing.* Falls Church, VA: American Society of Photogrammetry, 1975.

—**OBSCURANT** is a chemical agent that decreases the energy available for seekers, trackers, and vision-enhancement devices to carry out their functions. *See also:* Chemical Warfare.

References

Department of Defense, U.S. Army. *Deliberate Smoke Operations.* Field Manual FM 3-50. Washington, DC: Headquarters, Department of the Army, 1984.

—**OBSCURATION** is the effects of weather, battlefield dust, and debris or the use of smoke munitions to hamper observation and target-acquisition capabilities or to conceal activities or movement. *See also:* Smoke Screen.

References

Department of Defense, U.S. Army. *Operational Terms and Symbols.* Field Manual FM 101-5-1. Washington, DC: Headquarters, Department of the Army, 1985.

—**OBSCURATION FIRE** is a category of fire using smoke and white phosphorus directly on or near the enemy to hinder the observer and minimize his vision both within and beyond his position area. *See also:* Smoke Screen, White Phosphorus.

References

Department of Defense, U.S. Army. *Fire Support in Combined Arms Operations.* Field Manual FM 6-20. Washington, DC: Headquarters, Department of the Army, 1983.

—**OBSCURATION SMOKE** is smoke placed on or near enemy positions to minimize enemy observation both within and beyond the position area, or to cause its forces to vary speed, inadvertently change direction, deploy prematurely, or rely on nonoptical means of communication. *See also:* Screening Smoke, Smoke, Smoke Screen.

References

Department of Defense, U.S. Army. *Deliberate Smoke Operations*. Field Manual FM 3-50. Washington, DC: Headquarters, Department of the Army, 1984.

————. *Fire Support in Combined Arms Operations*. Field Manual FM 6-20. Washington, DC: Headquarters, Department of the Army, 1983.

————. *Operational Terms and Symbols*. Field Manual FM 101-5-1. Washington, DC: Headquarters, Department of the Army, 1985.

—**OBSERVATION.** There is a difference between *observation* and *sensing*. An *observation* is made when the effects of the round of ammunition are seen, but are not seen clearly enough to be absolutely certain whether or where the round hit the target. An observation of *lost* means that neither the tracer nor the effects of the round were seen after firing.

References

Department of Defense, U.S. Army. *Tank Gunnery*. Field Manual FM 17-12. Washington, DC: Headquarters, Department of the Army, 1984.

—**OBSERVATION AND FIELDS OF FIRE.** Contour and vegetation affect observation and fire. Where visibility is limited, direct fire weapons are less effective and movement entails less risk. Remote sensors can be used to cue artillery and to cover some areas that cannot be observed directly. Large forests, jungles, built-up areas, and tracts of broken ground limit observation and the effects of fire.

Fields of observation and fire differ according to weapon characteristics. Hilltops and the tops of buildings are excellent observation posts or radar sites, but are rarely satisfactory positions for direct fire weapon positions. Tanks, missiles, and machine guns must be positioned where their effects will be the greatest and dead space will be minimized.

The terrain should also be analyzed in terms of air observation and fire. In many cases, Army aircraft can overwatch from flanking positions in woods and valleys that are inaccessible to ground troops. Conversely, the enemy can also use explicit aerial avenues of approach for air reconnaissance and attacks.

References

Department of Defense, U.S. Army. *Operations*. Field Manual FM 100-5. Washington, DC: Headquarters, Department of the Army, 1986.

—**OBSERVATION HELICOPTER** is a helicopter used primarily for observation and reconnaissance but may be used for other functions.

References

Department of Defense, Joint Chiefs of Staff. *Department of Defense Dictionary of Military and Related Terms*. Washington, DC: GPO, 1986.

—**OBSERVATION POST (OP)** is a position from which military observations (i.e., visual, audible, or other means) are made, fire is directed or adjusted, and that possesses appropriate communications. The post may be airborne. *See also:* Observation Post/Listening Post.

References

Department of Defense, U.S. Army. *Operational Terms and Symbols*. Field Manual FM 101-5-1. Washington, DC: Headquarters, Department of the Army, 1985.

—**OBSERVATION POST/LISTENING POST (OP/ LP)** is a position occupied to observe and listen to the activities within a particular sector and to warn of an enemy approach.

References

Department of Defense, U.S. Army. *The Rifle Squads (Mechanized and Light Infantry)*. Training Circular TC 7-1. Washington, DC: Headquarters, Department of the Army, 1976.

—**OBSERVED FIRE** is fire for which the points of impact or burst can be seen by an observer. The fire can be controlled and adjusted based upon the observations. *See also:* Observed Fire Chart, Observed Fire Procedures, Observer Identification, Observer-Target Distance, Observer-Target Line, Observer-Target Range, Observing Angle, Observing Interval, Observing Line, Observing Point, Observing Sector.

References

Department of Defense, U.S. Army. *Operational Terms and Symbols*. Field Manual FM 101-5-1. Washington, DC: Headquarters, Department of the Army, 1985.

—**OBSERVED FIRE CHART** is a chart, usually on a grid, on which the relative locations of the batteries of a battalion and its targets are plotted from data that have been obtained after firing. *See also:* Observed Fire.

References

Department of Defense, U.S. Army. *Dictionary of United States Army Terms*. Army Regulation AR 310-25. Washington, DC: Headquarters, Department of the Army, 1986.

—**OBSERVED FIRE PROCEDURES** are standard procedures for use in adjusting indirect fire on a target. *See also:* Observed Fire.

References

Department of Defense, Joint Chiefs of Staff. *Department of Defense Dictionary of Military and Related Terms.* Washington, DC: GPO, 1986.

—**OBSERVER IDENTIFICATION,** in artillery, is the first element of a call for fire. It establishes communications and identifies the observer or spotter. *See also:* Observed Fire.

References

Department of Defense, Joint Chiefs of Staff. *Department of Defense Dictionary of Military and Related Terms.* Washington, DC: GPO, 1986.

—**OBSERVER-TARGET DISTANCE** is the distance along an imaginary straight line from the spotter or observer to the target. *See also:* Observed Fire.

References

Department of Defense, Joint Chiefs of Staff. *Department of Defense Dictionary of Military and Related Terms.* Washington, DC: GPO, 1986.

—**OBSERVER-TARGET (OT) LINE** is an imaginary straight line from the observer or spotter to the target. *See also:* Observed Fire.

References

Department of Defense, U.S. Army. *Operational Terms and Symbols.* Field Manual FM 101-5-1. Washington, DC: Headquarters, Department of the Army, 1985.

—**OBSERVER-TARGET RANGE** is the distance along an imaginary straight line from the observer/spotter to the target. *See also:* Observed Fire.

References

Department of Defense, Joint Chiefs of Staff. *Department of Defense Dictionary of Military and Related Terms.* Washington, DC: GPO, 1986.

—**OBSERVERS,** in a nuclear, biological, or chemical attack, give initial and follow-up information concerning an attack. The observing unit, usually a platoon or company, reports the attack to battalion headquarters by using a preformatted report (i.e., an NBC 1 report). The report is sent only by designated observers to division nuclear, biological, chemical centers and is part of the standardized nuclear, bio-

logical, chemical warning and reporting system *See also:* Biological Warfare, Chemical Warfare, Nuclear Warfare.

References

Department of Defense, U.S. Army. *NBC Operations.* Field Manual FM 3-100. Washington, DC: Headquarters, Department of the Army, 1985.

—**OBSERVING ANGLE** is an angle at the target between a line to the observer and a line to the gun or battery. It is the angular distance of an observer from the gun or battery. *See also:* Observed Fire.

References

Department of Defense, U.S. Army. *Dictionary of United States Army Terms.* Army Regulation AR 310-25. Washington, DC: Headquarters, Department of the Army, 1986.

—**OBSERVING INTERVAL** is the time between two successive observations that are made to secure firing data on a moving target. *See also:* Observed Fire.

References

Department of Defense, U.S. Army. *Dictionary of United States Army Terms.* Army Regulation AR 310-25. Washington, DC: Headquarters, Department of the Army, 1986.

—**OBSERVING LINE** is a simulated straight line from the observer to the target. *See also:* Observed Fire.

References

Department of Defense, U.S. Army. *Dictionary of United States Army Terms.* Army Regulation AR 310-25. Washington, DC: Headquarters, Department of the Army, 1986.

—**OBSERVING POINT** is the point on a target at which the observer sights to obtain firing data. *See also:* Observed Fire.

References

Department of Defense, U.S. Army. *Dictionary of United States Army Terms.* Army Regulation AR 310-25. Washington, DC: Headquarters, Department of the Army, 1986.

—**OBSERVING SECTOR.** (1) An observing sector is an area visible from the point of observation. (2) An observing sector is an area given to an assigned post for observation. *See also:* Observed Fire.

References

Department of Defense, U.S. Army. *Dictionary of United States Army Terms.* Army Regulation AR 310-25. Washington, DC: Headquarters, Department of the Army, 1986.

—**OBSOLETE ITEM** is an item or assemblage that is no longer acceptable for United States Army use.

References

Department of Defense, U.S. Army. *Dictionary of United States Army Terms.* Army Regulation AR 310-25. Washington, DC: Headquarters, Department of the Army, 1986.

—**OBSTACLE** is any natural or man-made obstruction that stops, delays, canalizes, restricts, or diverts the movement or maneuver of a force (e.g., abatis, antitank ditches, blown bridges, built-up areas, minefields, rivers, road craters, terrain, and wire). The effectiveness of an obstacle is enhanced considerably when it is covered by fire. Obstacles are classified as either existing or reinforcing. An existing obstacle is a natural or cultural restriction to movement that is part of the terrain when battle planning begins. A reinforcing obstacle is specifically constructed, emplaced, or detonated to tie together, strengthen, and extend existing obstacles.

A type of reinforcing obstacle is the standard obstacle. It is designed to simplify and expedite planning and logistics support, and is employed in multiples as necessary to conform to a specific target site. Reinforcing obstacles are listed in a guide that is normally prepared by the division engineer as an enclosure to the division standing operating procedures or as an annex to the operation plan. The guide lists all the types of obstacles that a unit may use and includes a drawing, a list of materials, and instructions for making them.

References

Department of Defense, U.S. Army. *Countermobility.* Field Manual FM 5-102. Washington, DC: Headquarters, Department of the Army, 1985.

————. *Operational Terms and Symbols.* Field Manual FM 101-5-1. Washington, DC: Headquarters, Department of the Army, 1985.

—**OBSTACLE APPROACH ANGLES** are the angles formed by the inclines at the base of a positive or the top of a negative vertical obstacle that a vehicle must negotiate to surmounting the obstacle.

References

Department of Defense, U.S. Army. *Dictionary of United States Army Terms.* Army Regulation AR 310-25. Washington, DC: Headquarters, Department of the Army, 1986.

—**OBSTACLE BASE WIDTH** is the distance across the bottom of an obstacle.

References

Department of Defense, U.S. Army. *Dictionary of United States Army Terms.* Army Regulation AR 310-25. Washington, DC: Headquarters, Department of the Army, 1986.

—**OBSTACLE COURSE** is an area filled with hurdles, fences, ditches, and other obstacles. It is used to train soldiers to surmount similar obstacles in the field, and to develop their quickness, endurance, and agility.

References

Department of Defense, U.S. Army. *Dictionary of United States Army Terms.* Army Regulation AR 310-25. Washington, DC: Headquarters, Department of the Army, 1986.

—**OBSTACLE LENGTH** is the length of the long axis of an obstacle.

References

Department of Defense, U.S. Army. *Dictionary of United States Army Terms.* Army Regulation AR 310-25. Washington, DC: Headquarters, Department of the Army, 1986.

—**OBSTACLE PLAN** is the part of an operation plan (or order) concerned with the use of obstacles to enhance friendly fires or to canalize, direct, restrict, delay, or stop the enemy movement. Obstacle plans are used at corps level and below. *See also:* Countermobility Operations, Logistic Constraint, Obstacle.

References

Department of Defense, U.S. Army. *Operational Terms and Symbols.* Field Manual FM 101-5-1. Washington, DC: Headquarters, Department of the Army, 1985.

—**OBSTACLE SPACING** is the horizontal distance between the contact edges of vertical obstacles.

References

Department of Defense, U.S. Army. *Dictionary of United States Army Terms.* Army Regulation AR 310-25. Washington, DC: Headquarters, Department of the Army, 1986.

—**OBSTACLE SPACING TYPE** is the pattern of obstacle locations. The two most common types are linear and random.

References

Department of Defense, U.S. Army. *Dictionary of United States Army Terms*. Army Regulation AR 310-25. Washington, DC: Headquarters, Department of the Army, 1986.

—**OBSTACLE STUDY** is a study performed at echelons above corps that is based upon a detailed analysis of the terrain and a broad concept for future operations in the area. It is designed to determine the most effective use of existing and reinforcing obstacles and the area's potential for combat operations. *See also:* Obstacle.

References

Department of Defense, U.S. Army. *Operational Terms and Symbols*. Field Manual FM 101-5-1. Washington, DC: Headquarters, Department of the Army, 1985.

—**OBSTACLE SYSTEM** is a coordinated series of obstacles designed or employed to canalize, direct, restrict, delay, or stop the movement of an opposing force, and to impose additional losses in personnel, time, and equipment on the opposing force.

References

Department of Defense, U.S. Army. *Dictionary of United States Army Terms*. Army Regulation AR 310-25. Washington, DC: Headquarters, Department of the Army, 1986.

—**OBSTACLE VERTICLE MAGNITUDE** is the distance from the base to the crest of the obstacle.

References

Department of Defense, U.S. Army. *Dictionary of United States Army Terms*. Army Regulation AR 310-25. Washington, DC: Headquarters, Department of the Army, 1986.

—**OBSTRUCTION.** (1) An obstruction is any object that rises far enough above the surrounding surface or above a specified height to create a hazard to aircraft in flight. (2) An obstruction is an object that rises far enough above the surrounding sea bed to create a hazard to navigation.

References

Department of Defense, Joint Chiefs of Staff. *Department of Defense Dictionary of Military and Related Terms*. Washington, DC: GPO, 1986.

—**OBSTRUCTION TO VISION** is any obstruction other than precipitation (e.g., fog, blowing snow, blowing sand, blowing dust, haze, and smoke).

References

Department of Defense, U.S. Army. *Weather Support for Army Tactical Operations*. Field Manual FM 34-81. Washington, DC: Headquarters, Department of the Army, 1984.

—**OCCULTER** is a shutter for closing off the beam of a searchlight when it is not being used so that it cannot be seen by the enemy.

References

Department of Defense, U.S. Army. *Dictionary of United States Army Terms*. Army Regulation AR 310-25. Washington, DC: Headquarters, Department of the Army, 1986.

—**OCCUPATION CLASP** is a metallic bar that denotes where the wearer performed occupational duty since 1945. *See also:* Accouterment.

References

Department of Defense, U.S. Army. *Dictionary of United States Army Terms*. Army Regulation AR 310-25. Washington, DC: Headquarters, Department of the Army, 1986.

—**OCCUPATION OF POSITION** is movement into and proper organization of an area to be used as a battle position.

References

Department of Defense, Joint Chiefs of Staff. *Department of Defense Dictionary of Military and Related Terms*. Washington, DC: GPO, 1986.

—**OCCUPIED BEDS** are beds currently assigned to patients as of midnight, including patients on passes that do not exceed 72 hours, and any bassinets assigned to newborn infants whose mothers are no longer hospitalized patients. Not included are patients on convalescent leave, on leave, absent without leave, absent sick or sick in quarters, subsisting elsewhere, and transient patients. *See also:* Operating Beds.

References

Department of Defense, U.S. Army. *Health Service Support in a Communications Zone (Test)*. Field Manual FM 8-21. Washington, DC: Headquarters, Department of the Army, 1981.

—**OCCUPIED TERRITORY** is an area under the authority and effective control of a belligerent armed force. The term is not applicable to territory being administered pursuant to peace terms, treaty, or other agreements, expressed or implied, with the civil authority of the territory. *See also:* Civil Affairs Agreement.

References

Department of Defense, Joint Chiefs of Staff. *Department of Defense Dictionary of Military and Related Terms.* Washington, DC: GPO, 1986.

—**OCONUS (OUTSIDE CONTINENTAL UNITED STATES) RESIDENT** is a person whose home of record is in any place other than in one of the 50 contiguous states of the United States or the District of Columbia.

References

Department of Defense, U.S. Army. *Dictionary of United States Army Terms.* Army Regulation AR 310-25. Washington, DC: Headquarters, Department of the Army, 1986.

—**OFFENSIVE** (PRINCIPLE OF WAR). The purpose of the offensive is to seize, retain, and exploit the initiative. The principle of offensive suggests that offensive action, or maintaining the initiative, is the most effective and decisive way to pursue and to attain a clearly defined, common goal. This is fundamentally true in the strategic, the operational, and the tactical senses. While it may be necessary to adopt a defensive posture, this should be only a temporary condition until the necessary means are available to resume offensive operations. An offensive spirit must be inherent in the conduct of all defensive operations, so that the defense is active not passive. This is because offensive action, whatever form it takes, is the means by which the nation or a military force captures and holds the initiative, maintains freedom of action, and achieves results. It permits the political leader or the military commander to capitalize on the initiative, impose his will on the enemy, set the terms and select the place of confrontation or battle, exploit vulnerabilities, and react to rapidly changing situations and unexpected developments. No matter what the level, the side that retains the initiative through offensive action forces the foe to react rather than to act. *See also:* Principles of War.

References

Department of Defense, U.S. Army. *The Army.* (Prepublication Issue.) Field Manual FM 100-1. Washington, DC: Headquarters, Department of the Army, 1986.

———. *Operations.* Field Manual FM 100-5. Washington, DC: Headquarters, Department of the Army, 1986.

—**OFFENSIVE AIR SUPPORT (OAS),** part of tactical air support of land operations, consists of tactical air reconnaissance, battlefield air interdiction, and close air support, that are conducted in direct support of land operations. OAS is a NATO term and is not used by the U.S. Army. *See also:* Tactical Air Reconnaissance.

References

Department of Defense, U.S. Army. *Attack Helicopter Operations.* Field Manual FM 17-50. Washington, DC: Headquarters, Department of the Army, 1984.

———. *Fire Support in Combined Arms Operations.* Field Manual FM 6-20. Washington, DC: Headquarters, Department of the Army, 1983.

———. *Operational Terms and Symbols.* Field Manual FM 101-5-1. Washington, DC: Headquarters, Department of the Army, 1985.

—**OFFENSIVE GRENADE** is a high explosive hand grenade used by troops who are advancing in the open. The body of the grenade is made of fiber so that fragments are not thrown when it explodes.

References

Department of Defense, U.S. Army. *Dictionary of United States Army Terms.* Army Regulation AR 310-25. Washington, DC: Headquarters, Department of the Army, 1986.

—**OFFENSIVE MINE COUNTERMEASURES** are measures intended to prevent the enemy from successfully laying mines. *See also:* Mine Warfare.

References

Department of Defense, Joint Chiefs of Staff. *Department of Defense Dictionary of Military and Related Terms.* Washington, DC: GPO, 1986.

—**OFFENSIVE RELIEF** means to bring fresh troops into the attack in order to maintain an offensive momentum. Such reliefs are most common as the force enters the exploitation or pursuit, but may also be necessary during the attack itself, if previously committed units have suffered so severely that they are unable to reach their objectives. Offensive reliefs may be conducted as reliefs in place, but ideally are conducted without a significant pause in offensive tempo. *See also:* Offensive (Principle of War).

References
Department of Defense, U.S. Army. *Operations*. Field Manual FM 100-5. Washington, DC: Headquarters, Department of the Army, 1986.

—**OFFENSIVE SMOKE SCREEN** is a blinding and harassing bombardment of enemy positions using smoke, during daylight or nighttime, to neutralize enemy firepower and mobility during tactical operations by friendly troops. *See also:* Smoke Screen.

References
Department of Defense, U.S. Army. *Operations*. Field Manual FM 100-5. Washington, DC: Headquarters, Department of the Army, 1986.

—**OFFICE OF RECORD.** (1) An office of record is the office officially designated to maintain the records for specified operations. (2) An office of record is the agency charged with maintaining the final accounting records for registered publications.

References
Department of Defense, U.S. Army. *Dictionary of United States Army Terms*. Army Regulation AR 310-25. Washington, DC: Headquarters, Department of the Army, 1986.

—**OFFICER** is a commissioned or warrant officer unless otherwise specified. *See also:* Commissioned Officer, Commission, Nonprior Service Personnel, Officer Accession System, Official Military Personnel File, Prior Service Personnel, Warrant Officer.

References
Department of Defense, U.S. Army. *Promotion of Officers on Active Duty*. Army Regulation AR 624-100. Washington, DC: Headquarters, Department of the Army, 1984.

—**OFFICER ACCESSION SYSTEM (OAS)** should provide officers of the requisite quantity, quality, and academic discipline to satisfy the requirements of the Active Army, Army National Guard, and the U.S. Army Reserve. Officers enter the Army through four precommissioning programs: The U.S. Military Academy, the U.S. Army Reserve Officers' Training Corps; the Officer Candidate School at Fort Benning, Georgia, and state National Guard officer candidate school programs.

References
Department of Defense, U.S. Army. *U.S. Army Policy Statement, 1988*. Washington, DC: Headquarters, Department of the Army, 1988.

—**OFFICER OF THE DAY** is an officer, acting directly under the commanding officer or field officer of the day, responsible on a given day for executing all orders of the commanding officer relating to guard duties and any other duties that may have been assigned.

References
Department of Defense, U.S. Army. *Guard Duty*. Field Manual FM 22-6. Washington, DC: Headquarters, Department of the Army, 1971.

—**OFFICERS' CALL** is a Department of the Army pamphlet published as-needed to keep Army officers informed on particular subjects.

References
Department of Defense, U.S. Army. *Dictionary of United States Army Terms*. Army Regulation AR 310-25. Washington, DC: Headquarters, Department of the Army, 1986.

—**OFFICERS' FIELD RATION DINING FACILITY** is an appropriated fund field ration dining facility established to feed commissioned and warrant officers.

References
Department of Defense, U.S. Army. *Dictionary of United States Army Terms*. Army Regulation AR 310-25. Washington, DC: Headquarters, Department of the Army, 1986.

—**OFFICIAL INFORMATION** is information owned by, produced for or by, or subject to the control of, the United States Government.

References
Department of Defense, Joint Chiefs of Staff. *Department of Defense Dictionary of Military and Related Terms*. Washington, DC: GPO, 1986.

—**OFFICIAL MILITARY PERSONNEL FILE (OMPF)** is the permanent, historical, and official record of a member's military service. It is usually maintained on microfiche, and is composed of a performance section, a service section, and, in some cases, a restricted section. *See also:* Member, Enlisted Person; Officer.

References
Department of Defense, U.S. Army. *Dictionary of United States Army Terms*. Army Regulation AR 310-25. Washington, DC: Headquarters, Department of the Army, 1986.

—**OFFICIAL TRAINING LITERATURE** includes manuals, technical manuals, training circulars, Reserve Officers' Training Corps manuals, and pamphlets, which are all published as Department of the Army documents.

References
Department of Defense, U.S. Army. *Dictionary of United States Army Terms*. Army Regulation AR 310-25. Washington, DC: Headquarters, Department of the Army, 1986.

—**OFF-LINE CRYPTO-OPERATION**, in communications security, means the encryption or decryption performed separately and at a different time than the time of transmission or decryption. It is done by manual or machine crypto-equipment that is not electrically connected to the signal line. *See also:* Communications Security.

References
Department of Defense, Defense Intelligence College. *Glossary of Intelligence Terms and Definitions*. Washington, DC: DIC, 1987.

—**OFF-ROUTE MINE** is an antitank horizontal action mine. *See also:* Mine Warfare.

References
Department of Defense, U.S. Army. *Mine/ Countermine Operations at the Company Level*. Field Manual FM 20-32. Washington, DC: Headquarters, Department of the Army, 1976.

—**OFFSET METHOD** is a way of describing locations on a map by giving the distance from the bottom of the map, and to the left or right of a secretly designated north or south line.

References
Department of Defense, U.S. Army. *Dictionary of United States Army Terms*. Army Regulation AR 310-25. Washington, DC: Headquarters, Department of the Army, 1986.

—**OFFSET PLOTTING** is a method of plotting firing data when different ranges and azimuths must be sent to each gun of a battery.

References
Department of Defense, U.S. Army. *Dictionary of United States Army Terms*. Army Regulation AR 310-25. Washington, DC: Headquarters, Department of the Army, 1986.

—**OFFSET REGISTRATION**, in field artillery operations, is registering from a supplementary position.

References
Department of Defense, U.S. Army. *Fire Support in Combined Arms Operations*. Field Manual FM 6-20. Washington, DC: Headquarters, Department of the Army, 1983.

—**OFFSHORE PROCUREMENT** is the purchase by military authorities in countries outside of the United States and its possessions, and Canada, with Regular Army funds of items for the International Cooperation Administration program, to be delivered to specified countries or for U.S. forces, wherever they are stationed.

References
Department of Defense, U.S. Army. *Dictionary of United States Army Terms*. Army Regulation AR 310-25. Washington, DC: Headquarters, Department of the Army, 1986.

—**OGIVE** is a curved forward part of a projectile. It goes up to and includes the pointed end of a projectile.

References
Department of Defense, U.S. Army. *Dictionary of United States Army Terms*. Army Regulation AR 310-25. Washington, DC: Headquarters, Department of the Army, 1986.

—**OLFACTORY DECEPTION.** Simulated battlefield odors can be used for deception. Pending the development and standardization of olfactory agents, munitions, and devices, it is left to the ingenuity and resourcefulness of commanders in the field to improvise the means for simulating battlefield odors.

References
Department of Defense, U.S. Army. *Tactical Deception*. Field Manual FM 90-2. Washington, DC: Headquarters, Department of the Army, 1978.

—**ON** is an element of a tank fire command. It directs the gunner to halt the traverse of the turret, and is usually preceded by the command "steady."

Reference
Department of Defense, U.S. Army. *Dictionary of United States Army Terms*. Army Regulation AR 310-25. Washington, DC: Headquarters, Department of the Army, 1986.

—**ON CALL** is a term used to signify that a prearranged concentration, air strike, or final protective fire may be called for. *See also:* Call for Fire.

References
Department of Defense, Joint Chiefs of Staff. *Department of Defense Dictionary of Military and Related Terms.* Washington, DC: GPO, 1986.

—**ON-CALL TARGET**, in fire support, is a planned target other than a scheduled target on which fire is delivered when requested. *See also:* Scheduled Target.

References
Department of Defense, U.S. Army. *Operational Terms and Symbols.* Field Manual FM 101-5-1. Washington, DC: Headquarters, Department of the Army, 1985.

—**ON-CALL TARGET** (NUCLEAR) is a planned nuclear target other than a scheduled nuclear target for which a need can be anticipated but that will be delivered on request rather than at a specific time. Coordination and warning of friendly troops and aircraft are mandatory. *See also:* Nuclear Warfare.

References
Department of Defense, Joint Chiefs of Staff. *Department of Defense Dictionary of Military and Related Terms.* Washington, DC: GPO, 1986.

—**ON-EQUIPMENT MATERIEL** are items of supply that, although they are not part of the equipment proper, are issued with an accompanying equipment (e.g., gun mounts, guns, radios, flashlights, fire extinguishers, sighting and fire control equipment, specified equipment (spare) parts, and tools for maintaining the equipment). They are required for equipment first echelon maintenance, operation, armament, fire protection, communications, and related elements.

References
Department of Defense, U.S. Army. *Dictionary of United States Army Terms.* Army Regulation AR 310-25. Washington, DC: Headquarters, Department of the Army, 1986.

—**ON GUARD.** (1) On guard is ready to defend or protect. (2) On guard is watching, as a member of the guard. (3) On guard is the first position of readiness in bayonet exercises.

References
Department of Defense, U.S. Army. *Dictionary of United States Army Terms.* Army Regulation AR 310-25. Washington, DC: Headquarters, Department of the Army, 1986.

—**ON HAND** is the quantity of an item physically available in a storage location and is part of the accountable property of an issuing activity.

References
Department of Defense, Joint Chiefs of Staff. *Department of Defense Dictionary of Military and Related Terms.* Washington, DC: GPO, 1986.

—**ON-LAUNCHER RELIABILITY** is the percentage of tactical missiles loaded on launchers for firing that are fired within the required time limits.

References
Department of Defense, U.S. Army. *Dictionary of United States Army Terms.* Army Regulation AR 310-25. Washington, DC: Headquarters, Department of the Army, 1986.

—**ON-LINE CRYPTO OPERATION**, in communications security, means the use of crypto-equipment that is directly connected to a signal line, so that encryption and transmission are accomplished simultaneously. *See also:* Communications; Off-Line Crypto-Operation.

References
Department of Defense, Defense Intelligence College. *Glossary of Intelligence Terms and Definitions.* Washington, DC: DIC, 1987.

—**ON-LOAD BASE** is an air base or airfield where support personnel and equipment are initially loaded on airlift aircraft.

References
Department of Defense, U.S. Army. *USA/USAF Doctrine for Joint Airborne and Tactical Airlift Operations.* Field Manual FM 100-27. Washington, DC: Headquarters, Department of the Army, 1985.

—**ON SITE INSPECTION** refers to procurement inspections conducted by the Military Department at the contractor's facilities to determine that supplies and services conform to the specifications and other controlling conditions cited in the contract. It includes transient and resident operations, source inspection of subcontractor, and clerical and supervisory functions related to inspection activities assigned solely to the contractor's facility.

References
Department of Defense, U.S. Army. *Dictionary of United States Army Terms.* Army Regulation AR 310-25. Washington, DC: Headquarters, Department of the Army, 1986.

—**ON-THE-JOB EXPERIENCE** is serving in the primary military occupational specialty or in a duty position that is authorized at the current or a higher grade.

References

Department of Defense, U.S. Army. *Enlisted Personnel Management System.* Army Regulation AR 600-200. Washington, DC: Headquarters, Department of the Army, 1984.

—**ON-THE-JOB TRAINING (OJT)** is an instruction process whereby students or trainees acquire knowledge and skills by actually performing the duties under competent supervision and in accordance with an approved plan program. *See also:* On-The-Job Experience.

References

Department of Defense, U.S. Army. *Enlisted Personnel Management System.* Army Regulation AR 600-200. Washington, DC: Headquarters, Department of the Army, 1984.

———. *How to Prepare and Conduct Military Training.* Field Manual FM 21-6. Washington, DC: Headquarters, Department of the Army, 1975.

—**ONE DAY'S SUPPLY** is a unit or quantity of supplies that has been adopted as a standard of measurement. It is used in estimating the average daily expenditure under stated conditions. It may also be expressed in terms of a factor (e.g., rounds of ammunition per weapon per day). *See also:* Standard Day of Supply.

References

Department of Defense, Joint Chiefs of Staff. *Department of Defense Dictionary of Military and Related Terms.* Washington, DC: GPO, 1986.

—**ONE HUNDRED PERCENT RECTANGLE** is an area that includes practically all the shot that has been fired by an artillery gun or battery at a target.

References

Department of Defense, U.S. Army. *Dictionary of United States Army Terms.* Army Regulation AR 310-25. Washington, DC: Headquarters, Department of the Army, 1986.

—**ONE SOLDIER POSITION** (deliberate), the individual soldier's basic defensive position, is a hole dug in the ground. This position allows flexibility in the use of cover because the hole only has to be long enough for one soldier and his gear. Since it does not have the security of a two-person position, it must allow a soldier to shoot to the front or oblique from behind frontal cover.

References

Department of Defense, U.S. Army. *Survivability.* Field Manual FM 5-103. Washington, DC: Headquarters, Department of the Army, 1985.

—**ONE-STATION UNIT TRAINING (OSUT)** is initial entry training in which elements of basic training and advanced individual training are provided in the same unit, under one cadre for the total period of training. In OSUT, elements of basic training and advanced individual training are either integrated and provided simultaneously, or are nonintegrated and provided in distinct basic training or advanced individual training phases.

References

Department of Defense, U.S. Army. *Enlisted Personnel.* Army Regulation AR 635-200. Washington, DC: Headquarters, Department of the Army, 1984.

—**ONE-TIME CRYPTOSYSTEM,** in communications security, means a cryptosystem that uses key variables only once. *See also:* Communications Security.

References

Department of Defense, Defense Intelligence College. *Glossary of Intelligence Terms and Definitions.* Washington, DC: DIC, 1987.

—**ONE-TIME SYSTEM** is a system of enciphering in which a nonrepeating key is used. *See also:* One-Time Crypto System.

References

Department of Defense, U.S. Army. *Dictionary of United States Army Terms.* Army Regulation AR 310-25. Washington, DC: Headquarters, Department of the Army, 1986.

—**ONE-TIME TAPE,** in communications security, is a punched paper tape that is used only once. It provides cryptovariables in certain machine cryptosystems. *See also:* Communications Security.

References

Department of Defense, Defense Intelligence College. *Glossary of Intelligence Terms and Definitions.* Washington, DC: DIC, 1987.

—**ONE-WAY ROUTE** is a path or roadway on which vehicles move in one direction only.

References

Department of Defense, U.S. Army. *Route Reconnaissance and Classification.* Field Manual FM 5-36. Washington, DC: Headquarters, Department of the Army, 1985.

—**OPEN** is a term used in a call for fire to indicate that the spotter or observer desires bursts to be separated by the maximum effective width of the burst of the shell fired.

References

Department of Defense, Joint Chiefs of Staff. *Department of Defense Dictionary of Military and Related Terms.* Washington, DC: GPO, 1986.

—**OPEN CODE** is a cryptographic system that uses an external text that has meaning. It is used in an attempt to disguise the hidden meaning. *See also:* CRYPTO.

References

Department of Defense, U.S. Army. *Dictionary of United States Army Terms.* Army Regulation AR 310-25. Washington, DC: Headquarters, Department of the Army, 1986.

—**OPEN COLUMN** is a motor march formation in which the vehicles are widely spaced as a passive defense measure. The normal vehicle distance is 75 to 100 meters. This permits vehicles that are not part of the march unit to overtake and enter the column, if necessary.

References

Department of Defense, U.S. Army. *The Infantry Rifle Company (Infantry, Airborne, Air Assault, Ranger).* Field Manual FM 7-10. Washington, DC: Headquarters, Department of the Army, 1982.

—**OPEN-END CONTRACT** is an order for goods or services that contains either no limit or varying limits of time and quantity, and that usually involves recurring orders and varying charges.

References

Department of Defense, U.S. Army. *Dictionary of United States Army Terms.* Army Regulation AR 310-25. Washington, DC: Headquarters, Department of the Army, 1986.

—**OPEN IMPROVED STORAGE SPACE** is an outside area that has been graded and hard surfaced or prepared with some suitable material so as to permit effective material handling operations.

References

Department of Defense, Joint Chiefs of Staff. *Department of Defense Dictionary of Military and Related Terms.* Washington, DC: GPO, 1986.

—**OPEN MESSES** are various nonappropriated activities that provide services essential for the dining, billeting, and recreation of officers, warrant officers, noncommissioned officers, and their families.

References

Department of Defense, U.S. Army. *Dictionary of United States Army Terms.* Army Regulation AR 310-25. Washington, DC: Headquarters, Department of the Army, 1986.

—**OPEN RANKS.** (1) Open ranks are an arrangement of ranks in close order drill in which the normal distance between ranks is increased by the length of a full step. (2) Open ranks is the preparatory command to take the position described above. *See also:* Close Ranks.

References

Department of Defense, U.S. Army. *Dictionary of United States Army Terms.* Army Regulation AR 310-25. Washington, DC: Headquarters, Department of the Army, 1986.

—**OPEN ROUTE** is a route that does not have traffic or movement control restrictions. The supervision on such a highway is ordinarily limited to control of traffic at intersections and is analogous to civilian control over rural roads carrying a small volume of traffic.

References

Department of Defense, U.S. Army. *Route Reconnaissance and Classification.* Field Manual FM 5-36. Washington, DC: Headquarters, Department of the Army, 1985.

—**OPEN SHEAF** is the lateral distribution of fire of two or more weapons so that the adjoining points of impact or points of burst are separated by the maximum effective width of burst of the type of shell that is being used. *See also:* Parallel Sheaf, Sheaf, Special Sheaf.

References

Department of Defense, Joint Chiefs of Staff. *Department of Defense Dictionary of Military and Related Terms.* Washington, DC: GPO, 1986.

Department of Defense, U.S. Army. *Dictionary of United States Army Terms.* Army Regulation AR 310-25. Washington, DC: Headquarters, Department of the Army, 1986.

—**OPEN-SOURCE INFORMATION** is a generic term describing information of potential intelligence value that is available to the public. *See also:* Classified Information.

References
Department of Defense, Joint Chiefs of Staff. *Department of Defense Dictionary of Military and Related Terms.* Washington, DC: GPO, 1986.

—**OPEN SOURCES** is a general intelligence term for primary and secondary source materials that are unclassified and may or may not be produced by the government. They are often the product of overt intelligence collection and often provide a valuable input to all source intelligence production. It is a common and valid observation that the availability of open-source material is much greater in open democratic societies than in closed, autocratic societies such as that in the Soviet Union and that this gives the latter an intelligence advantage. *See also:* Classified Information.

References
Oseth, John M. *Regulating U.S. Intelligence Operations: A Study in the Definition of the National Interest.* Frankfurt: University of Kentucky Press, 1985.

—**OPERATING ACTIVITY CENTER** is a center authorized and designated by Headquarters, Department of the Army, to perform, in a single location, a group of functionally related operational activities. *See also:* Installation.

References
Department of Defense, U.S. Army. *Dictionary of United States Army Terms.* Army Regulation AR 310-25. Washington, DC: Headquarters, Department of the Army, 1986.

—**OPERATING BEDS** are beds in a medical treatment facility that are currently set up and ready for the care of a patient. They must include the supporting space, equipment, and staff available under normal circumstances. Excluded from this category are transient patients' beds, incubators, bassinets, labor beds, and recovery beds. *See also:* Medical Treatment.

References
Department of Defense, U.S. Army. *Health Service Support in a Communications Zone (Test).* Field Manual FM 8-21. Washington, DC: Headquarters, Department of the Army, 1981.

—**OPERATING BUDGET** is the component of the operating program that details the financial plans in terms of costs (funded and unfunded) and obligations in support of the operating program for the budget year. At each level, the operating budget provides a financial plan to support the activities and function for which the commander is responsible. Operating budgets are used for administrative and management purposes and are not used to authorize the obligation of funds.

References
Department of Defense, U.S. Army. *Dictionary of United States Army Terms.* Army Regulation AR 310-25. Washington, DC: Headquarters, Department of the Army, 1986.

—**OPERATING BUILDING** is any structure, except a magazine, in which operations pertaining to manufacturing, processing, handling, loading, or assembling ammunition and explosives are performed. *See also:* Magazine.

References
Department of Defense, U.S. Army. *Ammunition and Explosives Safety Standards.* Army Regulation AR 385-64. Washington, DC: Headquarters, Department of the Army, 1987.

—**OPERATING FORCES** are the forces whose primary missions are to participate in combat and in the elements that support it. *See also:* Combat Forces, Combat Service Support Elements, Combat Support Elements.

References
Department of Defense, Joint Chiefs of Staff. *Department of Defense Dictionary of Military and Related Terms.* Washington, DC: GPO, 1986.

—**OPERATING HANDLE** is a handle or bar used to make the operating lever open and close the breech of the gun.

References
Department of Defense, U.S. Army. *Dictionary of United States Army Terms.* Army Regulation AR 310-25. Washington, DC: Headquarters, Department of the Army, 1986.

—**OPERATING LEVEL FACTOR** is a number used to identify the days of supply in the operating level. This factor, when divided into the total quantity demanded during the control period, equals the operating level quantity.

References

Department of Defense, U.S. Army. *Dictionary of United States Army Terms.* Army Regulation AR 310-25. Washington, DC: Headquarters, Department of the Army, 1986.

—OPERATING LEVEL OF SUPPLY refers to the quantities of materiel required to sustain operations between the time supplies are requisitioned for and their arrival. These quantities should be based upon the established replenishment period (e.g., monthly, quarterly, or other established period). *See also:* Level of Supply.

References

Department of Defense, Joint Chiefs of Staff. *Department of Defense Dictionary of Military and Related Terms.* Washington, DC: GPO, 1986.

—OPERATING LINE is a group of buildings, facilities, or related work stations that are arranged so that consecutive steps can be performed to manufacture an explosive, or to load, assemble, modify, and maintain ammunition.

References

Department of Defense, U.S. Army. *Ammunition and Explosives Safety Standards.* Army Regulation AR 385-64. Washington, DC: Headquarters, Department of the Army, 1987.

—OPERATING MAINTENANCE is the scheduled and unscheduled service and repair to vehicles and other equipment performed by the organization using them.

References

Department of Defense, U.S. Army. *Dictionary of United States Army Terms.* Army Regulation AR 310-25. Washington, DC: Headquarters, Department of the Army, 1986.

—OPERATING PERSONNEL are personnel who are allotted by Department of the Army personnel authorization vouchers and its major commands to perform functional, support, and overhead duties. These personnel are organized in table of distribution units except when specifically authorized as table of organization and equipment units by the Department of the Army. *See also:* Table of Distribution and Allowances, Table of Organization and Equipment.

References

Department of Defense, U.S. Army. *Dictionary of United States Army Terms.* Army Regulation AR 310-25. Washington, DC: Headquarters, Department of the Army, 1986.

—OPERATING PROGRAM is the program prepared by each Army command, agency, and installation that lists their annual objectives relating to the available resources (i.e., manpower, materiel, and money). *See also:* Operating Schedule.

References

Department of Defense, U.S. Army. *Dictionary of United States Army Terms.* Army Regulation AR 310-25. Washington, DC: Headquarters, Department of the Army, 1986.

—OPERATING SCHEDULE (1) Operating schedule is a time-phased plan prepared by a command, agency, or installation to indicate when certain accomplishments should occur. It is used to balance related activities and to prescribe a time sequence for objectives and for more efficient operating. (2) An operating schedule is a detailed schedule required in programming and budgeting that sets forth the time-phasing for a particular objective. *See also:* Operating Program.

References

Department of Defense, U.S. Army. *Dictionary of United States Army Terms.* Army Regulation AR 310-25. Washington, DC: Headquarters, Department of the Army, 1986.

—OPERATING STRENGTH refers to the present and absent strength of an organization that is classified under the "personnel status" of the Customary Army morning report heading as "permanent party." It does not include in-transit strength. Separately identifying operating strength provides strength data necessary for unit readiness reporting.

References

Department of Defense, U.S. Army. *Dictionary of United States Army Terms.* Army Regulation AR 310-25. Washington, DC: Headquarters, Department of the Army, 1986.

—OPERATION. (1) Operaton is a military action or a carrying out of a strategic, tactical, service, training, or administrative military mission. (2) Operation is the process of carrying on combat, including movement, supply, attack, defense, and maneuvers needed to gain the objectives of any battle or campaign.

References

Department of Defense, U.S. Army. *Operational Terms and Symbols.* Field Manual FM 101-5-1. Washington, DC: Headquarters, Department of the Army, 1985.

—**OPERATION AND MAINTENANCE (O & M), ARMY PROGRAM,** is a subdivision of the operation and maintenance, Army appropriation, as reflected in the Army management structure. There are nine such programs. *See also:* Army Management Structure.

References
Department of Defense, U.S. Army. *Dictionary of United States Army Terms.* Army Regulation AR 310-25. Washington, DC: Headquarters, Department of the Army, 1986.

—**OPERATION AND MAINTENANCE (O & M), ARMY SUBPROGRAM,** is a subdivision of an operation and maintenance, Army program, that is identified by the first two positions of the operation and maintenance, Army code in the Army management structure. There are fifteen such subprograms. *See also:* Operation and Maintenance, Army Program.

References
Department of Defense, U.S. Army. *Dictionary of United States Army Terms.* Army Regulation AR 310-25. Washington, DC: Headquarters, Department of the Army, 1986.

—**OPERATION AND MAINTENANCE (O&M) OF FACILITIES** are the functions generally performed for the common support of all organizations, activities, and units. These are listed and defined in the Army management structure. *See also:* Operation and Maintenance of Facilities Budget Activity Account.

References
Department of Defense, U.S. Army. *Dictionary of United States Army Terms.* Army Regulation AR 310-25. Washington, DC: Headquarters, Department of the Army, 1986.

—**OPERATION AND MAINTENANCE (O & M) OF FACILITIES BUDGET ACTIVITY ACCOUNT** Is a management account similar to a budget activity account and is used by the Department of the Army to indicate the operation and maintenance of facilities, a function, a mission, or an activity for the purpose of programming, budgeting, manpower utilization, accounting, and reporting. *See also:* Operation and Maintenance of Facilities.

References
Department of Defense, U.S. Army. *Dictionary of United States Army Terms.* Army Regulation AR 310-25. Washington, DC: Headquarters, Department of the Army, 1986.

—**OPERATION ANNEXES** are the supplemental instructions that are too voluminous, too technical, or too unusual to be included in the body of the plan or order. *See also:* Operation Plan.

References
Department of Defense, U.S. Army. *Operational Terms and Symbols.* Field Manual FM 101-5-1. Washington, DC: Headquarters, Department of the Army, 1985.

—**OPERATION ESTIMATE** (STAFF ESTIMATE) is the analysis of the factors affecting the mission to determine reasonable courses of action open to friendly forces. It provides a recommended course of action for accomplishing a mission. The operation estimate and the commander's estimate use the same format and generally have the same content; however, the operation estimate makes a recommendation rather than a decision.

References
Department of Defense, U.S. Army. *Staff Organization and Operations.* Field Manual FM 101-5. Washington, DC: Headquarters, Department of the Army, 1984.

—**OPERATION EXPOSURE GUIDE** is the maximum amount of nuclear radiation that the commander considers his unit may be permitted to receive while it is performing a specific mission or missions. *See also:* Nuclear Warfare.

References
Department of Defense, Joint Chiefs of Staff. *Department of Defense Dictionary of Military and Related Terms.* Washington, DC: GPO, 1986.

—**OPERATION HEADQUARTERS** is a headquarters primarily concerned with the command and control of the forces executing operational missions.

References
Department of Defense, U.S. Army. *Dictionary of United States Army Terms.* Army Regulation AR 310-25. Washington, DC: Headquarters, Department of the Army, 1986.

—**OPERATION MAP** is a map showing the location and strength of friendly forces involved in an operation. It may also indicate the predicted movement and location of enemy forces. *See also:* Map.

References

Department of Defense, U.S. Army. *Operational Terms and Symbols*. Field Manual FM 101-5-1. Washington, DC: Headquarters, Department of the Army, 1985.

—**OPERATION ORDER (OPORD or OPORDER)** is a directive issued by a commander to subordinate commanders to ensure the coordinated execution of an operation. It includes tactical movement orders. *See also:* Operation Plan.

References

Department of Defense, U.S. Army. *Air Defense Artillery Deployment: Chaparral/Vulcan/Stinger*. Field Manual FM 44-3. Washington, DC: Headquarters, Department of the Army, 1984.

———. *Operational Terms and Symbols*. Field Manual FM 101-5-1. Washington, DC: Headquarters, Department of the Army, 1985.

—**OPERATION ORDER FOR ROAD MOVEMENT** is an order containing instructions for moving personnel and prescribed equipment from one location to another within a stated period of time. These orders are issued by the authority having jurisdiction over the personnel who are involved in the order.

References

Department of Defense, U.S. Army. *Dictionary of United States Army Terms*. Army Regulation AR 310-25. Washington, DC: Headquarters, Department of the Army, 1986.

—**OPERATION OVERLAY** is an overlay showing the location, size, scheme of maneuver, and fires of friendly forces involved in an operation. It may indicate predicted movements and locations of enemy forces. It is usually substituted for an operation map at the lower echelons as an essential part of an operations order. *See also:* Map.

References

Department of Defense, U.S. Army. *Air Defense Artillery Deployment: Chaparral/Vulcan/Stinger*. Field Manual FM 44-3. Washington, DC: Headquarters, Department of the Army, 1984.

———. *Operational Terms and Symbols*. Field Manual FM 101-5-1. Washington, DC: Headquarters, Department of the Army, 1985.

—**OPERATION PLAN (OPLAN)** is a plan for a military operation or operations that extend over considerable space and time and is usually based upon stated assumptions. It covers a single op-eration or a series of connected operations that are to be carried out simultaneously or in succession, and implements operations derived from the campaign plan. When the time or conditions the plan based upon occur, the plan becomes an operation order. The OPLAN includes the following plans: (1) contingency, (2) supporting, (3) deployment, (4) employment, (5) consolidated, (6) base development, and (7) general. *See also:* Operation Order, Operation Plan in Complete Format, Operation Plan in Concept Format, Operation Planning.

References

Department of Defense, U.S. Army. *Air Defense Artillery Deployment: Chaparral/Vulcan/Stinger*. Field Manual FM 44-3. Washington, DC: Headquarters, Department of the Army, 1984.

———. *Operational Terms and Symbols*. Field Manual FM 101-5-1. Washington, DC: Headquarters, Department of the Army, 1985.

———. *Staff Organization and Operations*. Field Manual FM 101-5. Washington, DC: Headquarters, Department of the Army, 1984.

—**OPERATION PLAN (OPLAN) IN COMPLETE FORMAT** is an OPLAN for the execution of military operations that can be translated into an operation order with minimum alteration. The designation "plan" is often used instead of "order" in preparing for operations well in advance. Complete plans include deployment and employment phases, as appropriate. All areas of the plan are fully developed to include the complete tab (a type of appendix)/troop list and other essential annexes. *See also:* Operation Plan.

References

Department of Defense, U.S. Army. *Planning Logistics Support for Military Operations*. Field Manual FM 701-58. Washington, DC: Headquarters, Department of the Army, 1987.

—**OPERATION PLAN (OPLAN) IN CONCEPT FORMAT** is an abbrevitaed OPLAN that outlines the salient features or principles of a course of action. It is used to complete detailed planning and must be expanded prior to execution. *See also:* Operation Plan.

References

Department of Defense, U.S. Army. *Planning Logistics Support for Military Operations*. Field Manual FM 701-58. Washington, DC: Headquarters, Department of the Army, 1987.

—**OPERATION PLANNING.** Prepared by the commanders of unified and specified commands and their subordinate forces in response to requirements established by the Joint Chiefs of Staff, operation plans are developed for the conduct of military operations. Operation planning consists of developing deployment plans, which focus on the strategic mobility problem, and campaign plans, which focus on effectively employing military resources once they have arrived within the theater. Operation plans are designed to identify appropriate courses of action. Application of the principles of war to the joint operation planning process makes the plans simpler and more practical and provides a direct link to actual execution on the battlefield. *See also:* Operation Plan.

References

Department of Defense, U.S. Army. *The Army* (Prepublication Issue.) Field Manual FM 100-1. Washington, DC: Headquarters, Department of the Army, 1986.

—**OPERATIONAL.** In a medical treatment facility context, operational describes a medical treatment facility that is prepared to receive and treat patients. To attain this posture, the facility must have the minimum essential necessities for direct patient care. These necessities vary from one facility to another. As a practical operational technique, the patient care necessities are identified in advance and are normally included in the first element of the unit displaced when redeployment occurs. Specific requirements for each type of medical treatment facility and for other health service organizations are contained in appropriate Army training and evaluation programs.

References

Department of Defense, U.S. Army. *Health Service Support in a Communications Zone (Test).* Field Manual FM 8-21. Washington, DC: Headquarters, Department of the Army, 1981.

—**OPERATIONAL ART** is the employment of military forces to attain strategic goals in a theater of war or theater of operations through the design, organization, and execution of campaigns and major operations. A campaign is a series of joint actions designed to attain a strategic objective in a theater of war. Simultaneous campaigns may occur when the theater of war contains more than one theater of operation. Sequential campaigns in a single theater occur

when a large force changes or secures its original goal or when the conditions of the conflict change. An offensive campaign may follow a successful defensive campaign (e.g., as it did in Korea in 1950) or a new offensive campaign may be undertaken if strategic goals change or are not secured in the initial campaign. A major operation is composed of the coordinated actions of large forces in a single phase of a campaign or in a critical battle. Major operations decide the course of campaigns.

Operational art thus involves fundamental decisions about when and where to fight and whether to accept or decline battle. Its essence is the identification of the enemy's operational center-of-gravity—its source of strength or balance—and the concentration of superior combat power against that point to achieve a decisive success. No particular echelon of command is solely or uniquely concerned with operational art, but theater commanders and their chief subordinates usually plan and direct campaigns. Army groups and armies normally design the major ground operations of a campaign; corps and divisions normally execute those ground operations. *See also:* Doctrine, Strategy, Tactics.

References

Department of Defense, U.S. Army. *The Army.* (Prepublication Issue.) Field Manual FM 100-1. Washington, DC: Headquarters, Department of the Army, 1986.

———. *Operations.* Field Manual FM 100-5. Washington, DC: Headquarters, Department of the Army, 1986.

—**OPERATIONAL CHAIN OF COMMAND** is a hierarchy of authorities established for a particular operation or a series of continuing operations. *See also:* Administrative Chain of Command, Chain of Command.

References

Department of Defense, Joint Chiefs of Staff. *Department of Defense Dictionary of Military and Related Terms.* Washington, DC: GPO, 1986.

—**OPERATIONAL CHARACTERISTICS** are the military characteristics that pertain primarily to the functions to be performed by equipment, either alone or in conjunction with other equipment. For example, the operational characteristics for electronic equipment include such items as frequency coverage, channeling, type of modulation, and character of emission.

References

Department of Defense, Joint Chiefs of Staff. *Department of Defense Dictionary of Military and Related Terms.* Washington, DC: GPO, 1986.

—**OPERATIONAL COMMAND.** (1) Operational command is synonymous with operational control and is uniquely applied to the operational control exercised by the commanders of unified and specified commands over specified forces. (2) In NATO usage, operational command is the authority granted to commanders to deploy units, to reassign forces, and to retain or delegate operational or tactical control as necessary. It does not inherently include responsibility for the administration of logistics. *See also:* Operational Control.

References

Department of Defense, U.S. Army. *Air Defense Artillery Deployment: Chaparral/Vulcan/Stinger.* Field Manual FM 44-3. Washington, DC: Headquarters, Department of the Army, 1984.

—**OPERATIONAL CONTROL (OPCON)** is the authority delegated to a commander to direct the forces assigned to him so that he can accomplish specific missions and tasks that are usually limited by time, function, or location; to deploy these forces; and to retain or assign tactical control of these forces.

References

Department of Defense, Defense Intelligence College. *Glossary of Intelligence Terms and Definitions.* Washington, DC: DIC, 1987.

Department of Defense, U.S. Army. *Air Defense Artillery Deployment: Chaparral/Vulcan/Stinger.* Field Manual FM 44-3. Washington, DC: Headquarters, Department of the Army, 1984.

—**OPERATIONAL ELINT (ELECTRONIC INTELLIGENCE)** is a category of electronic intelligence concerned with the introduction, disposition, movement, use, tactics, and activity levels of known foreign noncommunications emitters and, where applicable, associated military systems. Operational electronic intelligence may be used for satisfying current intelligence requirements. *See also:* Electronic Intelligence.

References

Department of Defense, Defense Intelligence College. *Glossary of Intelligence Terms and Definitions.* Washington, DC: DIC, 1987.

—**OPERATIONAL EVOLUTION** is the test and analysis of a specific end-item or system, insofar as practicable under Service operating conditions, to determine if quantity production is warranted considering the increase in military effectiveness to be gained and its effectiveness as compared with currently available items or systems. Consideration is given to (1) personnel capabilities to maintain and operate the equipment; (2) size, weight, and location factors; and (3) enemy capabilities in the field.

References

Department of Defense, Joint Chiefs of Staff. *Department of Defense Dictionary of Military and Related Terms.* Washington, DC: GPO, 1986.

—**OPERATIONAL EXPOSURE GUIDE (OEG)** is the maximum amount of nuclear radiation that the commander considers his unit can receive while it is performing a particular mission or missions. *See also:* Radiation Status.

References

Department of Defense, U.S. Army. *Operational Terms and Symbols.* Field Manual FM 101-5-1. Washington, DC: Headquarters, Department of the Army, 1985.

—**OPERATIONAL INTELLIGENCE (OPINTEL).** (1) OPINTEL is the intelligence information needed to plan and execute operations. (2) OPINTEL is intelligence required to support the activities of intelligence agencies under the National Security Council. *See also:* Strategic Intelligence.

References

Department of Defense, Defense Intelligence College. *Glossary of Intelligence Terms and Definitions.* Washington, DC: DIC, 1987.

—**OPERATIONAL INTERCHANGEABILITY** is the ability to substitute one item for another of different composition or origin without losing effectiveness, accuracy, and safe performance.

References

Department of Defense, Joint Chiefs of Staff. *Department of Defense Dictionary of Military and Related Terms.* Washington, DC: GPO, 1986.

—**OPERATIONAL LEVEL OF WAR** is the theory of larger unit operations. It uses available military resources to attain strategic goals within a theater of war. It also involves planning and conducting campaigns. Campaigns are sustained operations designed to defeat an enemy force in a specified space and time with simultaneous and sequential battles. The disposition of forces, selection of objectives, and actions taken to weaken or to outmaneuver the enemy set the terms of the next battle and exploit tactical gains. They are all part of the operational level of war. In air-land battle doctrine, this level includes the marshalling of forces and logistical support, providing direction to ground and air maneuver, applying conventional and nuclear fires in depth, and employing unconventional and psychological warfare. *See also:* Principles of War.

References

Department of Defense, U.S. Army. *Psychological Operations.* Field Manual FM 33-1. Washington, DC: Headquarters, Department of the Army, 1979.

———. *Operations.* Field Manual FM 100-5. Washington, DC: Headquarters, Department of the Army, 1986.

———. *U.S. Army Operational Concept for Special Operations Forces*, TRADOC PAM 525-34. Washington, DC: Headquarters, Department of the Army, 1984.

—**OPERATIONAL MISSILE** is a missile that has been accepted by the using services for tactical or strategic use. *See also:* Operational Missile Launcher.

References

Department of Defense, Joint Chiefs of Staff. *Department of Defense Dictionary of Military and Related Terms.* Washington, DC: GPO, 1986.

—**OPERATIONAL MISSILE LAUNCHER** is a launcher that has been accepted by the using services and has been issued to them for tactical or strategic use.

References

Department of Defense, U.S. Army. *Dictionary of United States Army Terms.* Army Regulation AR 310-25. Washington, DC: Headquarters, Department of the Army, 1986.

—**OPERATIONAL ORDER (OPORD or OPORDER)** is a directive (usually formal) issued by a commander to his subordinate commanders to coordinate the execution of an operation.

References

Department of Defense, Joint Chiefs of Staff. *Department of Defense Dictionary of Military and Related Terms.* Washington, DC: GPO, 1986.

—**OPERATIONAL PLANNING** concentrates on the design of campaigns and major operations. At the theater level, campaign planning entails converting broad strategic guidance into a campaign plan for a joint or combined force. Operational planning within each theater of operations focuses on the execution of the campaign plan and on the staging, conduct, and exploitation of major operations. *See also:* Operational Plans.

References

Department of Defense, U.S. Army. *Operations.* Field Manual FM 100-5. Washington, DC: Headquarters, Department of the Army, 1986.

—**OPERATIONAL PLANS** are plans for a single or a series of connected operations that are to be carried out simultaneously or in succession.

References

Department of Defense, Joint Chiefs of Staff. *Department of Defense Dictionary of Military and Related Terms.* Washington, DC: GPO, 1986.

—**OPERATIONAL PROCEDURES** are the detailed methods by which headquarters and units carry out their operational tasks.

References

Department of Defense, Joint Chiefs of Staff. *Department of Defense Dictionary of Military and Related Terms.* Washington, DC: GPO, 1986.

—**OPERATIONAL PROJECT** is a Department of the Army-approved project authorizing the acquisition of stocks of equipment and supplies to support a specific requirement, which has been developed in accordance with the applicable Army regulations.

References

Department of Defense, U.S. Army. *Planning Logistics Support for Military Operations.* Field Manual FM 701-58. Washington, DC: Headquarters, Department of the Army, 1987.

—**OPERATIONAL PSYOP (PSYCHOLOGICAL OPERATIONS)** are psychological operations conducted to achieve mid-term objectives in support of campaigns and major operations. They are usually conducted at the theater level. *See also:* Psychological Operations.

References

Department of Defense, U.S. Army. *Psychological Operations.* Field Manual FM 33-1. Washington, DC: Headquarters, Department of the Army, 1979.

—**OPERATIONAL RATION** is a specially designed ration normally composed of nonperishable items for use under actual or simulated combat conditions. It is used in peacetime for emergencies, contingencies, travel, and training.

References

Department of Defense, U.S. Army. *Dictionary of United States Army Terms.* Army Regulation AR 310-25. Washington, DC: Headquarters, Department of the Army, 1986.

—**OPERATIONAL READINESS** is the capability of a unit, formation, weapon system, or equipment to perform the missions or functions for which it is organized or designed. The term may be used in a general sense or to express a level or degree of readiness. *See also:* Operational Readiness Evaluation, Operational Readiness Training.

References

Department of Defense, Joint Chiefs of Staff. *Department of Defense Dictionary of Military and Related Terms.* Washington, DC: GPO, 1986.

—**OPERATIONAL READINESS EVALUATION (ORE)** is an evaluation of the operational capability and effectiveness of a unit or any portion of a unit.

References

Department of Defense, Joint Chiefs of Staff. *Department of Defense Dictionary of Military and Related Terms.* Washington, DC: GPO, 1986.

—**OPERATIONAL READINESS FLOAT (ORF)** consists of selected end-items or major components that are stocked at support maintenance activities to increase their support capability. When customer equipment cannot be repaired in time to meet operational requirements, a replacement item may be issued from the ORF. The customer's equipment is retained by the maintenance activity, repaired, and made available for another ORF transaction.

References

Department of Defense, U.S. Army. *Organizational Maintenance Operations.* Field Manual FM 29-2. Washington, DC: Headquarters, Department of the Army, 1984.

—**OPERATIONAL READINESS TRAINING (ORT)** is a phase of training undertaken by units that have completed the formal phases of training and are assigned responsibility for maintaining the highest possible state of combat proficiency in order to accomplish their operational missions.

References

Department of Defense, U.S. Army. *How to Prepare and Conduct Military Training.* Field Manual FM 21-6. Washington, DC: Headquarters, Department of the Army, 1975.

—**OPERATIONAL RECORDS** help in the organizational control of equipment operators, operational planning, and the maximum use of equipment.

References

Department of Defense, U.S. Army. *Organizational Maintenance Operations.* Field Manual FM 29-2. Washington, DC: Headquarters, Department of the Army, 1984.

—**OPERATIONAL RESERVE** is an emergency reserve of men and material established to support a particular operation. *See also:* Reserve Supplies.

References

Department of Defense, U.S. Army. *Operational Terms and Symbols.* Field Manual FM 101-5-1. Washington, DC: Headquarters, Department of the Army, 1985.

—**OPERATIONAL ROUTE** is a land route allocated to a command for the execution of a specific operation and derived from the corresponding basic military route network.

References

Department of Defense, Joint Chiefs of Staff. *Department of Defense Dictionary of Military and Related Terms.* Washington, DC: GPO, 1986.

—**OPERATIONAL SECURITY (OPSEC)** refers to the measures designed to prevent unauthorized disclosure of information concerning planned, ongoing, or completed operations. *See also:* Communications Security.

References

Department of Defense, Defense Intelligence College. *Glossary of Intelligence Terms and Definitions.* Washington, DC: DIC, 1987.

—**OPERATIONAL SHIELD** is a barrier constructed at a particular location or around a particular machine or operating station to protect personnel, material, or equipment from the effects of a localized fire or explosion.

References

Department of Defense, U.S. Army. *Ammunition and Explosives Safety Standards.* Army Regulation AR 385-64. Washington, DC: Headquarters, Department of the Army, 1987.

—**OPERATIONAL STOCKS** are the stocks stored to meet operational requirements above the normal holdings and allowances. *See also:* War Reserves.

References

Department of Defense, Joint Chiefs of Staff. *Department of Defense Dictionary of Military and Related Terms.* Washington, DC: GPO, 1986.

—**OPERATIONAL SUPPLIES** are the supplies, above the normal allowances of an overseas theater, required to support the logistic and operational plans of a theater.

References

Department of Defense, U.S. Army. *Dictionary of United States Army Terms.* Army Regulation AR 310-25. Washington, DC: Headquarters, Department of the Army, 1986.

—**OPERATIONAL SUSTAINMENT** comprises the logistical and support activities required to sustain campaigns and major operations within a theater of operations. It extends from the theater sustaining base or bases that link strategic to theater support functions, to the forward combat service support units and facilities that are organic to major tactical formations. *See also:* Operational Supplies.

References

Department of Defense, U.S. Army. *Operations.* Field Manual FM 100-5. Washington, DC: Headquarters, Department of the Army, 1986.

—**OPERATIONAL TESTING** is a continuing process of evaluation that may be applied to either operational personnel or situations to determine their validity or reliability.

References

Department of Defense, Joint Chiefs of Staff. *Department of Defense Dictionary of Military and Related Terms.* Washington, DC: GPO, 1986.

—**OPERATIONAL TRAINING** is training that develops, maintains, or improves the operational readiness of individuals or units.

References

Department of Defense, Joint Chiefs of Staff. *Department of Defense Dictionary of Military and Related Terms.* Washington, DC: GPO, 1986.

—**OPERATIONAL USE OF TERRAIN.** Terrain forms the natural structure of the battlefield. Commanders must recognize its limitations and possibilities and use it to protect friendly opera-

tions and to put the enemy at a disadvantage. Terrain analysis, intelligence preparation of the battlefield, and engineer operations are key to the operational use of terrain.

References

Department of Defense, U.S. Army. *Operations.* Field Manual FM 100-5. Washington, DC: Headquarters, Department of the Army, 1986.

—**OPERATIONALLY READY.** (1) In reference to units or weapons systems, operationally ready means that the item can perform the missions or functions for which it was organized or designed. In this sense, both equipment and personnel readiness are included. (2) In respect to personnel, operationally ready means that an individual is available and qualified to perform his assigned missions or functions. (3) In respect to equipment, operationally ready means that an item is available and in condition to function as it was designed. *See also:* Operational Training.

References

Department of Defense, Joint Chiefs of Staff. *Department of Defense Dictionary of Military and Related Terms.* Washington, DC: GPO, 1986.

—**OPERATIONALLY READY MISSILE** is a missile on a serviceable launcher that is connected to serviceable firing control equipment.

References

Department of Defense, U.S. Army. *Dictionary of United States Army Terms.* Army Regulation AR 310-25. Washington, DC: Headquarters, Department of the Army, 1986.

—**OPERATIONS CODE** is a code used to encrypt tactical information. It is composed largely, though not exclusively, of single words and phrases. *See also:* CRYPTO.

References

Department of Defense, U.S. Army. *Communications Techniques: Electronics Countermeasures.* Field Manual FM 24-33. Washington, DC: Headquarters, Department of the Army, 1985.

—**OPERATIONS ORDERS (OPORDs)** are orders that provide for coordinated action to carry out the decision of a commander in the execution of an operation. "Operation order" includes tactical movement orders. Combat service support commanders also use operation orders to task their units. *See also:* Operation Plan.

References
Department of Defense, U.S. Army. *Staff Organiza-
tion and Operations.* Field Manual FM 101-5.
Washington, DC: Headquarters, Department of the
Army, 1984.

—**OPERATIONS RESEARCH** is the analytical study
of military problems to provide responsible
commanders and staff agencies with a scientific
basis for decisions on actions to improve military
operations.

References
Department of Defense, Joint Chiefs of Staff.
*Department of Defense Dictionary of Military and
Related Terms.* Washington, DC: GPO, 1986.

—**OPERATIONS SECURITY (OPSEC).** (1) In operations, OPSEC refers to the measures designed
to protect information concerning planned,
ongoing, or completed operations against unauthorized disclosure. It includes all the actions
that a command takes to deny the enemy information about friendly units and their operations. (2) In communications security, OPSEC
means the process of denying adversaries information about friendly capabilities and intentions by identifying, controlling, and protecting
the indicators associated with the planning and
execution of military operations and other activities.

References
Department of Defense, U.S. Army. *Operational
Terms and Symbols.* Field Manual FM 101-5-1.
Washington, DC: Headquarters, Department of the
Army, 1985.

————. *Support Operations: Echelons Above Corps.*
Field Manual FM 100-16. Washington, DC:
Headquarters, Department of the Army, 1986.

—**OPERATIONS SECURITY (OPSEC) INDICA-
TORS** are actions or information, classified or
unclassified, that if obtained by an adversary
would result in adversary operations, plans, and
actions that are harmful to achieving friendly
intentions and preserving friendly military capabilities. *See also:* Operations Security.

References
Department of Defense, Joint Chiefs of Staff.
*Department of Defense Dictionary of Military and
Related Terms.* Washington, DC: GPO, 1986.

—**OPERATIONS SECURITY (OPSEC) PROCESS** is
an Army tactical intelligence term that refers to
the procedures an Army entity employs to assure
or to enhance its OPSEC. The process involves
the continuous planning, data collection,
analysis, reporting, and execution of orders and
instructions. The process is cyclical, taking into
consideration the changing nature of both the
threat and friendly vulnerabilities. It is normally
composed of ten steps:

- Identifying the hostile intelligence
  collection threat;
- Identifying friendly force profiles and
  recommending essential elements of
  friendly information;
- Identifying friendly force vulnerabilities;
- Performing risk analysis and select
  essential elements of friendly information;
- Recommending OPSEC procedures;
- Selecting OPSEC measures;
- Applying the OPSEC measures;
- Directing the efforts to monitor the
  effectiveness of applied OPSEC
  measures;
- Monitoring the effectiveness of OPSEC
  measures; and
- Recommending adjustments to OPSEC
  measures.

See also: Communications Security.

References
Department of Defense, Joint Chiefs of Staff.
*Department of Defense Dictionary of Military and
Related Terms.* Washington, DC: GPO, 1986.

—**OPERATOR/CREW PREVENTIVE MAINTE-
NANCE CHECKS AND SERVICES.** The daily
preventive maintenance routine insures that the
readiness of all applicable equipment is checked
on a recurring basis and that a record is made of
faults that cannot be immediately corrected.

References
Department of Defense, U.S. Army. *Organizational
Maintenance Operations.* Field Manual FM 29-2.
Washington, DC: Headquarters, Department of the
Army, 1984.

—**OPERATOR'S SPRAYDOWN** is the process of
applying decontaminant onto unit equipment
control surfaces to stop contamination from
soaking into the surfaces. *See also:* Chemical
Warfare, Nuclear Warfare.

References
Department of Defense, U.S. Army. *NBC Decon-
tamination.* Field Manual FM 3-5. Washington,
DC: Headquarters, Department of the Army, 1985.

————. *NBC Operations.* Field Manual FM 3-100.
Washington, DC: Headquarters, Department of the
Army, 1985.

—**OPPOSING FORCES (OPFOR).** OPPOR units are trained and equipped to confront U.S. units with realistic opponents that look and fight like potential adversaries. Such realism enhances the value of training exercises. Well-equipped OPFOR units are skilled in tactics and techniques of a potential adversary. From them soldiers learn the potential adversary's tactics, doctrine, and weapon systems that they could successfully exploit in air-land battles. Additionally, OPFOR units encourage effective intelligence-gathering procedures; electronic warfare techniques; deception measures; and unconventional warfare techniques. *See also:* Opposing Forces Program.

References

Department of Defense, U.S. Army. *How to Conduct Training Exercises.* Field Manual FM 25-4. Washington, DC: Headquarters, Department of the Army, 1984.

—**OPPOSING FORCES PROGRAM** is an Army-wide training program that focuses peacetime preparedness training on the tactical vulnerabilities of potential adversaries. The opposing force program is designed to emphasize the competition inherent in battle by providing a credible, realistic opposing force in training, which uses doctrine, tactics, and weapons systems of actual potential adversaries.

References

Department of Defense, U.S. Army. *Army Exercises.* Army Regulation AR 350-28. Washington, DC: Headquarters, Department of the Army, 1985.

———. *Army Forces Training.* Army Regulation AR 350-41. Washington, DC: Headquarters, Department of the Army, 1986.

—**OPPOSITE NUMBERS** are officers (including foreign officers) having corresponding duty assignments within their respective military Services or establishments.

References

Department of Defense, Joint Chiefs of Staff. *Department of Defense Dictionary of Military and Related Terms.* Washington, DC: GPO, 1986.

—**OPSCOMM** is a communications link established for the routine informal exchange of information. *See also:* Communications Security.

References

Department of Defense, Joint Chiefs of Staff. *Department of Defense Dictionary of Military and Related Terms.* Washington, DC: GPO, 1986.

—**OPSEC (OPERATIONS SECURITY) SUPPORT** is an Army tactical intelligence term that refers to actions that support operations security measures. *See also:* Communications Security.

References

Department of Defense, Joint Chiefs of Staff. *Department of Defense Dictionary of Military and Related Terms.* Washington, DC: GPO, 1986.

—**OPSEC (OPERATIONS SECURITY) SURVEY,** in communications security, refers to a technique of data acquisition and analysis used to construct the sequence of events that are associated with time-definable operations and functions. The objective is to identify activity that could be exploited by the enemy to gain a military, technical, diplomatic, or economic advantage. It includes document reviews, interviews and observations, selected and communications security monitoring, and a review of all-source intelligence information that bears on the enemy threat. *See also:* Communications Security.

References

Department of Defense, Joint Chiefs of Staff. *Department of Defense Dictionary of Military and Related Terms.* Washington, DC: GPO, 1986.

—**OPTICAL INTELLIGENCE (OPTINT),** a subdiscipline of measurement and signature intelligence, is the portion of electro-optical intelligence that deals with visible light. *See also:* Intelligence.

References

Department of Defense, U.S. Army. *Counterintelligence.* Field Manual FM 34-60. Washington, DC: Headquarters, Department of the Army, 1985.

—**OPTICAL SIGHT** is a sight with lenses, prisms, or mirrors that is used in surveying or in laying weapons for bombing.

References

Department of Defense, U.S. Army. *Dictionary of United States Army Terms.* Army Regulation AR 310-25. Washington, DC: Headquarters, Department of the Army, 1986.

—**OPTIMUM HEIGHT** is the height of an explosion that will produce the maximum effect against a given target.

References

Department of Defense, Joint Chiefs of Staff. *Department of Defense Dictionary of Military and Related Terms.* Washington, DC: GPO, 1986.

—**OPTIMUM HEIGHT OF BURST.** For nuclear weapons, the optimum height of burst for a particular target or area is the altitude at which it is estimated that a weapon of a specified energy yield will produce a certain desired effect over the maximum possible area. *See also:* Nuclear Warfare.

References
Department of Defense, Joint Chiefs of Staff. *Department of Defense Dictionary of Military and Related Terms.* Washington, DC: GPO, 1986.

—**OPTIMUM UTILIZATION** is a method of assigning individuals to military positions that makes maximum use of their highest qualifications and abilities. *See also:* Military Operational Specialty.

References
Department of Defense, U.S. Army. *Enlisted Personnel Management System.* Army Regulation AR 600-200. Washington, DC: Headquarters, Department of the Army, 1984.

—**OPTIONAL CLOTHING** is a uniform or clothing that the individual is not required to own or wear but may be worn if the individual chooses to do so as prescribed by regulations.

References
Department of Defense, U.S. Army. *Wear and Appearance of Army Uniforms and Insignia.* Army Regulation AR 670-1. Washington, DC: Headquarters, Department of the Army, 1986.

—**ORAL TRADE TEST** is an oral examination to rate a person's knowledge in some type of work or trade.

References
Department of Defense, U.S. Army. *Dictionary of United States Army Terms.* Army Regulation AR 310-25. Washington, DC: Headquarters, Department of the Army, 1986.

—**ORANGE COMMANDER** is the officer designated to exercise operational control over orange forces for a specified period during an exercise. *See also:* Blue Commander, Orange Forces.

References
Department of Defense, Joint Chiefs of Staff. *Department of Defense Dictionary of Military and Related Terms.* Washington, DC: GPO, 1986.

—**ORANGE FORCES** are the forces used in an enemy role during NATO exercises. *See also:* Blue Forces, Force.

References
Department of Defense, Joint Chiefs of Staff. *Department of Defense Dictionary of Military and Related Terms.* Washington, DC: GPO, 1986.

—**ORDER** is a communication—written, oral, or by signal—that conveys instructions from a superior to a subordinate. In general, the terms "order" and "command" are synonymous. However, an order implies discretion as to the details of execution; a command does not.

References
Department of Defense, U.S. Army. *Operational Terms and Symbols.* Field Manual FM 101-5-1. Washington, DC: Headquarters, Department of the Army, 1985.

—**ORDER FOR INFORMATION** is composed of instructions or directives—applicable to all subordinate units—to prompt the collection of the information listed in the intelligence plan. *See also:* Intelligence Requirement.

References
Department of Defense, U.S. Army. *Dictionary of United States Army Terms.* Army Regulation AR 310-25. Washington, DC: Headquarters, Department of the Army, 1986.

—**ORDER-OF-BATTLE (OB)** is intelligence about the strength, identification, command structure, and disposition of the personnel, units, and equipment of any foreign force. In the Army tactical intelligence context, the Counter-Signals Intelligence section of the Military Intelligence unit develops order of battle data for enemy signals intelligence units and friendly order of battle as it pertains to the unit's electronic and communications systems. The data that make up an order of battle list include composition, disposition, strength, training status, tactics, communications-electronics emitters, logistics, combat effectiveness, and miscellaneous data, *See also:* Order-of-Battle Book, Order-of-Battle Card, Order-of-Battle Handbook.

References
Department of Defense, Defense Intelligence College. *Glossary of Intelligence Terms and Definitions.* Washington, DC: DIC, 1987.

Department of Defense, U.S. Army. *Intelligence Analysis.* Field Manual FM 34-3. Washington, DC: Headquarters, Department of the Army, 1986.

———. *Operational Terms and Symbols.* Field Manual FM 101-5-1. Washington, DC: Headquarters, Department of the Army, 1985.

———. *Support Operations: Echelons Above Corps.* Field Manual FM 100-16. Washington, DC: Headquarters, Department of the Army, 1986.

—**ORDER-OF-BATTLE (OB) BOOK** is a summary of all basic intelligence concerning the composition, disposition, identification, subordination, and strengths of a foreign nation's military forces. It includes all units from the various services that function in a ground or ground support role. OB books are normally published at echelons above corps by the service departments and the Defense Intelligence Agency. Allied nations, particularly the NATO nations, also publish OB books. *See also:* Order-of-Battle, Order-of-Battle Card, Order-of-Battle Handbook.

References

Department of Defense, U.S. Army. *Intelligence Analysis.* Field Manual FM 34-3. Washington, DC: Headquarters, Department of the Army, 1986.

—**ORDER-OF-BATTLE (OB) CARD** is a single, or master, standardized card that contains basic information on each enemy ground force unit or formation and provides all the pertinent OB information. *See also:* Order-of-Battle.

References

Department of Defense, Joint Chiefs of Staff. *Department of Defense Dictionary of Military and Related Terms.* Washington, DC: GPO, 1986.

—**ORDER-OF-BATTLE (OB) HANDBOOK,** often referred to as a "handbook of military forces," is a summary of basic intelligence on a foreign nation's political structure and military establishment, including its tactics and doctrine. It may include more technical data (e.g., the logistical system used and the characteristics of weapons and equipment). Like the OB book, the handbook is published by higher U.S. and allied commands. *See also:* Order-of-Battle.

References

Department of Defense, U.S. Army. *Intelligence Analysis.* Field Manual FM 34-3. Washington, DC: Headquarters, Department of the Army, 1986.

—**ORDER SHIP TIME** is the time between the initiation of a requisition by an activity and the receipt and recording by that activity of the material ordered. *See also:* Order Time.

References

Department of Defense, U.S. Army. *Support Operations: Echelons Above Corps.* Field Manual FM 100-16. Washington, DC: Headquarters, Department of the Army, 1986.

—**ORDER TIME.** (1) Order time is the time between the initiation of a stock replenishment action and the submittal or requisition of the order. (2) Order time is the time between the submittal of a requisition or order and the shipment of the materiel by the supplying activity.

References

Department of Defense, Joint Chiefs of Staff. *Department of Defense Dictionary of Military and Related Terms.* Washington, DC: GPO, 1986.

—**ORDERLY ROOM** is the office of a company in which the company's business is accomplished.

References

Department of Defense, U.S. Army. *Dictionary of United States Army Terms.* Army Regulation AR 310-25. Washington, DC: Headquarters, Department of the Army, 1986.

—**ORDERS** (GUARD). (1) A guard on post is governed by two types of orders: general orders and special orders. General orders outline the fundamental responsibilities of a guard; special orders instruct him in the actual performance of his duty while on a particular post. *See also:* Order.

References

Department of Defense, U.S. Army. *Guard Duty.* Field Manual FM 22-6. Washington, DC: Headquarters, Department of the Army, 1971.

—**ORDERS GROUP** is a standing group of key personnel who are requested to be present when a commander at any level issues his concept of the operation and his order.

References

Department of Defense, U.S. Army. *Operational Terms and Symbols.* Field Manual FM 101-5-1. Washington, DC: Headquarters, Department of the Army, 1985.

—**ORDINARY LEAVE** is an authorized absence from one's assigned duty. Military personnel accrue leave credit at the rate of 2.5 calendar days per month of active service. *See also:* Emergency Leave.

References
Department of Defense, U.S. Army. *Dictionary of United States Army Terms*. Army Regulation AR 310-25. Washington, DC: Headquarters, Department of the Army, 1986.

—**ORDINARY PRIORITY** is a category of immediate mission request lower than "urgent priority" but takes precedence over "search and attack priority." For example, a target that is delaying a unit's advance but not causing casualties would be assigned an ordinary priority. *See also:* Immediate Mission Request.

References
Department of Defense, Joint Chiefs of Staff. *Department of Defense Dictionary of Military and Related Terms*. Washington, DC: GPO, 1986.

—**ORDINARY TRANSPORT,** in railway terminology, is a load whose size, weight, or preparation does not entail special difficulties vis-à-vis the railway facilities or system that will be used.

References
Department of Defense, Joint Chiefs of Staff. *Department of Defense Dictionary of Military and Related Terms*. Washington, DC: GPO, 1986.

—**ORDNANCE** are explosives, chemicals, pyrotechnic, and similar stores (e.g., bombs, guns, ammunition, flares, smoke, and napalm). *See also:* Ordnance Officer, Ordnance Plan, Ordnance Service, Ordnance Staff Officer, Ordnance Troops.

References
Department of Defense, Joint Chiefs of Staff. *Department of Defense Dictionary of Military and Related Terms*. Washington, DC: GPO, 1986.

—**ORDNANCE OFFICER.** (1) An ordnance officer is an officer who is a member of the ordnance corps. (2) An ordnance officer is a special staff officer who advises commanders on the technical matters of ordnance. (3) An ordnance officer is an officer who has responsibilities concerning ordnance maintenance, ammunition, and general supply, including that of restoring captured enemy materiel to a usable condition. *See also:* Ordnance.

References
Department of Defense, U.S. Army. *Dictionary of United States Army Terms*. Army Regulation AR 310-25. Washington, DC: Headquarters, Department of the Army, 1986.

—**ORDNANCE PLAN** is a detailed statement on ordnance operations that is prepared for a commander, usually by the ordnance officer. It includes specific instructions for the use of ordnance units and deals with ordnance maintenance, ammunition, and restoring enemy equipment to a usable condition. *See also:* Ordnance.

References
Department of Defense, U.S. Army. *Dictionary of United States Army Terms*. Army Regulation AR 310-25. Washington, DC: Headquarters, Department of the Army, 1986.

—**ORDNANCE SERVICE** includes all the activities necessary to maintain the ordnance equipment of a command, and such other equipment as directed by proper authority, in usable condition. *See also:* Ordnance.

References
Department of Defense, U.S. Army. *Dictionary of United States Army Terms*. Army Regulation AR 310-25. Washington, DC: Headquarters, Department of the Army, 1986.

—**ORDNANCE STAFF OFFICER.** *See:* Ordnance Officer.

—**ORDNANCE TROOPS** are technically trained troops assigned or attached to a tactical unit to provide ordnance maintenance, supply, or a technical service. They also instruct in the use, maintenance, and adjustment of ordnance materiel. *See also:* Ordnance.

References
Department of Defense, U.S. Army. *Dictionary of United States Army Terms*. Army Regulation AR 310-25. Washington, DC: Headquarters, Department of the Army, 1986.

—**ORGANIC** is a unit that forms an essential part of an Army unit and is listed in its table of organization and equipment or table of distribution and allowances.

References
Department of Defense, U.S. Army. *Operational Terms and Symbols*. Field Manual FM 101-5-1. Washington, DC: Headquarters, Department of the Army, 1985.

———. *Staff Organization and Operations*. Field Manual FM 101-5. Washington, DC: Headquarters, Department of the Army, 1984.

—**ORGANIZATION.** (1) An organization is any military unit or larger command composed of two or more smaller units. In this meaning, a military element of a command is an organization in relation to its components and a unit in relation to higher commands. (2) Organization is the structure of a military element that is prescribed by a component authority such as a table of organization. *See also:* Unit.

References
Department of Defense, U.S. Army. *Operational Terms and Symbols.* Field Manual FM 101-5-1. Washington, DC: Headquarters, Department of the Army, 1985.

—**ORGANIZATION AND FUNCTIONS MANUAL** specifies the organization, functions, and responsibilities of every staff section within a command. It is the basis for assigning responsibility for staff actions and coordination. *See also:* Organization Chart.

References
Department of Defense, U.S. Army. *Staff Organizations and Operations.* Field Manual FM 101-5. Washington, DC: Headquarters, Department of the Army, 1984.

—**ORGANIZATION CHART** is a diagram showing the organization of units, offices, activities, or installations.

References
Department of Defense, U.S. Army. *Dictionary of United States Army Terms.* Army Regulation AR 310-25. Washington, DC: Headquarters, Department of the Army, 1986.

—**ORGANIZATION FOR EMBARKATION** is the administrative grouping of the landing force for an overseas movement. It includes, in any ship or embarkation group, the task organization that is established for landing, as well as additional forces embarked for purposes of transport or labor, or for distribution to achieve maximum security. *See also:* Organization for Landing.

References
Department of Defense, U.S. Army. *Dictionary of United States Army Terms.* Army Regulation AR 310-25. Washington, DC: Headquarters, Department of the Army, 1986.

—**ORGANIZATION FOR LANDING** is the specific tactical grouping of the landing force for the assault. *See also:* Landing Force.

References
Department of Defense, U.S. Army. *Dictionary of United States Army Terms.* Army Regulation AR 310-25. Washington, DC: Headquarters, Department of the Army, 1986.

—**ORGANIZATION OF THE GROUND** is the development of a defensive position by strengthening the natural defenses of the terrain and by assigning the occupying troops to specific localities.

References
Department of Defense, Joint Chiefs of Staff. *Department of Defense Dictionary of Military and Related Terms.* Washington, DC: GPO, 1986.

—**ORGANIZATION OF THE JOINT CHIEFS OF STAFF (OJCS)** is an element within the Department of Defense that includes the Joint Chiefs of Staff, the Office of the Chairman of the Joint Chiefs of Staff, and the directorates and agencies that have been designated as Joint Staff, or as supporting agencies or special offices of the Organization of the Joint Chiefs of Staff. *See also:* Joint Staff.

References
Department of Defense, Joint Chiefs of Staff. *Department of Defense Dictionary of Military and Related Terms.* Washington, DC: GPO, 1986.

—**ORGANIZATION PROPERTY** is the equipment authorized for a unit by a table of equipment and organization, a table of distribution and allowances, or a joint table of allowance. This equipment goes with the unit when it moves from one location to another. *See also:* Organization Property Book.

References
Department of Defense, U.S. Army. *Commander's Handbook for Property Accountability at the Unit Level.* Field Manual FM 10-14-1. Washington, DC: Headquarters, Department of the Army, 1984.

—**ORGANIZATION PROPERTY BOOK** is a record maintained to account for organization property that is not recorded on the individual clothing record or on the organizational clothing and equipment record.

References
Department of Defense, U.S. Army. *Dictionary of United States Army Terms.* Army Regulation AR 310-25. Washington, DC: Headquarters, Department of the Army, 1986.

—**ORGANIZATIONAL EQUIPMENT,** when referring to the method of use, signifies the equipment, other than individual equipment, used in the common mission of an organization or unit. *See also:* Equipment.

References

Department of Defense, Joint Chiefs of Staff. *Department of Defense Dictionary of Military and Related Terms.* Washington, DC: GPO, 1986.

—**ORGANIZATIONAL MAINTENANCE** is the maintenance that is the responsibility of and is performed by a using organization on its assigned equipment. Its phases normally consist of inspecting, servicing, lubricating, adjusting, and replacing parts, minor assemblies, and subassemblies. *See also:* Organizational Repair Parts.

References

Department of Defense, U.S. Army. *Intelligence and Electronic Warfare Operations.* Field Manual FM 34-1. Washington, DC: Headquarters, Department of the Army, 1987.

—**ORGANIZATIONAL REPAIR PARTS** are parts authorized to an organization for its own use.

References

Department of Defense, U.S. Army. *Dictionary of United States Army Terms.* Army Regulation AR 310-25. Washington, DC: Headquarters, Department of the Army, 1986.

—**ORGANIZATIONAL SUPPLY** is the service authorized for and performed by a using organization on its own equipment. This category incorporates the first and second echelons of supply as follows: *First echelon* of supply is performed by the individual user, wearer, or operator when he acquires the initial replacement or receives replenishment of supplies and equipment from unit supply. *Second echelon* of supply is performed by specially trained and assigned personnel from the user organization in acquiring, distributing, and accounting for the authorized initial replacement and replenishment of supplies and equipment at the organizational level.

References

Department of Defense, U.S. Army. *Dictionary of United States Army Terms.* Army Regulation AR 310-25. Washington, DC: Headquarters, Department of the Army, 1986.

—**ORGANIZED POSITION** is an area in which troops and weapons have been put in position for future action and in which field fortifications have been constructed.

References

Department of Defense, U.S. Army. *Dictionary of United States Army Terms.* Army Regulation AR 310-25. Washington, DC: Headquarters, Department of the Army, 1986.

—**ORGANIZED STRENGTH** is the actual, authorized, or programmed strength of all table of organization and equipment and table of distribution units of the Army, or subdivisions of the Army.

References

Department of Defense, U.S. Army. *Dictionary of United States Army Terms.* Army Regulation AR 310-25. Washington, DC: Headquarters, Department of the Army, 1986.

—**ORIENT.** (1) To orient is to place in the right position, or to place a map so that the arrow on it showing direction points *in* that direction, or so the meridian lines of a map point north. (2) To orient is to set the correct angular reading for a weapon or instrument so that it reads correctly for that location and for the direction the weapon or instrument is pointing. For some weapons and instruments, the elevation adjustment is included in this category. *See also:* Map.

References

Department of Defense, U.S. Army. *Dictionary of United States Army Terms.* Army Regulation AR 310-25. Washington, DC: Headquarters, Department of the Army, 1986.

—**ORIENTATION** is the turning of an instrument or map until a datum point or meridian is aligned with a datum point or a true meridian on the earth. *See also:* Map.

References

Department of Defense, U.S. Army. *Dictionary of United States Army Terms.* Army Regulation AR 310-25. Washington, DC: Headquarters, Department of the Army, 1986.

—**ORIENTATION ANGLE** is a horizontal clockwise angle from the line of fire to the orienting line.

References

Department of Defense, U.S. Army. *Dictionary of United States Army Terms.* Army Regulation AR 310-25. Washington, DC: Headquarters, Department of the Army, 1986.

—**ORIENTATION COURSE** is instruction that introduces a student to a particular technique or area of knowledge.

References
Department of Defense, U.S. Army. *Individual Military Education and Training.* Army Regulation AR 350-1. Washington, DC: Headquarters, Department of the Army, 1987.

—**ORIENTING LINE** is a line of known direction established on the ground and used as a reference line in aiming artillery pieces. *See also:* Orienting Station.

References
Department of Defense, U.S. Army. *Dictionary of United States Army Terms.* Army Regulation AR 310-25. Washington, DC: Headquarters, Department of the Army, 1986.

—**ORIENTING POINT** is a distant object sighted on with a gun in an aligning director or other instrument.

References
Department of Defense, U.S. Army. *Dictionary of United States Army Terms.* Army Regulation AR 310-25. Washington, DC: Headquarters, Department of the Army, 1986.

—**ORIENTING STATION** is a point on the orienting line near the gun position from which the battery may be oriented.

References
Department of Defense, U.S. Army. *Dictionary of United States Army Terms.* Army Regulation AR 310-25. Washington, DC: Headquarters, Department of the Army, 1986.

—**ORIGIN.** (1) An origin is a fixed point of reference on a graph, map, or chart. (2) The origin is the center of the muzzle of the gun at the instant of firing. *See also:* Map.

References
Department of Defense, U.S. Army. *Dictionary of United States Army Terms.* Army Regulation AR 310-25. Washington, DC: Headquarters, Department of the Army, 1986.

—**ORIGIN OF THE TRAJECTORY** is the center of the muzzle of the gun at the instant when the projectile leaves it.

References
Department of Defense, U.S. Army. *Dictionary of United States Army Terms.* Army Regulation AR 310-25. Washington, DC: Headquarters, Department of the Army, 1986.

—**ORIGINAL APPOINTMENT** is any appointment in a reserve or regular component of the armed forces that is neither a promotion nor a demotion. Officers may receive more than one "original appointment."

References
Department of Defense, U.S. Army. *Promotion of Officers on Active Duty.* Army Regulation AR 624-100. Washington, DC: Headquarters, Department of the Army, 1984.

—**ORIGINATING MEDICAL FACILITY** is a medical facility that initially transfers a patient to another medical facility. *See also:* Medical Treatment.

References
Department of Defense, Joint Chiefs of Staff. *Department of Defense Dictionary of Military and Related Terms.* Washington, DC: GPO, 1986.

—**ORIGINATOR** is the command by whose authority a message is sent. The originator's responsibilities include the responsibilities for the functions of both the drafter and the releasing officer. *See also:* Releasing Official.

References
Department of Defense, Joint Chiefs of Staff. *Department of Defense Dictionary of Military and Related Terms.* Washington, DC: GPO, 1986.

—**OTHER EQUIPMENT** are supplies that do not meet the criteria of capital property but cannot be classified as expendable.

References
Department of Defense, U.S. Army. *Dictionary of United States Army Terms.* Army Regulation AR 310-25. Washington, DC: Headquarters, Department of the Army, 1986.

—**OTHER FORCES FOR NATO** are forces that are not assigned or earmarked for a NATO command, but which might cooperate with NATO forces or be placed under the operational command or operational control of a NATO commander in certain specified circumstances. *See also:* Force.

References
Department of Defense, Joint Chiefs of Staff. *Department of Defense Dictionary of Military and Related Terms.* Washington, DC: GPO, 1986.

—**OTHER WAR RESERVE MATERIEL REQUIRE-MENT** level consists of the war reserve materiel requirement less the pre-positioned war reserve materiel requirement. *See also:* Other War Reserve Stock.

References

Department of Defense, Joint Chiefs of Staff. *Department of Defense Dictionary of Military and Related Terms.* Washington, DC: GPO, 1986.

—**OTHER WAR RESERVE MATERIEL REQUIRE-MENT, BALANCE,** is the portion of the other war reserve materiel requirement that has not been acquired or funded. This level consists of the other war reserve materiel requirement less the other war reserve materiel requirement, protectable. *See also:* Other War Reserve Stock.

References

Department of Defense, Joint Chiefs of Staff. *Department of Defense Dictionary of Military and Related Terms.* Washington, DC: GPO, 1986.

—**OTHER WAR RESERVE MATERIEL REQUIRE-MENT, PROTECTABLE,** is the portion of the other war reserve materiel requirement that is protected for purposes of procurement, funding, and inventory management. *See also:* Other War Reserve Stock.

References

Department of Defense, Joint Chiefs of Staff. *Department of Defense Dictionary of Military and Related Terms.* Washington, DC: GPO, 1986.

—**OTHER WAR RESERVE STOCK** is the quantity of an item that is acquired and placed in stock against the other war reserve materiel requirement. *See also:* Operational Stocks; Other War Reserve Materiel Requirement; Other War Reserve Materiel Requirement, Balance; Other War Reserve Materiel Requirement, Protectable; Preposition of Materiel Configured to Unit Sets.

References

Department of Defense, Joint Chiefs of Staff. *Department of Defense Dictionary of Military and Related Terms.* Washington, DC: GPO, 1986.

—**OUT** is a radiotelephone procedure proword that means "This is the end of my transmission to you and no answer is required or expected." *See also:* Proword.

References

Department of Defense, U.S. Army. *The Rifle Squads (Mechanized and Light Infantry).* Training Circular TC 7-1. Washington, DC: Headquarters, Department of the Army, 1976.

—**OUTLINE PLAN** is a preliminary plan that outlines the salient features or principles of a course of action prior to the initiation of detailed planning.

References

Department of Defense, U.S. Army. *Staff Organization and Operations.* Field Manual FM 101-5. Washington, DC: Headquarters, Department of the Army, 1984.

—**P-DAY** is the point in time when the rate of production of an item available for military consumption equals the rate at which the item is required by the armed forces. *See also:* P-Day Concept.

References
Department of Defense, Joint Chiefs of Staff. *Department of Defense Dictionary of Military and Related Terms.* Washington, DC: GPO, 1986.

—**P-DAY CONCEPT** is based upon the objective of procuring and storing the minimum amount of materiel necessary to equip, train, and sustain forces after D-day until production can continually meet the rate of consumption. P-day varies with each item because of the variation in consumption and in production capability for each item. *See also:* D-Day; P-Day.

References
Department of Defense, U.S. Army. *Dictionary of United States Army Terms.* Army Regulation AR 310-25. Washington, DC: Headquarters, Department of the Army, 1986.

—**P-HOUR** is the planned time that an airborne assault starts as the first jumper exits the aircraft over the objective drop zone. *See also:* Drop Zone.

References
Department of Defense, U.S. Army. *USA/USAF Doctrine for Joint Airborne and Tactical Airlift Operations.* Field Manual FM 100-27. Washington, DC: Headquarters, Department of the Army, 1985.

—**PACE,** for ground forces, is the regulated average speed a column or element moves. *See also:* Pacesetter.

References
Department of Defense, Joint Chiefs of Staff. *Department of Defense Dictionary of Military and Related Terms.* Washington, DC: GPO, 1986.

—**PACESETTER** is an individual, selected by the column commander, who travels in the lead vehicle or element to regulate the column speed and establish the pace necessary to meet the required movement order.

References
Department of Defense, U.S. Army. *The Infantry Rifle Company (Infantry, Airborne, Air Assault, Ranger).* Field Manual FM 7-10. Washington, DC: Headquarters, Department of the Army, 1982.

—**PACING ITEMS** are items so critical to the unit's mission that they have been selected for special emphasis (e.g., the tube-launched, optically tracked wire-guided missile and Dragon systems, the AH-1 helicopter, and the M60-series tank). They are continuously monitored and intensively managed at all levels of command.

References
Department of Defense, U.S. Army. *Organizational Maintenance Operations.* Field Manual FM 29-2. Washington, DC: Headquarters, Department of the Army, 1984.

—**PACKAGE** (NUCLEAR) is a discrete grouping of nuclear weapons by specific yield that is planned for employment in a specified area during a short time. *See also:* Nuclear Warfare.

References
Department of Defense, U.S. Army. *Fire Support in Combined Arms Operations.* Field Manual FM 6-20. Washington, DC: Headquarters, Department of the Army, 1983.

—**PACKAGE SHOWS** are live amateur or professional theatrical or musical attractions that are produced elsewhere and brought to an installation to perform for the troops.

References
Department of Defense, U.S. Army. *Dictionary of United States Army Terms.* Army Regulation AR 310-25. Washington, DC: Headquarters, Department of the Army, 1986.

—**PACKAGED FORCES** are forces of various sizes and compositions preselected for specific missions in order to facilitate planning and training.

References
Department of Defense, Joint Chiefs of Staff. *Department of Defense Dictionary of Military and Related Terms.* Washington, DC: GPO, 1986.

—**PACKAGED PETROLEUM PRODUCT** is a petroleum product (e.g., lubricant, oil, grease, or specialty item) that is normally packaged by a manufacturer and procured, stored, transported, and issued in containers having a fill capacity of 55 U.S. gallons (or 45 imperial gallons, or 205 liters) or less.

References
Department of Defense, Joint Chiefs of Staff. *Department of Defense Dictionary of Military and Related Terms.* Washington, DC: GPO, 1986.

—**PACKET** is a group of personnel who are similarly trained and selected for a specific assignment. *See also:* Regimental Affiliation.

References
Department of Defense, U.S. Army. *Dictionary of United States Army Terms.* Army Regulation AR 310-25. Washington, DC: Headquarters, Department of the Army, 1986.

—**PADLOCK** is a call indicating that one aircraft or one crew member is dedicated to maintain visual contact with the enemy.

References
Department of Defense, U.S. Army. *Air-to-Air Combat.* Field Manual FM 1-107. Washington, DC: Headquarters, Department of the Army, 1984.

—**PALLET** is a flat base for combining stores or carrying a single item to form a unit load for handling, transportation, and storage by materials handling equipment. *See also:* Palletized Unit Load.

References
Department of Defense, Joint Chiefs of Staff. *Department of Defense Dictionary of Military and Related Terms.* Washington, DC: GPO, 1986.

—**PALLETIZED UNIT LOAD** is a quantity of any item, packaged or unpackaged, that is specifically arranged on, and securely strapped or fastened to, a pallet so that the items and the pallet are handled as a unit.

References
Department of Defense, Joint Chiefs of Staff. *Department of Defense Dictionary of Military and Related Terms.* Washington, DC: GPO, 1986.

—**PANEL CODE** is a prearranged code designed for visual communications, usually between friendly units, by making use of marking panels. *See also:* Marking Panel.

References
Department of Defense, Joint Chiefs of Staff. *Department of Defense Dictionary of Military and Related Terms.* Washington, DC: GPO, 1986.

—**PANORAMIC AIR CAMERA,** in imagery and photoreconnaissance, refers to a camera that, through a system of moving optics or mirrors, scans a wide area of the terrain, usually from horizon to horizon. The camera can be mounted vertically or obliquely within the aircraft to scan across or along the line of flight. *See also:* Aerial Reconnaissance.

References
Department of Defense, Joint Chiefs of Staff. *Department of Defense Dictionary of Military and Related Terms.* Washington, DC: GPO, 1986.

—**PARABOMB** is a specially prepared equipment container equipped with a parachute that opens automatically after a delayed drop.

References
Department of Defense, U.S. Army. *Dictionary of United States Army Terms.* Army Regulation AR 310-25. Washington, DC: Headquarters, Department of the Army, 1986.

—**PARACAISSON** is a small, unassembled two-wheeled, hand-drawn vehicle whose body forms a container for artillery ammunition during air drops; upon being assembled, it becomes a utility cart.

References
Department of Defense, U.S. Army. *Dictionary of United States Army Terms.* Army Regulation AR 310-25. Washington, DC: Headquarters, Department of the Army, 1986.

—**PARACHUTE DEPLOYMENT HEIGHT** is the height above the intended impact point at which the parachute or parachutes are fully deployed.

References
Department of Defense, Joint Chiefs of Staff. *Department of Defense Dictionary of Military and Related Terms.* Washington, DC: GPO, 1986.

—**PARADE REST.** (1) Parade rest is a position that a soldier assumes in which the left foot is twelve inches to the left of the right foot, the legs are straight, and the hands are clasped behind the back. While at parade rest, the soldier remains motionless and silent. When a soldier has a rifle, parade rest is taken with the feet in this position, with the butt of the rifle on the ground, with the trigger to the front and the muzzle of the rifle in his right hand, extended forward, and with his left hand behind his back. (2) Parade rest is the command to assume the above stance.

References

Department of Defense, U.S. Army. *Dictionary of United States Army Terms*. Army Regulation AR 310-25. Washington, DC: Headquarters, Department of the Army, 1986.

—**PARADROP** is delivery by parachute of personnel or cargo from an aircraft in flight.

References

Department of Defense, Joint Chiefs of Staff. *Department of Defense Dictionary of Military and Related Terms*. Washington, DC: GPO, 1986.

—**PARALLAX.** Tank crewman are concerned with two types of parallax: external (or system) parallax and internal (or optical) parallax. *External parallax* is the apparent difference in position of an object when viewed from different positions. Since tank sights are necessarily offset from the bore, external parallax is present at all ranges other than the boresight range. Parallax is corrected automatically in advanced fire control systems (e.g., the M60A3 and XM1) but affects any other fire control system when firing by battlesight. Where applicable, the procedures to correct for external parallax are covered in the appropriate tank supplement. *Internal parallax* is present in a sight whenever the reticle and the target image are focused in different optical planes. (A reticle is a system of lines, dots, or other items that focuses the eyepiece of an optical instrument) This condition can be adjusted by the gunner, the turret mechanic, or direct support maintenance, but because of the properties of optical devices, it will only be correct for one range. Some residual internal parallax will always be present at other ranges. This residual effect can be minimized by careful adjustment of the headrest to provide consistent placement of the observer's eye relative to the sight. Electronic sights are not subject to internal parallax. *See also:* Parallax Correction, Parallax Error, Parallax in Altitude.

References

Department of Defense, U.S. Army. *Tank Gunnery*. Field Manual FM 17-12. Washington, DC: Headquarters, Department of the Army, 1984.

—**PARALLAX CORRECTION.** (1) A parallax correction is an allowance made for the difference in the position of a target as measured from the gun and as measured from the observer's position. (2) In air defense weapons, a parallax correction is that correction made to compensate for the displacement between remotely located equipment (e.g., radars and launchers) or from a battery directing or reference point (e.g., a target tracking radar). *See also:* Parallax.

References

Department of Defense, U.S. Army. *Dictionary of United States Army Terms*. Army Regulation AR 310-25. Washington, DC: Headquarters, Department of the Army, 1986.

—**PARALLAX ERROR.** (1) A parallax error is a mistake in an observation caused by making the observation from a position different from the normal one. (2) A parallax error is made by reading the dial of an instrument from a slant rather than from directly in front of the dial. *See also:* Parallax.

References

Department of Defense, U.S. Army. *Dictionary of United States Army Terms*. Army Regulation AR 310-25. Washington, DC: Headquarters, Department of the Army, 1986.

—**PARALLAX IN ALTITUDE** is the angle between the straight line from a celestial body to an observer, and the straight line from a celestial body to the center of the earth.

References

Department of Defense, U.S. Army. *Dictionary of United States Army Terms*. Army Regulation AR 310-25. Washington, DC: Headquarters, Department of the Army, 1986.

—**PARALLEL CLASSIFICATION,** in railway terminology, is the classification of ordinary transport military vehicles and equipment, based upon a comparative study of the main characteristics of those vehicles and equipment and of those of the ordinary flat wagons of a corresponding category onto which they can be loaded.

References

Department of Defense, Joint Chiefs of Staff. *Department of Defense Dictionary of Military and Related Terms*. Washington, DC: GPO, 1986.

—**PARALLEL SHEAF,** in artillery, is a sheaf in which the planes (lines) of fire of all firing pieces are parallel. *See also:* Sheaf.

References

Department of Defense, Joint Chiefs of Staff. *Department of Defense Dictionary of Military and Related Terms*. Washington, DC: GPO, 1986.

—**PARALLEL STAFF** is a staff in which one officer from each nation, or service is appointed to each post. *See also:* Combined Staff, Integrated Staff, Joint Staff.

References

Department of Defense, Joint Chiefs of Staff. *Department of Defense Dictionary of Military and Related Terms.* Washington, DC: GPO, 1986.

—**PARALLEL TRAINING** is a method of instruction in which an individual is given technical training, either basic or advanced, by an expert.

References

Department of Defense, U.S. Army. *Dictionary of United States Army Terms.* Army Regulation AR 310-25. Washington, DC: Headquarters, Department of the Army, 1986.

—**PARAMETRIC ESTIMATE** is a cost estimate developed by using the physical and performance characteristics of a system (e.g., speed, range, altitude, power/aperture product, endurance, and reliability) and comparing them with one's experience from similar or related systems.

References

Department of Defense, U.S. Army. *Dictionary of United States Army Terms.* Army Regulation AR 310-25. Washington, DC: Headquarters, Department of the Army, 1986.

—**PARAMILITARY FORCES** are forces or groups distinct from the regular armed forces of a country, but resemble them in organization, equipment, training, and mission. *See also:* Paramilitary Operation.

References

Department of Defense, U.S. Army. *Low Intensity Conflict.* Field Manual FM 100-20. Washington, DC: Headquarters, Department of the Army, 1981.

—**PARAMILITARY OPERATION** is "an operation that is undertaken by a paramilitary force." *See also:* Guerrilla, Guerrilla Operations, Guerrilla Warfare.

References

U.S. Congress. Senate. *Final Report of the Senate Select Committee to Study Government Operations With Respect to Intelligence Activities. Report 94-755. Book I, Foreign and Military Intelligence* (Church Committee Report). Washington, DC: GPO, 1976.

—**PARAMILITARY OPERATIONS** are operations that provide covert military assistance and guidance to unconventional and conventional foreign forces and organizations. *See also:* Guerrilla, Guerrilla Operations, Guerrilla Warfare.

References

Department of Defense, Joint Chiefs of Staff. *Department of Defense Dictionary of Military and Related Terms.* Washington, DC: GPO, 1986.

—**PARAPET POSITION** for air defense artillery provides improved protection for missile launcher equipment. Target acquisition equipment has special operational requirements that make it very difficult to protect. The requirement for it to "see" the battlefield precludes the use of dense protective materials (e.g., soil, concrete, and rock) in the construction of the position. *See also:* Parapet Position for a Self-Propelled Howitzer.

References

Department of Defense, U.S. Army. *Survivability.* Field Manual FM 5-103. Washington, DC: Headquarters, Department of the Army, 1985.

—**PARAPET POSITION FOR A SELF-PROPELLED HOWITZER** provides improved protection from near-miss indirect fire weapons effects and small caliber direct fire. The parapet is built from material that is removed from the excavation and is built low enough to permit direct howitzer fire.

References

Department of Defense, U.S. Army. *Survivability.* Field Manual FM 5-103. Washington, DC: Headquarters, Department of the Army, 1985.

—**PARAPETS** positioned at the front of or around major weapons systems provide improved protection from direct fire and from blast and fragments of indirect fire artillery, mortar, and rocket shells. At its base, the parapet has a thickness of at least eight feet. Further, the parapet functions as a standoff barrier for impact-detonating direct fire high explosive antitank and antitank guided missile projectiles. The parapet should cause the fuzes to activate, thereby increasing survivability for the protected vehicles. If the enemy uses kinetic energy direct-fire armor-piercing or hypervelocity projectiles, it is impossible to construct parapets thick enough for protection.

To protect against these projectiles, deep-cut, hull defilade, or turret defilade positions are prepared. *See also:* Parapet Position for Air Defense Artillery, Parapet Position for a Self-Propelled Howitzer.

References

Department of Defense, U.S. Army. *Survivability.* Field Manual FM 5-103. Washington, DC: Headquarters, Department of the Army, 1985.

—**PARENT STATION** is an organization or installation designated to furnish all or a portion of the common support requirements of another installation or separate organization.

References

Department of Defense, U.S. Army. *Dictionary of United States Army Terms.* Army Regulation AR 310-25. Washington, DC: Headquarters, Department of the Army, 1986.

—**PARENT UNIT.** (1) A parent unit is a table of organization and equipment unit, regardless of its size, that has a numerical designation and unit identification code assigned by the Department of the Army.

References

Department of Defense, U.S. Army. *Dictionary of United States Army Terms.* Army Regulation AR 310-25. Washington, DC: Headquarters, Department of the Army, 1986.

—**PARLIMENTAIRE** is an agent who represents a commander of belligerent forces in the field and who personally goes within the enemy lines to communicate or negotiate openly and directly with the enemy commander.

References

Department of Defense, Joint Chiefs of Staff. *Department of Defense Dictionary of Military and Related Terms.* Washington, DC: GPO, 1986.

—**PART** is an item forming part of an assembly or subassembly (e.g., a bracket, gear, switch, or potted circuit) that is not normally further broken down. *See also:* Part Number.

References

Department of Defense, Joint Chiefs of Staff. *Department of Defense Dictionary of Military and Related Terms.* Washington, DC: GPO, 1986.

Department of Defense, U.S. Army. *Dictionary of United States Army Terms.* Army Regulation AR 310-25. Washington, DC: Headquarters, Department of the Army, 1986.

—**PART NUMBER** is a combination of number, letters, and symbols assigned by a designer, a manufacturer, or a vendor to identify a specific part or item of materiel.

References

Department of Defense, Joint Chiefs of Staff. *Department of Defense Dictionary of Military and Related Terms.* Washington, DC: GPO, 1986.

—**PARTIAL DECONTAMINATION** is the removal or neutralization of all visible or detectable contamination from clothing and equipment and from surfaces of equipment that operators or crew members must contact in performing their mission. *See also:* Chemical Warfare, Nuclear Warfare.

References

Department of Defense, U.S. Army. *NBC Decontamination.* Field Manual FM 3-5. Washington, DC: Headquarters, Department of the Army, 1985.

—**PARTIAL JURISDICTION** is applied in instances where the federal government has been given the rights to exercise certain state authority, but where the state concerned reserves the right to exercise, by itself or concurrently with the United States, other authority constituting more than merely the right to serve civil or criminal process in the area.

References

Department of Defense, U.S. Army. *Dictionary of United States Army Terms.* Army Regulation AR 310-25. Washington, DC: Headquarters, Department of the Army, 1986.

—**PARTIAL MOBILIZATION** is expansion of the active Armed Forces resulting from action by Congress (up to full mobilization) or by the President (of not more than 1 million personnel) to mobilize Ready Reserve component units, individual reservists, and the resources needed for their support to meet the requirements of a war or other national emergency involving an external threat to the national security. *See also:* Mobilization.

References

Department of Defense, U.S. Army. *Officer Assignment Policies, Details, and Transfers.* Army Regulation AR 614-100. Washington, DC: Headquarters, Department of the Army, 1984.

—**PARTICIPATIVE LEADERSHIP** is a style of leadership in which the leader involves one or more subordinates in determining what to do and how to do it. He maintains final decisionmaking authority. *See also:* Leadership.

References
Department of Defense, U.S. Army. *Military Leadership.* Field Manual FM 22-100. Washington, DC: Headquarters, Department of the Army, 1983.

—**PARTS** are essential elements, components, or subassemblies of equipment. Parts are held in reserve to replace worn, damaged, lost, or destroyed elements of equipment so that the item can be restored to sound condition. *See also:* Parts Common, Parts Peculiar.

References
Department of Defense, U.S. Army. *Dictionary of United States Army Terms.* Army Regulation AR 310-25. Washington, DC: Headquarters, Department of the Army, 1986.

—**PARTS COMMON,** or common parts, are parts that can be widely adapted in the manufacture and maintenance of equipment because of their conventional design and standard physical characteristics.

References
Department of Defense, U.S. Army. *Dictionary of United States Army Terms.* Army Regulation AR 310-25. Washington, DC: Headquarters, Department of the Army, 1986.

—**PARTS PECULIAR** are parts whose design is controlled by a single manufacturer or whose use is restricted to items that are produced by a single manufacturer.

References
Department of Defense, U.S. Army. *Dictionary of United States Army Terms.* Army Regulation AR 310-25. Washington, DC: Headquarters, Department of the Army, 1986.

—**PASS.** (1) A pass is an authorized absence granted to personnel for a short period to provide a respite from work or for other specific reasons. At the end of the pass period, the person receiving the pass must be in his place of duty or in the location from which he regularly commutes to work. (2) A pass is one trip of a vehicle over a test course.

References
Department of Defense, U.S. Army. *Dictionary of United States Army Terms.* Army Regulation AR 310-25. Washington, DC: Headquarters, Department of the Army, 1986.

———. *Leaves and Passes.* Army Regulation AR 630-5. Washington, DC: Headquarters, Department of the Army, 1984.

—**PASS IN REVIEW** is to march in front of a reviewing officer during a ceremony. (2) Pass in review is the command given to start the above ceremony.

References
Department of Defense, U.S. Army. *Dictionary of United States Army Terms.* Army Regulation AR 310-25. Washington, DC: Headquarters, Department of the Army, 1986.

—**PASS TIME** is the time between the moment the first element passes a given point and the moment the last element passes the same point. *See also:* Pass Time (Road).

References
Department of Defense, U.S. Army. *The Infantry Rifle Company (Infantry, Airborne, Air Assault, Ranger).* Field Manual FM 7-10. Washington, DC: Headquarters, Department of the Army, 1982.

—**PASS TIME** (ROAD) is the time between the moment the leading vehicle of a column passes a given point and the moment the last vehicle passes the same point.

References
Department of Defense, Joint Chiefs of Staff. *Department of Defense Dictionary of Military and Related Terms.* Washington, DC: GPO, 1986.

—**PASSAGE LANE** is a lane through a unit or obstacle along which the company moves. It begins at a contact point and ends at a release point. *See also:* Contact Point, Release Point.

References
Department of Defense, U.S. Army. *The Infantry Rifle Company (Infantry, Airborne, Air Assault, Ranger).* Field Manual FM 7-10. Washington, DC: Headquarters, Department of the Army, 1982.

———. *Operational Terms and Symbols.* Field Manual FM 101-5-1. Washington, DC: Headquarters, Department of the Army, 1985.

—**PASSAGE OF COMMAND** is the exchange of responsibility for a sector or zone between the commanders of two units. The time of the exchange is mutually agreed upon by the two unit commanders unless it is determined by higher headquarters. *See also:* Passage of Lines, Relief in Place.

References

Department of Defense, U.S. Army. *Operational Terms and Symbols.* Field Manual FM 101-5-1. Washington, DC: Headquarters, Department of the Army, 1985.

—**PASSAGE OF LINES** is an operation in which one unit moves either forward or rearward through positions held by another friendly unit. During a passage of lines, both units are temporarily concentrated in a small area and are extremely vulnerable. For such passage to occur with the least disruption of either unit's tactical mission, the commanders must thoroughly coordinate troop movement, troop positions, combat support, and combat service support. *See also:* Passage Points.

References

Department of Defense, U.S. Army. *Armored and Mechanized Division Operations.* Field Manual FM 71-100. Washington, DC: Headquarters, Department of the Army, 1978.

———. *The Infantry Rifle Company (Infantry, Airborne, Air Assault, Ranger).* Field Manual FM 7-10. Washington, DC: Headquarters, Department of the Army, 1982.

———. *Operational Terms and Symbols.* Field Manual FM 101-5-1. Washington, DC: Headquarters, Department of the Army, 1985.

—**PASSAGE POINTS** are the commander-designated locations through which passing units should physically move.

References

Department of Defense, U.S. Army. *Armored and Mechanized Division Operations.* Field Manual FM 71-100. Washington, DC: Headquarters, Department of the Army, 1978.

———. *Operational Terms and Symbols.* Field Manual FM 101-5-1. Washington, DC: Headquarters, Department of the Army, 1985.

—**PASSENGER MILE** is a unit of measurement for transporting one passenger for one mile. Nautical miles are used for air and ocean transport; statute miles are used for rail, highway, and inland waterway transport in the United States.

References

Department of Defense, Joint Chiefs of Staff. *Department of Defense Dictionary of Military and Related Terms.* Washington, DC: GPO, 1986.

—**PASSING ACTION,** in general, identifies all types of supply transactions associated with materiel demands within supply distribution systems. The term applies when materiel demands (e.g., orders, referral orders, materiel release orders, and redistribution orders) are forwarded from one supply source to another.

References

Department of Defense, U.S. Army. *Dictionary of United States Army Terms.* Army Regulation AR 310-25. Washington, DC: Headquarters, Department of the Army, 1986.

—**PASSING ORDER** is an order used to pass an erroneously routed requisition to the appropriate depot or distribution point, and to pass a requisition from one distribution system to another.

References

Department of Defense, U.S. Army. *Dictionary of United States Army Terms.* Army Regulation AR 310-25. Washington, DC: Headquarters, Department of the Army, 1986.

—**PASSIVE,** in surveillance, describes actions or equipments that emit no energy capable of being detected. *See also:* Electronic Warfare.

References

Department of Defense, Joint Chiefs of Staff. *Department of Defense Dictionary of Military and Related Terms.* Washington, DC: GPO, 1986.

—**PASSIVE AIR DEFENSE** are measures other than active air defense that are taken to minimize the effects of hostile air action (e.g., cover, concealment, camouflage, dummy positions, dispersion, and protective construction).

References

Department of Defense, U.S. Army. *Air Defense Artillery Deployment: Chaparral/Vulcan/Stinger.* Field Manual FM 44-3. Washington, DC: Headquarters, Department of the Army, 1984.

———. *Air Defense Artillery Employment.* Field Manual FM 44-1. Washington, DC: Headquarters, Department of the Army, 1983.

———. *Air Defense Artillery Employment Hawk.* Field Manual FM 44-90. Washington, DC: Headquarters, Department of the Army, 1983.

———. *Operational Terms and Symbols.* Field Manual FM 101-5-1. Washington, DC: Headquarters, Department of the Army, 1985.

—**PASSIVE BALLISTIC MISSILE DEFENSE** encompasses all defensive measures other than active defense taken to minimize the effects of a hostile attack by ballistic missiles (e.g., the use of cover, concealment, camouflage, dispersion, and protective construction).

References

Department of Defense, Joint Chiefs of Staff. *Department of Defense Dictionary of Military and Related Terms.* Washington, DC: GPO, 1986.

—**PASSIVE COUNTERINTELLIGENCE,** in counterintelligence, counterinsurgency and counterespionage, attempts to counter potentially hostile covert operations. It involves personnel security briefings and other preventive measures. *See also:* Counterintelligence.

References

Department of Defense, Joint Chiefs of Staff. *Department of Defense Dictionary of Military and Related Terms.* Washington, DC: GPO, 1986.

—**PASSIVE DEFENSE** involves measures taken to reduce the probability of and to minimize the effects of damage caused by hostile action without the intention of taking the initiative.

References

Department of Defense, Joint Chiefs of Staff. *Department of Defense Dictionary of Military and Related Terms.* Washington, DC: GPO, 1986.

—**PASSIVE ELECTRONIC COUNTERMEASURES,** in electronic warfare, involve searching for and analyzing electromagnetic radiations to determine their origin and the pertinent characteristics of the radiations that the enemy may be using. *See also:* Electronic Countermeasures, Electronic Warfare.

References

Department of Defense, U.S. Army. *Operational Terms and Symbols.* Field Manual FM 101-5-1. Washington, DC: Headquarters, Department of the Army, 1985.

—**PASSIVE HOMING GUIDANCE** is a system of homing guidance wherein the receiver in the missile uses radiation from the target to direct the missile. *See also:* Guidance.

References

Department of Defense, Joint Chiefs of Staff. *Department of Defense Dictionary of Military and Related Terms.* Washington, DC: GPO, 1986.

—**PASSIVE JAMMING,** in electronic warfare, is using confusion reflectors to return spurious or confusing signals to the transmitting radar set. *See also:* Jammer.

References

Department of Defense, U.S. Army. *The Infantry Rifle Company (Infantry, Airborne, Air Assault, Ranger).* Field Manual FM 7-10. Washington, DC: Headquarters, Department of the Army, 1982.

—**PASSIVE SECURITY MEASURE** include camouflage, movement control, light and noise discipline, proper radiotelephone procedures, ground surveillance radars, and ground sensors. *See also:* Camouflage.

References

Department of Defense, U.S. Army. *The Infantry Rifle Company (Infantry. Airborne, Air Assault, Ranger).* Field Manual FM 7-10. Washington, DC: Headquarters, Department of the Army, 1982.

—**PASSIVE STANO (SURVEILLANCE, TARGET, ACQUISITION, NIGHT OBSERVATION) DEVICES** do not emit or project any signal, so their use cannot be detected. They collect and amplify external energy from certain sources (e.g., starlight, heat, infrared light, vibrations, and moving metal objects). These devices include starlight scopes (image intensification devices); the tube-launched, optically tracked, wire-guided missile night-sight, and the Dragon night tracker, which employ thermal imagery; and ground sensors.

References

Department of Defense, U.S. Army. *The Infantry Rifle Company (Infantry, Airborne, Air Assault, Ranger).* Field Manual FM 7-10. Washington, DC: Headquarters, Department of the Army, 1982.

—**PASSWORD** is a secret word or distinctive sound used to reply to a challenge. *See also:* Challenge, Countersign, Reply.

References

Department of Defense, Joint Chiefs of Staff. *Department of Defense Dictionary of Military and Related Terms.* Washington, DC: GPO, 1986.

—**PATCHING CENTRAL** is a facility in a communications system used to interconnect circuits temporarily, to fulfill circuit routing requirements, or to improve the quality of the circuits. Normally a part of a technical control center, it differs from a switching central, which temporarily interconnects established circuits in response to a subscriber's request. *See also:* Switching Central.

References

Department of Defense, U.S. Army. *Dictionary of United States Army Terms.* Army Regulation AR 310-25. Washington, DC: Headquarters, Department of the Army, 1986.

—**PATHFINDER BEACON** is a transmitting device utilizing electromagnetic radiation (e.g., visible light, infrared, ultraviolet, radar, or radio waves) that provides an identifiable point to assist in the guiding aircraft or assembling ground units.

References

Department of Defense, U.S. Army. *Dictionary of United States Army Terms.* Army Regulation AR 310-25. Washington, DC: Headquarters, Department of the Army, 1986.

—**PATHFINDER DETACHMENT** is an Army table of organization pathfinder organization. *See also:* Pathfinders.

References

Department of Defense, U.S. Army. *Dictionary of United States Army Terms.* Army Regulation AR 310-25. Washington, DC: Headquarters, Department of the Army, 1986.

—**PATHFINDER GUIDANCE** is aircraft guidance provided by pathfinders. *See also:* Pathfinders.

References

Department of Defense, U.S. Army. *Dictionary of United States Army Terms.* Army Regulation AR 310-25. Washington, DC: Headquarters, Department of the Army, 1986.

—**PATHFINDERS.** (1) Pathfinders are aircraft crews who lead a formation to the drop zone, release point, or target. (2) Pathfinders are teams dropped or airlanded at an objective to establish and operate navigational aids to guide aircraft to drop zones or landing zones. (3) Pathfinders are teams air delivered into enemy territory to determine the best approach and withdrawal lines, landing zones and sites for heliborne forces. *See also:* Drop Zone, Landing Zone, Pathfinder Beacon, Pathfinder Detachment, Pathfinder Guidance.

References

Department of Defense, U.S. Army. *Attack Helicopter Operations.* Field Manual FM 17-50. Washington, DC: Headquarters, Department of the Army, 1984.

———. *Operational Terms and Symbols.* Field Manual FM 101-5-1. Washington, DC: Headquarters, Department of the Army, 1985.

—**PATIENT** is a sick, injured, or wounded person who needs medical or dental care or treatment. *See also:* Medical Treatment.

References

Department of Defense, Joint Chiefs of Staff. *Department of Defense Dictionary of Military and Related Terms.* Washington, DC: GPO, 1986.

—**PATIENT ADMISSION RATE** is the average daily number of admissions per 1,000 average daily strength of an organization. It pertains to a specified portion of the total population that is served and is for a specified period or periods. Separate admission rates are always provided for wounded-in-action patients and disease and non-battle-injury patients. *See also:* Medical Treatment.

References

Department of Defense, U.S. Army. *Health Service Support in a Communications Zone (Test).* Field Manual FM 8-21. Washington, DC: Headquarters, Department of the Army, 1981.

———. *Planning for Health Service Support.* Field Manual FM 8-55. Washington, DC: Headquarters, Department of the Army, 1985.

—**PATIENT COLLECTING POINT** is a designated location at which patients are collected to await disposition after having received first aid or emergency medical care. Patient collecting points are normally established on or near the main routes of communication, in sites that provide the most feasible shelter against weather and protection against hostile fire. They are not treatment stations and medical personnel may or may not be present. *See also:* Medical Treatment.

References

Department of Defense, U.S. Army. *Dictionary of United States Army Terms.* Army Regulation AR 310-25. Washington, DC: Headquarters, Department of the Army, 1986.

—**PATIENT MORTALITY RATE** is a measure of the deaths occurring from a particular disease, injury, condition, or group of conditions. It shows the relationship between the number of patients with a particular condition and the number of deaths among these patients due to this condition. *See also:* Medical Treatment.

References

Department of Defense, U.S. Army. *Health Service Support in a Communications Zone (Test).* Field Manual FM 8-21. Washington, DC: Headquarters, Department of the Army, 1981.

—**PATIENTS REMAINING** are patients whether they are present or absent, who are carried on the rolls of a medical treatment facility. *See also:* Medical Treatment.

References

Department of Defense, U.S. Army. *Dictionary of United States Army Terms.* Army Regulation AR 310-25. Washington, DC: Headquarters, Department of the Army, 1986.

—**PATRIOT,** the Army's all-altitude missile system, is the centerpiece of the Army's theater air defense. The system's fast reaction capability, high firepower, and ability to operate in a severe electronic countermeasure environment are features that were not previously available in Nike Hercules and HAWK, the systems that Patriot is replacing. The Patriot design eases the field logistic burden, since its overall performance is achieved with less equipment, less operational manpower, and fewer repair parts than current systems. The combat element of the system is the fire unit that consists of a radar set, an engagement control station, a power plant, and up to eight remotely located launchers. The system is highly automated, combining high speed digital processing with various software routines to effectively control the battlespace. The single radar, using phased array technology, provides for all tactical functions of airspace surveillance, target detection and track, and support of missile guidance. The only manned element of the fire unit during an air battle is the engagement control station, which provides the human interface for control of automated operations. Each launcher contains four ready-to-fire missiles, sealed in canisters, that serve a dual purpose as shipping containers and launch tubes.

References

Weapons Systems: U.S. Army, Navy, and Air Force Directory, 1986-1988. Washington, DC: DCP, 1986.

Department of Defense, U.S. Army. *Air Defense Artillery Deployment: Chaparral/Vulcan/Stinger.* Field Manual FM 44-3. Washington, DC: Headquarters, Department of the Army, 1984.

———. *Patriot Battalion Operations.* Field Manual FM 44-15. Washington, DC: Headquarters, Department of the Army, 1984.

—**PATROL.** (1) A patrol is a detachment sent out to gather information or to carry out a destructive, harassing, mopping-up, or security mission.

(2) A patrol is a military police patrol, which normally consists of two military policemen. It performs enforcement duties in an assigned area during a specified time. It may be a foot, motor, train and terminal, water, or an air patrol, and may be conducted with civil police, personnel from other services, or with personnel from other nations. *See also:* Patrol Base.

References

Department of Defense, U.S. Army. *Operational Terms and Symbols.* Field Manual FM 101-5-1. Washington, DC: Headquarters, Department of the Army, 1985.

—**PATROL BASE** is a position set up when the patrol halts for an extended period. If the patrol halts for a long time in a place not protected by friendly troops, it takes active and passive security measures. *See also:* Patrol.

References

Department of Defense, U.S. Army. *The Infantry Rifle Company (Infantry, Airborne, Air Assault, Ranger).* Field Manual FM 7-10. Washington, DC: Headquarters, Department of the Army, 1982.

—**PATTERN ANALYSIS,** in Army tactical intelligence, refers to a detailed study of stereotyped actions that often occur in certain circumstances. Information in the Counter-Signals Intelligence data base that could give the enemy a clue to a unit's type, disposition, activity, or capability are reviewed, and if vulnerabilities are identified, corrective actions are taken. *See also:* Pattern Analysis (Counter-IMINT).

References

Department of Defense, U.S. Army. *Counterintelligence.* Field Manual FM 34-60. Washington, DC: Headquarters, Department of the Army, 1985.

———. *Counter-Signals Intelligence (C-SIGINT) Operations.* Field Manual FM 34-62. Washington, DC: Headquarters, Department of the Army, 1986.

———. *Military Intelligence Battalion (Combat Electronic Warfare Intelligence) (Division).* Field Manual FM 34-10. Washington, DC: Headquarters, Department of the Army, 1981.

———. *Military Intelligence Battalion Combat Electronic Warfare and Intelligence (Aerial Exploitation) (Corps).* Field Manual FM 34-22. Washington, DC: Headquarters, Department of the Army, 1984.

—**PATTERN ANALYSIS** (COUNTER-IMINT) is the detailed study of stereotyped actions that always occur in certain circumstances and that may cue the observer to the unit's type, disposition, activity, and capability. This process is applied against friendly units to assess how well the enemy intelligence collection system senses the friendly force's using imagery intelligence. Patterns usually result because of a unit's standing operating procedures. Examples of patterns include relocating fire support units forward before an attack; locating command posts and tactical operations centers in the same relative position to maneuver elements and to each other; and repeating reconnaissance overflights of areas that are planned for ground or air attack at about the same time before each operation.

References

Department of Defense, U.S. Army. *Counterintelligence.* Field Manual FM 34-60. Washington, DC: Headquarters, Department of the Army, 1985.

—**PATTERN LAYING,** in land mine warfare, is the laying of mines in a planned arrangement. *See also:* Mine Warfare.

References

Department of Defense, Joint Chiefs of Staff. *Department of Defense Dictionary of Military and Related Terms.* Washington, DC: GPO, 1986.

—**PATTERNS,** in Army tactical intelligence, refers to stereotyped actions that occur so habitually in certain circumstances that they cue an observer, well in advance, to the type of military unit or activity or to its identity, capabilities, or intent. Stereotyping occurs in a variety of ways (e.g., through communications deployment techniques or historical association). Such patterns must be unique and detectable to be of military significance. *See also:* Olfactory Deception.

References

Department of Defense, U.S. Army. *Counter-Signals Intelligence (C-SIGINT) Operations.* Field Manual FM 34-62. Washington, DC: Headquarters, Department of the Army, 1986.

———. *Military Intelligence Battalion (Combat Electronic Warfare Intelligence) (Division).* Field Manual FM 34-10. Washington, DC: Headquarters, Department of the Army, 1981.

———. *Military Intelligence Battalion Combat Electronic Warfare and Intelligence (Aerial Exploitation) (Corps).* Field Manual FM 34-22. Washington, DC: Headquarters, Department of the Army, 1984.

—**PAY.** *See:* Military Pay and Allowances.

—**PAY GRADE** is the pay grade established by the Career Compensation Act of 1949, as amended. *See also:* Military Pay and Allowances.

References

Department of Defense, U.S. Army. *Dictionary of United States Army Terms.* Army Regulation AR 310-25. Washington, DC: Headquarters, Department of the Army, 1986.

—**PAY PATIENT** is a patient who receives inpatient or outpatient health services at a medical or dental treatment facility and for whom the Department of the Army is reimbursed for the cost of the services, in accordance with Department of the Army regulatory directives. *See also:* Medical Treatment.

References

Department of Defense, U.S. Army. *Dictionary of United States Army Terms.* Army Regulation AR 310-25. Washington, DC: Headquarters, Department of the Army, 1986.

—**PAYLOAD.** (1) The payload is the sum of the weight of the passengers and cargo that an aircraft can carry. (2) A payload is a warhead, its container, and the activating devices in a military missile. (3) A payload is the load (expressed in tons of cargo or equipment, gallons of liquid, or numbers of passengers) that a vehicle is designed to transport under specified conditions of operation, in addition to its unladen weight.

References

Department of Defense, Joint Chiefs of Staff. *Department of Defense Dictionary of Military and Related Terms.* Washington, DC: GPO, 1986.

—**PEACE-KEEPING OPERATIONS (PKO)** are military operations conducted in support of diplomatic efforts to achieve, restore, or maintain peace in areas of potential or actual conflict. They include observation; surveillance and supervision; patrolling; complaint investigation; negotiation and mediation; and information gathering. The rules of engagement are based upon the principles of the minimum use of force, total impartiality, and the use of deadly force only when it is absolutely necessary and only as a last resort. *See also:* Low-Intensity Conflict.

References

Department of Defense, U.S. Army. *Psychological Operations.* Field Manual FM 33-1. Washington, DC: Headquarters, Department of the Army, 1979.

———. *U.S. Army Operational Concept for Special Operations Forces.* TRADOC PAM 525-34. Washington, DC: Headquarters, Department of the Army, 1984.

———. *U.S. Army Policy Statement, 1988.* Washington, DC: Headquarters, Department of the Army, 1988.

—**PEACETIME** is a situation where armed conflict does not exist or where armed conflict does exist, but the United States is not directly involved.

References

Department of Defense, U.S. Army. *Code of Conduct/Survival, Evasion, Resistance and Escape (SERE) Training.* Army Regulation AR 350-30. Washington, DC: Headquarters, Department of the Army, 1985.

—**PEACETIME CONTINGENCY OPERATIONS** are politically sensitive military operations that are normally characterized by the short-term rapid projection or use of forces in conditions short of conventional war (e.g., strikes, raids, rescues, recoveries, demonstrations, a show of force, unconventional warfare, or intelligence operations).

References

Department of Defense, U.S. Army. *Psychological Operations.* Field Manual FM 33-1. Washington, DC: Headquarters, Department of the Army, 1979.

———. *U.S. Army Operational Concept for Special Operations Forces.* TRADOC PAM 525-34. Washington, DC: Headquarters, Department of the Army, 1984.

———. *U.S. Army Policy Statement, 1988.* Washington, DC: Headquarters, Department of the Army, 1988.

—**PEACETIME ESTABLISHMENT,** or peacetime complement, is a table setting out the authorized peacetime manpower requirement for a unit, formation, or headquarters.

References

Department of Defense, Joint Chiefs of Staff. *Department of Defense Dictionary of Military and Related Terms.* Washington, DC: GPO, 1986.

—**PEACETIME FORCE MATERIEL ASSETS** is the portion of total materiel assets designated to meet the peacetime force materiel requirement. *See also:* War Reserves.

References

Department of Defense, Joint Chiefs of Staff. *Department of Defense Dictionary of Military and Related Terms.* Washington, DC: GPO, 1986.

—**PEACETIME FORCE MATERIEL REQUIREMENT** is the quantity of an item required to equip, provide a materiel pipeline, and sustain the U.S. force structure and the allied forces that are designated for U.S. peacetime support in the current Secretary of Defense guidance. The requirement includes approved supply support arrangements with foreign military sales countries and support through the scheduled establishment of normal appropriation and procurement lead-time periods.

References

Department of Defense, Joint Chiefs of Staff. *Department of Defense Dictionary of Military and Related Terms.* Washington, DC: GPO, 1986.

—**PEACETIME MATERIEL CONSUMPTION AND LOSSES** is the quantity of an item that is consumed, lost, or worn out beyond economical repair through normal appropriation and procurement lead-time periods.

References

Department of Defense, Joint Chiefs of Staff. *Department of Defense Dictionary of Military and Related Terms.* Washington, DC: GPO, 1986.

—**PEAK OVERPRESSURE** is the maximum amount of excessive pressure at a given location that is generally experienced at the instant the shock (or blast) wave reaches that location. *See also:* Shock Wave.

References

Department of Defense, Joint Chiefs of Staff. *Department of Defense Dictionary of Military and Related Terms.* Washington, DC: GPO, 1986.

—**PECUNIARY LIABILITY** is a personal, joint, or corporate monetary obligation to make good any lost, damaged, or destroyed property as a result of fault or neglect. It may also result from conditions stipulated in a contract or bond.

References

Department of Defense, U.S. Army. *Commander's Handbook for Property Accountability at the Unit Level.* Field Manual FM 10-14-1. Washington, DC: Headquarters, Department of the Army, 1984.

—**PEER TRAINING** is a technique of using fast learners to help slower learners perform successfully one or more training objectives.

References

Department of Defense, U.S. Army. *How to Prepare and Conduct Military Training.* Field Manual FM 21-6. Washington, DC: Headquarters, Department of the Army, 1975.

—**PEL** is the maximum time-weighted average airborne concentration (milligrams per cubic meter) of a chemical agent to which it is estimated that people in a specific location can be exposed for a specific period without experiencing adverse effects. *See also:* Chemical Warfare.

References
Department of Defense, U.S. Army. *Ammunition and Explosives Safety Standards.* Army Regulation AR 385-64. Washington, DC: Headquarters, Department of the Army, 1987.

—**PENCIL BEAM** is a searchlight beam reduced to, or set at, its minimum width.

References
Department of Defense, Joint Chiefs of Staff. *Department of Defense Dictionary of Military and Related Terms.* Washington, DC: GPO, 1986.

—**PENETRATION** is a form of offensive that seeks to break through the enemy's defense and disrupt its defensive system. It is used when enemy flanks are not assailable and when time does not permit some other form of maneuver. It attempts to rupture enemy defenses on a narrow front and thereby create both assailable flanks and access to the enemy's rear. Penetrations normally comprise three stages: initial rupture of enemy positions; roll-up of the flanks on either side of the gap; and exploitation to secure deep objectives. Because the penetration itself is vulnerable to flank attack, especially in its early stages, penetrating forces must move rapidly, and follow-on forces must be close behind to secure and widen the shoulders. Fire support must concentrate on suppressing enemy defenses quickly, and then shift to protecting the flanks of the attack.

References
Department of Defense, U.S. Army. *Operational Terms and Symbols.* Field Manual FM 101-5-1. Washington, DC: Headquarters, Department of the Army, 1985.

———. *Operations.* Field Manual FM 100-5. Washington, DC: Headquarters, Department of the Army, 1986.

—**PENETRATION** (INTELLIGENCE) is the recruitment of agents within, or the infiltration of agents or technical monitoring devices in, an organization or group in order to acquire information about or to influence its activities. *See also:* Intelligence.

References
Department of Defense, Joint Chiefs of Staff. *Department of Defense Dictionary of Military and Related Terms.* Washington, DC: GPO, 1986.

—**PEPTIZED FUEL** is thickened flamethrower fuel to which water or other chemicals are added before mixing to reduce the mixing time and to increase the storage stability. *See also:* Chemical Warfare.

References
Department of Defense, U.S. Army. *Dictionary of United States Army Terms.* Army Regulation AR 310-25. Washington, DC: Headquarters, Department of the Army, 1986.

—**PERCENTAGE CLEARANCE,** in mine warfare, is the estimated percentage of mines of specified characteristics that have been cleared from an area. *See also:* Mine Warfare.

References
Department of Defense, Joint Chiefs of Staff. *Department of Defense Dictionary of Military and Related Terms.* Washington, DC: GPO, 1986.

—**PERCUSSION.** (1) Percussion is a sharp, light blow, especially one that sets off an explosive. (2) Percussion is a command to set the time fuze of a projectile or bomb in a nonoperating position, to allow the projectile or bomb to be set off by the flow of impact.

References
Department of Defense, U.S. Army. *Dictionary of United States Army Terms.* Army Regulation AR 310-25. Washington, DC: Headquarters, Department of the Army, 1986.

—**PERCUSSION CHARGE** is a small high explosive charge that is set off by the blow of a firing pin. It is used to ignite the primer charge in order to fire the propelling charge of a gun.

References
Department of Defense, U.S. Army. *Dictionary of United States Army Terms.* Army Regulation AR 310-25. Washington, DC: Headquarters, Department of the Army, 1986.

—**PERCUSSION DETONATOR** is an item consisting of a blasting cap and explosive elements that is designed to detonate an explosive charge.

References
Department of Defense, U.S. Army. *Dictionary of United States Army Terms.* Army Regulation AR 310-25. Washington, DC: Headquarters, Department of the Army, 1986.

—**PERCUSSION MECHANISM** is a device that contains the firing pin assembly. It slides in the center bore of the breechlock of a gun.

References
Department of Defense, U.S. Army. *Dictionary of United States Army Terms*. Army Regulation AR 310-25. Washington, DC: Headquarters, Department of the Army, 1986.

—**PERCUSSION PRIMER** is a cap or cylinder containing a small charge of high explosive that may be set off by a blow. A percussion primer is used in all fixed and semifixed ammunition and in certain types of separate-loading ammunition to ignite the main propelling charge.

References
Department of Defense, U.S. Army. *Dictionary of United States Army Terms*. Army Regulation AR 310-25. Washington, DC: Headquarters, Department of the Army, 1986.

—**PERFORMANCE-ORIENTED TRAINING** is a training strategy in which learning is accomplished through the individual or collective performance of one or more tasks, under specified conditions, until the individual or team/unit can demonstrate the level of proficiency established as the training standard. Soldiers learn by doing a task, not by being told how to do it.

References
Department of Defense, U.S. Army. *Army Forces Training*. Army Regulation AR 350-41. Washington, DC: Headquarters, Department of the Army, 1986.

———. *How to Prepare and Conduct Military Training*. Field Manual FM 21-6. Washington, DC: Headquarters, Department of the Army, 1975.

—**PERFORMANCE TEST** is an evaluation tool that requires performance of a task under test conditions and is evaluated on a pass/fail (Go/No-Go) basis using a specified test standard. Performance tests are developed from information contained in the training objectives.

References
Department of Defense, U.S. Army. *How to Prepare and Conduct Military Training*. Field Manual FM 21-6. Washington, DC: Headquarters, Department of the Army, 1975.

—**PERIMETER DEFENSE** is a defense without an exposed flank consisting of forces deployed along the boundary of the defended area.

References
Department of Defense, Joint Chiefs of Staff. *Department of Defense Dictionary of Military and Related Terms*. Washington, DC: GPO, 1986.

—**PERIODIC INTELLIGENCE SUMMARY** (PERINTSUM) is a report on the intelligence situation in a tactical operation. It is normally produced at the corps level or higher and usually at 24-hour intervals, or as directed by the commander. *See also:* Intelligence.

References
Department of Defense, Joint Chiefs of Staff. *Department of Defense Dictionary of Military and Related Terms*. Washington, DC: GPO, 1986.

—**PERIODIC MONITORING** is the frequent check of the unit area for the presence of beta or gamma radiation. It is done if intelligence indicates that there is a threat concerning the possible use of nuclear weapons; if nuclear warfare has been initiated; if the dose rate falls below one centigray per hour; or if monitoring is ordered by the unit commander. *See also:* Nuclear Warfare.

References
Department of Defense, U.S. Army. *NBC Operations*. Field Manual FM 3-100. Washington, DC: Headquarters, Department of the Army, 1985.

—**PERIODIC REINVESTIGATION (PR),** or special background investigation-periodic reinvestigation, meets the periodic personnel reinvestigation requirements for access to sensitive compartmented information. Special background investigation-periodic reinvestigations are initiated at the four and one-half year point after the completion of the subject's last special background investigation. The special background investigation-periodic reinvestigation updates the information contained in the individual's file and recertifies him for access to sensitive compartmented information. *See also:* Special Background Investigation.

References
Department of Defense, Joint Chiefs of Staff. *Department of Defense Dictionary of Military and Related Terms*. Washington, DC: GPO, 1986.

—**PERIODIC REPORTS AND SUMMARIES** are submitted to a higher headquarters at prescribed times. Their content, which is specified by established standard operating procedures or orders, reports the information required at the end of the prescribed period, as well as any events and changes that have occurred since the previous report.

References
Department of Defense, U.S. Army. *Staff Organizations and Operations.* Field Manual FM 101-5. Washington, DC: Headquarters, Department of the Army, 1984.

—**PERIODICAL** is a regularly published publication that is issued more than once within a twelve-month period, but less frequently than daily. Its purpose is to disseminate professional, technical, or substantive information.

References
Department of Defense, Joint Chiefs of Staff. *Department of Defense Dictionary of Military and Related Terms.* Washington, DC: GPO, 1986.

—**PERIODS OF ESTIMATE** are progressive intervals or periods, measured in days, used by a medical facility to estimate its bed requirements. Normally, the estimates begin with the commencement of a military operation, and are calculated in periods of 30 days. Bed requirements are then calculated at the end of each time period.

References
Department of Defense, U.S. Army. *Planning for Health Service Support.* Field Manual FM 8-55. Washington, DC: Headquarters, Department of the Army, 1985.

—**PERIPHERAL COURSE** is a service school course that does not result in the award of a military occupational specialty, special, or additional qualification identifier; is not part of the education program leading to a commission or an appointment as a warrant officer; is not regarded as career schooling; or is not a part of an educational program for career development of officers or leadership development of enlisted personnel.

References
Department of Defense, U.S. Army. *Dictionary of United States Army Terms.* Army Regulation AR 310-25. Washington, DC: Headquarters, Department of the Army, 1986.

—**PERISHABLE CARGO** is cargo requiring refrigeration (e.g., meat, fruit, and fresh vegetables, and medical department biologicals).

References
Department of Defense, Joint Chiefs of Staff. *Department of Defense Dictionary of Military and Related Terms.* Washington, DC: GPO, 1986.

—**PERMANENT APPOINTMENT** is the appointment or promotion of an officer in the Regular Army, Army National Guard, or Army Reserve (as contrasted with a temporary appointment of an officer in the U.S. Army in time of war or national emergency). An officer may have permanent appointment in a grade in the Regular Army, Army National Guard, or Army Reserve, and a temporary appointment in a lower or higher grade in the U.S. Army. *See also:* Permanent Grade.

References
Department of Defense, U.S. Army. *Dictionary of United States Army Terms.* Army Regulation AR 310-25. Washington, DC: Headquarters, Department of the Army, 1986.

—**PERMANENT APPROPRIATION** is an established appropriation that is automatically renewed without further congressional action until it is altered or revoked.

References
Department of Defense, U.S. Army. *Dictionary of United States Army Terms.* Army Regulation AR 310-25. Washington, DC: Headquarters, Department of the Army, 1986.

—**PERMANENT CHANGE OF STATION (PCS).** (1) A PCS is the reassignment of a military member from one permanent station to another. It includes the change from home to first station when called to active duty, or the change from last station to home in connection with retirement or relief from active duty. (2) A PCS is the transfer of a unit from one permanent station to another. *See also:* Date Eligible to Return from Overseas, Expiration of Term of Service.

References
Department of Defense, U.S. Army. *Dictionary of United States Army Terms.* Army Regulation AR 310-25. Washington, DC: Headquarters, Department of the Army, 1986.

—**PERMANENT DUTY STATION.** *See:* Permanent Station.

—**PERMANENT ECHO** is any dense or fixed radar return caused by the reflection of energy from the earth's surface. It is distinguished from "ground clutter" by being from definable locations rather than from large areas. *See also:* Radar.

References

Department of Defense, Joint Chiefs of Staff. *Department of Defense Dictionary of Military and Related Terms.* Washington, DC: GPO, 1986.

—**PERMANENT EMPLACEMENT** is a fixed location for a gun. It is usually made of reinforced concrete, with the base plate and base ring set bolted in the concrete.

References

Department of Defense, U.S. Army. *Dictionary of United States Army Terms.* Army Regulation AR 310-25. Washington, DC: Headquarters, Department of the Army, 1986.

—**PERMANENT FOOD HANDLER** is a military or civilian person who is permanently assigned to duty in dining facilities, and to handle food, drink, or dining facility equipment. Dining facility managers and cooks are permanent food handlers.

References

Department of Defense, U.S. Army. *Dictionary* of *United States Army Terms.* Army Regulation AR 310-25. Washington, DC: Headquarters, Department of the Army, 1986.

—**PERMANENT GRADE,** or permanent rank, is a grade held by an enlisted person or an officer in the Regular Army, Army National Guard, or Army Reserve (as contrasted with the temporary grade of an enlisted person or an officer in the U.S. Army). *See also:* Permanent Appointment.

References

Department of Defense, U.S. Army. *Dictionary of United States Army Terms.* Army Regulation AR 310-25. Washington, DC: Headquarters, Department of the Army, 1986.

—**PERMANENT PARTIAL DISABILITY** is the complete loss of any member or part of the body or permanent impairment of any function of the body, other than total disability, that results from injury (occupational or otherwise). Such disabilities include disease and battle casualties. *See also:* Medical Treatment.

References

Department of Defense, U.S. Army. *Dictionary of United States Army Terms.* Army Regulation AR 310-25. Washington, DC: Headquarters, Department of the Army, 1986.

—**PERMANENT PARTY** is composed of the personnel assigned to an organization for the purpose of performing duty in the furtherance of the mission of the organization and who are properly chargeable against the personnel authorization of tables of organization and distribution. It includes personnel who are assigned for this purpose whose number exceeds the number authorized in such tables.

References

Department of Defense, U.S. Army. *Dictionary of United States Army Terms.* Army Regulation AR 310-25. Washington, DC: Headquarters, Department of the Army, 1986.

—**PERMANENT POST** is a permanent military installation established by the authority of the Secretary of the Army. It is normally called a "fort" (to distinguish it from a temporary installation for troops, which is normally called a "camp"). *See also:* Fort, Installation.

References

Department of Defense, U.S. Army. *Dictionary of United States Army Terms.* Army Regulation AR 310-25. Washington, DC: Headquarters, Department of the Army, 1986.

—**PERMANENT PROMOTION** is a promotion in the regular Army or in a reserve component of the Army. *See also:* Permanent Appointment, Permanent Grade.

References

Department of Defense, U.S. Army. *Dictionary of United States Army Terms.* Army Regulation AR 310-25. Washington, DC: Headquarters, Department of the Army, 1986.

—**PERMANENT PROPERTY** refers to the machinery, appliances, and apparatuses that are permanently installed and intended for lasting use at a military establishment.

References

Department of Defense, U.S. Army. *Dictionary of United States Army Terms.* Army Regulation AR 310-25. Washington, DC: Headquarters, Department of the Army, 1986.

—**PERMANENT STATION** is a post or station to which an officer or enlisted person is assigned to duty under orders that do not state when the assignment will end. *See also:* Permanent Change of Station.

References

Department of Defense, U.S. Army. *Dictionary of United States Army Terms.* Army Regulation AR 310-25. Washington, DC: Headquarters, Department of the Army, 1986.

—**PERMANENT TOTAL DISABILITY** is a condition that permanently and totally incapacitates a person from pursuing any gainful occupation. It is caused by disease, injury (occupational or otherwise), or battle. *See also:* Medical Treatment.

References

Department of Defense, U.S. Army. *Dictionary of United States Army Terms.* Army Regulation AR 310-25. Washington, DC: Headquarters, Department of the Army, 1986.

—**PERMEABLE PROTECTIVE CLOTHING** is clothing that has been treated (impregnated) with chemicals to protect against chemical agents. *See also:* Chemical Warfare.

References

Department of Defense, U.S. Army. *Dictionary of United States Army Terms.* Army Regulation AR 310-25. Washington, DC: Headquarters, Department of the Army, 1986.

—**PERMISSIVE ACTION LINKS (PALs)** are mechanical or electromechanical devices that, when in use, disenable a weapon by interrupting its assembly or firing sequence. Once disabled by a PAL, a weapon can be enabled only by enabling the device or by applying the proper combination to remove it. PALs are available for all U.S. Army nuclear weapons. *See also:* Nuclear Warfare.

References

Department of Defense, U.S. Army. *Operations for Nuclear-Capable Units.* Field Manual FM 100-50. Washington, DC: Headquarters, Department of the Army, 1980.

—**PERMISSIVE ATTACK LINK** is a device included in or attached to a nuclear weapon system to preclude arming and/or launching until the insertion of a prescribed discrete code or combination. The link may include equipment and cabling external to the weapon or weapon system to activate components within the weapon or weapons system. *See also:* Permissive Action Links.

References

Department of Defense, Joint Chiefs of Staff. *Department of Defense Dictionary of Military and Related Terms.* Washington, DC: GPO, 1986.

—**PERMISSIVE TDY (TEMPORARY DUTY)** is a nonchargeable absence to attend or participate in activities of a semi-official nature that are of benefit of the Department of the Army. *See also:* Temporary Duty.

References

Department of Defense, U.S. Army. *Leaves and Passes.* Army Regulation AR 630-5. Washington, DC: Headquarters, Department of the Army, 1984.

—**PERSHING II MISSILE SYSTEM** is a modular, evolutionary improvement to the Pershing 1A ballistic missile. It is more accurate than the P1A and has more than twice the range (1,800 km). The accuracy improvement is due to radar area correlation. As the Pershing II reentry vehicle descends in the area of the target, it compares live radar reflections from the target area with reference scenes that were stored in its system prior to its launch. It then makes course adjustments based upon the comparisons, producing almost pinpoint accuracy, and hence allowing the use of smaller nuclear warheads that produce less unwanted collateral damage. Pershing II also incorporates several other features that enhance its flexibility and decrease its operating costs. Pershing is truck-mounted, highly mobile, and rapid reacting. It is designated the MGM-31A.

References

Weapons Systems: U.S. Army, Navy, and Air Force Directory, 1986-1988. Washington, DC: DCP, 1986.

—**PERSISTENCY** is the ability of nuclear/biological/chemical weapons to remain lethal long after their release, both over the target where they were released and downwind for indefinite distances. Persistency depends on the physical and chemical properties of the agent, the weather, the methods of dissemination, and the terrain. *See also:* Biological Warfare, Chemical Warfare, Nuclear Warfare.

References

Department of Defense, U.S. Army. *NBC Operations.* Field Manual FM 3-100. Washington, DC: Headquarters, Department of the Army, 1985.

———. *NBC Protection.* Field Manual FM 3-4. Washington, DC: Headquarters, Department of the Army, 1985.

———. *Technical Escort Operations.* Field Manual FM 3-20. Washington, DC: Headquarters, Department of the Army, 1981.

—PERSONAL ERRORS are the differences in observations caused by the sighting limitations of an observer.

References
Department of Defense, U.S. Army. *Dictionary of United States Army Terms.* Army Regulation AR 310-25. Washington, DC: Headquarters, Department of the Army, 1986.

—PERSONAL LIAISON OFFICER, CHIEF OF STAFF, ARMY, is normally a Major General who is designated by the Chief of Staff, Army, to be his personal representative in a civil disturbance objective area. The personal liaison officer establishes and maintains liaison with responsible municipal, state, and Department of Defense officials in order to evaluate and keep the Chief of Staff apprised of existing conditions within the objective area.

References
Department of Defense, U.S. Army. *Dictionary of United States Army Terms.* Army Regulation AR 310-25. Washington, DC: Headquarters, Department of the Army, 1986.

—PERSONAL LOCATOR BEACON is an emergency radio locator beacon with a two-way speech facility that is carried by an aircrew, either on their persons or in their survival equipment. It is capable of providing homing signals to assist search and rescue operations.

References
Department of Defense, U.S. Army. *Dictionary of United States Army Terms.* Army Regulation AR 310-25. Washington, DC: Headquarters, Department of the Army, 1986.

—PERSONAL PROPERTY is property of any kind, except real property, records of the federal government, and naval vessels of the following categories: aircraft carriers, battleships, cruisers, destroyers, and submarines.

References
Department of Defense, Joint Chiefs of Staff. *Department of Defense Dictionary of Military and Related Terms.* Washington, DC: GPO, 1986.

—PERSONAL RESPONSIBILITY is the obligation of an individual for the proper use, care, and safekeeping of government property in his pos-

session. It applies to all property issued for, acquired for, or converted to the person's exclusive use, with or without a receipt.

References
Department of Defense, U.S. Army. *Commander's Handbook for Property Accountability at the Unit Level.* Field Manual FM 10-14-1. Washington, DC: Headquarters, Department of the Army, 1984.

—PERSONAL STAFF are the staff officers who the commander selects to coordinate and administer directly, instead of through the chief of staff. The commander's aides are members of his personal staff. *See also:* General Staff, Personal Staff Group, Special Staff, Staff.

References
Department of Defense, U.S. Army. *Dictionary of United States Army Terms.* Army Regulation AR 310-25. Washington, DC: Headquarters, Department of the Army, 1986.

—PERSONAL STAFF GROUP is the personal staff working under the immediate control of the commander and assisting him directly, instead of through the chief of staff or executive officer. Members of the personal staff include personnel specifically authorized by the table of organization and equipment and/or the table of distribution and allowances as personal assistants to the commander (e.g., aides-de-camp), personnel the commander desires to supervise directly, and personnel who by law or regulation have a special relationship to the commander. Typical personal staff members include the command sergeant major, inspector general, staff judge advocate, and the chaplain.

References
Department of Defense, U.S. Army. *Staff Organization and Operations.* Field Manual FM 101-5. Washington, DC: Headquarters, Department of the Army, 1984.

—PERSONAL WIPEDOWN is performed on the soldier's mask, hood, gloves, and essential gear. For chemical and biological contamination, the skin decon kit is used. Removal of chemical contamination from the battledress overgarment should not be attempted, since its special protective properties minimize the effects of chemical hazards. Radiological and biological contamination should be brushed from the overgarment. *See also:* Biological Warfare, Chemical Warfare, Nuclear Warfare.

References

Department of Defense, U.S. Army. *NBC Operations*. Field Manual FM 3-100. Washington, DC: Headquarters, Department of the Army, 1985.

—**PERSONNEL (PERS)** are the individuals required in either a military or civilian capacity to accomplish an assigned mission.

References

Department of Defense, Joint Chiefs of Staff. *Department of Defense Dictionary of Military and Related Terms*. Washington, DC: GPO, 1986.

—**PERSONNEL AND ADMINISTRATIVE (P&A) SERVICES** are the functions normally associated with adjutant general organizations and missions. Specific functions include personnel services, administrative services, postal services, and morale support activities.

References

Department of Defense, U.S. Army. *Support Operations: Echelons Above Corps*. Field Manual FM 100-16. Washington, DC: Headquarters, Department of the Army, 1986.

—**PERSONNEL (PERS) AUTHORIZATION.** *See:* Manpower Voucher.

—**PERSONNEL (PERS) CARRIER** is a motor vehicle, sometimes armored, used to transport troops and their equipment.

References

Department of Defense, U.S. Army. *Dictionary of United States Army Terms*. Army Regulation AR 310-25. Washington, DC: Headquarters, Department of the Army, 1986.

—**PERSONNEL (PERS) CEILING.** *See:* Manpower Voucher.

—**PERSONNEL (PERS) CENTER** is a Class I activity that provides administrative control over two or more of the following personnel processing activities: reception station, overseas replacement station, returnee assignment station, or transfer station.

References

Department of Defense, U.S. Army. *Dictionary of United States Army Terms*. Army Regulation AR 310-25. Washington, DC: Headquarters, Department of the Army, 1986.

—**PERSONNEL (PERS) CLASSIFICATION** is the process of evaluating and continuously reevaluating an individual's mental and physical abilities, interests, education, aptitudes, physical assignment limitations, occupational history, and military experience, so that he may be assigned to a duty that makes best use of his qualifications consistent with the needs of the Service.

References

Department of Defense, U.S. Army. *Dictionary of United States Army Terms*. Army Regulation AR 310-25. Washington, DC: Headquarters, Department of the Army, 1986.

—**PERSONNEL (PERS) ESTIMATE** (STAFF ESTIMATE) analyzes personnel and administration factors on soldier and unit effectiveness as they affect the accomplishment of a mission. From this estimate, conclusions are drawn and recommendations are made concerning troop preparedness, the feasibility of various courses of action from the G1 or S1 point of view, and the effects of each course of action on personnel operations.

References

Department of Defense, U.S. Army. *Staff Organization and Operations*. Field Manual FM 101-5. Washington, DC: Headquarters, Department of the Army, 1984.

—**PERSONNEL (PERS) IMMATERIEL POSITION** is a duty position that is not identified with one specific branch of the Army but is limited to officers whose branch is adjutant general or whose functional area is personnel management.

References

Department of Defense, U.S. Army. *Commissioned Officer Professional Development and Utilization*. Department of the Army Pamphlet 600-3. Washington, DC: Headquarters, Department of the Army, 1986.

—**PERSONNEL (PERS) INSECURITY** in communications security, means the capture, unauthorized absence, defection, or control by a hostile intelligence entity of an individual having knowledge of, or access to classified communications security information or material. *See also:* Communications Security.

References

Department of Defense, Joint Chiefs of Staff. *Department of Defense Dictionary of Military and Related Terms*. Washington, DC: GPO, 1986.

—**PERSONNEL (PERS) MANAGEMENT OFFICER** is an officer assigned to duty with an organization (e.g., army, corps, division, training activity, or similar unit or installation) in order to carry out the objectives of the military personnel management system within the assigned organization and its subordinate units.

References

Department of Defense, U.S. Army. *Dictionary of United States Army Terms.* Army Regulation AR 310-25. Washington, DC: Headquarters, Department of the Army, 1986.

—**PERSONNEL (PERS) MONITORING** is monitoring any part of an individual, his breath or excretions, or any part of his clothing.

References

Department of Defense, U.S. Army. *Dictionary of United States Army Terms.* Army Regulation AR 310-25. Washington, DC: Headquarters, Department of the Army, 1986.

—**PERSONNEL (PERS) OFFICER** is an officer in charge of keeping records pertaining to the personnel assigned to an organization. The assistant adjutant of a unit is often the personnel officer.

References

Department of Defense, U.S. Army. *Dictionary of United States Army Terms.* Army Regulation AR 310-25. Washington, DC: Headquarters, Department of the Army, 1986.

—**PERSONNEL (PERS) REACTION TIME** (NUCLEAR) is the time personnel require to take the prescribed protective measures after they receive a nuclear strike warning. *See also:* Nuclear Warfare.

References

Department of Defense, Joint Chiefs of Staff. *Department of Defense Dictionary of Military and Related Terms.* Washington, DC: GPO, 1986.

—**PERSONNEL (PERS) SECTION** is the subdivision of the staff of a unit that is concerned with matters relating to personnel as individuals.

References

Department of Defense, U.S. Army. *Dictionary of United States Army Terms.* Army Regulation AR 310-25. Washington, DC: Headquarters, Department of the Army, 1986.

—**PERSONNEL (PERS) SECURITY.** (1) Personnel security is the means or procedures (e.g., selective investigations, record checks, personal interviews, and supervisory controls) designed to provide reasonable assurance that people being considered for access to classified information are loyal and trustworthy. (2) A definition for personnel security that resulted from the Department of Defense response to Presidential Executive Order 12333, "United States Intelligence Activities," dated December 4, 1981, defined the types of activities that U.S. intelligence agencies could conduct in respect to U.S. citizens. It stated that "personnel security involves measures designed to insure that persons employed, or being considered for employment, in sensitive positions of trust are suitable for such employment with respect to loyalty, character, emotional stability, and reliability and that such employment is clearly consistent with the interests of national security. It includes measures designed to insure that persons granted access to classified information remain suitable for such access and that access is consistent with the interests of national security." *See also:* Personnel Security Investigation.

References

Department of Defense. *Activities of DoD Intelligence Components that Affect U.S. Persons.* (Department of Defense Directive 5240.1.) Washington, DC: Department of Defense, 1982.

Department of Defense, Defense Intelligence College. *Glossary of Intelligence Terms and Definitions.* Washington, DC: DIC, 1987.

—**PERSONNEL (PERS) SECURITY INVESTIGATION** is an inquiry into an individual's past to collect information about his loyalty, character, emotional stability, and reliability in order to ascertain his suitability for a position of trust. The Department of Defense implementation of Presidential Executive Order 12333, "United States Intelligence Activities," dated December 4, 1981, defines a personnel security investigation as

> (a) an inquiry into the activities of a person granted access to intelligence or other classified information; or a person who is being considered for access to intelligence or other classified information; including persons who are granted or may be granted access to facilities of the Depart-

ment of Defense components; or a person to be assigned or retained in a position with sensitive duties. The investigation is designed to develop information pertaining to the suitability, eligibility, and trustworthiness of the individual with respect to loyalty, character, emotional stability, and reliability.

(b) inquiries or other activities directed against Department of Defense employees or members of a Military Service to determine the facts of possible voluntary or involuntary compromise of classified information by them.

(c) the collection of information about or from military personnel in the course of tactical training exercises for security training purposes.

References

Department of Defense, Joint Chiefs of Staff. *Department of Defense Dictionary of Military and Related Terms.* Washington, DC: GPO, 1986.

—**PERSONNEL (PERS) SELECTION RESEARCH** is the development of psychological and psychometric methods through which the best candidates for successful training or job assignments are identified from a large applicant pool. The appropriateness of a selection approach to a personnel problem is contingent on such factors as the number of personnel who are needed for training or assignment, the number of personnel potentially available, the quality of personnel who are required for the job, and the importance of the job. *See also:* Personnel Utilization Research.

References

Department of Defense, U.S. Army. *Dictionary of United States Army Terms.* Army Regulation AR 310-25. Washington, DC: Headquarters, Department of the Army, 1986.

—**PERSONNEL SERVICES SUPPORT (PSS)** is the management of execution of all the division's personnel-related matters during combat. It includes personnel services, administrative services, strength accounting, replacement operations, casualty reporting, personnel records, administrative services, postal services, morale support services, finance/comptroller services, health services, chaplain activities, legal services, morale support activities, public affairs, and tactical general purpose automated data processing support.

References

Department of Defense, U.S. Army. *Combat Service Support Operations-Division.* Field Manual FM 63-2. Washington, DC: Headquarters, Department of the Army, 1983.

———. *Support Operations: Echelons Above Corps.* Field Manual FM 100-16. Washington, DC: Headquarters, Department of the Army, 1986.

—**PERSONNEL (PERS) UTILIZATION RESEARCH** concerns the development of human factors, knowledge, and techniques aimed at improving individual and group performance on the job. Such research considers the needed balance between people and machine capabilities, psychological and behavioral limits or working demands, and factors of the work environment, including unusual, as well as typical, conditions of the job. *See also:* Personnel Selection Research.

References

Department of Defense, U.S. Army. *Dictionary of United States Army Terms.* Army Regulation AR 310-25. Washington, DC: Headquarters, Department of the Army, 1986.

—**PERSONNEL (PERS) VULNERABILITY CONDITION** is the degree to which personnel are protected from nuclear weapon effects. Closely associated with degrees of risk are three conditions: protected, warned; exposed, warned; and exposed, unwarned.

References

Department of Defense, U.S. Army. *Dictionary of United States Army Terms.* Army Regulation AR 310-25. Washington, DC: Headquarters, Department of the Army, 1986.

—**PES** is the location of a quantity of explosives that will create a blast, fragment, thermal, or debris hazard if its contents accidentally explode. Quantity limitations for ammunition and explosives at a PES are determined by the distance to an exposed site.

References

Department of Defense, U.S. Army. *Ammunition and Explosives Safety Standards.* Army Regulation AR 385-64. Washington, DC: Headquarters, Department of the Army, 1987.

—**PETROLEUM INTERSECTIONAL SERVICE** is an intersectional or interzonal service in a theater of operations that operates pipelines and related facilities to supply bulk petroleum products to theater Army elements and other forces as directed.

References
Department of Defense, Joint Chiefs of Staff. *Department of Defense Dictionary of Military and Related Terms.* Washington, DC: GPO, 1986.

—**PETROLEUM, OILS, AND LUBRICANTS (POL)** is a broad term that includes all petroleum and associated products used by the armed forces.

References
Department of Defense, Joint Chiefs of Staff. *Department of Defense Dictionary of Military and Related Terms.* Washington, DC: GPO, 1986.

—**PHASE** is a specific part of an operation that is different from those that precede or follow it. Phasing assists in planning and controlling and may be indicated by time (e.g., preparatory fire phase), by distance (e.g., intermediate objective or report line), by terrain (e.g., crossing of an obstacle), or by occurrence of an event (e.g., commitment of a reserve). It is not to be confused with a phase line. It normally is associated with operations of larger units and with special operations (e.g., river crossing and airborne operations). *See also:* Operation, Phase Line.

References
Department of Defense, U.S. Army. *Operational Terms and Symbols.* Field Manual FM 101-5-1. Washington, DC: Headquarters, Department of the Army, 1985.

—**PHASE LINE (PL)** is used to control and coordinate military operations. It is usually a recognizable terrain feature (e.g., a ridgeline, stream or road) that extends across the zone of action. Units normally report when they cross phase lines, but do not halt unless they are specifically directed. PLs are often used to prescribe the timing of delay operations.

References
Department of Defense, U.S. Army. *Armored and Mechanized Division Operations.* Field Manual FM 71-100. Washington, DC: Headquarters, Department of the Army, 1978.

———. *The Infantry Rifle Company (Infantry, Airborne, Air Assault, Ranger).* Field Manual FM 7-10. Washington, DC: Headquarters, Department of the Army, 1982.

———. *Operational Terms and Symbols.* Field Manual FM 101-5-1. Washington, DC: Headquarters, Department of the Army, 1985.

—**PHASED EMPLOYMENT** is a method used by an attack helicopter unit commander to commit a portion of his assets into the battle for the most effective use of combat power. It involves a commitment of task-organized elements at planned times, and is often expressed in terms of predictable events or circumstances. *See also:* Attack Helicopter.

References
Department of Defense, U.S. Army. *Attack Helicopter Operations.* Field Manual FM 17-50. Washington, DC: Headquarters, Department of the Army, 1984.

—**PHASES.** Training exercises contain three phases: preexercise, execution, and postexercise. The preexercise phase covers planning and preparation. It ends with the start of the execution phase (STARTEX). The execution phase begins at STARTEX and concludes with the end of the exercise (ENDEX). During the execution phase, player units participate in the exercise, which is controlled and evaluated according to plans developed during the preexercise phase. The postexercise phase, beginning at ENDEX, covers reviews and reports. *See also:* Exercise.

References
Department of Defense, U.S. Army. *How to Conduct Training Exercises.* Field Manual FM 25-4. Washington, DC: Headquarters, Department of the Army, 1984.

—**PHASES OF MILITARY GOVERNMENT** are as follows:
- **Assault** is the period that commences with the first contact with civilians ashore and extends to the establishment of military government control ashore by the landing force.
- **Consolidation** is the period that commences with the establishment of military government control ashore by the landing force and extends to the establishment of control by occupation forces.
- **Occupation** is the period that commences when an area has been occupied in fact, and the military commander within that area is in a position to enforce public safety and order.

See also: Civil Affairs, Military Occupation.

References
Department of Defense, Joint Chiefs of Staff. *Department of Defense Dictionary of Military and Related Terms.* Washington, DC: GPO, 1986.

—**PHASES OF SMOKE.** There are four phases of smoke: (1) the individual streamer phase, during which smoke is generated from individual pots or generators; (2) the buildup phase, during which the individual smoke streamers start to merge; (3) the uniform phase, during which a uniformly obscuring smoke screen exists; and (4) the terminal phase, during which the screen thins out and the cover is no longer effective. *See also:* Smoke Screen.

References

Department of Defense, U.S. Army. *Dictionary of United States Army Terms.* Army Regulation AR 310-25. Washington, DC: Headquarters, Department of the Army, 1986.

—**PHASES OF TRAINING.** Training consists of five formal phases that are covered by separate Army training programs: basic combat training, advanced individual training, basic unit training, advanced unit training, and field exercises and maneuvers training. A sixth phase, operational readiness training, is entered into as determined by major commanders. *See also:* Operational Readiness Training.

References

Department of Defense, U.S. Army. *Dictionary of United States Army Terms.* Army Regulation AR 310-25. Washington, DC: Headquarters, Department of the Army, 1986.

—**PHONETIC ALPHABET** is a list of standard words used to identify letters in a message transmitted by radio or telephone. The following are the authorized words, listed in order, for each letter in the alphabet: Alfa, Bravo, Charlie, Delta, Echo, Foxtrot, Golf, Hotel, India, Juliet, Kilo, Lima, Mike, November, Oscar, Papa, Quebec, Romeo, Sierra, Tango, Uniform, Victor, Whiskey, X-ray, Yankee, and Zulu.

References

Department of Defense, Joint Chiefs of Staff. *Department of Defense Dictionary of Military and Related Terms.* Washington, DC: GPO, 1986.

—**PHONY MINEFIELDS** are used to deceive the enemy and degrade its mobility and to preserve friendly mobility. They are areas of ground that simulate live minefields and are used when a lack of time, personnel, or material prevents the use of real mines. Phony minefields can supplement or extend live minefields, and may be used as gaps in live minefields. To be effective, a phony minefield must be made to look like a live minefield by either burying metallic objects or by making the ground look as though mines are buried. *See also:* Mine Warfare.

References

Department of Defense, U.S. Army. *Countermobility.* Field Manual FM 5-102. Washington, DC: Headquarters, Department of the Army, 1985.

———. *Engineer Combat Operations.* Field Manual FM 5-100. Washington, DC: Headquarters, Department of the Army, 1984.

—**PHOSPHATE FINISH** is a black corrosion-resistant coating applied to small arms, artillery, or automotive components.

References

Department of Defense, U.S. Army. *Dictionary of United States Army Terms.* Army Regulation AR 310-25. Washington, DC: Headquarters, Department of the Army, 1986.

—**PHOTOGRAMMETRY.** *See:* Basic Cover (Photogrammetry).

—**PHOTOGRAPHIC COVERAGE** is the extent to which an area has been covered photographically by one mission or a series of missions or during a period of time. *See also:* Aerial Reconnaissance, Photographic Intelligence.

References

Department of Defense, Joint Chiefs of Staff. *Department of Defense Dictionary of Military and Related Terms.* Washington, DC: GPO, 1986.

—**PHOTOGRAPHIC FLIGHT LINE** is the prescribed path in space along which an air vehicle moves during the execution of a photo mission. *See also:* Aerial Reconnaissance, Photographic Intelligence.

References

Department of Defense, U.S. Army. *Dictionary of United States Army Terms.* Army Regulation AR 310-25. Washington, DC: Headquarters, Department of the Army, 1986.

—**PHOTOGRAPHIC INTELLIGENCE (PHOTINT)** is a category of imagery intelligence that involves the collected products of photographic interpretation that have been classified and interpreted for intelligence use. *See also:* Aerial Reconnaissance, Basic Cover (Photogrammetry), Photographic Coverage, Photographic Flight Line, Photographic Interpreter, Photographic Reading, Photographic Scale, Photographic Strip, Photography, Photomap.

References
Department of Defense, Defense Intelligence College. *Glossary of Intelligence Terms and Definitions.* Washington, DC: DIC, 1987.

—**PHOTOGRAPHIC INTERPRETATION (PI)** is a category of imagery interpretation and is the process of locating, recognizing, identifying, and describing objects, activities, and terrain from photographs. *See also:* Aerial Reconnaissance, Photographic Intelligence.

References
Department of Defense, Defense Intelligence College. *Glossary of Intelligence Terms and Definitions.* Washington, DC: DIC, 1987.

—**PHOTOGRAPHIC INTERPRETER (PI),** or photointerpreter, is an individual specially trained in photographic interpretation and therefore more qualified than the untrained observer to identify objects from their photographic images and to accurately and completely assess the significance of these objects. *See also:* Aerial Reconnaissance, Photographic Intelligence.

References
Department of Defense, Joint Chiefs of Staff. *Department of Defense Dictionary of Military and Related Terms.* Washington, DC: GPO, 1986.

—**PHOTOGRAPHIC READING** is the recognition of natural and man-made features from photographs that does not involve imagery interpretation techniques. *See also:* Aerial Reconnaissance, Photographic Intelligence.

References
Department of Defense, Joint Chiefs of Staff. *Department of Defense Dictionary of Military and Related Terms.* Washington, DC: GPO, 1986.

—**PHOTOGRAPHIC SCALE** is the ratio of the distance measured on a photograph or mosaic to the corresponding distance on the ground, classified as follows:

Very large scale	1:4,999 and higher
Large scale	1:5,000 to 1:9,999
Medium scale	1:10,00 to 1:14,999
Small scale	1:25,00 to 1:49,000
Very small scale	1:50,000 and lower

See also: Aerial Reconnaissance, Photographic Intelligence.

References
Department of Defense, Joint Chiefs of Staff. *Department of Defense Dictionary of Military and Related Terms.* Washington, DC: GPO, 1986.

—**PHOTOGRAPHIC STRIP** is a series of successive overlapping photographs that are taken along a selected course or direction. *See also:* Aerial Reconnaissance, Photographic Intelligence.

References
Department of Defense, Joint Chiefs of Staff. *Department of Defense Dictionary of Military and Related Terms.* Washington, DC: GPO, 1986.

—**PHOTOGRAPHY** is the process of using optical equipment to reproduce on film a viewed scene or object. *See also:* Aerial Reconnaissance, Photographic Intelligence.

References
Department of Defense, Joint Chiefs of Staff. *Department of Defense Dictionary of Military and Related Terms.* Washington, DC: GPO, 1986.

—**PHOTOMAP** is a reproduction of a photograph or photomosaic upon which the grid lines, marginal data, contours, place names, boundaries, and other data may have been added. *See also:* Aerial Reconnaissance, Photographic Intelligence.

References
Department of Defense, Joint Chiefs of Staff. *Department of Defense Dictionary of Military and Related Terms.* Washington, DC: GPO, 1986.

—**PHYSICAL CHARACTERISTICS** are the primarily physical military characteristics of equipment (e.g., weight, shape, volume, waterproofing, and sturdiness).

References
Department of Defense, Joint Chiefs of Staff. *Department of Defense Dictionary of Military and Related Terms.* Washington, DC: GPO, 1986.

—**PHYSICAL INSECURITY,** in communications security, means an occurrence (e.g., the loss, theft, loss of control, capture, recovery by salvage, tampering, unauthorized viewing, access, or photographing of material) that results in jeopardizing communications security material. *See also:* Communications Security.

References
Department of Defense, Joint Chiefs of Staff. *Department of Defense Dictionary of Military and Related Terms.* Washington, DC: GPO, 1986.

—**PHYSICAL INSPECTION.** (1) A physical inspection is a check made by direct observation or, when indicated, a partial examination, to ascertain the presence of an acute or chronic communicable disease, vermin infection, or any gross deterioration of physical status. (2) A physical inspection is a physical check of property to determine the amounts and the status of on-hand supply.

References

Department of Defense, U.S. Army. *Dictionary of United States Army Terms*. Army Regulation AR 310-25. Washington, DC: Headquarters, Department of the Army, 1986.

—**PHYSICAL INVENTORY ADJUSTMENT** is an accounting transaction used to correct a recorded balance when it disagrees with a validated physical count that has resulted from a scheduled or unscheduled inventory, materiel release, denial, location record audit, or erroneous capitalization or decapitalization action that reflects a true gain or loss action. Specifically excluded are adjustments resulting from reidentification, catalog data changes, purpose or condition code changes, and the condemnation of materiel resulting from rebuilding or surveillance programs. Accounting errors, errors attributed to computer malfunctions, and program errors are not categorized as physical inventory adjustments.

References

Department of Defense, U.S. Army. *Dictionary of United States Army Terms*. Army Regulation AR 310-25. Washington, DC: Headquarters, Department of the Army, 1986.

—**PHYSICAL PROFILE SERIAL** is an estimate of the overall ability of an individual to perform his military duties by considering his mental and physical condition. Six factors, designated PULHES, are expressed numerically: P—Physical capacity or stamina; U—upper extremities; L—lower extremities; H—hearing (including ear defects); E—eyes; and S—neuropsychiatric.

References

Department of Defense, U.S. Army. *Dictionary of United States Army Terms*. Army Regulation AR 310-25. Washington, DC: Headquarters, Department of the Army, 1986.

—**PHYSICAL SECURITY.** (1) Physical security, as a component of communications security, involves the physical measures used to protect classified equipment, material, and documents from disclosure to unauthorized persons. (2) Physical security is physical measures (e.g., safes, vaults, perimeter barriers, guard systems, alarms, and access controls) designed to safeguard installations against damage, disruption, or unauthorized entry; information or material against unauthorized access or theft; or specified personnel against harm. *See also:* Counterintelligence.

References

Department of Defense, Defense Intelligence College. *Glossary of Intelligence Terms and Definitions*. Washington, DC: DIC, 1987.

Department of Defense, U.S. Army. *Military Intelligence Battalion (CEWI) (Tactical Exploitation) (Corps): Counterintelligence, Interrogation, Electronic Warfare*. Field Manual FM 34-23. Washington, DC: Headquarters, Department of the Army, 1985.

———. *Operational Terms and Symbols*. Field Manual FM 101-5-1. Washington, DC: Headquarters, Department of the Army, 1985.

———. *Support Operations: Echelons Above Corps*. Field Manual FM 100-16. Washington, DC: Headquarters, Department of the Army, 1986.

—**PHYSICAL SECURITY INVESTIGATION** is a term that was developed when the Department of Defense responded to Presidential Executive Order 12333, "United States Intelligence Activities," dated December 4, 1981, which defined the types of activities that U.S. intelligence agencies could conduct concerning U.S. citizens. The term is defined as "all inquiries, inspections, or surveys of the effectiveness of controls and procedures designed to provide physical security; and all inquiries and other actions undertaken to obtain information pertaining to physical threats to Department of Defense personnel or property." *See also:* Physical Security.

References

Department of Defense, U.S. Army. *Support Operations: Echelons Above Corps*. Field Manual FM 100-16. Washington, DC: Headquarters, Department of the Army, 1986.

—**PICKUP FIELD** is an open area where aircraft in flight may approach the ground to snatch messages, other aircraft, personnel, or supplies into the air. *See also:* Pickup Message.

References

Department of Defense, U.S. Army. *Dictionary of United States Army Terms*. Army Regulation AR 310-25. Washington, DC: Headquarters, Department of the Army, 1986.

—**PICKUP MESSAGE** is a message that is picked up from the ground by a cable trailing from a low-flying aircraft.

References

Department of Defense, U.S. Army. *Dictionary of United States Army Terms*. Army Regulation AR 310-25. Washington, DC: Headquarters, Department of the Army, 1986.

—**PICKUP POINT** is a point on a trajectory visible to radar for which data have been obtained by computation or radar observation. *See also:* Radar.

References

Department of Defense, U.S. Army. *Dictionary of United States Army Terms*. Army Regulation AR 310-25. Washington, DC: Headquarters, Department of the Army, 1986.

—**PICKUP ZONE (PZ)** is a geographical area where troops and/or equipment are picked up by helicopter. *See also:* Pickup Point.

References

Department of Defense, U.S. Army. *Dictionary of United States Army Terms*. Army Regulation AR 310-25. Washington, DC: Headquarters, Department of the Army, 1986.

—**PIECEMEAL ATTACK** is an offensive action in which the various units are used as they become available, or where the timing of a planned action breaks down and the action is reduced to phases.

References

Department of Defense, U.S. Army. *Dictionary of United States Army Terms*. Army Regulation AR 310-25. Washington, DC: Headquarters, Department of the Army, 1986.

—**PIEZOELECTRIC CRYSTAL** is an initiating element that is found in many fuzes. When mechanically bent or stressed, it generates a voltage proportional to the stress that has been applied.

References

Department of Defense, U.S. Army. *Dictionary of United States Army Terms*. Army Regulation AR 310-25. Washington, DC: Headquarters, Department of the Army, 1986.

—**PILFERABLE ITEM** is an item that has resale value and therefore is especially subject to theft.

References

Department of Defense, U.S. Army. *Dictionary of United States Army Terms*. Army Regulation AR 310-25. Washington, DC: Headquarters, Department of the Army, 1986.

—**PILLARING** is the rapid vertical movement of smoke which sometimes results from the explosion of a white phosphorus bomb or projectile. The effect is undesirable because it does not obscure a large area. *See also:* Smoke Screen.

References

Department of Defense, U.S. Army. *Dictionary of United States Army Terms*. Army Regulation AR 310-25. Washington, DC: Headquarters, Department of the Army, 1986.

—**PILLBOX** is a small, low fortification that houses machine guns, antitank weapons, and other weapons. A pillbox is usually made of concrete, steel, or filled sandbags.

References

Department of Defense, Joint Chiefs of Staff. *Department of Defense Dictionary of Military and Related Terms*. Washington, DC: GPO, 1986.

—**PILOT/GUNNER** (ARMY AVIATION) is the crew member who controls the aircraft in flight and has the primary responsibility for firing stowed weapons.

References

Department of Defense, U.S. Army. *Gunnery Training for Attack Helicopters*. Training Circular TC 17-17. Washington, DC: Headquarters, Department of the Army, 1975.

—**PILOT-LINE OPERATION** is the production of the least amount of a military item in order to preserve or develop its production. Items selected for pilot-line operation are generally the most advanced items, or those whose production takes a long time to resume once their production has stopped. Pilot-line items generally have no current procurement objective, although a known or reasonable possible future procurement objective exists. *See also:* Prototype.

References

Department of Defense, U.S. Army. *Dictionary of United States Army Terms*. Army Regulation AR 310-25. Washington, DC: Headquarters, Department of the Army, 1986.

—**PILOT MATERIALS** are the minimum quantities of special materials, partially finished components, forgings, and castings used in specific production equipment and processes. Pilot materials are necessary to proof, tool, and test the manufacturing processes that produce the equipment in order to facilitate their later activation. *See also:* Prototype.

References

Department of Defense, U.S. Army. *Dictionary of United States Army Terms.* Army Regulation AR 310-25. Washington, DC: Headquarters, Department of the Army, 1986.

—**PILOT MODEL** is a prototype of an item that is usually handmade. Its primary purpose is to establish the suitability of the item from an engineering standpoint. *See also:* Prototype.

References

Department of Defense, U.S. Army. *Dictionary of United States Army Terms.* Army Regulation AR 310-25. Washington, DC: Headquarters, Department of the Army, 1986.

—**PINPOINT.** (1) A pinpoint is a precisely identified point, especially on the ground, that locates a very small target or a reference point for rendezvous, or is of value for other purposes. In this context, pinpoint is also the coordinates of that point. (2) Pinpoint is the ground position of aircraft that is determined by direct observation from the ground. *See also:* Pinpoint Target.

References

Department of Defense, Joint Chiefs of Staff. *Department of Defense Dictionary of Military and Related Terms.* Washington, DC: GPO, 1986.

—**PINPOINT TARGET,** in artillery, is a target that is less than 50 meters in diameter.

References

Department of Defense, Joint Chiefs of Staff. *Department of Defense Dictionary of Military and Related Terms.* Washington, DC: GPO, 1986.

—**PINTLE.** (1) A pintle is a vertical bearing about which a gun carriage revolves; it is a pin that is used as a hinge or axis. (2) A pintle is a hook, with a latch, on the rear of a towing vehicle to which a gun or trailer is attached by a lunette. *See also:* Pintle Center.

References

Department of Defense, U.S. Army. *Dictionary of United States Army Terms.* Army Regulation AR 310-25. Washington, DC: Headquarters, Department of the Army, 1986.

—**PINTLE CENTER** is an assumed center of a weapon upon which all firing data computations are based.

References

Department of Defense, U.S. Army. *Dictionary of United States Army Terms.* Army Regulation AR 310-25. Washington, DC: Headquarters, Department of the Army, 1986.

—**PIONEER AIRFIELD** is a selected area that permits operation of fixed or rotary-winged aircraft under favorable weather conditions and that contains at least minimum safety factors. A construction and maintenance effort may or may not be required to prepare a pioneer airfield.

References

Department of Defense, U.S. Army. *Dictionary of United States Army Terms.* Army Regulation AR 310-25. Washington, DC: Headquarters, Department of the Army, 1986.

—**PIPELINE,** in logistics, is the channel of support, or a specific portion of it, used to direct the flow of materiel or personnel from sources of procurement to their point of use.

References

Department of Defense, U.S. Army. *Dictionary of United States Army Terms.* Army Regulation AR 310-25. Washington, DC: Headquarters, Department of the Army, 1986.

—**PISTOL CLASP** is a metallic bar device worn on the uniform to denote a person's participation in a national or area pistol match.

References

Department of Defense, U.S. Army. *Dictionary of United States Army Terms.* Army Regulation AR 310-25. Washington, DC: Headquarters, Department of the Army, 1986.

—**PITCH** (ARMY AVIATION) is an in-cockpit call indicating that a pitch angle of 15 degrees up or down is desired. Pitch high or pitch low means a 25 degrees to 30 degrees pitch angle. To make pitch adjustments of less that 15 degrees, the words "climb" or "dive steeper" are used.

References

Department of Defense, U.S. Army. *Air-to-Air Combat.* Field Manual FM 1-107. Washington, DC: Headquarters, Department of the Army, 1984.

—**PITCH BACK** (ARMY AVIATION) is a wingover maneuver used to position an aircraft for an attack run.

References
Department of Defense, U.S. Army. *Air-to-Air Combat.* Field Manual FM 1-107. Washington, DC: Headquarters, Department of the Army, 1984.

—**PLAIN TEXT**, in communications, is normal text or language, or any sign or signal that conveys information without a hidden or secret meaning. According to the Church Committee, plain text is "unencrypted communications; specifically, the original message of a cryptogram, expressed in ordinary language." *See also:* CRYPTO.

References
Department of Defense, Defense Intelligence College. *Glossary of Intelligence Terms and Definitions.* Washington, DC: DIC, 1987.

U.S. Congress. Senate. *Final Report of the Senate Select Committee to Study Government Operations With Respect to Intelligence Activities. Report 94-755. Book I, Foreign and Military Intelligence* (Church Committee Report). Washington, DC: GPO, 1976.

—**PLAN** is a proposed method or a scheme to carry out a command decision or project. As part of the planning process, a plan represents the command's preparation in a specific area to meet a particular event. A plan may be written or oral. Although plans are based upon specific conditions or assumptions, they are not static; they are changed, refined, and updated as a result of continuing estimates and studies. *See also:* operation plan.

References
Department of Defense, U.S. Army. *Operational Terms and Symbols.* Field Manual FM 101-5-1. Washington, DC: Headquarters, Department of the Army, 1985.

—**PLAN FOR LOADING** is a collective term referring to all the individually prepared naval and landing force documents that, taken together, present in detail all the instructions for executing a ship-to-shore movement.

References
Department of Defense, U.S. Army. *Dictionary of United States Army Terms.* Army Regulation AR 310-25. Washington, DC: Headquarters, Department of the Army, 1986.

—**PLAN SUMMARY** is a required element of an operation plan that provides a brief recapitulation of the mission, the general situation, the concept of operations, the major forces required, the command arrangements, and the commander's appraisal of the logistics feasibility. *See also:* Operation Plan.

References
Department of Defense, U.S. Army. *Planning Logistics Support for Military Operations.* Field Manual FM 701-58. Washington, DC: Headquarters, Department of the Army, 1987.

—**PLANE OF DEPARTURE** is a vertical plane containing the path of a projectile as it leaves the muzzle of the weapon. *See also:* Plane of Fire, Plane of Position, Plane of Site.

References
Department of Defense, U.S. Army. *Dictionary of United States Army Terms.* Army Regulation AR 310-25. Washington, DC: Headquarters, Department of the Army, 1986.

—**PLANE OF FIRE** is a vertical plane containing the axis of the bore of a gun when it is ready to be fired.

References
Department of Defense, U.S. Army. *Dictionary of United States Army Terms.* Army Regulation AR 310-25. Washington, DC: Headquarters, Department of the Army, 1986.

—**PLANE OF POSITION** is a vertical plane of the gun and the target that contains a line of site.

References
Department of Defense, U.S. Army. *Dictionary of United States Army Terms.* Army Regulation AR 310-25. Washington, DC: Headquarters, Department of the Army, 1986.

—**PLANE OF SITE** is a plane made by two lines: one from the muzzle of the gun to the target, and the other horizontal but perpendicular to the first line at the muzzle of the gun.

References
Department of Defense, U.S. Army. *Dictionary of United States Army Terms.* Army Regulation AR 310-25. Washington, DC: Headquarters, Department of the Army, 1986.

—**PLANE TABLE MAP** is a large-scale map showing objects and their horizontal distances from each other. It is made without consideration of the curvature of the earth, and differs from a planimetric sketch because it shows relief.

References

Department of Defense, U.S. Army. *Dictionary of United States Army Terms*. Army Regulation AR 310-25. Washington, DC: Headquarters, Department of the Army, 1986.

—**PLANNED TARGET,** in artillery, is a target for prearranged fire.

References

Department of Defense, Joint Chiefs of Staff. *Department of Defense Dictionary of Military and Related Terms*. Washington, DC: GPO, 1986.

—**PLANNED TARGET** (NUCLEAR) is an area or point in which a nuclear bombing is anticipated. A planned nuclear target may be scheduled or on call, and firing data may or may not be determined in advance. Coordination with and warning of friendly troops and aircraft are mandatory. *See also:* Nuclear Warfare.

References

Department of Defense, Joint Chiefs of Staff. *Department of Defense Dictionary of Military and Related Terms*. Washington, DC: GPO, 1986.

—**PLANNING** is essential to the operation of the Army both in preparing for and in the conduct of war. Planning is both a science and an art. As a science, it deals with the specifics of manpower, arms, equipment, deployment capabilities, and monies, both actual and projected. However, since the future cannot be accurately predicted, planning is also an art. As such, it deals in unknowns. As a distillation of military art, the principles of war are particularly valuable as an aid to planning. *See also:* Planning Agent, Planning Chart, Planning Force, Principles of War.

References

Department of Defense, U.S. Army. *The Army* (Prepublication Issue). Field Manual FM 100-1. Washington, DC: Headquarters, Department of the Army, 1986.

—**PLANNING AGENT** is a subordinate headquarters of an Army component command designated to accomplish specific planning or execution tasks in support of contingency plans and requirements. A planning agent may be designated to accomplish the staging or marshalling, planning, deployment, or employment of forces. For example, an employment planning agent prepares a ground tactical plan or other

supporting plans, including the appropriate annexes to support the concept of operation of a unified command, Army component command, other commands, or a joint task force.

References

Department of Defense, U.S. Army. *Planning Logistics Support for Military Operations*. Field Manual FM 701-58. Washington, DC: Headquarters, Department of the Army, 1987.

—**PLANNING CHART** is a worldwide chart, usually with a scale of 1:5,000,000, that is used for route planning and for controlling tactical movements and developments. An aeronautical chart is one type of planning chart.

References

Department of Defense, U.S. Army. *Dictionary of United States Army Terms*. Army Regulation AR 310-25. Washington, DC: Headquarters, Department of the Army, 1986.

—**PLANNING FACTOR** (LOGISTICS) is a consideration or a multiplier used to estimate the amount and type of effort that will be needed in a contemplated operation. Planning factors are often expressed as rates, ratios, or lengths of time.

References

Department of Defense, U.S. Army. *Operational Terms and Symbols*. Field Manual FM 101-5-1. Washington, DC: Headquarters, Department of the Army, 1985.

—**PLANNING FORCE** is the force level required to reasonably assure the successful execution of the national strategy. It is sized for a specific scenario presented in the Joint Strategic Planning Document Supporting Analysis Part I and is keyed to a projected threat in the last year of the planning period. *See also:* Joint Strategic Planning Document.

References

Department of Defense, Joint Chiefs of Staff. *Department of Defense Dictionary of Military and Related Terms*. Washington, DC: GPO, 1986.

—**PLANNING GUIDANCE** refers to the policies, assumptions, directions, decisions, and instructions that have the effect of orders when they are received from higher authorities. National interests, objectives, priorities, and the anticipated actions of allies are aspects of planning guidance.

References

Collins, John M. *U.S.-Soviet Military Balance, 1980-1985.* Washington, DC: Congressional Research Service, 1985.

—**PLANNING POINT OF ORIGIN** is a geographic location in which forces, supplies, and equipment are assembled.

References

Department of Defense, U.S. Army. *Planning Logistics Support for Military Operations.* Field Manual FM 701-58. Washington, DC: Headquarters, Department of the Army, 1987.

—**PLASTIC EXPLOSIVE** is an explosive that, within normal ranges of temperature, can be molded into desired shapes.

References

Department of Defense, U.S. Army. *Dictionary of United States Army Terms.* Army Regulation AR 310-25. Washington, DC: Headquarters, Department of the Army, 1986.

—**PLASTICIZER** is a constituent of a propellent, high explosive, incendiary, or smoke composition that makes the finished product less brittle.

References

Department of Defense, U.S. Army. *Dictionary of United States Army Terms.* Army Regulation AR 310-25. Washington, DC: Headquarters, Department of the Army, 1986.

—**PLATOON (PLT)** is the basic combat unit capable of maneuvering to conduct combat operations. *See also:* Army, Battalion, Brigade, Company, Corps, Division, Regiment, Squad.

References

Department of Defense, U.S. Army. *The Mechanized Infantry Platoon and Squad.* Field Manual FM 7-7. Washington, DC: Headquarters, Department of the Army, 1984.

—**PLOTTING AND RELOCATING BOARD** is a board on which the field of fire of a battery is represented. On a plotting board, the observation stations, the base line, and the directing point or base piece are located to scale and in proper relation to each other. The plotting board is used to locate observed positions of the target and to make predictions so that the necessary firing data can be computed. *See also:* Plotting Board.

References

Department of Defense, U.S. Army. *Dictionary of United States Army Terms.* Army Regulation AR 310-25. Washington, DC: Headquarters, Department of the Army, 1986.

—**PLOTTING BOARD** is a device used to determine individual range and deflection corrections within the battery in order to obtain the desired sheaf and range spread. *See also:* Sheaf.

References

Department of Defense, U.S. Army. *Dictionary of United States Army Terms.* Army Regulation AR 310-25. Washington, DC: Headquarters, Department of the Army, 1986.

—**PNEUMATIC DECEPTION DEVICE** is a dummy tank, vehicle, or weapon, made of inflatable material. It is used to deceive enemy intelligence as to the location of friendly installations.

References

Department of Defense, U.S. Army. *Dictionary of United States Army Terms.* Army Regulation AR 310-25. Washington, DC: Headquarters, Department of the Army, 1986.

—**POINT AMBUSH** is positioned along the target's expected avenue of approach. How the ambush force deploys largely determines whether a point ambush will be able to deliver the heavy volume of highly concentrated fire necessary to isolate, trap, and destroy the target. *See also:* Ambush, Area Ambush, Armor Ambush.

References

Department of Defense, U.S. Army. *The Rifle Squads (Mechanized and Light Infantry).* Training Circular TC 7-1. Washington, DC: Headquarters, Department of the Army, 1976.

—**POINT CONTROL SYSTEM** is a traffic control system in which traffic posts are stationed at intersections of main roads that are being used for troop movements. Patrols control the traffic between the traffic posts.

References

Department of Defense, U.S. Army. *Dictionary of United States Army Terms.* Army Regulation AR 310-25. Washington, DC: Headquarters, Department of the Army, 1986.

—**POINT DEFENSE** is a posture designed to protect a limited area, and is normally the defense of vital elements of a force or the vital installations of the rear area. It is characterized by a priority of defense being given to specific assets, which can be either mobile or static and can be either organizations or installations. *See also:* Area Defense.

References

Department of Defense, U.S. Army. *U.S. Army Air Defense Employment*. Field Manual FM 44-1. Washington, DC: Headquarters, Department of the Army, 1983.

—**POINT DETONATING FUZE** is a fuze located in the nose of a projectile that is initiated upon impact. *See also:* Fuze (Specify Type).

References

Department of Defense, U.S. Army. *Dictionary of United States Army Terms*. Army Regulation AR 310-25. Washington, DC: Headquarters, Department of the Army, 1986.

—**POINT FEATURE** is an object whose location can be described by a single set of coordinates.

References

Department of Defense, U.S. Army. *Dictionary of United States Army Terms*. Army Regulation AR 310-25. Washington, DC: Headquarters, Department of the Army, 1986.

—**POINT MINEFIELDS** disorganize enemy forces and hinder their use of key areas. They are of irregular size and shape, and include all types of antitank and antipersonnel mines, and antihandling devices. They are used to add to and reinforce obstacles, or to rapidly block an enemy counterattack along an avenue of approach. *See also:* Mine Warfare.

References

Department of Defense, U.S. Army. *Countermobility*. Field Manual FM 5-102. Washington, DC: Headquarters, Department of the Army, 1985.

————. *Engineer Combat Operations*. Field Manual FM 5-100. Washington, DC: Headquarters, Department of the Army, 1984.

————. *The Infantry Rifle Company (Infantry, Airborne, Air Assault, Ranger)*. Field Manual FM 7-10. Washington, DC: Headquarters, Department of the Army, 1982.

————. *Operational Terms and Symbols*. Field Manual FM 101-5-1. Washington, DC: Headquarters, Department of the Army, 1985.

—**POINT OF BURST** is the point at which a projectile bursts.

References

Department of Defense, U.S. Army. *Dictionary of United States Army Terms*. Army Regulation AR 310-25. Washington, DC: Headquarters, Department of the Army, 1986.

—**POINT OF DEPARTURE (PD)** is the exact place where the company crosses the line of departure. A PD, normally used during limited visibility, may be designated for the company by either the company or the battalion commander. Guides may be posted at the PD to help the company find it and pass through friendly positions and obstacles. *See also:* Line of Departure.

References

Department of Defense, U.S. Army. *The Infantry Rifle Company (Infantry, Airborne, Air Assault, Ranger)*. Field Manual FM 7-10. Washington, DC: Headquarters, Department of the Army, 1982.

————. *Operational Terms and Symbols*. Field Manual FM 101-5-1. Washington, DC: Headquarters, Department of the Army, 1985.

—**POINT OF FALL,** or the level point, is a point in the curved path of a falling projectile that is level with the muzzle of the gun.

References

Department of Defense, U.S. Army. *Dictionary of United States Army Terms*. Army Regulation AR 310-25. Washington, DC: Headquarters, Department of the Army, 1986.

—**POINT OF IMPACT.** (1) The point of impact is the point on the drop zone where the first parachutist or air dropped cargo item lands or is expected to land. (2) The point of impact is the point at which a projectile, bomb, or reentry vehicle impacts or is expected to impact.

References

Department of Defense, Joint Chiefs of Staff. *Department of Defense Dictionary of Military and Related Terms*. Washington, DC: GPO, 1986.

—**POINT TARGET.** (1) A point target is a target that is so small that it requires the exact placement of ordnance in order to neutralize or destroy it. (2) A point target in nuclear warfare is one in which the ratio of the radius of damage to the target radius is equal to or greater than five.

References

Department of Defense, Joint Chiefs of Staff. *Department of Defense Dictionary of Military and Related Terms.* Washington, DC: GPO, 1986.

—**POINT TO POINT.** (1) Pertaining to communications, point to point is from one fixed station to another on a fixed channel. (2) Point to point pertains to a radio station operated by a communications agency for the transmission of public correspondence (e.g., government messages, press dispatches, commercial traffic, or personal messages). *See also:* Point to Point Line of Sight.

References

Department of Defense, U.S. Army. *Dictionary of United States Army Terms.* Army Regulation AR 310-25. Washington, DC: Headquarters, Department of the Army, 1986.

—**POINT TO POINT LINE OF SIGHT.** A point is within the line of sight of a sensor if the energy to which the sensor reacts can travel from the point to the sensor unobstructed by terrain, vegetation, or solid man-made objects. Spurious signal paths created by atypical conditions are not lines of sight.

References

Department of Defense, U.S. Army. *Dictionary of United States Army Terms.* Army Regulation AR 310-25. Washington, DC: Headquarters, Department of the Army, 1986.

—**POLAR COORDINATES,** in artillery, are the direction, distance, and vertical correction (shift) from the observer or spotter position to the target.

References

Department of Defense, Joint Chiefs of Staff. *Department of Defense Dictionary of Military and Related Terms.* Washington, DC: GPO, 1986.

—**POLE CHARGE** is a number of blocks of explosive that are tied together, capped, fuzed, mounted on the end of a pole, and are ready to be fired. The minimum weight of the charge is usually about fifteen pounds.

References

Department of Defense, U.S. Army. *Dictionary of United States Army Terms.* Army Regulation AR 310-25. Washington, DC: Headquarters, Department of the Army, 1986.

—**POLICY BOOK.** *See:* Policy file.

—**POLICY FILE** is a collection of the current policies of the commander and higher headquarters based upon existing orders, experience, and past command decisions. It is the basic operating principles for the staff section maintaining the file.

References

Department of Defense, U.S. Army. *Staff Organizations and Operations.* Field Manual FM 101-5. Washington, DC: Headquarters, Department of the Army, 1984.

—**POLITICAL INTELLIGENCE,** one component of strategic intelligence, is intelligence concerned with the dynamics of the internal and external political affairs of foreign countries, regional groups, multilateral treaty arrangements, and organizations and foreign political movements directed against or having an impact on established governments or authority. The primary producer of political intelligence is the Department of State.

The international position of any nation depends on such factors as the quality of its leadership; its domestic stability and economic position, manpower supply, and physical resources; its military power in relation to other countries; its position in international trade; its success in obtaining allies against possible future danger; and the influence in other countries of its culture and political system.

In studying the political aspects of strategic intelligence, the intelligence officer first considers the country's distribution and locus of political power, its political forces (dynamics), and its political equilibrium or stability. He often looks for the sources and sanctions of political power, since such power may be based upon authority provided in tradition, or it may derive from democratic choice, political magnetism (charisma), skill and superior competence in handling the affairs of government, monopoly of organized force, or a combination of these factors. An understanding of the nature and sources of authority is particularly important in studying non-Western societies, where institutions differ from those familiar to the Western-trained intelligence officer.

The intelligence analyst also looks at the way decisions are made, taking account of both formal and informal processes. A study of decisionmaking includes analyses of assigned responsibilities, personal and professional background and motivations of policymakers, mechanisms used to arrive at decisions, and information on which policymakers must act.

Adequate political intelligence provides valuable indications concerning the probable courses of action of foreign nations. Therefore, the form and internal dynamics of governments; their domestic and foreign policies; and their parties, institutions, administrative procedures, and political personalities be constantly studied.

Basic Principles of Government

The structures and processes of a government are based on certain principles. The intelligence analyst obtains a knowledge of these principles by studying the government's written constitutions and other documents in which they are expressed. The analyst also compares the origin, history, and interpretation of the government's basic law; the legal position of its legislative, judicial, and executive branches; and the civil and religious rights and privileges of its people. It is also important for the analyst to know the depth and extent of national devotion to the basic rights, privileges, and principles. Based upon all of the knowledge the analyst culls and analyzed, he is able to predict the government's future courses of action to some degree.

Governmental Structure

Governments are usually divided into central, regional, and local governments. Some nations also require a governmental structure for their colonies, possessions, dominions, mandates, and protectorates.

The intelligence analyst studies the operations of governmental organizations to determine their efficiency, integrity, and stability. Marked inefficiency and corruption in the operation of a government, if they indicate a change from past practices, may provide an opportunity for the emergence of new political forces. A long-term acceptance by the populace of such practices is indicative of widespread apathy. If the government becomes increasingly restrictive in regard to electoral procedures, the administration of justice, or the exercise of the basic rights and privileges of the people, it may mean that the government is embarking on a new course of action, either internal or international. Such action is often accompanied by a change in the governmental structure that will ease the direction and control of the new policy. Consequently, information regarding changes in the structure

or operation of a government is of great value in estimating the probable course of action of a nation.

Intelligence concerning the structural form of a government also contributes to the planning of the occupational phase that may follow the successful prosecution of a war. *See also:* Strategic Intelligence.

References
American Bar Association. *Oversight and Accountability of the U.S. Intelligence Agencies: An Evaluation.* Washington, DC: ABA, 1985.

Clauser, Jerome K., and Weir, Sandra M. *Intelligence Research Methodology.* State College, PA: HRB-Singer, 1975.

Department of Defense, Defense Intelligence College. *Glossary of Intelligence Terms and Definitions.* Washington, DC: DIC, 1987.

Godson, Roy, ed. *Intelligence Problems for the 1980s, Number 1: Elements of Intelligence.* Rev. ed. Washington, DC: National Strategy Information Center, 1983.

————. *Intelligence Problems for the 1980s, Number 4: Covert Action.* Washington, DC: National Strategy Information Center, 1981.

Kent, Sherman. *Strategic Intelligence for American World Policy.* Princeton, NJ: Princeton University Press, 1966.

Laqueur, Walter. *A World of Secrets.* New York: Basic Books, 1985.

Maurer, Alfred C.; Turnstall, Marion D.; and Keagle, James M. *Intelligence Policy and Process.* Boulder, CO: Westview Press, 1985.

Treverton, Gregory F. *Covert Action: The Limits of Intervention in the Postwar World.* New York: Basic Books, 1987.

Turner, Stansfield. *Secrecy and Democracy: The CIA in Transition.* Boston: Houghton Mifflin, 1985.

—**POLITICAL WARFARE** is the aggressive use of political means to achieve national objectives. *See also:* Political Intelligence.

References
Department of Defense, Joint Chiefs of Staff. *Department of Defense Dictionary of Military and Related Terms.* Washington, DC: GPO, 1986.

—**POLITICO-MILITARY ACTIVITIES** encompass military activities conducted primarily for their direct social, economic, political, and psychological impact. The activities, in their purest form, are the interaction of the military with the society-government. The operational concept involves such functions as community relations; civil affairs, psychological operations; certain aspects of informational activities; and coordination with other U.S. government agencies and friendly foreign governments. *See also:* Psychological Operations.

References
Department of Defense, U.S. Army. *Psychological Operations.* Field Manual FM 33-1. Washington, DC: Headquarters, Department of the Army, 1979.

—**POLITICO-MILITARY GAMING** is a simulation of situations involving the interaction of political, military, sociological, psychological, economic, scientific, and other appropriate factors.

References
Department of Defense, Joint Chiefs of Staff. *Department of Defense Dictionary of Military and Related Terms.* Washington, DC: GPO, 1986.

—**POOL.** (1) To pool is to maintain and control a supply of resources or personnel for other activities to draw upon. The primary purpose of a pool is to use pooled resources or personnel as efficiently as possible. (2) A pool is any combination of resources that serves a common purpose.

References
Department of Defense, Joint Chiefs of Staff. *Department of Defense Dictionary of Military and Related Terms.* Washington, DC: GPO, 1986.

—**POP** (ARMY AVIATION) is a maneuver used to achieve an immediate and rapid vertical change of altitude. *See also:* Pop-up Point.

References
Department of Defense, U.S. Army. *Air-to-Air Combat.* Field Manual FM 1-107. Washington, DC: Headquarters, Department of the Army, 1984.

—**POP-UP-POINT (PUP)** (ARMY AVIATION) is the location at which an aircraft quickly gains altitude for target acquisition and engagement. PUP occurs at the end of low-level terrain flight intended to avoid detection or to prevent effective engagement by the enemy.

References
Department of Defense, U.S. Army. *Air Defense Artillery Deployment: Chaparral/Vulcan/Stinger.* Field Manual FM 44-3. Washington, DC: Headquarters, Department of the Army, 1984.

———. *Air Defense Employment.* Field Manual FM 44-1. Washington, DC: Headquarters, Department of the Army, 1983.

———. *Attack Helicopter Operations.* Field Manual FM 17-50. Washington, DC: Headquarters, Department of the Army, 1984.

———. *Operational Terms and Symbols.* Field Manual FM 101-5-1. Washington, DC: Headquarters, Department of the Army, 1985.

—**PORT ARMS.** (1) Port arms is a position in which the weapon is held with the barrel up, diagonally across the body, along a line from the left shoulder to the right hip. (2) Port arms is the command to take this position.

References
Department of Defense, U.S. Army. *Dictionary of United States Army Terms.* Army Regulation AR 310-25. Washington, DC: Headquarters, Department of the Army, 1986.

—**PORT BERTHING CAPACITY** is the capacity of a port to receive and harbor ships.

References
Department of Defense, U.S. Army. *Dictionary of United States Army Terms.* Army Regulation AR 310-25. Washington, DC: Headquarters, Department of the Army, 1986.

—**PORT CALL** is a request from a loading agency for the movement of supplies, personnel, or units from the point of origin to a loading area (including the marshalling and staging areas). A port call includes the time that the cargo or personnel are to arrive at the port or terminal.

References
Department of Defense, U.S. Army. *Dictionary of United States Army Terms.* Army Regulation AR 310-25. Washington, DC: Headquarters, Department of the Army, 1986.

—**PORT COMMANDER** is an officer responsible for, and who has authority over, all activities at the marine port. He also commands all personnel assigned or are attached to the marine port organization.

References
Department of Defense, U.S. Army. *Dictionary of United States Army Terms.* Army Regulation AR 310-25. Washington, DC: Headquarters, Department of the Army, 1986.

—**PORT DISCHARGE CAPACITY** is the tonnage that can be discharged and the number of personnel that can be debarked from ships by a terminal or port. *See also:* Port Berthing Capacity.

References
Department of Defense, U.S. Army. *Dictionary of United States Army Terms.* Army Regulation AR 310-25. Washington, DC: Headquarters, Department of the Army, 1986.

—**PORT OF DEBARKATION (POD)** is a marine terminal at which troops, units, military sponsored personnel, unit impediments, and materiel board or are discharged from ships. Ports of debarkation normally act as ports of embarkation on return passenger and retrograde cargo shipments. *See also:* Army Terminals, Port of Embarkation.

References
Department of Defense, U.S. Army. *Support Operations: Echelons Above Corps.* Field Manual FM 100-16. Washington, DC: Headquarters, Department of the Army, 1986.

———. *Technical Escort Operations.* Field Manual FM 3-20. Washington, DC: Headquarters, Department of the Army, 1981.

—**PORT OF EMBARKATION** is a marine terminal at which troops, units, military sponsored personnel, unit impediments, and materiel board or are loaded aboard ships. Ports of embarkation normally act as ports of debarkation on return passenger and retrograde cargo shipments. *See also:* Army Terminals, Port of Debarkation.

References
Department of Defense, U.S. Army. *Technical Escort Operations.* Field Manual FM 3-20. Washington, DC: Headquarters, Department of the Army, 1981.

—**PORT RECEPTION AND ASSEMBLY CAPACITY** is the quantity of cargo that can be simultaneously received and assembled in covered and open assembly areas within a port or terminal area. *See also:* Port Berthing Capacity, Port Discharge Capacity.

References
Department of Defense, U.S. Army. *Dictionary of United States Army Terms.* Army Regulation AR 310-25. Washington, DC: Headquarters, Department of the Army, 1986.

—**PORT RECEPTION CAPACITY.** *See:* Port Berthing Capacity.

—**PORT SERIAL NUMBER** is the identification number assigned by loading marine terminals to all ships transporting military personnel or cargo. Numbers in sequence are assigned to each voyage prior to the commencement of the voyage.

References
Department of Defense, U.S. Army. *Dictionary of United States Army Terms.* Army Regulation AR 310-25. Washington, DC: Headquarters, Department of the Army, 1986.

—**PORT THROUGHPUT CAPACITY** is a planning factor used to determine the volume of cargo or passengers that a marine terminal can handle and process in one day. It is expressed as both loading and unloading capacity. Normally, the factor used represents the reception capacity, clearance capacity, or storage capacity, whichever presents the most severe terminal limitation. *See also:* Port Berthing Capacity.

References
Department of Defense, U.S. Army. *Dictionary of United States Army Terms.* Army Regulation AR 310-25. Washington, DC: Headquarters, Department of the Army, 1986.

—**POSITION.** (1) A position is the location or area occupied by a military unit. (2) A position is the location of a weapon, unit, or individual from which fire is delivered on a target. Positions may be classified as primary, alternate, or supplementary. (3) A position is the selection of an exact point within the operating area for the employment of antiair defense artillery units. (4) A position is the manner in which a weapon is held, as prescribed in the manual of arms. (5) A position is any of the standard postures that a soldier takes when firing a rifle or other weapon.

References
Department of Defense, U.S. Army. *Air Defense Artillery Employment Hawk.* Field Manual FM 44-90. Washington, DC: Headquarters, Department of the Army, 1983.

———. *Operational Terms and Symbols.* Field Manual FM 101-5-1. Washington, DC: Headquarters, Department of the Army, 1985.

—**POSITION CLASSIFICATION** is the process of isolating, describing, and coding the group of closely related duties, tasks, and responsibilities that normally constitute the primary duty assignment of one individual. The position is often classified in terms of the mental ability, skill, knowledge, aptitude, and occupational and military experience that are required for adequate performance in the position.

References
Department of Defense, U.S. Army. *Dictionary of United States Army Terms*. Army Regulation AR 310-25. Washington, DC: Headquarters, Department of the Army, 1986.

—**POSITION CORRECTION** is a correction applied to firing data to compensate for the difference in location of the individual pieces of a battery.

References
Department of Defense, U.S. Army. *Dictionary of United States Army Terms*. Army Regulation AR 310-25. Washington, DC: Headquarters, Department of the Army, 1986.

—**POSITION DEFENSE** is the type of defense in which the bulk of the defending force sent to selected tactical localities where the decisive battle is to be fought. Heavy reliance is placed on the force's ability to defend its positions and control the terrain.

References
Department of Defense, Joint Chiefs of Staff. *Department of Defense Dictionary of Military and Related Terms*. Washington, DC: GPO, 1986.

—**POSITION LIGHT** is a light or flare used to signal or show the position or direction of movement of an aircraft or of ground troops.

References
Department of Defense, U.S. Army. *Dictionary of United States Army Terms*. Army Regulation AR 310-25. Washington, DC: Headquarters, Department of the Army, 1986.

—**POSITION REQUIREMENTS CODE** is the identification of skills or qualifications required of an officer of appropriate grade to efficiently perform the duties of a position. *See also:* Position Classification.

References
Department of Defense, U.S. Army. *Dictionary of United States Army Terms*. Army Regulation AR 310-25. Washington, DC: Headquarters, Department of the Army, 1986.

—**POSITIVE CONTROL** is the operation of air traffic in a radar/non-radar-control environment in which the positive identification, tracking, and direction of aircraft within an airspace is conducted by an agency that has been assigned that authority and responsibility.

References
Department of Defense, U.S. Army. *Airspace Management and Army Air Traffic in a Combat Zone*. Field Manual FM 1-60. Washington, DC: Headquarters, Department of the Army, 1977.

—**POSITIVE MANAGEMENT** is a method of air battle management that relies on real-time data from radar, identification friend or foe, computer digital data link, and communications equipment to provide air defense command and control and airspace management. *See also:* Positive Control.

References
Department of Defense, U.S. Army. *Air Defense Artillery Employment Hawk*. Field Manual FM 44-90. Washington, DC: Headquarters, Department of the Army, 1983.

———. *Air Defense Employment*. Field Manual FM 44-1. Washington, DC: Headquarters, Department of the Army, 1983.

—**POSITIVE PHASE OF THE SHOCK WAVE** is the period during which the pressure rises very sharply to a value higher than the ambient pressure and then decreases rapidly to the ambient pressure. *See also:* Shock Wave.

References
Department of Defense, Joint Chiefs of Staff. *Department of Defense Dictionary of Military and Related Terms*. Washington, DC: GPO, 1986.

—**POSSIBLE** is a term used to qualify a statement made under conditions wherein some evidence exists to support the statement. This evidence is sufficient to warrant mention, but is insufficient to warrant assuming it to be true. *See also:* Probable.

References
Department of Defense, Joint Chiefs of Staff. *Department of Defense Dictionary of Military and Related Terms*. Washington, DC: GPO, 1986.

Department of Defense, U.S. Army. *Dictionary of United States Army Terms*. Army Regulation AR 310-25. Washington, DC: Headquarters, Department of the Army, 1986.

—**POST** (DRILLS AND CEREMONIES) is the correct place for an officer or noncommissioned officer to stand in a prescribed formation.

References
Department of Defense, U.S. Army. *Drills and Ceremonies*. Field Manual FM 22-5. Washington, DC: Headquarters, Department of the Army, 1986.

—**POST AND BASE COMMUNICATIONS** are communications provided for the operation of a military post, camp, base, installation, or station.

References

Department of Defense, U.S. Army. *Dictionary of United States Army Terms.* Army Regulation AR 310-25. Washington, DC: Headquarters, Department of the Army, 1986.

—**POST CEMETERY** is a military cemetery under the jurisdiction of the Department of the Army. It may be located on an active, inactive, or former Army installation.

References

Department of Defense, U.S. Army. *Dictionary of United States Army Terms.* Army Regulation AR 310-25. Washington, DC: Headquarters, Department of the Army, 1986.

—**POST EXCHANGE (PX)** is a trade name for the Exchange Service of the Army. It is commonly referred to as the "PX". *See also:* Army and Air Force Exchange Service.

References

Department of Defense, U.S. Army. *Dictionary of United States Army Terms.* Army Regulation AR 310-25. Washington, DC: Headquarters, Department of the Army, 1986.

—**POST FLAG** is the national flag used at posts and national cemeteries and is flown in fair weather except when the garrison flag is prescribed. The post flag is nineteen feet long (fly) by ten feet wide (hoist). *See also:* Garrison Flag.

References

Department of Defense, U.S. Army. *Dictionary of United States Army Terms.* Army Regulation AR 310-25. Washington, DC: Headquarters, Department of the Army, 1986.

—**POST PROPERTY** is real property (e.g., land and buildings) and supplies that are provided for use in garrisons as listed in the table of allowances for military installations.

References

Department of Defense, U.S. Army. *Dictionary of United States Army Terms.* Army Regulation AR 310-25. Washington, DC: Headquarters, Department of the Army, 1986.

—**POSTAL CONCENTRATION CENTER** is a post office or an agency of the U.S. Postal Service at which all mail for armed forces on maneuvers, afloat, or overseas is concentrated for sorting and delivery, or dispatch.

References

Department of Defense, U.S. Army. *Dictionary of United States Army Terms.* Army Regulation AR 310-25. Washington, DC: Headquarters, Department of the Army, 1986.

—**POSTAL FINANCE OFFICER** is an officer charged with maintaining supplies of postage stamps, stamped paper, money order forms, and other accountable and expendable items for issue to Army post offices that are operating within a specified overseas area.

References

Department of Defense, U.S. Army. *Dictionary of United States Army Terms.* Army Regulation AR 310-25. Washington, DC: Headquarters, Department of the Army, 1986.

—**POSTAL REGULATING DETACHMENT** is a table of organization and equipment organization established and operated according to the area or overseas command to provide intransit mail routing and redistribution services between Army post offices in the area served, and between Army post offices and serving base post offices.

References

Department of Defense, U.S. Army. *Dictionary of United States Army Terms.* Army Regulation AR 310-25. Washington, DC: Headquarters, Department of the Army, 1986.

—**POSTATTACK PERIOD,** in nuclear warfare, is the period between the termination of the final attack and the time political authorities agree to terminate hostilities. *See also:* Posthostilities Period, Transattack Period.

References

Department of Defense, Joint Chiefs of Staff. *Department of Defense Dictionary of Military and Related Terms.* Washington, DC: GPO, 1986.

—**POST-D-DAY PRODUCTION** is the quantity of an item that can be produced after D-day, as a result of D-day actions. These actions can accelerate the production from a production base that was established by a pre-D-day order. D-day actions can also result in the development or activation of new or additional production facilities after D-day. Post D-day production quantities are influenced by the production base temperature on D-day. *See also:* D-Day, Production Base Temperature.

References
Department of Defense, U.S. Army. *Dictionary of United States Army Terms*. Army Regulation AR 310-25. Washington, DC: Headquarters, Department of the Army, 1986.

—**POSTHOSTILITIES** is the period after the date of ratification by the political authorities of agreements to end hostilities. *See also:* Posthostilities Planning.

References
Department of Defense, Joint Chiefs of Staff. *Department of Defense Dictionary of Military and Related Terms*. Washington, DC: GPO, 1986.

—**POSTHOSTILITIES PLANNING** is the planning of the orderly dismantling of facilities and the redeploying of men and materiel that are no longer needed to support operations.

References
Department of Defense, U.S. Army. *Planning Logistics Support for Military Operations*. Field Manual FM 701-58. Washington, DC: Headquarters, Department of the Army, 1987.

—**POSTSTRIKE DAMAGE ESTIMATION** is a revised target analysis that is based upon new data (e.g., actual weapon yield, burst height, and ground zero) that are obtained by means other than direct assessment.

References
Department of Defense, Joint Chiefs of Staff. *Department of Defense Dictionary of Military and Related Terms*. Washington, DC: GPO, 1986.

—**POUCH KIT** is a pouch or cloth bag that holds the medical kit issued to members of the Army Medical Service for use in the field. *See also:* Medical Treatment.

References
Department of Defense, U.S. Army. *Dictionary of United States Army Terms*. Army Regulation AR 310-25. Washington, DC: Headquarters, Department of the Army, 1986.

—**POWDER TRAIN.** (1) A powder train usually consists of black powder used to activate older types of fuzes. (2) A powder train is a chain of explosives laid out for destruction by burning.

References
Department of Defense, U.S. Army. *Dictionary of United States Army Terms*. Army Regulation AR 310-25. Washington, DC: Headquarters, Department of the Army, 1986.

—**POWER TRAVERSE** is the turning of a gun to change the direction of fire by means of a power-driven mechanism, as in a tank, aircraft, or ship turret.

References
Department of Defense, U.S. Army. *Dictionary of United States Army Terms*. Army Regulation AR 310-25. Washington, DC: Headquarters, Department of the Army, 1986.

—**POWER TURRET** is a turret or enclosed gun mount turned by a power-driven mechanism, and is often found in tanks and aircraft. The gun or guns with the power turret move with it.

References
Department of Defense, U.S. Army. *Dictionary of United States Army Terms*. Army Regulation AR 310-25. Washington, DC: Headquarters, Department of the Army, 1986.

—**PRACTICAL EXERCISE** is a technique used during a training session that permits soldiers to acquire or practice the skills and knowledge that are necessary to perform successfully one or more training objectives. *See also:* Exercise.

References
Department of Defense, U.S. Army. *How to Prepare and Conduct Military Training*. Field Manual FM 21-6. Washington, DC: Headquarters, Department of the Army, 1975.

—**PRACTICE AMMUNITION** is ammunition used for target practice that has a propelling charge, but has either an inert filler or a low-explosive filler to serve as a spotting charge rather than actual ammunition.

References
Department of Defense, U.S. Army. *Dictionary of United States Army Terms*. Army Regulation AR 310-25. Washington, DC: Headquarters, Department of the Army, 1986.

—**PRACTICE MINE** is a close representation of a live mine that is used for exercise purposes. Its functioning may be scored visually, audibly, or electronically. *See also:* Mine Warfare.

References
Department of Defense, U.S. Army. *Mine/ Countermine Operations at the Company Level*. Field Manual FM 20-32. Washington, DC: Headquarters, Department of the Army, 1976.

—**PREARRANGED FIRE** is usually planned well in advance and executed at a predetermined time or during a predetermined period of time against targets or target areas of known location. *See also:* Scheduled Fire.

References

Department of Defense, U.S. Army. *Dictionary of United States Army Terms.* Army Regulation AR 310-25. Washington, DC: Headquarters, Department of the Army, 1986.

—**PREARRANGED MESSAGE CODE** is a code that has been adapted for the use of units that require a special or technical vocabulary. It is composed almost exclusively of groups representing complete or nearly complete sentences.

References

Department of Defense, U.S. Army. *Dictionary of United States Army Terms.* Army Regulation AR 310-25. Washington, DC: Headquarters, Department of the Army, 1986.

—**PREASSAULT OPERATIONS** are the endeavors conducted in the objective area prior to the assault (e.g., reconnaissance, minesweeping, shore bombardment, bombing, underwater demolitions, and destroying beach obstacles).

References

Department of Defense, Joint Chiefs of Staff. *Department of Defense Dictionary of Military and Related Terms.* Washington, DC: GPO, 1986.

—**PRECEDENCE.** (1) Precedence is the act or state of going before another. It is based especially upon military grade, and also upon position and date of appointment. (2) Precedence is the prescribed order in which medals and service ribbons are worn.

References

Department of Defense, U.S. Army. *Dictionary of United States Army Terms.* Army Regulation AR 310-25. Washington, DC: Headquarters, Department of the Army, 1986.

—**PRECEDENCE** (COMMUNICATIONS) is a designation assigned to a message by the originator to indicate to communications personnel the relative order of handling and to the addressee the order in which the message is to be routed. The types of precedence are emergency, flash, immediate, priority, and routine. The drafter is responsible for assigning the proper precedence to a message. The precedence should be no higher than that which is necessary to insure that the message will be delivered in time to accomplish the required action. Specifically, precedence indicates *to the drafter,* the required speed of delivery to the addressee; *to the telecommunications center personnel,* the relative order of processing, transmitting, and delivering the messages; and *to the addressee,* the relative order in which to note and take action on messages. *See also:* Precedence Categories.

References

Department of Defense, Defense Intelligence Agency. *Defense Intelligence Agency Manual.* Washington, DC: DIA, 1987.

Department of Defense, Defense Intelligence College. *Glossary of Intelligence Terms and Definitions.* Washington, DC: DIC, 1987.

Godson, Roy, ed., *Intelligence Problems for the 1980s, Number 1: Elements of Intelligence.* Rev. ed. Washington, DC: National Strategy Information Center, 1983.

—**PRECEDENCE** (RECONNAISSANCE) is a letter designation assigned by a unit requesting several reconnaissance missions to indicate their relative order of importance. *See also:* Aerial Reconnaissance.

References

Department of Defense, Joint Chiefs of Staff. *Department of Defense Dictionary of Military and Related Terms.* Washington, DC: GPO, 1986.

—**PRECEDENCE CATEGORIES** pertain to U.S. message transmission and are the means that govern how quickly a message will be transmitted. The content of the message determines the precedence that should be assigned, and the drafter of the message assigns the precedence to it. There are five precedence categories:

Emergency. This precedence may be used by only National Command Authorities, the Joint Chiefs of Staff, and certain designated commanders of Unified and Specified Commands. It is used for specifically designated emergency action command and control messages.

Flash. This precedence is reserved for initial enemy contact messages or operational combat messages of extreme urgency. Examples are (1) initial enemy contact reports; (2) messages recalling or diverting friendly aircraft that are about to bomb targets and that have been unexpectedly occupied by friendly forces, or messages taking emergency action to prevent conflict between friendly forces; (3) warning of imminent large-scale attacks; and (4) extremely urgent or critical intelligence messages.

Immediate. This precedence is reserved for messages relating to situations that gravely affect the security of national or allied forces or populations and that require immediate delivery to the addressee. Examples are (1) amplifying reports of initial enemy contact; (2) reports of unusual major movements of military forces of friendly powers in time of peace or strained relations; (3) messages that report enemy counterattack or that request or cancel additional support; (4) attack orders to commit a force in reserve without delay; (5) messages concerning logistical support of special weapons when essential to sustained operations; (6) reports of widespread civil disturbance; (7) reports of warning of grave natural disaster (e.g., earthquakes, floods, storms, hurricanes); (8) requests for, or directions concerning, distress assistance; (9) urgent intelligence or diplomatic messages; (10) aircraft movement reports (i.e., messages relating to requests for news of aircraft in flight, flight plans, and cancellation messages) to prevent unnecessary search and rescue actions; and (11) civil defense actions concerning the population and its survival.

Priority. This precedence is reserved for messages that require expeditious action by the addressee or furnish essential information for the conduct of operations in progress when "Routine" will not suffice. This is the highest precedence normally authorized for administrative messages. Examples are (1) situation reports on positions on the front where an attack is impending or where fire or air support will soon be placed; (2) orders to aircraft formations or units to coincide with ground or naval operations; (3) messages concerning the immediate movement of naval, air, or ground forces; and (4) administrative, logistic, and personnel matters of an urgent and time-sensitive nature.

Routine. This precedence is assigned to all types of messages that justify electrical transmission but that are not of sufficiently urgent or important to require a higher precedence. Examples are (1) messages concerning normal peacetime military operations, programs, or projects; (2) messages concerning stabilized tactical operations; (3) operational plans concerning projects; (4) periodic or consolidated intelligence reports; (5) troop or ship movement messages, except when time factors dictate the use of a higher precedence; (6) supply and equipment requisition and movement messages, except when time factors dictate the use of a higher precedence; and (7) administrative, logistic, and personnel matters.

Although the time necessary to process a message varies from command to command, the following guidelines, which are measured from the time the message is delivered to the transmitting center to the time it is available for delivery to the receiving center, are currently in effect: emergency overrides flash traffic; *flash* is handled as fast as possible, with the objective of less than ten minutes; *immediate* is handled within 30 minutes; *priority* is handled within three hours; and *routine* is handled within six hours. *See also:* Precedence.

References

Department of Defense, Defense Intelligence Agency. *Defense Intelligence Agency Manual.* Washington, DC: DIA, 1987.

—**PRECISION ADJUSTMENT** is a deliberate adjustment of the fire of one weapon in order to accurately place the mean point of impact on the target.

References

Department of Defense, U.S. Army. *Dictionary of United States Army Terms.* Army Regulation AR 310-25. Washington, DC: Headquarters, Department of the Army, 1986.

—**PRECISION FIRE** is fire in which the center of impact is accurately placed on a limited target. It is fire based upon precision adjustment. It is usually used to destroy enemy installations (e.g., gun emplacements, structures, and supply points). Precision fire differs from area fire, which is directed against a general area rather than against a given objective in the area. *See also:* Precision Adjustment.

References

Department of Defense, U.S. Army. *Dictionary of United States Army Terms.* Army Regulation AR 310-25. Washington, DC: Headquarters, Department of the Army, 1986.

—**PRECISION GUNNERY** is the most accurate type of direct fire and is used when time permits (e.g., when a tank is in defense or overwatch) or when a target is beyond the battlesight range. Using the tank's complete fire control system, precision gunnery can destroy any target that can be seen on the battlefield. Once a target is identified, the tank commander or gunner ranges on the target as accurately as possible, and the gunner makes a precise lay. The gunner moves his aiming cross to the center of the mass, making the last movement of his rectile up to the aiming point for the first round. This upward movement reduces the effect of any slack in the fire control system. If lead is required, the last movement may be in deflection to apply correct initial lead before engaging the target. If a round is preloaded, the engagement time is greatly decreased. *See also:* Precision Adjustment, Precision Fire.

References

Department of Defense, U.S. Army. *Tank Gunnery.* Field Manual FM 17-12. Washington, DC: Headquarters, Department of the Army, 1984.

—**PRECISION SWEEP,** in radar, is a small portion of a normal sweep, usually 2,000 meters, that is selected and expanded over the entire radar screen in order to permit precise range measurements. *See also:* Radar.

References

Department of Defense, U.S. Army. *Dictionary of United States Army Terms.* Army Regulation AR 310-25. Washington, DC: Headquarters, Department of the Army, 1986.

—**PRECLUSION OF DAMAGE** is a nuclear planning restriction used in conjunction with the least separation distance to avoid damage to important structures. If appropriate, it is included in the commander's guidance. *See also:* Least Separation Distance, Preclusion of Obstacles.

References

Department of Defense, U.S. Army. *Operational Terms and Symbols.* Field Manual FM 101-5-1. Washington, DC: Headquarters, Department of the Army, 1985.

—**PRECLUSION OF OBSTACLES** is a nuclear planning restriction used in conjunction with the least separation distance that, if appropriate, is included in the commander's guidance. It can include preclusion of fallout and tree blowdown. *See also:* Least Separation Distance, Preclusion of Damage.

References

Department of Defense, U.S. Army. *Operational Terms and Symbols.* Field Manual FM 101-5-1. Washington, DC: Headquarters, Department of the Army, 1985.

—**PRECLUSION ORIENTED ANALYSIS** is an analysis of the initial weapon sizes that are selected for the aimpoints that will maximize the lethal coverage of probable enemy locations within safety and collateral damage requirements. *See also:* Least Separation Distance.

References

Department of Defense, U.S. Army. *Operational Terms and Symbols.* Field Manual FM 101-5-1. Washington, DC: Headquarters, Department of the Army, 1985.

—**PRECLUSIVE BUYING** is the purchase in a neutral market, regardless of price, of vitally important materials to prevent them from falling into enemy hands.

References

Department of Defense, U.S. Army. *Dictionary of United States Army Terms.* Army Regulation AR 310-25. Washington, DC: Headquarters, Department of the Army, 1986.

—**PRECURSOR FRONT** is an air pressure wave that moves ahead of the main blast wave for some distance as a result of a nuclear explosion of appropriate yield and low-burst height over a heat-absorbing surface. The pressure at the precursor front increases more gradually than in a true (or ideal) shock wave, so that the behavior in the precursor region is said to be less than ideal. *See also:* Nuclear Warfare.

References

Department of Defense, Joint Chiefs of Staff. *Department of Defense Dictionary of Military and Related Terms.* Washington, DC: GPO, 1986.

—**PREDICTED CONCENTRATION** is step-by-step pointing. It is a series of successive concentrations that are fired at the same target. *See also:* Predicted Fire.

References

Department of Defense, U.S. Army. *Dictionary of United States Army Terms.* Army Regulation AR 310-25. Washington, DC: Headquarters, Department of the Army, 1986.

—**PREDICTED FIRE** is fire delivered without adjustment. The term is used to describe the ultimate delivery technique of applying accurately computed corrections (not corrections determined by firing) to standard firing data for all nonstandard conditions of the weapon-weather-ammunition combination and for rotation of the earth. It implies the capability of being able to deliver accurate surprise nonnuclear or nuclear fires on a target of known location in any direction from the weapon's position. It is limited in range only by the characteristics of the weapon and ammunition employed.

References

Department of Defense, Joint Chiefs of Staff. *Department of Defense Dictionary of Military and Related Terms.* Washington, DC: GPO, 1986.

Department of Defense, U.S. Army. *Dictionary of United States Army Terms.* Army Regulation AR 310-25. Washington, DC: Headquarters, Department of the Army, 1986.

—**PREDICTED FIRING** is firing at the point at which a moving target is expected to be when the projectile reaches it, according to predictions based upon observation. *See also:* Predicted Fire.

References

Department of Defense, U.S. Army. *Dictionary of United States Army Terms.* Army Regulation AR 310-25. Washington, DC: Headquarters, Department of the Army, 1986.

—**PREDICTED POINT** is a position at which it is expected that a moving target will arrive at the instant of firing; that is, the point that a moving target is expected to reach at the end of the dead time between the last observation and the moment of firing. It should not be confused with the set forward point, which is the predicted position of the target at the moment of impact. *See also:* Predicted Position.

References

Department of Defense, U.S. Army. *Dictionary of United States Army Terms.* Army Regulation AR 310-25. Washington, DC: Headquarters, Department of the Army, 1986.

—**PREDICTED POSITION** is the position at which it is expected that a moving target will arrive at the end of the time of flight of the projectile. *See also:* Predicted Point, Predicted Position Device, Predicting Interval, Prediction.

References

Department of Defense, U.S. Army. *Dictionary of United States Army Terms.* Army Regulation AR 310-25. Washington, DC: Headquarters, Department of the Army, 1986.

—**PREDICTED POSITION DEVICE** is a scale, ruler, chart, or predictor used to rapidly calculate the probable position of a moving target at a future instant.

References

Department of Defense, U.S. Army. *Dictionary of United States Army Terms.* Army Regulation AR 310-25. Washington, DC: Headquarters, Department of the Army, 1986.

—**PREDICTING DEAD TIME** is the time allowed for calculating and applying firing data, and is measured from the time of observation to the instant of firing.

References

Department of Defense, U.S. Army. *Dictionary of United States Army Terms.* Army Regulation AR 310-25. Washington, DC: Headquarters, Department of the Army, 1986.

—**PREDICTING INTERVAL** is the time between successive predictions of future positions of the target.

References

Department of Defense, U.S. Army. *Dictionary of United States Army Terms.* Army Regulation AR 310-25. Washington, DC: Headquarters, Department of the Army, 1986.

—**PREDICTION** is the process of determining what the probable future position of a moving target will be at a given time.

References

Department of Defense, U.S. Army. *Dictionary of United States Army Terms.* Army Regulation AR 310-25. Washington, DC: Headquarters, Department of the Army, 1986.

—**PREDICTION ANGLE** is the angle from the present line of sight to the gun line when it is properly pointed for a hit; that is, the angle by which the gun line must be offset to account for the lead angle, gravity drop, and velocity jump in order for the projectile to arrive at the predicted point of impact. *See also:* Predicted Point.

References

Department of Defense, U.S. Army. *Dictionary of United States Army Terms.* Army Regulation AR 310-25. Washington, DC: Headquarters, Department of the Army, 1986.

—**PREDICTION MECHANISM,** or predictor, is an instrument used in connection with a plotting board to determine the probable future location of a moving target in terms of direction and elevation from a position. *See also:* Predicted Fire.

References

Department of Defense, U.S. Army. *Dictionary of United States Army Terms.* Army Regulation AR 310-25. Washington, DC: Headquarters, Department of the Army, 1986.

—**PREDICTION SCALE** is an accurately graduated scale or rule used to measure the actual speed of a moving target. It is used together with a set forward rule or chart to locate, on the plotting board, the point at which the target will be when the gun is fired. *See also:* Predicted Position Device.

References

Department of Defense, U.S. Army. *Dictionary of United States Army Terms.* Army Regulation AR 310-25. Washington, DC: Headquarters, Department of the Army, 1986.

—**PREDICTOR.** (1) A predictor, or prediction mechanism, is an instrument used in connection with a plotting board to determine the probable future location of a moving target in terms of direction and elevation from a given position. (2) A predictor is a device used with a plotting board to calculate when a controlled underwater mine ought to be fired. Such a predictor indicates the exact moment when the target is over the mine. *See also:* Predicted Position Device.

References

Department of Defense, U.S. Army. *Dictionary of United States Army Terms.* Army Regulation AR 310-25. Washington, DC: Headquarters, Department of the Army, 1986.

—**PREEMPTIVE ATTACK** is an attack initiated on the basis of incontrovertible evidence that an enemy attack is imminent.

References

Department of Defense, Joint Chiefs of Staff. *Department of Defense Dictionary of Military and Related Terms.* Washington, DC: GPO, 1986.

—**PREENGRAVED ROTATING BAND** is a rotating band on a projectile that was machine-cut during manufacture so that the grooves and lands on the band match exactly the grooves and lands in the barrel of the weapon.

References

Department of Defense, U.S. Army. *Dictionary of United States Army Terms.* Army Regulation AR 310-25. Washington, DC: Headquarters, Department of the Army, 1986.

—**PRE-H-HOUR TRANSFER** is the transfer of control and tactical logistical parties from their parent ships to assigned control ships, and the transfer of the necessary troops and accompanying equipment from transports to landing ships or transports, in preparation for the ship-to-shore movement. *See also:* H-Hour.

References

Department of Defense, U.S. Army. *Dictionary of United States Army Terms.* Army Regulation AR 310-25. Washington, DC: Headquarters, Department of the Army, 1986.

—**PREINITIATION** is a premature detonation of a nuclear weapon resulting in a significantly reduced yield. *See also:* Nuclear Warfare.

References

Department of Defense, U.S. Army. *Nuclear Weapons Employment Doctrine and Procedures.* Field Manual FM 101-3-1. Washington, DC: Headquarters, Department of the Army, 1986.

———. *Operational Terms and Symbols.* Field Manual FM 101-5-1. Washington, DC: Headquarters, Department of the Army, 1985.

—**PRELANDING OPERATIONS** are the initial events of the assault phase. They include the continuation of similar preparation of the landing area that was begun by an advance force and the final preparations for the ship-to-shore movement. *See also:* Amphibious Operation.

References

Department of Defense, U.S. Army. *Dictionary of United States Army Terms.* Army Regulation AR 310-25. Washington, DC: Headquarters, Department of the Army, 1986.

—**PRE-LAUNCH SURVIVABILITY** is the probability that a delivery of a launch vehicle will survive an enemy attack under an established warning condition.

References

Department of Defense, Joint Chiefs of Staff. *Department of Defense Dictionary of Military and Related Terms.* Washington, DC: GPO, 1986.

—**PRELIMINARY DEMOLITION OBSTACLES** are not absolutely critical to the tactical commander's plan, and do not require a formal written demolition order. They can be detonated as soon as they are prepared or as the situation dictates. *See also:* Preliminary Demolition Target.

References

Department of Defense, U.S. Army. *Countermobility.* Field Manual FM 5-102. Washington, DC: Headquarters, Department of the Army, 1985.

—**PRELIMINARY DEMOLITION TARGET** is a target, other than a reserved demolition target, that is earmarked for demolition and can be destroyed immediately after preparation, provided that prior authority has been granted. *See also:* Reserved Demolition Target.

References
Department of Defense, Joint Chiefs of Staff. *Department of Defense Dictionary of Military and Related Terms.* Washington, DC: GPO, 1986.

—**PRELIMINARY FIRING** is training and practice in firing a gun. It is often done in order to find out which men are the best marksmen. Preliminary firing takes place before record firing, in which selected individuals are given additional training and a record is kept of their performance.

References
Department of Defense, U.S. Army. *Dictionary of United States Army Terms.* Army Regulation AR 310-25. Washington, DC: Headquarters, Department of the Army, 1986.

—**PREMATURE** is a type of malfunctioning in which a munition functions before the expected time.

References
Department of Defense, U.S. Army. *Dictionary of United States Army Terms.* Army Regulation AR 310-25. Washington, DC: Headquarters, Department of the Army, 1986.

—**PREPARATION,** or preparatory bombardment fire, is the heavy volume of prearranged ground, air, or naval fire that is delivered to destroy, disrupt, disorganize, and neutralize enemy positions, materiel, observation, communications, and command, and to demoralize and destroy the defending forces prior to the initiation of the attack of the assault echelon. *See also:* Preparation Fire.

References
Department of Defense, U.S. Army. *Dictionary of United States Army Terms.* Army Regulation AR 310-25. Washington, DC: Headquarters, Department of the Army, 1986.

—**PREPARATION FIRE** is fire delivered on targets in preparation of an assault. The preparation is planned by a direct support field artillery battalion or a higher echelon, and is an intense volume of fire delivered in accordance with a time schedule. The fires normally begin prior to H-hour and may extend beyond it, or they may start at another prescribed time or they may be held on-call. The duration of the preparation fire is influenced by factors such as the fire support needs of the entire force, the number of targets and firing assets, and the available ammunition.

References
Department of Defense, U.S. Army. *Operational Terms and Symbols.* Field Manual FM 101-5-1. Washington, DC: Headquarters, Department of the Army, 1985.

—**PREPARATION FOR OVERSEA MOVEMENT REQUISITION** is a requisition submitted to fill shortages existing in a unit that is scheduled for overseas deployment.

References
Department of Defense, U.S. Army. *Dictionary of United States Army Terms.* Army Regulation AR 310-25. Washington, DC: Headquarters, Department of the Army, 1986.

—**PREPARATORY COMMAND** is part of a drill command that states the movement or formation to be carried out. It is followed by the command of execution, which orders the command to be carried out. In the command, "forward, march," "forward" is the preparatory command, and "march" is the command of execution.

References
Department of Defense, U.S. Army. *Dictionary of United States Army Terms.* Army Regulation AR 310-25. Washington, DC: Headquarters, Department of the Army, 1986.

—**PREPARE FOR ACTION.** (1) To prepare for action is to put a gun into position for firing. (2) "Prepare for action" is a command to put a gun into position for firing. (3) To prepare for action is to put an armored vehicle in readiness for action. (4) "Prepare for action" is to put an armored vehicle in readiness for action.

References
Department of Defense, U.S. Army. *Dictionary of United States Army Terms.* Army Regulation AR 310-25. Washington, DC: Headquarters, Department of the Army, 1986.

—**PREPARED LAUNCHER** is a tactical launcher that is serviceable, assigned to a combat unit, and requires only positioning and loading to be ready for combat. *See also:* Prepared Missile.

References
Department of Defense, U.S. Army. *Dictionary of United States Army Terms.* Army Regulation AR 310-25. Washington, DC: Headquarters, Department of the Army, 1986.

—**PREPARED MISSILE** is a tactical missile, assembled and serviceable, that is assigned to a combat unit and requires only target designation programming and launching to be combat effective. *See also:* Prepared Launcher.

References
Department of Defense, U.S. Army. *Dictionary of United States Army Terms.* Army Regulation AR 310-25. Washington, DC: Headquarters, Department of the Army, 1986.

—**PREPLANNED AIR SUPPORT** is air support provided in accordance with a program that was planned in advance of the operation. *See also:* Air Support.

References
Department of Defense, Joint Chiefs of Staff. *Department of Defense Dictionary of Military and Related Terms.* Washington, DC: GPO, 1986.

—**PREPLANNED AIRLIFT** is an airlift planned in advance to meet a requirement for rapid, dependable transport of personnel, cargo, mail, and courier material on a regular basis. *See also:* Preplanned Airlift Requests.

References
Department of Defense, U.S. Army. *Repair Parts Supply for a Theater of Operations.* Field Manual FM 29-19. Washington, DC: Headquarters, Department of the Army, 1985.

—**PREPLANNED AIRLIFT REQUESTS** are requests that are generated to meet airlift requirements that can be forecast or where requirements can be anticipated and published in the Air Tasking Order. *See also:* Preplanned Airlift.

References
Department of Defense, U.S. Army. *USA/USAF Doctrine for Joint Airborne and Tactical Airlift Operations.* Field Manual FM 100-27. Washington, DC: Headquarters, Department of the Army, 1985.

—**PREPLANNED MISSION REQUEST** is a request for air support submitted in compliance with a schedule that permits detailed mission coordination and planning.

References
Department of Defense, U.S. Army. *Operational Terms and Symbols.* Field Manual FM 101-5-1. Washington, DC: Headquarters, Department of the Army, 1985.

—**PREPLANNED MISSION REQUEST** (RECONNAISSANCE) is a request for a reconnaissance mission on a target or in support of a maneuver that can be anticipated sufficiently in advance to allow detailed mission coordination and planning.

References
Department of Defense, Joint Chiefs of Staff. *Department of Defense Dictionary of Military and Related Terms.* Washington, DC: GPO, 1986.

—**PREPLANNED NUCLEAR SUPPORT** is support planned in advance of operations. *See also:* Nuclear Support.

References
Department of Defense, Joint Chiefs of Staff. *Department of Defense Dictionary of Military and Related Terms.* Washington, DC: GPO, 1986.

—**PREPLANNED SUPPLY** is a system by which supply requirements are computed by wholesale logistics activities, with participation of the supported command, for the initial support of forces through the development period on the basis of forecasted or established replacement factors/consumption rates and prior to the establishment of normal requisitioning capabilities. Supplies are incrementally shipped to the responsible supporting theater/task force logistics activity, on an as-required basis, to supplement and/or establish a theater/task force stock level to enable the activity to respond to requisitions that are submitted by supported units. *See also:* Preplanned Supply Packages; Pre-position; Pre-positioned Supplies; Pre-positioned War Reserve Materiel Requirement; Pre-positioned War Reserve Materiel Requirement, Balance; Pre-positioned War Reserve Materiel Requirement, Protectable; Pre-positioned War Reserve Materiel Stocks; Pre-positioned War Reserve Stock; Pre-positioning; Pre-positioned Organizational Materiel Configured in Unit Sets.

References
Department of Defense, U.S. Army. *Planning Logistics Support for Military Operations.* Field Manual FM 701-58. Washington, DC: Headquarters, Department of the Army, 1987.

—**PREPLANNED SUPPLY PACKAGES** are supplies that must arrive in the theater in time to maintain theater stockage objectives. *See also:* Preplanned Supply.

References
Department of Defense, U.S. Army. *Repair Parts Supply for a Theater of Operations.* Field Manual FM 29-19. Washington, DC: Headquarters, Department of the Army, 1985.

—**PRE-POSITION** is to place military units, equipment, or supplies at or near the point of planned use or at a designated location to reduce reaction time and to insure timely support of a specific force during the initial phases of an operation. *See also:* Preplanned Supply.

References
Department of Defense, Joint Chiefs of Staff. *Department of Defense Dictionary of Military and Related Terms.* Washington, DC: GPO, 1986.

—**PRE-POSITIONED SUPPLIES** are supplies located at or near the point of planned use or at other designated locations in order to reduce reaction time and insure resupply. *See also:* Preplanned Supply.

References
Department of Defense, U.S. Army. *Operational Terms and Symbols.* Field Manual FM 101-5-1. Washington, DC: Headquarters, Department of the Army, 1985.

—**PRE-POSITIONED WAR RESERVED MATERIEL REQUIREMENT** is that portion of the war reserve materiel requirement that the Secretary of Defense guidance dictates be reserved and positioned at or near the point of planned use or be issued to the user prior to hostilities. The goal is to reduce reaction time and to assure the timely support of a specific force or project until replenishment can be provided. *See also:* Preplanned Supply.

References
Department of Defense, Joint Chiefs of Staff. *Department of Defense Dictionary of Military and Related Terms.* Washington, DC: GPO, 1986.

—**PRE-POSITIONED WAR RESERVE MATERIEL REQUIREMENT, BALANCE,** is the portion of the pre-positioned war reserve materiel requirement that has not been acquired or funded. This level consists of the pre-positioned war reserve materiel requirement less the pre-positioned war reserve requirement, protectable. *See also:* Preplanned Supply.

References
Department of Defense, Joint Chiefs of Staff. *Department of Defense Dictionary of Military and Related Terms.* Washington, DC: GPO, 1986.

—**PRE-POSITIONED WAR RESERVE MATERIEL REQUIREMENT, PROTECTABLE,** is the portion of the pre-positioned war reserve materiel requirement that is protected for purposes of procurement, funding, and inventory management. *See also:* Preplanned Supply.

References
Department of Defense, Joint Chiefs of Staff. *Department of Defense Dictionary of Military and Related Terms.* Washington, DC: GPO, 1986.

—**PRE-POSITIONED WAR RESERVE MATERIEL STOCKS (PWRMS)** are the assets designated to satisfy the pre-positioned war reserve materiel requirement. PWRMS consist of overseas war reserves that include (1) theater war reserves to support initial combat consumption, (2) Department of the Army-approved operational stocks in overseas commands, that include pre-positioned materiel configured to unit sets, and (3) continental U.S. war reserves under the control of Army managers. *See also:* Preplanned Supply.

References
Department of Defense, U.S. Army. *Repair Parts Supply for a Theater of Operations.* Field Manual FM 29-19. Washington, DC: Headquarters, Department of the Army, 1985.

———. *Support Operations: Echelons Above Corps.* Field Manual FM 100-16. Washington, DC: Headquarters, Department of the Army, 1986.

—**PRE-POSITIONED WAR RESERVE STOCK (PWRS)** are the assets designated to satisfy the pre-positioned war reserve materiel requirement. *See also:* Preplanned Supply.

References
Department of Defense, Joint Chiefs of Staff. *Department of Defense Dictionary of Military and Related Terms.* Washington, DC: GPO, 1986.

—**PRE-POSITIONED ORGANIZATIONAL MATERIEL CONFIGURED IN UNIT SETS (POMCUS)** is organizational equipment stored in company- and battalion-size packages, in a ready-for-use condition. The purpose of

POMCUS is to position most of a unit's organizational equipment forward, so that in a crisis only unit personnel, with minimum equipment, will require airlift to meet the requirements of a NATO contingency. By placing equipment in the expected theater of operations, it does not need to be moved from the continental United States in an emergency. POMCUS is maintained by dedicated maintenance units until it is issued to the using organizations. *See also:* Preplanned Supply.

References

Department of Defense, U.S. Army. *Organizational Maintenance Operations.* Field Manual FM 29-2. Washington, DC: Headquarters, Department of the Army, 1984.

———. *U.S. Army Policy Statement, 1988.* Washington, DC: Headquarters, Department of the Army, 1988.

—**PRE-POSITIONING** is the storing of munitions and supplies in strategic positions to avoid the problems associated with resupply in the event of war. *See also:* Preplanned Supply.

References

Department of Defense, U.S. Army. *Support Operations: Echelons Above Corps.* Field Manual FM 100-16. Washington, DC: Headquarters, Department of the Army, 1986.

—**PRESCRIBED LOAD** is the quantity of combat-essential supplies and repair parts (other than ammunition) authorized by the major commanders for Class II and Class IV supplies to be on hand in units. The load, which is normally a fifteen-day level, is carried by the individuals or on the unit vehicles to enable the unit to sustain itself until resupply can be effected. Class II and IV supplies are designed for combat requirements and are supplemented for peacetime operations as required by adding items that do not fall into the category of combat-essential items. The quantities of Class I and III items are established by the major commanders. The prescribed load is continuously reconstituted as it is used. *See also:* Prescribed Load List.

References

Department of Defense, U.S. Army. *Operational Terms and Symbols.* Field Manual FM 101-5-1. Washington, DC: Headquarters, Department of the Army, 1985.

———. *Planning Logistics Support for Military Operations.* Field Manual FM 701-58. Washington, DC: Headquarters, Department of the Army, 1987.

—**PRESCRIBED LOAD LIST** is a composite listing of repair parts and special tools that are authorized for a unit so that it can perform organizational maintenance. *See also:* Prescribed Load.

References

Department of Defense, U.S. Army. *Planning Logistics Support for Military Operations.* Field Manual FM 701-58. Washington, DC: Headquarters, Department of the Army, 1987.

—**PRESCRIBED NUCLEAR LOAD (PNL)** is a specified quantity of nuclear weapons to be carried by a delivery unit. The establishment and replenishment of this load after such expenditure is a command decision and depends on the tactical situation; the nuclear logistic situation; and the capability of the unit to transport, protect, and use the load. It may vary from day to day and among similar delivery units. *See also:* Nuclear Weapon Package, Nuclear Weapon Subpackage.

References

Department of Defense, U.S. Army. *Nuclear Weapons Employment Doctrine and Procedures.* Field Manual FM 101-3-1. Washington, DC: Headquarters, Department of the Army, 1986.

———. *Operational Terms and Symbols.* Field Manual FM 101-5-1. Washington, DC: Headquarters, Department of the Army, 1985.

—**PRESCRIBED NUCLEAR STOCKAGE** is a specified quantity of nuclear weapons, components of nuclear weapons, and warhead test equipment that is to be stocked in special ammunition supply points or other logistical installations. Establishing and replenishing this stock is a command decision and depends on the tactical situation, the allocation, the capability of the logistical support unit to store and maintain the nuclear weapons, and the nuclear logistical situation. The prescribed stockage may vary from time to time and from unit to unit. *See also:* Nuclear Warfare.

References

Department of Defense, Joint Chiefs of Staff. *Department of Defense Dictionary of Military and Related Terms.* Washington, DC: GPO, 1986.

—**PRESENCE REPORT** is a report submitted by an incoming unit through the theater army to the host nation indicating that the unit has arrived in theater and is preparing to perform its operational mission.

References
Department of Defense, U.S. Army. *Support Operations: Echelons Above Corps.* Field Manual FM 100-16. Washington, DC: Headquarters, Department of the Army, 1986.

—**PRESIDENTIAL CALL** is an official order of the President of the United States that brings all or a part of the National Guard into the service of the United States in time of war or national emergency.

References
Department of Defense, U.S. Army. *Dictionary of United States Army Terms.* Army Regulation AR 310-25. Washington, DC: Headquarters, Department of the Army, 1986.

—**PRESIDENTIAL RELEASE** is a means of controlling the use of unconventional weapons. The President of the United States is the only individual authorized to permit the use of U.S. nuclear weapons, and only the President can order U.S. chemical warfare retaliation. The U.S. does not use biological agents in warfare. *See also:* Nuclear Warfare.

References
Department of Defense, U.S. Army. *NBC Operations.* Field Manual FM 3-100. Washington, DC: Headquarters, Department of the Army, 1985.

—**PRESIDENTIAL SALUTE** is a 21 gun salute that is given a President or ex-President of the United States when he visits a military establishment.

References
Department of Defense, U.S. Army. *Dictionary of United States Army Terms.* Army Regulation AR 310-25. Washington, DC: Headquarters, Department of the Army, 1986.

—**PRESIDENTIAL TESTIMONIAL** is a written testimonial by the President of the United States in appreciation of honorable service in the Armed Forces between 1940 and 1946.

References
Department of Defense, U.S. Army. *Dictionary of United States Army Terms.* Army Regulation AR 310-25. Washington, DC: Headquarters, Department of the Army, 1986.

—**PRESSURE FIRING DEVICE** is one of four types of firing devices used to initiate land mines and booby traps. It is detonated by exerting pressure or weight on a contrivance, and is essentially composed of a firing pin with a cocked trigger mechanism to which a blasting cap is attached. The cap initiates the main charge. *See also:* Mine Warfare.

References
Department of Defense, U.S. Army. *Dictionary of United States Army Terms.* Army Regulation AR 310-25. Washington, DC: Headquarters, Department of the Army, 1986.

—**PRESSURE FUZE** is a fuze that is designed to actuate when subjected to a given pressure or load. *See also:* Fuze (Specify Type).

References
Department of Defense, U.S. Army. *Mine/Countermine Operations at the Company Level.* Field Manual FM 20-32. Washington, DC: Headquarters, Department of the Army, 1976.

—**PRESSURE MINE** is a mine whose fuze responds to the direct pressure of a target. *See also:* Mine Warfare.

References
Department of Defense, U.S. Army. *Mine/Countermine Operations at the Company Level.* Field Manual FM 20-32. Washington, DC: Headquarters, Department of the Army, 1976.

—**PRESSURE-PULL FIRING DEVICE** is a firing device designed to go off when a pressure or pull is applied.

References
Department of Defense, U.S. Army. *Mine/Countermine Operations at the Company Level.* Field Manual FM 20-32. Washington, DC: Headquarters, Department of the Army, 1976.

—**PREVENTIVE ECCM (ELECTRONIC COUNTER COUNTERMEASURES) TECHNIQUES** are measures taken to reduce the vulnerability of friendly use of the electromagnetic spectrum to enemy efforts to disrupt or destroy that use. *See also:* Electronic Counter Countermeasures.

References
Department of Defense, U.S. Army. *Mine/Countermine Operations at the Company Level.* Field Manual FM 20-32. Washington, DC: Headquarters, Department of the Army, 1976.

—**PREVENTIVE MAINTENANCE (PM)** is the care and servicing of items or facilities by personnel for the purpose of maintaining equipment and facilities in satisfactory operating condition. PM includes systematic inspection, detection, and correction of incipient failures either before they occur or before they develop into major defects.

References

Department of Defense, Joint Chiefs of Staff. *Department of Defense Dictionary of Military and Related Terms.* Washington, DC: GPO, 1986.

—**PREVENTIVE MEDICINE COMPANY** is a unit organized to provide for the study, evaluation, and control of field environmental and other factors that can affect the health and morale of troops in the field army and the communications zone. *See also:* Medical Treatment.

References

Department of Defense, U.S. Army. *Dictionary of United States Army Terms.* Army Regulation AR 310-25. Washington, DC: Headquarters, Department of the Army, 1986.

—**PREVENTIVE MEDICINE OFFICER** is a medical corps officer with special training and experience in preventive medicine. He is assigned to a military command to initiate and supervise programs that prevent disease and nonbattle injuries and promote health. The preventive medicine officer is an assistant to the surgeon of the command and serves as a technical consultant on all matters pertaining to preventive medicine. *See also:* Medical Treatment.

References

Department of Defense, U.S. Army. *Dictionary of United States Army Terms.* Army Regulation AR 310-25. Washington, DC: Headquarters, Department of the Army, 1986.

—**PREVENTIVE WAR** is a war that is initiated in the belief that military conflict, while not imminent, is inevitable, and that to delay warfare would involve greater risk.

References

Department of Defense, Joint Chiefs of Staff. *Department of Defense Dictionary of Military and Related Terms.* Washington, DC: GPO, 1986.

—**PREWITHDRAWAL DEMOLITION TARGET** is a target that has been prepared for demolition prior to the withdrawal of forces. The target can be demolished at any time after the preparation, provided the demolition officer has ordered it destroyed.

References

Department of Defense, Joint Chiefs of Staff. *Department of Defense Dictionary of Military and Related Terms.* Washington, DC: GPO, 1986.

—**PRICE ANALYST** is a specialist on a contracting officer's negotiating team responsible for analyzing price information (e.g., cost breakdowns, market trends, comparable prices, cost engineering reports, and various accounting, engineering, and pricing data) to aid in negotiating reasonable contract prices.

References

Department of Defense, U.S. Army. *Dictionary of United States Army Terms.* Army Regulation AR 310-25. Washington, DC: Headquarters, Department of the Army, 1986.

—**PRIMACORD** is a flexible fabric tube that contains a filler of high explosive pentaerythritoltetranitrate that is used to transmit a detonation from the detonator to a booster or bursting charge. Primacord is the trade name for the type of detonating cord that is presently in use.

References

Department of Defense, U.S. Army. *Dictionary of United States Army Terms.* Army Regulation AR 310-25. Washington, DC: Headquarters, Department of the Army, 1986.

—**PRIMARY CENSORSHIP** is armed forces censorship performed by personnel of a company, battery, squadron, ship, station, base, or similar unit on the personal letters and communications of all persons assigned, attached, or otherwise under the jurisdiction of the unit. *See also:* Military Censorship.

References

Department of Defense, Joint Chiefs of Staff. *Department of Defense Dictionary of Military and Related Terms.* Washington, DC: GPO, 1986.

—**PRIMARY COGNIZANCE.** (1) Primary cognizance is a term used to indicate that a strategic planning team is responsible for preparing certain types of plans. (2) As applied to research and development, primary cognizance is the responsibility for the general management of a research and development program.

References

Department of Defense, U.S. Army. *Dictionary of United States Army Terms.* Army Regulation AR 310-25. Washington, DC: Headquarters, Department of the Army, 1986.

—**PRIMARY CONTROL OFFICER** is the officer who is embarked in a primary control ship and is responsible for controlling the movement of landing craft, amphibious vehicles, and landing ships to and from a beach. *See also:* Amphibious Operation.

References

Department of Defense, U.S. Army. *Dictionary of United States Army Terms*. Army Regulation AR 310-25. Washington, DC: Headquarters, Department of the Army, 1986.

—PRIMARY FIRE SECTOR is the principal area to be covered by gunfire from a particular weapon or unit.

References

Department of Defense, U.S. Army. *Dictionary of United States Army Terms*. Army Regulation AR 310-25. Washington, DC: Headquarters, Department of the Army, 1986.

—PRIMARY GUN is the principal or main gun, especially of a tank or armored vehicle.

References

Department of Defense, U.S. Army. *Dictionary of United States Army Terms*. Army Regulation AR 310-25. Washington, DC: Headquarters, Department of the Army, 1986.

—PRIMARY HAND RECEIPT is signed and given to the accountable officer by the person receiving the property and assuming responsibility for it.

References

Department of Defense, U.S. Army. *Commander's Handbook for Property Accountability at the Unit Level*. Field Manual FM 10-14-1. Washington, DC: Headquarters, Department of the Army, 1984.

—PRIMARY INTEREST is principal, although not exclusive, interest and responsibility for accomplishing a given mission. It includes the responsibility for reconciling the activities of other agencies that possess a collateral interest in the program. *See also:* Mission, Primary Mission.

References

Department of Defense, Joint Chiefs of Staff. *Department of Defense Dictionary of Military and Related Terms*. Washington, DC: GPO, 1986.

—PRIMARY MILITARY OCCUPATIONAL SPE-CIALTY (PMOS) denotes the military occupational skills in which an individual is best qualified. It is the MOS that is most important to the Army in terms of training, experience, demonstrated qualifications, and Army needs. *See also:* Military Occupational Specialty, Secondary Military Occupational Specialty.

References

Department of Defense, U.S. Army. *Enlisted Personnel Management System*. Army Regulation AR 600-200. Washington, DC: Headquarters, Department of the Army, 1984.

———. *Personnel Selection and Classification, Warrant Officer Occupational Specialties*. Army Regulation AR 611-112. Washington, DC: Headquarters, Department of the Army, 1987.

—PRIMARY MISSION is the principal purpose for which an organization was established. *See also:* Mission.

References

Department of Defense, U.S. Army. *Dictionary of United States Army Terms*. Army Regulation AR 310-25. Washington, DC: Headquarters, Department of the Army, 1986.

—PRIMARY PORT is a Department of the Army port of embarkation having the primary responsibility for the logistic support of an overseas command.

References

Department of Defense, U.S. Army. *Dictionary of United States Army Terms*. Army Regulation AR 310-25. Washington, DC: Headquarters, Department of the Army, 1986.

—PRIMARY POSITION is a place that provides the best means for a weapon, unit, or individual to fight to accomplish the assigned mission.

References

Department of Defense, U.S. Army. *Air Defense Artillery Deployment: Chaparral/Vulcan/Stinger*. Field Manual FM 44-3. Washington, DC: Headquarters, Department of the Army, 1984.

———. *Operational Terms and Symbols*. Field Manual FM 101-5-1. Washington, DC: Headquarters, Department of the Army, 1985.

—PRIMARY ROADS are made of a bitumen or concrete surface and are of a width greater than six meters. *See also:* Main Supply Route.

References

Department of Defense, U.S. Army. *Dictionary of United States Army Terms*. Army Regulation AR 310-25. Washington, DC: Headquarters, Department of the Army, 1986.

—PRIMARY SPECIALTY is the specialty assigned to an officer by Headquarters, Department of the Army, that will receive primary emphasis in the officer's professional development and use.

References
Department of Defense, U.S. Army. *Dictionary of United States Army Terms*. Army Regulation AR 310-25. Washington, DC: Headquarters, Department of the Army, 1986.

—**PRIMARY U.S. ARMY OVERSEA SUPPLY AGENCY** is a U.S. Army Oversea Supply Agency that has been assigned primary responsibility for the logistical support of a specific overseas area.

References
Department of Defense, U.S. Army. *Dictionary of United States Army Terms*. Army Regulation AR 310-25. Washington, DC: Headquarters, Department of the Army, 1986.

—**PRIMARY WEAPON** is a weapon that is the principal arm of a combat unit. The rifle, rather than grenades or chemical projectiles, is the primary or basic weapon of an infantry rifle company.

References
Department of Defense, U.S. Army. *Dictionary of United States Army Terms*. Army Regulation AR 310-25. Washington, DC: Headquarters, Department of the Army, 1986.

—**PRIMARY WEAPONS AND EQUIPMENT** are the major equipment essential to, and employed directly in, the accomplishment of assigned operational missions and tasks.

References
Department of Defense, U.S. Army. *Dictionary of United States Army Terms*. Army Regulation AR 310-25. Washington, DC: Headquarters, Department of the Army, 1986.

—**PRIME CONTRACT** is a contract agreement or purchase order entered into by a contractor and the U.S. government.

References
Department of Defense, U.S. Army. *Dictionary of United States Army Terms*. Army Regulation AR 310-25. Washington, DC: Headquarters, Department of the Army, 1986.

—**PRIME MOVER (PM)** is a vehicle, including heavy construction equipment, possessing military characteristics. It is designed primarily for towing heavy, wheeled weapons and frequently provides the facilities for transporting the crew of, and ammunition for, the weapon.

References
Department of Defense, Joint Chiefs of Staff. *Department of Defense Dictionary of Military and Related Terms*. Washington, DC: GPO, 1986.

—**PRIME CHARGE** is a charge completely ready for ignition.

References
Department of Defense, Joint Chiefs of Staff. *Department of Defense Dictionary of Military and Related Terms*. Washington, DC: GPO, 1986.

—**PRIMER** is a device used to initiate the functioning of an explosive or igniter train. It may be actuated by friction, a blow, pressure, or electricity. *See also:* Primer Detonator, Primer Pouch.

References
Department of Defense, U.S. Army. *Dictionary of United States Army Terms*. Army Regulation AR 310-25. Washington, DC: Headquarters, Department of the Army, 1986.

—**PRIMER DETONATOR** is an assembly consisting of a primer and a detonator. It may also have a delay element.

References
Department of Defense, U.S. Army. *Dictionary of United States Army Terms*. Army Regulation AR 310-25. Washington, DC: Headquarters, Department of the Army, 1986.

—**PRIMER LEAK** is a defect in a cartridge or shell that allows a partial escape of the hot propelling gases in a primer. It is caused by faulty construction or an excessive charge.

References
Department of Defense, U.S. Army. *Dictionary of United States Army Terms*. Army Regulation AR 310-25. Washington, DC: Headquarters, Department of the Army, 1986.

—**PRIMER POUCH** is a container that holds the primers used to fire separate loading ammunition. *See also:* Primer, Separate Loading Ammunition.

References
Department of Defense, U.S. Army. *Dictionary of United States Army Terms*. Army Regulation AR 310-25. Washington, DC: Headquarters, Department of the Army, 1986.

—**PRIMER SEAT** is a chamber in the breech mechanism of a gun that uses separate loading ammunition into which the primer is set. *See also:* Primer.

References

Department of Defense, U.S. Army. *Dictionary of United States Army Terms.* Army Regulation AR 310-25. Washington, DC: Headquarters, Department of the Army, 1986.

—**PRIMER SETBACK** is a defect in the firing of a round of fixed ammunition in which the explosion of the propelling charge forces the primer against the face of the bolt. Primer setback is due to a faulty bolt, a defective cartridge, or excessive pressure. *See also:* Primer.

References

Department of Defense, U.S. Army. *Dictionary of United States Army Terms.* Army Regulation AR 310-25. Washington, DC: Headquarters, Department of the Army, 1986.

—**PRIME-TIME FOR TRAINING** is an established period that is devoted entirely to mission-related training. Such training is done at the lowest level possible, with the maximum number of personnel present.

References

Department of Defense, U.S. Army. *How to Prepare and Conduct Military Training.* Field Manual FM 21-6. Washington, DC: Headquarters, Department of the Army, 1975.

—**PRIMING CHARGE** is an initial charge that transmits the detonation wave to the whole of the charge.

References

Department of Defense, Joint Chiefs of Staff. *Department of Defense Dictionary of Military and Related Terms.* Washington, DC: GPO, 1986.

—**PRIMING COMPOSITION** is a mixture of materials that is very sensitive to ignition by impact, percussion, or heat.

References

Department of Defense, U.S. Army. *Dictionary of United States Army Terms.* Army Regulation AR 310-25. Washington, DC: Headquarters, Department of the Army, 1986.

—**PRINCIPAL** is a military service or an agency of a military service that obtains supplies and services from another military service or agency.

References

Department of Defense, U.S. Army. *Dictionary of United States Army Terms.* Army Regulation AR 310-25. Washington, DC: Headquarters, Department of the Army, 1986.

—**PRINCIPAL DIRECTION OF FIRE** is the direction of fire assigned or designated as the main direction in which a weapon will be oriented. It is selected based upon the enemy, mission, terrain, and the weapon's capability.

References

Department of Defense, U.S. Army. *Operational Terms and Symbols.* Field Manual FM 101-5-1. Washington, DC: Headquarters, Department of the Army, 1985.

—**PRINCIPAL ITEMS** are end-items and replacement assemblies of such importance in the judgment of the Services that they require centralized individual item management techniques throughout the supply system, including depot level, base level, and items in the hands of the using units. Central inventory control of principal items includes centralized computation of requirements, central procurement, central direction of distribution, and central knowledge and control of all assets that are owned by the Services.

References

Department of Defense, Joint Chiefs of Staff. *Department of Defense Dictionary of Military and Related Terms.* Washington, DC: GPO, 1986.

—**PRINCIPAL OPERATIONAL INTEREST**, when used in connection with an established facility that is operated by one Service for joint use by two or more Services, indicates a requirement for the greatest need for the services of that facility. The term may be applied to a Service, but is more applicable to a command.

References

Department of Defense, Joint Chiefs of Staff. *Department of Defense Dictionary of Military and Related Terms.* Washington, DC: GPO, 1986.

—**PRINCIPAL SUBORDINATE COMMANDERS** is a designation that has been assigned to NATO commanders who are operationally responsible to major subordinate commanders for an allocated geographical area or function. *See also:* Major NATO Commanders, Major Subordinate Commanders, Subordinate Area Commanders.

References

Department of Defense, Joint Chiefs of Staff. *Department of Defense Dictionary of Military and Related Terms.* Washington, DC: GPO, 1986.

—**PRINCIPLES OF DETERRENCE** is a checklist, distilled from historical experience, that skilled strategists consider when developing concepts to persuade opponents that aggression of any kind is the least attractive alternatives; prevent undesired escalation if conflict occurs; and discourage allies of the opponent and the unaffiliated from pursuing courses of action that would adversely affect important plans or programs. *See also:* Principles of War.

References

Collins, John M. *U.S.-Soviet Military Balance, 1980-1985.* Washington, DC: Congressional Research Service, 1985.

—**PRINCIPLES OF WAR.** The U.S. Army published its first discussion of the principles of war in a 1921 Army training regulation. These principles were taken from the work of British Major General J.F.C. Fuller, who developed a set of principles of war during World War I to serve as guides for his own army. In the ensuing years, the original principles of war adopted by the U.S. Army have been slightly revised, but they have essentially stood the tests of analysis, experimentation, and practice. Today's Army recognizes the principles of objective, offensive, mass, economy of force, maneuver, unity of command, security, surprise, and simplicity.

Modern warfare requires the application of both the science and the art of war. The science of war is driven by new technological developments that can radically change the nature of the battlefield. The art of war, on the other hand, involves the critical historical analysis of warfare. The military professional derives from this analysis the fundamental principles—their combinations and applications—that have historically been successful on the battlefields. The principles of war, thus derived, belong to the art, rather than the science, of war. They are not immutable, and they do not provide precise mathematical formulae for success in battle. Their value lies in their usefulness in analyzing strategic, operational, and tactical issues. For the strategist, the principles of war provide a set of questions that should be considered if military strategy is to best serve the national interest. For campaign planners and tacticians, these prin-

ciples provide a conceptual framework for the military actions to be carried out. They are neither intended nor designed to be prescriptive; nor are they a substitute for the serious study of military history. The principles of war, when understood and applied properly, will stimulate thought and increase flexibility. *See also the following entries pertaining to principles of war:* Economy of Force, Maneuver, Objective, Offensive, Security, Simplicity, Surprise, Unity of Command, Mass.

References

Department of Defense, U.S. Army. *The Army.* (Prepublication Issue.) Field Manual FM 100-1. Washington, DC: Headquarters, Department of the Army, 1986.

————. *Operations.* Field Manual FM 100-5. Washington, DC: Headquarters, Department of the Army, 1986.

—**PRIOR SERVICE PERSONNEL** are in-service personnel with service before their current period of active duty. *See also:* Member, Enlisted Person, Officer.

References

Department of Defense, U.S. Army. *Army Reenlistment Program.* Army Regulation AR 601-28. Washington, DC: Headquarters, Department of the Army, 1984.

—**PRIORITY** is a value denoting a preferential rating or precedence in position that is used to discriminate between competing entities. In intelligence requirements, it is used to illustrate the relative importance of the requirements rather that an exclusive and final designation. It is to guide the actions planned, being planned, or in use to respond to the requirements. *See also:* Precedence.

References

Department of Defense, Defense Intelligence College. *Glossary of Intelligence Terms and Definitions.* Washington, DC: DIC, 1987.

—**PRIORITY DESIGNATOR (PD)** is a two-digit number (01 through 15) that indicates the priority of a requisition or shipment. PDs are based upon the force/activity designator of the requesting unit and the urgency of need for the item.

References

Department of Defense, U.S. Army. *Repair Parts Supply for a Theater of Operations.* Field Manual FM 29-19. Washington, DC: Headquarters, Department of the Army, 1985.

—**PRIORITY INTELLIGENCE REQUIREMENTS** are the requirements that a commander has anticipated and has assigned a priority in his planning and decisionmaking. *See also:* Information Requirements, Intelligence Cycle.

References
Department of Defense, Joint Chiefs of Staff. *Department of Defense Dictionary of Military and Related Terms.* Washington, DC: GPO, 1986.

—**PRIORITY MESSAGE** is a category of precedence reserved for messages that require expeditious action by the addressee(s) or that furnish essential information for the execution of operations that are in progress. It is used when a routine precedence will not suffice. *See also:* Precedence.

References
Department of Defense, Joint Chiefs of Staff. *Department of Defense Dictionary of Military and Related Terms.* Washington, DC: GPO, 1986.

—**PRIORITY NATIONAL INTELLIGENCE OB-JECTIVES (PNIOs)** are a guide for coordinating intelligence collection and production in response to requirements relating to formulating and executing national security policy. They are compiled annually by the Intelligence Community and flow directly from the intelligence mission as established by the National Security Council. They are specific enough to provide a basis for planning the allocation of collection and research resources, but are not so specific as to constitute in themselves research and collection requirements. *See also:* Information Requirements, Intelligence Cycle.

References
Department of Defense, Joint Chiefs of Staff. *Department of Defense Dictionary of Military and Related Terms.* Washington, DC: GPO, 1986.

—**PRIORITY OF FIRES** is a direction to a fire support planner to organize and use fire support means according to the importance of the supported unit's missions.

References
Department of Defense, U.S. Army. *Operational Terms and Symbols.* Field Manual FM 101-5-1. Washington, DC: Headquarters, Department of the Army, 1985.

—**PRIORITY OF PREPLANNED MISSION RE-QUESTS.** Mission requests are prioritized in the following categories: (1) targets capable of pre-

venting the execution of a plan of action; (2) targets capable of immediate serious interference with the plan of action; (3) targets capable of ultimate serious interference with the execution of a plan of action; and (4) targets capable of limited interference with the execution of a plan of action. *See also:* Preplanned Mission Requests.

References
Department of Defense, Joint Chiefs of Staff. *Department of Defense Dictionary of Military and Related Terms.* Washington, DC: GPO, 1986.

—**PRIORITY OF SUPPORT** are the priorities that have been set by the commander in his concept of the operation and during its execution to insure that combat support and combat service support are provided to subordinate elements in accordance with their relative importance to the accomplishment of the mission.

References
Department of Defense, U.S. Army. *Operational Terms and Symbols.* Field Manual FM 101-5-1. Washington, DC: Headquarters, Department of the Army, 1985.

—**PRIORITY SYSTEM FOR MISSION REQUESTS FOR TACTICAL RECONNAISSANCE.** *Priority I* requests take precedence over all other requests except previously assigned priority I items. The results of these requests are of paramount importance to the immediate battle situation or objective. *Priority II* are requests in support of the general battle situation and are accommodated as soon as possible after the priority I requests. These are requests to gain current battle information. *Priority III* are requests whose fulfillment updates the intelligence data base but does not affect the immediate battle situation. *Priority IV* requests are of a routine nature. These are fulfilled when the reconnaissance effort permits.

References
Department of Defense, Joint Chiefs of Staff. *Department of Defense Dictionary of Military and Related Terms.* Washington, DC: GPO, 1986.

—**PRIORITY TARGET** is a target on which the delivery of fires takes precedence over all other fires for the designated firing unit or element. The firing unit or element will prepare, as much as possible, for the engagement of such targets, and may be assigned only one such target.

References
Department of Defense, U.S. Army. *Operational Terms and Symbols.* Field Manual FM 101-5-1. Washington, DC: Headquarters, Department of the Army, 1985.

—**PRISONER.** (1) A prisoner is one who is deprived of his liberty; that is, one who has been placed in confinement or custody and has not been set at liberty by proper authority. (2) Prisoner refers to a category of personnel transferred or dropped from the rolls of their permanent organization but carried in a disciplinary or prisoner status. *See also:* Prisoner of War.

References
Department of Defense, U.S. Army. *Dictionary of United States Army Terms.* Army Regulation AR 310-25. Washington, DC: Headquarters, Department of the Army, 1986.

—**PRISONER OF WAR (POW)** is the status of all members of the U.S. Armed Forces who are forcibly detained by a foreign state or entity. Under international law, persons defined in the Geneva Convention, Article 4, have a right to POW status.

A POW is a detained person as defined in Articles 4 and 5 of the Geneva Convention Relative to the Treatment of Prisoners of War of August 12, 1949. In particular, he is one who is captured by the armed forces of the enemy while engaged in combat under orders of his government. As such, he is entitled to the combatant's privilege of immunity from the municipal law of the capturing state for warlike acts that do not amount to breaches of law of armed conflict. For example, a POW may be, but is not limited to, any person belonging to one of the following categories who has fallen into the power of the enemy: a member of the armed forces, organized militia or volunteer corps; a person who accompanies the armed forces without actually being a member of it; a member of a merchant marine or civilian aircraft crew not qualifying for more favorable treatment; or individuals who, on the approval of the enemy, spontaneously take up arms to resist the invading forces. *See also:* Prisoner of War Branch Camp, Prisoner of War Censorship, Prisoner of War Collecting Point, Prisoner of War Compound, Prisoner of War Enclosure, Prisoner of War Personnel Record, Prisoner of War Processing Company, Prisoners of War.

References
Department of Defense, U.S. Army. *Code of Conduct/Survival, Evasion, Resistance and Escape (SERE) Training.* Army Regulation AR 350-30. Washington, DC: Headquarters, Department of the Army, 1985.

—**PRISONER OF WAR (POW) BRANCH CAMP** is a subsidiary camp under the supervision and administration of a POW camp. *See also:* Prisoner of War, Prisoner of War Camp.

References
Department of Defense, Joint Chiefs of Staff. *Department of Defense Dictionary of Military and Related Terms.* Washington, DC: GPO, 1986.

—**PRISONER OF WAR (POW) CAGE** is a temporary construction, building, or enclosed area where prisoners of war are confined for interrogation and temporary detention pending further evacuation. *See also:* Prisoner of War.

References
Department of Defense, Joint Chiefs of Staff. *Department of Defense Dictionary of Military and Related Terms.* Washington, DC: GPO, 1986.

—**PRISONER OF WAR (POW) CAMP** is a semi-permanent camp established for the internment and complete administration of prisoners of war. It may be located on, or may be independent of, other military installations. *See also:* Prisoner of War.

References
Department of Defense, Joint Chiefs of Staff. *Department of Defense Dictionary of Military and Related Terms.* Washington, DC: GPO, 1986.

—**PRISONER OF WAR (POW) CENSORSHIP** is the censorship of the communications to and from prisoners of war and civilian internees who are held by the U.S. Armed Forces. *See also:* Prisoner of War.

References
Department of Defense, Joint Chiefs of Staff. *Department of Defense Dictionary of Military and Related Terms.* Washington, DC: GPO, 1986.

—**PRISONER OF WAR (POW) COLLECTING POINT** is a designated locality in a forward battle area where prisoners of war are assembled pending local examination for information of immediate tactical value and for subsequent evacuation. *See also:* Prisoner of War.

References
Department of Defense, Joint Chiefs of Staff.
*Department of Defense Dictionary of Military and
Related Terms.* Washington, DC: GPO, 1986.

—**PRISONER OF WAR (POW) COMPOUND** is a
subdivision of a POW enclosure. *See also:*
Prisoner of War, Prisoner of War Enclosure.

References
Department of Defense, Joint Chiefs of Staff.
*Department of Defense Dictionary of Military and
Related Terms.* Washington, DC: GPO, 1986.

—**PRISONER OF WAR (POW) ENCLOSURE** is a
subdivision of a POW camp. *See also:* Prisoner
of War.

References
Department of Defense, Joint Chiefs of Staff.
*Department of Defense Dictionary of Military and
Related Terms.* Washington, DC: GPO, 1986.

—**PRISONER OF WAR (POW) PERSONNEL
RECORD** is a form for recording a photograph
and fingerprints and other pertinent personal data
concerning the POW, including the information
required by the Geneva Convention. *See also:*
Prisoner of War.

References
Department of Defense, Joint Chiefs of Staff.
*Department of Defense Dictionary of Military and
Related Terms.* Washington, DC: GPO, 1986.

—**PRISONER OF WAR (POW) PROCESSING
COMPANY** is a military police unit that records
data concerning prisoners captured by the U.S.
Army. The information recorded includes the
person's name, POW serial number, photograph,
fingerprints, and an inventory of the person's
personal belongings. *See also:* Prisoner of War.

References
Department of Defense, U.S. Army. *Dictionary of
United States Army Terms.* Army Regulation AR
310-25. Washington, DC: Headquarters, Department of the Army, 1986.

—**PRISONERS OF WAR (POWs)** are persons as
defined in the Geneva Convention relative to
the Treatment of Prisoners of War of August 12,
1949. *See also:* Prisoner of War.

References
Department of Defense, Joint Chiefs of Staff.
*Department of Defense Dictionary of Military and
Related Terms.* Washington, DC: GPO, 1986.

—**PRIVACY.** (1) Privacy is the protection given to
information transmitted in a communications
system or network to conceal it from persons
within the system or network. It is also called
segregation. (2) Privacy means the short-term
protection given to unclassified communications
that require safeguarding, within existing laws,
from unauthorized persons.

References
Department of Defense, U.S. Army. *Dictionary of
United States Army Terms.* Army Regulation AR
310-25. Washington, DC: Headquarters, Department of the Army, 1986.

—**PROBABLE** is a term used to qualify a statement
made under conditions wherein the evidence
indicates but does not confirm that the statement
is true. *See also:* Possible.

References
Department of Defense, Joint Chiefs of Staff.
*Department of Defense Dictionary of Military and
Related Terms.* Washington, DC: GPO, 1986.

Department of Defense, U.S. Army. *Dictionary of
United States Army Terms.* Army Regulation AR
310-25. Washington, DC: Headquarters, Department of the Army, 1986.

—**PROBABLE ERROR IN HEIGHT (PEH) BRACKET**
is the distance above and below the desired
height of burst within which there is a 50-percent
probability that a nuclear weapon will detonate.
See also: Nuclear Warfare.

References
Department of Defense, U.S. Army. *Nuclear
Weapons Employment Doctrine and Procedures.*
Field Manual FM 101-3-1. Washington, DC:
Headquarters, Department of the Army, 1986.

—**PROBABILITY FACTOR** is a factor used as an
argument in entering probability tables. It is equal
to the error not to be exceeded, divided by the
probable error.

References
Department of Defense, U.S. Army. *Dictionary of
United States Army Terms.* Army Regulation AR
310-25. Washington, DC: Headquarters, Department of the Army, 1986.

—**PROBABILITY OF DAMAGE (PD)** is the probability that damage will occur to a target. It is
expressed as a percentage or as a decimal.

References
Department of Defense, Joint Chiefs of Staff.
*Department of Defense Dictionary of Military and
Related Terms.* Washington, DC: GPO, 1986.

—**PROBATIONER** is a prisoner who has been assigned to military training company. *See also:* Disciplinary Action.

References

Department of Defense, U.S. Army. *Dictionary of United States Army Terms.* Army Regulation AR 310-25. Washington, DC: Headquarters, Department of the Army, 1986.

—**PROCEDURAL ARRANGEMENTS** (COOPERATIVE LOGISTICS ARRANGEMENTS) are agreements between the U.S. Department of Defense and a foreign ministry of defense concerning the form and content of logistic support to be provided by the United States, and the related terms and conditions of the agreements.

References

Department of Defense, U.S. Army. *Dictionary of United States Army Terms.* Army Regulation AR 310-25. Washington, DC: Headquarters, Department of the Army, 1986.

—**PROCEDURAL CONTROL** is a type of airspace control accomplished by nonelectronic means. *See also:* Procedural Management.

References

Department of Defense, U.S. Army. *Airspace Management and Army Air Traffic in a Combat Zone.* Field Manual FM 1-60. Washington, DC: Headquarters, Department of the Army, 1977.

—**PROCEDURAL MANAGEMENT** is a method of air battle management that relies on the use of techniques such as segmenting airspace by volume and time and weapons control statuses. *See also:* Procedural Control.

References

Department of Defense, U.S. Army. *Air Defense Artillery Employment.* Field Manual FM 44-1. Washington, DC: Headquarters, Department of the Army, 1983.

———. *Air Defense Artillery Employment Hawk.* Field Manual FM 44-90. Washington, DC: Headquarters, Department of the Army, 1983.

—**PROCEDURE ANALYSIS** is the component of transmission security that determines trends in security and procedures violations, maintains a continual check on such occurrences, and initiates remedial and corrective measures when and where they are necessary. *See also:* Communications Security.

References

Department of Defense, U.S. Army. *Dictionary of United States Army Terms.* Army Regulation AR 310-25. Washington, DC: Headquarters, Department of the Army, 1986.

—**PROCEDURE MESSAGE** is a message in which the text contains only prosigns, operating signals, addressee designations, identification of messages, parts of messages, and amplifying data, as necessary. *See also:* Procedure Sign (Prosign).

References

Department of Defense, U.S. Army. *Dictionary of United States Army Terms.* Army Regulation AR 310-25. Washington, DC: Headquarters, Department of the Army, 1986.

—**PROCEDURE SIGN** (PROSIGN) is one or more letters or characters, or combinations of both, used to facilitate communication by conveying in condensed standard form, certain frequently used orders, instructions, requests, and communication-related information.

References

Department of Defense, U.S. Army. *Dictionary of United States Army Terms.* Army Regulation AR 310-25. Washington, DC: Headquarters, Department of the Army, 1986.

—**PROCEDURE WORD,** or proword, is a word or phrase that is limited to radiotelephone procedure and is used to facilitate communication by conveying information in a condensed standard form. A proword is used in lieu of a prosign. *See also:* Procedure Sign (Prosign).

References

Department of Defense, Joint Chiefs of Staff. *Department of Defense Dictionary of Military and Related Terms.* Washington, DC: GPO, 1986.

—**PROCESSING** is a step in the intelligence cycle where information becomes intelligence through evaluation, analysis, integration, and interpretation. *See also:* Intelligence.

References

U.S. Congress. Senate. *Final Report of the Senate Select Committee to Study Government Operations With Respect to Intelligence Activities. Report 94-755. Book I, Foreign and Military Intelligence* (Church Committee Report). Washington, DC: Government Printing Office, 1976.

—**PROCLAMATION** is a document published and issued to the inhabitants of an area that sets forth the basis of authority and scope of activities of a commander in a given area. It defines the obligations, liabilities, duties, and rights of the population that is affected.

References

Department of Defense, Joint Chiefs of Staff. *Department of Defense Dictionary of Military and Related Terms.* Washington, DC: GPO, 1986.

—**PROCUREMENT** is the process of obtaining personnel, services, supplies, and equipment. *See also:* Procurement Cost; Procurement Inspection; Procurement Objective; Procurement of Equipment and Munitions, Appropriations; Procurement Package; Procurement Rate; Procuring Activity; Producer Logistics.

References

Department of Defense, Joint Chiefs of Staff. *Department of Defense Dictionary of Military and Related Terms.* Washington, DC: GPO, 1986.

—**PROCUREMENT COST** is the total recurring and nonrecurring procurement appropriation expenditures required to produce and deploy a weapon system, plus associated initial spares and repair parts. Procurement cost includes all procurement appropriation expenditures attributable to the weapon system line item in the budget. Additional procurement costs (e.g., production base support, first destination transportation, and modifications) are not included, since they are contained in other budget line items. *See also:* Procurement.

References

Department of Defense, U.S. Army. *Dictionary of United States Army Terms.* Army Regulation AR 310-25. Washington, DC: Headquarters, Department of the Army, 1986.

—**PROCUREMENT INSPECTION** is an investigation into the performance of the procurement function and related activities, including all significant aspects of purchasing and contracting. *See also:* Procurement.

References

Department of Defense, U.S. Army. *Dictionary of United States Army Terms.* Army Regulation AR 310-25. Washington, DC: Headquarters, Department of the Army, 1986.

—**PROCUREMENT OBJECTIVE** is the amount required during a calendar year. The figure is approved in writing and is based upon firmly established trends. *See also:* Procurement.

References

Department of Defense, U.S. Army. *Dictionary of United States Army Terms.* Army Regulation AR 310-25. Washington, DC: Headquarters, Department of the Army, 1986.

—**PROCUREMENT OF EQUIPMENT AND MUNITIONS, APPROPRIATIONS,** is a term used to denote the five Army equipment appropriations: aircraft procurement, missile procurement, weapons procurement, procurement of tracked combat vehicles, and ammunition procurement; and other Army procurements. *See also:* Procurement.

References

Department of Defense, U.S. Army. *Dictionary of United States Army Terms.* Army Regulation AR 310-25. Washington, DC: Headquarters, Department of the Army, 1986.

—**PROCUREMENT PACKAGE** is the information required to obtain bids or proposals. It comprises a technical data package that describes the item or service, together with all applicable legal, administrative, and fiscal provisions necessary for a clear and complete description of the item or service that is to be procured. The proposed contract between the government and the supplier is also included in the package. *See also:* Procurement.

References

Department of Defense, U.S. Army. *Dictionary of United States Army Terms.* Army Regulation AR 310-25. Washington, DC: Headquarters, Department of the Army, 1986.

—**PROCUREMENT RATE** is the number of units of an item that are procured within a definite time period. *See also:* Procurement.

References

Department of Defense, U.S. Army. *Dictionary of United States Army Terms.* Army Regulation AR 310-25. Washington, DC: Headquarters, Department of the Army, 1986.

—**PROCURING ACTIVITY** is the agency responsible for purchasing supplies or services. Such activities include the U.S. Army Materiel Command; the zone interior armies; the National Guard Bureau; the Military District of Washington; the U.S. Army; and the overseas commands. *See also:* Procurement.

References

Department of Defense, U.S. Army. *Dictionary of United States Army Terms.* Army Regulation AR 310-25. Washington, DC: Headquarters, Department of the Army, 1986.

—**PRODUCER LOGISTICS** are the basic elements of logistics involving procurement and/or production of assets and their delivery to the user or customer. *See also:* Procurement.

References

Department of Defense, U.S. Army. *Dictionary of United States Army Terms.* Army Regulation AR 310-25. Washington, DC: Headquarters, Department of the Army, 1986.

—**PRODUCT.** (1) A product is an intelligence report that is disseminated to customers by an agency. (2) In signals intelligence, a product is intelligence information derived by analyzing signals intelligence materials. It is published as either a report or a translation for dissemination to customers. *See also:* Intelligence Cycle, Intelligence Production.

References

Department of Defense, Defense Intelligence College. *Glossary of Intelligence Terms and Definitions.* Washington, DC: DIC, 1987.

Department of Defense, U.S. Army. *Support Operations: Echelons Above Corps.* Field Manual FM 100-16. Washington, DC: Headquarters, Department of the Army, 1986.

U.S. Congress. Senate. *Final Report of the Senate Select Committee to Study Government Operations With Respect to Intelligence Activities. Report 94-755. Book I, Foreign and Military Intelligence* (Church Committee Report). Washington, DC: GPO, 1976.

—**PRODUCT IMPROVEMENT** is an engineering change or a modification to an item of materiel that has been classified as Standard A, B, and Limited Production to accomplish one or more of the following purposes: (1) to assure the safety of personnel; (2) to correct a performance deficiency discovered during troop usage that prohibits the use of an item for its intended purpose; (3) to prevent serious damage to equipment; (4) to break a serious production bottleneck; (5) to reduce significantly the total cost, when considering the total logistical functions; (6) to significantly increase the reliability or durability of an item; (7) to significantly improve or simplify maintenance; (8) to achieve greater equipment and component standardization; (9) to simplify design or operation; (10) to increase significantly the efficiency in use of materials; (11) to make equipment compatible with newer equipment with which it will be operated; (12) to enable an item to be utilized in a new role providing there is no degradation of the item's capability to perform its original role.

References

Department of Defense, U.S. Army. *Dictionary of United States Army Terms.* Army Regulation AR 310-25. Washington, DC: Headquarters, Department of the Army, 1986.

—**PRODUCTION.** (1) The U.S. Army's definition of production is "the conversion of information or intelligence information into finished intelligence through the integration, analysis, evaluation, and interpretation of all available data, and the preparation of intelligence reports in support of known or anticipated consumer requirements." (2) Production is part of the Intelligence Cycle. (3) Production, as defined by the Church Committee, is "the preparation of reports based on an analysis of information to meet the needs of intelligence users (consumers) within and outside of the Intelligence Community." *See also:* Intelligence Cycle, Intelligence Production.

References

Department of Defense, U.S. Army. *RDT&E Managers Intelligence and Threat Support Guide.* Alexandria, VA: Headquarters, Army Materiel Development and Readiness Command, 1983.

U.S. Congress. Senate. *Final Report of the Senate Select Committee to Study Government Operations With Respect to Intelligence Activities. Report 94-755. Book I, Foreign and Military Intelligence* (Church Committee Report). Washington, DC: GPO, 1976.

—**PRODUCTION BASE TEMPERATURE.** A production base is classified as hot or cold, depending on its rate of production on D-day. A production line operating at its maximum sustained production rate is a hot-base facility. A production facility that is available but is not producing is a cold-base facility. If a facility is producing at a minimum sustaining rate, it is generally referred to as a warm base. *See also:* Post D-Day Production.

References

Department of Defense, U.S. Army. *Dictionary of United States Army Terms.* Army Regulation AR 310-25. Washington, DC: Headquarters, Department of the Army, 1986.

—**PRODUCTION CONTROL** is the process of directing and controlling the work in a manufacturing plant or maintenance shop so that the most output of quality work results.

References

Department of Defense, U.S. Army. *Dictionary of United States Army Terms.* Army Regulation AR 310-25. Washington, DC: Headquarters, Department of the Army, 1986.

—**PRODUCTION EQUIPMENT** is equipment or machinery used in the production of goods or services to cut, abrade, grind, shape, form, join, measure, test, heat, or treat, production materials or "in process" products within a manufacturing, processing, assembling, or service establishment.

References

Department of Defense, U.S. Army. *Dictionary of United States Army Terms.* Army Regulation AR 310-25. Washington, DC: Headquarters, Department of the Army, 1986.

—**PRODUCTION LINE MAINTENANCE** is a system for repairing, overhauling, or rebuilding unserviceable materiel that flows in a definite sequence through a number of specific repair stations.

References

Department of Defense, U.S. Army. *Dictionary of United States Army Terms.* Army Regulation AR 310-25. Washington, DC: Headquarters, Department of the Army, 1986.

—**PRODUCTION MISSILE** is a complete missile that is accepted by the military or another governmental agency. It may be allocated for tactical or nontactical use. This category excludes prototype missiles.

References

Department of Defense, U.S. Army. *Dictionary of United States Army Terms.* Army Regulation AR 310-25. Washington, DC: Headquarters, Department of the Army, 1986.

—**PRODUCTION OF INTELLIGENCE** involves the collection and processing of information, the conversion of information into intelligence, and the dissemination of intelligence. *See also:* Intelligence.

References

Department of Defense, U.S. Army. *Staff Organizations and Operations.* Field Manual FM 101-5. Washington, DC: Headquarters, Department of the Army, 1984.

—**PRODUCTION OFFSET** is a term that represents the quantity of an item that is deliverable to users from post-D-day production to meet post-D-day consumption requirements for the forces identified by force planning codes that are authorized to receive production offsets. *See also:* D-to-P Concept.

References

Department of Defense, U.S. Army. *Dictionary of United States Army Terms.* Army Regulation AR 310-25. Washington, DC: Headquarters, Department of the Army, 1986.

—**PRODUCTION REQUIREMENTS** are the sum of authorized stock levels and pipeline needs, less stocks expected to become available; stocks on hand; stocks due in; returned stocks; and stocks from salvage, reclamation, rebuild, and other sources.

References

Department of Defense, U.S. Army. *Dictionary of United States Army Terms.* Army Regulation AR 310-25. Washington, DC: Headquarters, Department of the Army, 1986.

—**PRODUCTIVITY** is the average number of work units produced per person over a definite period of time.

References

Department of Defense, U.S. Army. *Dictionary of United States Army Terms.* Army Regulation AR 310-25. Washington, DC: Headquarters, Department of the Army, 1986.

—**PROFESSIONAL ARMY ETHIC** refers to the basic professional beliefs and values that should be held by all soldiers: loyalty to the ideals of the nation, loyalty to the unit, personal responsibility, and selfless service.

The professional Army ethic articulates American values, and applies to all members of the Department of the Army, active and reserve. The ethic sets the moral context for the Army in its service to the nation and inspires the sense of purpose necessary to preserve the nation even by the use of military force. From the moral values of the Constitution to the harsh realities of the battlefield, the professional Army ethic espouses resolutely those essential values that guide the way Army personnel lead their lives and perform their duties.

References

Department of Defense, U.S. Army. *The Army.* (Prepublication Issue.) Field Manual FM 100-1. Washington, DC: Headquarters, Department of the Army, 1986.

————. *Military Leadership.* Field Manual FM 22-100. Washington, DC: Headquarters, Department of the Army, 1983.

—**PROFESSIONAL DEVELOPMENT EDUCATION** is instruction that prepares commissioned officers, warrant officers, and enlisted personnel for assignment to positions of progressively greater responsibility. Such education includes West Point, civilian education degree programs, the U.S. Army Command and General Staff School, the Army War College, and equivalent colleges.

References

Department of Defense, U.S. Army. *Individual Military Education and Training.* Army Regulation AR 350-1. Washington, DC: Headquarters, Department of the Army, 1987.

—**PROFESSOR OF MILITARY SCIENCE.** (1) A professor of military science is a senior officer who is detailed by the Department of the Army for duty with a college-level civilian educational institution for the purpose of supervising instruction in authorized military subjects. (2) A professor of military science is a senior military instructor who is provided by the educational institution and approved by the Department of the Army for duty with the civilian educational institution sponsoring National Defense Cadet Corps units for the purpose of supervising instruction in authorized military subjects.

References

Department of Defense, U.S. Army. *Dictionary of United States Army Terms.* Army Regulation AR 310-25. Washington, DC: Headquarters, Department of the Army, 1986.

—**PROFICIENCY FLYING,** or combat readiness is proficiency flying, flying that is required of each Army aviator to maintain a safe minimum level of pilot skill.

References

Department of Defense, U.S. Army. *Dictionary of United States Army Terms.* Army Regulation AR 310-25. Washington, DC: Headquarters, Department of the Army, 1986.

—**PROFICIENCY FLYING STATUS** is flying accomplished under competent orders by rated personnel primarily to maintain basic flying skills while serving in assignments where such skills would normally not be required.

References

Department of Defense, U.S. Army. *Dictionary of United States Army Terms.* Army Regulation AR 310-25. Washington, DC: Headquarters, Department of the Army, 1986.

—**PROFICIENCY PAY (PP)** is the monthly amount of pay that may be awarded to an eligible soldier in addition to any pay and allowances to which he is entitled.

References

Department of Defense, U.S. Army. *Enlisted Personnel Management System.* Army Regulation AR 600-200. Washington, DC: Headquarters, Department of the Army, 1984.

—**PROFICIENCY RATING** is a classification that denotes a specific monthly rate of proficiency pay. *See also:* Proficiency Pay.

References

Department of Defense, U.S. Army. *Dictionary of United States Army Terms.* Army Regulation AR 310-25. Washington, DC: Headquarters, Department of the Army, 1986.

—**PROFILE** is an Army tactical intelligence term that refers to the picture formed through the identification and analysis of elements, actions, equipment, and details of military units or activity. Patterns plus signature equal profile. *See:* Signature.

References

Department of Defense, U.S. Army. *Counter-Signals Intelligence (C-SIGINT) Operations.* Field Manual FM 34-62. Washington, DC: Headquarters, Department of the Army, 1986.

————. *Military Intelligence Battalion (Combat Electronic Warfare Intelligence) (Division).* Field Manual FM 34-10. Washington, DC: Headquarters, Department of the Army, 1981.

————. *Military Intelligence Company (Combat Electronic Warfare and Intelligence) (Armored Cavalry Regiment/Separate Brigade).* Field Manual FM 34-30. Washington, DC: Headquarters, Department of the Army, 1983.

—**PROGRAM BUDGET ADVISORY COMMITTEE** is a committee composed of the principal staff officers of a command, agency, or installation headquarters. It is established to coordinate program and budget actions within the command.

References

Department of Defense, U.S. Army. *Dictionary of United States Army Terms.* Army Regulation AR 310-25. Washington, DC: Headquarters, Department of the Army, 1986.

—**PROGRAM CHANGE FACTOR,** a number used to adjust expected demands and returns over the forecast period, is a ratio reflecting planned changes in hours of operation, troop population, end-item densities, or other elements that may affect demands or returns in some future period.

References

Department of Defense, U.S. Army. *Dictionary of United States Army Terms.* Army Regulation AR 310-25. Washington, DC: Headquarters, Department of the Army, 1986.

—**PROGRAM COST** is the total recurring and nonrecurring expenditures from all appropriations that are required to develop, produce, and deploy a weapon system with the associated initial spares. It is composed of program acquisition cost, plus additional procurement costs (e.g., production base support, first destination transportation, and modifications and expenditures from other appropriations, including Army military personnel and Army operation and maintenance appropriations).

References

Department of Defense, U.S. Army. *Dictionary of United States Army Terms.* Army Regulation AR 310-25. Washington, DC: Headquarters, Department of the Army, 1986.

—**PROGRAM DECISION MEMORANDUM** is a document that provides the decisions of the Secretary of Defense on program objective memoranda and Joint Force memoranda. *See also:* Joint Force Memoranda.

References

Department of Defense, U.S. Army. *Dictionary of United States Army Terms.* Army Regulation AR 310-25. Washington, DC: Headquarters, Department of the Army, 1986.

—**PROGRAM MANAGEMENT** is the judicious use of resources, processes, and time in planning, executing, and appraising the results of administrative actions that are designed to accomplish a definitive objective. The term includes program development, program execution, program review and analysis, and program control.

References

Department of Defense, U.S. Army. *Dictionary of United States Army Terms.* Army Regulation AR 310-25. Washington, DC: Headquarters, Department of the Army, 1986.

—**PROGRAM OF INSTRUCTION** is the training management document that specifies the purpose, prerequisites, content, duration, and sequence of instruction for formal resident and nonresident courses at an educational institution.

References

Department of Defense, U.S. Army. *Dictionary of United States Army Terms.* Army Regulation AR 310-25. Washington, DC: Headquarters, Department of the Army, 1986.

—**PROGRAM OF TARGETS,** in fire support operations, is a number of targets of similar nature (e.g., counterfires). A program of fires may be designated by using the nature of the targets involved or a nickname. The targets are fired upon in a predetermined sequence.

References

Department of Defense, U.S. Army. *Fire Support in Combined Arms Operations.* Field Manual FM 6-20. Washington, DC: Headquarters, Department of the Army, 1983.

————. *Operational Terms and Symbols.* Field Manual FM 101-5-1. Washington, DC: Headquarters, Department of the Army, 1985.

—**PROGRAM SECTION** is the part of a program that pertains to the supplies or services of one of the agencies of the U.S. Army.

References

Department of Defense, U.S. Army. *Dictionary of United States Army Terms.* Army Regulation AR 310-25. Washington, DC: Headquarters, Department of the Army, 1986.

—**PROGRAM STOCK** are the repair parts and supplies stocked by a shop supply section for scheduled production line repair programs. Program stock is used primarily by intermediate maintenance units for scheduled equipment overhauls and for the maintenance of components or assemblies (e.g., engines and transmissions).

References

Department of Defense, U.S. Army. *Repair Parts Supply for a Theater of Operations.* Field Manual FM 29-19. Washington, DC: Headquarters, Department of the Army, 1985.

—**PROGRAMMED FORCES** are forces that exist for a fiscal year. They contain the major combat and tactical support forces that are expected to execute the national strategy within manpower, fiscal, and other constraints. *See also:* Current Force, Force, Intermediate Force Planning Level, Minimum Risk Force, Planning Force.

References

Department of Defense, Joint Chiefs of Staff. *Department of Defense Dictionary of Military and Related Terms.* Washington, DC: GPO, 1986.

—**PROGRAMMED STRENGTH** is the strength authorized for a given planning date or period to man the Army, command, or agency at a given structure, and to attain the prescribed degree of operational readiness or established goals, as appropriate. The authorized strength and structure are established for, and are included in, the Troop Program of the Army. *See also:* Programmed Forces, Troop Program.

References

Department of Defense, U.S. Army. *Dictionary of United States Army Terms.* Army Regulation AR 310-25. Washington, DC: Headquarters, Department of the Army, 1986.

—**PROGRESSIVE BURNING** is the burning of a propellent grain in which the burning surface increases with a resulting increase in pressure.

References

Department of Defense, U.S. Army. *Repair Parts Supply for a Theater of Operations.* Field Manual FM 29-19. Washington, DC: Headquarters, Department of the Army, 1985.

—**PROHIBITED AREA** is a specifically designated area at airfields, seadromes, or heliports in which all ammunition and explosives are prohibited.

References

Department of Defense, U.S. Army. *Ammunition and Explosives Safety Standards.* Army Regulation AR 385-64. Washington, DC: Headquarters, Department of the Army, 1987.

—**PROHIBITED ROUTE** (OR A PROHIBITED SECTION OF ROUTE) is a route or section of a route over which all traffic is prohibited.

References

Department of Defense, U.S. Army. *Route Reconnaissance and Classification.* Field Manual FM 5-36. Washington, DC: Headquarters, Department of the Army, 1985.

—**PROJECT** is a planned undertaking of a goal to be accomplished, produced, or constructed, and has a finite beginning and end. *See also:* Project Account Classification, Project Code.

References

Department of Defense, Joint Chiefs of Staff. *Department of Defense Dictionary of Military and Related Terms.* Washington, DC: GPO, 1986.

—**PROJECT ACCOUNT CLASSIFICATION** is a system of classifying actual or contemplated expenditures and the available funds in terms of the functions or activities involved.

References

Department of Defense, U.S. Army. *Repair Parts Supply for a Theater of Operations.* Field Manual FM 29-19. Washington, DC: Headquarters, Department of the Army, 1985.

—**PROJECT CODE** is a three-position alpha or numeric code that is used to identify (1) requisitions and related documents that are applicable to specific projects or programs or special exercises and maneuvers; (2) shipments of materiel for specific projects or programs; or (3) extraordinary programs that require identification at the requisitioner or supply level to satisfy program cost analysis.

References

Department of Defense, U.S. Army. *Planning Logistics Support for Military Operations.* Field Manual FM 701-58. Washington, DC: Headquarters, Department of the Army, 1987.

————. *Repair Parts Supply for a Theater of Operations.* Field Manual FM 29-19. Washington, DC: Headquarters, Department of the Army, 1985.

—**PROJECT STOCKS** are items of supply and equipment that are included in operational projects to support specific operations, contingencies, and/or war plans.

References

Department of Defense, U.S. Army. *Planning Logistics Support for Military Operations.* Field Manual FM 701-58. Washington, DC: Headquarters, Department of the Army, 1987.

—**PROJECTED SPECIALTY** is the career division's recommendation of the most appropriate specialty for a commissioned officer's next assignment to further his professional development, consistent with Army requirements. It normally is an officer's primary or alternate specialty.

References

Department of Defense, U.S. Army. *Planning Logistics Support for Military Operations.* Field Manual FM 701-58. Washington, DC: Headquarters, Department of the Army, 1987.

—**PROJECTILE** is an object projected by an applied exterior force and continuing in motion by virtue of its own inertia (e.g., bullet, shell, or grenade). The term is also applied to rockets and missiles. *See also:* Projectile Velocity.

References

Department of Defense, Joint Chiefs of Staff. *Department of Defense Dictionary of Military and Related Terms.* Washington, DC: GPO, 1986.

—**PROJECTILE VELOCITY** is (1) the velocity of the projectile along the line of departure or (2) the resultant of the muzzle velocity and the aircraft's velocity.

References

Department of Defense, U.S. Army. *Planning Logistics Support for Military Operations.* Field Manual FM 701-58. Washington, DC: Headquarters, Department of the Army, 1987.

—**PROMOTION.** *See:* Army Promotion List, Enlisted Evaluation System, Enlisted Grade Structure, Failed Selection for Promotion, Field Promotion Authority, Frocking, Promotion authority, Promotion Eligibility Date, Promotion List, Promotion Phase Points, Promotion Point Cutoff Score, Promotion Sequence Number, Promotion Zone, Selected for Promotion.

—**PROMOTION AUTHORITY** is a commander who has authority to promote enlisted members.

References

Department of Defense, U.S. Army. *Enlisted Personnel Management System.* Army Regulation AR 600-200. Washington, DC: Headquarters, Department of the Army, 1984.

—**PROMOTION ELIGIBILITY DATE (PED)** is the earliest date on which an officer who is recommended and selected may be promoted to the next higher grade. *See also:* Promotion Zone.

References

Department of Defense, U.S. Army. *Promotion of Officers on Active Duty.* Army Regulation AR 624-100. Washington, DC: Headquarters, Department of the Army, 1984.

—**PROMOTION LIST** is a list, provided by statute, of officers of the Regular Army by competitive category and below the permanent grade of brigadier general, in the order of standing for promotion. *See also:* Promotion Phase Points, Promotion Cutoff Score, Promotion Sequence Number.

References

Department of Defense, U.S. Army. *Promotion of Officers on Active Duty.* Army Regulation AR 624-100. Washington, DC: Headquarters, Department of the Army, 1984.

—**PROMOTION PHASE POINTS** influence the timing of promotions to a grade. They are expressed in terms of the length of time an officer must have served in the lower grade at the time of promotion to the higher grade. *See also:* Promotion List.

References

Department of Defense, U.S. Army. *Promotion of Officers on Active Duty.* Army Regulation AR 624-100. Washington, DC: Headquarters, Department of the Army, 1984.

—**PROMOTION POINT CUTOFF SCORE** is the minimum number of promotion points, by three-digit military occupational specialty, needed for promotion to the grades of E5 and E6 during a given time. *See also:* Promotion List.

References

Department of Defense, U.S. Army. *Enlisted Personnel Management System.* Army Regulation AR 600-200. Washington, DC: Headquarters, Department of the Army, 1984.

—**PROMOTION SEQUENCE NUMBER** is a number that shows the rank order of officers on the promotion list. *See also:* Promotion List.

References

Department of Defense, U.S. Army. *Promotion of Officers on Active Duty.* Army Regulation AR 624-100. Washington, DC: Headquarters, Department of the Army, 1984.

—**PROMOTION ZONE** is an eligibility category (defined by an announced range of dates of rank) of the zone of consideration that consists of commissioned officers on the active duty list of the same grade and competitive category, or warrant officers who *as lieutenant colonels or below* are eligible for promotion consideration for the first time (excluding any below the zone consideration); or *as colonels and brigadier generals* are eligible for promotion consideration, provided the officer (1) has not been recommended for promotion to the next higher grade when considered in the promotion zone or (2) has not been removed from a previous list of officers recommended for promotion to such grade if selected from in or above the promotion zone. *See also:* Above the Zone, Below the Zone, Promotion List, Zone of Consideration.

References
Department of Defense, U.S. Army. *Promotion of Officers on Active Duty.* Army Regulation AR 624-100. Washington, DC: Headquarters, Department of the Army, 1984.

—**PROMPT RADIATION** consists of gamma rays that are produced in fission and as a result of other neutron reactions and nuclear excitation of weapon materials that occur within one second or less after a nuclear explosion. The radiation from these sources are known either as prompt or instantaneous gamma rays. *See also:* Induced Radiation, Initial Radiation, Residual Nuclear Radiation (Residual Radioactivity).

References
Department of Defense, Joint Chiefs of Staff. *Department of Defense Dictionary of Military and Related Terms.* Washington, DC: GPO, 1986.

—**PRONE POSITION** (HASTY). (1) The prone fighting position is a further refinement of the skirmisher's trench. It serves as a good firing position for the soldier and provides better protection against direct fire weapons than the crater or skirmisher's trench. (2) The prone position is a posture of the body for firing from the ground. The stomach is flat against the ground, the legs are spread, and the insides of the feet are flat on the ground, but the head and shoulders are raised and are supported by the elbows, thus leaving the hands free to operate the gun.

References
Department of Defense, U.S. Army. *Survivability.* Field Manual FM 5-103. Washington, DC: Headquarters, Department of the Army, 1985.

—**PRONE SHELTER** is an open trench deep enough to protect a man lying flat (normally two feet by two feet by the length of the man) from small arms fire and from ground burst bombs and artillery shells. It gives little or no protection against airburst projectiles or against the crushing action of tanks.

References
Department of Defense, U.S. Army. *Dictionary of United States Army Terms.* Army Regulation AR 310-25. Washington, DC: Headquarters, Department of the Army, 1986.

—**PRONTO** means as quickly as possible.

References
Department of Defense, Joint Chiefs of Staff. *Department of Defense Dictionary of Military and Related Terms.* Washington, DC: GPO, 1986.

—**PROPAGANDA** is any form of communication (including information, ideas, doctrines, or special appeals that supports national objectives) and is designed to influence the opinions, emotions, attitudes, or behavior of any group in order to benefit the sponsor. *See also:* Propaganda Development, Propaganda Development Process.

References
Department of Defense, U.S. Army. *Psychological Operations.* Field Manual FM 33-1. Washington, DC: Headquarters, Department of the Army, 1979.

U.S. Congress. Senate. *Final Report of the Senate Select Committee to Study Government Operations With Respect to Intelligence Activities. Report 94-755. Book I, Foreign and Military Intelligence* (Church Committee Report). Washington, DC: GPO, 1976.

—**PROPAGANDA DEVELOPMENT** is the process of taking information, knowledge, and material, visualizing it, and expressing it as artwork, words, symbols, texts, manuscripts, and actions. *See also:* Propaganda.

References
Department of Defense, U.S. Army. *U.S. Army Operational Concept for Special Operations Forces,* TRADOC PAM 525-34. Washington, DC: Headquarters, Department of the Army, 1984.

—**PROPAGANDA DEVELOPMENT PROCESS** is a multistep procedure that concerns researching, designing, testing, producing, disseminating, and evaluating propaganda. *See also:* Propaganda.

References
Department of Defense, U.S. Army. *Psychological Operations.* Field Manual FM 33-1. Washington, DC: Headquarters, Department of the Army, 1979.

—**PROPELLANT** is the source that provides the energy required for propelling a projectile (i.e., an explosive charge for propelling a projectile, or a solid or liquid fuel used to propel a rocket or missile).

References
Department of Defense, Joint Chiefs of Staff. *Department of Defense Dictionary of Military and Related Terms.* Washington, DC: GPO, 1986.

—**PROPELLING CHARGE** is a powder charge that is set off in a weapon to propel a projectile from it. The burning of the confined propelling charge produces gases that force the projectile out of the weapon. *See also:* Propelling Increment.

References
Department of Defense, U.S. Army. *Dictionary of United States Army Terms.* Army Regulation AR 310-25. Washington, DC: Headquarters, Department of the Army, 1986.

—**PROPELLING INCREMENT** is a part of a propelling charge that is designed to be separated from the total charge. The increment can then be removed to enable the gunner to make range adjustments.

References
Department of Defense, U.S. Army. *Dictionary of United States Army Terms.* Army Regulation AR 310-25. Washington, DC: Headquarters, Department of the Army, 1986.

—**PROPERTY.** (1) Property is anything that may be owned. (2) In military terminology, property is usually confined to tangible property, including real estate and materiel. (3) For special purposes and in certain statutes, "property" excludes such items as public domain, certain lands, certain categories of naval ships, and the records of the federal government. *See also:* Property Account, Property Book Accountability, Property Book Officer, Property Custodian, Property Disposal Officer, Property Exchange, Property Officer, Property Voucher.

References
Department of Defense, Joint Chiefs of Staff. *Department of Defense Dictionary of Military and Related Terms.* Washington, DC: GPO, 1986.

—**PROPERTY ACCOUNT** is a formal record of property and property transactions in terms of quantity and/or cost, generally by item. An official record of government property must be maintained in accordance with Army regulations. *See also:* Property.

References
Department of Defense, Joint Chiefs of Staff. *Department of Defense Dictionary of Military and Related Terms.* Washington, DC: GPO, 1986.

—**PROPERTY BOOK ACCOUNTABILITY** is the obligation to maintain records, other than a stock record account, of certain classes of nonexpendable property and expendable (reportable) items listed under specified conditions or by specific instructions from Headquarters, Department of the Army. *See also:* Property.

References
Department of Defense, U.S. Army. *Dictionary of United States Army Terms.* Army Regulation AR 310-25. Washington, DC: Headquarters, Department of the Army, 1986.

—**PROPERTY BOOK OFFICER (PBO),** or vessel property book officer, is an individual designated to maintain accountability for property on property books. He has direct responsibility for property that is in his physical possession. *See also:* Property.

References
Department of Defense, U.S. Army. *Dictionary of United States Army Terms.* Army Regulation AR 310-25. Washington, DC: Headquarters, Department of the Army, 1986.

—**PROPERTY BOOKS** are accounting records of all nonexpendable property assigned to divisional and nondivisional organizations, table of distribution and allowances units, and separate companies. *See also:* Property.

References
Department of Defense, U.S. Army. *Commander's Handbook for Property Accountability at the Unit Level.* Field Manual FM 10-14-1. Washington, DC: Headquarters, Department of the Army, 1984.

—**PROPERTY CUSTODIAN** is an officer who acts as the agent of a military training institution for procuring, storing, issuing, and accounting for property belonging to, or issued to, the command. *See also:* Property.

References
Department of Defense, U.S. Army. *Dictionary of United States Army Terms.* Army Regulation AR 310-25. Washington, DC: Headquarters, Department of the Army, 1986.

—**PROPERTY DISPOSAL OFFICER** is the individual at an installation charged with the receipt, care, and authorized disposal of personal property. The property disposal officer is in charge of all salvage and disposal activities at an installation. He was formerly known as the salvage officer. *See also:* Property.

References

Department of Defense, U.S. Army. *Dictionary of United States Army Terms.* Army Regulation AR 310-25. Washington, DC: Headquarters, Department of the Army, 1986.

—**PROPERTY EXCHANGE** is replacing any item of property that is given by one unit to another. *See also:* Property.

References

Department of Defense, U.S. Army. *Dictionary of United States Army Terms.* Army Regulation AR 310-25. Washington, DC: Headquarters, Department of the Army, 1986.

—**PROPERTY OFFICER,** or supply officer, is a term used to indicate an officer who is responsible for the custody or issue of property. The term is not used to indicate an officer who has accountability for property unless he is expressly described as the "accountable property officer" (of an installation) or "accountable supply officer" (of a tactical organization). *See also:* Property.

References

Department of Defense, U.S. Army. *Dictionary of United States Army Terms.* Army Regulation AR 310-25. Washington, DC: Headquarters, Department of the Army, 1986.

—**PROPERTY VOUCHER** is any document that supports the transfer of property either from or to a stock record account. *See also:* Property.

References

Department of Defense, U.S. Army. *Dictionary of United States Army Terms.* Army Regulation AR 310-25. Washington, DC: Headquarters, Department of the Army, 1986.

—**PROPONENT.** (1) A proponent is an Army organization or staff that has been assigned primary responsibility for material or subject matter in an area of interest (e.g., a proponent school, a proponent staff agency, or a proponent center). *See also:* Proponent Agency.

References

Department of Defense, U.S. Army. *Dictionary of United States Army Terms.* Army Regulation AR 310-25. Washington, DC: Headquarters, Department of the Army, 1986.

—**PROPONENT AGENCY** is an Army organization or staff that has been assigned primary responsibility for material or subject matter in its area of interest.

References

Department of Defense, U.S. Army. *Army Forces Training.* Army Regulation AR 350-21. Washington, DC: Headquarters, Department of the Army, 1986.

—**PROPONENT SCHOOL** is an Army school that has been assigned responsibility to develop and review the instructional material relevant to its doctrinal, combat, or logistical training responsibility and is presented at one or more Army schools or training centers.

References

Department of Defense, U.S. Army. *Individual Military Education and Training.* Army Regulation AR 350-1. Washington, DC: Headquarters, Department of the Army, 1987.

—**PROTECTABLE MOBILIZATION RESERVE MATERIEL OBJECTIVE** is the portion of the total mobilization reserve materiel objective that represents the quantity of an item planned to be held in mobilization reserve inventories and procured for such inventories within the fund limitations of the current fiscal year. At the beginning of a fiscal year, the projectable mobilization reserve materiel objective will equal the total mobilization reserve stocks on hand or on order at the end of the prior fiscal year, plus augmentation planned (if any), with mobilization funds made available for the current fiscal year.

References

Department of Defense, U.S. Army. *Dictionary of United States Army Terms.* Army Regulation AR 310-25. Washington, DC: Headquarters, Department of the Army, 1986.

—**PROTECTED PERSONNEL** are civilian and military persons entitled to the benefits under any convention or treaty relating to the conduct of hostilities to which the opposing belligerents are parties. All protected persons who were described in the Geneva Convention of 1949 are included within this term.

References

Department of Defense, U.S. Army. *Dictionary of United States Army Terms.* Army Regulation AR 310-25. Washington, DC: Headquarters, Department of the Army, 1986.

—PROTECTED WIRELINE DISTRIBUTION SYSTEM, or an approved circuit, is a communications system to which electromagnetic and physical safeguards have been applied to permit secure electrical transmission of unencrypted classified information. The associated facilities include all equipment and wirelines so safeguarded. The major components are wirelines, subscriber sets, and terminal equipment.

References
Department of Defense, U.S. Army. *Dictionary of United States Army Terms.* Army Regulation AR 310-25. Washington, DC: Headquarters, Department of the Army, 1986.

—PROTECTING POWER is a neutral nation entrusted by a belligerent with the protection of the interests of the belligerent and its nationals in the territory of, or in territory occupied by, the enemy.

References
Department of Defense, U.S. Army. *Health Service Support in a Communications Zone (Test).* Field Manual FM 8-21. Washington, DC: Headquarters, Department of the Army, 1981.

—PROTECTION COMPLETE PENETRATION is penetration in which a fragment or fragments of either the impacting projectile or the plate are thrown to the rear of the plate with sufficient energy to perforate a .2-inch aluminum alloy, 24ST sheet, or its equivalent, when placed so as to receive those fragments passing from the rear of the plate. When it is possible to observe that these conditions are being met without the use of a sheet, as in heavier plate testing, the sheet is omitted.

References
Department of Defense, U.S. Army. *Dictionary of United States Army Terms.* Army Regulation AR 310-25. Washington, DC: Headquarters, Department of the Army, 1986.

—PROTECTION ELEMENT is a target intelligence term that pertains to the target that is to be destroyed. Protection elements are passive or active measures that are usually layered. Such elements have at least some measures that provide protection to all elements of a target. For example an antiair missile site would be a protection element for a radar site. *See also:* Target Intelligence, Targeting.

References
Department of Defense, U.S. Army. *Operations.* Field Manual FM 100-5. Washington, DC: Headquarters, Department of the Army, 1986.

—PROTECTION PARTIAL PENETRATION is penetration that approaches but does not fulfill the requirements for protection complete penetration. *See also:* Protection Complete Penetration.

References
Department of Defense, U.S. Army. *Dictionary of United States Army Terms.* Army Regulation AR 310-25. Washington, DC: Headquarters, Department of the Army, 1986.

—PROTECTIVE CLOTHING is clothing that is especially designed, fabricated, or treated to protect personnel against the hazards caused by extreme changes in the physical environment, dangerous working conditions, or enemy action.

References
Department of Defense, Joint Chiefs of Staff. *Department of Defense Dictionary of Military and Related Terms.* Washington, DC: GPO, 1986.

—PROTECTIVE COVER is an item or object that may be placed between an individual and a toxic chemical or biological agent spray source to prevent the agent from contacting the individual. *See also:* Biological Warfare, Chemical Warfare.

References
Department of Defense, U.S. Army. *Dictionary of United States Army Terms.* Army Regulation AR 310-25. Washington, DC: Headquarters, Department of the Army, 1986.

—PROTECTIVE FIRE is fire delivered by supporting guns and is directed against the enemy to hinder its fire or movement against friendly forces.

References
Department of Defense, U.S. Army. *Dictionary of United States Army Terms.* Army Regulation AR 310-25. Washington, DC: Headquarters, Department of the Army, 1986.

—PROTECTIVE MASK, formerly called a gas mask, is an item of individual protective equipment that consists of a facepiece with integral filter elements or an attached canister and carrier. The mask protects the wearer from inhaling toxic chemical agents, screening smokes, biological agents, and radioactive dust particles. *See also:* Biological Warfare, Chemical Warfare, Nuclear Warfare.

References
Department of Defense, U.S. Army. *Dictionary of United States Army Terms.* Army Regulation AR 310-25. Washington, DC: Headquarters, Department of the Army, 1986.

—**PROTECTIVE MINEFIELDS** aid units in local, close-in protection. There are two types of protective minefields: hasty and deliberate. *See also:* Mine Warfare.

References
Department of Defense, U.S. Army. *Countermobility.* Field Manual FM 5-102. Washington, DC: Headquarters, Department of the Army, 1985.

—**PROTECTIVE POSITION** protects the personnel and/or material not directly involved with fighting the enemy from attack or environmental extremes. *See also:* Protective Positions.

References
Department of Defense, U.S. Army. *Survivability.* Field Manual FM 5-103. Washington, DC: Headquarters, Department of the Army, 1985.

—**PROTECTIVE POSITIONS.** Vehicle protective positions are constructed for vehicles and weapons systems that do not provide direct fire against the enemy. The positions are neither hasty nor deliberate because they all require extensive engineer assets and construction materials to build. Unless separate overhead cover is constructed, the positions do not provide blast protection from indirect fire superquick, contact, or delay fuze shells. The positions do, however, provide medium artillery shell fragmentation protection from near-miss bursts greater than five feet from the position, and from direct fire high explosive antitank projectiles of 120 millimeters or less that are fired at the base of the position's eight-foot-thick parapet.

References
Department of Defense, U.S. Army. *Survivability.* Field Manual FM 5-103. Washington, DC: Headquarters, Department of the Army, 1985.

—**PROTECTIVE SECURITY** is a term used in counterespionage, counterintelligence, and counterinsurgency to describe an organized system of defensive measures that are instituted

and maintained at all levels of command to maintain the safety of people or objects. *See also:* Physical Security; Security.

References
Department of Defense, Joint Chiefs of Staff. *Department of Defense Dictionary of Military and Related Terms.* Washington, DC: GPO, 1986.

—**PROTECTIVE WALLS** are constructed to satisfy weather, topographical, tactical, and other military requirements. The walls range from simple ones, constructed with hand tools, to more difficult walls requiring specialized engineering and equipment capabilities.

Protection provided by the walls is restricted to stopping fragment and blast effects from near-miss explosions of mortar, rocket, or artillery shells; some direct fire protection is also provided. Overhead cover is not practical due to the size of the position surrounded by the walls.

References
Department of Defense, U.S. Army. *Survivability.* Field Manual FM 5-103. Washington, DC: Headquarters, Department of the Army, 1985.

—**PROTOTYPE** is a model used to evaluate design, performance, and production potential of equipment or other items being considered for possible manufacture.

References
Department of Defense, Joint Chiefs of Staff. *Department of Defense Dictionary of Military and Related Terms.* Washington, DC: GPO, 1986.

—**PROTOTYPE MISSILE** is a preliminary or early missile that is essentially the same design as the production missile. Prototype missiles are normally manufactured in small quantities to prove the production design and to establish production methods.

References
Department of Defense, U.S. Army. *Dictionary of United States Army Terms.* Army Regulation AR 310-25. Washington, DC: Headquarters, Department of the Army, 1986.

—**PROVISIONAL UNIT** is an assemblage of personnel and equipment that are temporarily organized in order to accomplish a specific mission.

References
Department of Defense, Joint Chiefs of Staff. *Department of Defense Dictionary of Military and Related Terms.* Washington, DC: GPO, 1986.

—**PROVOST COURT** is a military tribunal of limited jurisdiction that is convened in occupied territory that is under a military government. The provost court is usually composed of one officer. *See also:* Disciplinary Action.

References
Department of Defense, U.S. Army. *Dictionary of United States Army Terms.* Army Regulation AR 310-25. Washington, DC: Headquarters, Department of the Army, 1986.

—**PROVOST MARSHAL (PM) is** a staff officer who supervises all the activities of the military police of a command below the Headquarters, Department of the Army, and who advises the commander on military police matters, prisoners of war, military prisoners, and on other matters of concern to the commander and the provost marshal. *See also:* Military Police.

References
Department of Defense, U.S. Army. *Dictionary of United States Army Terms.* Army Regulation AR 310-25. Washington, DC: Headquarters, Department of the Army, 1986.

—**PROWORD.** *See:* Procedure Word.

—**PROXIMITY FUZE** is a fuze wherein primary initiation occurs by remotely sensing the presence, distance, and/or direction of a target or its associated environment by means of a signal that is generated by the fuze or emitted by the target, or by detecting a disturbance of a natural field surrounding the target. *See also:* Fuze (Specify Type).

References
Department of Defense, Joint Chiefs of Staff. *Department of Defense Dictionary of Military and Related Terms.* Washington, DC: GPO, 1986.

—**PROXY WAR** is a form of limited war in which great powers avoid a direct military confrontation by furthering their national security interests and objectives through conflict in which associates, not principles, participate. *See also:* Limited War.

References
Collins, John M. *U.S.-Soviet Military Balance, 1980-1985.* Washington, DC: Congressional Research Service, 1985.

—**PSYCHOLOGICAL ACTION** is using psychological media and supporting activities in peace and war to reduce the enemy's actual or potential prestige, while increasing friendly influence and feelings, in potentially hostile or neutral nations. *See also:* Psychological Warfare.

References
Department of Defense, U.S. Army. *Psychological Operations.* Field Manual FM 33-1. Washington, DC: Headquarters, Department of the Army, 1979.

—**PSYCHOLOGICAL CONSOLIDATION** involves actions intended to establish and maintain order and security in a combat zone and rear areas of friendly forces and to gain the support of the local population in a territory occupied by friendly forces. *See also:* Psychological Operations.

References
Department of Defense, Joint Chiefs of Staff. *Department of Defense Dictionary of Military and Related Terms.* Washington, DC: GPO, 1986.

—**PSYCHOLOGICAL CONSOLIDATION ACTIVITIES** are activities in peace and war that are designed to encourage the population that is located in areas under friendly control to support the military objectives and the operational freedom of the supported commanders. *See also:* Psychological Operations.

References
Department of Defense, U.S. Army. *Psychological Operations.* Field Manual FM 33-1. Washington, DC: Headquarters, Department of the Army, 1979.

—**PSYCHOLOGICAL MEDIA** are the technical and nontechnical media that establish any kind of communication with a target audience. *See also:* Psychological Operations.

References
Department of Defense, Joint Chiefs of Staff. *Department of Defense Dictionary of Military and Related Terms.* Washington, DC: GPO, 1986.

—**PSYCHOLOGICAL OBJECTIVE** is a statement of the measurable response that is expected from a target audience as a result of a psychological operation. The objective must accurately define the specific behavioral response or attitude change that is required. This, in turn, must support the psychological operation's goals. *See also:* Psychological Operations.

References
Department of Defense, U.S. Army. *Psychological Operations.* Field Manual FM 33-1. Washington, DC: Headquarters, Department of the Army, 1979.

—**PSYCHOLOGICAL OPERATIONS (PSYOPs)** are planned peacetime or wartime psychological activities directed toward influencing the behavior and attitudes of enemy, friendly, or neutral audiences in order to facilitate achieving one's political or military objectives. PSYSOPs include psychological action, psychological warfare, and psychological consolidation and encompass political, military, economic, ideological, and information activities designed to achieve a certain psychological effect. *See also:* Psychological Action, Psychological Consolidation, Psychological Consolidation Activities, Psychological Media, Psychological Objective, Psychological Operations Approach, Psychological Operations Campaign, Psychological Operations Estimate, Psychological Situation, Psychological Theme, Psychological Warfare, Psychological Warfare Consolidation.

References
Department of Defense, U.S. Army. *Psychological Operations*. Field Manual FM 33-1. Washington, DC: Headquarters, Department of the Army, 1979.

—**PSYCHOLOGICAL OPERATIONS (PSYOPs) APPROACH** is a technique used to induce a desired reaction on the part of the target audience. *See also:* Psychological Operations.

References
Department of Defense, U.S. Army. *Psychological Operations*. Field Manual FM 33-1. Washington, DC: Headquarters, Department of the Army, 1979.

—**PSYCHOLOGICAL OPERATIONS (PSYOPs) CAMPAIGN** is a series of planned propaganda and psychological actions that are undertaken to achieve a psychological objective or objectives. *See also:* Psychological Operations.

References
Department of Defense, U.S. Army. *Psychological Operations*. Field Manual FM 33-1. Washington, DC: Headquarters, Department of the Army, 1979.

—**PSYCHOLOGICAL OPERATIONS (PSYOPS) ESTIMATE** is an analysis of the current situation from a psychological perspective. It considers all of a commander's feasible courses of action, analyzes and compares them, and makes recommendations of key PSYOP factors that affect the accomplishment of the overall mission. *See also:* Psychological Operations.

References
Department of Defense, U.S. Army. *Psychological Operations*. Field Manual FM 33-1. Washington, DC: Headquarters, Department of the Army, 1979.

—**PSYCHOLOGICAL SITUATION** is the current emotional and mental state, or other behavioral motivation of a target audience. It is founded primarily on national, political, social, economic, and psychological peculiarities, but is subject to the influence of circumstances or events. *See also:* Psychological Operations.

References
Department of Defense, U.S. Army. *Psychological Operations*. Field Manual FM 33-1. Washington, DC: Headquarters, Department of the Army, 1979.

—**PSYCHOLOGICAL THEME** is an idea or topic upon which a psychological operation is based. *See also:* Psychological Operations.

References
Department of Defense, U.S. Army. *Psychological Operations*. Field Manual FM 33-1. Washington, DC: Headquarters, Department of the Army, 1979.

—**PSYCHOLOGICAL WARFARE.** (1) The official Army definition of psychological warfare is the use of the communications media and other psychological means, in a declared emergency or war, to bring psychological pressure to bear on the enemy and to favorably influence the attitudes of hostile groups and other target audiences in areas that are under enemy control. The primary goals are to weaken the enemy's will to engage in or to continue hostilities and to reduce his capacity for waging war. (2) Psychological warfare, as defined by the Church Committee, is the planned use of propaganda and other psychological actions to influence opinions, emotions, attitudes, and behavior of hostile foreign groups so as to support the achievement of national policy objectives. *See also:* Psychological Operations, Psychological Warfare Consolidation.

References
Department of Defense, U.S. Army. *Psychological Operations*. Field Manual FM 33-1. Washington, DC: Headquarters, Department of the Army, 1979.

U.S. Congress. Senate. *Final Report of the Senate Select Committee to Study Government Operations With Respect to Intelligence Activities. Report 94-755. Book I, Foreign and Military Intelligence* (Church Committee Report). Washington, DC: GPO, 1976.

—**PSYCHOLOGICAL WARFARE CONSOLIDA-TION** is psychological warfare that is directed toward people in friendly rear areas or in territory that is occupied by friendly military forces with the goal of facilitating military operations and promoting maximum cooperation among the civilian population. *See also:* Psychological Operations, Psychological Warfare.

References
Department of Defense, U.S. Army. *Psychological Operations.* Field Manual FM 33-1. Washington, DC: Headquarters, Department of the Army, 1979.

—**PUBLIC ACCESS EXCLUSION DISTANCE** is a calculated arc beyond which the presence of a chemical agent source is no more than 10.0, 4.3, and 150 milligrams per minute per cubic meter for GB, VX, and mustard chemical agents, respectively. *See also:* Chemical Warfare.

References
Department of Defense, U.S. Army. *Ammunition and Explosives Safety Standards.* Army Regulation AR 385-64. Washington, DC: Headquarters, Department of the Army, 1987.

—**PUBLIC AFFAIRS** are those public information and community relations activities directed toward the general public by the various elements of the Department of Defense. *See also:* Public Affairs Activities, Public Affairs Officer, Public Information, Public Information Activities, Public Information Agency.

References
Department of Defense, Joint Chiefs of Staff. *Department of Defense Dictionary of Military and Related Terms.* Washington, DC: GPO, 1986.

—**PUBLIC AFFAIRS ACTIVITIES** are all media relations activities designed to obtain the optimum national defense through internal and external support for the Army's role in a sound national military program. *See also:* Public Affairs.

References
Department of Defense, U.S. Army. *Dictionary of United States Army Terms.* Army Regulation AR 310-25. Washington, DC: Headquarters, Department of the Army, 1986.

—**PUBLIC AFFAIRS OFFICER (PAO)** is the staff officer who is responsible for the overall conduct of public affairs activities of a command, including public information, command information, and community relations. *See also:* Public Affairs.

References
Department of Defense, U.S. Army. *Dictionary of United States Army Terms.* Army Regulation AR 310-25. Washington, DC: Headquarters, Department of the Army, 1986.

—**PUBLIC INFORMATION.** (1) In general, public information is military-related information disseminated through public news media consistent with security constraints. Release of public information is considered desirable or nonobjectionable to the responsible releasing agency. (2) Public information is Army-related information released and disseminated to provide the people of the United States with facts about Army activities, missions, and objectives to further their understanding of Army activities. *See also:* Public Affairs.

References
Department of Defense, Joint Chiefs of Staff. *Department of Defense Dictionary of Military and Related Terms.* Washington, DC: GPO, 1986.

Department of Defense, U.S. Army. *Dictionary of United States Army Terms.* Army Regulation AR 310-25. Washington, DC: Headquarters, Department of the Army, 1986.

—**PUBLIC INFORMATION ACTIVITIES** are activities that: (1) prepare material for newspapers, periodicals, and other nonfederal publications; (2) distribute press releases and interview representatives of the press; (3) prepare materials (for broadcasting) and contracts (with broadcasting media); (4) prepare advertisements (i.e., paid or free) except those for acquiring or disposing of government property; (5) prepare, install, and circulate exhibits; (6) produce motion pictures and film strips, except for those used internally by the government; and (7) prepare publications that are neither legally required or required for the government's internal use. *See also:* Public Affairs.

References
Department of Defense, U.S. Army. *Dictionary of United States Army Terms.* Army Regulation AR 310-25. Washington, DC: Headquarters, Department of the Army, 1986.

—**PUBLIC INFORMATION AGENCY** is a press association, news, or pictorial feature service, newspaper, periodical, radio, or television broadcasting organization, or newsreel company that regularly collects and disseminates news to the public. *See also:* Public Affairs.

References

Department of Defense, Joint Chiefs of Staff. *Department of Defense Dictionary of Military and Related Terms.* Washington, DC: GPO, 1986.

Department of Defense, U.S. Army. *Dictionary of United States Army Terms.* Army Regulation AR 310-25. Washington, DC: Headquarters, Department of the Army, 1986.

—**PULL FIRING DEVICE** is a firing device designed to actuate when a given tensile effort is applied by a target.

References

Department of Defense, U.S. Army. *Mine/ Countermine Operations at the Company Level.* Field Manual FM 20-32. Washington, DC: Headquarters, Department of the Army, 1976.

—**PULL SUPPLY SYSTEM** is a system for disbursing supplies based upon requisitioning as needs are recognized.

References

Department of Defense, U.S. Army. *Support Operations: Echelons Above Corps.* Field Manual FM 100-16. Washington, DC: Headquarters, Department of the Army, 1986.

—**PULL-UP** (ARMY AVIATION) is a maneuver in which airspeed is traded for altitude (i.e., cyclic climb). *See also:* Pull-Up Point.

References

Department of Defense, U.S. Army. *Air-to-Air Combat.* Field Manual FM 1-107. Washington, DC: Headquarters, Department of the Army, 1984.

—**PULL-UP POINT** is the point at which an aircraft must start to increase altitude from a low-level approach in order to gain sufficient height from which to attack or to retire.

References

Department of Defense, U.S. Army. *Air Defense Artillery Deployment: Chaparral/Vulcan/Stinger.* Field Manual FM 44- 3. Washington, DC: Headquarters, Department of the Army, 1984.

—**PUNISHMENT BOOK** is a record kept by a company or similar unit commander, in which an account is recorded of minor offenses committed by soldiers and the punishment awarded in each case in accordance with Article 15, Non-Judicial Punishment, of the Uniform Code of Military Justice. *See also:* Disciplinary Action.

References

Department of Defense, U.S. Army. *Dictionary of United States Army Terms.* Army Regulation AR 310-25. Washington, DC: Headquarters, Department of the Army, 1986.

—**PUNITIVE ARTICLES** are the articles of the Uniform Code of Military Justice in which military crimes and offenses are enumerated. *See also:* Disciplinary Action.

References

Department of Defense, U.S. Army. *Dictionary of United States Army Terms.* Army Regulation AR 310-25. Washington, DC: Headquarters, Department of the Army, 1986.

—**PURCHASE CONTROL** is a term applied to a document (form) that directs the purchase of common items for services, agencies, and purposes other than Army technical supply.

References

Department of Defense, U.S. Army. *Dictionary of United States Army Terms.* Army Regulation AR 310-25. Washington, DC: Headquarters, Department of the Army, 1986.

—**PURCHASE PRICE VARIANCE** is an account maintained to accumulate the net difference between the actual cost and the standard price of purchased stock.

References

Department of Defense, U.S. Army. *Dictionary of United States Army Terms.* Army Regulation AR 310-25. Washington, DC: Headquarters, Department of the Army, 1986.

—**PURCHASE REQUEST** is a document for permission to obtain supplies prepared by an inventory control point, depot, or separate office, and forwarded to a procurement office.

References

Department of Defense, U.S. Army. *Dictionary of United States Army Terms.* Army Regulation AR 310-25. Washington, DC: Headquarters, Department of the Army, 1986.

—**PURCHASE RESPONSIBILITY** is that function of procurement that consists of contracting for (and may include final acceptance of) a given item or class of items, or manufacturing items in government-owned establishments.

References
Department of Defense, U.S. Army. *Dictionary of United States Army Terms.* Army Regulation AR 310-25. Washington, DC: Headquarters, Department of the Army, 1986.

—**PURE** is a company team that has only tank or mechanized infantry platoons assigned to it or a battalion task force that has only tank or mechanized infantry companies assigned to it.

References
Department of Defense, U.S. Army. *The Tank and Mechanized Infantry Battalion Task Force.* Field Manual FM 71-2. Washington, DC: Headquarters, Department of the Army, 1977.

—**PURGE** is an act or process of removing unwanted substances (e.g., contaminated air).

References
Department of Defense, U.S. Army. *NBC Protection.* Field Manual FM 3-4. Washington, DC: Headquarters, Department of the Army, 1985.

—**PURPLE HEART** is a decoration denoting the award of a citation certificate or wound chevron for wounds received in action against an enemy or as a direct result of an act of the enemy. *See also:* Valor.

References
Department of Defense, U.S. Army. *Dictionary of United States Army Terms.* Army Regulation AR 310-25. Washington, DC: Headquarters, Department of the Army, 1986.

—**PURSUIT** is an offensive operation against a retreating enemy force. It follows a successful attack or exploitation and is ordered when the enemy cannot conduct an organized defense and attempts to disengage. The objective is to maintain relentless pressure on the enemy and to completely destroy it. In pursuit, the attacker focuses on the major enemy force. Terrain objectives may be assigned to orient pursuing forces and are usually very deep into enemy-held territory. Pursuit operations require (1) a direct pressure force to deny enemy units a chance to rest, regroup, or resupply by keeping them in flight; and (2) an encircling force to envelop the fleeing force, cut its escape route, and in conjunction with the direct pressure force, attack to destroy the enemy force.

References
Department of Defense, U.S. Army. *The Tank and Mechanized Infantry Battalion Task Force.* Field Manual FM 71-2. Washington, DC: Headquarters, Department of the Army, 1977.

—**PUSH SUPPLY SYSTEM** is a process of shipping items without waiting for requisitions from the combat forces.

References
Department of Defense, U.S. Army. *Support Operations: Echelons Above Corps.* Field Manual FM 100-16. Washington, DC: Headquarters, Department of the Army, 1986.

—**PYROTECHNIC** is a mixture of chemicals that, when ignited, is capable of reacting exothermically to produce light, heat, smoke, sound, or gas. It may also be used to delay an explosive train because of its known burning time. Pyrotechnics are used for signalling or for lighting up an area at night. The term excludes propellants and explosives. *See also:* Pyrotechnic Delay.

References
Department of Defense, Joint Chiefs of Staff. *Department of Defense Dictionary of Military and Related Terms.* Washington, DC: GPO, 1986.

Department of Defense, U.S. Army. *Dictionary of United States Army Terms.* Army Regulation AR 310-25. Washington, DC: Headquarters, Department of the Army, 1986.

—**PYROTECHNIC DELAY** is a pyrotechnic device added to a firing system to transmit the ignition flame after a predetermined delay. *See also:* Pyrotechnic.

References
Department of Defense, Joint Chiefs of Staff. *Department of Defense Dictionary of Military and Related Terms.* Washington, DC: GPO, 1986.

—**PYROTECHNICS** are munitions containing chemicals that make a smoke or brilliant light while burning. They are used to signal or light up an area at night and are available in several types and colors. Pyrotechnic signals are prescribed in Army instructions. These signals are generally used for friendly units' identification, fire support control, target or position marking, and for ground-to-air communication. Their advantage is the speed with which information can be transmitted to large numbers of troops and isolated units.

References
Department of Defense, U.S. Army. *The Rifle Squads (Mechanized and Light Infantry).* Training Circular TC 7-1. Washington, DC: Headquarters, Department of the Army, 1976.

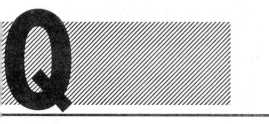

—**Q-D** is the quantity of explosives material and distance separation relationships that provide defined types of protection. These relationships are based upon levels of risk considered acceptable for the stipulated exposures and are tabulated in the appropriate Q-D tables. Separation distances are not absolute safe distances but are relative protective or safe distances. Greater distances than those shown in the tables are used whenever possible.

References
Department of Defense, U.S. Army. *Ammunition and Explosives Safety Standards*. Army Regulation AR 385-64. Washington, DC: Headquarters, Department of the Army, 1987.

—**QUADRANT ELEVATION** is the angle between the level base of the trajectory/horizontal and the axis of the weapon's bore when laid. It is the algebraic sum of the elevation, angle of site, and complementary angle of site.

References
Department of Defense, Joint Chiefs of Staff. *Department of Defense Dictionary of Military and Related Terms*. Washington, DC: GPO, 1986.

—**QUADRIPARTITE STANDARDIZATION AGREEMENT** is an agreement between the United States, the United Kingdom, Canada, and Australia. The equipment and procedures agreed upon often are marked with the prefix ABCA. The purpose is to standardize the equipping and operations of the four member nations to ensure interchangeability of equipment and operations regardless of the composition of the units or who is in command.

References
Department of Defense, U.S. Army. *NBC Operations*. Field Manual FM 3-100. Washington, DC: Headquarters, Department of the Army, 1985.

—**QUANTITY PER ACTION** is the quantity of a specific repair part expected to be used when maintenance is performed.

References
Department of Defense, U.S. Army. *Maintenance and Repair Parts Consumption Planning Guide for Contingency Operations*. Field Manual FM 42-9-23. Washington, DC: Headquarters, Department of the Army, 1980.

—**QUARTERING PARTY,** or advance party, is a group of unit representatives sent to a probable new site of operations to secure, reconnoiter, and organize the area before the unit's main body arrives. *See also:* Advance Party.

References
Department of Defense, U.S. Army. *Operational Terms and Symbols*. Field Manual FM 101-5-1. Washington, DC: Headquarters, Department of the Army, 1985.

—**QUARTERING WIND** is a wind that blows between tail and flank winds, toward the smoke objective. *See also:* Smoke Screen.

References
Department of Defense, U.S. Army. *Deliberate Smoke Operations*. Field Manual FM 3-50. Washington, DC: Headquarters, Department of the Army, 1984.

—**QUICK (HASTY) FIRING PLAN,** in fire support operations, is a fire plan prepared quickly at a lower echelon to support a tactical operation. It contains the necessary elements of a fire plan. *See also:* Fire Plan.

References
Department of Defense, U.S. Army. *Fire Support in Combined Arms Operations*. Field Manual FM 6-20. Washington, DC: Headquarters, Department of the Army, 1983.

—**QUICK FIX** is a tactical, heliborne jamming system configured in the EH-1H, EH-1X, and EH-60A helicopters. Each aircraft has the capability to intercept and jam radio communications, and the EH-1X and EH-60 versions can also locate (direction finding) communications transmitters. Quick Fix aircraft are organic to the division, brigade, and armored cavalry regiments.

References
Department of Defense, U.S. Army. *Military Intelligence Battalion Combat Electronic Warfare and Intelligence (Aerial Exploitation) (Corps)*. Field Manual FM 34-22. Washington, DC: Headquarters, Department of the Army, 1984.

—**QUICKLOOK** is an Army tactical intelligence airborne electronic intelligence collection and emitter location system. Mounted in the RV-1D Mohawk aircraft, Quicklook provides classification and location of electronic emitters to a ground-based data collection and emitter location facility via a digital downlink. Like Guardrail, Quicklook missions are flown in a stand-off mode. *See also:* Reconnaissance.

References

Department of Defense, U.S. Army. *Military Intelligence Battalion Combat Electronic Warfare and Intelligence (Aerial Exploitation) (Corps).* Field Manual FM 34-22. Washington, DC: Headquarters, Department of the Army, 1984.

—**QUICK SUPPLY STORE (QSS)** is a facility set up at the division level for over-the-counter issue of selected repair parts.

References

Department of Defense, U.S. Army. *Organizational Maintenance Operations.* Field Manual FM 29-2. Washington, DC: Headquarters, Department of the Army, 1984.

—**RACER** is a turntable that permits a heavy gun to be turned to the left or right.

References
Department of Defense, U.S. Army. *Dictionary of United States Army Terms*. Army Regulation AR 310-25. Washington, DC: Headquarters, Department of the Army, 1986.

—**RADAR (RADAR DETECTION AND RANGE)** is a term used in signals intelligence and signals analysis. Radar is an acronym for radio detection and ranging. It is a method, system, or a technique for using beamed, reflected, and timed electromagnetic radiation to detect, locate, or track objects, or to measure altitude. *See also:* Radar Coverage, Radar Discrimination, Radar Echo, Radar Exploitation Report, Radar Fire, Radar Horizon, Radar Intelligence, Radar Locating, Radar Netting, Radar Netting Station, Radar Netting Unit, Radar Range Calibration, Radar Ranging, Radar Reconnaissance, Radar Scan, Radar Silence, Radar Tracking Station.

References
Reeves, Robert; Anson, Abraham; and Landen, David. *Manual of Remote Sensing*. Falls Church, VA: American Society of Photogrammetry, 1975.

—**RADAR ABSORBENT MATERIAL,** in signals intelligence and signals analysis, is material used as a radar camouflage device to reduce the radar cross section or echo area of an object. *See also:* Radar.

References
Department of Defense, U.S. Army. *Dictionary of United States Army Terms*. Army Regulation AR 310-25. Washington, DC: Headquarters, Department of the Army, 1986.

—**RADAR COVERAGE** is the limits within which objects can be detected by one or more radar stations. *See also:* Radar.

References
Department of Defense, Joint Chiefs of Staff. *Department of Defense Dictionary of Military and Related Terms*. Washington, DC: GPO, 1986.

—**RADAR DISCRIMINATION** is the ability to distinguish separately on a radar scope objects that are close to each other. *See also:* Radar.

References
Department of Defense, U.S. Army. *Dictionary of United States Army Terms*. Army Regulation AR 310-25. Washington, DC: Headquarters, Department of the Army, 1986.

—**RADAR ECHO.** (1) A radar echo is the electromagnetic energy that is received after it is reflected off of an object. (2) A radar echo is the deflection or change of intensity on a cathode ray tube display that is produced by a radar echo. *See also:* Radar.

References
Department of Defense, Joint Chiefs of Staff. *Department of Defense Dictionary of Military and Related Terms*. Washington, DC: GPO, 1986.

—**RADAR EXPLOITATION REPORT (RADAR-EXREP),** in intelligence imagery and photoreconnaissance, is a report used to disseminate the results that have been obtained from the rapid analysis of radar imagery and from the debriefing of the air crew that flew the radar imagery mission. The report discusses the targets cited in the mission tasking, addressing each separately. *See also:* Radar.

References
Department of Defense. U.S. Army. *Intelligence Imagery*. Army Field Manual FM 34-55. Washington, DC: Headquarters, Department of the Army, 1985.

—**RADAR FIRE** is gunfire aimed at a target that is being tracked by radar. *See also:* Radar.

References
Department of Defense, Joint Chiefs of Staff. *Department of Defense Dictionary of Military and Related Terms*. Washington, DC: GPO, 1986.

—**RADAR HORIZON** is the locus of points at which the rays from a radar antenna become tangential to the earth's surface. On land, this locus varies according to the topographical features of the terrain. *See also:* Radar.

References
Department of Defense, Joint Chiefs of Staff. *Department of Defense Dictionary of Military and Related Terms*. Washington, DC: GPO, 1986.

—**RADAR IMAGERY** is imagery produced by recording radar waves that are reflected from a given target surface. *See also:* Radar.

References
Department of Defense, Joint Chiefs of Staff. *Department of Defense Dictionary of Military and Related Terms.* Washington, DC: GPO, 1986.

—**RADAR INTELLIGENCE (RADINT),** in intelligence imagery and photoreconnaissance, is intelligence information derived from information collected by radar. The vulnerability of platforms operating radars is generally offset by the penetrating capability, resolution, and geometric fidelity of radar over extreme distances. Because microwaves can penetrate virtually all atmospheric conditions, airborne radars are limited only by the ability of their platforms to operate in adverse weather conditions. *See also:* Radar.

References
Department of Defense, Defense Intelligence College. *Glossary of Intelligence Terms and Definitions.* Washington, DC: DIC, 1987.

Department of Defense, U.S. Army. *Counterintelligence.* Field Manual FM 34-60. Washington, DC: Headquarters, Department of the Army, 1985.

———. *Intelligence Imagery.* Army Field Manual FM 34-55. Washington, DC: Headquarters, Department of the Army, 1985.

—**RADAR LOCATING** is using radar to find the position of the burst of a projectile or of an enemy gun. *See also:* Radar.

References
Department of Defense, U.S. Army. *Dictionary of United States Army Terms.* Army Regulation AR 310-25. Washington, DC: Headquarters, Department of the Army, 1986.

—**RADAR NETTING** is the linking of several radars to a single center to provide integrated target information. *See also:* Radar.

References
Department of Defense, Joint Chiefs of Staff. *Department of Defense Dictionary of Military and Related Terms.* Washington, DC: GPO, 1986.

—**RADAR NETTING STATION** is a center that can receive data from radar tracking stations and exchange these data with other radar tracking stations, thus forming a radar netting system. *See also:* Radar, Radar Netting Unit, Radar Tracking Station.

References
Department of Defense, Joint Chiefs of Staff. *Department of Defense Dictionary of Military and Related Terms.* Washington, DC: GPO, 1986.

—**RADAR NETTING UNIT** is optional electronic equipment that converts the operations central of certain air defense fire distribution systems into a radar netting station. *See also:* Radar, Radar Netting Station.

References
Department of Defense, Joint Chiefs of Staff. *Department of Defense Dictionary of Military and Related Terms.* Washington, DC: GPO, 1986.

—**RADAR RANGE CALIBRATION** is the adjustment of a radar set so that when "on target," the radar set will indicate the correct range. *See also:* Radar.

References
Department of Defense, U.S. Army. *Dictionary of United States Army Terms.* Army Regulation AR 310-25. Washington, DC: Headquarters, Department of the Army, 1986.

—**RADAR RANGING** is the use of a radar transmission to determine the range to a target. *See also:* Radar.

References
Department of Defense, U.S. Army. *Dictionary of United States Army Terms.* Army Regulation AR 310-25. Washington, DC: Headquarters, Department of the Army, 1986.

—**RADAR RECONNAISSANCE,** an intelligence imagery and photoreconnaissance, is reconnaissance using radar to collect information on enemy activity and to determine the nature of the terrain. *See also:* Radar, Triangulation.

References
Department of Defense, Joint Chiefs of Staff. *Department of Defense Dictionary of Military and Related Terms.* Washington, DC: GPO, 1986.

—**RADAR SCAN** denotes the motion of a radio frequency beam through space as it searches for an echo. *See also:* Radar.

References
Department of Defense, U.S. Army. *Dictionary of United States Army Terms.* Army Regulation AR 310-25. Washington, DC: Headquarters, Department of the Army, 1986.

—**RADAR SILENCE** is an imposed discipline prohibiting the transmission by radar of electromagnetic signals on some or all frequencies. *See also:* Radar.

References

Department of Defense, Joint Chiefs of Staff. *Department of Defense Dictionary of Military and Related Terms.* Washington, DC: GPO, 1986.

—**RADAR TRACKING STATION** is a radar facility that has the capability of tracking moving targets. *See also:* Radar.

References

Department of Defense, Joint Chiefs of Staff. *Department of Defense Dictionary of Military and Related Terms.* Washington, DC: GPO, 1986.

—**RADIAC,** an acronym derived from the words "Radioactivity detection indication and computation," is an all-encompassing term to designate various types of radiological measuring instruments. *See also:* Nuclear Warfare, Radiac Dosimeter, Radiacmeters.

References

Department of Defense, Joint Chiefs of Staff. *Department of Defense Dictionary of Military and Related Terms.* Washington, DC: GPO, 1986.

—**RADIAC DOSIMETER** is an instrument used to measure the ionizing radiation absorbed by that instrument. *See also:* Radiac.

References

Department of Defense, U.S. Army. *NBC Operations.* Field Manual FM 3-100. Washington, DC: Headquarters, Department of the Army, 1985.

—**RADIACMETERS** are portable, battery-operated radiation detectors and indicators that are used to detect and measure beta and gamma radiations. *See also:* Radiac.

References

Department of Defense, U.S. Army. *NBC Operations.* Field Manual FM 3-100. Washington, DC: Headquarters, Department of the Army, 1985.

—**RADIATION DOSE** is the total amount of ionizing radiation, expressed in centigrays, that is absorbed by material or tissues. The term is often used in the sense of the exposure dose expressed in roentgens (i.e., a measure of the total amount of ionization that the quantity of radiation could produce in air). This could be distinguished from the absorbed dose, also given in rads, that represents the energy absorbed from the radiation per gram of specified body tissue. Further, the biological dose, in rems, is a measure of the biological effectiveness of the radiation exposure. *See also:* Radiation Dose Rate, Radiation Status.

References

Department of Defense, U.S. Army. *Operational Terms and Symbols.* Field Manual FM 101-5-1. Washington, DC: Headquarters, Department of the Army, 1985.

—**RADIATION DOSE RATE** is the radiation dose (dosage) absorbed per unit of time. A radiation dose rate can be set at some particular unit of time. For example, H+1 hour would be called the H+1 dose rate. *See also:* Radiation Dose.

References

Department of Defense, Joint Chiefs of Staff. *Department of Defense Dictionary of Military and Related Terms.* Washington, DC: GPO, 1986.

—**RADIATION EXPOSURE STATE** is the condition of a unit or an individual that is deduced from the cumulative whole body radiation dose(s) received. It is expressed as a symbol that indicates the potential for future operations and the degree of risk if exposed to additional nuclear radiation. *See also:* Radiation Dose.

References

Department of Defense, Joint Chiefs of Staff. *Department of Defense Dictionary of Military and Related Terms.* Washington, DC: GPO, 1986.

—**RADIATION INTELLIGENCE (RINT)** is a measurement and signature intelligence subdiscipline that concerns the functions and characteristics derived from information obtained from unintentional electromagnetic energy emanating from foreign sources. It does not include such energy emanating from nuclear detonations or radioactive sources. *See also:* Intelligence.

References

Department of Defense, U.S. Army. *Counterintelligence.* Field Manual FM 34-60. Washington, DC: Headquarters, Department of the Army, 1985.

—**RADIATION INTENSITY** is the radiation dose rate at a given time and place. It may be used, coupled with a figure, to denote the radiation intensity present at a given number of hours after a nuclear burst (e.g., RI-3 is a radiation intensity three hours after the time of burst). *See also:* Radiation Dose.

References
Department of Defense, Joint Chiefs of Staff. *Department of Defense Dictionary of Military and Related Terms.* Washington, DC: GPO, 1986.

—**RADIATION SICKNESS** is an illness resulting from excessive exposure to ionizing radiation. The earliest symptoms are nausea, vomiting, and diarrhea, which may be followed by loss of hair, hemorrhage, inflammation of the mouth and throat, and a general loss of energy. *See also:* Radiation Dose.

References
Department of Defense, Joint Chiefs of Staff. *Department of Defense Dictionary of Military and Related Terms.* Washington, DC: GPO, 1986.

—**RADIATION SITUATION MAP** shows the actual and/or predicted radiation situation in the area of interest. *See also:* Radiation Dose.

References
Department of Defense, Joint Chiefs of Staff. *Department of Defense Dictionary of Military and Related Terms.* Washington, DC: GPO, 1986.

—**RADIATION STATUS (RS)** is a means used to assist the commander in measuring unit exposure to radiation based upon total past cumulative dose in centigrays (cGy). The categories are
- *Radiation status 0 (RS-0):* No previous exposure history.
- *Radiation status 1 (RS-1):* Negligible radiation exposure history (more than 0, but less than 71 cGy).
- *Radiation status 2 (RS-2):* Significant but not a dangerous dose of radiation (more than 70, but less than 151 cGy).
- *Radiation status 3 (RS-3):* Unit has already received a dose of radiation that makes further exposure dangerous (more than 150 cGy).

See also: Radiation Dose.

References
Department of Defense, U.S. Army. *Operational Terms and Symbols.* Field Manual FM 101-5-1. Washington, DC: Headquarters, Department of the Army, 1985.

—**RADIO CALL SIGN** is a group of letters, numerals, or a combination of both that identifies a radio station. *See also:* Net Call Sign.

References
Department of Defense, U.S. Army. *Dictionary of United States Army Terms.* Army Regulation AR 310-25. Washington, DC: Headquarters, Department of the Army, 1986.

—**RADIO DAY** is the 24-hour period from midnight to midnight that is covered by a complete set of radio station records.

References
Department of Defense, U.S. Army. *Dictionary of United States Army Terms.* Army Regulation AR 310-25. Washington, DC: Headquarters, Department of the Army, 1986.

—**RADIO DECEPTION** is the use of radio to deceive the enemy (e.g., sending false dispatches, using deceptive headings, and using enemy call signs). *See also:* Electronic Warfare.

References
Department of Defense, Joint Chiefs of Staff. *Department of Defense Dictionary of Military and Related Terms.* Washington, DC: GPO, 1986.

—**RADIO DETECTION** is the detection of the presence of an object by radio-location without making a precise determination of its position. *See also:* Radio Direction Finding.

References
Department of Defense, Joint Chiefs of Staff. *Department of Defense Dictionary of Military and Related Terms.* Washington, DC: GPO, 1986.

—**RADIO DIRECTION FINDING (RDF),** in signals intelligence, communications security, communications intelligence, operations security, and signals analysis, is a radio location in which only the direction of a station, rather than its direction and distance, can be determined by means of its emissions. *See also:* Communications Security.

References
Department of Defense, Joint Chiefs of Staff. *Department of Defense Dictionary of Military and Related Terms.* Washington, DC: GPO, 1986.

—**RADIO DIRECTION FINDING DATA BASE (RDFDB)** is the aggregate of information acquired by airborne and surface means necessary to provide support to radio direction finding forces. *See also:* Radio Direction Finding.

References
Department of Defense, Joint Chiefs of Staff. *Department of Defense Dictionary of Military and Related Terms.* Washington, DC: GPO, 1986.

—**RADIO FIX,** in signals intelligence, communications security, communications intelligence, operations security, and signals analysis, is the location of a friendly or enemy radio transmitter.

It is determined by finding the direction of the transmitter from two or more listening stations. *See also:* Communications Security.

References

Department of Defense, Joint Chiefs of Staff. *Department of Defense Dictionary of Military and Related Terms.* Washington, DC: GPO, 1986.

—**RADIO LISTENING SILENCE** is a period during which all or certain radio equipment is kept in a receive-only mode on a given net except for the net control station. *See also:* Net (Communications), *Net* Control Station.

References

Department of Defense, U.S. Army. *Communications Techniques: Electronics Countermeasures.* Field Manual FM 24-33. Washington, DC: Headquarters, Department of the Army, 1985.

—**RADIO NAVIGATION GUIDANCE** is a technique in which the predetermined path of the missile can be adjusted laterally and in range by a device in the missile that navigates it along the desired path by the using radio signals from one or more external transmitters.

References

Department of Defense, U.S. Army. *Dictionary of United States Army Terms.* Army Regulation AR 310-25. Washington, DC: Headquarters, Department of the Army, 1986.

—**RADIO POSITION FINDING** is a process of locating a radio transmitter by plotting the intersection of its azimuths as determined by two or more radio direction finders. *See also:* Radio Direction Finding.

References

Department of Defense, U.S. Army. *Dictionary of United States Army Terms.* Army Regulation AR 310-25. Washington, DC: Headquarters, Department of the Army, 1986.

—**RADIO PROCEDURE** encompasses the standardized methods of transmission used by operators to save time and prevent confusion. By insuring uniformity, radio procedure increases security.

References

Department of Defense, U.S. Army. *Dictionary of United States Army Terms.* Army Regulation AR 310-25. Washington, DC: Headquarters, Department of the Army, 1986.

—**RADIO RANGE** is the radio range station and its system of marker beacons, or other radio directive devices, used as an aid in air navigation. *See also:* Radio Range Finding.

References

Department of Defense, U.S. Army. *Dictionary of United States Army Terms.* Army Regulation AR 310-25. Washington, DC: Headquarters, Department of the Army, 1986.

—**RADIO RANGE FINDING** is radio location in which the distance of an object is determined by means of its radio emissions, whether they are independent, reflected, or retransmitted on the same or another wave length.

References

Department of Defense, Joint Chiefs of Staff. *Department of Defense Dictionary of Military and Related Terms.* Washington, DC: GPO, 1986.

—**RADIO RECOGNITION** is a radio operator's determination by radio means of the friendly or enemy character, or the individuality, of another radio operator.

References

Department of Defense, Joint Chiefs of Staff. *Department of Defense Dictionary of Military and Related Terms.* Washington, DC: GPO, 1986.

—**RADIO RELAY (RADREL) SYSTEM** is a signal communication system that uses very high frequency and line-of-sight radio transmitters and receivers in lieu of trunk wire circuits. This system, when it is used in conjunction with carrier equipment, provides channels for both voice and teletype operations.

References

Department of Defense, U.S. Army. *Dictionary of United States Army Terms.* Army Regulation AR 310-25. Washington, DC: Headquarters, Department of the Army, 1986.

—**RADIO SILENCE** is a period during which all or certain radio equipment that is capable of radiation is kept inoperative.

References

Department of Defense, U.S. Army. *Communications Techniques: Electronics Countermeasures.* Field Manual FM 24-33. Washington, DC: Headquarters, Department of the Army, 1985.

—**RADIO TELEGRAPHY** is the transmission of telegraphic codes by radio. *See also:* Radio Telephony.

References
Department of Defense, Joint Chiefs of Staff.
Department of Defense Dictionary of Military and Related Terms. Washington, DC: GPO, 1986.

—**RADIO TELEPHONY** is the transmission of speech by modulated radio waves. *See also:* Radio Telegraphy.

References
Department of Defense, Joint Chiefs of Staff.
Department of Defense Dictionary of Military and Related Terms. Washington, DC: GPO, 1986.

—**RADIOACTIVITY** is the spontaneous emission of radiation, generally alpha or beta particles, that are often accompanied by gamma rays, from the nuclei of an unstable isotope. *See also:* Radiation Dose.

References
Department of Defense, Joint Chiefs of Staff.
Department of Defense Dictionary of Military and Related Terms. Washington, DC: GPO, 1986.

—**RADIOACTIVITY CONCENTRATION GUIDE** is the amount of any specified radioisotope that is acceptable in air and water for continuous human consumption. *See also:* Radiation Dose.

References
Department of Defense, Joint Chiefs of Staff.
Department of Defense Dictionary of Military and Related Terms. Washington, DC: GPO, 1986.

—**RADIOELECTRONIC COMBAT (REC)** means the total integration of electronic warfare with the physical destruction of resources in order to deny the enemy the use of its electronic control systems, while protecting one's own electronic control systems. *See also:* Electronic Warfare.

References
Department of Defense, U.S. Army. *Intelligence and Electronic Warfare Operations.* Field Manual FM 34-1. Washington, DC: Headquarters, Department of the Army, 1987.

———. *Military Intelligence Battalion (CEWI) (Operations) (Corps).* Field Manual 34-21. Washington, DC: Headquarters, Department of the Army, 1982.

———. *Military Intelligence Group (Combat Electronic Warfare and Intelligence) (Corps).* Field Manual FM 34-20. Washington, DC: Headquarters, U.S. Army, 1983.

—**RADIOLOGICAL AGENT** is any of a family of substances that produce casualties by emitting radiation. *See also:* Radiation Dose.

References
Department of Defense, U.S. Army. *Dictionary of United States Army Terms.* Army Regulation AR 310-25. Washington, DC: Headquarters, Department of the Army, 1986.

—**RADIOLOGICAL DEFENSE** encompasses the defensive measures taken against the radiation hazards that result from the use of nuclear or radiological weapons. *See also:* Radiation Dose.

References
Department of Defense, Joint Chiefs of Staff.
Department of Defense Dictionary of Military and Related Terms. Washington, DC: GPO, 1986.

—**RADIOLOGICAL OPERATION** is the use of radioactive materials or radiation-producing devices to cause casualties or restrict the use of terrain. It includes the intentional use of fallout from nuclear weapons. *See also:* Radiation Dose.

References
Department of Defense, U.S. Army. *Dictionary of United States Army Terms.* Army Regulation AR 310-25. Washington, DC: Headquarters, Department of the Army, 1986.

—**RADIOLOGICAL SAFETY** concerns the methods, plans, and procedures involved in establishing and exercising personnel protective measures against radiation hazards. The radiation hazards may result from various types of exposure (e.g., those associated with a nuclear explosion, handling or being in the vicinity of radioactive material, or radiation monitoring in a contaminated area). *See also:* Radiation Dose.

References
Department of Defense, U.S. Army. *Dictionary of United States Army Terms.* Army Regulation AR 310-25. Washington, DC: Headquarters, Department of the Army, 1986.

—**RADIOLOGICAL SURVEY** is the directed effort to determine the distribution and dose rates of radiation in an area. *See also:* Radiation Dose.

References
Department of Defense, Joint Chiefs of Staff.
Department of Defense Dictionary of Military and Related Terms. Washington, DC: GPO, 1986.

—**RADIOLOGICAL SURVEY INSTRUMENT** is an apparatus used to measure radiological contamination in an area. *See also:* Radiation Dose.

References

Department of Defense, U.S. Army. *Dictionary of United States Army Terms.* Army Regulation AR 310-25. Washington, DC: Headquarters, Department of the Army, 1986.

—**RADIOLOGICAL SURVEY PARTY** is the agency that carries out a radiological survey. *See also:* Radiation Dose.

References

Department of Defense, U.S. Army. *Dictionary of United States Army Terms.* Army Regulation AR 310-25. Washington, DC: Headquarters, Department of the Army, 1986.

—**RADIUS OF ACTION** is the maximum distance that a ship, aircraft, or vehicle can travel away from its base along a given course with normal combat loads and return without refueling, while allowing for all safety and operating factors.

References

Department of Defense, U.S. Army. *Operational Terms and Symbols.* Field Manual FM 101-5-1. Washington, DC: Headquarters, Department of the Army, 1985.

—**RADIUS OF DAMAGE (RD)** is the distance from ground zero at which there is a 50 percent probability of achieving the desired damage. *See also:* Collateral Damage (Nuclear).

References

Department of Defense, U.S. Army. *Nuclear Weapons Employment Doctrine and Procedures.* Field Manual FM 101-3-1. Washington, DC: Headquarters, Department of the Army, 1986.

———. *Operational Terms and Symbols.* Field Manual FM 101-5-1. Washington, DC: Headquarters, Department of the Army, 1985.

—**RADIUS OF SAFETY** is the horizontal distance from ground zero beyond which the effects of nuclear weapons on friendly troops are acceptable. *See also:* Nuclear Warfare.

References

Department of Defense, Joint Chiefs of Staff. *Department of Defense Dictionary of Military and Related Terms.* Washington, DC: GPO, 1986.

—**RADIUS OF TARGET (RT)** is the radius of a circular target area or an area target that is equated to a circle. *See also:* Target.

References

Department of Defense, U.S. Army. *Operational Terms and Symbols.* Field Manual FM 101-5-1. Washington, DC: Headquarters, Department of the Army, 1985.

—**RADIUS OF VULNERABILITY (RV)** is the radius of a circle within which friendly troops may become casualties or equipment may be damaged. *See also:* Target, Troop Safety.

References

Department of Defense, U.S. Army. *Operational Terms and Symbols.* Field Manual FM 101-5-1. Washington, DC: Headquarters, Department of the Army, 1985.

—**RAID** is a limited-objective attack into enemy territory for a specific purpose other than to gain or hold ground. Raids are often conducted to gain information, confuse the enemy, destroy key enemy installations and facilities, capture or free prisoners, or disrupt enemy command and control or support functions. The raiding force always withdraws from the objective area after completing its mission, and unless it is a stay-behind unit, it normally recovers to friendly lines.

References

Department of Defense, U.S. Army. *Operational Terms and Symbols.* Field Manual FM 101-5-1. Washington, DC: Headquarters, Department of the Army, 1985.

———. *Operations.* Field Manual FM 100-5. Washington, DC: Headquarters, Department of the Army, 1986.

—**RAID REPORT,** in air defense, is one of a series of related reports that are made in order to develop a plot that assists in the rapid evaluation of a tactical situation.

References

Department of Defense, Joint Chiefs of Staff. *Department of Defense Dictionary of Military and Related Terms.* Washington, DC: GPO, 1986.

—**RAIL LOADING** is the loading of personnel and equipment on railway rolling stock for shipment. *See also:* Railhead.

References

Department of Defense, U.S. Army. *Dictionary of United States Army Terms.* Army Regulation AR 310-25. Washington, DC: Headquarters, Department of the Army, 1986.

RAILHEAD is a point on a railway where loads are transferred between trains and other means of transport.

References
Department of Defense, Joint Chiefs of Staff. *Department of Defense Dictionary of Military and Related Terms.* Washington, DC: GPO, 1986.

RAILROAD TRANSPORTATION OFFICER, or railway transportation officer, is a military station agent at a railroad who assists the railhead officer in moving, releasing, and returning all railway rolling stock. *See also:* Railhead.

References
Department of Defense, U.S. Army. *Dictionary of United States Army Terms.* Army Regulation AR 310-25. Washington, DC: Headquarters, Department of the Army, 1986.

RAILWAY DIVISION is a geographic segment of a railroad in a theater of operations that is operated and maintained by the railway operations superintendent.

References
Department of Defense, U.S. Army. *Dictionary of United States Army Terms.* Army Regulation AR 310-25. Washington, DC: Headquarters, Department of the Army, 1986.

RAILWAY LINE CAPACITY is the maximum number of trains that can be moved in each direction over a specified section of track in a 24-hour period. *See also:* Route Capacity.

References
Department of Defense, Joint Chiefs of Staff. *Department of Defense Dictionary of Military and Related Terms.* Washington, DC: GPO, 1986.

RAILWAY LOADING RAMP is a sloping platform situated at the end or beside a track and rising to the level of the floor of the railcars or wagons.

References
Department of Defense, Joint Chiefs of Staff. *Department of Defense Dictionary of Military and Related Terms.* Washington, DC: GPO, 1986.

RAILWAY SERVICE is a military and operating agency of the Military Transportation Service that has been established in a theater of operations. It comprises Transportation Corps railway supervisory, operating, and maintenance units.

References
Department of Defense, U.S. Army. *Dictionary of United States Army Terms.* Army Regulation AR 310-25. Washington, DC: Headquarters, Department of the Army, 1986.

RAILWAY SHOP BATTALION is an organization of Transportation Corps personnel who are trained to operate railway shops. The battalion is capable of accomplishing depot heavy repair of railway equipment. Normally, one railway shop battalion can serve two or three railway operating battalions.

References
Department of Defense, U.S. Army. *Dictionary of United States Army Terms.* Army Regulation AR 310-25. Washington, DC: Headquarters, Department of the Army, 1986.

RAINFALL (NUCLEAR) is the water that falls from the base surge clouds after an underwater burst of a nuclear weapon. This rain is radioactive and is an important secondary effect of such a burst. *See also:* Nuclear Warfare.

References
Department of Defense, Joint Chiefs of Staff. *Department of Defense Dictionary of Military and Related Terms.* Washington, DC: GPO, 1986.

RAINOUT is radioactive material in the atmosphere that is brought down by precipitation. *See also:* Nuclear Warfare.

References
Department of Defense, Joint Chiefs of Staff. *Department of Defense Dictionary of Military and Related Terms.* Washington, DC: GPO, 1986.

RAISE PISTOL. (1) Raise pistol is a prescribed movement in the manual of the pistol that includes taking the pistol out of the holster and raising it as high as, and six inches in front of, the right shoulder. (2) Raise pistol is to perform the movement described above. (3) Raise pistol is the command to carry out this movement.

References
Department of Defense, U.S. Army. *Dictionary of United States Army Terms.* Army Regulation AR 310-25. Washington, DC: Headquarters, Department of the Army, 1986.

RALLY POINT is an easily identifiable point on the ground at which units can reassemble and reorganize if they become dispersed.

References

Department of Defense, U.S. Army. *Operational Terms and Symbols.* Field Manual FM 101-5-1. Washington, DC: Headquarters, Department of the Army, 1985.

—**RANDOM ACCESS.** (1) Random access pertains to the process of obtaining data from, or placing data into, computer storage where the time required for such access is independent of the location of the data most recently obtained or placed in storage. (2) Random access pertains to a storage device in which the access time is effectively independent of the location of the data. (3) Random access is an access mode in which specific logical records are obtained from, or are placed into, a mass storage file in a nonsequential manner.

References

Department of Defense, U.S. Army. *Dictionary of United States Army Terms.* Army Regulation AR 310-25. Washington, DC: Headquarters, Department of the Army, 1986.

—**RANDOM MINELAYING,** in mine warfare, is the laying of mines without regard to pattern. *See also:* Mine Warfare.

References

Department of Defense, Joint Chiefs of Staff. *Department of Defense Dictionary of Military and Related Terms.* Washington, DC: GPO, 1986.

—**RANDOM MIXED ALPHABET** is an alphabet in which the alphabet is constructed by randomly mixing the letters.

References

Department of Defense, U.S. Army. *Dictionary of United States Army Terms.* Army Regulation AR 310-25. Washington, DC: Headquarters, Department of the Army, 1986.

—**RANDOM OBSTACLE SPACING** is the mean distance between obstacles that do not cross the entire terrain unit and have a somewhat random location (e.g., stumps and logs).

References

Department of Defense, U.S. Army. *Dictionary of United States Army Terms.* Army Regulation AR 310-25. Washington, DC: Headquarters, Department of the Army, 1986.

—**RANGE.** (1) Range is the distance between any given point and an object or target. (2) Range is the extent or distance that limits the operation

or action of something (e.g., the range of an aircraft, ship, or gun). (3) Range is the distance that can be covered over a hard surface by a ground vehicle, with its rated payload, using the fuel in its tank and the cans that are normally carried as part of the vehicle's equipment. (4) Range is an area that has been equipped for practice in shooting at targets. In this meaning, it is also called a target range. *See also:* Range Adjustment, Range Angle, Range Card, Range Correction, Range Correction Board, Range Corrector Setting, Range Deviation, Range Difference, Range Disk, Range Dispersion Diagram, Range Drum, Range Error, Range Flag, Range Guard, Range Indicator, Range K, Range Markers, Range Resolution, Range Scale, Range Section, Range Spotting, Range Table, Range Wind, Ranging Sensing.

References

Department of Defense, U.S. Army. *Operational Terms and Symbols.* Field Manual FM 101-5-1. Washington, DC: Headquarters, Department of the Army, 1985.

—**RANGE ADJUSTMENT** involves successive changes of firing data so that the impact or burst will be on target with respect to range. *See also:* Range.

References

Department of Defense, U.S. Army. *Dictionary of United States Army Terms.* Army Regulation AR 310-25. Washington, DC: Headquarters, Department of the Army, 1986.

—**RANGE ANGLE,** or dropping angle, is the angle between the aircraft target line and the vertical line from the aircraft to the ground at the instant that the bomb is released. *See also:* Range.

References

Department of Defense, U.S. Army. *Dictionary of United States Army Terms.* Army Regulation AR 310-25. Washington, DC: Headquarters, Department of the Army, 1986.

—**RANGE CARD.** (1) A range card is a small chart on which ranges and directions to various targets and other important points in the area under fire are recorded. (2) A range card is a small chart showing the proper amount of charge to be used for various ranges within the limits of the weapon. (3) A range card is a rough sketch of the terrain around a weapon position. It is made for each automatic weapon and each antitank weapon, and shows the sectors of fire, the firing data for automatic weapons, targets, distances to targets, and target reference points. *See also:* Range.

References
Department of Defense, U.S. Army. *Military Police Team, Squad, Platoon Combat Operations.* Field Manual FM 19-4. Washington, DC: Headquarters, Department of the Army, 1984.

—**RANGE CORRECTION** involves the changes in firing data necessary to allow for deviations of range due to weather, ammunition, or other conditions. *See also:* Range.

References
Department of Defense, U.S. Army. *Dictionary of United States Army Terms.* Army Regulation AR 310-25. Washington, DC: Headquarters, Department of the Army, 1986.

—**RANGE CORRECTION BOARD** is a device with which the correction to be applied to the gun is computed mechanically. The correction that is obtained allows for all nonstandard conditions (e.g., variations in weather and ammunition). It is known as the ballistic correction. *See also:* Range.

References
Department of Defense, U.S. Army. *Dictionary of United States Army Terms.* Army Regulation AR 310-25. Washington, DC: Headquarters, Department of the Army, 1986.

—**RANGE CORRECTOR SETTING** is the degree to which the range scale of a position finding apparatus must be adjusted before use. *See also:* Range.

References
Department of Defense, U.S. Army. *Dictionary of United States Army Terms.* Army Regulation AR 310-25. Washington, DC: Headquarters, Department of the Army, 1986.

—**RANGE DEFLECTION PROTECTOR** is a device used to measure range deflection. *See also:* Range.

References
Department of Defense, U.S. Army. *Dictionary of United States Army Terms.* Army Regulation AR 310-25. Washington, DC: Headquarters, Department of the Army, 1986.

—**RANGE DEVIATION** is the distance by which a projectile misses the target. *See also:* Range.

References
Department of Defense, U.S. Army. *Dictionary of United States Army Terms.* Army Regulation AR 310-25. Washington, DC: Headquarters, Department of the Army, 1986.

—**RANGE DIFFERENCE** is the difference between the ranges from any two points to a third point. It is especially the difference between the ranges of a target from two different guns. *See also:* Range.

References
Department of Defense, U.S. Army. *Dictionary of United States Army Terms.* Army Regulation AR 310-25. Washington, DC: Headquarters, Department of the Army, 1986.

—**RANGE DISK** is a graduated disk used for range setting that is connected mechanically to the elevating mechanism of a gun. A range disk usually is graduated in meters of range and degrees of elevation. *See also:* Range.

References
Department of Defense, U.S. Army. *Dictionary of United States Army Terms.* Army Regulation AR 310-25. Washington, DC: Headquarters, Department of the Army, 1986.

—**RANGE DISPERSION DIAGRAM** is a chart indicating the expected percentage of shots that are fired with the same data which will fall into each of eight areas within the dispersion pattern for range. *See also:* Range.

References
Department of Defense, U.S. Army. *Dictionary of United States Army Terms.* Army Regulation AR 310-25. Washington, DC: Headquarters, Department of the Army, 1986.

—**RANGE DRUM** is a graduated cylinder-type indicator that is connected mechanically to the elevating mechanism of a gun and is used for range setting. *See also:* Range.

References
Department of Defense, U.S. Army. *Dictionary of United States Army Terms.* Army Regulation AR 310-25. Washington, DC: Headquarters, Department of the Army, 1986.

—**RANGE ERROR** is the difference between the range to the point of impact of a particular projectile and the range to the mean point of impact of a group of shots that are fired with the same data. *See also:* Range.

References

Department of Defense, U.S. Army. *Dictionary of United States Army Terms*. Army Regulation AR 310-25. Washington, DC: Headquarters, Department of the Army, 1986.

—**RANGE FLAG** is a red flag displayed on or near a target during firing practice. It warns that live firing is occurring. *See also:* Range.

References

Department of Defense, U.S. Army. *Dictionary of United States Army Terms*. Army Regulation AR 310-25. Washington, DC: Headquarters, Department of the Army, 1986.

—**RANGE GUARD** is a guard posted to keep people away from a target range while firing is occurring. *See also:* Range.

References

Department of Defense, U.S. Army. *Dictionary of United States Army Terms*. Army Regulation AR 310-25. Washington, DC: Headquarters, Department of the Army, 1986.

—**RANGE INDICATOR** is a card showing the distance in meters from the firing point to the target, and is used in target practice. Range indicators are attached to the parts of a landscape target to show the distances of points from the firer. *See also:* Range.

References

Department of Defense, U.S. Army. *Dictionary of United States Army Terms*. Army Regulation AR 310-25. Washington, DC: Headquarters, Department of the Army, 1986.

—**RANGE K,** in artillery fire, is a correction that is expressed in meters/1,000 meters range to correct for nonstandard conditions. *See also:* Range.

References

Department of Defense, U.S. Army. *Dictionary of United States Army Terms*. Army Regulation AR 310-25. Washington, DC: Headquarters, Department of the Army, 1986.

—**RANGE MARKERS** are two upright markers, which may be lighted at night, and placed so that when they are aligned, the direction they show can be used to aid in piloting. They may also be used in amphibious operations to assist in beaching landing ships and craft. *See also:* Range.

References

Department of Defense, Joint Chiefs of Staff. *Department of Defense Dictionary of Military and Related Terms*. Washington, DC: GPO, 1986.

—**RANGE RESOLUTION** is the ability of radar equipment to separate two reflecting objects on a similar bearing, but at different ranges from the antenna. This ability is determined primarily by the pulse length in use. *See also:* Range.

References

Department of Defense, Joint Chiefs of Staff. *Department of Defense Dictionary of Military and Related Terms*. Washington, DC: GPO, 1986.

—**RANGE SCALE.** (1) Range scale is a scale on the arm of a plotting board where the observed range of a moving target is recorded in finding firing data. (2) A range scale is a graduated scale on the sight or mount of a gun that is used to show the elevation of a gun. (3) A range scale is a table of firing data giving elevation settings corresponding to various ranges for the standard charges. *See also:* Range.

References

Department of Defense, U.S. Army. *Dictionary of United States Army Terms*. Army Regulation AR 310-25. Washington, DC: Headquarters, Department of the Army, 1986.

—**RANGE SECTION** consists of the personnel of a battery whose duty it is to observe range findings and to plot firing data for the guns. *See also:* Range.

References

Department of Defense, U.S. Army. *Dictionary of United States Army Terms*. Army Regulation AR 310-25. Washington, DC: Headquarters, Department of the Army, 1986.

—**RANGE SPOTTING** is watching the burst or impact of shots to note how much it missed the target. *See also:* Range.

References

Department of Defense, U.S. Army. *Dictionary of United States Army Terms*. Army Regulation AR 310-25. Washington, DC: Headquarters, Department of the Army, 1986.

—**RANGE SPREAD** is the technique used to place the mean point of impact of two or more units 100 meters apart on the gun-target line. *See also:* Range.

References

Department of Defense, Joint Chiefs of Staff. *Department of Defense Dictionary of Military and Related Terms.* Washington, DC: GPO, 1986.

—**RANGE TABLE** is a table that gives elevations corresponding to the ranges for a gun under various conditions. A range table is a part of a firing table. *See also:* Range.

References

Department of Defense, U.S. Army. *Dictionary of United States Army Terms.* Army Regulation AR 310-25. Washington, DC: Headquarters, Department of the Army, 1986.

—**RANGER MISSION** is a mission involving strike, tactical reconnaissance, and special light infantry operations. The execution of ranger missions is normally directed by the National Command Authority. Rangers also support operational level commanders during temporary operations when they are allocated or assigned by the theater commander. *See also:* National Command Authorities.

References

Department of Defense, U.S. Army. *U.S. Army Operational Concept for Special Operations Forces.* TRADOC PAM 525-34. Washington, DC: Headquarters, Department of the Army, 1984.

—**RANGING.** (1) Ranging is the process of establishing target distance. The types of ranging include echo, intermittent, manual, navigational, explosive echo, optical, and radar. (2) Ranging is wide scale scouting, especially by aircraft, designed to search an area systematically. Ranging is locating an enemy gun by watching its flash, listening to its report, or by a similar means. *See also:* Spot.

References

Department of Defense, Joint Chiefs of Staff. *Department of Defense Dictionary of Military and Related Terms.* Washington, DC: GPO, 1986.

Department of Defense, U.S. Army. *Dictionary of United States Army Terms.* Army Regulation AR 310-25. Washington, DC: Headquarters, Department of the Army, 1986.

—**RANGING SENSING** is observing the location of the striking or bursting point of a projectile with respect to range, and reporting it as a hit, over, short, lost, or doubtful. Range sensing does not include the accurate determination of distances. *See also:* Range.

References

Department of Defense, U.S. Army. *Dictionary of United States Army Terms.* Army Regulation AR 310-25. Washington, DC: Headquarters, Department of the Army, 1986.

—**RANK** is the order of precedence among members of the Armed Forces.

References

Department of Defense, U.S. Army. *Promotion of Officers on Active Duty.* Army Regulation AR 624-100. Washington, DC: Headquarters, Department of the Army, 1984.

—**RANK** (DRILLS AND CEREMONIES) is a line of men that is one element in depth.

References

Department of Defense, U.S. Army. *Drills and Ceremonies.* Field Manual FM 22-5. Washington, DC: Headquarters, Department of the Army, 1986.

—**RAPID FIRE** is a rate of firing small arms or automatic weapons. It is faster than slow fire, but slower than quick fire. *See also:* Slow Fire.

References

Department of Defense, U.S. Army. *Dictionary of United States Army Terms.* Army Regulation AR 310-25. Washington, DC: Headquarters, Department of the Army, 1986.

—**RAPPELING** is a means of moving quickly down very steep hills and cliffs. Rappeling involves sliding down a rope that has been anchored around a firm object, or anchor point (e.g., a tree, projecting rock, or piton at the top of the decline).

References

Department of Defense, U.S. Army. *Jungle Operations.* Field Manual FM 90-5. Washington, DC: Headquarters, Department of the Army, 1982.

—**RATE OF FIRE** is the number of rounds fired per weapon per minute. *See also:* Rapid Fire, Slow Fire.

References

Department of Defense, U.S. Army. *Operational Terms and Symbols.* Field Manual FM 101-5-1. Washington, DC: Headquarters, Department of the Army, 1985.

—**RATE OF MARCH** (SPEED) is the average number of miles or kilometers that are to be travelled in a given period, including all ordered halts. It is expressed in miles or kilograms per hour.

References

Department of Defense, U.S. Army. *Operational Terms and Symbols*. Field Manual FM 101-5-1. Washington, DC: Headquarters, Department of the Army, 1985.

———. *The Infantry Rifle Company (Infantry, Airborne, Air Assault, Ranger)*. Field Manual FM 7-10. Washington, DC: Headquarters, Department of the Army, 1982.

—**RATED LOAD** is the specified load for which equipment can safely operate under prescribed conditions.

References

Department of Defense, Joint Chiefs of Staff. *Department of Defense Dictionary of Military and Related Terms*. Washington, DC: GPO, 1986.

—**RATION** is the allowance of food for the subsistence of one person for one day. *See also:* Ration Article, Ration Basis of Issue, Ration Cycle, Ration Dense, Ration Factor, Ration Interval, Ration Return, Ration Scale, Ration Scales and National Groups, Ration Strength, Ration Supplements, Rations in Kind.

References

Department of Defense, U.S. Army. *Dictionary of United States Army Terms*. Army Regulation AR 310-25. Washington, DC: Headquarters, Department of the Army, 1986.

—**RATION ARTICLE** is the classification of the basic prescribed foods of the Army ration, and proper substitutes for them. *See also:* Ration.

References

Department of Defense, U.S. Army. *Dictionary of United States Army Terms*. Army Regulation AR 310-25. Washington, DC: Headquarters, Department of the Army, 1986.

—**RATION BASIS OF ISSUE** consists of ration articles issued for a given day that contain the quantity of food necessary for an equal number of breakfasts, lunches, and dinners. Normally these are only used in a theater of operations. *See also:* Ration.

References

Department of Defense, U.S. Army. *Dictionary of United States Army Terms*. Army Regulation AR 310-25. Washington, DC: Headquarters, Department of the Army, 1986.

—**RATION CYCLE** is the time covering one day's ration or three meals. It may begin with any meal. *See also:* Ration.

References

Department of Defense, U.S. Army. *Dictionary of United States Army Terms*. Army Regulation AR 310-25. Washington, DC: Headquarters, Department of the Army, 1986.

—**RATION DENSE** refers to foods which, through processing, have been reduced in volume and quantity to a small, compact package without appreciable loss of nutrients and have a high yield in relation to their volume. Dehydrates and concentrates are ration dense foods. *See also:* Ration.

References

Department of Defense, Joint Chiefs of Staff. *Department of Defense Dictionary of Military and Related Terms*. Washington, DC: GPO, 1986.

—**RATION FACTOR** is the average daily rate of issue per person of a subsistence item over a given period of time. It is usually expressed in pounds per 1,000 rations. *See also:* Ration.

References

Department of Defense, U.S. Army. *Dictionary of United States Army Terms*. Army Regulation AR 310-25. Washington, DC: Headquarters, Department of the Army, 1986.

—**RATION INTERVAL** is the time between the submission of a field ration request and the consumption of the food. *See also:* Ration.

References

Department of Defense, U.S. Army. *Dictionary of United States Army Terms*. Army Regulation AR 310-25. Washington, DC: Headquarters, Department of the Army, 1986.

—**RATION METHOD** is a method of determining the amount of reduction or enlargement needed to bring an air photograph to the scale of a mosaic map on which it is to be used. *See also:* Aerial Reconnaissance.

References

Department of Defense, U.S. Army. *Dictionary of United States Army Terms*. Army Regulation AR 310-25. Washington, DC: Headquarters, Department of the Army, 1986.

—**RATION RETURN** is the document by which monetary credit is claimed by an organization subsisting on the Monetary Allowance Ration System. *See also:* Ration.

References

Department of Defense, U.S. Army. *Dictionary of United States Army Terms.* Army Regulation AR 310-25. Washington, DC: Headquarters, Department of the Army, 1986.

—**RATION SCALE** is a subsistence requirement expressed as ration factors of a command for a given period of time. *See also:* Ration.

References

Department of Defense, U.S. Army. *Dictionary of United States Army Terms.* Army Regulation AR 310-25. Washington, DC: Headquarters, Department of the Army, 1986.

—**RATION SCALES FOR NATIONAL GROUPS** is a basic ration scale developed by commanders of overseas theaters for each of the national groups or other classes (except U.S. Armed Forces) that are being subsisted by the Army. The ration scale that is developed represents the national food habits of each group within the theater. *See also:* Ration.

References

Department of Defense, U.S. Army. *Dictionary of United States Army Terms.* Army Regulation AR 310-25. Washington, DC: Headquarters, Department of the Army, 1986.

—**RATION STRENGTH,** for field rations, is the actual number of persons who are present for meals. *See also:* Ration.

References

Department of Defense, U.S. Army. *Dictionary of United States Army Terms.* Army Regulation AR 310-25. Washington, DC: Headquarters, Department of the Army, 1986.

—**RATION SUPPLEMENTS** are items used as supplements to designated operational rations. A ration supplement, the sundries pack, is issued for use in the field to provide essential articles, tobacco, and confections prior to establishing adequate Army exchange or comparable sales facilities. *See also:* Ration.

References

Department of Defense, U.S. Army. *Dictionary of United States Army Terms.* Army Regulation AR 310-25. Washington, DC: Headquarters, Department of the Army, 1986.

—**RATIONALIZATION** is any action that increases the effectiveness of allied forces through more efficient or effective use of the defense resources that are committed to the alliance. Rationalization includes consolidation, reassignment of national priorities to higher alliance needs, standardization, specialization, mutual support or improved interoperability, and greater cooperation. Rationalization applies to both weapons/materiel resources and nonweapons military matters.

References

Department of Defense, U.S. Army. *Support Operations: Echelons Above Corps.* Field Manual FM 100-16. Washington, DC: Headquarters, Department of the Army, 1986.

—**RATIONS IN KIND** are cooked or uncooked food issued for consumption. *See also:* Ration.

References

Department of Defense, U.S. Army. *Dictionary of United States Army Terms.* Army Regulation AR 310-25. Washington, DC: Headquarters, Department of the Army, 1986.

—**RATLINE** is an organized effort to clandestinely move personnel or material across a denied area or border.

References

Department of Defense, Joint Chiefs of Staff. *Department of Defense Dictionary of Military and Related Terms.* Washington, DC: GPO, 1986.

—**RAW INTELLIGENCE** is collected intelligence information that has not yet been converted into intelligence. *See also:* Intelligence, Intelligence Cycle.

References

Department of Defense, Defense Intelligence College. *Glossary of Intelligence Terms and Definitions.* Washington, DC: Defense Intelligence College, 1987.

—**REACTION TIME.** (1) Reaction time is the time between the initiation of an action and the required response. (2) The reaction time is the time that is required between the receipt of an order directing an operation and the arrival of the initial element of the force concerned in the designated area.

References

Department of Defense, Joint Chiefs of Staff. *Department of Defense Dictionary of Military and Related Terms.* Washington, DC: GPO, 1986.

—**REACTIVE THREAT** is an Army intelligence term for devices, tactical techniques, and systems that could be adopted by a potential enemy in response to a U.S. system that is being developed.

References

Department of Defense, U.S. Army. *RDTGE Managers Intelligence and Threat Support Guide.* Alexandria, VA: Headquarters, Army Materiel Development and Readiness Command, 1983.

—**READINESS,** in peacetime, measures how well prepared combat, support, and mobility forces are to perform the functions that are designated, and how fast specified elements can arrive at specified places, given specified warning times. Superior marks demand trained personnel and serviceable equipment at or near authorized strengths. Intangibles (e.g., unit cohesion and high morale) are other indications of readiness. *See also:* Readiness Report.

References

Collins, John M. *U.S.-Soviet Military Balance, 1980-1985.* Washington, DC: Congressional Research Service, 1985.

—**READINESS REPORT** is a report submitted to the theater army by an incoming unit indicating that the unit has drawn all of its equipment, is self-sufficient, and is ready to perform its combat mission.

References

Department of Defense, U.S. Army. *Support Operations: Echelons Above Corps.* Field Manual FM 100-16. Washington, DC: Headquarters, Department of the Army, 1986.

—**READY** is the term used to indicate that a weapon is loaded, aimed, and prepared to fire.

References

Department of Defense, Joint Chiefs of Staff. *Department of Defense Dictionary of Military and Related Terms.* Washington, DC: GPO, 1986.

—**READY-FOR-ISSUE WEAPON** is an item that has been removed from preservation with all ancillary equipment (i.e., fire control, machine guns, radios, and mounts) installed. The vehicle has been fueled and basic issue items are aboard. No ammunition is aboard.

References

Department of Defense, U.S. Army. *Support Operations: Echelons Above Corps.* Field Manual FM 100-16. Washington, DC: Headquarters, Department of the Army, 1986.

—**READY MISSILE** is a tactical missile in the possession of a combat unit that is on a launcher and requires only a fire command to be put into use. *See also:* Ready Missile Rate.

References

Department of Defense, U.S. Army. *Dictionary of United States Army Terms.* Army Regulation AR 310-25. Washington, DC: Headquarters, Department of the Army, 1986.

—**READY MISSILE RATE** is the percentage of prepared missiles that are complete with warheads that are in a ready missile status. *See also:* Ready Missile.

References

Department of Defense, U.S. Army. *Dictionary of United States Army Terms.* Army Regulation AR 310-25. Washington, DC: Headquarters, Department of the Army, 1986.

—**READY POSITION,** in helicopter operations, is a designated place where a helicopter load of troops or equipment waits for pickup.

References

Department of Defense, Joint Chiefs of Staff. *Department of Defense Dictionary of Military and Related Terms.* Washington, DC: GPO, 1986.

—**READY RACK** is a rack for ammunition available for immediate use.

References

Department of Defense, U.S. Army. *Dictionary of United States Army Terms.* Army Regulation AR 310-25. Washington, DC: Headquarters, Department of the Army, 1986.

—**READY RESERVE (RR)** is the Selected Reserve and Individual Ready Reserve that can be called for active duty as prescribed by law. *See also:* Ready Reserve Mobilization Reinforcement Pool.

References

Department of Defense, Joint Chiefs of Staff. *Department of Defense Dictionary of Military and Related Terms.* Washington, DC: GPO, 1986.

—**READY RESERVE MOBILIZATION REIN- FORCEMENT POOL** is a collective term used to describe the members of the Ready Reserve who are assigned to Control Group (Annual Training), Control Group (Reinforcement), or staff and faculty U.S. Army Reserve schools. Members assigned to the staff and faculty of U.S. Army Reserve schools or are attached to reinforcement training units or U.S. Army Reserve school student detachments are subject to additional regulations and directives, but remain an element of the Ready Reserve Mobilization Reinforcement Pool.

References
Department of Defense, U.S. Army. *Dictionary of United States Army Terms.* Army Regulation AR 310-25. Washington, DC: Headquarters, Department of the Army, 1986.

—**READY RESERVE STRATEGIC ARMY FORCES** are reserve component division forces that have been selected for early mobilization and deployment. *See also:* Ready Reserve.

References
Department of Defense, U.S. Army. *Dictionary of United States Army Terms.* Army Regulation AR 310-25. Washington, DC: Headquarters, Department of the Army, 1986.

—**READY TO FIGHT** is a crewed, ready-for-issue weapon with ammunition stowed aboard. It is a weapon that has been boresighted and verified as operational. *See also:* Ready-to-Fight Weapon System.

References
Department of Defense, U.S. Army. *Support Operations: Echelons Above Corps.* Field Manual FM 100-16. Washington, DC: Headquarters, Department of the Army, 1986.

—**READY-TO-FIGHT WEAPON SYSTEM** is a completely processed weapon with crew. *See also:* Ready to Fight.

References
Department of Defense, U.S. Army. *Combat Service Support Operations-Division.* Field Manual FM 63-2. Washington, DC: Headquarters, Department of the Army, 1983.

—**REAL PROPERTY** consists of lands, buildings, structures, utilities, systems, and improvements and additions to them. It also includes the equipment attached to and made part of the buildings and structures (e.g., heating systems), but not moveable equipment. *See also:* Real Property Maintenance Activities.

References
Department of Defense, Joint Chiefs of Staff. *Department of Defense Dictionary of Military and Related Terms.* Washington, DC: GPO, 1986.

—**REAL PROPERTY MAINTENANCE ACTIVITIES (RPMA)** are actions taken to ensure that real estate is acquired, developed, maintained, and disposed of according to the objectives of the mission.

References
Department of Defense, U.S. Army. *Support Operations: Echelons Above Corps.* Field Manual FM 100-16. Washington, DC: Headquarters, Department of the Army, 1986.

—**REAL TIME** is the absence of delay, except for the time necessary to transmit the information, between the occurrence of an event and the receipt of the news at some other location. *See also:* Reporting Time Interval.

References
Department of Defense, Joint Chiefs of Staff. *Department of Defense Dictionary of Military and Related Terms.* Washington, DC: GPO, 1986.

—**REALLOCATION AUTHORITY** is an authority given to NATO commanders that is normally negotiated in peacetime. It permits them to reallocate in an "emergency in war," the national logistic resources controlled by the combat forces under their command, and made available by nations, in order to influence the battle logistically.

References
Department of Defense, Joint Chiefs of Staff. *Department of Defense Dictionary of Military and Related Terms.* Washington, DC: GPO, 1986.

—**REALTRAIN (REALISTIC TRAINING).** In REALTRAIN, unit leaders develop tactical scenarios based upon unit missions. The unit, which can range from a crew/fire team to a reinforced platoon, engages an opposing force as large as two platoons. Optical devices, telescopes, or plastic sighting plates are mounted on or in the weapons of the two opposing small unit forces. These devices are aligned with the weapon sights. Gunners shoot at targets by announcing the identification numbers worn by soldiers or displayed on vehicles while the target is aligned in their sights. Controllers remove simulated casualties and damaged or destroyed vehicles from the exercise. After the exercise, both forces meet for a post-action review and critique each other's performance.

References
Department of Defense, U.S. Army. *Unit Training Management.* Field Manual FM 25-2. Washington, DC: Headquarters, Department of the Army, 1984.

—**REAR AREA,** in Army tactical intelligence, means the area to the rear of the main battle area in which supply, maintenance, support, communication centers, and administrative echelons are located. For any particular command, the rear area extends rearward from the rear boundary of its main defense area to that command's rear boundaries. *See also:* Rear Area Combat Operations, Rear Area Operations Center, Rear Area Protection, Rear Area Security, Rear Area Security Control Center, Rear Area Security Controller, Rear Barrier, Rear Battle Threat Levels, Rear Combat Zone, Rear Operations Area, Rear Party.

References
Department of Defense, U.S. Army. *Operational Terms and Symbols.* Field Manual FM 101-5-1. Washington, DC: Headquarters, Department of the Army, 1985.

———. *Rear Battle.* Field Manual FM 90-14. Washington, DC: Headquarters, Department of the Army, 1985.

———. *Support Operations: Echelons Above Corps.* Field Manual FM 100-16. Washington, DC: Headquarters, Department of the Army, 1986.

—**REAR AREA COMBAT OPERATIONS (RACO)** are actions taken to prevent, neutralize, or destroy enemy forces in the rear area. *See also:* Rear Area.

References
Department of Defense, U.S. Army. *Support Operations: Echelons Above Corps.* Field Manual FM 100-16. Washington, DC: Headquarters, Department of the Army, 1986.

—**REAR AREA OPERATIONS CENTER (RAOC)** is the control center responsible for planning, coordinating, directing, and mounting the rear battle. *See also:* Rear Area, Rear Area Combat Operations.

References
Department of Defense, U.S. Army. *Operational Terms and Symbols.* Field Manual FM 101-5-1. Washington, DC: Headquarters, Department of the Army, 1985.

———. *Rear Battle.* Field Manual FM 90-14. Washington, DC: Headquarters, Department of the Army, 1985.

———. *Staff Organization and Operations.* Field Manual FM 101-5. Washington, DC: Headquarters, Department of the Army, 1984.

—**REAR AREA PROTECTION (RAP)** encompasses the actions taken to protect the rear areas from enemy operations and to prevent or minimize the damage from enemy attacks or natural disasters. RAP includes rear area combat operations. *See also:* Rear Area.

References
Department of Defense, U.S. Army. *Support Operations: Echelons Above Corps.* Field Manual FM 100-16. Washington, DC: Headquarters, Department of the Army, 1986.

—**REAR AREA SECURITY (RAS)** encompasses the measures taken prior to, during, and after an enemy airborne attack, sabotage action, infiltration, guerrilla action, and initiation of psychological warfare to minimize the effects of these operations. RAS measures are divided into three phases. *Phase I* measures include analyzing the available intelligence to determine the threat conditions, planning the dispersion of grouped activities, coordinating communications requirements, and setting area boundaries. *Phase II* measures include conducting reconnaissance, counterreconnaissance, surveillance, and counterintelligence; identifying and establishing RAS elements; organizing units for operational RAS missions; assigning sectors to RAS forces; and establishing communications and testing alert and warning systems. *Phase III* measures include defending units, bases, and critical terrain features; reinforcing ambushed convoys; and locating and eliminating small hostile forces. *See also:* Area Damage Control, Rear Area.

References
Department of Defense, U.S. Army. *Attack Helicopter Operations.* Field Manual FM 17-50. Washington, DC: Headquarters, Department of the Army, 1984.

—**REAR AREA SECURITY CONTROL CENTER** is the operating area through which the rear area security defense controller discharges responsibilities for rear area defense and area damage control. *See also:* Rear Area.

References
Department of Defense, U.S. Army. *Dictionary of United States Army Terms.* Army Regulation AR 310-25. Washington, DC: Headquarters, Department of the Army, 1986.

—**REAR AREA SECURITY CONTROLLER** is an officer appointed to assist in planning for, organizing, supervising, and conducting both rear area defense and area damage control. *See also:* Rear Area.

References

Department of Defense, U.S. Army. *Dictionary of United States Army Terms.* Army Regulation AR 310-25. Washington, DC: Headquarters, Department of the Army, 1986.

—**REAR BARRIER** is a barrier selected by an Army, corps, or division, behind which is established the next rearward defensive position. A rear barrier may also be established to protect critical terrain. *See also:* Rear Area.

References

Department of Defense, U.S. Army. *Dictionary of United States Army Terms.* Army Regulation AR 310-25. Washington, DC: Headquarters, Department of the Army, 1986.

—**REAR BATTLE (RB)** encompasses the actions, including area damage control, that are taken by all units (i.e., combat, combat support, combat service support, and host nation), singly or in a combined effort, to secure the force, neutralize or defeat enemy operations in the rear area, and insure freedom of action in the deep and close-in battles. *See also:* Area Damage Control, Rear Area.

References

Department of Defense, U.S. Army. *Operational Terms and Symbols.* Field Manual FM 101-5-1. Washington, DC: Headquarters, Department of the Army, 1985.

———. *Rear Battle.* Field Manual FM 90-14. Washington, DC: Headquarters, Department of the Army, 1985.

—**REAR BATTLE RESPONSE FORCES** are composed of military police response forces and tactical combat forces. Military *police response forces* are the MP forces assigned to respond to and conduct operations to close with and destroy attacking enemy forces that are beyond the combat capability of base defenses. Tactical combat forces are the forces assigned to defeat enemy airborne, air assault, amphibious, or ground infiltration attacks in the rear area. *See also:* Rear Area, Rear Battle.

References

Department of Defense, U.S. Army. *Operational Terms and Symbols.* Field Manual FM 101-5-1. Washington, DC: Headquarters, Department of the Army, 1985.

—**REAR BATTLE THREAT LEVELS.** Attacks in the rear area are classified as follows:

- **Level I** encompasses enemy controlled agent activity, sabotage by enemy sympathizers, and activities conducted by terrorist organizations.
- **Level II** encompasses diversionary operations and sabotage and reconnaissance missions conducted by enemy tactical units that are less than battalion size.
- **Level III** encompasses airborne, air assault, amphibious operations, or infiltration operations of battalion size or larger.

See also: Rear Area, Rear Battle.

References

Department of Defense, U.S. Army. *Operational Terms and Symbols.* Field Manual FM 101-5-1. Washington, DC: Headquarters, Department of the Army, 1985.

—**REAR COMBAT ZONE (RCZ)** is the portion of the combat zone that extends from the corps rear boundary to the Army group rear boundary. For rear battle purposes, the commanders of host nation territorial commands are responsible for the protection of facilities, installations, and areas assigned to their area of command. *See also:* Rear Area.

References

Department of Defense, U.S. Army. *Rear Battle.* Field Manual FM 90-14. Washington, DC: Headquarters, Department of the Army, 1985.

—**REAR COMMAND POST (CP).** A rear CP is normally established at the corps level and above. At the corps level, it is commanded by the deputy commander, and is intended to provide command and control for administrative and logistic support of combat operations. It also may serve as a focal point for rear area protection operations.

The rear CP consists of the staff activities concerned primarily with combat service support of the force, administrative support to the headquarters, and other activities that are not immediately concerned with current operations. Typical representatives within the rear echelon are elements of the G1 and G4 sections, G5, adjutant general, staff judge advocate, inspector general, provost marshal, supporting military intelligence elements concerned with counter-intelligence and prisoner of war interrogation activities, and the tactical airlift representative of the tactical air control party. Normally, rear CPs are near to or are collocated with combat service support units. *See also:* Command Post, Main Command Post, Rear Area, Tactical Command Post.

References

Department of Defense, U.S. Army. *Operational Terms and Symbols.* Field Manual FM 101-5-1. Washington, DC: Headquarters, Department of the Army, 1985.

———. *Staff Organizations and Operations.* Field Manual FM 101-5. Washington, DC: Headquarters, Department of the Army, 1984.

—**REAR ECHELON.** (1) Rear echelon is a generic term used to describe all the elements normally located in the rear area. (2) The rear echelon is composed of the units or elements that are not required in the airhead or beachhead. These units normally remain in the departure area. *See also:* Assault Echelon, Follow-Up Echelon, Rear Area.

References

Department of Defense, U.S. Army. *Operational Terms and Symbols.* Field Manual FM 101-5-1. Washington, DC: Headquarters, Department of the Army, 1985.

—**REAR GUARD** is a security detachment that protects the rear of a column from hostile forces. During a withdrawal, it delays the enemy by armed resistance, destroying bridges, and blocking roads.

References

Department of Defense, U.S. Army. *Cavalry.* Field Manual FM 17-95. Washington, DC: Headquarters, Department of the Army, 1977.

———. *Operational Terms and Symbols.* Field Manual FM 101-5-1. Washington, DC: Headquarters, Department of the Army, 1985.

—**REAR OPERATIONS,** at any echelon, comprise activities rearward of the elements in contact with the enemy. A rear operation is designed to assure freedom of maneuver and continuity of operations, including continuity of sustainment and command and control. Rear operations may have little immediate impact on close ground operations, but they are critical to subsequent operations, whether in exploiting success or re-couping failure. At the operational level, rear operations focus on preparing for the next phase of the campaign or major operation. At the tactical level, rear operations underwrite the tempo of combat, assuring the commander the agility to take immediate advantage of any op-portunity.

References

Department of Defense, U.S. Army. *Operations.* Field Manual FM 100-5. Washington, DC: Headquarters, Department of the Army, 1986.

—**REAR OPERATIONS AREA** is the area rearward of the tactical operations area rear boundary where airspace control is more definitive. The rear area dimensions are established by the joint force commander. *See also:* Rear Area.

References

Department of Defense, U.S. Army. *Airspace Management and Army Air Traffic in a Combat Zone.* Field Manual FM 1-60. Washington, DC: Headquarters, Department of the Army, 1977.

—**REAR PARTY** is a part of a rear guard that pro-tects the support and covers the withdrawal of the rear point. A rear party corresponds to the advance party of an advance guard. *See also:* Advance Guard, Advance Party, Rear Guard.

References

Department of Defense, U.S. Army. *Dictionary of United States Army Terms.* Army Regulation AR 310-25. Washington, DC: Headquarters, Depart-ment of the Army, 1986.

—**REAR POINT** is a group of soldiers in a rear guard who are farthest to the rear. The group observes enemy movements and discourages pursuit by using harassing fire against the en-emy. *See also:* Rear Guard.

References

Department of Defense, U.S. Army. *Dictionary of United States Army Terms.* Army Regulation AR 310-25. Washington, DC: Headquarters, Depart-ment of the Army, 1986.

—**REARMING.** (1) Rearming is an operation that replenishes the prescribed stores of ammunition, bombs, and other armaments for an aircraft, naval ship, tank, or armored vehicle, including replacement of defective ordnance equipment, in order to make it ready for combat service. (2) Rearming is resetting the fuze on a bomb, or an artillery, mortar, or rocket projectile, so that it will detonate at the desired time.

References
Department of Defense, Joint Chiefs of Staff. *Department of Defense Dictionary of Military and Related Terms.* Washington, DC: GPO, 1986.

—**REBUILD** is the restoration of an item to a standard that is as near as possible to its original condition in appearance, performance, and life expectancy. *See also:* Overhaul, Repair.

References
Department of Defense, Joint Chiefs of Staff. *Department of Defense Dictionary of Military and Related Terms.* Washington, DC: GPO, 1986.

—**RECALL TO ACTIVE DUTY.** *See:* Voluntary Order or Recall to Active Duty.

—**RECEDING LEG** is the portion of the target's course line in which the slant range increases for successive target positions.

References
Department of Defense, U.S. Army. *Dictionary of United States Army Terms.* Army Regulation AR 310-25. Washington, DC: Headquarters, Department of the Army, 1986.

—**RECEIPT** is a transmission made by a receiving station to indicate that a message has been satisfactorily received.

References
Department of Defense, Joint Chiefs of Staff. *Department of Defense Dictionary of Military and Related Terms.* Washington, DC: GPO, 1986.

—**RECEIPT INTO SUPPLY SYSTEM** is the time when the first contract item (or first quantity of the contract item) has been received at or is en route to the point of first delivery after inspection and acceptance. *See also:* Receiving Activity, Receiving Officer.

References
Department of Defense, Joint Chiefs of Staff. *Department of Defense Dictionary of Military and Related Terms.* Washington, DC: GPO, 1986.

—**RECEIVER** is the part of a gun that takes the charge from the magazine and holds it until it is seated in the breech.

References
Department of Defense, U.S. Army. *Dictionary of United States Army Terms.* Army Regulation AR 310-25. Washington, DC: Headquarters, Department of the Army, 1986.

—**RECEIVING ACTIVITY** is an activity that is authorized to physically receive shipments from a carrier and tallies in, inspects, and accepts material for the accounts of the military departments or other authorized agencies.

References
Department of Defense, U.S. Army. *Dictionary of United States Army Terms.* Army Regulation AR 310-25. Washington, DC: Headquarters, Department of the Army, 1986.

—**RECEIVING OFFICER** is the individual charged with the custody or storage of property received by means of a shipment. He is referred to as a receiving officer, as distinguished from the consignee on the bill of lading, since the consignee is usually the transportation officer. Usually the receiving officer is an accountable officer at the station or destination.

References
Department of Defense, U.S. Army. *Dictionary of United States Army Terms.* Army Regulation AR 310-25. Washington, DC: Headquarters, Department of the Army, 1986.

—**RECEPTACLE BOX** is the central electrical distribution box mounted on a gun carriage. It is the distributor of the fire control data received from the azimuth, elevation, and fuze setter in the director.

References
Department of Defense, U.S. Army. *Dictionary of United States Army Terms.* Army Regulation AR 310-25. Washington, DC: Headquarters, Department of the Army, 1986.

—**RECEPTEE** is an individual who is received for processing at a U.S. reception station. *See also:* Reception.

References
Department of Defense, U.S. Army. *Dictionary of United States Army Terms.* Army Regulation AR 310-25. Washington, DC: Headquarters, Department of the Army, 1986.

—**RECEPTION** encompasses all activities connected with classifying and caring for personnel until they are assigned to organizations. Reception includes completion of records, immunization, supplying of clothing and equipment, classification of skills, and assignment to units.

References

Department of Defense, U.S. Army. *Dictionary of United States Army Terms.* Army Regulation AR 310-25. Washington, DC: Headquarters, Department of the Army, 1986.

—**RECEPTION** (RADIO) is the quality of the signal received.

References

Department of Defense, U.S. Army. *Dictionary of United States Army Terms.* Army Regulation AR 310-25. Washington, DC: Headquarters, Department of the Army, 1986.

—**RECEPTION CAPACITY** is the number and types of ships that can be moved into a harbor or coastal area of a terminal per day. This capacity is an estimated tonnage that can be accommodated for discharge daily from the ships and is based solely upon an evaluation of the physical facilities of the terminal.

References

Department of Defense, U.S. Army. *Planning Logistics Support for Military Operations.* Field Manual FM 701-58. Washington, DC: Headquarters, Department of the Army, 1987.

—**RECEPTION PERIOD** is the initial portion of confinement devoted to the indoctrination and integration of newly arrived prisoners at correction installations. This period is also used to determine whether newly arrived prisoners have contagious diseases.

References

Department of Defense, U.S. Army. *Dictionary of United States Army Terms.* Army Regulation AR 310-25. Washington, DC: Headquarters, Department of the Army, 1986.

—**RECEPTION STATION** is an activity specifically designated to provide receiving, orientation, classification, testing, clothing, assignment, and movement of personnel enlisted, inducted, or ordered to active duty (including active duty for training). Reception stations are located in the continental United States and in Hawaii. *See also:* Receptee, Reception.

References

Department of Defense, U.S. Army. *Dictionary of United States Army Terms.* Army Regulation AR 310-25. Washington, DC: Headquarters, Department of the Army, 1986.

—**RECEPTIVITY** is the vulnerability of a target audience to a particular psychological operations media. *See also:* Psychological Operations.

References

Department of Defense, Joint Chiefs of Staff. *Department of Defense Dictionary of Military and Related Terms.* Washington, DC: GPO, 1986.

—**RECESS APPOINTMENT** is an appointment of a commissioned officer in the Regular Army that is tendered at the direction of the President while the Congress is in recess.

References

Department of Defense, U.S. Army. *Dictionary of United States Army Terms.* Army Regulation AR 310-25. Washington, DC: Headquarters, Department of the Army, 1986.

—**RECIPROCAL JURISDICTION** is the exercise of court-martial jurisdiction by one armed force over personnel of another armed force, pursuant to specific authorization by the President or by the Secretary of Defense. *See also:* Uniform Code of Military Justice.

References

Department of Defense, Joint Chiefs of Staff. *Department of Defense Dictionary of Military and Related Terms.* Washington, DC: GPO, 1986.

—**RECIPROCAL LAYING** is a method of making the planes of fire of two guns parallel by pointing the guns in a parallel direction. In reciprocal laying, the two guns sight on each other, then swing out through supplementary angles to produce equal deflections from the base line connecting the two pieces.

References

Department of Defense, U.S. Army. *Dictionary of United States Army Terms.* Army Regulation AR 310-25. Washington, DC: Headquarters, Department of the Army, 1986.

—**RECLAMA** is a request to duly constituted authority to reconsider its decision or its proposed action.

References

Department of Defense, Joint Chiefs of Staff. *Department of Defense Dictionary of Military and Related Terms.* Washington, DC: GPO, 1986.

—**RECLAMATION.** (1) Reclamation is the process of restoring to usefulness condemned, discarded, abandoned, or damaged materiel, or parts or components of them by repairing, refabricating, or renovating them, and returning them to supply channels. (2) Reclamation is a government requirement that a contractor make a reimburse or replace in kind for losses due to damage or spoiling of stores through his fault.

References
Department of Defense, U.S. Army. *Dictionary of United States Army Terms.* Army Regulation AR 310-25. Washington, DC: Headquarters, Department of the Army, 1986.

—**RECLASSIFICATION AUTHORITY** is the level of command or activity designated by Headquarters, Department of the Army, to change a primary military occupational specialty or secondary military occupational specialty or to withdraw any AMOS. *See also:* Military Occupational Specialty.

References
Department of Defense, U.S. Army. *Enlisted Personnel Management System.* Army Regulation AR 600-200. Washington, DC: Headquarters, Department of the Army, 1984.

—**RECLASSIFICATION MOS (MILITARY OCCUPATIONAL SPECIALTY)** is an action by a reclassification authority, with or without board action, that results in a change of an AMOS. *See also:* Military Occupational Specialty.

References
Department of Defense, U.S. Army. *Enlisted Personnel Management System.* Army Regulation AR 600-200. Washington, DC: Headquarters, Department of the Army, 1984.

—**RECLASSIFICATION TRAINING** is training that qualifies a soldier in a new military occupational specialty. *See also:* Military Occupational Specialty.

References
Department of Defense, U.S. Army. *Training for Mobilization and War.* Field Manual FM 25-5. Washington, DC: Headquarters, Department of the Army, 1985.

—**RECOGNITION.** (1) Recognition is the determination by any means of the individuality of persons, or of objects (e.g., aircraft, ships, or tanks), or of phenomena (e.g., communications-electronics patterns). (2) In ground combat operations, recognition is the determination that an object is categorically similar to an object already known (e.g., a tank, truck, or man, or person). *See also:* Recognition and Identification System, Recognition Signal.

References
Department of Defense, Joint Chiefs of Staff. *Department of Defense Dictionary of Military and Related Terms.* Washington, DC: GPO, 1986.

—**RECOGNITION AND IDENTIFICATION SYSTEM** is a system whereby friendly forces on land, sea, or air may recognize each other within or between the land, sea, or air.

References
Department of Defense, U.S. Army. *Dictionary of United States Army Terms.* Army Regulation AR 310-25. Washington, DC: Headquarters, Department of the Army, 1986.

—**RECOGNITION SIGNAL** is any prearranged signal by which individuals or units identify each other.

References
Department of Defense, Joint Chiefs of Staff. *Department of Defense Dictionary of Military and Related Terms.* Washington, DC: GPO, 1986.

—**RECOIL CYLINDER** is a fixed cylinder through which a piston attached to a gun is forced by the backward motion of the gun on firing. Recoil is cushioned by springs or by the slow passage of air or a fluid through holes in the piston.

References
Department of Defense, U.S. Army. *Dictionary of United States Army Terms.* Army Regulation AR 310-25. Washington, DC: Headquarters, Department of the Army, 1986.

—**RECOIL MECHANISM** is a mechanism designed to absorb the energy of recoil gradually and so avoid violent movement of the gun carriage. The recoil mechanism is usually hydraulic, pneumatic, or a spring-type shock absorber that permits the barrel assembly to move to the rear while resistance is progressively built up.

References
Department of Defense, U.S. Army. *Dictionary of United States Army Terms.* Army Regulation AR 310-25. Washington, DC: Headquarters, Department of the Army, 1986.

—**RECOIL OPERATED** is operated by the energy of recoil. The ejecting and loading mechanisms are actuated and the firing mechanism is positioned by the force of the barrel moving to the rear under pressure of the powder gases. Recoil-operated weapons are classified as *long recoil* when the barrel and breechblock, or bolt, recoil the entire distance together; and as *short recoil* when the breechblock, or bolt, is unlocked and the barrel is stopped after only a short distance of recoil.

References

Department of Defense, U.S. Army. *Dictionary of United States Army Terms.* Army Regulation AR 310-25. Washington, DC: Headquarters, Department of the Army, 1986.

—**RECOIL PIT** is a pit dug near the breech of a gun to provide space for the breech when it moves backward during recoil.

References

Department of Defense, U.S. Army. *Dictionary of United States Army Terms.* Army Regulation AR 310-25. Washington, DC: Headquarters, Department of the Army, 1986.

—**RECOILLESS** is a term applied to certain weapons employing high velocity gas ports (jets) to counteract recoil. *See also:* Recoilless Rifle (Heavy).

References

Department of Defense, U.S. Army. *Dictionary of United States Army Terms.* Army Regulation AR 310-25. Washington, DC: Headquarters, Department of the Army, 1986.

—**RECOILLESS RIFLE** (HEAVY) is a weapon capable of being fired from either a ground mount or a vehicle, and is capable of destroying tanks.

References

Department of Defense, Joint Chiefs of Staff. *Department of Defense Dictionary of Military and Related Terms.* Washington, DC: GPO, 1986.

—**RECONDITION** is to renovate, repair, overhaul, rebuild, or take any combination of these actions in order to return an item to working condition.

References

Department of Defense, U.S. Army. *Dictionary of United States Army Terms.* Army Regulation AR 310-25. Washington, DC: Headquarters, Department of the Army, 1986.

—**RECONNAISSANCE (RECCE or RECON or RCN).** (1) Reconnaissance is an operation intended to either gather information on the activities, resources or forces of a foreign nation, or on the meteorological, hydrographic, or geographic characteristics of an area. Reconnaissance can be through visual observation or

by other means. (2) Reconnaissance, in Army tactical intelligence, means a mission undertaken to obtain, by visual observation or other detection methods, information about the activities and resources of an enemy or a potential enemy; or to collect data concerning the meteorological, hydrographic, or geographic characteristics of a particular area.

References

Department of Defense, Defense Intelligence College. *Glossary of Intelligence Terms and Definitions.* Washington, DC: DIC, 1987.

Department of Defense, U.S. Army. *Operational Terms and Symbols.* Field Manual FM 101-5-1. Washington, DC: Headquarters, Department of the Army, 1985.

———. *Support Operations: Echelons Above Corps.* Field Manual FM 100-16. Washington, DC: Headquarters, Department of the Army, 1986.

—**RECONNAISSANCE AND SECURITY POSITIONS** are a series of outposts, roadblocks, and reconnaissance elements located on the principal approaches to, or on the dominating terrain outside of, an airhead.

References

Department of Defense, U.S. Army. *Dictionary of United States Army Terms.* Army Regulation AR 310-25. Washington, DC: Headquarters, Department of the Army, 1986.

—**RECONNAISSANCE BROADCAST** is a radio broadcast operated by the ground liaison officer with a reconnaissance unit to disseminate the results of visual, photographic, or radar reconnaissance. This broadcast is monitored by Army, corps, divisions, and any other interested party.

References

Department of Defense, U.S. Army. *Dictionary of United States Army Terms.* Army Regulation AR 310-25. Washington, DC: Headquarters, Department of the Army, 1986.

—**RECONNAISSANCE BY FIRE** is a method of reconnaissance in which fire is placed on a suspected enemy position to cause the enemy to disclose his presence by movement or return fire.

References

Department of Defense, U.S. Army. *Operational Terms and Symbols.* Field Manual FM 101-5-1. Washington, DC: Headquarters, Department of the Army, 1985.

—**RECONNAISSANCE EXPLOITATION REPORT (RECCEXREP)** is an intelligence imagery and photoreconnaissance term for the format used to report the results of a tactical air reconnaissance mission. Whenever possible, it includes the interpretation of sensor imagery resulting from the mission. It provides the first rapid analysis of imagery and debriefing of the air crew that flew the reconnaissance mission. The report discusses the targets that were requested in the mission tasking, addressing each one separately. *See also:* Reconnaissance.

References

Department of Defense, Joint Chiefs of Staff. *Department of Defense Dictionary of Military and Related Terms.* Washington, DC: GPO, 1986.

—**RECONNAISSANCE IN FORCE (RIF).** (1) RIF in intelligence imagery and photoreconnaissance, refers to an offensive operation that is intended to discover or test the enemy's strength or to obtain other information. (2) RIF is a limited-objective operation conducted by a large force to discover and test the enemy's dispositions and strengths, or to develop other intelligence. Even when the commander is executing a RIF to gather information, he must be alert to any opportunity to exploit tactical success. If the enemy situation must be developed along a broad front, the RIF may consist of strong probing actions to determine the enemy situation at selected points. The enemy's reactions may reveal weaknesses in its defensive system. Because RIF is primarily an information-gathering operation, commanders must carefully evaluate the risks involved, and must make provisions in advance to either extricate the force or exploit its success. *See also:* Reconnaissance.

References

Department of Defense, U.S. Army. *Operational Terms and Symbols.* Field Manual FM 101-5-1. Washington, DC: Headquarters, Department of the Army, 1985.

——. *Operations.* Field Manual FM 100-5. Washington, DC: Headquarters, Department of the Army, 1986.

—**RECONNAISSANCE OF POSITION** is a detailed examination of the terrain in order to provide a basis for selecting advantageous locations for guns and troops.

References

Department of Defense, U.S. Army. *Dictionary of United States Army Terms.* Army Regulation AR 310-25. Washington, DC: Headquarters, Department of the Army, 1986.

—**RECONNAISSANCE OPERATIONS** gain information about the terrain and the enemy. They are termed route, zone, and area. The techniques for reconnoitering are generally the same for all three: the mission indicates the type of information that is sought.

References

Department of Defense, U.S. Army. *The Tank and Mechanized Infantry Battalion Task Force.* Field Manual FM 71-2. Washington, DC: Headquarters, Department of the Army, 1977.

—**RECONNAISSANCE PATROL** (AREA OR ZONE) is a patrol that collects information or confirms or disproves the accuracy of information that was previously gained. *See also:* Patrol, Reconnaissance.

References

Department of Defense, U.S. Army. *The Infantry Rifle Company (Infantry, Airborne, Air Assault, Ranger).* Field Manual FM 7-10. Washington, DC: Headquarters, Department of the Army, 1982.

—**RECONNAISSANCE PATROL** (GROUND) is a small patrol used to gain information about the enemy, preferably without its knowledge. *See also:* Patrol, Reconnaissance.

References

Department of Defense, U.S. Army. *Operational Terms and Symbols.* Field Manual FM 101-5-1. Washington, DC: Headquarters, Department of the Army, 1985.

—**RECONNAISSANCE PHOTOGRAPHY,** in intelligence imagery and photoreconnaissance, is photography that has been taken to obtain information on the results of bombing, or on enemy movements, concentrations, activities, or forces. *See also:* Reconnaissance.

References

Department of Defense, Joint Chiefs of Staff. *Department of Defense Dictionary of Military and Related Terms.* Washington, DC: GPO, 1986.

—**RECONNAISSANCE STRIP** is a series of overlapping photographs that, when joined together, provide a rough continuous picture of the area photographed. A reconnaissance strip is generally used in studying a long, narrow piece of terrain (e.g., a river or a road). *See also:* Aerial Reconnaissance.

References

Department of Defense, U.S. Army. *Dictionary of United States Army Terms.* Army Regulation AR 310-25. Washington, DC: Headquarters, Department of the Army, 1986.

—**RECONNAISSANCE SYSTEM TURNAROUND** is the activity of an imagery inspection and the preparation and clearance of a reconnaissance system for the next sortie. *See also:* Aerial Reconnaissance.

References

Department of Defense, U.S. Army. *Dictionary of United States Army Terms.* Army Regulation AR 310-25. Washington, DC: Headquarters, Department of the Army, 1986.

—**RECONSTITUTE.** (1) To reconstitute is to replace on the rolls of the Army in an inactive status, a table of organization and equipment unit that has been disbanded. This can be done only by the authority of the Secretary of the Army. (2) To reconstitute is to restore water to dehydrated foods. (3) To reconstitute is to reform or remake (e.g., to reconstitute a reserve). (4) To reconstitute is to revitalize medical assemblages through replacing outdated deteriorating items, including new items, and repackaging containers, when appropriate. *See also:* Medical Treatment.

References

Department of Defense, U.S. Army. *Dictionary of United States Army Terms.* Army Regulation AR 310-25. Washington, DC: Headquarters, Department of the Army, 1986.

—**RECONSTITUTION** is the total process of keeping a force supplied with various supply classes, services, and replacement personnel, and the equipment required to maintain the desired level of combat effectiveness. It also includes restoring units that are not combat effective to the desired level of combat effectiveness by replacing critical equipment and personnel. Reconstitution encompasses unit regeneration and sustaining support. *See also:* Rehabilitation.

References

Department of Defense, U.S. Army. *Combat Service Support Operations-Division.* Field Manual FM 63-2. Washington, DC: Headquarters, Department of the Army, 1983.

———. *Operations.* Field Manual FM 100-5. Washington, DC: Headquarters, Department of the Army, 1986.

———. *Planning Logistics Support for Military Operations.* Field Manual FM 701-58. Washington, DC: Headquarters, Department of the Army, 1987.

———. *Support Operations: Echelons Above Corps.* Field Manual FM 100-16. Washington, DC: Headquarters, Department of the Army, 1986.

—**RECONSTITUTION SITE** is a location selected by the surviving command authority as the site at which a damaged or destroyed headquarters can be reformed from survivors of the attack or from personnel from other sources who have been predesignated as replacements. *See also:* Reconstitution.

References

Department of Defense, Joint Chiefs of Staff. *Department of Defense Dictionary of Military and Related Terms.* Washington, DC: GPO, 1986.

—**RECORD AS TARGET,** in artillery, is the order used to denote that the target is to be recorded for future engagement or reference.

References

Department of Defense, Joint Chiefs of Staff. *Department of Defense Dictionary of Military and Related Terms.* Washington, DC: GPO, 1986.

—**RECORD FIRING** is target practice in which a record is kept. For small arms, this record is the basis of a soldier's classification in marksmanship.

References

Department of Defense, U.S. Army. *Dictionary of United States Army Terms.* Army Regulation AR 310-25. Washington, DC: Headquarters, Department of the Army, 1986.

—**RECORDED,** in artillery, is the response used to indicate that the action taken to "record as target" has been completed. *See also:* Record as Target.

References

Department of Defense, Joint Chiefs of Staff. *Department of Defense Dictionary of Military and Related Terms.* Washington, DC: GPO, 1986.

—**RECORDING,** in Army tactical intelligence, is a step in the signals intelligence process. *See also:* SIGINT Process.

References

Department of Defense, U.S. Army. *Counter-Signals Intelligence (C-SIGINT) Operations.* Field Manual FM 34-62. Washington, DC: Headquarters, Department of the Army, 1986.

—**RECORDS** are any papers, photographs (including film), photographic copies, or maps, regardless of their physical form or characteristics, that are accumulated or maintained in filing equipment, boxes, or on shelves, and occupy office or storage space. Records do not include blank forms that are maintained for supply purposes. This term has the same meaning as files, except that it is more inclusive and more generalized. *See also:* Records Administrator, Records Center, Records Holding Area, Records Management, Records Management Officer.

References
Department of Defense, U.S. Army. *Dictionary of United States Army Terms.* Army Regulation AR 310-25. Washington, DC: Headquarters, Department of the Army, 1986.

—RECORDS ADMINISTRATOR is an individual designated to supervise records management throughout a command and serve as staff officer on all matters relating to records management. Records administrators are designated by the commanders of major commands, the commanders of intermediate commands, and the heads of Headquarters, Department of the Army, offices who have installations or off-post activities under their command. *See also:* Records.

References
Department of Defense, U.S. Army. *Dictionary of United States Army Terms.* Army Regulation AR 310-25. Washington, DC: Headquarters, Department of the Army, 1986.

—RECORDS CENTER. (1) A records center is an activity established in the continental United States for receiving, maintaining, servicing, and disposing records that are required to be retired from active offices of the Department of the Army, records-holding areas, and overseas records centers in accordance with retirement standards because they can be maintained and administered more efficiently in a central facility. (2) A records center is an activity established in a major overseas command to hold cutoff files in less desirable space and low cost filing equipment pending their destruction or retirement to a records center in the continental United States. *See also:* Records.

References
Department of Defense, U.S. Army. *Dictionary of United States Army Terms.* Army Regulation AR 310-25. Washington, DC: Headquarters, Department of the Army, 1986.

—RECORDS HOLDING AREA is a facility established at an installation or a major activity that is located off an installation of the Army field command in the continental United States. Its purpose is to hold cutoff files in less desirable space and low-cost filing equipment pending their destruction or their retirement to a records center in the continental United States. *See also:* Records.

References
Department of Defense, U.S. Army. *Dictionary of United States Army Terms.* Army Regulation AR 310-25. Washington, DC: Headquarters, Department of the Army, 1986.

—RECORDS MANAGEMENT is the application of management techniques in the creation, transmission, maintenance, use, preservation, and disposition of records. Records management is synonymous with records administration and paperwork management. *See also:* Records.

References
Department of Defense, U.S. Army. *Dictionary of United States Army Terms.* Army Regulation AR 310-25. Washington, DC: Headquarters, Department of the Army, 1986.

—RECORDS MANAGEMENT OFFICER is the individual designated to supervise the internal records management function in a Headquarters, Department of the Army, office; a major or intermediate command headquarters; an installation; or an off-post activity. *See also:* Records.

References
Department of Defense, U.S. Army. *Dictionary of United States Army Terms.* Army Regulation AR 310-25. Washington, DC: Headquarters, Department of the Army, 1986.

—RECOUPMENT (1) Recoupment is a payment to an individual for expenses. (2) Recoupment is a payment to the government by an individual for losses that are a person's fault or are due to his carelessness. It is the repayment or recovery of money.

References
Department of Defense, U.S. Army. *Dictionary of United States Army Terms.* Army Regulation AR 310-25. Washington, DC: Headquarters, Department of the Army, 1986.

—RECOVER. (1) To recover is to go back to a position that was just held in a drill or practice. (2) Recover is a command to go back to any such position. (3) To recover is to solve or reconstruct cryptographic data or plain text. (4) To recover is to return damaged, unserviceable, or abandoned materiel to supply or maintenance channels. It is usually applicable only to the combat zone. *See also:* Recovery.

References

Department of Defense, U.S. Army. *Dictionary of United States Army Terms.* Army Regulation AR 310-25. Washington, DC: Headquarters, Department of the Army, 1986.

—**RECOVERABLE ITEM** is an item that normally is not consumed in use and is subject to return for repair or disposal. *See also:* Repairable Item.

References

Department of Defense, Joint Chiefs of Staff. *Department of Defense Dictionary of Military and Related Terms.* Washington, DC: GPO, 1986.

—**RECOVERY** encompasses the following: it returns immobilized equipment to operation; it retrieves equipment for repair and reissue; it retrieves equipment so that it may be used as a source of repair parts through controlled exchange or cannibalization; it retrieves abandoned materiel for further use; it prevents enemy capture of materiel; and it obtains enemy materiel for intelligence exploitation or for use by U.S. or allied forces.

References

Department of Defense, U.S. Army. *Operational Terms and Symbols.* Field Manual FM 101-5-1. Washington, DC: Headquarters, Department of the Army, 1985.

———. *Organizational Maintenance Operations.* Field Manual FM 29-2. Washington, DC: Headquarters, Department of the Army, 1984.

—**RECOVERY AND RECONSTITUTION** encompass the actions taken by a nation prior to, during, and following an attack by an enemy nation to minimize the effects of the attack, rehabilitate the national economy, provide for the welfare of the people, and maximize the combat potential of the remaining forces and supporting activities.

References

Department of Defense, Joint Chiefs of Staff. *Department of Defense Dictionary of Military and Related Terms.* Washington, DC: GPO, 1986.

—**RECOVERY AREA** is an area from which evaders and escapees are evacuated. *See also:* Evasion and Escape.

References

Department of Defense, U.S. Army. *Individual Military Education and Training.* Army Regulation AR 350-1. Washington, DC: Headquarters, Department of the Army, 1987.

—**RECOVERY PARTY.** (1) A recovery party is a group sent to locate and bring back damaged materiel that can be repaired and used again. (2) A recovery party is a surveying party that is sent to locate identifiable features of the terrain and to mark them on air photographs of the area for use as controls in mapmaking.

References

Department of Defense, U.S. Army. *Dictionary of United States Army Terms.* Army Regulation AR 310-25. Washington, DC: Headquarters, Department of the Army, 1986.

—**RECOVERY SITE**, in evasion and escape usage, is an area from which an evader or an escapee can be evacuated. *See also:* Evasion and Escape.

References

Department of Defense, Joint Chiefs of Staff. *Department of Defense Dictionary of Military and Related Terms.* Washington, DC: GPO, 1986.

—**RECOVERY VEHICLE, MEDIUM,** is a full-tracked vehicle designed for rescuing crews and recovering tanks and other vehicles under battlefield conditions. It is designated as M88A1.

References

Department of Defense, Joint Chiefs of Staff. *Department of Defense Dictionary of Military and Related Terms.* Washington, DC: GPO, 1986.

—**RECREATION CENTER** is a hotel or other improved facility offering billeting and messing accommodations for military personnel who are on leave or pass. In addition, such a center usually provides recreational, social, and entertainment programs.

References

Department of Defense, U.S. Army. *Dictionary of United States Army Terms.* Army Regulation AR 310-25. Washington, DC: Headquarters, Department of the Army, 1986.

—**RECREATION SERVICES.** (1) Recreation services is a term used to denote a functional grouping of certain morale and welfare services. The term normally includes entertainment, service clubs, libraries, crafts, sports, and rest, leave, and relaxation. (2) Recreation services embrace the personnel services established and controlled by military authorities, and designed to contribute to the physical and mental effectiveness of military personnel and authorized family members and civilian employees.

References

Department of Defense, U.S. Army. *Dictionary of United States Army Terms.* Army Regulation AR 310-25. Washington, DC: Headquarters, Department of the Army, 1986.

—**RECRUITING DISTRICT** is a geographical subdivision of an Army area in the continental United States that is established to administer recruiting activities. *See also:* Recruiting Main Station, Recruiting Main Objective, Recruiting Service, Recruiting Station.

References

Department of Defense, U.S. Army. *Dictionary of United States Army Terms.* Army Regulation AR 310-25. Washington, DC: Headquarters, Department of the Army, 1986.

—**RECRUITING MAIN STATION** is an installation established, as required, under each recruiting district for the purpose of processing enlistees.

References

Department of Defense, U.S. Army. *Dictionary of United States Army Terms.* Army Regulation AR 310-25. Washington, DC: Headquarters, Department of the Army, 1986.

—**RECRUITING OBJECTIVE** is a goal that establishes the number of personnel to be enlisted by the recruiting service in a given period.

References

Department of Defense, U.S. Army. *Dictionary of United States Army Terms.* Army Regulation AR 310-25. Washington, DC: Headquarters, Department of the Army, 1986.

—**RECRUITING SERVICE** is the field service force that operates the recruiting program for the U.S. Army.

References

Department of Defense, U.S. Army. *Dictionary of United States Army Terms.* Army Regulation AR 310-25. Washington, DC: Headquarters, Department of the Army, 1986.

—**RECRUITING STATION** is an installation established under each recruiting main station. It is where prospective recruits are contacted and are preliminarily screened for enlistment.

References

Department of Defense, U.S. Army. *Dictionary of United States Army Terms.* Army Regulation AR 310-25. Washington, DC: Headquarters, Department of the Army, 1986.

—**RECTANGLE OF DISPERSION** is an area, assumed to be rectangular, in which the projectiles of a weapon will fall when the weapon is fired with the same firing data under apparently identical conditions.

References

Department of Defense, U.S. Army. *Dictionary of United States Army Terms.* Army Regulation AR 310-25. Washington, DC: Headquarters, Department of the Army, 1986.

—**RECTANGULAR COORDINATES** are a system of lines drawn parallel to two fixed lines of reference at known distances from them. A point may be located in such a system by the intersection of two such lines drawn parallel to, and at known distances from, the two known perpendicular reference lines.

References

Department of Defense, U.S. Army. *Dictionary of United States Army Terms.* Army Regulation AR 310-25. Washington, DC: Headquarters, Department of the Army, 1986.

—**RECURRING COST** is the sum of the expenses for personnel, materiel consumed in use, operating, overhead, support services, and other items that are incurred on an annual or recurring basis.

References

Department of Defense, U.S. Army. *Dictionary of United States Army Terms.* Army Regulation AR 310-25. Washington, DC: Headquarters, Department of the Army, 1986.

—**RECURRING DEMAND** is a request by an authorized requisitioner to satisfy a materiel requirement for consumption or stock replenishment that is anticipated to recur periodically. Demand whose future occurrence is unknown is considered recurring. Recurring demands are considered by the supporting supply system in order to procure, store, and distribute materiel to meet similar future demands.

References

Department of Defense, Joint Chiefs of Staff. *Department of Defense Dictionary of Military and Related Terms.* Washington, DC: GPO, 1986.

—**RECURRING INVESTMENT** is a cost category containing the cost elements that occur repeatedly in the production of a weapon or support system, or its components. It includes the costs incurred to deliver the weapon or support system or its components to the user.

References

Department of Defense, U.S. Army. *Dictionary of United States Army Terms*. Army Regulation AR 310-25. Washington, DC: Headquarters, Department of the Army, 1986.

—**RECURRING ISSUE** is an issue made on a cyclical basis to replenish materiel that is consumed or worn out through fair wear and tear in operations. Each issue is made to a consignee who is eligible to request further replenishment, when required, in the foreseeable future.

References

Department of Defense, U.S. Army. *Dictionary of United States Army Terms*. Army Regulation AR 310-25. Washington, DC: Headquarters, Department of the Army, 1986.

—**RECYCLE** is the cycling of an individual within a course of instruction that will result in increased training time beyond the normal course length.

References

Department of Defense, U.S. Army. *Individual Military Education and Training*. Army Regulation AR 350-1. Washington, DC: Headquarters, Department of the Army, 1987.

—**REDEPLOYMENT** is the transfer of a unit, an individual, or supplies deployed in one area to another area, or to another location within the area, or to the zone of interior for the purpose of further employment.

References

Department of Defense, Joint Chiefs of Staff. *Department of Defense Dictionary of Military and Related Terms*. Washington, DC: GPO, 1986.

—**REDESIGNATE** is to change the official name or number of a unit. The redesignation has the effect of removing the original designation from current records and substituting the new designation.

References

Department of Defense, U.S. Army. *Dictionary of United States Army Terms*. Army Regulation AR 310-25. Washington, DC: Headquarters, Department of the Army, 1986.

—**REDESIGNATED SITE** is a surviving facility that may be redesignated as the command center to carry out the functions of an incapacitated alternate headquarters or facility.

References

Department of Defense, Joint Chiefs of Staff. *Department of Defense Dictionary of Military and Related Terms*. Washington, DC: GPO, 1986.

—**REDEYE** is a lightweight, man-portable, shoulder-fired air defense artillery weapon for low altitude air defense of forward combat area troops. It is designated the FIM-43.

References

Department of Defense, U.S. Army. *U.S. Army Air Defense Employment*. Field Manual FM 44-1. Washington, DC: Headquarters, Department of the Army, 1983.

—**REDISTRIBUTION** is the act of transferring control, use, or the location of material between units or activities within or among the military services or between the military services and other government agencies. *See also:* Redistribution Order.

References

Department of Defense, Joint Chiefs of Staff. *Department of Defense Dictionary of Military and Related Terms*. Washington, DC: GPO, 1986.

—**REDISTRIBUTION ORDER.** (1) A redistribution order is an order issued by a responsible inventory manager to an accountable supply distribution activity within the manager's supply distribution complex, directing the release of materiel to another supply redistribution activity within the same supply complex. (2) For intraservice use, a redistribution order is used by inventory managers or major subordinate commanders to direct the release and shipment of materiel from an accountable post, camp, station, or base, to another similar accountable activity in order to satisfy a specific command.

References

Department of Defense, U.S. Army. *Dictionary of United States Army Terms*. Army Regulation AR 310-25. Washington, DC: Headquarters, Department of the Army, 1986.

—**REDUCED CHARGE** is a charge that uses a reduced amount of propellent to fire a gun at a short range (as compared with normal range). *See also:* Normal Charge.

References

Department of Defense, Joint Chiefs of Staff. *Department of Defense Dictionary of Military and Related Terms*. Washington, DC: GPO, 1986.

—**REDUCED DIET** is a diet consistent with the food requirements for sedentary conditions. It is authorized for use with prisoners in disciplinary segregation. *See also:* Disciplinary Action.

References

Department of Defense, U.S. Army. *Dictionary of United States Army Terms.* Army Regulation AR 310-25. Washington, DC: Headquarters, Department of the Army, 1986.

—**REDUCED LIGHTNING** is the reduction in brightness of ground vehicle lights by either reducing the power or by screening the lamps in such a way that the intensity of any visible light is limited.

References

Department of Defense, Joint Chiefs of Staff. *Department of Defense Dictionary of Military and Related Terms.* Washington, DC: GPO, 1986.

—**REDUCED STRENGTH UNIT** is a unit organized at the minimum organizational strength, consistent with the demands of a long noncombatant period and a limited period of combat.

References

Department of Defense, U.S. Army. *Dictionary of United States Army Terms.* Army Regulation AR 310-25. Washington, DC: Headquarters, Department of the Army, 1986.

—**REDUCTION** is a change in a soldier's status to a lower pay grade. *See also:* Reduction Authority, Reduction Board.

References

Department of Defense, U.S. Army. *Enlisted Personnel Management System.* Army Regulation AR 600-200. Washington, DC: Headquarters, Department of the Army, 1984.

—**REDUCTION AUTHORITY** is a commander who has the authority to reduce enlisted members in pay grade.

References

Department of Defense, U.S. Army. *Enlisted Personnel Management System.* Army Regulation AR 600-200. Washington, DC: Headquarters, Department of the Army, 1984.

—**REDUCTION BOARD** is a local board tasked to recommend whether an enlisted member should be reduced in pay grade for inefficiency or civil conviction.

References

Department of Defense, U.S. Army. *Enlisted Personnel Management System.* Army Regulation AR 600-200. Washington, DC: Headquarters, Department of the Army, 1984.

—**REDUCTION COEFFICIENT** is the ratio of observer target distance to the gun target distance. It is a number by which an observed deviation is multiplied in order to correct the firing data at the guns.

References

Department of Defense, U.S. Army. *Dictionary of United States Army Terms.* Army Regulation AR 310-25. Washington, DC: Headquarters, Department of the Army, 1986.

—**REDUCTION IN FORCE (RIF)** is an involuntary reduction of civilian personnel in a military organization.

References

Department of Defense, U.S. Army. *Dictionary of United States Army Terms.* Army Regulation AR 310-25. Washington, DC: Headquarters, Department of the Army, 1986.

—**REENLISTMENT** is a second or subsequent voluntary enrollment in the Army. *See also:* Immediate Reenlistment, Reenlistment Bonus, Reenlistment Leave, Reenlistment Rate.

References

Department of Defense, U.S. Army. *Dictionary of United States Army Terms.* Army Regulation AR 310-25. Washington, DC: Headquarters, Department of the Army, 1986.

—**REENLISTMENT BONUS** is a bonus paid to an enlisted member who reenlists within 90 days or three months from his date of honorable discharge for service that is to be performed after the reenlistment.

References

Department of Defense, U.S. Army. *Dictionary of United States Army Terms.* Army Regulation AR 310-25. Washington, DC: Headquarters, Department of the Army, 1986.

—**REENLISTMENT LEAVE** is leave granted to enlisted personnel as a result of reenlistment. *See also:* Reenlistment.

References

Department of Defense, U.S. Army. *Leaves and Passes.* Army Regulation AR 630-5. Washington, DC: Headquarters, Department of the Army, 1984.

—**REENLISTMENT RATE** is the ratio of total reenlistments occurring in a given period to total number of individuals who were eligible to reenlist in the same period.

References

Department of Defense, U.S. Army. *Dictionary of United States Army Terms.* Army Regulation AR 310-25. Washington, DC: Headquarters, Department of the Army, 1986.

—**REFER.** To refer is to bring the gun sights on a chosen aiming point without moving an artillery piece that has been laid for direction.

References

Department of Defense, U.S. Army. *Dictionary of United States Army Terms.* Army Regulation AR 310-25. Washington, DC: Headquarters, Department of the Army, 1986.

—**REFERENCE LINE** is a convenient and readily identifiable line used by the observer or spotter as the line to which he spots the target.

References

Department of Defense, Joint Chiefs of Staff. *Department of Defense Dictionary of Military and Related Terms.* Washington, DC: GPO, 1986.

—**REFERENCE NUMBER.** (1) A reference number is one of a series of numbers chosen to represent the values of units of measure, especially in fire control, to avoid the use of plus, minus, up, down, right, and left. (2) In the Federal Cataloging System, a reference number is a number, except an activity stock number, used to identify an item of production or is a number used with other identifying numbers to identify a supply item. Reference numbers include manufacturer's, part, drawing, model, type, source-controlling, and specification-controlling numbers; the manufacturer's trade name, when the manufacturer identifies the item by trade name only; NATO stock numbers; and specification or standard part, drawing, or type numbers.

References

Department of Defense, U.S. Army. *Dictionary of United States Army Terms.* Army Regulation AR 310-25. Washington, DC: Headquarters, Department of the Army, 1986.

—**REFERENCE PIECE** is one gun of a battery that is selected as the standard with which to compare the firing of other guns. Each of the other guns is called a test piece.

References

Department of Defense, U.S. Army. *Dictionary of United States Army Terms.* Army Regulation AR 310-25. Washington, DC: Headquarters, Department of the Army, 1986.

—**REFERENCE POINT** is a prominent, easily located point in the terrain.

References

Department of Defense, U.S. Army. *Operational Terms and Symbols.* Field Manual FM 101-5-1. Washington, DC: Headquarters, Department of the Army, 1985.

—**REFERRAL ORDER** is an order used between depots, inventory managers, or managers in a supply distribution system to pass routed requisitions for supplies to another supply source when the initial one cannot fulfill the demand.

References

Department of Defense, U.S. Army. *Dictionary of United States Army Terms.* Army Regulation AR 310-25. Washington, DC: Headquarters, Department of the Army, 1986.

—**REFERRING POINT** is a new aiming point on which gunners are to refer an artillery piece that has been laid for direction.

References

Department of Defense, U.S. Army. *Dictionary of United States Army Terms.* Army Regulation AR 310-25. Washington, DC: Headquarters, Department of the Army, 1986.

—**REFLECTED SHOCK WAVE** occurs when a shock wave traveling in a medium strikes the interface between this medium and a denser medium. At this time, part of the energy of the shock wave induces a shock wave in the denser medium and the remainder of the energy results in the formation of a reflected shock wave that travels back through the less dense medium. *See also:* Shock Wave.

References

Department of Defense, Joint Chiefs of Staff. *Department of Defense Dictionary of Military and Related Terms.* Washington, DC: GPO, 1986.

—**RE-FORM** is a command to restore the previous element or formation and is used only during drill instructions.

References

Department of Defense, U.S. Army. *Drills and Ceremonies.* Field Manual FM 22-5. Washington, DC: Headquarters, Department of the Army, 1986.

—**REFUGEE** is a term used in clandestine and covert intelligence operations to describe a person who is outside the country or area of his former residence and who, because of fear of being prosecuted or because of hostilities in that area or country, is unwilling or unable to return to it.

References

Department of Defense, Defense Intelligence College. *Glossary of Intelligence Terms and Definitions.* Washington, DC: DIC, 1987.

—**REGENERATION** is the rebuilding of a unit through the large-scale replacement of personnel, equipment, and supplies; the reestablishment of command and control; and the conduct of mission-essential training for replacement personnel. Usually a unit undergoing regeneration must be withdrawn from the enemy. *See also:* Reconstitution, Rehabilitation, Sustaining Support.

References

Department of Defense, U.S. Army. *Operations.* Field Manual FM 100-5. Washington, DC: Headquarters, Department of the Army, 1986.

—**REGIMENT (REGT)** is a grouping of like-type continental U.S. and outside continental U.S. battalions with the same regimental designation that is formed to allow recurring assignments over the length of a soldier's career. Organizationally, it is an administrative and tactical unit, on a command level below a division or brigade and above a battalion, the entire organization of which is prescribed by a table of organization. The commanding officer of a regiment is usually a colonel. *See also:* Army, Battalion, Brigade, Company, Corps, Division, Platoon, Squad.

References

Department of Defense, U.S. Army. *Army Forces Training.* Army Regulation AR 350-41. Washington, DC: Headquarters, Department of the Army, 1986.

—**REGIMENTAL AFFILIATION** is the close and continuous association or identification of an officer with one regiment throughout his career.

References

Department of Defense, U.S. Army. *Officer Assignment Policies, Details, and Transfers.* Army Regulation AR 614-100. Washington, DC: Headquarters, Department of the Army, 1984.

—**REGIMENTAL LANDING TEAM (RLT)**, in amphibious operations, is a task organization of an infantry regiment, battle group, or similar unit, reinforced by the elements required for initiating combat operations ashore. This is normally composed of the assault battalion landing teams and a regimental landing team in reserve. *See also:* Amphibious Operation.

References

Department of Defense, U.S. Army. *Operations.* Field Manual FM 100-5. Washington, DC: Headquarters, Department of the Army, 1986.

—**REGIONAL MAINTENANCE REPRESENTATIVE** is a military or a civil service representative who makes periodic visits to all military users of equipment to assist in improving organizational and field maintenance; report unsatisfactory performance of materiel and materiel design deficiencies; assist in inspecting equipment for repair feasibility upon request; assisting in evacuating unserviceable equipment; provide on-the-job training; and investigate tools, parts, and test equipment problems.

References

Department of Defense, U.S. Army. *Dictionary of United States Army Terms.* Army Regulation AR 310-25. Washington, DC: Headquarters, Department of the Army, 1986.

—**REGIONAL PURCHASE** is the purchase of supplies or equipment in the United States by a designated regional purchasing office to fill the supply requirements of installations located within a geographic area of responsibility.

References

Department of Defense, U.S. Army. *Dictionary of United States Army Terms.* Army Regulation AR 310-25. Washington, DC: Headquarters, Department of the Army, 1986.

—**REGIONAL REINFORCING FORCE** is a force made available to a major NATO commander, which is then allocated by him to a specific major subordinate commander for employment.

References

Department of Defense, Joint Chiefs of Staff. *Department of Defense Dictionary of Military and Related Terms.* Washington, DC: GPO, 1986.

—**REGIONAL RESERVE** is a reinforcing force, made available through a major NATO commander to a major subordinate commander, that is not yet committed to a specific task, but is available as required for employment or engagement on order within the major subordinate commander's area of responsibility. *See also:* Regional Reinforcing Force.

References
Department of Defense, Joint Chiefs of Staff. *Department of Defense Dictionary of Military and Related Terms.* Washington, DC: GPO, 1986.

—**REGIONAL SUPPORT** is combat service support that includes transportation and supply direct support, maintenance direct support and general support, personnel, finance, and troop welfare administration, military justice, responsibility for coordinating area communications and group development, and dissemination of intelligence and nuclear, biological, chemical reporting and warning to all tenant units. Regional support does not include health services. *See also:* Combat Service Support , Direct Support, General Support.

References
Department of Defense, U.S. Army. *Support Operations: Echelons Above Corps.* Field Manual FM 100-16. Washington, DC: Headquarters, Department of the Army, 1986.

—**REGISTERED CRYPTOMATERIAL** is cryptomaterial that is accountable to the office of record and is issued on receipt, transfer, and destruction, as well as on a quarterly basis. *See also:* CRYPTO.

References
Department of Defense, U.S. Army. *Dictionary of United States Army Terms.* Army Regulation AR 310-25. Washington, DC: Headquarters, Department of the Army, 1986.

—**REGISTERED DOCUMENT** is a classified document bearing a short title and a register number for which periodic inventory is established.

References
Department of Defense, U.S. Army. *Dictionary of United States Army Terms.* Army Regulation AR 310-25. Washington, DC: Headquarters, Department of the Army, 1986.

—**REGISTRATION** is the adjustment of fire to determine firing data corrections. *See also:* Registration Fire, Registration Point.

References
Department of Defense, Joint Chiefs of Staff. *Department of Defense Dictionary of Military and Related Terms.* Washington, DC: GPO, 1986.

—**REGISTRATION FIRE** is fire delivered to obtain accurate data for the subsequent target accuracy.

References
Department of Defense, U.S. Army. *Operational Terms and Symbols.* Field Manual FM 101-5-1. Washington, DC: Headquarters, Department of the Army, 1985.

—**REGISTRATION POINT** is a terrain feature or other designated point on which fire is adjusted so corrections can be made to firing data.

References
Department of Defense, U.S. Army. *Operational Terms and Symbols.* Field Manual FM 101-5-1. Washington, DC: Headquarters, Department of the Army, 1985.

—**REGRADE** is to determine that certain classified information requires, in the interests of national defense, a higher or lower degree of protection against unauthorized disclosure than is currently provided, coupled with changing the classification designation to reflect such a higher or lower degree (e.g., a document might be regraded from SECRET to CONFIDENTIAL and then sorted in a less secure area or container). *See also:* Downgrade.

References
Department of Defense, Joint Chiefs of Staff. *Department of Defense Dictionary of Military and Related Terms.* Washington, DC: GPO, 1986.

—**REGULAR ARMY (RA)** is the permanent army that is maintained in peacetime as well as in war. It is the standing army, and one of the components of the U.S. Army. *See also:* Active Army, Army Composition, Army National Guard, Reserve Components, United States Army, United States Army Reserve.

References
Department of Defense, U.S. Army. *Dictionary of United States Army Terms.* Army Regulation AR 310-25. Washington, DC: Headquarters, Department of the Army, 1986.

—**REGULAR ARMY PROMOTION LIST NUMBER (RAPLN)** is a number that denotes rank order of Regular Army warrant officers on active duty.

References
Department of Defense, U.S. Army. *Personnel Selection and Classification, Warrant Officer Occupational Specialties.* Army Regulation AR 611-112. Washington, DC: Headquarters, Department of the Army, 1987.

————. *Promotion of Officers on Active Duty.* Army Regulation AR 624-100. Washington, DC: Headquarters, Department of the Army, 1984.

—**REGULAR CONVOY PHASE** is the periodic shipping of supplies according to a preplanned schedule.

References
Department of Defense, U.S. Army. *Dictionary of United States Army Terms.* Army Regulation AR 310-25. Washington, DC: Headquarters, Department of the Army, 1986.

—**REGULARLY SCHEDULED UNIT TRAINING ASSEMBLY (RSUTA),** in the Army Reserve, is training time for which pay and retirement point credit are authorized.

References
Department of Defense, U.S. Army. *Information Pamphlet for the Career Development of Enlisted Members of the U.S. Army Reserve.* Department of the Army Pamphlet DA PAM 140-8. Washington, DC: Headquarters, Department of the Army, 1986.

—**REGULARLY SUPERCEDED KEYING MATERIAL,** in communications security, refers to the keying material that is designated for use during a specific period of time, and is superceded regardless of whether the key is used. *See also:* Communications Security.

References
Department of Defense, U.S. Army. *Dictionary of United States Army Terms.* Army Regulation AR 310-25. Washington, DC: Headquarters, Department of the Army, 1986.

—**REGULATED ITEM** is any item whose distribution is closely supervised because there is a shortage of the item, it is costly, or it is highly technical or hazardous. *See also:* Critical Item, Critical Supplies, Materiel.

References
Department of Defense, Joint Chiefs of Staff. *Department of Defense Dictionary of Military and Related Terms.* Washington, DC: GPO, 1986.

—**REGULATED SUPPLIES,** or command regulated supplies, and are supplies that the commander has decided must be closely controlled because of their scarcity or high cost, or because of mission need. Any item or group of items can be designated as regulated, but normally some items in supply classes II, III (bulk), IV, V, and VII are regulated. If an item is regulated, the commander designating the item must approve its release before issue. *See also:* Classes of Supply.

References
Department of Defense, U.S. Army. *Operational Terms and Symbols.* Field Manual FM 101-5-1. Washington, DC: Headquarters, Department of the Army, 1985.

—**REGULATING OFFICER** is an officer in command of a regulating station who is responsible for the smooth and orderly movement of troops and materiel within the area under his control. *See also:* Regulating Station.

References
Department of Defense, U.S. Army. *Dictionary of United States Army Terms.* Army Regulation AR 310-25. Washington, DC: Headquarters, Department of the Army, 1986.

—**REGULATING STATION** is a command agency established to control all movements of personnel and supplies into or out of a given area.

References
Department of Defense, Joint Chiefs of Staff. *Department of Defense Dictionary of Military and Related Terms.* Washington, DC: GPO, 1986.

—**REGULATING UNIT** is a unit within a marching column that sets the pace for the rest of the column.

References
Department of Defense, U.S. Army. *Dictionary of United States Army Terms.* Army Regulation AR 310-25. Washington, DC: Headquarters, Department of the Army, 1986.

—**REGULATORY SIGN** is a sign used by a competent authority to regulate and control traffic.

References
Department of Defense, Joint Chiefs of Staff. *Department of Defense Dictionary of Military and Related Terms.* Washington, DC: GPO, 1986.

—**REHABILITATION.** (1) Rehabilitation is the processing, usually in a relatively quiet area, of units that, or individuals who, have been recently withdrawn from combat or arduous duty. During rehabilitation, equipment is reconditioned, and the units rested and restored with replacements, issued replacement supplies and equipment, given training, and generally made ready for use in future operations. (2) Rehabilitation is the action performed to restore an installation to its authorized design standards. (3) Rehabilitation is the action taken to restore to a serviceable condition materiel that has deteriorated. (4) Rehabilitation is the action taken to prepare individuals who have been immobilized due to illness, injury, or enforced incarceration for return to military duty or useful civilian employment. *See also:* Reconstitution, Regeneration, Sustaining Support.

References
Department of Defense, U.S. Army. *Dictionary of United States Army Terms.* Army Regulation AR 310-25. Washington, DC: Headquarters, Department of the Army, 1986.

—**REHABILITATION TRAINING CENTER** is an Army correctional treatment facility used in national emergencies as a vehicle for rehabilitating and restoring prisoners to duty. Overseas detention and rehabilitation training centers, disciplinary training centers, and disciplinary training companies are included. *See also:* Disciplinary Action.

References
Department of Defense, U.S. Army. *Dictionary of United States Army Terms.* Army Regulation AR 310-25. Washington, DC: Headquarters, Department of the Army, 1986.

—**REHEARSAL** is an exercise that rehearses the plans that have been developed for a specific combat mission.

References
Department of Defense, U.S. Army. *Dictionary of United States Army Terms.* Army Regulation AR 310-25. Washington, DC: Headquarters, Department of the Army, 1986.

—**REIMBURSABLE PERSONNEL.** There are two classifications of reimbursables: (1) all military personnel authorized to, and performing with, a governmental agency other than those of the Department of Defense for whose services the Department of the Army is reimbursed from the using agency; and (2) personnel who are furnished by the Department of the Army to activities that are classified as civil functions by the Department.

References
Department of Defense, U.S. Army. *Dictionary of United States Army Terms.* Army Regulation AR 310-25. Washington, DC: Headquarters, Department of the Army, 1986.

—**REINFORCEMENT TRAINING UNIT** is a U.S. Army Reserve nontroop program consisting of attached personnel from the Ready Reserve mobilization reinforcing pool, organized to provide Reserve duty training in nonpay training status for its members. *See also:* Ready Reserve Mobilization Reinforcement Pool.

References
Department of Defense, U.S. Army. *Dictionary of United States Army Terms.* Army Regulation AR 310-25. Washington, DC: Headquarters, Department of the Army, 1986.

—**REINFORCEMENTS** are members of the Army Ready Reserve who are assigned to the Inactive National Guard and to designated U.S. Army Reserve nontroop program elements. These reinforcements are used to bring Active Army and reserve component units to full table of organization and equipment or table of distribution strength upon mobilization.

References
Department of Defense, U.S. Army. *Dictionary of United States Army Terms.* Army Regulation AR 310-25. Washington, DC: Headquarters, Department of the Army, 1986.

—**REINFORCEMENTS** (ENEMY ORDER OF BATTLE STRENGTH COMPUTATION) are the enemy forces whose area of possible use against the friendly force depends on the friendly selection of a specific course of action and on enemy capabilities. Reinforcements include all known enemy forces that are not committed against a friendly force or outside the friendly zone or sector, but that can be reasonably considered capable of closing with the friendly force in time to affect the accomplishment of the mission. *See also:* Order of Battle.

References
Department of Defense, U.S. Army. *Intelligence Analysis.* Field Manual FM 34-3. Washington, DC: Headquarters, Department of the Army, 1986.

—**REINFORCING,** in Army tactical intelligence, means providing support to one Military Intelligence unit by another. Such support is responsive to the needs of the reinforced unit. The reinforcing Military Intelligence unit is under the operational control of the reinforced unit. *See also:* Intelligence.

References
Department of Defense, U.S. Army. *Operational Terms and Symbols*. Field Manual FM 101-5-1. Washington, DC: Headquarters, Department of the Army, 1985.

—**REINFORCING** (ARTILLERY) is a tactical mission in which one artillery unit augments the fire of another artillery unit. Artillery fire is delivered on-call from the reinforcement unit by an artillery unit that is assigned the reinforcing mission. *See also:* Direct Support Artillery, General Support Artillery, General Support Reinforcing.

References
Department of Defense, U.S. Army. *Operational Terms and Symbols*. Field Manual FM 101-5-1. Washington, DC: Headquarters, Department of the Army, 1985.

—**REINFORCING OBSTACLES** are placed on a battlefield and are designed to strengthen the existing terrain to slow, stop, or canalize the enemy. Their use is only limited by imagination, time, manpower, or logistic constraints. They include blowing a road crater, constructing a log crib, or installing a minefield. Scatterable mines are reinforcing obstacles that are emplaced by various delivery systems such as artillery or aircraft. The two categories of reinforcing obstacles are conventional obstacles and dynamic obstacles. Additionally, there are five types of reinforcing obstacles: demolition; constructed; land mine; contamination; and expedient obstacles. *See also:* Obstacles.

References
Department of Defense, U.S. Army. *Countermobility*. Field Manual FM 5-102. Washington, DC: Headquarters, Department of the Army, 1985.

—**RELATERAL TELL** is the relay of information between facilities through the use of a third facility. This type of telling is appropriate between automated facilities in a degraded communications environment.

References
Department of Defense, Joint Chiefs of Staff. *Department of Defense Dictionary of Military and Related Terms*. Washington, DC: GPO, 1986.

—**RELATIVE BEARING** is the direction expressed as a horizontal angle normally measured clockwise from the forward point of the longitudinal axis of the vehicle to an object or body.

References
Department of Defense, Joint Chiefs of Staff. *Department of Defense Dictionary of Military and Related Terms*. Washington, DC: GPO, 1986.

—**RELATIVE BIOLOGICAL EFFECTIVENESS.** The ratio of the number of rads of gamma radiation of a certain energy that will produce a specified biological effect to the number of rads of another radiation required to produce the same effect is the biological effectiveness of the latter radiation. *See also:* Nuclear Warfare.

References
Department of Defense, Joint Chiefs of Staff. *Department of Defense Dictionary of Military and Related Terms*. Washington, DC: GPO, 1986.

—**RELEASE FROM ACTIVE DUTY** is the end of active duty status, and transfer or reversion to an Army National Guard or a U.S. Army Reserve component not on active duty. Personnel enlisted or inducted who have a Reserve obligation under Title 10 of the United States Code, the Military Service Act of 1967, as amended, or any other provision of law are transferred to a U.S. Army Reserve Control Group. Unit members of the U. S. Army National Guard and U.S. Army Reserve revert from active duty status to their components to complete unexpired enlistments or unfilled obligations. *See also:* Obligated Reservist, Obligated Volunteer Officer, Obligation, Retirement, Separation, Service Obligation.

References
Department of Defense, U.S. Army. *Enlisted Personnel*. Army Regulation AR 635-200. Washington, DC: Headquarters, Department of the Army, 1984.

————. *Information Pamphlet for the Career Development of Enlisted Members of the U.S. Army Reserve*. Department of the Army Pamphlet DA PAM 140-8. Washington, DC: Headquarters, Department of the Army, 1986.

————. *Processing Personnel for Separation*. Army Regulation AR 635-10. Washington, DC: Headquarters, Department of the Army, 1984.

—**RELEASE POINT.** (1) A release point is a clearly defined point on a route at which specific elements of a column of ground vehicles or flight of aircraft revert to their respective commanders, each one of these elements continuing its movement toward its own appropriate destination. (2) In dismounted attacks, especially at night, the release point is the point at which a commander releases control of subordinate units to their commanders or leaders. *See also:* Start Point.

References

Department of Defense, U.S. Army. *The Infantry Rifle Company (Infantry, Airborne, Air Assault, Ranger).* Field Manual FM 7-10. Washington, DC: Headquarters, Department of the Army, 1982.

————. *Operational Terms and Symbols.* Field Manual FM 101-5-1. Washington, DC: Headquarters, Department of the Army, 1985.

—**RELEASE UNIT** is a shipment unit that, because of a specific commodity designation, weight, size, or mode of transportation, must be assigned to a movement control activity before being placed into a transportation system. *See also:* Movement Control Authority.

References

Department of Defense, U.S. Army. *Dictionary of United States Army Terms.* Army Regulation AR 310-25. Washington, DC: Headquarters, Department of the Army, 1986.

—**RELEASED,** in air defense, frees weapons and crews from commitments and states of readiness. When they are released, they are given a time at which the state of readiness will be resumed.

References

Department of Defense, Joint Chiefs of Staff. *Department of Defense Dictionary of Military and Related Terms.* Washington, DC: GPO, 1986.

—**RELEASING COMMANDER** (NUCLEAR WEAPONS) is a commander who has been delegated the authority to approve the use of nuclear weapons within prescribed limits. *See also:* Executing Commander (Nuclear Weapons).

References

Department of Defense, Joint Chiefs of Staff. *Department of Defense Dictionary of Military and Related Terms.* Washington, DC: GPO, 1986.

—**RELEASING OFFICIAL.** In message preparation, a releasing official is a person who has been authorized to approve a message for electrical transmission. He is the last person to read a message before it is sent. As a result, he must be certain that (1) the message is necessary and should be sent; (2) that the information it contains is sufficiently important or time sensitive to require it to be sent by message; and (3) that the message has been given the appropriate security classification. *See also:* Intelligence.

References

Department of Defense, Defense Intelligence Agency. *Defense Intelligence Agency Manual.* Washington, DC: DIA, 1984.

—**RELIABILITY** is the ability of an item to perform a required function under stated conditions for a specified period of time.

References

Department of Defense, Joint Chiefs of Staff. *Department of Defense Dictionary of Military and Related Terms.* Washington, DC: GPO, 1986.

Department of Defense, U.S. Army. *Dictionary of United States Army Terms.* Army Regulation AR 310-25. Washington, DC: Headquarters, Department of the Army, 1986.

—**RELIEF** are the inequities of evaluation and the configuration of land features on the surface of the earth that may be represented on maps and charts by contours, hypsometric tints, shading, or spot elevations. *See also:* Map.

References

Department of Defense, Joint Chiefs of Staff. *Department of Defense Dictionary of Military and Related Terms.* Washington, DC: GPO, 1986.

—**RELIEF COMMANDER** is the next senior noncommissioned officer of the guard. He instructs and posts sentries, changes reliefs, and is in charge of one of the reliefs.

References

Department of Defense, U.S. Army. *Guard Duty.* Field Manual FM 22-6. Washington, DC: Headquarters, Department of the Army, 1971.

—**RELIEF IN PLACE** is an operation in which, by direction of higher authority, all or part of a unit is replaced in an area by an incoming unit. The responsibilities of the replaced elements for the mission and the assigned zone of operations are transferred to the incoming unit. The incoming unit continues the operation as ordered.

References

Department of Defense, U.S. Army. *Armored and Mechanized Division Operations.* Field Manual FM 71-100. Washington, DC: Headquarters, Department of the Army, 1978.

————. *Operational Terms and Symbols.* Field Manual FM 101-5-1. Washington, DC: Headquarters, Department of the Army, 1985.

—**RELIGIOUS PROGRAM** consists of the activities employed by the commander to provide for the religious, spiritual, moral, and ethical well-being of all military personnel in the command. *See also:* Chaplain.

References

Department of Defense, U.S. Army. *The Chaplain and Chaplain Assistant in Combat Operations.* Field Manual FM 16-5. Washington, DC: Headquarters, Department of the Army, 1984.

—**RELOCATION.** (1) Relocation is determining the range and azimuth from one station to a target when the range and azimuth from another station to the target are known. (2) Relocation is determining the range and azimuth of a future position of a moving target. *See also:* Relocation Clock.

References

Department of Defense, U.S. Army. *Dictionary of United States Army Terms.* Army Regulation AR 310-25. Washington, DC: Headquarters, Department of the Army, 1986.

—**RELOCATION CLOCK** is a circular diagram used in fire adjustment to show accurately the positions of a moving target and the deviations of shots as reported by observers.

References

Department of Defense, U.S. Army. *Dictionary of United States Army Terms.* Army Regulation AR 310-25. Washington, DC: Headquarters, Department of the Army, 1986.

—**REMAINING FORCES** are the total surviving U.S. forces at any given stage of combat operations.

References

Department of Defense, Joint Chiefs of Staff. *Department of Defense Dictionary of Military and Related Terms.* Washington, DC: GPO, 1986.

—**REMAINING VELOCITY** is the speed of a projectile at any point along its path of fire. The remaining velocity is usually measured in feet per second.

References

Department of Defense, U.S. Army. *Dictionary of United States Army Terms.* Army Regulation AR 310-25. Washington, DC: Headquarters, Department of the Army, 1986.

—**REMANUFACTURE** is a modification applied when an object, such as an item of equipment is being rebuilt to incorporate current technology to increase the capacity and productivity of industrial plant equipment.

References

Department of Defense, U.S. Army. *Dictionary of United States Army Terms.* Army Regulation AR 310-25. Washington, DC: Headquarters, Department of the Army, 1986.

—**REMEDIAL ELECTRONIC COUNTER COUNTERMEASURES TECHNIQUES** are actions taken to reduce the effectiveness of enemy efforts to jam the friendly use of the electromagnetic spectrum. *See also:* Electronic Counter Countermeasures.

References

Department of Defense, U.S. Army. *Communications Techniques: Electronics Countermeasures.* Field Manual FM 24-33. Washington, DC: Headquarters, Department of the Army, 1985.

—**REMOTE AREA OPERATIONS** are undertaken in contested or insurgent-controlled areas to establish operating bases and government strongholds. These areas may be populated by ethnic, religious, or other isolated minority groups. Such operations may be conducted to establish bases in unpopulated areas where insurgent forces have established staging areas, training areas, rest areas, logistical facilities, or command posts. The remote area may be in interior regions of the country or near border areas where major infiltration routes exist. Such operations are normally conducted by specially trained and selected units. *See also:* Low Intensity Conflict.

References

Department of Defense, U.S. Army. *Low Intensity Conflict.* Field Manual FM 100-20. Washington, DC: Headquarters, Department of the Army, 1981.

———. *U.S. Army Operational Concept for Special Operations Forces.* TRADOC PAM 525-34. Washington, DC: Headquarters, Department of the Army, 1984.

—**REMOTE-ARMING SYSTEM** is a system designed to arm or disarm mines by remote control devices. *See also:* Mine Warfare.

References

Department of Defense, U.S. Army. *Mine/Countermine Operations at the Company Level.* Field Manual FM 20-32. Washington, DC: Headquarters, Department of the Army, 1976.

—**REMOTE DELIVERY,** in mine operations, is the delivery of mines to a target area by any means other than direct emplacement. The exact position of the mines so laid may not be known. *See also:* Mine Warfare.

References

Department of Defense, Joint Chiefs of Staff. *Department of Defense Dictionary of Military and Related Terms.* Washington, DC: GPO, 1986.

—**REMOTE SENSING** is an intelligence imagery and photoreconnaissance term for measuring or acquiring information about some property or phenomenon by a recording device that is not in physical or intimate contact with the subject of the study. *See also:* Remotely Employed Sensors.

References

Reeves, Robert; Anson, Abraham; and Landen, David. *Manual of Remote Sensing.* Falls Church, VA: American Society of Photogrammetry, 1975.

—**REMOTELY EMPLOYED SENSORS (REMS)** are remotely monitored devices implanted in an area to monitor personnel or vehicle activity. A sensor system consists of REMs, sensor relays, and sensor monitoring equipment. This term has replaced the term "unattended ground sensors."

References

Department of Defense, U.S. Army. *Operational Terms and Symbols.* Field Manual FM 101-5-1. Washington, DC: Headquarters, Department of the Army, 1985.

—**REMOTELY FIRED MINE** is a mine designed to be fired by remote control. *See also:* Mine Warfare.

References

Department of Defense, U.S. Army. *Mine/ Countermine Operations at the Company Level.* Field Manual FM 20-32. Washington, DC: Headquarters, Department of the Army, 1976.

—**REMOTELY PILOTED VEHICLE (RPV)** is an unmanned air vehicle capable of being controlled by a person from a distant location through a communications link. It is normally used for airborne reconnaissance, surveillance, or target acquisition and designation, because it can provide timely and accurate intelligence and it can locate targets. It is designed to be recoverable.

References

Department of Defense, U.S. Army. *Air Defense Artillery Deployment: Chaparral/Vulcan/Stinger.* Field Manual FM 44-3. Washington, DC: Headquarters, Department of the Army, 1984.

————. *Operational Terms and Symbols.* Field Manual FM 101-5-1. Washington, DC: Headquarters, Department of the Army, 1985.

—**RENDEZVOUS** is a prearranged meeting scheduled for a specific time and location from which an action or phase of an operation begins. It is also where and when to return after an operation.

References

Department of Defense, Joint Chiefs of Staff. *Department of Defense Dictionary of Military and Related Terms.* Washington, DC: GPO, 1986.

—**RENDEZVOUS POINT** is a place where a company assembles after a movement. *See also:* Rendezvous.

References

Department of Defense, U.S. Army. *The Infantry Rifle Company (Infantry, Airborne, Air Assault, Ranger).* Field Manual FM 7-10. Washington, DC: Headquarters, Department of the Army, 1982.

—**RENEGOTIATION** is a proceeding that is intended to determine the existence of, and secure repayment to the government for, excessive profits, if any, for a fiscal year or other period, that were received or accrued under contracts or subcontracts that are subject to statutory renegotiation. *See also:* Renegotiation Agreement.

References

Department of Defense, U.S. Army. *Dictionary of United States Army Terms.* Army Regulation AR 310-25. Washington, DC: Headquarters, Department of the Army, 1986.

—**RENEGOTIATION AGREEMENT** is a voluntary contractual understanding that results from renegotiation to provide for repayment of certain profits found to be excessive, or for price reductions, or for both.

References

Department of Defense, U.S. Army. *Dictionary of United States Army Terms.* Army Regulation AR 310-25. Washington, DC: Headquarters, Department of the Army, 1986.

—**REORDER POINT.** (1) The reorder point when a stock replenishment requisition is submitted to maintain the predetermined or calculated stockage objective. (2) The sum of the safety level of supply plus the level of order and shipping time equals the reorder point.

References
Department of Defense, Joint Chiefs of Staff. *Department of Defense Dictionary of Military and Related Terms.* Washington, DC: GPO, 1986.

—**REORGANIZATION.** Reorganization is an action that shifts resources within an attrited unit to increase its level of combat effectiveness (e.g., internal redistribution of equipment and personnel and the formation of composite units).

References
Department of Defense, U.S. Army. *Operations.* Field Manual FM 100-5. Washington, DC: Headquarters, Department of the Army, 1986.

—**REORGANIZE** is to change from one type of unit to another within an arm or service, or to change personnel and equipment within a unit in accordance with newly published or revised tables of organization.

References
Department of Defense, U.S. Army. *Dictionary of United States Army Terms.* Army Regulation AR 310-25. Washington, DC: Headquarters, Department of the Army, 1986.

—**REPAIR** is the restoration of an item to serviceable condition by correcting a specific failure or unserviceable condition. *See also:* Overhaul, Rebuild, Repair Cycle, Repair Cycle Float, Repair Kit, Repair Leadtime, Repair Part, Repair Parts and Special Tools List, Repair Time, Repair Versus Recovery Decision, Repairable Item.

References
Department of Defense, Joint Chiefs of Staff. *Department of Defense Dictionary of Military and Related Terms.* Washington, DC: GPO, 1986.

—**REPAIR BACKLOG** is the existing workload that is beyond the capability of an organization or a segment of an organization to accomplish in a given period of time. *See also:* Repair.

References
Department of Defense, U.S. Army. *Dictionary of United States Army Terms.* Army Regulation AR 310-25. Washington, DC: Headquarters, Department of the Army, 1986.

—**REPAIR CYCLE** are the stages through which a repairable item passes from the time it is removed or replaced until it is reinstalled or replaced in stock in serviceable condition. *See also:* Repair.

References
Department of Defense, U.S. Army. *Support Operations: Echelons Above Corps.* Field Manual FM 100-16. Washington, DC: Headquarters, Department of the Army, 1986.

—**REPAIR CYCLE FLOAT** is an additional quantity of end-items of mission essential maintenance significant equipment that is specified to be stocked in the supply system and withdrawn when necessary to allow for scheduled overhauls without detracting from the unit's readiness condition. *See also:* Repair.

References
Department of Defense, U.S. Army. *Dictionary of United States Army Terms.* Army Regulation AR 310-25. Washington, DC: Headquarters, Department of the Army, 1986.

—**REPAIR KIT** generally refers to a group of parts issued together under one stock number and used for reconditioning a subassembly. *See also:* Repair.

References
Department of Defense, U.S. Army. *Dictionary of United States Army Terms.* Army Regulation AR 310-25. Washington, DC: Headquarters, Department of the Army, 1986.

—**REPAIR LEADTIME** is the time between the awarding of a work order or contract and the completed repair of the item for the first scheduled shipment. *See also:* Repair.

References
Department of Defense, U.S. Army. *Dictionary of United States Army Terms.* Army Regulation AR 310-25. Washington, DC: Headquarters, Department of the Army, 1986.

—**REPAIR PART** is a part, subassembly, assembly, or component that is required to be installed in the maintenance or repair of an end-item, subassembly, or component. *See also:* Repair.

References
Department of Defense, U.S. Army. *Dictionary of United States Army Terms.* Army Regulation AR 310-25. Washington, DC: Headquarters, Department of the Army, 1986.

—**REPAIR PARTS AND SPECIAL TOOLS LIST** is a list of repair parts; special tools; and test, measurement, and diagnostic equipment that is required for maintaining a specified number of end-items or systems for a specified period of time for each level of authorized maintenance. *See also:* Repair.

References

Department of Defense, U.S. Army. *Dictionary of United States Army Terms.* Army Regulation AR 310-25. Washington, DC: Headquarters, Department of the Army, 1986.

—**REPAIR TIME** is the interval between the time that repair or overhaul of an item commences and the time that the item is restored to a serviceable condition. *See also:* Repair.

References

Department of Defense, U.S. Army. *Dictionary of United States Army Terms.* Army Regulation AR 310-25. Washington, DC: Headquarters, Department of the Army, 1986.

—**REPAIR-VERSUS-RECOVERY DECISION** is a decision made on a case-by-case basis whenever equipment becomes inoperable. Equipment should be repaired on site when possible, since this is generally the quickest and least costly alternative. However, the tactical situation, the extent of damage to the equipment, the availability of personnel, tools and repair parts, and other factors may require that the item be repaired at a maintenance activity. *See also:* Repair.

References

Department of Defense, U.S. Army. *Organizational Maintenance Operations.* Field Manual FM 29-2. Washington, DC: Headquarters, Department of the Army, 1984.

—**REPAIRABLE ITEM** is an item that can be reconditioned or economically repaired for reuse when it becomes unserviceable. *See also:* Recoverable Item.

References

Department of Defense, Joint Chiefs of Staff. *Department of Defense Dictionary of Military and Related Terms.* Washington, DC: GPO, 1986.

—**REPEAT,** in artillery, is an order or request to fire again the same number of rounds with the same method of fire.

References

Department of Defense, Joint Chiefs of Staff. *Department of Defense Dictionary of Military and Related Terms.* Washington, DC: GPO, 1986.

—**REPEATER JAMMER** is a jamming transmitter used to confuse or deceive the enemy by causing its equipment to present false information. This is done by a system that intercepts and reradiates a signal on the frequency of the enemy's equipment. The reradiated signal is modified, causing the enemy's equipment to present an erroneous range, azimuth, or number of targets. *See also:* Jammer.

References

Department of Defense, Joint Chiefs of Staff. *Department of Defense Dictionary of Military and Related Terms.* Washington, DC: GPO, 1986.

—**REPLACEMENT** is an individual assigned or earmarked for assignment to fill a vacancy in an organization. The term includes hospitalized personnel, previously dropped from the rolls of an organization, when they are discharged from a hospital for return to duty. *See also:* Loss Replacement.

References

Department of Defense, U.S. Army. *Dictionary of United States Army Terms.* Army Regulation AR 310-25. Washington, DC: Headquarters, Department of the Army, 1986.

—**REPLACEMENT COMPANY** is a company in which personnel are received, administered, and provided appropriate training before they are assigned to units.

References

Department of Defense, U.S. Army. *Dictionary of United States Army Terms.* Army Regulation AR 310-25. Washington, DC: Headquarters, Department of the Army, 1986.

—**REPLACEMENT DEMAND** is a demand for the replacement of items that have been consumed or are worn out.

References

Department of Defense, Joint Chiefs of Staff. *Department of Defense Dictionary of Military and Related Terms.* Washington, DC: GPO, 1986.

—REPLACEMENT FACTOR is the estimated percentage of equipment or repair parts in use that will have to be replaced during a given period because they will have worn out, be beyond repair, have been abandoned or stolen, have been destroyed by the enemy, or have been victim to causes other than catastrophes. *See also:* Replacement Issues.

References
Department of Defense, Joint Chiefs of Staff. *Department of Defense Dictionary of Military and Related Terms.* Washington, DC: GPO, 1986.

—REPLACEMENT ISSUES are the portion of issues made to using agencies in order to replace equipment that has been previously supplied. This is done to maintain the standards of efficiency and quantity, as prescribed by the equipment allocation documents. Such issues replace equipment that has worn out beyond economical repair, as well as equipment that has been abandoned, destroyed, lost during enemy action, or stolen. The following issues do not constitute replacement issues: in-transit losses attributable to sinking; losses of clothing caused by the separation of personnel from the services; issues transferred between depots; issues that replace unserviceable but economically repairable equipment; and issues to an organization to replace serviceable equipment that has been withdrawn from that organization.

References
Department of Defense, U.S. Army. *Dictionary of United States Army Terms.* Army Regulation AR 310-25. Washington, DC: Headquarters, Department of the Army, 1986.

—REPLACEMENTS are personnel who are required to perform the duties of others who are departing the unit.

References
Department of Defense, Joint Chiefs of Staff. *Department of Defense Dictionary of Military and Related Terms.* Washington, DC: GPO, 1986.

—REPLENISHMENT CYCLE QUANTITY is the amount of materiel required to sustain normal operations during the interval between successive replenishments. Under normal conditions, it is equal to the operating level quantity.

References
Department of Defense, U.S. Army. *Dictionary of United States Army Terms.* Army Regulation AR 310-25. Washington, DC: Headquarters, Department of the Army, 1986.

—REPLY is an answer to a challenge. *See also:* Challenge, Countersign, Password.

References
Department of Defense, Joint Chiefs of Staff. *Department of Defense Dictionary of Military and Related Terms.* Washington, DC: GPO, 1986.

—REPORT; GENERAL, MISSION REVIEW, OR SECOND PHASE, is an intelligence report containing information on all targets that have been covered in one photographic sortie. *See also:* Aerial Reconnaissance, Intelligence.

References
Department of Defense, U.S. Army. *Dictionary of United States Army Terms.* Army Regulation AR 310-25. Washington, DC: Headquarters, Department of the Army, 1986.

—REPORT LINE is a line at which troops, after having reached it, must report to their command echelon.

References
Department of Defense, Joint Chiefs of Staff. *Department of Defense Dictionary of Military and Related Terms.* Washington, DC: GPO, 1986.

—REPORT OF CHARGES is a detailed summary of an investigation conducted by a surveying officer of the loss of property and a separate review of the findings and recommendations.

References
Department of Defense, U.S. Army. *Commander's Handbook for Property Accountability at the Unit Level.* Field Manual FM 10-14-1. Washington, DC: Headquarters, Department of the Army, 1984.

—REPORT OF INVESTIGATION is an official written record of all pertinent information obtained in an inquiry concerning a crime, offense, accident, allegation, or personal background. *See also:* Uniform Code of Military Justice.

References
Department of Defense, U.S. Army. *Dictionary of United States Army Terms.* Army Regulation AR 310-25. Washington, DC: Headquarters, Department of the Army, 1986.

—REPORT OF SEPARATION is a written report provided to military personnel upon release from active duty, discharge, retirement, or dismissal, documentary evidence of active duty or active duty for training. *See also:* Retirement, Separation.

References
Department of Defense, U.S. Army. *Dictionary of United States Army Terms.* Army Regulation AR 310-25. Washington, DC: Headquarters, Department of the Army, 1986.

—**REPORT OF SHIPMENT (REPSHIP)** is notification by the shipper to the consignee that a specific shipment is en route.

References
Department of Defense, U.S. Army. *Transportation Reference Data.* Field Manual FM 55-15. Washington, DC: Headquarters, Department of the Army, 1986.

—**REPORT OF SURVEY** is an official report used to record the circumstances concerning the loss, unserviceability, or destruction of property. It serves as, or supports, a voucher for dropping items from the property records on which they are listed. It also serves to determine all questions of responsibility (pecuniary or otherwise) for the loss or the condition of the articles.

References
Department of Defense, U.S. Army. *Dictionary of United States Army Terms.* Army Regulation AR 310-25. Washington, DC: Headquarters, Department of the Army, 1986.

—**REPORT, PHOTOGRAPHIC INTERPRETATION,** is a general term for any form of report issued as a result of the interpretation of photography. *See also:* Aerial Reconnaissance.

References
Department of Defense, U.S. Army. *Dictionary of United States Army Terms.* Army Regulation AR 310-25. Washington, DC: Headquarters, Department of the Army, 1986.

—**REPORTED UNIT** is a unit designation that has been mentioned in an agent report, captured document, or interrogation report, but for which there is insufficient information to include the unit in the accepted order of battle holdings.

References
Department of Defense, Joint Chiefs of Staff. *Department of Defense Dictionary of Military and Related Terms.* Washington, DC: GPO, 1986.

—**REPORTING TIME INTERVAL.** (1) In surveillance, the reporting time interval is the interval between when an event was detected and news of its occurrence has been reported. (2) In communications, the reporting time interval is the time of transmission of a report from the originating terminal to the end receiver.

References
Department of Defense, Joint Chiefs of Staff. *Department of Defense Dictionary of Military and Related Terms.* Washington, DC: GPO, 1986.

—**REQUEST FOR ISSUE OR TURN-IN** is a form authorized for use by a unit, organization, or activity to request supplies or to turn in supplies to a supply officer, accountable officer, or property disposal officer.

References
Department of Defense, U.S. Army. *Dictionary of United States Army Terms.* Army Regulation AR 310-25. Washington, DC: Headquarters, Department of the Army, 1986.

—**REQUEST FOR PAY ACTION** is a form used by a member of the Army to request payment of less than the total pay that he is due; payment by check; partial pay; advance pay; or advance payment of a travel allowance.

References
Department of Defense, U.S. Army. *Dictionary of United States Army Terms.* Army Regulation AR 310-25. Washington, DC: Headquarters, Department of the Army, 1986.

—**REQUEST MODIFY**, in artillery, is a request for a modification by any person other than the person who is authorized to make modifications to a fire plan.

References
Department of Defense, Joint Chiefs of Staff. *Department of Defense Dictionary of Military and Related Terms.* Washington, DC: GPO, 1986.

—**REQUIRED DELIVERY DATE.** (1) The required delivery date is the calendar date that specifies when materiel is actually required to be delivered to the requisitioner and is always a date that is earlier or later than the computed standard delivery date. (In other words, a required delivery date cannot equal exactly a computed standard delivery date.) (2) The required delivery date is the date that a unit is required to arrive at the main battle area in support of a specific operations plan.

References
Department of Defense, Joint Chiefs of Staff. *Department of Defense Dictionary of Military and Related Terms.* Washington, DC: GPO, 1986.

Department of Defense, U.S. Army. *Dictionary of United States Army Terms*. Army Regulation AR 310-25. Washington, DC: Headquarters, Department of the Army, 1986.

—REQUIRED MILITARY FORCE is composed of the armed forces that are necessary to carry out a military mission for a specified period of time.

References

Department of Defense, Joint Chiefs of Staff. *Department of Defense Dictionary of Military and Related Terms*. Washington, DC: GPO, 1986.

—REQUIRED SUPPLY RATE (RSR) is the amount of ammunition, expressed in rounds per weapon per day for ammunition items that are fired by weapons, and in terms of other units of measure per day for bulk allotment and other items that are estimated to be required to sustain the operations of any designated force without restriction for a specified period. The RSR is based on the type of operation to be conducted, the type and number of weapon systems to be armed, and the number of enemy targets one expects to engage. *See also:* Controlled Supply Rate.

References

Department of Defense, U.S. Army. *Operational Terms and Symbols*. Field Manual FM 101-5-1. Washington, DC: Headquarters, Department of the Army, 1985.

—REQUIREMENTS MANAGEMENT, in Army tactical intelligence, means the translation of the commander's guidance and the concept of the operation into basic intelligence, electronic warfare, counterintelligence, and operations security requirements; and the general planning, direction, and control that are necessary to satisfy those requirements. *See also:* Intelligence.

References

Department of Defense, Department of the Army. *Intelligence and Electronic Warfare Operations*. Field Manual FM 34-1. Washington, DC: Headquarters, Department of the Army, 1987.

———. *Military Intelligence Group (Combat Electronic Warfare and Intelligence) (Corps)*. Field Manual FM 34-20. Washington, DC: Headquarters, Department of the Army, 1983.

———. *Military Intelligence Battalion (CEWI) (Operations) (Corps)*. Field Manual FM 34- 21. Washington, DC: Headquarters, Department of the Army, 1982.

—REQUIRING DEPARTMENT is a department originating a requisition or procurement request for supplies or services to be purchased by another department.

References

Department of Defense, U.S. Army. *Dictionary of United States Army Terms*. Army Regulation AR 310-25. Washington, DC: Headquarters, Department of the Army, 1986.

—REQUISITION. (1) A requisition is an authoritative demand or request, especially for personnel, supplies, or services that are authorized but are not made available without a specific request. A requisition makes such a request. (2) To requisition is to demand or require services from an invaded or conquered nation.

References

Department of Defense, Joint Chiefs of Staff. *Department of Defense Dictionary of Military and Related Terms*. Washington, DC: GPO, 1986.

—REQUISITIONING OBJECTIVE is the maximum quantities of materiel to be maintained on hand and on order so that current operations can be sustained. It consists of the sum of the stocks that are represented by the operating level, safety level, and the order and shipping time or procurement time, as appropriate. *See also:* Level of Supply.

References

Department of Defense, Joint Chiefs of Staff. *Department of Defense Dictionary of Military and Related Terms*. Washington, DC: GPO, 1986.

—RESCHEDULED TRAINING is instruction that is placed on the unit training schedule for subsections of the unit or for individuals at a time, date, and location other than the normal assembly area. Pay and retirement point credit are authorized for such training.

References

Department of Defense, U.S. Army. *Army Exercises*. Army Regulation AR 350-28. Washington, DC: Headquarters, Department of the Army, 1985.

———. *Individual Military Education and Training*. Army Regulation AR 350-1. Washington, DC: Headquarters, Department of the Army, 1987.

—RESCIND concerns published directives. To rescind is to denote the cancellation in whole or in part as of the announced date in the retraction.

It is not retroactive, and a replacement of the cancelled portions of the directive may or may not be provided in the retraction.

References

Department of Defense, U.S. Army. *Dictionary of United States Army Terms*. Army Regulation AR 310-25. Washington, DC: Headquarters, Department of the Army, 1986.

—**RESEARCH AND DEVELOPMENT (R & D) COSTS** are a cost category that includes the costs resulting from applied research engineering design, analysis, development, and testing that can be related to a specific weapon or support system work breakdown structure component. The effort from which these costs derive usually occurs within advanced development, engineering development, and operational systems development.

References

Department of Defense, U.S. Army. *Dictionary of United States Army Terms*. Army Regulation AR 310-25. Washington, DC: Headquarters, Department of the Army, 1986.

—**RESEARCH AND DEVELOPMENT (R & D) MISSILE** is a missile that has been produced for research, development, testing, or evaluation purposes. It may be a preliminary design missile, a test vehicle, or a production missile that has been allocated for test and evaluation projects. This category includes portions of production-type missiles that have been allocated to space projects.

References

Department of Defense, U.S. Army. *Dictionary of United States Army Terms*. Army Regulation AR 310-25. Washington, DC: Headquarters, Department of the Army, 1986.

—**RESECTION** is a method of locating a point by computation or by plotting the intersection of rays that have been obtained from sights taken from three or more points of known location.

References

Department of Defense, U.S. Army. *Dictionary of United States Army Terms*. Army Regulation AR 310-25. Washington, DC: Headquarters, Department of the Army, 1986.

—**RESERVE.** (1) The reserve is that portion of a body of troops that is kept to the rear, or withheld from action at the beginning of an engagement, and is available for a decisive mo-

ment. (2) The Reserve are members of the military Services who are not in active service but who are subject to call to active duty. (3) A reserve is a portion of an appropriation or contract authorization that is held or set aside for future operations or contingencies and for which administrative authorization to incur commitments or obligations has been withheld. *See also:* General Reserve, Operational Reserve, Reserve Supplies.

References

Department of Defense, U.S. Army. *Operational Terms and Symbols*. Field Manual FM 101-5-1. Washington, DC: Headquarters, Department of the Army, 1985.

—**RESERVE CENTER SUPPLY OFFICER** is an officer or civilian employee, located on or near a U.S. Army Reserve Center. He is under the jurisdiction of the U.S. Army Corps commander, and serves as a satellite installation supply officer. When a Reserve Center supply officer is made responsible for supplying a number of Army Reserve Centers, he will be designated as the area supply officer.

References

Department of Defense, U.S. Army. *Dictionary of United States Army Terms*. Army Regulation AR 310-25. Washington, DC: Headquarters, Department of the Army, 1986.

—**RESERVE COMPONENTS (RCs).** The Reserve Components of the U.S. Army are the Army Reserve, and the Army National Guard of the United States. In each, there are three reserve categories: a Ready Reserve; a Standby Reserve; and a Retired Reserve. Each reservist is placed in one of these categories. *See also:* Reserve Components Contingency Force.

References

Department of Defense, Joint Chiefs of Staff. *Department of Defense Dictionary of Military and Related Terms*. Washington, DC: GPO, 1986.

—**RESERVE COMPONENTS CONTINGENCY FORCE** is a group of selected divisions and the supporting elements that are designated to reconstitute an effective Ready Reserve Strategic Army Force.

References

Department of Defense, U.S. Army. *Dictionary of United States Army Terms*. Army Regulation AR 310-25. Washington, DC: Headquarters, Department of the Army, 1986.

—**RESERVE FORCE,** in an overseas operation, is a subordinate task organization of a joint expeditionary force consisting of ships carrying reserve troops that are usually formed into a landing force that is capable of being landed in accordance with the general scheme of maneuver or as the tactical situation dictates.

References

Department of Defense, U.S. Army. *Dictionary of United States Army Terms.* Army Regulation AR 310-25. Washington, DC: Headquarters, Department of the Army, 1986.

—**RESERVE OFFICER** is a duly commissioned male or female officer or warrant officer of the Reserve components.

References

Department of Defense, U.S. Army. *Dictionary of United States Army Terms.* Army Regulation AR 310-25. Washington, DC: Headquarters, Department of the Army, 1986.

—**RESERVE REQUIREMENTS** are the supplies and equipment necessary to meet the emergency situations that may be expected in a military campaign. *See also:* Reserve Supplies.

References

Department of Defense, U.S. Army. *Dictionary of United States Army Terms.* Army Regulation AR 310-25. Washington, DC: Headquarters, Department of the Army, 1986.

—**RESERVE SUPPLIES,** or reserves, are the on-hand supplies in excess of immediate needs. Their purpose is to insure the continuity of an adequate supply of such items. *See also:* Battle Reserves, Individual Reserves, Unit Reserves.

References

Department of Defense, U.S. Army. *Planning Logistics Support for Military Operations.* Field Manual FM 701-58. Washington, DC: Headquarters, Department of the Army, 1987.

—**RESERVED AREA** is a land or water area that has been set apart by Presidential Executive order for purposes of national defense. Admittance to such an area without authorization is either prohibited or restricted.

References

Department of Defense, U.S. Army. *Dictionary of United States Army Terms.* Army Regulation AR 310-25. Washington, DC: Headquarters, Department of the Army, 1986.

—**RESERVED DEMOLITION OBSTACLES** (NON-NUCLEAR) are the obstacles or demolition targets that the commander deems to be critical to the tactical plan. The authority to execute the obstacle is reserved by the authorizing commander through a formal order known as a demolition order. *See also:* Repair.

References

Department of Defense, U.S. Army. *Countermobility.* Field Manual FM 5-102. Washington, DC: Headquarters, Department of the Army, 1985.

—**RESERVED DEMOLITION TARGET** is a target for demolition whose destruction must be controlled at a specific level of command because it plays a vital part in the tactical or strategic plan, because of the importance of the structure itself, or because the demolition may be accomplished in the face of the enemy. *See also:* Reserved Demolition Obstacles.

References

Department of Defense, Joint Chiefs of Staff. *Department of Defense Dictionary of Military and Related Terms.* Washington, DC: GPO, 1986.

—**RESERVED ROUTE** (A FORM OF CONTROLLED ROUTE), in road traffic, is a specified route that is allocated exclusively to an authority or a formation (e.g., a route reserved exclusively for a division), or is intended to meet a particular requirement (e.g., a route reserved exclusively for evacuation).

References

Department of Defense, U.S. Army. *Route Reconnaissance and Classification.* Field Manual FM 5-36. Washington, DC: Headquarters, Department of the Army, 1985.

—**RESIDENT SCHOOL CREDIT** is the granting of credit by the commandant of a school or college to persons who have successfully completed a resident course of instruction.

References

Department of Defense, U.S. Army. *Dictionary of United States Army Terms.* Army Regulation AR 310-25. Washington, DC: Headquarters, Department of the Army, 1986.

—**RESIDUAL CONTAMINATION** is contamination that remains after steps have been taken to remove it. These steps may consist of nothing more than allowing the contamination to decay normally. *See also:* Nuclear Warfare.

References
Department of Defense, U.S. Army. *NBC Protection.* Field Manual FM 3-4. Washington, DC: Headquarters, Department of the Army, 1985.

—**RESIDUAL FORCES** are unexpended portions of the remaining U.S. forces that have an immediate combat potential for continued military operations, and that have deliberately been withheld.
References
Department of Defense, Joint Chiefs of Staff. *Department of Defense Dictionary of Military and Related Terms.* Washington, DC: GPO, 1986.

—**RESIDUAL NUCLEAR RADIATION** (RESIDUAL RADIOACTIVITY) is nuclear radiation caused by fallout, radioactive material dispersed artificially, or irradiation that results from a nuclear explosion and persists longer than one minute after burst. Sources of such radioactivity that are created by nuclear explosions include fission fragments and radioactive matter that is created primarily by neutron activation, but also by gamma and other radiation activation. Other possible sources of residual radioactivity include radioactive material that was created and dispersed by means other than a nuclear explosion. *See also:* Contamination, Induced Radiation, Initial Radiation.
References
Department of Defense, U.S. Army. *Nuclear Weapons Employment Doctrine and Procedures.* Field Manual FM 101-3-1. Washington, DC: Headquarters, Department of the Army, 1986.
———. *Operational Terms and Symbols.* Field Manual FM 101-5-1. Washington, DC: Headquarters, Department of the Army, 1985.

—**RESISTANCE** is a mental defense against enemy attempts to coerce prisoners of war by interrogation, indoctrination, and exploitation through propaganda or other means so as to further the enemy's war effort. Resistance includes the use of mental and physical techniques to withstand the effects of enemy-imposed psychological pressure, physical mistreatment, dietary deficiencies, or medical neglect during captivity.
References
Department of Defense, U.S. Army. *Code of Conduct/Survival, Evasion, Resistance and Escape (SERE) Training.* Army Regulation AR 350-30. Washington, DC: Headquarters, Department of the Army, 1985.

—**RESISTANCE FORCE,** in unconventional warfare, is the portion of the population of a country engaged in a resistance movement. The force can be composed of guerrillas, auxiliaries, or members of the underground.
References
Department of Defense, U.S. Army. *Dictionary of United States Army Terms.* Army Regulation AR 310-25. Washington, DC: Headquarters, Department of the Army, 1986.

—**RESISTANCE MOVEMENT** is an organized effort by some portion of the civil population of a country to resist the legally established government or an occupying power and to disrupt civil order and stability.
References
Department of Defense, Joint Chiefs of Staff. *Department of Defense Dictionary of Military and Related Terms.* Washington, DC: GPO, 1986.

—**RESOLUTION** is a measurement of the smallest detail that can be distinguished by a sensor system under specific conditions.
References
Department of Defense, Joint Chiefs of Staff. *Department of Defense Dictionary of Military and Related Terms.* Washington, DC: GPO, 1986.

—**RESOLUTION** (PHOTOGRAPHIC) is the ability of the entire photographic system, including the lens, exposure, and film processing, to render a sharply defined image. *See also:* Aerial Reconnaissance.
References
Department of Defense, U.S. Army. *Operational Terms and Symbols.* Field Manual FM 101-5-1. Washington, DC: Headquarters, Department of the Army, 1985.

—**RESOLUTION IN AZIMUTH** is the angle by which two targets must be separated in azimuth in order to be distinguished by a radar set when the targets are at the same range. *See also:* Radar.
References
Department of Defense, U.S. Army. *Dictionary of United States Army Terms.* Army Regulation AR 310-25. Washington, DC: Headquarters, Department of the Army, 1986.

—**RESOLUTION IN RANGE** is how far apart two targets must be separated in range in order to be distinguished by a radar set when the targets are on the same azimuth line.

References

Department of Defense, U.S. Army. *Dictionary of United States Army Terms*. Army Regulation AR 310-25. Washington, DC: Headquarters, Department of the Army, 1986.

—**RESOURCE MANAGEMENT** is the process of efficient acquisition, allocation, and use of resources, including manpower, money, materials, and services, in order to effectively accomplish assigned missions. The process is cyclical and includes planning, programming, distribution, usage, accounting, reprogramming, and redistribution.

References

Department of Defense, U.S. Army. *Dictionary of United States Army Terms*. Army Regulation AR 310-25. Washington, DC: Headquarters, Department of the Army, 1986.

—**RESOURCES** are the manpower, funds, materiel, space, and time available for or required to accomplish specific tasks or to realize specific objectives. Included in this concept of materiel are all objects, including equipment, tools, and systems.

References

Department of Defense, U.S. Army. *Support Operations: Echelons Above Corps*. Field Manual FM 100-16. Washington, DC: Headquarters, Department of the Army, 1986.

—**RESPIRATOR** is a device that regulates the counter-recoil mechanism on a weapon.

References

Department of Defense, U.S. Army. *Dictionary of United States Army Terms*. Army Regulation AR 310-25. Washington, DC: Headquarters, Department of the Army, 1986.

—**RESPONSE TIME,** in intelligence usage, is the time lapse between the initiation of a request for information and the receipt of that information.

References

Department of Defense, U.S. Army. *Dictionary of United States Army Terms*. Army Regulation AR 310-25. Washington, DC: Headquarters, Department of the Army, 1986.

—**RESPONSIBILITY.** (1) Responsibility is the obligation to carry forward an assigned task to a successful conclusion. With responsibility goes the authority to direct and take the necessary action to insure success. (2) Responsibility is the obligation of a person for the proper care, custody, use, and safekeeping of government property or funds that are entrusted to his possession or supervision. *See also:* Indications and Warning.

References

Department of Defense, U.S. Army. *Commander's Handbook for Property Accountability at the Unit Level*. Field Manual FM 10-14-1. Washington, DC: Headquarters, Department of the Army, 1984.

—**RESPONSIBLE OFFICER** is an officer who is answerable by law and regulations for the discharge of a duty. He may or may not be accountable in the supply sense. *See also:* Accountable Officer.

References

Department of Defense, U.S. Army. *Dictionary of United States Army Terms*. Army Regulation AR 310-25. Washington, DC: Headquarters, Department of the Army, 1986.

—**REST.** (1) In artillery, rest is a command indicating that the unit(s) or gun(s) to which it is addressed shall not follow up fire orders during the time that the order is in force. (2) A rest is a mechanical support for a gun that is used when one is aiming or firing. (3) Rest is a command that allows soldiers to move, talk, or smoke in ranks, but requires them to keep one foot in place.

References

Department of Defense, Joint Chiefs of Staff. *Department of Defense Dictionary of Military and Related Terms*. Washington, DC: GPO, 1986.

Department of Defense, U.S. Army. *Dictionary of United States Army Terms*. Army Regulation AR 310-25. Washington, DC: Headquarters, Department of the Army, 1986.

—**REST AND RECUPERATION (R&R)** is the withdrawal of soldiers from combat or duty in a combat area for short periods of rest and recuperation. This is commonly referred to as R&R. *See also:* Rehabilitation.

References

Department of Defense, Joint Chiefs of Staff. *Department of Defense Dictionary of Military and Related Terms*. Washington, DC: GPO, 1986.

—**REST AND RECUPERATION (R&R) LEAVE— DESIGNATED AREAS** is chargeable leave granted in conjunction with R&R programs that are established in the areas that are designated for hostile fire/imminent danger pay. It must be determined that operational military considerations preclude the full execution of ordinary leave programs. *See also:* Rest and Recuperation.

References

Department of Defense, U.S. Army. *Code of Conduct/Survival, Evasion, Resistance and Escape (SERE) Training.* Army Regulation AR 350-30. Washington, DC: Headquarters, Department of the Army, 1985.

—**RESTART AT . . .** , in artillery, is a command used to restart a fire plan after "dwell at . . . ," or "check firing," or "cease loading," has been ordered.

References

Department of Defense, Joint Chiefs of Staff. *Department of Defense Dictionary of Military and Related Terms.* Washington, DC: GPO, 1986.

—**RESTATED MISSION** results from the commander's mission analysis. It is a clear, concise statement of the task (or tasks) to be accomplished by the command and the goal to be achieved. *See also:* Mission Analysis.

References

Department of Defense, U.S. Army. *Staff Organization and Operations.* Field Manual FM 101-5. Washington, DC: Headquarters, Department of the Army, 1984.

—**RESTORATION** is repair of damaged facilities to a condition that is similar to their original construction.

References

Department of Defense, U.S. Army. *Support Operations: Echelons Above Corps.* Field Manual FM 100-16. Washington, DC: Headquarters, Department of the Army, 1986.

—**RESTRAINT** is confinement to a civilian or military correctional facility, or restriction or confinement to quarters or another specified area.

References

Department of Defense, U.S. Army. *Processing Personnel for Separation.* Army Regulation AR 635-10. Washington, DC: Headquarters, Department of the Army, 1984.

—**RESTRAINT OF LOADS** is the process of binding, lashing, and wedging items into one unit or into a transporter in a manner that will insure that the items do not move while they are in transit. *See also:* Lashing Point, Lashings.

References

Department of Defense, Joint Chiefs of Staff. *Department of Defense Dictionary of Military and Related Terms.* Washington, DC: GPO, 1986.

—**RESTRICTED AREA (RA).** (1) A restricted area is a land, sea, or air area in which special restrictive measures are used to prevent or minimize interference between friendly forces. (2) A restricted area is an area under military jurisdiction in which special security measures are used to prevent unauthorized entry. *See also:* Controlled Firing Area.

References

Department of Defense, Joint Chiefs of Staff. *Department of Defense Dictionary of Military and Related Terms.* Washington, DC: GPO, 1986.

—**RESTRICTED DATA (RD)** is all information concerning: (1) the design, manufacture, or use of nuclear weapons; (2) the production of special nuclear material; (3) the use of special nuclear material in the production of energy. Restricted data do not include data that were declassified or removed from the restricted data category pursuant to Section 142 of the Atomic Energy Act of 1954, as amended. *See also:* Nuclear Warfare.

References

Department of Defense, Joint Chiefs of Staff. *Department of Defense Dictionary of Military and Related Terms.* Washington, DC: GPO, 1986.

—**RESTRICTED OPERATIONS AREA** is an airspace of defined dimensions designated by the airspace control authority, in response to specific operational situations or requirements, within which the operation of one or more airspace users is restricted. These areas are established by the airspace control authority in response to the requests of local ground force commanders. Such areas can be declared for either aircraft or antiaircraft defense artillery (ADA). When they are established for *aircraft*, they are done to maximize effectiveness, in which case the normal weapons control status is WEAPONS FREE. Restricted operations areas for *ADA* are established to maximize aircraft effectiveness, in which case, the normal ADA weapons control status is WEAPONS HOLD. The Patriot system has the capability to display restricted, prohibited, and weapons control volumes. *See also:* Patriot.

References
Department of Defense, U.S. Army. *Patriot Battalion Operations.* Field Manual FM 44-15. Washington, DC: Headquarters, Department of the Army, 1984.

—**RESTRICTED TRAFFIC** is traffic over a route controlled by regulations that limit speeds, the types of vehicles permitted, the maximum weights allowed, and the hours at which the route is open to different types of traffic. *See also:* Traffic Management.

References
Department of Defense, U.S. Army. *Dictionary of United States Army Terms.* Army Regulation AR 310-25. Washington, DC: Headquarters, Department of the Army, 1986.

—**RESTRICTION** is a punitive restraint imposed on a person who is subject to military law by nonjudicial punishment or a military court. It restricts a person to the limits prescribed in the order. *See also:* Administrative Restriction.

References
Department of Defense, U.S. Army. *Dictionary of United States Army Terms.* Army Regulation AR 310-25. Washington, DC: Headquarters, Department of the Army, 1986.

—**RESTRICTIVE FIRE AREA (RFA)** is an area in which specific restrictions are imposed and into which fires that exceed those restrictions may not be delivered without prior coordination with the establishing headquarters. *See also:* Restrictive Fire Plan.

References
Department of Defense, U.S. Army. *Operational Terms and Symbols.* Field Manual FM 101-5-1. Washington, DC: Headquarters, Department of the Army, 1985.

—**RESTRICTIVE FIRE LINE (RFL)** is a line established between converging friendly forces that may or may not be moving. It prohibits fires or effects from fires across the line without coordination with the effected force. It is established by the commander of the converging forces. *See also:* Restrictive Fire Plan.

References
Department of Defense, U.S. Army. *Armored and Mechanized Division Operations.* Field Manual FM 71-100. Washington, DC: Headquarters, Department of the Army, 1978.

————. *Operational Terms and Symbols.* Field Manual FM 101-5-1. Washington, DC: Headquarters, Department of the Army, 1985.

—**RESTRICTIVE FIRE PLAN (RFP)** is a safety measure for friendly aircraft. It establishes airspace that is reasonably safe from friendly surface-delivered nonnuclear fires. *See also:* Restrictive Fire Area, Restrictive Fire Line.

References
Department of Defense, Joint Chiefs of Staff. *Department of Defense Dictionary of Military and Related Terms.* Washington, DC: GPO, 1986.

—**RESUME**, in air intercept usage, is a code meaning "Resume last patrol ordered."

References
Department of Defense, Joint Chiefs of Staff. *Department of Defense Dictionary of Military and Related Terms.* Washington, DC: GPO, 1986.

—**RESUPPLY** is the act of replenishing stocks in order to maintain the required levels of supply.

References
Department of Defense, Joint Chiefs of Staff. *Department of Defense Dictionary of Military and Related Terms.* Washington, DC: GPO, 1986.

—**RESUPPLY OF EUROPE** is the NATO shipping of supplies to Europe during the period from the outbreak of the war until the end of such a requirement. These supplies exclude any material already located in Europe, but include other supplies irrespective of their origin or location.

References
Department of Defense, Joint Chiefs of Staff. *Department of Defense Dictionary of Military and Related Terms.* Washington, DC: GPO, 1986.

—**RESUSCITATIVE AND STABILIZING MEDICAL TREATMENT** is medical or surgical treatment provided to patients to save life or limb and to prepare them for evacuation without jeopardizing their well-being or prolonging their morbidity. *See also:* Medical Treatment.

References
Department of Defense, U.S. Army. *Dictionary of United States Army Terms.* Army Regulation AR 310-25. Washington, DC: Headquarters, Department of the Army, 1986.

—**RETAINED ENEMY PERSONNEL** are certain enemy-protected personnel (e.g., medical personnel, chaplains, under certain circumstances, members of National Red Cross Societies and other recognized volunteer aid societies) who are retained in prisoner-of-war camps to assist prisoners-of-war. Although these people are retained, they are not considered prisoners-of-war but they receive at least the protection prisoners-of-war receive.

References

Department of Defense, U.S. Army. *Dictionary of United States Army Terms*. Army Regulation AR 310-25. Washington, DC: Headquarters, Department of the Army, 1986.

—**RETARD** is a request from a spotter indicating that the illuminating projectile burst is desired later in relation to the subsequent bursts of high explosive projectiles.

References

Department of Defense, Joint Chiefs of Staff. *Department of Defense Dictionary of Military and Related Terms*. Washington, DC: GPO, 1986.

—**RETENTION LIMIT** is the maximum quantity of an item authorized for retention in the Army supply system.

References

Department of Defense, U.S. Army. *Dictionary of United States Army Terms*. Army Regulation AR 310-25. Washington, DC: Headquarters, Department of the Army, 1986.

—**RETENTIONS** are ships assigned to the control of a theater commander for moving cargo from point-to-point within the theater or between theaters. Retentions include local fleet retentions assigned for an indefinite period, and rotational retentions, which include all other retentions.

References

Department of Defense, U.S. Army. *Dictionary of United States Army Terms*. Army Regulation AR 310-25. Washington, DC: Headquarters, Department of the Army, 1986.

—**RETIRED LIST** is a list of officers who have been released from active service in a military force because of age, disability, or for another cause, and who are qualified to receive retired pay.

References

Department of Defense, U.S. Army. *Dictionary of United States Army Terms*. Army Regulation AR 310-25. Washington, DC: Headquarters, Department of the Army, 1986.

—**RETIRED RESERVE** consists of the individuals whose names are placed on the Reserve Retired list by proper authority in accordance with law and regulations. Members of the Retired Reserve may, if qualified, be ordered to active duty involuntarily in time of war or a national emergency that is declared by Congress, or when otherwise authorized by law, and then only when it is determined by the Secretary of the Army that adequate numbers of qualified individuals in the required categories are not readily available in the Ready Reserve or in an active status in the Standby Reserve.

References

Department of Defense, U.S. Army. *Dictionary of United States Army Terms*. Army Regulation AR 310-25. Washington, DC: Headquarters, Department of the Army, 1986.

—**RETIRED SERVICEMEN'S FAMILY PROTECTION PLAN** is a survivor annuity plan available to Army members, both men and women, who may elect to receive a reduced amount of retired pay in order to provide an annuity that is payable monthly to their survivors if the members dies.

References

Department of Defense, U.S. Army. *Dictionary of United States Army Terms*. Army Regulation AR 310-25. Washington, DC: Headquarters, Department of the Army, 1986.

—**RETIREE RECALL PROGRAM.** Army retirees represent one of the largest sources of pretrained manpower. In the event of mobilization, more than 100,000 retirees will report within seven days to a variety of locations in the continental United States either to fill positions that are needed specifically for mobilization or to occupy positions that were previously held by soldiers, thereby freeing them for deployment. Additionally, retirees living in West Germany and Korea are preassigned to duties in those countries.

References

Department of Defense, U.S. Army. *U.S. Army Policy Statement, 1988*. Washington, DC: Headquarters, Department of the Army, 1988.

—**RETIREMENT.** (1) Retirement is the orderly withdrawal of troops according to their own plan and without pressure from the enemy. (2) Retirement is release from active military service because of age, length of service, disability, or another cause, in accordance with Army regulations and applicable laws, and with or without the entitlement to receive retired pay. This includes both temporary and permanent disability retirements. *See also:* Continuous Active Duty, Delaying Action, Disengagement, Nonduty Status, Release From Active Duty, Report of Separation, Retired List, Retired Reserve, Retiree Recall Program, Retirement for Length of Service, Retirement for Physical Disability, Retrograde Movement, Separation, Statement of Service, Temporary Disability Retired List.

References

Department of Defense, U.S. Army. *Dictionary of United States Army Terms.* Army Regulation AR 310-25. Washington, DC: Headquarters, Department of the Army, 1986.

—**RETIREMENT FOR LENGTH OF SERVICE** is the retirement of soldiers who have served twenty or more years in the active military service.

References

Department of Defense, U.S. Army. *Processing Personnel for Separation.* Army Regulation AR 635-10. Washington, DC: Headquarters, Department of the Army, 1984.

—**RETIREMENT FOR PHYSICAL DISABILITY** is a retirement classification that concerns the retirement of soldiers from the Active Army because of physical disability. Such soldiers are placed on either the permanent or the temporary disability retired list as directed by the Secretary of the Army.

References

Department of Defense, U.S. Army. *Processing Personnel for Separation.* Army Regulation AR 635-10. Washington, DC: Headquarters, Department of the Army, 1984.

—**RETIREMENT ROUTE** is the track or series of tracks along which helicopters move from a specific landing site or landing zone. *See also:* Helicopter Lane.

References

Department of Defense, Joint Chiefs of Staff. *Department of Defense Dictionary of Military and Related Terms.* Washington, DC: GPO, 1986.

—**RETIREMENTS** are rearward movements away from the enemy by a force that is not in contact. They are normally covered by the security forces of another unit to their rear and are conducted as a tactical road movement. Retiring units must be organized to fight, but they do so only in self-defense. A retiring unit may be attacked by guerrillas, air strikes, air assaults, or long-range fires, and its commander must have plans for dealing with such contingencies. Security and speed are the most important factors in a retirement. *See also:* Delaying Operation, Retrograde Operation.

References

Department of Defense, U.S. Army. *Operational Terms and Symbols.* Field Manual FM 101-5-1. Washington, DC: Headquarters, Department of the Army, 1985.

———. *Operations.* Field Manual FM 100-5. Washington, DC: Headquarters, Department of the Army, 1986.

—**RETRAINING** is training intended to qualify an individual in another military occupational specialty. Upon the satisfactory completion of such training, the new military occupational specialty will be awarded to the soldier and will be designated as his primary occupational specialty. Retraining normally occurs when a requirement for a member's current military occupational specialty no longer exists, or when a soldier can no longer perform in his current specialty because of a change in his physical condition. *See also:* Military Occupational Specialty.

References

Department of Defense, U.S. Army. *Individual Military Education and Training.* Army Regulation AR 350-1. Washington, DC: Headquarters, Department of the Army, 1987.

—**RETRAINING BRIGADE** is a correctional treatment facility for confining, retraining, and restoring prisoners as more highly motivated soldiers. When applicable, it also prepares prisoners for their return to civilian life. *See also:* Disciplinary Action.

References

Department of Defense, U.S. Army. *Dictionary of United States Army Terms.* Army Regulation AR 310-25. Washington, DC: Headquarters, Department of the Army, 1986.

—**RETRANSMISSION (REXMIT)** is the use of a radio communication set to rebroadcast a message on a different frequency simultaneously with the original broadcast. This is done by means of an electrically operated device that links the receiver and the transmitter of a set.

References
Department of Defense, U.S. Army. *Dictionary of United States Army Terms*. Army Regulation AR 310-25. Washington, DC: Headquarters, Department of the Army, 1986.

—**RETROFIT ACTION** is action that modifies a piece of equipment that is currently in service. *See also:* Retrofit Change Kit.

References
Department of Defense, Joint Chiefs of Staff. *Department of Defense Dictionary of Military and Related Terms*. Washington, DC: GPO, 1986.

—**RETROFIT CHANGE KIT** is a kit of parts needed to modify a piece of equipment that is currently in service.

References
Department of Defense, U.S. Army. *Dictionary of United States Army Terms*. Army Regulation AR 310-25. Washington, DC: Headquarters, Department of the Army, 1986.

—**RETROGRADE.** (1) Retrograde is a movement of materiel that is contrary to the normal flow. (2) Retrograde is a condition designation for materiel (e.g., ammunition) that is earmarked for movement to a rear depot or to an off-shore facility. *See also:* Retrograde Cargo, Retrograde Movement, Retrograde Operation, Retrograde Personnel.

References
Department of Defense, U.S. Army. *Dictionary of United States Army Terms*. Army Regulation AR 310-25. Washington, DC: Headquarters, Department of the Army, 1986.

—**RETROGRADE CARGO** is cargo that is being returned to the United States from an overseas command. *See also:* Retrograde.

References
Department of Defense, U.S. Army. *Planning Logistics Support for Military Operations*. Field Manual FM 701-58. Washington, DC: Headquarters, Department of the Army, 1987.

—**RETROGRADE MOVEMENT** is any movement of a command to the rear or away from the enemy. It may be forced by the enemy or may be made voluntarily. Such movements may be classified as a withdrawal, a retirement, or a delaying action. *See also:* Delaying Operation, Disengagement, Retirements.

References
Department of Defense, U.S. Army. *Operations*. Field Manual FM 100-5. Washington, DC: Headquarters, Department of the Army, 1986.

—**RETROGRADE OPERATION** is a movement to the rear or away from the enemy. It may be forced or voluntary, but in either case, the higher commander must approve it. Retrograde operations gain time, preserve forces, avoid combat under undesirable conditions, or draw the enemy into an unfavorable position. Commanders use these operations to harass, to exhaust, to resist, to delay, and to damage an enemy. Retrograde operations are also used in operational maneuvers to reposition forces, to shorten lines of communications, or to permit the withdrawal of another force for use elsewhere. The three types of retrograde operations are delays, withdrawals, and retirements. In *delays*, units give up ground to gain time. Delaying units inflict the greatest possible damage on an enemy while preserving their freedom of action. In *withdrawals*, all or part of a committed force disengages from the enemy voluntarily to preserve the force or free it for a new mission. In *retirements*, a force that is not in active combat with the enemy conducts a movement to the rear, normally as a tactical road march. *See also:* Retrograde.

References
Department of Defense, U.S. Army. *Operations*. Field Manual FM 100-5. Washington, DC: Headquarters, Department of the Army, 1986.

—**RETROGRADE PERSONNEL** are personnel who are evacuated from a theater of operations, and may include noncombatants and civilians. *See also:* Retrograde.

References
Department of Defense, Joint Chiefs of Staff. *Department of Defense Dictionary of Military and Related Terms*. Washington, DC: GPO, 1986.

—**RETROGRADE RIVER CROSSING** is made when enemy advances threaten to overwhelm a division, causing it to retrograde and subjecting it to enemy pursuit. In this situation, the crossing is made to establish a defense on the exit bank, or to continue the retrograde to defensive positions that are beyond the river. *See also:* Retrograde.

References
Department of Defense, U.S. Army. *River Crossing Operations.* Field Manual FM 90-13. Washington, DC: Headquarters, Department of the Army, 1978.

—**RETURN LOAD** is composed of personnel and/or cargo that are to be transported by a returning carrier.

References
Department of Defense, Joint Chiefs of Staff. *Department of Defense Dictionary of Military and Related Terms.* Washington, DC: GPO, 1986.

—**RETURN PISTOL** is a command to put a pistol back in the holster. Return pistol is a prescribed command in the Army's pistol manual.

References
Department of Defense, U.S. Army. *Dictionary of United States Army Terms.* Army Regulation AR 310-25. Washington, DC: Headquarters, Department of the Army, 1986.

—**RETURN PROGRAM** is a planned operation to accomplish the financial disposition of the remains of U.S. Armed Forces personnel as mutually arranged for, and executed by the joint commander and the Deputy Chief of Staff for Logistics. A return program may be possible during the combat phase of isolated military operations, depending on the tactical and logistical situation, and provided it does not conflict with the national policy. *See also:* Killed in Action.

References
Department of Defense, U.S. Army. *Dictionary of United States Army Terms.* Army Regulation AR 310-25. Washington, DC: Headquarters, Department of the Army, 1986.

—**RETURNED MATERIEL** are quantities of supplies that were issued previously and are being returned to the control of the responsible agency.

References
Department of Defense, U.S. Army. *Dictionary of United States Army Terms.* Army Regulation AR 310-25. Washington, DC: Headquarters, Department of the Army, 1986.

—**RETURNEE REASSIGNMENT STATION** is an activity adjacent to a major continental U.S. Army transportation terminal that has been established to provide administrative processing for personnel who are returning to the continental United States from an overseas command.

References
Department of Defense, U.S. Army. *Dictionary of United States Army Terms.* Army Regulation AR 310-25. Washington, DC: Headquarters, Department of the Army, 1986.

—**RETURNS LIST** is a list of essential items (i.e., critical and intensively managed secondary items and repair parts) that is prepared by national inventory control points. It also lists recoverable items that are selected for automatic returns. *See also:* Recoverable Item.

References
Department of Defense, U.S. Army. *Dictionary of United States Army Terms.* Army Regulation AR 310-25. Washington, DC: Headquarters, Department of the Army, 1986.

—**RETURNS WITH CREDIT** are materiel accepted by an entity of the Army Stock Fund or Defense Supply Agency (Defense Stock Fund) for which an allowance is made based upon the stated condition.

References
Department of Defense, U.S. Army. *Dictionary of United States Army Terms.* Army Regulation AR 310-25. Washington, DC: Headquarters, Department of the Army, 1986.

—**REUTILIZATION ASSIGNMENT** is the assignment of previously trained graduates of military or civilian schools to positions that require such training. In most cases, these personnel will have already served an initial utilization tour.

References
Department of Defense, U.S. Army. *Dictionary of United States Army Terms.* Army Regulation AR 310-25. Washington, DC: Headquarters, Department of the Army, 1986.

—**REVENUE-PRODUCING ACTIVITY** is a self-sustained nonappropriated fund activity established to sell merchandise and services to military and civilian personnel at Army installations and to provide financial support to welfare funds. *See also:* Nonappropriated Fund Activity.

References
Department of Defense, U.S. Army. *Dictionary of United States Army Terms.* Army Regulation AR 310-25. Washington, DC: Headquarters, Department of the Army, 1986.

—**REVERSE** (ARMY AVIATION) refers to turns only and indicates reversing the direction and severity of the desired turn. A reverse call made while an aircraft is in a turn will result in an immediate hard turn in the opposite direction.

References

Department of Defense, U.S. Army. *Air-to-Air Combat*. Field Manual FM 1-107. Washington, DC: Headquarters, Department of the Army, 1984.

—**REVERSE PLANNING** is a planning method used by leaders to prepare their men for a given mission. Working from a known deadline, the leader plans backward from that deadline, allocating the available time to preparations and actions that contribute to accomplishing the mission.

References

Department of Defense, U.S. Army. *Military Police Team, Squad, Platoon Combat Operations*. Field Manual FM 19-4. Washington, DC: Headquarters, Department of the Army, 1984.

—**REVERSE SLOPE** is a position on the ground that is not exposed to direct fire or observation. It may be a slope that descends away from the enemy. *See also:* Reverse Slope Defense.

References

Department of Defense, U.S. Army. *Operational Terms and Symbols*. Field Manual FM 101-5-1. Washington, DC: Headquarters, Department of the Army, 1985.

—**REVERSE SLOPE DEFENSE** is a defense area organized on any ground not exposed to direct fire or observation. It may be on a slope that descends away from the enemy.

References

Department of Defense, U.S. Army. *Operational Terms and Symbols*. Field Manual FM 101-5-1. Washington, DC: Headquarters, Department of the Army, 1985.

—**REVIEW.** (1) A review is a formal inspection of an organization. (2) A review is a ceremony to honor an official or dignitary, or to present decorations to military personnel.

References

Department of Defense, U.S. Army. *Dictionary of United States Army Terms*. Army Regulation AR 310-25. Washington, DC: Headquarters, Department of the Army, 1986.

—**REVIEWING AUTHORITY.** (1) A reviewing authority is a person who, or appellate agency that, must approve and affirm the findings and sentence of a courtmartial before the sentence may be carried out. (2) A reviewing authority is the office authorized to take final action on Reports of Survey by the authority of the Secretary of the Army. *See also:* Disciplinary Action.

References

Department of Defense, U.S. Army. *Dictionary of United States Army Terms*. Army Regulation AR 310-25. Washington, DC: Headquarters, Department of the Army, 1986.

—**RIB RIFLING** is rifling of the bore of a gun in which the lands and grooves are of equal width.

References

Department of Defense, U.S. Army. *Dictionary of United States Army Terms*. Army Regulation AR 310-25. Washington, DC: Headquarters, Department of the Army, 1986.

—**RIBBON OR RIBBON BAR** is a portion of the suspension ribbon of a medal that is worn in lieu of the medal and is made in the form of a bar.

References

Department of Defense, U.S. Army. *Wear and Appearance of Army Uniforms and Insignia*. Army Regulation AR 670-1. Washington, DC: Headquarters, Department of the Army, 1986.

—**RICOCHET BURST** is the near-surface burst of a high explosive projectile after the projectile strikes the surface obliquely and is deflected at an angle. A ricochet burst is used effectively against enemy personnel, instead of the common airburst that is secured by a time fuze before the projectile strikes. *See also:* Airburst, Ricochet Fire.

References

Department of Defense, U.S. Army. *Dictionary of United States Army Terms*. Army Regulation AR 310-25. Washington, DC: Headquarters, Department of the Army, 1986.

—**RICOCHET FIRE** is fire in which the projectile glances from a surface after impact. It is sometimes used in artillery to obtain airbursts after the initial impact. *See also:* Airburst.

References

Department of Defense, U.S. Army. *Dictionary of United States Army Terms*. Army Regulation AR 310-25. Washington, DC: Headquarters, Department of the Army, 1986.

—**RIFLE CLASP** is a metallic bar that denotes the bearer's participation in a national or area rifle match.

References
Department of Defense, U.S. Army. *Dictionary of United States Army Terms*. Army Regulation AR 310-25. Washington, DC: Headquarters, Department of the Army, 1986.

—**RIFLE GRENADE** is a grenade or small bomb designed to be shot from a special launcher device attached to the muzzle of a rifle or carbine. It is propelled by a special blank cartridge that is fired in the rifle or carbine. The three types of rifle grenades are fragmentation, antitank, and smoke grenades.

References
Department of Defense, U.S. Army. *Dictionary of United States Army Terms*. Army Regulation AR 310-25. Washington, DC: Headquarters, Department of the Army, 1986.

—**RIFLE SALUTE** is a salute defined in the manual of arms, in which the rifle is held at the right shoulder arms or the order arms position, and the left hand is carried smartly across the body to the rifle, the forearm is horizontal, the palm is down, and the fingers are together and are extended.

References
Department of Defense, U.S. Army. *Dictionary of United States Army Terms*. Army Regulation AR 310-25. Washington, DC: Headquarters, Department of the Army, 1986.

—**RIGHT FACE.** (1) In close-order drill, right face is a movement made from the halted position of attention. The soldier turns on the heel of the right foot and the ball of the left foot in order to face 90 degrees to the right of the original position. (2) Right face is the command to execute the above movement.

References
Department of Defense, U.S. Army. *Dictionary of United States Army Terms*. Army Regulation AR 310-25. Washington, DC: Headquarters, Department of the Army, 1986.

—**RIGHT FLANK.** (1) The right flank is the entire right side of a command from the leading element to the rearmost element as it faces the enemy. (2) The "right flank" is a preparatory command to have every soldier in a formation change direction 90 degrees to the right of the original direction of march. All men in the formation change at the same time.

References
Department of Defense, U.S. Army. *Dictionary of United States Army Terms*. Army Regulation AR 310-25. Washington, DC: Headquarters, Department of the Army, 1986.

—**RIGHT (LEFT) FLANK, MARCH,** is a two-part command that directs every soldier in a formation to change the direction of march 90 degrees to the left or right of the original direction of march.

References
Department of Defense, U.S. Army. *Dictionary of United States Army Terms*. Army Regulation AR 310-25. Washington, DC: Headquarters, Department of the Army, 1986.

—**RIGHT SHOULDER ARMS.** (1) Right shoulder arms is a movement in the manual of the rifle in which the rifle is placed on the right shoulder, barrel up, and is inclined at a 45 degree angle. (2) Right shoulder arms is the command to execute the above movement.

References
Department of Defense, U.S. Army. *Dictionary of United States Army Terms*. Army Regulation AR 310-25. Washington, DC: Headquarters, Department of the Army, 1986.

—**RIGHT TO RIGHT** (ARMY AVIATION) is a call that tells the pilots of both aircraft that are approaching each other head-on to alter their course to the left so as to keep each other in sight on their right. Additionally, during a head-on pass, an aircraft with a nose-high altitude passes high (nose high, goes high). This is a nonstandard procedure. After the initiating aircraft calls "Right-to-right pass," the other aircraft acknowledges, "Roger, right-to-right pass."

References
Department of Defense, U.S. Army. *Airspace Management and Army Air Traffic in a Combat Zone*. Field Manual FM 1-60. Washington, DC: Headquarters, Department of the Army, 1977.

—**RIGIDITY OF THE TRAJECTORY** is the assumption that the trajectory may be tilted up or down through small angles of sites without materially affecting its shape.

References

Department of Defense, U.S. Army. *Dictionary of United States Army Terms.* Army Regulation AR 310-25. Washington, DC: Headquarters, Department of the Army, 1986.

—**RING AND BEAD SIGHT** is a type of gunsight in which the front sight is a bead or post and the rear sight is a ring. *See also:* Ring Sight.

References

Department of Defense, U.S. Army. *Dictionary of United States Army Terms.* Army Regulation AR 310-25. Washington, DC: Headquarters, Department of the Army, 1986.

—**RING SIGHT** is any gunsight having a ring through which one looks. Ring sights are usually used as rear sights.

References

Department of Defense, U.S. Army. *Dictionary of United States Army Terms.* Army Regulation AR 310-25. Washington, DC: Headquarters, Department of the Army, 1986.

—**RIOT CONTROL AGENT (RCA)** is a chemical that produces temporary irritating or disabling effects when it comes in contact with the eyes or when it is inhaled.

References

Department of Defense, Joint Chiefs of Staff. *Department of Defense Dictionary of Military and Related Terms.* Washington, DC: GPO, 1986.

—**RIOT CONTROL OPERATIONS** involve the use of riot control agents and special tactics, formations, and equipment to control violent disorders.

References

Department of Defense, Joint Chiefs of Staff. *Department of Defense Dictionary of Military and Related Terms.* Washington, DC: GPO, 1986.

—**RIOT GUN** is any shotgun with a short barrel, especially a short-barrelled shotgun that is used in guard duty or to scatter rioters. A riot gun usually has a twenty-inch cylinder barrel.

References

Department of Defense, U.S. Army. *Dictionary of United States Army Terms.* Army Regulation AR 310-25. Washington, DC: Headquarters, Department of the Army, 1986.

—**RIPE**, in mine warfare, is a word that once was used to mean "armed." *See also:* Mine Warfare.

References

Department of Defense, Joint Chiefs of Staff. *Department of Defense Dictionary of Military and Related Terms.* Washington, DC: GPO, 1986.

—**RIPPLE FIRE** (AIR DEFENSE) is the firing of two missiles from one or more launchers, with a predetermined time between the launches. It is used when the commander wants to engage multiple targets at a short range. Ripple fire is preferred over multiple fire when engaging multiple targets because of the high probability that if the first missile destroys the first target, the second missile will be guided toward a second aircraft in the same formation.

References

Department of Defense, U.S. Army. *Air Defense Artillery Deployment: Chaparral/Vulcan/Stinger.* Field Manual FM 44-3. Washington, DC: Headquarters, Department of the Army, 1984.

———. *Air Defense Artillery Employment Hawk.* Field Manual FM 44-90. Washington, DC: Headquarters, Department of the Army, 1983.

———. *Air Defense Employment.* Field Manual FM 44-1. Washington, DC: Headquarters, Department of the Army, 1983.

———. *Patriot Battalion Operations.* Field Manual FM 44-15. Washington, DC: Headquarters, Department of the Army, 1984.

—**RISK.** There are at least two types of risk in combat. One is the risk of losing men and equipment to accomplish a mission. The other is that a chosen course of action may not be successful, or even if it is successful, it may fail to achieve the desired results. All leaders must take risks of both types prudently and independently, basing their decisions upon their own judgment.

References

Department of Defense, U.S. Army. *Operations.* Field Manual FM 100-5. Washington, DC: Headquarters, Department of the Army, 1986.

—**RISK ANALYSIS** is the process of determining the risks to operations when no operations security measures are applied to protect or control friendly vulnerabilities from hostile intelligence collection, and of comparing these risks to the cost of implementing the operations security measures (in terms of time, equipment, funds, and manpower) and their probable effectiveness.

References

Department of Defense, U.S. Army. *Intelligence Analysis.* Field Manual FM 34-3. Washington, DC: Headquarters, Department of the Army, 1986.

———. *Intelligence and Electronic Warfare Operations.* Field Manual FM 34-1. Washington, DC: Headquarters, Department of the Army, 1987.

—**RIVER BANK CONDITION** is the height, slope, and soil composition of far-shore and near-shore riverbanks. *See also:* River State.

References

Department of Defense, U.S. Army. *Weather Support for Army Tactical Operations.* Field Manual FM 34-81. Washington, DC: Headquarters, Department of the Army, 1984.

—**RIVER CROSSING** is an operation conducted as part of and in conjunction with other operations to quickly overcome a water obstacle. The tactical objectives that are assigned by higher headquarters may or may not include terrain objectives within the bridgehead; however, terrain objectives or space are required to ensure the security of the force and the crossing sites. *See also:* Deliberate River Crossing, Hasty River Crossing.

References

Department of Defense, U.S. Army. *Operational Terms and Symbols.* Field Manual FM 101-5-1. Washington, DC: Headquarters, Department of the Army, 1985.

—**RIVER LINE.** (1) The river line is the water's edge on the defender's side of a stream. (2) A river line is any tactical line that is marked by a stream.

References

Department of Defense, U.S. Army. *Dictionary of United States Army Terms.* Army Regulation AR 310-25. Washington, DC: Headquarters, Department of the Army, 1986.

—**RIVER STATE** is the elevation of the water surface in a stream as measured by a river gauge with reference to some arbitrarily selected zero datum.

References

Department of Defense, U.S. Army. *Weather Support for Army Tactical Operations.* Field Manual FM 34-81. Washington, DC: Headquarters, Department of the Army, 1984.

—**RIVERINE AREA** is an inland or coastal area comprising both land and water. It is characterized by limited land lines of communication and has extensive water surface or inland waterways that provide natural routes for surface transportation and communications. *See also:* Riverine Operations.

References

Department of Defense, Joint Chiefs of Staff. *Department of Defense Dictionary of Military and Related Terms.* Washington, DC: GPO, 1986.

—**RIVERINE OPERATIONS** are operations designed to cope with and exploit the unique characteristics of a riverine area, to locate and destroy hostile forces, and to achieve or maintain control of the riverine area. Joint riverine operations combine land, naval, and air operations, as appropriate, and are suited to the nature of the specific riverine area in which the operations are to be conducted.

References

Department of Defense, Joint Chiefs of Staff. *Department of Defense Dictionary of Military and Related Terms.* Washington, DC: GPO, 1986.

—**ROAD BLOCK** is a barrier or obstacle, usually covered by fire, that is used to block, or limit the movement of, hostile vehicles along a route.

References

Department of Defense, Joint Chiefs of Staff. *Department of Defense Dictionary of Military and Related Terms.* Washington, DC: GPO, 1986.

—**ROAD CAPACITY** is the maximum traffic flow attainable on a given roadway, using all available lanes. It is usually expressed in vehicles per hour or vehicles per day. *See also:* Traffic Management.

References

Department of Defense, Joint Chiefs of Staff. *Department of Defense Dictionary of Military and Related Terms.* Washington, DC: GPO, 1986.

—**ROAD CLEARANCE DISTANCE** is the total distance the head of a motor column must travel for the entire column to have passed a given section of road. *See also:* Road Clearance Time.

References

Department of Defense, U.S. Army. *Dictionary of United States Army Terms.* Army Regulation AR 310-25. Washington, DC: Headquarters, Department of the Army, 1986.

—**ROAD CLEARANCE TIME** is the total time a column needs to travel over and to pass by a section of road. *See also:* Road Clearance Distance.

References

Department of Defense, Joint Chiefs of Staff. *Department of Defense Dictionary of Military and Related Terms.* Washington, DC: GPO, 1986.

—**ROAD DISCIPLINE** is the orderly, systematic movement of troops, vehicles, and mounts using a road. Road discipline prevents confusion and delay. *See also:* Traffic Management.

References

Department of Defense, U.S. Army. *Dictionary of United States Army Terms.* Army Regulation AR 310-25. Washington, DC: Headquarters, Department of the Army, 1986.

—**ROAD DISTANCE** is the distance from one point to another point on a road. It is usually expressed in miles.

References

Department of Defense, U.S. Army. *Dictionary of United States Army Terms.* Army Regulation AR 310-25. Washington, DC: Headquarters, Department of the Army, 1986.

—**ROAD MARCH** is a type of unit movement that is made when the unit is not in contact with the enemy.

References

Department of Defense, U.S. Army. *Military Police Team, Squad, Platoon Combat Operations.* Field Manual FM 19-4. Washington, DC: Headquarters, Department of the Army, 1984.

—**ROAD MOVEMENT GRAPH** is a time space diagram used in planning and controlling both road and foot marches, and in preparing or checking road movement tables. *See also:* Road Movement Table, Traffic Management.

References

Department of Defense, U.S. Army. *Dictionary of United States Army Terms.* Army Regulation AR 310-25. Washington, DC: Headquarters, Department of the Army, 1986.

—**ROAD MOVEMENT TABLE** is a composite list showing the general organization and time and space schedule for a march movement. It is generally published as an annex to an operation order for road movement.

References

Department of Defense, U.S. Army. *Dictionary of United States Army Terms.* Army Regulation AR 310-25. Washington, DC: Headquarters, Department of the Army, 1986.

—**ROAD NET** is the system of roads that exists within a particular locality or area.

References

Department of Defense, Joint Chiefs of Staff. *Department of Defense Dictionary of Military and Related Terms.* Washington, DC: GPO, 1986.

—**ROAD RECONNAISSANCE REPORT** is a report that contains the detailed information necessary for accurately classifying a road.

References

Department of Defense, U.S. Army. *Dictionary of United States Army Terms.* Army Regulation AR 310-25. Washington, DC: Headquarters, Department of the Army, 1986.

—**ROAD SCREEN** is anything used to conceal the traffic movement along a road from enemy observation. It pertains particularly to artificial concealment and camouflage.

References

Department of Defense, U.S. Army. *Dictionary of United States Army Terms.* Army Regulation AR 310-25. Washington, DC: Headquarters, Department of the Army, 1986.

—**ROAD SPACE** is the length of roadway allocated to, and actually occupied by, a column on a route. It is expressed in miles or kilometers.

References

Department of Defense, Joint Chiefs of Staff. *Department of Defense Dictionary of Military and Related Terms.* Washington, DC: GPO, 1986.

—**ROCKET** is a self-propelled vehicle whose trajectory or course, while in flight, cannot be controlled. *See also:* Rocket-Assisted Projectile.

References

Department of Defense, Joint Chiefs of Staff. *Department of Defense Dictionary of Military and Related Terms.* Washington, DC: GPO, 1986.

—**ROCKET-ASSISTED PROJECTILE (RAP)** is a projectile that has been modified with a post-launch boost to give it greater range.

References

Department of Defense, U.S. Army. *Dictionary of United States Army Terms.* Army Regulation AR 310-25. Washington, DC: Headquarters, Department of the Army, 1986.

—**ROCKET LAUNCHER (RL)** is a device (e.g., a barrel, tube, rail, or platform) from which rockets are projected.

References

Department of Defense, U.S. Army. *Dictionary of United States Army Terms.* Army Regulation AR 310-25. Washington, DC: Headquarters, Department of the Army, 1986.

—**ROCKET MOTOR.** (1) A rocket motor is a chamber in which the rocket propellant is burned to provide a propelling force. (2) A rocket motor is a propulsion device that consists essentially of a thrust chamber and an exhaust nozzle and that carries its own fuel combination from which hot gases are generated by combustion and are expanded through a nozzle.

References

Department of Defense, U.S. Army. *Dictionary of United States Army Terms.* Army Regulation AR 310-25. Washington, DC: Headquarters, Department of the Army, 1986.

—**ROGER** is a radiotelephone procedure proword that means "I have received your last transmission satisfactorily." *See also:* Proword.

References

Department of Defense, U.S. Army. *The Rifle Squads (Mechanized and Light Infantry).* Training Circular TC 7-1. Washington, DC: Headquarters, Department of the Army, 1976.

—**ROLAND MISSILE SYSTEM** provides all-weather, short-range, low-altitude air defense. It complements medium-to-high altitude air defense systems, as well as low-altitude gun and missile systems, in providing an integrated air defense throughout an area of operations. It is radar guided (with an optical backup capability) and is mounted entirely on one wheeled vehicle. A single Roland unit can track and destroy as many as ten aircraft in minutes.

References

Department of Defense, U.S. Army. *Air Defense Employment.* Field Manual FM 44-1. Washington, DC: Headquarters, Department of the Army, 1983.

———. *Weapons Systems: U.S. Army, Navy, and Air Force Directory, 1986-1988.* Washington, DC: DCP, 1986.

—**ROLE NUMBER,** in the medical field, is the classification of treatment facilities according to their different capabilities. *See also:* Medical Treatment.

References

Department of Defense, Joint Chiefs of Staff. *Department of Defense Dictionary of Military and Related Terms.* Washington, DC: GPO, 1986.

—**ROLL BACK** is the process of progressive destruction and/or neutralization of the opposing defenses, starting at the periphery and working inward, to permit deeper penetration of succeeding defense positions.

References

Department of Defense, Joint Chiefs of Staff. *Department of Defense Dictionary of Military and Related Terms.* Washington, DC: GPO, 1986.

—**ROLLING BARRAGE** is a barrage in which the fire of units or subunits progresses by leapfrogging.

References

Department of Defense, U.S. Army. *Dictionary of United States Army Terms.* Army Regulation AR 310-25. Washington, DC: Headquarters, Department of the Army, 1986.

—**ROLLING RESERVES** are reserve supplies held close to troop units. They are stored in railroad cars or in trucks that are ready for immediate transportation, so that supply remains responsive to the needs of the operating forces.

References

Department of Defense, U.S. Army. *Dictionary of United States Army Terms.* Army Regulation AR 310-25. Washington, DC: Headquarters, Department of the Army, 1986.

—**ROLL-ON/ROLL-OFF (RORO)** is ocean shipping in which wheeled or tracked vehicles are driven aboard a special ship, secured for the voyage, and driven off at the destination port.

References

Department of Defense, U.S. Army. *Planning Logistics Support for Military Operations.* Field Manual FM 701-58. Washington, DC: Headquarters, Department of the Army, 1987.

—**ROLL-UP** is the process for the orderly dismantling of facilities that are no longer required to support current operations, thus making them available for transfer to other areas.

References
Department of Defense, Joint Chiefs of Staff.
*Department of Defense Dictionary of Military and
Related Terms.* Washington, DC: GPO, 1986.

—**ROSETTE** is a lapel device made by gathering
the suspension ribbon of a medal into a circular
shape. It is worn on civilian clothing.

References
Department of Defense, U.S. Army. *Wear and
Appearance of Army Uniforms and Insignia.* Army
Regulation AR 670-1. Washington, DC: Headquar-
ters, Department of the Army, 1986.

—**ROTATING BAND** is a soft metal band around
a projectile and near its base. It makes the projectile fit tightly in the bore by centering it. It
also prevents gas from escaping, and gives the
projectile its spin.

References
Department of Defense, U.S. Army. *Dictionary of
United States Army Terms.* Army Regulation AR
310-25. Washington, DC: Headquarters, Department of the Army, 1986.

—**ROTATING UNIT** is a unit that is engaged in
cyclical movements between an overseas area
and the continental United States.

References
Department of Defense, U.S. Army. *Dictionary of
United States Army Terms.* Army Regulation AR
310-25. Washington, DC: Headquarters, Department of the Army, 1986.

—**ROTOR DISK MASKING** (Army Aviation) is a
situation in which an aircraft's rotor disk prevents
the air crew from using the plane's weapons
upward in order to engage an aircraft above it.

References
Department of Defense, U.S. Army. *Airspace
Management and Army Air Traffic in a Combat
Zone.* Field Manual FM 1-60. Washington, DC:
Headquarters, Department of the Army, 1977.

—**ROUND OF AMMUNITION** comprises all the
components necessary to fire a weapon one time.
In general, these components are the primer,
propellent, the container or holder for the propellent (cartridge case or bag), and the projectile
(with a fuze or booster if these are necessary for
the proper functioning of the projectile). *See also:*
Ammunition.

References
Department of Defense, U.S. Army. *Dictionary of
United States Army Terms.* Army Regulation AR
310-25. Washington, DC: Headquarters, Department of the Army, 1986.

—**ROUNDS COMPLETE,** in artillery, is used to
report that the number of rounds that were
specified in the order "fire for effect" have been
fired.

References
Department of Defense, Joint Chiefs of Staff.
*Department of Defense Dictionary of Military and
Related Terms.* Washington, DC: GPO, 1986.

—**ROUTE** is the prescribed course to be travelled
from a specific point of origin to a specific
destination. The route's beginning is designated
as the starting point, and its end is the release
point. A starting point and a release point time
may be set for control when more than one unit
will use the same route. Maneuver units, support
units, and company trains may use different
routes. A route is normally used behind the line
of departure, but may be used in night attacks or
other special operations. *See also:* Line of Departure, Release Point, Start Point.

References
Department of Defense, U.S. Army. *The Infantry
Rifle Company (Infantry, Airborne, Air Assault,
Ranger).* Field Manual FM 7-10. Washington, DC:
Headquarters, Department of the Army, 1982.

———. *Operational Terms and Symbols.* Field
Manual FM 101-5-1. Washington, DC: Headquarters, Department of the Army, 1985.

—**ROUTE CAPACITY.** (1) The route capacity is the
maximum traffic flow of vehicles in one direction at the most restricted point on a given route.
(2) The route capacity is the maximum number
of metric tons that can be moved in one direction over a particular route in one hour. It is the
product of the maximum traffic flow and the
average payload of the vehicles using the route.
See also: Railway Line Capacity, Route Classification.

References
Department of Defense, Joint Chiefs of Staff.
*Department of Defense Dictionary of Military and
Related Terms.* Washington, DC: GPO, 1986.

—**ROUTE CLASSIFICATION** is a classification assigned to a route that is based upon such factors as minimum width, worst route type, least bridge, raft, or culvert military classification, and obstructions to traffic flow. *See also:* Military Load Classification, Route Capacity.

References
Department of Defense, U.S. Army. *Operational Terms and Symbols.* Field Manual FM 101-5-1. Washington, DC: Headquarters, Department of the Army, 1985.

—**ROUTE COLUMN.** (1) A route column is a close order formation for troops, and is suitable for marching. (2) A route column is a flexible formation that is adopted during the contact remote phase of a movement to contact. During this phase, troops need not be tactically grouped, and may move by various means of transportation and by different routes.

References
Department of Defense, U.S. Army. *Dictionary of United States Army Terms.* Army Regulation AR 310-25. Washington, DC: Headquarters, Department of the Army, 1986.

—**ROUTE MARCH** is a march in which the troops are allowed to break step, talk, or sing.

References
Department of Defense, U.S. Army. *Dictionary of United States Army Terms.* Army Regulation AR 310-25. Washington, DC: Headquarters, Department of the Army, 1986.

—**ROUTE OF ADVANCE (ROA)** shows the assigned route of march and is labeled with a number, letter, or name. The start point and release point may also be shown. *See also:* Release Point, Start Point.

References
Department of Defense, U.S. Army. *Armored and Mechanized Division Operations.* Field Manual FM 71-100. Washington, DC: Headquarters, Department of the Army, 1978.

—**ROUTE ORDER** is a manner in which a route march is made when mounted on horseback or travelling in vehicles. Talking, smoking, and relaxing are permitted, provided that there is no straggling or loss of positions.

References
Department of Defense, U.S. Army. *Dictionary of United States Army Terms.* Army Regulation AR 310-25. Washington, DC: Headquarters, Department of the Army, 1986.

—**ROUTE RECONNAISSANCE** is reconnaissance along a specific line of communications (e.g., a road, railway, or waterway) in order to provide new or updated information on route conditions (e.g., road and bridge classification, terrain, and obstacles) and activities (e.g., the existence of chemical or radiological contamination, and enemy emplacements) along the route. It is often done by aircraft. *See also:* Aerial Reconnaissance.

References
Department of Defense, U.S. Army. *Operational Terms and Symbols.* Field Manual FM 101-5-1. Washington, DC: Headquarters, Department of the Army, 1985.

————. *The Tank and Mechanized Infantry Battalion Task Force.* Field Manual FM 71-2. Washington, DC: Headquarters, Department of the Army, 1977.

—**ROUTE STEP.** (1) A route step is a way of marching in which the troops are allowed to break step, talk, or sing, and carry their guns as they please. (2) Route step is the preparatory command to march in this manner.

References
Department of Defense, U.S. Army. *Dictionary of United States Army Terms.* Army Regulation AR 310-25. Washington, DC: Headquarters, Department of the Army, 1986.

—**ROUTE TRANSPOSITION** is a cryptographic system in which the transposition is accomplished by following, within a matrix, a prearranged route connecting adjacent letters. *See also:* CRYPTO.

References
Department of Defense, U.S. Army. *Dictionary of United States Army Terms.* Army Regulation AR 310-25. Washington, DC: Headquarters, Department of the Army, 1986.

—**ROUTES OF COMMUNICATION** are a network of roads over which supplies are carried and combat movements are made. They include navigable waterways, aircraft landing facilities, and rail facilities.

References
Department of Defense, U.S. Army. *Route Reconnaissance and Classification.* Field Manual FM 5-36. Washington, DC: Headquarters, Department of the Army, 1985.

—**ROUTINE** is an ordered set of instructions that may have some general or frequent use.

References

Department of Defense, U.S. Army. *Dictionary of United States Army Terms.* Army Regulation AR 310-25. Washington, DC: Headquarters, Department of the Army, 1986.

—**ROUTINE AMMUNITION MAINTENANCE** is maintenance operations not involving disassembling ammunition or replacing components, and comprising chiefly cleaning and protecting exterior surfaces of individual items, packages of ammunition, ammunition components, and explosives.

References

Department of Defense, U.S. Army. *Dictionary of United States Army Terms.* Army Regulation AR 310-25. Washington, DC: Headquarters, Department of the Army, 1986.

—**ROUTINE ECONOMIC AIRLIFT** is a logistic program, operational worldwide, employing computerized formulas to select items for movement to and from overseas theaters routinely by air. The program involves air shipment of replenishment items, regardless of their requisition priority. The additional costs of routine use of premium transportation will be offset by savings that are realized through reductions in the pipeline and inventory.

References

Department of Defense, U.S. Army. *Dictionary of United States Army Terms.* Army Regulation AR 310-25. Washington, DC: Headquarters, Department of the Army, 1986.

—**ROUTINE IDENTIFIER** is a three-position code that identifies a specific supply and distribution organization as to its military service or governmental ownership and its geographical location.

References

Department of Defense, U.S. Army. *Dictionary of United States Army Terms.* Army Regulation AR 310-25. Washington, DC: Headquarters, Department of the Army, 1986.

—**ROUTINE MESSAGE** is a category of precedence that is to be used for all types of messages that are important enough to warrant their transmission by electronic means, but are not of sufficient urgency to require a higher precedence. *See also:* Precedence.

References

Department of Defense, Joint Chiefs of Staff. *Department of Defense Dictionary of Military and Related Terms.* Washington, DC: GPO, 1986.

—**ROUTINE REPLENISHMENT** is the supply of a deployed force after the termination of preplanned supply. It is based upon the requisitions submitted by the task force or theater commander.

References

Department of Defense, U.S. Army. *Planning Logistics Support for Military Operations.* Field Manual FM 701-58. Washington, DC: Headquarters, Department of the Army, 1987.

—**ROUTINE SUPPLY** is supply that consists of replacement and consumption supplies delivered to the airhead in bulk. It is based upon the actual need for distribution by normal supply procedures plus reserve supplies to build up reserves to a desired level.

References

Department of Defense, U.S. Army. *USA/USAF Doctrine for Joint Airborne and Tactical Airlift Operations.* Field Manual FM 100-27. Washington, DC: Headquarters, Department of the Army, 1985.

—**ROUTING INDICATOR** is a group of letters assigned to indicate (1) the geographic location of the station; (2) a fixed headquarters of a command, activity, or unit at a geographic location; and (3) the general location of a tape relay or tributary station to facilitate the routing of traffic over the tape relay networks.

References

Department of Defense, Joint Chiefs of Staff. *Department of Defense Dictionary of Military and Related Terms.* Washington, DC: GPO, 1986.

—**ROVING FIELD ARTILLERY** is field artillery that is withdrawn from its regular position and assigned to special missions. Roving field artillery is usually moved about and fired from different positions to deceive the enemy as to one's own position and strength. *See also:* Roving Gun.

References

Department of Defense, U.S. Army. *Dictionary of United States Army Terms.* Army Regulation AR 310-25. Washington, DC: Headquarters, Department of the Army, 1986.

—**ROVING GUN** is a gun that is moved about and fired from different positions to mislead and harass the enemy. It is generally used for registration when the location of the battery position must remain secret.

References
Department of Defense, U.S. Army. *Dictionary of United States Army Terms.* Army Regulation AR 310-25. Washington, DC: Headquarters, Department of the Army, 1986.

—**ROW MARKERS,** in land mine warfare, are natural, artificial, or specially installed markers, that are located at the start and finish of a mine row. They are used where mines are laid by individual rows. *See also:* Mine Warfare.

References
Department of Defense, Joint Chiefs of Staff. *Department of Defense Dictionary of Military and Related Terms.* Washington, DC: GPO, 1986.

—**RULES OF ENGAGEMENT (ROE).** (1) Rules of engagement are directives issued by a competent military authority. They specify the circumstances and the limitations under which forces will initiate or continue combat engagement with the enemy forces they encounter. (2) In air defense, the rules of engagement are directives that delineate the circumstances under which weapons can be used to fire at aircraft. The right of self-defense is always preserved.

References
Department of Defense, U.S. Army. *Air Defense Artillery Deployment: Chaparral/Vulcan/Stinger.* Field Manual FM 44-3. Washington, DC: Headquarters, Department of the Army, 1984.

———. *Operational Terms and Symbols.* Field Manual FM 101-5-1. Washington, DC: Headquarters, Department of the Army, 1985.

—**RUNNING FIRE** (ARMY AVIATION) is fire delivered from an aircraft in forward terrain flight.

References
Department of Defense, U.S. Army. *Gunnery Training for Attack Helicopters.* Training Circular TC 17-17. Washington, DC: Headquarters, Department of the Army, 1975.

—**RUNNING KEY SYSTEM.** (1) A running key system is a cipher system in which previously agreed upon plain text or book serves as the source of successive letters for encipherment. (2) A running key system is a cipher system using a long keying sequence that is used only once in a given message. *See also:* CRYPTO.

References
Department of Defense, U.S. Army. *Dictionary of United States Army Terms.* Army Regulation AR 310-25. Washington, DC: Headquarters, Department of the Army, 1986.

—**RUNNING SPARE** is a repair part that is packaged and shipped with an operable set of equipment in addition to the parts needed for initial operation in order to provide replacements as they become necessary. Vacuum tubes, dry batteries, and brushes are often included as running spares.

References
Department of Defense, U.S. Army. *Dictionary of United States Army Terms.* Army Regulation AR 310-25. Washington, DC: Headquarters, Department of the Army, 1986.

—**RUPTURE.** (1) To rupture is to quickly create a gap in the enemy defense positions. (2) A rupture is a complete or partial circular break in the metal of a fired cartridge case. A rupture causes loss of power and difficult extraction or jamming. (3) A rupture is the breaking of the earth or another substance by the explosion of a projectile or other charge below the surface.

References
Department of Defense, U.S. Army. *Operational Terms and Symbols.* Field Manual FM 101-5-1. Washington, DC: Headquarters, Department of the Army, 1985.

—**RUPTURE FORCE,** in breakout operations, is the force that penetrates the enemy forces and opens a gap for the remainder of the force to push through.

References
Department of Defense, U.S. Army. *Dictionary of United States Army Terms.* Army Regulation AR 310-25. Washington, DC: Headquarters, Department of the Army, 1986.

—**RUSES** are tricks intended to deceive the enemy. Generally they are single actions and may be planned or may be impromptu. They may be employed by tactical units to cause the enemy to disclose its intentions, state of morale, or combat readiness. *See also:* Deception Operations, Displays, Feint.

References
Department of Defense, U.S. Army. *Operational Terms and Symbols.* Field Manual FM 101-5-1. Washington, DC: Headquarters, Department of the Army, 1985.

—**S-DAY** is a date used in the wartime manpower planning system data base to denote the first mobilization manpower action in the scenario (e.g., the first 100,000-man call-up) when this first action does not coincide with M-day. *See also:* C-Day, D-day, H-hour, M-Day.

References

Department of Defense, Joint Chiefs of Staff. *Department of Defense Dictionary of Military and Related Terms.* Washington, DC: GPO, 1986.

—**SABOT.** (1) A sabot is an aluminum body of a high velocity armor piercing tracer projectile having a tungsten carbide core. In this case, the core may be considered as the subcalibre projectile. (2) A sabot is a lightweight carrier in which a projectile is centered to permit firing the projectile in the larger caliber weapon. The carrier fills the bore of the weapon from which the projectile is fired. The sabot is normally discarded a short distance from the muzzle.

References

Department of Defense, Joint Chiefs of Staff. *Department of Defense Dictionary of Military and Related Terms.* Washington, DC: GPO, 1986.

Department of Defense, U.S. Army. *Dictionary of United States Army Terms.* Army Regulation AR 310-25. Washington, DC: Headquarters, Department of the Army, 1986.

—**SABOTAGE.** (1) Sabotage is an action against material, premises, or utilities or their production, that injures, interferes with or obstructs the national security or ability of a nation to prepare for or wage a war. (2) Sabotage is a counterintelligence term used in the context of automatic data system security and refers to a situation in which "sleeper" agents who have been blended into the mainstream of society are issued orders to sabotage critical Department of Defense computer facilities prior to or during the outbreak of hostilities. Such agents could physically attack power sources, air conditioning systems, and water supplies. Although access to such facilities is tightly controlled, few installations are hardened to withstand the effects of well-placed, high explosive demolitions. (3) Sabotage is an act or acts with intent to injure, interfere with, or obstruct the national defense of a country by willfully injuring or destroying, or attempting to injure or destroy, material, premises, or utilities, to include human and natural resources. *See also:* Sabotage and Espionage Directed Against the Army, Terrorism Counteraction.

References

Department of Defense, Defense Intelligence College. *Glossary of Intelligence Terms and Definitions.* Washington, DC: DIC, 1987.

Department of Defense, U.S. Army. *Support Operations: Echelons Above Corps.* Field Manual FM 100-16. Washington, DC: Headquarters, Department of the Army, 1986.

—**SABOTAGE AND ESPIONAGE DIRECTED AGAINST THE ARMY (SAEDA)** is an educational program oriented toward members and employees of the U.S. Army. It attempts to improve security by training people to recognize and report approaches by hostile agents. Successful SAEDA efforts may result in the initiation of other special operations. *See also:* Sabotage, Terrorism Counteraction.

References

Department of Defense, U.S. Army. *Counterintelligence.* Field Manual FM 34-60. Washington, DC: Headquarters, Department of the Army, 1985.

—**SAFE.** (1) As applied to explosives, safe is a condition indicating an explosive device is in an unarmed position; or a condition during which detonation cannot occur by fuze action. (2) Safe means so constituted and set so as not to detonate accidentally. (3) Safe means the opposite of armed.

References

Department of Defense, U.S. Army. *Dictionary of United States Army Terms.* Army Regulation AR 310-25. Washington, DC: Headquarters, Department of the Army, 1986.

—**SAFE AREA** is a designated area in hostile territory that offers the evader or escapee a reasonable chance of avoiding capture and surviving until he can be evacuated. *See also:* Safe Area Intelligence Brief.

References

Department of Defense, Joint Chiefs of Staff. *Department of Defense Dictionary of Military and Related Terms.* Washington, DC: GPO, 1986.

—**SAFE AREA INTELLIGENCE BRIEF (SAIB)** is a briefing about a safe area within a hostile area. It is presented to those who may be in danger of being captured to help them avoid apprehension.

References

Department of Defense, Joint Chiefs of Staff. *Department of Defense Dictionary of Military and Related Terms*. Washington, DC: GPO, 1986.

—**SAFE BURST HEIGHT** is the height of burst at or above which the level of fallout, or damage to ground installations, is at a predetermined level that is acceptable to the military commander. *See also:* Nuclear Warfare.

References

Department of Defense, Joint Chiefs of Staff. *Department of Defense Dictionary of Military and Related Terms*. Washington, DC: GPO, 1986.

—**SAFE CONDUCT** is a document similar to a passport and issued by a military authority. A person must have such a document if he wishes to enter or remain in a restricted area. A safe conduct may also enable the holder to move goods to or from places within the area and to engage in trade that would otherwise be forbidden.

References

Department of Defense, U.S. Army. *Dictionary of United States Army Terms*. Army Regulation AR 310-25. Washington, DC: Headquarters, Department of the Army, 1986.

—**SAFE HAVEN.** (1) A safe haven is a designated area or areas to which noncombatants who are the U.S. government's responsibility, and commercial vehicles and materiel, may be evacuated during a domestic or other valid emergency. (2) A safe haven is a temporary storage provided to Department of Energy classified shipment transporters at Department of Defense facilities in order to assure the safety and security of nuclear material or nonnuclear classified material. This classification also includes parking for commercial vehicles carrying Class A or Class B explosives.

References

Department of Defense, Joint Chiefs of Staff. *Department of Defense Dictionary of Military and Related Terms*. Washington, DC: GPO, 1986.

—**SAFE LEVEL OF SUPPLY** is the quantity of materiel, in addition to the operating level of supply, required to be on hand to permit continu-ous operations in the event of a minor interruption in normal replenishment or unpredictable fluctuations in demand. *See also:* Level of Supply.

References

Department of Defense, Joint Chiefs of Staff. *Department of Defense Dictionary of Military and Related Terms*. Washington, DC: GPO, 1986.

—**SAFE SEPARATION DISTANCE** is the minimum distance between the delivery system and the weapon beyond which the hazards associated with functioning (detonation) are acceptable.

References

Department of Defense, Joint Chiefs of Staff. *Department of Defense Dictionary of Military and Related Terms*. Washington, DC: GPO, 1986.

—**SAFEGUARD.** (1) Safeguard is a written order issued by a commander for the protection of persons or property from molestation by troops. A safeguard may be issued for reasons of military discipline, personal consideration, public policy, or humanity. Forcing a safeguard is disregarding and violating such an order, and in time of war is punishable by death. (2) Safeguard is a soldier or detachment that is detailed to protect people, places, or property. (3) Safeguard is a lock on a door or gate for the protection of people, places, or property.

References

Department of Defense, U.S. Army. *Dictionary of United States Army Terms*. Army Regulation AR 310-25. Washington, DC: Headquarters, Department of the Army, 1986.

—**SAFETY.** (1) A safety is a locking or cutoff device that prevents a weapon from being fired accidentally. (2) Safety is freedom from or protection against hazardous conditions that have the potential to cause injury, illness, or death to personnel, or damage to or loss of equipment or property.

References

Department of Defense, U.S. Army. *Dictionary of United States Army Terms*. Army Regulation AR 310-25. Washington, DC: Headquarters, Department of the Army, 1986.

—**SAFETY CARD** is a card issued for a particular battery position for a particular time, prescribing the area into which fire may safely be placed both laterally and in depth.

References
Department of Defense, U.S. Army. *Dictionary of United States Army Terms*. Army Regulation AR 310-25. Washington, DC: Headquarters, Department of the Army, 1986.

—**SAFETY DEVICE** is a device in or on the fuze or firing device to prevent an accidental detonation or arming. *See also:* Fuze (Specify Type).

References
Department of Defense, U.S. Army. *Mine/ Countermine Operations at the Company Level*. Field Manual FM 20-32. Washington, DC: Headquarters, Department of the Army, 1976.

—**SAFETY DIAGRAM** is a geographic representation, usually an overlay, depicting the areas into which fire may safely be placed. *See also:* Safety Card.

References
Department of Defense, U.S. Army. *Dictionary of United States Army Terms*. Army Regulation AR 310-25. Washington, DC: Headquarters, Department of the Army, 1986.

—**SAFETY DISTANCE** (ROAD) is the distance between vehicles traveling in a column that is specified by the command in light of safety requirements.

References
Department of Defense, Joint Chiefs of Staff. *Department of Defense Dictionary of Military and Related Terms*. Washington, DC: GPO, 1986.

—**SAFETY FACTOR.** (1) A safety factor is an increase in range or elevation that must be set on a gun so that friendly troops, over whose heads fire is to be delivered, will not be endangered. (2) A safety factor is an overload factor in a design to ensure the equipment's safe operation.

References
Department of Defense, U.S. Army. *Dictionary of United States Army Terms*. Army Regulation AR 310-25. Washington, DC: Headquarters, Department of the Army, 1986.

—**SAFETY FORK.** (1) Safety fork is a metal clip that fits over the cover of the fuze in a mine and prevents the mine from being set off accidentally. Its function is the same as that of a safety pin or safety level in a grenade, bomb, or projectile. (2) A safety fork is the metal clip part of the quick parachute release assembly that prevents accidental release of the parachute harness. *See also:* Mine Warfare.

References
Department of Defense, U.S. Army. *Dictionary of United States Army Terms*. Army Regulation AR 310-25. Washington, DC: Headquarters, Department of the Army, 1986.

—**SAFETY FUZE** is a pyrotechnic contained in a flexible and weatherproof sheath burning at a timed and constant rate. It is used to transmit a flame to a detonator. *See also:* Fuze (Specify Type).

References
Department of Defense, Joint Chiefs of Staff. *Department of Defense Dictionary of Military and Related Terms*. Washington, DC: GPO, 1986.

—**SAFETY LEVEL OF SUPPLY** is the quantity of materiel, in addition to the operating level of supply, required to be on hand to permit continuous operations in the event of a minor interruption in normal replenishment or unpredictable fluctuations in demand. *See also:* Level of Supply.

References
Department of Defense, Joint Chiefs of Staff. *Department of Defense Dictionary of Military and Related Terms*. Washington, DC: GPO, 1986.

—**SAFETY LEVER.** (1) A safety lever prevents the accidental firing of a grenade so long as it remains locked in position. Its function is the same as that of the safety fork in projectiles, bombs, and mines. (2) A safety lever sets the safety mechanism on certain types of automatic weapons.

References
Department of Defense, U.S. Army. *Dictionary of United States Army Terms*. Army Regulation AR 310-25. Washington, DC: Headquarters, Department of the Army, 1986.

—**SAFETY LIMIT.** (1) A safety limit is the line marking off the zone or area in front of friendly troops, over whose heads gunfire is delivered. Shots must clear this zone if the troops are not to be endangered. (2) A safety limit consists of the bounds that are set around a target area on a firing range, within which there is a danger from shell fragments or ricocheting shells.

References
Department of Defense, U.S. Army. *Dictionary of United States Army Terms*. Army Regulation AR 310-25. Washington, DC: Headquarters, Department of the Army, 1986.

—**SAFETY LINE,** in land mine warfare, is the demarcation line for trip wire or wire-actuated mines in a minefield. It serves to protect the minelaying personnel. After the minefield is laid, this line is neither marked on the ground nor plotted on the minefield record. *See also:* Mine Warfare.

References
Department of Defense, Joint Chiefs of Staff. *Department of Defense Dictionary of Military and Related Terms.* Washington, DC: GPO, 1986.

—**SAFETY LOCK** is a locking device that prevents a gun from being fired accidentally.

References
Department of Defense, U.S. Army. *Dictionary of United States Army Terms.* Army Regulation AR 310-25. Washington, DC: Headquarters, Department of the Army, 1986.

—**SAFETY OFFICER.** (1) Safety officer is an officer who supervises field practice in gunnery to make sure that persons and property are not endangered. He is the assistant to the officer in charge of firing. (2) A safety officer is the officer who administers and directs organizational safety program activities.

References
Department of Defense, U.S. Army. *Dictionary of United States Army Terms.* Army Regulation AR 310-25. Washington, DC: Headquarters, Department of the Army, 1986.

—**SAFETY PROGRAM** is a program to reduce and keep to a minimum personnel accidents and the resultant monetary losses, thus providing a more efficient utilization of resources and advancing the combat effectiveness of the Army.

References
Department of Defense, U.S. Army. *Dictionary of United States Army Terms.* Army Regulation AR 310-25. Washington, DC: Headquarters, Department of the Army, 1986.

—**SAFETY SHOES.** (1) Safety shoes are special shoes designed to prevent foot injuries. (2) Safety shoes are special shoes (with conductive or nonconductive soles) that prevent sparks when one is working with explosives or other hazardous material.

References
Department of Defense, U.S. Army. *Dictionary of United States Army Terms.* Army Regulation AR 310-25. Washington, DC: Headquarters, Department of the Army, 1986.

—**SAFETY STAKE** is one of the stakes set in the ground to mark the right or left limit of safety fire of a gun.

References
Department of Defense, U.S. Army. *Dictionary of United States Army Terms.* Army Regulation AR 310-25. Washington, DC: Headquarters, Department of the Army, 1986.

—**SAFETY ZONE,** is a land, sea, or air area reserved for noncombat operations of friendly aircraft, surface ships, submarines, or ground forces.

References
Department of Defense, Joint Chiefs of Staff. *Department of Defense Dictionary of Military and Related Terms.* Washington, DC: GPO, 1986.

—**SAFING,** as applied to weapons and ammunition, is the changing from a state of readiness to a safe condition. *See also:* Safety, Safety Lever, Safety Lock.

References
Department of Defense, Joint Chiefs of Staff. *Department of Defense Dictionary of Military and Related Terms.* Washington, DC: GPO, 1986.

—**SAFING AND ARMING MECHANISM** prevents the unintended functioning of the main charge of the ammunition prior to the completion of the arming delay, and, conversely, allows the ammunition explosive train to function after arming. *See also:* Safing.

References
Department of Defense, U.S. Army. *Dictionary of United States Army Terms.* Army Regulation AR 310-25. Washington, DC: Headquarters, Department of the Army, 1986.

—**SALES OFFICER** is an officer or civilian employee who has been designated by the installation commander to manage the sales of supplies, equipment, and services involving appropriated funds. He also reports charges for communication service, taxes, and telegrams. Sales officers include repairs and utilities sales officers, post signal or communications officers, property disposal officers, clothing sales officers, medical officers, laundry officers, and self-service supply center officers.

References
Department of Defense, U.S. Army. *Dictionary of United States Army Terms.* Army Regulation AR 310-25. Washington, DC: Headquarters, Department of the Army, 1986.

—**SALIENT** is an outward bend in the trace of the forward line of friendly troops or on the outside bend of a river.

References

Department of Defense, U.S. Army. *Operational Terms and Symbols.* Field Manual FM 101-5-1. Washington, DC: Headquarters, Department of the Army, 1985.

—**SALLY PORT** is a large gate or passage in a fortified place.

References

Department of Defense, U.S. Army. *Dictionary of United States Army Terms.* Army Regulation AR 310-25. Washington, DC: Headquarters, Department of the Army, 1986.

—**SALTED WEAPON** is a nuclear weapon that has, in addition to its normal components, certain elements or isotopes that capture neutrons at the time of the explosion and produce radioactive products over and above the usual radioactive debris. *See also:* Minimum Residual Radioactivity Weapon, Nuclear Warfare.

References

Department of Defense, Joint Chiefs of Staff. *Department of Defense Dictionary of Military and Related Terms.* Washington, DC: GPO, 1986.

—**SALUTE** is a mnemonic term for a report format: Size, Activity, Location, Unit, Time, Equipment.

References

Department of Defense, U.S. Army. *The Infantry Rifle Company (Infantry, Airborne, Air Assault, Ranger).* Field Manual FM 7-10. Washington, DC: Headquarters, Department of the Army, 1982.

—**SALUTE TO THE UNION** *See:* National Salute.

—**SALUTING DISTANCE** is a distance, generally between six and 30 paces, at which salutes are given. Because recognizing insignia is difficult beyond 30 paces, 30 paces is set as the maximum distance.

References

Department of Defense, U.S. Army. *Dictionary of United States Army Terms.* Army Regulation AR 310-25. Washington, DC: Headquarters, Department of the Army, 1986.

—**SALUTING GUN** is a cannon used to fire salutes.

References

Department of Defense, U.S. Army. *Dictionary of United States Army Terms.* Army Regulation AR 310-25. Washington, DC: Headquarters, Department of the Army, 1986.

—**SALVAGE.** (1) Salvage is property that has some value in excess of its basic material content but that is in such condition that it has no reasonable prospect of use for any purpose as a unit and its rehabilitation or repair for a unit is clearly impractical. (2) Salvaging is the saving or rescuing of condemned, discarded, or abandoned property, and of the materials contained therein for reuse, refabrication, or scrapping. *See also:* Salvage Procedure.

References

Department of Defense, Joint Chiefs of Staff. *Department of Defense Dictionary of Military and Related Terms.* Washington, DC: GPO, 1986.

—**SALVAGE PROCEDURE** is the recovery, evacuation, and reclamation of damaged, discarded, condemned, or abandoned allied or enemy materiel, ships, craft, and floating equipment for reuse, repair, refabrication, or scrapping.

References

Department of Defense, Joint Chiefs of Staff. *Department of Defense Dictionary of Military and Related Terms.* Washington, DC: GPO, 1986.

—**SALVO,** in close air support and air interdiction operations, is a method of delivering fire in which the release mechanisms of weapons are operated to release or fire all ordnance of a specific type simultaneously. *See also:* Salvo Fire (Air Defense Method of Engagement).

References

Department of Defense, Joint Chiefs of Staff. *Department of Defense Dictionary of Military and Related Terms.* Washington, DC: GPO, 1986.

—**SALVO FIRE** (AIR DEFENSE METHOD OF ENGAGEMENT) is firing two missiles from two separate launchers with a minimum amount of time between launches. Salvo fire is selected when the commander wants an extremely high kill assurance against a single pop-up target. This is the least desirable firing method when engaging multiple targets due to the high probability of destroying only one aircraft with the missiles. *See also:* Pop-up Target.

References
Department of Defense, U.S. Army. *Patriot Battalion Operations*. Field Manual FM 44-15. Washington, DC: Headquarters, Department of the Army, 1984.

—**SALVO RIGHT (LEFT)** is an element of fire command to obtain salvo fire from automatic grenade launchers beginning with the portion of the system mounted on the right (left) side of the combat vehicle M551 (i.e., armored reconnaissance airborne assault vehicle).

References
Department of Defense, U.S. Army. *Dictionary of United States Army Terms*. Army Regulation AR 310-25. Washington, DC: Headquarters, Department of the Army, 1986.

—**SANCTUARY** is a nation or area near or contiguous to a combat area that by tacit agreement between the warring powers is exempt from attack and therefore serves as a refuge for staging, logistic, or other activities of the combatant powers.

References
Department of Defense, Joint Chiefs of Staff. *Department of Defense Dictionary of Military and Related Terms*. Washington, DC: GPO, 1986.

—**SANITIZATION** is the process of editing or otherwise altering intelligence information or reports in order to protect sensitive intelligence sources, methods, capabilities, analytical procedures, or privileged information so that the document can be disseminated more widely. *See also:* Intelligence.

References
Department of Defense, U.S. Army. *Support Operations: Echelons Above Corps*. Field Manual FM 100-16. Washington, DC: Headquarters, Department of the Army, 1986.

—**SANITIZE.** *See:* Sanitization.

—**SANITIZED AREA** is an area from which all sensitive compartmented information has been removed so that individuals who have not been indoctrinated for it can enter the area for legitimate reasons and on a temporary basis. These personnel, who may be accomplishing janitorial, maintenance, or other legitimate business, must be escorted at all times while in the area by an individual who has been indoctrinated for the information. *See also:* Intelligence.

References
Department of Defense, U.S. Army. *Support Operations: Echelons Above Corps*. Field Manual FM 100-16. Washington, DC: Headquarters, Department of the Army, 1986.

—**SATCHEL CHARGE** is a number of blocks of explosive taped to a board that has been fitted with a rope or wire loop for carrying and attaching it. The minimum weight of the charge is usually about fifteen pounds. It is sometimes incorrectly called a satchel bomb.

References
Department of Defense, U.S. Army. *Dictionary of United States Army Terms*. Army Regulation AR 310-25. Washington, DC: Headquarters, Department of the Army, 1986.

—**SATELLITE** is a unit or activity of a government agency, military department, or command that is not a tenant but that is dependent on a designated installation for specified support, either as assigned by higher authority or through a mutually developed written support agreement.

References
Department of Defense, U.S. Army. *Dictionary of United States Army Terms*. Army Regulation AR 310-25. Washington, DC: Headquarters, Department of the Army, 1986.

—**SATELLITE DINING FACILITY** is a dining facility that receives menu items either totally or partially prepared from a central food preparation facility for final preparation and serving to authorized persons.

References
Department of Defense, U.S. Army. *Dictionary of United States Army Terms*. Army Regulation AR 310-25. Washington, DC: Headquarters, Department of the Army, 1986.

—**SATELLIZATION AUTHORITY** is the designation of a specific Army installation, subinstallation, or activity to provide all or a portion of the support requirements to one or more designated installations, subinstallations, or separate organizations. This designation may occur by direction of higher authority or through a written interdepartmental, interservice, or intraservice support agreement. *See also:* Satellite.

References
Department of Defense, U.S. Army. *Dictionary of United States Army Terms.* Army Regulation AR 310-25. Washington, DC: Headquarters, Department of the Army, 1986.

—**SAY AGAIN** is a radiotelephone procedure proword that means "Say again all of your last transmission." *See also:* Proword.

References
Department of Defense, U.S. Army. *The Rifle Squads (Mechanized and Light Infantry).* Training Circular TC 7-1. Washington, DC: Headquarters, Department of the Army, 1976.

—**SCABBING.** (1) Scabbing is the breaking off of fragments of hard material inside a wall due to the impact or explosion of a projectile outside of the wall. (2) Scabbing is the material used to fill excess space along the length of railway freight cars or ammunition cars.

References
Department of Defense, U.S. Army. *Dictionary of United States Army Terms.* Army Regulation AR 310-25. Washington, DC: Headquarters, Department of the Army, 1986.

—**SCALE.** (1) Scale is a thin flat triangle-shaped strip of wood, plastic, or metal, with one or more edges graduated in units of linear measurements (e.g., inches, centimeters, feet, yards, or meters) and in fractional or decimal subdivisions thereof. The units may be in various scale ratios, and the scale is used in drafting to plot and measure linear distances. (2) A scale is the ratio between the distance on a map, chart, or photograph and the corresponding distance on the surface of the earth. *See also:* Photographic Scale.

References
Department of Defense, Joint Chiefs of Staff. *Department of Defense Dictionary of Military and Related Terms.* Washington, DC: GPO, 1986.

Department of Defense, U.S. Army. *Dictionary of United States Army Terms.* Army Regulation AR 310-25. Washington, DC: Headquarters, Department of the Army, 1986.

—**SCALE FACTOR** is a value by which an actual ground distance is multiplied in order to compensate for map distortion when determining the ground distance as represented on a map.

References
Department of Defense, U.S. Army. *Dictionary of United States Army Terms.* Army Regulation AR 310-25. Washington, DC: Headquarters, Department of the Army, 1986.

—**SCALE OF AN EXERCISE** is the size of an exercise in terms of the resources that are required or allocated. It may be categorized as large, medium, or small. *See also:* Exercise.

References
Department of Defense, Joint Chiefs of Staff. *Department of Defense Dictionary of Military and Related Terms.* Washington, DC: GPO, 1986.

—**SCAN.** (1) A scan, in electronic warfare, is the movement of an electronic beam through space as it searches for a target. Scanning is done by moving the radar antenna or by lobe watching. (2) A scan, as defined by the Church Committee, is "one complete rotation of an antenna in the electromagnetic and acoustic contexts." *See also:* Electronic Warfare.

References
Department of Defense, Joint Chiefs of Staff. *Department of Defense Dictionary of Military and Related Terms.* Washington, DC: GPO, 1986.

U.S. Congress. Senate. *Final Report of the Senate Select Committee to Study Government Operations With Respect to Intelligence Activities. Report 94-755. Book I, Foreign and Military Intelligence* (Church Committee Report). Washington, DC: GPO, 1976.

—**SCANNING** is the process of directing the radio frequency energy propagated by a radar antenna successively over all points in a given region or area. *See also:* Scan.

References
Department of Defense, U.S. Army. *Dictionary of United States Army Terms.* Army Regulation AR 310-25. Washington, DC: Headquarters, Department of the Army, 1986.

—**SCATTER** (ARMY AVIATION) is a call to indicate that the flight should break up according to a prearranged plan.

References
Department of Defense, U.S. Army. *Air-to-Air Combat.* Field Manual FM 1-107. Washington, DC: Headquarters, Department of the Army, 1984.

—**SCATTER PLAN** (ARMY AVIATION) is a prearranged formation breakup and rendezvous plan.

References

Department of Defense, U.S. Army. *Air-to-Air Combat*. Field Manual FM 1-107. Washington, DC: Headquarters, Department of the Army, 1984.

—**SCATTERABLE MINES** are mines designed to self-destruct after a set period of time. With the exception of the wide angle side penetrating system, which is directly emplaced, scatterable mines are remotely delivered ground systems, artillery, helicopters, and high performance aircraft. The term should not be used to describe conventional mines that have been laid without regard to a pattern. *See also:* Mine Warfare.

References

Department of Defense, U.S. Army.
Countermobility. Field Manual FM 5-102. Washington, DC: Headquarters, Department of the Army, 1985.

————. *Mine/Countermine Operations at the Company Level*. Field Manual FM 20-32. Washington, DC: Headquarters, Department of the Army, 1976.

————. *Operational Terms and Symbols*. Field Manual FM 101-5-1. Washington, DC: Headquarters, Department of the Army, 1985.

—**SCHEDULE CONTROL SYSTEM** is a system of traffic control in which a truck column and troops are dispatched over fixed routes at given rates of speed according to a time system.

References

Department of Defense, U.S. Army. *Dictionary of United States Army Terms*. Army Regulation AR 310-25. Washington, DC: Headquarters, Department of the Army, 1986.

—**SCHEDULE OF FIRE** encompasses groups of fires or series of fires that are fired in a definite sequence according to a definite program. The time of starting the schedule may be ON CALL. For identification purposes, schedules may be referred to by a code name or other identification.

References

Department of Defense, Joint Chiefs of Staff.
Department of Defense Dictionary of Military and Related Terms. Washington, DC: GPO, 1986.

—**SCHEDULE OF TARGETS,** in artillery, are individual targets, or groups or series of targets, that are to be fired on in a definite sequence according to a definite program.

References

Department of Defense, Joint Chiefs of Staff.
Department of Defense Dictionary of Military and Related Terms. Washington, DC: GPO, 1986.

—**SCHEDULED FIRE** is a type of prearranged fire that is executed at a predetermined time.

References

Department of Defense, Joint Chiefs of Staff.
Department of Defense Dictionary of Military and Related Terms. Washington, DC: GPO, 1986.

—**SCHEDULED INVENTORY** is a physical inventory that is to be conducted on a group of items within a specified period of time according to an established plan. The items may be selected on a specific basis (e.g., on a cycle, sample, special, or complete basis).

References

Department of Defense, U.S. Army. *Dictionary of United States Army Terms*. Army Regulation AR 310-25. Washington, DC: Headquarters, Department of the Army, 1986.

—**SCHEDULED MAINTENANCE** is the periodic prescribed inspection and servicing of equipment done on a calendar, mileage, or hours of operation basis. *See also:* Organizational Maintenance.

References

Department of Defense, Joint Chiefs of Staff.
Department of Defense Dictionary of Military and Related Terms. Washington, DC: GPO, 1986.

—**SCHEDULED SUPPLIES** are requirements for items that can be reasonably predicted. A scheduled supply normally will not require a requisition to be submitted by the user for its replenishment. Requirements are based upon troop strength, equipment density, forecasts, or daily usage factors. Supply classes I, III (bulk), V, and VI are normally treated as scheduled supplies. *See also:* Scheduled Supply.

References

Department of Defense, U.S. Army. *Operational Terms and Symbols*. Field Manual FM 101-5-1. Washington, DC: Headquarters, Department of the Army, 1985.

—**SCHEDULED SUPPLY** is a system whereby any user or supplier unit is furnished some or all of its supply requirements by a previously planned schedule that specifies the items, quantities, time, and place of delivery. *See also:* Scheduled Supplies.

References

Department of Defense, U.S. Army. *Planning Logistics Support for Military Operations.* Field Manual FM 701-58. Washington, DC: Headquarters, Department of the Army, 1987.

—**SCHEDULED TARGET,** in artillery, is a planned target on which fire is to be delivered at a specific time. *See also:* Scheduled

References

Department of Defense, U.S. Army. *Operational Terms and Symbols.* Field Manual FM 101-5-1. Washington, DC: Headquarters, Department of the Army, 1985.

—**SCHEDULED TARGET** (NUCLEAR) is a planned target on which a nuclear weapon is to be delivered at a specific time during the operation of a supported force. The time is specified in terms of minutes before or after a designated time or in terms of the accomplishment of a predetermined movement or task. Coordination and warning of friendly troops and aircraft are mandatory before the attack occurs. *See also:* Nuclear Warfare.

References

Department of Defense, Joint Chiefs of Staff. *Department of Defense Dictionary of Military and Related Terms.* Washington, DC: GPO, 1986.

—**SCHEME OF COMMAND** is a plan for the control of all elements of a command during a military operation, including providing for communications, observation, and the location of the command post.

References

Department of Defense, U.S. Army. *Dictionary of United States Army Terms.* Army Regulation AR 310-25. Washington, DC: Headquarters, Department of the Army, 1986.

—**SCHEME OF MANEUVER** is the part of a tactical plan that is to be executed by a maneuver force to achieve its assigned objectives or to hold its assigned area.

References

Department of Defense, U.S. Army. *Operational Terms and Symbols.* Field Manual FM 101-5-1. Washington, DC: Headquarters, Department of the Army, 1985.

—**SCHOOL CENTER** is a center authorized and designated by the Headquarters, Department of the Army, to accomplish combat developments and to provide guidance for education and training within a clearly delineated branch or specialty area of the Army. *See also:* Learning Center.

References

Department of Defense, U.S. Army. *Dictionary of United States Army Terms.* Army Regulation AR 310-25. Washington, DC: Headquarters, Department of the Army, 1986.

—**SCHOOL YEAR** is fifty weeks and is based upon a fiscal calendar (October 1 to September 30).

References

Department of Defense, U.S. Army. *Individual Military Education and Training.* Army Regulation AR 350-1. Washington, DC: Headquarters, Department of the Army, 1986.

—**SCIENTIFIC AND ENGINEERING PROGRAM PERSONNEL** are enlisted personnel who possess a baccalaureate degree and work experience or a master's degree in a scientific and engineering specialization that is directly usable by the Army in the field of research and development.

References

Department of Defense, U.S. Army. *Dictionary of United States Army Terms.* Army Regulation AR 310-25. Washington, DC: Headquarters, Department of the Army, 1986.

—**SCIENTIFIC AND TECHNICAL INTELLIGENCE (S&T or S&TI),** one of the eight components of strategic intelligence, is intelligence that concerns foreign developments in basic and applied scientific and technical research and development. This includes engineering and production techniques, new technology, and weapon systems and their capabilities and characteristics. It also includes intelligence that requires that the analyst have scientific or technical expertise (e.g., medicine, physical health studies, and behavioral expertise). The Defense Intelligence Agency, the various service scientific and technological organizations, and the Central Intelligence Agency all have responsibilities in the production of scientific and technical intelligence.

General

Scientific and technical intelligence is the study of the scientific and technical capacities and activities of all nations. No significant changes are likely to occur in the techniques of modern war or in the production of new weapons without the aid of science. Hence, the intelligence officer learns about the activities of foreign scientists, the research and development programs and scientific organization of foreign nations, the funds available for scientific study and the discoveries and inventions that result from these activities. Scientific intelligence, moreover, is contributory to other components of strategic intelligence, especially economic, telecommunications, and armed forces intelligence.

Scientific activities may be divided into basic or pure research and applied science. The military research and development program is a particular phase of the latter that is of primary interest to the intelligence analyst. Applied science is of most importance to the military and is often identified as technical intelligence. Pure scientific research, however, is a key national potential.

Potential

The history and traditions of a nation's scientific endeavor largely determine the government's attitude toward science. A knowledge of this attitude helps the intelligence officer estimate the role of the scientists in the country under consideration and the fields of research that are receiving major attention. An important factor in determining scientific potential is the rate at which a country is training its new scientists and the quality of their training.

New Weapons and Equipment

An important task of scientific and technical intelligence is forecasting new weapons and equipment of foreign armed forces. A study of the scientific research being accomplished in a country will reveal discoveries that may later be applied to develop new weapons. These discoveries occur in such areas as electronics and atomic energy. However, important discoveries also occur in other fields and should not be ignored. For example, the discoveries that led to the development of synthetic materials or substitutes have allowed nations to wage war in spite of shortages in materials that were previously considered essential to conduct war (e.g., synthetic fuels, lubricants, and synthetic rubber).

Scientific and technical intelligence is concerned with all scientific developments that may have military application until such developments result in weapons that are adopted by a foreign nation as standard equipment. The weapons then become the concern of the armed forces intelligence analyst.

Collection

Collecting scientific and technical information is usually complicated by the fact that most countries take extreme measures to conceal scientific and technical activities. The problem is further aggravated by the lack of sufficient technically trained personnel for fieldwork. The scientific researcher must depend to a large extent on information that is furnished to him by observers who are not specialists in this field.

Scientific and technical intelligence should identify the main research and development organizations of a nation and their types; their interrelationships and how their efforts are coordinated; and where and how research projects originate. The researcher must ascertain the governmental structure that controls or supervises scientific research and development, both within and outside the armed forces.

National academies of science can provide valuable material for the intelligence analyst. The membership roster of an academy lists the nation's leading scientists, and the academy frequently publishes scholarly papers that reveal trends in its research programs. This applies also to organizations that sponsor or engage in research. Another source is technical publications, which frequently report on the latest scientific developments in a country.

Colleges and universities, especially those with outstanding scientific or technical schools, also can be sources of valuable intelligence information. The types of science stressed in their curricula may yield valuable information on the items that the nation is emphasizing in its research and development programs.

In many countries, there are privately owned research organizations. Their relationship with the government, their significance and caliber, and the types of research in which they are engaged should be carefully studied. Also, it should be determined whether the research organizations have any international affiliations. The research projects that are receiving major attention may be conspicuous by the allocation of both public and private funds. The information will be even more valuable if the intelligence analyst can ascertain what amounts are allocated to specific projects or to individual scientists. Citations accompanying prizes, scholarships, and other awards often recite the accomplishments for which the honor was conferred.

Other targets that can be exploited for possible scientific and technical intelligence include evidence of (1) the exporting and importing of materials or equipment that pertain to a specific type of scientific research or development; (2) the stockpiling of certain raw materials; (3) the erection or expansion of facilities that are appropriate to specific categories of research or manufacture; (4) the imposition of extreme security precautions around an installation; and (5) the awarding of higher wages or other inducements to certain types of scientists or workers.

The whereabouts of scientists is especially important, for the location of specialists is often a key to the type of research activity being conducted by a particular installation.

Scientists in one country frequently correspond and exchange visits with scientists in other countries, including those of the Soviet bloc. This type of scientific contact can often be exploited to obtain useful or significant information on Soviet bloc scientific activities.

Of particular importance to the military aspects of scientific and technical intelligence is the development of new collection techniques, based upon scientific principles that can be used to collect important technical information.

Conclusions

The key functions of scientific and technical intelligence are to project the future threat potential against the United States; to aid in U.S. research and development; to evaluate the vulnerability and survivability of U.S. weapons; and to aid in the development of U.S. countermeasures.

The key sources of scientific and technical information on a given nation are
- *Human intelligence*, which should be helpful in providing intelligence on the nation's policy, military strategy, military requirements, research, specifications and tests, production, and facilities construction. In addition, it should provide even better information, which is of medium value (potentially useful) in the production of intelligence in the areas of the nation's design and development focus and its military operations.
- *Open literature*, which can provide low value (helpful) information on the nation's military requirements, resource allocation, threat assessment, and military operations, medium value (potentially useful) information in the areas of policy, military strategy, design and development, specifications and tests, and technology exploitation, and high value (virtually sufficient) data on the nation's research.
- *Photography*, which can provide medium value (potentially useful) data on the nation's design and development operations, military operations, and its production, and high value (virtually sufficient) data on facilities construction.
- *Communications intelligence*, which can provide low value (helpful) data on military requirements, resource allocation, and specifications and tests, medium value (potentially useful) information on design and development, military operations, and facilities construction, and high value (virtually sufficient) information on production.
- *Material exploitation*, which can provide medium value (potentially useful) information on design and development and on production.

See also: Strategic Intelligence.

References

Clauser, Jerome K., and Weir, Sandra M. *Intelligence Research Methodology*. State College, PA: HRB-Singer, 1975.

Department of Defense, Defense Intelligence College. *Glossary of Intelligence Terms and Definitions*. Washington, DC: DIC, 1987.

—**SCISSORS** (ARMY AVIATION) is an evasive maneuver used to avoid an enemy aircraft that is gaining the six-o'clock position.

References

Department of Defense, U.S. Army. *Air-to-Air Combat*. Field Manual FM 1-107. Washington, DC: Headquarters, Department of the Army, 1984.

—**SCRAMBLE.** (1) In telephony, scramble means to make unintelligible to casual interception. (2) Scramble, in cryptology, means to mix in random or quasi-random fashion. (3) Scramble, in air operations, means the emergency dispatch of aircraft for interception. *See also:* CRYPTO.

References

Department of Defense, U.S. Army. *Dictionary of United States Army Terms*. Army Regulation AR 310-25. Washington, DC: Headquarters, Department of the Army, 1986.

—**SCREEN.** (1) In surveillance, a screen is camouflage and concealment. It is any natural or artificial material placed between the collection sensor and the object to be camouflaged or concealed. (2) A screen is a security element whose primary task is to observe, identify, and report information. It only fights in self-protection. (3) A screen is a wire mesh gauze or sieve.

References

Department of Defense, Joint Chiefs of Staff. *Department of Defense Dictionary of Military and Related Terms.* Washington, DC: GPO, 1986.

Department of Defense, U.S. Army. *Dictionary of United States Army Terms.* Army Regulation AR 310-25. Washington, DC: Headquarters, Department of the Army, 1986.

—**SCREENING** is a preselection early in the selection process to identify who in the available supply of personnel meet the minimum qualifications for a given assignment. It is selection in which those below the minimum qualifying score on a preliminary evaluating instrument are not considered further for a particular assignment.

References

Department of Defense, U.S. Army. *Dictionary of United States Army Terms.* Army Regulation AR 310-25. Washington, DC: Headquarters, Department of the Army, 1986.

—**SCREENING FIRE** is a category of fire using smoke or other obscurants used on the battlefield between enemy observation points and friendly units. Its purpose is to mask friendly maneuvers or to deceive and confuse the enemy as to the nature of friendly operations. *See also:* Fire.

References

Department of Defense, U.S. Army. *Dictionary of United States Army Terms.* Army Regulation AR 310-25. Washington, DC: Headquarters, Department of the Army, 1986.

—**SCREENING FORCE** maintains surveillance, provides early warning to the main body, impedes and harasses the enemy with supporting indirect fires, and destroys the enemy reconnaissance elements that are within its capability. *See also:* Screen.

References

Department of Defense, U.S. Army. *Operational Terms and Symbols.* Field Manual FM 101-5-1. Washington, DC: Headquarters, Department of the Army, 1985.

—**SCREENING SMOKE** is smoke used in areas of friendly operation or in areas between friendly and enemy forces to conceal ground movement, breaching, and recovery operations, key assembly areas, supply routes, and logistic facilities. It reduces enemy ground and aerial observation. *See also:* Identification Smoke, Obscuration Smoke, Smoke.

References

Department of Defense, U.S. Army. *Deliberate Smoke Operations.* Field Manual FM 3-50. Washington, DC: Headquarters, Department of the Army, 1984.

————. *Operational Terms and Symbols.* Field Manual FM 101-5-1. Washington, DC: Headquarters, Department of the Army, 1985.

—**SCREW PICKET** is a metal post with a spiral point resembling a corkscrew. It is used as a support for a wire entanglement or as an anchor for a cable.

References

Department of Defense, U.S. Army. *Dictionary of United States Army Terms.* Army Regulation AR 310-25. Washington, DC: Headquarters, Department of the Army, 1986.

—**SEA LINE OF COMMUNICATION (SLOC)** is an ocean route that connects an operating military force with a base of operations.

References

Department of Defense, U.S. Army. *Support Operations: Echelons Above Corps.* Field Manual FM 100-16. Washington, DC: Headquarters, Department of the Army, 1986.

—**SEA TAIL** is the part of an airborne or air transported unit that is not committed to combat by air and will join the organization by sea travel.

References

Department of Defense, U.S. Army. *Dictionary of United States Army Terms.* Army Regulation AR 310-25. Washington, DC: Headquarters, Department of the Army, 1986.

—**SEALED ORDERS** are secret or confidential orders in a sealed envelope that are given to a commander of troops or of a ship. He is instructed not to open them until a given time or until he arrives at a specified designation.

References

Department of Defense, U.S. Army. *Dictionary of United States Army Terms.* Army Regulation AR 310-25. Washington, DC: Headquarters, Department of the Army, 1986.

—**SEARCH** is a step in the Army tactical intelligence process of signals intelligence. *See also:* Signals Intelligence.

References

Department of Defense, U.S. Army. *Military Intelligence Battalion Combat Electronic Warfare and Intelligence (Aerial Exploitation) (Corps)*. Field Manual FM 34-22. Washington, DC: Headquarters, Department of the Army, 1984.

—**SEARCH SECTOR** is an area in the sky or on the surface of the earth assigned to be covered by searchlight, radar, or another detecting device for the purpose of detecting and locating targets.

References

Department of Defense, U.S. Army. *Dictionary of United States Army Terms*. Army Regulation AR 310-25. Washington, DC: Headquarters, Department of the Army, 1986.

—**SEASHORE CONDITION** is the height, slope, beach width (low and high tide), and soil composition of the far and the near seashore.

References

Department of Defense, U.S. Army. *Weather Support for Army Tactical Operations*. Field Manual FM 34-81. Washington, DC: Headquarters, Department of the Army, 1984.

—**SEASON CRACKING** is cracking caused by age since manufacture. Ammunition materiel subject to season cracking has an established cure date for inspection requirements.

References

Department of Defense, U.S. Army. *Dictionary of United States Army Terms*. Army Regulation AR 310-25. Washington, DC: Headquarters, Department of the Army, 1986.

—**SECOND DESTINATION TRANSPORTATION** is the relocation of property from its original point of storage to another point of storage.

References

Department of Defense, U.S. Army. *Dictionary of United States Army Terms*. Army Regulation AR 310-25. Washington, DC: Headquarters, Department of the Army, 1986.

—**SECOND OR SUBSEQUENT TERMER** is a soldier who has reenlisted one or more times and is, therefore, on his second or subsequent term of active federal military service. A soldier who has prior service in another branch of the Armed Forces enters the Army as a "second or subsequent termer." *See also:* First Timer.

References

Department of Defense, U.S. Army. *Army Reenlistment Program*. Army Regulation AR 601-280. Washington, DC: Headquarters, Department of the Army, 1984.

—**SECOND STRIKE** is the first counterblow of a war. It is generally associated with nuclear weapons. *See also:* Nuclear Warfare.

References

Department of Defense, Joint Chiefs of Staff. *Department of Defense Dictionary of Military and Related Terms*. Washington, DC: GPO, 1986.

—**SECOND STRIKE CAPABILITY** is the ability to survive a first strike with sufficient resources to deliver an effective counterblow. It is generally associated with nuclear weapons. *See also:* Nuclear Warfare, Second Strike.

References

Department of Defense, Joint Chiefs of Staff. *Department of Defense Dictionary of Military and Related Terms*. Washington, DC: GPO, 1986.

—**SECONDARY ARMY TERMINAL** is an Army terminal that is acting in the capacity of a shipping agent for a primary Army terminal. *See also:* Army Terminal.

References

Department of Defense, U.S. Army. *Dictionary of United States Army Terms*. Army Regulation AR 310-25. Washington, DC: Headquarters, Department of the Army, 1986.

—**SECONDARY ELEMENTS,** in target intelligence, are the parts of the target that are not directly relevant to the principal mission or functions of target. Thus, leaving the secondary elements undamaged does not affect the outcome of the mission. For example, if a radar site is a target, the radar facility and its support facilities are the critical primary elements of the target because they are critical to the site's mission; the mess hall, in this case is a secondary element.

References

Department of Defense, Joint Chiefs of Staff. *Department of Defense Dictionary of Military and Related Terms*. Washington, DC: GPO, 1986.

—**SECONDARY FIRE SECTOR** are areas not in a fire sector, but can be swept by fire if necessary. Such areas are located close to the flanks in the fire sectors of adjacent units.

References
Department of Defense, U.S. Army. *Dictionary of United States Army Terms.* Army Regulation AR 310-25. Washington, DC: Headquarters, Department of the Army, 1986.

—**SECONDARY ITEM** is a class of supplies that includes end-items, replacement assemblies, parts, and consumables, other than principal items.

References
Department of Defense, U.S. Army. *Dictionary of United States Army Terms.* Army Regulation AR 310-25. Washington, DC: Headquarters, Department of the Army, 1986.

—**SECONDARY LANDING** is a landing usually made outside the designated landing area in order to directly or indirectly support the main landing. *See also:* Amphibious Operations.

References
Department of Defense, U.S. Army. *Dictionary of United States Army Terms.* Army Regulation AR 310-25. Washington, DC: Headquarters, Department of the Army, 1986.

—**SECONDARY MOS (MILITARY OCCUPATIONAL SPECIALTY) (SMOS)** is an AMOS in a specialty that is different from the primary military occupational specialty. It is second in importance to the Army when it is evaluating training, experience, demonstrated qualifications, and the Army's needs. *See also:* Military Occupational Specialty, Primary Military Occupational Specialty.

References
Department of Defense, U.S. Army. *Enlisted Personnel Management System.* Army Regulation AR 600-200. Washington, DC: Headquarters, Department of the Army, 1984.

—**SECONDARY POSITION SPECIALTY CODE** is the code of the specialty that corresponds to the secondary requirements of a commissioned officer position.

References
Department of Defense, U.S. Army. *Dictionary of United States Army Terms.* Army Regulation AR 310-25. Washington, DC: Headquarters, Department of the Army, 1986.

—**SECONDARY RADAR** is radar using automatic retransmission on the same or a different radio frequency. *See also:* Radar.

References
Department of Defense, U.S. Army. *Dictionary of United States Army Terms.* Army Regulation AR 310-25. Washington, DC: Headquarters, Department of the Army, 1986.

—**SECONDARY ROAD.** (1) A secondary road is a road supplementing a main road. It is usually wide enough and suitable for two-way, all-weather traffic at moderate or slow speeds. (2) A secondary road is a linear surface feature making an open way for vehicles on an artificially made surface of gravel, bitumen, or concrete, and of a width between four and six meters.

References
Department of Defense, Joint Chiefs of Staff. *Department of Defense Dictionary of Military and Related Terms.* Washington, DC: GPO, 1986.
Department of Defense, U.S. Army. *Dictionary of United States Army Terms.* Army Regulation AR 310-25. Washington, DC: Headquarters, Department of the Army, 1986.

—**SECONDARY SOURCE OF SUPPLY** is any source of supply that supplements an initial source of supply by means of an extract requisition, shipping order, or purchase request.

References
Department of Defense, U.S. Army. *Dictionary of United States Army Terms.* Army Regulation AR 310-25. Washington, DC: Headquarters, Department of the Army, 1986.

—**SECONDARY STATION.** (1) A secondary station is the observation post at the end of a base line that is farthest from the gun or directing point. (2) A secondary station is any station in a radio net other than the net control station. *See also:* Net Control Station.

References
Department of Defense, U.S. Army. *Dictionary of United States Army Terms.* Army Regulation AR 310-25. Washington, DC: Headquarters, Department of the Army, 1986.

—**SECONDARY TARGET** is a target against which fire is directed when the main fire mission has been accomplished, or when it has become impossible or impractical for the gun or battery to carry out the main fire mission.

References
Department of Defense, U.S. Army. *Dictionary of United States Army Terms.* Army Regulation AR 310-25. Washington, DC: Headquarters, Department of the Army, 1986.

—**SECONDARY WEAPON** is a supporting or aux-iliary weapon or a unit, vehicle, position, or aircraft. It is generally a gun of smaller caliber than the primary weapon, and its purpose is to protect or supplement the fire of the primary weapon.

References

Department of Defense, U.S. Army. *Dictionary of United States Army Terms.* Army Regulation AR 310-25. Washington, DC: Headquarters, Depart-ment of the Army, 1986.

—**SECRETARY OF THE ARMY** is the head of the Department of the Army, who administers that department as a individual executive department within the Department of Defense, and who retains all powers and duties relating to the Department that have not been specifically conferred upon the Secretary of Defense as head of the Department of Defense.

References

Department of Defense, U.S. Army. *Dictionary of United States Army Terms.* Army Regulation AR 310-25. Washington, DC: Headquarters, Depart-ment of the Army, 1986.

—**SECTION (SEC).** (1) A SEC is a subdivision of an office, installation, territory, works, or organi-zation (especially a major subdivision of a staff). (2) A SEC is a tactical unit of the Army. It is smaller than a platoon and larger than a squad. In some organizations, the section, rather than the squad, is the basic tactical unit. (3) A SEC is an area in a warehouse extending from one wall to the next. It is usually the largest subdivision of one floor.

References

Department of the Army. *Operational Terms and Symbols.* Field Manual FM 101-5-1. Washington, DC: Headquarters, Department of the Army, 1985.

—**SECTOR** is an area designated by boundaries within which a unit operates and for which it is responsible. Normally, sectors are used in de-fensive operations. *See also:* Area of Influence, Sector Attack, Sector Commander, Sector Con-troller, Zone of Action.

References

Department of the Army. *Operational Terms and Symbols.* Field Manual FM 101-5-1. Washington, DC: Headquarters, Department of the Army, 1985.

—**SECTOR ATTACK** is an attack option in which the area of operation, including the target and the avenues of approach, is sectored. Each ele-ment of the staff is allotted a specific operating sector. In this way, the groups can work autono-mously within their own sectors while still providing each other mutual support so that the team can saturate the target area. Sector attacks reduce problems associated with aircraft coor-dination, ordnance fan, and fragmentation clearance, and once organized by sectors, the team can function even during intense electronic warfare jamming. *See also:* Sector.

References

Department of Defense, U.S. Army. *Operational Terms and Symbols.* Field Manual FM 101-5-1. Washington, DC: Headquarters, Department of the Army, 1985.

—**SECTOR COMMANDER** is an officer respon-sible for the tactical control of air defense forces and the operations of facilities within a specified sector of an air defense area.

References

Department of Defense, Joint Chiefs of Staff. *Department of Defense Dictionary of Military and Related Terms.* Washington, DC: GPO, 1986.

—**SECTOR CONTROLLER.** Sector controller is an officer in charge of the sector control post in a sector and responsible to the area damage control center. He is appointed to act on behalf of a sector commander in the sector operations center, and is responsible for the operational control of all active air defenses in the sector area in coordination with those of adjacent sectors. In these tasks he is under the overall direction of the group or command controller.

References

Department of Defense, Joint Chiefs of Staff. *Department of Defense Dictionary of Military and Related Terms.* Washington, DC: GPO, 1986.

Department of Defense, U.S. Army. *Dictionary of United States Army Terms.* Army Regulation AR 310-25. Washington, DC: Headquarters, Depart-ment of the Army, 1986.

—**SECTOR OF FIRE** is an area, limited by bound-aries, that is required to be covered by obser-vation or fire by an individual weapon or unit. Sectors of fire and primary target lines are established to assist in the distribution of antiair defense artillery fires. Sectors of fire are normally designated at the battalion level after a review of fire unit radar coverage diagrams. They enable the commander to specify which fire unit is preferred to engage targets within designated areas. The primary target line is the center of a unit's sector of fire. Sectors of fire and primary target lines serve as guides for target assignment by battalion tactical directors. Secondary target lines can also be established. *See also:* Secondary Target.

References

Department of Defense, U.S. Army. *The Infantry Rifle Company (Infantry, Airborne, Air Assault, Ranger).* Field Manual FM 7-10, Washington, DC: Headquarters, Department of the Army, 1982.

————. *Operational Terms and Symbols.* Field Manual FM 101-5-1. Washington, DC: Headquarters, Department of the Army, 1985.

————. *Patriot Battalion Operations.* Field Manual FM 44-15, April 1984. Washington, DC: Headquarters, U.S. Army, 1984.

—**SECURE** is to gain possession of a position or terrain feature, with or without force, and to deploy in a manner that prevents its destruction or loss to enemy action. *See also:* Denial Measure.

References

Department of the Army. *Operational Terms and Symbols.* Field Manual FM 101-5-1. Washington, DC: Headquarters, Department of the Army, 1985.

—**SECURE AREA,** in intelligence security and counterintelligence, refers to an authorized facility used for storing, handling, discussing, and processing sensitive compartmented information. *See also:* Sensitive Compartmented Intelligence Facility.

References

Department of Defense, U.S. Army. *Operational Terms and Symbols.* Field Manual FM 101-5-1. Washington, DC: Headquarters, Department of the Army, 1985.

—**SECURE PHONE** is a phone equipped with scramblers or other devices so that conversations cannot be monitored.

References

Department of Defense, U.S. Army. *Operational Terms and Symbols.* Field Manual FM 101-5-1. Washington, DC: Headquarters, Department of the Army, 1985.

—**SECURE TELECOMMUNICATIONS FACILITY,** in communications security, refers to a telecommunications facility that uses cryptomaterial to protect the transmission of national security information. *See also:* Communications Security.

References

Department of Defense, U.S. Army. *Operational Terms and Symbols.* Field Manual FM 101-5-1. Washington, DC: Headquarters, Department of the Army, 1985.

—**SECURITY.** (1) In the general sense, security involves establishing and maintaining protective measures that are intended to insure a state of inviolability from hostile acts and influences. The types of security include automatic data processing system security; communications security; computer security; cryptographic security; electronic emission security; electronic security; emanation security; emission security; information security; multilevel security; national security; operations security; personnel security; physical security; signals security; transmission security; and uni-level security. (2) In Army tactical intelligence, security has three meanings: (a) the measures taken by a military unit, activity, or installation to protect itself against acts that are designed to, or that may, impair its effectiveness; (b) a condition that results from establishing and maintaining protective measures that insure a state of inviolability from hostile acts or influences; (c) with respect to classified matter, a condition that prevents unauthorized persons from having access to official information that is safeguarded in the interests of national security. *See also:* Access, Classification, Classified Information, Declassification, Downgrade, Need-to-Know, Need-to-Know Principle, Sanitization, Sanitize, Sanitized Area, Security Certification, Security Classification, Sensitive Compartmented Information, Sensitive Compartmented Information Facility.

References

Department of Defense, U.S. Army. *Counter-Signals Intelligence (C-SIGINT) Operations.* Field Manual FM 34-62. Washington, DC: Headquarters, Department of the Army, 1986.

—**SECURITY** (PRINCIPLE OF WAR): Never permit the enemy to acquire an unexpected advantage.

Security reduces friendly vulnerability to hostile acts, influence, and surprise. At the strategic level, security requires that active and passive measures be taken to protect the United States and its armed forces against espionage, subversion, and strategic intelligence collection.

Security is also necessary to plan and conduct campaigns. Security measures, however, should not be allowed to interfere with flexibility of thought and action, since rigidity and dogmatism increase the vulnerability to enemy surprise. A thorough knowledge and understanding of enemy strategy, tactics, and doctrine, and detailed staff planning can improve security and reduce the vulnerability to surprise.

At the tactical level, security is essential to the protection and husbanding of combat power. It results from the measures taken by a command to protect itself from surprise, observation, detection, interference, espionage, sabotage, and annoyance. Security may be achieved by establishing and maintaining protective measures against hostile acts or influence; or it may be assured by establishing deception operations designed to confuse and dissipate enemy attempts to interfere with the force that is being secured. Risk is an inherent condition of war, and the application of security does not suggest overcautiousness or the avoidance of calculated risk. *See also:* Principles of War.

References

Department of Defense, U.S. Army. *Operations.* Field Manual FM !00-5. Washington, DC: Headquarters, Department of the Army, 1986.

————. *Support Operations: Echelons Above Corps.* Field Manual FM 100-16. Washington, DC: Headquarters, U.S. Army, 1986.

—**SECURITY ALERT TEAM** is composed of two or more security force members who form the initial reinforcing element responding to security alarms, emergencies, or irregularities.

References

Department of Defense, Joint Chiefs of Staff. *Department of Defense Dictionary of Military and Related Terms.* Washington, DC: GPO, 1986.

—**SECURITY ASSISTANCE** is all of the activities that the U.S. government carries out under the authority of the Foreign Assistance Act or Foreign Military Sales Act or related appropriation acts and other related authorities. Under this authority, the United States provides defense articles, military training, and other defense-related services, by grant, credit, or cash sales, in furtherance of national policies and objectives.

References

Department of Defense, U.S. Army. *Civil Affairs Operations.* Field Manual FM 41-10. Washington, DC: Headquarters, Department of the Army, 1985.

—**SECURITY ASSISTANCE FORCE (SAF)** is a specially trained, area-oriented, partially language-qualified, ready force that is available to the commander of a unified command to support operations in situations that are less than open hostilities and in limited and general war. SAF organizations vary in size and capabilities according to theater requirements.

References

Department of Defense, U.S. Army. *Low Intensity Conflict.* Field Manual FM 100-20. Washington, DC: Headquarters, Department of the Army, 1981.

—**SECURITY CERTIFICATION** is a form of authorization issued by a competent national authority indicating that a person has been investigated and is eligible for access to classified material to the extent stated on the certification. *See also:* Security Classification.

References

Department of Defense, Joint Chiefs of Staff. *Department of Defense Dictionary of Military and Related Terms.* Washington, DC: GPO, 1986.

—**SECURITY CLASSIFICATION** is a categorization of national security information and material by assigning a level of security that provides adequate safety for the information contained in the item. There are three security categories:

TOP SECRET is assigned to national security information or material that requires the most protection. Its unauthorized disclosure could reasonably be expected to cause exceptionally grave damage to the national security. Examples of "exceptionally grave damage" include armed hostilities against the United States or its allies; disruption of foreign relations vitally affecting the national security; the compromise of vital defense plans or complex cryptologic and communications intelligence systems; the revelation of sensitive intelligence operations; and the disclosure of scientific or technological developments vital to national security.

SECRET is assigned to national security information that requires a substantial degree of protection. Its unauthorized disclosure could reasonably be expected to cause serious damage to the national security. Examples of "serious damage" include disruption of foreign relations significantly affecting the national security; significantly impairing a program or policy directly related to the national security; revealing significant military plans or intelligence operations; and compromising significant scientific or technological developments relating to the national security.

CONFIDENTIAL is assigned to national security information that requires protection. Its unauthorized disclosure could reasonably be expected to cause damage to the national security. *See also:* Sensitive Compartmented Information.

References

Department of Defense, Joint Chiefs of Staff. *Department of Defense Dictionary of Military and Related Terms.* Washington, DC: GPO, 1986.

—**SECURITY CLEARANCE** is an administrative determination that an individual is eligible, from a security standpoint, for access to classified information.

References

Department of Defense, Joint Chiefs of Staff. *Department of Defense Dictionary of Military and Related Terms.* Washington, DC: GPO, 1986.

—**SECURITY COGNIZANCE** is the responsibility for implementing the Department of Defense industrial security program for a facility.

References

Department of Defense, U.S. Army. *Dictionary of United States Army Terms.* Army Regulation AR 310-25. Washington, DC: Headquarters, Department of the Army, 1986.

—**SECURITY CONTROL OFFICER** is an officer, warrant officer, or responsible civilian official who is appointed in each command or agency to exercise staff supervision over the safeguarding of defense information.

References

Department of Defense, U.S. Army. *Dictionary of United States Army Terms.* Army Regulation AR 310-25. Washington, DC: Headquarters, Department of the Army, 1986.

—**SECURITY COUNTERMEASURES**, in counterintelligence, counterespionage, and counterinsurgency, are measures designed to impair the effectiveness of an unfriendly or hostile attack upon security. *See also:* Counterintelligence.

References

Department of Defense, Joint Chiefs of Staff. *Department of Defense Dictionary of Military and Related Terms.* Washington, DC: GPO, 1986.

—**SECURITY ELEMENT** is the early warning and security part of an ambush patrol. It secures and blocks enemy avenues of approach into and out of the ambush site. *See also:* Security Force.

References

Department of Defense, U.S. Army. *The Infantry Rifle Company (Infantry, Airborne, Air Assault, Ranger).* Field Manual FM 7-10. Washington, DC: Headquarters, Department of the Army, 1982.

—**SECURITY FORCE** is the early warning or security portion of a point ambush. In a patrol, the security element is the security force. *See also:* Ambush Force, Assault Element (Ambush).

References

Department of Defense, U.S. Army. *The Rifle Squads (Mechanized and Light Infantry).* Training Circular TC 7-1. Washington, DC: Headquarters, Department of the Army, 1976.

—**SECURITY-IN-DEPTH** is a term used to describe the sum of security measures that are placed in layers around a facility or an installation. Security-in-depth includes the use of local security measures, perimeter defense techniques, and internal security measures.

References

Department of Defense, U.S. Army. *Military Police Team, Squad, Platoon Combat Operations.* Field Manual FM 19-4. Washington, DC: Headquarters, Department of the Army, 1984.

—**SECURITY INTELLIGENCE** is intelligence on the identity, capabilities, and intentions of hostile organizations or individuals who are, or may be, engaged in espionage, sabotage, subversion, or terrorism. *See also:* Counterintelligence, Intelligence, Security.

References

Department of Defense, Joint Chiefs of Staff. *Department of Defense Dictionary of Military and Related Terms.* Washington, DC: GPO, 1986.

—**SECURITY MEASURES**, as defined by the Church Committee, are "steps taken by the government and intelligence departments and agencies, among others, for protection from espionage, observation, sabotage, annoyance, or surprise. With respect to classified materials, it is the condition that prevents unauthorized persons from having access to official information which is safeguarded in the interests of national defense."

References

U.S. Congress. Senate. *Final Report of the Senate Select Committee to Study Government Operations With Respect to Intelligence Activities. Report 94-755. Book I, Foreign and Military Intelligence* (Church Committee Report). Washington, DC: GPO, 1976.

—**SECURITY OPERATIONS** protect the battalion task force from tactical surprise. To accomplish their mission, security forces must find the enemy before the enemy finds the battalion task force. When done properly, security operations give the battalion task force commander sufficient time to move to concentrate against the enemy force on advantageous terrain.

Security operations are designed to obtain information about the enemy and provide reaction time, maneuver space, and protection to the main body. They are characterized by aggressive reconnaissance to reduce terrain and enemy unknowns, gaining and maintaining contact with the enemy to insure continuous information, and providing early and accurate reporting of information to the protected force. Security operations include screening operations, guard operations, covering force operations, and area security operations. Area security operations are normally associated with rear battle operations. The other types of security operations may be oriented in any direction from a stationary or moving force. A force conducting security operations is designated as a screening force, a guard force, a covering force, or an area security force.

References

Department of Defense, U.S. Army. *The Tank and Mechanized Infantry Battalion Task Force.* Field Manual FM 71-2. Washington, DC: Headquarters, Department of the Army, 1977.

—**SEDITION** is the willful making or conveying of reports or statements with the intent to interfere with the operation or the success of the U.S. Armed Forces or to promote the success of its enemies; the willful causing of insubordination, disloyalty, mutiny or refusal of duty in the Armed Forces; or willful obstruction of recruitment of enlistment service of the United States.

References

Department of Defense, U.S. Army. *Dictionary of United States Army Terms.* Army Regulation AR 310-25. Washington, DC: Headquarters, Department of the Army, 1986.

—**SEEKER** (ARMY AVIATION) is the operational signal-receiving end of an infrared missile.

References

Department of Defense, U.S. Army. *Air-to-Air Combat.* Field Manual FM 1-107. Washington, DC: Headquarters, Department of the Army, 1984.

—**SEEN FIRE** is fire continuously aimed at the future position of an aircraft, the aim being derived from visual observation. *See also:* Fire.

References

Department of Defense, U.S. Army. *Dictionary of United States Army Terms.* Army Regulation AR 310-25. Washington, DC: Headquarters, Department of the Army, 1986.

—**SEGMENT** is a portion of a mine strip extending in a straight line from one strip marker to a change of strip direction or from one change of direction to a marker. *See also:* Mine Warfare.

References

Department of Defense, U.S. Army. *Mine/Countermine Operations at the Company Level.* Field Manual FM 20-32. Washington, DC: Headquarters, Department of the Army, 1976.

—**SEIZE** is to clear a designated area and to take control of it. *See also:* Seizure.

References

Department of Defense, U.S. Army. *Operational Terms and Symbols.* Field Manual FM 101-5-1. Washington, DC: Headquarters, Department of the Army, 1985.

—**SEIZURE**, as an operational purpose, is the capture of a restricted portion of an enemy-controlled territory. The capture of an isolated landmass (e.g., an island) is usually categorized as a seizure.

References

Department of Defense, U.S. Army. *Dictionary of United States Army Terms.* Army Regulation AR 310-25. Washington, DC: Headquarters, Department of the Army, 1986.

—**SELECTED AREA** is an area to be concealed by smoke. *See also:* Smoke Screen.

References
Department of Defense, U.S. Army. *Deliberate Smoke Operations.* Field Manual FM 3-50. Washington, DC: Headquarters, Department of the Army, 1984.

—**SELECTED FOR PROMOTION** is an officer who has been recommended for promotion by a Department of the Army promotion board, or a Department of the Army special selection board, and whose promotion has been approved by proper authority.

References
Department of Defense, U.S. Army. *Promotion of Officers on Active Duty.* Army Regulation AR 624-100. Washington, DC: Headquarters, Department of the Army, 1984.

—**SELECTED-ITEM INVENTORY** is an unscheduled physical inventory that must be accomplished for a given Federal Stock Number or otherwise identified item. It is done, for example, when accountable activity records reflect a zero balance and/or a back-order position, and an attempt is being made to satisfy a high-priority requisition.

References
Department of Defense, U.S. Army. *Dictionary of United States Army Terms.* Army Regulation AR 310-25. Washington, DC: Headquarters, Department of the Army, 1986.

—**SELECTED-ITEM MANAGEMENT SYSTEM** is a system used to intensively manage and control selected critical or essential items of materiel that represent the Army's greatest procurement costs and inventory monetary value.

References
Department of Defense, U.S. Army. *Dictionary of United States Army Terms.* Army Regulation AR 310-25. Washington, DC: Headquarters, Department of the Army, 1986.

—**SELECTED ITEMS** are items assigned or are susceptible to being assigned line item numbers. They include Class II, Class IIa, Class IV, and Class IVa supplies which require continuing part support, and Class V and Va supplies. *See also:* Supplies.

References
Department of Defense, U.S. Army. *Dictionary of United States Army Terms.* Army Regulation AR 310-25. Washington, DC: Headquarters, Department of the Army, 1986.

—**SELECTED RESERVE** is the portion of the Ready Reserve consisting of units and, as designated by the Secretary concerned, of individual reservists who are required to participate in inactive duty training periods and annual training, both of which are in a pay status. The Selected Reserve also includes persons performing initial active duty for training. *See also:* Ready Reserve.

References
Department of Defense, Joint Chiefs of Staff. *Department of Defense Dictionary of Military and Related Terms.* Washington, DC: GPO, 1986.

—**SELECTIVE MOBILIZATION** is the expansion of the Armed Forces resulting from an action by Congress or the President to mobilize reserve components, individual ready reservists, and the resources needed for their support to meet the requirements of a domestic emergency that is not the result of an enemy attack. *See also:* Mobilization.

References
Department of Defense, Joint Chiefs of Staff. *Department of Defense Dictionary of Military and Related Terms.* Washington, DC: GPO, 1986.

—**SELF-AUTHENTICATION** is a procedure by which a transmitting communications station establishes its own validity to the station it is calling.

References
Department of Defense, U.S. Army. *Dictionary of United States Army Terms.* Army Regulation AR 310-25. Washington, DC: Headquarters, Department of the Army, 1986.

—**SELF-DESCRIPTION FORM** is a form on which an individual gives information concerning his background, attitudes, beliefs, and personality reactions. Scores computed from the information are useful in predicting the individual's likelihood of on-the-job success.

References
Department of Defense, U.S. Army. *Dictionary of United States Army Terms.* Army Regulation AR 310-25. Washington, DC: Headquarters, Department of the Army, 1986.

—**SELF-DESTROYING FUZE** is a fuze designed to burst a projectile before the end of its flight. *See also:* Fuze (Specify Type).

References

Department of Defense, Joint Chiefs of Staff. *Department of Defense Dictionary of Military and Related Terms.* Washington, DC: GPO, 1986.

—**SELF-PACED** is a training technique that permits each soldier to learn at a rate consistent with his ability.

References

Department of Defense, U.S. Army. *How to Prepare and Conduct Military Training.* Field Manual FM 21-6. Washington, DC: Headquarters, Department of the Army, 1975.

—**SELF-PROTECTION JAMMING,** in electronic warfare, is the jamming an aircraft performs to protect itself. *See also:* Electronic Warfare, Jamming.

References

Department of Defense, Joint Chiefs of Staff. *Department of Defense Dictionary of Military and Related Terms.* Washington, DC: GPO, 1986.

—**SELF-SERVICE SUPPLY CENTER (SSSC)** is a distribution point for consumable and expendable supplies (e.g., certain hand tools, gasket material, and hardware). The SSSC operates much like a commercial supermarket.

References

Department of Defense, U.S. Army. *Organizational Maintenance Operations.* Field Manual FM 29-2. Washington, DC: Headquarters, Department of the Army, 1984.

—**SELF-STERILIZING FUZE** is a fuze designed to become inoperative automatically after a predetermined period of time. *See also:* Fuze (Specify Type).

References

Department of Defense, U.S. Army. *Mine/ Countermine Operations at the Company Level.* Field Manual FM 20-32. Washington, DC: Headquarters, Department of the Army, 1976.

—**SEMIACTIVE INSTALLATION.** (1) A semiactive installation is an installation that is not in continuous use by Army organizations other than by an Active Army garrison required to support the intermittent use of the installation for reserve component or field exercise requirements. (2) A semiactive installation is an installation in the custody of a non-Army agent who is charged with supporting reserve component training or maintaining the installation as a mobilization base.

References

Department of Defense, U.S. Army. *Dictionary of United States Army Terms.* Army Regulation AR 310-25. Washington, DC: Headquarters, Department of the Army, 1986.

—**SEMIAUTOMATIC SUPPLY** is a system by which certain supplies needed by units, activities, or forces are periodically shipped by the responsible supply agencies on the basis of reports of the status of stocks on hand and en route to the using agency. All other supplies are furnished on the basis of requisitions that are initiated by the using agency.

References

Department of Defense, U.S. Army. *Dictionary of United States Army Terms.* Army Regulation AR 310-25. Washington, DC: Headquarters, Department of the Army, 1986.

—**SEMIAUTOMATIC TEST EQUIPMENT** is any testing device that requires human participation in the decisionmaking, control, or evaluative functions of the item being tested.

References

Department of Defense, U.S. Army. *Dictionary of United States Army Terms.* Army Regulation AR 310-25. Washington, DC: Headquarters, Department of the Army, 1986.

—**SEMIFIXED AMMUNITION** is ammunition in which the cartridge case is not permanently attached to the projectile. *See also:* Ammunition.

References

Department of Defense, Joint Chiefs of Staff. *Department of Defense Dictionary of Military and Related Terms.* Washington, DC: GPO, 1986.

—**SEMIMOBILE UNIT** is a unit that does not have enough vehicles of its own to transport all of the assigned personnel and equipment from one point to another in one trip. *See also:* Mobile Unit.

References

Department of Defense, U.S. Army. *Dictionary of United States Army Terms.* Army Regulation AR 310-25. Washington, DC: Headquarters, Department of the Army, 1986.

—**SENIOR ARMY AVIATOR** is an aeronautical designation awarded by the Chief of Staff, United States Army, or such officers as he may designate, to members of the Army.

References

Department of Defense, U.S. Army. *Dictionary of United States Army Terms*. Army Regulation AR 310-25. Washington, DC: Headquarters, Department of the Army, 1986.

—**SENSING** is a mental notation by the gunner or tank commander of where the round that has been fired goes in relation to the target and the target aiming point in the rectile at the time of firing. The most accurate sensing is when the gunner can see the tracer of the round being fired as it passes by the target, or strikes the ground short of the target, or as it strikes the target.

References

Department of Defense, U.S. Army. *Tank Gunnery*. Field Manual FM 17-2-C2. Washington, DC: Headquarters, Department of the Army, 1980.

—**SENSITIVE** indicates that the subject (e.g., an agency, installation, person, position, document, material, or activity) requires special protection from disclosure in order to avoid a compromise or a threat to the security of the sponsor. *See also:* Sensitive Compartmented Information.

References

Department of Defense, Defense Intelligence College. *Glossary of Intelligence Terms and Definitions*. Washington, DC: DIC, 1987.

—**SENSITIVE AREA** is a specific location that has become a center of activity of intelligence interest. *See also:* Intelligence.

References

Department of Defense, U.S. Army. *Dictionary of United States Army Terms*. Army Regulation AR 310-25. Washington, DC: Headquarters, Department of the Army, 1986.

—**SENSITIVE COMPARTMENTED INFORMATION (SCI)** is information requiring special controls, access requirements, and restricted handling within compartmented intelligence systems and for which compartmentation has been established. Such data is normally given a code word to indicate a specific project or program. *See also:* Sensitive Compartmented Information Facility.

References

Department of Defense, U.S. Army. *Support Operations: Echelons Above Corps*. Field Manual FM 100-16. Washington, DC: Headquarters, Department of the Army, 1986.

—**SENSITIVE COMPARTMENTED INFORMATION FACILITY (SCIF)** is an authorized area, room, group of rooms, or installation where sensitive compartmented information may be stored, used, discussed, and/or electronically processed. Sensitive compartmented information procedural and physical measures prevent people from having free access to information unless they have been formally indoctrinated for the particular sensitive compartmented information that is authorized for use and storage within the SCIF.

Authorization of the facility as an SCIF is a continuous process, with periodic reinspections of the facility's physical, emissions, and personnel security measures. The key individual in this process is the special security/special activities officer, who is the point of contact for the special access programs. *See also:* Sensitive Compartmented Information.

References

Department of Defense, Defense Intelligence College. *Glossary of Intelligence Terms and Definitions*. Washington, DC: DIC, 1987.

Department of Defense, Joint Chiefs of Staff. *Department of Defense Dictionary of Military and Related Terms*. Washington, DC: GPO, 1986.

—**SENSITIVE INTELLIGENCE SOURCES AND METHODS** refers to intelligence that has been developed from information from a single, very vulnerable source or from a very vulnerable method. Revealing the intelligence enables the enemy to easily identify the source or the method from which it was obtained, and to take measures that stop the passage of further information. Leaks of this type of information are among the most devastating, because not only is the information compromised, but the source from which the information originated or the method by which it was obtained may be permanently destroyed. Such damage usually extends into the future if alternative sources are not developed to provide the information.

References

Department of Defense, Defense Intelligence College. *Glossary of Intelligence Terms and Definitions*. Washington, DC: DIC, 1987.

Department of Defense, Joint Chiefs of Staff. *Department of Defense Dictionary of Military and Related Terms*. Washington, DC: GPO, 1986.

—**SENSITIVE ITEM** is materiel that requires a high degree of protection. Fragile, delicate, and hazardous items, and special weapons except ammunition, narcotics, and highly technical items are considered sensitive items.

References

Department of Defense, U.S. Army. *Dictionary of United States Army Terms*. Army Regulation AR 310-25. Washington, DC: Headquarters, Department of the Army, 1986.

—**SENSITIVE POSITION** is any position within the Department of the Army that carries great responsibility concerning the national security. Such positions include any duty or responsibility that requires access to top secret, secret, or confidential information or material, or any other position so designated by the Secretary of the Army or his designee.

References

Department of Defense, U.S. Army. *Dictionary of United States Army Terms*. Army Regulation AR 310-25. Washington, DC: Headquarters, Department of the Army, 1986.

—**SENSOR,** or technical sensor, is a technical device designed to detect and respond to one or more particular stimulae and upon detection, may record or transmit a resultant impulse for interpretation or measurement. "Special sensor" is an unclassified term used to refer to a highly classified or controlled technical sensor.

References

Department of Defense, U.S. Army. *Operational Terms and Symbols*. Field Manual FM 101-5-1. Washington, DC: Headquarters, Department of the Army, 1985.

—**SENTENCED PRISONER** is a prisoner whose sentence to confinement has been ordered to be carried out. *See also:* Disciplinary Action.

References

Department of Defense, U.S. Army. *Dictionary of United States Army Terms*. Army Regulation AR 310-25. Washington, DC: Headquarters, Department of the Army, 1986.

—**SENTINEL** is an individual of the guard whose duties are prescribed by general and/or special orders. He is also referred to as a guard, sentry, or lookout. *See also:* Guard, Guard Operations, Sentry.

References

Department of Defense, U.S. Army. *Guard Duty*. Field Manual FM 22-6. Washington, DC: Headquarters, Department of the Army, 1971.

—**SENTRY** is a guard, sentinel, or lookout. He is a soldier who has been assigned to duty as a member of a guard, to keep watch, maintain order, protect persons or places against surprise, or warn of enemy attack.

References

Department of Defense, U.S. Army. *Guard Duty*. Field Manual FM 22-6. Washington, DC: Headquarters, Department of the Army, 1971.

—**SEPARATE** pertains to an activity financed and operated entirely within a department and without any formal coordination with any other department.

References

Department of Defense, U.S. Army. *Dictionary of United States Army Terms*. Army Regulation AR 310-25. Washington, DC: Headquarters, Department of the Army, 1986.

—**SEPARATE BATTALION** is a battalion that does not form part of a regiment and that operates as an independent unit in the field. It is an administrative as well as a tactical unit. *See also:* Battalion.

References

Department of Defense, U.S. Army. *Dictionary of United States Army Terms*. Army Regulation AR 310-25. Washington, DC: Headquarters, Department of the Army, 1986.

—**SEPARATE BATTERY** is a field artillery battery that does not form part of a battalion and that operates as an independent unit in the field. *See also:* Battery.

References

Department of Defense, U.S. Army. *Dictionary of United States Army Terms*. Army Regulation AR 310-25. Washington, DC: Headquarters, Department of the Army, 1986.

—**SEPARATE COMPANY** is a company that does not form part of a battalion and that operates as an independent unit in the field. *See also:* Company.

References

Department of Defense, U.S. Army. *Dictionary of United States Army Terms.* Army Regulation AR 310-25. Washington, DC: Headquarters, Department of the Army, 1986.

—**SEPARATE LOADING AMMUNITION** is a type of ammunition in which the projectile and the charge are separately loaded into a gun. *See also:* Ammunition.

References

Department of Defense, U.S. Army. *Guard Duty.* Field Manual FM 22-6. Washington, DC: Headquarters, Department of the Army, 1971.

—**SEPARATED AMMUNITION** is a type of ammunition in which the projectile and its propelling charge are sealed in a cartridge case. Both are loaded into a weapon in one operation. *See also:* Separate Loading Ammunition.

References

Department of Defense, U.S. Army. *Dictionary of United States Army Terms.* Army Regulation AR 310-25. Washington, DC: Headquarters, Department of the Army, 1986.

—**SEPARATION** is a term that refers to personnel actions resulting from a release from active duty, a discharge, a retirement, a dropping from the rolls, a release from military control of people without a military status, or a death. *See also:* Retirement.

References

Department of Defense, U.S. Army. *Enlisted Personnel.* Army Regulation AR 635-200. Washington, DC: Headquarters, Department of the Army, 1984.

———. *Promotion of Officers on Active Duty.* Army Regulation AR 624-100. Washington, DC: Headquarters, Department of the Army, 1984.

—**SEPARATION ZONE** is an area between two adjacent horizontal or vertical areas.

References

Department of Defense, Joint Chiefs of Staff. *Department of Defense Dictionary of Military and Related Terms.* Washington, DC: GPO, 1986.

—**SEQUELS TO THE CAMPAIGN PLAN.** Actions after a battle (i.e., sequels) is over are an important means of anticipating the enemy course of action and of accelerating its decision cycle. Preplanned sequels to a future battle are based upon possible outcomes—victory, defeat, or stalemate. They establish the general dispositions, objectives, and missions for subordinate units after the battle, which can be amended as necessary and ordered into effect.

References

Department of Defense, U.S. Army. *Operations.* Field Manual FM 100-5. Washington, DC: Headquarters, Department of the Army, 1986.

—**SEQUENTIAL ATTACK** is a basic option that is applicable when the target area is small and the attack avenues are limited. This situation may preclude all members of the attack team from engaging the target at the same time. In this case, each element is assigned the target area for a specific period of time, and during this time, it works to destroy the target. Strike aircraft and attack helicopters continue to sequence in and out of the target area until the target is destroyed or fuel or ordnance shortages dictate egress. This option works well when the attack aircraft flight enters the battle and engages the targets as the attack helicopters maneuver to new firing positions. The attack helicopters then engage the target as the aircraft momentarily exit the target area. The elements support each other as constant pressure is applied on enemy positions. *See also:* Attack Helicopters.

References

Department of Defense, U.S. Army. *Attack Helicopter Operations.* Field Manual FM 17-50. Washington, DC: Headquarters, Department of the Army, 1984.

—**SERGEANT (SGT)** is a mobile, inertially guided, solid-propellant, surface-to-surface missile, with a nuclear warhead capability, designed to attack targets up to a range of 75 nautical miles. It is designated the MGM-29A.

References

Department of Defense, Joint Chiefs of Staff. *Department of Defense Dictionary of Military and Related Terms.* Washington, DC: GPO, 1986.

—**SERGEANT OF THE GUARD** is the senior noncommissioned officer of the guard. He supervises the enlisted members of the guard and is responsible to the commander of the guard. *See also:* Guard.

References

Department of Defense, U.S. Army. *Guard Duty.* Field Manual FM 22-6. Washington, DC: Headquarters, Department of the Army, 1971.

—**SERIAL.** (1) A serial is a group of march units under a single commander; it is a given number or letter designation to aid in planning and control. (2) A serial is a troop unit or an integral part of it, with accompanying equipment, that is assigned a numerical designation for scheduling convenience or in order to control its ship-to-shore movement in amphibious operations. *See also:* Serial (Air Force).

References

Department of Defense, U.S. Army. *The Infantry Rifle Company (Infantry, Airborne, Air Assault, Ranger).* Field Manual FM 7-10. Washington, DC: Headquarters, Department of the Army, 1982.

—**SERIAL** (AIR FORCE) is any number of aircraft under one commander, usually conveying one air-transportable unit or subunit to the same objective. It is usually separated from other formations by time and space.

References

Department of Defense, U.S. Army. *USA/USAF Doctrine for Joint Airborne and Tactical Airlift Operations.* Field Manual FM 100-27. Washington, DC: Headquarters, Department of the Army, 1985.

—**SERIAL NUMBER.** (1) A serial number is a number assigned to a document by the originating office in order to count the copies prepared and to control their distribution. It differs from a register number in that the latter is used for accounting purposes. (2) A serial number is a number of a message in a series. (3) A serial number is a specific number or symbol of a series assigned to an individual item of materiel for identification. (4) A serial number is an arbitrary number assigned to each unit or grouping and its equipment based upon how it is being organized for transport (i.e., embarked entirely in one ship; to be landed as a unit on one beach or helicopter landing zone; and to be landed at approximately the same time). *See also:* Serial.

References

Department of Defense, U.S. Army. *Dictionary of United States Army Terms.* Army Regulation AR 310-25. Washington, DC: Headquarters, Department of the Army, 1986.

—**SERIES OF FIRES** is a number of groups or concentrations of fires that support a maneuver phase.

References

Department of Defense, U.S. Army. *Dictionary of United States Army Terms.* Army Regulation AR 310-25. Washington, DC: Headquarters, Department of the Army, 1986.

—**SERIES OF TARGETS**, in fire support, is a number of targets or groups of targets that support a maneuver phase in a predetermined time sequence. A series of targets is indicated by a code name or nickname.

References

Department of Defense, U.S. Army. *Operational Terms and Symbols.* Field Manual FM 101-5-1. Washington, DC: Headquarters, Department of the Army, 1985.

—**SERIOUSLY ILL.** A patient is seriously ill when his illness is so severe that there is cause for immediate concern but there is no imminent danger that he will die. *See also:* Medical Treatment.

References

Department of Defense, Joint Chiefs of Staff. *Department of Defense Dictionary of Military and Related Terms.* Washington, DC: GPO, 1986.

—**SERIOUSLY WOUNDED** is a stretcher case (a person who must be transported by others). *See also:* Medical Treatment.

References

Department of Defense, Joint Chiefs of Staff. *Department of Defense Dictionary of Military and Related Terms.* Washington, DC: GPO, 1986.

—**SERVICE (SER) or (SVC).** (1) Service pertains to a branch of the Army or an organization whose primary function is to render noncombatant support to other organizations rather than to engage in combat. (2) Service encompasses all the activities of a unit or a command other than combat activities. (3) A service is one of the components of the U.S. Armed Forces (i.e., Army, Navy, Air Force, or Marine Corps). (4) In communications, service refers to the notes covering the routing instructions, time of delivery or receipt, radio frequency used, the operator's identifying sign, or similar information that is written on a message blank by the sending and receiving operators. *See also:* Combat Service Support, Military Service, Service of the Piece, Special Branches.

References
Department of Defense, Joint Chiefs of Staff. *Department of Defense Dictionary of Military and Related Terms.* Washington, DC: GPO, 1986.

—SERVICE AMMUNITION is ammunition intended for combat, rather than for training purposes.

References
Department of Defense, Joint Chiefs of Staff. *Department of Defense Dictionary of Military and Related Terms.* Washington, DC: GPO, 1986.

—SERVICE AREA is an area in which the administrative services of a major military organization (e.g., an army or air force installation) are located. The communications zone is the service area for a theater of operations. *See also:* Communications Zone.

References
Department of Defense, U.S. Army. *Dictionary of United States Army Terms.* Army Regulation AR 310-25. Washington, DC: Headquarters, Department of the Army, 1986.

—SERVICE CALLS are regular calls given by a bugle, drum, or other means, to assemble men for formation or routine duties. It is the largest classification of bugle calls, including calls not classified as warning calls, formation calls, or alarm calls. *See also:* Adjutant's Call.

References
Department of Defense, U.S. Army. *Dictionary of United States Army Terms.* Army Regulation AR 310-25. Washington, DC: Headquarters, Department of the Army, 1986.

—SERVICE CAP is a uniform cap of authorized material and a visor.

References
Department of Defense, U.S. Army. *Dictionary of United States Army Terms.* Army Regulation AR 310-25. Washington, DC: Headquarters, Department of the Army, 1986.

—SERVICE CHEVRON. *See:* War Service Chevron.

—SERVICE CLUB is a facility designed to provide a balanced program of recreation and social activities. It is primarily for enlisted personnel and their families at a military installation. It is administered and operated by professional service club personnel under the supervision of the special services officer.

References
Department of Defense, U.S. Army. *Dictionary of United States Army Terms.* Army Regulation AR 310-25. Washington, DC: Headquarters, Department of the Army, 1986.

—SERVICE COMPONENT COMMANDER. Each service component commander is responsible for recommending the proper employment of his forces and for accomplishing operational tasks that are assigned by the joint commander. He is also responsible for his service in matters of internal administration and discipline; training in own service doctrine, techniques, and tactics; designation of specific units to meet joint requirements; logistics functions normal to the component; tactical employment of service component forces; and service intelligence matters.

References
Department of Defense, U.S. Army. *Operations.* Field Manual FM 100-5. Washington, DC: Headquarters, Department of the Army, 1986.

———. *U.S. Army Operational Concept for Special Operations Forces.* TRADOC PAM 525-34. Washington, DC: Headquarters, Department of the Army, 1984.

—SERVICE ECHELON is a subdivision of a military command that is responsible for supplying, evacuating, maintaining, and administering the command. *See also:* Echelon.

References
Department of Defense, U.S. Army. *Dictionary of United States Army Terms.* Army Regulation AR 310-25. Washington, DC: Headquarters, Department of the Army, 1986.

—SERVICE MAGAZINE is a building used for the intermediate storage of explosive materials.

References
Department of Defense, U.S. Army. *Ammunition and Explosives Safety Standards.* Army Regulation AR 385-64. Washington, DC: Headquarters, Department of the Army, 1987.

—SERVICE MARKING is composed of symbols, numerals, or letters that are painted, stenciled, or stamped onto supplies or ammunition to give information that is needed for the proper handling, storage, or use of the item.

References

Department of Defense, U.S. Army. *Dictionary of United States Army Terms*. Army Regulation AR 310-25. Washington, DC: Headquarters, Department of the Army, 1986.

—SERVICE MEDAL is an award made to those who have participated in designated wars, campaigns, and expeditions or who have fulfilled specified service requirements in a credible manner. *See also:* Accouterment.

References

Department of Defense, U.S. Army. *Wear and Appearance of Army Uniforms and Insignia*. Army Regulation AR 670-1. Washington, DC: Headquarters, Department of the Army, 1986.

—SERVICE MESSAGE is a message between communications personnel pertaining to any phase of traffic handling, communications facilities, or circuit conditions. *See also:* Message.

References

Department of Defense, U.S. Army. *Dictionary of United States Army Terms*. Army Regulation AR 310-25. Washington, DC: Headquarters, Department of the Army, 1986.

—SERVICE NUMBER is a combination of numbers and letters assigned to each individual in the military service as a means of positive personal identification.

References

Department of Defense, U.S. Army. *Dictionary of United States Army Terms*. Army Regulation AR 310-25. Washington, DC: Headquarters, Department of the Army, 1986.

—SERVICE OBLIGATION is an obligation to perform military service for a period of time. It is incurred by law or a voluntary undertaking (e.g., receiving training, accepting promotion, making a change of station, or an agreement). For example, an obligation is incurred under the Universal Military Training and Service Act, as amended, by persons who become members of an armed force for the first time. The obligation dates from induction, initial enlistment, or appointment. It may be for either six or eight years

service, Active and Reserve combined, depending on the time of entry into service and other factors.

References

Department of Defense, U.S. Army. *Dictionary of United States Army Terms*. Army Regulation AR 310-25. Washington, DC: Headquarters, Department of the Army, 1986.

—SERVICE OF THE PIECE is the operation and maintenance of a gun or another piece of equipment by its crew. *See also:* Servicing.

References

Department of Defense, U.S. Army. *Dictionary of United States Army Terms*. Army Regulation AR 310-25. Washington, DC: Headquarters, Department of the Army, 1986.

—SERVICE-PECULIAR LOGISTICS CAPABILITIES are the logistic support activities that are organic to a particular military service and that must be performed by that military service to insure the successful accomplishment of the missions that have been assigned. Such capabilities are used when considering interservice support activities.

References

Department of Defense, U.S. Army. *Dictionary of United States Army Terms*. Army Regulation AR 310-25. Washington, DC: Headquarters, Department of the Army, 1986.

—SERVICE PRACTICE is part of the training program for artillery units consisting primarily of practical problems in preparing, executing, and conducting fire with service or practice ammunition. *See also:* Service Ammunition.

References

Department of Defense, U.S. Army. *Dictionary of United States Army Terms*. Army Regulation AR 310-25. Washington, DC: Headquarters, Department of the Army, 1986.

—SERVICE RECORD is a form on which a record of military service is maintained on enlisted personnel. It is opened upon enlistment, reenlistment after a lapse of more than 24 hours, or induction. It is closed at the time of separation, at which point it is forwarded to Headquarters, Department of the Army, for filing as a permanent record. *See also:* Member, Enlisted Person.

References

Department of Defense, U.S. Army. *Dictionary of United States Army Terms*. Army Regulation AR 310-25. Washington, DC: Headquarters, Department of the Army, 1986.

—**SERVICE SCHOOL COURSE** is the part of a program at a specific skill level that is conducted in an Army service school or Army training center. *See also:* Service School Training.

References
Department of Defense, U.S. Army. *Individual Military Education and Training.* Army Regulation AR 350-1. Washington, DC: Headquarters, Department of the Army, 1987.

—**SERVICE SCHOOL TRAINING** is institutional training, either individual or collective, that is conducted in Army schools or Army training centers. *See also:* Service School Course.

References
Department of Defense, U.S. Army. *Individual Military Education and Training.* Army Regulation AR 350-1. Washington, DC: Headquarters, Department of the Army, 1987.

—**SERVICE STATION TECHNIQUE** is a method of resupply in which combat vehicles move to a central location to receive supplies.

References
Department of Defense, U.S. Army. *Commander's Handbook for Property Accountability at the Unit Level.* Field Manual FM 10-14-1. Washington, DC: Headquarters, Department of the Army, 1984.

———. *Division Headquarters and Headquarters Detachments, Supply and Transport Battalions and Supply and Service Battalions.* Field Manual FM 29-7. Washington, DC: Headquarters, Department of the Army, 1984.

———. *Organizational Maintenance Operations.* Field Manual FM 29-2. Washington, DC: Headquarters, Department of the Army, 1984.

—**SERVICE STOCK** is a predetermined list of items and the specific quantities of them that are needed for the normal operation of a given subordinate or off-station supply activity that does not obtain these same items from other sources.

References
Department of Defense, U.S. Army. *Dictionary of United States Army Terms.* Army Regulation AR 310-25. Washington, DC: Headquarters, Department of the Army, 1986.

—**SERVICE STRIPE** is a stripe worn on the left sleeve of the shirt or coat of an enlisted person. Each stripe indicates a three-year period of military service. *See also:* Accouterment.

References
Department of Defense, U.S. Army. *Dictionary of United States Army Terms.* Army Regulation AR 310-25. Washington, DC: Headquarters, Department of the Army, 1986.

—**SERVICE TROOPS** are the units designed to provide supply, maintenance, transportation, evacuation, hospitalization, and other services needed by air and ground combat units to carry out their combat missions effectively. *See also:* Service-Peculiar Logistics Capabilities, Service Stock.

References
Department of Defense, Joint Chiefs of Staff. *Department of Defense Dictionary of Military and Related Terms.* Washington, DC: GPO, 1986.

—**SERVICE UNIFORM** is the uniform worn daily in the garrison environment when the utility or dress uniforms are not required or appropriate. Service uniforms are the Army green uniforms and the AG 388 uniforms. *See also:* Service Cap.

References
Department of Defense, U.S. Army. *Wear and Appearance of Army Uniforms and Insignia.* Army Regulation AR 670-1. Washington, DC: Headquarters, Department of the Army, 1986.

—**SERVICE UNIT** is a unit or organization designed primarily to render noncombat support to other units or for the theater as a whole to insure the continuity of operations. *See also:* Service Troops.

References
Department of Defense, U.S. Army. *Dictionary of United States Army Terms.* Army Regulation AR 310-25. Washington, DC: Headquarters, Department of the Army, 1986.

—**SERVICEABILITY STANDARDS** are standards that materiel must meet prior to issue. Serviceability is designated as Serviceable Group A (i.e., it is ready for issue), Serviceable Group B (i.e., it is ready for issue and with minor repair), Serviceable Group C (i.e., it is ready for issue and economically repairable or serviceable), or Serviceable Group D (i.e., it is ready for issue but not economically repairable). *See also:* Maintenance Serviceability Standards.

References
Department of Defense, U.S. Army. *Dictionary of United States Army Terms.* Army Regulation AR 310-25. Washington, DC: Headquarters, Department of the Army, 1986.

SERVICEABLE EQUIPMENT is equipment that meets the maintenance standards in the training manual and other Department of the Army technical publications and is capable of performing its prescribed function at rated capacity for 90 days under combat conditions.

References

Department of Defense, U.S. Army. *Planning Logistics Support for Military Operations*. Field Manual FM 701-58. Washington, DC: Headquarters, Department of the Army, 1987.

SERVICES are the functions of administrative support that are supplementary to the major services of transport, health, supply, and maintenance. Services include laundry, postal, mortuary, food service, and salvage services. They may be subdivided into personnel services and logistics services according to the practice of each army.

References

Department of Defense, U.S. Army. *Dictionary of United States Army Terms*. Army Regulation AR 310-25. Washington, DC: Headquarters, Department of the Army, 1986.

SERVICING is work on a motor vehicle that consists of clearing, refueling, lubricating, and replenishing the cooling agent and the air in the tires, so that the vehicle will continue to perform properly.

References

Department of Defense, U.S. Army. *Dictionary of United States Army Terms*. Army Regulation AR 310-25. Washington, DC: Headquarters, Department of the Army, 1986.

SET FORWARD is the forward movement of component parts within a projectile, missile, or bomb when impact occurs. *See also:* Setback.

References

Department of Defense, U.S. Army. *Dictionary of United States Army Terms*. Army Regulation AR 310-25. Washington, DC: Headquarters, Department of the Army, 1986.

SETBACK is a rearward jerk, caused by inertia, of free-moving parts in a projectile when it is fired. This force is used to push back a spring or plunger in the time fuze and start the operation of the fuze. *See also:* Set Forward.

References

Department of Defense, U.S. Army. *Dictionary of United States Army Terms*. Army Regulation AR 310-25. Washington, DC: Headquarters, Department of the Army, 1986.

SETTING RING is part of a mechanical fuze setter that takes hold of a fixed ring on the fuze of a projectile. It then rotates the entire projectile, except for a small ring, or setting element in the fuze. This setting element is kept from turning by the adjusting ring in the fuze setter just long enough to make the desired change in the setting of the fuze. *See also:* Fuze (Specify Type).

References

Department of Defense, U.S. Army. *Dictionary of United States Army Terms*. Army Regulation AR 310-25. Washington, DC: Headquarters, Department of the Army, 1986.

SETTING ROUNDS are rounds of ammunition fired at various angles of elevation to seat the spade and base plate of a gun mount firmly in the ground.

References

Department of Defense, U.S. Army. *Dictionary of United States Army Terms*. Army Regulation AR 310-25. Washington, DC: Headquarters, Department of the Army, 1986.

SEVERANCE ALLOWANCE is an allowance provided to enlisted personnel who are separated from the Army to pay for an individual's clothing and equipment. *See also:* Military Pay and Allowances.

References

Department of Defense, U.S. Army. *Dictionary of United States Army Terms*. Army Regulation AR 310-25. Washington, DC: Headquarters, Department of the Army, 1986.

SHALLOW FORDING is the crossing of a water obstacle by a self-propelled gun or ground vehicle equipped with built-in waterproofing, with its wheels or tracks in contact with the ground and without the use of a special waterproofing kit. *See also:* Deep Fording.

References

Department of Defense, Joint Chiefs of Staff. *Department of Defense Dictionary of Military and Related Terms*. Washington, DC: GPO, 1986.

—**SHAPED CHARGE** is a charge shaped so that its explosive force will be concentrated in a specific direction.

References
Department of Defense, Joint Chiefs of Staff. *Department of Defense Dictionary of Military and Related Terms.* Washington, DC: GPO, 1986.

—**SHEAF**, in artillery, are planned planes (lines) of fire that produce a desired pattern of bursts from rounds fired by two or more weapons.

References
Department of Defense, Joint Chiefs of Staff. *Department of Defense Dictionary of Military and Related Terms.* Washington, DC: GPO, 1986.

—**SHEAR LINK ASSEMBLY** is a device designed to break at a specified mechanical load.

References
Department of Defense, Joint Chiefs of Staff. *Department of Defense Dictionary of Military and Related Terms.* Washington, DC: GPO, 1986.

—**SHEET EXPLOSIVE** is plastic explosive provided in sheet form.

References
Department of Defense, Joint Chiefs of Staff. *Department of Defense Dictionary of Military and Related Terms.* Washington, DC: GPO, 1986.

—**SHELF LIFE.** (1) Shelf life is the length of time during which an item of supply, subject to deterioration or having a limited life that cannot be renewed, is considered serviceable while stored. (2) Shelf life is the total period of time, beginning with the date of manufacture, cure, or assembly, that an item may remain in the combined wholesale and retail storage system and be suitable for issue to, and use by, the end user. The shelf life should not be confused with service life, which is a measurement of the anticipated total in-use time. *See also:* Storage Life.

References
Department of Defense, Joint Chiefs of Staff. *Department of Defense Dictionary of Military and Related Terms.* Washington, DC: GPO, 1986.

Department of Defense, U.S. Army. *Dictionary of United States Army Terms.* Army Regulation AR 310-25. Washington, DC: Headquarters, Department of the Army, 1986.

—**SHELF-LIFE CODE** is a code assigned to a shelf-life item to identify the period of time that begins with the date the item was manufactured, cured,

or assembled, and ends with the date by which the item must be used or inspected, tested, restored or disposed of. *See also:* Shelf Life.

References
Department of Defense, U.S. Army. *Dictionary of United States Army Terms.* Army Regulation AR 310-25. Washington, DC: Headquarters, Department of the Army, 1986.

—**SHELF-LIFE ITEM** is a supply item that has deteriorative or unstable characteristics that necessitate it being assigned a storage time period to insure that the item will perform satisfactorily in service. For a medical commodity, the definition of a shelf-life item refers only to expiration-dated items. Medical items that have not been assigned a medical potency expiration date are defined as estimated storage life items.

There are two types of shelf life items. *Type I* is an item that through an examination of test data or through actual experience is determined to have a definite nonextendable period of shelf life. *Type II* covers items that have an assigned shelf life period that may be extended after the completion of a prescribed inspection, test, or restorative action. *See also:* Shelf Life.

References
Department of Defense, U.S. Army. *Dictionary of United States Army Terms.* Army Regulation AR 310-25. Washington, DC: Headquarters, Department of the Army, 1986.

—**SHELL.** (1) A shell is a hollow projectile that is filled with an explosive, a chemical, or with another material, as opposed to a shot, which is a solid projectile. (2) A shell is a shotgun cartridge. *See also:* Shell (Specify Type).

References
Department of Defense, U.S. Army. *Dictionary of United States Army Terms.* Army Regulation AR 310-25. Washington, DC: Headquarters, Department of the Army, 1986.

—**SHELL** (SPECIFY TYPE) is a command or request indicating the type of projectile that is to be used.

References
Department of Defense, Joint Chiefs of Staff. *Department of Defense Dictionary of Military and Related Terms.* Washington, DC: GPO, 1986.

—**SHELL DESTROYING TRACER** is an igniter element that is placed between the explosive in an air defense projectile and the tracer element.

It is designed to permit the activation of the explosive by the tracer element after the projectile has passed the target point but is still high enough to be harmless to ground troops.

References

Department of Defense, U.S. Army. *Dictionary of United States Army Terms.* Army Regulation AR 310-25. Washington, DC: Headquarters, Department of the Army, 1986.

—**SHELL WAVE** is an audible disturbance or wave that is emitted from shells moving at supersonic speeds.

References

Department of Defense, U.S. Army. *Dictionary of United States Army Terms.* Army Regulation AR 310-25. Washington, DC: Headquarters, Department of the Army, 1986.

—**SHELLING REPORT** is any report of enemy shelling containing information on caliber, direction, time, density, or the area shelled.

References

Department of Defense, Joint Chiefs of Staff. *Department of Defense Dictionary of Military and Related Terms.* Washington, DC: GPO, 1986.

—**SHELTERS** are constructed primarily to protect soldiers, equipment, and supplies from enemy action and the weather. They are usually constructed near fighting positions, and differ from fighting positions because there are usually no provisions for firing weapons from them.

References

Department of Defense, U.S. Army. *Survivability.* Field Manual FM 5-103. Washington, DC: Headquarters, Department of the Army, 1985.

—**SHIELDED ENCLOSURE,** in communications security, means an area (a room or a container) that is specifically designed to attenuate electromagnetic radiation or acoustic emanations that originate from either inside or outside of the area. *See also:* Communications Security.

References

Department of Defense, Joint Chiefs of Staff. *Department of Defense Dictionary of Military and Related Terms.* Washington, DC: GPO, 1986.

—**SHIELDING.** (1) Shielding is material of suitable thickness and physical characteristics used to protect personnel from radiation during the manufacture, handling, and transportation of fissionable and radioactive materials. (2)

Shielding consists of obstructions that tend to protect personnel or materials from the effects of a nuclear explosion.

References

Department of Defense, Joint Chiefs of Staff. *Department of Defense Dictionary of Military and Related Terms.* Washington, DC: GPO, 1986.

—**SHIFT.** (1) A shift is the transfer of fire from one target to another. (2) To shift is to transfer fire from one target to another. (3) Shift is the deflection difference from one designated point to another, and is used when opening or closing the sheaf of field artillery or mortar units. *See also:* Sheaf.

References

Department of Defense, U.S. Army. *Dictionary of United States Army Terms.* Army Regulation AR 310-25. Washington, DC: Headquarters, Department of the Army, 1986.

—**SHIFTING FIRE** is fire delivered at a constant range and at varying deflections. It is used to cover the width of a target that is too great to be covered by an open sheaf. *See also:* Sheaf.

References

Department of Defense, Joint Chiefs of Staff. *Department of Defense Dictionary of Military and Related Terms.* Washington, DC: GPO, 1986.

—**SHILLELAGH** is a missile system mounted on the main battle tank and assault reconnaissance vehicle for use against enemy armor, troops, and field fortifications. It is designated as MGM-51.

References

Department of Defense, Joint Chiefs of Staff. *Department of Defense Dictionary of Military and Related Terms.* Washington, DC: GPO, 1986.

—**SHIPMENT.** (1) A consolidated shipment is two or more items moving to a break bulk point or ultimate consignee under a single key transportation control number. (2) A partial shipment is one that has been separated at a shipping activity into two or more increments for onward movement with separate documentation for each shipment. (3) A split shipment is one that has been separated at a transshipment point into two or more increments for onward movement with separate documentations for each increment. (4) A unit consists of one or more line-item requisitions for shipment to one ultimate consignee under a single key transportation control number. *See also:* Break Bulk Point, Shipment Number, Shipment Planning, Shipment Sponsor, Shipment Status, Shipment Unit.

References

Department of Defense, U.S. Army. *Dictionary of United States Army Terms.* Army Regulation AR 310-25. Washington, DC: Headquarters, Department of the Army, 1986.

—**SHIPMENT IDENTIFIER** is a group of letters used to identify certain individuals or groups who travel wholly by air under overseas travel orders that employ this method.

References

Department of Defense, U.S. Army. *Dictionary of United States Army Terms.* Army Regulation AR 310-25. Washington, DC: Headquarters, Department of the Army, 1986.

—**SHIPMENT NUMBER** is the number assigned by the contractor to a shipment that is being made under a shipment order or contract. *See also:* Shipment.

References

Department of Defense, U.S. Army. *Dictionary of United States Army Terms.* Army Regulation AR 310-25. Washington, DC: Headquarters, Department of the Army, 1986.

—**SHIPMENT PLANNING** is the concurrent planning of the warehousing, packaging, and transportation functions at shipment or transshipment points to effectively manage the actions essential for preparing shipments to be transported efficiently and timely. *See also:* Shipment.

References

Department of Defense, U.S. Army. *Dictionary of United States Army Terms.* Army Regulation AR 310-25. Washington, DC: Headquarters, Department of the Army, 1986.

—**SHIPMENT SPONSOR** is the military department authorizing the movement of material in the Department of Defense transportation system. *See also:* Shipment.

References

Department of Defense, U.S. Army. *Dictionary of United States Army Terms.* Army Regulation AR 310-25. Washington, DC: Headquarters, Department of the Army, 1986.

—**SHIPMENT STATUS** is positive information about a shipment, including the date of shipment, the mode by which it was shipped, and the transportation control number. *See also:* Shipment.

References

Department of Defense, U.S. Army. *Dictionary of United States Army Terms.* Army Regulation AR 310-25. Washington, DC: Headquarters, Department of the Army, 1986.

—**SHIPMENT UNIT** consists of one or more items for shipment to one ultimate consignee under a single key transportation control number. *See also:* Shipment.

References

Department of Defense, U.S. Army. *Dictionary of United States Army Terms.* Army Regulation AR 310-25. Washington, DC: Headquarters, Department of the Army, 1986.

—**SHOCK ACTION** is the combined destructive physical and psychological effect on the enemy produced by the violent impact of mounted and motor armor-protected firepower of tanks and supporting troops. *See also:* Shock Front, Shock Wave.

References

Department of Defense, U.S. Army. *Dictionary of United States Army Terms.* Army Regulation AR 310-25. Washington, DC: Headquarters, Department of the Army, 1986.

—**SHOCK FRONT** refers to the boundaries between the pressure disturbance created by an explosion in the air, water, or earth and the ambient atmosphere.

References

Department of Defense, Joint Chiefs of Staff. *Department of Defense Dictionary of Military and Related Terms.* Washington, DC: GPO, 1986.

—**SHOCK WAVE** is a continuously propagated pressure pulse formed from an explosion in air, under water, or under ground. *See also:* Blast Wave.

References

Department of Defense, Joint Chiefs of Staff. *Department of Defense Dictionary of Military and Related Terms.* Washington, DC: GPO, 1986.

—**SHOOT-LOOK-SHOOT,** an air defense method of engagement, is the firing of missiles against a single target, one at a time, with a kill assessment being automatically performed by the computer after each firing and prior to the launch of the second missile at the target. This is the only method used by the computer for automatic engagements, since it provides the most effective use of missiles considering the high probability of kill by a single missile. It is normally the preferred method of firing.

References

Department of Defense, U.S. Army. *Patriot Battalion Operations.* Field Manual FM 44-15. Washington, DC: Headquarters, Department of the Army, 1984.

—**SHOP STOCK** consists of repair parts and consumable supplies stocked in a support-level maintenance activity for its internal use. The two types of shop stocks are demand-supported stock and bench stock. *See also:* Bench Stock Supply, Shop Supplies.

References

Department of Defense, U.S. Army. *Repair Parts Supply for a Theater of Operations.* Field Manual FM 29-19. Washington, DC: Headquarters, Department of the Army, 1985.

—**SHOP SUPPLIES** are expendable items consumed in operation and maintenance (e.g., oils, solvents, tape, packing, flux, and welding rods). *See also:* Shop Stock.

References

Department of Defense, U.S. Army. *Dictionary of United States Army Terms.* Army Regulation AR 310-25. Washington, DC: Headquarters, Department of the Army, 1986.

—**SHOP SUPPLY** is the element of a maintenance unit charged with providing the repair parts, assemblies, components, and maintenance materials that are needed by unit shops to accomplish the unit's maintenance mission.

References

Department of Defense, U.S. Army. *Dictionary of United States Army Terms.* Army Regulation AR 310-25. Washington, DC: Headquarters, Department of the Army, 1986.

—**SHORAD SYSTEMS,** or short-range air defense systems, currently include all man portable air defense systems (Redeye and Stinger), and Duster, Vulcan, Roland, and Chaparral. They cover the low-altitude approaches into the battlefield and prevent the enemy's attack of friendly ground forces, air bases, and logistical centers by providing a high volume of accurate fire. *See also:* HIMAD (High-to-Medium Altitude Air Defense).

References

Department of Defense, U.S. Army. *Air Defense Artillery Employment Hawk.* Field Manual FM 44-90. Washington, DC: Headquarters, Department of the Army, 1983.

————. *Air Defense Employment.* Field Manual FM 44-1. Washington, DC: Headquarters, Department of the Army, 1983.

—**SHORE-TO-SHORE OPERATION** is a land force operation involving a water crossing in assault craft, or in assault craft and aircraft in order to establish a force on, or to withdraw a force from, a far shore. It is usually an operation conducted by one service. *See also:* Amphibious Operation.

References

Department of Defense, U.S. Army. *Dictionary of United States Army Terms.* Army Regulation AR 310-25. Washington, DC: Headquarters, Department of the Army, 1986.

—**SHORT,** in artillery, is a spotting or an observation used by an observer to indicate that bursts have occurred short of the target in relation to the spotting line. *See also:* Spotting Line.

References

Department of Defense, Joint Chiefs of Staff. *Department of Defense Dictionary of Military and Related Terms.* Washington, DC: GPO, 1986.

—**SHORT GUARD.** (1) Short guard is a prescribed guard position in bayonet drill in which the point of the bayonet is directed at the opponent's stomach, and the right hand holds the small of the stock near the right hip. (2) Short guard is the command to take the above position. *See also:* Guard.

References

Department of Defense, U.S. Army. *Dictionary of United States Army Terms.* Army Regulation AR 310-25. Washington, DC: Headquarters, Department of the Army, 1986.

—**SHORT-LIFE ITEM** is an item whose estimated average service life is less than five years. *See also:* Consumption Rate.

References
Department of Defense, U.S. Army. *Dictionary of United States Army Terms*. Army Regulation AR 310-25. Washington, DC: Headquarters, Department of the Army, 1986.

—**SHORT-RANGE AIR DEFENSE ENGAGEMENT ZONE (SHORADEZ)** is established to define the airspace within which short-range air defense systems will operate. Because the centralized control of short-range air defense systems may not be possible, these zones must be clearly defined and disseminated so that friendly aircraft can avoid them. *See also:* HIMAD (High-to-Medium Altitude Air Defense), SHORAD (Short-Range Air Defense).

References
Department of Defense, U.S. Army. *Patriot Battalion Operations*. Field Manual FM 44-15. Washington, DC: Headquarters, Department of the Army, 1984.

—**SHORT-RANGE BALLISTIC MISSILE (SRBM)** is a ballistic missile with a range of up to about 600 miles. *See also:* Medium-Range Ballistic Missile.

References
Department of Defense, Joint Chiefs of Staff. *Department of Defense Dictionary of Military and Related Terms*. Washington, DC: GPO, 1986.

—**SHORT RANGE RADAR.** A short range radar is a radar equipment whose maximum range on a reflecting target of one square meter normal to the signal path exceeds 50 miles but is less than 150 miles, provided that a line of sight exists between the target and the radar. *See also:* Very Short Range Radar.

References
Department of Defense, U.S. Army. *Dictionary of United States Army Terms*. Army Regulation AR 310-25. Washington, DC: Headquarters, Department of the Army, 1986.

—**SHORT ROUND** is the inadvertent delivery of ordnance on friendly troops, installations, or civilians.

References
Department of Defense, Joint Chiefs of Staff. *Department of Defense Dictionary of Military and Related Terms*. Washington, DC: GPO, 1986.

—**SHORT SHIPMENT** is freight that is listed and manifested, but is not received.

References
Department of Defense, U.S. Army. *Dictionary of United States Army Terms*. Army Regulation AR 310-25. Washington, DC: Headquarters, Department of the Army, 1986.

—**SHORT SUPPLY.** An item is in short supply when the total on-hand stock and anticipated receipts during a given period are less than the total estimated demand during that period.

References
Department of Defense, Joint Chiefs of Staff. *Department of Defense Dictionary of Military and Related Terms*. Washington, DC: GPO, 1986.

—**SHORT-TERM PSYOP (PSYCHOLOGICAL OPERATIONS) CAMPAIGN** consists of propaganda and psychological actions conducted to support tactical objectives and are directed at a relatively small target audience. The intent is to achieve short-term psychological objectives when an immediate response is required. *See also:* Psychological Operations.

References
Department of Defense, U.S. Army. *Psychological Operations*. Field Manual FM 33-1. Washington, DC: Headquarters, Department of the Army, 1979.

—**SHORT THRUST** is a bayonet thrust in which the arm is extended and the body thrown forward with the weight shifted to the leading foot. A short lunge, it is delivered at a distance of about three feet.

References
Department of Defense, U.S. Army. *Dictionary of United States Army Terms*. Army Regulation AR 310-25. Washington, DC: Headquarters, Department of the Army, 1986.

—**SHORT TOUR AREA** is an overseas area in which the prescribed tour length is less than 36 months if family members are present and 24 months for all other types of tours. *See also:* Tour of Duty.

References
Department of Defense, U.S. Army. *Dictionary of United States Army Terms*. Army Regulation AR 310-25. Washington, DC: Headquarters, Department of the Army, 1986.

—**SHORTCOMING** is an imperfection or malfunction occurring during the life cycle of equipment. Although it will not cause an immediate breakdown, jeopardize safe operation, or materially reduce the usability of the materiel or end product, it should be reported and corrected to increase efficiency and to render the equipment completely serviceable. If it occurs during test phases, the shortcoming should be corrected if this can be done without unduly complicating the item or inducing another undesirable characteristic (e.g., increased cost and weight).

References

Department of Defense, U.S. Army. *Dictionary of United States Army Terms.* Army Regulation AR 310-25. Washington, DC: Headquarters, Department of the Army, 1986.

—**SHORTFALL** is the lack of forces, equipment, personnel, materiel, or capability, apportioned to and identified as a plan requirement, that would adversely affect the command's ability to accomplish its mission.

References

Department of Defense, Joint Chiefs of Staff. *Department of Defense Dictionary of Military and Related Terms.* Washington, DC: GPO, 1986.

—**SHOT**, in artillery, is a report that indicates a gun or guns have been fired.

References

Department of Defense, Joint Chiefs of Staff. *Department of Defense Dictionary of Military and Related Terms.* Washington, DC: GPO, 1986.

—**SHOW OF FORCE** is a mission carried out to demonstrate U.S. resolve, whereby U.S. forces are deployed to defuse a situation that may be detrimental to U.S. interests or national objectives. *See also:* Military Mission Options.

References

Collins, John M. *U.S.-Soviet Military Balance, 1980-1985.* Washington, DC: Congressional Research Service, 1985.

Department of Defense, U.S. Army. *Operational Terms and Symbols.* Field Manual FM 101-5-1. Washington, DC: Headquarters, Department of the Army, 1985.

—**SHOWDOWN INSPECTION** is an inspection of all individual clothing and equipment and organizational equipment to insure their completeness and serviceability.

References

Department of Defense, U.S. Army. *Dictionary of United States Army Terms.* Army Regulation AR 310-25. Washington, DC: Headquarters, Department of the Army, 1986.

—**SHUTTLE MARCHING** is alternate riding and marching in a troop movement. It is usually done because there are not enough vehicles to transport the entire unit.

References

Department of Defense, U.S. Army. *Dictionary of United States Army Terms.* Army Regulation AR 310-25. Washington, DC: Headquarters, Department of the Army, 1986.

—**SHUTTLING.** (1) Shuttling is transporting troops, equipment, and supplies by a series of round trips of the same vehicles. It may be done by hauling a load the entire distance and then returning for another load; or it may be done by carrying successive portions of the marching force for short distances while the remaining portions continue on foot. (2) In tractor semitrailer and truck-trailer operations, shuttling is repeated trips of tractors or trucks to move semitrailers or trailers between locations. *See also:* Shuttle Marching.

References

Department of Defense, U.S. Army. *Dictionary of United States Army Terms.* Army Regulation AR 310-25. Washington, DC: Headquarters, Department of the Army, 1986.

—**SICK CALL.** (1) Sick call is the daily assembly when all sick and injured, other than those in the hospital, report to a medical officer for examination and treatment. (2) Sick call is a bugle call or signal for assembly. *See also:* Medical Treatment.

References

Department of Defense, U.S. Army. *Dictionary of United States Army Terms.* Army Regulation AR 310-25. Washington, DC: Headquarters, Department of the Army, 1986.

—**SIDE-LOOKING AIRBORNE RADAR (SLAR)** is an airborne radar, viewing at right angles to the axis of the vehicle, that produces a presentation of terrain or targets. SLAR can provide stand-off surveillance of large areas, has a near-all weather capability, is equally effective day or night, and has a stand-off capability, that places it out of range of enemy forward defense systems. *See also:* Standoff.

References

Department of Defense, Defense Intelligence College. *Glossary of Intelligence Terms and Definitions.* Washington, DC: DIC, 1987.

—**SIDE SPRAY** are fragments of a bursting shell that are thrown sideways from the line of flight. *See also:* Base Spray, Nose Spray.

References
Department of Defense, U.S. Army. *Dictionary of United States Army Terms.* Army Regulation AR 310-25. Washington, DC: Headquarters, Department of the Army, 1986.

—**SIDE STEP** is a single step twelve inches to the right or left of a given standing position.

References
Department of Defense, U.S. Army. *Dictionary of United States Army Terms.* Army Regulation AR 310-25. Washington, DC: Headquarters, Department of the Army, 1986.

—**SIGHT BASE** is a mount for a gun sight.

References
Department of Defense, U.S. Army. *Dictionary of United States Army Terms.* Army Regulation AR 310-25. Washington, DC: Headquarters, Department of the Army, 1986.

—**SIGHT BLADE** is a thin, flat, metal post used as a front sight on some firearms.

References
Department of Defense, U.S. Army. *Dictionary of United States Army Terms.* Army Regulation AR 310-25. Washington, DC: Headquarters, Department of the Army, 1986.

—**SIGHT BRACKET** is a clamp used to hold a detachable sight in position when it is mounted on a gun.

References
Department of Defense, U.S. Army. *Dictionary of United States Army Terms.* Army Regulation AR 310-25. Washington, DC: Headquarters, Department of the Army, 1986.

—**SIGHT COVER** is a protective metal cover fastened about a sight to guard it from being moved out of adjustment by jars and blows.

References
Department of Defense, U.S. Army. *Dictionary of United States Army Terms.* Army Regulation AR 310-25. Washington, DC: Headquarters, Department of the Army, 1986.

—**SIGHT LEAF** is a moveable hinged part of a rear sight of a gun that can be raised and set to a desired range or snapped down when it is not in use.

References
Department of Defense, U.S. Army. *Dictionary of United States Army Terms.* Army Regulation AR 310-25. Washington, DC: Headquarters, Department of the Army, 1986.

—**SIGHTING BAR** is a wooden device with enlarged front and rear sights, an eyepiece, and a movable target. It is used to train men in the proper method of aiming a small arms weapon. The eyepiece forces the student to hold his eye in the proper position. Because of the size of the sights, errors of aiming are very apparent.

References
Department of Defense, U.S. Army. *Dictionary of United States Army Terms.* Army Regulation AR 310-25. Washington, DC: Headquarters, Department of the Army, 1986.

—**SIGHTING DISK** is a cardboard or metal disk with a small bull's-eye painted on it and an attached handle. With a gun in a fixed position, a sighting disk is used in aiming practice. The instructor moves the disk across a sheet of paper as the student directs, until the student believes that it is in line with the sights. He then marks the position. Three such marks make up a shot group or aiming group.

References
Department of Defense, U.S. Army. *Dictionary of United States Army Terms.* Army Regulation AR 310-25. Washington, DC: Headquarters, Department of the Army, 1986.

—**SIGHTING SHOT** is a trial shot fired from a gun to find out whether the sights are properly adjusted.

References
Department of Defense, U.S. Army. *Dictionary of United States Army Terms.* Army Regulation AR 310-25. Washington, DC: Headquarters, Department of the Army, 1986.

—**SIGINT (SIGNALS INTELLIGENCE) ACTIVITY** is an activity conducted in order to produce signals intelligence. *See also:* Signals Intelligence.

References
Department of Defense, Defense Intelligence College. *Glossary of Intelligence Terms and Definitions.* Washington, DC: DIC, 1987.

—**SIGINT (SIGNALS INTELLIGENCE) DIRECT SERVICE** is a reporting procedure intended to provide SIGINT to a military commander or other authorized recipient in response to SIGINT requirements. The product may vary from recurring, serialized reports produced by the National Security Agency/Central Security Service to instantaneous a periodic reports that are provided to the command or other recipient, usually from a fixed SIGINT activity that collects and processes SIGINT. *See also:* Signals Intelligence.

References
Department of Defense, Joint Chiefs of Staff. *Department of Defense Dictionary of Military and Related Terms.* Washington, DC: GPO, 1986.

—**SIGINT (SIGNALS INTELLIGENCE) DIRECT SERVICE ACTIVITY** is a SIGINT activity composed of collection and associated resources that normally perform in a direct service role under the SIGINT operational control of the Director, National Security Agency/Chief, Central Security Service. *See also:* Signals Intelligence.

References
Department of Defense, Joint Chiefs of Staff. *Department of Defense Dictionary of Military and Related Terms.* Washington, DC: GPO, 1986.

—**SIGINT (SIGNALS INTELLIGENCE) DIRECT SUPPORT** is the provision of SIGINT information to a military commander by a SIGINT direct support unit in direct response to SIGINT operational tasking that has been ordered by that commander. *See also:* Signals Intelligence.

References
Department of Defense, Joint Chiefs of Staff. *Department of Defense Dictionary of Military and Related Terms.* Washington, DC: GPO, 1986.

—**SIGINT (SIGNALS INTELLIGENCE) DIRECT SUPPORT UNIT** is a SIGINT unit that is usually mobile and is designed to perform a SIGINT direct support role for a military commander under delegated authority from the Director, National Security Agency/Chief, Central Security Service. *See also:* Signals Intelligence.

References
Department of Defense, Joint Chiefs of Staff. *Department of Defense Dictionary of Military and Related Terms.* Washington, DC: GPO, 1986.

—**SIGINT (SIGNALS INTELLIGENE) OPERATIONAL CONTROL** is the authoritative direction of SIGINT activities, including the tasking and allocation of effort, and the authoritative prescription of the uniform techniques and standards by which SIGINT information is collected, processed, and reported. *See also:* Signals Intelligence.

References
Department of Defense, Joint Chiefs of Staff. *Department of Defense Dictionary of Military and Related Terms.* Washington, DC: GPO, 1986.

—**SIGINT (SIGNALS INTELLIGENCE) OPERATIONAL TASKING** is the authoritative operational direction and direct ordering of SIGINT requirements by a military commander on designated SIGINT resources. These requirements are directive, irrespective of other priorities, and are conditioned only by the capability of the resources to produce such information. Operational tasking includes the authority to deploy and redeploy all or part of the SIGINT resources for which SIGINT operational tasking authority has been delegated. *See also:* Signals Intelligence.

References
Department of Defense, Joint Chiefs of Staff. *Department of Defense Dictionary of Military and Related Terms.* Washington, DC: GPO, 1986.

—**SIGINT (SIGNALS INTELLIGENCE) OPERATIONAL TASKING AUTHORITY (SOTA)** is a military commander's authority to operationally direct and order SIGINT requirements on designated SIGINT resources. These requirements are directive, irrespective of other priorities, and are conditioned only by the capability of those resources to produce such information. Operational tasking authority includes the authority to deploy and redeploy all or part of the SIGINT resources for which SIGINT operational tasking authority has been delegated. *See also:* Signals Intelligence.

References
Department of Defense, U.S. Army. *Support Operations: Echelons Above Corps.* Field Manual FM 100-16. Washington, DC: Headquarters, Department of the Army, 1986.

—**SIGINT (SIGNALS INTELLIGENCE) PROCESS.** The process used to perform SIGINT in the Army tactical intelligence context involves search, identification, direction finding, recording, analysis, and dissemination. Each of these steps are defined as follows:
  • **Search** is the beginning of the SIGINT

process. In this step, intercept operators are assigned a portion of the frequency spectrum and are told to look for signals of interest. Once a signal is intercepted, the intelligence portion of the process begins.

- **Identification** is the analysis of the content of the communications or signal characteristics of the emitter in order to identify the signal for further exploitation. Analysis can be as simple as identifying a language or as complicated as determining a special code that is being used by a unit.
- **Direction finding** is the determining of an emitter's location. It is used to determine the approximate direction or bearing of a transmitting antenna. When the direction finding station obtains a line of bearing, it provides an approximate direction to the emitter, but not the distance. Two or three lines of bearing are needed to provide a more definite location. (The exception is the single station locator system, which can provide a location with one bearing.)
- **Recording** is the placing of all intercepted traffic with other associated data in the appropriate files or logging information in a way that it can be easily retrieved, collated, or cross-referenced. This information can then be used in analysis.
- **Analysis** is a systematic examination of intercepted data in order to identify significant facts and derive conclusions. All information on the intercepted signals, including messages and traffic from communications emitters, is passed to an analysis center. There, it is combined with information gathered from numerous sources and analyzed to determine the enemy's locations, make-up, capabilities, and intentions.
- **Dissemination** is rapidly passing usable information and intelligence to the decisionmaker, for use in developing plans or for immediate action.

See also: Signals Intelligence.

References

Department of Defense, U.S. Army. *Counter-Signals Intelligence (C-SIGINT) Operations.* Field Manual FM 34-62. Washington, DC: Headquarters, Department of the Army, 1986.

———. *Support Operations: Echelons Above Corps.* Field Manual FM 100-16. Washington, DC: Headquarters, Department of the Army, 1986.

—SIGINT (SIGNALS INTELLIGENCE)-RELATED ACTIVITY is any operation intended primarily for a purpose other than producing SIGINT, but which can be used to produce SIGINT or produces SIGINT as a by-product of its principal purpose. *See also:* SIGINT Activity.

References

Department of Defense, Defense Intelligence College. *Glossary of Intelligence Terms and Definitions.* Washington, DC: DIC, 1987.

—SIGINT (SIGNALS INTELLIGENCE) RESOURCES are the personnel (with the appropriate equipment) of any unit, activity, or organizational element who are engaged in SIGINT activities. *See also:* Signals Intelligence.

References

Department of Defense, Joint Chiefs of Staff. *Department of Defense Dictionary of Military and Related Terms.* Washington, DC: GPO, 1986.

—SIGINT (SIGNALS INTELLIGENCE) SUPPORT PLANS are plans prepared by the National Security Agency/Central Security Service, in coordination with concerned elements of the U.S. SIGINT system, which specify how the resources of the system will be aligned in crisis or war to support military operations that are covered by certain Joint Chiefs of Staff and unified and specified command operation plans. *See also:* Signals Intelligence.

References

Department of Defense, Joint Chiefs of Staff. *Department of Defense Dictionary of Military and Related Terms.* Washington, DC: GPO, 1986.

—SIGINT (SIGNALS INTELLIGENCE) TECHNICAL INFORMATION is information concerning or derived from intercepted foreign transmissions or radiations. It is technical information as opposed to intelligence and requires further collection or analysis before it becomes SIGINT. *See also:* Signals Intelligence.

References

Department of Defense, Defense Intelligence College. *Glossary of Intelligence Terms and Definitions.* Washington, DC: DIC, 1987.

—SIGN OFF is a proword that denotes the end of a transmission.

References
Department of Defense, U.S. Army. *Dictionary of United States Army Terms*. Army Regulation AR 310-25. Washington, DC: Headquarters, Department of the Army, 1986.

—**SIGNAL.** (1) A signal is anything intentionally transmitted by visual, electromagnetic, nuclear, or acoustic methods for either communications or noncommunications purposes. (2) As defined by the Church Committee and applied to electronics, a signal is any transmitted electrical impulse. (3) A signal is a pyrotechnic item that is designed to produce a sign by means of illumination, smoke, sound, or a combination of these effects to provide identification, location, or a warning.

References
Department of Defense, Defense Intelligence College. *Glossary of Intelligence Terms and Definitions*. Washington, DC: DIC, 1987.

U.S. Congress. Senate. *Final Report of the Senate Select Committee to Study Government Operations With Respect to Intelligence Activities. Report 94-755. Book I. Foreign and Military Intelligence* (Church Committee Report). Washington, D.C.: GPO, 1976.

—**SIGNAL AXIS** is a line or route on which lie the starting position and the probable future locations of the command post of a unit during a troop movement. It is the main route along which messages are relayed or sent to and from combat units in the field.

References
Department of Defense, U.S. Army. *Dictionary of United States Army Terms*. Army Regulation AR 310-25. Washington, DC: Headquarters, Department of the Army, 1986.

—**SIGNAL CENTER** is a group of signal communication facilities operated by the Army in the field and that consist of a communications center, a telephone switching central, and the appropriate means of signal communications. *See also:* Communications Center.

References
Department of Defense, Joint Chiefs of Staff. *Department of Defense Dictionary of Military and Related Terms*. Washington, DC: GPO, 1986.

—**SIGNAL COMMUNICATIONS** are any means of transmitting messages in plain or encrypted text other than by direct conversation or mail.

References
Department of Defense, U.S. Army. *Dictionary of United States Army Terms*. Army Regulation AR 310-25. Washington, DC: Headquarters, Department of the Army, 1986.

—**SIGNAL OPERATION INSTRUCTIONS** are a series of orders issued for technical control and coordination of a command's signal communications activities.

References
Department of Defense, Joint Chiefs of Staff. *Department of Defense Dictionary of Military and Related Terms*. Washington, DC: GPO, 1986.

—**SIGNAL SECURITY,** in Army tactical intelligence, encompasses all of the measures taken to protect friendly electromagnetic emissions from exploitation by the enemy. It is a generic term that includes both communications security and electronic security. *See also:* Communications Security, Electronic Security.

References
Department of Defense, U.S. Army. *Intelligence and Electronic Warfare Operations*. Field Manual FM 34-1. Washington, DC: Headquarters, Department of the Army, 1987.

———. *Military Intelligence Battalion (CEWI) (Operations) (Corps)*. Field Manual FM 34-21. Washington, DC: Headquarters, Department of the Army, 1982.

—**SIGNAL SERVICE** is an organization, installation, or operation of a unit's signal communications.

References
Department of Defense, U.S. Army. *Dictionary of United States Army Terms*. Army Regulation AR 310-25. Washington, DC: Headquarters, Department of the Army, 1986.

—**SIGNAL STRENGTH** usually refers to the magnitude of a received signal, in volts, that is induced across the input terminals of a receiver.

References
Department of Defense, U.S. Army. *Dictionary of United States Army Terms*. Army Regulation AR 310-25. Washington, DC: Headquarters, Department of the Army, 1986.

—**SIGNAL SYSTEM** is an integrated arrangement of communication components that provide a means of signal communications. *See also:* Signal System Control Center.

References
Department of Defense, U.S. Army. *Dictionary of United States Army Terms*. Army Regulation AR 310-25. Washington, DC: Headquarters, Department of the Army, 1986.

—SIGNAL SYSTEMS CONTROL CENTER is a central communications activity, established by a signal corps unit, to accomplish detailed signal system planning and engineering, including traffic analysis and traffic engineering. It coordinates, directs, and controls the implementation, integration, and operation of a signal communication system, including the allocation of radio frequencies, and it provides a signal information service. The operational control of the signal communications system is normally exercised through subordinate signal systems control centers and communications technical control centers.

References
Department of Defense, U.S. Army. *Dictionary of United States Army Terms*. Army Regulation AR 310-25. Washington, DC: Headquarters, Department of the Army, 1986.

—SIGNAL-TO-JAMMING RATIO is the ratio of the strength of a desired signal to that of a jamming signal at a selected point in a circuit. *See also:* Jamming.

References
Department of Defense, U.S. Army. *Communications Techniques: Electronics Countermeasures*. Field Manual FM 24-33. Washington, DC: Headquarters, Department of the Army, 1985.

—SIGNAL TROOPS are troops of the Signal Corps, especially those who are assigned to divisions and corps, and who maintain and operate communications systems.

References
Department of Defense, U.S. Army. *Dictionary of United States Army Terms*. Army Regulation AR 310-25. Washington, DC: Headquarters, Department of the Army, 1986.

—SIGNALING PANEL is a strip of cloth used to send code signals between the ground and airborne aircraft.

References
Department of Defense, U.S. Army. *Dictionary of United States Army Terms*. Army Regulation AR 310-25. Washington, DC: Headquarters, Department of the Army, 1986.

—SIGNALING SMOKE is smoke used to relay prearranged communications on the battlefield. It is frequently used to identify targets, evacuation points, and friendly unit perimeters.

References
Department of Defense, U.S. Army. *Deliberate Smoke Operations*. Field Manual FM 3-50. Washington, DC: Headquarters, Department of the Army, 1984.

—SIGNALS ANALYSIS (SA) is a step in the Army tactical intelligence signals intelligence process. *See also:* SIGINT (SIGNALS INTELLIGENCE) Process.

References
Department of Defense, U.S. Army. *Counter-Signals Intelligence (C-SIGINT) Operations*. Field Manual FM 34-62. Washington, DC: Headquarters, Department of the Army, 1986.

—SIGNALS INTELLIGENCE (SIGINT). (1) SIGINT is intelligence information composed of any or all of the following: communications intelligence, electronics intelligence, and foreign instrumentation signals intelligence, regardless of how this information is transmitted. (2) SIGINT, as defined by the Church Committee, is "the general term for the foreign intelligence mission of the National Security Agency/Central Security Service (NSA/CSS). SIGINT involves the interception, processing, analysis, and dissemination of information that is derived from foreign electrical communications and other signals. It is composed of three elements: Communications Intelligence (COMINT), Electronics Intelligence (ELINT), and Telemetry Intelligence (TELINT). Most SIGINT is collected by personnel of the Service Cryptologic Agencies."

References
Department of Defense, U.S. Army. *Support Operations: Echelons Above Corps*. Field Manual FM 100-16. Washington, DC: Headquarters, Department of the Army, 1986.

U.S. Congress. Senate. *Final Report of the Senate Select Committee to Study Government Operations With Respect to Intelligence Activities. Report 94-755. Book I, Foreign and Military Intelligence* (Church Committee Report). Washington, DC: GPO, 1976.

—SIGNALS SECURITY (SIGSEC) ACQUISITION AND ANALYSIS, in communications security, is collecting and analyzing electronic emissions in order to determine the susceptibility of these emissions to interception and exploitation by hostile intelligence services. It includes cataloging the transmission spectrum and taking signal parameter measurements as required. It does not include acquiring information that is carried on the system, which is in the realm of signals security surveillance. *See also:* Signals Security Surveillance.

References

Department of Defense, Defense Intelligence College. *Glossary of Intelligence Terms and Definitions.* Washington, DC: DIC, 1987.

—**SIGNALS SECURITY (SIGSEC) SURVEILLANCE,** in electronic warfare, signals intelligence, communications security, operations security, and signals analysis, involves systematically surveilling one's own electronic emissions in order to determine if the existing signals security measures are adequate, to provide data from which to predict the effectiveness of proposed signals security measures, and to confirm that these measures are adequate after they are implemented. *See also:* Communications Security, Operations Security, Signals Intelligence.

References

Department of Defense, Defense Intelligence College. *Glossary of Intelligence Terms and Definitions.* Washington, DC: DIC, 1987.

—**SIGNALS SECURITY (SIGSEC) SURVEY** is the primary means for accomplishing a SIGSEC vulnerability assessment, which is a SIGSEC support function that is performed to determine the extent to which U.S. military noncommunications and communications emitter systems and electromagnetic radiations from those systems can be exploited and disrupted. It compares enemy communications intelligence and electronic intelligence collection capabilities with friendly force electromagnetic profiles, and identifies friendly force vulnerabilities to the enemy collection threat. This function involves identifying the vulnerabilities and providing follow-on assistance in developing and implementing countermeasures. The procedure for estimating the electromagnetic vulnerability of a unit or activity is the electromagnetic vulnerability assessment. *See also:* Communications Security.

References

Department of Defense, U.S. Army. *Counterintelligence.* Field Manual FM 34-60. Washington, DC: Headquarters, Department of the Army, 1985.

—**SIGNALS SUPPORT** is the provision of personnel and equipment from other forces for establishing a special or supplementary communications system.

References

Department of Defense, Joint Chiefs of Staff. *Department of Defense Dictionary of Military and Related Terms.* Washington, DC: GPO, 1986.

—**SIGNATURE.** (1) In communications and communications security, signature refers to the touch of a wireless radio operator which indicates his personal transmitting pattern. Each operator has certain aspects to his touch that are so idiosyncratic that an experienced receiver can tell immediately if the operator has been switched. (2) In Army tactical intelligence, signature means the identification of a military unit or activity resulting from the unique and detectable, visual, imagery, electromagnetic, olfactory, or acoustical display of key equipment that is normally associated with that type of unit or activity. Signatures fall into four categories: imagery (visual, photographic, or infrared); electromagnetic (communications and noncommunications); acoustical; and olfactory. Signatures are detected because different units have different types of equipment, are of differing sizes, emit different electromagnetic signals, deploy differently, and have different noises and smells associated with them. Detection of individual signatures can be used by enemy analysts to locate entire units, key activities, groups, and so forth. (3) In weaponry, a signature is the visible effect (e.g., smoke, flame, or debris) that is produced at a firing position when a weapon is fired. *See also:* Communications Security.

References

Department of Defense, U.S. Army. *Air Defense Artillery Deployment: Chaparral/Vulcan/Stinger.* Field Manual FM 44-3. Washington, DC: Headquarters, Department of the Army, 1984.

———. *Counter-Signals Intelligence (C-SIGINT) Operations.* Field Manual FM 34-62. Washington, DC: Headquarters, Department of the Army, 1986.

———. *Operational Terms and Symbols.* Field Manual FM 101-5-1. Washington, DC: Headquarters, Department of the Army, 1985.

—**SIGNED ROUTE** is a route along which a unit has placed directional signs that bear its unit identification symbol. The signs are for the unit's use only and must comply with movement regulations.

References

Department of Defense, U.S. Army. *Route Reconnaissance and Classification.* Field Manual FM 5-36. Washington, DC: Headquarters, Department of the Army, 1985.

—**SIGNIFICANT TRACKS** (AIR DEFENSE) are tracks (paths) of aircraft or missiles that behave in an unusual manner that warrants attention and can pose a threat to a defended area.

References

Department of Defense, Joint Chiefs of Staff. *Department of Defense Dictionary of Military and Related Terms.* Washington, DC: GPO, 1986.

—**SIGSEC (SIGNALS SECURITY) VULNERABILITY ASSESSMENT** is a SIGSEC support function. It is performed to determine the extent to which U.S. military noncommunications and communications emitter systems and the electromagnetic radiations from those systems can be exploited and disrupted. *See also:* Signals Security Survey.

References

Department of Defense, U.S. Army. *Counterintelligence.* Field Manual FM 34-60. Washington, DC: Headquarters, Department of the Army, 1985.

—**SILHOUETTE TARGET.** (1) A silhouette target is a target whose shape is outlined against a light background although its body features cannot be clearly seen. (2) A silhouette target is a practice target consisting of the dark image of a person or object that is outlined against a light background.

References

Department of Defense, U.S. Army. *Dictionary of United States Army Terms.* Army Regulation AR 310-25. Washington, DC: Headquarters, Department of the Army, 1986.

—**SIMPLICITY** (PRINCIPLE OF WAR). Simplicity, in a principle of war context, means to prepare clear, uncomplicated plans and clear, concise orders to insure thorough understanding. In the strategic, operational, and tactical dimensions, guidance, plans, and orders should be as simple and direct as the attainment of the objective will allow. The strategic importance of the principle of simplicity goes well beyond its more traditional military application. It is an important element in the development and enhancement of public support. If the U.S. people are to commit their lives and resources to a military operation, they must understand the purpose that is to be achieved. Political and military objectives and operations must therefore be presented in clear, concise, understandable terms: simple and direct plans and orders cannot compensate for ambiguous and cloudy objectives. In its military application, this principle promotes strategic flexibility by encouraging broad strategic guidance rather than detailed and involved instruction.

At the operational and tactical levels, simplicity of plans and instructions contributes to successful operations. Direct, simple plans, and clear, concise orders are essential to reduce the chances for misunderstanding and confusion. Other factors being equal, a simple plan executed promptly is to be preferred over a complex plan executed later. *See also:* Principles of War.

References

Department of Defense, U.S. Army. *Operational Terms and Symbols.* Field Manual FM 101-5-1. Washington, DC: Headquarters, Department of the Army, 1985.

———. *Operations.* Field Manual FM 100-5. Washington, DC: Headquarters, Department of the Army, 1986.

—**SIMULATED MUSTARD** is a harmless substance composed of molasses residuum that is used in training to simulate toxic liquid chemical agents. *See also:* Chemical Warfare.

References

Department of Defense, U.S. Army. *Dictionary of United States Army Terms.* Army Regulation AR 310-25. Washington, DC: Headquarters, Department of the Army, 1986.

—**SIMULATION** is a representation of a portion of a system, the operation of the system, the environment in which the system operates, and the environment in which command and staff are trained to perform wartime functions.

References

Department of Defense, U.S. Army. *Training for Mobilization and War.* Field Manual FM 25-5. Washington, DC: Headquarters, Department of the Army, 1985.

—**SIMULATORS** is a generic term for systems-specific devices that train individuals or crews in system use and maintenance.

References

Department of Defense, U.S. Army. *Training for Mobilization and War.* Field Manual FM 25-5. Washington, DC: Headquarters, Department of the Army, 1985.

—**SIMULTANEOUS ENGAGEMENT** is the concurrent engagement of hostile targets by a combination of interceptor aircraft and surface-to-air missiles.

References

Department of Defense, Joint Chiefs of Staff. *Department of Defense Dictionary of Military and Related Terms.* Washington, DC: GPO, 1986.

—**SINGLE-CHAMBER STORAGE SITE** is an evacuated chamber with its own access to the natural ground surface. It is not connected to any other storage chamber.

References

Department of Defense, U.S. Army. *Ammunition and Explosives Safety Standards.* Army Regulation AR 385-64. Washington, DC: Headquarters, Department of the Army, 1987.

—**SINGLE ENVELOPMENT** is a maneuver made against one flank or around one flank and to the rear of the initial disposition of the enemy. *See also:* Double Envelopment, Envelopment, Turning Movement.

References

Department of Defense, U.S. Army. *Operational Terms and Symbols.* Field Manual FM 101-5-1. Washington, DC: Headquarters, Department of the Army, 1985.

—**SINGLE FLOW ROUTE** is a route at least one-and-a-half lanes wide allowing the passage of a column of vehicles, and permitting isolated vehicles to pass or travel in the opposite direction at predetermined points. *See also:* Limited Access Route.

References

Department of Defense, Joint Chiefs of Staff. *Department of Defense Dictionary of Military and Related Terms.* Washington, DC: GPO, 1986.

—**SINGLE INTEGRATED OPERATIONS PLAN** (SIOP) is the U.S. contingency plan for strategic retaliatory strikes in event of nuclear war. Targets, timing, tactics, and force requirements are considered for a variety of responses. It is pre-pared by the Joint Strategic Target Planning Staff, which is collocated with SAC Headquarters at Offutt Air Force Base outside of Omaha, Nebraska. *See also:* Nuclear Warfare.

References

Collins, John M. *U.S.-Soviet Military Balance, 1980-1985.* Washington, DC: Congressional Research Service, 1985.

—**SINGLE MANAGER** is a military department or agency that is designated by the Secretary of Defense to be responsible for managing specified commodities or common service activities on a Department of Defense-wide basis.

References

Department of Defense, Joint Chiefs of Staff. *Department of Defense Dictionary of Military and Related Terms.* Washington, DC: GPO, 1986.

—**SINGLE MEMBER SPONSOR** is a member of the regular or reserve components of the Army who has no spouse or is legally separated from a spouse, but has physical and legal custody of or responsibility for one or more children under the age of eighteen or family members who are incapable of self-care regardless of their age.

References

Department of Defense, U.S. Army. *Dictionary of United States Army Terms.* Army Regulation AR 310-25. Washington, DC: Headquarters, Department of the Army, 1986.

—**SINGLE PERFORATED GRAIN** is a cylindrical propellent grain with a single perforation located on its axis.

References

Department of Defense, U.S. Army. *Dictionary of United States Army Terms.* Army Regulation AR 310-25. Washington, DC: Headquarters, Department of the Army, 1986.

—**SINGLE SECTION CHARGE** is a propelling charge in separate loading ammunition that is loaded into a single bag. A single section charge cannot be reduced or increased for changes of range, as a multisection charge can be. *See also:* Separate Loading Ammunition.

References

Department of Defense, U.S. Army. *Dictionary of United States Army Terms.* Army Regulation AR 310-25. Washington, DC: Headquarters, Department of the Army, 1986.

SINGLE SHOT HIT PROBABILITY is the probability that a single projectile fired against a target will hit that target under a given set of conditions regardless of whether the target is defeated or destroyed by the single hit. *See also:* Single Shot Kill Probability.

References
Department of Defense, U.S. Army. *Dictionary of United States Army Terms.* Army Regulation AR 310-25. Washington, DC: Headquarters, Department of the Army, 1986.

SINGLE SHOT KILL PROBABILITY is the probability that a single projectile fired at a target will destroy or effectively disable it. *See also:* Single Shot Hit Probability.

References
Department of Defense, U.S. Army. *Dictionary of United States Army Terms.* Army Regulation AR 310-25. Washington, DC: Headquarters, Department of the Army, 1986.

SINGLE STATION METHOD is a method of locating a target in which both the direction and the distance to the target are determined from only one station.

References
Department of Defense, U.S. Army. *Dictionary of United States Army Terms.* Army Regulation AR 310-25. Washington, DC: Headquarters, Department of the Army, 1986.

SITE is the placement of individual items of equipment on selected spots within the position. *See also:* Position.

References
Department of Defense, U.S. Army. *Air Defense Artillery Employment.* Field Manual FM 44-1. Washington, DC: Headquarters, Department of the Army, 1983.
——. *Air Defense Artillery Employment Hawk.* Field Manual FM 44-90. Washington, DC: Headquarters, Department of the Army, 1983.

SITUATION is the total of all the conditions and circumstances that affect a unit or command at any given time. *See also:* Situation Map, Situation Report, Situational Template.

References
Department of Defense, U.S. Army. *Dictionary of United States Army Terms.* Army Regulation AR 310-25. Washington, DC: Headquarters, Department of the Army, 1986.

SITUATION MAP (SITMAP), in Army tactical intelligence, refers to maps that graphically depict the current, known dispositions, and major activities of friendly and enemy forces. The basic SITMAP provides a format for accurate notations of friendly and enemy forces relative to friendly boundaries. Electronic order of battle overlays are used to graphically depict communications and noncommunications emitters and associated units, facilities, and activities. *See also:* Order of Battle.

References
Department of Defense, U.S. Army. *Counter-Signals Intelligence (C-SIGINT) Operations.* Field Manual FM 34-62. Washington, DC: Headquarters, Department of the Army, 1986.
——. *Operational Terms and Symbols.* Field Manual FM 101-5-1. Washington, DC: Headquarters, Department of the Army, 1985.

SITUATION REPORT (SITREP) is a narrative report prepared by a subordinate commander for his superiors to inform them of his evaluation of the significant factors that substantially improve or impair his operational readiness.

References
Department of Defense, Joint Chiefs of Staff. *Department of Defense Dictionary of Military and Related Terms.* Washington, DC: GPO, 1986.

SITUATIONAL TEMPLATE is a series of projections based upon enemy doctrine that portray the most probable disposition and location of enemy forces within constraints imposed by weather and terrain.

References
Department of Defense, U.S. Army. *Operational Terms and Symbols.* Field Manual FM 101-5-1. Washington, DC: Headquarters, Department of the Army, 1985.

SITUATIONAL TRAINING EXERCISES comprise a training package that is easily tailored to assist in training critical tasks and missions. The package provides training methods and procedures, resource requirements, situations, and scenarios.

References
Department of Defense, U.S. Army. *Army Forces Training.* Army Regulation AR 350-41. Washington, DC: Headquarters, Department of the Army, 1986.

—**SKATE MOUNT** is a mounting of a machine gun that permits it to travel on a continuous track extending around the inside of the body of a vehicle. The gun can be locked in any position for use.

References

Department of Defense, U.S. Army. *Dictionary of United States Army Terms.* Army Regulation AR 310-25. Washington, DC: Headquarters, Department of the Army, 1986.

—**SKELETON CREW** is the smallest number of men that can operate and care for equipment.

References

Department of Defense, U.S. Army. *Dictionary of United States Army Terms.* Army Regulation AR 310-25. Washington, DC: Headquarters, Department of the Army, 1986.

—**SKI MINE** is an antipersonnel, pressure-type mine designed for emplacement in ski trails. *See also:* Mine Warfare.

References

Department of Defense, U.S. Army. *Dictionary of United States Army Terms.* Army Regulation AR 310-25. Washington, DC: Headquarters, Department of the Army, 1986.

—**SKILL** identifies a requirement and an officer possessing specialized skills to perform duties of specific position that may require significant education, training, and experience. A skill can be related to more than one branch or functional area. An officer may have more than one skill. *See also:* Area of Concentration, Branch, Functional Area.

References

Department of Defense, U.S. Army. *Dictionary of United States Army Terms.* Army Regulation AR 310-25. Washington, DC: Headquarters, Department of the Army, 1986.

—**SKILL EVALUATION TEST** is a performance-oriented written test that is used to evaluate a soldier's military occupational specialty and skill level proficiency in performing the soldier's manual tasks. Results of the test provide objective information on soldier strengths and weaknesses for the commander to use when making training management decisions. *See also:* Skill Qualification Test.

References

Department of Defense, U.S. Army. *Training for Mobilization and War.* Field Manual FM 25-5. Washington, DC: Headquarters, Department of the Army, 1985.

—**SKILL LEVEL** is a level of proficiency required to perform a specific military job and the level of proficiency at which an individual qualifies in that military occupational specialty.

References

Department of Defense, U.S. Army. *Dictionary of United States Army Terms.* Army Regulation AR 310-25. Washington, DC: Headquarters, Department of the Army, 1986.

—**SKILL PROGRESSION COURSE** is a course designed to train military personnel in skills related to a specific military occupational specialty. This is training that provides commissioned officers, warrant officers, and enlisted personnel with the knowledge and skills they need to perform at higher skill levels or in supervisory positions. Included are officer advanced courses, senior warrant officer courses, and primary, basic, advanced, and senior level noncommissioned officer education system courses.

References

Department of Defense, U.S. Army. *Individual Military Education and Training.* Army Regulation AR 350-1. Washington, DC: Headquarters, Department of the Army, 1987.

—**SKILL QUALIFICATION TEST (SQT)** is a formally administered written performance-oriented test that provides an indication of a soldier's proficiency in a military occupational specialty and skill level. The results are used for training and personnel management purposes. *See also:* Skill Evaluation Test.

References

Department of Defense, U.S. Army. *Army Forces Training.* Army Regulation AR 350-41. Washington, DC: Headquarters, Department of the Army, 1986.

———. *Enlisted Personnel Management System.* Army Regulation AR 600-200. Washington, DC: Headquarters, Department of the Army, 1984.

—**SKIN DECON** is a basic soldier survival skill that involves removing contamination from exposed skin. *See also:* Skin Decon Technique.

References
Department of Defense, U.S. Army. *NBC Operations*. Field Manual FM 3-100. Washington, DC: Headquarters, Department of the Army, 1985.

—**SKIN DECON TECHNIQUE** is the process of removing or neutralizing contamination on the skin within one minute of contamination to prevent it from penetrating the skin.

References
Department of Defense, U.S. Army. *NBC Decontamination*. Field Manual FM 3-5. Washington, DC: Headquarters, Department of the Army, 1985.

—**SKIRMISHER'S TRENCH** (HASTY) is a shallow position that provides a hasty prone fighting position for the individual soldier. When an immediate shelter from enemy fire is needed and existing defilade firing positions are not available, soldiers lie prone or on their side, scrape the soil with an entrenching tool, and pile the soil in a low parapet between themselves and the enemy. In this manner, a shallow body-length pit is quickly formed in all but the hardest ground. The trench is oriented so it is oblique to enemy fire. A soldier presents a low silhouette in this type of position and is protected to a limited extent from small caliber fire.

References
Department of Defense, U.S. Army. *Survivability*. Field Manual FM 5-103. Washington, DC: Headquarters, Department of the Army, 1985.

—**SKIRTING ARMOR** is the outermost plate or piece of a spaced armor structure.

References
Department of Defense, U.S. Army. *Dictionary of United States Army Terms*. Army Regulation AR 310-25. Washington, DC: Headquarters, Department of the Army, 1986.

—**SKY COVER** is the portion of the sky covered completely by clouds and obscurations.

References
Department of Defense, U.S. Army. *Weather Support for Army Tactical Operations*. Field Manual FM 34-81. Washington, DC: Headquarters, Department of the Army, 1984.

—**SKY GLOW** is illumination caused by weapon firing from a defiladed position. *See also:* Defilade.

References
Department of Defense, U.S. Army. *Dictionary of United States Army Terms*. Army Regulation AR 310-25. Washington, DC: Headquarters, Department of the Army, 1986.

—**SLANT PLANE** in artillery, is the plane containing the target course line and the pintle center of the gun.

References
Department of Defense, U.S. Army. *Dictionary of United States Army Terms*. Army Regulation AR 310-25. Washington, DC: Headquarters, Department of the Army, 1986.

—**SLANT RANGE.** (1) Slant range is the distance in a straight line from the center of a burst of weapon at the instant of detonation (zero point) to a target. (2) Slant range is the distance in a straight line from a gun, point of observation, or radar set to a target, especially an air target.

References
Department of Defense, U.S. Army. *Dictionary of United States Army Terms*. Army Regulation AR 310-25. Washington, DC: Headquarters, Department of the Army, 1986.

—**SLANT RANGE VISIBILITY** is the maximum distance on a slant at which ordinary objects can be seen and identified. This visibility is normally observed from an airborne aircraft, though it can be a surface-observed parameter.

References
Department of Defense, U.S. Army. *Weather Support for Army Tactical Operations*. Field Manual FM 34-81. Washington, DC: Headquarters, Department of the Army, 1984.

—**SLATE** is a report used by the military services for listing petroleum requirements. The petroleum products written slate is a stock status and planned requirements report compiled monthly by an overseas commander to requisition bulk petroleum products and certain packaged fuel. The petroleum products message slate is an advanced requirements report that is submitted by electrical transmission by the joint petroleum office and later is confirmed by a written slate. *See also:* Slated Items.

References
Department of Defense, U.S. Army. *Dictionary of United States Army Terms*. Army Regulation AR 310-25. Washington, DC: Headquarters, Department of the Army, 1986.

—**SLATED ITEMS** are bulk petroleum and packaged items that are requisitioned for overseas use by means of a consolidated requirement document, prepared and submitted through joint petroleum office channels. Packaged petroleum items are requisitioned in accordance with normal requisitioning procedures. *See also:* Slate.

References

Department of Defense, Joint Chiefs of Staff. *Department of Defense Dictionary of Military and Related Terms.* Washington, DC: GPO, 1986.

—**SLATING** is the process that matches officers who have been selected through the centralized command or school selection system to a specific command or school.

References

Department of Defense, U.S. Army. *Officer Assignment Policies, Details, and Transfers.* Army Regulation AR 614-100. Washington, DC: Headquarters, Department of the Army, 1984.

—**SLEEVE EMBLEM** is a cloth insignia worn on the sleeve to indicate the wearer's status. Civilian employees and civilian members of military missions wear sleeve emblems.

References

Department of Defense, U.S. Army. *Dictionary of United States Army Terms.* Army Regulation AR 310-25. Washington, DC: Headquarters, Department of the Army, 1986.

—**SLEEVE TARGET** is a tubular open-ended bag that fills with air and bellies out when towed by an aircraft in flight. It is used as a target.

References

Department of Defense, U.S. Army. *Dictionary of United States Army Terms.* Army Regulation AR 310-25. Washington, DC: Headquarters, Department of the Army, 1986.

—**SLEIGH** is part of a gun carriage that supports the recoil mechanism and barrel of the gun, and slides with the gun on recoil, guiding it in runways in the cradle.

References

Department of Defense, U.S. Army. *Dictionary of United States Army Terms.* Army Regulation AR 310-25. Washington, DC: Headquarters, Department of the Army, 1986.

—**SLICE** is an average logistic planning factor used to obtain estimates of the requirements for personnel and materiel. A personnel slice, for example, generally consists of the total strength of the stated basic combatant elements, plus its proportional share of all supporting and higher headquarters personnel.

References

Department of Defense, Joint Chiefs of Staff. *Department of Defense Dictionary of Military and Related Terms.* Washington, DC: GPO, 1986.

—**SLIGHTLY WOUNDED** is a person who has been wounded, but who is able to sit or walk. *See also:* Medical Treatment.

References

Department of Defense, Joint Chiefs of Staff. *Department of Defense Dictionary of Military and Related Terms.* Washington, DC: GPO, 1986.

—**SLING ARMS** is to place a rifle or another weapon in a position with its sling over the carrier's shoulder.

References

Department of Defense, U.S. Army. *Dictionary of United States Army Terms.* Army Regulation AR 310-25. Washington, DC: Headquarters, Department of the Army, 1986.

—**SLIVERS** are pieces of propellant grains of triangular cross section that remain unburned when the web of multi-perforated grains has been burned through. Slivers are also produced by unburned portions of a combustible cartridge case.

References

Department of Defense, U.S. Army. *Dictionary of United States Army Terms.* Army Regulation AR 310-25. Washington, DC: Headquarters, Department of the Army, 1986.

—**SLOPE** is the angle a surface makes with the horizontal (measured in either percent or degrees).

References

Department of Defense, U.S. Army. *Dictionary of United States Army Terms.* Army Regulation AR 310-25. Washington, DC: Headquarters, Department of the Army, 1986.

—**SLOPE OF FALL** is the ratio between the drop of a projectile and its horizontal movement. It is the tangent of the angle of fall.

References

Department of Defense, U.S. Army. *Dictionary of United States Army Terms.* Army Regulation AR 310-25. Washington, DC: Headquarters, Department of the Army, 1986.

—**SLOW FIRE** is a type of gunnery fire used to instruct beginners and in record practice. In slow fire, no time limit is set for completing a score. *See also:* Rapid Fire.

References

Department of Defense, U.S. Army. *Dictionary of United States Army Terms.* Army Regulation AR 310-25. Washington, DC: Headquarters, Department of the Army, 1986.

—**SMALL ARMS** are all arms, including automatic weapons, up to and including 20 millimeter (.787 inch) weapons. *See also:* Small Arms Ammunition.

References

Department of Defense, Joint Chiefs of Staff. *Department of Defense Dictionary of Military and Related Terms.* Washington, DC: GPO, 1986.

—**SMALL ARMS AMMUNITION** is ammunition for small arms (i.e., all ammunition up to and including 20 millimeters, or .787 inches).

References

Department of Defense, Joint Chiefs of Staff. *Department of Defense Dictionary of Military and Related Terms.* Washington, DC: GPO, 1986.

—**SMALL BORE PRACTICE** is practice in firing with small arms using .22 caliber ammunition instead of the standard service rounds.

References

Department of Defense, U.S. Army. *Dictionary of United States Army Terms.* Army Regulation AR 310-25. Washington, DC: Headquarters, Department of the Army, 1986.

—**SMALL-LOT STORAGE** is generally a quantity of less than one pallet stack, stacked to maximum storage height. The term refers to a lot consisting of from one container to two or more pallet loads, but is not of sufficient quantity to form a complete pallet column.

References

Department of Defense, Joint Chiefs of Staff. *Department of Defense Dictionary of Military and Related Terms.* Washington, DC: GPO, 1986.

—**SMALL MINE BLOCK** is a group of mines, from a few clusters to up to a few dozen mines. The block is usually not laid in a pattern and is intended to constitute a narrow barrier across a road, a crossing, a defile, or other area. *See also:* Mine Warfare.

References

Department of Defense, U.S. Army. *Mine/Countermine Operations at the Company Level.* Field Manual FM 20-32. Washington, DC: Headquarters, Department of the Army, 1976.

—**SMALL OF THE STOCK** is the part of the stock on a small arms weapon that is ordinarily gripped by the right hand. It is the part of the stock immediately behind the receiver and trigger assembly, and is the pistol grip in some styles of stocks.

References

Department of Defense, U.S. Army. *Dictionary of United States Army Terms.* Army Regulation AR 310-25. Washington, DC: Headquarters, Department of the Army, 1986.

—**SMALL-SCALE MAP** is a map having a scale smaller than 1:600,000. *See also:* Map.

References

Department of Defense, Joint Chiefs of Staff. *Department of Defense Dictionary of Military and Related Terms.* Washington, DC: GPO, 1986.

—**SMOKE.** (1) Smoke is a particulate of solid or liquid particles of low vapor pressure that settles slowly under gravity. In general, smoke particles range downward from about 5 micrometers in diameter to less than 0.1 micrometer in diameter. (2) Smoke is a suspension of small liquid or solid particles in air. (3) Smoke is a filling for smoke munitions (e.g., bombs, shells, and grenades). (4) Smoke is to produce signaling or screening smoke with any munition. (5) Smoke, in a general sense, is any artificial aerosol. Smoke is classified in three general categories: identification smoke, obscuration smoke, and screening smoke. *See also:* Identification Smoke, Obscuration Smoke, Screening Smoke, Smoke Screen.

References

Department of Defense, U.S. Army. *Deliberate Smoke Operations.* Field Manual FM 3-50. Washington, DC: Headquarters, Department of the Army, 1984.

———. *Operational Terms and Symbols.* Field Manual FM 101-5-1. Washington, DC: Headquarters, Department of the Army, 1985.

—**SMOKE AGENT** is a substance that, through its chemical or physical properties, produces a screening or signal smoke. *See also:* Smoke Screen.

References

Department of Defense, U.S. Army. *Deliberate Smoke Operations.* Field Manual FM 3-50. Washington, DC: Headquarters, Department of the Army, 1984.

—**SMOKE AND FLASH DEFILADE** (1) Smoke and flash defilade is a condition in which the smoke and flash of a gun are concealed from enemy observation by an intervening obstacle (e.g., a hill or ravine). (2) Smoke and flash defilade is the vertical distance by which the smoke and flash of a gun are concealed from enemy observation.

References

Department of Defense, U.S. Army. *Deliberate Smoke Operations.* Field Manual FM 3-50. Washington, DC: Headquarters, Department of the Army, 1984.

—**SMOKE BLANKET** is a dense concentration of smoke established over and around friendly areas to protect them from air visual observation and visual precision bombing attack, or established over enemy area to protect attacking aircraft from air defense fire. Blankets can also be used at night to prevent enemy-observed air attack by flare light. *See also:* Smoke Screen, Terminal Phase.

References

Department of Defense, U.S. Army. *Deliberate Smoke Operations.* Field Manual FM 3-50. Washington, DC: Headquarters, Department of the Army, 1984.

—**SMOKE CANDLE** is a munition that produces smoke by vaporizing fog oil. *See also:* Smoke Screen.

References

Department of Defense, U.S. Army. *Deliberate Smoke Operations.* Field Manual FM 3-50. Washington, DC: Headquarters, Department of the Army, 1984.

—**SMOKE CONTROL POINT** is the point from which the technical control of a smoke screen is exercised. *See also:* Smoke Screen.

References

Department of Defense, U.S. Army. *Deliberate Smoke Operations.* Field Manual FM 3-50. Washington, DC: Headquarters, Department of the Army, 1984.

—**SMOKE CURTAIN** is a vertical smoke screen placed between friendly and hostile troops or installations to prevent enemy ground observation. *See also:* Smoke Screen.

References

Department of Defense, U.S. Army. *Deliberate Smoke Operations.* Field Manual FM 3-50. Washington, DC: Headquarters, Department of the Army, 1984.

—**SMOKE EMPLACEMENT** is a fortified or prepared position for a mechanical smoke generator or smoke pot. *See also:* Smoke Screen.

References

Department of Defense, U.S. Army. *Deliberate Smoke Operations.* Field Manual FM 3-50. Washington, DC: Headquarters, Department of the Army, 1984.

—**SMOKE GENERATOR** is a mechanical device that vaporizes fog oil and releases it to condense in the air as a white smoke that is useful for large-area screening. *See also:* Smoke Screen.

References

Department of Defense, U.S. Army. *Deliberate Smoke Operations.* Field Manual FM 3-50. Washington, DC: Headquarters, Department of the Army, 1984.

—**SMOKE HAZE** is a light concentration of smoke placed over friendly installations to restrict accurate enemy observation and fire but it is not dense enough to hamper friendly operations. The density of the haze is equal to that of a light fog. *See also:* Smoke Screen.

References

Department of Defense, U.S. Army. *Deliberate Smoke Operations.* Field Manual FM 3-50. Washington, DC: Headquarters, Department of the Army, 1984.

—**SMOKE LINE** is a series of smoke positions or emplacements established to accomplish a mission. It may be fixed or mobile, straight or irregular. *See also:* Smoke Screen.

References

Department of Defense, U.S. Army. *Deliberate Smoke Operations.* Field Manual FM 3-50. Washington, DC: Headquarters, Department of the Army, 1984.

—**SMOKE MUNITION** is a device that produces a screening or signal smoke. *See also:* Smoke Screen.

References

Department of Defense, U.S. Army. *Deliberate Smoke Operations.* Field Manual FM 3-50. Washington, DC: Headquarters, Department of the Army, 1984.

—**SMOKE POSITION** is the location of a smoke pot or mechanical smoke generator. *See also:* Smoke Screen.

References

Department of Defense, U.S. Army. *Deliberate Smoke Operations.* Field Manual FM 3-50. Washington, DC: Headquarters, Department of the Army, 1984.

—**SMOKE POT** is an expendable bucket or pot-like ammunition that produces a dense smoke by burning a smoke mixture. *See also:* Smoke Screen.

References

Department of Defense, U.S. Army. *Deliberate Smoke Operations.* Field Manual FM 3-50. Washington, DC: Headquarters, Department of the Army, 1984.

—**SMOKE PROJECTILE,** or smoke shell, is any projectile containing a smoke-producing agent released on impact or burst. *See also:* Smoke Screen.

References

Department of Defense, U.S. Army. *Deliberate Smoke Operations.* Field Manual FM 3-50. Washington, DC: Headquarters, Department of the Army, 1984.

—**SMOKE SCREEN** is smoke placed on the battlefield to deceive or confuse the enemy as to the activities of friendly maneuvering elements. It is used in friendly operational areas or between friendly and enemy forces. It degrades enemy ground and aerial observation and defeats or degrades enemy electro-optical systems. Screening smoke also conceals ground maneuver, breaching, and recovery operations, key assembly areas, and supply routes. The three types of smoke screens are blanket, screen, and curtain. *See also:* Smoke, Smoke Agent, Smoke Blanket, Smoke Candle, Smoke Control Point, Smoke Curtain, Smoke Emplacement, Smoke Generator, Smoke Haze, Smoke Line, Smoke Munition, Smoke Position, Smoke Pot, Smoke Projectile, Smoke Screen, Smoke Shell.

References

Department of Defense, U.S. Army. *Deliberate Smoke Operations.* Field Manual FM 3-50. Washington, DC: Headquarters, Department of the Army, 1984.

———. *NBC Operations.* Field Manual FM 3-100. Washington, DC: Headquarters, Department of the Army, 1985.

—**SMOKE SHELL.** *See:* Smoke Projectile.

—**SMOKELESS PROPELLENT** is a propellent for which there is little or no visible smoke on firing.

References

Department of Defense, U.S. Army. *Dictionary of United States Army Terms.* Army Regulation AR 310-25. Washington, DC: Headquarters, Department of the Army, 1986.

—**SNAKE** is a specially constructed explosive charge used to clear paths through minefields. It is constructed so that it may be pulled near the obstacle, then pushed into place by a tank. *See also:* Mine Warfare.

References

Department of Defense, U.S. Army. *Dictionary of United States Army Terms.* Army Regulation AR 310-25. Washington, DC: Headquarters, Department of the Army, 1986.

—**SNIPERSCOPE** is a device that combines a sniperscope and a carbine or other firearm. This enables the operator to see and shoot at targets in the dark. *See also:* Snooperscope.

References

Department of Defense, U.S. Army. *Dictionary of United States Army Terms.* Army Regulation AR 310-25. Washington, DC: Headquarters, Department of the Army, 1986.

—**SNOOPERSCOPE** is a hand-carried device that combines a source of infrared rays with a viewer to enable the operator to see in the dark. *See also:* Sniperscope.

References

Department of Defense, U.S. Army. *Dictionary of United States Army Terms.* Army Regulation AR 310-25. Washington, DC: Headquarters, Department of the Army, 1986.

—**SNOW DEPTH** is the actual depth of snow on the ground at any instant during a storm or after any single snowstorm or a series of snowstorms.

References
Department of Defense, U.S. Army. *Direction Finding Operations.* Field Manual FM 34-88. Washington, DC: Headquarters, Department of the Army, 1984.

————. *Long-Range Reconnaissance Patrol Company.* Field Manual FM 31-18. Washington, DC: Headquarters, Department of the Army, 1968.

—**SOCIOLOGICAL INTELLIGENCE,** one of the eight components of strategic intelligence, is concerned with social stratification, value systems, beliefs, and other social characteristics of selected populations. The Department of State is the primary producer of sociological intelligence.

General

The Intelligence Community believes that sociology is the study of society, as well as of the groups within society, their composition, organization, purposes, and habits, and the role of the individual in relation to social institutions. Each foreign society should be viewed as a distinctive culture with its own combination of social and cultural features, including history, language, and values.

From this, the Community believes that the factors influencing the group behavior of human beings are best studied through examining a nation's social institutions and culture. These include social groupings with special reference to stratification and mobility, the churches, national morality, and taboos; national traditions and habits of thought; and slow or rapid trends toward change.

Factors that affect the cohesion and stability of societies may be seen in the means whereby societies transmit information, influence, and authority—which may be through a variety of social channels ranging from distinctive ways of inculcating values and habits in rearing children to elaborate systems of mass communication for developing viewpoints and attitudes.

For strategic intelligence purposes, the Intelligence Community states that the sociological relating to groups of people may be studied under six headings: demography (i.e., the study of population, manpower and labor); social characteristics; public opinion; education; religion; and public welfare.

Demography

Demographic intelligence consists primarily of statistics that describe the size, distribution, and characteristics of a population, together with the changes in these aspects. Such statistics are normally derived from censuses and vital statistics covering the entire population being described or from a survey of a sample of the population. Estimates derived in other ways have proven to be highly inaccurate and are of little value for intelligence purposes. Fortunately, the international apparatus for gathering and integrating these statistics has steadily improved, and in general it can be said that from the point of view of intelligence, the problems involved are more those of interpretation than of collection.

On another level, demography should be understood to include the study of factors that affect rates of population growth. Social conditions, such as the standard of living, may have marked effects. Medical conditions may diminish death rates with striking results. Governmental policies, furthermore, may strengthen or weaken these factors, or, as through propaganda and suggestion, exert influence upon trends in the population. Information about these factors is less readily available and they require attention in the field.

Certainly the size and rate of growth of the total population, taken in conjunction with resources, trade and existing technology, determine the level of economic well-being in the country. The rate of population growth and the rate of economic growth determine the rate of per capita economic growth. The level of economic well-being and the rate of per capita economic growth are, in turn, major factors in a country's military potential and political power.

Statistics on the characteristics and the distribution of the population can be compiled by using a variety of categories. Among the most useful are age-and-sex groups, geographical groups, geographical categories, proportions living in urban and rural areas, ethnic categories, educational categories, proportion participating in the labor force, and the distribution of the labor force among the various types of economic activity. Among the most important characteristics of a population are its birth and death rates, its rates of marriage and divorce, and its rates of internal and external migration.

In addition to the significance of these rates for population growth, they can provide the demographic specialist with a wealth of information about the economic, social, and cultural characteristics of the population to which they refer.

Social Characteristics

Intelligence on this subject includes considering both the physical and cultural characteristics of a people and their national attitudes and social organization. Physical characteristics of most peoples can be readily studied in reference works, but intelligence should take note of variable factors such as physical vigor, and perhaps also stature and carriage. The cultural characteristics include command and distribution of languages and dialects; social stratification, including cleavages and divisions and their effects on the political and military solidarity of the national society; and trends in the composition and size of social groups and levels. Business and professional groups, secret societies, including revolutionary movements, and military and aristocratic orders are considered under this heading.

Public Opinion

Public opinion is the expression of attitudes of significant segments of the population on questions of general interest to the state and society. It is not monolithic, since it may be made up of many conflicting viewpoints. Nor should it necessarily be identified with a majority consensus on a distinctive set of opinions. Intelligence should therefore pay attention to the opinions of minority groups, especially of groups that are capable of exerting pressure on governments by virtue of their organized energy, politico-economic power, para-military resources, special influence, personal contacts, or articulateness.

Given understanding of the basic attitudes that are prevalent in a society, propagandists, particularly in totalitarian countries, can direct the flow of opinion into channels that lead to powerful mass movements, forceful national action, and even war. The role and formulation of public opinion (and its political consequences) vary considerably in different societies. Consequently, it is important to secure intelligence on both the basic social attitudes of a country and the ease with which these attitudes are directed toward certain preconceived aims or are susceptible to being so directed.

The mechanism that shapes opinion requires observation at three levels. *Intelligence production* is largely a matter of biographic intelligence about editors, writers, and information staffs, including specialized advisers such as psychologists. *Dissemination* is accomplished by the media, including the press, radio, magazines, movies, and educational institutions, but front organizations and other interest or pressure groups may also play an important role. Finally, *the content of the information or propaganda* naturally caps the structure. Sophisticated techniques have been developed for analyzing the substance of public opinion, and the intelligence collector must take account of those techniques in order to avoid many pitfalls.

Education

A study of the level of education is required for estimating the possible future progress of a nation in political development, economics, and science. Public policy concerning education is one major element of this estimate, because public authorities at the local or often the national level closely supervise the school system and some paramilitary training at an early stage. Intelligence focuses on the general level and character of education in a country and the quality of its secondary schools, trade schools, colleges, and graduate schools. It includes statistics on literacy, the philosophy of education and training, the quality of artistic and cultural interest, the number of students who go to foreign countries, the extent to which foreign languages are taught, and the values and attitudes that the schools seek to inculcate.

Religion

The distribution of adherents to various religions, the presence or absence of an official state church, the attitude of church groups toward the government, and the attitude of the government toward religious groups have an important bearing on national psychology, public opinion, and education. The type of religious organization and the extent to which religious values and codes are operative also must be considered.

Some religions glorify war, others vilify it, and there are myriad attitudes between these two extremes. The intelligence analyst tries to remain constantly aware of the enormous extent to which religion pervades every aspect of life in certain countries. These countries' leaders and their policies cannot be understood outside of the context of their religion.

Public Welfare

Public welfare concerns matters such as health, living conditions, organizations for social service, social insurance, and social problems that have a bearing on national strength and stability. These problems include the extent and significance of divorce, broken homes, slums, narcotics, crime, and the ways in which a society copes with these problems.

Intelligence in the field of public welfare has many uses outside the purely sociological interest. National health, for example, is a key to the vitality of a nation and its people. It affects the industrial potential of a nation, the effects of a possible blockade and restrictive buying programs, and the degree to which a nation may withstand the rigors of war. Moreover, the status of public health and sanitization in a foreign country would be of paramount importance to U.S. planning if U.S. troops were required to conduct operations there. *See also:* Strategic Intelligence.

References

Clauser, Jerome K., and Weir, Sandra M. *Intelligence Research Methodology.* State College, PA: HRB-Singer, 1975.

—**SOFT MISSILE BASE** is a launching base that is not protected against the attack of nuclear weapons. *See also:* Nuclear Warfare.

References

Department of Defense, Joint Chiefs of Staff. *Department of Defense Dictionary of Military and Related Terms.* Washington, DC: GPO, 1986.

—**SOFT TARGET** is a target that is not protected against the blast, heat, and radiation produced by nuclear explosions. There are many degrees of softness. Some missiles and aircraft, for example, are built to ward off certain effects, but they are "soft" compared with shelters and silos. *See also:* Nuclear Warfare.

References

Collins, John M. *U.S.-Soviet Military Balance, 1980-1985.* Washington, DC: Congressional Research Service, 1985.

—**SOLDIER, ENLISTED PERSON,** is an enlisted man or woman in the Army. The term includes all persons enlisted in any component of the Army, in active federal service, or active duty for training unless otherwise indicated or obviously inappropriate. *See also:* Member, Enlisted Person.

References

Department of Defense, U.S. Army. *Enlisted Personnel.* Army Regulation AR 635-200. Washington, DC: Headquarters, Department of the Army, 1984.

—**SOLDIER SUPPORT MISSION AREA** includes the items that directly support the individual soldier. This mission area includes organizational clothing and individual equipment, chemical-biological defense equipment, night vision devices, and individual weapons.

References

Weapons Systems: U.S. Army, Navy, and Air Force Directory, 1986—1988. Washington, DC: DCP, 1986.

—**SOLDIER'S AND SAILOR'S CIVIL RELIEF ACT** is a federal statute that gives civil and legal protection to members of the Armed Forces by suspending the enforcement of certain civil liabilities. It is also called the Civil Relief Act.

References

Department of Defense, U.S. Army. *Dictionary of United States Army Terms.* Army Regulation AR 310-25. Washington, DC: Headquarters, Department of the Army, 1986.

—**SOLDIER'S DEPOSITS** are funds of enlisted personnel deposited with a finance and accounting officer through their personnel officer.

References

Department of Defense, U.S. Army. *Dictionary of United States Army Terms.* Army Regulation AR 310-25. Washington, DC: Headquarters, Department of the Army, 1986.

—**SOLDIER'S MANUALS** are a series of field manuals that describe the skills a soldier must be able to perform to be proficient in his military occupational specialty. They contain standardized training objectives for critical individual tasks in a given military occupational specialty and skill level. Commanders and soldiers use the manuals to plan training, arrange for training transport, and evaluate training and proficiency. Trainers use them to conduct training and to prepare soldiers for qualifying examinations. Soldiers use them to prepare for all aspects of their military occupational specialty.

References
Department of Defense, U.S. Army. *Individual Military Education and Training.* Army Regulation AR 350-1. Washington, DC: Headquarters, Department of the Army, 1986.

————. *The Rifle Squads (Mechanized and Light Infantry).* Training Circular TC 7-1. Washington, DC: Headquarters, Department of the Army, 1976.

————. *Unit Training Management.* Field Manual FM 25-2. Washington, DC: Headquarters, Department of the Army, 1984.

—SOLDIER'S TRAINING PUBLICATIONS (STPs) are replacing field manuals as the publication medium for soldiers. They present tasks for individual training and unit evaluation. They include soldier's manuals, job books, and trainer's guides.

References
Department of Defense, U.S. Army. *Army Forces Training.* Army Regulation AR 350-41. Washington, DC: Headquarters, Department of the Army, 1986.

————. *Individual Military Education and Training.* Army Regulation AR 350-1. Washington, DC: Headquarters, Department of the Army, 1986.

————. *Training for Mobilization and War.* Field Manual FM 25- 5. Washington, DC: Headquarters, Department of the Army, 1985.

—SONIC DECEPTION is the projection of sounds to produce battlefield noises. It is directed against the enemy's sound ranging set and the human ear, and is used to support a deception story. *See also:* Deception.

References
Department of Defense, U.S. Army. *Tactical Deception.* Field Manual FM 90-2. Washington, DC: Headquarters, Department of the Army, 1978.

—SORTIE is the set of photographs taken on a photographic mission. *See also:* Aerial Reconnaissance.

References
Department of Defense, U.S. Army. *Dictionary of United States Army Terms.* Army Regulation AR 310-25. Washington, DC: Headquarters, Department of the Army, 1986.

—SORTIE (AIR). (1) A sortie is a sudden attack made from a defensive position. In this context, it sometimes called a sally. (2) A sortie is an operational flight by one aircraft.

References
Department of Defense, U.S. Army. *Operational Terms and Symbols.* Field Manual FM 101-5-1. Washington, DC: Headquarters, Department of the Army, 1985.

—SORTIE NUMBER, in photoreconnaissance and imagery intelligence collection, is a reference number used to identify all the imagery taken by all of the sensors during one air reconnaissance sortie. *See also:* Aerial Reconnaissance, Sortie.

References
Department of Defense, U.S. Army. *Dictionary of United States Army Terms.* Army Regulation AR 310-25. Washington, DC: Headquarters, Department of the Army, 1986.

—SOUND AND FLASH (RANGING) are two distinct and separate but supplementary systems of locating enemy weapons and secondarily, adjusting friendly counterfire by observation by sonic devices on the sound produced by the enemy weapons in firing; or by the friendly projectile in exploding; or by visual observation of the flash produced by the enemy weapon or friendly projectile.

References
Department of Defense, U.S. Army. *Dictionary of United States Army Terms.* Army Regulation AR 310-25. Washington, DC: Headquarters, Department of the Army, 1986.

—SOUND DISCIPLINE is observing the official restrictions on the sounds that may be made in a particular location. It is often applied near a listening or sound locator post.

References
Department of Defense, U.S. Army. *Dictionary of United States Army Terms.* Army Regulation AR 310-25. Washington, DC: Headquarters, Department of the Army, 1986.

—SOUND OFF is a command given at parade and guard mount when the band is to play a short series of chords before beginning to play the march.

References
Department of Defense, U.S. Army. *Dictionary of United States Army Terms.* Army Regulation AR 310-25. Washington, DC: Headquarters, Department of the Army, 1986.

—**SOUND RANGING** (SOUND LOCATING) is a method of locating the source of a sound (e.g., that of a gun report or a shell burst) by calculations based upon the intervals between the reception of the sound at various previously oriented microphone stations. *See also:* Sound Ranging Adjustment, Sound Ranging Plotting Board.

References

Department of Defense, U.S. Army. *Weather Support for Army Tactical Operations.* Field Manual FM 34-81. Washington, DC: Headquarters, Department of the Army, 1984.

—**SOUND-RANGING ADJUSTMENT** is the adjustment of the fire of a friendly gun or battery by sound-ranging methods applied to the sound of the gun's or battery's shell bursts.

References

Department of Defense, U.S. Army. *Dictionary of United States Army Terms.* Army Regulation AR 310-25. Washington, DC: Headquarters, Department of the Army, 1986.

—**SOUND RANGING PLOTTING BOARD** is a standard plotting board used to locate the source of a sound. *See also:* Plotting Board.

References

Department of Defense, U.S. Army. *Dictionary of United States Army Terms.* Army Regulation AR 310-25. Washington, DC: Headquarters, Department of the Army, 1986.

—**SOURCE.** (1) A source is a person, device, system, or activity from which intelligence information is obtained. (2) In clandestine activity, a source is an agent, normally a foreign national, who works for an intelligence activity. (3) In interrogation activities, a source is any person who furnishes intelligence information, either with or without the knowledge that the information is being used for intelligence purposes. (4) An uncontrolled source is a voluntary contributor of information who may or may not know that the information will be used for intelligence purposes. (5) Source, as defined by the Church Committee, is "a person, thing, or activity which provides intelligence information. In clandestine activities, the term applies to an agent or asset, normally a foreign national, being used in an intelligence activity for intelligence purposes. In interrogations, it refers to a person who furnishes intelligence information with or without

knowledge that the information is being used for intelligence purposes." *See also:* Human Source.

References

Clancy, Tom. *The Cardinal of the Kremlin.* New York: Putnam, 1988.

Department of Defense, Defense Intelligence College. *Glossary of Intelligence Terms and Definitions.* Washington, DC: DIC, 1987.

U.S. Congress. Senate. *Final Report of the Senate Select Committee to Study Government Operations With Respect to Intelligence Activities. Report 94-755. Book I, Foreign and Military Intelligence* (Church Committee Report). Washington, DC: GPO, 1976.

—**SOURCE EMISSION LISTS** are the amount of chemical agent that may be released at a particular point based upon the effects of natural dilution, ventilation, and meteorological conditions.

References

Department of Defense, U.S. Army. *Ammunition and Explosives Safety Standards.* Army Regulation AR 385-64. Washington, DC: Headquarters, Department of the Army, 1987.

—**SOURCE, MAINTENANCE, AND RECOVERY CODE** is a code indicating the parts that have been selected to satisfy maintenance or repair requirements. It is the most efficient and practical source or method of supplying a selected repair part.

References

Department of Defense, U.S. Army. *Dictionary of United States Army Terms.* Army Regulation AR 310-25. Washington, DC: Headquarters, Department of the Army, 1986.

—**SPACED ARMOR** is a protective armor consisting of two or more plates or pieces of the same or different material, with intervening unfilled space or spaces.

References

Department of Defense, U.S. Army. *Dictionary of United States Army Terms.* Army Regulation AR 310-25. Washington, DC: Headquarters, Department of the Army, 1986.

—**SPALL** are fragments that are torn from either the outer or the inner surface of an armor plate as a result of a complete or partial penetration of the armor by an explosive or projectile, or by the dynamic effects of an explosive charge.

References
Department of Defense, U.S. Army. *Dictionary of United States Army Terms.* Army Regulation AR 310-25. Washington, DC: Headquarters, Department of the Army, 1986.

—**SPAN OF DETONATION** (ATOMIC DEMOLITION MUNITION EMPLOYMENT) is the total period of time, resulting from a timer error, between the earliest and the latest possible detonation time. (1) Early time is the earliest possible time that an atomic demolition munition can detonate. (2) Fire time is the time that the atomic demolition munition will detonate if the timers function precisely without error. (3) Late time is the latest possible time that an atomic demolition munition can detonate. *See also:* Nuclear Warfare.

References
Department of Defense, Joint Chiefs of Staff. *Department of Defense Dictionary of Military and Related Terms.* Washington, DC: GPO, 1986.

—**SPAR BRIDGE** is a bridge that is built of timbers that are lashed together.

References
Department of Defense, U.S. Army. *Dictionary of United States Army Terms.* Army Regulation AR 310-25. Washington, DC: Headquarters, Department of the Army, 1986.

—**SPARE** is an individual part, subassembly, or assembly that is supplied for the maintenance of repair systems or equipment.

References
Department of Defense, Joint Chiefs of Staff. *Department of Defense Dictionary of Military and Related Terms.* Washington, DC: GPO, 1986.

—**SPECIAL ACTIVE DUTY FOR TRAINING HOURS** are full-time duty, on a voluntary basis, in the active federal military service of the United States under 10 U.S.C. § 672 (d) in connection with projects relating to the reserve components of the Armed Forces programs, including support of operations of training camps, training ships, and unit conversions to new weapons systems when the Secretary of the Army determines that appropriate personnel in the Active Army are not available for the duties to be performed. Such duties are essential to the organization and training programs of the reserve components, and such services are beyond that which the Active Army normally provides for the support of the reserve component programs.

References
Department of Defense, U.S. Army. *Dictionary of United States Army Terms.* Army Regulation AR 310-25. Washington, DC: Headquarters, Department of the Army, 1986.

—**SPECIAL ACTIVITIES** are the units and elements whose missions are to handle activities of an international, joint, liaison, diplomatic, political, research, or other special-purpose nature, including informational, recreational, and morale activities that are provided for the benefit of the Armed Forces as a whole.

References
Department of Defense, U.S. Army. *Dictionary of United States Army Terms.* Army Regulation AR 310-25. Washington, DC: Headquarters, Department of the Army, 1986.

—**SPECIAL AMMUNITION** are ammunition items so designated by the Department of the Army because of requirements for extraordinary control, handling, or security. This term includes

- Nuclear and nonnuclear warhead sections, atomic demolition munitions, nuclear projectiles, and associated spotting rounds, propelling charges, and repair parts;
- Missile bodies (except for missiles that combine high-density, low-maintenance, and conventional ammunition features), related components of missile bodies (less repair parts), and missile propellants, certain items that are supplied through special ammunition Class V channels (e.g., associated test and handling equipment and special tools);
- Lethal and incapacitating chemical agents and ammunition.

See also: Chemical Warfare, Nuclear Warfare, Special Ammunition Load, Special Ammunition Supply Point.

References
Department of Defense, U.S. Army. *Dictionary of United States Army Terms.* Army Regulation AR 310-25. Washington, DC: Headquarters, Department of the Army, 1986.

—**SPECIAL AMMUNITION LOAD** is the specific quantity of special ammunition to be carried by a delivery unit. Establishing and replenishing this load after each expenditure are command decisions and depend on the mission, the tactical and logistical situation, and the capacity of the unit to transport and to use the load. It may vary from day to day and among similar delivery units. *See also:* Special Ammunition.

References

Department of Defense, U.S. Army. *Dictionary of United States Army Terms.* Army Regulation AR 310-25. Washington, DC: Headquarters, Department of the Army, 1986.

—**SPECIAL AMMUNITION SUPPLY POINT** (SASP) is a mobile supply point where special ammunition is stored and issued to delivery points. *See also:* Special Ammunition.

References

Department of Defense, U.S. Army. *Support Operations: Echelons Above Corps.* Field Manual FM 100-16. Washington, DC: Headquarters, Department of the Army, 1986.

—**SPECIAL AREA** is a vital area that is to be defended by artillery over which friendly aircraft are prohibited from flying at all times.

References

Department of Defense, U.S. Army. *Dictionary of United States Army Terms.* Army Regulation AR 310-25. Washington, DC: Headquarters, Department of the Army, 1986.

—**SPECIAL BACKGROUND INVESTIGATION** (SBI) is an inquiry into an individual's background history. In addition to the information verified for a background investigation, the subject's employment and records are checked for fifteen years and his reputation is checked through visits to his neighborhood. When completed, the SBI meets the investigative requirements for access to sensitive compartmented information. *See also:* Background Investigation, Sensitive Compartmented Information.

References

Allen, Thomas B., and Polmar, Norman. *Merchants of Treason: America's Secrets for Sale.* New York: Delacorte Press, 1988.

Department of Defense, U.S. Army. *Counterintelligence.* Field Manual FM 34-60. Washington, DC: Headquarters, Department of the Army, 1985.

—**SPECIAL BRANCHES** are a grouping of branches and officers who are primarily concerned with providing combat service support or administration to the Army as a whole but are managed separately from combat service support

branches. The special branches include Army Medical Department, Chaplains, and the Judge Advocate General. *See also:* Combat Service Support, Service.

References

Department of Defense, U.S. Army. *Officer Assignment Policies, Details, and Transfers.* Army Regulation AR 614-100. Washington, DC: Headquarters, Department of the Army, 1984.

————. *Overseas Service.* Army Regulation AR 614-30. Washington, DC: Headquarters, Department of the Army, 1984.

—**SPECIAL CAREER PROGRAMS** are programs of personnel management designed to develop and utilize officers who are particularly well-qualified in certain functional areas. These areas are of critical Army-wide importance, but do not fall within the development patterns of any single career branch.

References

Department of Defense, U.S. Army. *Dictionary of United States Army Terms.* Army Regulation AR 310-25. Washington, DC: Headquarters, Department of the Army, 1986.

—**SPECIAL CARGO** is cargo that requires special handling or protection (e.g., pyrotechnics and precision instruments).

References

Department of Defense, U.S. Army. *Transportation Reference Data.* Field Manual FM 55-15. Washington, DC: Headquarters, Department of the Army, 1986.

—**SPECIAL CATEGORY (SPECAT) MESSAGES** are messages identified with specific projects or subjects that require security protection or handling that is not guaranteed by the normal security classification. SPECAT messages must be handled and viewed only by specially cleared or authorized personnel.

References

Department of Defense, U.S. Army. *Dictionary of United States Army Terms.* Army Regulation AR 310-25. Washington, DC: Headquarters, Department of the Army, 1986.

—**SPECIAL CHEMICAL, BIOLOGICAL, AND RADIOLOGICAL SENTINEL** is a specially trained and equipped sentry who is posted at a protective shelter, contaminated area, or other critical installation to enforce chemical, biological, and radiological discipline in order to minimize the effects of an enemy chemical, biological, or radiological attack. *See also:* Biological Warfare, Chemical Warfare, Nuclear Warfare.

References
Department of Defense, U.S. Army. *Dictionary of United States Army Terms.* Army Regulation AR 310-25. Washington, DC: Headquarters, Department of the Army, 1986.

—**SPECIAL COMMUNICATIONS.** (1) Special communications are nontactical telecommunications systems, networks, facilities, service, and equipment used to support special commands and task forces or missions and programs. (2) Special communications are post and base communications, defense communications, system communications, or tactical communications.

References
Department of Defense, U.S. Army. *Dictionary of United States Army Terms.* Army Regulation AR 310-25. Washington, DC: Headquarters, Department of the Army, 1986.

—**SPECIAL CORRECTIONS.** (1) Special corrections is a term used in a fire message to indicate that an accurately computed sheaf is desired. (2) Special corrections is a fire command indicating that position corrections are to be applied to form a regular sheaf. *See also:* Sheaf.

References
Department of Defense, U.S. Army. *Dictionary of United States Army Terms.* Army Regulation AR 310-25. Washington, DC: Headquarters, Department of the Army, 1986.

—**SPECIAL COURT-MARTIAL** is a court-martial consisting of at least three members, having jurisdiction to try any person subject to military law for any crime or offense that is not capital but is made punishable by the Uniform Code of Military Justice. A special court-martial may impose sentences of not more than six months' confinement at hard labor and forfeitures of two-thirds pay per month for a like period, except that a bad conduct discharge may be imposed in addition to the authorized punishments when approved by the officer exercising general court-martial jurisdiction over the accused, and subject to review by the Judge Advocate General and appellate agencies in his office. *See also:* General Court-Martial, Summary Court-Martial.

References
Department of Defense, U.S. Army. *Dictionary of United States Army Terms.* Army Regulation AR 310-25. Washington, DC: Headquarters, Department of the Army, 1986.

—**SPECIAL DUTY** is duty performed with an organization other than the organization to which one is assigned, while continuing to be administered by, and reporting daily to, the organization of assignment. *See also:* Borrowed Military Manpower.

References
Department of Defense, U.S. Army. *Enlisted Personnel Management System.* Army Regulation AR 600-200. Washington, DC: Headquarters, Department of the Army, 1984.

—**SPECIAL FOOD ALLOWANCE** is a prescribed quantity of food, defined by components, quantity, or monetary value, that is required to support operational missions whenever the use of a basic daily food allowance is impracticable. *See also:* Basic Daily Food Allowance.

References
Department of Defense, U.S. Army. *Dictionary of United States Army Terms.* Army Regulation AR 310-25. Washington, DC: Headquarters, Department of the Army, 1986.

—**SPECIAL FORCES OPERATIONAL BASE (SFOB),** in unconventional warfare, is a provisional organization established within a friendly area by elements of a special forces group to provide command, administration, training, logistical support, and intelligence for operational apecial forces detachments and for any other forces that may be placed under its operational control.

References
Department of Defense, U.S. Army. *Operational Terms and Symbols.* Field Manual FM 101-5-1. Washington, DC: Headquarters, Department of the Army, 1985.

—**SPECIAL FUND** is a fund, restricted in use or expenditure to the purpose designated by law, into which U.S. government receipts are deposited. These receipts have come to the government from specific sources that are designated by law.

References
Department of Defense, U.S. Army. *Operational Terms and Symbols.* Field Manual FM 101-5-1. Washington, DC: Headquarters, Department of the Army, 1985.

—**SPECIAL GUARD** is a soldier or a group of soldiers detailed for various guard duties and who have not been assigned to the main guard. Guards of honor and other guards who are posted to protect personnel, as well as the interior guard of a command, are assigned to the special guard. *See also:* Guard.

References

Department of Defense, U.S. Army. *Operational Terms and Symbols.* Field Manual FM 101-5-1. Washington, DC: Headquarters, Department of the Army, 1985.

—**SPECIAL INTELLIGENCE (SI)** is an unclassified term used to describe a category of sensitive compartmented information. *See also:* Sensitive Compartmented Information.

References

Allen, Thomas B., and Polmar, Norman. *Merchants of Treason: America's Secrets for Sale.* New York: Delacorte Press, 1988.

Department of Defense, Defense Intelligence College. *Glossary of Intelligence Terms and Definitions.* Washington, DC: DIC, 1987.

—**SPECIAL INTELLIGENCE COMMUNICATIONS (SPINTCOMM)** is a communications network designed to handle all special intelligence and consists of the facilities under the operational and technical control of the chief of intelligence of each of the military departments, under the management of the Defense Intelligence Agency, and under the technical and security specification criteria that have been established and are monitored by the National Security Agency. *See also:* Sensitive Compartmented Information.

References

Department of Defense, Defense Intelligence College. *Glossary of Intelligence Terms and Definitions.* Washington, DC: DIC, 1987.

—**SPECIAL INVENTORY** is a scheduled physical inventory of a specific item as a result of a special requirement (e.g., a location audit) or for any reason deemed appropriate by the accountable activity.

References

Department of Defense, U.S. Army. *Operational Terms and Symbols.* Field Manual FM 101-5-1. Washington, DC: Headquarters, Department of the Army, 1985.

—**SPECIAL OPERATING AGENCY** is a headquarters that receives allocations from the Comptroller of the Army and has limited authority to suballocate funds to designated operating agencies under its command jurisdiction.

References

Department of Defense, U.S. Army. *Operational Terms and Symbols.* Field Manual FM 101-5-1. Washington, DC: Headquarters, Department of the Army, 1985.

—**SPECIAL OPERATIONS (SO)** are conducted by specially trained, equipped, and organized Department of Defense forces against strategic and tactical targets in pursuit of national military, political, economic, or psychological objectives. So operations may be conducted during peace or war. They may support conventional operations or may be waged independently if the use of conventional forces is either inappropriate or unfeasible. Sensitive peacetime operations, except for training, are normally authorized by the National Command Authority and are conducted either under its direction or under that of a designated commander. Special operations may include unconventional warfare, counterterrorist operations, collective security, psychological operations, and civil affairs measures. *See also:* Special Operations Forces.

References

Department of Defense, U.S. Army. *Operational Terms and Symbols.* Field Manual FM 101-5-1. Washington, DC: Headquarters, Department of the Army, 1985.

———. *Psychological Operations.* Field Manual FM 33-1. Washington, DC: Headquarters, Department of the Army, 1979.

—**SPECIAL OPERATIONS FORCES (SOF)** perform unconventional warfare. They consist of U.S. Army Special Forces, other special operating forces, or native insurgents. They operate deep in the enemy's rear area and can disrupt enemy operations by conducting either unconventional warfare or unilateral operations. Normally, preestablished command arrangements determine how the unified commander assigns missions to his SOF. SOF can also provide support to lower level commanders when their elements are located in such a commander's area of interest.

References

Department of Defense, U.S. Army. *The Army Terrorism Counteraction Program.* Army Regulation AR 525-13. Washington, DC: Headquarters, Department of the Army, 1988.

————. *Operations.* Field Manual FM 100-5. Washington, DC: Headquarters, Department of the Army, 1986.

—**SPECIAL PSYOP (PSYCHOLOGICAL OPERA-TIONS) STUDY,** in PSYOP, is a prescribed collection of specific information pertaining to a given area or element that is developed from available information and intelligence prior to or during hostilities. *See also:* Psychological Operations.

References

Department of Defense, U.S. Army. *Psychological Operations.* Field Manual FM 33-1. Washington, DC: Headquarters, Department of the Army, 1979.

—**SPECIAL PURPOSE AMMUNITION** includes white phosphorus and target practice rounds. Target practice rounds are used for gunnery practice. White phosphorus rounds are used to hide movement and mark targets, and are designed to burst when they hit, forming a thick white cloud of smoke. When white phosphorus hits the skin, it sticks and burns.

References

Department of Defense, U.S. Army. *Tank Gunnery.* Field Manual FM 17-12. Washington, DC: Headquarters, Department of the Army, 1984.

—**SPECIAL-PURPOSE VEHICLE** is a vehicle that incorporates a special chassis and design to meet a specialized requirement. *See also:* Vehicle.

References

Department of Defense, Joint Chiefs of Staff. *Department of Defense Dictionary of Military and Related Terms.* Washington, DC: GPO, 1986.

—**SPECIAL-PURPOSE WEAPONS,** which include fuel-air munitions and flamethrowers, disperse fuel into the atmosphere and form a fuel-air mixture that is detonated. The fuel is usually contained in a metal canister and is dispersed by detonating a central burster charge carried within the canister. Upon proper dispersion, the fuel-air mixture is detonated, and peak pressures within the detonated cloud reach 300 pounds per square inch. *See also:* Chemical Warfare.

References

Department of Defense, U.S. Army. *Survivability.* Field Manual FM 5-103. Washington, DC: Headquarters, Department of the Army, 1985.

—**SPECIAL QUALIFICATION IDENTIFIER** is a digit added to a military operational specialty code to identify the qualifications needed to perform a specific type of military activity over and above individual military occupational specialty requirements.

References

Department of Defense, U.S. Army. *Individual Military Education and Training.* Army Regulation AR 350-1. Washington, DC: Headquarters, Department of the Army, 1987.

—**SPECIAL REACTION TEAM (SRT)** is a specially trained team of military and security personnel who serve as the installation commander's primary response force in a major disruption or threat situation on the installation. The SRT is armed and equipped to isolate, contain, gather information concerning, and, if necessary, neutralize a special threat. Mission employment of the SRT may include resolving barricaded criminal situations, resolving sniper situations, rescuing hostages, apprehending suspects, and collecting and reporting intelligence during special threat situations.

References

Department of Defense, U.S. Army. *The Army Terrorism Counteraction Program.* Army Regulation AR 525-13. Washington, DC: Headquarters, Department of the Army, 1988.

—**SPECIAL SECURITY GROUP (SSG),** which controls the dissemination of sensitive compartmented information to the U.S. Army worldwide, became part of the U.S. Army Intelligence and Security Command in 1980. *See also:* Sensitive Compartmented Information.

References

Finnegan, John P. *Military Intelligence: A Picture History.* Arlington, VA: U.S. Army Intelligence and Security Command, 1984.

—**SPECIAL SECURITY OFFICER (SSO)** is the control point for security procedures within any activity that is authorized to have sensitive compartmented information. The most significant duties of the Special Security Officer are to:

- Supervise the operation of the Special Security Office and administer the sensitive compartmented information security program, including sensitive compartmented information security oversight for other local sensitive compartmented information facilities that are under his jurisdiction;
- Maintain all relevant directives, regulations, manuals, and guidelines needed to adequately fulfill the SSO responsibilities;
- Insure that sensitive compartmented information is properly used, accounted for, controlled, safeguarded, packaged, transmitted, and destroyed;
- Provide advice and assistance concerning sensitive compartmented information classification, control systems, sanitization, downgrading, decompartmentation, operational use, and emergency use;
- Insure that sensitive compartmented information is disseminated only to those who are authorized to have access to the material and have a need to know;
- Manage the sensitive compartmented information personnel, communications/TEMPEST, and physical security procedures and actions;
- Maintain the command's sensitive compartmented information billet structure;
- Conduct security briefings, education programs, indoctrinations and debriefings, obtain signed nondisclosure agreements and perform other related personnel security actions pertaining to sensitive compartmented information programs;
- Annually inspect all subordinate sensitive compartmented information facilities, document the inspection results, recommend corrective actions, and follow up on the corrective measures;
- Insure that each subordinate SSO and other security personnel perform an annual self-inspection of their facilities;
- Investigate security infractions, make recommendations, and prepare the required reports;
- Maintain listings of available products and assure the dissemination of products to authorized users;
- Provide privacy communications support to general/flag officers residing in or transiting temporarily at the installation;
- Maintain a telephone log of special security office personnel; and
- Develop a continuing security education training and awareness program.

See also: Sensitive Compartmented Information, Sensitive Compartmented Information Facility.

References

Department of Defense, Defense Intelligence College. *Glossary of Intelligence Terms and Definitions.* Washington, DC: DIC, 1987.

—**SPECIAL SECURITY OFFICER (SSO) SYSTEM** is a system through which the Director, Defense Intelligence Agency, the service intelligence chiefs, and the unified and specified commands perform their responsibilities concerning the security, use, and dissemination of sensitive compartmented information including both physical and electrical means. The acronym SSO is used to refer to both the office and the officer. *See also:* Sensitive Compartmented Information, Sensitive Compartmented Information Facility.

References

Department of Defense, Defense Intelligence College. *Glossary of Intelligence Terms and Definitions.* Washington, DC: DIC, 1987.

—**SPECIAL SENSOR** is an unclassified term that refers to a highly classified or controlled technical sensor.

References

Department of Defense, U.S. Army. *Support Operations: Echelons Above Corps.* Field Manual FM 100-16. Washington, DC: Headquarters, Department of the Army, 1986.

—**SPECIAL SHEAF**, in artillery, is any sheaf other than one that is parallel, converged, or open. *See also:* Sheaf.

References

Department of Defense, Joint Chiefs of Staff. *Department of Defense Dictionary of Military and Related Terms.* Washington, DC: GPO, 1986.

—**SPECIAL STAFF** is composed of all staff officers who have duties at a headquarters and are not included in the general (coordinating) staff group or in the personal staff group. The special staff includes certain technical specialists and heads of services (e.g., the quartermaster officer, the antiaircraft officer, or the transportation officer). *See also:* General Staff, Personal Staff, Special Staff Group, Staff.

References
Department of Defense, Joint Chiefs of Staff. *Department of Defense Dictionary of Military and Related Terms*. Washington, DC: GPO, 1986.

—**SPECIAL STAFF GROUP** is composed of special staff officers who assist the commander in professional, technical, and other functional areas. They generally are organized into sections according to their professional, technical, or functional area of interest in the command. The specific number and duties of special staff officers vary at each level of command and are based upon tables of equipment and organization and tables of distribution and allowances authorizations, the desires of the commander, and the size and level of the command. In some cases, a special staff officer is a unit commander (e.g., a division artillery commander). *See also:* Special Staff.

References
Department of Defense, U.S. Army. *Staff Organizations and Operations*. Field Manual FM 101-5. Washington, DC: Headquarters, Department of the Army, 1984.

—**SPECIAL TEST AND HANDLING EQUIPMENT** is an item that has limited application and is specifically designed for use in conjunction with the operation, care, calibration, or maintenance of another end-item. Materials handling equipment are not included in this category.

References
Department of Defense, U.S. Army. *Operational Terms and Symbols*. Field Manual FM 101-5-1. Washington, DC: Headquarters, Department of the Army, 1985.

—**SPECIAL THREAT** is any situation involving a sniper, barricaded criminal, hostage taker, or any terrorist incident that requires a special response, reaction, manpower management, training, and equipment.

References
Department of Defense, U.S. Army. *The Army Terrorism Counteraction Program*. Army Regulation AR 525-13. Washington, DC: Headquarters, Department of the Army, 1988.

—**SPECIAL TOOL AND EQUIPMENT** are usually designed concurrently with an end-item and are designed and developed to perform maintenance, test/calibration, diagnostic/prognostic analysis, and other related support for a specific end-item.

References
Department of Defense, U.S. Army. *Operational Terms and Symbols*. Field Manual FM 101-5-1. Washington, DC: Headquarters, Department of the Army, 1985.

—**SPECIAL TROOPS** are troops assigned to the headquarters of a division or a larger unit.

References
Department of Defense, U.S. Army. *Operational Terms and Symbols*. Field Manual FM 101-5-1. Washington, DC: Headquarters, Department of the Army, 1985.

—**SPECIAL WEAPON CONTROL INSTRUCTIONS** are the means of disseminating air defense weapons control engagement and disengagement instructions on specific airborne objects.

References
Department of Defense, U.S. Army. *Operational Terms and Symbols*. Field Manual FM 101-5-1. Washington, DC: Headquarters, Department of the Army, 1985.

—**SPECIAL WEAPONS** is a term used to indicate weapons that are grouped for special procedures, security, or other reasons. However, specific terminology (e.g., nuclear weapons or guided missiles) is preferable.

References
Department of Defense, Joint Chiefs of Staff. *Department of Defense Dictionary of Military and Related Terms*. Washington, DC: GPO, 1986.

—**SPECIALIST INTELLIGENCE REPORT** is a category of specialized, technical reports that are used to disseminate intelligence. *See also:* Intelligence Reporting.

References
Department of Defense, Joint Chiefs of Staff. *Department of Defense Dictionary of Military and Related Terms*. Washington, DC: GPO, 1986.

—**SPECIALIST, SCIENTIFIC AND PROFESSIONAL LINGUISTIC PERSONNEL** are civilian personnel who have technical skills that have a military occupational specialty counterpart and for which the Army has a current need. In general, these military occupational specialties are highly technical and require long-term training to perform the skills associated with those specialties.

References

Department of Defense, U.S. Army. *Operational Terms and Symbols*. Field Manual FM 101-5-1. Washington, DC: Headquarters, Department of the Army, 1985.

—**SPECIALIZATION** is an arrangement within an alliance wherein the individual or group of individuals most suited because of their technical skills, location, or other qualifications assumes greater responsibility for a specific task or a significant portion of a specific task than one or more other members.

References

Department of Defense, Joint Chiefs of Staff. *Department of Defense Dictionary of Military and Related Terms*. Washington, DC: GPO, 1986.

—**SPECIALIZED SKILL TRAINING** is individual training that provides commissioned officers, warrant officers, and enlisted personnel with skill progression and functional training.

References

Department of Defense, U.S. Army. *Individual Military Education and Training*. Army Regulation AR 350-1. Washington, DC: Headquarters, Department of the Army, 1987.

—**SPECIALTY** is a professional military career field for training, using, and developing commissioned officers.

References

Department of Defense, U.S. Army. *Individual Military Education and Training*. Army Regulation AR 350-1. Washington, DC: Headquarters, Department of the Army, 1987.

—**SPECIALTY CLINIC** is a medical treatment facility that was established as a part of an Army health clinic or of the Department of Clinics and Community Health Care Services of an Army hospital. There, patients receive treatment or care from personnel in clinics that are classified into the basic specialties and subspecialties of medicine. *See also:* Medical Treatment.

References

Department of Defense, U.S. Army. *Operational Terms and Symbols*. Field Manual FM 101-5-1. Washington, DC: Headquarters, Department of the Army, 1985.

—**SPECIALTY SCHOOL** is an Army school that conducts formal resident and nonresident professional education in skilled progressional and functional courses or courses that are not part of a structured and sequential education system. These courses are designed to provide the professional and technical skills needed by individuals for duty in one of the officer, warrant officer, or enlisted military occupational specialties.

References

Department of Defense, U.S. Army. *Individual Military Education and Training*. Army Regulation AR 350-1. Washington, DC: Headquarters, Department of the Army, 1987.

—**SPECIFIC IMPULSE,** or specific thrust, is a performance parameter of a rocket propellent expressed in seconds, equal to weight in pounds per second.

References

Department of Defense, U.S. Army. *Operational Terms and Symbols*. Field Manual FM 101-5-1. Washington, DC: Headquarters, Department of the Army, 1985.

—**SPECIFIC INTELLIGENCE COLLECTION RE-QUIREMENT (SICR)** is an identified gap in intelligence that can be satisfied only by collection of more information. It must be validated by the appropriate requirements control authority. *See also:* Intelligence Requirement.

References

Department of Defense, Defense Intelligence College. *Glossary of Intelligence Terms and Definitions*. Washington, DC: DIC, 1987.

—**SPECIFIED COMMAND.** A specified command is a command that has a broad continuing mission and is normally composed of one service. The specified commands are (1) Strategic Air Command (SAC), a command with responsibility for worldwide strategic nuclear operations; and (2) Force Command (FORSCOM), the strategic land force reserve of the free world, provides a reserve of combat-ready ground forces to reinforce the other unified and specified commands, and plans for the defense of the United States and Alaska.

The unified and specified commands are force packages that are to be employed in military operations. The operational chain of command proceeds from the President to the Secretary of Defense through the Chairman of the Joint Chiefs of Staff to the unified and specified commands to their component commands. This concept is difficult for many to understand, because of the popular belief that the Services control and command their own forces and commands. The Services do in terms of administration and maintenance, but do not in terms of operational employment.

The unified and specified command concept emerged in the years following World War II, as the U.S. military realized that the nature of warfare had progressed beyond theater warfare, where the several military forces could operate in isolation. The development of modern weapons meant that warfare in one theater could affect drastically the events in another theater. It was realized that what was needed was combined arms package that could provide adequate coordination among the several forces operating in a given region. The unified and specified command approach was the response to this problem. *See also:* Unified Command.

References
Department of Defense, U.S. Army. *Operational Terms and Symbols*. Field Manual FM 101-5-1. Washington, DC: Headquarters, Department of the Army, 1985.

—**SPECTRUM OF WAR** is a term that encompasses the full range of conflict (i.e., cold, limited, and general war).

References
Department of Defense, Joint Chiefs of Staff. *Department of Defense Dictionary of Military and Related Terms*. Washington, DC: GPO, 1986.

—**SPEED OF ADVANCE** is, in land warfare, the speed that is expected to be covered over the ground.

References
Department of Defense, U.S. Army. *Dictionary of United States Army Terms*. Army Regulation AR 310-25. Washington, DC: Headquarters, Department of the Army, 1986.

—**SPEED RING SIGHT** is a reticular sight, which may be metallic or an optiprismatic apparatus, with concentric ring elements by which the values of lead angles required for certain target speeds can be determined.

References
Department of Defense, U.S. Army. *Dictionary of United States Army Terms*. Army Regulation AR 310-25. Washington, DC: Headquarters, Department of the Army, 1986.

—**SPIN STABILIZATION** is the directional stability of a projectile obtained by the action of gyroscopic forces that result from the spinning of a body about its axis of symmetry.

References
Department of Defense, Joint Chiefs of Staff. *Department of Defense Dictionary of Military and Related Terms*. Washington, DC: GPO, 1986.

—**SPLASH.** (1) Splash, in artillery, is a word that is transmitted to an observer or a spotter five seconds before the estimated time of the impact of a salvo or round. (2) In air interception, splash means the destruction of a target that has been verified by visual or radar means.

References
Department of Defense, Joint Chiefs of Staff. *Department of Defense Dictionary of Military and Related Terms*. Washington, DC: GPO, 1986.

—**SPLINTERPROOF SHELTER** is a shelter that protects against rifle and machine-gun fire, splinters of high explosive shells, and grenades, but not against direct hits by three-inch shells or larger.

References
Department of Defense, U.S. Army. *Dictionary of United States Army Terms*. Army Regulation AR 310-25. Washington, DC: Headquarters, Department of the Army, 1986.

—**SPLIT** (ARMY AVIATION) is a 180-degree turn away from the flight. The call is given with a direction (left or right).

References
Department of Defense, U.S. Army. *Air-to-Air Combat*. Field Manual FM 1-107. Washington, DC: Headquarters, Department of the Army, 1984.

—**SPLIT CAMERAS,** in intelligence imagery and photoreconnaissance, is an assembly of two cameras that are positioned at a fixed overlapping angle relative to each other. *See also:* Fan Camera Photography, Sortie Number.

References
Department of Defense, Defense Intelligence College. *Glossary of Intelligence Terms and Definitions*. Washington, DC: DIC, 1987.

—**SPLIT PHASE** (ARMY AVIATION) exists when members of a flight are operating at 90 degrees from each other during an engagement.

References
Department of Defense, U.S. Army. *Air-to-Air Combat*. Field Manual FM 1-107. Washington, DC: Headquarters, Department of the Army, 1984.

—**SPLIT PLANE** (ARMY AVIATION) exists when members of a flight are operating at different altitudes during an engagement.

References
Department of Defense, U.S. Army. *Air-to-Air Combat*. Field Manual FM 1-107. Washington, DC: Headquarters, Department of the Army, 1984.

—**SPLIT TURN** (ARMY AVIATION) is a maneuver in which members of the flight turn 180 degrees from each other.

References
Department of Defense, U.S. Army. *Air-to-Air Combat*. Field Manual FM 1-107. Washington, DC: Headquarters, Department of the Army, 1984.

—**SPLIT UNIT** is an element of a unit that is stationed at a location different from that of the main portion of the unit.

References
Department of Defense, U.S. Army. *Dictionary of United States Army Terms*. Army Regulation AR 310-25. Washington, DC: Headquarters, Department of the Army, 1986.

—**SPLIT VERTICAL PHOTOGRAPHY,** in intelligence imagery and photoreconnaissance, is photographs that are taken simultaneously by two cameras that are mounted at an angle from the vertical. One camera is tilted to the left, and one to the right, in order to obtain a small overlap. *See also:* Sortie Number.

References
Department of Defense, Defense Intelligence College. *Glossary of Intelligence Terms and Definitions*. Washington, DC: DIC, 1987.

—**SPOILING ATTACKS** are conducted to destroy a portion of the enemy force, throw the enemy off balance, cause it to alter its plans, gain time for a larger force, or deny the enemy its ability to surveil the battle area. Although the spoiling attack is an offensive operation, it is normally used while the division is defending. It is conducted much like a hasty attack in a movement to contact. On contact, the attacking elements develop the situation, employ fire and maneuver, and close with the enemy to inflict maximum loses. *See also:* Hasty Attack.

References
Department of Defense, U.S. Army. *Armored and Mechanized Division Operations*. Field Manual FM 71-100. Washington, DC: Headquarters, Department of the Army, 1978.

————. *Engineer Combat Operations*. Field Manual FM 5-100. Washington, DC: Headquarters, Department of the Army, 1984.

————. *Operational Terms and Symbols*. Field Manual FM 101-5-1. Washington, DC: Headquarters, Department of the Army, 1985.

—**SPONSON** is a hollow enlargement on the side of the hull of a tank. It is used for storing ammunition, or as a space for radio equipment or guns.

References
Department of Defense, U.S. Army. *Dictionary of United States Army Terms*. Army Regulation AR 310-25. Washington, DC: Headquarters, Department of the Army, 1986.

—**SPOT.** (1) To spot is to determine, by observation, deviations of ordnance from the target for the purpose of supplying necessary information for adjustment of fire. (2) To spot is to place in a proper location. *See also:* Adjustment of Fire.

References
Department of Defense, U.S. Army. *Fire Support in Combined Arms Operations*. Field Manual FM 6-20. Washington, DC: Headquarters, Department of the Army, 1983.

—**SPOT INTELLIGENCE REPORT (SPIREP)** is a narrative report submitted by the unified and specified commands, the military services, and military organizations of the divisional (two-star) level whenever critical developments appear imminent or are of potentially high interest to U.S. national-level decisionmakers. Its purpose is to give the Joint Chiefs of Staff, the National Military Intelligence Center, the unified and specified commands and selected government agencies timely intelligence information on developments that could have an immediate and significant effect on current planning and operations. The initial SPIREP will not be delayed for verifying the information or for getting more details. Rather, amplifying or clarifying information should be transmitted in a follow-up SPIREP. *See also:* Dissemination, Intelligence Cycle.

References
Department of Defense, Defense Intelligence
College. *Glossary of Intelligence Terms and
Definitions.* Washington, DC: DIC, 1987.

—**SPOT JAMMING,** in electronic warfare, is
jamming a specific frequency or channel. *See
also:* Jamming.

References
Department of Defense, Defense Intelligence
College. *Glossary of Intelligence Terms and
Definitions.* Washington, DC: DIC, 1987.

—**SPOT REPORT** is a concise narrative report of
essential information covering events or conditions that may have an immediate and significant
effect on current planning and operations. A
spot report is given the fastest means of transmission. *See also:* Dissemination, Intelligence
Cycle.

References
Department of Defense, Defense Intelligence
College. *Glossary of Intelligence Terms and
Definitions.* Washington, DC: DIC, 1987.

Department of Defense, U.S. Army. *Operational
Terms and Symbols.* Field Manual FM 101-5-1.
Washington, DC: Headquarters, Department of the
Army, 1985.

—**SPOT REQUISITION** are items of civilian supply, essential or supplemental. They are not,
however, included in agreed plans requisitioned
by theater commanders.

References
Department of Defense, U.S. Army. *Dictionary of
United States Army Terms.* Army Regulation AR
310-25. Washington, DC: Headquarters, Department of the Army, 1986.

—**SPOTTER.** (1) A spotter is a small, black metal
disk attached to a target in practice shooting to
show the marksman exactly where the target
was hit. (2) A spotter is an observer who is stationed to observe and report the results of naval
gunfire to the firing agency and who also may
be used in designating targets. *See also:* Field
Artillery Observer.

References
Department of Defense, Joint Chiefs of Staff.
*Department of Defense Dictionary of Military and
Related Terms.* Washington, DC: GPO, 1986.

—**SPOTTING** is a process of determining by visual or electronic observation deviations of artillery or naval gunfire from the target in relation
to a spotting line for the purpose of supplying
the information needed to adjust or analyze the
fire. *See also:* Spotting Board.

References
Department of Defense, Joint Chiefs of Staff.
*Department of Defense Dictionary of Military and
Related Terms.* Washington, DC: GPO, 1986.

—**SPOTTING BOARD** is a device used to determine the direction and size of deviations from
the target. It converts the readings of spotters
into usable firing data. *See also:* Spotting.

References
Department of Defense, U.S. Army. *Dictionary of
United States Army Terms.* Army Regulation AR
310-25. Washington, DC: Headquarters, Department of the Army, 1986.

—**SPOTTING CHARGE** is a low-explosive charge
used in practice ammunition to show the striking point of a projectile or bomb.

References
Department of Defense, U.S. Army. *Dictionary of
United States Army Terms.* Army Regulation AR
310-25. Washington, DC: Headquarters, Department of the Army, 1986.

—**SPOTTING LINE** is either the gun-target line,
the observer-target line, or a reference line used
by the spotter or observer to make spot corrections. *See also:* Gun Target Line, Observer-Target Distance, Observer-Target Range, Reference
Line.

References
Department of Defense, Joint Chiefs of Staff.
*Department of Defense Dictionary of Military and
Related Terms.* Washington, DC: GPO, 1986.

—**SPRINGING CHARGE** is a small explosive
charge used to enlarge (spring) the diameter of a
borehole, or to form a chamber at the bottom of
a borehole in which a larger charge may be
placed.

References
Department of Defense, U.S. Army. *Dictionary of
United States Army Terms.* Army Regulation AR
310-25. Washington, DC: Headquarters, Department of the Army, 1986.

—**SQUAD (SQD)** is the basic subdivision of the platoon. *See also:* Army, Battalion, Brigade, Company, Corps, Division, Platoon, Regiment.

References

Department of Defense, U.S. Army. *Dictionary of United States Army Terms.* Army Regulation AR 310-25. Washington, DC: Headquarters, Department of the Army, 1986.

—**SQUAD AUTOMATIC WEAPON (M249)** provides a lightweight, one-man-portable, base of fire for infantry squads. This role was filled during World War II and Korea by the Browning automatic rifle, during the 1960s by the M14A1 rifle, and during the 1970s by the M16A1 rifle, which was equipped with a bipod and fired in the automatic mode. There are two M249s to each Army Corps infantry squad.

References

Department of Defense, U.S. Army. *U.S. Army Policy Statement, 1988.* Washington, DC: Headquarters, Department of the Army, 1988.

———. *Weapons Systems: U.S. Army, Navy, and Air Force Directory, 1986-1988.* Washington, DC: DCP, 1986.

—**SQUAD COLUMN** is an extended order formation in which the personnel in a squad are arranged in an irregular column behind the leader, usually about five paces apart. *See also:* Squad.

References

Department of Defense, U.S. Army. *Dictionary of United States Army Terms.* Army Regulation AR 310-25. Washington, DC: Headquarters, Department of the Army, 1986.

—**SQUAD COMBAT OPERATIONS EXERCISE SIMULATED (SCOPES)** is an engagement simulation training technique used in individual and collective tactical training whereby inexpensive 6X-power telescopes are mounted on rifles and numbers are placed on the helmets of the participants to provide a near-real time method of casualty assessment. The "kill" or "be killed" feature of SCOPES adds realism to tactical training and reinforces techniques that permit success and survival on the modern battlefield.

References

Department of Defense, U.S. Army. *How to Prepare and Conduct Military Training.* Field Manual FM 21-6. Washington, DC: Headquarters, Department of the Army, 1975.

—**SQUADRON** is the basic administrative aviation unit of the Army, Navy, Marine Corps, and Air Force.

References

Department of Defense, Joint Chiefs of Staff. *Department of Defense Dictionary of Military and Related Terms.* Washington, DC: GPO, 1986.

—**SQUARE BASE** is the rear-end of a projectile that is cylindrically shaped and does not taper off from the rotating band to the end, as does a projectile having a boattail.

References

Department of Defense, U.S. Army. *Dictionary of United States Army Terms.* Army Regulation AR 310-25. Washington, DC: Headquarters, Department of the Army, 1986.

—**STABILITY (AMMUNITION)** is a measure of the ammunition's ability to resist deterioration or change by chemical decomposition of a chemical, incendiary, smoke, or other explosive materiel while in storage for long periods of time.

References

Department of Defense, U.S. Army. *Dictionary of United States Army Terms.* Army Regulation AR 310-25. Washington, DC: Headquarters, Department of the Army, 1986.

—**STABILIZED TOUR** is a continental U.S. tour for which a mandatory period of duty has been established. *See also:* Tour of Duty.

References

Department of Defense, U.S. Army. *Dictionary of United States Army Terms.* Army Regulation AR 310-25. Washington, DC: Headquarters, Department of the Army, 1986.

—**STABILIZER,** in ammunition, is a material added to a propellant, chemical, incendiary, or smoke composition to inhibit or reduce deterioration or change by chemical decomposition of its explosive materials while it is in storage.

References

Department of Defense, U.S. Army. *Dictionary of United States Army Terms.* Army Regulation AR 310-25. Washington, DC: Headquarters, Department of the Army, 1986.

—**STABILIZING FIN** is a fin on the tail of some projectiles and bombs that helps to maintain balance during flight so that the projectile or bomb strikes nose first.

References
Department of Defense, U.S. Army. *Dictionary of United States Army Terms.* Army Regulation AR 310-25. Washington, DC: Headquarters, Department of the Army, 1986.

—**STACK ARMS.** (1) Stack arms means to put a number of rifles in groups, upright with their butts on the ground. Three of them are linked together with the stacking swivels. Additional rifles are stacked leaning against this group. (2) Stack arms means the command to do the above operation.

References
Department of Defense, U.S. Army. *Dictionary of United States Army Terms.* Army Regulation AR 310-25. Washington, DC: Headquarters, Department of the Army, 1986.

—**STAFF** are officers specially ordered or detailed to assist the commander exercise his command. The staff provides information for the commander; continuously studies the situation for anticipatory planning; submits recommendations as to plans and orders on its own initiative or in response to directives; translates decisions of the commander into orders and provides for their dissemination; and supervises, as directed, the execution of orders to insure adherence to and successful execution of the intentions and policies of the commander. *See also:* Army General Staff, Army Staff, Personal Staff.

References
Department of Defense, U.S. Army. *Dictionary of United States Army Terms.* Army Regulation AR 310-25. Washington, DC: Headquarters, Department of the Army, 1986.

—**STAFF AND ADMINISTRATIVE RESERVE** is a section of the Army Reserve consisting of staff specialist branch personnel who serve in positions that are not peculiar to any particular branch of service assignments. These personnel are trained in managing military operations that are not strategical or tactical.

References
Department of Defense, U.S. Army. *Dictionary of United States Army Terms.* Army Regulation AR 310-25. Washington, DC: Headquarters, Department of the Army, 1986.

—**STAFF AUTHORITY.** The commander specifically delegates authority to the staff or a particular staff officer. He normally delegates authority to the staff to take final action on matters within command policy. The authority delegated to individual staff officers varies with the level and mission of the command, the immediacy of the operations, and the relationship of the staff officer's area of interest to the primary mission of the command. *See also:* Staff.

References
Department of Defense, U.S. Army. *Staff Organization and Operations.* Field Manual FM 101-5. Washington, DC: Headquarters, Department of the Army, 1984.

—**STAFF CHANNEL** is the staff-to-staff link between headquarters for coordination and transmission of information.

References
Department of Defense, U.S. Army. *Staff Organization and Operations.* Field Manual FM 101-5. Washington, DC: Headquarters, Department of the Army, 1984.

—**STAFF CONFERENCE** is a meeting of staff officers who are normally principal staff officers or their representatives, and are either from one or several headquarters. Other elements of the staff may be present. *See also:* Staff.

References
Department of Defense, U.S. Army. *Staff Organization and Operations.* Field Manual FM 101-5. Washington, DC: Headquarters, Department of the Army, 1984.

—**STAFF COORDINATION** is the action required within a staff to insure that the various staff officers act in harmony or agreement in carrying out the plans of the commanders, and that conflicts and duplications are avoided by making necessary adjustments in plans and policies prior to their implementation. *See also:* Staff.

References
Department of Defense, U.S. Army. *Staff Organization and Operations.* Field Manual FM 101-5. Washington, DC: Headquarters, Department of the Army, 1984.

—**STAFF DIVISION** is an organizational unit, usually nonoperating, established to assist the commanding general or a higher command in discharging responsibilities. Personnel of staff divisions formulate plans, advise operating units about their work, and follow through on the execution of approved programs. *See also:* Staff.

References

Department of Defense, U.S. Army. *Staff Organization and Operations*. Field Manual FM 101-5. Washington, DC: Headquarters, Department of the Army, 1984.

—**STAFF DUTY** is service on the staff of a commander. *See also:* Staff.

References

Department of Defense, U.S. Army. *Staff Organization and Operations*. Field Manual FM 101-5. Washington, DC: Headquarters, Department of the Army, 1984.

—**STAFF ESTIMATES** are the staff officers' evaluations of how factors in their particular fields of interest will influence the courses of action under consideration by the commander. *See also:* Staff.

References

Department of Defense, U.S. Army. *Operational Terms and Symbols*. Field Manual FM 101-5-1. Washington, DC: Headquarters, Department of the Army, 1985.

———. *Staff Organizations and Operations*. Field Manual FM 101-5. Washington, DC: Headquarters, Department of the Army, 1984.

—**STAFFING GUIDE** is a manual that provides guidance for determining the number and kind of personnel required to operate table of distribution units.

References

Department of Defense, U.S. Army. *Staff Organization and Operations*. Field Manual FM 101-5. Washington, DC: Headquarters, Department of the Army, 1984.

—**STAFF INSPECTIONS** are made by individual officers or teams, as directed by the commander. These inspections normally are conducted to determine certain conditions within a subordinate unit (e.g., compliance or conformity with policies and regulations).

References

Department of Defense, U.S. Army. *Staff Organization and Operations*. Field Manual FM 101-5. Washington, DC: Headquarters, Department of the Army, 1984.

—**STAFF INTELLIGENCE** is intelligence prepared by any department or agency through the correlation and interpretation of all intelligence materials available to it in order to meet its specific requirements and responsibilities.

References

Department of Defense, Defense Intelligence College. *Glossary of Intelligence Terms and Definitions*. Washington, DC: Defense Intelligence College, 1987.

—**STAFF PLANNING FACTOR** is a properly selected multiplier, based upon experience, used in planning to estimate the amount and type of effort that will be needed in a contemplated operation.

References

Department of Defense, U.S. Army. *Dictionary of United States Army Terms*. Army Regulation AR 310-25. Washington, DC: Headquarters, Department of the Army, 1986.

—**STAFF RESEARCH** is the collection and evaluation of the facts necessary to solve problems or to provide information. *See also:* Staff.

References

Department of Defense, U.S. Army. *Staff Organization and Operations*. Field Manual FM 101-5. Washington, DC: Headquarters, Department of the Army, 1984.

—**STAFF RESPONSIBILITY.** The assignment of staff responsibility carries no connotation of command authority over other staff officers or over any other elements of the command. Although the commander retains overall responsibility, the staff officer is responsible for the manner in which delegated authority is exercised and for the results obtained. *See also:* Staff.

References

Department of Defense, U.S. Army. *Staff Organization and Operations*. Field Manual FM 101-5. Washington, DC: Headquarters, Department of the Army, 1984.

—**STAFF SECTION WORKSHEET** is an indexed assembly of extracts from current orders, messages, directives, and decisions used to prepare estimates, plans, orders, and periodic reports. *See also:* Staff.

References

Department of Defense, U.S. Army. *Dictionary of United States Army Terms*. Army Regulation AR 310-25. Washington, DC: Headquarters, Department of the Army, 1986.

—**STAFF STUDY** is a staff officer's analysis of and his recommended solution to a specific problem or problem area. The purpose of the staff study, like the estimate of a situation, is to collect and to analyze relevant information in order to develop the most effective solution to a problem. *See also:* Staff.

References

Department of Defense, U.S. Army. *Staff Organization and Operations.* Field Manual FM 101-5. Washington, DC: Headquarters, Department of the Army, 1984.

—**STAFF SUPERVISION** is the process of advising other staff officers and individuals who are subordinate to the commander of the commander's plans and policies, interpreting those plans and policies, assisting such subordinates in carrying them out, determining the extent to which they are being followed, and advising the commander of the results. *See also:* Staff.

References

Department of Defense, Joint Chiefs of Staff. *Department of Defense Dictionary of Military and Related Terms.* Washington, DC: GPO, 1986.

—**STAFF SUPPORT ACTIVITY** is an organization that exists to assist the headquarters to which it reports. Staff support activities assist in the formulation of policies and procedures or provide the necessary administrative and/or logistical support. *See also:* Staff.

References

Department of Defense, U.S. Army. *Dictionary of United States Army Terms.* Army Regulation AR 310-25. Washington, DC: Headquarters, Department of the Army, 1986.

—**STAFF SUPPORT AGENCY** is an agency at Headquarters, Department of the Army, level that exists primarily to support and assist in the formulation of policies and procedures or provides necessary administrative and/or logistical support for the Headquarters. *See also:* Agency.

References

Department of Defense, U.S. Army. *Dictionary of United States Army Terms.* Army Regulation AR 310-25. Washington, DC: Headquarters, Department of the Army, 1986.

—**STAFF VISITS** are by staff officers to subordinate units to get information for the commander, to observe the execution of orders and instructions, and to provide advice and assistance in their areas of responsibility. *See also:* Staff.

References

Department of Defense, U.S. Army. *Staff Organization and Operations.* Field Manual FM 101-5. Washington, DC: Headquarters, Department of the Army, 1984.

—**STAGE.** (1) To stage is to process, in a specified area, troops who are in transit from one locality to another. (2) Stage is the part of the air route from one air staging unit to the next. *See also:* Marshalling, Staging Area.

References

Department of Defense, Joint Chiefs of Staff. *Department of Defense Dictionary of Military and Related Terms.* Washington, DC: GPO, 1986.

—**STAGE FIELD** is a predetermined area where aircraft assemble prior to conducting an air assault operation.

References

Department of Defense, U.S. Army. *Operational Terms and Symbols.* Field Manual FM 101-5-1. Washington, DC: Headquarters, Department of the Army, 1985.

—**STAGING.** During a campaign, lines of communication often become overextended. This may require the staging of sustaining bases forward as the combat forces advance or the rapid evacuation of those bases if friendly forces withdraw. Routes, rail lines, airfields, ports, and pipelines of the lines of communication are also affected by such moves. Additional construction, route improvement, and movement control measures accompany any staging of forward bases and how close to the battle the commander will bring his bases. Control of the airspace, transportation limitations, requirements of the force, and the availability of combat service support units and military police affect the location and movement of bases and lines of communication.

References

Department of Defense, U.S. Army. *Operations.* Field Manual FM 100-5. Washington, DC: Headquarters, Department of the Army, 1986.

—**STAGING AREA.** (1) A staging area is a general locality between the mounting area and the objective of an amphibious or an airborne operation. It is the area through which a force or parts of a force pass after mounting or refueling, regrouping its ships, inspection, and the redistribution of troops. (2) A staging area is a general locality, containing accommodations for troops, that is established for the concentration of troop units and transient personnel between movements over the lines of communication. In this context, it is also referred to as an intermediate staging area or an intermediate staging base. *See also:* Mounting Area, Staging.

References

Department of Defense, U.S. Army. *Operational Terms and Symbols.* Field Manual FM 101-5-1. Washington, DC: Headquarters, Department of the Army, 1985.

—**STAGING STATION** is an installation or activity established to provide accommodations during a temporary retention of troops. It is necessary for movement control as the troops move from one location to another prior to, and in preparation for, an overseas movement.

References

Department of Defense, U.S. Army. *Dictionary of United States Army Terms.* Army Regulation AR 310-25. Washington, DC: Headquarters, Department of the Army, 1986.

—**STAND FAST.** (1) Stand fast is a command used in artillery units. It directs all movements of men and materiel to stop. (2) Stand fast is a command given to prevent the movement of the indicated units while the others move.

References

Department of Defense, Joint Chiefs of Staff. *Department of Defense Dictionary of Military and Related Terms.* Washington, DC: GPO, 1986.

Department of Defense, U.S. Army. *Dictionary of United States Army Terms.* Army Regulation AR 310-25. Washington, DC: Headquarters, Department of the Army, 1986.

—**STANDARD A** is a combat-acceptable item that will fill an operational requirement and is being produced to fill existing shortages. *See also:* Standard B.

References

Department of Defense, U.S. Army. *Dictionary of United States Army Terms.* Army Regulation AR 310-25. Washington, DC: Headquarters, Department of the Army, 1986.

—**STANDARD B** is an item that will satisfactorily fill an operational requirement, but which is being, or has been, replaced by a newer generation or series of the item. *See also:* Standard A.

References

Department of Defense, U.S. Army. *Dictionary of United States Army Terms.* Army Regulation AR 310-25. Washington, DC: Headquarters, Department of the Army, 1986.

—**STANDARD B RATION** is a nonperishable substance used to feed troops during field operations where kitchen facilities, with the exception of refrigeration, are not available. *See also:* Meal Ready to Eat, Individual.

References

Department of Defense, U.S. Army. *Staff Organizations and Operations.* Field Manual FM 101-5. Washington, DC: Headquarters, Department of the Army, 1984.

—**STANDARD BALLISTIC CONDITIONS** are a set of ballistic conditions that are arbitrarily assumed as a standard for computing firing tables/range tables.

References

Department of Defense, U.S. Army. *Dictionary of United States Army Terms.* Army Regulation AR 310-25. Washington, DC: Headquarters, Department of the Army, 1986.

—**STANDARD CIVIL TIME** is the mean solar time. It is based upon the movement of the sun over a certain specified meridian, called the time meridian, and is adopted for use over a considerable area. With a few exceptions, standard time is based upon some meridian that differs by a multiple of 15 degrees from the meridian of Greenwich. Civil time begins at midnight.

References

Department of Defense, U.S. Army. *Staff Organization and Operations.* Field Manual FM 101-5. Washington, DC: Headquarters, Department of the Army, 1984.

—**STANDARD DAY OF SUPPLY** is the total amount of supplies required for an average day based upon Standing Group NATO rates and/or on national rates, as appropriate. *See also:* One Day's Supply.

References
Department of Defense, Joint Chiefs of Staff. *Department of Defense Dictionary of Military and Related Terms.* Washington, DC: GPO, 1986.

—**STANDARD DETENTION UNIT** is a standard 48-cell unit that is used in Army prison installations for segregating prisoners as a disciplinary or protective measure. *See also:* Disciplinary Action.

References
Department of Defense, U.S. Army. *Dictionary of United States Army Terms.* Army Regulation AR 310-25. Washington, DC: Headquarters, Department of the Army, 1986.

—**STANDARD FIGHTING TRENCH** is developed from the crawl trench with an increased depth of five and one-half feet. It is sometimes constructed with fighting bays or with a fighting step. Fighting positions are constructed on both sides of the trench to provide alternative positions to fight to the rear, step-off areas for foot traffic in the trench, and protection against lengthwise firing into the trench. Overhead cover also provides additional protection. Although this trench is primarily a fighting position, it is also used for communications, supply, evacuation, and troop movement. *See also:* Crawl Trench.

References
Department of Defense, U.S. Army. *Survivability.* Field Manual FM 5-103. Washington, DC: Headquarters, Department of the Army, 1985.

—**STANDARD IGLOO MAGAZINE** is an earth-covered, arch-type magazine, with or without a separate door barricade, that is constructed according to standards established by the U.S. Army. *See also:* Magazine.

References
Department of Defense, U.S. Army. *Ammunition and Explosives Safety Standards.* Army Regulation AR 385-64. Washington, DC: Headquarters, Department of the Army, 1987.

—**STANDARD MUZZLE VELOCITY** is the speed at which a given projectile is supposed to leave the muzzle of a gun. The speed is calculated on the basis of the particular gun, the propelling charge used, and the type of projectile fired from the gun. Firing tables are based upon standard muzzle velocity.

References
Department of Defense, U.S. Army. *Dictionary of United States Army Terms.* Army Regulation AR 310-25. Washington, DC: Headquarters, Department of the Army, 1986.

—**STANDARD OPERATING PROCEDURE, OR STANDING OPERATING PROCEDURE, (SOP),** is a standing set of instructions that cover features of operations that lend themselves to standardized procedures without a loss of effectiveness. The procedure is applicable unless it is ordered otherwise.

References
Department of Defense, U.S. Army. *Staff Organization and Operations.* Field Manual FM 101-5. Washington, DC: Headquarters, Department of the Army, 1984.

—**STANDARD PATTERN,** in land mine warfare, is the agreed pattern to which mines are normally laid. *See also:* Mine Warfare.

References
Department of Defense, Joint Chiefs of Staff. *Department of Defense Dictionary of Military and Related Terms.* Washington, DC: GPO, 1986.

—**STANDARD SCORE** is a score that permits a comparison between an individual's test results and those of a group taking the same test. Raw scores on all Army tests are converted to standard scores in order to make scores on a variety of tests directly comparable. Army standard scores range approximately from 40 to 160 with an average of 100.

References
Department of Defense, U.S. Army. *Dictionary of United States Army Terms.* Army Regulation AR 310-25. Washington, DC: Headquarters, Department of the Army, 1986.

—**STANDARD TACTICAL MISSIONS** are missions that apply to all types of air defense artillery units, assign mutual responsibilities, and define specific command relationships between supported and supporting units. The four air defense artillery standard tactical missions are general support; general support-reinforcing; reinforcing; and direct support. *See also:* Direct Support, General Support, General Support Reinforcing, Reinforcing.

References

Department of Defense, U.S. Army. *U.S. Army Air Defense Artillery Employment Hawk.* Field Manual FM 44-90. Washington, DC: Headquarters, Department of the Army, 1983.

————. *U.S. Army Air Defense Employment.* Field Manual FM 44-1. Washington, DC: Headquarters, Department of the Army, 1983.

—**STANDARD TRAJECTORY** is the calculated path through the air that a projectile is expected to follow under given conditions of weather, position, and materiel, including the particular fuze, projectile, and propelling charge that are used. Firing tables are based upon standard trajectories.

References

Department of Defense, U.S. Army. *Dictionary of United States Army Terms.* Army Regulation AR 310-25. Washington, DC: Headquarters, Department of the Army, 1986.

—**STANDARD TRENCH** is a trench of uniform cross section that can be used either as a fire or communications trench. *See also:* Trench.

References

Department of Defense, U.S. Army. *Dictionary of United States Army Terms.* Army Regulation AR 310-25. Washington, DC: Headquarters, Department of the Army, 1986.

—**STANDARD TYPE** is a broad term used to designate the most advanced and satisfactory items that have been adopted as standard.

References

Department of Defense, U.S. Army. *Dictionary of United States Army Terms.* Army Regulation AR 310-25. Washington, DC: Headquarters, Department of the Army, 1986.

—**STANDARD-USE ARMY AIRCRAFT ROUTES** are established outside of minimum risk routes/low-level transit routes to enable Army rotary wing aircraft to enter and leave the combat zone from the corps rear boundary to the brigade rear boundary with minimum danger of collision with high-speed aircraft.

References

Department of Defense, U.S. Army. *Patriot Battalion Operations.* Field Manual FM 44-15. Washington, DC: Headquarters, Department of the Army, 1984.

—**STANDARDIZATION** is the process by which member nations achieve the closest practicable cooperation among forces, the most efficient use of research, development, and production resources; and agree to adopt, on the broadest possible basis, the use of: (1) common or compatible operational, administrative, and logistics procedures; (2) common or compatible technical procedures and criteria; (3) common, compatible, or interchangeable supplies, components, weapons, or equipment; and (4) common or compatible tactical doctrine with corresponding organizational compatibility. *See also:* Standardization Agreement.

References

Department of Defense, U.S. Army. *Support Operations: Echelons Above Corps.* Field Manual FM 100-16. Washington, DC: Headquarters, Department of the Army, 1986.

—**STANDARDIZATION AGREEMENT (STANAG)** is the record of an agreement among several nations to adopt the same or similar military equipment; ammunition; supplies and stores; and operational, administrative, and logistics procedures. It is the acronym for North Atlantic Treaty Organization (NATO) standardization agreement. NATO consists of fifteen member nations allied together for military interoperability in both equipment and methods of operations. As each STANAG is adopted, it becomes part of each nation's unilateral procedures and is incorporated into national doctrinal and procedural publications.

References

Department of Defense, U.S. Army. *NBC Operations.* Field Manual FM 3-100. Washington, DC: Headquarters, Department of the Army, 1985.

————. *Support Operations: Echelons Above Corps.* Field Manual FM 100-16. Washington, DC: Headquarters, Department of the Army, 1986.

—**STANDARDIZATION PROGRAM** contains the operational, tactical, logistical, administrative, and training tasks, drills, and procedures that are performed the same way throughout the entire Army.

References

Department of Defense, U.S. Army. *Training for Mobilization and War.* Field Manual FM 25-5. Washington, DC: Headquarters, Department of the Army, 1985.

—**STANDBY.** (1) Standby is a command to troops to take posts without delay and be ready for action. (2) Standby is a condition in which electronic equipment (e.g., radios, radars, and computers) is kept in readiness for instantaneous action to overcome the warm-up time required by most vacuum tubes. (3) Standby is a warning order given to an observer five seconds before the expected time of a burst.

References
Department of Defense, U.S. Army. *Dictionary of United States Army Terms.* Army Regulation AR 310-25. Washington, DC: Headquarters, Department of the Army, 1986.

—**STANDBY RESERVE** are the units and members of the Reserve components (other than those in the Ready Reserve or Retired Reserve) who are liable for active duty only as provided in 10 U.S.C. §§ 273, 672, and 674.

Reservists classified active status, standby reserve are those who (1) are completing their statutory military service obligation, (2) are being retained in an active status under 10 U.S.C. § 1006, (3) were screened from the Ready Reserve as being key personnel and requested assignment to the active status list, or (4) may be temporarily assigned to the standby reserve for hardship or for another cogent reason determined by the Secretary concerned, with the expectation of their being returned to Ready Reserve.

Individuals classified inactive status, standby reserve are those who are not required by law or regulation to remain members of an active status program but who (1) desire to retain their Reserve affiliation in a nonparticipating status and (2) have skills that may be of possible future use to the military department concerned.

References
Department of Defense, Joint Chiefs of Staff. *Department of Defense Dictionary of Military and Related Terms.* Washington, DC: GPO, 1986.

—**STANDBY STATUS** (UNIT) is a nonoperating condition caused by extreme personnel shortages. In standby status the unit's equipment is placed in administrative storage and a minimum of personnel is retained to perform essential safeguards against fire and theft.

References
Department of Defense, U.S. Army. *Dictionary of United States Army Terms.* Army Regulation AR 310-25. Washington, DC: Headquarters, Department of the Army, 1986.

—**STANDBY STORAGE** is a storage classification for supplies and equipment that are intended for withdrawal at a time sometime after 90 days, but before three years.

References
Department of Defense, U.S. Army. *Dictionary of United States Army Terms.* Army Regulation AR 310-25. Washington, DC: Headquarters, Department of the Army, 1986.

—**STANDBY SUPPLIES** are items of supply, excluding repair parts, that are needed to safeguard health, to insure the uninterrupted operation of the installation's facilities, or to prevent the destruction of property, and for which requisitioning objectives cannot be established either because of stockage restrictions or because of insufficient demand. Such stocks are limited to the quantity required to meet anticipated emergencies and will be included in the installation stockage list and will be so identified.

References
Department of Defense, U.S. Army. *Dictionary of United States Army Terms.* Army Regulation AR 310-25. Washington, DC: Headquarters, Department of the Army, 1986.

—**STANDING OPERATING PROCEDURE.** *See:* Standard Operating Procedure.

—**STANDING ORDER** is a promulgated order that remains in force until it is amended or cancelled.

References
Department of Defense, Joint Chiefs of Staff. *Department of Defense Dictionary of Military and Related Terms.* Washington, DC: GPO, 1986.

—**STANDING PATROL.** The strength of a standing patrol varies and is determined by the commander allotting the task. The patrol's task may be reconnaissance, listening, fighting, or a combination of these missions. It differs from reconnaissance, fighting, or listening patrols in that, having taken up its allotted position, it is not free to maneuver in the performance of its task without permission. *See also:* Patrol.

References
Department of Defense, Joint Chiefs of Staff. *Department of Defense Dictionary of Military and Related Terms.* Washington, DC: GPO, 1986.

—**STANDING SIGNAL INSTRUCTIONS** are a series of instructions explaining the use of items included in the signal operation instructions. They may also include the other technical instructions needed to coordinate and control the communications-electronics operations of the command.

References

Department of Defense, U.S. Army. *Dictionary of United States Army Terms.* Army Regulation AR 310-25. Washington, DC: Headquarters, Department of the Army, 1986.

—**STANDOFF (ARMY AVIATION).** (1) Standoff, as it pertains to shaped charge ammunition, is the distance between the base of the liner and the target at the time of initiation. (2) Standoff is the maximum range of a weapon that is to be employed. It is the desirable characteristic of a weapon system that permits the attacking aircraft to launch an attack on the target at a safe distance, which is usually outside the range of counterfire.

References

Department of Defense, U.S. Army. *Air-to-Air Combat.* Field Manual FM 1-107. Washington, DC: Headquarters, Department of the Army, 1984.

———. *Mine/Countermine Operations at the Company Level.* Field Manual FM 20-32. Washington, DC: Headquarters, Department of the Army, 1976.

—**STAND-TO** is an evolution held both morning and evening to insure that every man adjusts to the changing light and noise conditions, and is dressed, equipped, and ready for action. The stand-to should start before first light in the morning and continue until after light. It should start before dark in the evening and last until after dark. The starting and ending times should vary to prevent establishing a pattern, but the stand-to must last long enough to accomplish its purpose.

References

Department of Defense, U.S. Army. *The Infantry Rifle Company (Infantry, Airborne, Air Assault, Ranger).* Field Manual FM 7-10. Washington, DC: Headquarters, Department of the Army, 1982.

—**STANO (SURVEILLANCE, TARGET, ACQUISITION, NIGHT OBSERVATION) DEVICES** may be either active or passive and are designed to help units perform one or more of these tasks:

- **Surveillance:** the continuous, all-weather, day-and-night watch over the battlefield.
- **Target acquisition:** the detection, identification, and location of targets so they can be hit by organic or supporting weapons, day or night, in any type of weather.

- **Night observation:** the observation conducted at night and at other times when visibility is poor.

References

Department of Defense, U.S. Army. *The Infantry Rifle Company (Infantry, Airborne, Air Assault, Ranger).* Field Manual FM 7-10. Washington, DC: Headquarters, Department of the Army, 1982.

—**STAR GAUGE** is the instrument for measuring the diameter of the bore of a gun.

References

Department of Defense, U.S. Army. *Dictionary of United States Army Terms.* Army Regulation AR 310-25. Washington, DC: Headquarters, Department of the Army, 1986.

—**STAR SHELL** is a projectile that contains a chemical that is ignited when the projectile bursts. The chemical burns with a brilliant flame and is used to illuminate targets at night.

References

Department of Defense, U.S. Army. *Dictionary of United States Army Terms.* Army Regulation AR 310-25. Washington, DC: Headquarters, Department of the Army, 1986.

—**START POINT (SP)** is a well-defined point on a route at which a movement of vehicles begins to be under the control of the commander of the movement. It is at this point that the column is formed by the successive passing, at an appointed time, of each of the elements composing the column. In addition to the principal start point of a column, there may be secondary start points for its different elements.

References

Department of Defense, U.S. Army. *The Infantry Rifle Company (Infantry, Airborne, Air Assault, Ranger).* Field Manual FM 7-10. Washington, DC: Headquarters, Department of the Army, 1982.

———. *Operational Terms and Symbols.* Field Manual FM 101-5-1. Washington, DC: Headquarters, Department of the Army, 1985.

—**STATE OF ALERT,** as used in air defense, is the combat readiness that is maintained by a fire unit. It is expressed in terms of the period of time within which the unit must be capable of launching at least one missile. States of alert are: battle stations (fire within 30 seconds), five-minute, fifteen-minute, thirty-minute, one-hour, and three-hour.

References
Department of Defense, U.S. Army. *Dictionary of United States Army Terms.* Army Regulation AR 310-25. Washington, DC: Headquarters, Department of the Army, 1986.

—**STATE OF READINESS-STATE 1** (SAFE) is the state of a demolition target when the demolition charge that it contains has been placed and secured. The firing or initiating circuits have been installed, but have not been connected to the demolition charge, and the detonators or initiators have not been installed or connected. *See also:* State of Readiness-State 2-(Armed).

References
Department of Defense, Joint Chiefs of Staff. *Department of Defense Dictionary of Military and Related Terms.* Washington, DC: GPO, 1986.

—**STATE OF READINESS-STATE 2** (ARMED) is the state of a demolition target when the demolition charges are in place, the firing or priming circuits are installed, complete, and are ready for firing. *See also:* State of Readiness-State 1-(Safe).

References
Department of Defense, Joint Chiefs of Staff. *Department of Defense Dictionary of Military and Related Terms.* Washington, DC: GPO, 1986.

—**STATE OF THE GROUND** is a description of landscape properties (e.g., snow covered, icy, dry, dusty, or muddy).

References
Department of Defense, U.S. Army. *Weather Support for Army Tactical Operations.* Field Manual FM 34-81. Washington, DC: Headquarters, Department of the Army, 1984.

—**STATE OF THE SEA** is a description of the properties of the wind-generated waves on the sea surface.

References
Department of Defense, U.S. Army. *Weather Support for Army Tactical Operations.* Field Manual FM 34-81. Washington, DC: Headquarters, Department of the Army, 1984.

—**STATEMENT OF CHARGES** is a form listing the items of property that have been issued to a military person which he has lost, damaged, or destroyed, and for which he must reimburse the government.

References
Department of Defense, U.S. Army. *Dictionary of United States Army Terms.* Army Regulation AR 310-25. Washington, DC: Headquarters, Department of the Army, 1986.

—**STATEMENT OF SERVICE** is a letter-type brief of an officer's official military service during his entire career. This letter is usually prepared for public relations use or on request of federal, state, or local officials. *See also:* Retirement.

References
Department of Defense, U.S. Army. *Dictionary of United States Army Terms.* Army Regulation AR 310-25. Washington, DC: Headquarters, Department of the Army, 1986.

—**STATIC EMPLOYMENT** is employment of air defense artillery in defense of permanent or semipermanent installations. *See also:* Mobile Employment.

References
Department of Defense, U.S. Army. *Dictionary of United States Army Terms.* Army Regulation AR 310-25. Washington, DC: Headquarters, Department of the Army, 1986.

—**STATIC LINE** (AIR TRANSPORT) is a line attached to a parachute pack and to a strop or anchor cable in an aircraft so that when the load is dropped, the parachute is deployed automatically.

References
Department of Defense, Joint Chiefs of Staff. *Department of Defense Dictionary of Military and Related Terms.* Washington, DC: GPO, 1986.

—**STATIC TEST** is the test of a device in a stationary or hold-down position.

References
Department of Defense, U.S. Army. *Dictionary of United States Army Terms.* Army Regulation AR 310-25. Washington, DC: Headquarters, Department of the Army, 1986.

—**STATIC TEST STAND** is a location on which liquid propellent engines or solid propellent motors are tested while remaining in place.

References
Department of Defense, U.S. Army. *Ammunition and Explosives Safety Standards.* Army Regulation AR 385-64. Washington, DC: Headquarters, Department of the Army, 1987.

—**STATION.** (1) Station is a general term meaning any military or naval activity at a fixed land location. (2) A station is a particular kind of activity to which other activities or individuals may come for a specific service, which is often of a technical nature. (3) A station is an assigned area in an approach, contact, or battle disposition. (4) Station is any place of duty or post or position in the field to which an individual, or group of individuals, or a unit may be assigned. (5) Station is one or more transmitters or receivers or a combination of transmitters and receivers, including the accessory equipment necessary for carrying on radio communication service. Each station is classified by the service in which it operates permanently or temporarily. (6) Station is, in survey, a marked location on the earth's surface, the coordinates of which are to be determined, assumed, or known. *See also:* Station Complement, Station Designator.

References

Department of Defense, Joint Chiefs of Staff. *Department of Defense Dictionary of Military and Related Terms.* Washington, DC: GPO, 1986.

Department of Defense, U.S. Army. *Dictionary of United States Army Terms.* Army Regulation AR 310-25. Washington, DC: Headquarters, Department of the Army, 1986.

—**STATION COMPLEMENT** means the operating personnel who are permanently assigned to an installation to perform all housekeeping and administrative duties required to maintain and operate the physical facilities. The station complement also provides supplies and services for all other permanently assigned personnel, as well as for the nonoperating personnel attached to the installation for training and processing.

References

Department of Defense, U.S. Army. *Dictionary of United States Army Terms.* Army Regulation AR 310-25. Washington, DC: Headquarters, Department of the Army, 1986.

—**STATION DESIGNATOR** is a combination of two or three call letters used to identify a radio station.

References

Department of Defense, U.S. Army. *Dictionary of United States Army Terms.* Army Regulation AR 310-25. Washington, DC: Headquarters, Department of the Army, 1986.

—**STATION HOSPITAL** is a fixed medical treatment facility. *See also:* Hospital.

References

Department of Defense, U.S. Army. *Dictionary of United States Army Terms.* Army Regulation AR 310-25. Washington, DC: Headquarters, Department of the Army, 1986.

—**STATION LIST** is a directory that gives the location of the various headquarters elements of a command.

References

Department of Defense, U.S. Army. *Dictionary of United States Army Terms.* Army Regulation AR 310-25. Washington, DC: Headquarters, Department of the Army, 1986.

—**STATION LOG** is a diary kept by a station operator. It is a report of the stations with which the operator has been in communication and of the messages handled.

References

Department of Defense, U.S. Army. *Dictionary of United States Army Terms.* Army Regulation AR 310-25. Washington, DC: Headquarters, Department of the Army, 1986.

—**STATION PROPERTY** is property, except table of organization and equipment property, that is authorized for use at an installation. In the event of emergencies or other circumstances that establish a temporary requirement for unauthorized table of organization and equipment items, such items, on approval by a major commander, may be issued as installation property for the duration of such temporary periods. Items so issued are accounted for on the installation property book.

References

Department of Defense, U.S. Army. *Dictionary of United States Army Terms.* Army Regulation AR 310-25. Washington, DC: Headquarters, Department of the Army, 1986.

—**STATION STOCK** (LEVEL) is the maximum quantity of supplies, expressed in days of supply, permitted to be on hand or due in at any time at a military installation. This level is based upon actual past issues and anticipated demands. It represents the requisitioning objective.

References

Department of Defense, U.S. Army. *Dictionary of United States Army Terms.* Army Regulation AR 310-25. Washington, DC: Headquarters, Department of the Army, 1986.

—**STATION TIME** is the time when the aircrew, passengers, and materiel are to be in the aircraft and prepared for the flight. The passengers are to be seated, the loads are to be tied down, and the aircrews are to have completed their briefing and preflight inspection.

References
Department of Defense, U.S. Army. *USA/USAF Doctrine for Joint Airborne and Tactical Airlift Operations.* Field Manual FM 100-27. Washington, DC: Headquarters, Department of the Army, 1985.

—**STATIONARY HOVERING FIRE** (ARMY AVIATION) is fire delivered from any altitude that permits effective target engagement while the firing aircraft remains stationary over a point on the ground.

References
Department of Defense, U.S. Army. *Gunnery Training for Attack Helicopters.* Training Circular TC 17-17. Washington, DC: Headquarters, Department of the Army, 1975.

—**STAYBEHIND** is an agent or agent organization established in a given country that is to be activated in the event of a hostile overrun or other circumstances under which normal access would be denied. *See also:* Staybehind Force.

References
Department of Defense, Joint Chiefs of Staff. *Department of Defense Dictionary of Military and Related Terms.* Washington, DC: GPO, 1986.

—**STAYBEHIND FORCE** is a force that is left in position to conduct a specified mission when the remainder of the force withdraws or retires from the area.

References
Department of Defense, Joint Chiefs of Staff. *Department of Defense Dictionary of Military and Related Terms.* Washington, DC: GPO, 1986.

—**STAYING POWER** (AN ELEMENT OF FORCE READINESS). Commanders must anticipate severe personnel and equipment casualties, restricted mobility, constrained logistic resupply capabilities, and reduced reaction times. The side that can best sustain combat operations and retain its combat effectiveness is likely to win. Throughout the conflict, combat engagements are often quick, intense, destructive, and decisive. Therefore, the Army's concept of sustained land combat embraces:

- Development of modern and properly balanced combat, combat support, and combat service support forces that will give the greatest opportunity for victory. These forces must be able to conduct joint and combined combat operations over extended frontages for lengthy periods of time without significant initial reinforcement other than by tactical air forces.
- Maintenance of a strong continental base to support these forces.
- Readiness for timely response to any mission—from land warfare by forward-deployed forces to selective contingency operations in a jungle or desert environment, from armored and mechanized infantry combat to special operations and amphibious or airborne assaults.

References
Department of Defense, U.S. Army. *The Army.* (Prepublication Issue.) Field Manual FM 100-1. Washington, DC: Headquarters, Department of the Army, 1986.

—**STEADY ON** is an element of a tank fire command. It is obeyed until "on", the command to stop traversing, is given. *See also:* On.

References
Department of Defense, U.S. Army. *Dictionary of United States Army Terms.* Army Regulation AR 310-25. Washington, DC: Headquarters, Department of the Army, 1986.

—**STEERING BRAKE** is a means of turning, stopping, or holding a tracked vehicle.

References
Department of Defense, U.S. Army. *Dictionary of United States Army Terms.* Army Regulation AR 310-25. Washington, DC: Headquarters, Department of the Army, 1986.

—**STEP.** (1) Step is the prescribed distance measure from one heel to the other heel of a marching soldier. (2) Step is a place in walking or marching. A full step is 30 inches, a half step is fifteen inches in quick-time marching. (3) Step means to move a cipher element (e.g., a rotor or key tape) from one enciphering position to another.

References
Department of Defense, U.S. Army. *Drills and Ceremonies.* Field Manual FM 22-5. Washington, DC: Headquarters, Department of the Army, 1986.

—**STEP HEIGHT** is the perpendicular height of a slope facet.

References

Department of Defense, U.S. Army. *Dictionary of United States Army Terms.* Army Regulation AR 310-25. Washington, DC: Headquarters, Department of the Army, 1986.

—**STEREOSCOPIC COVER** is an intelligence imagery and photoreconnaissance term. Stereoscopic cover involves taking photography with sufficient overlap to permit a complete stereoscopic examination. *See also:* Aerial Reconnaissance, Sortie Number, Stereoscopic Pair, Stereoscopic Vision, Stereoscopy.

References

Reeves, Robert; Anson, Abraham; and Landen, David. *Manual of Remote Sensing.* Falls Church, VA: American Society of Photogrammetry, 1975.

—**STEREOSCOPIC PAIR** is an intelligence imagery and photoreconnaissance term for two photographs with sufficient overlap of detail that it is possible to make a stereoscopic examination of an object or an area that appears in both photographs. *See also:* Aerial Reconnaissance, Sortie Number.

References

Reeves, Robert; Anson, Abraham; and Landen, David. *Manual of Remote Sensing.* Falls Church, VA: American Society of Photogrammetry, 1975.

—**STEREOSCOPIC VISION**, an intelligence imagery and photoreconnaissance term, is the capability to perceive three dimensional images. *See also:* Aerial Reconnaissance, Sortie Number.

References

Reeves, Robert; Anson, Abraham; and Landen, David. *Manual of Remote Sensing.* Falls Church, VA: American Society of Photogrammetry, 1975.

—**STEREOSCOPY** is an intelligence imagery and photoreconnaissance term for the science that concerns three-dimensional effects and how these effects are produced. *See also:* Aerial Reconnaissance, Sortie Number.

References

Reeves, Robert; Anson, Abraham; and Landen, David. *Manual of Remote Sensing.* Falls Church, VA: American Society of Photogrammetry, 1975.

—**STERILIZE** is to return an armed mine fuze to an inactive state. *See also:* Mine Warfare.

References

Department of Defense, U.S. Army. *Mine/Countermine Operations at the Company Level.* Field Manual FM 20-32. Washington, DC: Headquarters, Department of the Army, 1976.

—**STICK.** (1) A stick is a number of paratroopers who jump from one aperture or door of an aircraft during one run over the drop zone. (2) A stick is a succession of missiles that are fired or release separately at predetermined intervals from a single aircraft. *See also:* Stick Commander (Air Transport).

References

Department of Defense, U.S. Army. *USA/USAF Doctrine for Joint Airborne and Tactical Airlift Operations.* Field Manual FM 100-27. Washington, DC: Headquarters, Department of the Army, 1985.

—**STICK COMMANDER** (AIR TRANSPORT) is a designated individual who controls parachutists from the time they enter the aircraft until they exit. *See also:* Jumpmaster.

References

Department of Defense, Joint Chiefs of Staff. *Department of Defense Dictionary of Military and Related Terms.* Washington, DC: GPO, 1986.

—**STICKY CHARGE** is an improvised explosive charge, covered with heavy grease, tar, or other adhesive material, that is thrown against or stuck on an object by hand. It is incorrectly called a sticky bomb.

References

Department of Defense, U.S. Army. *Dictionary of United States Army Terms.* Army Regulation AR 310-25. Washington, DC: Headquarters, Department of the Army, 1986.

—**STINGER MISSILE SYSTEM** is a short-range, man-portable, shoulder-fired, infrared homing (heat-seeking) air defense guided missile system. It is designed to counter high-speed, low-level, ground-attack aircraft. As a shoulder-fired missile system, it provides air defense coverage to even the smallest combat units. The missile homes in on the heat that is emitted by either jet or propeller-driven fixed-wing aircraft or helicopters and uses a proportional navigational system that allows it to fly an intercept course to the target. A Stinger crew sights its target and electronically interrogates it to determine if it is a friend. The missile notifies the gunner when it has locked on the target. It is then fired from the tube by a small launch motor. Once it has travelled a safe distance from the gunner, its main engine ignites and propels it to the target. Stinger is stored in a steel tube, requires no maintenance in the field, and is designed to withstand the rigors of the battlefield.

References
Department of Defense, U.S. Army. *Air Defense Employment*. Field Manual FM 44-1. Washington, DC: Headquarters, Department of the Army, 1983.
———. *Weapons Systems: U.S. Army, Navy, and Air Force Directory, 1986-1988*. Washington, DC: DCP, 1986.

—**STOCK ACCOUNTING** is the establishment and maintenance of formal records of the materiel that is in stock. The records reflect such information as quantities, values, condition, and other data, as required. *See also:* Stock Accounting Activity, Stock Control.

References
Department of Defense, U.S. Army. *Dictionary of United States Army Terms*. Army Regulation AR 310-25. Washington, DC: Headquarters, Department of the Army, 1986.

—**STOCK ACCOUNTING ACTIVITY** is an activity assigned the responsibility of maintaining a stock record account.

References
Department of Defense, U.S. Army. *Dictionary of United States Army Terms*. Army Regulation AR 310-25. Washington, DC: Headquarters, Department of the Army, 1986.

—**STOCK CONTROL** is the process of maintaining inventory data on the quantity, location, and condition of supplies that are due in, on hand, and due out to determine quantities of material and equipment that are available and are required for issue and to facilitate the distribution and management of materiel. *See also:* Inventory Control.

References
Department of Defense, Joint Chiefs of Staff. *Department of Defense Dictionary of Military and Related Terms*. Washington, DC: GPO, 1986.

—**STOCK COORDINATION** is a supply management function that is usually exercised at the department level. It controls the assignment of material cognizance for items or categories of material to inventory managers.

References
Department of Defense, Joint Chiefs of Staff. *Department of Defense Dictionary of Military and Related Terms*. Washington, DC: GPO, 1986.

—**STOCK FUND DIVISION** is a chartered element of the Army Stock Fund that is established, operated, and managed as an independent corporate entity of the fund for all financial and supply management purposes. *See also:* Stock Fund Materiel.

References
Department of Defense, U.S. Army. *Dictionary of United States Army Terms*. Army Regulation AR 310-25. Washington, DC: Headquarters, Department of the Army, 1986.

—**STOCK FUND MATERIEL** are items of materiel that are authorized for stock funding financing. The items are designated in regulatory media.

References
Department of Defense, U.S. Army. *Dictionary of United States Army Terms*. Army Regulation AR 310-25. Washington, DC: Headquarters, Department of the Army, 1986.

—**STOCK MANAGEMENT** is the direction and supervision of stock distribution from the time it becomes available until it is expended, declared surplus, or sent to disposal.

References
Department of Defense, U.S. Army. *Dictionary of United States Army Terms*. Army Regulation AR 310-25. Washington, DC: Headquarters, Department of the Army, 1986.

—**STOCK RECORD OF ACCOUNT** is a basic record showing by item the receipt and issuance of property, the balances on hand, and other identifying or stock control data as required by the proper authority.

References
Department of Defense, Joint Chiefs of Staff. *Department of Defense Dictionary of Military and Related Terms*. Washington, DC: GPO, 1986.

—**STOCKADE** is a correctional facility under the jurisdiction of an installation commander and used for confining military prisoners. *See also:* Disciplinary Action.

References
Department of Defense, U.S. Army. *Guard Duty*. Field Manual FM 22-6. Washington, DC: Headquarters, Department of the Army, 1971.

—**STOCKAGE LEVEL** is the quantity of supplies authorized or directed to be kept on hand and on order to support future demands. *See also:* Stockage List.

References

Department of Defense, U.S. Army. *Repair Parts Supply for a Theater of Operations*. Field Manual FM 29-19. Washington, DC: Headquarters, Department of the Army, 1985.

—**STOCKAGE LIST** is a list of all items authorized to be stocked at a specified supply echelon. *See also:* Stockage Level, Stockage List Code, Stockage List Item, Stockage List Item Supply Code.

References

Department of Defense, U.S. Army. *Planning Logistics Support for Military Operations*. Field Manual FM 701-58. Washington, DC: Headquarters, Department of the Army, 1987.

—**STOCKAGE LIST CODE** is a letter code that denotes the status of the item in relation to the authorized stockage list. *See also:* Stockage List.

References

Department of Defense, U.S. Army. *Dictionary of United States Army Terms*. Army Regulation AR 310-25. Washington, DC: Headquarters, Department of the Army, 1986.

—**STOCKAGE LIST ITEM** is an item of supply authorized to be stocked by a particular unit and is included in the authorized stockage list of that unit. *See also:* Stockage List.

References

Department of Defense, U.S. Army. *Dictionary of United States Army Terms*. Army Regulation AR 310-25. Washington, DC: Headquarters, Department of the Army, 1986.

—**STOCKAGE LIST ITEM SUPPLY CODE** is a code used in conjunction with authorized stockage lists to indicate the normal source of supply for a supply item. *See also:* Stockage List.

References

Department of Defense, U.S. Army. *Dictionary of United States Army Terms*. Army Regulation AR 310-25. Washington, DC: Headquarters, Department of the Army, 1986.

—**STOCKAGE OBJECTIVE** consists of the maximum quantities of materiel to be maintained on hand in order to sustain current operations. It consists of the sum of stocks that are represented by the operating level and the safety level. *See also:* Level of Supply.

References

Department of Defense, U.S. Army. *Repair Parts Supply for a Theater of Operations*. Field Manual FM 29-19. Washington, DC: Headquarters, Department of the Army, 1985.

—**STOCKPILE.** (1) Stockpile is a stock of strategic or critical materials that are stored and maintained for use during emergencies. (2) Stockpile means quantities of supplies and equipment that are authorized to be procured for current operations. Stockpiles are established in lieu of, or in addition to, normal levels of supply, usually because procurement economics, procurement difficulties, or unpredictable issue demands such action. (3) Stockpile means stores of special ammunition, usually major assemblies of weapons (both nuclear and nonnuclear) that are in the custody of the Department of Defense.

References

Department of Defense, U.S. Army. *Dictionary of United States Army Terms*. Army Regulation AR 310-25. Washington, DC: Headquarters, Department of the Army, 1986.

—**STOCKPILE TO TARGET SEQUENCE.** (1) Stockpile to target sequence is the order of events involved in removing a nuclear weapon from storage, and assembling, testing, transporting, and delivering it on the target. (2) Stockpile to target sequence means a document that defines the logistical and employment concepts and related physical environments that are involved in transporting a nuclear weapon from the stockpile and delivering it on the target. It may also define the logistical flow that is involved in moving nuclear weapons to and from the stockpile for quality assurance testing, modification, and retrofit, and the recycling of limited-life components. *See also:* Nuclear Warfare.

References

Department of Defense, Joint Chiefs of Staff. *Department of Defense Dictionary of Military and Related Terms*. Washington, DC: GPO, 1986.

—**STOCKS** are the quantities of supplies that are on hand and ready to use.

References

Department of Defense, Joint Chiefs of Staff. *Department of Defense Dictionary of Military and Related Terms*. Washington, DC: GPO, 1986.

—STOP FIRE (AIR DEFENSE FIRE CONTROL OR-DER) is the command used to temporarily halt the engagement sequence due to internally unsafe fire unit conditions. It is seldom transmitted outside the firing battery. This command can be given by anyone in the fire unit who observes an unsafe condition. The engagement continues after the unsafe condition has been corrected.

References
Department of Defense, U.S. Army. *Air Defense Artillery Employment Hawk.* Field Manual FM 44-90. Washington, DC: Headquarters, Department of the Army, 1983.

———. *Air Defense Employment.* Field Manual FM 44-1. Washington, DC: Headquarters, Department of the Army, 1983.

———. *Patriot Battalion Operations.* Field Manual FM 44-15. Washington, DC: Headquarters, Department of the Army, 1984.

—STOPPAGE is a failure of an automatic or semi-automatic firearm to extract or eject a spent case, or to load or fire a new round.

References
Department of Defense, U.S. Army. *Dictionary of United States Army Terms.* Army Regulation AR 310-25. Washington, DC: Headquarters, Department of the Army, 1986.

—STORAGE LIFE is the length of time for which an item of supply including explosives given specific storage conditions, may be expected to remain serviceable and, if relevant, safe. *See also:* Shelf Life.

References
Department of Defense, Joint Chiefs of Staff. *Department of Defense Dictionary of Military and Related Terms.* Washington, DC: GPO, 1986.

—STORAGE PARK is an area where vehicles are put away when they are not in daily use.

References
Department of Defense, U.S. Army. *Dictionary of United States Army Terms.* Army Regulation AR 310-25. Washington, DC: Headquarters, Department of the Army, 1986.

—STORM FLAG is a national flag used at posts and national cemeteries and flown in lieu of the post flag in inclement weather. The storm flag is nine and one-half feet fly (long) by five feet hoist (wide). This flag may be used in lieu of the interment flag to drape the casket of the honored dead in a military funeral. *See also:* Garrison Flag, Post Flag.

References
Department of Defense, U.S. Army. *Dictionary of United States Army Terms.* Army Regulation AR 310-25. Washington, DC: Headquarters, Department of the Army, 1986.

—STRADDLE TRENCH is a trench used as a latrine during field operations and combat.

References
Department of Defense, U.S. Army. *Dictionary of United States Army Terms.* Army Regulation AR 310-25. Washington, DC: Headquarters, Department of the Army, 1986.

—STRADDLING is sensing that is applied to deflection only when too many rights and lefts (overs and shorts) result in a group of shots fired or for other disposition. *See also:* Sensing.

References
Department of Defense, U.S. Army. *Dictionary of United States Army Terms.* Army Regulation AR 310-25. Washington, DC: Headquarters, Department of the Army, 1986.

—STRAGGLER COLLECTING POINT is a location that is manned and operated by military police. It is where stragglers are assembled and processed for return to their units or for other disposition. *See also:* Straggler Line, Stragglers.

References
Department of Defense, U.S. Army. *Dictionary of United States Army Terms.* Army Regulation AR 310-25. Washington, DC: Headquarters, Department of the Army, 1986.

—STRAGGLER LINE is a military police control line that may be manned or unmanned. It extends across the zone of action or sector of defense, is usually in the rear of division medium artillery positions, and is designated by a commander for the apprehension of stragglers, line crossers, and infiltrators. It may consist of fixed posts or patrols when it is manned.

References
Department of Defense, U.S. Army. *Dictionary of United States Army Terms.* Army Regulation AR 310-25. Washington, DC: Headquarters, Department of the Army, 1986.

—STRAGGLERS are any personnel, vehicles, or aircraft that, without apparent purpose or assigned mission, become separated from their unit, column, or formation.

References
Department of Defense, Joint Chiefs of Staff. *Department of Defense Dictionary of Military and Related Terms.* Washington, DC: GPO, 1986.

—**STRAIGHT-LINE METHOD OF COMPUTING REPLACEMENT FACTORS** means to divide the replacement issues of an item that have been made during a given period of time by the average quantity of the item in use during that period. This method is particularly applicable when the age distribution of a group of items has become sufficiently stabilized so that the same percent of an item is replaced during each period of time. This percentage should equal the replacement factor period divided by the average life of the item. *See also:* Consumption Rate.

References
Department of Defense, U.S. Army. *Dictionary of United States Army Terms.* Army Regulation AR 310-25. Washington, DC: Headquarters, Department of the Army, 1986.

—**STRATEGIC AEROMEDICAL EVACUATION.** (1) Strategic aeromedical evacuation is the phase of aeromedical evacuation that provides airlift for patients from overseas areas or from theaters of active operations to NATO countries or to a temporary safe area. (2) Strategic aeromedical evacuation is the phase of evacuation that provides airlift for patients out of the theater of operations to a main support area. *See also:* Medical Treatment.

References
Department of Defense, U.S. Army. *Dictionary of United States Army Terms.* Army Regulation AR 310-25. Washington, DC: Headquarters, Department of the Army, 1986.

—**STRATEGIC AIR INTELLIGENCE** is intelligence that is synthesized specifically to appraise such elements of enemy capabilities and vulnerabilities as are necessary for the establishment of national policy and counsel on air preparedness and air operations. *See also:* Intelligence.

References
Department of Defense, U.S. Army. *Dictionary of United States Army Terms.* Army Regulation AR 310-25. Washington, DC: Headquarters, Department of the Army, 1986.

—**STRATEGIC AIRLIFT** is the continuous or sustained movement of units, personnel, and materiel in support of all Department of Defense agencies between area commands; between the continental U.S. and overseas areas; or within an area of command. Strategic airlift resources possess a capability to airland or airdrop troops, supplies, and equipment to augment tactical forces when required.

References
Department of Defense, U.S. Army. *USA/USAF Doctrine for Joint Airborne and Tactical Airlift Operations.* Field Manual FM 100-27. Washington, DC: Headquarters, Department of the Army, 1985.

—**STRATEGIC CONCENTRATION** is an assembly of forces in areas from which they will begin campaign operations.

References
Department of Defense, Joint Chiefs of Staff. *Department of Defense Dictionary of Military and Related Terms.* Washington, DC: GPO, 1986.

—**STRATEGIC CONCEPT** is the course of action that is accepted as a result of an estimate of the strategic situation. It is a statement of what is to be done in broad terms that are sufficiently flexible to permit its use in framing military, diplomatic, economic, psychological, and other measures. *See also:* Basic Undertakings.

References
Department of Defense, Joint Chiefs of Staff. *Department of Defense Dictionary of Military and Related Terms.* Washington, DC: GPO, 1986.

—**STRATEGIC DEFENSE** is the strategy and forces that are designed primarily to protect a national homeland, including its people, production base, institutions, and other assets, against armed attacks. *See also:* Strategic Offense.

References
Collins, John M. *U.S.-Soviet Military Balance, 1980-1985.* Washington, DC: Congressional Research Service, 1985.

—**STRATEGIC DEFENSIVE** is a large-scale defensive action of a nation at war, as opposed to tactical defense, which refers to a particular operation. *See also:* Strategic Defense.

References
Department of Defense, U.S. Army. *Dictionary of United States Army Terms.* Army Regulation AR 310-25. Washington, DC: Headquarters, Department of the Army, 1986.

—**STRATEGIC INTELLIGENCE** is the intelligence needed for formulating policy and military plans at the national and international levels. It differs primarily from tactical intelligence in the level of its use, but may also vary in scope and detail. The components of strategic intelligence are biographic intelligence, economic intelligence, sociological intelligence, transportation and telecommunications intelligence, military geographic intelligence, armed forces intelligence, political intelligence, and scientific and technical intelligence. *See also:* Entries under each of these titles.

References
Department of Defense, Defense Intelligence College. *Glossary of Intelligence Terms and Definitions.* Washington, DC: DIC, 1987.

Department of Defense, U.S. Army. *Psychological Operations.* Field Manual FM 33-1. Washington, DC: Headquarters, Department of the Army, 1979.

——. *Support Operations: Echelons Above Corps.* Field Manual FM 100-16. Washington, DC: Headquarters, Department of the Army, 1986.

—**STRATEGIC LEVEL OF WAR** is a military strategy employing the armed forces of a nation to secure the objectives of national policy by applying force or the threat of force. Military strategy sets the fundamental conditions for operations.

References
Department of Defense, U.S. Army. *Psychological Operations.* Field Manual FM 33-1. Washington, DC: Headquarters, Department of the Army, 1979.

——. *U.S. Army Operational Concept for Special Operations Forces.* TRADOC PAM 525-34. Washington, DC: Headquarters, Department of the Army, 1984.

—**STRATEGIC LOGISTICS** means all military actions concerned with providing logistics support to a theater of operations.

References
Department of Defense, U.S. Army. *Dictionary of United States Army Terms.* Army Regulation AR 310-25. Washington, DC: Headquarters, Department of the Army, 1986.

—**STRATEGIC MAP** is a map of medium scale or smaller, used for planning operations, including moving, concentrating, and supplying troops. *See also:* Map.

References
Department of Defense, Joint Chiefs of Staff. *Department of Defense Dictionary of Military and Related Terms.* Washington, DC: GPO, 1986.

—**STRATEGIC MISSION** is a mission directed at one or more of a selected series of enemy targets with the purpose of progressive destruction and disintegration of the enemy's war-making capacity and its will to make war. Targets of the mission include key manufacturing systems, sources of raw material, critical material, stockpiles, power systems, transportation systems, communication facilities, and other such target systems. As opposed to tactical operations, strategic operations are designed to have a long-range, rather than an immediate, effect on the enemy and its military forces.

References
Department of Defense, Joint Chiefs of Staff. *Department of Defense Dictionary of Military and Related Terms.* Washington, DC: GPO, 1986.

—**STRATEGIC MOBILITY** is the capability to deploy and sustain military forces worldwide in support of national strategy. *See also:* Mobility.

References
Department of Defense, Joint Chiefs of Staff. *Department of Defense Dictionary of Military and Related Terms.* Washington, DC: GPO, 1986.

—**STRATEGIC OFFENSE** is an offensive action in which the strategy and forces are designed primarily to destroy the enemy's war-making capacity during a general war or to so degrade it that the enemy's opposition collapses. *See also:* Strategic Defense.

References
Collins, John M. *U.S.-Soviet Military Balance, 1980-1985.* Washington, DC: Congressional Research Service, 1985.

—**STRATEGIC OFFENSIVE** is a large-scale offensive action of a nation at war, as opposed to a tactical offensive, which refers to a particular operation. *See also:* Strategic Offense.

References
Department of Defense, U.S. Army. *Dictionary of United States Army Terms.* Army Regulation AR 310-25. Washington, DC: Headquarters, Department of the Army, 1986.

—**STRATEGIC PLAN** provides for the overall conduct of war.

References

Department of Defense, U.S. Army. *Staff Organization and Operations*. Field Manual FM 101-5. Washington, DC: Headquarters, Department of the Army, 1984.

—**STRATEGIC PSYCHOLOGICAL ACTIVITIES** normally are conducted both in peace and in war to gain the support of friendly and neutral nations and to reduce the will and capacity of hostile or potentially hostile nations to wage war. *See also:* Psychological Operations.

References

Department of Defense, U.S. Army. *Psychological Operations*. Field Manual FM 33-1. Washington, DC: Headquarters, Department of the Army, 1979.

—**STRATEGIC PSYCHOLOGICAL WARFARE** involves actions that pursue long-term and primarily political objectives, in a declared emergency or war. They are designed to undermine the enemy's will to fight and to reduce its capacity for waging war. It can be directed against the enemy (e.g., the dominating political group, the government, and the executive agencies), toward the population as a whole, or toward certain elements of it. *See also:* Psychological Operations.

References

Department of Defense, Joint Chiefs of Staff. *Department of Defense Dictionary of Military and Related Terms*. Washington, DC: GPO, 1986.

—**STRATEGIC PSYOP (PSYCHOLOGICAL OPERATIONS)** is conducted to advance broad or long-term objectives and to create a psychological environment that is favorable to military operations. *See also:* Psychological Operations.

References

Department of Defense, U.S. Army. *Psychological Operations*. Field Manual FM 33-1. Washington, DC: Headquarters, Department of the Army, 1979.

—**STRATEGIC RECONNAISSANCE** means a search over side areas, usually by air, to gain information of enemy concentrations or movements that should aid in making strategic or large-scale decisions.

References

Department of Defense, U.S. Army. *Dictionary of United States Army Terms*. Army Regulation AR 310-25. Washington, DC: Headquarters, Department of the Army, 1986.

—**STRATEGIC RESERVE.** (1) A strategic reserve is an external reinforcing force that is not committed in advance to a specific major subordinate command, but that can be deployed to any region for a mission chosen by the major NATO commander. (2) Strategic reserve is the portion of a military force that is withheld from action with a primary mission of preparing for immediate employment in order to execute strategic missions.

References

Department of Defense, U.S. Army. *Dictionary of United States Army Terms*. Army Regulation AR 310-25. Washington, DC: Headquarters, Department of the Army, 1986.

—**STRATEGIC SEALIFT** is composed of naval and merchant ships, together with their crews. It is used to move armed forces, equipment, and supplies over long distances, especially intercontinentally.

References

Collins, John M. *U.S.-Soviet Military Balance, 1980-1985*. Washington, DC: Congressional Research Service, 1985.

—**STRATEGIC STABILITY** is a state of equilibrium that encourages prudence by opponents facing the possibility of general war. Tendencies toward an arms race are restrained, since neither side has an undue advantage.

References

Collins, John M. *U.S.-Soviet Military Balance, 1980-1985*. Washington, DC: Congressional Research Service, 1985.

—**STRATEGIC TELECOMMUNICATIONS** are continental, intercontinental, and intercommand telecommunications facilities and services that are owned, leased, operated, or controlled by the Department of the Army. They are a means of exercising command and control, and logistic and administrative support of elements of the Department, down to the Army component commander within the theater of operations, and other Department of Defense and governmental agencies as directed.

References

Department of Defense, U.S. Army. *Dictionary of United States Army Terms*. Army Regulation AR 310-25. Washington, DC: Headquarters, Department of the Army, 1986.

—**STRATEGIC VULNERABILITY** is the suscepti-bility of vital elements of national power to being seriously decreased or adversely changed by actions within the capability of another nation. Strategic vulnerability may pertain to political, geographic, economic, scientific, sociological, or military factors.

References
Department of Defense, Joint Chiefs of Staff.
Department of Defense Dictionary of Military and Related Terms. Washington, DC: GPO, 1986.

—**STRATEGIC WARNING** is a notification that enemy-initiated hostilities may be imminent. This notification may be received from minutes to hours, to days, or longer, prior to the initiation of hostilities. It is intelligence information or intelligence concerning the threat of the initia-tion of hostilities against the United States or of hostilities in which U.S. forces may become involved. *See also:* Strategic Warning Lead Time, Strategic Warning Postdecision Time, Strategic Warning Predecision Time, Tactical Warning.

References
Department of Defense, Defense Intelligence College. *Glossary of Intelligence Terms and Definitions.* Washington, DC: DIC, 1987.
Department of Defense, Joint Chiefs of Staff.
Department of Defense Dictionary of Military and Related Terms. Washington, DC: GPO, 1986.

—**STRATEGIC WARNING LEAD TIME,** in indi-cations and warning, is the time between the receipt of strategic warning and the beginning of hostilities. This time may include two action periods: strategic warning predecision time and strategic warning postdecision time. *See also:* Indications and Warning, Strategic Concept, Strategic Warning, Strategic Warning Postdecision time, Strategic Warning Predecision time.

References
Department of Defense, Joint Chiefs of Staff.
Department of Defense Dictionary of Military and Related Terms. Washington, DC: GPO, 1986.

—**STRATEGIC WARNING POSTDECISION TIME** is the time that begins after the decision, made at the highest levels of government in response to a strategic warning, is ordered executed and ends with the start of hostilities or the termina-tion of the threat. It is the part of strategic warning lead time that is available for executing

prehostility actions to strengthen the national strategic posture. *See also:* Strategic Warning, Strategic Warning Lead Time.

References
Department of Defense, Joint Chiefs of Staff.
Department of Defense Dictionary of Military and Related Terms. Washington, DC: GPO, 1986.

—**STRATEGIC WARNING PREDECISION TIME** is the time that begins upon receipt of a strategic warning and ends when a decision is ordered executed. It is the part of strategic warning lead time available to the highest levels of government to decide on a strategic course of action. *See also:* Strategic Warning.

References
Department of Defense, Joint Chiefs of Staff.
Department of Defense Dictionary of Military and Related Terms. Washington, DC: GPO, 1986.

—**STRATEGIST POSITION** is an authorized Army position on Army, joint, or combined staffs, or in other appropriate agencies and activities. The incumbent of the position is responsible for formulating, articulating, or instructing strategic concepts, initiatives, and views. His assigned duties involve the assessment of the impact of political, economic, psychological, sociological, and military elements of national power on the international environment and the potential impact of the elements of national power of other countries on U.S. interests and objectives, and the development and articulation of ways in which military power can effectively support national interests and the attainment of national objectives.

References
Department of Defense, U.S. Army. *Dictionary of United States Army Terms.* Army Regulation AR 310-25. Washington, DC: Headquarters, Depart-ment of the Army, 1986.

—**STRATEGY,** according to the Joint Chiefs of Staff, is the art and science of developing and using political, economic, psychological, and military forces as necessary during peace and war to afford the maximum support to policies in order to increase the probabilities and favorable consequences of victory and to lessen the chances of defeat. *See also:* Doctrine, Military Strategy, National Strategy, Operational Art, Tactics.

References

Department of Defense, U.S. Army. *Operations*. Field Manual FM 100-5. Washington, DC: Headquarters, Department of the Army, 1986.

—**STREAMER** is the smoke cloud formed by a single smoke source. *See also:* Smoke Screen.

References

Department of Defense, U.S. Army. *Deliberate Smoke Operations*. Field Manual FM 3-50. Washington, DC: Headquarters, Department of the Army, 1984.

—**STRENGTH** (ORDER OF BATTLE FACTOR) describes a unit of force in terms of men, weapons, and equipment. Information concerning strength provides the commander with an indication of enemy capabilities and helps determine the probable courses of action or options that are open to the enemy. A lack of strength or a preponderance of strength has the effect of lowering or raising the estimate of the capabilities of an enemy force. Likewise, a marked concentration or buildup of units in an area gives the commander certain indications of enemy objectives and probable courses of action. During peacetime, changes in the strength of a potential enemy force is an important indication of its intention to wage war. *See also:* Strength Accountability.

References

Department of Defense, U.S. Army. *Intelligence Analysis*. Field Manual FM 34-3. Washington, DC: Headquarters, Department of the Army, 1986.

—**STRENGTH ACCOUNTABILITY** is a function of a command comprising accountability to competent higher authority for the strength of military personnel under the commander's assignment jurisdiction and for the strength of units attached to it when conditions make it impracticable for units to forward morning reports to the command of assignment for processing.

References

Department of Defense, U.S. Army. *Combat Service Support Operations-Division*. Field Manual FM 63-2. Washington, DC: Headquarters, Department of the Army, 1983.

—**STRESS** is a memory device used by the military police to remember the actions that they take when collecting enemy prisoners of war. STRESS stands for search, tag, report, evacuate, segregate, and safeguard.

References

Department of Defense, U.S. Army. *Military Police Team, Squad, Platoon Combat Operations*. Field Manual FM 19-4. Washington, DC: Headquarters, Department of the Army, 1984.

—**STRIKE.** (1) Strike is an attack intended to inflict damage on, seize, or destroy an objective. (2) Strike means to take down, remove, or prepare for transfer, especially a flag, a tent, or a camp.

References

Department of Defense, Joint Chiefs of Staff. *Department of Defense Dictionary of Military and Related Terms*. Washington, DC: GPO, 1986.

Department of Defense, U.S. Army. *Dictionary of United States Army Terms*. Army Regulation AR 310-25. Washington, DC: Headquarters, Department of the Army, 1986.

—**STRIKE CAMPAIGN** includes combat operations in zones under insurgent control or in contested zones. They are targeted against insurgent tactical forces and bases outside areas of government control. Other internal defense activities may support tactical forces during combat operations. Strike forces normally do not remain in the area of operations after the mission is accomplished.

References

Department of Defense, U.S. Army. *Low Intensity Conflict*. Field Manual FM 100-20. Washington, DC: Headquarters, Department of the Army, 1981.

—**STRIKE FORCE AREA** is the portion of the defensive sector, in the mobile defense, that lies behind the forward defense area. *See also:* Forward Defense Area.

References

Department of Defense, U.S. Army. *Dictionary of United States Army Terms*. Army Regulation AR 310-25. Washington, DC: Headquarters, Department of the Army, 1986.

—**STRIKE PHOTOGRAPHY** is photography taken during an air strike. It is valuable in assessing the success of the strike. *See also:* Sortie Number.

References

Department of Defense, U.S. Army. *Dictionary of United States Army Terms*. Army Regulation AR 310-25. Washington, DC: Headquarters, Department of the Army, 1986.

—**STRING.** (1) A string is a series of radio messages sent from one station to another. The receiving station does not signal receipt of each one individually, but waits until the whole series is given to acknowledge receipt. (2) A string is a given number of shots fired within a certain time interval.

References
Department of Defense, U.S. Army. *Dictionary of United States Army Terms.* Army Regulation AR 310-25. Washington, DC: Headquarters, Department of the Army, 1986.

—**STRIP MARKER** is a marker—natural, artificial, or specially installed—that locates the start and the finish of a mine strip. *See also:* Mine Warfare.

References
Department of Defense, U.S. Army. *Mine/ Countermine Operations at the Company Level.* Field Manual FM 20-32. Washington, DC: Headquarters, Department of the Army, 1976.

—**STRIP MOSAIC** is a mosaic consisting of one strip of air photographs that were taken on a single flight. *See also:* Aerial Reconnaissance.

References
Department of Defense, U.S. Army. *Dictionary of United States Army Terms.* Army Regulation AR 310-25. Washington, DC: Headquarters, Department of the Army, 1986.

—**STRONG SIDE** (ARMY AVIATION) is the side of a flight formation that provides the greatest protection against a threat. In an echelon right formation, the strong side is on the right.

References
Department of Defense, U.S. Army. *Air-to-Air Combat.* Field Manual FM 1-107. Washington, DC: Headquarters, Department of the Army, 1984.

—**STRONGPOINTS.** The strongpoint is essentially an antitank "nest" that cannot be quickly overrun or bypassed by tanks, and that can be reduced by enemy infantry only if it expends much time and overwhelming forces. A strongpoint is located on a terrain feature that is critical to the defense or on one that must be denied to the enemy. It is the cork in the bottleneck that was formed by terrain, obstacles, and units. In some cases, division or brigade commanders may direct that a strongpoint be emplaced by a mechanized unit, usually a battalion.

References
Department of Defense, U.S. Army. *Armored and Mechanized Division Operations.* Field Manual FM 71-100. Washington, DC: Headquarters, Department of the Army, 1978.

———. *Operational Terms and Symbols.* Field Manual FM 101-5-1. Washington, DC: Headquarters, Department of the Army, 1985.

—**STRUCTURE OF MODERN WARFARE.** War is a national undertaking that must be coordinated from the highest levels of policymaking to the lowest levels of execution. Military strategy, operational art, and tactics are the broad divisions of activity in preparing for and conducting war. Successful military strategy achieves national and alliance political aims at the lowest possible cost in lives and treasure. Operational art translates those aims into effective military operations and campaigns. Sound tactics win the battles and engagements that produce successful campaigns and operations. While the principles of war apply equally to strategy, operational art, and tactics, they apply differently to each level of war. *See also:* Principles of War.

References
Department of Defense, U.S. Army. *Operations.* Field Manual FM 100-5. Washington, DC: Headquarters, Department of the Army, 1986.

—**STRUCTURE STRENGTH** is the strength required to sustain performance of a general war mission for table of organization and equipment units, or the prescribed mission of table of distribution and allowances units.

References
Department of Defense, U.S. Army. *Dictionary of United States Army Terms.* Army Regulation AR 310-25. Washington, DC: Headquarters, Department of the Army, 1986.

—**STRUT.** (1) A strut is part of the lock mechanism in automatic pistols and revolvers that puts pressure on the hammer. (2) A strut is a brace or supporting piece, especially in an aircraft or an artillery piece.

References
Department of Defense, U.S. Army. *Dictionary of United States Army Terms.* Army Regulation AR 310-25. Washington, DC: Headquarters, Department of the Army, 1986.

—**STUDY** is a detailed consideration of a specific condition or situation that is based upon a careful evaluation of information and factual data already available.

References

Department of Defense, U.S. Army. *Dictionary of United States Army Terms.* Army Regulation AR 310-25. Washington, DC: Headquarters, Department of the Army, 1986.

—**SUBACTIVITY** is a subordinate element of an activity that shares the unit identification code and manpower and equipment authorizations that are included in the table of distribution and allowances or the table of organization and equipment of a parent unit. *See also:* Activity.

References

Department of Defense, U.S. Army. *Dictionary of United States Army Terms.* Army Regulation AR 310-25. Washington, DC: Headquarters, Department of the Army, 1986.

—**SUBALLCATION** is a fund allocation made by a special operation agency to designated operating agencies for allotment purposes. *See also:* Allocation.

References

Department of Defense, U.S. Army. *Dictionary of United States Army Terms.* Army Regulation AR 310-25. Washington, DC: Headquarters, Department of the Army, 1986.

—**SUBALLOTMENT.** (1) A suballotment is an authorization from allotted funds. It makes a designated portion available for obligation. Fiscal accounting records and fiscal reports must be maintained and rendered. (2) A suballotment is the transfer of personnel or property to a subordinate command. *See also:* Allotment.

References

Department of Defense, U.S. Army. *Dictionary of United States Army Terms.* Army Regulation AR 310-25. Washington, DC: Headquarters, Department of the Army, 1986.

—**SUBASSEMBLY** is a portion of an assembly, consisting of two or more parts, that can be provided and replaced as an entity. *See also:* Assembly, Component, Part.

References

Department of Defense, Joint Chiefs of Staff. *Department of Defense Dictionary of Military and Related Terms.* Washington, DC: GPO, 1986.

—**SUBCALIBER AMMUNITION** is practice ammunition of a smaller caliber than the standard for the gun being used for practice. Subcaliber ammunition is economical and may be fired in relatively crowded areas. It is used with special subcaliber equipment to simulate firing conditions with standard ammunition.

References

Department of Defense, U.S. Army. *Dictionary of United States Army Terms.* Army Regulation AR 310-25. Washington, DC: Headquarters, Department of the Army, 1986.

—**SUBCLASSES OF SUPPLY** provides subclassifications within specific classes of supply based upon the following considerations: (1) specialized transportation requirements, (2) specialized packaging requirements, (3) peculiar storage and handling characteristics, (4) commodity characteristics, (5) intended usage characteristics, and (6) chemical/radiological sensitivity hazards. Subclasses of supply are depicted by alphabetic or numeric codes.

References

Department of Defense, U.S. Army. *Dictionary of United States Army Terms.* Army Regulation AR 310-25. Washington, DC: Headquarters, Department of the Army, 1986.

—**SUBCOURSE** is a nonresident course of military instruction that pertains to one subject.

References

Department of Defense, U.S. Army. *Individual Military Education and Training.* Army Regulation AR 350-1. Washington, DC: Headquarters, Department of the Army, 1987.

—**SUB-HAND RECEIPT** is a hand receipt between the primary hand receipt holder and any person subsequently being given the property for his use. A sub-hand receipt does not transfer the direct responsibility for the property to the sub-hand receipt holder.

References

Department of Defense, U.S. Army. *Commander's Handbook for Property Accountability at the Unit Level.* Field Manual FM 10-14-1. Washington, DC: Headquarters, Department of the Army, 1984.

—**SUBINSTALLATION** is under the command of, and receives support from, the commander of another installation that is geographically distant. *See also:* Installation.

References
Department of Defense, U.S. Army. *Dictionary of United States Army Terms.* Army Regulation AR 310-25. Washington, DC: Headquarters, Department of the Army, 1986.

—**SUBMUNITION** is any item, device, or munition that dispenses from or is carried in projectiles, dispensers, or cluster bomb units and is intended to be fired. Rockets are not considered submunitions.

References
Department of Defense, U.S. Army. *Dictionary of United States Army Terms.* Army Regulation AR 310-25. Washington, DC: Headquarters, Department of the Army, 1986.

—**SUBORDINATE AREA COMMANDERS** is a designation that has been assigned to NATO commanders who are operationally responsible to Allied Commander-in-Chief Channel for an allocated geographical area. *See also:* Major NATO Commanders, Major Subordinate Commanders, Principal Subordinate Commanders.

References
Department of Defense, Joint Chiefs of Staff. *Department of Defense Dictionary of Military and Related Terms.* Washington, DC: GPO, 1986.

—**SUBPACKAGE** (NUCLEAR) means groupings of division and lower echelon nuclear weapons. They are employment schemes for a portion of a corps package. *See also:* Package (Nuclear).

References
Department of Defense, U.S. Army. *Dictionary of United States Army Terms.* Army Regulation AR 310-25. Washington, DC: Headquarters, Department of the Army, 1986.

—**SUBSATURATION DIVING** is exposure of personnel to ambient pressure greater than 1 bar absolute for durations that will not require the use of saturation decompression procedures.

References
Department of Defense, U.S. Army. *Dictionary of United States Army Terms.* Army Regulation AR 310-25. Washington, DC: Headquarters, Department of the Army, 1986.

—**SUBSEQUENT OPERATIONS PHASE** is the phase of an airborne, air assault, or amphibious operation conducted after the assault phase. Operations in the objective area may consist of offense, defense, linkup, or withdrawal. *See also:* Air Movement Phase, Assault Phase, Mounting Phase.

References
Department of Defense, U.S. Army. *Operational Terms and Symbols.* Field Manual FM 101-5-1. Washington, DC: Headquarters, Department of the Army, 1985.

—**SUBSISTENCE** is food for, and provisions to be used in, feeding military personnel and animals. *See also:* Subsistence Quality, Subsistence Wholesomeness.

References
Department of Defense, U.S. Army. *Dictionary of United States Army Terms.* Army Regulation AR 310-25. Washington, DC: Headquarters, Department of the Army, 1986.

—**SUBSISTENCE QUALITY** pertains to type, class, or grade of subsistence of food and any other attribute except wholesomeness. *See also:* Subsistenced.

References
Department of Defense, U.S. Army. *Dictionary of United States Army Terms.* Army Regulation AR 310-25. Washington, DC: Headquarters, Department of the Army, 1986.

—**SUBSISTENCE WHOLESOMENESS** pertains to health and medical aspects or other conditions that may render subsistence food unacceptable for consumption. *See also:* Subsistence.

References
Department of Defense, U.S. Army. *Dictionary of United States Army Terms.* Army Regulation AR 310-25. Washington, DC: Headquarters, Department of the Army, 1986.

—**SUBSTITUTE ITEM** is an item authorized for issue in lieu of a standard item of like nature and quality. *See also:* Substitute Standard.

References
Department of Defense, U.S. Army. *Dictionary of United States Army Terms.* Army Regulation AR 310-25. Washington, DC: Headquarters, Department of the Army, 1986.

—**SUBSTITUTE STANDARD.** Substitute standard type designates an item that is not as satisfactory as a standard type, but is a usable substitute and may be procured to supplement the supply of a standard type.

References

Department of Defense, U.S. Army. *Dictionary of United States Army Terms.* Army Regulation AR 310-25. Washington, DC: Headquarters, Department of the Army, 1986.

—**SUBSURFACE BURST** is a nuclear burst that is generally used to damage underground targets and structures and to make craters as barriers and obstacles. Shallow subsurface bursts may produce a significant amount of fallout. *See also:* Nuclear Warfare.

References

Department of Defense, U.S. Army. *Nuclear Weapons Employment Doctrine and Procedures.* Field Manual FM 101-3-1. Washington, DC: Headquarters, Department of the Army, 1986.

—**SUBUNITS** are subordinate elements of parent units that are separately identified in authorization documents by name, numbers, or letters. They include companies or battalions, platoons, or detachments of separate companies.

References

Department of Defense, U.S. Army. *Dictionary of United States Army Terms.* Army Regulation AR 310-25. Washington, DC: Headquarters, Department of the Army, 1986.

—**SUBVERSION** is an action designed to undermine the military, economic, psychological, and political strength or morale of a regime. *See also:* Unconventional Warfare.

References

Department of Defense, Joint Chiefs of Staff. *Department of Defense Dictionary of Military and Related Terms.* Washington, DC: GPO, 1986.

—**SUCCESSION OF COMMAND** occurs when a subordinate commander substitutes for and assumes the authority, duties, and functions of a senior disabled commander.

References

Department of Defense, U.S. Army. *Planning Logistics Support for Military Operations.* Field Manual FM 701-58. Washington, DC: Headquarters, Department of the Army, 1987.

—**SUCCESSIVE FORMATION** is formation in which the various units move into their positions, one after another.

References

Department of Defense, U.S. Army. *Dictionary of United States Army Terms.* Army Regulation AR 310-25. Washington, DC: Headquarters, Department of the Army, 1986.

—**SUCCESSIVE LEVEL TRAINING** is a training concept under which a low-skill military occupational specialty is established as a base from which the highest caliber military personnel are selected and trained into a higher skill military occupational specialty without interruption.

References

Department of Defense, U.S. Army. *Dictionary of United States Army Terms.* Army Regulation AR 310-25. Washington, DC: Headquarters, Department of the Army, 1986.

—**SUCCESSIVE OBJECTIVES** are objectives in sequence where one objective is initially assaulted by a portion of the main force, supported by the remainder. As soon as the commander is assured the assaulting force can mop up the initial objective, other portions of the command attack the next objective. This process can be continued until the final objective is reached. This approach usually applies to armored units.

References

Department of Defense, U.S. Army. *Dictionary of United States Army Terms.* Army Regulation AR 310-25. Washington, DC: Headquarters, Department of the Army, 1986.

—**SUCCESSIVE POSITIONS** are defensive fighting positions that are located one after the other on the battlefield. A force can conduct a delaying action from successive delay positions. *See also:* Delay From Alternate Positions.

References

Department of Defense, U.S. Army. *Operational Terms and Symbols.* Field Manual FM 101-5-1. Washington, DC: Headquarters, Department of the Army, 1985.

—**SUFFICIENCY** is a force structure standard that demands capabilities that are adequate to attain the desired ends without undue waste. Superiority thus is essential in some circumstances; parity/essential equivalence suffices under less demanding conditions; and inferiority, qualitative as well as quantitative, is sometimes acceptable. *See also:* Superiority.

References

Collins, John M. *U.S.-Soviet Military Balance, 1980-1985*. Washington, DC: Congressional Research Service, 1985.

—**SUMMARY COURT-MARTIAL** is a court-martial composed of one officer. It may impose punishment of confinement up to one month, hard labor without confinement up to 45 days, restriction up to two months, and forfeitures up to two-thirds of one month's pay. *See also:* General Court-Martial, Special Court-Martial.

References

Department of Defense, U.S. Army. *Dictionary of United States Army Terms*. Army Regulation AR 310-25. Washington, DC: Headquarters, Department of the Army, 1986.

—**SUMMARY COURT OFFICER** is an officer who is appointed to perform the duties of a summary court-martial and to administer oaths under the Uniform Code of Military Justice, Article 136. *See also:* Summary Court-Martial.

References

Department of Defense, U.S. Army. *Dictionary of United States Army Terms*. Army Regulation AR 310-25. Washington, DC: Headquarters, Department of the Army, 1986.

—**SUMMIT** is the highest altitude above mean sea level that a projectile reaches in its flight from the gun to the target. It is the algebraic sum of the maximum ordinate and the altitude of the gun.

References

Department of Defense, Joint Chiefs of Staff. *Department of Defense Dictionary of Military and Related Terms*. Washington, DC: GPO, 1986.

—**SUNDRY FUND ACTIVITY** is a nonappropriated fund activity not defined as a welfare or revenue-producing activity. It pertains to self-sustained funds and to associations whose active membership is composed of limited groups of military personnel on active duty and eligible civilian employees, or any combination of such membership.

References

Department of Defense, U.S. Army. *Dictionary of United States Army Terms*. Army Regulation AR 310-25. Washington, DC: Headquarters, Department of the Army, 1986.

—**SUPER HIGH DOLLAR VALUE ITEMS** are a relatively small group of selected end-items and repair parts whose dollar value (annual demands and/or unit cost) represents a considerable investment for the Department of the Army.

References

Department of Defense, U.S. Army. *Dictionary of United States Army Terms*. Army Regulation AR 310-25. Washington, DC: Headquarters, Department of the Army, 1986.

—**SUPERCHARGE** (WEAPONS, AND AMMUNITION) is a propelling charge that is intended to give the highest standard muzzle velocity authorized for the projectile in the weapon from which it is fired. It is sometimes used as an identifying weapon designation when more than one type of charge is available for a weapon.

References

Department of Defense, U.S. Army. *Dictionary of United States Army Terms*. Army Regulation AR 310-25. Washington, DC: Headquarters, Department of the Army, 1986.

—**SUPERCRITICAL** (NUCLEAR) is a condition of fissionable material in which a chain reaction multiplies with such speed as to cause an explosion. *See also:* Nuclear Warfare.

References

Department of Defense, U.S. Army. *Dictionary of United States Army Terms*. Army Regulation AR 310-25. Washington, DC: Headquarters, Department of the Army, 1986.

—**SUPERELEVATION** is an added positive angle in air defense gunnery that compensates for the fall of the projectile during the time of flight due to the pull of gravity.

References

Department of Defense, U.S. Army. *Dictionary of United States Army Terms*. Army Regulation AR 310-25. Washington, DC: Headquarters, Department of the Army, 1986.

—**SUPERENCIPHERMENT** is the result of subjecting cipher text to more enciphering. *See also:* Superencryption.

References

Department of Defense, U.S. Army. *Dictionary of United States Army Terms*. Army Regulation AR 310-25. Washington, DC: Headquarters, Department of the Army, 1986.

—**SUPERENCRYPTION** is a further encryption of encrypted text for privacy or increased security. *See also:* Superencipherment.

References

Department of Defense, U.S. Army. *Dictionary of United States Army Terms.* Army Regulation AR 310-25. Washington, DC: Headquarters, Department of the Army, 1986.

—**SUPERIMPOSED** is a term used in fire planning to indicate that an artillery unit is augmenting fire on a target and its fire may be lifted from that target by the authority implicit in its fire support role.

References

Department of Defense, Joint Chiefs of Staff. *Department of Defense Dictionary of Military and Related Terms.* Washington, DC: GPO, 1986.

—**SUPERIOR PERFORMANCE QUALIFICATION SCORE** is the military occupational specialty evaluation score established and announced by Headquarters, Department of the Army, as a means of identifying personnel in a particular primary military occupational specialty and skill level who may be selected by the unit commander for award of proficiency pay (superior performance). *See also:* Military Operational Specialty.

References

Department of Defense, U.S. Army. *Dictionary of United States Army Terms.* Army Regulation AR 310-25. Washington, DC: Headquarters, Department of the Army, 1986.

—**SUPERIORITY** is a force structure standard that demands capabilities that are markedly greater than those of the opponent.

References

Collins, John M. *U.S.-Soviet Military Balance, 1980-1985.* Washington, DC: Congressional Research Service, 1985.

—**SUPERNUMERARY** is an extra member of the guard who is used when needed to replace a guard or to perform duties prescribed by local directives. *See also:* Guard.

References

Department of Defense, U.S. Army. *Guard Duty.* Field Manual FM 22-6. Washington, DC: Headquarters, Department of the Army, 1971.

—**SUPERQUICK FUZE,** or instantaneous fuze, is a fuze that functions immediately upon the impact of the missile with the target. This type of fuze is the quickest possible: the firing pin is driven into the primer immediately upon first contact of the missile with the target; hence, the missile functions at the surface of the target. *See also:* Fuze (Specify Type).

References

Department of Defense, U.S. Army. *Dictionary of United States Army Terms.* Army Regulation AR 310-25. Washington, DC: Headquarters, Department of the Army, 1986.

—**SUPERSENSITIVE FUZE** is a fuze that quickly sets off a projectile when it strikes even a very light target (e.g., an airplane wing). *See also:* Fuze (Specify Type).

References

Department of Defense, U.S. Army. *Dictionary of United States Army Terms.* Army Regulation AR 310-25. Washington, DC: Headquarters, Department of the Army, 1986.

—**SUPERVISED ON-THE-JOB TRAINING (SOJT)** is a training process whereby personnel acquire knowledge and skills through the actual performance of duties under competent supervision, in accordance with an approved, planned program.

References

Department of Defense, U.S. Army. *Army Forces Training.* Army Regulation AR 350-41. Washington, DC: Headquarters, Department of the Army, 1986.

—**SUPERVISED ROUTE** (A FORM OF CONTROLLED ROUTE) is a route controlled by traffic control posts, traffic patrols, or both. A movement credit card is required for convoys of ten or more vehicles or for individual vehicles of exceptional size or weight. *See also:* Route.

References

Department of Defense, U.S. Army. *Route Reconnaissance and Classification.* Field Manual FM 5-36. Washington, DC: Headquarters, Department of the Army, 1985.

—**SUPERVISORY RESPONSIBILITY** is the obligation of a supervisor for the proper use, care, and safekeeping of government property that is issued to or used by his subordinates.

References
Department of Defense, U.S. Army. *Commander's Handbook for Property Accountability at the Unit Level.* Field Manual FM 10-14-1. Washington, DC: Headquarters, Department of the Army, 1984.

—**SUPPLEMENT** is a separate publication related to a basic publication prepared to provide additional information or summaries. It may include extracts from the basic publication.

References
Department of Defense, Joint Chiefs of Staff. *Department of Defense Dictionary of Military and Related Terms.* Washington, DC: GPO, 1986.

—**SUPPLEMENTAL CIVILIAN SUPPLIES** are civilian supplies, provided during the military period, that are not considered essential and that are financed and programmed through civilian agencies, if approved by the theater command.

References
Department of Defense, U.S. Army. *Dictionary of United States Army Terms.* Army Regulation AR 310-25. Washington, DC: Headquarters, Department of the Army, 1986.

—**SUPPLEMENTAL FIRE CONTROL MEASURES** are procedural management measures issued by proper military authority that delineate or modify hostile criteria, delegate identification authority, or serve directly as aids in fire distribution or airspace control. The five supplemental fire control measures are (1) air defense operations area; (2) weapons engagement zone; (3) high density airspace control zone; (4) temporary airspace restrictions; and (5) sectors of fire and primary target lines. *See also:* Air Defense Operations Area, High Density Airspace Control Zone, Sector of Fire, Temporary Airspace Restrictions, Weapon Engagement Zone.

References
Department of Defense, U.S. Army. *Patriot Battalion Operations.* Field Manual FM 44-15. Washington, DC: Headquarters, Department of the Army, 1984.

—**SUPPLEMENTAL FOOD ALLOWANCE** is a prescribed quantity of food, defined by components and monetary value, that is required in addition to the basic daily food allowance due to unusual or extraordinary circumstances.

References
Department of Defense, U.S. Army. *Dictionary of United States Army Terms.* Army Regulation AR 310-25. Washington, DC: Headquarters, Department of the Army, 1986.

—**SUPPLEMENTAL PROGRAMMED INTERPRETATION REPORT (SUPIR)** is a standardized imagery interpretation report that provides information on significant targets that were covered by a mission that has not been previously included in other reports. It may also be submitted when supplementary information is required. *See also:* Aerial Reconnaissance.

References
Department of Defense, Joint Chiefs of Staff. *Department of Defense Dictionary of Military and Related Terms.* Washington, DC: GPO, 1986.

—**SUPPLEMENTARY CHARGE** is a cylindrical container, the filler of which is normally trinitrotoluene, used in a deep-cavity projectile to fill the void between the ordinary fuze and booster combination and the bursting charge.

References
Department of Defense, U.S. Army. *Dictionary of United States Army Terms.* Army Regulation AR 310-25. Washington, DC:Headquarters, Department of the Army, 1986.

—**SUPPLEMENTARY POSITION** is a site that provides the best means to accomplish a task that cannot be accomplished from the primary or alternate positions. It is often to the right or rear of the primary position and lets the platoon defend against an attack on an avenue of approach that is not covered by the primary position. A supplementary position may be assigned when the platoon covers more than one avenue of approach. *See also:* Alternate Position, Battle Position, Position, Successive Positions.

References
Department of Defense, U.S. Army. *Air Defense Artillery Deployment: Chaparral/Vulcan/Stinger.* Field Manual FM 44-3. Washington, DC: Headquarters, Department of the Army, 1984.

————. *Air Defense Artillery Employment.* Field Manual FM 44-1. Washington, DC: Headquarters, Department of the Army, 1983.

————. *The Infantry Rifle Company (Infantry, Airborne, Air Assault, Ranger).* Field Manual FM 7-10. Washington, DC: Headquarters, Department of the Army, 1982.

———. *Operational Terms and Symbols.* Field Manual FM 101-5-1. Washington, DC: Headquarters, Department of the Army, 1985.

—**SUPPLEMENTARY TARGET** is a target other than the original target assigned to a gun or battery. It is a target on which fire is delivered when the original targets have been destroyed, or when it is impossible to deliver effective fire on them.

References

Department of Defense, U.S. Army. *Dictionary of United States Army Terms.* Army Regulation AR 310-25. Washington, DC: Headquarters, Department of the Army, 1986.

—**SUPPLIES** are all the items necessary to equip, maintain, and operate a military command. They include food, clothing, equipment, arms, ammunition, fuel, materials, and machinery of all kinds. For planning and administrative purposes, supplies are divided as noted below. The subclassification materiel designators (A through T) may be used in combination with the designated subclassifications to further define a portion of a class of supply for planning purposes (e.g., Class V AL might be used to designate ammunition, air missile). Additional codes may be used by the Services to satisfy a specific requirement. This additional permissive coding is not to be used in lieu of that designated for the major classification and subclassification.

- **Class I**—Subsistence, including gratuitous health and welfare items; subclassifications: A—air (in-flight rations); R—refrigerated subsistence; S—nonrefrigerated subsistence (less combat rations); C—combat rations (including gratuitous health and welfare items).
- **Class II**—Clothing, individual equipment, tentage, organization tool sets and tool kits, hand tools, administrative, and housekeeping supplies and equipment; subclassifications: B—ground support materiel (includes power generators and construction, barrier, bridging, firefighting, petroleum, and mapping equipment); E—general supplies; F—clothing and textiles; M—weapons; T—industrial supplies, including bearings, block and tackle, cable, chain, wire, rope, screws, bolts, studs, steel rods, plates, and bars.
- **Class III**—Petroleum, oil, and lubricants, hydraulic and insulating oils, preservatives, liquid and compressed gases, bulk chemical products, coolants, de-icing and antifreeze compounds (together with components and additives of such products) and coal; subclassifications: A—air; W—ground (surface).
- **Class IV**—Construction materials, including installed equipment, and all fortification/barrier materials; no subclassifications.
- **Class V**—Ammunition of all types (including chemical, biological, radiological, and special weapons), bombs, explosives, mines, fuzes, detonators, pyrotechnics, missiles, rockets, propellants, and other associated items; subclassifications: A—air; and W—ground.
- **Class VI**—Personal-demand items (nonmilitary sales items); no subclassifications.
- **Class VII**—End-items that are ready for their intended use (e.g., launchers, tanks, mobile machine shops, or vehicles); subclassifications: A—air; B-ground support materiel (includes power generators and construction, barrier, bridging, fire fighting, petroleum, and mapping equipment); D—administrative vehicles (commercial vehicles used in administrative motor pools); G—electronics; K—tactical vehicles; L—missiles, M—weapons; and N—special weapons.
- **Class VIII**—Medical materiel, including medical peculiar repair parts; no subclassifications.
- **Class IX**—Repair parts and components, includes kits, assemblies, and sub-assemblies, repairable and nonrepairable, that are required for maintenance of all equipment; subclassifications: are the same as Class VII with addition of T—industrial supplies (includes bearings, block and tackle, cable, chain, wire rope, screws, bolts, studs, steel rods, plates, and bars).
- **Class X**—materiel to support nonmilitary programs (e.g., agricultural and economic development) that are not included in Classes I-IX; no subclassifications.

See also: Supply.

References

Department of Defense, Joint Chiefs of Staff. *Department of Defense Dictionary of Military and Related Terms.* Washington, DC: GPO, 1986.

—**SUPPLY** is the process of providing all the items necessary to equip, maintain, and operate a military command. It involves procuring, distributing, maintaining, and salvaging supplies. There are two phases to supply. The *producer phase* extends from the determination of procurement schedules to the acceptance of finished supplies by the Army. The *consumer phase* extends from the receipt of finished supplies by the Army through the issues of the supplies for use or consumption.

References
Department of Defense, U.S. Army. *Combat Service Support Operations-Division.* Field Manual FM 63-2. Washington, DC: Headquarters, Department of the Army, 1983.

—**SUPPLY AND EVACUATION SECTION** is a staff division that prepares and carries out policies that are established for supplying, evacuating, and transporting personnel and materiel belonging to a command.

References
Department of Defense, U.S. Army. *Dictionary of United States Army Terms.* Army Regulation AR 310-25. Washington, DC: Headquarters, Department of the Army, 1986.

—**SUPPLY CONTROL** is the process by which a supply item is controlled within the supply system. It includes requisitioning, receiving, storing, controlling stock, identifying, and accounting. *See also:* Supply, Supply Control Review.

References
Department of Defense, Joint Chiefs of Staff. *Department of Defense Dictionary of Military and Related Terms.* Washington, DC: GPO, 1986.

—**SUPPLY CONTROL REVIEW** is the process of computing a new requirements forecast and comparing it with the latest asset information in order to determine the exact supply position on a given item. It involves the manual preparation of a supply control study or a mechanized review. *See also:* Supply.

References
Department of Defense, U.S. Army. *Dictionary of United States Army Terms.* Army Regulation AR 310-25. Washington, DC: Headquarters, Department of the Army, 1986.

—**SUPPLY CREDIT** is an assignment of an item to an organization and against which requisitions are to be applied. It is subject to the organization commander's call of a definite quantity of supply, services, or personnel for a prescribed period of time. *See also:* Supply.

References
Department of Defense, U.S. Army. *Dictionary of United States Army Terms.* Army Regulation AR 310-25. Washington, DC: Headquarters, Department of the Army, 1986.

—**SUPPLY DEPOT** is an installation or facility assigned a wholesale or intermediate (overseas) supply mission that includes the receipt, storage, issue, care, preservation, and rewarehousing of materiel in storage, packing and shipping; set assembly/disassembly, inventory control, quality control, traffic management, and administrative support functions. *See also:* Supply.

References
Department of Defense, U.S. Army. *Dictionary of United States Army Terms.* Army Regulation AR 310-25. Washington, DC: Headquarters, Department of the Army, 1986.

—**SUPPLY ECONOMY** is the practice of conserving material by every individual in the Armed Forces. It is developed through training and practice until it becomes a habit. It includes conserving, maintaining, safeguarding, recovering, repairing, and salvaging food, fuel, clothing, weapons, transport, and all materiel. *See also:* Supply.

References
Department of Defense, U.S. Army. *Dictionary of United States Army Terms.* Army Regulation AR 310-25. Washington, DC: Headquarters, Department of the Army, 1986.

—**SUPPLY MANUALS** are a series of publications that contain information pertaining to the supply of items in the Army supply system.

References
Department of Defense, U.S. Army. *Dictionary of United States Army Terms.* Army Regulation AR 310-25. Washington, DC: Headquarters, Department of the Army, 1986.

—**SUPPLY POINT DISTRIBUTION** is a method of distributing supplies to the receiving unit at a supply point, railhead, or truckhead. The unit then moves the supplies to its own area using its own transportation. *See also:* Supply.

References
Department of Defense, U.S. Army. *Combat Service Support Operations-Division*. Field Manual FM 63-2. Washington, DC: Headquarters, Department of the Army, 1983.

—**SUPPLY SUPPORT ACTIVITY** encompasses activities assigned a Department of Defense activity address code and have a supply support mission (e.g., direct support units, missile support elements, maintenance general support units, supply and transportation battalions, supply and service units, repair and utility accounts, installation supply divisions, service schools, materiel management centers, technical supply agencies, self-service supply centers, clothing sales stores, tables of distribution and allowances maintenance shops, central issue facilities, and clothing initial issue points). *See also:* Supply.

References
Department of Defense, U.S. Army. *Dictionary of United States Army Terms*. Army Regulation AR 310-25. Washington, DC: Headquarters, Department of the Army, 1986.

—**SUPPLY SUPPORT REQUEST** is a request submitted by an activity that is responsible for supporting an end-item being provisioned to an inventory manager who is a manager of some of the support items or is a potential manager of some new support items that are used in the end-item. *See also:* Supply.

References
Department of Defense, U.S. Army. *Dictionary of United States Army Terms*. Army Regulation AR 310-25. Washington, DC: Headquarters, Department of the Army, 1986.

—**SUPPLY TRANSACTION REPORTING** is reporting to the appropriate supply accounting activity on individual transactions that affect the stock status of materiel. The reporting is done as each of these transactions occur.

References
Department of Defense, Joint Chiefs of Staff. *Department of Defense Dictionary of Military and Related Terms*. Washington, DC: GPO, 1986.

—**SUPPORT.** (1) Support is the action of a force that aids, protects, complements, or sustains another force in accordance with a directive that requires such action. (2) Support is a unit that helps another unit in battle. Aviation, artil-lery, or naval gunfire may be used as a support for infantry. A support relationship is established by assigning a tactical mission to the supporting unit. Such support may be expressed as direct support, general support, or general support reinforcing. (3) Support is any part of any unit that is held back at the beginning of an attack as a reserve. (4) A support is an element of a command that assists, protects, or supplies other forces in combat. *See also:* Direct Support, General Support, General Support Reinforcing.

References
Department of Defense, U.S. Army. *Operational Terms and Symbols*. Field Manual FM 101-5-1. Washington, DC: Headquarters, Department of the Army, 1985.

—**SUPPORT AREA** is a designated area in which combat service support elements, some staff elements, and other elements are located to support a unit. Company, battalion, brigade, and division support areas are geographical areas that are generally located toward the rear of the unit(s) they support.

References
Department of Defense, U.S. Army. *Air Defense Artillery Deployment: Chaparral/Vulcan/Stinger*. Field Manual FM 44-3. Washington, DC: Headquarters, Department of the Army, 1984.

———. *Combat Service Support Operations-Division*. Field Manual FM 63-2. Washington, DC: Headquarters, Department of the Army, 1983.

———. *Operational Terms and Symbols*. Field Manual FM 101-5-1. Washington, DC: Headquarters, Department of the Army, 1985.

—**SUPPORT CARGO** are all supplies and equipment necessary to establish and maintain Army personnel in overseas bases. It includes cargo for approved Department of the Army operational development and construction projects.

References
Department of Defense, U.S. Army. *Dictionary of United States Army Terms*. Army Regulation AR 310-25. Washington, DC: Headquarters, Department of the Army, 1986.

—**SUPPORT CRAFT** are naval craft designed for the seaward employment of rockets, mortars, and automatic weapons at close range both in support of an assault against enemy-held beaches and in the continuation of the attack. *See also:* Amphibious Operation.

References
Department of Defense, U.S. Army. *Dictionary of United States Army Terms.* Army Regulation AR 310-25. Washington, DC: Headquarters, Department of the Army, 1986.

—**SUPPORT ECHELON** is composed of elements that furnish logistical assistance to combat units. (2) A support echelon is the units that support by fire the commander's plan of maneuver. *See also:* Base of Fire.

References
Department of Defense, U.S. Army. *Operational Terms and Symbols.* Field Manual FM 101-5-1. Washington, DC: Headquarters, Department of the Army, 1985.

—**SUPPORT ELEMENT** (AMBUSH) is the part of a patrol that supports the assault element by firing into and around the kill zone. The support element moves into position prior to the assault element. From its position, it suppresses the objective and shifts its fire when the assault starts. It normally covers the withdrawal of the assault element from the immediate area of the objective, and then withdraws on an order or a signal. *See also:* Kill Zone.

References
Department of Defense, U.S. Army. *The Infantry Rifle Company (Infantry, Airborne, Air Assault, Ranger).* Field Manual FM 7-10. Washington, DC: Headquarters, Department of the Army, 1982.

—**SUPPORT FACILITIES** are ammunition and explosives storage or operations that solely support the functions of tactical or using units. This function distinguishes them from storage depots or manufacturing facilities.

References
Department of Defense, U.S. Army. *Ammunition and Explosives Safety Standards.* Army Regulation AR 385-64. Washington, DC: Headquarters, Department of the Army, 1987.

—**SUPPORT FORCE** is composed of the forces charged with providing intense direct overwatching fires to the assault and breaching forces.

References
Department of Defense, U.S. Army. *Operational Terms and Symbols.* Field Manual FM 101-5-1. Washington, DC: Headquarters, Department of the Army, 1985.

—**SUPPORT ITEMS,** are items (e.g., spares, repair parts, tools, test equipment, or sundry materiels) that are subordinate to or associated with an end-item and are required to operate or overhaul an end-item.

References
Department of Defense, Joint Chiefs of Staff. *Department of Defense Dictionary of Military and Related Terms.* Washington, DC: GPO, 1986.

—**SUPPORT RELATIONSHIPS** are established to define the specific responsibilities between supporting and supported units. The command responsibilities, the responsibility for logistic support, and the authority to reorganize or reassign the component elements of a supporting force remain with the higher headquarters or parent unit, unless otherwise specified. *See also:* Direct Support, General Support, General Support Reinforcing.

References
Department of Defense, U.S. Army. *Operational Terms and Symbols.* Field Manual FM 101-5-1. Washington, DC: Headquarters, Department of the Army, 1985.

—**SUPPORT UNIT** is a unit that acts with, and assists or protects another unit, but does not act under the orders of the commander of the protected unit, of which it is not an organic part.

References
Department of Defense, U.S. Army. *Dictionary of United States Army Terms.* Army Regulation AR 310-25. Washington, DC: Headquarters, Department of the Army, 1986.

—**SUPPORTABILITY** is the characteristic of a piece of materiel that quantifies its ability to adapt to changing supply and maintenance concepts.

References
Department of Defense, U.S. Army. *Dictionary of United States Army Terms.* Army Regulation AR 310-25. Washington, DC: Headquarters, Department of the Army, 1986.

—**SUPPORTED CINC (COMMANDER IN CHIEF)** is a commander of a unified or specified command who is assigned a mission in the standing joint plan or by directive of the Joint Chiefs of Staff for the conduct of operations. He prepares operation plans for the conduct of such operations.

References

Department of Defense, U.S. Army. *Planning Logistics Support for Military Operations*. Field Manual FM 701-58. Washington, DC: Headquarters, Department of the Army, 1987.

—**SUPPORTING ARMS** are air, sea, and land weapons of all types used to support ground units. *See also:* Supporting Arms Coordinator.

References

Department of Defense, Joint Chiefs of Staff. *Department of Defense Dictionary of Military and Related Terms*. Washington, DC: GPO, 1986.

—**SUPPORTING ARMS COORDINATOR** is the officer in charge of the supporting arms coordination center. He is the direct representative of the Navy commander who is charged with supporting fires coordination at the time. He integrates the fire plans of the supporting arms to insure their most effective use in furthering the landing force scheme of maneuver ashore.

References

Department of Defense, U.S. Army. *Dictionary of United States Army Terms*. Army Regulation AR 310-25. Washington, DC: Headquarters, Department of the Army, 1986.

—**SUPPORTING ARTILLERY** executes fire missions in support of a specific unit (usually an artillery unit). However, it remains under the command of the next higher artillery commander.

References

Department of Defense, Joint Chiefs of Staff. *Department of Defense Dictionary of Military and Related Terms*. Washington, DC: GPO, 1986.

—**SUPPORTING ATTACK** is an offensive operation carried out in conjunction with a main attack and is designed to achieve one or more of the following: (1) to deceive the enemy; (2) to destroy or pin down enemy forces that could interfere with the main attack; (3) to control ground which, if it were occupied by the enemy, would hinder the main attack; or (4) to force the enemy to commit reserves prematurely or in an indecisive area.

References

Department of Defense, U.S. Army. *Operational Terms and Symbols*. Field Manual FM 101-5-1. Washington, DC: Headquarters, Department of the Army, 1985.

—**SUPPORTING CINC (COMMANDER IN CHIEF)** is a commander of a unified or specified command who provides forces to a supported commander of a unified or specified command.

References

Department of Defense, U.S. Army. *Planning Logistics Support for Military Operations*. Field Manual FM 701-58. Washington, DC: Headquarters, Department of the Army, 1987.

—**SUPPORTING DISTANCE.** (1) Supporting distance is the distance between two units that can be traveled in time for one to come to the aid of the other. (2) Supporting distance means, for small infantry units, the distance between them that can be effectively covered by their mutual fire.

References

Department of Defense, U.S. Army. *Operational Terms and Symbols*. Field Manual FM 101-5-1. Washington, DC: Headquarters, Department of the Army, 1985.

—**SUPPORTING ESTABLISHMENT** is the Active Army less the operating forces. This area comprises the supporting forces, special activities, training forces, and transients and patients.

References

Department of Defense, U.S. Army. *Dictionary of United States Army Terms*. Army Regulation AR 310-25. Washington, DC: Headquarters, Department of the Army, 1986.

—**SUPPORTING FIRE** is delivered by supporting units to assist and protect a unit in combat. *See also:* Close Supporting Fire, Deep Supporting Fire, Direct Supporting Fire.

References

Department of Defense, Joint Chiefs of Staff. *Department of Defense Dictionary of Military and Related Terms*. Washington, DC: GPO, 1986.

—**SUPPORTING FORCES.** (1) Supporting forces are stationed in, or are deployed to, an area of operations in order to provide support for the execution of an operation order. The operational command of supporting forces is not passed to the supported commander. (2) Supporting forces are the units and elements whose missions are to perform logistical, intelligence, and administrative functions. They are not a part of the operating forces. This category is largely in the continental United States but includes some installations and dependent personnel support in overseas theaters.

References
Department of Defense, U.S. Army. *Planning Logistics Support for Military Operations.* Field Manual FM 701-58. Washington, DC: Headquarters, Department of the Army, 1987.

—**SUPPORTING PLAN** is a category of the operation plan. It is an operation that is prepared by either a supporting commander or a subordinate commander to satisfy the requests or requirements of the supported commander's plan. *See also:* Operation Plan.

References
Department of Defense, U.S. Army. *Planning Logistics Support for Military Operations.* Field Manual FM 701-58. Washington, DC: Headquarters, Department of the Army, 1987.

—**SUPPORTING RANGE** is the distance within which effective fires can be delivered by available weapons.

References
Department of Defense, U.S. Army. *Dictionary of United States Army Terms.* Army Regulation AR 310-25. Washington, DC: Headquarters, Department of the Army, 1986.

—**SUPPORTING WEAPON** is any weapon used to assist or protect a unit of which it is not an organic part.

References
Department of Defense, U.S. Army. *Dictionary of United States Army Terms.* Army Regulation AR 310-25. Washington, DC: Headquarters, Department of the Army, 1986.

—**SUPPRESS ENEMY AIR DEFENSE FIRES** in fire support operations, are fires used to suppress enemy air defenses while friendly aircraft operate in an area.

References
Department of Defense, U.S. Army. *Dictionary of United States Army Terms.* Army Regulation AR 310-25. Washington, DC: Headquarters, Department of the Army, 1986.

—**SUPPRESSION.** Suppression is the temporary or transient degrading of a weapons system's performance by an enemy force, so that the system performs below the level needed to fulfill its mission objectives. Suppression may be accomplished by direct and indirect fires, electronic countermeasures, or smoke that is brought to bear on enemy personnel, weapons, and equipment. When these measures are lifted, the enemy may once again be fully effective. *See also:* Suppression Mission.

References
Department of Defense, U.S. Army. *Air Defense Artillery Deployment: Chaparral/Vulcan/Stinger.* Field Manual FM 44-3. Washington, DC: Headquarters, Department of the Army, 1984.

———. *Attack Helicopter Operations.* Field Manual FM 17-50. Washington, DC: Headquarters, Department of the Army, 1984.

———. *Operational Terms and Symbols.* Field Manual FM 101-5-1. Washington, DC: Headquarters, Department of the Army, 1985.

—**SUPPRESSION MISSION** is conducted to suppress an actual or suspected weapons system in order to degrade its performance below the level needed to fulfill its mission objectives at a specific time for a specific period of time.

References
Department of Defense, Joint Chiefs of Staff. *Department of Defense Dictionary of Military and Related Terms.* Washington, DC: GPO, 1986.

—**SUPPRESSION OF ENEMY AIR DEFENSES** (SEAD) is any action that temporarily destroys, degrades, or obscures an enemy's surface air defense to enhance the effectiveness of friendly air operations. Joint suppression of enemy air defenses is that portion of SEAD that requires joint interaction to suppress enemy surface-to-air defense systems having an influence on the tactical air-land battle area. *See also:* Suppression.

References
Department of Defense, U.S. Army. *Air Defense Artillery Deployment: Chaparral/Vulcan/Stinger.* Field Manual FM 44-3. Washington, DC: Headquarters, Department of the Army, 1984.

———. *Attack Helicopter Operations.* Field Manual FM 17-50. Washington, DC: Headquarters, Department of the Army, 1984.

———. *Operational Terms and Symbols.* Field Manual FM 101-5-1. Washington, DC: Headquarters, Department of the Army, 1985.

———. *Operations.* Field Manual FM 100-5. Washington, DC: Headquarters, Department of the Army, 1986.

—**SUPPRESSIVE FIRE** is fire on or about a weapons system. It is intended to degrade the system's performance below the level needed to fulfill its mission.

References

Department of Defense, Joint Chiefs of Staff. *Department of Defense Dictionary of Military and Related Terms*. Washington, DC: GPO, 1986.

—**SURE-PAY** is an acronym that has been adopted by the Army to represent the check-to-financial organization pay option. It became the standard pay method for all soldiers entering service after October 1, 1985.

References

Department of Defense, U.S. Army. *Army Forces Training*. Army Regulation AR 350-41. Washington, DC: Headquarters, Department of the Army, 1986.

———. *U.S. Army Policy Statement, 1988*. Washington, DC: Headquarters, Department of the Army, 1988.

—**SURFACE LINE** is a telephone or telegraph line laid on the ground hastily during the early stages of an attack or a defense. In an organized area, surface lines are replaced by more permanent installations.

References

Department of Defense, U.S. Army. *Dictionary of United States Army Terms*. Army Regulation AR 310-25. Washington, DC: Headquarters, Department of the Army, 1986.

—**SURFACE MISSION** is the mission of air defense artillery to attack ground or naval targets.

References

Department of Defense, U.S. Army. *Dictionary of United States Army Terms*. Army Regulation AR 310-25. Washington, DC: Headquarters, Department of the Army, 1986.

—**SURFACE OF IMPACT** is the plane tangent to the ground or coincides with the surface of the target at the point of impact of a projectile.

References

Department of Defense, U.S. Army. *Dictionary of United States Army Terms*. Army Regulation AR 310-25. Washington, DC: Headquarters, Department of the Army, 1986.

—**SURFACE OF RUPTURE** is an area on the surface of the ground that is broken up by the explosion of an underground charge.

References

Department of Defense, U.S. Army. *Dictionary of United States Army Terms*. Army Regulation AR 310-25. Washington, DC: Headquarters, Department of the Army, 1986.

—**SURFACE-TO-AIR MISSILE (SAM)** is a surface-launched missile designed to operate against a target that is above the earth's surface. *See also:* Surface-to-Air Missile Envelope, Surface-to-Air-Missile Installation, Surface-to-Surface Missile.

References

Department of Defense, Joint Chiefs of Staff. *Department of Defense Dictionary of Military and Related Terms*. Washington, DC: GPO, 1986.

—**SURFACE-TO-AIR MISSILE (SAM) ENVELOPE** is the air space within the kill capabilities of a specific surface-to-air missile system. *See also:* Surface-to-Air Missile.

References

Department of Defense, Joint Chiefs of Staff. *Department of Defense Dictionary of Military and Related Terms*. Washington, DC: GPO, 1986.

—**SURFACE-TO-AIR MISSILE (SAM) INSTALLATION** is a surface-to-air missile site with the surface-to-air missile system hardware installed. *See also:* Surface-to-Air Missile.

References

Department of Defense, Joint Chiefs of Staff. *Department of Defense Dictionary of Military and Related Terms*. Washington, DC: GPO, 1986.

—**SURFACE-TO-AIR MISSILE (SAM) SITE** is a plot of ground prepared in such a manner that it will readily accept the hardware used in a surface-to-air missile system. *See also:* Surface-to-Air Missile.

References

Department of Defense, Joint Chiefs of Staff. *Department of Defense Dictionary of Military and Related Terms*. Washington, DC: GPO, 1986.

—**SURFACE-TO-SURFACE MISSILE (SSM)** is a surface-launched missile designed to operate against a target on the surface. *See also:* Surface-to-Air Missile.

References

Department of Defense, Joint Chiefs of Staff. *Department of Defense Dictionary of Military and Related Terms*. Washington, DC: GPO, 1986.

—**SURGEON** is a senior medical officer, usually a staff officer, who advises the commander on health services matters. *See also:* Health Services.

References
Department of Defense, U.S. Army. *Dictionary of United States Army Terms.* Army Regulation AR 310-25. Washington, DC: Headquarters, Department of the Army, 1986.

—**SURGICAL TEAM** is a component of a professional services unit. It augments the surgical staff of the medical unit to which it is attached. *See also:* Medical Treatment.

References
Department of Defense, U.S. Army. *Dictionary of United States Army Terms.* Army Regulation AR 310-25. Washington, DC: Headquarters, Department of the Army, 1986.

—**SURPLUS PROPERTY** is any excess property not required for the needs and for the discharge of the responsibilities of any federal agencies, including the Department of Defense. Such property is designated by the General Services Administration.

References
Department of Defense, Joint Chiefs of Staff. *Department of Defense Dictionary of Military and Related Terms.* Washington, DC: GPO, 1986.

—**SURPRISE** (PRINCIPLE OF WAR) is to strike the enemy at a time or place, or in a manner, for which it is unprepared.

To a large degree, the principle of surprise is the reciprocal of the principle of security. Concealing one's own capabilities and intentions creates the opportunity to strike the enemy when it is unaware or unprepared. However, strategic surprise is difficult to achieve. Rapid advances in strategic surveillance technology make it increasingly more difficult to mask or to cloak the large-scale marshalling or movement of manpower and equipment. This problem is compounded in an open society such as the United States, where freedom of the press and information are highly valued. However, the United States can achieve a degree of psychological surprise due to its strategic capability. The rapid deployment of U.S. combat forces into a crisis area can forestall or upset the plans and preparations of an enemy. This capability can give the United States the advantage in both a physical and psychological sense by denying the enemy the initiative.

Surprise is important at the operational and tactical levels, because it can decisively affect the outcome of battles. With surprise, success out of proportion to the effort expended may be obtained. Surprise results from going against an enemy at a time or place or in a manner for which it is unprepared. It is not essential that the enemy be taken unaware, but only that it become aware too late to react effectively. Factors contributing to surprise include speed and alacrity, employment of unexpected factors, effective intelligence, deception operations of all kinds, variations of tactics and methods of operations, and operations security. *See also:* Principles of War.

References
Department of Defense, U.S. Army. *The Army.* (Prepublication Issue.) Field Manual FM 100-1. Washington, DC: Headquarters, Department of the Army, 1986.

———. *Operations.* Field Manual FM 100-5. Washington, DC: Headquarters, Department of the Army, 1986.

—**SURPRISE DOSAGE ATTACK** is a chemical attack that delivers a dose of chemical on a target sufficient to produce the desired casualties before the troops can mask or otherwise protect themselves. *See also:* Chemical Warfare.

References
Department of Defense, Joint Chiefs of Staff. *Department of Defense Dictionary of Military and Related Terms.* Washington, DC: GPO, 1986.

—**SURVEILLANCE (SURVL).** (1) In a general sense, surveillance is the systematic observation or monitoring of places, persons, or things by visual, aural, electronic, photographic, or other means. (2) Surveillance, in Army tactical intelligence, means the all-weather, day and night systematic observation of a battle area for intelligence purposes. (3) Surveillance is the systematic observation of airspace, surface, or subsurface areas; places; persons; or things by visual, aural, electronic, photographic, or other means. *See also:* Surveillance and Reconnaissance Missions.

References
Department of Defense, Defense Intelligence College. *Glossary of Intelligence Terms and Definitions.* Washington, DC: DIC, 1987.

Department of Defense, U.S. Army. *Military Intelligence Group (Combat Electronic Warfare and Intelligence) (Corps).* Field Manual FM 34-20. Washington, DC: Headquarters, Department of the Army, 1983.

———. *Support Operations: Echelons Above Corps.* Field Manual FM 100-16. Washington, DC: Headquarters, Department of the Army, 1986.

—**SURVEILLANCE AND RECONNAISSANCE MISSIONS** collect information from airborne, orbital, and surface-based sensors. Air Force and Navy surveillance and reconnaissance efforts are a part of the national intelligence-gathering and systematic observation process. These operations provide a wide variety of information necessary to the development of national security policy, force postures, planning actions, force employment, and informed responses in times of crisis.

Surveillance operations collect information continuously from the air, land, and sea. Reconnaissance operations are directed toward specific targets. Through surveillance and reconnaissance, varied data (e.g., meteorological, hydrographic, geographic, electronic, and communications characteristics) can be collected on any given area of the earth's surface. The products of reconnaissance and surveillance activities have strategic, operational, and tactical applications in both peace and war. Strategic and operational/tactical surveillance and reconnaissance provide timely notification of hostile intent and actions as well as other information that is vital to the National Command Authority and combat commanders. These operations are instrumental in identifying the composition and capability of hostile and potentially hostile forces. As a result, the total capability of foreign nations to conduct war can be assessed and U.S. forces can be tailored to effectively counter the threat.

References

Department of Defense, U.S. Army. *Long-Range Surveillance.* Field Manual FM 7-93. Washington, DC: Headquarters, Department of the Army, 1987.

———. *Operations.* Field Manual FM 100-5. Washington, DC: Headquarters, Department of the Army, 1986.

—**SURVEYING OFFICER** is an officer who is authorized to make an inquiry and fix responsibility for the damage, destruction, or loss (not due to fair wear and tear) of government property.

References

Department of Defense, U.S. Army. *Dictionary of United States Army Terms.* Army Regulation AR 310-25. Washington, DC: Headquarters, Department of the Army, 1986.

—**SURVIVABILITY** is the development of fighting and protective positions, using natural and improved terrain features as well as man-made structures, to improve the survivability and effectiveness of a friendly force. *See also:* Survivability Operations, Survivability Training.

References

Department of Defense, U.S. Army. *Support Operations: Echelons Above Corps.* Field Manual FM 100-16. Washington, DC: Headquarters, Department of the Army, 1986.

—**SURVIVABILITY OPERATIONS** are developing and constructing protective positions (e.g., earth berms, dug-in positions, and overhead protection) and enacting countersurveillance means to reduce the effectiveness of enemy weapon systems.

References

Department of Defense, U.S. Army. *Operational Terms and Symbols.* Field Manual FM 101-5-1. Washington, DC: Headquarters, Department of the Army, 1985.

———. *Support Operations: Echelons Above Corps.* Field Manual FM 100-16. Washington, DC: Headquarters, Department of the Army, 1986.

—**SURVIVABILITY TRAINING** insures proficiency during intense and continuous combat and that individual soldiers and teams can operate effectively in a variety of situations. It involves routine tasks that units must perform well to insure their survival. Examples of such training include operations in nuclear, biological, or chemical environments; operations in hostile electronic warfare environments; operations using various command post configurations; operations that are required to feed, arm, fuel, and maintain the units' command and control elements; procedures for succession of command; limited visibility operations; activation of alternate communication methods; activation of alternate command posts; the hands-off between command posts (tactical command post to main command post); passive air defense; and local security, to include calls for indirect fire and close air support.

References

Department of Defense, U.S. Army. *How to Conduct Training Exercises.* Field Manual FM 25-4. Washington, DC: Headquarters, Department of the Army, 1984.

—**SURVIVAL** is the act of living through a period of hardship (e.g., evading the enemy, being interned as a prisoner of war, or handling a passive survival situation with slight or no risk of detection by the enemy). It includes using fieldcraft techniques to live off the land, maintaining physical health and developmental vigor under adverse conditions, and developing the will to survive. It also includes a combination of these factors that results in positive actions taken by isolated individuals or prisoners of war to return to friendly control with health, dignity, and honor as soon as possible.

References
Department of Defense, U.S. Army. *Code of Conduct/Survival, Evasion, Resistance and Escape (SERE) Training.* Army Regulation AR 350-30. Washington, DC: Headquarters, Department of the Army, 1985.

—**SUSCEPTIBILITY.** (1) Susceptibility is the degree to which a device, equipment, or weapons system is open to effective attack due to one or more inherent weaknesses. (2) Susceptibility is the vulnerability of a target audience to particular forms of psychological operations research.

References
Department of Defense, Joint Chiefs of Staff. *Department of Defense Dictionary of Military and Related Terms.* Washington, DC: GPO, 1986.

Department of Defense, U.S. Army. *Counter-Signals Intelligence (C-SIGINT) Operations.* Field Manual FM 34-62. Washington, DC: Headquarters, Department of the Army, 1986.

—**SUSPECT BATTERY.** (1) A suspect battery is a hostile battery that is known to exist, but cannot be accurately located. (2) A suspect battery is an accurately located position that may or may not be occupied, or may be a dummy position.

References
Department of Defense, U.S. Army. *Dictionary of United States Army Terms.* Army Regulation AR 310-25. Washington, DC: Headquarters, Department of the Army, 1986.

—**SUSPECT TRUCK AND CAR SITE** is a designated location for placing trucks and railcars containing ammunition or explosives that are suspected of being in hazardous condition. These sites are also used for trucks and railcars that may be in a condition that is hazardous to their contents.

References
Department of Defense, U.S. Army. *Ammunition and Explosives Safety Standards.* Army Regulation AR 385-64. Washington, DC: Headquarters, Department of the Army, 1987.

—**SUSPEND** is to deprive an officer of some of the privileges of his rank (e.g., sitting as a member of a court-martial, selecting quarters, or exercising command) as a punishment for some offense. Suspending an officer does not deprive him of the right to promotion.

References
Department of Defense, U.S. Army. *Dictionary of United States Army Terms.* Army Regulation AR 310-25. Washington, DC: Headquarters, Department of the Army, 1986.

—**SUSPENSION.** (1) Suspension is the act of suspending and officer as a punishment for an offense, or the act of suspending the execution, in whole or in part, of the sentence of a court-martial. (2) Suspension is a mechanical linkage that provides spring or flexible support between the ground contacting members of a vehicle and the chassis or hull. (3) Suspension refers to finely divided particles floating in a fluid.

References
Department of Defense, U.S. Army. *Dictionary of United States Army Terms.* Army Regulation AR 310-25. Washington, DC: Headquarters, Department of the Army, 1986.

—**SUSPENSION OF ARMS** is a short truce arranged by location commanders for a special purpose (e.g., to collect the wounded, to bury the dead, or to arrange for an exchange of prisoners).

References
Department of Defense, U.S. Army. *Dictionary of United States Army Terms.* Army Regulation AR 310-25. Washington, DC: Headquarters, Department of the Army, 1986.

—**SUSPENSION OF FAVORABLE PERSONNEL ACTION** are controls that suspend favorable personnel actions affecting Army members.

References
Department of Defense, U.S. Army. *Commissioned Officer Professional Development and Utilization.* Department of the Army Pamphlet 600-3. Washington, DC: Headquarters, Department of the Army, 1986.

—**SUSPENSION OF FLYING** is the withdrawal of an individual's authority to participate in regular and frequent air flights.

References

Department of Defense, U.S. Army. *Dictionary of United States Army Terms*. Army Regulation AR 310-25. Washington, DC: Headquarters, Department of the Army, 1986.

—**SUSPENSION OF VOUCHERS** is an action taken by the General Accounting Office when it withholds credit for a voucher in the accounts of a disbursing officer because there is doubt regarding the legality of the payment, lack of supporting papers, or other administrative omission and technicalities.

References

Department of Defense, U.S. Army. *Dictionary of United States Army Terms*. Army Regulation AR 310-25. Washington, DC: Headquarters, Department of the Army, 1986.

—**SUSPENSION RIBBON** is a distinctly colored cloth strip from which a metal pendant is suspended by a fastening device.

References

Department of Defense, U.S. Army. *Dictionary of United States Army Terms*. Army Regulation AR 310-25. Washington, DC: Headquarters, Department of the Army, 1986.

—**SUSTAINABILITY** is the ability to maintain the necessary level and duration of combat activity to achieve national objectives. It is a function of providing and maintaining the levels of force, materiel, and consumables necessary to support a military effort.

References

Department of Defense, Joint Chiefs of Staff. *Department of Defense Dictionary of Military and Related Terms*. Washington, DC: GPO, 1986.

—**SUSTAINED RATE OF FIRE** is the actual rate of fire that a weapon can continue to deliver for an indefinite period of time without seriously overheating.

References

Department of Defense, U.S. Army. *Operational Terms and Symbols*. Field Manual FM 101-5-1. Washington, DC: Headquarters, Department of the Army, 1985.

—**SUSTAINER** (MISSILE) is a propulsion system that travels with, and does not separate from, the missile.

References

Department of Defense, U.S. Army. *Dictionary of United States Army Terms*. Army Regulation AR 310-25. Washington, DC: Headquarters, Department of the Army, 1986.

—**SUSTAINING BASE** is the pool of personnel resources for available overseas assignments.

References

Department of Defense, U.S. Army. *Overseas Service*. Army Regulation AR 614-30. Washington, DC: Headquarters, Department of the Army, 1984.

—**SUSTAINING SUPPLY** is the materiel required to support a unit after it arrives in a theater from the time its accompanying supplies and pre-war stocks are anticipated to run out until regular resupply commences.

References

Department of Defense, U.S. Army. *Planning Logistics Support for Military Operations*. Field Manual FM 701-58. Washington, DC: Headquarters, Department of the Army, 1987.

—**SUSTAINING SUPPORT** are the continuous resupply and service actions that maintain a unit at a desired level of combat effectiveness. These actions include replenishing all classes of supply and the transportation required to accomplish resupply, essential maintenance, recovery and evacuation of nonoperational equipment, medical treatment and evacuation, and individual personnel replacement and services required to sustain the unit.

References

Department of Defense, U.S. Army. *Combat Service Support Operations-Division*. Field Manual FM 63-2. Washington, DC: Headquarters, Department of the Army, 1983.

———. *Support Operations: Echelons Above Corps*. Field Manual FM 100-16. Washington, DC: Headquarters, Department of the Army, 1986.

—**SUSTAINMENT.** The sole measurement of successful sustainment has always been the generation of combat power at the decisive time and place. Because the environment for this has never been more demanding, today's units must be as simple and as rugged as possible. They must also use complex weapons and consume large stocks of materiel to fight a sophisticated enemy. High- and mid-intensity operations are therefore characterized by a high consumption of military materiel; by a great diversity of equipment types; by the expansion of the battle area resulting from both sides employing sophisticated weapons, communications, and sensors; and by extending lines of support within and outside the theater of operations. Sustainment on this enlarged, materiel-intensive, electronically sensitive, and lethal battlefield presents an unprecedented challenge.

Sustainment of the operational and tactical efforts in this environment comprises six key sustainment functions: manning, arming, fueling, fixing, transporting the supported force, and protecting the sustainment system itself from attack.

References

Department of Defense, U.S. Army. *Operations.* Field Manual FM 100-5. Washington, DC: Headquarters, Department of the Army, 1986.

—**SUSTAINMENT TRAINING** is individual and collective training conducted in unit or resident schools, units, and organizations to insure continued expertise on operation, maintenance, and employment or fielded systems or equipment. The frequency of such training varies with individual and collective tasks; with the role, location, and personnel who man the unit; and the wishes of the commander.

References

Department of Defense, U.S. Army. *Army Forces Training.* Army Regulation AR 350-41. Washington, DC: Headquarters, Department of the Army, 1986.

———. *Training for Mobilization and War.* Field Manual FM 25-5. Washington, DC: Headquarters, Department of the Army, 1985.

—**SWEEP JAMMING** is a narrow band of jamming that is swept back and forth over a relatively wide operating band of frequencies. *See also:* Jammer.

References

Department of Defense, Joint Chiefs of Staff. *Department of Defense Dictionary of Military and Related Terms.* Washington, DC: GPO, 1986.

—**SWEEPING FIRE** is fire, especially from automatic weapons, that shifts gradually in elevation or direction. *See also:* Fire.

References

Department of Defense, U.S. Army. *Dictionary of United States Army Terms.* Army Regulation AR 310-25. Washington, DC: Headquarters, Department of the Army, 1986.

—**SWIMMING CAPABILITY,** as applied to vehicles, is the ability of a vehicle to negotiate water obstacles by propelling itself across water bodies without being in contact with the bottom. *See also:* Swimming Device.

References

Department of Defense, U.S. Army. *Dictionary of United States Army Terms.* Army Regulation AR 310-25. Washington, DC: Headquarters, Department of the Army, 1986.

—**SWIMMING DEVICE** is a device attached to a vehicle to make it float. A provision must also be made to propel the floating vehicle through the water.

References

Department of Defense, U.S. Army. *Dictionary of United States Army Terms.* Army Regulation AR 310-25. Washington, DC: Headquarters, Department of the Army, 1986.

—**SWINGING TRAVERSE** is a type of fire used against dense troop formations that are moving toward a machine-gun position or rapidly moving targets. In this fire, the traverse clamp is loosened so that a gunner makes rapid changes by exerting pressure against the pistol grip.

References

Department of Defense, U.S. Army. *Dictionary of United States Army Terms.* Army Regulation AR 310-25. Washington, DC: Headquarters, Department of the Army, 1986.

—**SWITCH POSITION** is a defense position diagonal to, and connecting, successive defensive positions that are parallel to the front.

References

Department of Defense, U.S. Army. *Dictionary of United States Army Terms.* Army Regulation AR 310-25. Washington, DC: Headquarters, Department of the Army, 1986.

—**SWITCH TRENCH** is a trench diagonal to, and connecting, successive trenches that are parallel to the front.

References
Department of Defense, U.S. Army. *Dictionary of United States Army Terms.* Army Regulation AR 310-25. Washington, DC: Headquarters, Department of the Army, 1986.

—**SWITCHING CENTRAL** is a facility in a communication system that is used to temporarily manually or automatically interconnect telephone, teletypewriter, data, or radio telephone circuits in response to a subscriber request.

References
Department of Defense, U.S. Army. *Dictionary of United States Army Terms.* Army Regulation AR 310-25. Washington, DC: Headquarters, Department of the Army, 1986.

—**SYLLABARY,** or spelling table, in a code book, is a list of individual letters or a combination of letters or syllables, accompanied by their equivalent code groups, used to spell out words or proper names that are not included in the vocabulary of a code.

References
Department of Defense, U.S. Army. *Dictionary of United States Army Terms.* Army Regulation AR 310-25. Washington, DC: Headquarters, Department of the Army, 1986.

—**SYMBOL** is a sign composed of a diagram, number, abbreviation, color, or combination of them, used to identify and distinguish a particular military unit, activity, or installation.

References
Department of Defense, U.S. Army. *Operational Terms and Symbols.* Field Manual FM 101-5-1. Washington, DC: Headquarters, Department of the Army, 1985.

—**SYMPATHETIC ACTUATION** is the detonation of a mine fuze that is caused by a nearby explosion. *See also:* Mine Warfare.

References
Department of Defense, U.S. Army. *Mine/Countermine Operations at the Company Level.* Field Manual FM 20-32. Washington, DC: Headquarters, Department of the Army, 1976.

—**SYMPATHETIC DETONATION** is the detonation of a charge by exploding another charge adjacent to it.

References
Department of Defense, Joint Chiefs of Staff. *Department of Defense Dictionary of Military and Related Terms.* Washington, DC: GPO, 1986.

—**SYNCHRO** is a self-synchronous device used in fire control equipment that converts mechanical angular position data into an electrical sign, or vice versa. It is also known as a selsyn, a self-synchronous unit, an autosyn, or a magslip (British).

References
Department of Defense, U.S. Army. *Dictionary of United States Army Terms.* Army Regulation AR 310-25. Washington, DC: Headquarters, Department of the Army, 1986.

—**SYNCHRONIZATION** is the arrangement of battlefield activities in time, space, and purpose to produce maximum relative combat power at the decisive point. Synchronization is both a process and a result. Commanders synchronize activities, and in doing so they produce synchronized operations.

Synchronization includes but is not limited to the actual concentration of forces and fires at the point of decision. Some of the activities that must be synchronized in an operation (e.g., interdiction with maneuver, or the shifting of reserves with the rearrangement of air defense) must occur before the decisive moment and may occur at locations distant from each other. While separated in time and space, however, these activities are synchronized if their combined consequences are to be felt at the decisive time and place.

References
Department of Defense, U.S. Army. *Operations.* Field Manual FM 100-5. Washington, DC: Headquarters, Department of the Army, 1986.

—**SYNTHESIS,** in intelligence, is the examining and combining of processed information with other information and intelligence prior to the final interpretation of the material. *See also:* Intelligence.

References
Department of Defense, Joint Chiefs of Staff. *Department of Defense Dictionary of Military and Related Terms.* Washington, DC: GPO, 1986.

—**SYNTHETIC EXERCISE** is an exercise in which the enemy and/or friendly forces are generated, displayed, and moved by electronic or other means on simulators, radar scopes, or other training devices. *See also:* Exercise.

References

Department of Defense, Joint Chiefs of Staff. *Department of Defense Dictionary of Military and Related Terms*. Washington, DC: GPO, 1986.

—**SYSTEM (SYS).** (1) A weapon system is composed of equipment, skills, and techniques, the composite of which forms an instrument of combat. The complete weapon system includes all related facilities, equipment, materials, services, and personnel required solely for its operation, so that the instrument of combat becomes a self-sufficient unit of striking power in its intended operational environment. (2) A support system is a composite of equipment, skills, and techniques that, while not an instrument of combat, is capable of performing a clearly defined function in support of a mission. A complete support system includes all the related facilities, equipment, materials, services, and personnel required for operation of the system, so that it can be considered a self-sufficient unit in its intended operational environment. (3) A system is any organized assembly of resources and procedures united and regulated by interaction or interdependence to accomplish a set of specific functions.

References

Department of Defense, Joint Chiefs of Staff. *Department of Defense Dictionary of Military and Related Terms*. Washington, DC: GPO, 1986.

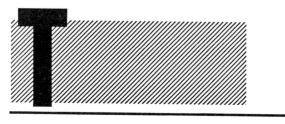

—**TABARD** is a silk banner that is attached to a bugle or trumpet.

References

Department of Defense, U.S. Army. *Dictionary of United States Army Terms.* Army Regulation AR 310-25. Washington, DC: Headquarters, Department of the Army, 1986.

—**TABLE OF ALLOWANCE (TOA)** is an equipment allowance document that prescribes basic allowances of organizational equipment and provides the control to develop, revise, or change equipment authorization inventory data. *See also:* Table of Distribution and Allowances, Table of Organization and Equipment, Table of Organization/Table of Distribution Structure Strength.

References

Department of Defense, Joint Chiefs of Staff. *Department of Defense Dictionary of Military and Related Terms.* Washington, DC: GPO, 1986.

—**TABLE OF DISTRIBUTION AND ALLOW-ANCES (TDA)** is a table that prescribes the mission, organizational structure, personnel, and equipment authorizations, and requirements of a military unit to perform a specific mission for which there is no appropriate table of organization and equipment. *See also:* Table of Organization and Equipment.

References

Department of Defense, U.S. Army. *Organizational Maintenance Operations.* Field Manual FM 29-2. Washington, DC: Headquarters, Department of the Army, 1984.

—**TABLE OF ORGANIZATION AND EQUIPMENT (TOE)** details manpower and equipment authorizations for individual units. It provides a basis for further development of official authorization documents for specific units. These are Department of the Army-published modified tables of organization and equipment. *See also:* Modification Table of Organization and Equipment.

References

Department of Defense, U.S. Army. *Armored and Mechanized Division Operations.* Field Manual FM 71-100. Washington, DC: Headquarters, Department of the Army, 1978.

———. *Organizational Maintenance Operations.* Field Manual FM 29-2. Washington, DC: Headquarters, Department of the Army, 1984.

—**TABLE OF ORGANIZATION/TABLE OF DIS-TRIBUTION STRUCTURE STRENGTH** is the full table of organization and equipment strength (or type B or Cadre strength, when appropriate) for units organized under F or earlier series tables of organization and equipment; level 1 strength (or type B or Cadre strength when appropriate) for units organized under G or later series table of organization and equipment; and the authorized strength of units organized under tables of distribution and allowances. *See also:* Type B (Strength Order).

References

Department of Defense, U.S. Army. *Dictionary of United States Army Terms.* Army Regulation AR 310-25. Washington, DC: Headquarters, Department of the Army, 1986.

—**TAC TURN** (ARMY AVIATION) is a formation maneuver involving 60 to 120 degrees of turn. The tac turn usually involves a change in formation position and is usually given with direction (left or right).

References

Department of Defense, U.S. Army. *Air-to-Air Combat.* Field Manual FM 1-107. Washington, DC: Headquarters, Department of the Army, 1984.

—**TACTICAL** pertains to the employment of units in combat.

References

Department of Defense, U.S. Army. *Dictionary of United States Army Terms.* Army Regulation AR 310-25. Washington, DC: Headquarters, Department of the Army, 1986.

—**TACTICAL AIR COMMAND.** (1) A tactical air command is an Air Force organization designed to conduct offensive and defensive air operations in conjunction with land or sea forces. (2) A tactical air command is a designation of one of the subordinate commands of the Air Force.

References
Department of Defense, U.S. Army. *Attack Helicopter Operations*. Field Manual FM 17-50. Washington, DC: Headquarters, Department of the Army, 1984.

—**TACTICAL AIR CONTROL CENTER (TACC)** is the principal air operations installation (land- or ship-based) from which all aircraft and all air warning functions of tactical air operations are controlled.

References
Department of Defense, U.S. Army. *Attack Helicopter Operations*. Field Manual FM 17-50. Washington, DC: Headquarters, Department of the Army, 1984.

—**TACTICAL AIR CONTROL PARTY (TACP)**, in amphibious warfare operations, is a subordinate Marine or Air Force operational component of the landing force tactical air control system that is designed to provide air liaison functions and to control aircraft from a forward observation post. Tactical air control parties operate at the division, regimental, and battalion levels. Thus located at each appropriate command echelon of the supported ground force, they advise and assist the commander, request and coordinate tactical air support, and meet other requirements of the ground force that they are supporting. A TACP consists of experienced air crews and technicians, ground and airborne vehicles, and the communications equipment that is needed to obtain, coordinate, and control tactical air support of ground operations. *See also:* Air Liaison Officer, Forward Air Controller, Tactical Air Control Center, Tactical Air Control Party Support Team.

References
Department of Defense, U.S. Army. *Attack Helicopter Operations*. Field Manual FM 17-50. Washington, DC: Headquarters, Department of the Army, 1984.
————. *Operational Terms and Symbols*. Field Manual FM 101-5-1. Washington, DC: Headquarters, Department of the Army, 1985.

—**TACTICAL AIR CONTROL PARTY (TACP) SUPPORT TEAM** is an Army team organized to provide armored combat or special-purpose vehicles and crews to certain tactical air control parties.

References
Department of Defense, U.S. Army. *Attack Helicopter Operations*. Field Manual FM 17-50. Washington, DC: Headquarters, Department of the Army, 1984.

—**TACTICAL AIR COORDINATION ELEMENT (TACE)** is a U.S. Air Force element that operates with a corps tactical operations center. The TACE plans and controls Air Force missions in support of corps forces and assists Army planners on matters related to air operations.

References
Department of Defense, U.S. Army. *Attack Helicopter Operations*. Field Manual FM 17-50. Washington, DC: Headquarters, Department of the Army, 1984.

—**TACTICAL AIR COORDINATOR, AIRBORNE (TACA)**, is an Air Force term for an Air Force officer who operates from a fixed-wing aircraft to coordinate the employment of in-bound close air support flights. He provides close air support pilots with battle information and directions to the target area. When necessary, he acts as a relay from the forward air controller or the ground force commander. *See also:* Close Air Support.

References
Department of Defense, U.S. Army. *Attack Helicopter Operations*. Field Manual FM 17-50. Washington, DC: Headquarters, Department of the Army, 1984.

—**TACTICAL AIR DIRECTION CENTER (TADC)**, in amphibious warfare operations, is an air operations installation that is under the overall control of the tactical air control command center. It is from the TADC that aircraft and aircraft warning service functions of tactical air operations in an area of responsibility are directed. *See also:* Amphibious Operation.

References
Department of Defense, U.S. Army. *Attack Helicopter Operations*. Field Manual FM 17-50. Washington, DC: Headquarters, Department of the Army, 1984.

—**TACTICAL AIR DOCTRINE** encompasses the fundamental principles designed to provide guidance for the use of air power in tactical air operations to attain established objectives. *See also:* Tactical Air Operation.

References

Department of Defense, U.S. Army. *Attack
Helicopter Operations*. Field Manual FM 17-50.
Washington, DC: Headquarters, Department of the
Army, 1984.

—**TACTICAL AIR FORCE (TAF)** is an air force that
is charged with carrying out tactical air operations in coordination with ground or naval forces.
See also: Tactical Air Operation.

References

Department of Defense, U.S. Army. *Attack
Helicopter Operations*. Field Manual FM 17-50.
Washington, DC: Headquarters, Department of the
Army, 1984.

—**TACTICAL AIR OPERATION** is an air operation
involving the use of air power in coordination
with ground forces to (1) gain and maintain air
superiority; (2) prevent the movement of enemy
forces into and within the objective area and to
seek out and destroy those forces and their
supporting installations; and (3) join with ground
forces in operations within the objective area in
order to assist directly in the attainment of their
immediate objective.

References

Department of Defense, Joint Chiefs of Staff.
*Department of Defense Dictionary of Military and
Related Terms*. Washington, DC: GPO, 1986.

—**TACTICAL AIR OPERATIONS** is an Air Force
term for operations involving six combat functions: counterair, close air support, air interdiction, tactical air reconnaissance, tactical airlift
operations (including air evacuation), and special operations (including surveillance and reconnaissance) that are performed by tactical air
forces. *See also:* Air Interdiction, Counterair,
Tactical Air Support.

References

Department of Defense, U.S. Army. *Attack
Helicopter Operations*. Field Manual FM 17-50.
Washington, DC: Headquarters, Department of the
Army, 1984.

———. *Operational Terms and Symbols*. Field
Manual FM 101-5-1. Washington, DC: Headquarters, Department of the Army, 1985.

———. *Operations*. Field Manual FM 100-5.
Washington, DC: Headquarters, Department of the
Army, 1986.

—**TACTICAL AIR OPERATIONS CENTER (TAOC),**
in amphibious warfare operations, is a subordinate operational component of the Marine Air

Control System that is designed for control and
direction of air defense. It is under the operational control of a tactical air command or direction center, as appropriate. *See also:* Tactical
Air Operation.

References

Department of Defense, U.S. Army. *Attack
Helicopter Operations*. Field Manual FM 17-50.
Washington, DC: Headquarters, Department of the
Army, 1984.

—**TACTICAL AIR RECONNAISSANCE** is the use
of vehicles to obtain information concerning
terrain, weather, and the disposition, composition, movement, installations, lines of communication, and the electronic and communications
emissions of enemy forces. In addition, such
reconnaissance aids in artillery gunfire adjustment and in the systematic and random observation of ground battle areas, targets, and airspace sectors.

References

Department of Defense, U.S. Army. *Attack
Helicopter Operations*. Field Manual FM 17-50.
Washington, DC: Headquarters, Department of the
Army, 1984.

———. *Operational Terms and Symbols*. Field
Manual FM 101-5-1. Washington, DC: Headquarters, Department of the Army, 1985.

—**TACTICAL AIR SUPPORT** is a U.S. Air Force
term for air operations that directly support the
land battle (e.g., close air support, tactical air
reconnaissance, battlefield air interdiction
(NATO), and tactical airlift). *See also:* Tactical Air
Operation.

References

Department of Defense, U.S. Army. *Attack
Helicopter Operations*. Field Manual FM 17-50.
Washington, DC: Headquarters, Department of the
Army, 1984.

—**TACTICAL AIR SUPPORT ELEMENT** is an element of the Army division or corps tactical operations center consisting of G2 and G3 air
personnel who coordinate and integrate tactical
air support with current tactical ground operations. *See also:* Tactical Air Operation.

References

Department of Defense, U.S. Army. *Attack
Helicopter Operations*. Field Manual FM 17-50.
Washington, DC: Headquarters, Department of the
Army, 1984.

—**TACTICAL AIR TRANSPORT OPERATIONS** involve carrying passengers and cargo within a theater by means of (1) airborne operations (including parachute assault, helicopter-borne assault, and air landing); (2) air logistic support; (3) special missions; and (4) aeromedical evacuation missions.

References
Department of Defense, Joint Chiefs of Staff. *Department of Defense Dictionary of Military and Related Terms.* Washington, DC: GPO, 1986.

—**TACTICAL AIRLIFT** (INTERTHEATER AIRLIFT) is the movement of personnel and materiel by Air Force aircraft. It provides air movement and delivery of combat troops and supplies directly into objective areas through airlanding, extraction, air drop, or other delivery techniques. It is also used for air transport in direct support of airborne assault, carriage of air transported forces, tactical air supply, evacuation of casualties from forward airfields, and special operations. *See also:* Tactical Air Transport Operations.

References
Department of Defense, U.S. Army. *Operational Terms and Symbols.* Field Manual FM 101-5-1. Washington, DC: Headquarters, Department of the Army, 1985.

———. *USA/USAF Doctrine for Joint Airborne and Tactical Airlift Operations.* Field Manual FM 100-27. Washington, DC: Headquarters, Department of the Army, 1985.

—**TACTICAL AREA OF RESPONSIBILITY** (TAOR) is a defined area of land for which responsibility is specifically assigned to the commander of the area as a measure for control of assigned forces and coordination of support.

References
Department of Defense, U.S. Army. *Long-Range Reconnaissance Patrol Company.* Field Manual FM 31-18. Washington, DC: Headquarters, Department of the Army, 1968.

—**TACTICAL CALL SIGN** is a call sign that identifies a tactical command or tactical communications facility. *See also:* Call Sign.

References
Department of Defense, Joint Chiefs of Staff. *Department of Defense Dictionary of Military and Related Terms.* Washington, DC: GPO, 1986.

—**TACTICAL COLLECTIVE TRAINING** is training designed to prepare teams, crews, squads, and units to properly employ the concepts and techniques that are appropriate for a given tactical situation.

References
Department of Defense, U.S. Army. *How to Prepare and Conduct Military Training.* Field Manual FM 21-6. Washington, DC: Headquarters, Department of the Army, 1975.

—**TACTICAL COMBAT FORCES (TCF)** are the combat forces the commander assigns the mission of defeating rear battle threat forces.

References
Department of Defense, U.S. Army. *Rear Battle.* Field Manual FM 90-14. Washington, DC: Headquarters, Department of the Army, 1985.

—**TACTICAL COMMAND** is the authority delegated to the commander to assign tasks to forces under his command for the accomplishment of the mission that has been assigned by higher authority.

References
Department of Defense, Joint Chiefs of Staff. *Department of Defense Dictionary of Military and Related Terms.* Washington, DC: GPO, 1986.

—**TACTICAL COMMAND, CONTROL AND COMMUNICATIONS MISSION AREA** includes resources for providing effective command and control, automation, and communications support for combat units. For a commander to effectively control his tactical elements, he must know where they are located and must have a means to talk to them even if the enemy is conducting electronic countermeasures. The systems included in this mission area provide this capability.

References
Weapons Systems: U.S. Army, Navy, and Air Force Directory, 1986-1988. Washington, DC: DCP, 1986.

—**TACTICAL COMMAND POST (TACCP)** is the forward echelon of a headquarters. The TACCP may consist of a G2, G3, fire support, tactical air control party, air defense artillery, and combat service support liaison (G1 and G4 elements). It is located well forward on the battlefield so that the commander is near subordinate commanders and can directly influence operations. At the division level, the TACCP is located within FM radio range of the committed brigades. *See also:* Command Post, Main Command Post, Rear Command Post.

References
Department of Defense, U.S. Army. *Operational Terms and Symbols.* Field Manual FM 101-5-1. Washington, DC: Headquarters, Department of the Army, 1985.

—**TACTICAL COMMUNICATIONS** are communications provided by, or are under the operational control of, commanders of combat forces, combat troops, combat support troops, or forces that have been assigned a combat service support mission.

References
Department of Defense, U.S. Army. *Dictionary of United States Army Terms.* Army Regulation AR 310-25. Washington, DC: Headquarters, Department of the Army, 1986.

—**TACTICAL CONCEPT** is a statement, in broad outline, that provides a common basis for the future development of tactical doctrine.

References
Department of Defense, Joint Chiefs of Staff. *Department of Defense Dictionary of Military and Related Terms.* Washington, DC: GPO, 1986.

—**TACTICAL CONTROL** is the detailed (usually local) direction and control of the movements or maneuvers necessary to accomplish assigned missions or tasks.

References
Department of Defense, U.S. Army. *Support Operations: Echelons Above Corps.* Field Manual FM 100-16. Washington, DC: Headquarters, Department of the Army, 1986.

—**TACTICAL COUNTERINTELLIGENCE** are actions designed to thwart the enemy's intelligence collection by denying and shielding friendly intentions and actions.

References
Department of Defense, U.S. Army. *Operational Terms and Symbols.* Field Manual FM 101-5-1. Washington, DC: Headquarters, Department of the Army, 1985.

—**TACTICAL DAMAGE ASSESSMENT** is a direct examination of an actual strike area by air observation, air photography, or direct ground observation.

References
Department of Defense, U.S. Army. *Dictionary of United States Army Terms.* Army Regulation AR 310-25. Washington, DC: Headquarters, Department of the Army, 1986.

—**TACTICAL DATA INFORMATION LINK (TADIL)-A** is a netted link in which one unit acts as a net control station and interrogates each unit by roll call. Once interrogated, the unit transmits its data to the net (i.e., each unit receives all of the information that is transmitted). This is a direct retransfer of data and no relaying is involved. *See also:* Net (Communications), Tactical Data Information Link-B.

References
Department of Defense, Joint Chiefs of Staff. *Department of Defense Dictionary of Military and Related Terms.* Washington, DC: GPO, 1986.

—**TACTICAL DATA INFORMATION LINK (TADIL)-B** is a point-to-point data link between two units that provides for simultaneous transmission and reception of data (duplex). *See also:* Tactical Data Information Link-A.

References
Department of Defense, Joint Chiefs of Staff. *Department of Defense Dictionary of Military and Related Terms.* Washington, DC: GPO, 1986.

—**TACTICAL DECEPTION** encompasses the actions taken to surprise or mislead the enemy on current or intended operations for a specified time. The objective of the deception is to keep the enemy misinformed, causing him to react in a way that is favorable to friendly forces, or to not react at all. Deception operations portray logical activities that disguise, conceal, or draw attention away from true activities.

References
Department of Defense, U.S. Army. *The Tank and Mechanized Infantry Battalion Task Force.* Field Manual FM 71-2. Washington, DC: Headquarters, Department of the Army, 1977.

—**TACTICAL DRILL EXERCISE** is an exercise used to prepare a unit to perform a tactical technique or procedure. It can be conducted on a parade ground or over actual terrain. The key is to begin slowly by executing the action by-the-numbers. It allows the unit or team to progress step by step until the members operate as a team and can perform the task at normal speed. *See also:* Tactical.

References
Department of Defense, U.S. Army. *How to Prepare and Conduct Military Training.* Field Manual FM 21-6. Washington, DC: Headquarters, Department of the Army, 1975.

—**TACTICAL EMPLOYMENT OF NUCLEAR WEAPONS,** as used in field manuals, is a term that refers to the use of nuclear weapons by the battlefield commander, usually the corps or division commander, in support of maneuver forces in his command. *See also:* Nuclear Warfare.

References
Department of Defense, U.S. Army. *Support Operations: Echelons Above Corps.* Field Manual FM 100-16. Washington, DC: Headquarters, Department of the Army, 1986.

—**TACTICAL EXERCISE WITHOUT TROOPS (TEWT)** is a low-cost, low-overhead exercise conducted in the field on actual terrain that is suitable for training units for specific missions. Using a few support troops, TEWTs are used by commanders to train subordinate leaders and battle staffs at any echelon to analyze terrain, employ units according to the terrain analysis, emplace weapon systems to best support the unit's mission, conduct the unit mission, and coach subordinates on the best use of terrain and the proper employment of all combat arms. *See also:* Exercise.

References
Department of Defense, U.S. Army. *How to Conduct Training Exercises.* Field Manual FM 25-4. Washington, DC: Headquarters, Department of the Army, 1984.
————. *How to Prepare and Conduct Military Training.* Field Manual FM 21-6. Washington, DC: Headquarters, Department of the Army, 1975.

—**TACTICAL EXPLOITATION OF NATIONAL CAPABILITIES (TENCAP)** allows the services to use the products from national reconnaissance programs for tactical purposes. The national programs have capabilities that far exceed those of the service tactical organizations and can provide the information at much less cost than can the services. The purpose of the TENCAP is to allow the services to exploit the current and future capabilities of the national systems and to permit the integration of this information into tactical decisionmaking as quickly as possible.

References
Department of Defense, Joint Chiefs of Staff. *Department of Defense Dictionary of Military and Related Terms.* Washington, DC: GPO, 1986.

—**TACTICAL FACILITIES** are prepared locations with an assigned combat mission (e.g., missile launch facilities, alert aircraft parking areas, or fixed-gun positions).

References
Department of Defense, U.S. Army. *Ammunition and Explosives Safety Standards.* Army Regulation AR 385-64. Washington, DC: Headquarters, Department of the Army, 1987.

—**TACTICAL INFORMATION PROCESSING AND INTERPRETATION SYSTEM (TIPI)** is a tactical, mobile, land-based, automated information handling system designed to store and retrieve intelligence information and to process and interpret imagery or nonimagery data.

References
Department of Defense, Joint Chiefs of Staff. *Department of Defense Dictionary of Military and Related Terms.* Washington, DC: GPO, 1986.

—**TACTICAL INSPECTION** is an inspection to evaluate the combat efficiency of a unit.

References
Department of Defense, U.S. Army. *Dictionary of United States Army Terms.* Army Regulation AR 310-25. Washington, DC: Headquarters, Department of the Army, 1986.

—**TACTICAL INTELLIGENCE (TACINT or TACINTEL)** (1) Tactical intelligence is foreign intelligence produced under the aegis of the Secretary of Defense and is intended primarily to respond to the needs of military field commanders so that they can maintain the readiness of operating forces for combat operations and to support the planning and conduct of combat operations. (2) Tactical intelligence, as defined by the Church Committee, is "intelligence supporting military plans and operations at the military unit level. Tactical intelligence and strategic intelligence differ only in scope, point of view, and level of employment." (3) Tactical intelligence, in the indications and warning context, means intelligence that is required for planning and conducting tactical operations. Essentially tactical intelligence and strategic intelligence differ only in scope, point of view, and level of employment. *See also:* Combat Intelligence, Intelligence, Strategic Intelligence.

References

Department of Defense, Defense Intelligence College. *Glossary of Intelligence Terms and Definitions.* Washington, DC: DIC, 1987.

Department of Defense, U.S. Army. *Psychological Operations.* Field Manual FM 33-1. Washington, DC: Headquarters, Department of the Army, 1979.

U.S. Congress. Senate. *Final Report of the Senate Select Committee to Study Government Operations With Respect to Intelligence Activities. Report 94-755. Book I, Foreign and Military Intelligence* (Church Committee Report). Washington, DC: GPO, 1976.

—**TACTICAL INTELLIGENCE AND RELATED ACTIVITIES (TIARA)** are activities outside of the National Foreign Intelligence Program that (1) respond to operational commanders' tasking for time-sensitive information on foreign entities; (2) respond to national intelligence community tasking of systems whose primary mission is to support operating forces; (3) train personnel for intelligence duties; (4) provide an intelligence reserve; and (5) are devoted to research and development of intelligence or related capabilities. Specifically excluded from TIARA are programs so closely integrated with a weapon system that their primary function is to provide immediate-use targeting data. *See also:* Tactical Intelligence.

References

Department of Defense, Joint Chiefs of Staff. *Department of Defense Dictionary of Military and Related Terms.* Washington, DC: GPO, 1986.

—**TACTICAL INTELLIGENCE ASSET** is an intelligence asset that is funded in Department of Defense programs. Its primary purpose is to collect or process intelligence information or to produce tactical intelligence. *See also:* Intelligence Asset, Tactical Intelligence.

References

Department of Defense, Defense Intelligence College. *Glossary of Intelligence Terms and Definitions.* Washington, DC: DIC, 1987.

—**TACTICAL INTELLIGENCE READINESS TRAINING** is an Army-wide program conducted by national-level intelligence agencies and activities. The training is designed to maintain and improve the technical and foreign language skills of tactical intelligence personnel. *See also:* Tactical Intelligence.

References

Department of Defense, U.S. Army. *Army Forces Training.* Army Regulation AR 350-41. Washington, DC: Headquarters, Department of the Army, 1986.

—**TACTICAL LAYING CAPACITY** is the actual mine-laying performance, in use, of mine-laying equipment, taking into account the time required for resupply, charging, and related tasks. *See also:* Mine Warfare.

References

Department of Defense, U.S. Army. *Mine/Countermine Operations at the Company Level.* Field Manual FM 20-32. Washington, DC: Headquarters, Department of the Army, 1976.

—**TACTICAL LEAD** (ARMY AVIATION) is an aircraft in a flight that has the best grasp of the tactical situation. The tactical lead may change several times during a mission.

References

Department of Defense, U.S. Army. *Air-to-Air Combat.* Field Manual FM 1-107. Washington, DC: Headquarters, Department of the Army, 1984.

—**TACTICAL LEVEL OF WAR.** Tactics are the specific techniques that smaller units use to win battles and engagements that support operational objectives. Tactics employ all available combat, combat support, and combat service support forces. They involve moving and positioning forces on the battlefield in relation to the enemy, providing fire support, and logistically supporting forces prior to, during, and after engagements with the enemy. At the corps and division levels, the operational and tactical levels are not clearly separable, but are guided by the same principles. An operation designed to defeat any enemy force in an extended area does so through operational maneuver and a series of tactical actions. *See also:* Tactics.

References

Department of Defense, U.S. Army. *Operations.* Field Manual FM 100-5. Washington, DC: Headquarters, Department of the Army, 1986.

———. *Psychological Operations.* Field Manual FM 33-1. Washington, DC: Headquarters, Department of the Army, 1979.

————. *U.S. Army Operational Concept for Special Operations Forces.* TRADOC PAM 525-34. Washington, DC: Headquarters, Department of the Army, 1984.

—**TACTICAL LOCALITY** is an area of terrain that possesses a tactical significance in the particular circumstances existing at a particular time because of its location or features.

References
Department of Defense, Joint Chiefs of Staff. *Department of Defense Dictionary of Military and Related Terms.* Washington, DC: GPO, 1986.

—**TACTICAL LOGISTICS** is the provision of logistics support to combat forces that are deployed within a theater of operations. *See also:* Theater of Operations.

References
Department of Defense, U.S. Army. *Dictionary of United States Army Terms.* Army Regulation AR 310-25. Washington, DC: Headquarters, Department of the Army, 1986.

—**TACTICAL MAP** is a large-scale map used for tactical and administrative purposes. *See also:* Map.

References
Department of Defense, Joint Chiefs of Staff. *Department of Defense Dictionary of Military and Related Terms.* Washington, DC: GPO, 1986.

—**TACTICAL MINEFIELDS** are emplaced as a part of an obstacle plan. These minefields channelize, delay, and disrupt enemy attacks; reduce enemy mobility; block enemy penetrations; increase the effectiveness of friendly fire; deny the enemy the ability to withdraw its forces; prevent enemy reinforcement; protect friendly flanks; and destroy or disable enemy vehicles and personnel. Tactical minefields are emplaced using conventional or scatterable mines, and the density and depth of the field depends on the tactical situation. All types of mines and antihandling devices can be used in such fields, and they often have a standard pattern and density. The mines can be laid by hand or by using the M57 mine dispersing system. *See also:* Mine Warfare.

References
Department of Defense, U.S. Army. *Countermobility.* Field Manual FM 5-102. Washington, DC: Headquarters, Department of the Army, 1985.

————. *Engineer Combat Operations.* Field Manual FM 5-100. Washington, DC: Headquarters, Department of the Army, 1984.

—**TACTICAL MISSILE (TA)** is a missile that has been produced for combat use. *See also:* Tactical Missile Inventory.

References
Department of Defense, U.S. Army. *Dictionary of United States Army Terms.* Army Regulation AR 310-25. Washington, DC: Headquarters, Department of the Army, 1986.

—**TACTICAL MISSILE INVENTORY** is the total number of existing tactical missiles that are held at all combat and support levels, including missiles in depots and in transit, basic loads, and reserve stocks.

References
Department of Defense, U.S. Army. *Dictionary of United States Army Terms.* Army Regulation AR 310-25. Washington, DC: Headquarters, Department of the Army, 1986.

—**TACTICAL MOVEMENT** is the movement of troops and equipment. It is related to a tactical mission and occurs under combat conditions but at a time when the troops are not in direct ground contact with the enemy.

References
Department of Defense, U.S. Army. *Dictionary of United States Army Terms.* Army Regulation AR 310-25. Washington, DC: Headquarters, Department of the Army, 1986.

—**TACTICAL NUCLEAR DOCTRINE** is a term that identifies both the tactical use of nuclear weapons and the conduct of maneuver operations in an integrated environment. *See also:* Nuclear Warfare.

References
Department of Defense, U.S. Army. *Support Operations: Echelons Above Corps.* Field Manual FM 100-16. Washington, DC: Headquarters, Department of the Army, 1986.

—**TACTICAL NUCLEAR WEAPON EMPLOYMENT** is the use of nuclear weapons against enemy forces and enemy supporting installations or facilities. The weapons are used to support operations that contribute to accomplishing a military mission of limited scope or in support of the commander's scheme of maneuver. Their planned use is usually limited to the area of military operations. *See also:* Nuclear Warfare.

References

Department of Defense, Joint Chiefs of Staff. *Department of Defense Dictionary of Military and Related Terms*. Washington, DC: GPO, 1986.

—**TACTICAL OPERATIONS** are the conduct of battles and engagements within the context of campaigns and major operations. They are the domain of corps and smaller units. They are supported by higher echelons of the command that set the terms of battle and provide support for it. Brigades and smaller units may fight engagements—smaller, separate actions—either as part of a battle or as separate actions. Tactical success is measured by the success or failure to achieve the aims set by higher commanders.

References

Department of Defense, U.S. Army. *Operations*. Field Manual FM 100-5. Washington, DC: Headquarters, Department of the Army, 1986.

—**TACTICAL OPERATIONS AREA** is the area between the fire support coordination line and the rear operations area where maximum flexibility in the use of airspace is needed to assure mission accomplishment. The rear boundary of the tactical operations area should normally be at or near the rear boundary of the frontline divisions. *See also:* Fire Support Coordination Line.

References

Department of Defense, U.S. Army. *Airspace Management and Army Air Traffic in a Combat Zone*. Field Manual FM 1-60. Washington, DC: Headquarters, Department of the Army, 1977.

—**TACTICAL OPERATIONS CENTER (TOC)** is a group of the elements of an Army general or special staff concerned with current tactical operations and current tactical support. The group's staff activities are functionally grouped into elements or cells.

References

Department of Defense, U.S. Army. *Operational Terms and Symbols*. Field Manual FM 101-5-1. Washington, DC: Headquarters, Department of the Army, 1985.

—**TACTICAL PLAN** is the plan for a particular combat operation, exclusive of arrangements for supply, evacuation, maintenance, or administration. *See also:* Tactical Planning.

References

Department of Defense, U.S. Army. *Dictionary of United States Army Terms*. Army Regulation AR 310-25. Washington, DC: Headquarters, Department of the Army, 1986.

—**TACTICAL PLANNING** centers on the preparation of battles and engagements. Like operational planning, tactical planning begins with the assignment of a mission or with the commander's recognition of a requirement, and continues until the mission is complete. In essence, it requires a full definition of the mission, collection of all pertinent information, development and analysis of options, and, finally, a decision that forms the basis for a plan or order. This process is a continuous cycle, and is as thorough as time allows. The key to successful planning is anticipating future events and preparing for contingencies.

References

Department of Defense, U.S. Army. *Operations*. Field Manual FM 100-5. Washington, DC: Headquarters, Department of the Army, 1986.

—**TACTICAL PSYCHOLOGICAL WARFARE** involves actions designed to bring pressure to bear on enemy forces and civilians in support of tactical military ground, air, or sea operations in areas where these operations are planned or conducted. It must conform to the overall strategic psychological warfare policy, but will be conducted as an integral part of combat operations. It is conducted to achieve relatively immediate or short-term objectives in support of tactical commanders. *See also:* Psychological Operations.

References

Department of Defense, Joint Chiefs of Staff. *Department of Defense Dictionary of Military and Related Terms*. Washington, DC: GPO, 1986.

—**TACTICAL RANGE** is a range in which realistic targets are in use and a certain freedom of maneuver is allowed.

References

Department of Defense, Joint Chiefs of Staff. *Department of Defense Dictionary of Military and Related Terms*. Washington, DC: GPO, 1986.

—**TACTICAL RESERVE** is a part of a force that is held under the control of the commander. It is to be used as a maneuvering force to influence future action.

References
Department of Defense, Joint Chiefs of Staff.
Department of Defense Dictionary of Military and Related Terms. Washington, DC: GPO, 1986.

—**TACTICAL STANDARD MOBILITY** is the second highest level of mobility and includes the requirement for occasional cross-country movement.

References
Department of Defense, U.S. Army. *Dictionary of United States Army Terms*. Army Regulation AR 310-25. Washington, DC: Headquarters, Department of the Army, 1986.

—**TACTICAL SUB-CONCEPT** is a statement, in broad outline, for a specific field of military capability within a tactical concept that provides a common basis both for equipment and weapon system development and for future development of tactical doctrine.

References
Department of Defense, Joint Chiefs of Staff.
Department of Defense Dictionary of Military and Related Terms. Washington, DC: GPO, 1986.

—**TACTICAL SUPPORT MOBILITY** is a level of mobility designating the requirement for infrequent off-road operations over selected terrain with most of the movement on primary and secondary roads.

References
Department of Defense, U.S. Army. *Dictionary of United States Army Terms*. Army Regulation AR 310-25. Washington, DC: Headquarters, Department of the Army, 1986.

—**TACTICAL SURVEILLANCE OFFICER** is an assistant on the staff of each corps, Army group, and theater headquarters who is especially trained in the capabilities and limitations of tactical air reconnaissance and photographic reconnaissance in air/ground operations. *See also:* Tactical Air Reconnaissance.

References
Department of Defense, U.S. Army. *Dictionary of United States Army Terms*. Army Regulation AR 310-25. Washington, DC: Headquarters, Department of the Army, 1986.

—**TACTICAL SUSTAINMENT** includes all the combat support service activities necessary to support battles and engagements and the tactical activities that precede and follow them.

Tactical units from corps to battalion are sustained by organic or supporting combat service support that provide for their routine requirements and that can be reinforced to give them additional strength for operations. *See also:* Combat Service Support.

References
Department of Defense, U.S. Army. *Operations*.
Field Manual FM 100-5. Washington, DC: Headquarters, Department of the Army, 1986.

—**TACTICAL TRAINING** is the training of troops in all phases of combat operations related to offensive, defensive, and retrograde operations.

References
Department of Defense, U.S. Army. *How to Prepare and Conduct Military Training*. Field Manual FM 21-6. Washington, DC: Headquarters, Department of the Army, 1975.

—**TACTICAL TROOPS** are combat troops, together with any service troops who are required for their direct support, who are organized under one commander to operate as a unit and engage the enemy in combat. *See also:* Troops.

References
Department of Defense, Joint Chiefs of Staff.
Department of Defense Dictionary of Military and Related Terms. Washington, DC: GPO, 1986.

—**TACTICAL UNIT** is an organization of troops, aircraft, or ships intended to serve as a single unit in combat. It may include service units required for its direct support. *See also*: Service.

References
Department of Defense, Joint Chiefs of Staff.
Department of Defense Dictionary of Military and Related Terms. Washington, DC: GPO, 1986.

—**TACTICAL WARNING.** (1) Tactical warning is a notification that the enemy has initiated hostilities. Such warning may be received at any time from the launching of the attack until the attack reaches it target. (2) In satellite missile surveillance, tactical warning is a notification to operational command centers that a specific threat is occurring. The component elements that describe events are (1) country of origin (i.e., the country or countries initiating the hostilities); (2) event type and size (i.e., identification of the type of event and the determination of its size or the number of weapons); (3) country under attack (which is determined by observing the trajectory of an object and predicting its impact point); and (4) event time (i.e., the time that the hostile event occurred). *See also:* Indications and Warning.

References

Department of Defense, Joint Chiefs of Staff. *Department of Defense Dictionary of Military and Related Terms.* Washington, DC: GPO, 1986.

—**TACTICAL WHEELED VEHICLE FLEET** refers to motor vehicles used in direct support of combat or tactical operations. The fleet includes vehicles (of military design and commercial) in the combat, combat support, and combat service support tables(s) of organization and equipment. The tactical wheeled vehicle fleet is one of two categories of the wheeled vehicle fleet; the other category is the nontactical wheeled vehicle fleet. *See also:* Nontactical Wheeled Vehicle Fleet.

References

Department of Defense, U.S. Army. *Dictionary of United States Army Terms.* Army Regulation AR 310-25. Washington, DC: Headquarters, Department of the Army, 1986.

—**TACTICAL WIRE** are wire entanglements used to break up the attack formations of the enemy and hold it in areas that can be covered by intense defensive fire.

References

Department of Defense, U.S. Army. *Dictionary of United States Army Terms.* Army Regulation AR 310-25. Washington, DC: Headquarters, Department of the Army, 1986.

—**TACTICS** are the employment of units in combat, and the ordered arrangement and maneuver of units in relation to each other and to the enemy in order to use their full potentialities. Tactics require the specific application of doctrinal principles.

While operational art sets the objectives and pattern of military activities, tactics is the art by which corps and smaller unit commanders translate potential combat power into victorious battles and engagements. Engagements are small conflicts between opposing maneuver forces and can be conducted by covering forces, guard forces, patrols, units in defense, and units moving to contact fight engagements when they encounter the enemy. They are normally conflicts of a few hours' duration that are fought between divisions or smaller units, and they may or may not bring on a battle.

Sound tactics win battles and engagements by moving forces on the battlefield to gain a positional advantage over the enemy; by applying fire support to facilitate and exploit that advantage; and by assuring the sustainment of friendly forces before, during, and after an engagement with the enemy. Sound tactics employ all available combat, combat support, and combat service support forces where they will make the greatest contribution to the effort. *See also:* Doctrine, Operational Art, Strategy.

References

Department of Defense, U.S. Army. *The Army.* (Prepublication Issue.) Field Manual FM 100-1. Washington, DC: Headquarters, Department of the Army, 1986.

———. *Operations.* Field Manual FM 100-5. Washington, DC: Headquarters, Department of the Army, 1986.

———. *Air Defense Artillery Employment.* Field Manual FM 44-1. Washington, DC: Headquarters, Department of the Army, 1983.

—**TAIL WIND** is a wind that blows toward the smoke objective from behind the smoke source.

References

Department of Defense, U.S. Army. *Deliberate Smoke Operations.* Field Manual FM 3-50. Washington, DC: Headquarters, Department of the Army, 1984.

—**TAILGATE MEDICAL SUPPORT** is an economy-of-force device employed primarily to retain maximum deployability responsiveness during movement halts or to avoid the time and effort required to set up a formal, operational treatment facility. Tailgate medical support consists of dispensing medications, bandages, and splints, and performing simple emergency life-sustaining measures. It is literally performed at the "tailgate" of a vehicle or in a structure of other area using an easily reached set of medical supplies and equipment to insure promptness and efficiency. The mobility of the unit is not affected by this support, and only three to five minutes are required to open or close this service. *See also:* Medical Treatment.

References

Department of Defense, U.S. Army. *Health Service Support in a Communications Zone (Test).* Field Manual FM 8-21. Washington, DC: Headquarters, Department of the Army, 1981.

—**TAILGATE TECHNIQUE** is a method of resupply. Combat vehicles remain in their hide or fight positions and the supplies are brought to them.

References
Department of Defense, U.S. Army. *Tank Platoon Division 86 (Test).* Field Manual FM 17-5. Washington, DC: Headquarters, Department of the Army, 1984.

—**TAIL CHASE** (ARMY AVIATION) is a maneuver on the enemy's six-o'clock position at a 200- to 500-foot distance.

References
Department of Defense, U.S. Army. *Air-to-Air Combat.* Field Manual FM 1-107. Washington, DC: Headquarters, Department of the Army, 1984.

—**TALLY** (ARMY AVIATION) refers to a visual contact with an enemy aircraft or flight (e.g., "Tally" or "No Tally").

References
Department of Defense, U.S. Army. *Air-to-Air Combat.* Field Manual FM 1-107. Washington, DC: Headquarters, Department of the Army, 1984.

—**TANK, COMBAT, FULL-TRACKED, 90-MM GUN (M48A3),** is a fully armored combat vehicle that provides mobile fire power and crew protection for offensive combat. It is armed with one 90-mm gun, one 50-caliber machine gun, and one 7.62-mm machine gun.

References
Department of Defense, Joint Chiefs of Staff. *Department of Defense Dictionary of Military and Related Terms.* Washington, DC: GPO, 1986.

—**TANK, COMBAT, FULL-TRACKED, 105-MM GUN (M-60),** is a heavy, fully armored combat vehicle that provides mobile fire power and crew protection for offensive combat. It is armed with one 105-mm gun, one 50-caliber machine gun, and one 7.62-mm gun.

References
Department of Defense, Joint Chiefs of Staff. *Department of Defense Dictionary of Military and Related Terms.* Washington, DC: GPO, 1986.

—**TANK, COMBAT, FULL-TRACKED, 152-MM GUN,** is a heavy, fully armored combat vehicle that provides mobile fire power and crew protection for offensive combat. It is armed with one 152-mm gun/launcher capable of firing Shillelagh missiles or conventional combustible ammunition, one 50-caliber machine gun, and one 7.62-mm machine gun. *See also:* Shillelagh.

References
Department of Defense, Joint Chiefs of Staff. *Department of Defense Dictionary of Military and Related Terms.* Washington, DC: GPO, 1986.

—**TANK HEAVY** is a company team that has more tank platoons than mechanized infantry platoons or a battalion task force that has more tank companies than mechanized infantry companies.

References
Department of Defense, U.S. Army. *The Tank and Mechanized Infantry Battalion Task Force.* Field Manual FM 71-2. Washington, DC: Headquarters, Department of the Army, 1977.

—**TANK LANDING SHIP (LST)** is a naval ship designed to transport land and amphibious vehicles, tanks, combat vehicles, and equipment in an amphibious assault. *See also:* Amphibious Operation.

References
Department of Defense, Joint Chiefs of Staff. *Department of Defense Dictionary of Military and Related Terms.* Washington, DC: GPO, 1986.

—**TANK, MAIN BATTLE,** is a tracked vehicle that provides mobile firepower and area protection for offensive combat.

References
Department of Defense, Joint Chiefs of Staff. *Department of Defense Dictionary of Military and Related Terms.* Washington, DC: GPO, 1986.

—**TANK RANGE CARDS.** A range card is a sketch or diagram of a tank position on which possible target areas and terrain features have been plotted in relation to the tank. Primarily, the range card enables the crew to engage with the auxiliary fire control instruments targets that cannot be engaged with the direct-fire sights because of poor visibility or where illumination is not available. It is the tank crew's fire plan.

References
Department of Defense, U.S. Army. *Tank Gunnery.* Field Manual FM 17-12. Washington, DC: Headquarters, Department of the Army, 1984.

—**TANK RECOVERY VEHICLE** is a full-tracked motor vehicle, usually armored, designed to remove disabled or abandoned heavy vehicles from a battlefield to a collection point or maintenance establishment.

References

Department of Defense, U.S. Army. *Dictionary of United States Army Terms.* Army Regulation AR 310-25. Washington, DC: Headquarters, Department of the Army, 1986.

—**TANK TRANSPORTER** is a special-purpose wheeled vehicle, or a combination of vehicles, designed to transport tanks and other heavy vehicles over highway and natural terrain. It has the ability to load and unload disabled vehicles without supplemental assistance.

References

Department of Defense, U.S. Army. *Dictionary of United States Army Terms.* Army Regulation AR 310-25. Washington, DC: Headquarters, Department of the Army, 1986.

—**TANK VEHICLE** is a vehicle, normally wheeled, incorporating, in lieu of body, a tank-type container for transporting bulk liquid. It normally includes dispensing valves and may include pumps, hoses, and/or devices for segregating water and impurities from fuel.

References

Department of Defense, U.S. Army. *Dictionary of United States Army Terms.* Army Regulation AR 310-25. Washington, DC: Headquarters, Department of the Army, 1986.

—**TARGET.** (1) A target is a country, area, installation, organization, weapon system, military force, political or economic situation, signal, person, or other entity against which intelligence operations are conducted. (2) A target is a target intelligence term that pertains to the target to be destroyed. In this context, it is a geographic area, complex, or installation planned for capture or destruction by military forces or an area that has been designated to receive future firing. (3) A target, as defined by the Church Committee, is a person, agency, facility, area, or country against which intelligence operations are directed. (4) In artillery, a target is an impact burst that hits the target. *See also:* Acquire, Target Acquisition.

References

Department of Defense, Defense Intelligence College. *Glossary of Intelligence Terms and Definitions.* Washington, DC: DIC, 1987.

Department of Defense, U.S. Army. *Operational Terms and Symbols.* Field Manual FM 101-5-1. Washington, DC: Headquarters, Department of the Army, 1985.

————. *Support Operations: Echelons Above Corps.* Field Manual FM 100-16. Washington, DC: Headquarters, Department of the Army, 1986.

Reeves, Robert; Anson, Abraham; and Landen, David. *Manual of Remote Sensing.* Falls Church, VA: American Society of Photogrammetry, 1975.

U.S. Congress. Senate. *Final Report of the Select Committee to Study Government Operations With Respect to Intelligence Activities. Report 94-755. Book I, Foreign and Military Intelligence* (Church Committee Report). Washington, DC: GPO, 1976.

—**TARGET ACQUISITION** is a target intelligence term pertaining to the target to be destroyed. It is detecting, identifying, and locating a target in sufficient detail to permit the effective use of weapons against it. *See also:* Targeting.

References

Department of Defense, U.S. Army. *Operational Terms and Symbols.* Field Manual FM 101-5-1. Washington, DC: Headquarters, Department of the Army, 1985.

—**TARGET ACQUISITION SYSTEM** consists of the equipment and personnel necessary to detect, identify, and locate ground targets in sufficient detail to permit an effective attack, or to orient or cue other devices or intelligence sources on a specific area or areas. *See also:* Targeting.

References

Department of Defense, U.S. Army. *Field Artillery Target Acquisition.* Field Manual FM 6-121. Washington, DC: Headquarters, Department of the Army, 1978.

—**TARGET ALLOCATION,** in air defense, is the process, following weapon assignment, of allocating a particular target or area to a specific surface-to-air missile unit or interceptor aircraft.

References

Department of Defense, Joint Chiefs of Staff. *Department of Defense Dictionary of Military and Related Terms.* Washington, DC: GPO, 1986.

—**TARGET ANALYSIS (TA)** is a target intelligence term pertaining to the target to be destroyed. It is an examination of potential targets to determine their relative military importance so that they can be prioritized and the weapons that will be required to incur the desired level of damage or casualties. *See also:* Targeting.

References
Department of Defense, U.S. Army. *Operational Terms and Symbols.* Field Manual FM 101-5-1. Washington, DC: Headquarters, Department of the Army, 1985.

—**TARGET ANALYST** is a nuclear and chemical analyst who is qualified for duty in a unit with a table of organization and equipment/position requiring knowledge of the techniques and procedures for nuclear and chemical target analysis. *See also:* Targeting.

References
Department of Defense, U.S. Army. *Nuclear Weapons Employment Doctrine and Procedures.* Field Manual FM 101-3-1. Washington, DC: Headquarters, Department of the Army, 1986.

—**TARGET AREA DESIGNATED GRID** is a grid system that uses numbers and letters for an area designation of targets: numbers for indicating a 1,000-meter square and letters for indicating a 200-meter square within the numbered square. *See also:* Targeting.

References
Department of Defense, U.S. Army. *Dictionary of United States Army Terms.* Army Regulation AR 310-25. Washington, DC: Headquarters, Department of the Army, 1986.

—**TARGET AREA GRID** is a simplification of the military grid used for rapid point designation when great accuracy is not required. *See also:* Targeting.

References
Department of Defense, U.S. Army. *Dictionary of United States Army Terms.* Army Regulation AR 310-25. Washington, DC: Headquarters, Department of the Army, 1986.

—**TARGET AREA OF INTEREST** is an area or point along a corridor, the successful interdiction of which will cause the enemy to either abandon a particular course of action or require it to use specialized engineer support to continue its operations.

References
Department of Defense, U.S. Army. *Operational Terms and Symbols.* Field Manual FM 101-5-1. Washington, DC: Headquarters, Department of the Army, 1985.

—**TARGET AREA SURVEY** is the portion of a survey concerned principally with the location of targets and observation posts. *See also:* Target Area of Interest.

References
Department of Defense, U.S. Army. *Dictionary of United States Army Terms.* Army Regulation AR 310-25. Washington, DC: Headquarters, Department of the Army, 1986.

—**TARGET AREA SURVEY BASE** is a base line used to locate targets or other points by the intersection of observations from two stations located at opposite ends on the line.

References
Department of Defense, Joint Chiefs of Staff. *Department of Defense Dictionary of Military and Related Terms.* Washington, DC: GPO, 1986.

—**TARGET ARRAY** is a graphic representation of enemy forces, personnel, and facilities in a specific situation. It is accompanied by a target analysis.

References
Department of Defense, U.S. Army. *Operational Terms and Symbols.* Field Manual FM 101-5-1. Washington, DC: Headquarters, Department of the Army, 1985.

—**TARGET AUDIENCE** is an individual or group selected for influence or attack by means of psychological operations.

References
Department of Defense, Joint Chiefs of Staff. *Department of Defense Dictionary of Military and Related Terms.* Washington, DC: GPO, 1986.

—**TARGET BASE LINE** is a line connecting prime targets along the periphery of a geographic area. *See also:* Targeting.

References
Department of Defense, Joint Chiefs of Staff. *Department of Defense Dictionary of Military and Related Terms.* Washington, DC: GPO, 1986.

—**TARGET CHARACTERISTICS** is a target intelligence term pertaining to the target to be destroyed. Every target has many distinctive characteristics by which it can be detected, located, and identified for future action. Such characteristics generally are classified as being functional, physical, environmental, or psycho-social. Additional information is often provided concerning the mobility of the target. *See also:* Target Intelligence, Targeting.

References
Department of Defense, Joint Chiefs of Staff. *Department of Defense Dictionary of Military and Related Terms.* Washington, DC: GPO, 1986.

—**TARGET CHART** is a large-scale map or diagram showing the target or targets that have been assigned to bombing aircraft. A target chart is one type of aeronautical chart. *See also:* Targeting.

References
Department of Defense, U.S. Army. *Dictionary of United States Army Terms.* Army Regulation AR 310-25. Washington, DC: Headquarters, Department of the Army, 1986.

—**TARGET COMPLEX** is a geographically integrated series of target concentrations. *See also:* Target.

References
Department of Defense, Joint Chiefs of Staff. *Department of Defense Dictionary of Military and Related Terms.* Washington, DC: GPO, 1986.

—**TARGET CONCENTRATION** is a grouping of geographically proximate targets. *See also:* Target, Target Complex.

References
Department of Defense, Joint Chiefs of Staff. *Department of Defense Dictionary of Military and Related Terms.* Washington, DC: GPO, 1986.

—**TARGET CORRELATION** is a target intelligence term pertaining to the target to be destroyed. It occurs when information from one or more than one source is used to determine targeting data. This normally requires only a short time to verify. *See also:* Target Intelligence, Targeting.

References
Department of Defense, U.S. Army. *Military Intelligence Battalion (CEWI) (Tactical Exploitation) (Corps): Counterintelligence, Interrogation, Electronic Warfare.* Field Manual FM 34-23. Washington, DC: Headquarters, Department of the Army, 1985.

———. *Military Intelligence Company (Combat Electronic Warfare and Intelligence) (Armored Cavalry Regiment/Separate Brigade).* Field Manual FM 34-30. Washington, DC: Headquarters, Department of the Army, 1983.

———. *Military Intelligence Group (Combat Electronic Warfare and Intelligence) (Corps).* Field Manual FM 34-20. Washington, DC: Headquarters, Department of the Army, 1983.

—**TARGET DATA INVENTORY (TDI)** is a basic targeting program that provides standardized target data in support of the requirements of the Joint Chiefs of Staff, military departments, and unified and specified commands for target planning coordination and weapons application. *See also:* Targeting.

References
Department of Defense, Joint Chiefs of Staff. *Department of Defense Dictionary of Military and Related Terms.* Washington, DC: GPO, 1986.

—**TARGET DATE** is the date on which an action is planned to be accomplished or initiated. *See also:* Targeting.

References
Department of Defense, Joint Chiefs of Staff. *Department of Defense Dictionary of Military and Related Terms.* Washington, DC: GPO, 1986.

—**TARGET DESIGNATING SYSTEM** is a means of transmitting to one instrument the position of a target that has been located by another instrument. *See also:* Targeting.

References
Department of Defense, U.S. Army. *Dictionary of United States Army Terms.* Army Regulation AR 310-25. Washington, DC: Headquarters, Department of the Army, 1986.

—**TARGET DEVELOPMENT** is an Army tactical intelligence term that refers to a process in intelligence analysis. It includes locating, identifying, and tracking targets to permit engaging them at the greatest possible range. Target development is essential to the delay, attrition, and destruction of second-echelon and other follow-on forces. *See also:* Targeting.

References
Department of Defense, U.S. Army. *Military Intelligence Battalion (CEWI) (Tactical Exploitation) (Corps): Counterintelligence, Interrogation, Electronic Warfare.* Field Manual FM 34-23. Washington, DC: Headquarters, Department of the Army, 1985.

———. *Military Intelligence Company (Combat Electronic Warfare and Intelligence) (Armored Cavalry Regiment/Separate Brigade).* Field Manual FM 34-30. Washington, DC: Headquarters, Department of the Army, 1983.

———. *Military Intelligence Group (Combat Electronic Warfare and Intelligence) (Corps)*. Field Manual FM 34-20. Washington, DC: Headquarters, Department of the Army, 1983.

—**TARGET DISCRIMINATION** is the ability of a surveillance or guidance system to identify or engage any one target when multiple targets are present. *See also:* Targeting.

References
Department of Defense, Joint Chiefs of Staff. *Department of Defense Dictionary of Military and Related Terms.* Washington, DC: GPO, 1986.

—**TARGET DOSSIER** is a file of assembled target intelligence about a specific geographic area. *See also:* Target Intelligence, Targeting.

References
Department of Defense, Joint Chiefs of Staff. *Department of Defense Dictionary of Military and Related Terms.* Washington, DC: GPO, 1986.

—**TARGET ECHO** is a radio signal that is reflected by an air or other target and received by the radar station that transmitted the original signal.

References
Department of Defense, U.S. Army. *Dictionary of United States Army Terms.* Army Regulation AR 310-25. Washington, DC: Headquarters, Department of the Army, 1986.

—**TARGET EVALUATION** is an examination of targets to determine their military importance and their relative priority for attack. *See also:* Targeting.

References
Department of Defense, U.S. Army. *Dictionary of United States Army Terms.* Army Regulation AR 310-25. Washington, DC: Headquarters, Department of the Army, 1986.

—**TARGET FOLDER** is a folder containing target intelligence and related materials. It is prepared for planning and executing action against a specific target. *See also:* Targeting.

References
Department of Defense, Joint Chiefs of Staff. *Department of Defense Dictionary of Military and Related Terms.* Washington, DC: GPO, 1986.

—**TARGET GRID** is a device for converting the observer's target locations and corrections with respect to the observer target line to target locations and corrections with respect to the gun target line. *See also:* Targeting.

References
Department of Defense, Joint Chiefs of Staff. *Department of Defense Dictionary of Military and Related Terms.* Washington, DC: GPO, 1986.

—**TARGET INDICATING SYSTEM** is a system that allows the tracker of an air defense automatic weapon to detect the direction of approach of a suitable target, or the approach of a new target after engagement with one target has been broken off. The operation of this system requires the tracker to slew his weapon in the indicated direction, locate his target, and begin tracking. *See also:* Targeting.

References
Department of Defense, U.S. Army. *Dictionary of United States Army Terms.* Army Regulation AR 310-25. Washington, DC: Headquarters, Department of the Army, 1986.

—**TARGET INDICATOR (TI)** is a possible target that requires further information before it is considered a target. *See also:* Targeting.

References
Department of Defense, U.S. Army. *Dictionary of United States Army Terms.* Army Regulation AR 310-25. Washington, DC: Headquarters, Department of the Army, 1986.

—**TARGET INFORMATION CENTER** is an intelligence center set up afloat or ashore for assembly, evaluation, interpretation, dissemination, and coordination of target information for supporting artillery, naval gunfire, or air weapons. *See also:* Targeting.

References
Department of Defense, U.S. Army. *Dictionary of United States Army Terms.* Army Regulation AR 310-25. Washington, DC: Headquarters, Department of the Army, 1986.

—**TARGET INTELLIGENCE (TI)** portrays and locates the components of a target or target complex and indicates its identification, vulnerability, and relative importance. Target intelligence is special-purpose military intelligence derived from all sources to support decisionmakers, operational forces, and supporting staff functions in planning for and executing strikes and attacks against selected enemy forces, facilities, and functions. Such intelligence also supports the development of U.S. policy and planning guidance and military planners who are engaged in weapons acquisition and force structure decisionmaking. Target intelligence is included in automated data bases and in imagery-based products (e.g., automated tactical target graphics). *See also:* Targeting.

References

Department of Defense, Joint Chiefs of Staff. *Department of Defense Dictionary of Military and Related Terms.* Washington, DC: GPO, 1986.

—**TARGET LIST.** (1) A target list is a tabulation of confirmed or suspected targets. It is maintained by any echelon for information and fire support planning purposes. (2) A target list is an appendix to an obstacle index of an operation order/operation plan. It lists the obstacles by number, type, location, and executing unit and is used ❡ plan and monitor the execution of the obstacle plan. *See also:* Targeting.

References

Department of Defense, U.S. Army. *Fire Support in Combined Arms Operations.* Field Manual FM 6-20. Washington, DC: Headquarters, Department of the Army, 1983.

———. *Operational Terms and Symbols.* Field Manual FM 101-5-1. Washington, DC: Headquarters, Department of the Army, 1985.

—**TARGET NODE** is a target that includes a communications terminal shared by to two or more branches (e.g., a switched communications network). It includes switching points, patching points, retransmission stations, and command and control facilities.

References

Department of Defense, U.S. Army. *Attack Helicopter Operations.* Field Manual FM 17-50. Washington, DC: Headquarters, Department of the Army, 1984.

—**TARGET NUMBER** is the reference number given to a target by a fire control unit. *See also:* Targeting.

References

Department of Defense, Joint Chiefs of Staff. *Department of Defense Dictionary of Military and Related Terms.* Washington, DC: GPO, 1986.

—**TARGET OF OPPORTUNITY.** (1) A target of opportunity is an unplanned target that appears during combat and can be reached by ground fire, naval fire, or aircraft fire. (2) In clandestine intelligence, target of opportunity is an entity that becomes available to an intelligence service or agency by chance. It provides the opportunity

to collect needed information. (3) A target of opportunity, as defined by the Church Committee, is "a term describing an entity (e.g., governmental entity, installation, political organization, or individual) that becomes available to an intelligence agency or service by chance, and provides the opportunity for the collection of needed information." (4) In the context of nuclear warfare, a target of opportunity is a nuclear target observed or detected after an operation begins but that was not previously considered, analyzed, or planned. Generally fleeting in nature, it should be attacked as soon as possible within the time limitations that have been imposed for coordinating with and warning friendly troops and aircraft.

References

Department of Defense, U.S. Army. *Fire Support in Combined Arms Operations.* Field Manual FM 6-20. Washington, DC: Headquarters, Department of the Army, 1983.

———. *Operational Terms and Symbols.* Field Manual FM 101-5-1. Washington, DC: Headquarters, Department of the Army, 1985.

U.S. Congress. Senate. *Final Report of the Senate Select Committee to Study Government Operations With Respect to Intelligence Activities. Report 94-755. Book I, Foreign and Military Intelligence* (Church Committee Report). Washington, DC: GPO, 1976.

—**TARGET-ORIENTED ANALYSIS** is analysis of initial aimpoints that are chosen to determine whether the weapons available to attack a confirmed target are capable of and appropriate for meeting the commander's requirements. *See also:* Circular Error Probable, Damage Estimation, Least Separation Distance, Target, Troop Safety.

References

Department of Defense, U.S. Army. *Operational Terms and Symbols.* Field Manual FM 101-5-1. Washington, DC: Headquarters, Department of the Army, 1985.

—**TARGET OVERLAY** is an overlay on a map showing the locations of friendly artillery units, targets, boundaries, and fire support coordination measures. It enables the fire support coordinator to view graphically all targets that are planned to support the maneuver force and to determine the best fire support agency to engage the listed targets.

References
Department of Defense, U.S. Army. *Operational Terms and Symbols.* Field Manual FM 101-5-1. Washington, DC: Headquarters, Department of the Army, 1985.

—**TARGET PREDICTION** is a "best guess" about a target's location. *See also:* Targeting.

References
Department of Defense, U.S. Army. *Field Artillery Target Acquisition.* Field Manual FM 6-121. Washington, DC: Headquarters, Department of the Army, 1978.

—**TARGET PRIORITY** is a grouping of targets with the indicated sequence of attack. *See also:* Targeting.

References
Department of Defense, Joint Chiefs of Staff. *Department of Defense Dictionary of Military and Related Terms.* Washington, DC: GPO, 1986.

—**TARGET PRODUCTION** is the processing needed to develop a target. In its simplest form, target production could be the mere passing of combat information from a known, accurate, and reliable source to the fire control element for attack. In its more complex form, it is the synthesis and analysis of data from diverse sources into estimating a target location that is sufficiently accurate to permit attack. *See also:* Targeting.

References
Department of Defense, U.S. Army. *Field Artillery Target Acquisition.* Field Manual FM 6-121. Washington, DC: Headquarters, Department of the Army, 1978.

—**TARGET REFERENCE POINT (TRP)** is an easily recognizable point on the ground that is either natural or man-made and is used to identify enemy targets or controlling fires. TRPs are usually designated by company commanders or platoon leaders for company teams, platoons, sections, or individual weapons. They can also designate the center of an area where the commander plans to rapidly distribute or converge the fires of all his weapons. TRPs are designated by using the standard target symbol and target numbers issued by the fire support team or fire support officer. Once designated, a TRP also constitutes an indirect fire target and is identified by two letters and four numbers in the same manner as the indirect fire targets.

References
Department of Defense, U.S. Army. *The Infantry Rifle Company (Infantry, Airborne, Air Assault, Ranger).* Field Manual FM 7-10. Washington, DC: Headquarters, Department of the Army, 1982.

———. *Operational Terms and Symbols.* Field Manual FM 101-5-1. Washington, DC: Headquarters, Department of the Army, 1985.

—**TARGET RESPONSE** (NUCLEAR) is the effect on men, material, and equipment of the blast, heat, light, and nuclear radiation resulting from the explosion of a nuclear weapon. *See also:* Nuclear Warfare.

References
Department of Defense, Joint Chiefs of Staff. *Department of Defense Dictionary of Military and Related Terms.* Washington, DC: GPO, 1986.

—**TARGET SELECTION STANDARDS** are criteria by which all targeting data must be evaluated to determine if the data will lead to the production of a valid target. Target selection standards are dynamic (i.e., they are changed as the enemy situation changes to reflect the most up-to-date information about the enemy). *See also:* Targeting.

References
Department of Defense, U.S. Army. *Field Artillery Target Acquisition.* Field Manual FM 6-121. Washington, DC: Headquarters, Department of the Army, 1978.

—**TARGET SELECTOR** is a component of both a target designation system and a target indicating system. It is an off-carriage observing instrument used to select an initial or new target. It is electrically connected to the gun mount in such a manner as to slew the gun to the approximate azimuth and elevation of a selected target (when the selector is a component of a target designating system) and to give the tracker an indication of the direction of approach of a selected target (when the selector is a component of a target indicating system). *See also:* Targeting.

References
Department of Defense, U.S. Army. *Dictionary of United States Army Terms.* Army Regulation AR 310-25. Washington, DC: Headquarters, Department of the Army, 1986.

—**TARGET SIGNATURES.** Most weapons and vehicles produce telltale signs, a result of design or the environment in which the equipment is used. For example, firing a tank main gun on dry sandy soil raises a dust cloud and a tank driving in built-up areas makes more noise than one moving through an open field. Sight, hearing, smell, and sometimes touch and taste assist in detecting and identifying signatures that lead to target location, identification, and rapid engagement. Examples of Signatures are the following:

- *Soldier signatures,* which include foxholes, trash, torn-up vegetation (used for camouflage), and fires.
- *Track vehicle signatures,* which are the most obvious in open areas and rolling terrain. They include tank tracks on ground, tank track and engine noise, dust clouds, diesel smoke, loud sharp reports followed by white smoke, and a bright white flash at night.
- *Antitank signatures,* which are often seen in open areas where tanks are likely to be used. They include "swish" of a missile launch; long, thin wires from previously fired antitank guided missiles; tracers of slow flying antitank guided missiles; sharp crack of an antitank gun; and dismounted gunner up to 80 meters away from a launching rail.
- *Artillery signatures,* which include a loud dull report, grayish-white cloud of smoke, bright orange flash and black smoke from airbursts, and rushing noise heard several seconds prior to the impact of a round.
- *Aircraft signatures,* which are often seen where terrain masks (e.g., ridges or forests) are available for aircraft to hide behind. They include aircraft noise, glare of sun from aircraft canopies and rotor blades, vapor trails from aircraft or fired missiles, dust and movement of foliage from hovering helicopters
- *Obstacles and mines,* which are to be expected between uncrossable terrain features and will probably be covered by enemy fire (usually infantry with antitank weapons). An example is loose or disturbed dirt in a regular pattern.

See also: Targeting.

References

Department of Defense, U.S. Army. *Field Artillery Target Acquisition.* Field Manual FM 6-121. Washington, DC: Headquarters, Department of the Army, 1978.

———. *Operational Terms and Symbols.* Field Manual FM 101-5-1. Washington, DC: Headquarters, Department of the Army, 1985.

—**TARGET SYSTEM** is a target intelligence term pertaining to the target to be destroyed. It is all the targets situated in a particular geographic area that are functionally related. *See also:* Targeting.

References

Department of Defense, Joint Chiefs of Staff. *Department of Defense Dictionary of Military and Related Terms.* Washington, DC: GPO, 1986.

—**TARGET SYSTEM COMPONENTS** is a target intelligence term pertaining to the target to be destroyed. These are a set of targets belonging to one or more groups of industries and basic utilities, which are required to produce component parts of an end-product or system. A ball bearing factory would be a component of a target system pertaining to enemy tank production. *See also:* Targeting.

References

Department of Defense, U.S. Army. *Field Artillery Target Acquisition.* Field Manual FM 6-121. Washington, DC: Headquarters, Department of the Army, 1978.

———. *Military Intelligence Group (Combat Electronic Warfare and Intelligence) (Corps).* Field Manual FM 34-20. Washington, DC: Headquarters, Department of the Army, 1983.

———. *Operational Terms and Symbols.* Field Manual FM 101-5-1. Washington, DC: Headquarters, Department of the Army, 1985.

—**TARGET TRACKING RADAR** is a precision tracking radar that is an integral part of a weapon system and is used to track the target. Its function is to furnish target-position data to the computer when used in a command guidance system. In a beam rider system, the radar provides coordinate information to permit the guidance of the missile to the target by the onboard computer. This radar also serves to illuminate the target in a missile system that utilizes semi-active homing guidance.

References

Department of Defense, U.S. Army. *Dictionary of United States Army Terms.* Army Regulation AR 310-25. Washington, DC: Headquarters, Department of the Army, 1986.

—**TARGETING.** (1) Targeting is a key function during peace, exercises, crises, and war. It includes policy, operations, logistics, cartography, demography, intelligence, and automated data processing personnel, products, processes, and procedures. Complementary aspects of targeting are performed at each level of the air, ground, naval, and joint headquarters. The intelligence targeting function is the bridge that unifies and links these many disciplines, levels of command, and air, ground, and naval offensive forces and operations. During peacetime, it is the daily task of targeting personnel to plan for occurrences that might be deterred but for which preparations must be made nevertheless. For targeting to be done well during hostilities, preparation during peacetime and training during exercises are at least as important as target selection during a war. Without extensive, coordinated preparation, targeting will not be accomplished effectively when it is most critical, thus squandering valuable resources and potentially resulting in defeat. Targeting is the process of selecting targets and matching them with the operational capabilities in order to support the commander's stated concept of operations. The *targeting process* is a logical sequence of interdependent planning functions that occur at all levels of command and that result in offensive plans and operations that are the most likely to succeed. *Target intelligence* is an integral part of every stage of the targeting process, since it may continually provide data that either justify the continued validity of the target or indicate that the target is no longer valid. Target intelligence may also be crucial in planning the type of operation to be conducted against the target. The targeting process has the following major steps:

- *A concept of operations,* which is a verbal or graphic statement, in broad outline, of a commander's assumptions or intentions concerning an operation or a series of operations. It is reviewed and used as guidance for the remainder of the process.
- *Target development* includes systematically identifying and analyzing target systems and the component installations, sites, and entities in order to determine which critical and vulnerable elements friendly military operations should be directed against in order to achieve the specified tactical or strategic objective.
- *Weaponeering* is the process of estimating the quantity of specific types of munitions, fuzing, and delivery vehicles required to achieve the desired damage to a specific target or type of target, while minimizing the damage to friendly forces and civilian objects, property, and people.

- *Force and weapon availability and application* involve matching offensive delivery assets and weapons against the proposed targets, based upon weaponeering recommendations, in order to apply the offensive, destructive systems as effectively, economically, and quickly as possible.
- *Execution* occurs when friendly forces attack the target.
- *Assessment* is the final phase. It involves analyzing the mission results to determine if the mission was accomplished. Assessment goes beyond bomb damage assessment and includes determining the capability of the target to continue functioning or to recover.

The objectives of targeting are to deter; to decimate enemy forces and capabilities; to retaliate; to send a signal; to deny the enemy the ability to achieve its aims; to inhibit enemy reconstruction; to terminate hostilities on terms favorable to the United States and its allies; or to obtain a better peace.

(2) In communications intelligence, targeting is the intentional selection or collection of telecommunications for intelligence purposes. *See also:* Target, Target Acquisition, Target Analysis, Target Characteristics, Target Correlation, Target Development, Target Intelligence, Target System, Target System Components.

References

Department of Defense, Defense Intelligence College. *Glossary of Intelligence Terms and Definitions.* Washington, DC: DIC, 1987.

Department of Defense, U.S. Army. *Field Artillery Target Acquisition.* Field Manual FM 6-121. Washington, DC: Headquarters, Department of the Army, 1978.

———. *Military Intelligence Group (Combat Electronic Warfare and Intelligence) (Corps).* Field Manual FM 34-20. Washington, DC: Headquarters, Department of the Army, 1983.

—**TASK FORCE (TF).** (1) In operations, a task force is a temporary grouping of units under one commander. It is formed to carry out a specific operation or mission. (2) A task force is a temporary organization of units under one commander assembled to carry out an ongoing specific task. Units may be TFs, regardless of attachments, whenever they are on a semipermanent mission. Brigade and higher units normally are not designated as TFs unless the operation or mission requires joint airborne, amphibious or other special, semi-independent operations. (3) Based upon the organization, a task force can be a battalion-sized unit of combat arms, consisting of a battalion control headquarters, with at least one of its major subordinate elements, and the attachment of at least one company-sized element or another combat or combat support arm (e.g., an infantry battalion headquarters; one or more of its organic companies; and the attachment of one or more of the following: a tank company, an armored cavalry troop, or an engineer company). *See also:* Battalion Task Force, Task Organization.

References

Department of Defense, U.S. Army. *Operational Terms and Symbols*. Field Manual FM 101-5-1. Washington, DC: Headquarters, Department of the Army, 1985.

—**TASK ORGANIZATION** is a temporary grouping of forces designed to accomplish a particular mission. It involves distributing assets to subordinate control headquarters by attachment or by placing them in direct support or under the operational control of the subordinate.

References

Department of Defense, U.S. Army. *Air Defense Artillery Deployment: Chaparral/Vulcan/Stinger*. Field Manual FM 44-3. Washington, DC: Headquarters, Department of the Army, 1984.

———. *Operational Terms and Symbols*. Field Manual FM 101-5-1. Washington, DC: Headquarters, Department of the Army, 1985.

—**TASKS** are specific Army, Navy, and Air Force assignments that must be done to successfully implement the phased concept of operations stemming from the overall strategic concept. In stating the tasks, an appropriate amount of information concerning the who, what, when, where, why, and how is given. There are two categories of tasks: initial operations and subsequent operations. *See also:* Initial Operating Capability, Subsequent Operations Phase.

References

Department of Defense, U.S. Army. *Dictionary of United States Army Terms*. Army Regulation AR 310-25. Washington, DC: Headquarters, Department of the Army, 1986.

—**TEAM.** The company team is a combined arms team. It combines tank and mechanized infantry platoons under the single command of a tank company or mechanized infantry company

headquarters. It is the smallest combined arms team that can also have in it other combat arms elements. A wide range of engineer, signal, and logistics support is available and may from time to time be part of the company team. It is normally supported by mortars, artillery, and sometimes by attack helicopters and Air Force tactical fighter bombers.

References

Department of Defense, U.S. Army. *The Tank and Mechanized Infantry Company Team*. Field Manual FM 71-1. Washington, DC: Headquarters, Department of the Army, 1977.

—**TEAR DOWN,** or strip, is the breakdown of a major assembly into its component parts. *See also:* Assembly.

References

Department of Defense, U.S. Army. *Dictionary of United States Army Terms*. Army Regulation AR 310-25. Washington, DC: Headquarters, Department of the Army, 1986.

—**TECHNICAL BULLETIN** is a publication that contains information pertaining to weapons, equipment, and professional techniques.

References

Department of Defense, U.S. Army. *Dictionary of United States Army Terms*. Army Regulation AR 310-25. Washington, DC: Headquarters, Department of the Army, 1986.

—**TECHNICAL CHANNEL.** (1) A technical channel is a method used by the chiefs of service, within the limits and in the manner prescribed by the commander, to handle routine technical reports and instructions not involving variations from command policies and directives. (2) A technical channel is the technical link between two commands used to transmit technical instructions. It is used by the commanders and staff officers who have been given the authority to do so due to the technical nature of the activities within their assigned areas of responsibility.

References

Department of Defense, U.S. Army. *Dictionary of United States Army Terms*. Army Regulation AR 310-25. Washington, DC: Headquarters, Department of the Army, 1986.

———. *Staff Organization and Operations*. Field Manual FM 101-5. Washington, DC: Headquarters, Department of the Army, 1984.

—**TECHNICAL CHARACTERISTICS** are characteristics of equipment that pertain primarily to the engineering principles involved in producing equipment with desired military characteristics. For example, the technical characteristics of electronic equipment include such items as circuitry and the types and arrangements of its components.

References
Department of Defense, U.S. Army. *Dictionary of United States Army Terms.* Army Regulation AR 310-25. Washington, DC: Headquarters, Department of the Army, 1986.

—**TECHNICAL COMMITTEE** is a committee established and maintained by the chief of each developing agency to assure adequate coordination among the developing and using agencies during classification and procurement activities.

References
Department of Defense, U.S. Army. *Dictionary of United States Army Terms.* Army Regulation AR 310-25. Washington, DC: Headquarters, Department of the Army, 1986.

—**TECHNICAL CONTROL** is the specialized professional guidance and direction exercised by an authority in technical matters.

References
Department of Defense, U.S. Army. *Dictionary of United States Army Terms.* Army Regulation AR 310-25. Washington, DC: Headquarters, Department of the Army, 1986.

—**TECHNICAL DAMAGE ASSESSMENT** is an assessment conducted by special teams to obtain technical information.

References
Department of Defense, U.S. Army. *Dictionary of United States Army Terms.* Army Regulation AR 310-25. Washington, DC: Headquarters, Department of the Army, 1986.

—**TECHNICAL DATA PACKAGE** is a description of an item or service that is sufficiently comprehensive that it can be used for procurement purposes. It consists of all applicable technical data (e.g., plans, drawings and associated lists, specifications, purchase descriptions, standards, models, performance requirements, quality assurance provisions, and packing data).

References
Department of Defense, U.S. Army. *Dictionary of United States Army Terms.* Army Regulation AR 310-25. Washington, DC: Headquarters, Department of the Army, 1986.

—**TECHNICAL ELINT (ELECTRONIC INTELLIGENCE)** is a term that describes the technical characteristics of a given emitter. It is used to estimate the emitter's primary function, capabilities, modes of operation (including malfunctions), and role within a complex weapons system or defense network. *See also:* Electronic Intelligence.

References
Department of Defense, U.S. Army. *Operational Terms and Symbols.* Field Manual FM 101-5-1. Washington, DC: Headquarters, Department of the Army, 1985.

—**TECHNICAL ESCORT** is the accompanying of a shipment of sensitive materials (e.g., chemical agents or munitions, biological, or etiological materials or munitions, or radioactive material) by personnel qualified and equipped to assure the safety and security for the shipment. *See also:* Biological Warfare, Chemical Warfare, Nuclear Warfare.

References
Department of Defense, U.S. Army. *Technical Escort Operations.* Field Manual FM 3-20. Washington, DC: Headquarters, Department of the Army, 1981.

—**TECHNICAL INFORMATION** is information, including scientific information, that relates to the research, development, engineering, test, evaluation, production, operation, use, and maintenance of munitions and other military supplies and equipment.

References
Department of Defense, Joint Chiefs of Staff. *Department of Defense Dictionary of Military and Related Terms.* Washington, DC: GPO, 1986.

—**TECHNICAL INSPECTION.** (1) Technical inspection is inspection of equipment and weapons to determine whether they are serviceable for continued use or whether repairs are necessary. (2) A technical inspection is the initial, in-process, and final inspections performed within a maintenance unit on materiel needing repair. It is performed to determine the condition, deficiencies, parts requirements, the nature of the necessary repairs, and whether the item will be repaired locally, salvaged, or evacuated (initial inspection); to determine whether repairs in process are being performed properly (in-process inspection); and to determine, before a disposition is made of a repaired item, whether all required repairs were performed satisfactorily (final inspection). *See also:* In-Process Review.

References

Department of Defense, U.S. Army. *Dictionary of United States Army Terms.* Army Regulation AR 310-25. Washington, DC: Headquarters, Department of the Army, 1986.

—**TECHNICAL INTELLIGENCE (TI)** is intelligence on the characteristics and performance of foreign weapons and equipment. It is a part of scientific and technical intelligence and is distinct from order of battle. *See also:* Order-of-Battle, Scientific and Technical Intelligence.

References

Department of Defense, Defense Intelligence College. *Glossary of Intelligence Terms and Definitions.* Washington, DC: DIC, 1987.

—**TECHNICAL MANUAL** is a publication that discusses in detail the subjects considered necessary for the full accomplishment of required training. It also contains descriptions of materiel and instructions for the operation, handling, maintenance, and repair of the materiel; and information and instructions on technical procedures. *See also:* Field Manuals, Field Service Regulations.

References

Department of Defense, U.S. Army. *Dictionary of United States Army Terms.* Army Regulation AR 310-25. Washington, DC: Headquarters, Department of the Army, 1986.

—**TECHNICAL MANUALS (TMs)** are equipment-oriented manuals. They assist the squad in maintaining its weapons, vehicles, and equipment.(Maintenance plays a large part in training the squad for combat.)

References

Department of Defense, U.S. Army. *The Rifle Squad (Mechanized and Light Infantry).* Training Circular TC 7-1. Washington, DC: Headquarters, Department of the Army, 1976.

—**TECHNICAL OBSERVER** is the civilian technical expert of a commercial firm who accompanies troops to observe and report on the operation of mechanical equipment or armament under field conditions.

References

Department of Defense, U.S. Army. *Dictionary of United States Army Terms.* Army Regulation AR 310-25. Washington, DC: Headquarters, Department of the Army, 1986.

—**TECHNICAL PROFICIENCY INSPECTION** is an inspection of a nuclear weapons storage support or delivery organization to determine its capability to meet operational commitments in nuclear weapons as directed in its current mission, while adhering to standard procedures in storage, maintenance, safety testing, handling, and assembly.

References

Department of Defense, U.S. Army. *Dictionary of United States Army Terms.* Army Regulation AR 310-25. Washington, DC: Headquarters, Department of the Army, 1986.

—**TECHNICAL RATE OF LAYING** is the rate of mine emplacement that is achievable by any system. It does not take into account the time required for resupply and recharging. *See also:* Mine Warfare.

References

Department of Defense, U.S. Army. *Mine/ Operations at the Company Level.* Field Manual FM 20-32. Washington, DC: Headquarters, Department of the Army, 1976.

—**TECHNICAL SERVICE CONTRACT** is a contract in which civilian personnel perform technical services for the Department of the Army.

References

Department of Defense, U.S. Army. *Dictionary of United States Army Terms.* Army Regulation AR 310-25. Washington, DC: Headquarters, Department of the Army, 1986.

—**TECHNICAL SERVICE MATERIAL POSITION** is a duty position requiring an officer to have chemical, engineer, ordnance, quartermaster, signal, or transportation as his basic branch. It is not identified with, or limited to, a specific branch.

References

Department of Defense, U.S. Army. *Dictionary of United States Army Terms.* Army Regulation AR 310-25. Washington, DC: Headquarters, Department of the Army, 1986.

—**TECHNICAL SIGINT (SIGNALS INTELLIGENCE)** is intelligence information that provides a detailed description of the technical characteristics of a given emitter, thus permitting estimates to be made about its primary function, capabilities, modes of operation (including malfunctions), and state-of-the-art characteristics, as well as its specific role within a complex weapon system or defense network. Technical SIGINT contributes to technical intelligence. *See also:* Technical Intelligence.

References

Department of Defense, Defense Intelligence College. *Glossary of Intelligence Terms and Definitions.* Washington, DC: DIC, 1987.

—**TECHNICAL SUPPLY OPERATIONS** are performed by supply units or technical supply elements of supply and maintenance units in acquiring, accounting for, storing, and issuing Class II and IV items that are needed by supported units and maintenance activities. *See also:* Supplies.

References

Department of Defense, Joint Chiefs of Staff. *Department of Defense Dictionary of Military and Related Terms.* Washington, DC: GPO, 1986.

—**TECHNICAL SURVEILLANCE COUNTERMEASURES (TSCM) SURVEY** is a thorough physical, electronic, and visual examination by special agents in and about an area in order to detect technical surveillance devices, technical security hazards, and physical security weaknesses. TSCM surveys differ from TEMPEST surveys in that the latter are limited to investigation and studies of compromising emanations, whereas the TSCM surveys are basically designed to prevent the technical penetration efforts of hostile intelligence services. *See also:* Technical Surveillance Measures, TEMPEST.

References

Department of Defense, Joint Chiefs of Staff. *Department of Defense Dictionary of Military and Related Terms.* Washington, DC: GPO, 1986.

—**TECHNICAL SURVEILLANCE MEASURES (TSM)** are specialized techniques (e.g., the polygraph, electronic surveillance, use of locks and locking devices, and technical surveillance countermeasures). All of these may be used in the support of any counter-human intelligence operation.

References

Department of Defense, U.S. Army. *Counterintelligence.* Field Manual FM 34-60. Washington, DC: Headquarters, Department of the Army, 1985.

—**TECHNICIAN** (RESERVE COMPONENT) is a full-time career civilian employee of the Army National Guard or Army Reserve. He is normally a military member of the unit for which he is employed and provides day-to-day continuity of operations. Technicians support functions for which the National Guard or Reserve commanders are responsible, but which cannot be performed by unit personnel during the regularly scheduled training periods.

References

Department of Defense, U.S. Army. *Dictionary of United States Army Terms.* Army Regulation AR 310-25. Washington, DC: Headquarters, Department of the Army, 1986.

—**TECHNIQUE** is an accepted and established way to perform an act (e.g., the detailed methods used by troops or commanders to perform assigned tasks). Technique refers to the basic methods of using equipment and personnel. For example, "tactics and technique" often refers to the general and detailed methods used by commanders and forces to carry out their assignments.

References

Department of Defense, U.S. Army. *Dictionary of United States Army Terms.* Army Regulation AR 310-25. Washington, DC: Headquarters, Department of the Army, 1986.

—**TECHNIQUE OF TARGET ATTACK** (ARMY AVIATION) is the combination of flight mode (i.e., profile) and type of fire (i.e., relationship of weapon to target) that is appropriate to the engagement of a given target.

References

Department of Defense, U.S. Army. *Gunnery Training for Attack Helicopters.* Training Circular TC 17-17. Washington, DC: Headquarters, Department of the Army, 1975.

—**TELEVISION IMAGERY** is imagery acquired by a television camera and recorded or transmitted electronically. *See also:* Aerial Reconnaissance.

References
Department of Defense, Joint Chiefs of Staff. *Department of Defense Dictionary of Military and Related Terms.* Washington, DC: GPO, 1986.

—**TEMPEST** is an unclassified short title referring to investigations and studies of compromising examinations from friendly forces. As commonly used in the Army, "TEMPEST" is synonymous with emanations security and/or control of compromising emanations. TEMPEST activities include providing technical support on the selection of TEMPEST-approved or compliant electric classified information processing equipment and on installation criteria. *See also:* Tempest Test.

References
Department of Defense, U.S. Army. *Counterintelligence.* Field Manual FM 34-60. Washington, DC: Headquarters, Department of the Army, 1985.

—**TEMPEST TEST** is a laboratory or on-site (i.e., field) test to determine the nature and amplitude of conducted or radiated signals containing compromising information. A test normally includes the detection and measurement of these signals and an analysis to determine the correlation between received signals and potentially compromising transmitted signals. *See also:* TEMPEST.

References
Department of Defense, U.S. Army. *Dictionary of United States Army Terms.* Army Regulation AR 310-25. Washington, DC: Headquarters, Department of the Army, 1986.

—**TEMPLATE** is an Army tactical intelligence term that means a graphic illustration of an enemy capability drawn to scale. It is an analytical tool that integrates enemy doctrine, capabilities, and vulnerabilities and applies them to specific terrain, weather, and tactical scenarios. There are several types of templates. Among them are the following:

- *A doctrinal template,* which depicts how the enemy would like to fight if it were not restricted by terrain and weather.
- *A situation template,* which depicts how the enemy might adjust its doctrine to fit terrain and weather constraints.
- *An event template,* which depicts time-related, logically sequenced indications or events that are keyed to a series of situation templates. Event templating determines the what, when, and where of collection planning.
- *A decision support template,* which is keyed to the event template and identifies critical events that are relative to time, location, and the current situation and that require tactical decisions.

References
Department of Defense, Department of the Army. *Intelligence and Electronic Warfare Operations.* Field Manual FM 34-1. Washington, DC: Headquarters, Department of the Army, 1984.

———. *Military Intelligence Battalion (CEWI) (Operations) (Corps).* Field Manual FM 34-21. Washington, DC: Headquarters, Department of the Army, 1982.

—**TEMPORARY AIRSPACE RESTRICTIONS** are requirements that can be imposed on segments of airspace-defined dimensions in response to specific situations and needs. These restrictions can be applied to search and rescue operations, air refueling areas, high density airspace control zones, concentrated interdiction areas, areas declared air defense artillery weapons control status WEAPONS FREE, and areas that are used for combat air patrols. Declaring such restrictions includes identifying (1) the airspace user being restricted; (2) the period, area, altitude, and height of restriction; and (3) the procedures for canceling or modifying the restriction in event of a communications loss. The three common temporary restrictions are restricted operations areas, minimum risk route/low-level transit routes, and standard-use Army aircraft routes.

References
Department of Defense, U.S. Army. *Patriot Battalion Operations.* Field Manual FM 44-15. Washington, DC: Headquarters, Department of the Army, 1984.

—**TEMPORARY DISABILITY RETIRED LIST** is a list of officers and enlisted personnel who are released from active service because of permanent disability (the degree of which has not been established) who are required to undergo periodic medical examinations at intervals of eighteen months or less, but who are entitled to receive retired pay for a period of five years if they are not removed from the list before that time. *See also:* Retirement.

References
Department of Defense, U.S. Army. *Dictionary of United States Army Terms*. Army Regulation AR 310-25. Washington, DC: Headquarters, Department of the Army, 1986.

—**TEMPORARY DUTY (TDY)** is duty at one or more locations, other than the member's permanent station. The member is under orders that direct the performance of official duties.

References
Department of Defense, U.S. Army. *Leaves and Passes*. Army Regulation AR 630-5. Washington, DC: Headquarters, Department of the Army, 1984.

—**TEMPORARY EXPEDIENT EQUIPMENT LIST** is a list of the minimum equipment necessary for meaningful unit training before total authorized allowances have been received.

References
Department of Defense, U.S. Army. *Dictionary of United States Army Terms*. Army Regulation AR 310-25. Washington, DC: Headquarters, Department of the Army, 1986.

—**TEMPORARY HAND RECEIPT** is the temporary issue or loan of property for no more than 30 days by the unit property book officer. The receiving individual assumes responsibility by signing a receipt.

References
Department of Defense, U.S. Army. *Commander's Handbook for Property Accountability at the Unit Level*. Field Manual FM 10-14-1. Washington, DC: Headquarters, Department of the Army, 1984.

—**TEMPORARY TOURS OF ACTIVE DUTY** are terms of voluntary active duty performed for a prescribed period by the Army National Guard and U.S. Army Reserve soldiers in support of an Active Army mission. Normally, such tours do not exceed 139 days. *See also:* Temporary Duty.

References
Department of Defense, U.S. Army. *Information Pamphlet for the Career Development of Enlisted Members of the U.S. Army Reserve*. Department of the Army Pamphlet DA PAM 140-8. Washington, DC: Headquarters, Department of the Army, 1986.

—**TENANT** is a unit or activity of one government agency, military department, or command that occupies facilities or an installation of another military department or command and receives supplies or other support services from that installation. *See also:* Tenant Activity.

References
Department of Defense, U.S. Army. *Dictionary of United States Army Terms*. Army Regulation AR 310-25. Washington, DC: Headquarters, Department of the Army, 1986.

—**TENANT ACTIVITY** is an organization, activity, or unit located at an installation or subinstallation belonging to another command, and from which it is receiving specified types of supply or other services. *See also:* Tenant.

References
Department of Defense, U.S. Army. *Dictionary of United States Army Terms*. Army Regulation AR 310-25. Washington, DC: Headquarters, Department of the Army, 1986.

—**TENTACLE FUZE** is a fuze that is actuated only when pressure is applied simultaneously to two tentacles connected to opposite sides of it. *See also:* Fuze (Specify Type).

References
Department of Defense, U.S. Army. *Operational Terms and Symbols*. Field Manual FM 101-5-1. Washington, DC: Headquarters, Department of the Army, 1985.

—**TENTATIVE TABLE OF ORGANIZATION AND EQUIPMENT** is a table prescribed for a unit. Its organization is considered experimental: for the personnel, the equipment, or both. *See also:* Table of Organization and Equipment.

References
Department of Defense, U.S. Army. *Dictionary of United States Army Terms*. Army Regulation AR 310-25. Washington, DC: Headquarters, Department of the Army, 1986.

—**TERMINAL** are the military and commercial facilities where cargo or personnel are loaded, unloaded, and handled while in transit by various modes of transportation.

References
Department of Defense, U.S. Army. *Dictionary of United States Army Terms*. Army Regulation AR 310-25. Washington, DC: Headquarters, Department of the Army, 1986.

—**TERMINAL BALLISTICS** is a subdivision within ballistics that deals with the effects of missiles at the target. *See also:* Ballistics.

References

Department of Defense, U.S. Army. *Dictionary of United States Army Terms*. Army Regulation AR 310-25. Washington, DC: Headquarters, Department of the Army, 1986.

—**TERMINAL COMMAND** is a transportation corps unit that provides a command headquarters for a terminal or base area in which one or more terminals are located. *See also*: Terminal.

References

Department of Defense, U.S. Army. *Dictionary of United States Army Terms*. Army Regulation AR 310-25. Washington, DC: Headquarters, Department of the Army, 1986.

—**TERMINAL LEAVE** is ordinary leave granted to assist separating members with their personal affairs. *See also:* Ordinary Leave.

References

Department of Defense, U.S. Army. *Leaves and Passes*. Army Regulation AR 630-5. Washington, DC: Headquarters, Department of the Army, 1984.

—**TERMINAL PHASE** is the stage of a smoke screen when the screen has thinned out and the cover is no longer effective. *See also:* Smoke Blanket.

References

Department of Defense, U.S. Army. *Deliberate Smoke Operations*. Field Manual FM 3-50. Washington, DC: Headquarters, Department of the Army, 1984.

—**TERMINAL POSTAL OFFICER** is the commanding officer of a U.S. Army military mail terminal who acts as a liaison officer with the accountable postmaster, postal concentration center officials, and postal inspectors on Army post office matters. This includes furnishing information on the distribution of Army post office mail and the opening and closing of Army post offices and units.

References

Department of Defense, U.S. Army. *Dictionary of United States Army Terms*. Army Regulation AR 310-25. Washington, DC: Headquarters, Department of the Army, 1986.

—**TERMINAL SERVICE COMPANY** is a transportation corps unit trained and equipped to perform cargo and passenger loading and unloading operations on ships, aircraft, railcars, or trucks to perform cargo segregation operations.

References

Department of Defense, U.S. Army. *Dictionary of United States Army Terms*. Army Regulation AR 310-25. Washington, DC: Headquarters, Department of the Army, 1986.

—**TERMINAL THROUGHPUT CAPACITY (TTC)** is an estimate of the total tonnage or personnel an existing terminal can receive, process, and clear in one day.

References

Department of Defense, U.S. Army. *Planning Logistics Support for Military Operations*. Field Manual FM 701-58. Washington, DC: Headquarters, Department of the Army, 1987.

—**TERMINAL VALUE** is the expected value of existing facilities and other assets or projected facilities and other assets, at the end of their economic life.

References

Department of Defense, U.S. Army. *Dictionary of United States Army Terms*. Army Regulation AR 310-25. Washington, DC: Headquarters, Department of the Army, 1986.

—**TERRAIN ANALYSIS** is the process of interpreting a geographic area to determine the effect of the natural and man-made features on military operations. Understanding the limitations and opportunities of terrain is a fundamental military skill. Terrain analysis varies among levels of command. Leaders of small tactical units concentrate on woodlines, streams, and individual hills. Division and corps commanders analyze road nets, aerial avenues of movement, drainage patterns, and hill systems.

At the operational level, campaign planners consider terrain from an even broader perspective. Commanders perform terrain analyses in light of their units' missions. They evaluate the terrain's potential for cover and concealment, its impact on their own and enemy mobility, and its use for observation and direct fire effect. The able commander recognizes the battlefield's natural structure and acts to improve or overcome it as necessary to accomplish the mission. Such analysis must include a unit's assigned area of responsibility, the surrounding terrain that may affect operations, and the airspace immediately over it. Fire, maneuver, and obstacle plans are designed as an integrated whole fitted to the terrain on which the operation is to be conducted.

The key elements of terrain analysis are summarized in the OCOKA (i.e., observation and fields of fire, cover and concealment, obstacles and movement, key terrain, and avenues of approach).

References

Department of Defense, U.S. Army. *Operational Terms and Symbols.* Field Manual FM 101-5-1. Washington, DC: Headquarters, Department of the Army, 1985.

————. *Staff Organization and Operations.* Field Manual FM 101-5. Washington, DC: Headquarters, Department of the Army, 1984.

—**TERRAIN BREAK ANGLE** is the angle between two adjacent slope facets that may or may not constitute an obstacle. *See also:* Obstacle.

References

Department of Defense, U.S. Army. *Dictionary of United States Army Terms.* Army Regulation AR 310-25. Washington, DC: Headquarters, Department of the Army, 1986.

—**TERRAIN EXERCISE** is a tactical exercise in which the disposition and movement of simulated groups are planned and discussed on a particular piece of ground (the troops are imaginary and the solution is usually written). It is an excellent exercise to train squad and platoon leaders how to analyze terrain for the planning and conduct of an operation. *See also:* Exercise.

References

Department of Defense, U.S. Army. *How to Prepare and Conduct Military Training.* Field Manual FM 21-6. Washington, DC: Headquarters, Department of the Army, 1975.

—**TERRAIN FACTOR** is any attribute of the ground that can be adequately described at any point (or instant of time) by a single measurable value (e.g., a slope or an obstacle height). *See also:* Terrain Analysis.

References

Department of Defense, U.S. Army. *Dictionary of United States Army Terms.* Army Regulation AR 310-25. Washington, DC: Headquarters, Department of the Army, 1986.

—**TERRAIN FLIGHT** is the tactic of using helicopters to take advantage of the terrain, vegetation, and man-made objects in order to degrade the enemy's ability to visually, optically, or electronically detect or locate the helicopter. This tactic involves a constant awareness of the capabilities and positions of the enemy's weapons and detection means in relation to available masking terrain features and flight routes. Terrain flying involves flights close to the earth's surface and includes the tactical application of low-level, contour, and nap-of-the-earth flight techniques. A low-level flight is carried out above the obstacles but at an altitude where detection by an enemy force is avoided or minimized. It is, therefore, at a constant indicated altitude and airspeed. *See also:* Contour Flight (Army Aviation).

References

Department of Defense, U.S. Army. *Air Defense Artillery Deployment: Chaparral/Vulcan/Stinger.* Field Manual FM 44-3. Washington, DC: Headquarters, Department of the Army, 1984.

————. *Attack Helicopter Operations.* Field Manual FM 17-50. Washington, DC: Headquarters, Department of the Army, 1984.

————. *Operational Terms and Symbols.* Field Manual FM 101-5-1. Washington, DC: Headquarters, Department of the Army, 1985.

—**TERRAIN INTELLIGENCE** is information on the military significance of natural and man-made characteristics of an area. The commander acquaints himself with the terrain to the fullest extent possible before combat. Because maps are sometimes inaccurate or incomplete, commanders should conduct detailed reconnaissance, issuing orders from vantage points on the ground itself whenever possible. The intelligence staff officer (G2 or S2) is responsible for assembling information on the terrain and estimating its effect on operations. Sources of terrain intelligence include military, civilian, and engineer maps; topographical studies; civilian officials and area residents; prisoners of war; and air, space, and ground reconnaissance units. *See also:* Terrain Analysis.

References

Department of Defense, U.S. Army. *Staff Organizations and Operations.* Field Manual FM 101-5. Washington, DC: Headquarters, Department of the Army, 1984.

—**TERRAIN MASKING** refers to the characteristics of terrain features that allow an object to be hidden.

References

Department of Defense, U.S. Army. *Dictionary of United States Army Terms*. Army Regulation AR 310-25. Washington, DC: Headquarters, Department of the Army, 1986.

—**TERRAIN MODEL EXERCISE** is a tactical exercise in which a sandtable or some other type of terrain model is substituted for the actual terrain. It is an excellent exercise to train leaders how to plan and conduct a tactical operation and to demonstrate how to conduct an operation to the entire unit. *See also:* Terrain Modeling.

References

Department of Defense, U.S. Army. *How to Prepare and Conduct Military Training*. Field Manual FM 21-6. Washington, DC: Headquarters, Department of the Army, 1975.

—**TERRAIN MODELING** is the mathematical modeling of the physical shape of a portion of the earth's surface (terrain) by fitting functions to the elevation status.

References

Department of Defense, U.S. Army. *Dictionary of United States Army Terms*. Army Regulation AR 310-25. Washington, DC: Headquarters, Department of the Army, 1986.

—**TERRAIN PROFILE** is a geometric representation of terrain surface (e.g., an elevation versus distance curve).

References

Department of Defense, U.S. Army. *Dictionary of United States Army Terms*. Army Regulation AR 310-25. Washington, DC: Headquarters, Department of the Army, 1986.

—**TERRAIN REINFORCEMENT** is the development of terrain using obstacles to degrade enemy mobility or to enhance friendly survivability through the construction of fighting positions and cover. It is a combined arms operation in which engineers and other units participate. Engineers install tank ditches, minefields, abatis, craters, and demolitions to canalize enemy movement, to hold the enemy in areas where it can be destroyed by fire, and to protect the flanks of maneuvering forces. Artillery, aviation, and close air support units emplace scatterable mines on targets of opportunity to suppress threat to air defense and artillery units and to interdict follow-on threat formations. Defending units emplace minefields around their own positions and usually construct their own fighting positions. Engineers operating with leading maneuver elements clear obstacles, construct bridges and rafts, and support countermine operations. *See also:* Countermobility Operations, Survivability Operations.

References

Department of Defense, U.S. Army. *Operational Terms and Symbols*. Field Manual FM 101-5-1. Washington, DC: Headquarters, Department of the Army, 1985.

————. *Staff Organization and Operations*. Field Manual FM 101-5. Washington, DC: Headquarters, Department of the Army, 1984.

—**TERRAIN RETURN** is radiation reflected from the ground and returned as an echo to the radar set.

References

Department of Defense, U.S. Army. *Dictionary of United States Army Terms*. Army Regulation AR 310-25. Washington, DC: Headquarters, Department of the Army, 1986.

—**TERRAIN SPOTTING** is positive spotting of a round that is not on the observer target line, but is based upon a knowledge of the terrain near the target.

References

Department of Defense, U.S. Army. *Dictionary of United States Army Terms*. Army Regulation AR 310-25. Washington, DC: Headquarters, Department of the Army, 1986.

—**TERRAIN STUDY** is an analysis and interpretation of the natural and man-made features of an area, their effects on military operations, and the effect of weather and climate on these features. *See also:* Terrain Analysis.

References

Department of Defense, Joint Chiefs of Staff. *Department of Defense Dictionary of Military and Related Terms*. Washington, DC: GPO, 1986.

—**TERRORISM** is the unlawful use of force or violence against persons or property to intimidate or coerce a government, the civilian population or any segment thereof, in furtherance of political or social objectives. It is the calculated use of violence or the threat of violence to attain goals that are political, religious, or ideological. This is done through intimidation, coercion, or instilling fear. Terrorism involves a criminal act that is often symbolic and is intended to influence an audience beyond its immediate victims.

References

Department of Defense, Defense Intelligence College. *Glossary of Intelligence Terms and Definitions.* Washington, DC: DIC, 1987.

Department of Defense, U.S. Army. *The Army Terrorism Counteraction Program.* Army Regulation AR 525-13. Washington, DC: Headquarters, Department of the Army, 1988.

—**TERRORISM COUNTERACTION** is action taken to counter a terrorist threat. It includes antiterrorism (defensive measures taken to reduce vulnerability to terrorist attack) and counterterrorism (offensive measures taken in response to terrorist acts).

Defeating terrorism requires the development of national-level policy and offensive and defensive capabilities. For the U.S. Army, terrorism counteractions require an effective program, intelligence gathering and threat analysis, and the reduction of the vulnerability of military forces.

References

Department of Defense, U.S. Army. *The Army Terrorism Counteraction Program.* Army Regulation AR 525-13. Washington, DC: Headquarters, Department of the Army, 1988.

———. *U.S. Army Operational Concept for Special Operations Forces.* TRADOC PAM 525-34. Washington, DC: Headquarters, Department of the Army, 1984.

———. *U.S. Army Policy Statement, 1988.* Washington, DC: Headquarters, Department of the Army, 1988.

—**TERRORIST GROUP** is a group that is politically, religious, or ideologically oriented and uses terrorism as its prime mode of operations.

References

Department of Defense, U.S. Army. *The Army Terrorism Counteraction Program.* Army Regulation AR 525-13. Washington, DC: Headquarters, Department of the Army, 1988.

—**TERRORIST ORGANIZATION** is a group that engages in terrorist activities.

References

Department of Defense, U.S. Army. *Dictionary of United States Army Terms.* Army Regulation AR 310-25. Washington, DC: Headquarters, Department of the Army, 1986.

—**TERRORIST THREAT CONDITION (THREATCON)** is a level of terrorist threat to U.S. military facilities and personnel. There are three levels of THREATCON:

- *THREATCON WHITE* means that there is a nonspecific terrorist threat against U.S. military personnel or facilities in a general geographic area. The threat may be based upon information that the terrorist elements in the area have general plans against military facilities.
- *THREATCON YELLOW* means that there is a specific threat against U.S. military personnel or facilities in a particular geographic area. This threat may be based upon information that terrorist elements are actively preparing for operations in a particular area.
- *THREATCON RED* means that there is an imminent threat of terrorist acts against specific U.S. military personnel or facilities. This threat may be based upon information regarding plans or preparations for terrorist attacks against specific persons or facilities.

References

Department of Defense, Joint Chiefs of Staff. *Department of Defense Dictionary of Military and Related Terms.* Washington, DC: GPO, 1986.

—**TEST CONTROL OFFICER** is an individual appointed to control the issue and use of test materials. Under the Enlisted Evaluation System, the individual must be a commissioned or warrant officer who is appointed by the installation commander and supervises the operation of the installation of Enlisted Evaluation System within a designated area. *See also:* Enlisted Evaluation System.

References

Department of Defense, U.S. Army. *Dictionary of United States Army Terms.* Army Regulation AR 310-25. Washington, DC: Headquarters, Department of the Army, 1986.

—**TEST EQUIPMENT** is electric, electronic, mechanical, hydraulic, or pneumatic equipment (automatic, manual, or a combination of the two) that checks the ability of other equipment to function.

References

Department of Defense, U.S. Army. *Dictionary of United States Army Terms.* Army Regulation AR 310-25. Washington, DC: Headquarters, Department of the Army, 1986.

—**TEST, MEASUREMENT, AND DIAGNOSTIC EQUIPMENT (TMDE)** is electronic, mechanical, hydraulic, or pneumatic equipment (automatic, manual, or a combination of the two) that checks out or ascertains the calibration function of other equipment. *See also:* Test Equipment.

References
Department of Defense, U.S. Army. *Support Operations: Echelons Above Corps.* Field Manual FM 100-16. Washington, DC: Headquarters, Department of the Army, 1986.

—**TEST PIECE** is a gun used to compare with another gun in calibration. The gun used as the basis of comparison is the "reference piece," the gun adjusted accurately with reference to it is the "test piece."

References
Department of Defense, U.S. Army. *Dictionary of United States Army Terms.* Army Regulation AR 310-25. Washington, DC: Headquarters, Department of the Army, 1986.

—**TETRYTOL** is a binary explosive consisting of a mixture of tetryl and TNT.

References
Department of Defense, U.S. Army. *Dictionary of United States Army Terms.* Army Regulation AR 310-25. Washington, DC: Headquarters, Department of the Army, 1986.

—**THEATER** is a geographical area outside of the continental United States for which a commander of a unified or specified command has been assigned military responsibility. *See also:* Theater Army.

References
Department of Defense, Joint Chiefs of Staff. *Department of Defense Dictionary of Military and Related Terms.* Washington, DC: GPO, 1986.

—**THEATER ADP (AUTOMATED DATA PROCESSING) SERVICE CENTER** is a fully mobile, militarized computer center that processes Standard Army Multicommand Management Information Systems and command-unique software in support of theater army wartime force development and combat service support functions. Each center is managed, operated, and maintained by military personnel.

References
Department of Defense, U.S. Army. *Support Operations: Echelons Above Corps.* Field Manual FM 100-16. Washington, DC: Headquarters, Department of the Army, 1986.

—**THEATER AIR DEFENSE FORCES** are interceptor aircraft and surface-to-surface missiles that are designed primarily to support tactical forces. Some can be adapted for strategic intelligence. *See also:* Strategic Intelligence.

References
Collins, John M. *U.S.-Soviet Military Balance, 1980-1985.* Washington, DC: Congressional Research Service, 1985.

—**THEATER ARMY** is normally the Army service component command in a unified command. As an echelon above the corps organization, it provides combat, combat support, and combat service support forces in the theater. It is tailored to each theater. Third U.S. Army, Eighth U.S. Army (Korea), and U.S. Army, Europe, are examples of current theater armies. The theater army as the service component has both operational and support responsibilities. Its exact tasks are assigned by the theater commander-in-chief and may be operational missions, logistic tasks, or a combination of both.

Theater army commanders are responsible to the unified commander in a theater for recommending how the U.S. Army forces assigned to them should be allocated and employed. Their support responsibilities include the requirements to organize and maintain Army forces in the theater.

The organization of theater armies varies between theaters according to the size of the U.S. Army component in a force and with the factors of mission, enemy, terrain, troops, and time available. Other levels of command also perform theater army functions. For example, a corps staff could perform the theater army function if only a single corps is committed to a contingency area. A larger separate staff may be necessary to handle the administrative, legal, logistical, personnel, intelligence, operations, and communications tasks of a large force deployed overseas. Liaison between a theater army and another headquarters employing its forces must be performed whenever theater armies release operational command of their units. *See also:* Army, Corps, Theater.

References
Department of Defense, U.S. Army. *Operational Terms and Symbols.* Field Manual FM 101-5-1. Washington, DC: Headquarters, Department of the Army, 1985.

———. *Staff Organization and Operations.* Field Manual FM 101-5. Washington, DC: Headquarters, Department of the Army, 1984.

———. *Support Operations: Echelons Above Corps.* Field Manual FM 100-16. Washington, DC: Headquarters, Department of the Army, 1986.

—**THEATER ARMY AIR COMMAND (TAACOM)** is the key logistics operator in the communications zone. He functions as a major subordinate command under the theater army. The TAACOM is organized to provide direct support to units located in or passing through his assigned area and specified general support to all Army and other units in the theater as directed by the theater army commander.

References
Department of Defense, U.S. Army. *Combat Service Support Operations-Theater.* Field Manual FM 63-4. Washington, DC: Headquarters, Department of the Army, 1984.

—**THEATER ARMY LOGISTICAL COMMAND** is the command, located in the communications zone, that has the responsibility for providing administrative support, except personnel replacement and civil affairs, to all U.S. Army Forces located in a theater of operations and to the theater Navy, theater Air Force, allied, and other forces that have been assigned to it. *See also:* Communications Zone.

References
Department of Defense, U.S. Army. *Dictionary of United States Army Terms.* Army Regulation AR 310-25. Washington, DC: Headquarters, Department of the Army, 1986.

—**THEATER ARMY MOVEMENT CONTROL AGENCY (TAMCA)** is the U.S. theater Army organization responsible for coordinating and administering transportation policy. The functional element under the theater Army movement control agency for movement control is the theater Army movement control center.

References
Department of Defense, U.S. Army. *Support Operations: Echelons Above Corps.* Field Manual FM 100-16. Washington, DC: Headquarters, Department of the Army, 1986.

—**THEATER DEPOT** is an installation, normally under communication zone control, that has the missions of receiving, storing, and issuing supplies for the theater or major subordinate commands. This term also applies to any overseas depot or other major supply activity that relies

on facilities located in the continental United States for its resupply. *See also:* Communication Zone.

References
Department of Defense, U.S. Army. *Dictionary of United States Army Terms.* Army Regulation AR 310-25. Washington, DC: Headquarters, Department of the Army, 1986.

—**THEATER FORECAST OF REQUISITIONS** is a quarterly report submitted by an overseas command that forecasts the quantities of standard stock list items estimated to be requisitioned and shipped from the United States during each of the succeeding four calender quarters.

References
Department of Defense, U.S. Army. *Dictionary of United States Army Terms.* Army Regulation AR 310-25. Washington, DC: Headquarters, Department of the Army, 1986.

—**THEATER INVENTORY CONTROL POINT** is an activity, designated by the overseas theater commander, assigned the responsibility for the centralized or integrated management and control of stocks stored and issued from theater depots and/or storage points.

References
Department of Defense, U.S. Army. *Dictionary of United States Army Terms.* Army Regulation AR 310-25. Washington, DC: Headquarters, Department of the Army, 1986.

—**THEATER MANAGEMENT FORCE (TMF)** is an installation's action force that responds to major disruptions at the installation. The TMF should be of sufficient size to manage the disruption and usually involves a command element, security element, negotiation team, special reaction team, and a logistical element.

References
Department of Defense, U.S. Army. *The Army Terrorism Counteraction Program.* Army Regulation AR 525-13. Washington, DC: Headquarters, Department of the Army, 1988.

—**THEATER MEDICAL EVACUATION POLICY** is the maximum period, established by the Secretary of Defense with the advice of the Joint Chiefs of Staff, that patients may be held within the theater for treatment. The theater Army commander normally establishes intratheater evacuation (holding) policies for the combat zone and the communications zone. The policy establishes, in terms of the number of days, the maximum period of hospitalization and convalescence that patients may be held within the theater for treatment. The policy does not require that a patient be held in the theater for the entire period of noneffectiveness. A patient who is not expected to be ready for return to duty within the period established in the policy is evacuated to the continental United States or some other safe area. This is done as soon as the treating physicians determine that such evacuation will not aggravate the patient's disabilities or medical condition. This policy is not a substitute for clinical judgment in the management of individual patients. *See also:* Medical Treatment.

References

Department of Defense, U.S. Army. *Planning for Health Service Support.* Field Manual FM 8-55. Washington, DC: Headquarters, Department of the Army, 1985.

———. *Planning Logistics Support for Military Operations.* Field Manual FM 701-58. Washington, DC: Headquarters, Department of the Army, 1987.

—**THEATER NUCLEAR FORCES, WEAPONS, OPERATIONS** is nuclear combat power expressly designed for the deterrent, offensive, and defensive purposes that contribute to accomplishing localized military missions through the threatened or actual application of such power. They may be employed in general as well as in limited wars. *See also:* General War, Limited War.

References

Collins, John M. *U.S.-Soviet Military Balance, 1980-1985.* Washington, DC: Congressional Research Service, 1985.

—**THEATER OF OPERATIONS** is normally divided into a combat zone and a communications zone. However, the situation and international agreements might dictate a further division of the combat zone into a forward and a rear combat zone. The combat zone is the part of the theater of operations that the combat forces need to conduct operations. It contains the necessary organic combat support and combat service support facilities. It includes the geographical area extending from the rear boundary of the corps into the enemy-controlled area. The communications zone extends from the corps

rear boundary to the theater boundaries designated by higher authority. *See also:* Combat Support, Combat Service Support, Combat Zone, Communications Zone, Operations.

References

Department of Defense, U.S. Army. *Combat Service Support Operations-Theater.* Field Manual FM 63-4. Washington, DC: Headquarters, Department of the Army, 1984.

—**THEATER RESERVE STOCKS** are materials, equipment, and items that are authorized each theater in terms of days of supply to support initial combat consumption until resupply can be accomplished.

References

Department of Defense, U.S. Army. *Support Operations: Echelons Above Corps.* Field Manual FM 100-16. Washington, DC: Headquarters, Department of the Army, 1986.

—**THEATER STOCK LEVEL** is a quantity of supplies authorized by Headquarters, Department of the Army, to be maintained in a theater of operations as stock-on-hand ready-for-use.

References

Department of Defense, U.S. Army. *Dictionary of United States Army Terms.* Army Regulation AR 310-25. Washington, DC: Headquarters, Department of the Army, 1986.

—**THEATER WAR RESERVES** are the portion of the mobilization reserve materiel objective authorized each theater in days of supply to support initial combat consumption until surface resupply becomes effective.

References

Department of Defense, U.S. Army. *Dictionary of United States Army Terms.* Army Regulation AR 310-25. Washington, DC: Headquarters, Department of the Army, 1986.

—**THERMAL EFFECTS.** (1) Thermal effects are the energy emitted from the fireball as thermal radiation. (2) Thermal effects are the heat and light produced by a nuclear explosion. *See also:* Thermal Radiation.

References

Department of Defense, U.S. Army. *NBC Operations.* Field Manual FM 3-100. Washington, DC: Headquarters, Department of the Army, 1985.

—**THERMAL IMAGERY** (INFRARED) is imagery produced by measuring and recording electronically the thermal radiation of objects. *See also:* Thermal Radiation.

References
Department of Defense, Joint Chiefs of Staff. *Department of Defense Dictionary of Military and Related Terms.* Washington, DC: GPO, 1986.

—**THERMAL RADIATION.** (1) Thermal radiation consists of the heat and light produced by a nuclear explosion. (2) Thermal radiation is electromagnetic radiations emitted from a heat or light source as a consequence of its temperature. It consists essentially of ultraviolet, visible, and infrared radiations. *See also:* Flash Blindness (Dazzle).

References
Department of Defense, Joint Chiefs of Staff. *Department of Defense Dictionary of Military and Related Terms.* Washington, DC: GPO, 1986.

—**THERMATE** is a secondary incendiary agent used as a filling for incendiary munitions. It is a mixture of thermite (iron oxide and aluminum) and other oxidizing agents that burn at about 4,300 degrees Fahrenheit. *See also:* Thermite.

References
Department of Defense, U.S. Army. *Dictionary of United States Army Terms.* Army Regulation AR 310-25. Washington, DC: Headquarters, Department of the Army, 1986.

—**THERMITE** is a commercial welding mixture of iron oxide and aluminum. It is used as an incendiary for some munitions.

References
Department of Defense, U.S. Army. *Dictionary of United States Army Terms.* Army Regulation AR 310-25. Washington, DC: Headquarters, Department of the Army, 1986.

—**THERMONUCLEAR WEAPON** is a weapon in which very high temperatures are used to bring about the fusion of light nuclei (e.g., hydrogen isotopes such as deuterium and tritium) with the accompanying release of energy. The high temperatures required are obtained through fission. *See also:* Nuclear Warfare.

References
Department of Defense, Joint Chiefs of Staff. *Department of Defense Dictionary of Military and Related Terms.* Washington, DC: GPO, 1986.

—**THICKENED FUEL** is gasoline with a thickener (i.e., gelling agent) added. It is used as an incendiary fuel in flamethrowers and firebombs. *See also:* Chemical Warfare.

References
Department of Defense, U.S. Army. *Dictionary of United States Army Terms.* Army Regulation AR 310-25. Washington, DC: Headquarters, Department of the Army, 1986.

—**THICKENING** is the reinforcing of units during a defense action in order to concentrate forces and thus attain a desired combat ratio. In the thickening of main battle area units, reinforcing elements may come from the covering force reserve units or laterally from other forces in the main battle area. Thickening may also include the adjusting of boundaries in order to concentrate more forces in a smaller area. *See also:* Main Battle Area.

References
Department of Defense, U.S. Army. *Operational Terms and Symbols.* Field Manual FM 101-5-1. Washington, DC: Headquarters, Department of the Army, 1985.

—**THIN NATURAL SCREEN** is a natural growth left in front of entrenchments and emplacements to aid in concealing them.

References
Department of Defense, U.S. Army. *Dictionary of United States Army Terms.* Army Regulation AR 310-25. Washington, DC: Headquarters, Department of the Army, 1986.

—**THIRD STATE NATIONAL** is a non-United States citizen who is not a citizen of the country in which he is employed and who has been brought into that country to be employed under special employment conditions by the United States Army.

References
Department of Defense, U.S. Army. *Dictionary of United States Army Terms.* Army Regulation AR 310-25. Washington, DC: Headquarters, Department of the Army, 1986.

—**THREAT.** (1) A threat is a force or activity that is viewed as being inimicable to the interests of a nation. In terms of a nation's armed forces, a threat is usually the armed forces of another nation. Often, however, the threat from a nation's internal forces is viewed as more serious than any external threat. This is particularly true in Third World countries. The threat is usually the object of a nation's major intelligence effort, because it is through intelligence that the threat is defined and measured. This, in turn, drives most decisions concerning such areas as the defense budget, strength of the armed forces, military deployments, and modernization. For these reasons, the threat is an important starting point in the intelligence process. (2) Threat is a communications security term that means the technical or operational capability of a hostile entity to detect, exploit, or subvert friendly telecommunications and the demonstrated, presumed, or inferred intent of that entity to conduct such activity. (3) Threat is an Army tactical intelligence term that refers to the technical and operational capability of an enemy to detect, exploit, or subvert friendly telecommunications and the demonstrated, presumed, or inferred intent of that enemy to conduct such activity. In this concept, there are two aspects to threat: the threat from and the threat to. *The threat from* is represented by the general or "generic" threat posed by a hostile signals intelligence capability. *The threat to* is the identification of a specific threat that is targeted against a specific unit or activity. The threat to is derived from analysis of the generic threat (templates) and available information concerning signals intelligence capabilities and intentions that are facing a unit or activity. (4) Threat is an indications and warning term that refers to the extant military, economic, and/or political capability of a foreign country, coupled with aggressive intentions to use this capability to perform an action that could be detrimental to the United States. *See also:* Threat Analysis.

References

Collins, John M. *U.S.-Soviet Military Balance, 1980-1985.* Washington, DC: Congressional Research Service, 1985.

Department of Defense, Defense Intelligence College. *Glossary of Intelligence Terms and Definitions.* Washington, DC: DIC, 1987.

Department of Defense, U.S. Army. *Counter-Signals Intelligence (C-SIGINT) Operations.* Field Manual FM 34-62. Washington, DC: Headquarters, Department of the Army, 1986.

————. *RDTGE Managers Intelligence and Threat Support Guide.* Alexandria, VA: Headquarters, Army Materiel Development and Readiness Command, 1983.

—**THREAT ANALYSIS** is the process of using analytic techniques to develop plausible alternative representations of foreign environments and capabilities.

References

Department of Defense, U.S. Army. *Support Operations: Echelons Above Corps.* Field Manual FM 100-16. Washington, DC: Headquarters, Department of the Army, 1986.

—**THREAT APPROVAL** is an Army intelligence term that means validation (in the Army context). It is done at the Headquarters, Department of the Army, Intelligence and Threat Analysis Center (U.S. Army), or Major Army Command level. *See also:* Threat.

References

Department of Defense, U.S. Army. *RDTGE Managers Intelligence and Threat Support Guide.* Alexandria, VA: Headquarters, Army Materiel Development and Readiness Command, 1983.

—**THREAT STUDY** is an authoritative intelligence assessment of enemy capabilities (i.e., combat materiel, employment doctrine, environment, and force structures) that would affect general U.S. planning or developments. A threat study has two aspects: (1) an assessment of the level of development that the economy, technology, and/or forces of the country have achieved or a forecast of what they can be expected to achieve in the future; and (2) a recasting of existing assessments and forecasts that provide a statement of the threat as it relates to a specific research or combat developments project. *See also:* Threat.

References

Department of Defense, U.S. Army. *Dictionary of United States Army Terms.* Army Regulation AR 310-25. Washington, DC: Headquarters, Department of the Army, 1986.

—**THREAT VALIDATION** is an Army intelligence term that refers to the Defense Intelligence Agency's evaluation of, and concurrence with, threat documentation. Defense Intelligence Agency evaluations of Service-produced threats stress the appropriateness and completeness of the intelligence, accuracy of the judgments, the consistency with existing intelligence positions, the logic of the extrapolations from existing intelligence, and the suitability of the methodologies that have been used. Validation indicates the general acceptability of the intelligence for use in support of a specific plan, program, study, materiel acquisition milestone, or combat development activity. *See also:* Threat.

References
Department of Defense, U.S. Army. *RDTGE Managers Intelligence and Threat Support Guide.* Alexandria, VA: Headquarters, Army Materiel Development and Readiness Command, 1983.

—**THRESHOLD** is an intangible and adjustable line between levels and types of conflict (e.g., the separation between nuclear and nonnuclear warfare). The greater the reluctance to use nuclear weapons, the higher the threshold.

References
Collins, John M. *U.S.-Soviet Military Balance, 1980-1985.* Washington, DC: Congressional Research Service, 1985.

—**THROUGHPUT DISTRIBUTION.** (1) Throughput distribution is used to describe shipments that bypass intermediate installations. (2) Throughput distribution is the bypassing of one or more intermediate supply echelons in the supply system, thereby avoiding multiple handling.

References
Department of Defense, U.S. Army. *Operational Terms and Symbols.* Field Manual FM 101-5-1. Washington, DC: Headquarters, Department of the Army, 1985.
———. *Support Operations: Echelons Above Corps.* Field Manual FM 100-16. Washington, DC: Headquarters, Department of the Army, 1986.

—**THRUST LINE** is a line forming the base of all coordinates in the thrust line system of locating the position of objects on a map. It is a commander-designated line that is located on the map by two reference points, or by a reference point and a direction. Somewhere on the thrust line is a base point, also designated by the commander, from which all coordinates are measured. Points are located by giving their distance along the thrust line, forward or back of the base point, and their distance is perpendicular to the thrust line.

References
Department of Defense, U.S. Army. *Dictionary of United States Army Terms.* Army Regulation AR 310-25. Washington, DC: Headquarters, Department of the Army, 1986.

—**TIARA.** *See:* Tactical Intelligence and Related Activities.

—**TIE DOWN** is the fastening or securing of a load to its carrier by using ropes, cables, or other means to prevent it from shifting during transport. Tie down is also used as a noun to describe the material used to secure a load.

References
Department of Defense, Joint Chiefs of Staff. *Department of Defense Dictionary of Military and Related Terms.* Washington, DC: GPO, 1986.

—**TILT ROD FUZE** is a fuze designed to actuate when a rod forming part of the fuze is displaced by contact with the target.

References
Department of Defense, U.S. Army. *Operations.* Field Manual FM 100-5. Washington, DC: Headquarters, Department of the Army, 1986.

—**TIME DISTANCE** is the time it takes the head of a column to move from one point to another at a given pace.

References
Department of Defense, U.S. Army. *The Infantry Rifle Company (Infantry, Airborne, Air Assault, Ranger).* Field Manual FM 7-10. Washington, DC: Headquarters, Department of the Army, 1982.

—**TIME FIRE** is fire in which fuzes are set to activate after a fixed time interval and before impact. *See also:* Fire.

References
Department of Defense, U.S. Army. *Dictionary of United States Army Terms.* Army Regulation AR 310-25. Washington, DC: Headquarters, Department of the Army, 1986.

—**TIME FUZE** is a fuze containing a device that regulates the time that the fuze will function. *See also:* Fuze (Specify Type).

References
Department of Defense, Joint Chiefs of Staff. *Department of Defense Dictionary of Military and Related Terms.* Washington, DC: GPO, 1986.

—**TIME GAP** is the sum of the intervals between columns and elements of the columns. It is expressed in minutes. *See also:* Column, Element.

References

Department of Defense, U.S. Army. *Dictionary of United States Army Terms.* Army Regulation AR 310-25. Washington, DC: Headquarters, Department of the Army, 1986.

—**TIME INTERVAL** is the time that elapses between successive elements of a column as they pass a given point.

References

Department of Defense, U.S. Army. *Dictionary of United States Army Terms.* Army Regulation AR 310-25. Washington, DC: Headquarters, Department of the Army, 1986.

—**TIME LAG** is the time difference between how fast a bomb released under given conditions falls compared with the time of fall for an ideal bomb released under identical conditions.

References

Department of Defense, U.S. Army. *Dictionary of United States Army Terms.* Army Regulation AR 310-25. Washington, DC: Headquarters, Department of the Army, 1986.

—**TIME OF ATTACK** is the hour at which the attack is to be launched. If a line of departure is prescribed, it is the hour at which the line is to be crossed by the leading elements of the attack. *See also:* Line of Departure.

References

Department of Defense, U.S. Army. *Operational Terms and Symbols.* Field Manual FM 101-5-1. Washington, DC: Headquarters, Department of the Army, 1985.

—**TIME OF FLIGHT,** in artillery, is the time in seconds from the instant a weapon is fired, launched, or released from the delivery vehicle or weapons system to the instant it strikes or detonates.

References

Department of Defense, Joint Chiefs of Staff. *Department of Defense Dictionary of Military and Related Terms.* Washington, DC: GPO, 1986.

—**TIME ON TARGET (TT OR TOT).** (1) Time on target is a method of firing on a target in which various artillery units, mortars, and/or naval gunfire support ships fire their initial rounds to strike the target simultaneously at the time required. (2) Time on target is the time when aircraft are scheduled to attack or photograph the target. (3) Time on target is the actual time at which aircraft attack or photograph a target. (4) Time on target is the time at which a nuclear detonation is planned at a specified desired ground zero. *See also:* Targeting.

References

Department of Defense, U.S. Army. *Attack Helicopter Operations.* Field Manual FM 17-50. Washington, DC: Headquarters, Department of the Army, 1984.

————. *Operational Terms and Symbols.* Field Manual FM 101-5-1. Washington, DC: Headquarters, Department of the Army, 1985.

—**TIME-PHASED FORCE DEPLOYMENT DATA (TPFDD)** refers to the computer-supported data base portion of an operation plan. It contains time-phased force data, non-unit-related cargo and personnel data, and movement data for the operation plan, including (1) in-place units; (2) units to be deployed to support the operation plan with a priority indicating the desired sequence for their arrival at the port of debarkation; (3) the routing of forces to be deployed; (4) movement data associated with deploying forces; (5) estimates of non-unit-related cargo and personnel movements to be conducted concurrently with the deployment of forces; and (6) an estimate of transportation requirements that must be fulfilled by common-user lift resources as well as the requirements that can be fulfilled by assigned or attached transportation resources. *See also:* Time-Phased Force and Deployment List, Time-Phased Transportation Requirements List.

References

Department of Defense, U.S. Army. *Planning Logistics Support for Military Operations.* Field Manual FM 701-58. Washington, DC: Headquarters, Department of the Army, 1987.

—**TIME-PHASED FORCE AND DEPLOYMENT LIST (TPFDL)** identifies the types and/or actual units required to support the operation plan, indicates the origin and the ports of debarkation or ocean area, and provides data concerning their destination. It may also be generated as a computer listing from the time-phased force and deployment data. *See also:* Time-Phased Force and Deployment Data, Time-Phased Transportation Requirements List.

References

Department of Defense, U.S. Army. *Planning Logistics Support for Military Operations.* Field Manual FM 701-58. Washington, DC: Headquarters, Department of the Army, 1987.

—**TIME-PHASED TRANSPORTATION REQUIRE-MENTS LIST (TPTRL)** is part of the Time-Phased Force and Deployment data that defines the movement requirements and includes a time-phased listing by type units/mobility echelons, fillers and replacement personnel, and bulk supplies that are to be transported by air or sea to support an operations plan. It provides mobility data that are related to these deployments and estimates movement requirements to be fulfilled by both common-user lift resources and assigned transportation resources. *See also:* Time-Phased Force and Deployment Data, Time-Phased Force and Deployment List.

References
Department of Defense, U.S. Army. *Planning Logistics Support for Military Operations*. Field Manual FM 701-58. Washington, DC: Headquarters, Department of the Army, 1987.

—**TIME-SENSITIVE TARGETS** are the targets requiring immediate response because they pose (or will soon pose) a clear and present danger to friendly forces or are highly lucrative, fleeting targets of opportunity.

References
Department of Defense, Joint Chiefs of Staff. *Department of Defense Dictionary of Military and Related Terms*. Washington, DC: GPO, 1986.

—**TIP-OFF** is an Army tactical intelligence term that means data that can be used for fire or maneuver decisions as it is received without further processing, interpretation, or integration with other data.

References
Department of Defense, U.S. Army. *Counter-Signals Intelligence (C-SIGINT) Operations*. Field Manual FM 34-62. Washington, DC: Headquarters, Department of the Army, 1986.

—**TILTING STRIP,** in intelligence imagery and photoreconnaissance, is the information that is added to photographic negatives or positives to identify them and provide reference information. *See also:* Imagery Intelligence.

References
Department of Defense, Joint Chiefs of Staff. *Department of Defense Dictionary of Military and Related Terms*. Washington, DC: GPO, 1986.

—**TNT EQUIVALENT** is a measure of the energy released from the detonation of a nuclear weapon, or from the explosion of a given quantity of fissionable material, in terms of the amount of TNT (trinitrotoluene) that could release the same amount of energy when exploded. *See also:* Nuclear Warfare.

References
Department of Defense, Joint Chiefs of Staff. *Department of Defense Dictionary of Military and Related Terms*. Washington, DC: GPO, 1986.

—**TO ACCOMPANY TROOPS** refers to items of military equipment, authorized by tables of organization and equipment, that deploying units must carry with them (e.g., organizational clothing, protective masks, and individual weapons). *See also:* Table of Organization and Equipment.

References
Department of Defense, U.S. Army. *Support Operations: Echelons Above Corps*. Field Manual FM 100-16. Washington, DC: Headquarters, Department of the Army, 1986.

—**TO THE COLORS** is a bugle call sounded as a salute to the color, to the President, the Vice President, an ex-President, or a foreign chief magistrate. *See also:* Color.

References
Department of Defense, U.S. Army. *Dictionary of United States Army Terms*. Army Regulation AR 310-25. Washington, DC: Headquarters, Department of the Army, 1986.

—**TOLERANCE DOSE** is the amount of radiation that may be received by an individual within a specified period of time negligible to the individual. *See also:* Nuclear Warfare.

References
Department of Defense, Joint Chiefs of Staff. *Department of Defense Dictionary of Military and Related Terms*. Washington, DC: GPO, 1986.

—**TOMAHAWK** is an air-, land-, ship-, or submarine-launched cruise missile with three variants: land attack with conventional capability; land attack with nuclear capability; and tactical anti-ship with conventional warhead.

References
Department of Defense, Joint Chiefs of Staff. *Department of Defense Dictionary of Military and Related Terms*. Washington, DC: GPO, 1986.

—**TON-MILES** is a unit of measure expressed in the number of short tons moved over a specific distance in miles.

References

Department of Defense, U.S. Army. *Transportation Reference Data.* Field Manual FM 55-15. Washington, DC: Headquarters, Department of the Army, 1986.

—**TONE DOWN,** in camouflage and concealment, is the process of making an object or surface less conspicuous by reducing its contrast to the surroundings or background.

References

Department of Defense, Joint Chiefs of Staff. *Department of Defense Dictionary of Military and Related Terms.* Washington, DC: GPO, 1986.

—**TOP SECRET CONTROL (TSC)** is a system that controls the storage, accountability, and dissemination of top secret material. The system includes physical security (in that the material can only be retained in approved areas), dissemination (in that only those who have been cleared for access to top secret material can be allowed to see it and must sign on a sheet that they have seen it), and accountability (in that periodic inventories must be taken to account for all the top secret material). *See also:* Top Secret Control Officer.

References

Department of Defense, Joint Chiefs of Staff. *Department of Defense Dictionary of Military and Related Terms.* Washington, DC: GPO, 1986.

—**TOP SECRET CONTROL OFFICER (TSCO)** is an officer, warrant officer, or responsible civilian official appointed in each command or agency to be responsible for the receipt, custody, and distribution of top secret material within the local command and the transmission of top secret material outside the immediate organization. He is responsible for the physical security of the command's top secret information and, unless he is given an exemption, must conduct an inventory of all top secret materials at least annually.

References

U.S. Department of Defense. Information Security Oversight Office. *Directive No. 1: National Security Information.* (Reprinted in *Federal Register,* June 25, 1982, at 27836-27841.)

—**TOPOGRAPHIC CREST** is the highest point of a hill, ridge, or mountain. *See also:* Military Crest.

References

Department of Defense, U.S. Army. *Operational Terms and Symbols.* Field Manual FM 101-5-1. Washington, DC: Headquarters, Department of the Army, 1985.

————. *S2 Reference Guide.* Training Circular TC 30-28. Washington, DC: Headquarters, Department of the Army, 1977.

—**TORPEX** is a high explosive consisting of TNT, cyclonite, and aluminum powder, and is often used in mines. *See also:* Mine Warfare.

References

Department of Defense, U.S. Army. *Dictionary of United States Army Terms.* Army Regulation AR 310-25. Washington, DC: Headquarters, Department of the Army, 1986.

—**TOTAL ALLOWANCE** is based upon a table of organization and equipment, or a table of distribution and allowances, as applicable. Such allowances do not apply to repair parts, and changes to total allowances require the approval of Headquarters, Department of the Army. *See also:* Table of Distribution and Allowances, Table of Organization and Equipment.

References

Department of Defense, U.S. Army. *Dictionary of United States Army Terms.* Army Regulation AR 310-25. Washington, DC: Headquarters, Department of the Army, 1986.

—**TOTAL ARMY,** within the Army, is the total force policy as a total Army bond among the Active Army, Army National Guard, Army Reserve, and the civilian work force. It is expressed in the balance of the Army's force structure and in equipment modernization programs. Total Army planning reflects active cooperation and affiliation between the Service's active and reserve component units. It increases the mobilization potential of reserve units and insures their timely availability in wartime. *See also:* Active Army, Reserve Components.

References

Department of Defense, U.S. Army. *The Army.* (Prepublication Issue.) Field Manual FM 100-1. Washington, DC: Headquarters, Department of the Army, 1986.

—**TOTAL ARMY COMMUNITY** is a diverse community consisting of soldiers on active duty, soldiers in the reserve components, retired soldiers, supporting civilian employees, and the families of all such personnel. It is also called the Army Community.

References
Department of Defense, U.S. Army. *Dictionary of United States Army Terms*. Army Regulation AR 310-25. Washington, DC: Headquarters, Department of the Army, 1986.

—**TOTAL ARMY PERSONNEL MODEL (TAPM)** is a conceptual framework for developing programs, policies, and procedures to be used by all Army personnel in preparing for war and during peacetime. The programs developed within TAPM cover the complete Army lifecycle. They include accessing, training, sustaining, and transitioning all military and civilian personnel into and between the active and reserve components.

References
Department of Defense, U.S. Army. *U.S. Army Policy Statement, 1988*. Washington, DC: Headquarters, Department of the Army, 1988.

—**TOTAL DOSAGE ATTACK** is a chemical attack/fire mission used to build up the dosage needed to incapacitate enemy personnel over an extended period of time. It is normally employed against troops who have no protection available. *See also:* Surprise Dosage Attack.

References
Department of Defense, Joint Chiefs of Staff. *Department of Defense Dictionary of Military and Related Terms*. Washington, DC: GPO, 1986.

—**TOTAL FEDERAL OFFICER SERVICE** is all periods of commissioned/warrant officer service, active and reserve, creditable for basic pay (time since basic entry date), minus any period(s) of enlisted service creditable for basic pay.

References
Department of Defense, U.S. Army. *Dictionary of United States Army Terms*. Army Regulation AR 310-25. Washington, DC: Headquarters, Department of the Army, 1986.

—**TOTAL FORCE.** In national security planning, U.S. active and reserve component forces and allied forces are conceived as an entity, the total force. This force has a military effectiveness greater than the sum of its parts. In practical terms, this means that the Department of Defense and the individual Services consider the capabilities of these forces, both in their primary and alternate roles, when structuring U.S. forces or planning their employment. Total force planning, budgeting, and operations can increase employment options for specific weapon systems, expand the effective roles of Reserve and National Guard forces, take allied defense efforts more fully into account, and promote interservice and intra-alliance support.

References
Department of Defense, U.S. Army. *The Army*. (Prepublication Issue.) Field Manual FM 100-1. Washington, DC: Headquarters, Department of the Army, 1986.

—**TOTAL MOBILIZATION** is the expansion of the Armed Forces resulting from an action by Congress and the President to organize and/or generate additional units or personnel beyond the existing force structure, and the resources needed for their support, to meet the total requirements of a war or other national emergency involving an external threat to the national security.

References
Department of Defense, Joint Chiefs of Staff. *Department of Defense Dictionary of Military and Related Terms*. Washington, DC: GPO, 1986.

—**TOTAL OPERATIONAL FLYING DUTY CREDIT** is flying performed under orders by rated or designated members while serving in assignments in which basic flying skills normally are maintained in the performance of assigned duties. The flying is performed by members in training and leads to the award of an aeronautical rating or designation.

References
Department of Defense, U.S. Army. *Dictionary of United States Army Terms*. Army Regulation AR 310-25. Washington, DC: Headquarters, Department of the Army, 1986.

—**TOUCHDOWN**, in amphibious operations, is the initial landing of the first element of the assault forces on a hostile beach. *See also:* Amphibious Operation.

References
Department of Defense, U.S. Army. *Dictionary of United States Army Terms*. Army Regulation AR 310-25. Washington, DC: Headquarters, Department of the Army, 1986.

—**TOUR OF DUTY.** (1) Tour of duty is the period in which assigned military personnel remain at one station or geographical location. (2) Tour of duty is a continental U.S. tour for which a mandatory period of duty has been established. *See also:* All-Others Tour, Command-Sponsored Dependents, Dependent Restricted Tour, Long Tour Area, Obligated Tour, Short Tour Area, Stabilized Tour.

References

Department of Defense, U.S. Army. *Dictionary of United States Army Terms.* Army Regulation AR 310-25. Washington, DC: Headquarters, Department of the Army, 1986.

—**TOW MISSILE SYSTEM** is a component of a tube-launched, optically tracked, wire-command link guided (TOW) missile weapon system that is crew-portable. It is the most powerful antitank weapon used by the infantry. It is found at battalion level in ground units and is also mounted on the Bradley Fighting Vehicle, Improved TOW Vehicle, the high mobility, multipurpose, wheeled vehicle, and on the AH-1S Cobra Helicopter. *See also:* Tow 2.

References

Weapons Systems: U.S. Army, Navy, and Air Force Directory, 1986-1988. Washington, DC: DCP, 1986.

—**TOW 2** is an improved TOW (tube-launched, optically tracked, wire-command, link-guided) missile designed to retain the TOW capabilities against recent threat innovations in the area of reactive armor and electro-optical countermeasures. The TOW 2 provides a more lethal six-inch warhead, greater speed, and improved guidance.

References

Department of Defense, U.S. Army. *U.S. Army Policy Statement, 1988.* Washington, DC: Headquarters, Department of the Army, 1988.

—**TOWED ARTILLERY** is an artillery weapon designed to be towed by a motor vehicle.

References

Department of Defense, U.S. Army. *Dictionary of United States Army Terms.* Army Regulation AR 310-25. Washington, DC: Headquarters, Department of the Army, 1986.

—**TOXIC AREA** is a defined area in which SCG K ammunition or Class 6 chemical agents are handled or stored. *See also:* Chemical Warfare.

References

Department of Defense, U.S. Army. *Ammunition and Explosives Safety Standards.* Army Regulation AR 385-64. Washington, DC: Headquarters, Department of the Army, 1987.

—**TOXIC CHEMICAL, BIOLOGICAL, OR RADIOLOGICAL ATTACK** is an attack directed at man, animals, or crops using injurious agents of radiological, biological, or chemical origin. *See also:* Biological Warfare, Chemical Warfare, Nuclear Warfare.

References

Department of Defense, Joint Chiefs of Staff. *Department of Defense Dictionary of Military and Related Terms.* Washington, DC: GPO, 1986.

—**TOXIN AGENT** is a poison secreted by a vegetable or animal organism (as distinguished from inorganic poisons). Such poisons can also be manufactured by synthetic processes. *See also:* Biological Warfare, Chemical Warfare.

References

Department of Defense, Joint Chiefs of Staff. *Department of Defense Dictionary of Military and Related Terms.* Washington, DC: GPO, 1986.

—**TOXINS,** as defined by the Church Committee, "are chemicals which are not living organisms, but are produced by living organisms and are lethal." *See also:* Biological Warfare.

References

U.S. Congress. Senate. *Final Report of the Senate Select Committee to Study Government Operations With Respect to Intelligence Activities. Report 94-755. Book I, Foreign and Military Intelligence* (Church Committee Report). Washington, DC: GPO, 1976.

—**TRACING** is the act of requesting the location of a shipment to expedite its movement or to establish its delivery time.

References

Department of Defense, U.S. Army. *Transportation Reference Data.* Field Manual FM 55-15. Washington, DC: Headquarters, Department of the Army, 1986.

—**TRACK.** (1) A track is a series of related contacts that are displayed on a plotting board. (2) To track means to display or record the successive positions of a moving object. (3) To track means to lock onto a point of radiation and obtain guidance from it. (4) To track means to keep a gun properly aimed and to point a target-locating instrument continuously at a moving target. (5) A track is the actual path of an aircraft above the surface of the earth. The course is the path that is planned; the track is the path that is taken. (6) A track is one of the endless belts on which a full-track or half-track vehicle runs. (7) A track is a metal part forming a path for a moving object (e.g., the track around the inside of a vehicle for moving a mounted gun).

References
Department of Defense, Joint Chiefs of Staff. *Department of Defense Dictionary of Military and Related Terms.* Washington, DC: GPO, 1986.

—**TRACK HANDOVER,** in air defense, is the process of transferring the responsibility for production of a track from one track production area to another. *See also:* Track.

References
Department of Defense, Joint Chiefs of Staff. *Department of Defense Dictionary of Military and Related Terms.* Washington, DC: GPO, 1986.

—**TRACK OFF** is a deliberate underestimation or overestimation of the predicted path of a target in order to bring about an eventual intersection of the line of fire with the target.

References
Department of Defense, U.S. Army. *Dictionary of United States Army Terms.* Army Regulation AR 310-25. Washington, DC: Headquarters, Department of the Army, 1986.

—**TRACK PRODUCTION** is a function of a surveillance organization in which the active and passive radar inputs are correlated into coherent position reports, together with historical positions, identity, height, strength, and direction.

References
Department of Defense, Joint Chiefs of Staff. *Department of Defense Dictionary of Military and Related Terms.* Washington, DC: GPO, 1986.

—**TRACK-LAYING VEHICLE** is a vehicle that travels upon two or more endless tracks mounted on each side of the vehicle. A tracked vehicle (e.g., a tank) has high mobility and maneuverability, is usually armed and frequently armored, and is intended for tactical use.

References
Department of Defense, U.S. Army. *Dictionary of United States Army Terms.* Army Regulation AR 310-25. Washington, DC: Headquarters, Department of the Army, 1986.

—**TRACTION CAPABILITY** is the ability of a soil to provide sufficient resistance between the soil and the tread, or track of a vehicle, to furnish the necessary forward thrust for a vehicle to move forward.

References
Department of Defense, U.S. Army. *Dictionary of United States Army Terms.* Army Regulation AR 310-25. Washington, DC: Headquarters, Department of the Army, 1986.

—**TRAFFIC,** as defined by the Church Committee, are "messages that are carried over a communications network." *See also:* Traffic Analysis.

References
U.S. Congress. Senate. *Final Report of the Senate Select Committee to Study Government Operations With Respect to Intelligence Activities. Report 94-755. Book I, Foreign and Military Intelligence* (Church Committee Report). Washington, DC: GPO, 1976.

—**TRAFFIC ANALYSIS (TA)** is a cryptologic discipline that develops information from communications about the composition and operation of communication systems and the organizations that they serve. The process involves studying the traffic and related materials and reconstructing communication plans in order to produce signals intelligence. *See also:* Signals Intelligence.

References
Department of Defense, Defense Intelligence College. *Glossary of Intelligence Terms and Definitions.* Washington, DC: DIC, 1987.

—**TRAFFIC ASSOCIATION,** in cryptology, is the relation of the flow of a particular type of traffic with the geographical points of origin and destination.

References
Department of Defense, U.S. Army. *Dictionary of United States Army Terms.* Army Regulation AR 310-25. Washington, DC: Headquarters, Department of the Army, 1986.

—**TRAFFIC CIRCULATION MAP,** or circulation map, is a map showing traffic routes and the measures for traffic regulation. It indicates the roads for use by certain classes of traffic, the location of traffic control stations, and the directions in which traffic may move. *See also:* Map, Traffic Control Police (Road Transport).

References

Department of Defense, Joint Chiefs of Staff. *Department of Defense Dictionary of Military and Related Terms.* Washington, DC: GPO, 1986.

—**TRAFFIC CONTROL POINT (TCP)** is a point on the ground or road network. It is a static, garrison-type environment, where the military police control the traffic flow. *See also:* Traffic Control Police (Road Transport).

References

Department of Defense, U.S. Army. *Operational Terms and Symbols.* Field Manual FM 101-5-1. Washington, DC: Headquarters, Department of the Army, 1985.

—**TRAFFIC CONTROL POLICE** (ROAD TRANSPORT) are individuals ordered by a military commander or by national authorities to facilitate the movement of traffic and to prevent or report any breach of road traffic regulations. *See also:* Traffic Circulation Map, Traffic Density, Traffic Flow, Traffic Headquarters, Traffic Management, Traffic Map, Traffic Regulating Line, Trafficability, Trafficability Sampler.

References

Department of Defense, Joint Chiefs of Staff. *Department of Defense Dictionary of Military and Related Terms.* Washington, DC: GPO, 1986.

—**TRAFFIC DENSITY** is the average number of vehicles that occupy 1 kilometer or 1 mile of road space, expressed in vehicles per kilometer or vehicles per mile. *See also:* Traffic Control Police (Road Transport).

References

Department of Defense, U.S. Army. *The Infantry Rifle Company (Infantry, Airborne, Air Assault, Ranger).* Field Manual FM 7-10. Washington, DC: Headquarters, Department of the Army, 1982.

—**TRAFFIC FLOW** is the total number of vehicles passing a given point in a given time. Traffic flow is expressed as vehicles per hour. *See also:* Traffic Control Police (Road Transport).

References

Department of Defense, Joint Chiefs of Staff. *Department of Defense Dictionary of Military and Related Terms.* Washington, DC: GPO, 1986.

—**TRAFFIC FLOW SECURITY,** in communications security, means the capability of certain on-line, machine cryptosystems to conceal the presence of valid message traffic. *See also:* Communications Security.

References

Department of Defense, Joint Chiefs of Staff. *Department of Defense Dictionary of Military and Related Terms.* Washington, DC: GPO, 1986.

—**TRAFFIC HEADQUARTERS** are headquarters exercising highway traffic regulation. Its duties include planning, routing, scheduling, and directing the actual use of the highways by vehicles, personnel afoot (including troops, refugees, and other civilians), and animals so that highway transportation, facilities, and equipment are used most effectively and in accordance with assigned tasks. *See also:* Traffic Control Police (Road Transport).

References

Department of Defense, U.S. Army. *Dictionary of United States Army Terms.* Army Regulation AR 310-25. Washington, DC: Headquarters, Department of the Army, 1986.

—**TRAFFIC MANAGEMENT** is the direction, control, and supervision of all functions incident to procuring and using freight and passenger transportation services. *See also:* Traffic Control Police (Road Transport).

References

Department of Defense, Joint Chiefs of Staff. *Department of Defense Dictionary of Military and Related Terms.* Washington, DC: GPO, 1986.

—**TRAFFIC MAP** is a map used in planning and regulating the flow of traffic. It includes routes, road data, the direction of movement, and the amount of moving traffic. *See also:* Traffic Control Police (Road Transport).

References

Department of Defense, U.S. Army. *Dictionary of United States Army Terms.* Army Regulation AR 310-25. Washington, DC: Headquarters, Department of the Army, 1986.

—**TRAFFIC REGULATING LINE** is a control measure used to delineate the areas of responsibility for traffic regulation and control of different command elements during a river crossing operation.

References
Department of Defense, U.S. Army. *Military Police Team, Squad, Platoon Combat Operations*. Field Manual FM 19-4. Washington, DC: Headquarters, Department of the Army, 1984.

—**TRAFFICABILITY** is the capability of the terrain to bear traffic and refers to the extent that terrain will permit the continued movement of all types of traffic. *See also:* Traffic Control Police (Road Transport).

References
Department of Defense, U.S. Army. *Operational Terms and Symbols*. Field Manual FM 101-5-1. Washington, DC: Headquarters, Department of the Army, 1985.

—**TRAFFICABILITY SAMPLER** is an instrument that is a piston-type soil sampler for securing soft soil samples. The design of the sampler is such that constant-volume samples can be taken, thereby facilitating the rapid determination of soil mass density. *See also:* Traffic Control Police (Road Transport).

References
Department of Defense, U.S. Army. *Dictionary of United States Army Terms*. Army Regulation AR 310-25. Washington, DC: Headquarters, Department of the Army, 1986.

—**TRAIL.** The components of trail are broken down as follows: (1) *Trail distance*, which is the horizontal distance between the point of impact of the bomb and a point vertically below the aircraft at the instant of impact. (2) *Cross trail*, or *deflection component of trail*, which is the distance the bomb falls downwind on a line perpendicular to the aircraft's track projected from the point of release. (3) *Range component of trail*, which is the horizontal distance from the point vertically below the aircraft at the instant of bomb impact to the point where the cross trail cuts the track. (4) *Trail angle*, which is the angle between the vertical and the line joining the point of impact to the aircraft at the instant of impact. (5) *Cross trail angle*, which is the angle in the horizontal plane measured between the aircraft track projected from the point of release and a line joining the release point to the point of impact. (6) *Range component of cross trail*, which is a horizontal distance along the track that is equal to the difference between trail distance and the range component of trail.

References
Department of Defense, U.S. Army. *Dictionary of United States Army Terms*. Army Regulation AR 310-25. Washington, DC: Headquarters, Department of the Army, 1986.

—**TRAIL FORMATION,** or column formation, means vehicles that are proceeding one behind the other at designated intervals.

References
Department of Defense, U.S. Army. *Dictionary of United States Army Terms*. Army Regulation AR 310-25. Washington, DC: Headquarters, Department of the Army, 1986.

—**TRAIN** is a service force (or group of service elements) that provides logistic support (e.g., the vehicles and operating personnel that furnish supply, evacuation, and maintenance services to a land unit). (2) A train means bombs dropped in short intervals or sequence. *See also:* Battalion Trains, Brigade Trains, Company Trains, Field Train.

References
Department of Defense, Joint Chiefs of Staff. *Department of Defense Dictionary of Military and Related Terms*. Washington, DC: GPO, 1986.

—**TRAIN HEADWAY** is the interval of time between two trains boarded by the same unit at the same point.

References
Department of Defense, Joint Chiefs of Staff. *Department of Defense Dictionary of Military and Related Terms*. Washington, DC: GPO, 1986.

—**TRAIN PATH,** in railway terminology, is the timing of a possible movement of a train along a given route. All the train paths on a given route constitute a timetable.

References
Department of Defense, Joint Chiefs of Staff. *Department of Defense Dictionary of Military and Related Terms*. Washington, DC: GPO, 1986.

—**TRAIN-UP TRAINING** is the process of increasing the skills and knowledge of an individual to a higher skill level in an military occupational specialty. It may involve certification.

References
Department of Defense, U.S. Army. *Training for Mobilization and War*. Field Manual FM 25-5. Washington, DC: Headquarters, Department of the Army, 1985.

—**TRAINEES.** *See:* Training Forces.

—**TRAINERS.** *See:* Training Forces.

—**TRAINER'S GUIDE** is a field manual that provides information required by training managers and trainers to meet their responsibilities in the overall training plan for a particular military occupational specialty. It indicates where each task is initially trained and where additional training is conducted. The trainer guide explains the training manager's and trainer's responsibilities for the soldier's military occupational specialty training and evaluation. A trainer's guide may be a separate manual or a part of the higher skill level soldiers manual. It is the primary planning document for individual training in units. *See also:* Training Aids.

References

Department of Defense, U.S. Army. *Army Forces Training.* Army Regulation AR 350-41. Washington, DC: Headquarters, Department of the Army, 1986.

————. *Unit Training Management.* Field Manual FM 25-2. Washington, DC: Headquarters, Department of the Army, 1984.

—**TRAINING AIDS** are items developed and/or procured primarily to assist in training and the process of learning. *See also:* Trainer's Guide.

References

Department of Defense, Joint Chiefs of Staff. *Department of Defense Dictionary of Military and Related Terms.* Washington, DC: GPO, 1986.

—**TRAINING AIRCRAFT** are small sturdy aircraft used to train flyers.

References

Department of Defense, U.S. Army. *Dictionary of United States Army Terms.* Army Regulation AR 310-25. Washington, DC: Headquarters, Department of the Army, 1986.

—**TRAINING AMMUNITION MANAGEMENT INFORMATION SYSTEM (TAMIS)** is a computer system that provides a data link to Headquarters, Department of the Army, from installations and divisions in order to exchange information on ammunition authorizations and usage data by training events. *See also:* Training Ammunition Information System.

References

Department of Defense, U.S. Army. *Army Forces Training.* Army Regulation AR 350-41. Washington, DC: Headquarters, Department of the Army, 1986.

—**TRAINING AMMUNITION MANAGEMENT SYSTEM** is an Army-wide program that determines training ammunition requirements, justifies the requirements and supporting funds, and provides command involvement in managing and controlling training ammunition. *See also:* Training Ammunition Management Information System.

References

Department of Defense, U.S. Army. *Army Forces Training.* Army Regulation AR 350-41. Washington, DC: Headquarters, Department of the Army, 1986.

—**TRAINING AND AUDIOVISUAL SUPPORT OFFICER** is the manager for training and audiovisual support activities at the installation level.

References

Department of Defense, U.S. Army. *Army Forces Training.* Army Regulation AR 350-41. Washington, DC: Headquarters, Department of the Army, 1986.

—**TRAINING BASE.** (1) Soldiers start their careers, receive their first orientation to the Army, participate in soldierization, and learn basic skills at the training base. They return to the learning base throughout their careers to learn more advanced technical skills and leadership techniques. The training base includes service schools; training centers; U.S. Army Reserve schools; major Army command, installation, and unit schools; colleges and universities; and Army National Guard academies. (2) A training base consists of the activities, facilities, equipment, and personnel that make up the Army training centers, Army schools and courses, and units specifically established or directed to conduct individual training on a recurring basis.

References

Department of Defense, U.S. Army. *Unit Training Management.* Field Manual FM 25-2. Washington, DC: Headquarters, Department of the Army, 1984.

—**TRAINING CENTER** is authorized and designated by Headquarters, Department of the Army, to conduct basic individual training, basic combat training, advanced individual training, combat support training, and/or other specialized training.

References
Department of Defense, U.S. Army. *How to Prepare and Conduct Military Training.* Field Manual FM 21-6. Washington, DC: Headquarters, Department of the Army, 1975.

—**TRAINING CIRCULAR (TC)** promulgates temporary training directives, policies, or information that are too frequently revised for inclusion in permanent training literature. It is also used to promulgate new training doctrines, tactics, or techniques that must be disseminated immediately.

References
Department of Defense, U.S. Army. *The Rifle Squads (Mechanized and Light Infantry).* Training Circular TC 7-1. Washington, DC: Headquarters, Department of the Army, 1976.

—**TRAINING DEVICE** is any three-dimensional object that has been developed, fabricated, or procured specifically for improving the learning process. Training devices are categorized as systems devices or nonsystems devices. *Systems devices* are designed for use with a system or an item of equipment including subassemblies or components (e.g., training devices for the TOW missile system and M60 series tank). *Nonsystems devices* are designed to support general military training or training that is not directly related to a specific material system. They are used in garrisons and at local and major training areas to help achieve and maintain individual and collective proficiency at reduced cost. *See also:* Training Aids.

References
Department of Defense, U.S. Army. *Army Forces Training.* Army Regulation AR 350-41. Washington, DC: Headquarters, Department of the Army, 1986.
———. *Unit Training Management.* Field Manual FM 25-2. Washington, DC: Headquarters, Department of the Army, 1984.

—**TRAINING EFFECTIVENESS** is the part of the evaluation process that seeks to determine how well the trainer used training resources to accomplish the assigned training objectives. *See also:* Training Efficiency.

References
Department of Defense, U.S. Army. *Army Forces Training.* Army Regulation AR 350-41. Washington, DC: Headquarters, Department of the Army, 1986.
———. *How to Prepare and Conduct Military Training.* Field Manual FM 21-6. Washington, DC: Headquarters, Department of the Army, 1975.

—**TRAINING EFFICIENCY** is the part of the evaluation process that seeks to determine how efficiently the trainer used training resources to accomplish the assigned training objectives. *See also:* Training Effectiveness.

References
Department of Defense, U.S. Army. *Army Forces Training.* Army Regulation AR 350-41. Washington, DC: Headquarters, Department of the Army, 1986.

—**TRAINING EXTENSION COURSE (TEC)** consists of validated, interactive, performance-oriented, self-study training materials that are developed and fielded under the sole direction of the U.S. Army Training Support Center. The courses are designed to provide active army and reserve components commanders with the capability to upgrade the quality of individual training and military occupational specialty proficiency in their units. The TEC includes training objectives and a diagnostic test. The lessons use audiovisual and audio materials, as well as written material formats, and focus on preparing soldiers to perform specific tasks required by their jobs.

References
Department of Defense, U.S. Army. *Army Forces Training.* Army Regulation AR 350-41. Washington, DC: Headquarters, Department of the Army, 1986.
———. *Individual Military Education and Training.* Army Regulation AR 350-1. Washington, DC: Headquarters, Department of the Army, 1987.
———. *The Rifle Squads (Mechanized and Light Infantry).* Training Circular TC 7-1. Washington, DC: Headquarters, Department of the Army, 1976.

—**TRAINING FORCES** is a category of personnel consisting of trainees, students (permanent change of station as shown in the force structure), and trainers. (1) *Trainees* are personnel assigned to training centers and other miscellaneous training activities in order to receive instruction. (2) *Students* are personnel assigned to formal Army schools and courses, schools of other services or allied armed forces, and joint colleges and projects, and personnel attending civilian institutions for the purpose of receiving instruction. (This excludes personnel on temporary duty.) (3) *Trainers* are personnel who instruct or provide training advice to units and individuals, or who provide essential administrative support in schools, training centers, military districts, and other miscellaneous training activities.

References

Department of Defense, U.S. Army. *Dictionary of United States Army Terms*. Army Regulation AR 310-25. Washington, DC: Headquarters, Department of the Army, 1986.

—**TRAINING GOAL** is a broad statement of the desired individual or unit proficiency regarding a capability required to be prepared to accomplish the mission.

References

Department of Defense, U.S. Army. *Army Forces Training*. Army Regulation AR 350-41. Washington, DC: Headquarters, Department of the Army, 1986.

———. *How to Prepare and Conduct Military Training*. Field Manual FM 21-6. Washington, DC: Headquarters, Department of the Army, 1975.

—**TRAINING LITERATURE** is the body of writings published to inform all concerned as to the doctrine, tactics, techniques, and procedures that have been adopted for use in training individuals and units of the U.S. Army. *See also:* Official Training Literature.

References

Department of Defense, U.S. Army. *How to Prepare and Conduct Military Training*. Field Manual FM 21-6. Washington, DC: Headquarters, Department of the Army, 1975.

—**TRAINING MANAGEMENT** is the art of applying limited resources (human, physical, financial, and time) in a manner that permits the efficient and effective development of individuals and units so that they can successfully accomplish their peacetime and wartime missions. *See also:* Training Management Control System, Training Manager.

References

Department of Defense, U.S. Army. *How to Prepare and Conduct Military Training*. Field Manual FM 21-6. Washington, DC: Headquarters, Department of the Army, 1975.

—**TRAINING MANAGEMENT CONTROL SYSTEM** is an automated aid to help unit commanders plan training, evaluate how resources affect training, and record the accomplishments and the resources that were used during training.

References

Department of Defense, U.S. Army. *Army Forces Training*. Army Regulation AR 350-41. Washington, DC: Headquarters, Department of the Army, 1986.

—**TRAINING MANAGER** is a person responsible for planning, organizing, conducting, and evaluating training, including the development of the training program. Training managers include any commander who develops a training program or who provides guidance to commanders who do. Under present Army policies, battalion and separate company commanders are the principal training managers. However, company commanders or the operations/training officers of commands developing training programs are also training managers.

References

Department of Defense, U.S. Army. *Army Forces Training*. Army Regulation AR 350-41. Washington, DC: Headquarters, Department of the Army, 1986.

———. *How to Prepare and Conduct Military Training*. Field Manual FM 21-6. Washington, DC: Headquarters, Department of the Army, 1975.

—**TRAINING MINE** is a mine that looks identical to a live mine, but does not have an explosive charge. There are three types: the insert mine, the practice mine, and the drill mine. *See also:* Mine Warfare.

References

Department of Defense, U.S. Army. *Mine/ Countermine Operations at the Company Level*. Field Manual FM 20-32. Washington, DC: Headquarters, Department of the Army, 1976.

—**TRAINING OBJECTIVE** is a three-part statement that specifies (1) *task* (i.e., a statement that specifies an action to be performed by an individual or team/unit); (2) *condition(s)* (i.e., statement(s) that specify the circumstances under which a particular task is to be performed, including the information and equipment to be provided or denied for the performance of the task); and (3) *training standard* (i.e., a statement that specifies the minimum acceptable proficiency required of an individual or team/unit in the performance of a particular task).

References
Department of Defense, U.S. Army. *Army Forces Training*. Army Regulation AR 350-41. Washington, DC: Headquarters, Department of the Army, 1986.

————. *How to Prepare and Conduct Military Training*. Field Manual FM 21-6. Washington, DC: Headquarters, Department of the Army, 1975.

—**TRAINING-PAY CATEGORY** is a designation that identifies the number of days of training and pay required for members of the reserve components.

References
Department of Defense, Joint Chiefs of Staff. *Department of Defense Dictionary of Military and Related Terms*. Washington, DC: GPO, 1986.

—**TRAINING PROGRAM** is the training document that outlines the general plan for conducting individual and collective training in an organization for specified periods of time. It is prepared and disseminated for the information of all personnel concerned with training.

References
Department of Defense, U.S. Army. *Army Forces Training*. Army Regulation AR 350-41. Washington, DC: Headquarters, Department of the Army, 1986.

————. *How to Prepare and Conduct Military Training*. Field Manual FM 21-6. Washington, DC: Headquarters, Department of the Army, 1975.

—**TRAINING PUBLICATIONS** are printed or reproduced material used by the Army to train individuals or units. The term "training publications" is an overall term that includes training literature, both official and unofficial.

References
Department of Defense, U.S. Army. *Dictionary of United States Army Terms*. Army Regulation AR 310-25. Washington, DC: Headquarters, Department of the Army, 1986.

—**TRAINING RECORDS** are informal records maintained at the unit level that are not subject to formal inspection. They include information about the training and test results of individuals, crews, teams, and units. They assist training managers and trainers to develop training programs and to prepare and conduct training.

References
Department of Defense, U.S. Army. *Army Forces Training*. Army Regulation AR 350-41. Washington, DC: Headquarters, Department of the Army, 1986.

————. *How to Prepare and Conduct Military Training*. Field Manual FM 21-6. Washington, DC: Headquarters, Department of the Army, 1975.

—**TRAINING RESOURCES** are the resources (i.e., human, physical, financial, and time) used to conduct or support training. They may be internally controlled by a unit or externally controlled by a headquarters that allocates their use to units as required.

References
Department of Defense, U.S. Army. *Army Forces Training*. Army Regulation AR 350-41. Washington, DC: Headquarters, Department of the Army, 1986.

—**TRAINING SUPPORT PACKAGE** is a composite lesson plan and associated student handout materials used by the instructor to support formal training.

References
Department of Defense, U.S. Army. *Individual Military Education and Training*. Army Regulation AR 350-1. Washington, DC: Headquarters, Department of the Army, 1986.

—**TRAJECTORY** is the flight path of a bomb, projectile, or missile from its release to its impact.

References
Department of Defense, U.S. Army. *Dictionary of United States Army Terms*. Army Regulation AR 310-25. Washington, DC: Headquarters, Department of the Army, 1986.

—**TRAJECTORY CHART** is a diagram of a side view of the paths of projectiles fired at various elevations under standard conditions. The trajectory chart is different for different guns, projectiles, and fuzes.

References
Department of Defense, U.S. Army. *Dictionary of United States Army Terms*. Army Regulation AR 310-25. Washington, DC: Headquarters, Department of the Army, 1986.

—**TRAJECTORY SCORER** is a device capable of continuously defining the position of a missile in a sphere whose center coincides with the origin of the target's coordinate axes. The time history record of the intercept must provide both range and angular position of the missile with respect to a target that meets the scoring requirements.

References

Department of Defense, U.S. Army. *Dictionary of United States Army Terms.* Army Regulation AR 310-25. Washington, DC: Headquarters, Department of the Army, 1986.

—**TRAJECTORY SHIFT** is the degree to which the trajectory of a projectile under the action of a thrust mechanism departs from a purely ballistic trajectory.

References

Department of Defense, U.S. Army. *Dictionary of United States Army Terms.* Army Regulation AR 310-25. Washington, DC: Headquarters, Department of the Army, 1986.

—**TRANSATTACK PERIOD.** (1) In nuclear warfare, the transattack period is from the initiation of the attack to its termination. (2) As applied to the Single Integrated Operational Plan, the transattack period extends from execution (or enemy attack, whichever is sooner) to termination of the Single Integrated Operational Plan. *See also:* Post-Attack Period, Single Integrated Operational Plan.

References

Department of Defense, Joint Chiefs of Staff. *Department of Defense Dictionary of Military and Related Terms.* Washington, DC: GPO, 1986.

—**TRANSFER** is relief from assignment in one component, branch, category, or administrative entity of the Army with concurrent assignment to another component, branch, category, or administrative entity.

References

Department of Defense, U.S. Army. *Dictionary of United States Army Terms.* Army Regulation AR 310-25. Washington, DC: Headquarters, Department of the Army, 1986.

—**TRANSFER ACTIVITY,** or transfer station, or transfer point, is a designated, centralized activity established to process the transfers of military personnel.

References

Department of Defense, U.S. Army. *Dictionary of United States Army Terms.* Army Regulation AR 310-25. Washington, DC: Headquarters, Department of the Army, 1986.

—**TRANSFER LIMIT** is the maximum difference in direction and range from the location of a checkpoint. Within these limits, corrections computed for the checkpoints are assumed to be sufficiently accurate to warrant application to any target, thereby justifying its attack by a transfer of fire.

References

Department of Defense, U.S. Army. *Dictionary of United States Army Terms.* Army Regulation AR 310-25. Washington, DC: Headquarters, Department of the Army, 1986.

—**TRANSFER ORDER** is an order by the Secretary of Defense to the Secretary of the Army, Secretary of the Navy, and/or Secretary of the Air Force generally transferring certain functions, powers, and duties from one to the other.

References

Department of Defense, U.S. Army. *Dictionary of United States Army Terms.* Army Regulation AR 310-25. Washington, DC: Headquarters, Department of the Army, 1986.

—**TRANSFER POINT** is a centralized activity at an installation designed by proper authority to process the transfers of military personnel who are assigned to activities at the same installation, satellites of this installation, and other personnel as may be assigned to that activity.

References

Department of Defense, U.S. Army. *Dictionary of United States Army Terms.* Army Regulation AR 310-25. Washington, DC: Headquarters, Department of the Army, 1986.

—**TRANSFER PROCESSING** are the final procedures (i.e., an orientation, medical and dental examination, records processing interview, personnel information interview, outgoing records check, departure ceremony, and final pay) necessary to process the release of military personnel from active duty by discharge, retirement, or placement on the temporary disability retired list.

References

Department of Defense, U.S. Army. *Dictionary of United States Army Terms.* Army Regulation AR 310-25. Washington, DC: Headquarters, Department of the Army, 1986.

—**TRANSFER STANDARD** refers to the time periods when files are transferred to records-holding areas or overseas records centers, from one command or activity to another command or activity or to another government agency.

References

Department of Defense, U.S. Army. *Dictionary of United States Army Terms.* Army Regulation AR 310-25. Washington, DC: Headquarters, Department of the Army, 1986.

—**TRANSFER STATION** is a training, transient, and patient activity designated by Headquarters, Department of the Army, to process the transfers of overseas returnees who are returning for separation; who are military personnel reassigned to that activity specifically for separation; or who are onpost personnel stationed at an installation containing such an activity. *See also:* Separation.

References

Department of Defense, U.S. Army. *Dictionary of United States Army Terms.* Army Regulation AR 310-25. Washington, DC: Headquarters, Department of the Army, 1986.

—**TRANSIENT.** (1) Transients are personnel who are stopping temporarily at a post or station to which they are not assigned or attached before moving on to their destination elsewhere. (2) A transient is an individual awaiting orders or transport at a post or station to which he is not attached or assigned. *See also:* Transient Billeting Facility, Transient Dining Facility.

References

Department of Defense, Joint Chiefs of Staff. *Department of Defense Dictionary of Military and Related Terms.* Washington, DC: GPO, 1986.

—**TRANSIENT BILLETING FACILITY** is a facility operated primarily for the temporary billeting of military, civilian, and retired military personnel and their family members who are en route to or from a permanent duty station; on temporary duty; on leave; or are there for rest and recreation. This includes all activities conducted within the premises of such a facility that are integral parts of the facility.

References

Department of Defense, U.S. Army. *Dictionary of United States Army Terms.* Army Regulation AR 310-25. Washington, DC: Headquarters, Department of the Army, 1986.

—**TRANSIENT DINING FACILITY** is designated by the installation commander to feed individuals authorized to be provided for without reimbursement because they are awaiting orders or transportation at an installation to which they are not assigned or attached and have a destination elsewhere; or because of duty requirements, consume meals in a dining facility located at an installation other than the installation to which they are assigned or attached.

References

Department of Defense, U.S. Army. *Dictionary of United States Army Terms.* Army Regulation AR 310-25. Washington, DC: Headquarters, Department of the Army, 1986.

—**TRANSIENT FIELD RATION MESS** is a dining facility designated by the commanders of major units where installations feed individuals who are authorized to receive food in kind and are present in the major unit or installation during meal hours, but are not a part of the morning report strength of the major unit or installation.

References

Department of Defense, U.S. Army. *Dictionary of United States Army Terms.* Army Regulation AR 310-25. Washington, DC: Headquarters, Department of the Army, 1986.

—**TRANSIENT FORCES** are the forces that pass or stage through, or are based temporarily within, the area of responsibility of another command but are not under its operational control.

References

Department of Defense, Joint Chiefs of Staff. *Department of Defense Dictionary of Military and Related Terms.* Washington, DC: GPO, 1986.

—**TRANSIENT INSTALLATION CONFINEMENT FACILITY** is a facility established, operated, and specifically authorized by the Provost Marshal General for the temporary confinement of prisoners at installations where exceptional circumstances preclude the establishment or economical operation of an installation confinement facility. *See also:* Disciplinary Action.

References

Department of Defense, U.S. Army. *Dictionary of United States Army Terms.* Army Regulation AR 310-25. Washington, DC: Headquarters, Department of the Army, 1986.

—**TRANSIENT TARGET**, or fleeting target, is a moving target that remains within the observing and firing distance for such a short period that it affords little time for deliberate adjustment and fire against it. Transient targets may be aircraft, vehicles, ships, or marching troops.

References
Department of Defense, U.S. Army. *Dictionary of United States Army Terms.* Army Regulation AR 310-25. Washington, DC: Headquarters, Department of the Army, 1986.

—**TRANSITION TRAINING** is unit training that stresses changes in equipment, doctrine, or organization. It trains individuals assigned to the unit who have no prior experience with the subject that has been changed. It also provides general and continuous training to the unit concerning the new individual and collective skills that are required because of the changes.

References
Department of Defense, U.S. Army. *Army Forces Training.* Army Regulation AR 350-41. Washington, DC: Headquarters, Department of the Army, 1986.

———. *Training for Mobilization and War.* Field Manual FM 25-5. Washington, DC: Headquarters, Department of the Army, 1985.

—**TRANSMISSION SECURITY (TRANSEC)** is a component of communications security. It results from all of the measures designed to protect transmissions from interception and exploitation by means other than cryptanalysis. In the Army tactical environment, this includes using only authorized operations procedures on radiotelephone nets; maintaining net discipline at all times; using authentication procedures; encrypting all classified and sensitive information before transmitting it; and using radio and telephone only for official business and keeping all conversations (transmissions) as brief as possible. *See also:* Communications Security.

References
Department of Defense, Defense Intelligence College. *Glossary of Intelligence Terms and Definitions.* Washington, DC: Defense Intelligence College, 1987.

Department of Defense, U.S. Army. *Counterintelligence.* Field Manual FM 34-60. Washington, DC: Headquarters, Department of the Army, 1985.

———. *Support Operations: Echelons Above Corps.* Field Manual FM 100-16. Washington, DC: Headquarters, Department of the Army, 1986.

—**TRANSPORT CAPACITY** is the number of persons, weight, or volume of the load that can be carried under given conditions. *See also:* Payload, Transportation Management.

References
Department of Defense, Joint Chiefs of Staff. *Department of Defense Dictionary of Military and Related Terms.* Washington, DC: GPO, 1986.

—**TRANSPORT STREAM** is composed of transport vehicles proceeding in a trail formation. *See also:* Transportation Management.

References
Department of Defense, Joint Chiefs of Staff. *Department of Defense Dictionary of Military and Related Terms.* Washington, DC: GPO, 1986.

—**TRANSPORT VEHICLE** is a motor vehicle designed and used without modification to the chassis to transport personnel and cargo. *See also:* Vehicle.

References
Department of Defense, Joint Chiefs of Staff. *Department of Defense Dictionary of Military and Related Terms.* Washington, DC: GPO, 1986.

—**TRANSPORTABILITY** is the capability of material to be moved by towing, self-propulsion, or carrier via any means (e.g., railways, highways, pipelines, oceans, and airways). *See also:* Transportation Management.

References
Department of Defense, Joint Chiefs of Staff. *Department of Defense Dictionary of Military and Related Terms.* Washington, DC: GPO, 1986.

—**TRANSPORTABLE COMSEC (COMMUNICATIONS SECURITY) FACILITY** contains classified COMSEC material and can be readily moved from one location to another. It is not, however, equipped to be operated while it is in motion. *See also:* Communications Security.

References
Department of Defense, Joint Chiefs of Staff. *Department of Defense Dictionary of Military and Related Terms.* Washington, DC: GPO, 1986.

—**TRANSPORTATION AND TELECOMMUNICATIONS INTELLIGENCE,** one of the eight components of strategic intelligence, examines transportation networks, including the highways, railroads, inland waterways, and civil air capability, as well as a nation's telephone, telegraph, and civil broadcast capabilities. The Defense Intelligence Agency has primary responsibility for the production of transportation and communications intelligence.

General

Transportation intelligence is concerned with the operation and facilities of transportation systems in foreign countries. This subject includes railways, highways, inland waterways, petroleum pipelines, ports, the merchant marine, and aviation.

Telecommunications intelligence is concerned with the operation and facilities of fixed military communications systems in foreign countries. This includes radio, television, telephone, telegraph, submarine cable, and related communications media. The ultimate purpose of this intelligence is to permit evaluation of (1) the military potential and vulnerability of a country's total telecommunications systems and (2) the compatibility between local communications equipment and U.S. equipment.

These systems are closely tied to the nation's social and economic life. The more interdependent they are, the more vulnerable they are to all forms of attack. Conversely, the more complex and diversified they are, the more flexible they are and consequently the more difficult to destroy. Similarly, the more extensive and well-integrated transportation systems are, the less vulnerable they are to attack. Integration means the effective interconnection of the various regional systems.

Thus, a transportation system may be extensive if it covers a large area, but will not be well integrated unless it is interconnected, and the rail gauges, weight-carrying capacities, and operating techniques are common throughout the system. The same is true in the case of a telecommunications system. A complex, dispersed, and diversified telecommunications system is less vulnerable to destruction and provides more flexibility in operation.

In measuring the effectiveness of a transportation or a telecommunications system from a military point of view, it must be recognized that the military uses of these systems in wartime will be superimposed upon the normal domestic requirements. For example, a comparison of the number of telephones and the number of miles of telephone wire in a country with those of another country is meaningless unless the degree to which each country depends on these

systems to support its normal domestic economy is also compared. This necessity for comparison on the basis of need and capacity is equally important in evaluating all types of transportation and telecommunications facilities.

The possibility of substituting an alternate means must also be considered. The overall vulnerability of a transportation system is lessened if adequate alternative means exist, as in the case where railroads are supplemented by inland waterways. The same is true of telecommunications if telephone and telegraph can be rerouted through other systems or readily supplemented by radio in the event of bombing, sabotage, or local disruption.

There is usually a close affinity between the telecommunications and transportation systems of a country. Major telecommunications routes almost invariably follow the basic pattern of transportation routes. This is true because (1) telecommunications emerged in the nineteenth century, after the transportation routes had been established; (2) the location of the major economic centers determined the transportation routes and subsequently the telecommunications routes; and (3) telecommunications routes are easier to construct, maintain, supply, and repair if they are located along the readily accessible transportation routes.

In the Middle East, the overall pattern of some telecommunications does not differ appreciably from the transportation pattern that was established over 7,000 years ago. The major exception to this parallel pattern is found in radio relay systems, which are beginning to depart from the established transportation routes. Individual towers can be placed on high ground, reached by helicopter, and spaced many miles apart. These factors lessen the requirements for easy road access and mile-by-mile servicing, which are mandatory in the case of pole lines. Line-of-sight characteristics of the radio relay systems tend to follow the shortest straight distance between major terminals and avoid the frequently winding routes of the transportation system.

Operationally, telecommunications have enormously increased the tonnage capacities of transportation systems by providing speedier scheduling, and coordination and control of shipments. Reciprocally, the control lines along transportation routes may provide additional communications circuits in a military emergency. As an index to the volume of military requirements on telecommunications, over 100,000 telephone calls may be required in the production, assembly, and shipment of one modern prototype aircraft.

Transportation

Railroads. A well-integrated and efficiently operated railway system is a vital necessity to the economy of a modern highly industrialized nation. The size and efficiency of the railway network are important indices of the economic and military potential of a country. An expanding railway system is often indicative of an expanding economy. Railroad construction without apparent economic justification, or the apparently needless duplication of railway facilities, is often important evidence of strategic military planning.

Railway traffic flow studies are essential in estimating the economic position and potential of a nation in peace and war. Sensitive railway junctions, bridges, tunnels, yards, and control facilities must be studied carefully from the standpoint of the acute effect of their loss to the economy and military capabilities of a nation. Knowledge of their susceptibility to interdiction by military action or sabotage provides an index to their vulnerability. In addition, data are required on routes, mileage, gauges, multiplicity of track, curves and grades, the condition and composition of roadbeds, spurs, rolling stock, repair facilities, classification yards, lubricants, and supplies of all kinds.

Highways. A well-integrated and extensive highway net is essential to any country with a highly developed economy. Most of the general remarks concerning railways in the preceding paragraph are applicable to the study of highway systems. The highways of a country include its primary and secondary road nets, overland routes, and trails.

To assess the adequacy of a country's highways, it is necessary to collect extensive data on capacities both as to weight and volume, surface conditions, the effect of water and climate on the surfaces, constructions, defiles, bridges, and by-passes. Operational data required include numbers and types of motor vehicles available, repair facilities, and supplies. Traffic density studies provide valuable information concerning the normal level of use of highways and provide a valuable means of measuring changes in the character of highway activity.

Inland Waterways. Inland waterways may be of prime importance to a nation's economy. Although operating at slow speeds, inland waterway carriers have great weight-carrying capacities and often supplement both the rail and highway transportation systems. To determine the importance of waterways to the peacetime economy of a nation and to estimate the degree to which traffic may be increased in time of war, it is necessary to collect the same type of data required for rail and highway transport. In addition, data peculiar to waterways (e.g., depths of channels; locations of dams, locks, bridges, inland ports; and the availability of ships and boats) must be considered.

Air Transport. Although air transport is only a supplementary mode of transportation providing a high-speed, long-distance medium with definite weight-carrying limitations, it is becoming increasingly important in relation to older forms of transportation. Some countries lacking adequate railways, highways, and waterways depend to a great extent on air transport to support an expanding economy. This is particularly true of countries that have undergone extensive economic development since the advent of the airplane.

In addition, commercial aviation provides a ready means of reinforcing military aviation in time of war. Necessary data on air transport include organization, personnel, airline companies, air and ground equipment, repair facilities, fuel, routes, navigational aids, and airports.

Pipelines. Pipelines are practical only for the transportation of extremely limited types of materials in great bulk over comparatively long distances. The materials transported are primarily liquid and gaseous (e.g., petroleum products, chemicals, and illuminating gas). However, pipelines provide a speedy means of transporting their specialized loads over difficult terrain in mountainous and desert areas. Because pipelines are generally laid in straight lines, the distances they traverse are often shorter than they are for other means of transportation.

Although pipelines are extremely vulnerable to sabotage, they can usually be camouflaged since they can be buried or covered with vegetation. The length, diameter, capacity, type of construction, type of material transported, and the location and type of pumping stations are important factors concerning pipelines.

Merchant Marine. Sea transport is a basic necessity for the participation of any nation in world trade. Nations that do not possess adequate shipping facilities must depend on the merchant marines of other countries. Nearly every nation of the world would be seriously hampered in both peace and war if it were denied the use of maritime shipping facilities. Moreover, the nation possessing a strong merchant fleet has an important auxiliary to its navy in wartime. The importance of any merchant marine depends on the size of its fleet, the quality of its seamanship, the newness of its ships, the adequacy and extent of repair and construction facilities, the distribution of its shipping, and its routes and ports of call.

Ports and Harbors. Although the study of ports and harbors is a part of transportation and telecommunications intelligence, it is also an important aspect of economic intelligence. In wartime, this factor becomes even more important since, in addition to their normal peacetime significance, there is their added importance to the attacker, who needs to capture port facilities to support his landings, and for the subsequent supply of the ground, naval, and air offensives.

To estimate the value of a port, it is necessary to know its location, the type of shelter afforded, the average length, channels, bottom and silting, hydrographic conditions, warehousing facilities, types of piers and wharves, tonnage capacities for both long and short periods, availability of marine supplies, and the extent of repair and construction facilities.

The development of modern engineering techniques, which permit the construction of emergency port facilities at beach locations for temporary wartime use, has not detracted from the basic necessity to control conventional harbors and ports.

Telecommunications

Telecommunications can be defined as any means or method for transmitting information by use of electrical energy or the electromagnetic spectrum. Any portion of this spectrum might be used in a telecommunications system (e.g., radio frequencies, audible frequencies, visible light, infrared and ultraviolet). Theoretically, even alpha, beta, gamma, or cosmic rays could be used to transmit information. The most common types of telecommunications equipment appearing in modern civil systems are the telephone, telegraph, radio and television, and submarine cable. Many combinations (e.g., radiotelegraph, variants such as wired broadcasting and facsimile, or specialized developments such as microwave relay equipment) are becoming prevalent. Variations in telecommunications systems are almost infinite. For example, a communication between two distant cities may begin with one individual speaking into a telephone, travel over a coaxial cable, be amplified at a repeater station, be relayed by microwave relay towers, be carried on overhead lines, thence underwater by submarine cable, before finally reaching a listener at another city. These variations, while increasing the technical problem, actually decrease the vulnerability of the system as a whole, because alternate routes and facilities are available for rerouting messages in the event of damage to a part of the system.

In wartime, if these means for rapid communication were destroyed or even interrupted, all types of surface and air transportation might be seriously impaired. Modern nations have become so dependent on telecommunications for government, industry, education, propaganda, coordination, and control purposes that they would be paralyzed if their telecommunications system were destroyed.

Intelligence on telecommunications should provide an overall picture showing its background and its significance to the nation, as well as information on its top administration and control. This picture should be supported by detailed data on all existing civil equipment, facilities, and systems (both domestic and international). Connections with surrounding countries and electronic warfare (jamming and electronic countermeasures) aspects are especially important. Details should include accurate locations, routes, capacities, technical characteristics of equipment, vulnerability, repair and maintenance, facilities, administration, and usage patterns in peace and war. *See also:* Strategic Intelligence.

References

Clauser, Jerome K., and Weir, Sandra M. *Intelligence Research Methodology.* State College, PA: HRB-Singer, 1975.

Department of Defense, Defense Intelligence College. *Glossary of Intelligence Terms and Definitions.* Washington, DC: DIC, 1987.

Department of Defense, Joint Chiefs of Staff. *Department of Defense Dictionary of Military and Related Terms.* Washington, DC: GPO, 1986.

—**TRANSPORTATION CONTROL AND MOVE-MENT DOCUMENT** is the basic document for all cargo movements. It contains the basic information necessary to make movement management decisions through the worldwide Department of Defense transportation system. *See also:* Transportation Management.

References

Department of Defense, U.S. Army. *Transportation Reference Data.* Field Manual FM 55-15. Washington, DC: Headquarters, Department of the Army, 1986.

—**TRANSPORTATION ENGINEERING** is the science of evaluating the requirements for, and planning the layout and functional aspects of, transportation facilities. It also involves developing the most efficient relationships with respect to transportation equipment, transportation facilities, and traffic movement patterns to insure adequate, safe, and efficient movement by all modes of transportation. *See also:* Transportation Management.

References

Department of Defense, U.S. Army. *Dictionary of United States Army Terms.* Army Regulation AR 310-25. Washington, DC: Headquarters, Department of the Army, 1986.

—**TRANSPORTATION MANAGEMENT** is the performance of command and/or staff functions related to (1) planning, coordinating, evaluating, and analyzing all aspects of water, rail, highway, and air transportation systems; (2) developing transportation policies and doctrine; (3) assessing capabilities in terms of current and projected transport requirements; (4) allocating and monitoring the use of transportation resources in accordance with established priorities; and (5) preparing contingency transportation plans. *See also:* Transport Capacity, Transport Stream, Transport Vehicle, Transportability, Transportation Control and Movement Document, Transportation Engineering, Transportation Movement Release, Transportation Movement Requirements Data, Transportation Network, Transportation Operating Agencies, Transportation Priorities.

References

Department of Defense, U.S. Army. *Dictionary of United States Army Terms.* Army Regulation AR 310-25. Washington, DC: Headquarters, Department of the Army, 1986.

—**TRANSPORTATION MOVEMENT RELEASE** consists of the shipping instructions issued by a movement control authority in response to a cargo offering. *See also:* Transportation Management.

References

Department of Defense, U.S. Army. *Transportation Reference Data.* Field Manual FM 55-15. Washington, DC: Headquarters, Department of the Army, 1986.

—**TRANSPORTATION MOVEMENT REQUIREMENTS DATA (TMRD)** is a listing or card deck of supplies in shipping configuration that will be shipped in support of a contingency operation. The supplies will be identified by class of supply, weight, dimensions, special handling characteristics, mode(s) of transportation, markings (project code) to be used, supply source, and recommended aerial port of embarkation. *See also:* Transportation Management.

References

Department of Defense, U.S. Army. *Planning Logistics Support for Military Operations.* Field Manual FM 701-58. Washington, DC: Headquarters, Department of the Army, 1987.

—**TRANSPORTATION NETWORK** is the complete system of the routes pertaining to all means of transport available in a particular area. It is made up of the network peculiar to each means of transport. *See also:* Transportation Management.

References

Department of Defense, Joint Chiefs of Staff. *Department of Defense Dictionary of Military and Related Terms.* Washington, DC: GPO, 1986.

Department of Defense, U.S. Army. *Support Operations: Echelons Above Corps.* Field Manual FM 100-16. Washington, DC: Headquarters, Department of the Army, 1986.

————. *Transportation Reference Data.* Field Manual FM 55-15. Washington, DC: Headquarters, Department of the Army, 1986.

—**TRANSPORTATION OPERATING AGENCIES** is a generic term used to describe the various transportation agencies: (1) *Military:* Traffic Management Command, under the Department of the Army; the Military Sealift Command, under the Department of the Navy; and the Military Airlift Command, under the Department of the

Air Force. (2) *Civil*: The federal agencies responsible under national emergency conditions for the operational direction of one or more forms of transportation. These are also referred to as Federal Modal Agencies or Federal Transport Agencies. *See also:* Transportation Management.

References
Department of Defense, Joint Chiefs of Staff. *Department of Defense Dictionary of Military and Related Terms.* Washington, DC: GPO, 1986.

Department of Defense, U.S. Army. *Support Operations: Echelons Above Corps.* Field Manual FM 100-16. Washington, DC: Headquarters, Department of the Army, 1986.

———. *Transportation Reference Data.* Field Manual FM 55-15. Washington, DC: Headquarters, Department of the Army, 1986.

—**TRANSPORTATION PRIORITIES** are indicators assigned to eligible traffic that establish its movement precedence. Appropriate priority systems apply to the movement of traffic by sea and air. In times of emergency, priorities may be applicable to continental United States movements by land, water, or air. *See also:* Transportation Management.

References
Department of Defense, Joint Chiefs of Staff. *Department of Defense Dictionary of Military and Related Terms.* Washington, DC: GPO, 1986.

—**TRANSSHIPMENT ACTIVITY** is a transportation activity responsible for receiving, processing, and forwarding shipments within the Department of Defense transportation system.

References
Department of Defense, U.S. Army. *Dictionary of United States Army Terms.* Army Regulation AR 310-25. Washington, DC: Headquarters, Department of the Army, 1986.

—**TRAP MINE** is designed to explode unexpectedly when enemy personnel attempt to move an object. *See also:* Mine Warfare.

References
Department of Defense, U.S. Army. *Dictionary of United States Army Terms.* Army Regulation AR 310-25. Washington, DC: Headquarters, Department of the Army, 1986.

—**TRAVEL ALLOWANCE** is a reimbursement for expenses incurred by an Army member traveling under orders issued by a competent authority.

References
Department of Defense, U.S. Army. *Dictionary of United States Army Terms.* Army Regulation AR 310-25. Washington, DC: Headquarters, Department of the Army, 1986.

—**TRAVELING** is a movement technique used when speed is necessary and contact with enemy forces is not likely. All elements of the unit move simultaneously with the unit leader located where he can best control the units. It is the fastest but the least secure movement technique and is used when speed is important and enemy contact is not likely. Movement is continuous, and interval and dispersion are maintained between vehicles as the terrain and administrative restrictions permit.

References
Department of Defense, U.S. Army. *Cavalry.* Field Manual FM 17-95. Washington, DC: Headquarters, Department of the Army, 1977.

———. *Operational Terms and Symbols.* Field Manual FM 101-5-1. Washington, DC: Headquarters, Department of the Army, 1985.

—**TRAVELING OVERWATCH** is a movement technique used when contact with enemy forces is possible. The lead and trail elements of a unit move together, but distance separates the lead and trail elements to improve security. Traveling overwatch is used when contact is possible, but speed is desirable. The lead element moves continually along the most covered and concealed routes for protection from possible enemy observation and direct fire. The trail element moves at variable speeds, continuously overwatching. The trail element must maintain visual contact with the lead element, staying close enough to provide suppressive fire and to maneuver for support, yet far enough from the rear that enemy direct fire engagement of the lead element does not prevent its delivery of suppressive fires or interfere with its maneuverability. *See also:* Bound, Bounding Overwatch, Leapfrog.

References
Department of Defense, U.S. Army. *Cavalry.* Field Manual FM 17-95. Washington, DC: Headquarters, Department of the Army, 1977.

———. *Operational Terms and Symbols.* Field Manual FM 101-5-1. Washington, DC: Headquarters, Department of the Army, 1985.

—**TRAVERSE.** (1) To traverse is to turn a weapon to the right or left on its mount. (2) Traverse is a method of surveying in which lengths and directions of lines between points of the earth are obtained by or from field measurements. It is used in determining the positions of the points.

References
Department of Defense, Joint Chiefs of Staff. *Department of Defense Dictionary of Military and Related Terms.* Washington, DC: GPO, 1986.

—**TRAVERSE LEVEL** is that vertical height above low-level air defense systems at which aircraft can safely cross the area. It is expressed as both a height and an altitude.

References
Department of Defense, Joint Chiefs of Staff. *Department of Defense Dictionary of Military and Related Terms.* Washington, DC: GPO, 1986.

—**TREADWAY BRIDGE** is a bridge whose roadway is formed by two tracks or treadways.

References
Department of Defense, U.S. Army. *Dictionary of United States Army Terms.* Army Regulation AR 310-25. Washington, DC: Headquarters, Department of the Army, 1986.

—**TREMBLER FIRING DEVICE** is a firing device designed to actuate when vibrated or shaken.

References
Department of Defense, U.S. Army. *Mine/Countermine Operations at the Company Level.* Field Manual FM 20-32. Washington, DC: Headquarters, Department of the Army, 1976.

—**TRENCH.** Trenches are holes in the ground excavated to connect individual fighting positions and weapons positions in the progressive development of a defensive area. They protect and conceal personnel moving between fighting positions or in and out of the area. Two basic trenches are the crawl trench and the standard fighting trench.

References
Department of Defense, U.S. Army. *Survivability.* Field Manual FM 5-103. Washington, DC: Headquarters, Department of the Army, 1985.

—**TRENCH BURIAL** is a method of burial resorted to when casualties are heavy. A trench is prepared and the individual remains are laid in it side by side, thus obviating the necessity of digging and filling in individual graves.

References
Department of Defense, Joint Chiefs of Staff. *Department of Defense Dictionary of Military and Related Terms.* Washington, DC: GPO, 1986.

—**TRIAGE.** (1) Triage is the medical sorting of patients according to type and seriousness of injury, likelihood of survival, and the establishment of priority for treatment and/or evacuation to assure medical care of the greatest benefit to the largest number. The categories are *minimal* (i.e., those who require limited treatment and can be returned to duty); *immediate* (i.e., patients requiring immediate care to save a life or limb); *delay* (i.e., patients who, after emergency treatment, incur little additional risk by delay of further treatment); and *expectant* (i.e., patients so critically injured that only complicated and prolonged treatment will improve life expectancy). (2) Triage is a medical term that applies to maintenance (i.e., the sorting of equipment to determine the fastest repair method or level, and whether to cannibalize a piece of equipment). *See also:* Medical Treatment.

References
Department of Defense, U.S. Army. *Support Operations: Echelons Above Corps.* Field Manual FM 101-5. Washington, DC: Headquarters, Department of the Army, 1986.

—**TRIAL ELEVATION**, in terrestrial fire, is the elevation at which fire for effect is begun.

References
Department of Defense, U.S. Army. *Dictionary of United States Army Terms.* Army Regulation AR 310-25. Washington, DC: Headquarters, Department of the Army, 1986.

—**TRIANGLE EXERCISE** is a form of rifle target practice in which the rifleman fires three shots, making three holes as close together as possible. *See also:* Exercise.

References
Department of Defense, U.S. Army. *Dictionary of United States Army Terms.* Army Regulation AR 310-25. Washington, DC: Headquarters, Department of the Army, 1986.

—**TRIANGULATION** is a method of surveying in which the locations of the different terrain features are found by a system of triangles, each of whose baselines is established accurately as to location and length. As locations of new points are determined, new baselines are established and the locations of other points are determined from them.

References

Department of Defense, U.S. Army. *Dictionary of United States Army Terms*. Army Regulation AR 310-25. Washington, DC: Headquarters, Department of the Army, 1986.

—**TRI-CAMERA PHOTOGRAPHY,** in imagery and photoreconnaissance, is photography obtained by the simultaneous exposure of film from three cameras that have been systematically placed at fixed overlapping angles that are relative to each other. The purpose of such photography is to cover a wide field. *See also:* Titling Strip.

References

Department of Defense, Joint Chiefs of Staff. *Department of Defense Dictionary of Military and Related Terms*. Washington, DC: GPO, 1986.

—**TRIG LIST,** published by Army units, includes essential information on accurately located survey points.

References

Department of Defense, Joint Chiefs of Staff. *Department of Defense Dictionary of Military and Related Terms*. Washington, DC: GPO, 1986.

—**TRIGGERING SCREENS** are separately built or are added on to existing structures. They are used to activate the fuze of an incoming shell at a "standoff" distance from the structure. The screen initiates detonation at a distance where only fragments reach the structure. A variety of materials are usually used to detonate both super-quick fuze shells and delay fuze shells up to and including 130 millimeters. Super-quick shell detonation requires only enough material to activate the fuze. Delay shells require more material to both limit penetration and activate the fuze.

References

Department of Defense, U.S. Army. *Survivability*. Field Manual FM 5-103. Washington, DC: Headquarters, Department of the Army, 1985.

—**TRIPWIRE** is a largely symbolic force positioned on an ally's soil to signal a nation's commitment to a particular country or coalition of countries. Attacks against the token contingent would trigger retaliation.

References

Collins, John M. *U.S.-Soviet Military Balance, 1980-1985*. Washington, DC: Congressional Research Service, 1985.

—**TROOP** is a subordinate unit of the cavalry squadron. The troop has both administrative and tactical functions. It is equivalent to a company or battery.

References

Department of Defense, U.S. Army. *Dictionary of United States Army Terms*. Army Regulation AR 310-25. Washington, DC: Headquarters, Department of the Army, 1986.

—**TROOP BASIS** is an approved list of the military units and individuals (including civilians), who are required for the performance of a particular mission by numbers, organization, and equipment, and, in the case of larger commands, deployment.

References

Department of Defense, Joint Chiefs of Staff. *Department of Defense Dictionary of Military and Related Terms*. Washington, DC: GPO, 1986.

—**TROOP ISSUE SUBSISTENCE ACTIVITY** is the element of an installation responsible for acquiring, storing, issuing, selling, and accounting for subsistence supplies that are used for personnel who are authorized to eat in appropriated fund dining facilities, and by organizations and activities, including reserve components, that are authorized to purchase them. Its functions are administered by a troop issue subsistence officer. *See also:* Troop Issue Subsistence Officer.

References

Department of Defense, U.S. Army. *Dictionary of United States Army Terms*. Army Regulation AR 310-25. Washington, DC: Headquarters, Department of the Army, 1986.

—**TROOP ISSUE SUBSISTENCE OFFICER** is an individual who has been appointed by the installation commander to be responsible and accountable for troop issue subsistence operations. He controls the requisition, receipt, storage, and issue/sale of specification subsistence items.

References

Department of Defense, U.S. Army. *Dictionary of United States Army Terms*. Army Regulation AR 310-25. Washington, DC: Headquarters, Department of the Army, 1986.

—**TROOP LEADING PROCEDURES** are the process a leader goes through to prepare his unit to accomplish a tactical mission. It is a process repeated each time he is alerted for a mission. *See also:* Troop Leading Steps.

References

Department of Defense, U.S. Army. *The Mechanized Infantry Platoon and Squad.* Field Manual FM 7-7. Washington, DC: Headquarters, Department of the Army, 1984.

——. *Tank Platoon Division 86 (Test).* Field Manual FM 17-5. Washington, DC: Headquarters, Department of the Army, 1984.

—**TROOP LEADING STEPS** are the established actions to be performed in order to respond to the requirements of the commander as stated in the operations order. They are (1) receive the mission, (2) issue the warning order, (3) make a tentative plan to accomplish the mission, (4) initiate the necessary movement sequence, (5) reconnoiter, (6) complete the plan, (7) issue orders, and (8) supervise and refine. *See also*: Troop Leading Procedures.

References

Department of Defense, U.S. Army. *Air Defense Artillery Employment Hawk.* Field Manual FM 44-90. Washington, DC: Headquarters, Department of the Army, 1983.

——. *Air Defense Employment.* Field Manual FM 44-1. Washington, DC: Headquarters, Department of the Army, 1983.

—**TROOP MEDICAL CLINIC** is a medical treatment activity designed to accomplish sick call, as well as limited treatment within the capacity of the activity and referral of patients to a health clinic, hospital, or dental clinic. It normally provides limited treatment, immunization services, medical examinations, physical profiling, and limited pharmacy dispensing facilities. *See also:* Medical Treatment.

References

Department of Defense, U.S. Army. *Dictionary of United States Army Terms.* Army Regulation AR 310-25. Washington, DC: Headquarters, Department of the Army, 1986.

—**TROOP PROGRAM** is the planning blueprint of the Department of the Army that defines the projected size, structure, and deployment of the Army, together with the civilian personnel, for use in budgetary, logistical, training, and organizational personnel planning. *See also:* Troop Program Unit.

References

Department of Defense, U.S. Army. *Dictionary of United States Army Terms.* Army Regulation AR 310-25. Washington, DC: Headquarters, Department of the Army, 1986.

—**TROOP PROGRAM UNIT (TPU)** is a term used to describe a unit of the selected reserve in training and pay category A (paid drill), which has been programmed and organized under a table of organization and equipment or a table of distribution and allowances. It serves as a unit on mobilization or one that is assigned a mobilization mission. The "unit" in this case is the largest separate unit prescribed by the table of organization and equipment or table of distribution and allowances.

References

Department of Defense, U.S. Army. *Dictionary of United States Army Terms.* Army Regulation AR 310-25. Washington, DC: Headquarters, Department of the Army, 1986.

——. *Information Pamphlet for the Career Development of Enlisted Members of the U.S. Army Reserve.* Department of the Army Pamphlet DA PAM 140-8. Washington, DC: Headquarters, Department of the Army, 1986.

—**TROOP SAFETY** means the limiting requirements used in calculating the minimum safe distance needed to protect friendly troops. It is included in the commander's guidance and is divided into three degrees of risk: negligible; moderate; and emergency. The degree of risk is used to express personnel vulnerability as unwarned, exposed personnel; warned, exposed personnel; and warned, protected personnel. *See also:* Minimum Safe Distance; Moderate Risk (Nuclear); Negligible Risk (Nuclear); Radius of Vulnerability; Target-Oriented Analysis; Unwarned Exposed; Warned Protected.

References

Department of Defense, Joint Chiefs of Staff. *Department of Defense Dictionary of Military and Related Terms.* Washington, DC: GPO, 1986.

—**TROOP SUPPORT AGENCY** is a field operating agency under the supervision of Headquarters, Department of the Army. It is concerned with the management and standardization of procedures for the worldwide operation of the Army food service program, troop issue subsistence, laundry and dry cleaning activities, central issue facilities, clothing sales stores, and clothing initial issue points.

References
Department of Defense, U.S. Army. *Dictionary of United States Army Terms*. Army Regulation AR 310-25. Washington, DC: Headquarters, Department of the Army, 1986.

—**TROOP TEST** is a test conducted in the field for the purpose of evaluating operational or organizational concepts, doctrine, tactics, and techniques, or to gain further information on material.

References
Department of Defense, Joint Chiefs of Staff. *Department of Defense Dictionary of Military and Related Terms*. Washington, DC: GPO, 1986.

—**TROOPS** is a collective term for uniformed military personnel. *See also:* Airborne Troops, Combat Service Support Elements, Combat Support Troops, Service Troops, Tactical Troops.

References
Department of Defense, Joint Chiefs of Staff. *Department of Defense Dictionary of Military and Related Terms*. Washington, DC: GPO, 1986.

—**TROPHY OF WAR** is any item of captured enemy equipment, that can be retained by its captors without violating international law, federal law, or current Army regulations.

References
Department of Defense, U.S. Army. *Dictionary of United States Army Terms*. Army Regulation AR 310-25. Washington, DC: Headquarters, Department of the Army, 1986.

—**TROUBLE SHOOTING** is the process of investigating and detecting the cause of an aircraft's or equipment's malfunctioning.

References
Department of Defense, U.S. Army. *Dictionary of United States Army Terms*. Army Regulation AR 310-25. Washington, DC: Headquarters, Department of the Army, 1986.

—**TRUE AZIMUTH** is an azimuth referenced to true north or true south.

References
Department of Defense, U.S. Army. *Dictionary of United States Army Terms*. Army Regulation AR 310-25. Washington, DC: Headquarters, Department of the Army, 1986.

—**TRUE COURSE** is the course of an aircraft, tank, or ship, as indicated by the horizontal angle between the true north-south line and the direction of motion.

References
Department of Defense, U.S. Army. *Dictionary of United States Army Terms*. Army Regulation AR 310-25. Washington, DC: Headquarters, Department of the Army, 1986.

—**TRUMP LINE** is a kind of sling formed by a strap strung over the forehead or chest. It is used by a person who is carrying a pack on his back.

References
Department of Defense, U.S. Army. *Dictionary of United States Army Terms*. Army Regulation AR 310-25. Washington, DC: Headquarters, Department of the Army, 1986.

—**TUBE ARTILLERY** refers to howitzers and guns, whether they are towed or self-propelled (as opposed to rockets and missiles).

References
Collins, John M. *U.S.-Soviet Military Balance, 1980-1985*. Washington, DC: Congressional Research Service, 1985.

—**TUNGSTEN CARBIDE CORE** is the heavy, hard core used in hyper-velocity armor-piercing projectiles.

References
Department of Defense, U.S. Army. *Dictionary of United States Army Terms*. Army Regulation AR 310-25. Washington, DC: Headquarters, Department of the Army, 1986.

—**TURN-IN SLIP** is a form used for local returns of excess or unserviceable property.

References
Department of Defense, U.S. Army. *Dictionary of United States Army Terms*. Army Regulation AR 310-25. Washington, DC: Headquarters, Department of the Army, 1986.

—**TURNAROUND** is the length of time between arriving at a point and being ready to depart from that point. It is used in this sense for loading, unloading, refueling, and rearming vehicles, aircraft, and ships.

References
Department of Defense, Joint Chiefs of Staff. *Department of Defense Dictionary of Military and Related Terms*. Washington, DC: GPO, 1986.

—**TURNING MOVEMENT** is a variation of the envelopment in which the attacker attempts to avoid the defense entirely, instead seeking to secure key terrain deep in the enemy's rear and along his lines of communication. Faced with a major threat to his rear, the enemy is thus "turned" out of his defensive positions and is forced to attack rearward at a disadvantage. *See also:* Double Envelopment, Envelopment, Single Envelopment.

References

Department of Defense, U.S. Army. *Operational Terms and Symbols.* Field Manual FM 101-5-1. Washington, DC: Headquarters, Department of the Army, 1985.

———. *Operations.* Field Manual FM 100-5. Washington, DC: Headquarters, Department of the Army, 1986.

—**TURNING POINT**, in land mine warfare, is a point on the centerline of a mine strip or row where strips or rows change direction. *See also:* Mine Warfare.

References

Department of Defense, Joint Chiefs of Staff. *Department of Defense Dictionary of Military and Related Terms.* Washington, DC: GPO, 1986.

—**TURRET-DOWN POSITION** is when an entire vehicle is behind cover, but the commander can still observe to the front from the turret hatch or cupola. Even in the most intense combat situations a tank will not need to fire constantly. Most of the time the tank crew will be observing to acquire targets. In turret-down position, the main gun and coax machine gun can be fired. Stationary or moving, the turret-down positions are used when observing and acquiring targets. *See also:* Hide, Hull-Down Position.

References

Department of Defense, U.S. Army. *Operational Terms and Symbols.* Field Manual FM 101-5-1. Washington, DC: Headquarters, Department of the Army, 1985.

———. *Tank Gunnery.* Field Manual FM 17-12. Washington, DC: Headquarters, Department of the Army, 1984.

—**TWENTY-FIVE PERCENT RECTANGLE** is a rectangle eight probable deflection errors wide and one range probable error deep, within which will fall 25 percent of a large number of shots fired with the same setting. One range limit of this rectangle is the center of impact of a large number of shots that are fired with the same setting. There are two 25 percent rectangles, one on either side of the center of impact. These two rectangles form the 50 percent rectangle.

References

Department of Defense, U.S. Army. *Dictionary of United States Army Terms.* Army Regulation AR 310-25. Washington, DC: Headquarters, Department of the Army, 1986.

—**TWO-ELEMENT DIFFERENTIAL** is a characteristic incorporated in certain codes in which the groups differ from one another by a minimum of two elements, either in their identity or in the position they occupy. When the elements are letters, the characteristic is called a two-letter differential; when the elements are digits, it is called a two-figure differential.

References

Department of Defense, U.S. Army. *Dictionary of United States Army Terms.* Army Regulation AR 310-25. Washington, DC: Headquarters, Department of the Army, 1986.

—**TWO-MAN RULE**, or two-man concept, or two-man policy; refers to a policy that a minimum of two authorized persons, each capable of detecting incorrect or unauthorized procedures with respect to the task being performed and each familiar with applicable safety and security requirements, must be present during any operation that affords access to material (nuclear weapons and certain designated components) requiring protection under the two-man rule.

References

Department of Defense, Joint Chiefs of Staff. *Department of Defense Dictionary of Military and Related Terms.* Washington, DC: GPO, 1986.

Department of Defense, U.S. Army. *Operations for Nuclear-Capable Units.* Field Manual FM 100-50. Washington, DC: Headquarters, Department of the Army, 1980.

—**TWO-PART CODE** is a code consisting of two sections or parts: (1) an encoding section in which the vocabulary items are arranged in alphabetical or other systematic order, accompanied by their code equivalents arranged in nonalphabetical or random order; and (2) a decoding section in which the code groups are arranged in alphabetical or numerical order and are accompanied by their plain text meanings, that are now in a mixed order. *See also:* CRYPTO.

References

Department of Defense, U.S. Army. *Dictionary of United States Army Terms.* Army Regulation AR 310-25. Washington, DC: Headquarters, Department of the Army, 1986.

—**TWO-SOLDIER POSITION WITH OVERHEAD COVER** (DELIBERATE) provides protection from airburst weapons fragments and allows soldiers to fire from beneath it. It is an improvement over the open two-soldier position.

References

Department of Defense, U.S. Army. *Survivability.* Field Manual FM 5-103. Washington, DC: Headquarters, Department of the Army, 1985.

—**TWO-UP** is a formation with two elements disposed abreast and the remaining elements in the rear.

References

Department of Defense, Joint Chiefs of Staff. *Department of Defense Dictionary of Military and Related Terms.* Washington, DC: GPO, 1986.

—**TYPE B-STRENGTH ORDER** is a column in the personnel section of a table of organization and equipment that authorizes only the minimum of U.S. military command, supervisory, technical, and necessary maintenance personnel positions that are required to perform the stated mission of the unit when augmented by available non-U.S. personnel.

References

Department of Defense, U.S. Army. *Dictionary of United States Army Terms.* Army Regulation AR 310-25. Washington, DC: Headquarters, Department of the Army, 1986.

—**TYPE EQUIPMENT METHOD LOAD** is a method designed for use by staff planners at the division and higher levels. It provides a rapid method of determining aircraft requirements for general planning purposes. The critical factor is that the number of vehicles and towed weapons to be transported largely determines the number of aircraft that are required for a unit.

References

Department of Defense, U.S. Army. *Dictionary of United States Army Terms.* Army Regulation AR 310-25. Washington, DC: Headquarters, Department of the Army, 1986.

—**TYPE OF OPTIONS** are methods by which countries, participating in the Foreign Military Sales program, advise supply sources by coded entry on requisitions, as to whether materiel shipments should be released without prior notice to country representatives or freight forwarders. *Type A* depicts automatic shipment without prior notice. *Type Y* advises the Foreign Military Sales country representative or freight

forwarder that Foreign Military Sales materiel will be shipped on the fifteenth day subsequent to the date of the notice of availability, unless alternate shipping instructions are received. *Type Z* advises the Foreign Military Sales country representative or freight forwarder that Foreign Military Sales materiel is ready for shipment and specific shipping instructions are required.

References

Department of Defense, U.S. Army. *Dictionary of United States Army Terms.* Army Regulation AR 310-25. Washington, DC: Headquarters, Department of the Army, 1986.

—**TYPE TABLE OF DISTRIBUTION AND ALLOWANCE** is a document published by Headquarters, Department of the Army, that serves as a model in developing tables of distribution and allowances for select reserve component and mobilization units. It shows the organizational structure and personnel and equipment requirements for a common type table of distribution and allowances unit.

References

Department of Defense, U.S. Army. *Dictionary of United States Army Terms.* Army Regulation AR 310-25. Washington, DC: Headquarters, Department of the Army, 1986.

—**TYPE UNIT** is a type of organizational entity established within the Armed Forces and is uniquely identified by a type code.

References

Department of Defense, Joint Chiefs of Staff. *Department of Defense Dictionary of Military and Related Terms.* Washington, DC: GPO, 1986.

Department of Defense, U.S. Army. *Planning Logistics Support for Military Operations.* Field Manual FM 701-58. Washington, DC: Headquarters, Department of the Army, 1987.

—**TYPE UNIT DATA (TUCHA) (FILE)** provides the standard planning data on movement characteristics for personnel, cargo, and accompanying supplies associated with deployable type units of fixed composition. The file contains the weight and cube of selected cargo categories, the physical characteristics of the cargo, and the number of personnel requiring nonorganic transportation. *See also:* Type Unit.

References

Department of Defense, U.S. Army. *Planning Logistics Support for Military Operations.* Field Manual FM 701-58. Washington, DC: Headquarters, Department of the Army, 1987.

—**UH-60 BLACKHAWK** is a helicopter that is highly maneuverable in all geographical environments and can carry up to eleven combat-equipped soldiers or an equal cargo load.

References

Department of Defense, U.S. Army. *U.S. Army Policy Statement, 1988.* Washington, DC: Headquarters, Department of the Army, 1988.

—**UNATTENDED AIR SENSOR** is any airborne sensor designed primarily for automatic operations and remote monitoring. *See also:* Aerial Reconnaissance.

References

Department of Defense, U.S. Army. *Dictionary of United States Army Terms.* Army Regulation AR 310-25. Washington, DC: Headquarters, Department of the Army, 1986.

—**UNATTENDED GROUND SENSOR** is any sensor, except those mounted on air platforms, designed primarily for automatic operations and remote monitoring. *See also:* Unattended Air Sensor.

References

Department of Defense, U.S. Army. *Dictionary of United States Army Terms.* Army Regulation AR 310-25. Washington, DC: Headquarters, Department of the Army, 1986.

—**UNCLASSIFIED MATTER** is official material that does not require security safeguards, but whose disclosure may be controlled for other reasons.

References

Department of Defense, Joint Chiefs of Staff. *Department of Defense Dictionary of Military and Related Terms.* Washington, DC: GPO, 1986.

—**UNCOMMITTED FORCE** is a force that is not in contact with an enemy and is not deployed on a specific mission or course of action.

References

Department of Defense, U.S. Army. *Operational Terms and Symbols.* Field Manual FM 101-5-1. Washington, DC: Headquarters, Department of the Army, 1985.

—**UNCONVENTIONAL MINE** is a mine fabricated at or near its point of use from other explosives (e.g., a bomb, artillery shell, or TNT blocks). *See also:* Mine Warfare.

References

Department of Defense, U.S. Army. *Mine/ Countermine Operations at the Company Level.* Field Manual FM 20-32. Washington, DC: Headquarters, Department of the Army, 1976.

—**UNCONVENTIONAL WARFARE (UW)** involves a broad spectrum of military and paramilitary operations conducted in enemy-held, enemy-controlled, or politically sensitive territory. Unconventional warfare includes, but is not limited to, the interrelated fields of guerrilla warfare, evasion and escape, subversion, sabotage, and other operations of a low visibility, covert, or clandestine nature. These interrelated aspects of unconventional warfare may be performed singly or collectively by predominantly indigenous personnel, usually supported and directed in varying degrees by an external source during all conditions of war and peace. *See also:* Guerrilla Warfare.

References

Department of Defense, Joint Chiefs of Staff. *Department of Defense Dictionary of Military and Related Terms.* Washington, DC: GPO, 1986.

Department of Defense, U.S. Army. *Operational Terms and Symbols.* Field Manual FM 101-5-1. Washington, DC: Headquarters, Department of the Army, 1985.

———. *Psychological Operations.* Field Manual FM 33-1. Washington, DC: Headquarters, Department of the Army, 1979.

—**UNCONVENTIONAL WARFARE FORCES** are U.S. military forces that have an existing unconventional warfare capability and consist of Army Special forces and any Navy, Air Force, or Marine units assigned to these operations. *See also:* Guerrilla Warfare.

References

Department of Defense, Joint Chiefs of Staff. *Department of Defense Dictionary of Military and Related Terms.* Washington, DC: GPO, 1986.

—**UNCOVER.** (1) To uncover is to remove a hat, cap, or helmet. (2) To uncover is to move certain designated soldiers of a formation to either side in order to get more space between individuals. In physical training, at the command "UNCOVER," each even numbered (or odd numbered) individual makes a sideways step.

(3) Uncover is a command to move in the above manner. (4) Uncover is to expose or leave unprotected by movement or maneuver. *See also:* Service Cap.

References

Department of Defense, U.S. Army. *Dictionary of United States Army Terms.* Army Regulation AR 310-25. Washington, DC: Headquarters, Department of the Army, 1986.

—**UNDER SECRETARY OF THE ARMY** is a civilian appointed by the President, with the consent of the Senate, to perform the duties prescribed by the Secretary and Assistant Secretaries of the Army.

References

Department of Defense, U.S. Army. *Dictionary of United States Army Terms.* Army Regulation AR 310-25. Washington, DC: Headquarters, Department of the Army, 1986.

—**UNDESIRABLE DISCHARGE** is a form of discharge given to an enlisted member of the Army under conditions that are other than honorable. It may be issued for unfitness, misconduct, homosexuality, or security reasons. *See also:* Unsuitable Personnel, Untrainable Personnel.

References

Department of Defense, U.S. Army. *Dictionary of United States Army Terms.* Army Regulation AR 310-25. Washington, DC: Headquarters, Department of the Army, 1986.

—**UNEXPLODED EXPLOSIVE DEVICE** is explosive ordnance that has been primed, fuzed, armed, or otherwise prepared for action and has been fired, dropped, launched, projected, or placed in such a manner as to constitute a hazard to operations, installations, personnel, or material. It remains unexploded for malfunction or design reasons or for any other cause.

References

Department of Defense, Joint Chiefs of Staff. *Department of Defense Dictionary of Military and Related Terms.* Washington, DC: GPO, 1986.

—**UNIFIED ACTION ARMED FORCES** is a publication setting forth the principles, doctrines, and functions governing the activities and performance of the Armed Forces of the United States when two or more Services or elements of them are acting together.

References

Department of Defense, Joint Chiefs of Staff. *Department of Defense Dictionary of Military and Related Terms.* Washington, DC: GPO, 1986.

—**UNIFIED COMMAND.** A Unified Command is one with a broad continuing mission under a single commander and composed of significant assigned components of two or more services. The Unified and Specified Commands are force packages that are to be employed in military operations. The operational chain of command proceeds from the President to the Secretary of Defense to the Chairman of the Joint Chiefs of Staff to the Unified and Specified Commands to their component commands. This concept is difficult for many to understand, because the popular belief is that the Services control and command their own forces and commands. The Services do in terms of administration and maintenance, but do not in terms of operational employment. Rather, the above-described chain-of-command prevails.

The Unified and Specified Command concept emerged in the years following World War II, as the United States realized that the nature of warfare had progressed beyond theater warfare, where the several military forces could operate in isolation. The development of modern weapons meant that warfare in one theater could affect drastically the events in another theater. It was realized that what was needed was the combined arms package that could provide adequate coordination among the several forces operating in a given region. The Unified and Specified Command approach was the response to this problem. The Unified Commands are the following:

- *U.S. Atlantic Command (USLANTCOM),* which defends the eastern approaches to the United States and the sea lines of communication in the Atlantic area. The Commander-in-Chief, Atlantic is also Supreme Allied Commander, Atlantic, a major NATO commander.
- *U.S. Southern Command (USSOUTHCOM)* defends the Panama Canal and fulfills U.S. military responsibilities throughout the Latin American region.
- *U.S. European Command (USEUCOM)* is responsible for the United States contribution to NATO and for commanding U.S. forces assigned to Europe.

Its area of responsibility also includes the Middle East and the African states bordering on the Mediterranean. The Commander-in-Chief, U.S. Forces Europe, is also Supreme Allied Commander, Europe, a major NATO commander, and as such is responsible for Allied Command Europe.

- *U.S. Pacific Command (USPACOM)* is responsible for the defense of the United States from attack in the Pacific, and for United States defense interests in the Pacific and Indian Ocean areas.
- *U.S. Central Command (USCENTCOM)* is responsible primarily for the Southwest Asia area for the conduct of operational planning for contingencies.
- *U.S. Special Operations Command (USSOCOM)* is responsible for providing combat-ready special operations forces for rapid deployment to the other Unified Commands.
- *U.S. Space Command (USSPACECOM)* is responsible for space control, directing space support operations for assigned systems, and operating Joint Chiefs of Staff-designated space systems in support of the National Command Authorities, the Joint Chiefs of Staff, and other Unified and Specified Commands.
- *U.S. Transportation Command (USTRANSCOM)* is responsible for providing common-user airlift, sealift, terminal services, and U.S. commercial air and land transportation to deploy, employ, and sustain U.S. forces worldwide.

Where the United States has no significant forces assigned, unified operations, if required, would be conducted by deploying a joint task force headquarters to provide the necessary command and control. *See also:* Specified Command.

References

Department of Defense, Joint Chiefs of Staff. *Department of Defense Dictionary of Military and Related Terms.* Washington, DC: GPO, 1986.

Department of Defense, U.S. Army. *Operational Terms and Symbols.* Field Manual FM 101-5-1. Washington, DC: Headquarters, Department of the Army, 1985.

————. *Psychological Operations.* Field Manual FM 33-1. Washington, DC: Headquarters, Department of the Army, 1979.

"The Unified and Specified Commands." *Defense 87* (Nov.-Dec. 1987): 2-58.

—**UNIFIED LOGISTIC SUPPORT** is the provision of logistic support to two or more military services, or their elements, by a single agency or service, by any appropriate method (e.g., joint, common, or cross-servicing support).

References

Department of Defense, U.S. Army. *Dictionary of United States Army Terms.* Army Regulation AR 310-25. Washington, DC: Headquarters, Department of the Army, 1986.

—**UNIFORM CODE OF MILITARY JUSTICE (UCMJ)** is a code of laws governing the conduct of all people in the Armed Forces, as well as those who are subject to military law. *See also:* General Court-Martial, Non-Judicial Punishment, Special Court-Martial, Summary Court-Martial.

References

Department of Defense, U.S. Army. *Dictionary of United States Army Terms.* Army Regulation AR 310-25. Washington, DC: Headquarters, Department of the Army, 1986.

—**UNIFORM PHASE** is a phase of smoke during which the uniformly obscuring screen of smoke exists. *See also:* Smoke Screen.

References

Department of Defense, U.S. Army. *Deliberate Smoke Operations.* Field Manual FM 3-50. Washington, DC: Headquarters, Department of the Army, 1984.

—**UNIFORMED SERVICES** are the Army, Navy, Air Force, Marine Corps, Coast Guard, National Oceanic and Atmospheric Administration, and Public Health Service.

References

Department of Defense, Joint Chiefs of Staff. *Department of Defense Dictionary of Military and Related Terms.* Washington, DC: GPO, 1986.

Department of Defense, U.S. Army. *Promotion of Officers on Active Duty.* Army Regulation AR 624-100. Washington, DC: Headquarters, Department of the Army, 1984.

—**UNILATERAL EXERCISE** is an exercise involving forces of only one nation and service. *See also:* Exercise.

References

Department of Defense, U.S. Army. *Army Exercises.* Army Regulation AR 350-28. Washington, DC: Headquarters, Department of the Army, 1985.

—**UNI-SERVICE COMMAND** is a command composed of forces from only one service.

References
Department of Defense, Joint Chiefs of Staff. *Department of Defense Dictionary of Military and Related Terms.* Washington, DC: GPO, 1986.

—**UNIT.** (1) A unit is any military element whose structure is prescribed by competent authority (e.g., a table of equipment and organization). Specifically, it is a part of an organization. (2) A unit is an organization title of a subdivision of a group in a task force. (3) A unit is a standard of basic quantity into which an item of supply is divided, issued, or used. In this meaning, it is called a "unit of issue." (4) A unit is an organization of the Selective Reserve that is organized, equipped, and trained to be mobilized and to serve on active duty as an organization. *See also:* Organization.

References
Department of Defense, U.S. Army. *Operational Terms and Symbols.* Field Manual FM 101-5-1. Washington, DC: Headquarters, Department of the Army, 1985.

—**UNIT ASSEMBLY** is a combination of machine parts that constitutes a complete auxiliary part of an end-item, performs a specific auxiliary function, and may be removed from the parent item without itself being disassembled.

References
Department of Defense, U.S. Army. *Dictionary of United States Army Terms.* Army Regulation AR 310-25. Washington, DC: Headquarters, Department of the Army, 1986.

—**UNIT AWARD** is an award made to an operating unit and worn by members of that unit who participated in the cited action (permanent unit award). Unit awards may also be authorized for temporary wear by other personnel while actually serving in the cited unit (temporary unit awards).

References
Department of Defense, U.S. Army. *Wear and Appearance of Army Uniforms and Insignia.* Army Regulation AR 670-1. Washington, DC: Headquarters, Department of the Army, 1986.

—**UNIT CATEGORIES.** Units are classified into the following three categories.

Category I is a unit, organized under a table of organization and equipment, whose primary mission is to engage and inflict casualties and equipment damage on the enemy by use of weapons. Category I status extends to the unit's corresponding headquarters and service companies, whose mission is to support and provide assistance to it, and to the command and control headquarters habitually operating in the forward portion of the active combat area (forward of the brigade rear boundary). Category I units normally operate in the forward position of the active combat area, but may, because of the range of their primary weapons and positioning requirements, operate in the division and corps rear areas.

Category II is a unit, organized under a table of organization and equipment, whose mission is primarily to provide command and control, combat support, or combat service support and assistance to category I units. It operates in the combat zone, normally between the brigade and corps rear boundaries.

Category III is a unit, organized under a table of organization and equipment, whose mission is primarily to provide service and assistance to the units operating in the combat zone area and operating agencies of the communications zone. The unit functions habitually in the communications zone or along the lines of communications leading to the communications zone. *See also:* Unit.

References
Department of Defense, U.S. Army. *Dictionary of United States Army Terms.* Army Regulation AR 310-25. Washington, DC: Headquarters, Department of the Army, 1986.

—**UNIT COVERAGE** is the religious support provided by a unit ministry team to all personnel assigned or attached to a unit, regardless of the religious affiliation of either the chaplain or the unit member. *See also:* Chaplain.

References
Department of Defense, U.S. Army. *The Chaplain and Chaplain Assistant in Combat Operations.* Field Manual FM 16-5. Washington, DC: Headquarters, Department of the Army, 1984.

—**UNIT DESIGNATION LIST (UDL)** is a list of the units designated to fulfill requirements of a force list. *See also:* Unit.

References

Department of Defense, U.S. Army. *Planning Logistics Support for Military Operations.* Field Manual FM 701-58. Washington, DC: Headquarters, Department of the Army, 1987.

—**UNIT DISTRIBUTION** is a method of distributing supplies by which the issuing agency delivers issued supplies to the receiving unit.

References

Department of Defense, U.S. Army. *Combat Service Support Operations-Division.* Field Manual FM 63-2. Washington, DC: Headquarters, Department of the Army, 1983.

———. *Operational Terms and Symbols.* Field Manual FM 101-5-1. Washington, DC: Headquarters, Department of the Army, 1985.

—**UNIT IDENTIFICATION CODE (UIC)** is a six-character, alphanumeric code that uniquely identifies each Active, Reserve, and National Guard unit of the Armed Forces. *See also:* Unit.

References

Department of Defense, U.S. Army. *Planning Logistics Support for Military Operations.* Field Manual FM 701-58. Washington, DC: Headquarters, Department of the Army, 1987.

—**UNIT-LEVEL HEALTH SERVICE SUPPORT** has the primary functions of evacuating the sick and wounded from battle areas, providing emergency medical treatment following acquisition of enemy territory, and evacuating patients, as necessary. *See also:* Medical Treatment.

References

Department of Defense, U.S. Army. *Combat Service Support Operations-Theater.* Field Manual FM 63-4. Washington, DC: Headquarters, Department of the Army, 1984.

—**UNIT LEVEL MAINTENANCE.** *See:* Unit Maintenance.

—**UNIT LOADING** is the loading of troop units and their equipment and supplies in the same vessels, aircraft, or land vehicles.

References

Department of Defense, Joint Chiefs of Staff. *Department of Defense Dictionary of Military and Related Terms.* Washington, DC: GPO, 1986.

—**UNIT MAINTENANCE,** or unit-level maintenance. The mission of unit maintenance is to repair by replacement and to perform other minor repairs (e.g., adjust, clean, lubricate, and tighten). It is characterized by quick turnaround and is normally performed by all table of organization and equipment units in the Army, regardless of their location in the theater or within the continental United States.

References

Department of Defense, U.S. Army. *Combat Service Support Operations-Theater.* Field Manual FM 63-4. Washington, DC: Headquarters, Department of the Army, 1984.

———. *Repair Parts Supply for a Theater of Operations.* Field Manual FM 29-19. Washington, DC: Headquarters, Department of the Army, 1985.

—**UNIT MANNING SYSTEM (UMS).** The Active Army implemented a UMS to improve combat effectiveness by reducing personnel turbulence and fostering unit cohesion, esprit, and loyalty in Army units. The program consists of two major subsystems: Cohesion Operational Readiness Training Unit Replacement for the U.S. Army, and the U.S. Army Regimental System. Initially, only the infantry, armor, and cannon field artillery combat arms were involved in the program. Combat support and combat service support have been integrated into the program where practicable and necessary. *See also:* Regimental Affiliation, Unit.

References

Department of Defense, U.S. Army. *U.S. Army Policy Statement, 1988.* Washington, DC: Headquarters, Department of the Army, 1988.

—**UNIT MINISTRY TEAM** consists of the chaplain and chaplain assistant, who are assigned to a battalion or brigade-size unit. *See also:* Chaplain.

References

Department of Defense, U.S. Army. *The Chaplain and Chaplain Assistant in Combat Operations.* Field Manual FM 16-5. Washington, DC: Headquarters, Department of the Army, 1984.

—**UNIT OF ISSUE,** in its special storage meaning, refers to the quantity of an item (i.e. each number, dozen, gallon, pair, pound, ream, or yard). It is usually termed unit of issue in order to distinguish it from "unit price."

References

Department of Defense, Joint Chiefs of Staff. *Department of Defense Dictionary of Military and Related Terms.* Washington, DC: GPO, 1986.

—**UNIT PATHFINDERS** are personnel selected from ground units or installations who are trained in pathfinder techniques. *See also:* Pathfinders.

References
Department of Defense, U.S. Army. *Dictionary of United States Army Terms.* Army Regulation AR 310-25. Washington, DC: Headquarters, Department of the Army, 1986.

—**UNIT REGENERATION** involves the replacement, reorganization, and redistribution actions necessary to restore an attrited unit that is no longer combat effective to the desired level of combat effectiveness. *See also:* Unit.

References
Department of Defense, U.S. Army. *Combat Service Support Operations-Theater.* Field Manual FM 63-4. Washington, DC: Headquarters, Department of the Army, 1984.

———. *Support Operations: Echelons Above Corps.* Field Manual FM 100-16. Washington, DC: Headquarters, Department of the Army, 1986.

—**UNIT-RELATED EQUIPMENT AND SUPPLIES** are all the equipment and supplies assigned to a specific unit and must be transported to an area of operations or that are designated as accompanying supplies.

References
Department of Defense, U.S. Army. *Planning Logistics Support for Military Operations.* Field Manual FM 701-58. Washington, DC: Headquarters, Department of the Army, 1987.

—**UNIT REPLACEMENT** is the movement of a Cohesion Operational Readiness Training unit from a location inside the continental United States to one outside the United States and its disestablishment at the end of its life cycle and replacement with a newly deployed unit. *See also:* Regimental Affiliation.

References
Department of Defense, U.S. Army. *Army Forces Training.* Army Regulation AR 350-41. Washington, DC: Headquarters, Department of the Army, 1986.

—**UNIT RESERVES** are prescribed quantities of supplies carried by a unit as a reserve to cover emergencies.

References
Department of Defense, Joint Chiefs of Staff. *Department of Defense Dictionary of Military and Related Terms.* Washington, DC: GPO, 1986.

—**UNIT STRENGTH,** as applied to a friendly or enemy unit, relates to the number of personnel, amount of supplies, armament, equipment and vehicles, and the total logistic capability. *See also:* Unit Strength Maintenance.

References
Department of Defense, Joint Chiefs of Staff. *Department of Defense Dictionary of Military and Related Terms.* Washington, DC: GPO, 1986.

—**UNIT STRENGTH MAINTENANCE** (STAFF RESPONSIBILITY). The area of unit strength maintenance involves two duties. The first is to maintain a current personnel estimate of the situation in coordination with other staff officers by: (1) Collecting, analyzing, and presenting command data indicating authorized, assigned, and attached strength in relation to the commander's planned course of action with which to evaluate the personnel situation and allocate resources. Sources of data include daily personnel status reports, gain and loss estimates, health services reports, provost marshall reports, and critical military operational specialty shortages. (2) Maintaining continuous personnel loss estimates to update requisitions for personnel replacements. (3) Monitoring, collecting, and analyzing data affecting soldier readiness (e.g., morale, organizational climate, commitment, and cohesion) and recommending policies and procedures to eliminate problems and deficiencies and to enhance morale readiness.
The second duty is to develop plans through assessing strength data, both current and projected, and soldier readiness posture to maintain strength. *See also:* Unit Strength.

References
Department of Defense, U.S. Army. *Staff Organizations and Operations.* Field Manual FM 101-5. Washington, DC: Headquarters, Department of the Army, 1984.

—**UNIT TEST** is a component of the mission training plan that provides a methodology to conduct a formal external evaluation at the discretion of the commander to provide a "snapshot" of unit proficiency. *See also:* Unit.

References
Department of Defense, U.S. Army. *Army Forces Training.* Army Regulation AR 350-41. Washington, DC: Headquarters, Department of the Army, 1986.

—**UNIT TRAINING** is training (individual, collective, and joint or combined) that is conducted in a unit. *See also:* Unit Training Assembly, Unit Training Cycle.

References

Department of Defense, U.S. Army. *Army Exercises.* Army Regulation AR 350-28. Washington, DC: Headquarters, Department of the Army, 1985.

———. *Army Forces Training.* Army Regulation AR 350-41. Washington, DC: Headquarters, Department of the Army, 1986.

———. *Training for Mobilization and War.* Field Manual FM 25- 5. Washington, DC: Headquarters, Department of the Army, 1985.

—**UNIT TRAINING ASSEMBLY** is an authorized and scheduled training assembly of at least four hours. It is mandatory for all troop program unit members.

References

Department of Defense, Joint Chiefs of Staff. *Department of Defense Dictionary of Military and Related Terms.* Washington, DC: GPO, 1986.

—**UNIT TRAINING CYCLE** is the time provided in the unit training program, from the start of basic individual training until the completion of the field exercise and maneuver phase, for units participating in maneuvers; or until the end of unit training for those who do not participate in maneuvers.

References

Department of Defense, U.S. Army. *Dictionary of United States Army Terms.* Army Regulation AR 310-25. Washington, DC: Headquarters, Department of the Army, 1986.

—**UNIT TRAINS** are combat service support personnel and equipment that are organic or attached to a force that provides supply, evacuation, and maintenance services. Unit trains, whether or not echeloned, are under unit control and no portion of them is released to the control of a higher headquarters. Trains are normally echeloned into combat and field trains. *See also:* Combat Trains; Field Train.

References

Department of Defense, U.S. Army. *Armored and Mechanized Division Operations.* Field Manual FM. 71-100. Washington, DC: Headquarters, Department of the Army, 1978.

———. *Staff Organization and Operations.* Field Manual FM 101-5. Washington, DC: Headquarters, Department of the Army, 1986.

—**UNIT TYPE CODE (UTC)** is a five-character alphanumeric code associated with and allows each type unit/organization to be categorized into a kind or class having common distinguishing characteristics. *See also:* Unit.

References

Department of Defense, U.S. Army. *Planning Logistics Support for Military Operations.* Field Manual FM 701-58. Washington, DC: Headquarters, Department of the Army, 1987.

—**UNIT VACANCY** is a position authorized by paragraph and line number of a table of equipment and organization or table of distribution and allowance (for U.S. Army Reserve units) that is unoccupied or is filled by an officer of a lower grade than that authorized for the position (and provided that an officer in the grade of the position is not assigned as over strength). *See also:* Unit.

References

Department of Defense, Joint Chiefs of Staff. *Department of Defense Dictionary of Military and Related Terms.* Washington, DC: GPO, 1986.

—**UNITED STATES ARMED FORCES** is used to denote collectively only the regular components of the Army, Navy, Air Force, Marine Corps, and Coast Guard.

References

Department of Defense, Joint Chiefs of Staff. *Department of Defense Dictionary of Military and Related Terms.* Washington, DC: GPO, 1986.

—**UNITED STATES ARMY (USA) OR ARMY OF THE UNITED STATES (AUS).** These terms mean the Army or Armies referred to in the U.S. Constitution, less that part established by law as the U.S. Air Force. "United States Army" is used in preference to "Army of the United States." The United States Army includes the Regular Army, the National Guard of the United States, and the Army Reserve; all persons appointed, enlisted, or inducted in the Army without specification of component; and all persons serving in the Army under call or conscription under any provision of law, including members of the National Guard of the states, territories, and the District of Columbia, when in the service of the United States pursuant to call as provided by law. In certain instances, however, "United States Army" has been used in statutes to mean the Regular Army.

References

Department of Defense, U.S. Army. *Dictionary of United States Army Terms.* Army Regulation AR 310-25. Washington, DC: Headquarters, Department of the Army, 1986.

—**UNITED STATES ARMY DOMESTIC INTELLIGENCE OPERATIONS.** During the upheavals of the 1960s, the Army was directed to increase its surveillance of dissident groups. It responded by establishing files on several groups and by harassing some of them. The program was terminated in 1974. *See also:* United States Army Intelligence (G-2).

References

Breckinridge, Scott D. *The CIA and the U.S. Intelligence System.* Boulder, CO: Westview Press, 1986.

—**UNITED STATES ARMY INTELLIGENCE (G-2)** provides intelligence to the U.S. Army and to the Department of Defense. In this capacity, it (1) is responsible for collecting, producing, and disseminating military and military-related foreign intelligence, including intelligence on indications and warning, capabilities, weapons, and equipment; (2) conducts counterintelligence operations and produces and disseminates counterintelligence reports; and (3) develops, buys, and manages tactical intelligence systems and equipment.

The major components of Army Intelligence are the Army Intelligence and Security Command (which performs the necessary signals intelligence, human intelligence, and counterintelligence functions) and the Army Intelligence Agency. In addition to its headquarters staff, the Army Intelligence Agency is composed of the Missile and Space Intelligence Center (located at Redstone Arsenal, Huntsville, Alabama), the Intelligence Threat and Analysis Center (located in the Washington Navy Yard, Washington, DC) and the Foreign Science and Technology Center (located in Charlottesville, Virginia). *See also:* United States Army Domestic Intelligence Operations, United States Army Intelligence Agency, United States Army Intelligence and Security Command, United States Army Intelligence and Threat Analysis Center, United States Army Intelligence Center and School, United States Army Intelligence Command.

References

Department of Defense, Joint Chiefs of Staff. *Department of Defense Dictionary of Military and Related Terms.* Washington, DC: GPO, 1986.

Finnegan, John P. *Military Intelligence: A Picture History.* Arlington, VA: U.S. Army Intelligence and Security Command, 1984.

—**UNITED STATES ARMY INTELLIGENCE AGENCY (USAINTA OR USAIA)** was responsible for the Army's counterintelligence program until 1977, when USAINTA was merged with the U.S. Army Security elements to form the U.S. Army Intelligence and Security Command. It was reactivated in 1985 as the Army Intelligence Agency. Presently composed of the Intelligence and Threat Analysis Center, the Foreign Science and Technology Center, and the Missile and Space Intelligence Center, it provides intelligence users with short- to long-range scientific and technological as well as general military intelligence assessments. Serving tactical and strategic planners, policy-makers, and weapons developers, the Army Intelligence Agency's all-source analysis is significant in U.S. force modernization, operational planning, materiel acquisition, weapons modeling, strategic space systems, technology transfer, arms control, and operations security. *See also:* United States Army Intelligence.

References

Breckinridge, Scott D. *The CIA and the U.S. Intelligence System.* Boulder, CO: Westview Press, 1986.

Department of Defense, U.S. Army. *AIA: Threat Analysis.* Falls Church, VA: U.S. Army Intelligence Agency, 1987.

Finnegan, John P. *Military Intelligence: A Picture History.* Arlington, VA: U.S. Army Intelligence and Security Command, 1984.

—**UNITED STATES ARMY INTELLIGENCE AND SECURITY COMMAND (USAINSCOM)** was created on January 1, 1977, as the result of a reorganization that was intended to improve the Army's intelligence activities. It combined certain elements of the Army Security Agency, the U.S. Army Intelligence Agency, the U.S. Army Forces Command, and the Assistant Chief of Staff, Department of the Army.

INSCOM is under the direction of the Army's Deputy Chief of Staff for Intelligence and other national authorities. Its mission is to accomplish intelligence, security, and electronic warfare operations for Army echelons above the corps level. It produces Army-level general intelligence and threat analysis, and monitors intelligence and threat production by other Army elements. It is also responsible for responding to actions from the Department of the Army. INSCOM has more than 16,000 military and civilian employees.

INSCOM has three basic types of units. Its *field stations* are part of the worldwide U.S. communications network and provide rapid relay and secure communications. Its *single disciplinary military intelligence units* provide intelligence and security support to the Army. The *multidiscipline military intelligence units* provide security support to deployable and deployed Army forces, and have resources such as counterintelligence, operations security support, and signals security support units.

In addition, INSCOM has several unique units. Its Army Russian Institute in Garmisch, Federal Republic of Germany, provides the Army with Russian area specialists. The Institute's program includes Soviet area studies, travel in the Soviet Union, and two years of advanced Russian language training.

INSCOM's Central Security Facility, located at Fort George Meade, Maryland, provides information to more than 400 requesters worldwide, including the Defense Investigative Service. The facility also processes requests that are submitted under the Freedom of Information Act.

Finally, the Command's Special Security Group, headquartered at Arlington Hall Station, Virginia, provides the secure means to disseminate sensitive compartmented information to Army organizations.

INSCOM is currently headquartered at Arlington Hall Station, Virginia, and at Fort George Meade, Maryland, with field stations in Germany, Japan, Korea, Panama, Turkey, and the United States, and military intelligence units in Panama, Korea, Germany, Japan, and the United States. *See also:* United States Army Intelligence.

References

Department of Defense, U.S. Army, Headquarters, U.S. Army Intelligence and Security Command. *INSCOM: United States Army Intelligence and Security Command.* Arlington Hall Station, VA: Public Affairs Office, U.S. Army Intelligence and Security Command, 1985.

—**UNITED STATES ARMY INTELLIGENCE AND THREAT CENTER (ITAC).** ITAC was created in 1977, as the merger of six independent Army intelligence organizations. A further consolidation occurred in 1985, when ITAC was joined with the Foreign Science and Technology Center and the Missile and Space Intelligence Center to form the Army Intelligence Agency.

ITAC's mission is to provide the Department of the Army and the Department of Defense with comprehensive general intelligence and counterintelligence analysis and production reflecting the capabilities, vulnerabilities, and current and future threats to the Army from foreign military and security forces. In accomplishing its mission, ITAC produces studies that analyze the military capabilities of foreign forces against conventional and unconventional attack, project hostile capabilities in certain geographic areas, and assess the political and military environments that can influence Army force and operations planning.

Organization. ITAC is composed of a command element (with the Command Office, a Special Security detachment, a Special Research detachment, an administrative office, and management office), and six divisions. The names and purposes of these divisions are as follows:

- *The Automated Services Division* provides automation and operations research analytical support. It establishes and administers all ITAC computer systems, and oversees the design, development, and use of the Automated Threat Intelligence Production System.

- *The Counterintelligence and Terrorism Division* collates, analyzes, and evaluates information of counterintelligence significance and prepares estimates and studies of foreign intelligence services and international terrorist activities. It supports the U.S. Army Subversion and Espionage Directed Against the U.S.Army and Operational Security programs through studies and analyses of the multidisciplinary threat that is posed by foreign intelligence services. It supports contingency planning and major exercises through hostile intelligence threat assessments. The division provides assessments in support of the Army's technology transfer control program. It also monitors the internal security situation of key countries and gives spot security evaluations to high-level Army travelers prior to their departure overseas.

- *The Imagery Division* produces detailed imagery exploitation reports and keys on foreign ground forces equipment and weaponry and responds to imagery-exploitation support requirements from the Department of the Army, Department of Defense, and other agencies. Exploitation and retasking of targets of Army interest is performed daily. Many capabilities of weapon systems can be deduced from the imagery analysis and mensuration provided by division analysts. Imagery reports are produced for users at all levels in addition to supporting projects for other ITAC divisions and Army Intelligence Agency centers. This information supplies imagery-derived intelligence to contingency forces in times of crisis.

- *The Regional Division* conducts research and analysis on assigned areas of the world where U.S. forces may be employed, and produces short-, mid-, and long-range forecasts and assessments of these areas. These studies cover military capabilities as well as the political, economic, demographic, sociological, cultural, and geographic aspects of certain countries (e.g., long-range planning estimates are made to determine U.S. strategic requirements and to develop and prioritize force capabilities and structures). Additionally, this division participates in the Department of Defense-delegated production programs for ground order of battle and associated installations. In this capacity, it has a major input into the Defense Intelligence Agency ground order of battle estimates.
- *The Warsaw Pact Division* conducts research and analysis of Soviet and Warsaw Pact forces, tactics, operations, and materiel. It produces short-, mid-, and long-range forecasts of Warsaw Pact organization tactics, operational art, and strategy. Projections are made as far as twenty years into the future to assess the threats the Army may encounter. When considering the cost of major Army materiel development systems, it is essential that they not become prematurely obsolete through corresponding enemy countermeasures that could have been forecast.
- *A Special Research Detachment* is collocated with the National Security Agency at Fort Meade, Maryland. It is responsible for all-source, signals-intelligence-intensive research, analysis, and production on the Warsaw Pact, Latin American, and Middle Eastern countries. The detachment focuses on specific intelligence issues dealing with current and near-term national security questions. It also provides direct support to other ITAC divisions when required and provides analytical assistance for high interest study task forces.

- *A Production Support Division* provides editorial, graphic, photographic, audiovisual, printing, and research support.

See also: United States Army Intelligence.

References

Department of Defense, U.S. Army. *United States Army Intelligence and Threat Analysis Center.* Washington, DC: U.S. Army Intelligence Threat and Analysis Center, 1987.

—**UNITED STATES ARMY INTELLIGENCE CENTER AND SCHOOL (USAICS)** is located at Fort Huachuca, Arizona. The school offers courses in intelligence collection, counterintelligence, intelligence and imagery analysis, terrorism, interrogation, and all source intelligence. *See also:* United States Army Intelligence.

References

Defense Intelligence Agency. *Training Compendium for General Defense Career Development Program (IDCP) Personnel DOD 1430.10M3-TNG.* Washington, DC: DIA, 1986.

—**UNITED STATES ARMY INTELLIGENCE COMMAND (USAINTC OR USAIC)** was established in 1965 and took control of the seven counterintelligence groups in the continental United States. As a result of the significant disturbances in U.S. cities in the 1960s, USAINTC became deeply involved in domestic intelligence collection operations. When the command's role was revealed in the early 1970s, there was a significant public reaction. USAINTC's responsibilities concerning conducting background investigations of prospective government intelligence employees were given to the newly formed Defense Intelligence Service. Since these duties accounted for about 90 percent of the command's workload, it ceased to have a mission. It was finally discontinued in 1977, and was replaced by the U.S. Army Intelligence Agency. *See also:* United States Army Intelligence.

References

Finnegan, John P. *Military Intelligence: A Picture History.* Arlington, VA: U.S. Army Intelligence and Security Command, 1984.

—**UNITED STATES ARMY REGIMENTAL SYSTEM (USARS)** is designed to enhance combat effectiveness by providing the opportunity for affiliation. Affiliation develops loyalty and commitment, fosters an extended sense of belonging, improves unit esprit, and institutionalizes a warfighting spirit. A regiment within the USARS is defined as a single unit or a group of like-type units designed with a unique regimental color and formed for the purpose of providing an affiliated soldier with an opportunity for long-term identification, the potential for recurring assignments, and the basis to perpetuate customs and traditions. *See also:* Regimental Affiliation.

References
Department of Defense, U.S. Army. *U.S. Army Policy Statement, 1988*. Washington, DC: Headquarters, Department of the Army, 1988.

—**UNITED STATES ARMY RESERVE (USAR)** is a federal force consisting of individual reinforcements and combat, combat support, support, and training-type units organized and maintained to provide military training in peacetime and a reservoir of trained units and individual reservists to be ordered to active duty in the event of a national emergency. *See also:* Active Army, Army Composition, Army National Guard, United States Army, United States Army Reserve Center.

References
Department of Defense, U.S. Army. *Dictionary of United States Army Terms*. Army Regulation AR 310-25. Washington, DC: Headquarters, Department of the Army, 1986.

—**UNITED STATES ARMY RESERVE CENTER (USARC)** is a home station facility, activity, or installation used for administering to and training U.S. Army Reserve units and personnel. *See also:* United States Army Reserve.

References
Department of Defense, U.S. Army. *Dictionary of United States Army Terms*. Army Regulation AR 310-25. Washington, DC: Headquarters, Department of the Army, 1986.

—**UNITED STATES ARMY RESERVE FORCES SCHOOL** is a table of distribution and allowance unit specifically organized for the purpose of presenting Army service school courses and selected military occupational specialty training. *See also:* United States Army Reserve School.

References
Department of Defense, U.S. Army. *Individual Military Education and Training*. Army Regulation AR 350-1. Washington, DC: Headquarters, Department of the Army, 1987.

—**UNITED STATES ARMY RESERVE SCHOOL** is a table of distribution and allowance unit specifically organized for the purpose of presenting Army service school courses and selected military occupational specialty training for reserve component personnel during reserve and annual active duty training periods. *See also:* United States Army Reserve Forces School.

References
Department of Defense, U.S. Army. *Dictionary of United States Army Terms*. Army Regulation AR 310-25. Washington, DC: Headquarters, Department of the Army, 1986.

—**UNITED STATES ARMY SCHOOL OF THE AMERICAS (USARSA)** is the U.S. Army Training and Doctrine Command school with the principal responsibility for training military students from Latin America. Its primary objectives are to conduct military education and training for Latin American military personnel in Spanish, to foster greater cooperation among the Armed Forces of the Americas, and to increase the level of understanding about the United States among Latin American military personnel.

References
Department of Defense, U.S. Army. *U.S. Army Policy Statement, 1988*. Washington, DC: Headquarters, Department of the Army, 1988.

—**UNITED STATES ARMY SPECIAL FORCES (SF)** is composed of military personnel with cross-training in basic and specialized military skills, organized into small, multipurpose detachments with the mission to train, organize, supply, direct, and control indigenous forces in guerrilla warfare and counterinsurgency operations, and to conduct unconventional warfare operations. *See also:* Guerilla Warfare, Unconventional Warfare.

References
Department of Defense, Joint Chiefs of Staff. *Department of Defense Dictionary of Military and Related Terms*. Washington, DC: GPO, 1986.

—**UNITED STATES ARMY TRAINING CENTER** is a nonservice school activity that conducts basic combat training for nonprior service enlisted personnel and advanced individual training given to personnel after basic training in order to qualify them for the award of a military occupational specialty.

References
Department of Defense, U.S. Army. *Dictionary of United States Army Terms.* Army Regulation AR 310-25. Washington, DC: Headquarters, Department of the Army, 1986.

—**UNITED STATES ARMY WAR COLLEGE (AWC),** located at Carlisle Barracks, Pennsylvania, offers a 44-week course of instruction for military officers of the ranks of lieutenant colonel or colonel (O5 and O6) and civilians of equivalent rank. The course is intended to prepare the student for senior command and staff positions in the Army and the Department of Defense, and to promote an understanding of the art and science of land warfare. It includes an examination of the national and international environment, national security policy formulation, and the decisionmaking process within the Department of Defense and a detailed study of land warfare, including the historical aspects of warfare, development of U.S. military strategy, force planning and structuring, command, management and employment of Army forces, and future considerations for the conduct of land battle. *See also:* National Defense University.

References
Defense Intelligence Agency. *Training Compendium for General Defense Career Development Program (IDCP) Personnel DOD 1430.10M3-TNG.* Washington, DC: DIA, 1986.

—**UNITED STATES GOVERNMENT LIFE INSUR-ANCE** is government life insurance that was available upon application to persons who fulfilled active military service from October 6, 1917 to October 8, 1940. Between October 8, 1940 and April 25, 1951, it was available to persons who served on active duty between October 6, 1917 and July 2, 1921. After April 25, 1951, it is available only to the following groups of individuals meeting specific requirements: (1) individuals who surrendered permanent plans of United States Government Life Insurance for cash while on active duty between April 25, 1951 and January 1, 1957; (b) individuals who had term United States Government Life Insurance and the term expired prior to January 1, 1957 while the person was on active duty or within 120 days after separation. *See also:* National Service Life Insurance.

References
Department of Defense, U.S. Army. *Dictionary of United States Army Terms.* Army Regulation AR 310-25. Washington, DC: Headquarters, Department of the Army, 1986.

—**US ROLAND** is a short-range, low-altitude, all-weather Army air defense artillery surface-to-air missile system that is under development. It is based upon the Franco-German Roland III missile system.

References
Department of Defense, Joint Chiefs of Staff. *Department of Defense Dictionary of Military and Related Terms.* Washington, DC: GPO, 1986.

—**UNITIZED LOAD** is a single item, or a number of items packaged, packed, or arranged in a specific manner and capable of being handled as a unit. Unitization may be accomplished by placing the item or items in a container or banding them securely together.

References
Department of Defense, Joint Chiefs of Staff. *Department of Defense Dictionary of Military and Related Terms.* Washington, DC: GPO, 1986.

—**UNITY OF COMMAND** (PRINCIPLE OF WAR). For every objective, a unity of effort is to be insured under one responsible commander.

At the national level, the U.S. Constitution provides for unity of command by appointing the President as Commander-in-Chief of the Armed Forces. He is assisted in this role by the national security organization, which includes the Secretary of Defense and the Joint Chiefs of Staff at the strategic level, and the Unified and Specified Commands and joint task forces at the operational level.

Unity of command helps to focus effort on a common goal. At the strategic level, this common goal equates to the political purpose of the United States and the broad strategic objectives that flow from it.

In both the operational and tactical dimensions, military forces should be employed to develop their full combat power, which requires unity of command. Coordination may be achieved by cooperation; it is, however, best achieved by vesting a single commander with the requisite authority over all forces employed in pursuit of a common goal. *See also:* Principles of War.

References

Department of Defense, U.S. Army. *The Army.* (Prepublication Issue.) Field Manual FM 100-1. Washington, DC: Headquarters, Department of the Army, 1986.

————. *Operational Terms and Symbols.* Field Manual FM 101-5-1. Washington, DC: Headquarters, Department of the Army, 1985.

————. *Operations.* Field Manual FM 100-5. Washington, DC: Headquarters, Department of the Army, 1986.

—**UNIVERSAL MISSION LOAD** constitutes the part of the mission load of combat essential Classes II and IV materiel that can be universally applied with support capability as stated in the table of organization and equipment for units whose specific mission assignment cannot be predetermined. It may lack items applicable (peculiar) to a specific supported unit or theater due to specialization of standardization. It becomes the mission load when the items are adjusted either prior to or after unit deployment in support of specific units. The universal mission load is an integral part of the authorized stockage list for continental U.S. table of organization and equipment support-type units. The authorized stockage list will continue to be maintained in accordance with current regulations.

References

Department of Defense, U.S. Army. *Dictionary of United States Army Terms.* Army Regulation AR 310-25. Washington, DC: Headquarters, Department of the Army, 1986.

—**UNKNOWN.** (1) Unknown is a code meaning that the information is not available. (2) Unknown is an unidentified target. *See also:* Bogey, Bogey Dope.

References

Department of Defense, Joint Chiefs of Staff. *Department of Defense Dictionary of Military and Related Terms.* Washington, DC: GPO, 1986.

—**UNOBSERVED FIRE** is fire for which the points of impact or burst are not seen.

References

Department of Defense, U.S. Army. *Operational Terms and Symbols.* Field Manual FM 101-5-1. Washington, DC: Headquarters, Department of the Army, 1985.

—**UNSERVICEABLE SUPPLIES.** (1) Unserviceable supplies are all supplies that require repair, reprocessing, or modification prior to being included in stock-on-hand ready-for-issue. (2) Unserviceable supplies are quantities that cannot be used because they are obsolete, worn, damaged, or otherwise not suitable for their intended purpose.

References

Department of Defense, U.S. Army. *Dictionary of United States Army Terms.* Army Regulation AR 310-25. Washington, DC: Headquarters, Department of the Army, 1986.

—**UNSUITABLE PERSONNEL** are persons who may exhibit their unsuitability through interests or habits detrimental to the maintenance of good order and discipline and who may have records of minor misconduct requiring repetitive corrective or disciplinary action. *See also:* Untrainable Personnel.

References

Department of Defense, U.S. Army. *Army Reenlistment Program.* Army Regulation AR 601-28. Washington, DC: Headquarters, Department of the Army, 1984.

—**UNTRAINABLE PERSONNEL** are persons who are found to be lacking in the abilities and aptitudes to the extent that they require frequent or continued special instruction or supervision. *See also:* Unsuitable Personnel.

References

Department of Defense, U.S. Army. *Army Reenlistment Program.* Army Regulation AR 601-28. Washington, DC: Headquarters, Department of the Army, 1984.

—**UNWARNED EXPOSED** pertains to the vulnerability of friendly forces to nuclear weapon effects. In this condition, personnel are assumed to be standing in the open at burst time, but have dropped to a prone position by the time the blast wave arrives. They are expected to have areas of bare skin exposed to direct thermal radiation. *See also:* Warned Exposed, Warned Protected.

References

Department of Defense, Joint Chiefs of Staff. *Department of Defense Dictionary of Military and Related Terms.* Washington, DC: GPO, 1986.

—**UP.** (1) In artillery, up is a term used in a call for fire to indicate that the target is higher in altitude than the point that has been used as a reference point for the target location. (2) Up is a correction used by an observer or a spotter in time fire to indicate that an increase in the height of burst is desired.

References
Department of Defense, U.S. Army. *Operational Terms and Symbols.* Field Manual FM 101-5-1. Washington, DC: Headquarters, Department of the Army, 1985.

—**URBAN AREA OPERATIONS** are characterized by close coordination between the armed forces, police forces, paramilitary forces, and other security forces for the protection of critical installations and control of subversive activities. Operations in an urban area also may be part of a consolidation campaign or a continuing effort not specifically designated as a campaign.

References
Department of Defense, U.S. Army. *Low Intensity Conflict.* Field Manual FM 100-20. Washington, DC: Headquarters, Department of the Army, 1981.

—**URGENT PRIORITY** is a category of immediate mission request that is lower than emergency priority but takes precedence over ordinary priority (e.g., enemy artillery or mortar fire falling on friendly troops and causing casualties). *See also:* Emergency Priority.

References
Department of Defense, Joint Chiefs of Staff. *Department of Defense Dictionary of Military and Related Terms.* Washington, DC: GPO, 1986.

—**USABLE RATE OF FIRE** is the normal rate of fire of a gun in actual use measured in units of shots per minute. The usable rate of fire is considerably less than a gun's maximum rate of fire, which is a theoretical value based solely upon the mechanical operation of the weapon.

References
Department of Defense, U.S. Army. *Dictionary of United States Army Terms.* Army Regulation AR 310-25. Washington, DC: Headquarters, Department of the Army, 1986.

—**USAGE PROFILE** is a situational outline that specifies environmental and performance characteristics of an end-item in a given wartime situation.

References
Department of Defense, U.S. Army. *Maintenance and Repair Parts Consumption Planning Guide for Contingency Operations.* Field Manual FM 42-9-23. Washington, DC: Headquarters, Department of the Army, 1980.

—**UTILITY UNIFORMS** are fatigue uniforms normally worn in the field, in training, or in performing duties where it is not practical or appropriate to wear a service uniform. Utility uniforms include the temperate and hot weather uniform, fatigues, and the optional jungle fatigues (where authorized). *See also:* Service Uniform.

References
Department of Defense, U.S. Army. *Wear and Appearance of Army Uniforms and Insignia.* Army Regulation AR 670-1. Washington, DC: Headquarters, Department of the Army, 1986.

—**UTILIZATION TOUR** is service in a designated position to offset the officer's obligation to the Army for partially or fully funded civil or military schooling.

References
Department of Defense, U.S. Army. *Officer Assignment Policies, Details, and Transfers.* Army Regulation AR 614-100. Washington, DC: Headquarters, Department of the Army, 1984.

—**VALOR** is heroism under combat conditions. *See also:* Above and Beyond the Call of Duty.

References

Department of Defense, U.S. Army. *Military Awards.* Army Regulation AR 672-5-1. Washington, DC: Headquarters, Department of the Army, 1984.

—**VECTOR GUNSIGHT** is a device on the gun that computes the vector required for the projectile to strike the target.

References

Department of Defense, U.S. Army. *Dictionary of United States Army Terms.* Army Regulation AR 310-25. Washington, DC: Headquarters, Department of the Army, 1986.

—**VECTORED ATTACK** is an attack in which an air, surface, or subsurface weapon carrier, not holding contact on the target, is vectored to the weapon delivery point by a unit that holds contact on the target.

References

Department of Defense, Joint Chiefs of Staff. *Department of Defense Dictionary of Military and Related Terms.* Washington, DC: GPO, 1986.

—**VEE** is an arrangement of vehicles or personnel for movement or combat in the shape of a vee. It may be used when the enemy situation is vague and the leader requires firepower to the front and flanks. *See also:* Column, Line, Wedge.

References

Department of Defense, U.S. Army. *Operational Terms and Symbols.* Field Manual FM 101-5-1. Washington, DC: Headquarters, Department of the Army, 1985.

—**VEHICLE** is a self-propelled, boosted, or towed conveyance for transporting personnel or cargo or other material on land, sea, or through air or space. *See also:* Amphibious Vehicle, Combat Vehicle, Special-Purpose Vehicle.

References

Department of Defense, Joint Chiefs of Staff. *Department of Defense Dictionary of Military and Related Terms.* Washington, DC: GPO, 1986.

—**VEHICLE CARGO** is wheeled or tracked equipment, including weapons, that require certain deck space, head room, and other definite clearance.

References

Department of Defense, Joint Chiefs of Staff. *Department of Defense Dictionary of Military and Related Terms.* Washington, DC: GPO, 1986.

—**VEHICLE CONE INDEX** is the minimum cone index of soil strength that will permit the vehicle to complete a given number of passes.

References

Department of Defense, U.S. Army. *Dictionary of United States Army Terms.* Army Regulation AR 310-25. Washington, DC: Headquarters, Department of the Army, 1986.

—**VEHICLE DISTANCE** is the clearance between vehicles in a column measured from the rear of one vehicle to the front of the following vehicle. *See also:* Accordion Effect.

References

Department of Defense, U.S. Army. *The Infantry Rifle Company (Infantry, Airborne, Air Assault, Ranger).* Field Manual FM 7-10. Washington, DC: Headquarters, Department of the Army, 1982.

—**VEHICLE LANES.** After the first breach is made in a minefield, foot lanes may be widened to one-way vehicle lanes at least eight meters wide. Vehicle lanes also may be breached separately from foot lanes. Existing roads are used when possible, and mines are cleared along their entire width. *See also:* Breach, Mine Warfare.

References

Department of Defense, U.S. Army. *Engineer Combat Operations.* Field Manual FM 5-100. Washington, DC: Headquarters, Department of the Army, 1984.

—**VEHICLE NOMENCLATURE.** The U.S. Army Ordnance Department uses the following system. The designation T1, T2, etc., indicates that the item is a developmental item. While in the developmental stage, when a major change is incorporated, the item will take the designation T1E1, T1E2, etc. Such a designation indicates a change affecting the military characteristics or installation. When an item has been adopted as a standard by the Ordnance Technical Committee, the item is given the designation M1, M2, etc. When a major change occurs in an item adopted as standard, such as one that affects military characteristics, installations, manufacture, storage or use, the designation changes to M1A1, M1A2, etc. The designation M1A1-B1, M1A1-B2, etc., indicates that a different type of material is used that constitutes a major change in production because of the scarcity of material. When a standard article has been modified by the development of an experimental nonstandard process or procedure, it takes the designation M1E1, M1E2, etc. If the item thus modified is adopted as standard by the Ordnance Department, it takes a designation in the proper sequence of the M1A series. For example, an item designated as M1E6 may become M1A4 if it is the fourth item adopted as standard in that type of material.

References

Hoffscmidt, E.J., and Tantum, W.H., eds. *Tank Data 2.* Old Greenwich, CT: WE, Inc., 1966.

—**VEHICLE SUMMARY AND PRIORITY TABLE** is a table listing all vehicles by priority of debarkation from a combat-loaded ship. It includes the nomenclature, dimensions, square feet, cubic feet, weight, and stowage location of each vehicle, the cargo loaded in each vehicle, and the name of the unit to which the vehicle belongs. *See also:* Administrative Loading.

References

Department of Defense, U.S. Army. *Staff Organization and Operations.* Field Manual FM 101-5. Washington, DC: Headquarters, Department of the Army, 1986.

—**VEHICLE WASHDOWN** is the process of flushing contamination off of equipment surfaces to limit its spread, to reduce the overall amounts of contamination, and to speed weathering. *See also:* Decontamination, Weathering.

References

Department of Defense, U.S. Army. *NBC Decontamination.* Field Manual FM 3-5. Washington, DC: Headquarters, Department of the Army, 1985.

—**VERY LIGHT** is a colored signal flare fired from a special pistol. *See also:* Very Pistol.

References

Department of Defense, U.S. Army. *Dictionary of United States Army Terms.* Army Regulation AR 310-25. Washington, DC: Headquarters, Department of the Army, 1986.

—**VERY LONG RANGE RADAR.** (1) Very long range radar is equipment whose range on a reflecting target of one square meter normal to the signal path exceeds 965 kilometers, provided that a line of sight exists between the target and the radar. (2) It is equipment whose maximum theoretical range exceeds 400 nautical miles. *See also:* Radar, Very Short Range Radar.

References

Department of Defense, U.S. Army. *Dictionary of United States Army Terms.* Army Regulation AR 310-25. Washington, DC: Headquarters, Department of the Army, 1986.

—**VERY PISTOL** is a special pistol used to fire colored signal flares. *See also:* Very Light.

References

Department of Defense, U.S. Army. *Dictionary of United States Army Terms.* Army Regulation AR 310-25. Washington, DC: Headquarters, Department of the Army, 1986.

—**VERY SHORT RANGE RADAR** is equipment whose range on a reflecting target of one square meter is less than 50 miles, provided that a line of sight exists between the target and the radar. *See also:* Radar, Very Long Range Radar.

References

Department of Defense, U.S. Army. *Dictionary of United States Army Terms.* Army Regulation AR 310-25. Washington, DC: Headquarters, Department of the Army, 1986.

—**VESICANT AGENT** is a chemical that acts on a person's eyes and lungs and blisters the skin. *See also:* Chemical Warfare.

References

Department of Defense, U.S. Army. *Technical Escort Operations.* Field Manual FM 3-20. Washington, DC: Headquarters, Department of the Army, 1981.

—**VETERINARIAN** is the senior veterinary officer of an organization who is in charge of all veterinary personnel and activities.

References

Department of Defense, U.S. Army. *Dictionary of United States Army Terms.* Army Regulation AR 310-25. Washington, DC: Headquarters, Department of the Army, 1986.

—**VICE CHIEF OF STAFF** is the principal adviser and assistant to the Chief of Staff, United States Army, who acts for the Chief of Staff in his absence.

References

Department of Defense, U.S. Army. *Dictionary of United States Army Terms.* Army Regulation AR 310-25. Washington, DC: Headquarters, Department of the Army, 1986.

—**VICTORY MEDALS** are medals awarded to all personnel who served in the Armed Forces of the United States during World War I and II. *See also:* Accouterment.

References

Department of Defense, U.S. Army. *Dictionary of United States Army Terms.* Army Regulation AR 310-25. Washington, DC: Headquarters, Department of the Army, 1986.

—**VISIBILITY** is the distance at which it is just possible to distinguish a prominent object against the background with the unaided eye. *See also:* Weather VAT (B), Weather Information, Weather Intelligence, Weather Minimum.

References

Department of Defense, U.S. Army. *Deliberate Smoke Operations.* Field Manual FM 3-50. Washington, DC: Headquarters, Department of the Army, 1984.

—**VISION SLIT** is any narrow opening or slit in armor through which one can look. It applies particularly to slits in tanks or other armored vehicles.

References

Department of Defense, U.S. Army. *Dictionary of United States Army Terms.* Army Regulation AR 310-25. Washington, DC: Headquarters, Department of the Army, 1986.

—**VISITING CORRESPONDENT** is a journalist, writer, radio correspondent, or photographer who is given authority by the Secretary of the Army or the Commander in Chief to visit a field of operations and to publish material only after the visit ends. The correspondent is not attached to a headquarters and does not wear a uniform. Accredited correspondents differ from visiting correspondents in that they are permitted to carry on their work in a theater of operations, or a base command; are attached to a headquarters, and wear an officer's uniform without insignia. *See also:* Censorship.

References

Department of Defense, U.S. Army. *Dictionary of United States Army Terms.* Army Regulation AR 310-25. Washington, DC: Headquarters, Department of the Army, 1986.

—**VISUAL** (ARMY AVIATION) refers to visual contact with one's own flight or wingman. For example, "visual" or "no visual."

References

Department of Defense, U.S. Army. *Air-to-Air Combat.* Field Manual FM 1-107. Washington, DC: Headquarters, Department of the Army, 1984.

—**VISUAL DECEPTION.** Two items that are commonly used in visual deception are dummies and decoys. A *dummy* is an imitation of something on the battlefield. A *decoy* is used to draw the attention of the enemy away from a more important area. When a dummy is used to draw the enemy's attention from some other area, it is also termed a decoy. *See also:* Decoy.

References

Department of Defense, U.S. Army. *Tactical Deception.* Field Manual FM 90-2. Washington, DC: Headquarters, Department of the Army, 1978.

—**VISUAL ELEVATION** is the distance above the target at which the white tracer streak from a machine gun must appear in order to allow for the drop in the trajectory.

References

Department of Defense, U.S. Army. *Dictionary of United States Army Terms.* Army Regulation AR 310-25. Washington, DC: Headquarters, Department of the Army, 1986.

—**VISUAL METEOROLOGICAL CONDITIONS** are meteorological conditions expressed in terms of visibility, cloud distance, and ceiling. *See also:* Weather VAT (B), Weather Information, Weather Intelligence, Weather Minimum.

References

Department of Defense, U.S. Army. *Airspace Management and Army Air Traffic in a Combat Zone.* Field Manual FM 1-60. Washington, DC: Headquarters, Department of the Army, 1977.

—**VITAL AREA** is a designated area or installation to be defended by air defense units.

References

Department of Defense, Joint Chiefs of Staff. *Department of Defense Dictionary of Military and Related Terms.* Washington, DC: GPO, 1986.

—**VOLLEY.** (1) Volley is a method of artillery firing in which each piece fires the specified number of rounds without any attempt to synchronize with the other pieces. (2) A volley is a burst of fire, especially a salute that is fired by a detachment of riflemen. *See also:* Volley Fire.

References

Department of Defense, U.S. Army. *Dictionary of United States Army Terms.* Army Regulation AR 310-25. Washington, DC: Headquarters, Department of the Army, 1986.

—**VOLLEY FIRE** is artillery fire in which each piece fires a specific number of rounds without regard to the other pieces and as fast as accuracy will permit.

References

Department of Defense, U.S. Army. *Dictionary of United States Army Terms.* Army Regulation AR 310-25. Washington, DC: Headquarters, Department of the Army, 1986.

—**VOLUNTARY ORDER OR RECALL TO ACTIVE DUTY** is the ordering or calling of individual members of the reserve components of the Army or retired Army personnel for full time duty in the active military service of their country with their consent.

References

Department of Defense, U.S. Army. *Dictionary of United States Army Terms.* Army Regulation AR 310-25. Washington, DC: Headquarters, Department of the Army, 1986.

—**VOLUNTARY TRAINING** is training in a nonpay status for Individual Ready Reservists and active status Standby Reservists. Participation in voluntary training is for retirement points only and may be achieved by training with Selected Reserve or Voluntary Training units; by active duty for training; by completion of authorized military correspondence courses; by attending designated courses of instruction; by performing equivalent duty; by participating in special military and professional events designated by the Military Departments; or by participating in authorized Civil Defense activities. *See also:* Voluntary Training Unit.

References

Department of Defense, Joint Chiefs of Staff. *Department of Defense Dictionary of Military and Related Terms.* Washington, DC: GPO, 1986.

—**VOLUNTARY TRAINING UNIT** is a reserve unit formed by volunteers to provide inactive duty training in a nonpay status for individual Ready Reservists and active status Standby Reservists who are attached under competent orders and participate in such units for retirement points. *See also:* Voluntary Training.

References

Department of Defense, Joint Chiefs of Staff. *Department of Defense Dictionary of Military and Related Terms.* Washington, DC: GPO, 1986.

—**VOMITING AGENT** is a chemical agent that causes vomiting and may also cause coughing, sneezing, pain in the nose and throat, nasal discharge, or tears. Headaches often follow exposure to the agent. *See also:* Chemical Warfare.

References

Department of Defense, U.S. Army. *Dictionary of United States Army Terms.* Army Regulation AR 310-25. Washington, DC: Headquarters, Department of the Army, 1986.

—**V SERIES** (CHEMICAL AGENTS) are a group of toxic chemical agents that generally are colorless and odorless. In liquid or aerosol form, they affect the body in a manner that is similar to that of other nerve agents, such as G series agents. *See also:* Chemical Warfare.

References

Department of Defense, U.S. Army. *Dictionary of United States Army Terms.* Army Regulation AR 310-25. Washington, DC: Headquarters, Department of the Army, 1986.

—**VULCAN** is an Army air defense artillery gun that provides low-altitude air defense and has a direct fire capability against surface targets. The gun is a six-barreled, air-cooled, 20-mm rotary-fixed weapon. *See also:* Vulcan Gun M163, Vulcan Gun M167.

References

Department of Defense, Joint Chiefs of Staff. *Department of Defense Dictionary of Military and Related Terms.* Washington, DC: GPO, 1986.

—**VULCAN GUN M163** is a full-tracked, light-weight, lightly armored, six-barreled, 20-mm gun system designed for deployment in the forward combat area to provide air defense against the low-altitude air threat. *See also:* Vulcan Gun, Vulcan Gun M167.

References

Department of Defense, U.S. Army. *Air Defense Artillery Employment.* Field Manual FM 44-1. Washington, DC: Headquarters, Department of the Army, 1983.

—**VULCAN GUN M167** is a towed, six-barrel, 20-mm gun system designed for deployment in the forward area to provide air defense against the low-altitude air threat. *See also:* Vulcan Gun, Vulcan Gun M163.

References

Department of Defense, U.S. Army. *Air Defense Artillery Employment.* Field Manual FM 44-1. Washington, DC: Headquarters, Department of the Army, 1983.

—**VULNERABILITY.** (1) Vulnerability is a susceptibility in the presence of a threat. (Susceptibility in the absence of a threat does not constitute a vulnerability.) Vulnerabilities are those profiles which disclose indicators of a unit's planning or operational procedures that, unless adequate operations security procedures are implemented, will be detected by hostile collection resources. If collected, these vulnerabilities could comprise the unit's essential elements of friendly information, thus jeopardizing the success of the plan or operation. Vulnerabilities may include any activity that is undertaken by a military unit, and are determined by comparing the friendly force profile (all indicators key to the current operation) to the hostile collection threat. Time, date, location, and type of collector are the first important factors when considering vulnerability. (2) Vulnerability can be specified in the following manner. An *enemy vulnerability* is any condition or circumstance of the enemy situation or the area of operations that makes the enemy especially liable to damage, deception, or defeat. *National vulnerabilities* are those susceptibilities of a nation to any action, by any means, in peace or war through which its war potential may be reduced or its will to fight diminished. *See also:* Essential Elements of Friendly Information, Operations Security, Susceptibility.

References

Department of Defense, U.S. Army. *Counter-Signals Intelligence (C-SIGINT) OPERATIONS.* Field Manual FM 34-62. Washington, DC: Headquarters, Department of the Army, 1986.

———. *U.S. Army Operational Concept for Special Operations Forces.* TRADOC PAM 525-34. Washington, DC: Headquarters, Department of the Army, 1984.

—**VULNERABILITY PROGRAM** is a program conducted in order to determine the degree of, and to remedy insofar as possible, any existing susceptibility of nuclear weapons to enemy countermeasures, accidental fire, and accidental shock.

References

Department of Defense, Joint Chiefs of Staff. *Department of Defense Dictionary of Military and Related Terms.* Washington, DC: GPO, 1986.

—**VULNERABILITY STUDY** is an analysis of the capabilities and limitations of a force in a specific situation to determine those vulnerabilities that can be exploited by an opposing force. *See also:* Essential Elements of Friendly Information, Operations Security, Susceptibility, Vulnerability.

References

Department of Defense, Joint Chiefs of Staff. *Department of Defense Dictionary of Military and Related Terms.* Washington, DC: GPO, 1986.

—**VULNERABLE AREA** *See:* Vital Area.

—**VULNERABLE CRITICAL ELEMENTS** is a target intelligence term that pertains to the target to be destroyed. These elements are targeted for attack, because their destruction means the most economic, effective, and safe way to negate the principal functions of an installation, site, or entity. *See also:* Vulnerable Elements.

References

Department of Defense, Joint Chiefs of Staff. *Department of Defense Dictionary of Military and Related Terms.* Washington, DC: GPO, 1986.

—**VULNERABLE ELEMENTS** is a target intelligence term that pertains to the target to be destroyed. Such elements are susceptible to detection, identification, collection, or neutralization. *See also:* Vulnerable Critical Elements.

References

Department of Defense, Joint Chiefs of Staff. *Department of Defense Dictionary of Military and Related Terms.* Washington, DC: GPO, 1986.

—**VULNERABLE POINT.** *See:* Vital Area.

—**WALKING PATIENT** is a patient who does not require a litter while in transit to medical care. *See also:* Died of Wounds, Killed in Action, Wounded in Action.

References
Department of Defense, Joint Chiefs of Staff. *Department of Defense Dictionary of Military and Related Terms.* Washington, DC: GPO, 1986.

—**WALLOW COURSE,** or mud line slurry course, is a wide trench filled with a decontaminating chemical, usually chlorinated lime mixed with mud. Vehicles that have come in contact with chemical agents are driven through or wallowed through this trench so that they can be freed from the agents. *See also:* Chemical Warfare.

References
Department of Defense, U.S. Army. *Dictionary of United States Army Terms.* Army Regulation AR 310-25. Washington, DC: Headquarters, Department of the Army, 1986.

—**WAR CRIME** is a violation by an individual or an organization of the accepted laws and customs of war.

References
Department of Defense, U.S. Army. *Dictionary of United States Army Terms.* Army Regulation AR 310-25. Washington, DC: Headquarters, Department of the Army, 1986.

—**WAR DAMAGE REPAIR** are the actions, including emergency repair and restoration, taken to remedy the damage that was done to facilities by combat.

References
Department of Defense, U.S. Army. *Support Operations: Echelons Above Corps.* Field Manual FM 100-16. Washington, DC: Headquarters, Department of the Army, 1986.

—**WAR-FIGHTING** involves combat actions (as opposed to deterrence actions, which are intended to prevent rather than prosecute wars). *See also:* Deterrence.

References
Collins, John M. *U.S.-Soviet Military Balance, 1980-1985.* Washington, DC: Congressional Research Service, 1985.

—**WAR GAME** is a simulation of a military operation involving two or more opposing forces. In the game, rules, data, and procedures that are designed to depict an actual or assumed real life situation are used. *See also:* Exercise.

References
Department of Defense, Joint Chiefs of Staff. *Department of Defense Dictionary of Military and Related Terms.* Washington, DC: GPO, 1986.

—**WAR RESERVE MODE (WARM)** is an intentional change in observable electromagnetic emitter parameters or operational procedures that are intended to reduce the effectiveness of electronic warfare equipment or other detection, classification, and support activities of opposing forces. These modes are deliberately held in reserve for wartime or emergency use and are seldom if ever intercepted or observed prior to use. *See also:* Electronic Warfare.

References
Department of Defense, Joint Chiefs of Staff. *Department of Defense Dictionary of Military and Related Terms.* Washington, DC: GPO, 1986.

—**WAR RESERVE STOCKAGE LIST (WARSL)** is a listing of principal and secondary end-items that are authorized by command for stockage in war reserves for use by U.S. forces. The list is used to compute war reserve requirements that are essential to sustain combat or to support sudden mobilization requirements. It also may be used as the basis for selecting repair parts that are essential to supporting end-items in combat. *See also*: Operational Stocks; Other War Reserve Materiel Requirement; Other War Reserve Materiel Requirement, Balance; Other War Reserve Materiel Requirement, Protectable; Prepositioned Supplies; Prepositioned War Reserve Materiel Requirement, Balance; Prepositioned War Reserve Materiel Requirement, Protectable; Prepositioned War Reserve Materiel Requirement, Stocks; Prepositioning; Preposition of Materiel Configured to Unit Sets; War Reserve Stocks; War Reserve Storage Areas; War Reserves.

References

Department of Defense, U.S. Army. *Planning Logistics Support for Military Operations.* Field Manual FM 701-58. Washington, DC: Headquarters, Department of the Army, 1987.

———. *Repair Parts Supply for a Theater of Operations.* Field Manual FM 29-19. Washington, DC: Headquarters, Department of the Army, 1985.

—**WAR RESERVE STOCKS (WRS)** are established in strategic locations worldwide. These will provide an immediate supply of ammunition, weapons, fuel, and secondary items during the initial days of combat. They are intended for wartime consumption until the supply pipeline can be filled from U.S. depots and manufacturers. *See also:* War Reserve Stockage List.

References

Department of Defense, U.S. Army. *U.S. Army Policy Statement, 1988.* Washington, DC: Headquarters, Department of the Army, 1988.

—**WAR RESERVE STORAGE AREAS** are areas that have been designated by Headquarters, Department of the Army, for stockpiling war reserves in various specified states of preservation. *See also:* War Reserve Stockage List.

References

Department of Defense, U.S. Army. *Support Operations: Echelons Above Corps.* Field Manual FM 100-16. Washington, DC: Headquarters, Department of the Army, 1986.

—**WAR RESERVES** are stocks of materiel that are acquired in peacetime in order to meet the increased military requirements that will occur in wartime. These reserves are intended to provide support to sustain operations until wartime resupply can be accomplished. War reserve stocks are composed of (1) pre-positioned war materiel stocks, (2) CONSSTOCS, (3) priority mobilization war reserves for early mission reserve components, (4) full Army mobilization war reserves, (5) war reserve stocks for allies, (6) special contingency stockpile, (7) operational project stocks, and (8) other war reserve materiel stocks. *See also:* War Reserve Stockage List.

References

Department of Defense, U.S. Army. *Planning Logistics Support for Military Operations.* Field Manual FM 701-58. Washington, DC: Headquarters, Department of the Army, 1987.

—**WAR ROOM** is a room at headquarters where current information is maintained on situation maps or charts together with such other pertinent data as may be desired. It is primarily an orientation, briefing, and conference room. *See also:* National Military Command Center.

References

Department of Defense, U.S. Army. *Dictionary of United States Army Terms.* Army Regulation AR 310-25. Washington, DC: Headquarters, Department of the Army, 1986.

—**WAR SERVICE CHEVRON** is a V-shaped cloth device denoting service in a theater of operations between 1917 and 1920. A gold-colored chevron was awarded for each full six months of service and a blue-colored chevron was awarded for three months' of service or less. *See also:* Accouterment.

References

Department of Defense, U.S. Army. *Dictionary of United States Army Terms.* Army Regulation AR 310-25. Washington, DC: Headquarters, Department of the Army, 1986.

—**WARHEAD** is the part of a missile, projectile, torpedo, rocket, or other munition that contains either the nuclear or thermonuclear system, high-explosive system, chemical or biological agents, or inert materials that are intended to inflict damage. *See also:* Warhead Mating, Warhead Section.

References

Department of Defense, Joint Chiefs of Staff. *Department of Defense Dictionary of Military and Related Terms.* Washington, DC: GPO, 1986.

—**WARHEAD MATING** is the act of attaching a warhead section to a rocket or missile body, torpedo, airframe, motor, or guidance section. *See also:* Warhead, Warhead Section.

References

Department of Defense, Joint Chiefs of Staff. *Department of Defense Dictionary of Military and Related Terms.* Washington, DC: GPO, 1986.

—**WARHEAD SECTION** is a completely assembled warhead, including the appropriate skin sections and related components. *See also:* Warhead, Warhead Mating.

References

Department of Defense, Joint Chiefs of Staff. *Department of Defense Dictionary of Military and Related Terms.* Washington, DC: GPO, 1986.

—**WARN** refers to attack signals to alert personnel that they should take protective action to prevent chemical injuries. *See also:* Chemical Warfare.

References

Department of Defense, U.S. Army. *NBC Operations.* Field Manual FM 3-100. Washington, DC: Headquarters, Department of the Army, 1985.

—**WARNED EXPOSED** is the vulnerability of friendly forces to the effects of nuclear weapons. In this condition, personnel are assumed to be prone with all skin covered and with thermal protection of at least that which is provided by a two-layer summer uniform. *See also:* Unwarned Exposed, Warned Protected.

References

Department of Defense, Joint Chiefs of Staff. *Department of Defense Dictionary of Military and Related Terms.* Washington, DC: GPO, 1986.

—**WARNED PROTECTED** is the vulnerability of friendly forces to nuclear weapons effects. In this condition, personnel are assumed to have some protection against heat, blast, and radiation such as that afforded in closed armored vehicles or crouched in fox holes with improvised overhead shielding. *See also:* Unwarned Exposed, Warned Exposed.

References

Department of Defense, Joint Chiefs of Staff. *Department of Defense Dictionary of Military and Related Terms.* Washington, DC: GPO, 1986.

—**WARNING,** in indications and warning, is a notification of impending activities on the part of a foreign power or powers, including hostilities, that may affect U.S. military forces or security interests. *See also:* Indications and Warning.

References

Department of Defense, Joint Chiefs of Staff. *Department of Defense Dictionary of Military and Related Terms.* Washington, DC: GPO, 1986.

—**WARNING INTELLIGENCE,** in indications and warning, is an intelligence product upon which one can base or justify a notification of impending activities by foreign powers, including hostilities, that may adversely affect U.S. military forces or security interests. *See also:* Indications and Warning, Warning Intelligence Appraisal.

References

Department of Defense, Joint Chiefs of Staff. *Department of Defense Dictionary of Military and Related Terms.* Washington, DC: GPO, 1986.

—**WARNING INTELLIGENCE APPRAISAL** is produced by the Defense Intelligence Agency. It is an alerting document on a developing intelligence and warning situation, providing a more in-depth analysis and assessment than the Defense Intelligence Notice. The Warning Appraisal is prepared, printed, and disseminated on an urgent basis whenever a short assessment of an imminent development is of considerable interest to high-level U.S. officials. *See also:* Indications and Warning, Warning Intelligence.

References

Von Hoene, John P. A. *Intelligence User's Guide.* Washington, DC: DIA, 1983.

—**WARNING NET,** in intelligence and warning, is a communications system that is established to disseminate warning information of enemy movements or actions to all interested commands. *See also:* Indications and Warning, Warning Intelligence, Warning Intelligence Appraisal.

References

Von Hoene, John P.A. *Intelligence User's Guide.* Washington, DC: DIA, 1983.

—**WARNING ORDERS** are preliminary notices of actions or orders that are to follow. These are usually brief oral or written messages, and are intended to give subordinates the time to make the necessary plans and preparations.

References

Department of Defense, U.S. Army. *Operational Terms and Symbols.* Field Manual FM 101-5-1. Washington, DC: Headquarters, Department of the Army, 1985.

————. *Staff Organization and Operations.* Field Manual FM 101-5. Washington, DC: Headquarters, Department of the Army, 1986.

—**WARRANT OFFICER** is an officer who has been appointed, by warrant, by the Secretary of the Army. He is a highly skilled technician who is provided to fill a position above the enlisted level that is too specialized in scope to permit the effective development and continued utilization of a broadly trained, branch-qualified commissioned officer. His rank and precedence are below that of a second lieutenant, but above those of a cadet.

References
Department of Defense, U.S. Army. *Personnel Selection and Classification, Warrant Officer Occupational Specialties.* Army Regulation AR 611-112. Washington, DC: Headquarters, Department of the Army, 1987.

—**WATCH CENTER,** in indications and warning, is a center for the review of all incoming intelligence information and that possesses, or has access to, extensive communications for alerting local intelligence personnel and contacting appropriate external reporting sources and other nodes in the Department of Defense Indications and Warning System. *See also:* Indications and Warning, Warning Intelligence, Warning Intelligence Appraisal.

References
Von Hoene, John P.A. *Intelligence User's Guide.* Washington, DC: DIA, 1983.

—**WEAK SIDE** (ARMY AVIATION) is the side of a flight formation that provides the least protection against a threat. In an echelon right formation, the weak side is to the left.

References
Department of Defense, U.S. Army. *Air-to-Air Combat.* Field Manual FM 1-107. Washington, DC: Headquarters, Department of the Army, 1984.

—**WEAPON AND PAYLOAD IDENTIFICATION** is (1) the determination of the type of weapon that is being used in an attack; (2) the discrimination of a re-entry vehicle from penetration aids being used with the reentry vehicle. *See also:* Weapon System.

References
Department of Defense, Joint Chiefs of Staff. *Department of Defense Dictionary of Military and Related Terms.* Washington, DC: GPO, 1986.

—**WEAPON CONTROL STATUS.** *See:* Air Defense Weapons Control Status.

—**WEAPON DELIVERY** is the total action required to locate the target, establish the necessary release conditions, and maintain guidance to the target, if this is required. It includes detecting, recognizing, and acquiring the target, the weapon's release, and weapon guidance. *See also:* Weapon System.

References
Department of Defense, U.S. Army. *Dictionary of United States Army Terms.* Army Regulation AR 310-25. Washington, DC: Headquarters, Department of the Army, 1986.

—**WEAPON ENGAGEMENT ZONE (WEZ),** in air defense, is airspace of defined dimensions within which the responsibility for engagement normally rests with a particular air defense weapon system. Use of WEZs does not preclude engagement of high-priority targets by more than one type of weapon system if centralized control of each weapon system involved is available. Activating a WEZ can be used to delegate identification authority to respective subordinate units by specifying different (usually more stringent) hostile criteria within the WEZ than outside the WEZ. Commonly used WEZs include the fighter engagement zone, missile engagement zone, and short-range air defense engagement zone. *See also:* Air Defense, Fighter Engagement Zone, Missile Engagement Zone, Short-Range Air Defense Engagement Zone.

References
Department of Defense, U.S. Army. *Patriot Battalion Operations.* Field Manual FM 44-15. Washington, DC: Headquarters, Department of the Army, 1984.

—**WEAPON SELECTOR** is a circular scale used to relate nuclear damage radii to a target on a map. *See also:* Nuclear Warfare.

References
Department of Defense, U.S. Army. *Dictionary of United States Army Terms.* Army Regulation AR 310-25. Washington, DC: Headquarters, Department of the Army, 1986.

—**WEAPON SIGNATURE** is any smoke, vapor trail, noise, heat, flash, tracer, or flight characteristic that denotes a specific weapon system. *See also:* Signature.

References
Department of Defense, U.S. Army. *Operational Terms and Symbols.* Field Manual FM 101-5-1. Washington, DC: Headquarters, Department of the Army, 1985.

—**WEAPON SYSTEM** is a delivery vehicle and weapon combination including all related equipment, materials, services, and personnel required so that the system becomes self-sufficient in its intended operational environment. *See also:* Weapon and Payload Identification,

Weapon Delivery, Weapon System Employment Concept, Weapon System Management, Weapon System Replacement Operations, Weapons Assignment, Weapons List, Weapons Readiness State, Weapons Recommendation Sheet.

References

Department of Defense, U.S. Army. *Support Operations: Echelons Above Corps.* Field Manual FM 100-16. Washington, DC: Headquarters, Department of the Army, 1986.

—**WEAPON SYSTEM EMPLOYMENT CONCEPT** is a description in broad terms, based upon established outline characteristics, of the application of a particular equipment or weapon system within the framework of a tactical concept and future doctrines. *See also:* Weapon System.

References

Department of Defense, Joint Chiefs of Staff. *Department of Defense Dictionary of Military and Related Terms.* Washington, DC: GPO, 1986.

—**WEAPON SYSTEM MANAGEMENT** is the efficient and best use of the number of operational weapon systems required in the battalions of a division according to the command's or General Staff's fill priorities. *See also:* Weapon System.

References

Department of Defense, U.S. Army. *Combat Service Support Operations-Division.* Field Manual FM 63-2. Washington, DC: Headquarters, Department of the Army, 1983.

—**WEAPON SYSTEM REPLACEMENT OPERA-TIONS (WSRO)** is a management tool used to mate personnel and equipment at the communications zone or the corps or division support areas as a "ready to fight" weapon system. It is the management of the total weapon system, such as a tank, with its crew. It allows commanders to rapidly zero-in combat power at the decisive time and place on the battlefield. *See also:* Weapon System.

References

Department of Defense, U.S. Army. *Combat Service Support Operations-Division.* Field Manual FM 63-2. Washington, DC: Headquarters, Department of the Army, 1983.

————. *Support Operations: Echelons Above Corps.* Field Manual FM 100-16. Washington, DC: Headquarters, Department of the Army, 1986.

—**WEAPON-TARGET LINE** is an imaginary straight line from a weapon to a target.

References

Department of Defense, Joint Chiefs of Staff. *Department of Defense Dictionary of Military and Related Terms.* Washington, DC: GPO, 1986.

—**WEAPONS ASSIGNMENT,** in air defense, is the process by which weapons are assigned to individual air weapons controllers for use in accomplishing an assigned mission. *See also:* Weapon System.

References

Department of Defense, Joint Chiefs of Staff. *Department of Defense Dictionary of Military and Related Terms.* Washington, DC: GPO, 1986.

—**WEAPONS CONTROL STATUSES.** There are three degrees of weapons fire control that are used by the commander to control the fires of air defense weapons. They are WEAPONS FREE, WEAPONS TIGHT, and WEAPONS HOLD. *See also:* Weapons Free, Weapons Hold, Weapons Tight.

References

Department of Defense, U.S. Army. *Air Defense Artillery Employment.* Field Manual FM 44-1. Washington, DC: Headquarters, Department of the Army, 1983.

—**WEAPONS FREE,** in air defense, is a weapon control status that is used to indicate that weapons systems may be fired at any target that is not positively identified as friendly. *See also:* Weapons Control Statuses.

References

Department of Defense, U.S. Army. *Operational Terms and Symbols.* Field Manual FM 101-5-1. Washington, DC: Headquarters, Department of the Army, 1985.

—**WEAPONS HOLD,** in air defense, is a weapon control status that is used to indicate that weapons systems may be fired only in self-defense or in response to a formal order. *See also:* Weapons Control Statuses.

References

Department of Defense, U.S. Army. *Operational Terms and Symbols.* Field Manual FM 101-5-1. Washington, DC: Headquarters, Department of the Army, 1985.

—**WEAPONS LIST** is a list of weapons authorized and on hand within tactical or other units employed in a combat role. It includes hand-carried weapons, towed, artillery, and weapons mounted on wheeled or tracked vehicles. *See also:* Weapon System.

References
Department of Defense, U.S. Army. *Dictionary of United States Army Terms.* Army Regulation AR 310-25. Washington, DC: Headquarters, Department of the Army, 1986.

—**WEAPONS OF MASS DESTRUCTION,** in arms control usage, are weapons that are capable of massive destruction and of killing large numbers of people. These can be nuclear, chemical, biological, and radiological weapons. The term excludes the means of transporting or propelling the weapon where such means are a separable and divisible part of the weapon. *See also:* Biological Warfare, Chemical Warfare, Nuclear Warfare.

References
Department of Defense, Joint Chiefs of Staff. *Department of Defense Dictionary of Military and Related Terms.* Washington, DC: GPO, 1986.

—**WEAPONS READINESS STATE** is the degree of readiness of air defense weapons that can become airborne or be launched to carry out an assigned task. Weapons readiness states are expressed in numbers of weapons and numbers of minutes. Weapons readiness states are defined as follows:

- **Two minutes**—Weapons can be released within two minutes.
- **Five minutes**—Weapons can be released within five minutes.
- **Fifteen minutes**—Weapons can be released within fifteen minutes.
- **Thirty minutes**—Weapons can be released within thirty minutes.
- **One hour**—Weapons can be released within one hour.
- **Three hours**—Weapons can be released within three hours.
- **Released**—Weapons are released from defense commitment for a specified period of time.

See also: Weapon System.

References
Department of Defense, Joint Chiefs of Staff. *Department of Defense Dictionary of Military and Related Terms.* Washington, DC: GPO, 1986.

—**WEAPONS RECOMMENDATION SHEET (WRS)** is a sheet or chart that defines the intention of the attack and recommends the nature of weapons and resulting damage that is expected, as well as the tonnage, fuzing, spacing, desired mean points of impact, and intervals of reattack. *See also:* Weapon System.

References
Department of Defense, Joint Chiefs of Staff. *Department of Defense Dictionary of Military and Related Terms.* Washington, DC: GPO, 1986.

—**WEAPONS TIGHT,** in air defense, is a weapon control status that is used to indicate that weapons systems may be fired only at targets identified as hostile. *See also:* Weapons Control Statuses.

References
Department of Defense, U.S. Army. *Operational Terms and Symbols.* Field Manual FM 101-5-1. Washington, DC: Headquarters, Department of the Army, 1985.

—**WEAR** is the change in the internal measurements of a barrel of a weapon that results from firing. *See also:* Wear Tables.

References
Department of Defense, U.S. Army. *Dictionary of United States Army Terms.* Army Regulation AR 310-25. Washington, DC: Headquarters, Department of the Army, 1986.

—**WEAR TABLES** are tables indicating the decreases in muzzle velocity that are expected as the result of tube wear due to firing. *See also:* Wear.

References
Department of Defense, U.S. Army. *Dictionary of United States Army Terms.* Army Regulation AR 310-25. Washington, DC: Headquarters, Department of the Army, 1986.

—**WEATHER (VAT B)** is a short form weather report that gives the following:
V—visibility in miles.
A—amount of clouds in eights.
T—height of cloud top, in thousands of feet.
B—height of cloud base, in thousands of feet.
(The reply is a series of four numbers preceded by the word "weather." An unknown item is reported as "unknown.") *See also:* Visibility, Weather Information, Weather Intelligence, Weather Minimum.

References
Department of Defense, Joint Chiefs of Staff. *Department of Defense Dictionary of Military and Related Terms.* Washington, DC: GPO, 1986.

—**WEATHER INFORMATION** is information concerning the state of the atmosphere and its military implications. It is data concerning forecasts, summaries, and climatology. *See also:* Visibility, Weather VAT (B), Weather Information, Weather Intelligence, Weather Minimum.

References
Department of Defense, U.S. Army. *Weather Support for Army Tactical Operations.* Field Manual FM 34-81. Washington, DC: Headquarters, Department of the Army, 1984.

—**WEATHER INTELLIGENCE** is an analysis of the effect of weather on the plans and operations of both friendly and enemy forces. *See also:* Weather Information.

References
Department of Defense, U.S. Army. *Weather Support for Army Tactical Operations.* Field Manual FM 34-81. Washington, DC: Headquarters, Department of the Army, 1984.

—**WEATHER MINIMUM** is the worst weather conditions under which aviation operations may be conducted under either visual or instrument flight rules. It is usually prescribed by directives and standing operating procedures in terms of minimum ceiling, visibility, or specific hazards to flight. *See also:* Weather Information.

References
Department of Defense, Joint Chiefs of Staff. *Department of Defense Dictionary of Military and Related Terms.* Washington, DC: GPO, 1986.

—**WEATHER SUPPORT** includes weather observing, forecasting, briefings, climatological support, and solar geophysical data. *See also:* Weather Information.

References
Department of Defense, U.S. Army. *Dictionary of United States Army Terms.* Army Regulation AR 310-25. Washington, DC: Headquarters, Department of the Army, 1986.

—**WEATHER SUPPORT FORCE** is the air weather service organization that provides joint weather support to the Army and Air Force in the field. *See also:* Weather Information.

References
Department of Defense, U.S. Army. *Weather Support for Army Tactical Operations.* Field Manual FM 34-81. Washington, DC: Headquarters, Department of the Army, 1984.

—**WEATHER SUPPORT PRODUCTS** include weather observations, forecasts of general weather conditions, specific meteorological data elements, solar geophysical information, climatological studies and analyses, and weather briefings. *See also:* Weather Information.

References
Department of Defense, U.S. Army. *Dictionary of United States Army Terms.* Army Regulation AR 310-25. Washington, DC: Headquarters, Department of the Army, 1986.

—**WEATHERING** is gradual decontamination by evaporating or decomposing the chemical agent. *See also:* Chemical Warfare.

References
Department of Defense, U.S. Army. *NBC Operations.* Field Manual FM 3-100. Washington, DC: Headquarters, Department of the Army, 1985.

—**WEDGE** is a formation of vehicles or personnel that (1) permits excellent fire to the front and good fire to each flank, (2) facilitates control, (3) permits sustained effort and provides flank security, (4) lends itself readily to fire and movement, and (5) is often used when the enemy situation is vague and contact is imminent. *See also:* Column, Line, Vee.

References
Department of Defense, U.S. Army. *Operational Terms and Symbols.* Field Manual FM 101-5-1. Washington, DC: Headquarters, Department of the Army, 1985.

—**WEIGHTING** involves the actions taken by the commander to increase the capabilities of a unit (e.g., allocating additional forces, allocating priorities of fire, or reducing the size of the unit's area of responsibility).

References
Department of Defense, U.S. Army. *Operational Terms and Symbols.* Field Manual FM 101-5-1. Washington, DC: Headquarters, Department of the Army, 1985.

—**WELFARE FUNDS** are nonappropriated funds that are established and maintained primarily from income derived from revenue-producing activities. They are used to supplement morale, welfare, and recreational facilities and services provided from appropriated funds. Recreation-type articles and services procured from these funds may be used concurrently by military personnel and their family members. They may be used specifically for military personnel minor family members when such expenditures are secondary in priority to recreational requirements for military personnel. In overseas areas, these funds may also be expended for the incidental benefit of civilian employees and their family members. Civilian welfare funds are used to provide certain recreational and limited welfare services considered essential by an installation commander to the morale of civilian personnel. Welfare funds also may be established for prisoners in correctional facilities.

References
Department of Defense, U.S. Army. *Dictionary of United States Army Terms.* Army Regulation AR 310-25. Washington, DC: Headquarters, Department of the Army, 1986.

—**WET-BULB-GLOBE TEMPERATURE (WBGT) INDEX** is an indicator of the loss of physical effectiveness that is due to a combination of temperature, humidity, and wind. *See also:* Wet-Bulb-Temperature.

References
Department of Defense, U.S. Army. *Weather Support for Army Tactical Operations.* Field Manual FM 34-81. Washington, DC: Headquarters, Department of the Army, 1984.

—**WET-BULB-TEMPERATURE** is the lowest temperature to which air can be cooled by evaporating water into it at constant pressure, when the heat required for evaporation is supplied by the cooling of the air. The temperature is given by a well-ventilated, wet-bulb thermometer. *See also:* Wet-Bulb-Globe-Temperature Index.

References
Department of Defense, U.S. Army. *Weather Support for Army Tactical Operations.* Field Manual FM 34-81. Washington, DC: Headquarters, Department of the Army, 1984.

—**WHAT STATE** (Army Aviation) is a report of the amount of armament and fuel remaining. For example, two Alphas (Stinger missiles), four Bravos (TOW missiles), three Charlies (HELLFIRE missiles), two Deltas (gunshots times 100), and 500 pounds (fuel) or time in hours and minutes (zero plus three zero).

References
Department of Defense, U.S. Army. *Air-to-Air Combat.* Field Manual FM 1-107. Washington, DC: Headquarters, Department of the Army, 1984.

—**WHITE LISTS** contain the identities and locations of individuals who have been identified as being of intelligence or counterintelligence interest and are expected to be able to provide information or assistance in existing or new areas of intelligence interest. They are usually in accord with, or are favorably inclined toward, U.S. policies. Their contributions are based upon a voluntary and cooperative attitude. Decisions to place individuals on the white list may be affected by the combat situation, critical need for specialists in scientific fields, and periodic theater intelligence needs. Examples of individuals who may be included in this category are (1) former political leaders of a hostile state who were deposed by the hostile political leaders; (2) intelligence agents who are employed by the United States or by allied intelligence agencies; (3) key civilians in areas of scientific research, which may include faculty members of universities and staffs of industrial or national research facilities, whose bonafides have been established; (4) leaders of religious groups and other humanitarian groups; and (5) other persons who can materially and significantly aid the political, scientific, and military objectives of the United States and whose bonafides have been established. *See also:* Black Lists, Gray Lists.

References
Department of Defense, U.S. Army. *Counterintelligence.* Field Manual FM 34-60. Washington, DC: Headquarters, Department of the Army, 1985.

—**WHITE PHOSPHORUS (WP)** is a yellow, waxy chemical that ignites spontaneously when it is exposed to the air. It is used as a filling for various projectiles, and as a smoke-producing agent. It has an incendiary effect. *See also:* Smoke Screen.

References
Department of Defense, U.S. Army. *Dictionary of United States Army Terms.* Army Regulation AR 310-25. Washington, DC: Headquarters, Department of the Army, 1986.

—**WHOLE BODY DOSE** is the total amount of ionizing radiation that has been received by a person. *See also:* Nuclear Warfare.

References

Department of Defense, U.S. Army. *Technical Escort Operations*. Field Manual FM 3-20. Washington, DC: Headquarters, Department of the Army, 1981.

—**WILCO** is a radiotelephone procedure proword that means "I have received your message, understand it, and will comply." *See also:* Acknowledge.

References

Department of Defense, U.S. Army. *The Rifle Squads (Mechanized and Light Infantry)*. Training Circular TC 7-1. Washington, DC: Headquarters, Department of the Army, 1976.

—**WINDAGE JUMP** is a velocity jump that is due to the cross-wind coupling with muzzle velocity. It usually is a very small error with fixed gunnery, but may have a large effect in flexible gunnery. *See also:* Wind Sensitivity.

References

Department of Defense, U.S. Army. *Dictionary of United States Army Terms*. Army Regulation AR 310-25. Washington, DC: Headquarters, Department of the Army, 1986.

—**WINDAGE SCALE,** or wind gauge, is a scale of adjusting a sight to allow for the effect of wind on a bullet in flight. *See also*: Wind Sensitivity.

References

Department of Defense, U.S. Army. *Dictionary of United States Army Terms*. Army Regulation AR 310-25. Washington, DC: Headquarters, Department of the Army, 1986.

—**WINDCHILL FACTOR** (INDEX) is the cooling effect of any combination of temperature and wind that is expressed as the loss of body heat in kilogram calories per hour per square meter of skin surface. *See also:* Weather Information.

References

Department of Defense, U.S. Army. *Weather Support for Army Tactical Operations*. Field Manual FM 34-81. Washington, DC: Headquarters, Department of the Army, 1984.

—**WIRE ENTANGLEMENT** is an obstacle of barbed wire. It is used to hold the enemy to areas that can be covered by gunfire, and to delay or prevent an assault. *See also:* Wire Roll.

References

Department of Defense, U.S. Army. *Dictionary of United States Army Terms*. Army Regulation AR 310-25. Washington, DC: Headquarters, Department of the Army, 1986.

—**WIRE HEAD** is the forward limit of telephone or telegraph communications in a command.

References

Department of Defense, U.S. Army. *Dictionary of United States Army Terms*. Army Regulation AR 310-25. Washington, DC: Headquarters, Department of the Army, 1986.

—**WIRE ROLL** is an antimechanized barrier consisting of a roll of steel wire wound in a continuous spiral which becomes entangled in, and jams, the propelling wheels or tracks of a vehicle. It is a wire roll that is similar to a concertina. *See also:* Wire Entanglement.

References

Department of Defense, U.S. Army. *Dictionary of United States Army Terms*. Army Regulation AR 310-25. Washington, DC: Headquarters, Department of the Army, 1986.

—**WITHDRAWAL NOT UNDER PRESSURE** occurs when a unit disengages and moves to the rear while the enemy is not attacking. The unit must be ready to fight its way to the rear or to resume the defense if the enemy attacks. A withdrawal not under pressure is conducted with secrecy and deception. It is best done at night or during other periods of limited visibility (e.g., fog, snow, rain, or smoke). Usually all platoons move to the rear at the same time. However, the company leaves a security force (formerly called the detachment left in contact), which is part of the battalion security force, to cover the withdrawal by deception and by fire and maneuver when required. *See also:* Withdrawal to the Objective Rally Point; Withdrawal Under Pressure.

References

Department of Defense, U.S. Army. *The Infantry Rifle Company (Infantry, Airborne, Air Assault, Ranger)*. Field Manual FM 7-10. Washington, DC: Headquarters, Department of the Army, 1982.

—**WITHDRAWAL TO THE OBJECTIVE RALLY POINT.** The objective rally point is far enough from the ambush site that it will not be overrun if the enemy attacks the ambush. Routes of withdrawal to the objective rally point are reconnoitered. If the situation permits, each man walks the route that he is to use and picks out checkpoints. When the ambush is to be executed at night, each man must be able to follow his route in the dark. *See also:* Withdrawal Not Under Pressure.

References
Department of Defense, U.S. Army. *The Rifle Squads (Mechanized and Light Infantry)*. Training Circular TC 7-1. Washington, DC: Headquarters, Department of the Army, 1976.

—WITHDRAWAL UNDER PRESSURE is conducted when a unit is directed to withdraw from a sector or is forced from its defensive positions by the enemy. In a withdrawal under pressure, the company disengages and moves to the rear while the enemy is attacking. The company disengages by fighting its way to the rear. The unit may move to another position to continue the defense or may disengage and move elsewhere for another mission. Each company tries to disengage from the enemy by fire and maneuver to the rear. Once a company has disengaged and moved to the rear of its original position, the battalion commander directs what it is to do next. This may include covering the rearward movement of other companies, occupying a new defensive position, or moving to perform another mission. *See also:* Withdrawal Not Under Pressure.

References
Department of Defense, U.S. Army. *The Infantry Rifle Company (Infantry, Airborne, Air Assault, Ranger)*. Field Manual FM 7-10. Washington, DC: Headquarters, Department of the Army, 1982.

—WITHDRAWALS. Commanders conduct withdrawals to remove subordinate units from combat, adjust defensive positions, or relocate their entire force. Whether withdrawing locally or as a part of a general withdrawal, committed forces voluntarily disengage from the enemy and move to the rear. Withdrawals may be conducted under or free from enemy pressure and with or without the assistance of friendly units. Whatever the case, withdrawals will always begin under the threat of enemy interference. *See also:* Delaying Operation, Disengagement, Retirement, Retrograde, Withdrawal Not Under Pressure, Withdrawal to the Objective Rally Point, Withdrawal Under Pressure.

References
Department of Defense, U.S. Army. *Armored and Mechanized Division Operations*. Field Manual FM 71-100. Washington, DC: Headquarters, Department of the Army, 1978.

———. *Operational Terms and Symbols*. Field Manual FM 101-5-1. Washington, DC: Headquarters, Department of the Army, 1985.

———. *Operations*. Field Manual FM 100-5. Washington, DC: Headquarters, Department of the Army, 1986.

—WITHHOLD (NUCLEAR) is the limiting authority to use nuclear weapons by denying their use within specified geographical areas or certain countries. *See also:* Nuclear Warfare.

References
Department of Defense, Joint Chiefs of Staff. *Department of Defense Dictionary of Military and Related Terms*. Washington, DC: GPO, 1986.

—WORKBOOK is an informal, indexed collection of information that is obtained from written or oral orders, messages, journal entries, and conferences. A staff workbook aids in the staff officer's information collection effort, assists in maintaining a current estimate of the situation in the particular staff officer's field of interest, and serves as a ready reference for preparing plans, orders and reports. *See also:* Journal.

References
Department of Defense, U.S. Army. *Staff Organization and Operations*. Field Manual FM 101-5. Washington, DC: Headquarters, Department of the Army, 1986.

—WORK ORDER (WO) is a specific or blanket authorization to perform certain work. It is usually broader in scope than a job order, but is sometimes used synonymously with job order.

References
Department of Defense, Joint Chiefs of Staff. *Department of Defense Dictionary of Military and Related Terms*. Washington, DC: GPO, 1986.

—WORLDWIDE MILITARY COMMAND AND CONTROL SYSTEM (WWMCCS), according to the Joint Chiefs of Staff, is "the system that provides the means for operational direction and technical administrative support involved in the function of command and control of U.S. military forces." Components of the system are (1) the National Military Command System; (2) the WWMCCS-related management/information systems of the headquarters of the military departments; (3) the command and control systems of the headquarters of the Service component commands; and (4) the command and control support systems of Department of Defense agencies.

The requirement for the system was identified in the Defense Reorganization Act of 1958, and was subsequently formalized as a system that established a set of command and control capabilities that were to support the national command authorities, the Joint Chiefs of Staff, and the major field commanders. The goal of the system was to assure effective connectivity among the national command authorities, Joint Chiefs of Staff, and other components of the National Military Command System down to the service component commanders.

The system provides a multipath channel of secure communications to transmit information from primary sources to those who must make decisions (including the President) and to transmit their decisions, in the form of military orders, to their subordinates.

WWMCCS is not a single system, nor are there plans for it to become one. It is a system of systems that range from the national to the theater level. Some of the systems are unique to WWMCCS, but most were designed, developed, bought, and used to satisfy the command and control requirements of the services or the commands that normally use them. Their primary function is to support the national level command and control function.

There are five elements of the WWMCCS: warning systems; communications; data collection and processing; executive aids; and facilities. Each of these permeates various levels of command and control, and together, their operation forms a worldwide information system. Finally, the system supports four basic functional areas: resource and unit monitoring; conventional planning and execution; nuclear planning and execution; and tactical warning and attack assessment. *See also:* Indications and Warning, Worldwide Warning Indicator Monitoring System.

References

Department of Defense, National Defense University, *Joint Staff Officer's Guide, 1986.* Washington, DC: GPO, 1986.

Department of Defense, U.S. Army. *Planning Logistics Support for Military Operations.* Field Manual FM 701-58. Washington, DC: Headquarters, Department of the Army, 1987.

—**WOUND CHEVRON** is a gold-colored cloth design shaped like a V, to indicate wounds received in action in World War I. It is worn with its point down on the lower part of the right sleeve. *See also:* Accouterment.

References

Department of Defense, U.S. Army. *Dictionary of United States Army Terms.* Army Regulation AR 310-25. Washington, DC: Headquarters, Department of the Army, 1986.

—**WOUNDED IN ACTION (WIA)** is a battle casualty other than "killed in action" who has received an injury from an external agent or cause. The term encompasses all types of wounds and other injuries that are received in action, where there is a piercing of the body, as in a penetrating or perforated wound, or none, as in a contused wound. All fractures, blast concussions, effects of chemical or biological warfare agents, effects of ionizing radiation, or any other destructive weapon or agent are also included. Battle casualties who require admission to a military treatment facility or who die of their wounds after reaching one are reported as WIA. The WIA category includes the died of wounds received in action, but excludes the killed in action. Individual medical records and morbidity reports that are received by the Surgeon General include, in addition to WIA, all other individuals wounded or injured in action and treated at military treatment facilities without requiring hospital admission. This includes persons admitted and then returned to duty at military treatment facilities forward of the corps level hospitals as well as persons who are treated on an outpatient status. *See also:* Died of Wounds, Killed in Action.

References

Department of Defense, U.S. Army. *Planning Logistics Support for Military Operations.* Field Manual FM 701-58. Washington, DC: Headquarters, Department of the Army, 1987.

—**WRONG** is a proword meaning, "Your last transmission was incorrect, the correct version is _____." *See also:* Proword.

References

Department of Defense, Joint Chiefs of Staff. *Department of Defense Dictionary of Military and Related Terms.* Washington, DC: GPO, 1986.

—**ZENITH** is the point in the celestial sphere exactly overhead (as opposed to nadir). *See also:* Nadir.

References

Department of Defense, Joint Chiefs of Staff. *Department of Defense Dictionary of Military and Related Terms.* Washington, DC: GPO, 1986.

—**ZERO DEFLECTION** is the adjustment of a sight exactly parallel to the axis of the bore of the gun to which it is attached.

References

Department of Defense, U.S. Army. *Dictionary of United States Army Terms.* Army Regulation AR 310-25. Washington, DC: Headquarters, Department of the Army, 1986.

—**ZERO HEIGHT OF BURST** is the condition obtained when rounds fired with the same fuze setting and the same quadrant elevation result in an equal number of airs and grazes.

References

Department of Defense, U.S. Army. *Dictionary of United States Army Terms.* Army Regulation AR 310-25. Washington, DC: Headquarters, Department of the Army, 1986.

—**ZEROING** establishes a definite relationship between the trajectory of a given round and the line of sight at the zero range. It is the next logical step to boresighting any weapon. With a properly zeroed weapon, the trajectory of a given round will intersect the line of sight at the zero range.

References

Department of Defense, U.S. Army. *Tank Gunnery.* Field Manual FM 17-2-C2. Washington, DC: Headquarters, Department of the Army, 1980.

—**ZIPPER** (ARMY AVIATION) is two clicks of a mike button that is used to acknowledge instructions.

References

Department of Defense, U.S. Army. *Air-to-Air Combat.* Field Manual FM 1-107. Washington, DC: Headquarters, Department of the Army, 1984.

—**ZONE I** (NUCLEAR) is a circular area, determined by using minimum safe distance I as a radius and the desired ground zero as the center, from which all armed forces are evacuated. If the evacuation is not possible or if a commander elects a higher degree of risk, maximum protective measures will be required. *See also:* Zone II (Nuclear); Zone III (Nuclear).

References

Department of Defense, Joint Chiefs of Staff. *Department of Defense Dictionary of Military and Related Terms.* Washington, DC: GPO, 1986.

—**ZONE II** (NUCLEAR) is a circular area (less zone I), determined by using minimum safe distance II as a radius and the desired ground zero as the center, in which all personnel require maximum protection. Maximum protection denotes that armed forces personnel are in "buttoned up" tanks or crouched in foxholes with improvised overhead shielding. *See also:* Zone I (Nuclear); Zone III (Nuclear).

References

Department of Defense, Joint Chiefs of Staff. *Department of Defense Dictionary of Military and Related Terms.* Washington, DC: GPO, 1986.

—**ZONE III** (NUCLEAR) is a circular area (less zones I and II), determined by using minimum safe distance III as the radius and the desired ground zero as the center, in which all personnel require minimum protection. Minimum protection denotes that armed forces personnel are prone on open ground with all skin areas covered and with an overall thermal protection at least equal to that provided by a two-layer uniform. *See also:* Zone I (Nuclear); Zone II (Nuclear).

References

Department of Defense, Joint Chiefs of Staff. *Department of Defense Dictionary of Military and Related Terms.* Washington, DC: GPO, 1986.

—**ZONE FIRE** is composed of field artillery fires delivered in a constant direction at several quadrant elevations. *See also:* Area Fire.

References

Department of Defense, U.S. Army. *Fire Support in Combined Arms Operations.* Field Manual FM 6-20. Washington, DC: Headquarters, Department of the Army, 1983.

—**ZONE OF ACTION** is a tactical subdivision of a larger area, the responsibility for which is assigned to a tactical unit. A zone of action is generally applied to offensive action.

References

Department of Defense, U.S. Army. *Operational Terms and Symbols.* Field Manual FM 101-5-1. Washington, DC: Headquarters, Department of the Army, 1985.

—**ZONE OF CONSIDERATION** pertains to commissioned and warrant officers who are on active duty and are eligible for promotion. Eligibility is based upon date of rank or longevity and the zone consists of period of time with specific dates. The zone consists of the promotion zone, above the zone, and below the zone. *See also:* Above the Zone; Below the Zone.

References

Department of Defense, U.S. Army. *Promotion of Officers on Active Duty.* Army Regulation AR 624-100. Washington, DC: Headquarters, Department of the Army, 1984.

—**ZONE OF FIRE** is an area within which a designated ground unit or fire support ship delivers, or is prepared to deliver, fire support. Fire may or may not be observed.

References

Department of Defense, Joint Chiefs of Staff. *Department of Defense Dictionary of Military and Related Terms.* Washington, DC: GPO, 1986.

—**ZONE OF INTERIOR (ZI)** is the part of the national territory that is not included in the theater of operations.

References

Department of Defense, U.S. Army. *Dictionary of United States Army Terms.* Army Regulation AR 310-25. Washington, DC: Headquarters, Department of the Army, 1986.

—**ZONE RECONNAISSANCE** is a directed effort to obtain detailed information concerning all routes, obstacles (including chemical or radiological contamination), terrain, and enemy forces within a zone defined by boundaries. A zone reconnaissance normally is assigned when the enemy situation is vague or when information concerning cross-country trafficability is desired. *See also:* Area Reconnaissance; Route Reconnaissance.

References

Department of Defense, U.S. Army. *Operational Terms and Symbols.* Field Manual FM 101-5-1. Washington, DC: Headquarters, Department of the Army, 1985.

—**ZULU TIME (Z)** is Greenwich Mean Time. *See also:* Local Mean Time.

References

Department of Defense, Joint Chiefs of Staff. *Department of Defense Dictionary of Military and Related Terms.* Washington, DC: GPO, 1986.

Bibliography

Allen, Thomas B., and Polmar, Norman. *Merchants of Treason: America's Secrets for Sale.* New York: Delacorte Press, 1988.

American Bar Association. *Oversight and Accountability of the U.S. Intelligence Agencies: An Evaluation.* Washington, DC: ABA, 1985.

Bamford, James. *The Puzzle Palace: A Report on America's Most Secret Agency.* New York: Penguin Books, 1983.

Becket, Henry S.A. *The Dictionary of Espionage: Spookspeak Into English.* New York: Stein and Day, 1986.

Blackburn, N. Glenn. "Computers: A Counterintelligence Concern." Unpublished paper provided to the editors. Washington, DC: 1987.

Breckenridge, Scott D. *The CIA and the U.S. Intelligence System.* Boulder, CO: Westview Press, 1986.

Clancy, Tom. *The Cardinal of the Kremlin.* New York: Putnam, 1988.

Collins, John M. *U.S.-Soviet Military Balance, 1980-1985.* Washington, DC: Congressional Research Service, 1985.

Corson, William R. *The Armies of Ignorance: The Rise of the American Intelligence Empire.* New York: Dial Press, 1977.

Deacon, Richard. *Spyclopedia: An Encyclopedia of Spies, Secret Services, Operations, Jargon, and All Subjects Related to the World of Espionage.* London: MacDonald, 1987.

Godson, Roy, ed. *Intelligence Problems for the 1980s, Number 1: Elements of Intelligence.* Rev. ed. Washington, DC: National Strategy Information Center, 1983.

Hoffschmidt, E.J., and Tantum, W.H., eds. *Tank Data 2.* Old Greenwich, CT: WE, Inc., 1966.

———. *Intelligence Problems for the 1980s, Number 3: Counterintelligence.* Washington, DC: National Strategy Information Center, 1980.

———. *Intelligence Problems for the 1980s, Number 4: Covert Action.* Washington, DC: National Strategy Information Center, 1981.

———. *Intelligence Problems for the 1980s, Number 5: Clandestine Collection.* Washington, DC: National Strategy Information Center, 1982.

Kent, Sherman. *Strategic Intelligence for American World Policy.* Princeton, NJ: Princeton University Press, 1966.

Kessler, Ronald. *Spy vs. Spy: Stalking Soviet Spies in America.* New York: Charles Scribner's Sons, 1988.

Laqueur, Walter. *A World of Secrets.* New York: Basic Books, 1985.

Lowenthal, Mark M. *U.S. Intelligence: Evolution and Anatomy.* New York: Praeger, 1984.

Martin, Paul H. "Communications-Computer Security." *Journal of Electronic Defense* (June 1987).

Maurer, Alfred C.; Turnstall, Marion D.; and Keagle, James M. *Intelligence Policy and Process.* Boulder, CO: Westview Press, 1985.

Muzerall, Joseph V., and Carty, Thomas P. "COMSEC and Its Need for Key Management." *DP&CS* (Spring 1987).

Oseth, John M. "Intelligence and Low Intensity Conflict." *Naval War and College Review.* (Nov.-Dec. 1984): 19-36.

———. *Regulating U.S. Intelligence Operations: A Study in the Definition of the National Interest.* Frankfurt, KY: University of Kentucky Press, 1985.

Poyer, David. *The Med.* New York: St. Martin's Press, 1988.

Reeves, Robert; Anson, Abraham; and Landen, David. *Manual of Remote Sensing.* Falls Church, VA: American Society of Photogrammetry, 1975.

Treverton, Gregory F. *Covert Action: The Limits of Intervention in the Postwar World.* New York: Basic Books, 1987.

Turner, Stansfield. *Secrecy and Democracy: The CIA in Transition.* Boston: Houghton Mifflin, 1985.

Ware, Willis H. "Information Systems, Security, and Privacy." *EDUCOM Bulletin* (Summer 1984).

Watson, Bruce W., and Dunn, Peter M., eds. *American Intervention in Grenada: The Implications of Operation "Urgent Fury."* Boulder, Colorado: Westview Press, 1985.

Weapons Systems: U.S. Army, Navy, and Air Force Directory, 1986-1988. Washington, DC: DCP, 1986.

Government Documents

Clauser, Jerome K., and Weir, Sandra M. *Intelligence Research Methodology.* State College, PA: HRB-Singer, Inc., 1975.

Department of Defense. *Activities of DoD Intelligence Components That Affect U.S. Persons.* (Department of Defense Directive 5240.1) Washington, DC: Department of Defense, 1982.

Department of Defense. Defense Intelligence Agency. *Training Compendium for General Defense Career Development Program (IDCP) Personnel DOD 1430.10M3-TNG.* Washington, DC: DIA, 1986.

Department of Defense, Defense Intelligence College. *Glossary of Intelligence Terms and Definitions.* Washington, DC: DIC, 1987.

Department of Defense. Information Security Oversight Office. *Directive No. 1: National Security Information.* (Reprinted in *Federal Register,* June 25, 1982, at 27836-27841.)

Department of Defense, Joint Chiefs of Staff. *Department of Defense Dictionary of Military and Related Terms.* Washington, DC: GPO, 1986.

Department of Defense, National Defense University. *Joint Staff Officer's Guide, 1986.* Washington, DC: GPO, 1986.

Department of Defense, U.S. Army, Headquarters, U.S. Army Intelligence and Security Command. *INSCOM: United States Army Intelligence and Security Command.* Arlington Hall Station, VA: Public Affairs Office, U.S. Army Intelligence and Security Command, 1985.

Department of Defense, U.S. Army. *AIA: Threat Analysis.* Falls Church, VA: U.S. Army Intelligence Agency, 1987.

————. *Air Cavalry Combat Brigade.* Field Manual FM 17-47. Washington, DC: Headquarters, Department of the Army, 1982.

————. *Air Defense Artillery Deployment: Chaparral/Vulcan/ Stinger.* Field Manual FM 44-3. Washington, DC: Headquarters, Department of the Army, 1984.

————. *Air-to-Air Combat.* Field Manual FM 1-107. Washington, DC: Headquarters, Department of the Army, 1984.

————. *Airspace Management and Army Air Traffic in a Combat Zone.* Field Manual FM 1-60. Washington, DC: Headquarters, Department of the Army, 1977.

————. *Ammunition and Explosives Safety Standards.* Army Regulation AR 385-64. Washington, DC: Headquarters, Department of the Army, 1987.

————. *Ammunition Handbook.* Field Manual FM 9-13. Washington, DC: Headquarters, Department of the Army, 1981.

————. *Armored and Mechanized Division Operations.* Field Manual FM 71-100. Washington, DC: Headquarters, Department of the Army, 1978.

————. *The Army* (Prepublication Issue.) Field Manual FM 100-1. Washington, DC: Headquarters, Department of the Army, 1986.

————. *Army Exercises.* Army Regulation AR 350-28. Washington, DC: Headquarters, Department of the Army, 1985.

————. *Army Forces in Amphibious Operations.* Field Manual FM 31-12. Washington, DC: Headquarters, Department of the Army, 1961.

————. *Army Forces Training.* Army Regulation AR 350-41. Washington, DC: Headquarters, Department of the Army, 1986.

————. *Army Reenlistment Program.* Army Regulation AR 601-28. Washington, DC: Headquarters, Department of the Army, 1984.

————. *The Army Terrorism Counteraction Program.* Army Regulation AR 525-13. Washington, DC: Headquarters, Department of the Army, 1988.

————. *Attack Helicopter Operations.* Field Manual FM 17-50. Washington, DC: Headquarters, Department of the Army, 1984.

————. *Cavalry.* Field Manual FM 17-95. Washington, DC: Headquarters, Department of the Army, 1977.

————. *The Chaplain and Chaplain Assistant in Combat Operations.* Field Manual FM 16-5. Washington, DC: Headquarters, Department of the Army, 1984.

————. *Civil Affairs Operations.* Field Manual FM 41-10. Washington, DC: Headquarters, Department of the Army, 1985.

————. *Code of Conduct/Survival, Evasion, Resistance and Escape (SERE) Training.* Army Regulation AR 350-30. Washington, DC: Headquarters, Department of the Army, 1985.

————. *Combat Communications.* Field Manual FM 24-1. Washington, DC: Headquarters, Department of the Army, 1976.

————. *Combat Service Support.* Field Manual FM 100-10. Washington, DC: Headquarters, Department of the Army, 1983.

————. *Combat Service Support Operations-Corps.* Field Manual FM 63-3J. Washington, DC: Headquarters, Department of the Army, 1985.

————. *Combat Service Support Operations-Division.* Field Manual FM 63-2. Washington, DC: Headquarters, Department of the Army, 1983.

————. *Combat Service Support Operations-Theater.* Field Manual FM 63-4. Washington, DC: Headquarters, Department of the Army, 1984.

————. *Combat Service Support Operations-Theater Army.* Field Manual FM 63-5. Washington, DC: Headquarters, Department of the Army, 1985.

————. *Commander's Handbook for Property Accountability at the Unit Level.* Field Manual FM 10-14-1. Washington, DC: Headquarters, Department of the Army, 1984.

————. *Commissioned Officer Professional Development and Utilization.* Department of the Army Pamphlet 600-3. Washington, DC: Headquarters, Department of the Army, 1986.

————. *Communications-Electronics Operation Instructions "The CEOI."* Training Circular TC 24-1. Washington, DC: Headquarters, Department of the Army, 1982.

————. *Communications Techniques: Electronics Countermeasures.* Field Manual FM 24-33. Washington, DC: Headquarters, Department of the Army, 1985.

————. *Counterintelligence.* Field Manual FM 34-60. Washington, DC: Headquarters, Department of the Army, 1985.

————. *Countermobility.* Field Manual FM 5-102. Washington, DC: Headquarters, Department of the Army, 1985.

————. *Counter-Signals Intelligence (C-SIGINT) Operations.* Field Manual FM 34-62. Washington, DC: Headquarters, Department of the Army, 1986.

————. *Deliberate Smoke Operations.* Field Manual FM 3-50. Washington, DC: Headquarters, Department of the Army, 1984.

————. *Department of Army Policy Statement, 1988.* Washington, DC: Headquarters, Department of the Army, 1988.

————. *Dictionary of United States Army Terms.* Army Regulation AR 310-25. Washington, DC: Headquarters, Department of the Army, 1986.

————. *Direction Finding Operations.* Field Manual FM 34-88. Washington, DC: Headquarters, Department of the Army, 1984.

————. *Division Artillery, Field Artillery Brigade, and Field Artillery Section (Corps)*. Field Manual FM 6-20-2. Washington, DC: Headquarters, Department of the Army, 1981.

————. *Division Headquarters and Headquarters Detachments, Supply and Transport Battalions and Supply and Service Battalions*. Field Manual FM 29-7. Washington, DC: Headquarters, Department of the Army, 1984.

————. *Drills and Ceremonies*. Field Manual FM 22-5. Washington, DC: Headquarters, Department of the Army, 1986.

————. *Engineer Combat Operations*. Field Manual FM 5-100. Washington, DC: Headquarters, Department of the Army, 1984.

————. *Enlisted Personnel*. Army Regulation AR 635-200. Washington, DC: Headquarters, Department of the Army, 1984.

————. *Enlisted Personnel Management System*. Army Regulation AR 600-200. Washington, DC: Headquarters, Department of the Army, 1984.

————. *Explosive Ordnance Disposal Service and Unit Operations*. Field Manual FM 95-5. Washington, DC: Headquarters, Department of the Army, 1984.

————. *Field Artillery Target Acquisition*. Field Manual FM 6-121. Washington, DC: Headquarters, Department of the Army, 1978.

————. *Fire Support in Combined Arms Operations*. Field Manual FM 6-20. Washington, DC: Headquarters, Department of the Army, 1983.

————. *40-MM Grenade Launchers M203 and M79*. Field Manual FM 23-31. Washington, DC: Headquarters, Department of the Army, 1972.

————. *Glossary of Terms—Nuclear Weapon Phenomena and Effects*. DASIAC-SR-208. Washington, DC: Headquarters, Department of the Army, 1985.

————. *Guard Duty*. Field Manual FM 22-6. Washington, DC: Headquarters, Department of the Army, 1971.

————. *Gunnery Training for Attack Helicopters*. Training Circular TC 17-17. Washington, DC: Headquarters, Department of the Army, 1975.

————. *Health Service Support in a Communications Zone (Test)*. Field Manual FM 8-21. Washington, DC: Headquarters, Department of the Army, 1981.

————. *Health Service Support in the Theater of Operations*. Field Manual FM 8-10. Washington, DC: Headquarters, Department of the Army, 1978.

————. *How to Conduct Training Exercises*. Field Manual FM 25-4. Washington, DC: Headquarters, Department of the Army, 1984.

————. *How to Prepare and Conduct Military Training*. Field Manual FM 21-6. Washington, DC: Headquarters, Department of the Army, 1975.

————. *Individual Military Education and Training*. Army Regulation AR 350-1. Washington, DC: Headquarters, Department of the Army, 1987.

————. *Infantry, Airborne, and Air Assault Brigade Operations*. Field Manual FM 7-30. Washington, DC: Headquarters, Department of the Army, 1981.

————. *The Infantry Battalion (Infantry, Airborne, Air Assault)*. Field Manual FM 7-20. Washington, DC: Headquarters, Department of the Army, 1984.

————. *The Infantry Rifle Company (Infantry, Airborne, Air Assault, Ranger)*. Field Manual FM 7-10. Washington, DC: Headquarters, Department of the Army, 1982.

————. *Information Pamphlet for the Career Development of Enlisted Members of the U.S. Army Reserve*. Department of the Army Pamphlet DA PAM 140-8. Washington, DC: Headquarters, Department of the Army, 1986.

————. *Intelligence Analysis*. Field Manual FM 34-3. Washington, DC: Headquarters, Department of the Army, 1986.

————. *Intelligence and Electronic Warfare Operations*. Field Manual FM 34-1. Washington, DC: Headquarters, Department of the Army, 1987.

————. *Intelligence Imagery*. Field Manual FM 34-55. Washington, DC: Headquarters, Department of the Army, 1985.

————. *Intelligence Interrogation*. Field Manual FM 34-52. Washington, DC: Headquarters, Department of the Army, 1987.

———. *Jungle Operations*. Field Manual FM 90-5. Washington, DC: Headquarters, Department of the Army, 1982.

———. *The Law of War*. Training Circular TC 27-10-3. Washington, DC: Headquarters, Department of the Army, 1985.

———. *Leadership and Command at Senior Levels*. Field Manual FM 22-103. Washington, DC: Headquarters, Department of the Army, 1987.

———. *Leaves and Passes*. Army Regulation AR 630-5. Washington, DC: Headquarters, Department of the Army, 1984.

———. *Light Infantry Battalion Task Force*. Field Manual FM 7-72. Washington, DC: Headquarters, Department of the Army, 1987.

———. *Long-Range Reconnaissance Patrol Company*. Field Manual FM 31-18. Washington, DC: Headquarters, Department of the Army, 1968.

———. *Long-Range Surveillance*. Field Manual FM 7-93. Washington, DC: Headquarters, Department of the Army, 1987.

———. *Low Intensity Conflict*. Field Manual FM 100-20. Washington, DC: Headquarters, Department of the Army, 1981.

———. *M16A1 Rifle and Rifle Marksmanship*. Field Manual FM 23-9. Washington, DC: Headquarters, Department of the Army, 1974.

———. *Machinegun 7.62-MM, M60*. Field Manual FM 23-67. Washington, DC: Headquarters, Department of the Army, 1964.

———. *Maintenance and Repair Parts Consumption Planning Guide for Contingency Operations*. Field Manual FM 42-9-23. Washington, DC: Headquarters, Department of the Army, 1980.

———. *Management of Stress in Army Operations*. Field Manual FM 26-2. Washington, DC: Headquarters, Department of the Army, 1986.

———. *Map Reading*. Field Manual FM 21-26. Washington, DC: Headquarters, Department of the Army, 1969.

———. *The Mechanized Infantry Platoon and Squad*. Field Manual FM 7-7. Washington, DC: Headquarters, Department of the Army, 1984.

———. *Military Awards*. Army Regulation AR 672-5-1. Washington, DC: Headquarters, Department of the Army, 1984.

———. *Military Convoy Operations in the Continental United States*. Field Manual FM 55-312. Washington, DC: Headquarters, Department of the Army, 1981.

———. *Military Intelligence Battalion Combat Electronic Warfare and Intelligence (Aerial Exploitation) (Corps)*. Field Manual FM 34-22. Washington, DC: Headquarters, Department of the Army, 1984.

———. *Military Intelligence Battalion (Combat Electronic Warfare Intelligence) (Division)*. Field Manual FM 34-10. Washington, DC: Headquarters, Department of the Army, 1981.

———. *Military Intelligence Battalion (CEWI) (Operations) (Corps)*. Field Manual FM 34-21. Washington, DC: Headquarters, Department of the Army, 1982.

———. *Military Intelligence Battalion (CEWI) (Tactical Exploitation) (Corps): Counterintelligence, Interrogation, Electronic Warfare*. Field Manual FM 34-23. Washington, DC: Headquarters, Department of the Army, 1985.

———. *Military Intelligence Company (Combat Electronic Warfare and Intelligence) (Armored Cavalry Regiment/Separate Brigade)*. Field Manual FM 34-30. Washington, DC: Headquarters, Department of the Army, 1983.

———. *Military Intelligence Group (Combat Electronic Warfare and Intelligence) (Corps)*. Field Manual FM 34-20. Washington, DC: Headquarters, Department of the Army, 1983.

———. *Military Leadership*. Field Manual FM 22-100. Washington, DC: Headquarters, Department of the Army, 1983.

———. *Military Operations on Urbanized Terrain (MOUT)*. Field Manual FM 90-10. Washington, DC: Headquarters, Department of the Army, 1979.

———. *Military Police Support for the Airland Battle*. Field Manual FM 19-1. Washington, DC: Headquarters, Department of the Army, 1983.

———. *Military Police Team, Squad, Platoon Combat Operations*. Field Manual FM 19-4. Washington, DC: Headquarters, Department of the Army, 1984.

———. *Military Symbols.* Field Manual FM 21-30. Washington, DC: Headquarters, Department of the Army, 1970.

———. *Mine/Countermine Operations at the Company Level.* Field Manual FM 20-32. Washington, DC: Headquarters, Department of the Army, 1976.

———. *NBC Decontamination.* Field Manual FM 3-5. Washington, DC: Headquarters, Department of the Army, 1985.

———. *NBC Operations.* Field Manual FM 3-100. Washington, DC: Headquarters, Department of the Army, 1985.

———. *NBC Protection.* Field Manual FM 3-4. Washington, DC: Headquarters, Department of the Army, 1985.

———. *Nuclear Weapons Employment Doctrine and Procedures.* Field Manual FM 101-3-1. Washington, DC: Headquarters, Department of the Army, 1986.

———. *Officer Assignment Policies, Details, and Transfers.* Army Regulation AR 614-100. Washington, DC: Headquarters, Department of the Army, 1984.

———. *Operational Terms and Symbols.* Field Manual FM 101-5-1. Washington, DC: Headquarters, Department of the Army, 1985.

———. *Operations.* Field Manual FM 100-5. Washington, DC: Headquarters, Department of the Army, 1986.

———. *Operations for Nuclear-Capable Units.* Field Manual FM 100-50. Washington, DC: Headquarters, Department of the Army, 1980.

———. *Organizational Maintenance Operations.* Field Manual FM 29-2. Washington, DC: Headquarters, Department of the Army, 1984.

———. *Overseas Service.* Army Regulation AR 614-30. Washington, DC: Headquarters, Department of the Army, 1984.

———. *Patriot Battalion Operations.* Field Manual FM 44-15. Washington, DC: Headquarters, Department of the Army, 1984.

———. *Personnel Selection and Classification, Warrant Officer Occupational Specialties.* Army Regulation AR 611-112. Washington, DC: Headquarters, Department of the Army, 1987.

———. *Planning for Health Service Support.* Field Manual FM 8-55. Washington, DC: Headquarters, Department of the Army, 1985.

———. *Planning Logistics Support for Military Operations.* Field Manual FM 701-58. Washington, DC: Headquarters, Department of the Army, 1987.

———. *Processing Personnel for Separation.* Army Regulation AR 635-10. Washington, DC: Headquarters, Department of the Army, 1984.

———. *Promotion of Officers on Active Duty.* Army Regulation AR 624-100. Washington, DC: Headquarters, Department of the Army, 1984.

———. *Psychological Operations.* Field Manual FM 33-1. Washington, DC: Headquarters, Department of the Army, 1979.

———. *RDT&E Managers Intelligence and Threat Support Guide.* Alexandria, VA: Headquarters, Army Materiel Development and Readiness Command, 1983.

———. *Rear Battle.* Field Manual FM 90-14. Washington, DC: Headquarters, Department of the Army, 1985.

———. *Repair Parts Supply for a Theater of Operations.* Field Manual FM 29-19. Washington, DC: Headquarters, Department of the Army, 1985.

———. *The Rifle Squads (Mechanized and Light Infantry).* Training Circular TC 7-1. Washington, DC: Headquarters, Department of the Army, 1976.

———. *River Crossing Operations.* Field Manual FM 90-13. Washington, DC: Headquarters, Department of the Army, 1978.

———. *Route Reconnaissance and Classification.* Field Manual FM 5-36. Washington, DC: Headquarters, Department of the Army, 1985.

———. *S2 Reference Guide.* Training Circular TC 30-28. Washington, DC: Headquarters, Department of the Army, 1977.

———. *Selection of Enlisted Soldiers for Training and Assignment.* Army Regulation AR 614-200. Washington, DC: Headquarters, Department of the Army, 1984.

———. *Staff Organization and Operations.* Field Manual FM 101-5. Washington, DC: Headquarters, Department of the Army, 1986.

———. *Support Operations: Echelons Above Corps.* Field Manual FM 100-16. Washington, DC: Headquarters, Department of the Army, 1986.

———. *Survivability.* Field Manual FM 5-103. Washington, DC: Headquarters, Department of the Army, 1985.

———. *Tactical Deception.* Field Manual FM 90-2. Washington, DC: Headquarters, Department of the Army, 1978.

———. *Tactical Single Channel Radio Communications Techniques.* Field Manual FM 24-18. Washington, DC: Headquarters, Department of the Army, 1984.

———. *Tactics, Techniques, and Concepts of Antiarmor Warfare.* Field Manual FM 23-3. Washington, DC: Headquarters, Department of the Army, 1972.

———. *The Tank and Mechanized Infantry Battalion Task Force.* Field Manual FM 71-2. Washington, DC: Headquarters, Department of the Army, 1977.

———. *The Tank and Mechanized Infantry Company Team.* Field Manual FM 71-1. Washington, DC: Headquarters, Department of the Army, 1977.

———. *Tank Gunnery.* Field Manual FM 17-12. Washington, DC: Headquarters, Department of the Army, 1984.

———. *Tank Gunnery.* Field Manual FM 17-2-C2. Washington, DC: Headquarters, Department of the Army, 1980.

———. *Tank Platoon Division 86 (Test).* Field Manual FM 17-5. Washington, DC: Headquarters, Department of the Army, 1984.

———. *Technical Escort Operations.* Field Manual FM 3-20. Washington, DC: Headquarters, Department of the Army, 1981.

———. *Training for Mobilization and War.* Field Manual FM 25-5. Washington, DC: Headquarters, Department of the Army, 1985.

———. *Training Management in Battalions.* Field Manual FM 21-5-7. Washington, DC: Headquarters, Department of the Army, 1977.

———. *Transportation Reference Data.* Field Manual FM 55-15. Washington, DC: Headquarters, Department of the Army, 1986.

———. *Unit Training Management.* Field Manual FM 25-2. Washington, DC: Headquarters, Department of the Army, 1984.

———. *U.S. Army Air Defense Artillery Employment.* Field Manual FM 44-1. Washington, DC: Headquarters, Department of the Army, 1983.

———. *U.S. Army Air Defense Artillery Employment Hawk.* Field Manual FM 44-90. Washington, DC: Headquarters, Department of the Army, 1983.

———. *U.S. Army Air Defense Employment.* Field Manual FM 44-1. Washington, DC: Headquarters, Department of the Army, 1983.

———. *United States Army Intelligence and Threat Analysis Center.* Washington, DC: United States Army Intelligence Threat and Analysis Center, 1987.

———. *U.S. Army Operational Concept for Special Operations Forces,* TRADOC PAM 525-34. Washington, DC: Headquarters, Department of the Army, 1984.

———. *U.S. Army Policy Statement, 1988.* Washington, DC: Headquarters, Department of the Army, 1988.

———. *USA/USAF Doctrine for Joint Airborne and Tactical Airlift Operations.* Field Manual FM 100-27. Washington, DC: Headquarters, Department of the Army, 1985.

———. *Wartime Casualty Reporting.* Field Manual FM 12-15. Washington, DC: Headquarters, Department of the Army, 1983.

———. *Wear and Appearance of Army Uniforms and Insignia.* Army Regulation AR 670-1. Washington, DC: Headquarters, Department of the Army, 1986.

————. *Weather Support for Army Tactical Operations.* Field Manual FM 34-81. Washington, DC: Headquarters, Department of the Army, 1984.

Finnegan, John P. *Military History: A Picture History.* Arlington, VA: U.S. Army Intelligence and Security Command, 1984.

Laubenthal, Sanders A. "Preparing 'the Team': Defense Attache Training." *DIC Newsletter* (Winter 1986): 1-4.

National Security Agency. *Limitations and Procedures in Signals Intelligence Operations of the USSS.* Washington, DC: GPO, 1976.

Office of the President of the United States. *Executive Order 12036 U.S. Intelligence Activities.* Washington, DC, 1978.

"The United and Specified Commands." *Defense 87* (Nov.-Dec. 1987): 2-58.

U.S. Congress. *Central Intelligence Information Act.* Public Law 98-477, October 15, 1984. Washington, DC: GPO, 1984.

U.S. Congress. *Intelligence Identities Protection Act of 1982.* Public Law 97-200. Washington, DC: GPO, 1982.

U.S. Congress, Senate. *Final Report, Senate Select Committee on Intelligence.* Washington, DC: GPO, 1976.

U.S. Congress. Senate. *Final Report of the Senate Select Committee to Study Government Operations With Respect to Intelligence Activities. Report 94-755. Book I, Foreign and Military Intelligence* (Church Committee Report). Washington, DC: GPO, 1976.

Von Hoene, John P.A. *Intelligence User's Guide.* Washington, DC: DIA, 1983.

About the Editors

Peter G. Tsouras is an analyst at the U.S. Army Intelligence and Threat Analysis Center, Washington, D.C., and a lieutenant colonel in the U.S. Army Reserve. He has written extensively on Soviet naval matters, and is the author of an incisive series of articles on Russian military history. Currently he is writing a comprehensive study of ground-based military power since World War II and an encyclopedia of military quotations that illustrate the art of war. He will soon begin a series of studies on German military strategy in World War II.

Commander Bruce W. Watson, U.S. Navy (Retired) served as a naval intelligence officer for twenty-two years. He currently is an Adjunct Professor at the Defense Intelligence College at the University of Virginia, and is a freelance writer and consultant on defense matters. Dr. Watson has served as Vice Chairman and as Chairman, Comparative Foreign Policy Section, International Studies Association. The series editor of the Garland Series of U.S. Military Affairs, he has coedited three other volumes in that series. The author of *Red Navy at Sea*, he has coedited three books on the Soviet Navy and has written several articles on the subject, as well as having written or coedited seven books on defense and national security matters. He has just completed a comprehensive study of sea power since World War II, is editing a study on the December 1989 U.S. military intervention in Panama, and is writing a second book on Soviet naval operations.

Susan M. Watson has a sustained interest in national security affairs and U.S. defense policy. Her work has appeared in the U.S. Naval Institute *Proceedings* and she has coedited *The Soviet Navy: Strengths and Liabilities* and *The Soviet Naval Threat to Europe: Military and Political Dimensions*. This is her second coedited volume in the Garland Series on Military Affairs.